MAKE THE
MOST OF YOUR
TIME ON
EARTH

A ROUGH GUIDE TO THE WORLD

D1421692

ROUGH
GUIDES

PUBLISHING INFORMATION

This compact edition published January 2010 by
Rough Guides Ltd, 80 Strand, London WC2R 0RL
14 Local Shopping Centre, Panchsheel Park, New Delhi 110017, India
Distributed by the Penguin Group
Penguin Books Ltd, 80 Strand, London WC2R 0RL
Penguin Group (USA) 375 Hudson Street, NY 10014, USA
Penguin Group (Australia) 250 Camberwell Road, Camberwell, Victoria 3124, Australia
Penguin Books Canada Ltd, 10 Alcorn Avenue, Toronto, Ontario, Canada M4V 1E4
Penguin Group (NZ) 67 Apollo Drive, Mairangi Bay, Auckland 1310, New Zealand
Typeset in Serifa and Helvetica Neue to an original design by Diana Jarvis
Printed and bound by South China Printing Ltd
© Rough Guides 2010

608pp includes index
A catalogue record for this book is available from the British Library
ISBN: 978-1-84836-557-5

The publishers and authors have done their best to ensure the accuracy and currency of all the information in
Make the Most of Your Time on Earth: A Rough Guide to the World, however, they can accept no responsibility
for any loss, injury, or inconvenience sustained by any traveller as a result of information or advice contained in the guide.

3   5   7   9   8   6   4   2

CREDITS AND ACKNOWLEDGEMENTS

Editors: Keith Drew, AnneLise Sorensen **Design:** Diana Jarvis **Cartography:** Ed Wright **Picture editor:** Jj Luck **Production:** Rebecca Short

Thanks above all are due to all our writers, without whose relentless curiosity, great writing and capacity for enjoying themselves this book could not exist. Also to the talented host of people who put the whole thing together: Keith Drew and AnneLise Sorensen for a superb editing job; Carole Mansur, Andy McCulloch, Jan McCann for proofreading; Diana Jarvis for her latest – and perhaps greatest – design creation; Ed Wright for his elegant maps; Jj Luck for her great eye for an image; Róisín Cameron for last-minute proofreading, indexing, and, er, just about everything; Andrew Rosenberg and Kate Berens for sage advice and good writing; Lucy White, Karoline Densley, Helena Smith and James Smart for editorial work in the UK; Steven Horak, Amy Hegarty, April Isaacs, Anna Owens and Ella Steim for editorial work in the US; Helen Phillips and Alison Murchie for various last-minute fixes; Scott Stickland for his cool head and technical acumen; Michelle Bhatia and Sarel Mayer for layout; Chloë Roberts for a great cover; and finally to Coralie Bickford-Smith for her unwittingly wonderful title.

CONTENTS

Introduction...4
Britain & Ireland 6
Western Europe 40
Iberian Peninsula......................................78
Scandinavia...108
Southeast Europe 124
Eastern Europe 166
North Africa 186
West Africa...206
Central & East Africa 222
Southern Africa.......................................242
The Middle East......................................268
USA...292
Canada...328
The Caribbean 348
Mexico & Central America....................364
South America...392
Central & Northern Asia 432
The Indian Subcontinent.......................470
Southeast Asia...503
Australia, New Zealand & the South Pacific 532
The Polar Regions...................................579
Small print 585
Things you need to know 586
Index...603

INTRODUCTION

Experiences have always been at the heart of the Rough Guide concept. When we started writing Rough Guides we wanted to share the kind of travel that we had been doing ourselves. Our aim was to put a destination's culture at centre stage: to highlight the clubs and bars where you could hear local music, eat and drink with people you hadn't come on holiday with, watch the local football, join in with the festivals. And we wanted to push travel a bit further, inspiring our readers to get away from the established routes and seek something that little bit more special and authentic – in short, to settle for nothing less than an ultimate travel experience.

What makes the best kind of travel experience? Well, it should be something you would recommend to others, something you would want tell your friends or family about: an experience that you'll always remember. It could be about the sense of awe you felt the first time you set eyes on an iconic building or looked out across a special landscape; it might be the camaraderie of joining the locals at a village fiesta – or the epic train ride you took to get there; perhaps an adrenaline-inducing physical activity – rainforest zipwiring, or soaring over the desert in a hot-air balloon; or even just enjoying a simple meal with new people in a perfect setting.

It's possible to have some of the best travel experiences without going very far at all. Travel isn't only about distance and long-haul flights. However, the most meaningful often take place when we move away from the familiar, out of our comfort zone, where even the most run-of-the-mill situations and events take on an exotic quality. It's no coincidence that so many of the experiences we feature in this book have some degree of cultural engagement. They're driven by taste, but also opportunity: some are very easy to do; others less so; they can be seasonal events that happen once each year; they can be almost wilfully remote. What they have in common is that they are all Rough Guide writers' personal recommendations, accumulated over the 25 years of our existence. And they are designed to evoke the same excitement in you that they originally did in us.

Finally, at Rough Guides we have always been conscious of the double-edged nature of travel – of the consequences to local communities, to the environment, and to ourselves. We believe that most of the time the benefits far outweigh the drawbacks, and that a world made up of nations that keep themselves to themselves would be a less interesting and perhaps more dangerous place. Our planet is rich and diverse, and it is one of the pleasures of life to see and understand as much of it as we can. Everyone wants to make the most of their time on earth. This book will hopefully provide some inspiring ideas for how to go about it.

Martin Dunford
Publishing Director, Rough Guides

MAKING THE MOST OF OUR READERS

Of course you can't reduce all the world has to offer into 1000 experiences – and each of us has our own ideas of what should be included. If there's something that you have done and that you feel should have been in this book, we'd love to hear from you. We'll be doing a new edition of Make the Most of Your Time on Earth before long, and we'd like to include your feedback, accounts and photos – both in the book and on the Rough Guide website. Send in your experiences and suggestions to makethemost@roughguides.com or to one of the addresses on p.2.

SOAKING UP THE EDINBURGH FESTIVAL • GO WEST: HIKING THE PEMBROKESHIRE COAST PATH • GET LOST IN THE BALTI TRIANGLE • **WALKING THE WALLS OF CONWY CASTLE** • HOGMANAY: BRINGING IN THE NEW YEAR SCOTTISH STYLE • A TASTE OF SKYE • WATCHING THE HURLING AT CROKE PARK • ENJOYING THE SEASONS OF THE SCILLIES • PAINTING THE TOWN GREEN ON ST PATRICK'S DAY • A TASTE OF RUM IN KINLOCH CASTLE • HUNTING GHOSTS IN YORK • GUNPOWDER, TREASON AND PLOT LEWES BONFIRE NIGHT • FISH AND CHIPS: THE TRUE ENGLISH FAVOURITE • SUPPING GUINNESS IN DUBLIN • WANDERING BORROWDALE IN THE LAKE DISTRICT • BE HUMBLED IN DURHAM • DRESSING UP FOR ROYAL ASCOT • BARGING DOWN THE BARROW • SURFING THE SEVERN BORE • **ON THE FIDDLE: ATTENDING A TRADITIONAL IRISH MUSIC SESSION** • HIKING THE PENNINE WAY • FOLLOWING THE OYSTER TRAIL IN GALWAY • HOLKHAM MAGIC • TOASTING BAD WEATHER IN THE SCOTTISH HIGHLANDS • HORSING ABOUT AT THE COMMON RIDINGS • MOUNTAIN BIKING WELSH TRAILS • LEARNING TO SURVIVE IN DEEPEST DORSET • BURNING RUBBER AT THE ISLE OF MAN TT • EXPERIENCE GLASTONBURY • FINDING HEAVEN ON EARTH IN CORNWALL • **HOARDING BOOKS IN HAY–ON–WYE** • WALKING IN THE MOUNTAINS OF MOURNE • FEELING INSIGNIFICANT AT THE BRITISH MUSEUM • DAYDREAMING IN OXFORD • CYCLING IN THE NEW FOREST • **CALLING IN THE HEAVIES AT THE HIGHLAND GAMES** • SEE THE BELFAST MURALS • SURFING IN NEWQUAY • PLAYING THE OLD COURSE AT ST ANDREWS • PUNTING ON THE CAM • BREATHING IN THE SEA AIR IN TOBERMORY • GETTING AWAY FROM IT ALL ON SKELLIG MICHAEL • GIGGING IN GLASGOW • **HITTING THE STREETS FOR THE NOTTING HILL CARNIVAL** • CLUBBING IN LONDON • WALKING ON DARTMOOR • TRUNDLING ALONG THE WEST HIGHLANDS RAILWAY • WINNING THE PREHISTORIC LOTTERY • LOSING YOURSELF IN CONNEMARA • HIKING IN SNOWDONIA • **WATCHING FOOTBALL AT THE THEATRE OF DREAMS** • INTO THE VALLEY: HEARING A WELSH CHOIR • TAKE A STROLL FROM ST PAUL'S TO TATE MODERN • CHASING CHEESE IN GLOUCESTER • CATCHING THE LAST NIGHT OF THE PROMS • POUNDING THE STREETS OF LONDON • SOAKING UP THE EDINBURGH FESTIVAL • GO WEST: HIKING THE PEMBROKESHIRE COAST PATH • GET LOST IN THE BALTI TRIANGLE • HOGMANAY: BRINGING IN THE NEW YEAR SCOTTISH STYLE • A TASTE OF SKYE • **GUNPOWDER, TREASON AND PLOT: LEWES BONFIRE NIGHT** • WATCHING THE HURLING AT CROKE PARK • ENJOYING THE SEASONS OF THE SCILLIES • PAINTING THE TOWN GREEN ON ST PATRICK'S DAY • A TASTE OF RUM IN KINLOCH CASTLE • HUNTING GHOSTS IN YORK • FISH AND CHIPS: THE TRUE ENGLISH FAVOURITE • SUPPING GUINNESS IN DUBLIN • WANDERING BORROWDALE IN THE LAKE DISTRICT • BE HUMBLED IN DURHAM • DRESSING UP FOR ROYAL ASCOT • **BARGING DOWN THE BARROW** • SURFING THE SEVERN BORE • HIKING THE PENNINE WAY • FOLLOWING THE OYSTER TRAIL IN GALWAY • HOLKHAM MAGIC • TOASTING BAD WEATHER IN THE SCOTTISH HIGHLANDS • HORSING ABOUT AT THE COMMON RIDINGS • MOUNTAIN BIKING WELSH TRAILS • **PLAYING THE OLD COURSE AT ST ANDREWS** • LEARNING TO SURVIVE IN DEEPEST DORSET • ON THE FIDDLE: ATTENDING A TRADITIONAL IRISH MUSIC SESSION • CALLING IN THE HEAVIES AT THE HIGHLAND GAMES • BURNING RUBBER AT THE ISLE OF MAN TT • EXPERIENCE GLASTONBURY • FINDING HEAVEN ON EARTH IN CORNWALL • WALKING IN THE MOUNTAINS OF MOURNE • FEELING INSIGNIFICANT AT THE BRITISH MUSEUM • DAYDREAMING IN OXFORD • CYCLING IN THE NEW FOREST • SEE THE BELFAST MURALS • **PUNTING ON THE CAM** • SURFING IN NEWQUAY • BREATHING IN THE SEA AIR IN TOBERMORY • GETTING AWAY FROM IT ALL ON SKELLIG MICHAEL • GIGGING IN GLASGOW • CLUBBING IN LONDON • WALKING ON DARTMOOR • TRUNDLING ALONG THE WEST HIGHLANDS RAILWAY • WINNING THE PREHISTORIC LOTTERY • LOSING YOURSELF IN CONNEMARA • HIKING IN SNOWDONIA • INTO THE VALLEY: HEARING

BRITAIN & IRELAND

001–059

SCOTLAND

PLAYING
040 THE OLD COURSE
AT ST ANDREWS

CALLING IN THE HEAVIES
AT THE HIGHLAND GAMES 034

ON THE FIDDLE:
ATTENDING A
TRADITIONAL IRISH 033
MUSIC SESSION

NORTHERN
IRELAND

REPUBLIC
OF
IRELAND

WATCHING FOOTBALL
055 AT THE THEATRE OF DREAMS

WALKING THE WALLS
OF CONWY CASTLE 005

BARGING DOWN THE BARROW 029

WALES   ENGLAND

HOARDING BOOKS
020 IN HAY-ON-WYE

001 PUNTING ON THE CAM

HITTING THE STREETS FOR
THE NOTTING HILL CARNIVAL 036

GUNPOWDER, TREASON AND PLOT:
LEWES BONFIRE NIGHT 017

ENGLAND The experienced professional punter – propelling boatloads of tourists along Cambridge's river Cam – speaks of the simple sensory pleasure to be found in the interaction of the firm riverbed, the massive pole (wielded with a masterful delicacy) and the punt itself, pushing against the springy upthrust of the gentle waters. In fact, it is like driving a people carrier with a joystick from a seat where the luggage would usually go. Your punt will naturally be attracted to other punts, blocking the river under the sarcastic gaze of the city's youth, who stop to watch your ineptitude from one of the many pretty bridges. Your response should be to affect an ironic detachment; something achieved more easily when you console yourself with the idea that perhaps punting was never meant to be done well. The point is to drift with languorous unconcern, admiring the beautiful college gardens and architecture, while disguising incompetence as abstraction and reverie.

This slow river is lined with some of the grandest architecture in the country. You recline almost at the water's level as the great buildings rear around you in a succession of noble set-pieces. Perhaps the two most notable sights are the chapel at King's College, a structure of forbidding single-minded authority, and Christopher Wren's library for Trinity College, which has the same rigorous perfection that some may find refreshing (or overwhelming).

When you're done punting, the colleges are wonderful places to explore, if they'll let you in; the rules of access vary from college to college and season to season, although you can always behave as if you have a perfect right to walk wherever you like and see what happens.

001
PUNTING
ON THE CAM

002 WATCHING THE HURLING AT CROKE PARK

IRELAND The player leaps like a basketball star through a crowd of desperate opponents and flailing sticks. Barely visible to the naked eye, the arcing ball somehow lodges in his upstretched palm. Dropping to the ground, he shimmies his way out of trouble, the ball now delicately balanced on the flat end of his hurley, then bang! With a graceful, scything pull, he slots the ball through the narrow uprights, seventy yards away.

Such is the stuff of Irish boyhood dreams, an idealized sequence of hurling on continual rewind. With similarities to lacrosse and hockey – though it's not really like either – hurling is a thrilling mix of athleticism, timing, outrageous bravery and sublime skill. Said to be the fastest team game in the world, it can be readily enjoyed by anyone with an eye for sport.

The best place to watch a match is Dublin's Croke Park, the headquarters of the GAA (Gaelic Athletic Association). In this magnificent, 80,000-seater stadium, you'll experience all the colour, banter and passion of inter-county rivalry. And before the game, you can visit the excellent GAA Museum to get up to speed on hurling and its younger brother, Gaelic football, ancient sports whose renaissance was entwined with the struggle for Irish independence. Here, you'll learn about the first Bloody Sunday in 1920, when British troops opened fire on a match at this very ground, killing twelve spectators and one of the players. You'll be introduced to the modern-day descendants of Cúchulain, the greatest warrior-hero of Irish mythology, who is said to have invented hurling: star players of the last century including flat-capped Christy Ring of Cork and more recent icons such as Kilkenny's D.J. Carey. And finally, you can attempt to hit a hurling ball yourself – after a few fresh-air shots, you'll soon appreciate the intricate skills the game requires.

003 RAMBLING ON DARTMOOR

ENGLAND In the middle of that most genteel of counties, Devon, it comes as something of a shock to encounter the 365 square miles of raw granite, barren bogland and rippling seas of heather that make up Dartmoor. The feeling of space is intimidating. If you want to de-clutter your mind and energize your body, the recipe is simple: invest in a pair of hiking boots, switch off your mobile and set out on an adventure into the primitive heart of Britain. The briefest of journeys onto the moor will be enough to take in the dusky umbers of the landscape, flecked by yellow gorse and purple heather, or the verdant patchwork of greens threaded by flashes of moorland stream, all washed in a moist and misty light. Even the gathering haze that precedes rain appears otherworldly, while the moor under a mantle of snow and illuminated by a crisp wintry light is spellbinding.

Your walk will take you from picturesque, hideaway hamlets such as Holne and Buckland-in-the-Moor to bare wilderness and blasted crag within a few strides. There are some surprising examples of architecture, too, including the authentically Norman Okehampton Castle and the wholly fake Castle Drogo, built by Lutyens in the early twentieth century in the style of a medieval fortress. But by far the most stirring man-made relics to be found are the Bronze and Iron Age remains, a surprising testimony to the fact that this desolate expanse once hummed with activity: easily accessible are the grand hut circles of Grimspound, where Conan Doyle set a scene from his Sherlock Holmes yarn, *The Hound of the Baskervilles*.

The best way to explore the moor is on an organized walk led by a knowledgeable guide, often focusing on a theme, from birdwatching to orienteering to painting. It's a first-rate way to get to grips with the terrain, and discover facets of this vast landscape that you'd never encounter on your own. Alternatively, equip yourself with a decent map and seek out your own piece of Dartmoor. You may not see another soul for miles, but you'll soon absorb its slow, soothing rhythm.

004 A TASTE OF SKYE

SCOTLAND The young waitress with soft skin and a lilting Hebridean accent handed over the menu and drew my attention to the day's specials chalked up on the blackboard above the mantelpiece.

I was in a window seat – though the windows of the rebuilt croft house were small, dating from days when glass was an inconceivable luxury and insulation was provided by thick stone walls and a thatch of reeds and bracken. My view included said reeds and bracken, growing thickly near the seaweed-tangled shore, a patch of steel-coloured water and green land beyond, rounded and speckled with sheep at first, then rising to broad-shouldered slopes and the more ragged shapes of higher hills.

I hadn't expected the menu to compare to the scenery, but it did – and read like a mini-guidebook. Crab fresh from Bracadale, langoustines caught in a Loch Dunvegan creel, scallops hand-dived near Sconser, wild venison from the Cuillin. There were woodland mushrooms, berries gathered from local gardens and doused in heather honey, creamy soft cheeses from Lochalsh, and oatcakes made on a traditional flat skillet in the kitchen. Afterwards, I sampled a tangy whisky distilled and aged in the salty coastal air at Talisker.

You come to a place as magical as Skye to discover the struggles of its history, the charm of its rugged shores, the drama of the jagged mountain tops and the seductive allure of the wonderfully green (but hardly fertile) landscape. You look out for a soaring golden eagle or a darting otter, tramp along mossy paths and scramble over tumbledown castle ruins. Skye fills the senses and tugs at your emotions, but it's a very pleasant realization that it can also fill your belly.

005 Walking the walls of
CONWY CASTLE

WALES Up on Conwy Castle battlements the wind whips around the eight solid towers that have stood on this rocky knoll for over seven hundred years. It's a superb spot with long views out across the surrounding landscape, but look down from the castle's magnificent curtain walls and you'll see all the elements that combined to make Conwy one of the most impressive fortresses of its day.

The castle occupies an important site, beside the tidal mud flats of the Conwy Estuary where pearl mussels have been harvested for centuries. To the south lie the northern peaks of Snowdonia, the mountains where the Welsh have traditionally sought refuge from invaders such as the Norman English, who built this castle around 1283. Conwy formed a crucial link in Edward I's "Iron ring" of eight castles around North Wales, designed to finally crush the last vestiges of Welsh resistance to his rule. Gazing upon this imposing fortress, which took just five years to build and is still largely intact, it isn't hard to understand why he was successful.

A key part of the castle's design was its integration with the town, so that the two could support each other, and from the battlements a three-quarter-mile ring of intact town walls, punctuated with 21 towers, loops out from the base of the castle, encircling Conwy's old town. For centuries, the Welsh were forced to live outside the town walls while the English prospered within; the latter left behind a fine legacy in the form of the fourteenth-century half-timbered Aberconwy House and Plas Mawr, Britain's best-preserved Elizabethan townhouse.

Finish off the day by heading into town and walking a circuit of the thirty-foot-high town walls. Start at the very highest point (tower 13), where you get a superb view across the slate roofs of the town to the castle, and wander down towards the river where a pint on the quay outside the *Liverpool Arms* is de rigueur on a fine evening.

006 HOGMANAY: SEEING THE YEAR IN, SCOTTISH STYLE

SCOTLAND Like all the best celebrations, Hogmanay has its feet firmly planted in the pagan past. A traditional festival of hedonistic misrule, it's designed to blast away the mid-winter blues and is celebrated with passionate intensity in Scotland, from the borders to the farthest-flung islands.

Though the general idea is now a miasma of drunkenness topped off with some fireworks, the festival as it is celebrated in Scotland has some very particular customs. It is traditionally a time to settle your affairs, and then welcome luck into your home by first footing – visiting your neighbours with gifts, originally a lump of coal. The luckiest visitor is considered to be a tall, dark-haired man, perhaps for obvious reasons.

Even the smallest village will host some sort of Hogmanay celebration – while these can be of a churningly sentimental tartan nature, you can also get lucky and hear great live music. A good option is to find a genuine ceilidh, where musicians improvise around standard folk songs, often to wild, exhilarating effect. And nothing will help you shed your inhibitions like a bit of Scottish country dancing – a caller shouts instructions, but taking a wrong turn in an eightsome reel is half the fun.

Scotland's major Hogmanay magnet, though, is the city of Edinburgh, where the once chaotic celebrations have been transformed into a major ticketed event, with bands, dancing and 100,000 people on the streets. The bells at midnight are the signal to start the fireworks, the floodlit castle and the jagged silhouette of the old town providing the most dramatic of backdrops. At this point, strangers will grab your hands, pump your arms up and down, and bellow out *Auld Lang Syne*, and any last shreds of Scottish Presbyterian reserve are abandoned.

007 GET LOST IN THE BALTI TRIANGLE

ENGLAND The Balti Triangle is one of Birmingham's leading culinary assets – over fifty restaurants all competing to serve the best, simplest, no-nonsense and, above all, cheapest Indian food. The apex of the fabled Triangle is where Moseley Road meets Stratford Road – two major crossroads are Highgate Road and Taunton Road – and two of the busiest balti boulevards are Ladypool Road and Stoney Lane. Balti as we know it was born in Birmingham's large Pakistani and Kashmiri communities in the 1970s and is really a testament to their business acumen rather than any fancy gastronomic impulse. As restaurateurs, they saw the merits of a style of eating that linked the British love of curry with some shortcuts in the kitchen. Each dish is finished to order, so the customer always gets the combination of ingredients they want – "meat-peas-spinach" or "chicken-king prawn-extra hot". Other defining elements of balti are the use of bits torn from a huge naan bread to eat with rather than cutlery – less cutlery means less washing up; a bring-your-own-alcohol policy – less licensing hassle; and low, low prices, enabled by turning the tables at a phenomenal rate.

There are lots of restaurants to choose from, but some in particular stand out; *Adil*'s, founded in 1977, was one of the first balti restaurants in the country and is very traditional, even for a balti house – try the balti meat with chickpeas and extra methi. Award-winning *Al Frash* serves a deliciously spicy balti called "Afrodesia" – minced chicken and king prawn with ground ginger and garlic. *Zeb's Miripuri Cuisine* lost its frontage during a tornado in 2004 and is much smarter now, but the cooking is as good as ever – it does a mean balti chicken jalfrezi. Otherwise, just wander into the Triangle and take pot luck in any restaurant that looks busy. Just remember to take your own alcohol.

008 GO WEST: HIKING THE PEMBROKESHIRE COAST PATH

WALES The Pembrokeshire Coast Path fringes Britain's only coastal national park, which has resisted the onslaught of the 21st century in all but a few hotspots such as Tenby and St David's (and even these remain remarkably lovely). Get out and stride along part of the 143-mile trail and you'll soon appreciate this evocative and spectacular edge of Wales.

Long golden surf beaches easily rival those of California; the clear green seas are the habitat of seals, whales, dolphins, sharks and, in summer, exotic species such as sunfish and even seahorses; further offshore, you'll spot islands that are home to internationally important seabird colonies; you can wander atop the highest sea cliffs in Wales, bent into dramatic folds by ancient earth movements; and in the hamlets, harbours and villages you pass through along the way, there are plenty of charming pubs and restaurants at which to refuel.

This variety is one of the best things about the coast path, which offers something for everyone – and not just in summer. The off-season can provide the thrilling spectacle of mighty Atlantic storms dashing thirty-foot waves against the sea cliffs as you fight your way along an exhilaratingly wind-lashed beach, whilst the next day the sun could be glittering in a clear blue sky with seabirds wheeling and screeching overhead. Take time out from your hike to relax and enjoy views across the Atlantic, which, other than the occasional lighthouse dotting the horizon, have remained unchanged since St Patrick sailed from Whitesands Beach to Ireland.

To walk the full length of the path takes up to two weeks and, surprisingly, involves more ascent than climbing Mount Everest, but even just a half-day outing along the trail is worth the effort, and acts as a reminder that Britain boasts some of the finest coastline in the world.

009 ENJOYING THE SEASONS OF THE SCILLIES

ENGLAND It's no exaggeration to say that, from London, you can get to the Caribbean quicker than the Scillies. But then, that's part of the appeal. You take the night train down to Penzance and then hop on the Scillonian ferry (not for the queasy) or the helicopter out over the Atlantic.

What awaits depends very much on the weather. The Scillies out of season are bracing, as wind and rain batter these low island outcrops. Wrapped in waterproofs, you can still have fun, squelching over wet bracken and spongy turf to odd outcrops of ruined castles, or picking through the profusion of shells on the beaches. And if you can afford a room at the *Hell Bay Hotel* on Bryher, then you can top off the day with a first-rate meal while gazing at original sculptures and paintings by Barbara Hepworth and Ivor Hitchens.

In summer, when the sun's out, it's a very different scene, and you can swim, go boating, even learn to scuba dive – the water is crystal clear and there are numerous wrecks. It can be a cheap holiday, too, since for only a few pounds you can pitch a tent at the Bryher campsite and enjoy one of the loveliest views in Europe. From there, wander down to the *Fraggle Rock* pub for a pint of Timothy Taylors and a crab sandwich, and then, if the tide's right, wade across to the neighbouring island of Tresco, and explore the subtropical Abbey Gardens.

I keep stressing Bryher, as that's my island. Scilly-fans are fiercely loyal. But you can have almost as good a time on St Martin's, which has arguably the best beaches, and a brilliantly sited pub, *The Turk's Head*, or on the diminutive St Agnes (population 72), with its wind-sculpted granite. St Mary's doubtless has devotees, too, but with the islands' main town, regular roads and cars, it lacks essential isolated romance. For that, you'll find me on Bryher.

FISH AND CHIPS: THE TRUE ENGLISH FAVOURITE

ENGLAND Whatever you may think of fish and chips – that it's been surpassed as the true English dish by chicken vindaloo, that it's a stodgy recipe for a sure heart attack – there's something undeniably appealing about it. This hot, greasy, starchy mess, smothered with salt and drenched in vinegar, can satisfy like little else.

Quite frankly, you'll probably be served a lot of awful fish and chips along the way. This despite the fact that fish and chips is on a bit of a roll, even, heaven forbid, nearly fashionable.

All kinds of chefs, buoyed by the renaissance in British cuisine, have been trying their hand at dressing up the humble dish. Indeed, noted gourmet Rick Stein – who has his own fish and chips restaurant on the southwest coast in Padstow – has compared serving up good fish and chips to presenting a plate of Helford oysters with a bottle of premier cru Chablis.

Fish and chips has pretty much always meant cod, and it's still far and way the favourite (though now we're told the world is running out), followed by traditional substitutes such as skate, plaice, haddock and bottom-feeding rock salmon (the appealing way of saying "catfish" or "dogfish"), but gurnard and monkfish are both getting their daring turns in the fryer. As for the batter that invariably coats the fish, flour and water is standard, though you might find yeast and beer batter or matzo meal in the most outré of places. What's the basic chip? Thick-cut potatoes, preferably cooked in beef drippings – and, of course, coated in a light layer of grease and liberal lashings of salt and vinegar.

So maybe that heart attack is coming. Hang the health issues and stuff the cod crisis. Just get stuck in.

011 SUPPING GUINNESS IN DUBLIN

IRELAND Rain lashing a grey Dublin Friday. *The Palace*, etched in glass, promises refuge. In quick. No trouble catching the barman's eye, "A pint, please". As he slowly begins to pour, time to take in the handsome room: mirrored screens sectioning the bar discreetly, Victorian mahogany twirling everywhere. I eavesdrop while the half-poured Guinness stands to one side to settle: the Dublin–Mayo match on Sunday, brutal tailbacks on the M50, bin charges. More patience needed when the glass is full, waiting for the black-and-white turmoil to calm itself; drawings of writers Flann O'Brien and Patrick Kavanagh, old *Palace* regulars, stare down.

I settle myself in the back room, under a glass roof that floods light in and noisily reminds me of the drenching I'm missing. Clutching my pint, I think of the philosopher, struggling with the problem of consciousness, who compared beer in a glass to the brain, the mind or soul to the froth on top – same physical stuff, but in essence quite different. Surely he can't have been Irish – this dark, malty liquid seems barely on speaking terms with the creamy, white top. A twist in the tale, perhaps only possible in "God's own country": as I sup my way through the black stuff, the froth persists, sinking slowly down the glass.

Same again? A fine pint, but was it the best Guinness in Dublin – and so, I suppose, the world? Some say it's better round the corner at *Mulligan*'s, where it's been sanctified by generations of *Irish Times* journalists. Or is the travel-shy liquid happier at *Ryan*'s, just across the river from the brewery? And what about the brewery's own panoramic bar? There you get a manicured pint, as its maker intended, with views over the city and the Wicklow Mountains thrown in.

Now, what was I meant to be doing this afternoon?

012 WANDERING BORROWDALE IN THE LAKE DISTRICT

ENGLAND Eighteenth-century Romantic poet Thomas Gray described the narrowest part of Borrowdale – the so-called Jaws of Borrowdale – as "a menacing ravine whose rocks might, at any time, fall and crush a traveller". Gray obviously didn't get out much, for more than anything Borrowdale is characterized by its sylvan beauty, the once glaciated hills smoothed off by the ancient ice. Some have dubbed it the most beautiful valley in England, and it's easy to see why on the gentle walks that weave across the flat valley floor. Some of the best are around Derwentwater, its mountain backdrop, wooded slopes and quaint ferry service making it one of the prettiest lakes in the area.

Ever since Victorian times, visitors have flocked to the Bowder Stone, a two-thousand-ton glacial erratic probably carried south from Scotland in the last Ice Age. This cube of andesitic lava is perched so precariously on one edge that it looks ready to topple at any moment. Wooden steps give access to its thirty-foot summit where the rock is worn smooth by hundreds of thousands of feet.

Immediately north, a circular walk takes in an area boasting the densest concentration of superb views in the Lake District. The most spectacular is from Walla Crag – vistas stretch over Derwentwater up to the Jaws of Borrowdale.

North of the Bowder Stone, a small tumbling stream is spanned by Ashness Bridge, an ancient stone-built structure designed for packhorses. With its magnificent backdrop of Derwentwater and the rugged beauty of northern fells, it's one of the most photographed scenes in the entire Lake District.

013 BE HUMBLED IN DURHAM

ENGLAND Durham Cathedral is now something of a celebrity to millions who've never even set foot in the Northeast, having appeared as Hogwart's detention hall, courtyard and Quidditch practice arena in the Harry Potter films. This recent brush with fame, however, is a mere blink in the cathedral's centuries-old history, as Durham stands as one of the greatest and most enduring achievements of Norman architectural engineering.

Looming over this university city like a gentle giant, the cathedral offers a haven of calm from the narrow, bustling streets. Boasting the enormous lion-shaped Sanctuary door knocker that, when rapped, would guarantee desperate fugitives 37 days of refuge, the North Porch Door opens onto the broad Norman nave, flanked by immense pillars, deeply carved with geometric grooves. Lighting up the east wall of the cathedral is the magnificent Rose window, below which you'll find the final resting place of the north's popular saint, St Cuthbert; the monk from Lindisfarne, famed for his healing hands, was deposited here in 1104 after a protracted and somewhat unceremonious tour of the country in his coffin (he had died in 687).

A hike up the Central Tower is worth the wear on the thigh muscles; 325 steps spiral up for 223 feet, where you're greeted with a superb panoramic view of the surrounding county, Wearside – claustrophobics be warned: the steps are extremely steep and narrow. The entrance to the tower is in the South Transept, next to Prior Castell's colourful sixteenth-century clock, decorated with a Scottish thistle: the last remaining testament to Durham's sticky involvement in the Civil War, when Cromwell used the cathedral to imprison 3000 Scottish soldiers.

At night, the Cathedral takes on an entirely new persona; bathed in artificial light, it dominates the skyline in haunting magnitude. To experience the cathedral in all its auricular glory, aim to visit around 5pm for the Evensong service, when you can enjoy the enchanting refrains of the university choristers. And if you're after more magic – this time in the culinary sense – the Almshouses café is located just across the grassy Palace Green (a perennial stage for streaking students). Sublime. The cake selection that is, not the streakers.

014 PAINTING THE TOWN GREEN ON ST PATRICK'S DAY

IRELAND There's something about the words "party" and "Ireland". In a country that turns death into a two-day piss-up (someone once observed that the only difference between an Irish wake and an Irish wedding was that there was one less drunk person), the national holiday just had to be something special. No one does it quite like the Irish, especially on their home turf, and no one in Ireland does St Patrick's Day quite as good as Dublin.

The events surrounding the festival – from street theatre to acrobatics, and drumming to puppet shows – change by the year, but the St Patrick's Day Parade itself (always held on March 17) is a constant, and the backbone of the celebrations. As many as 700,000 green-tinged festivalgoers descend en masse into the city centre to drink and dance the day away, and cheer on the assorted marching bands and themed pageants and floats. The parade starts at around noon at St Patrick's Cathedral on Patrick Street, winding its way north through town before finishing by the Black Church near Dorset Street Upper. To get a really good view, it's best to secure a place as near to O'Connell Bridge, at the southern end of O'Connell Street, as early in the day as possible.

The official face of the festival may be the street parade, but the soul of the business – the real "craic", as the Irish would say – is in the pubs of the city, where some of the antics would make Bacchus himself blanch. After the parade, most of the revellers make their way to Earlsfort Terrace, at the southeastern corner of St Stephen's Green, for the hugely popular Céilí Mór (literally "Great Dance Event") – a veritable orgy of Irish dance to live bands – where the alcohol-fuelled exuberance of the crowd is tempered only by the trained dancers who try to forge some semblance of choreography from the increasingly malleable mass.

015 A TASTE OF RUM IN KINLOCH CASTLE

SCOTLAND Scotland isn't a country that's short of fairy-tale castles, and you don't have to be a prince or a prisoner to get to stay in one. Some have been transformed into smart hotels or holiday lets, but it's worth remembering that romantic medieval digs can be rather more compromised by draughts, awkward layouts and endless staircases than your average *Holiday Inn*.

Top of the pile of weird and wonderful piles must come Kinloch Castle on Rum, a spectacular but sparsely populated island just south of Skye. Named not by pirates but by the Vikings, who described it as "wide", its empty glens and distinctive peaks once formed a noted sporting estate. In the late nineteenth century, one particularly extravagant owner, Sir George Bullough, set about building a grand castle to house himself and his wealthy chums whenever they fancied bagging a few stags and living it up with their mistresses and racing cars. Built in red sandstone with crenellations, turrets and all kinds of early mod - cons including double glazing, central heating and electricity, Kinloch Castle was as extravagant as it was out of place. Not many of the rugged Hebridean islands can boast a billiard room, a barrel organ and palm houses.

Between the wars the spendthrift aristos retreated to places less wild and remote, and both Rum and Kinloch Castle are now in the hands of the conservation body Scottish Natural Heritage. The castle is a bit of a millstone, in truth, a unique piece of architecture but now falling to bits. The interiors remain largely intact with their threadbare Edwardian furnishings, and the servants' quarters are used as a hostel for visitors and volunteer conservation workers. A few larger rooms act as communal lounges and by special arrangement it's still possible to stay in grander style in some of the original guest bedrooms. You'll feel sympathetic to the castle's plight more than overwhelmed by its opulence, bewildered by its eccentricity rather than enchanted. But there is, after all, a shadow side to all fairy tales.

016 HUNTING GHOSTS IN YORK

ENGLAND Roman and Viking history, the Minster and Betty's Tearooms may be visitor staples during the day, but there are some rather different experiences to be had on the backstreets of York after dark. At night, at various points around the city, groups of tourists gather, some nervously wringing their hands, others cracking jokes to ease their apprehension. As the Minster bell tolls, their guide arrives, clad in funereal black, and a hushed silence falls upon the group. Leading his flock down the shadowy streets, the ghoulish journey begins.

With its turbulent history, it's not surprising that York is such a hangout for things that go bump in the night. Founded by the Romans in 71 AD as "Eboracum", the city has suffered Viking invasion, Civil War, the Black Death and a cholera epidemic. With its narrow lanes, twisting alleyways and dark, looming Tudor buildings, it's a decidedly spooky place to wander in the dark. The Shambles (originally the Anglo-Saxon "Fleshammels" – meaning "Street of the Butchers") is an obligatory stop-off for any "hunting party", one of the city's oldest streets, and mentioned in the Domesday Book. Ghostly apparitions that have appeared here include a headless Sir Thomas Percy, Earl of Northumberland, who was executed in 1572 for plotting against Queen Elizabeth 1; and a forlorn Margaret Clitherow, crushed to death by the authorities for illegally harbouring Catholic priests in 1586. Another stop is The Treasurer's House, reputedly the most haunted building in Britain. Legless Roman soldiers, a murderous wife and sallow-faced children are all said to lurk in the corridors of the house, built in 1419. The ghosts are not just limited to humans though: a large black hound with red glowing eyes is also said to patrol the city's gloomy snickleways and passages.

You have been warned.

ENGLAND The first week of November sees one of the eccentric English's most irresponsible, unruly and downright dangerous festivals – Bonfire Night. Up and down the country, human effigies are burned in back gardens and fireworks are set off – all in the name of Guy Fawkes' foiled attempt to blow up the Houses of Parliament in 1605 – but in the otherwise peaceful market town of Lewes, things are taken to extremes. Imagine a head-on collision between Halloween and Mardi Gras and you're well on your way to picturing Bonfire Night, Lewes-style.

Throughout the night, smoke fills the Lewes air, giving the steep and narrow streets an eerie, almost medieval feel. As the evening draws on, rowdy torch-lit processions make their way through the streets, pausing to hurl barrels of burning tar into the River Ouse before dispersing to their own part of town to stoke up their bonfires.

Establishment propaganda in the aftermath of the so-called Gunpowder Plot ensured that Fawkes' name was forever associated with treason and treachery, and that "bone fires" – featuring burnings in effigy of villains of the day – became inextricably linked with his name. As the societies head for their own bonfires, they are each trailed by huge papier-mâché figures. Crammed full of fireworks themselves, these "guys" are defended by a number of "prelates", who fearlessly bat the rockets thrown at them by members of rival societies back into the crowd.

Forget the limp burgers of mainstream displays and lame sparklers suitable for use at home – for a real pyrotechnic party, Lewes is king.

017

GUNPOWDER, TREASON AND PLOT:
LEWES BONFIRE NIGHT

018 EXPERIENCE GLASTONBURY

ENGLAND "Glastonbury" – the name conjures up so many images. It's both a place and an event; only now the latter has absorbed the mystical, mythical associations of the Glastonbury of Arthurian and early Christian fame – both closely entwined with the story of the Holy Grail – to become the granddaddy of all festivals. Like the legendary town of Brigadoon, it makes a brief, enchanted appearance at the end of June and then it's gone, leaving a plethora of scarcely believable stories in its wake. Did you survive Glastonbury? Were you one of the chosen few who managed to get a ticket? (Incredibly, they are invariably sold out even before the line-up is announced.) Sure, there are bigger, brasher festivals, but Glasto is the oldest, wildest, coolest one around, where, uniquely, music makes up only part of the event. Here, the vibe is everything, and though it attracts the biggest names – and the greatest range of acts from Bowie to REM to Rolf Harris to the English National Opera – it's what happens away from the stages that really counts. Naked fertility rites, surreal costumes, fire-dancing, yoga at dawn, and – too often – mud, glorious mud, exploding toilets and losing your tent. It's hippies meets rave culture; travellers meets stockbrokers; and, for the most part, smiley, happy people, and not only on account of the enormous quantities of drugs consumed. Even with the arrival of CCTV, the double-perimeter fence and the watchtowers, still the spirit lives on. Eccentric, bolshie, comical, trans-generational, carnivalesque – there's something for everyone. You can visit the circus; listen to a stand-up show; watch *Hamlet*; have an Indian head massage; take a pottery class; attend a ceilidh; go shopping; watch a movie; learn to drum; get married, or be a guest at someone else's wedding; sleep in the dance tent; lose your friends (physically, that is); and – occasionally – watch a band. It's deeply traditional, and always contemporary – like a medieval midsummer fayre with mobile phones. Arrive with no preconceptions and let the spirit of the festival take you. Will you survive Glastonbury?

019 WALKING IN THE MOUNTAINS OF MOURNE

NORTHERN IRELAND The mountains rise above the seaside town of Newcastle like green giants, with Slieve Donard the highest, almost three thousand feet above the sandy strand of Dundrum Bay. Donard is just one of more than twenty peaks in County Down's Kingdom of Mourne (as the tourist office likes to call it), with a dozen of them towering over two thousand feet. Conveniently grouped together in a range that is just seven miles broad and about fourteen miles long, they are surprisingly overlooked – especially by many locals. On foot, in a landscape with no interior roads, you feel as if you have reached a magical oasis of high ground, a pure space that is part Finian's Rainbow and part Middle Earth.

Cutting across the heart of the Mournes is a dry-stone wall, part of a 22-mile barrier built in the 1920s to keep livestock out of the water catchment for the Silent Valley Reservoir. When a mist rolls off the sea, or a rain squall hits hard, the wall is a shelter, and a guide.

This is a wet place where the Glen River flows from the flanks of Slieve Commedagh and through the Donard wood. Some slopes are bog, and ragged black-faced sheep shelter behind clumps of golden gorse. Up here, peregrines ride on the wind and sharp-beaked ravens hope to scavenge the corpse of a lamb or two. Tied to the earth, you can follow the Brandy Pad, a scenic smuggler's track leading over the mountains from the Bloody River through Hare's gap and down again to Clonachullion. This is ancient land, and prehistoric cairns and stone graves – said to mark the resting place of Irish chiefs – dot the hills, peering through the mist to meet you.

020 HOARDING BOOKS IN HAY-ON-WYE

WALES Though a drive through the electrically green countryside that surrounds Hay-on-Wye makes for a perfectly lovely afternoon, the more potent draw is the sleepy Welsh town's mouthwatering amount of printed matter: with over a million books crammed into its aging stores, quaint, cobblestoned Hay-on-Wye (Y Gelli, in Welsh) is a bibliophilic Mecca to be reckoned with.

Dusty volumes are packed in like sardines, occupying everywhere the eyes roam. Moldering British cookbooks fight for shelf space – some of them in shops down tucked-away alleys verdant with moss and mildew – with plant-taxonomy guides, romance novels and pricey but lavishly produced first-editions.

To unearth these treasures, the intrepid bookhunter need only meander into one of the many bookshops that liberally dot the town. And with a human-to-bookstore ratio of around 40:1, there's a lot of choice. Mystery aficionados should check out Murder & Mayhem, while a visit to The Poetry Bookshop is de rigueur for fans of verse. One of the largest and most diverse collections can be found at the Hay Cinema Bookshop – rickety mini-stairways, two sprawling floors and a labyrinthine series of rooms loosely divided by subject matter create a unique book-browsing space that seems to exist outside the space-time continuum for the way in which it can so wholly consume an afternoon. Stay long enough and your faith that there's an underlying logic to the bookshelves' progression from "Fifteenth-century Russian History" to "British Water Fowl" to "Erotica" will grow wonderfully, psychotically strong.

Topic-driven pilgrimages aside, a visit to the two outdoor used bookstores in front of crumbling Hay Castle is unmissable. Ringed by stone ramparts, the castle – nearly 1000 years old – provides a striking backdrop as you rifle through scads of books eclectic in appearance as much as theme.

021 FEELING INSIGNIFICANT AT THE BRITISH MUSEUM

ENGLAND The first thing that strikes you about the British Museum is its enormous size. From the moment you step through the gates into the sprawling front courtyard and gaze up at the imposing Greek Revival portico with its towering Ionic columns, you are humbled. With 2.5 miles of exhibits that span civilizations across the globe from ancient times to the modern day, this museum is not to be sniffed at.

Head to the Great Court, where gleaming white stone and sleek marble floors reflect the light streaming down through the state-of-the-art glass-and-steel roof; the bright white glare reflecting off every shiny surface is almost blinding. Straight ahead, the central Round Reading Room, a remnant of the British Library that originally resided here, offers old-fashioned solace in the midst of this stark modernity. Its small door beckons you in to a space of wood-panelled, book-lined walls enclosed by an immense dome, which towers overhead in soothing hues of pale sky blue and eggshell white.

Move on to the exhibit galleries, where you'll encounter an entirely different type of largesse; here, in the endless labyrinth of display rooms, the achievements of past civilizations cannot fail to instil a sense of awe. As you crane your neck to take in the full height of the Greeks' gargantuan statues and admire the skilfully carved friezes Lord Elgin pilfered from the Parthenon, it's easy to feel belittled by the sheer grandeur of it all; cowering in front of the perfectly preserved Egyptian mummies and soaking up the significance of the code-breaking Rosetta Stone, you can almost feel the vast weight of history pressing down upon you. Hours later you re-enter the modern world through the colonnaded portico feeling exhausted and a great deal less important, yet exhilarated by the marvels mankind has wrought.

022 HIKING IN SNOWDONIA

WALES Though the mountains of Snowdonia rarely poke above 3000ft, they exhibit a rugged majesty quite out of keeping with that statistic. This tightly packed kernel of soaring cliff faces, jagged pinnacles and plunging waterfalls fills only a tiny corner of North Wales, and yet people find enough great hiking here to keep them coming back for years.

As you'd expect, the focus is on Snowdon itself, the highest mountain south of the Scottish Grampians. Its peak is at the apex of a grand cirque whose lofty peaks are linked by knife-edge ridges. Half a dozen well-trodden paths lead to the top, some following gentle grassy slopes, others taking increasingly intricate routes that demand good balance and a head for heights.

Snowdon is undoubtedly one of Britain's finest mountains, but hardened hikers are often heard complaining about the cog railway that runs from the town of Llanberis to the café, bar and post office at the top. No matter that it's been there for a century, they'd rather hike something less tainted. And they don't come much purer than Tryfan (3200ft), allegedly the only mountain in Wales you can't climb without using your hands. At the blocky summit mound, you'll find Adam and Eve, two monoliths about six feet high and three feet apart. They say if you jump between them you will gain the "Freedom of Tryfan". The jump itself is trivial enough, but the consequences of overshooting don't bear thinking about.

023 DAYDREAMING IN OXFORD

ENGLAND Christchurch meadow at dusk and my timing is impeccable. The light is perfect – the harsh midday sun has softened, and now, rather than glinting off the spires and turrets of Merton and Corpus Christi colleges, it seems almost to embrace them, revealing their sharp angles and intricate carvings. They jut proudly above the quiet parklands and sports grounds, and the majestic Tom Tower of Christchurch presides graciously over the centre of Oxford. The noise of the city centre (just minutes to the north) has melted away, and I pause for a second, hoping to preserve the moment. This is Oxford University at its best; the time when its touristy title "the city of dreaming spires" doesn't seem so overblown after all.

Such fleeting glimpses of this centuries-old seat of learning, right in the midst of a thoroughly modern city, are both disarming and exhilarating. For a brief time, the colleges shed any contemporary associations and you can imagine what it would have been like to study here, long before cars clogged the narrow streets and camera-toting tourists swarmed amongst the cloisters. The spires acquire a greater significance, appearing to reach up, high into the sky, almost signifying the pursuit of knowledge.

Back at ground level there's plenty more to stimulate the imagination and fire up the intellect. Wander down Oxford's narrow alleys and into its quiet corners, where you'll feel the presence of generations of scholars who've gone before. Duck into the Eagle and Child pub, where J.R.R. Tolkien and C.S. Lewis hobnobbed; stroll the echoing walkways of Magdalen College, through which politician William Hague and Nobel Laureate Seamus Heaney rushed to tutorials; and visit the cavernous dining hall at Christchurch, where the likes of John Locke and Albert Einstein once ate but which is now more famous as Hogwart's hall in the Harry Potter films. In Oxford, however, facts are far better than fiction.

ENGLAND Is Holkham Bay in north Norfolk the best beach in Britain? It must certainly be the broadest. At high tide, you follow the private road from Holkham Hall, walk through a stretch of woods and expect to find the sea at your feet. But it is – literally – miles away: two miles at the very least, shimmering beyond a huge expanse of dunes, pools, flat sands and salt marsh. If it's your first visit, it may seem oddly familiar – for this was the location for Gwyneth Paltrow's walk along the sands, as Viola, at the end of *Shakespeare in Love*.

The amazing thing about Holkham is that, even with the filming of a Hollywood movie in full swing, you could have wandered onto the beach and not noticed. It is that big. You saunter off from the crowds near the road's end and within a few minutes you're on your own, splashing through tidal pools, picking up the odd shell, or – if it's warm enough – diving into the sea. You can walk along the beach all the way to Wells (to the east) or Overy Staithe (west), or drop back from the sea and follow trails through woods of Corsican pines. Just beware going out onto the sandbanks when there's a rising tide; it comes in alarmingly fast.

Birdlife is exceptional around Holkham – which is a protected reserve – and you'll see colonies of Brent geese, chattering and little terns, and many other birds. And if you head down the coast to Cley-next-the-Sea or to Blakeney, you'll find even more riches, accompanied by rows of twitchers, camped behind binoculars. Take time to walk out to the hides at Cley Marshes, or for a boat ride to Blakeney Point, where you can watch up to 400 common and grey seals basking on the mud.

HOLKHAM MAGIC

024

025 TOASTING BAD WEATHER IN THE SCOTTISH HIGHLANDS

SCOTLAND First, be glad that it rains so much in Scotland. Without the rain the rivers here wouldn't run – the Livet, the Fiddich, the Spey. Without the rain the glens wouldn't be green and the barley wouldn't grow tall and plump.

Be glad it's damp here in Scotland. Peat needs a few centuries sitting in a bog to come out right. Then a breeze, and a wee bit of sun, to dry it. You burn it, with that delicious reek – the aroma – to dry the malted barley. Earth, wind and fire.

And be glad it's cold here too. Whisky was being made in these hills for centuries before refrigeration. Cool water to condense the spirit. After all, if you're going to leave liquid sitting around in wooden barrels for ten or more years, you don't want it too warm. The evaporation – the angels' share – is bad enough. Still, it makes the idea of "taking the air" in Speyside rather more appealing.

And if it weren't cold and wet and damp, you wouldn't appreciate being beside that roaring fire and feeling the taste for something to warm the cockles. Here's a heavy glass for that dram, that measure. How much? More than a splash, not quite a full pour. Look at the colour of it: old gold.

Taste it with your nose first; a whisky expert is called a "noser" rather than a "taster". Single malts have all sorts of smells and subtleties and flavours: grass, biscuits, vanilla, some sweet dried fruit, a bit of peat smoke. Drinking it is just the final act.

Aye, with a wee splash of water. The spirit overpowers your tastebuds otherwise. A drop, to soften it, unlock the flavours. Not sacrilege – the secret. Water.

Is it still raining?

Let me pour you another.

026 MOUNTAIN BIKING WELSH TRAILS

WALES It's not often that the modest mountains of Wales can compete with giants like the Alps or the Rockies, but when it comes to mountain biking, the trails that run through the craggy peaks of Snowdonia, the high moorlands of the Cambrian Mountains, and the deep, green valleys of South Wales are more than a match for their loftier counterparts. Indeed, the International Mountain Biking Association has long rated Wales as one of the planet's top destinations.

Over the last decade or so, a series of purpose-built mountain-biking centres has been created throughout the Principality, providing world-class riding for everyone from rank beginner through to potential world-cup downhiller. From easy, gently undulating trails along former rail lines that once served the heavy industry of the South Wales valleys to the steep, rooty, rocky single tracks that run through the cloud-shadowed hills of North Wales, this is mountain biking at its finest.

Take a centre such as Coed-y-Brenin in Snowdonia National Park. You can ride all day here through deep pine forests, beside tumbling cascades, and alongside open pastures whose vistas stretch from the blue-green water of the Irish Sea to the misty mountain tops of the Snowdon range – and that will just cover a couple of trails at only one of seven mountain-bike centres located around the country.

The tracks have been designed to be ridden year round – despite the country's (somewhat) undeserved reputation for inclement weather, Welsh trails, like Welsh riders, can deal with anything that's thrown at them, and they remain open in all conditions. That's not to say you should wait for the next downpour – hit the trails when the sun is shining, when the views stretch far into the distance, and you'll begin to understand why this really is some of the finest mountain biking on earth.

027 HORSING ABOUT AT THE COMMON RIDINGS

SCOTLAND The Common Ridings of the Scottish Border towns of Hawick, Selkirk, Jedburgh and Lauder are one of Britain's best-kept secrets. Commemorating the days when the Scots needed early warnings of attacks from their expansionist neighbours, the focus of each event is a dawn horseback patrol of the commons and fields that mark each town's boundaries – an equestrian extravaganza that combines the danger of Pamplona's Fiesta de San Fermin and the drinking of Munich's Oktoberfest. Selkirk may boast the largest number of riders, and Lauder might be the oldest event, but Hawick is always the first – and the best attended – of them all.

At dawn on each day of the ridings, a colourful and incredibly noisy drum and fife band marches around the streets to shake people from their sleep and, more importantly, to allow plenty of time for the riders, and virtually the entire town population,

to get down to the pub – they open at 6am – and stock up on the traditional breakfast of "Curds and Cream" (rum and milk). Suitably fortified, the riders – numbering some two hundred, and all exquisitely attired in cream jodhpurs, black riding boots, tweed jackets and white silk neckerchiefs – mount their horses and gallop at breakneck speed around the ancient lanes and narrow streets of town, before heading out into the fields to continue the racing in a slightly more organized manner.

By early evening, and with the racing done for the day, the spectators and riders stagger back into Harwick to re-acquaint themselves with the town's pubs, an activity that most people approach with gusto. Stumbling out onto the street at well past midnight, you should have just enough time for an hour or two of shuteye before the fife band strikes up once more and it's time to do it all over again.

028 DRESSING UP FOR ROYAL ASCOT

ENGLAND Picture the scene: the pop and fizz of hundreds of champagne bottles, the sweet smell of trampled grass, show-stopping millinery, royalty and celebrities mingling cheerfully with the crowds, and, of course, the steaming coats of snorting, cavorting thoroughbreds. You couldn't be anywhere other than Royal Ascot.

Featuring the very best horses and jockeys from all over the globe, Royal Ascot is the cream of British horseracing – speed, agility and nail-biting finishes, this is entertainment in pure equine form. None of the five days' races are commercially sponsored, and many reflect their regal origins: the Queen Anne Stakes (the first race of the meeting, in honour of the course's founder), the Coronation Stakes and the Queen's Vase (named for the accession of Queen Victoria). Each day at 2pm sharp, the present-day queen, a racehorse owner herself, helps put the "Royal" in "Royal Ascot" as she arrives in an open-top horse-drawn carriage, leading a procession from Windsor Castle down the middle of the course.

Ascot may be the world's finest horseracing meet, but the majority of people are here for the social scene, the fine dining and the fashion show. Come equipped with a killer outfit – and an equally killer hat (the bigger, and more outrageous, the better) – and you'll fit right in. All that remains is to pack a sumptuous picnic, to be munched with friends by the side of the car (preferably a Porsche). But if you'd rather avoid the stress of providing your own fancy fodder, dine on lobster, smoked salmon or beef in one of the restaurants, accompanied by a bottle of champagne – just one of the 170,000 that'll be quaffed that day. Good going, isn't it?

029 BARGING DOWN THE BARROW

IRELAND There's a point on the river Barrow in County Kildare, about halfway between the country towns of Athy and Carlow, when you realize that you're in the middle of absolutely nowhere. A quick flick of the engine into neutral and you're surrounded by silence, nothing but the soothing slosh of water as the barge's bow glides slowly through the reeds. Flanked on both sides by trees and rolling fields of verdant emerald green, there's only one thing to do: sit back and soak up the solitude.

For nearly two hundred years, steel-boarded barges have plied the Grand Canal network, first transporting peat to Dublin and beyond, and latterly ferrying holidaymakers through the languid countryside. A week spent cruising along the Grand Canal and down the river Barrow, one of the most beautiful navigable stretches in Europe, is time spent recharging the soul: after a few early-morning maintenance checks, just undo the moorings, start up the engine and off you go, slowly chugging your way to the next ruined castle or cosy local.

Idle days make for idle ways, and the beauty of barging is that you have to do very little to keep your thirty-foot vessel on the straight and narrow. Manoeuvring through a set of double locks without taking the whole thing with you provides a brief lull in the languor – racks have to be cranked, sluices opened and pawls closed, all while the driver holds the barge steady to avoid getting beached on the back sill – but the rest of the day is spent cruising the backwaters of middle Ireland at a leisurely 5mph.

But if you're going to get nowhere fast, there can surely be fewer places better than the Barrow. Yellow iris, cuckooflower and heavily scented meadowsweet line the river banks, herons let your barge get tantalizingly close before launching off across the water, and there's a traditional pub at every turn, each serving finer Guinness than the last.

030 SURFING THE SEVERN BORE

ENGLAND Autumn mist swirls across the placid waters of the River Severn, and a kingfisher flits along the riverbank in a spark of colour. Gradually, from downriver, a noise like the murmuring of a distant crowd develops into a roar, then suddenly a mighty brown wave of water appears across the entire width of the river, topped here and there by a creamy curl where the wave is racing to get ahead of itself.

This is the Severn Bore, one of the longest and biggest tidal bores in the world. It's an alarming sight when you're watching from the riverbank. If you're actually in the river, it can be terrifying.

The river, though, is where you'll be if you choose to surf the Bore. Since the Sixties, surfers from all over the world have made their way to the Severn to catch this remarkable wave. It occurs on the biggest tides of the year when Atlantic waters from the Bristol Channel surge up the Severn estuary at as much as 12mph and become funnelled between the ever-narrowing river banks to create one of the UK's most bizarre natural spectacles.

If the equinoxes coincide with big Atlantic swells, the wave may be as much as six feet high, tearing off overhanging tree branches, sweeping away sections of river bank and providing a ride that can last for several miles. It's a challenge even for a competent surfer. Non-surfers will want to stay bankside, from where the Bore is simply a strange and magnificent sight.

031
HIKING THE
PENNINE
WAY

ENGLAND After two weeks' walking through rain and shine (and with moods to match), the final day of the Pennine Way, Britain's oldest and longest long-distance footpath, is upon you: a 27-mile marathon over the desolate Cheviot Hills. It's a challenging finale but the narcotic effects of mounting euphoria ought to numb your multiple aches. Anyway, if you're one of the few who've made it this far, you'll not give up now.

The Pennine Way begins at the village of Edale in Derbyshire's Peak District and meanders 270 miles north to Kirk Yetholm beneath the Cheviot Hills and a mile across the Scottish border. Along its course, it leads through some of England's most beautiful and least crowded countryside. In the early stages, it passes the birthplace of the English Industrial Revolution, and today stone slabs from the derelict mills and factories have been recycled into winding causeways over the once notorious moorland peat bogs. This is Brontë country, too, grim on a dank, misty day but bleakly inspiring when the cloud lifts.

The mires subside to become the rolling green pastures and dry-stone walls of the Yorkshire Dales that rise up to striking peaks like the 2278-ft (694m) high Pen y ghent – the "Mountain of the Winds".

The limestone Dales in turn become the wilder northern Pennines, where no one forgets stumbling onto the astounding glaciated abyss of High Cup Nick. The Way's final phase begins with an invigorating stage along the 2000-year-old Hadrian's Wall before ending with the calf-wrenching climax over the Cheviots.

Walking the wilds is exhilarating but staying in pretty villages along the way is also a highlight. Again and again you'll find yourself transported back to a bygone rural idyll of village shops, church bells and, of course, the pub. Memories of mud and glory will pass before your eyes as you stagger the last few yards onto Kirk Yetholm's village green, stuff your reviled backpack in the garbage and turn towards the inviting bar at the *Border Hotel*.

032 LEARNING TO SURVIVE IN DEEPEST DORSET

ENGLAND It looked like something Bilbo Baggins might have kept his compost in. But for me, and the couple of other bushcraft students, the forest pod proved a very cosy shelter indeed. We'd spent most of the previous afternoon learning how to build it from deadwood gathered off the floor of our coppice in Dorset. Clad in leafy branches of beech and chestnut, with a low opening as an entrance, it must have been pretty close to what our ancestors would have put together on hunting trips thousands of years ago.

Reviving lost survival techniques as a means to getting closer to nature is very much the underlying goal of Bushcraft Week. Our instructor, Andy "Woody" Wood, is an ex-military man who has spent years living, travelling and hunting with indigenous people, from the polar ice cap to the Kalahari, soaking up their wilderness skills and, in the process, re-kindling in himself a more intimate relationship with his native British environment.

Under Woody's expert guidance we learn the correct way to lay fires and how to use naturally flammable fungus to light them; how to dig out an earth oven to cook in; and select wood that becomes hot coals instead of tinder when lit. For implements, we're taught Scandinavian carving methods and shown ways to turn brass picture-framing wire into lethal rabbit snares. Thankfully, these are never laid, but one day we're given a sack of dead bunnies to skin, dress and cook, along with pot herbs we gather from the forest.

After a week amid the greenery, I emerge a more contented creature than I was before, smelling strongly of woodsmoke and roast rabbit but seeing the world – or, at least, the bits of it covered in trees instead of tarmac – in an altogether different light. And you never know: in these times of melting icebergs and rising water levels, with skills that might just come in useful one day.

033 ON THE FIDDLE: ATTENDING A TRADITIONAL IRISH MUSIC SESSION

IRELAND I've lost count of the times I've asked a publican in Ireland where to find a decent music session only to hear the sighing retort, "Ah, you should have been here last night", usually conjoined with the opinion that "the craic was doing ninety". The "craic" in question is a reference to taking your spirits to a higher plain, though not by pharmaceutical methods – it's simply an indefinable moment when good company, conversation, laughter and music all combine into one hell of an evening.

Truth be told, you can follow the "official" sessions listings and hang around the best festivals until the end of time, but you'll rarely encounter that moment when cooking whisky becomes the finest malt. For the best sessions happen when you least expect them, and often in the unlikeliest places.

I'd been up in North Donegal, investigating the bluff and breezy headlands, and decided to pitch my tent on a campsite near Downings, a place blessed by a glorious swirling curve of sandy beach. The midges were at their hungriest, but once my evening meal was done and dusted, I decided to investigate the harbour. It was a pleasant spot indeed, and, on the way back, I called into a local pub. I left eight hours later. Memories are blurred, but I do recall an inordinate number of conversations about everything from US foreign policy to the price of fish in Kilkeel. But the ultimate and utter high point of the evening was provided by a group of musicians who unexpectedly turned up at around 10.30pm and proceeded to play and sing to their hearts' delight well into the small hours.

We sang, we danced and I ended up sleeping in the wrong tent, but that was OK, since the person I'd usurped slept in mine.

034 CALLING IN THE HEAVIES AT THE
HIGHLAND GAMES

SCOTLAND Throughout Scotland, not just in the Highlands, summer signals the onset of the Highland Games, from the smallest village get-togethers to the Giant Cowal Highland Gathering in Dunoon, which draws a crowd of 10,000. Urbanistas might blanch at the idea of al fresco Scottish country dancing, but with dog trials, tractors, fudge stalls and more cute animals than you could toss a caber at, the Highland Games are a guaranteed paradise for kids.

It's thought that the games originated in the eleventh century as a means of selecting soldiers through trials of strength and endurance. These events were formalized in the nineteenth century, partly as a result of Queen Victoria's romantic attachment to Highland culture, a culture that had in reality been brutally extinguished following the defeat of the Jacobites at Culloden.

The military origins of the games are recalled in displays of muscle - power by bulky be-kilted local men, from tossing the caber (ie tree trunk) to hurling hammers and stones, and pitching bales of straw over a raised pole. Music and dance are also integral to the games, with pipe bands and small girls – kitted out in waistcoats, kilts and long woolly socks – performing reels and sword dances. You might also see horsejumping, as well as sheepdogs being put through their paces, while the agricultural shows feature prize animals, from sleek ponies with intricate bows tied in their manes and tails to curly horned-rams.

035 BURNING RUBBER AT THE ISLE OF MAN TT

ENGLAND For fifty weeks of the year, the Isle of Man is a sleepy little place. Locals leave their doors unlocked, they stop to chat in the street, and they know the name of their next-door neighbour's cat. But for two weeks in summer, everything changes, as forty thousand visitors – with twelve thousand motorcycles – cross the Irish Sea and turn this quiet island into a rubber-burning, beer-swilling, eardrum-busting maelstrom of a motorcycle festival.

The TT (Tourist Trophy) has been screeching round the Isle of Man for a hundred years, but only came about thanks to the island's political peculiarity. The Isle of Man is a Crown dependency but not a part of the UK or the EU – it has its own parliament and its own laws. And so when, in the early days of the automobile, the UK forbade motor racing on its public roads and imposed a speed limit of 20mph, race organizers made their way over the water.

And they've never left, although the race they devised in 1907 would be impossible to initiate today. It's the kind of event that drives health and safety officers to drink: the 37-mile Mountain Course, which competitors lap several times, is no carefully cambered track – it's an ordinary road that winds its way through historic towns, screams along country roads, climbs hills and takes in two hundred bends, many of which are not lined by grass or pavement but by bone-mashing, brain-spilling brick walls. And the fastest riders complete the course at an average speed of 120mph.

Sad to say, they don't all reach the finish line. Around two hundred riders have taken their final tumble on the roads of the TT, and islanders will delight in describing the details to you over a pint of local Bushey's beer. They'll also tell you that, while many of their fellow Manx folk love the adrenalin, the triumph and the tragedy of those two weeks in summer, others are less enthusiastic. The combination of road closures and roistering bikers drives these malcontents to blow the dust from their door keys, to lock up their homes and seek refuge elsewhere – taking their daughters with them.

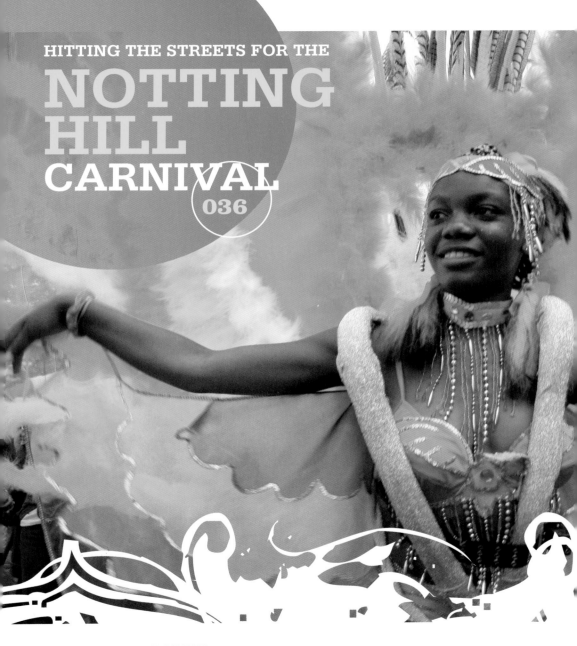

HITTING THE STREETS FOR THE
NOTTING HILL CARNIVAL
036

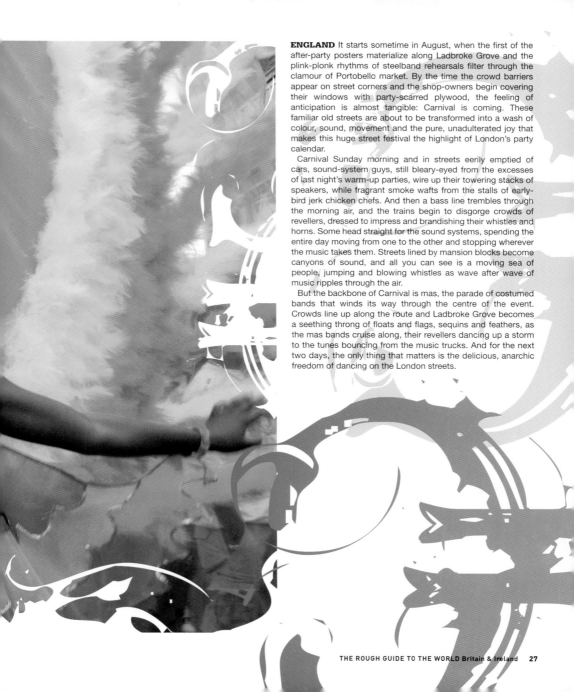

ENGLAND It starts sometime in August, when the first of the after-party posters materialize along Ladbroke Grove and the plink-plonk rhythms of steelband rehearsals filter through the clamour of Portobello market. By the time the crowd barriers appear on street corners and the shop-owners begin covering their windows with party-scarred plywood, the feeling of anticipation is almost tangible: Carnival is coming. These familiar old streets are about to be transformed into a wash of colour, sound, movement and the pure, unadulterated joy that makes this huge street festival the highlight of London's party calendar.

Carnival Sunday morning and in streets eerily emptied of cars, sound-system guys, still bleary-eyed from the excesses of last night's warm-up parties, wire up their towering stacks of speakers, while fragrant smoke wafts from the stalls of early-bird jerk chicken chefs. And then a bass line trembles through the morning air, and the trains begin to disgorge crowds of revellers, dressed to impress and brandishing their whistles and horns. Some head straight for the sound systems, spending the entire day moving from one to the other and stopping wherever the music takes them. Streets lined by mansion blocks become canyons of sound, and all you can see is a moving sea of people, jumping and blowing whistles as wave after wave of music ripples through the air.

But the backbone of Carnival is mas, the parade of costumed bands that winds its way through the centre of the event. Crowds line up along the route and Ladbroke Grove becomes a seething throng of floats and flags, sequins and feathers, as the mas bands cruise along, their revellers dancing up a storm to the tunes bouncing from the music trucks. And for the next two days, the only thing that matters is the delicious, anarchic freedom of dancing on the London streets.

037 CYCLING IN THE NEW FOREST

ENGLAND Covering a wedge of land between Bournemouth, Southampton and the English Channel, the New Forest offers some of Britain's most exhilarating cycling country, with a chance to lose yourself amid a network of roads, gravelled paths and bridleways, and 150 miles of car-free cycle tracks. Here, you can indulge your wild side, surrounded by a leafy world remote from modern-day stresses. Spring brings budding growth to the area and the ground is swathed in delicate colour, while autumn paints the forest in gorgeous hues of red and brown. Your travels will take you past tidy thatched cottages on quiet wooded lanes onto exposed heathland with magnificent views and dotted with deer. The 40mph speed limit on forest roads makes for a safe and unhassled ride, picnic spots are ubiquitous, and the occasional pub provides more substantial refreshment.

England's newest national park has been a protected wilderness for nigh on a thousand years: William the Conqueror appropriated the area as a hunting reserve (his son, William Rufus, was killed here by an arrow in an apparent accident). The area has changed little since Norman times, and is a superb place to spot wildlife: amid terrain ranging from thick woodland to bogs, heath and grassland strewn with bracken and gorse, the forest is home to around 2000 fallow, roe, red and sika deer, not to mention some 3000 wild ponies, and numerous sheep, cattle, pigs and donkeys.

Park up the car, and pedal off; go fast or take your time; map out routes or ride at random – you're the boss on this invigorating escape into freedom.

038 SEE THE BELFAST MURALS

NORTHERN IRELAND Mention the Falls Road and Shankill districts of Belfast, and up flash images of bitter sectarian street battles between the pro-British, Protestant Loyalists and the pro-Irish, largely Catholic Republicans.

These close neighbours have long used wall paintings to stake territorial claims, and now that Belfast is back on the tourist agenda, the murals have become a star attraction.

Walking west from central Belfast to the Republican Falls Road, you can't miss the huge painted images adorning almost all end-terrace walls. Some are tributes to the fallen, while others commemorate specific incidents such as the 1981 prison hunger strike when Bobby Sands became a Republican martyr, along with nine comrades. Elsewhere, "Free Ireland" slogans depict wrists shackled by manacles labelled "Made in Britain". The message could hardly be clearer.

A few steps up the side streets north of the Falls Road you

hit the Peace Line, a fortified boundary of razor wire and CCTV cameras that separates the road from Loyalist Shankill. The heavy steel gates are now left open, hopefully permanently.

There's an altogether more militaristic feel to Shankill, with guns on almost every mural. Union Jacks are ubiquitous, even on the kerbstones, and one whole housing estate is ringed by red, white and blue kerbing. Most murals also bear the red hand of Ulster, which forms the centrepiece of the Ulster Flag and features on the emblems of both the UVF and UDA paramilitary organizations.

In these districts, passions run high and you'd think it would feel unsettling being a rubbernecking tourist in a place that has witnessed so much bloodshed. But most people are just pleased that you're interested. If you feel at all intimidated or want a deeper insight, opt for one of the excellent taxi tours that visit both districts.

039 SURFING IN NEWQUAY

ENGLAND With surf culture currently enjoying a huge upsurge in Britain, the time is right to wax down your board and slip on a wetsuit. New punters and dedicated surf dudes alike are finding breaks in all kinds of unlikely places, but the Cornwall town of Newquay retains its place as capital of the UK surf scene. Its eleven beaches of fine sand stretching over seven miles are regularly pounded by mighty Atlantic swell, which has travelled over 3000 uninterrupted miles to provide surfers with the kind of rides that make all the salt spray, paddling and "pearls" (tumbling off the front of the board when trying to stand up) worthwhile. It may not have the climate of Bondi, Malibu or Waikiki, but wind, tide and currents combine here to create perfect conditions, making Newquay the venue for regular competitions that draw pros from Australia, the US and Japan, as well as Europe.

Newquay's beaches accommodate every level: serious aficionados and intermediates head for west-facing Fistral, which has waves at all stages but is best at low tide – beachside showers here add to its appeal – while novices, body boarders and Malibu boarders find the sheltered beaches of Towan, Great Western, Tolcarne and Lusty Glaze more appealing. These town beaches mostly face north or northwest and so get fewer breaks than Fistral, although a big southwest swell can pick things up considerably. When these shores get too congested for comfort, head up to Watergate Bay, home to the Extreme Academy (for more hardcore outdoor activities such as kitesurfing and waveskiing), a couple of funky restaurants and acres of empty sands. Such is the lure of surf that people come to Newquay with a bucket and spade, and leave with a board.

PLAYING THE OLD COURSE AT ST ANDREWS

SCOTLAND There are a several places where you have to play a round at least once to call yourself a true golf devotee – Pine Valley, Pebble Beach and Augusta National – but the Old Course at St Andrews is still the one. Just walking out onto the first tee sends shivers down the spine, thinking how many feet, legendary or otherwise, have squared up to send a ball hurtling into the blustery winds before you.

St Andrews is the "home of golf", the game's equivalent of Wembley or Wimbledon, a venue that is part of the mythology of the sport. The contemporary view may be that golf courses should be manufactured, created and sculpted, but St Andrews had a very special designer: Mother Nature. The landscape is the course. It may not have the charm or the aesthetics of its American counterparts but it has real character. There's barely a tree to be seen, which makes it differ atmospherically from many modern courses. Similarly, there's little water around,

aside from Swilcan Burn that has to be traversed on the 18th fairway and the adjacent bruise-black waters of the North Sea. This perceived lack of obstacles doesn't mean there's little to test the most experienced of players; the course is filled with hidden humps, bumps and dips, and there are man-made challenges, too – the infamous Road Hole Bunker on the 17th being the most notorious. Any obstacle that requires a ladder to escape from must be pretty hardcore.

They've been teeing off here for around three hundred years and you'd guess it hasn't changed much at all, which is one of the things that makes this such a unique sporting experience. Be sure to take a local caddie, though – that way, he can worry about whether you should be using a 9-iron or a pitching wedge, and you can concentrate on absorbing the significance of it all.

041 BREATHING IN THE SEA AIR IN TOBERMORY

SCOTLAND On the old stone fishing pier in Tobermory on the island of Mull, a very affordable indulgence is available: queue at the fish and chip van and order a scallop supper. It'll be served in brown paper, just like the classic (but more mundane) takeaway fish and chips, and you'll probably have to perch on the harbour wall to eat them, but you get a meal of steaming chips and sweet, tender scallops, gathered from the surrounding waters a few hours previously, as well as free views across the prettiest port on the west coast of Scotland.

Close by, fishing boats are tied up at the pier, pyramids of lobster creels piled up in their sterns. Out in the bay, yachts sit on their moorings, while large inflatable boats with deep-throated outboard engines circle near the jetty, ready to take passengers on an evening spin out into the surrounding waters to look for seals, porpoises, dolphins, basking sharks and, quite possibly, minke or killer whales.

Along the waterfront, prominent tall houses are painted in vibrant blue, pink, yellow, red or gleaming white. No matter what the weather, they're an uplifting, if slightly garish, sight. The rest of the village – the grand castellated hotel, cosy guesthouses, the arts centre with its background vibe of uplifting Gaelic songs – is perched on a hillside that rises sharply from the water. Toil up the short but steep switchback roads of the upper village and you'll be treated to increasingly impressive views of the bay, the wave-creased Sound of Mull and empty hills beyond. Venture even further, across the heathery golf course on the fringes of the village, and dramatic glimpses of the strewn islands and ragged coast to the north and west begin to appear. It's not a bad way to walk off supper.

042 SOAKING UP THE EDINBURGH FESTIVAL

SCOTLAND People talk about culture vultures flocking to the Edinburgh Festival in August, but the truth is that for an event this big you need the stamina of an ox, the appetite of a hippo and the nocturnal characteristics of an owl. The sheer scale and diversity of what's going on in the Scottish capital each August can be hard to digest properly – over half a dozen separate festivals taking place simultaneously, some 1500 different shows each day, across 200 different venues. Not to mention the street acts, the buskers, the bizarrely dressed leafleters – and the simple fascination to be had just watching it all swirl around you.

How do you do the Festival without fear of disappointment or exhaustion? Book early for something significant in the International Festival, perhaps one of the world's great Philharmonic orchestras at the Usher Hall. Wander into the tented Book Festival in gracious Charlotte Square and enjoy a reading and erudite discussion with a favourite author. Take a chance on an intriguing-sounding piece of theatre by a company you've never heard of in a venue you struggle to find. After all, you've scoured the reviews in the papers over a couple of cappuccinos in a pleasant café and found a four-star show you can fit in before the new film by that director you've admired for a while.

Pick up a last-minute offer on cheap tickets for a comedian you've seen do a nearly hilarious slot on telly, then join the crowds shuffling up the Royal Mile to the nightly Military Tattoo, thrilling its multinational audience with pomp, ceremony and massed pipe bands, rounded off with fireworks crashing around the castle's battlements.

Time for more? There's probably a risqué cabaret going on at one of the Fringe venues, or a crazy Hungarian folk band stomping its way into the wee small hours in a folk club. But if you're going to do it all again tomorrow, then find a quiet corner of a cosy, wood-panelled pub and order a dram of whisky. Good stuff, this culture.

043 LOSING YOURSELF IN CONNEMARA

IRELAND On the far western edge of Europe, the starkly beautiful region of Connemara is a great place to get lost. Cut off from the rest of Ireland by the 25-mile barrier of Lough Corrib, the lie of the land at first looks simple, with two statuesque mountain ranges, the Maam Turks and the Twelve Bens, bordered by the deep fjord of Killary Harbour to the north. The coast, however, is full of jinks and tricks, a hopeless maze of inlets, peninsulas and small islands. Dozens of sparkling lakes and vast blanket bogs covered in purple moor grass further blur the distinction between land and water. Throw in a fickle climate, which can turn from blazing sunshine to grey, soaking mist in the time it takes to buy a loaf of bread, and the carefree sense of disorientation is complete.

This austere, infertile land was brutally depopulated by starvation, eviction and emigration during the Great Famine of the 1840s. Even when dramatist J.M. Synge visited in the early twentieth century, he considered any farming here to be like "the freak of an eccentric". Today, these wild and lonely margins are the ultimate fulfilment of visitors' romantic dreams of Ireland, with enough variety to warrant weeks of exploration.

Cycling on the quiet backroads – many of which were built to provide employment during the Famine – is probably the best way to get to know the area. At an even gentler pace, the outlandishly contorted geology provides great diversity for walkers, ranging from tough, high-level treks in the mountains to scenic hikes up isolated hummocks such as Errisbeg and Tully Hill.

044 CLUBBING IN LONDON

ENGLAND From superclubs to sweaty backrooms, hiphop to hardcore, there's a London club-night guaranteed to get you throwing shapes on the dance floor. Institutions such as *Fabric* and *Ministry of Sound* are pricey, but well worth it to experience world-famous DJs on knee-tremblingly loud sound systems: buy tickets in advance to avoid the three-hour queues. For a less commercial, more spontaneous vibe, keep an ear cocked for pounding bass lines next time you're strolling past Festival Pier, on the South Bank. When the tide is out, free parties periodically pop up on the grubby strip of sand, attracting a diverse mix of grungy ravers and passing tourists.

North, south, east or west? Partisan local opinion is divided. In a trio of clubs hidden north amongst the industrial wasteland behind King's Cross, a smart international crowd go mad for any kind of house music, whether funky or Ibiza euphoric.

South of the river, the holy meets the hedonistic in the crypt beneath Brixton's St Matthew's Church, which hosts regular drum 'n' bass, hard tech house and trance nights. Clubbing out east veers on the theatrical, with trendy Hoxtonites striding out in vintage frocks, flat caps and dramatic make-up, as indie, pop and electro collide in weird and wonderful ways. Meanwhile, small venues and scruffy boho chic are the order of the day west in Notting Hill, with an eclectic soundtrack of soulful funk, broken beat and world music.

After-parties used to be word-of-mouth affairs, but thanks to 24-hour licensing there's now a whole host of excuses to avoid going to bed. Amongst the dedicated party people who've been out since Friday, you'll spot a fair few fresh faces who have got up on Sunday morning to go straight to a club. Whatever day of the week, there's absolutely no excuse for staying in.

045 GETTING AWAY FROM IT ALL O N SKELLIG MICHAEL

IRELAND The jagged twin pyramids of the Skellig Islands rise abruptly out of the Atlantic Ocean, six miles off the southwest tip of Ireland. Little Skellig is a teeming, noisy bird sanctuary, home to around 50,000 gannets and now officially full (the excess have had to move to another island off County Wexford). In tranquil contrast, neighbouring Skellig Michael shelters one of the most remarkable hermitages in the world.

In the late seventh or early eighth century, a monastery was somehow built on this inhospitable outcrop, in imitation of the desert communities of the early Church fathers – and indeed, continuing the practices of Ireland's druids, who would spend long periods alone in the wilderness. Its design is a miracle of ingenuity and devotion. On small artificial terraces, the dry-stone beehive huts were ringed by sturdy outer walls, which deflected the howling winds and protected the vegetable patch made of bird droppings; channels crisscrossed the settlement to funnel rainwater into cisterns. Monks – up to fifteen of them

at a time – lived here for nearly five hundred years, withstanding anything the Atlantic could throw at them – including numerous Viking raids. In the twelfth century, however, a climatic change made the seas even rougher, while pressure was brought to bear on old, independent monasteries such as Skellig Michael to conform, and eventually the fathers adopted the Augustinian rule and moved to the mainland.

The beauty of a visit to the island is that it doesn't require a huge leap to imagine how the monks might have lived. You still cross over from the mainland on small, slow boats, huddling against the spray. From the quay, 650 steps climb almost vertically to the monastery, whose cells, chapels and refectory remain largely intact after 1300 years. The island even has residents, at least in the summer: friendly guides, employed by the Office of Public Works to give talks to visitors, stay out here for weeks at a time, making the most of the spiritual solitude.

046 TRUNDLING ALONG THE WEST HIGHLANDS RAILWAY

SCOTLAND Even in a country as scenic as Scotland, you don't expect to combine travelling by train with classic views of the Scottish Highlands; the tracks are down in the glens, after all, tracing the lower contours of the steep-sided scenery. On the other hand, you might be craning your neck, but at least you don't have to keep your eyes on the road. And you can always get out; in fact, some of the stations on the West Highland line are so remote that no public road connects them. At each stop, a handful of deerstalkers, hikers, mountain bikers, photographers or day-trippers might get on or off. It'll be a few hours until the next train comes along, but that's not a problem. There's a lot to take in.

The scenery along the West Highland Railway is both epic in its breadth and compelling in its imagery. You travel at a very sedate pace in a fairly workaday train carriage from the centre of Glasgow and its bold Victorian buildings, along the banks of

the gleaming Clyde estuary, up the thickly wooded loch shores of Argyll, across the desolate heathery bogs of Rannoch Moor and deep into the grand natural architecture of the Central Highlands, their dappled birch forests fringing green slopes and mist-enveloped peaks.

After a couple of hours, the train judders gently into the first of its destinations, Fort William, set at the foot of Britain's highest peak, Ben Nevis. The second leg of the journey is a gradual pull towards the Hebrides. At Glenfinnan, the train glides over an impressive 21-arch viaduct most famous these days for conveying Harry Potter on the *Hogwarts Express*. Not long afterwards, the line reaches the coast, where there are snatched glimpses of bumpy islands and silver sands, before you pull into the fishing port of Mallaig, with seagulls screeching overhead in the stiff, salty breeze, and the shape of Skye emerging from across the sea.

ENGLAND It's not difficult to find Tate Modern. As befits a former power station, the place is huge, forbidding and boasts a 325-foot chimney that towers over the most central section of the Thames. If you're a first timer, however, you need some guidance in order to get the maximum "wow factor" out of your initiation. You don't want to sidle up to the place from the nearest tube (Southwark), and enter via the north door. No, no, no. The right approach is crucial. Get yourself to St Paul's Cathedral, turn your back on Wren's masterpiece and head down Peter's Hill, which leads straight to the Millennium Bridge, perfectly framing the South Bank's cathedral of modern art.

The Millennium Bridge itself is a miracle of sorts: London's first new Thames crossing since Tower Bridge, and the capital's first-ever pedestrian-only bridge. Of course, its greatest claim to fame is as the "wobbly bridge". Unfortunately, the wobbling, which saw the bridge closed for nearly two years just days after its millennial opening, has now been cured, though if there's enough of you, you can always put it to the test.

Once across the river, make your way to Tate Modern's western entrance, from which a long, sloping ramp will take you into the gallery's awe-inspiring Turbine Hall. Each year, the Tate commissions a colossal installation to fill this unique space, everything from a giant winter sun and ceiling mirrors to a curly matrix of oversized playground slides. Inside the main galleries, you'll find every twentieth-century "-ism" represented, from late Impressionism and early Cubism to Abstract Expressionism and Super-Realism, and every major artist, from Monet and Picasso to Joseph Beuys and Mark Rothko. Be warned: by all means dip your feet in, but don't try to see everything at once, and leave enough time to visit the seventh-floor café (for the views).

TAKE A STROLL FROM ST PAUL'S TO TATE MODERN

047

048 CHASING CHEESE IN GLOUCESTER

ENGLAND Cooper's Hill Cheese-Rolling, an organized bout of chasing cheese down a grassy mound in Gloucestershire, is one of Britain's best-known festivals, and possibly its most bizarre – a totem, somehow, of a country of eccentric and long-established events. It's certainly in the best spirit of British amateurism: anyone can enter, and all they have to do is fling themselves down the precipitous hill after an eighteen-pound wheel of Double Gloucester. The first one to reach it wins – and no prizes for guessing what.

049 FREE-DIVING IN THE ROYAL NAVY'S SETT

ENGLAND It's 100 feet deep and filled with warm, clear water. The Royal Navy Submarine Escape Training Tank (SETT) in Gosport does what it says on the label, but it's a perfect place to practise free-diving, with safety ropes for swimmers to hold onto as they fin down in preparation for trying the sport in the sea. Fans of Luc Besson's cult movie *Le Grand Bleu*, spearfishermen and scuba divers all get drawn to free-diving, because it is a purer, simpler form of experiencing the tranquillity of the underwater world – you just hold your breath and go. The training tank is like a giant space rocket filled with shimmering water, luring you to dive into the depths.

050 CATCHING THE LAST NIGHT OF THE PROMS

ENGLAND As much a part of the British summer as strawberries and cream, the Proms can also lay claim to being the biggest classical music festival on the planet, watched by millions around the globe. Eight weeks of daily concerts culminate in the raucous end-of-term party that is the Last Night, when after a relatively light programme of popular classics a 5000-strong audience – including a core of die-hard "Prommers", armed with Union Jacks and klaxons and sporting straw boaters – attempts to raise the roof of London's Royal Albert Hall with rousing patriotic sing-alongs in the *Rule Britannia* vein. Tickets are not easy to get. To apply for Last Night tickets in advance, you need to book for at least six other concerts. If this seems like overkill, join the misty-eyed, flag-waving hordes at the open-air Proms in the Park for big-screen link-ups to the main event in Hyde Park and now in other cities around Britain too. All together now: *"Land of Hope and Glory..."*.

051 WINNING THE PREHISTORIC LOTTERY

IRELAND Every year in Ireland, thousands of people do the Newgrange lottery. Entry is by application form, with the draw made in October by local schoolchildren. And the prize? The lucky winners are invited to a bleak, wintry field in the middle of County Meath on the longest night of the year, to huddle into a dank and claustrophobic tunnel and wait for the sun to come up.

It's not just any old field, though, but part of Brú na Boinne, one of Europe's most important archeological sites. A slow bend in the River Boyne cradles this extraordinary ritual landscape of some forty Neolithic mounds, which served not only as graves but also as spiritual and ceremonial meeting places for the locals, five thousand years ago. The tunnel belongs to the most famous passage mound, Newgrange, which stretches over 273 feet in diameter, weighs 200,000 tons in total and is likely to have taken forty years to build. The lottery winners get to experience the annual astronomical event

for which the tomb's passage was precisely and ingeniously designed: through a roofbox over the entrance, the first rays of the rising sun on the winter solstice shine unerringly into the burial chamber, 65 feet away at the end of the passage in the heart of the mound.

Not everyone gets to win the lottery, of course, so throughout the year as part of an entertaining guided tour of the Newgrange mound, visitors are shown an electrically powered simulation of the solstice dawn in the central chamber. Once you've taken the tour and seen the impressive visitor centre at Brú na Boinne, the perfect complement is then to drive 19 miles west to the Loughcrew Cairns, a group of thirty similar mounds that are largely unexcavated. Here, you borrow a torch and the key to the main passage tomb, Cairn T, and you'll almost certainly have the place to yourself. With views of up to sixteen counties on a clear day, you can let your imagination run wild in an unspoilt and enigmatic landscape.

052 GIGGING IN GLASGOW

SCOTLAND Pop stars, travelling from coach to bar and from plane to arena, are notoriously oblivious about the city they happen to be performing in. There are countless stories of frontmen bellowing "Hello, Detroit!" when they're actually in Toronto. But some places have a genuine buzz about them. London is fine, but all too often its crowds sit back and wait to be impressed. If you want real passion, vibrant venues and bands who really play out of their skin, Glasgow is where it's at.

Scotland's biggest city has an alternative rock pedigree that few can match. Primal Scream, Franz Ferdinand, the Jesus & Mary Chain, Simple Minds, Snow Patrol and Belle & Sebastian have all sprung from a city that *Time* magazine has described as Europe's "secret capital" of rock music. Its gig scene, which stretches from gritty pubs to arty student haunts, marvellous church halls to cavernous arenas, is enthusiastic, vociferous and utterly magnetic. Nice 'N' Sleazy and King Tut's Wah Wah Hut (where Alan McGee first spotted Oasis) are legendary in their own right, but if one venue really defines the city, it's the Barrowland.

Opened in the 1930s as a ballroom (which explains the fine acoustics), it was the hunting ground of the killer known as "Bible John" in the late Sixties. It's still a fairly rough-and-ready place – the Barras market is just outside, and its location in the Celtic heartland of Glasgow's East End makes it a favoured venue for rambunctious traditional bands. Shane McGowan's been there, drinking lurid cocktails, his slurred vocals drowned out by a roaring crowd. So have Keane, flushed at the success of their piano-pop debut, and looking bemused at the small fights that broke out near the front at their performance.

Of course, most gigs finish without the drama getting violent. With a 2000 capacity that's atmospheric but intimate, and without any seats or barriers to get in the way of the music or the pogoing, the Barrowland is a wonderful place to see a live performance, full of energy and expectation. I've seen PJ Harvey transfix the crowd, the Streets provoke wall-to-wall grins, the Mars Volta prompt walkouts, Leftfield play spine-shaking bass and Echo and the Bunnymen cement their return with dark majesty. Go get some memories of your own.

053 POUNDING THE STREETS OF LONDON

ENGLAND Running the London Marathon for charity is perhaps the ultimate tick-off-the-list event, something that most people promise themselves they'll do – one day, when they've got a bit more time and when the New Year's resolution lasts longer than mid-January.

But despite all those that fall by the wayside, nearly 100,000 apply each year, for less than half that number of spaces. And it's easy to see why. Running on one of the finest courses in the world is incentive enough – the 26.2 miles take you over Tower

Bridge, under Canary Wharf and past the Tower of London, Big Ben and Buckingham Palace – but it's the million spectators lining very inch of the route that make London really special.

Only with their unceasing support can you make it all the way to the end, and those last few unforgettable yards outside Buckingham Palace – when, after running nonstop for some four and a half hours, you're pipped to the finish post by a man dressed as a rhino.

054 INTO THE VALLEY: HEARING A WELSH CHOIR

WALES The road into Senghenydd from the imposing Welsh castle town of Caerphilly snakes along the side of a steep slope that drops into a rocky valley. Lined with red-toned terraced houses constructed from local stone, the village almost clings to the hillside, and though coal mining died out here long ago, the landscape still bears its scars. You may need to pause on the high street to allow stray sheep to cross the road – this is Britain at its most rural.

Senghenydd is home to the Aber Valley Male Voice Choir, and though the choir gives concerts all over the world, it is here in the village's ex-servicemen's club that the sound is created and honed to perfection. The 61 men, many of them second- or third-generation choristers, perform everything from sombre hymns to the Bohemian Rhapsody. Singing in both English and Welsh, their voices swell in four-part harmonies, as rich and complex as an orchestra.

Male voice choirs are a Welsh institution, part of the lives of thousands of working men from Snowdonia to the Rhondda. The choirs grew from the companionship and community spirit forged by the men who worked down the mines of the south and the quarries of the north.

Times have changed, but they are still going strong. The choir in Senghenydd practises twice a week (the men come as much for the camaraderie as for the music), and visitors are welcome to drop in on a rehearsal – a moving and intimate experience. The high proportion of silver hair in the choir ranks might raise concern about whether the younger generation will carry on the tradition. But with nearly 150 male voice choirs in a land of just 2.9 million people, this unique part of Welsh life is in no danger of disappearing.

055 WATCHING FOOTBALL AT THE THEATRE OF DREAMS

ENGLAND "U-NI-TED!" the chant starts at the top of the Stretford End. "U-NI-TED!" the chorus engulfs the rest of the stand, rolling out around the ground. "U-NI-TED!" 70,000 voices singing as one. "U-NI-TED!" And the team hasn't even left the dressing room yet.

Watching a match at Old Trafford, Manchester United's self-styled "Theatre of Dreams", is the biggest thrill in spectator sport. The stadium (76,000 capacity) is massive, and full at every game with the Red faithful – not just from Manchester, but from all over Britain, as well as huge contingents from Ireland and Scandinavia.

They come to see a team that is truly legendary. One that, for all Chelsea's millions, or Barcelona's brilliance, remains by far the biggest name in European football. And why is that? Let's start with some history. In 1958, United lost the heart of the decade's most glorious team in the Munich Air Disaster (the clock in the South Stand still bears the fateful time) and became, overnight, a national icon. Then, ten years later,

they lived the dream, becoming the first English team to win the European Cup. It was a trophy achieved with football of utter romance – forged by the great Bobby Charlton and the world's first football superstar, George Best – and the legend has never quite let up. The club lapsed for a while, but since the inauguration of the Premiership in 1992, manager Sir Alex Ferguson's team has dominated English football, winning nine league titles, four FA Cups and, in 1999, their second European Cup, part of an unprecedented "Treble".

They have done so playing inspired, entertaining football – nothing less would be tolerated at Old Trafford. And today, as always, the inspiration comes from the wings – where Cristiano Ronaldo and Ryan Giggs ply their trickery – and from a great centre forward, Wayne Rooney, the most talented English footballer of his generation. To see this trio live, calling for the ball, racing down the pitch, takes your breath away. Or, as the massed ranks sing, "We are the pride of all Europe, the cock of the north...".

056 FOLLOWING THE OYSTER TRAIL IN GALWAY

IRELAND A canny bit of marketing may lie behind the origins of the Galway International Oyster Festival, but Ireland's longest-running and greatest gourmet extravaganza continues to celebrate the arrival of the new oyster season in the finest way possible: with a three-day furore of drinking, dancing and crustacean guzzling.

Just after midday in Eyre Square, Galway's mayor cracks open the first oyster of the season, knocks it back in one gulp, and declares the festival officially open – just as he has done since the 1950s, when the festival's devisers were searching for something that could extend the tourist season into September. A parade of marching bands, vintage cars, oyster openers, dignitaries and the like then makes its way down the town's main street and along the bank of the River Corrib, its destination the festival marquee, and the World Oyster Opening Championship.

All this pomp, however, is purely a sideshow, albeit a colourful one, to the weekend's main attraction, the Guinness Oyster Trail – the real backbone of the party and one of the greatest Irish pub crawls ever devised. The Trail consists of some thirty boozers dotted around the town, each providing a host of live music, comedy and dance acts over the entire period and, more importantly, offering free oysters with a pint of Guinness – every pub on the Oyster Trail employs a full-time oyster-opener throughout the weekend, who frantically and ceaselessly liberates the delicious creatures from their shells.

The traditional objective is to down a pint and a couple of oysters in every pub along the Trail over the three days – that's around thirty pints and up to one hundred oysters. If you can do this and still make it down for breakfast on the Sunday morning, you need never prove yourself again.

057 FLYING WITH BA TO BARRA AND BEYOND

SCOTLAND BA8855 is perhaps the oddest scheduled domestic flight in Britain. It is a twenty-seater propeller plane that takes off daily from Glasgow and lands an hour later directly on the beach at Barra, the southernmost island of the Western Isles, also known as the Outer Hebrides. There is no airstrip, nor are there even any lights on the sand, and the flight times shift to fit in with the tide tables, because at high tide the runway is submerged.

Even if Barra were a dreary destination, the flight would be worth taking simply for the views it gives of Scotland's beautiful west coast and the islands of Mull, Skye, Rum and Eigg. It's probably also the only British Airways flight on which the woman who demonstrates the safety procedures then turns round, gets into the cockpit and flies the plane.

The Western Isles is the only part of Britain – and one of only a few in the world – where you can experience truly stunning landscape and solitude at the same time, a hundred-mile-long archipelago consisting of a million exquisitely beautiful acres with a population that would leave Old Trafford stadium two-thirds empty.

Give yourself a week to drive slowly up through the island chain, from Barra to Eriskay, site of the famous "Whisky Galore" shipwreck (both the real and the fictional one), from South Uist to Benbecula to North Uist, then finally to Harris and Lewis. Some islands are linked by causeways (all of which have "Beware: Otters Crossing" traffic signs), others by car ferries. Stop if you can at the Scarista Inn, a gourmet paradise set in the midst of a walker's Eden alongside a stunning, vast, perpetually empty white sandy beach.

058 HIGHLAND FLING: GETTING PERSONAL WITH BEN NEVIS

SCOTLAND Scots delight in telling you that Ben Nevis means "venomous hill" in Gaelic, and the name seemed spot on that bleak February morning, with clouds blanketing the peak and an icy wind whistling across from the Atlantic. At 4406ft, Britain's highest mountain is a bairn by Alpine standards, but hiking the Highland giant is not to be scoffed at; the trail ascends relentlessly from sea level past murky lochans, boulder-strewn plateaux and jaw-dropping gullies. Guidebooks say it's best to walk "The Ben" in summer, but if you're prepared for Artic conditions, there's nothing like winter for a wee adventure.

The dewy greenery of Glen Nevis slowly faded and Highland cattle shrunk to specks on the landscape as I scaled the rocky track skirting Meall an t-Suidhe hill. Each step took me closer to a brooding sky; clouds occasionally peeled back to reveal snow-clad Glencoe and the steely waters of Loch Linnhe. After a steady climb into the gloom, a wave of relief washed over me as I glimpsed the halfway lochan – prematurely perhaps, as soon after I hit the snow. I'd expected a light dusting at the summit, but certainly not two hours of stomping through knee-deep, hard-packed powder on the plateau. The trail had all but vanished in the white, my toes were numb, and only frozen footprints were left to guide me.

Exhausted yet exhilarated, I plopped myself down next to the cairn at the top just in time to see the sun pierce a hole in the clouds. As if on cue, shafts of light illuminated the rolling Munroes and the deep blue lochs studding the valley, casting shadows on the distant crags of the Cairngorms. It only lasted for a few minutes but made all the hard slog worth it. In the late afternoon, climbers were still scrambling up the treacherous North Face. But I'd done my intrepid bit. Now it was time to kick back and enjoy the view from my balcony over Britain.

FINDING HEAVEN ON
EARTH
IN CORNWALL

ENGLAND A disused clay pit may seem like an odd location for Britain's very own ecological paradise, but then everything about Cornwall's Eden Project is refreshingly far from conventional. From the conception of creating a unique ecosystem that could showcase the diversity of the world's plant life, through to the execution – a set of alien-like, temperate biomes, gigantic geodesic conservatories wedged into the hillside – the designers have never been less than innovative.

The humid tropics biome, the largest conservatory in the world, is kept at a constant 30°c and, besides housing trees and creepers scaling its full 160ft height, takes visitors on a journey through tropical agriculture, from coffee growing to the banana trade, rice production to a cure for leukemia. There's even a life-size replica of a Malaysian jungle home made from bamboo, and a raffia African rondavel (a makeshift straw hut field workers use when tending their crops and animals).

The smaller biome reconstitutes the Mediterranean, California and parts of South Africa under one roof (well, "ETFE cushions"),

showing how arid regions have been cultivated for centuries in order to fill the shelves of the world's supermarkets. There's also a well-informed introduction to the evils of the tobacco trade (the dangers of nicotine aside, tobacco plant cultivation depletes the soil's fertility and requires a huge array of sprays and fertilizers to keep production up with world demand), but the centrepiece is a homage to the god of wine, Bacchus, with wild, twisting sculptural installations of a Bacchanalian orgy surrounded by vines. The outdoor biome continues the focus on sustainable ethics, with an introduction to biofuels, such as rapeseed, which can be used to create biodiesel, and willow coppicing, a sustainable way of obtaining wood.

Perhaps all this research and construction represents how future generations will exist? You'd better Adam'n'Eve-it. Maybe we've already taken our chunk of the apple or maybe, with a visit to the Eden Project, we've enough information to create change in our everyday lives and live in harmony with our very own biome: Planet Earth.

MISCELLANY

FIVE GREAT FILMS

How Green Was My Valley (1941). You can almost imagine you're in South Wales in Western director John Ford's family saga, even though he filmed it in California.

Brief Encounter (1945). Elegant romance set in stiff-upper-lip 1940s England; a chance meeting at a train station sparks a deep but impossible love affair between two married people.

Withnail and I (1987). Bruce Robinson's mordant cult comedy is a classic 1960s period piece that moves from London via a wonderfully deserted M1 to the Lake District.

Trainspotting (1996). Witty, brilliant adaptation of Irvine Welsh's druggy novel set in an Edinburgh far from the tourist picture book.

The Wind That Shakes the Barley (2006). Palm D'Or-winning drama about the Irish Civil War of the 1920s.

WHAT'S IN A NAME?

The **British Isles** is a term that encompasses the whole of England, Scotland, Wales and Ireland. **Britain** (or Great Britain if you prefer) refers only to Scotland, England and Wales. The United Kingdom (UK), on the other hand, is a political term and includes all of Britain and Northern Ireland. **Éire** is the official (Gaelic) term for the **Republic of Ireland** (all of Ireland, except Northern Ireland).

LANGUAGES

English is spoken throughout Britain and Ireland. However, **Welsh** is spoken by around 600,000 people, with **Scottish Gaelic** hanging in there with just under 60,000 speakers. **Irish Gaelic** is the official language of the Irish Republic (English being the second), and is understood by about 40 percent of the population, though it is the mother tongue of only around 80,000 people. In the cities across Britain and Ireland, you'll also hear an abundance of languages being spoken, with as many as **300** spoken in London.

FIVE TOP TOURIST ATTRACTIONS

Blackpool Pleasure Beach (England; 6.2 million visitors per year)
Edinburgh Castle (Scotland; 1.5 million visitors)
Guinness Storehouse, Dublin (Ireland; 750,000 visitors)
St Fagans Natural History Museum, near Cardiff (Wales; 600,000 visitors)
Giant's Causeway, Antrim (Northern Ireland; 500,000 visitors)

KNOW YOUR RIGHTS

A series of misguided battles in France in 1215 left King John squeezing his subjects for funding through extortionate taxes. As a result, the English barons rebelled, captured London and forced him to sign the **Magna Carta**, a series of concessions from the king guaranteeing rights and privileges for the barons. For the first time, the powers of the king over his subjects were limited by a written contract. This was the initial step in a lengthy process leading to the current system of a constitutional monarchy, where the queen remains a symbolic Head of State, but has little real power. Since 1993, she has even had to pay tax herself on her private income from the Duchy of Lancaster – although she still manages to avoid paying inheritance tax.

THE NATIONAL HEALTH SERVICE

The **NHS**, which was set up in 1948 to run the UK's public hospitals and health clinics, is the third biggest employer in the world, after the Chinese army and the Indian State Railways, employing four percent of the working population in England alone.

KINGS AND QUEENS OF ENGLAND

Dynasty	Monarch (Accession date)
Normandy 1066–1154	William I (William the Conqueror) (1066), William II (1087), Henry I (1100), Stephen (1135)
Plantagenet 1154–1399	Henry II (1154), Richard I (1189), John (1199), Henry III (1216), Edward I (1272), Edward II (1307), Edward III (1327), Richard II (1377)
Lancaster 1399–1461	Henry IV (1399), Henry V (1413), Henry VI (1422)
York 1461–1485	Edward IV (1461), Edward V (1483), Richard III (1483)
Tudor 1485–1558	Henry VII (1485), Henry VIII (1509), Edward VI (1547), Jane (1553), Mary I (1553), Elizabeth I (1558)
Stuart 1603–1649	James I (VI of Scotland) (1603), Charles I (1625)
In 1649, Charles I was beheaded and the Commonwealth declared. Oliver Cromwell became Lord Protector (1653–58), then Richard Cromwell (1658–59). The monarchy was restored in 1660.	
Stuart 1660–1714	Charles II (1660), James II (VII of Scotland) (1685), William III and Mary II (1689), Anne (1702)
Hanover 1714–1901	George I (1714), George II (1727), George III (1760), George IV (1820), William IV (1830), Victoria (1837)
Saxe-Coburg-Gotha 1901–1917	Edward VII (1901), George V (1910)
George V took the name Windsor in 1917, during the First World War.	
Windsor 1917–present	Edward VIII (1936), George VI (1936), Elizabeth II (1952)

WORLD'S LONGEST PLACE NAME

Llanfairpwllgwyngyllgogerychwyrndr obwyll-llandysiliogogogoch is a town in Anglesey, North Wales. The name translates as "The Church of St Mary in the hollow of white hazel near a rapid whirlpool and the Church of St Tysilio near the red cave". However, only the first five syllables are authentic; the rest was invented in the 1880s in order to draw tourists – as, indeed, it has.

FIVE LUXURIOUS COUNTRY RETREATS

Babington House, Frome, England
Trendy country-house hotel set in acres of impressive grounds, and featuring a bar, restaurant, cinema, pool room and spa. Ⓦ www.babingtonhouse.co.uk.

Dalhousie Castle, Midlothian, Scotland
Historic thirteenth-century castle where guests can dine in the *Dungeon Restaurant*, and handle hawks and owls in the Falconry. Ⓦ www.dalhousiecastle.co.uk.

The Devonshire Arms, Skipton, England
Luxurious country retreat, occupying an old coaching house in the heart of the beautiful Yorkshire Dales. Ⓦ www .thedevonshirearms.co.uk.

St Ervan Manor, Padstow, England
Luxurious B&B with an elegant restaurant situated in a nineteenth-century Grade II-listed building. Ⓦ www .stervanmanor.co.uk.

Ballymaloe House, near Cork, Ireland
Charming family-run country house hotel set on a 200-acre farm that is just as famous for its award-winning restaurant. Ⓦ www. ballymaloe.ie.

THE TOWN THAT CAME IN FROM THE COLD

Berwick-upon-Tweed is the northernmost town in England – in fact, it's so far north its football team plays in the Scottish league. A quintessential border town, it changed hands fourteen times before being finally relinquished by the Scots in 1482. An apocryphal story has it that when the Crimean War broke out against Russia in 1853, the declaration of war was signed by Queen Victoria in the name of Britain, Ireland and Berwick-upon-Tweed. However, at the end of the war the peace treaty was only signed by Britain and Ireland, meaning Berwick remained officially at war with Russia. Berwick wasn't actually mentioned

in either declaration, but in 1966 a Soviet official put the matter to rest when he signed a peace treaty with the Mayor of Berwick.

WILD BEASTS

The most fearsome land mammal in Britain and Ireland today is the **fox**, while the largest is the **red deer**. So not much to worry about there then. Of course, the islands once boasted a much wider variety of mammals: **wolves** survived in Scotland and Ireland up until the eighteenth century, and **brown bears** and **lynxes** used to roam the countryside in pre-Roman times. More recently, a semi-wild herd of **reindeer** (wiped out in the Middle Ages) has returned to the Scottish Highlands, and the **beaver** is currently being reintroduced to Argyll. Although lynxes were last seen in the British Isles approximately two thousand years ago, many people believe there are still big cats roaming the wild in Britain. The most notorious is the so-called **Beast of Bodmin Moor**, a black, panther-like creature which reputedly lives in Cornwall.

SUMMER MUSIC FESTIVALS

Barely a week goes by over the summer months when there isn't some sort of outdoor shindig going on. The big names – **Reading** and **Leeds** (now known jointly as the Carling Weekend), and relative newcomers such as Scotland's **T in the Park** and the two **V** events – tend to draw the largest crowds and most currently favoured acts, while other mid-sized newbies such as the revived **Isle of Wight Festival** and its late-season Isle of Wight brother, **Bestival**, fill in the gaps. August's **The Big Chill** is, as you might expect, a more laid-back, family-orientated affair. Then there's the niche and specialist dos, including Reading's well-established world-music extravaganza, **WOMAD**, and the notoriously hard-to-get-tickets-to **Cambridge Folk Festival**, both held in July; others include **Creamfields** – house and die-hard dance fans only; and the **Brecon Jazz Festival** for cool jazz sounds.

A SPOOKY STAY

The *Schooner Hotel* in Alnmouth has twice been named the **Most Haunted Hotel in Britain** by The Poltergeist Society. The 400-year-old hotel has 32 rooms – and an estimated 60 ghostly guests. Paranormal reports include sightings and doors operating on their own, the appearance of orbs, cold spots, and phantom apparitions. Rooms 16, 28 and 30 allegedly receive the most activity.

LAW OF THE LAND

Britain possesses a long and rich history that stretches back over thousands of years, and many of the laws that exist today date back just as far; though, sadly, they are rarely upheld:

• It is illegal to enter the Houses of Parliament dressed in a suit of armour.

• By law, all London taxi drivers must ask their passengers if they have smallpox or the plague.

• A law passed in 1366 forbids English people from marrying Irish people.

• If a dead whale is found anywhere on the British coast the tail belongs to the Queen, in case she needs the bones for a corset.

FIVE GREAT READS

Great Expectations Charles Dickens
Semi-autobiographical tale of a young orphan boy who unexpectedly comes into money. With an array of larger-than-life characters, the story moves from the wind-swept marshes of Kent to the excitement and bustle of London.

Dubliners James Joyce
Fifteen sharply drawn and sometimes poignant stories evoking the rich variety of the Irish capital and its inhabitants at the beginning of the twentieth century.

To the Lighthouse Virginia Woolf
A family holiday in Scotland is the starting point for this experimental novel, which explores the nature of time, aspiration and personal relationships in vivid and poetic language.

The Prime of Miss Jean Brodie Muriel Spark
Set in an Edinburgh school in the 1930s, this witty novel is centred around the influence – benign and otherwise – of charismatic teacher Jean Brodie on her most favoured pupils.

Collected Stories Dylan Thomas
Wales's most famous poet was also an occasional writer of prose. This collection gathers up his best pieces, including *A Child's Christmas in Wales* and *Quite Early One Morning*, which he later turned into his famous radio play *Under Milk Wood*.

CYCLING IN THE DUTCH COUNTRYSIDE • THE FRIEDRICHSBAD: THE BEST BATHS IN BADEN-BADEN • ART AFTER DARK: AN EVENING IN THE LOUVRE • CLIMBING MONT ST-MICHEL • LORDING IT IN THE LOIRE VALLEY • SWIMMING UNDER THE PONT DU GARD • TASTING WINES THAT ARE FIT FOR A PRINCE • **LISTENING TO MOZART IN SALZBURG** • CANOEING DOWN THE DORDOGNE • BUNGEEING OFF THE VERZASCA DAM • CHAMPAGNE TASTING IN ÉPERNAY • DOWNING A STEIN OR TEN AT THE OKTOBERFEST • COOL CAMPING IN THE FRENCH PYRENEES • LOUNGING ABOARD THE GLACIER EXPRESS • SLOPING OFF TO THE FRENCH ALPS • PLAYBOYS AND PETROLHEADS: THE MONACO GRAND PRIX • FEELING THE LOVE IN BERLIN • **BRAVING THE HEIGHTS OF BONIFACIO** • CATCHING THE CULTURAL ZEITGEIST IN GRAZ • LIVING THE HIGH LIFE IN ST-TROPEZ • ON THE ART TRAIL IN THE CÔTE D'AZUR • GATHERING FRIENDS FOR A SWISS FONDUE • GETTING NAKED IN CAP D'AGDE • TAKING A TRIP UP THE EIFFEL TOWER • KAFFEE UND KÜCHEN IN A VIENNESE KAFFEEHAUS • FREEWHEELING IN THE UPPER DANUBE VALLEY • **JOINING THE GILLES AT BINCHE CARNIVAL** • GOING UNDERGROUND IN THE CASEMENTS DU BOCK • MAKING A STATEMENT AT A GAME OF TREIZE • PARAGLIDING IN THE ZILLERTAL • LUNCH IN A RURAL RESTAURANT • IMPRESSIONIST PAINTINGS AT THE MUSÉE D'ORSAY • THE JEWEL OF BERRY: CATHÉDRALE ST-ETIENNE • COMMUNING WITH CARNAC'S PREHISTORIC PAST • **ASSEMBLING A PICNIC FROM SARLAT MARKET** • BATTLING THE ELEMENTS ON THE BRITTANY COAST • GORGING ON CHOCOLATE IN BRUSSELS • MUSH! MUSH! HUSKY SLEDDING IN THE SWISS ALPS • **GOING UNDERGROUND IN THE CASEMENTS DU BOCK** • SCHLOSS NEUSCHWANSTEIN: THE ULTIMATE FAIRYTALE CASTLE • WASHING IT DOWN WITH CIDER IN NORMANDY • HIKING CORSICA'S GR20 • HAVING A BEER IN BRUSSELS • SNOW WONDER: PODDING IT UP IN THE SWISS ALPS • CRANKING UP THE VOLUME ON QUEEN'S DAY • PAYING YOUR RESPECTS IN NORMANDY • SHAKEN AND STIRRED IN MONTE-CARLO • MACAROONS FIT FOR HER MAJESTY • **LIVING THE HIGH LIFE IN ST-TROPEZ** PARTYING THE NIGHT AWAY AT A SUMMER FÊTE • WINE-TASTING IN BORDEAUX • CATHAR CASTLES OF LANGUEDOC-ROUSSILLON • EXPLORING THE PREHISTORIC CAVE ART OF PECH-MERLE • DELUXE DINING IN PARIS • GOING TO THE MEDIEVAL MOVIES • SPENDING A DAY IN AMSTERDAM'S MUSEUM QUARTER • BERLIN BY NIGHT • **THE CRESTA RUN: SLEDGING WITH A DIFFERENCE** • KAYAKING ACROSS BORDERS ON LAKE CONSTANCE • BIG FOOT: SNOWSHOEING THROUGH THE BLACK FOREST • TREATING YOUR SENSES AT A CHRISTKINDLMARKTS • DEFYING GRAVITY ON THE SEMMERING RAILWAY • COW FIGHTING AT THE COMBATS DES REINES • THE SUPER-HUMAN RACE • SKIING THE STREIF • GETTING GROOVY AT THE MONTREUX JAZZ FESTIVAL • **CYCLING IN THE DUTCH COUNTRYSIDE** • THE FRIEDRICHSBAD: THE BEST BATHS IN BADEN-BADEN • ART AFTER DARK: AN EVENING IN THE LOUVRE • CLIMBING MONT ST-MICHEL • LORDING IT IN THE LOIRE VALLEY • SWIMMING UNDER THE PONT DU GARD • **TASTING WINES THAT ARE FIT FOR A PRINCE** • CANOEING DOWN THE DORDOGNE • BUNGEEING OFF THE VERZASCA DAM • CHAMPAGNE TASTING IN ÉPERNAY • DOWNING A STEIN OR TEN AT THE OKTOBERFEST • COOL CAMPING IN THE FRENCH PYRENEES • LOUNGING ABOARD THE GLACIER EXPRESS • SLOPING OFF TO THE FRENCH ALPS • PLAYBOYS AND PETROLHEADS: THE MONACO GRAND PRIX • **FEELING THE LOVE IN BERLIN** • BRAVING THE HEIGHTS OF BONIFACIO • CATCHING THE CULTURAL ZEITGEIST IN GRAZ • • ON THE ART TRAIL IN THE CÔTE D'AZUR • GATHERING FRIENDS FOR A SWISS FONDUE • LISTENING TO MOZART IN SALZBURG • GETTING NAKED IN CAP D'AGDE • TAKING A TRIP UP THE EIFFEL TOWER • KAFFEE UND KÜCHEN IN A VIENNESE KAFFEEHAUS • FREEWHEELING IN THE UPPER DANUBE VALLEY • JOINING THE GILLES AT BINCHE CARNIVAL • MAKING A STATEMENT AT A GAME OF TREIZE •

WESTERN EUROPE

060–126

060 CYCLING IN THE DUTCH COUNTRYSIDE

NETHERLANDS

FEELING THE LOVE IN BERLIN **080**

GERMANY

BELGIUM

JOINING THE GILLES
AT BINCHE CARNIVAL **087**

062 GOING UNDERGROUND
IN THE CASEMENTS DU BOCK

LUXEMBOURG

LIECHTENSTEIN

LISTENING TO MOZART
IN SALZBURG

FRANCE

TASTING WINES THAT ARE
FIT FOR A PRINCE **094**

073

AUSTRIA

123 THE CRESTA RUN:
SLEDGING WITH A DIFFERENCE

105 ASSEMBLING A PICNIC
FROM SARLAT MARKET

SWITZERLAND

LIVING THE HIGH LIFE
IN ST-TROPEZ **090**

MONACO

081 BRAVING THE HEIGHTS
OF BONIFACIO

THE NETHERLANDS If you like the idea of cycling, but would rather cut off both arms and legs than bike up a mountain, then perhaps The Netherlands is the place for you – especially if you're also scared of traffic. The most cycle-friendly country in the world, Holland has a fantastically well-integrated network of cycle paths that make it simple for even the rawest cycling greenhorns to get around by bike, and to enjoy its under-rated and sometimes swooningly beautiful vast skies, flat pastures and huge expanses of water. If you don't want to go far, get hold of a Dutch-style bike, gearless and with back-pedal brakes or bring your own and follow the country's network of 26 well-signposted long-distance or LF paths ('landelijke fietroutes'), which connect up the whole country so you never have to go near a main road. The Netherlands is a small country and it's easy to cover 50km or so a day, maybe more if you're fit enough and have a decent bike – the sit-upand-beg Dutch variety are only really suitable for short distances. The only thing holding you back may be the wind, which can whip across the Dutch dykes and polders. But there's nothing quite like the feeling of your first Heineken of the evening after a long day's cycle. Tot ziens!

060 CYCLING IN THE DUTCH COUNTRYSIDE

061 COW-FIGHTING AT THE COMBAT DES REINES

SWITZERLAND A peculiarly Swiss sport, cowfighting is said to have originated when the villages of the Valais region used to get together to see whose cow was the most suited to lead the herd up to summer pasture. Nowadays, it's a far more serious business, with farmers breeding animals specifically to fight for the cash – and kudos – that taking the prestigious Queen of the Herd title entails. Despite the image of two heavyweight heifers going at it, it's a rather civilized event: no one gets hurt, least of all the cows, and spectating is accompanied by a good (and rather un-Swiss-like) amount of roaring and drinking.

But the real showpiece of the season, the top battle of the bovines, is the Combat de Reines. Held in Martigny's large ancient Roman amphitheatre, it's the culmination of hundreds of cattle fights that have been going on all summer, the winner of which brings a whole new (literal) meaning to the term "cash cow".

062 GOING UNDERGROUND IN THE CASEMENTS DU BOCK

LUXEMBOURG The network of dark, damp tunnels below Luxembourg City's tenth-century castle – the Rocher du Bock – remains a legacy of the country's strategic position within Europe. Narrow stone staircases twist down under ground, leading into a maze of cave-like chambers and passageways. The Spanish began the casements in 1644, carving them out of the rock to house soldiers and cannons – fortifications that successive European powers continued to build upon. Eventually spanning twenty-three kilometres, the tunnels were partially destroyed after military withdrawal, though they later provided vital shelter for the people of Luxembourg during both world wars. Now a World Heritage site, what remains of the underground ramparts is eerie, claustrophobic, and utterly fascinating.

063 HORSING ABOUT AT THE POLO WORLD CUP ON SNOW

SWITZERLAND Polo may not be the "Sport of Kings", but you have to have money to play it – and possibly even more to follow it. But all good glitterati make the pilgrimage to St Moritz on the last weekend of January for the sport's top tournament: the annual Polo World Cup on Snow.

Held on the town's frozen lake, the event pulls in aristocratic punters from all over Europe to sip champagne and cheer on one of the four teams battling it out for the coveted championship title and the Cartier trophy. Competition is ferocious, and the players hurl themselves and their steeds into some spectacular duels, but the biggest bonus is that they're doing it all on an icy, snow-covered surface. Start saving now and you may just have enough money to treat your grandchildren to a trip.

064 DEFYING GRAVITY ON THE SEMMERING RAILWAY

AUSTRIA You don't need a train spotter to tell you that the Semmering Railway is a little bit special. Running forty-two kilometres between the towns of Gloggnitz and Murzzuschlag, the line – a World Heritage site – winds though the last surge of the eastern Austrian Alps before they taper off into the Hungarian plains. Of course, the mountain landscape is spectacular, but the railway itself rightly grabs your attention.

Built between 1848 and 1854, it is a daring feat of civil engineering that uses sixteen viaducts (several supported by two-storey arches), fifteen tunnels and over one hundred curved stone bridges to surmount the 460-metre difference in height. The engineer was Carlo di Ghega, a man who pushed the technical boundaries during the pioneering heyday of railway construction.

The track had to rise up over a kilometre-high mountain pass – which then became the highest altitude that could be reached by railroad in the world – and overcome extreme radii and upward gradients. Twenty thousand workmen laboured to carve the vision from the limestone rock; such was the feat that afterwards it was triumphantly claimed that there was now nowhere that a railway could not be built.

The Semmering Railway is a harmonious blend of technology and nature. It created the first modern tourism phenomenon, as the rural idyll became readily accessible to the Viennese elite. The steam engines that once worked the rails were replaced by electricity in 1959, but the architecture of the grand old line remains. The quality of the tunnels and viaducts mean they have been used continuously and, as you make the ninety-minute journey, it takes little to imagine you're inside a stately old engine as it curves around the exhilarating Kalte Rinne or Krauselklause viaducts.

065 CHAMPAGNE TASTING IN ÉPERNAY

FRANCE Champagne is an exclusive drink, in all senses of the word, what with its upmarket associations and the fact that it can be made only from the grapes grown in the Champagne region of northern France. The centre of champagne production is Épernay, a town that's made much of its association with the fizzy stuff, and where all the maisons of the well-known brands are lined up along the appropriately named Avenue de Champagne.

All of these champagne houses offer tours and tastings, and one of the best places to indulge is at the maison of Moët et Chandon, arguably the best-known brand in the world. The splendid, cathedral-like cellars afford suitable dignity to this most regal of drinks, while the multilingual guides divulge the complexities of blending different grapes and vintages to maintain a consistency of flavour from one year to the next. During the tasting, an enthusiastic sommelier explains the subtleties of flavour in the different cuvées, and although the whole experience can feel rather impersonal, it's nonetheless an essential part of any visit to the region.

For an altogether more exclusive experience, head 15km or so north of Épernay to the village of Bligny. Here, the eighteenth-century Château de Bligny is the only one in France still producing its own champagne and, if you call ahead, you can arrange a private tour. Driving through the wrought-iron gates and up the scrunchy gravel driveway, a sense of understated class strikes you immediately, and things only get classier as you're taken through the tastefully furnished rooms and vaulted cellars, and shown the family's cherished champagne flute collection. A tasting of several prize-winning vintages, taken in the opulent drawing room, is of course included, and as you savour your second glass, you'll doubtless conclude that there's no better place to get a flavour of the heady world of champagne than the home ground of this "drink of kings".

066 DOWNING A STEIN OR TEN AT THE OKTOBERFEST

GERMANY The world's largest public festival, the Munich Oktoberfest, kicks off on the third Saturday in September and keeps pumping day after day for a full two weeks. Known locally as the "Wies'n" after the sprawling Theresienwiese park in which it takes place, it was first held to celebrate the wedding of local royalty but is now an unadulterated celebration of beer and Bavarian life, attracting seven million visitors and seeing over four million litres of beer disappear in sixteen days.

At the heart of the festival are fourteen enormous beer tents where boisterous crowds sit at long benches, elbow to elbow, draining one huge litre-capacity glass or "stein" after another. If you're up for annihilation, head to the Hofbrau tent at a weekend, go for the ten-stein challenge and join the thousands of youngbloods braying for beer. If you actually want to remember your time in Munich, or to encounter some real Germans, pitch up midweek and take in two or three of the other beer tents. Whenever and wherever you go, you can count on one thing – within two steins you'll be laughing with your neighbours like long-lost buddies and banging the table in time with the Oompah bands.

The busiest time to visit Oktoberfest is the first weekend, when the "Grand Entry of the Oktoberfest Landlords and Breweries" starts the whole thing off as participants attired in Bavarian finery (lederhosen, basically), decorated carriages, curvaceous waitresses on horse-drawn floats and booming brass bands from each of the beer tents parade through town, joined by several thousand thirsty locals and international partygoers.

The local mayor gets things going by tapping the first barrel of Oktoberfest beer at the park's entrance and declaring "Ozapftis", which means "it's been tapped", but translates more accurately as, "Why doesn't everybody get as wasted as possible in my town for the next two weeks and don't worry about the mess because we'll clear up?" Huge cheers rise up from the crowd as the mad dash to the cavernous beer tents begins.

FRANCE Summer trips to France often mean le camping: a couple of weeks in a high-density site amid ranks of über-equipped German RVs and the pervasive whiff of shower gel from the dreaded sanitary block. There are, however, alternatives.

One of a new breed of cooler, greener, environmentally friendlier sites, set up so you can camp without the burden of bringing your own tents, is Tipis Indiens, a tiny farm-based campsite at Gèdre, deep in the Pyrenees. Set on a glorious natural balcony at 1300 metres, looking straight up the valley to the jaw-dropping Cirque de Gavarnie, the site consists of four Native American tipis, well spaced and simply furnished with beds, lanterns and traditional Native American decor. Each has its own little campfire (logs provided) and an uninterrupted, chocolate-box view of the mountains, while a stone barn nearby houses a kitchen and dining room, complete with a long pine table.

Gèdre is slap in the middle of one of the most dramatic parts of the Pyrenees, perfectly placed for day walks around the green, barn-studded foothills, or more serious treks up to the watershed above Gavarnie and the wild Saugué Plateau. You can catch buses further afield to visit the grottoes at Luz Saint Saveur, Trabés and Lourdes.

In terms of your carbon footprint, this is a particularly sound holiday choice because it's one that can – if you're starting out from the UK, at least – be made without needing to get in a plane or car. Fast train services run all the way to Lourdes, from where regular buses shuttle up the valley to Gèdre. Once on site, it's possible to get around with a combination of buses, the occasional taxi, and lots of healthy, zero-carbon walking through glorious scenery.

COOL CAMPING IN THE
FRENCH PYRENEES

067

068 CLIMBING MONT ST-MICHEL

FRANCE Wondrously unique yet as recognizable as the Eiffel Tower, Mont St-Michel and its harmonious blend of natural and man-made beauty has been drawing tourists and pilgrims alike to the Normandy coast for centuries. Rising some eighty metres from the waters of the bay that bears its name, this glowering granite outcrop has an entire commune clinging improbably to its steep boulders, its tiers of buildings topped by a magnificent Benedictine abbey.

From a few kilometres away, the sheer scale of the Mont provides an almost surreal backdrop to the rural tranquillity of Normandy – a startling welcome for the first-time visitor. And as you approach along the causeway that connects the Mont to the rest of France, the grandeur of this World Heritage Site becomes all the more apparent. Up close, the narrow, steepening streets offer an architectural history lesson, with Romanesque and Gothic buildings seemingly built one on top of the other.

Perched at the summit is the abbey itself, gushingly described by Guy de Maupassant as "the most wonderful Gothic building ever made for God on this earth". Although the first church was founded here in 709, today's abbey was constructed between the eleventh and thirteenth centuries, under Norman and subsequently French patronage. And as much as it's an aesthetic delight, the abbey is also a place of serenity: less than a third of the 3.5 million tourists that flock here each year actually climb all the way up to see it, and it remains a perfect place to be still and contemplate the Mont's glorious isolation.

Looking out from Mont St-Michel, as you watch the tides rolling in around its base – "like a galloping horse", said Victor Hugo – you can understand why medieval pilgrims would risk drowning to reach it, and why no invading force has ever succeeded in capturing the rock. It's a panorama to be savoured – as fine a sight as that of the Mont itself, and one that'll stay with you for a long time.

069 LORDING IT IN THE LOIRE VALLEY

FRANCE You can't translate the word château. "Castle" is too warlike, "palace" too regal – and besides, they're all so different: some are grim and broken keeps, others lofty Gothic castles or exquisite Renaissance manor houses. Many are elegant country residences whose tall, shuttered windows overlook swathes of rolling parkland. And a few – the finest – are magnificent royal jewels set in acre upon acre of prime hunting forest.

Today, the aristocracy no longer lord it over every last village in France, but a surprising number still cling to their ancestral homes. Some eke out a living offering tours, and the most fascinating châteaux are not always the grandest palaces but the half-decrepit country homes of faded aristocrats who will show off every stick of furniture, or tell you stories of their ancestors in the very chapel where they themselves will one day be buried.

Some owners, enticingly, even offer bed and breakfast. You get a vividly personal sense of France's patrician past when you wake up and see the moonlight shining through the curtains of your original, seventeenth-century four-poster – as at the château de Brissac in Anjou. Or when you gaze from your leaded window down an ancient forest ride in the Manoir de la Renomonière in Touraine, or draw a chair up to the giant stone bedroom fireplace at the perfectly tumbledown château de Chémery, near Blois.

As for the great royal residences, most are now cold and empty. National monuments like Chambord, a "hunting lodge" with a chimney for every day of the year, or Fontainebleau, where the Mona Lisa once hung in the royal bathroom, are the stunning but faded fruits of a noble culture that cherished excellence and had the money to pay for it in spades. But thanks to the tourist trade, many châteaux are recovering their former glory. The French state now scours auction houses all over the world for the fine furnishings flogged off by the wagon-load after the Revolution. Once empty and echoing, the royal palaces will soon be gilded once more – if not, perhaps, occupied.

070 SHAKEN BUT NOT STIRRED IN MONTE-CARLO

MONACO There are lots of casinos along the French Riviera, but only one Casino de Monte-Carlo. The Lilliputian royal palace of the ruling Grimaldi family may be the official heart of Monaco, but in splendour and fame it's quite outgunned by the Casino de Monte-Carlo, easily the world's most historic and magnificent homage to gambling.

Well into the twentieth century, it was the Casino's coffers that kept the precarious little statelet of Monaco financially viable, and it was the Casino that made the Grimaldis glamorous enough to marry into Hollywood royalty in 1956, when Prince Rainier wed ice-cool Grace Kelly.

The building glitters and sparkles in the Mediterranean sunshine like the belle époque jewel it is; the architect, Charles Garnier, also designed the Paris opera house, and was not a man to leave any stone unturned – or any rocaille ungilded – in his quest for showy magnificence. Once inside, you show your ID and check in coats and bags – and if your clothing is deemed inappropriate, you won't get any further. But this isn't a place to visit in beachwear, anyway: better to wear your finest and wander its salons with Bond-like insouciance. At certain times, your entrance fee will be reimbursed in chips for the tables, which is enough to make even the most sceptical of visitors feel part of the action.

Most go no further than the Salons Europe, the first in a series of increasingly discreet and opulent rooms leading from the grand lobby which culminate in the inner sanctum of the Salons Privés.

But even the Salons Europe have a certain mystique. Despite the incongruous ranks of bleeping, flashing slot machines, it's the roulette table that takes centre stage. Sombre, serious and more than a little obsessive, the faces of the serious gamblers around the table betray intense concentration. Hard though it is to banish thoughts of Ian Fleming's fictional alter ego, few real gamblers bear much resemblance to 007. Lately, they've built a Monte Carlo Resort and Casino in Las Vegas. But Monaco's jewel remains the real Casino Royale.

071 SWIMMING UNDER THE PONT DU GARD

FRANCE A monumentally graceful section of the Roman aqueduct that once supplied Nîmes with fresh water, the Pont du Gard is an iconic structure, a tribute both to the engineering prowess of its creators and, with its lofty, elegant triple-tiered arches, to their aesthetic sensibilities. Though mostly long-gone today, the aqueduct originally cut boldly through the countryside for a staggering 50km, across hills, through a tunnel and over rivers. The bridge has endured, though, providing inspiration for the masons and architects who, over the centuries, travelled from all over France to see it, meticulously carving their names and home towns into the weathered, pale gold stone.

A fancy visitor centre gives you the lowdown on the construction of the bridge, but a better way to get up close and personal to this architectural marvel is to follow the hundreds of French visitors who descend on a sunny day: make for the rocky banks of the River Gard, don your swimming gear and take to the water. The tiers of arches rise high above you and to either side, with just one of the six lower arches making a superbly confident step across the river. Propelled by the gentle current of the reassuringly shallow Gard, you can float right under the arch, which casts a dense shadow onto the turquoise water. Beyond the bridge the river widens, and fearless kids leap from the rocks adjoining the aqueduct into the deepening waters, while families tuck into lavish picnics on the banks.

The splendour of the Pont du Gard made eighteenth-century philosopher and aqueduct enthusiast Rousseau wish he'd been born a Roman – perhaps he chose to ignore the fact that the bridge was built by slave labour. Better to be a twenty-first-century visitor – the only labour you'll have to expend is a bit of backstroke as you look up at what is still, after 2000 years, one of France's most imposing monuments.

072 LOUNGING ABOARD THE GLACIER EXPRESS

SWITZERLAND The Swiss are often chided for not being much good at, say, football, jokes or wars – but two things they do better than just about anyone are mountains and trains. Combine the two, and you're onto a winner.

We were booked on the Glacier Express; there were pristine blue skies that morning at St Moritz and our state-of-the-art panoramic carriage awaited. Vast windows extended from knee level right up around the top of the coach; from any seat the views were all-encompassing. As we got going, we didn't feel like passengers, stuck behind glass, but rather travellers, engaged in the scenery.

The journey started under sparkling sunshine beside the River Inn, whose waters tumble east to join the Danube; here, amidst the wild Alpine forests, it's the slenderest of mountain brooks. Every sightline was dominated by sky-blue, snow-white and pine-green. By mid-morning, we were rolling on alongside the young Rhine, crossable here by a single stepping-stone.

As forests, wild gorges, snowy peaks and huddled villages trundled past, the train climbed effortlessly into the bleak high country, above the treeline. After lunch onboard, we downed a warming schnapps as we crested the Oberalp Pass – 2033m above sea level, though still dwarfed by a thousand more metres of craggy cliffs. Rolling down the other side, the snow lay thick on the village roofs below.

By mid-afternoon, our carriage was quiet: fingers were laced over bellies and there were a few yawns. But still the scenery was compulsive: we gazed down into a bottomless ravine and then craned our necks to take in the soaring summits, framed against a still-perfect Alpine blue sky.

As the train pulled into the little village of Zermatt, we caught our first glimpse of the iconic, pyramidal Matterhorn, and celebrated our arrival – with a Toblerone, naturally.

073 LISTENING TO MOZART IN SALZBURG

AUSTRIA Wolfgang Amadeus Mozart was the original musical prodigy, an eighteenth-century pop idol whose fame took him to Vienna, Prague and the capitals of Europe, and in the years since his death he has become an industry. No Mozart connection, however slight, is ignored. There are Mozart views to savour, Mozart chocolates to devour and any amount of Mozart kitsch to consume. Brushing all that aside, however, the music remains. And there's no better place to hear it than in Mozart's beautiful, Baroque home town.

Mozart was the Salzburg-born son of a court musician who swiftly recognized his son's musical ability – junior gave his first performance before the court of Prince-Archbishop Sigismund Graf von Schrattenbach, amid the splendour of the Salzburg Residenz, at the tender age of six. These days, the best opportunity for serious fans to hear Mozart in Salzburg is during the annual Mozartwoche (Mozart Week), which takes place at the Mozarteum and the Festspielhaus around the time of the composer's birthday (27 January), and which each year focuses on a particular aspect of the composer's work.

You can hear his music in glorious historic surroundings at any time of the year. Much the most luxurious are the candlelit Mozart dinner concerts in the hall of the *Stiftskeller St Peter* restaurant in the St Peter monastery, where you eat food prepared according to recipes from the 1900s while opera singers in eighteenth-century costume perform arias and duets from Don Giovanni, the Marriage of Figaro and the Magic Flute. Occasional dinner concerts are also held in the mighty medieval fortress that towers above the city. But if you're in more reflective mood, the Mozart Requiem is regularly performed at the Kollegienkirche, the university church whose Baroque magnificence matches in stone the splendour of Mozart's genius.

074 GETTING NAKED IN CAP D'AGDE

FRANCE Awkward to pronounce, difficult to place on a map and virtually impossible to describe to friends when you return home, Cap d'Agde's legendary nudist resort is one of the world's most unique places to stay. Of a size and scale befitting a small town, the Cap offers an ostentatious expression of alternative living. But this is no sect. The 60,000-odd naked people who come here during the height of summer often have nothing more in common than sunburnt bottoms and a desire to express themselves in unconventional ways.

The resort's sprawling campsite is generally the domain of what the French like to call bios: the hardy souls who arrive at the Cap when the nights are still chilly and leave when the last leaves have fallen from the trees. They love their body hair as much as they hate their clothes, are invariably the naked ones in the queue at the post office, and don't mind the odd strand of spaghetti getting tangled up in their short and curlies at lunch. These textile-loathing bios share the Cap with a very different breed, who are occasionally found at the campsite, but usually prefer the privacy of apartments or hotel rooms. During the day, these libertines gather at the northern end of the Cap's two-kilometre-long beach. For them, being naked is a fashion statement as much as a philosophy: smooth bodies, strategically placed tattoos and intimate piercings are the order of the day – and sex on the beach is not necessarily a cocktail.

In the evenings, the bios prefer to play a game of pétanque, cook dinner and go to bed early. Meanwhile, as the last camp stoves are cooling down, a few couples might be spotted slipping out of the campsite dressed in leather, PVC, lacy lingerie and thigh-high stiletto boots to join the throngs of more adventurous debauchees who congregate nightly in the Cap's bars, restaurants and notoriously wild swingers' clubs for a night of uninhibited fun and frolicking.

TAKING A
TRIP UP THE
EIFFEL TOWER

075

FRANCE You catch glimpses of it all day as you stroll around the city: toytown-small from the Sacré-Coeur in the morning; pylon-sized as you saunter by the Seine after lunch; and looming omnipresent over the skyline as you linger over drinks in St Germain, trying to time your assault to coincide with the golden-pink dusk that everyone says provides the best backdrop to the views from the top. A short Metro ride and suddenly you're there. The excruciating wait in the throng underneath ticks away as you crane your neck to look up through the golden-lit tangle of metal and into the darkening sky, a perspective that enhances the tower's stature like no other can.

The smooth glide to the top is shared with swarms of schoolchildren and camera-wielding fellow tourists, but they all seem to fade away as you step out of the packed lift and walk around the tower's four sides, the wind whistling past your ears and stinging your eyes into dampness.

The city unfurls like a blanket below as you strain to distinguish less familiar landmarks nestling between the Louvre and the Champs-Elysées, and try to imagine the chic Parisian lives being played out behind the many lit windows.

On the hour, thousands of sodium lights fizz and pop all over the rusty-red metal, turning the tower into a crackling, lit-up version of itself. Locals and hardened travellers alike may scoff at the kitschy, magical illuminations, yet they seem to complete what remains the quintessential Parisian experience.

CANOEING DOWN THE DORDOGNE

076

FRANCE Have you ever fancied paddling in speckled sunlight past ancient châteaux and honey-hued villages, stopping off for a spot of gentle sightseeing and ending the day with a well-earned gastronomic extravaganza? If so, then canoeing down the Dordogne river of southwest France is just the ticket.

For a 170-kilometre stretch from Argentat down to Mauzac the river provides classic canoeing. The scenery is glorious and varied, there are umpteen first-class sights within a stone's throw of the water and the choice of accommodation ranges from convivial campsites and rustic, village inns to luxury hotels in converted châteaux. The free-flowing river also offers a variety of canoeing conditions to suit beginners upwards, and though it's hardly white-water rafting, some of the Dordogne's rapids are sufficiently challenging, particularly in spring and early summer, to give at least a frisson of excitement.

Keen canoeists should start at Argentat, from where it takes roughly ten days to paddle downstream. The river here is fast, fun and more or less crowd-free. Beyond Beaulieu the current eases back as the river widens, and the first limestone outcrops and sandy beaches – perfect for a picnic lunch – start to appear. Souillac marks the beginning of the most famous – and busiest – stretch of river. If you can only spare one day, then paddle from Souillac, or Domme, to Beynac where the river loops beneath beetling cliffs from which medieval fortresses keep watch from their dizzying eyries. At water level you glide past walnut orchards, duck farms and houses drenched in geraniums.

The crowds fall behind as you slip past Beynac. There are fewer sights and the scenery is more mellow, though the Dordogne has one final treat in store at Limeuil where it splits into two great channels that meander across the floodplain. Leave your canoe behind and head for the limestone cliffs for a bird's-eye view of this classic Dordogne scene.

077 SLOPING OFF TO THE FRENCH ALPS

FRANCE While no one country offers the perfect skiing experience, France does come pretty close: from Chamonix's towering off-piste swells to Portes du Soleil's Swiss Wall, so steep that even the piste-bashing machines can't get down it, the country has enough of the tough stuff to keep the most hardcore skiers and boarders happy. Few things are as thrilling as shivering at the top of an icy pinnacle and realizing that – unless you want to spend the night there – the only way is down, pulling long carves through glistening snow, taking bumps and jumps on loose knees and grinning as the world rushes by.

Of course, you don't have to be a boy racer to enjoy the French Alps. There are gentle, rolling pistes aplenty, as well as restaurants doling out immense portions of melted raclette cheese to vin chaud-supping French scenesters who never seem to get their skis wet. And the epic scope of what's on offer here is continually inspiring: in Val Thorens, the Alps boast the highest resort in Europe; the many glaciers here mean you can ski year-round; and Les Trois Vallées offers the world's largest ski area.

And if the desire to leave the grubby, humdrum lower world behind is as central to skiing and snowboarding as the need for speed, this glorious scale makes the French Alps a splendid place to escape to. Most people who come here return again and again and, before too many seasons are up, find themselves swearing like a native, discovering an unforeseen affection for unflattering jumpsuits and slipping into the amorphous lift queues with proper Gallic carelessness.

078 THE FRIEDRICHSBAD: THE BEST BATHS IN BADEN-BADEN

GERMANY Time does strange things in southwest Germany. Even before Einstein hit on his Theory of Relativity in Ülm, Mark Twain had realized something was up after taking to the waters in the smart spa town of Baden-Baden. "Here at the Friedrichsbad," he wrote, "you lose track of time within ten minutes and track of the world within twenty."

Nearly 2000 years after the Romans tapped curative waters in this corner of the Black Forest, Twain swore that he left his rheumatism in Baden-Baden (literally, the "Baths of Baden"). England physios also considered Friedrichsbad sessions good enough to fast-track the return of injured striker Wayne Rooney for the World Cup in 2006. But regardless of whether a visit to the Roman-Irish mineral baths is for relaxation or rheumatism, as Twain noted, minutes melt into hours once inside. Midway through the full sixteen-stage programme, schedules are mere memories as you float in the circular pool of the Kuppelbad, whose marble walls and columns, creamy caryatids and sculpted cupola make it seem more minor Renaissance cathedral than spa centrepiece. By the final stage, time is meaningless and locations are a blur, as you drift prune-like and dozy between a sequence of mineral water baths, showers, scrubs and saunas of ever-decreasing temperatures.

If time warps inside the Friedrichsbad, the spa itself is a throwback to when Baden-Baden was a high rollers' playground – Kaisers and Tzars flocked here for the summer season, Queen Victoria promenaded parks planted in ball-gown colours, Strauss and Brahms staged gala concerts, and Dostoevsky tried his luck in a Versailles-styled casino. With such esteemed visitors, the town's steam room suddenly looked rather frumpy. So in 1877, Grand Duke Friedrich I cut the opening ribbons to his spa, the most modern bathing house in Europe but with all the palatial trimmings: hand-painted tiles or arches and colonnades that alluded to the decadence of antiquity.

Be warned: for all its stately appearance, you need to leave your inhibitions at the Friedrichsbad door: bathing is nude and frequently mixed. Which can be just as much of a shock as the penultimate plunge into 18˚C waters. Or the realization as you emerge tingling and light-headed, that, actually, the five hours you thought you spent inside were only three.

079 SKIING THE STREIF

AUSTRIA It never looked this icy on TV. And it certainly never looked this steep. But then cameras have a way of warping reality: they make people look ever so slightly bigger; and they make downhill-skiing runs look a lot, lot tamer.

And Kitzbühel's "Streif" is far from tame. A legendary downhill course that makes up one third of the Hahnenkammrennen, the most popular series of races on the skiing World Cup circuit, Streif is a challenging run in the same way that Everest is a difficult climb.

Buoyed by the bravado of a late-night gluwein, you have somehow talked yourself into giving it a crack. But now your legs are gone, and you can't seem to shake the image of an alpine rescue team scraping you off the slopes.

3, 2, 1. And you plunge down the slope, scooping up powder in the widest snowplough the course has ever scene. The Mausefalle (Mousetrap) is swiftly negotiated – too swiftly for your liking – and you're on your way, the rushing wind making your eyes stream as you whizz through Steilhang and down Alte Schneise. Perfect edging and exact timing is the key to success here. Most amateurs have neither, and sure enough you skitter across an icy patch, your trailing ski almost catching an edge. There isn't time to think of the mess you'd have made if it had done.

Building up sufficient speed to carry you through Brückenschuß and Gschößwiese, a section of the course most commentators maliciously describe as "flat", you descend on the Hausbergkante – a jump, followed by a difficult left-hand turn over a large rise in the terrain – and then its down the Rasmusleitn, to the finish line. You punch the air and wave to the imaginary crowd. Piece of cake.

GERMANY Every year, over a million people head for the steaming techno music fest that is Berlin's Love Parade, which has grown to become one of the world's largest free music festivals. Everything about the event is of epic proportions, but the highlight is the Parade itself, which kicks off at 2pm on Saturday and lasts throughout the evening. A procession of floats, bands, mobile sound systems, dancers, skinheads, ravers and DJ trucks moves along the Strasse des 17 Juni, slowly making a circuit between the Siegessäule, at the heart of massive Tiergarten park, and finally the famous Brandenburg Gate at its eastern end.

FEELING THE
LOVE IN
BERLIN

080

BRAVING THE HEIGHTS OF
BONIFACIO

FRANCE A mere eleven kilometres separate the northernmost extremity of Sardinia from the iconic white cliffs of Bonfiacio, on Corsica's wild southern tip. In fine weather, the straits can seem languid, like a lake of sapphire-coloured oil. But when the weather is up, as it was the first time I made the ferry crossing from Santa Teresa di Gallura, the ferocity of the currents ripping through this treacherous sea lane remind you that, to generations of mariners, Bonifacio was a symbol of salvation.

Rearing vertically from the waves, the striated chalk escarpments form a wall of dazzling brilliance, even on dull, stormy days. A row of ancient Genoese houses squeezes close to their edge, looking aloof and not a little smug – despite the fact the chalk beneath has crumbled away in colossal chunks, leaving the structures hanging precariously over expanses of cobalt sea and razor-sharp rock.

Rounding the harbour mouth, the waves grow suddenly still and the ferry seems to glide the last couple of hundred metres into port. Under the vast, sand-coloured ramparts of Bonifacio's citadel, tourists stroll along a quayside lined with rows of luxury yachts and pretty stone tenements sporting pastel-painted shutters. Wafts of coffee, grilled fish and freshly baked bread drift out of the waterfront cafés as you climb from the port up the steps of the Montée Rastello to Bonifacio's haute ville.

Most people are in a hurry to peak inside the gateway at the top, at the narrow alleyways, tiny cobbled squares and delicate campanile of the Église Sainte-Marie-Majeur. But the town never looks quite as wonderful as it does from the cliffs around it. Follow the path that strikes left of the Montée into the maquis, an ocean of scrub rolling away to the mountains inland, and – as your ferry pitches and rolls its way out of the harbour and back across the straits to Santa Teresa – you'll be rewarded with one of the most magnificent seascapes in the entire Mediterranean.

081

082 BUNGEEING OFF THE VERZASCA DAM

SWITZERLAND Sweaty palms. I had sweaty palms then, looking out over the edge, and I still get sweaty palms just thinking about it.

It was a fresh, sunny afternoon, and I'd driven up from Locarno, on the Swiss shores of Lake Maggiore. As the road climbed through sun-dappled pine forest, the giant wall of the Verzasca Dam came into view. I parked and walked out onto the dam.

To my right lay a calm blue lake, framed by wooded slopes, with the high, snowy Alps looming in the distance. But on my left the ground fell away into a dry, yawning chasm; between me and a valley mouth was empty air – not forgetting the razor-sharp rocks littering the ravine far below. And, halfway along the dam, people were flinging themselves off into this space.

Switzerland has a reputation as a placid place, docile even. It's all cheese, chocolate and cowbells. Swiss people – so the stereotype would have it – don't take risks; they exploit calculated investment opportunities.

The Verzasca Dam blows that stereotype into thin air. Never mind Australia or New Zealand – this is the world's highest bungee jump, fully 220m (722ft) high. If you've seen *Goldeneye*, you might remember it from the opening sequence. But 007 used a stunt double. You don't.

It's a mind-bending prospect. While I was watching, one jumper took a look over the edge and retreated; another was sitting quietly, trying to gather her courage. People who did leap seemed to take an age to fall, swan-diving out into nothingness, their howls echoing up off the dam.

I wish I could report that I met the Verzasca challenge. But I didn't. Sweaty palms, you see. Just standing on the edge looking down was challenging enough for me.

083 ON THE ART TRAIL IN THE CÔTE D'AZUR

FRANCE Like most of Renoir's work, it's instantly appealing, with a dazzling range of colour and a warmth that radiates out from the canvas. A hazy farmhouse at the end of a driveway, framed by leafy trees and bathed in sunny pastel tones, *La Ferme des Collettes* is one of the artist's most famous paintings, perfectly evoking a hot, balmy day in the south of France.

But what makes this watercolour extra special is its location: it's one of eleven on show in the actual ferme depicted in the painting, a mansion in Cagnes-sur-Mer where the celebrated Impressionist lived and worked from 1907 until his death, and which is now the Musée Renoir. Step outside and you step right into the picture, bathed in the same bright light and warm Mediterranean air.

And then there's Picasso. Probably the greatest painter of the twentieth century, he spent a prolific year at the Château Grimaldi in Antibes, a short drive south of Nice. Now the Musée Picasso, it's packed with work from that period – the creative energy of *Ulysses and his Sirens*, a four metre-high representation of the Greek hero tied to the mast of his ship, is simply overwhelming. But it's hard to stare at something this intense for long, and you'll soon find yourself drifting to the windows – and the same spectacular view of the ocean that inspired Picasso sixty years ago.

Ever since pointillist Paul Signac beached his yacht at St-Tropez in the 1880s, the Côte d'Azur has inspired more writers, sculptors and painters than almost anywhere on the planet. If you want to follow in their footsteps, Nice is the place to start, home to Henri Matisse for much of his life. Resist the temptations of the palm-fringed promenade and head inland to the Musée Matisse, a striking maroon-toned building set in the heart of an olive grove. Among the exotic works on display, Nature morte aux grenades offers a particularly powerful insight into the intense emotional connection Matisse established with this part of France, his vibrant use of raw, bold colour contrasting beautifully with the rough, almost clumsy style.

084 CATCHING THE CULTURAL ZEITGEIST IN GRAZ

AUSTRIA Throughout 2006, when most of Austria was celebrating the 250th birthday of a baby-faced composer in a curly wig, visitors to the southern city of Graz were confronted with jumbo-sized posters declaring the area "a Mozart-free zone". Graz has good reason to get cheeky about Austria's heritage industry. In recent years this quaint Habsburg town has reinvented itself as a trendy twenty-first-century destination, thanks in large part to the Kunsthaus Graz, a landmark exhibition centre opened in 2003 to celebrate the city's one-year reign as European Capital of Culture.

Nicknamed the "friendly alien", the curvy Kunsthaus billows up above the city's baroque buildings like the back of a leaping urban whale. Resembling the cargo hold of an interplanetary spacecraft, the interior could easily double as the set for one of local boy Arnold Schwarzenegger's sci-fi movies. It's certainly well suited to the ground-breaking art exhibitions that have established the Kunsthaus as a must-visit destination for anyone interested in central European art.

After stroking your chin at the Kunsthaus, you can cross the river Mur to check out yet more contemporary exhibitions at the Neue Galerie, before striding uphill to see what's going on at the Forum Stadtpark, a bunker-like gallery in the city park which has been a major focus of mad-cap cultural happenings since the 1960s.

Graz is also famous for being the host city of the Steierischer Herbst (Styrian Autumn), one of Europe's most delightfully baffling festivals of contemporary art, music and new media. Visit while its on and not only will you collide with crowds of culture-freaks but you'll also be able to join in celebrations of Styria's pumpkin harvest. The love lavished on this locally grown vegetable is another addition to the city's growing armoury of eccentricities.

085 KAFFEE UND KÜCHEN IN A VIENNESE KAFFEEHAUS

AUSTRIA As refined as afternoon tea and as sacred as the Japanese tea ceremony, Kaffee und Kuchen – coffee and cake – is the most civilized of Viennese rituals. It is not an experience to be rushed, and should you try, the archetypal grumpy Viennese waiter will surely sabotage your efforts. Kaffee und Kuchen is as much a cultural as a culinary experience.

The cafés are destinations in their own right: the grand, nineteenth-century *Café Central*, the suave *Café Landtmann* and the gloomy, bohemian *Café Hawelka* are as distinct from each other as Topfenstrudel is from Gugelhupf. In these memorable surroundings, there are newspapers to be read, cigarettes to be smoked – for the Austrians lag behind other European Union members in banishing the habit – and, very likely, fevered artistic or political discussions to be had. Trotsky, it is said, planned world revolution over kaffee und kuchen in Vienna, though the contrast between the revolutionary intent and the bourgeois trappings must have been richly comic.

The coffee-and-cake culture is unique to Austria. For coffee, you may order a cappuccino, but you'll endear yourself to your waiter if instead you go for a mélange, which is the closest Austrian equivalent. The choice is bewildering: there are Einspänner, kleiner or grosser Brauner, and even the Kaisermélange with egg yolk and brandy. Whatever you order, you'll most likely also get a small glass of water with your coffee.

The cakes are made with care from high-quality ingredients. It doesn't make them any healthier, but at least it ensures that the assault on your arteries is usually an enjoyable one. Apfelstrudel and the unexpectedly bitter chocolate Sachertorte are reliable and ubiquitous, ideally eaten with a heap of schlagobers (whipped cream) on the side. More exotic creations include the multi-layered almond-sponge Esterhazytorte and the caramel-topped Dobostorte.

For all their sugary delights, an air of gloom pervades many Viennese cafés: part nostalgia for vanished imperial glories, part tobacco smoke, but also surely an acknowledgement of the transitory nature of sensual pleasure. Because finishing a hot, pungently sour cherry strudel is a small death, the last delicious forkful as full of sorrow and yearning as anything by Mahler.

086 BATTLING THE ELEMENTS ON THE BRITTANY COAST

FRANCE There's no better place to prepare for Brittany's wild and ragged coast than St-Malo. Fresh off the ferry from England, it's easy to imagine that you've been transported back to a time when pirates drank in the taverns and swaggered through the cobbled streets of the old citadel. Head up onto the ramparts and you'll hear the angry sea seething below and feel drops of water smack against your face as a black cloud passes overhead on its way down the Breton coast towards Finistère.

With a name that translates as "the end of the world", Finistère is one of the most isolated parts of France. Its bleak and beautiful sense of loneliness hits you with every gust of wind that blows in off the sea and sweeps across the heather-covered headlands, ruffling your hair, watering your eyes and filling your lungs with fresh, moist air. Roscoff, Finistère's second-largest port, looks like a sleepy outpost compared with St-Malo, its forlorn fishing boats stuck in the mud at low tide and shafts of light piercing through dark clouds that forever threaten rain.

Southeast of Roscoff, and marking Finistère's (and France's) Land's End, Pointe du Raz is one of Brittany's busiest spots. But even though a million people visit each year, you don't have to walk for too long before the windswept paths that weave precariously around the promontory become deserted, and it's just you and the ocean. Only now, the sea that bubbled beneath St-Malo's ramparts is crashing ferociously against the precipitous cliffs that bring France to such a sudden and dramatic end. "In chasmal beauty looms that wild weird western shore", wrote Thomas Hardy of the Cornish cliffs across the Channel, but his inspiration could just as easily have come from this powerful and strangely seductive swathe of coastline.

087 JOINING THE GILLES AT THE BINCHE CARNIVAL

BELGIUM Taking place in February or March, the four-hundred-year-old Binche Carnival is a magic combination of the country's national preoccupation with beer – outdoor beer tents are stacked high with a huge variety of Belgian brews – and a bizarre tradition that dates back to the Middle Ages.

The spectacular March of the Gilles is a parade of six hundred peculiarly and identically dressed men – the Gilles – strange, giant-like figures who dominate this event, all wearing the same wax masks, along with green glasses and moustaches, apparently in the style of Napoleon III.

On Mardi Gras, groups of Gilles gather in the Grand-Place to dance around in a huge circle, or rondeau, holding hands and tapping their wooden-clogged feet in time to the beat of the drum. The drummers, or tamboureurs, are situated in the middle of the circle, as a smaller rondeau of petits gilles. Get inside the circles if you can; here, you're perfectly placed to get dragged in with Gilles as they head into the town hall to ritually remove their masks. In the afternoon, they emerge to lead the Grand Parade, sporting tall hats elaborately adorned with ostrich feathers, and clutching wooden baskets filled with oranges, which they throw with gusto into the crowd, covering everyone in blood-red juice and pulp. Be warned, though, that this ferocious "battle" is a decidedly one-sided affair – it's not done to throw them back.

088 MAKING A STATEMENT AT A GAME OF TREIZE

FRANCE Most people associate the French with rugby union and the Six Nations, but they also play rugby league in the southeast – a sport that was famously banned by the Vichy government and is only now making a comeback. As such, going to a game is as much a political act as anything.

"Treize", as it's known, is most popular in the Languedoc regions and through the Aude, Roussillon and Corbiéres. Its temples are in Limoux, standing astride the twisting river Aude and birthplace of the world's first sparkling wine; Villenueve-sur-Lot, hometown of the first rugby league club in France and of Jean Galia, the revered pioneer of treize whose statue stands in Ille-sur-Têt; and Carcassonne, famous for its preserved medieval Cité and the Château Comtal, but better known to treizistes as the home of Puig-Aubert, or "Pipette", the chain-smoking star of France's tours to Australia in the 1950s. His statue stands at the gates of the Stade Albert Domec where

AS Carcassonne, the most successful rugby league club in the country, plays. Visit *Chez Felix*, the bar where treizistes and players congregate, at 11 rue Carnot, and stay at the *Hotel Terminus* opposite the station, traditional home to touring international squads.

And then there's Perpignan, deep in Catalonia, home to Union Treiziste Catalan (UTC), the biggest club name in French rugby league. Spend the morning viewing the thirteenth-century Palais des Rois de Majorque and St Jean's Cathedral, built of stones taken from the nearby river, then take the long walk up the dusty Avenue du Maréchal Foch to the Stade Gilbert Brutus, home of UTC – who, under the nom de plume of the Catalan Dragons, have started playing in the British Super League in an attempt to raise the profile of their sport to a French public weaned on only the union code. The spiritual heirs of Galia and Puig-Aubert intend to ride again...

089 FREEWHEELING IN THE UPPER DANUBE VALLEY

GERMANY When Germans wax lyrical about the Rhine and Bavarian Alps, they're just trying to keep you out of the Upper Danube Valley. Few know that Strauss' beloved Blue Danube waltzes into the picture in the Black Forest; and fewer still that one of its most awe-inspiring stretches is tucked away in rural Swabia. Here, limestone pinnacles and cave-riddled crags force you to look up.

Looking up, I discovered, is tempting but treacherous if you're pedaling along the banks, lose your balance and barely manage to escape a head-on collision with a cliff. Breathtaking – in every sense of the word. I freewheeled from Fridingen, following the loops and bends of the Danube through evergreen valleys speckled with purple thistles. There's something special about a place that, for all its beauty, remains untouched by tourism. Aside from the odd farmer bidding me "Guten Tag", I was alone

in discovering this Daliesque landscape; where surreal rock formations and deep crevasses punctuate shady pine and birch forests. A soft breeze blew across the cliffs and I could hear the distant hammering of woodpeckers.

Pulling up at a bend in the river, I paused to dangle my toes into the tingling water streaked pink and gold. Towering two hundred metres above was the gravity-defying Burg Bronnen, a medieval castle clinging precipitously to a rocky outcrop and seemingly hanging on for dear life. There was no way I was going to be able to lug my bike up there. No matter, I might still make it to the Benedictine abbey in Beuron if I notched it up a gear. Then again, maybe not. Out here in the sticks, time no longer mattered. I slipped back into my saddle and slowly continued to trace the Danube's curves; the late-afternoon sun silhouetted turrets, pinnacles and treetops.

090 LIVING THE HIGH LIFE IN ST-TROPEZ

FRANCE The Côte d'Azur has always been as much myth as reality, but if one place lives up to the image of luxurious excess, it's St-Tropez. Fifty years after Bardot transformed it into a symbol of youth and sex, it is still, for the duration of the summer season, the European capital of irresponsible, irrepressible hedonism, a place where people wear Prada to the harbour, sunglasses to the bars, and barely anything at all to the beach.

St-Tropez has history and culture; it has one of the most remarkable art museums in the South of France. But no-one really comes here to improve their mind – or even, for that matter, their tan. St-Tropez is about flaunting whatever it is you've got.

There is undeniably something slightly absurd about it all. Physically, St-Tropez is still a small fishing village, peculiarly ill-adapted to the trappings of modern wealth. The Hummers and Bentleys get jammed in the narrow lanes, the huge motor yachts block the views of the harbour, and the stylish restaurant and bar concessions almost obliterate the sand along the Plage

de Pampelonne. Cafés that doubtless started modestly enough have expanded to department store dimensions, and if there's one word that sums the place up, it's excess: too much money, too much jewellery, too-much champagne. Call it St-Trop, as the French do: Saint-Too-Much.

But there's also an irresistible party atmosphere. This is the perfect place to be young, rich and beautiful – and if you're not all of those things, then a successful visit requires careful planning. Calculate how much you can afford to spend each day, then double it. Make sure your hair, clothes and credit rating are in tip-top condition. It's very important to be able to affect insouciance: of *course* your tiny portion of sushi is worth a small fortune; of *course* you always pay obscene amounts for a vodka and tonic. The clubbing isn't the wildest in the Mediterranean, but it is surely the most glamorous: you won't wind up dancing next to P Diddy or Elton John in Ayia Napa, but you might just at the Caves du Roy.

AUSTRIA The sweet, heady tang of gluwein penetrates the frosty air, fairy lights twinkle in the dwindling light and children scurry past munching on delicious vanillekipel (vanilla cookies coated in sugar): I'm standing in the middle of an Austrian Christkindlmarkt, absorbing the festive, merry atmosphere. Even though it's freezing cold, I'm reluctant to cover my nose with my thick woollen scarf – the smells swirling around this little wonderland are just too good to miss.

In the weeks leading up to Christmas, market places across the country fill with stalls selling arts and crafts and delicious Austrian delicacies. I wander through the hustle and bustle, from stall to stall, occasionally munching on a bit of strudel and sipping my warming gluwein. I should probably take some home as Christmas gifts, but I have a funny feeling that these just might not make it as far as the wrapping paper.

091
TREATING YOUR SENSES AT A CHRISTKINDLMARKT

092 COMMUNING WITH CARNAC'S PREHISTORIC PAST

FRANCE Created around 3300 BC, Carnac's three alignments of over two thousand menhirs comprise the greatest concentration of standing stones in the world. Come here in the summer and you'll encounter crowds and boundary ropes. But visit during the winter and you can wander among them freely – and if you arrive just after sunrise, when the mist still clings to the coast, you'll be accompanied by nothing but the birds and the sounds of the local farms waking up.

Just to the north of town, where the stones of the Le Ménec alignment are at their tallest, you can walk between broken megalithic walls that stand twice your height. Stretching for more than one hundred metres from one side to the other and extending for over a kilometre, the rows of stones might first seem part of a vast art installation. Each is weathered and worn by five thousand years of Atlantic storms, and their stark individuality provides a compelling contrast to the symmetry of the overall arrangement. But it's hard to believe there wasn't something religious about them.

It's possible that the stones had some sort of ritual significance, linked to the numerous tombs and dolmens in the area; or they may have been the centre of a mind-blowing system to measure the precise movements of the moon – we simply don't know. At the northwest end of the third and final alignment, Kerlescan, don't turn back as most visitors do. Keep walking to where the stones peter out in the thick, damp woodland of Petit Ménec, and the moss- and lichen-smothered menhirs seem even more enchanting, half hidden in the leaves. There's something incredibly stirring about these rows of megalithic monuments, and something mystical – it's that feeling you get when you walk into a quiet church, the sense of being in a spiritual place. And the knowledge that they were placed here for reasons we don't understand sends shivers down your spine.

093 GATHERING FRIENDS FOR A SWISS FONDUE

SWITZERLAND No one takes cheese as seriously as the Swiss. Elsewhere, cheese is one element within a more complex meal. In Switzerland, cheese is the meal – and fondue is the classic cheese feast.

Pick a cold night and gather some friends: fondue is a sociable event, designed to ward off the Alpine chill with hot comfort food, warming alcohol and good company. No Swiss would dream of tackling one alone.

In French, fondre means "to melt": fondue essentially comprises a pot of molten cheese that is brought to the table and kept bubbling over a tiny burner. To eat it, you spear a little cube of bread or chunk of potato with a long fork, swirl it through the cheese, twirl off the trailing ends and pop it into your mouth.

Those are the basics. But you'll find there's a whole ritual surrounding fondue consumption that most Swiss take alarmingly seriously. To start with, no one can agree on ingredients: the classic style is a moitié-moitié, or "half-and-half" – a mixture of Gruyère and Emmental – but many folk insist on nutty Vacherin Fribourgeois playing a part, and hardy types chuck in a block of stinking Appenzeller. Then there's the issue of what kind of alcohol to glug into the pot: kirsch (cherry spirit) is common, but French-speaking Swiss prefer white wine, while German speakers from the Lake Constance orchards stick firmly to cider.

Once that's decided and the pot is bubbling, everyone drinks a toast, the Swiss way: with direct eye contact as you say the other person's name – no mumbling or general clinking allowed! Then give your bread a good vigorous spin through the cheese (it helps stop the mixture separating), but lose it off your fork and the drinks are on you.

If the whole thing sounds like a recipe for a stomachache, you'd be spot-on: imagine roughly 250g (half a pound) of molten cheese solidifying inside you. There's a reason for the traditional coup de milieu – everyone downing a shot of alcohol halfway through the meal: if it doesn't help things settle, at least it masks the discomfort.

094 TASTING WINES THAT ARE FIT FOR A PRINCE

LIECHTENSTEIN Sandwiched between Switzerland and Austria, the principality of Liechtenstein may be pint sized, but it has plenty of treats up its Alpine sleeves. There's the scenic mountain backdrop, for one, and the appealingly stodgy cuisine – the highlight being käsknöpfle (cheese-laden dumplings), which are as good a way as any to line your stomach for a visit to the prince's wine cellars. Prince Hans-Adam II, resident of the mountaintop medieval castle that looks down imperiously on the state's capital, Vaduz, boasts one of the finest vineyards in the Rhine Valley, with optimum conditions for growing Pinot Noir and Chardonnay. If you fail to score a personal invitation to the castle, a tour of the prince's Hofkellerei winery – culminating in a tasting of five vintages in the royal cellars – is a highly satisfying second best.

095 VOGEL GRYFF: THERE'S NO PLACE LIKE BASEL

SWITZERLAND It might look like a bizarre remake of The Wizard of Oz, but the Vogel Gryff has more than 400 years of history behind it – a time-honoured festival from the Middle Ages that is focused around the mascots of Basel's neighbourhoods: a dancing lion, a tree-carrying "wild man" and the Vogel Gryff itself, a griffin that bears an uncanny resemblance to Sesame Street's Big Bird.

Their entrance is grand enough – the three heraldic creatures make their way down the Rhine on a makeshift raft – but it's the procession through town that draws the huge crowd, a sort of costumed conga-line dance meets pub-crawl that careers around town long into the night.

096 ART AFTER DARK: AN EVENING IN THE LOUVRE

FRANCE If getting up close to the *Mona Lisa* was never easy, in the wake of *Da Vinci Code* fever it's now almost as challenging as the puzzle at the heart of Dan Brown's blockbuster. But come on a Wednesday or Friday evening for one of the Louvre's late openings, and you'll find things considerably quieter.

Make your way along the shadowy, labyrinthine corridors to the outstanding Italian collection, where the famous Grande Galerie, its blonde parquet stretching into the dark distance, displays all the great names in Italian Renaissance art: Mantegna, Botticelli, Titian, Bellini, Raphael, Veronese. And then, of course, there's Leonardo's *Mona Lisa* herself – without the daytime swarms, you may get the opportunity to truly appreciate this strange and beguiling painting.

097 GETTING GROOVY AT THE MONTREUX JAZZ FESTIVAL

SWITZERLAND Backed by craggy hills and jutting out into the eastern tip of Lake Geneva, Montreux's setting is almost as stylish as its famous festival. But then few things are quite as cool as the Montreux Jazz Festival, one of Europe's most prestigious music events and a showcase for emerging talent as much as established stars.

This is jazz, but not as you may know it – everything from hip-hop to acid jazz, gospel, techno, reggae and African jazz get an airing, and you can groove the days away on samba and salsa boats that head out on to the town's lake every afternoon. Jazz runs deep in Montreux – one of the venues is called the Miles Davis Hall – and the festival continues to expand and diversify, featuring a bewildering range of workshops and an A-List line-up. Herbie Hancock and John McLaughlin are just two of the more regular artists from a cast of around two thousand.

098 ARS ELECTRONICA CENTRE: LOSING GRIP ON REALITY

AUSTRIA Pegging yourself as the Museum of the Future is, in our ever-changing world, bold. Brash, even. And that's exactly what the Ars Electronica Centre in Linz is. Dedicated to new technology, and its influence within the realms of art, few museums on earth have their fingers quite as firmly on the pulse.

The Ars features over fifty interactive installations, from warring robots to displays that enable you to create your own cyberspace project, but everyone comes here for the CAVE (Cave Automatic Visual Environment), the only exhibition of its kind that's open to the public. This cubed room, measuring – cutely enough – 3 x 3 x 3, is at the cutting-edge of virtual reality; the simulation uses technology so advanced – 3-D projections dance across the walls and along the floor, as you navigate through virtual solar systems and across artificial landscapes – that you feel like you're part of the installation.

There's also a cool rooftop cybercafé. After all that virtual reality, you're going to need a strong coffee to bring you back down to earth.

FRANCE A world apart from piles of old stones, paintings of curly-wigged fat men or pungent-smelling chateaux, seeing the Bayeux Tapestry is more like going to the movies than trotting round a traditional tourist sight. Wrapped around a half-lit wall like a medieval IMAX theatre, it's protected by a glass case and dim lighting, while a deep, movie-trailer voice gives a blow-by-blow headphone commentary of the kings, shipwrecks and gory battles depicted in the comic-strip-like scenes.

The nuns who are thought to have embroidered this seventy-metre strip of linen chronicling William of Normandy's conquest of England could hardly have guessed that, nearly a millennium later, people would be lining up to marvel at their meticulous artwork and impeccable storytelling.

But like Shakespeare's plays, the Bayeux Tapestry is one of history's timeless treasures. Okay, so the characters are two-dimensional, the ancient colours hardly HD and the scenes difficult to decipher without the commentary, but it's captivating

nonetheless. William looks every bit the superhero on the back of his huge horse, while King Harold, with his dastardly moustache, appears the archetypal villain, his arrow in the eye a just dessert.

The wonderful detail adds intriguing layers to the main theme: the appearance of Halley's Comet as a bad omen when Harold is crowned king builds up the suspense, while the apparent barbecuing of kebabs on the beach has led some historians to argue that the tapestry is considerably newer than first thought. Whether this is true is of no great importance – the images are as engrossing now as they ever were, and on exiting the theatre, even the staunchest of Brits might feel enthused enough to be secretly pleased that a brave Frenchman crossed the Channel to give Harold his comeuppance. And in this way, the Bayeux Tapestry has lost none of its power as one of the finest pieces of propaganda the world has ever seen.

099
GOING TO THE
MEDIEVAL
MOVIES

Lunch
IN A RURAL RESTAURANT

100

FRANCE Picture a village square with tables set out under ancient trees, and dappled sunlight playing on waiters bearing plates of local delicacies whose heady aromas fill the air. While this archetypal image of a restaurant in rural France is of course a cliché, such places do still exist – just ask around, or keep your eyes open as you drive through the villages. Then take your place at the table and give your tastebuds a treat.

The most traditional of rural restaurants won't offer a choice – you simply sit down and the food starts to arrive. To whet the appetite, you help yourself from a tureen of soup, one of those wonderful "everlasting" concoctions whose flavours become ever more complex by the day.

Depending on the region, your next course is likely to be a selection of charcuterie or crudités, a slice of savoury tart or perhaps mussels if you're near the coast. The main dish will almost always be meat: a juicy steak, a hearty beef or game stew, or maybe roast pork or lamb laced with herbs and a hefty dose of garlic. Though fried potatoes and green beans are the usual accompaniment, you may get something more interesting such as a vegetable gratin or fragrant wild mushrooms.

Then it's a green salad and the cheese board, hopefully a sampler of local specialities: soft, creamy rounds of Brie or Brillat-Savarin; aromatic, blue-veined wedges of Roquefort; and goats' cheese in herb-crusted pyramids. You're now on the home straight.

If space allows, dessert could be a simple sorbet or bowl of summer-sweet seasonal fruits, or a more elaborate confectionery such as clafoutis (upside-down cake), croustade (apple tart laced with armagnac) or the classic, totally irresistible chocolate mousse. No French meal is complete without a coffee – black and strong – and after such an extravaganza you may feel the need for a brandy or other digestif. Then it's time to pay up and find a shady spot for your siesta.

101 IMPRESSIONIST PAINTINGS AT THE MUSÉE D'ORSAY

FRANCE Forget the Louvre, it's not a patch on the Musée d'Orsay – or so you'll be told. Maybe this is down to continued bitterness toward futuristic glass pyramids, but it's probably more about the understated elegance of the Musée d'Orsay itself. Handsomely located in a renovated turn-of-the-century railway station, the museum's splendid collection of vibrant Impressionist canvases are displayed in much more intimate surroundings, right up under the roof in a wing whose attic-like feel is far less formal and imposing than the Louvre.

A wander through the compact Impressionist and Post-Impressionist galleries provides an astonishingly comprehensive tour of the best paintings of the period, the majority of them easily recognizable classics like Van Gogh's *Starry Night* or Renoir's *Dance at Le Moulin de la Galette*. Even better, these are paintings you can really engage with, their straightforward style and vibrant, life-like scenes drawing you into the stories they tell. It's easy to forget where you are and, transfixed, reach

out a finger to trace the chunky swirls of paint that make up Van Gogh's manic skies; you might even catch yourself imitating the movements of Degas' delicate ballerinas as they dance across the walls, sweeping their arms in arcs above their heads and pointing their tiny toes.

When the intricate grandeur of Monet's Rouen Cathedral looms above you and reinstates a sense of decorum, it's almost as if you were standing under the imposing bulk of the old building itself. Exhilaration returns as you're transported to the tropics by Gauguin's disarming Tahitian maids, who eye you coyly from the depths of the jungle. But don't get so caught up in the stories that you forget the incredible artistic prowess on display; stick your nose right up to Seurat's dotted Cirque, then inch slowly backwards and, as the yellow-clad acrobats appear with their white horse, you'll feel the immense genius of the pioneer of pointillism.

102 MUSH! MUSH! HUSKY SLEDDING IN THE SWISS ALPS

SWITZERLAND I don't think he actually said "Mush! Mush!" – all I caught was a little click of the teeth and a high-pitched cry – but the dogs still howled and yapped and took off through the snow like hounds out of hell.

We were up at 3000m, whisking across the snowfields on a sled drawn by eight huskies yoked in pairs. Earlier, the musher, René, had pointed out the different breeds to us – most were regular huskies, with their pale coats and blue eyes, but he also had several stocky, dark-pelted Greenlands. It was about ten degrees below freezing, under a crystal-clear blue sky – really too warm for them: these dogs prefer temperatures nearer minus thirty.

The sled was a simple affair, a couple of metres long, with

a platform at the back for the musher to stand on with reins in hand and us sitting below, facing the bobbing tails of the rearmost pair of dogs. We whooshed along: what a great way to travel! Human and dog working together, in a spectacular natural setting of high peaks and grand panoramas.

Even on that short ride, we could see the pack at work: René had yoked an adolescent trainee alongside one of the old matriarchs at the front, and she was doling out some training of her own, with the odd nip to keep the young'un in line.

As we arrived back at base, the rest of the pack set up a frantic howling to greet the returnees, who stood, tongues out, panting clouds of steamy breath. They looked fantastic – I wanted to set off again into the wilderness and never come back.

103 THE JEWEL OF BERRY: CATHÉDRALE ST-ETIENNE

FRANCE A flat plain at the very heart of France, stranded between the verdant Loire valley and the abundant hillsides of Burgundy, the Berry region has become a byword for provincial obscurity. This really is la France profonde, the cherished "deep France", whose peasant traditions continue to resist the modernization that threatens – so they say – to engulf the nation. You can drive for miles here without seeing anything except open fields and modest farmhouses.

As you approach the miniature regional capital of Bourges, however, a mighty landmark begins to reveal itself. Looming over the fields, allotments and low houses is a vast Gothic cathedral, its perfect skeleton of flying buttresses and keel-like roof giving it the look of a huge ship in dry dock. A stupendous relic of the inexorable, withdrawing tide of power and belief, its preposterous size and wealth of detailing prove that the Berry was not always a backwater. In the early thirteenth century, when the cathedral was built, this was a powerful and wealthy region – and Bourges' archbishops wanted all the world to know it.

At the foot of the impossibly massive west front, five great portals yawn open, their deep arches fringed by sculptures. You could spend hours gazing at the central portal, which depicts the Last Judgement in appalling detail, complete with snake-tailed and wing-arsed devils, and damned souls – some wearing bishops' mitres – screaming from the bottom of boiling cauldrons.

Inside, the prevailing mood is one of quieter awe. The magnificent nave soars to an astonishing 38 metres, and is ringed by two tall aisles. No matter where you look, smooth-as-bone columns power their way from marble floor to tent-like vault, their pale stone magically dappled with colours cast by some of Europe's finest, oldest and deepest-hued stained glass. Behind the high altar, at the very heart of the cathedral and at the very centre of France, the apse holds these jewels of the Berry: precious panels of coloured glass, their images of the Crucifixion, the Last Judgement, the Apocalypse and of Joseph and his coat glowing like gemstones.

104 WASHING IT DOWN WITH CIDER IN NORMANDY

FRANCE Normandy is to cider what Bordeaux is to wine. Sparkling, crisp and refreshing, it's the perfect foil to the artery-clogging food that Normans also do rather well – and as some of France's best food and drink comes from the rolling hills and green meadows of Normandy's Pays d'Auge, dining at a country restaurant in these parts is an experience not to miss.

The bottle of cider plonked down by your waiter may look as distinguished as a fine champagne, but don't stand on ceremony: open it quickly and take a good swig while it's still cold.

Norman cider is typically sweeter and less alcoholic than its English cousin, but it's the invigorating fizz that tickles the back of the throat and bubbles up through the nose that you'll remember.

You could try a kir normand: cider mixed with cassis – a more sophisticated and delicious French take on that old student favourite, "snakebite and black".

Make sure that you have a full glass ready for the arrival of your andouilles starter: although it won't necessarily enhance the taste of assorted blood and guts in a sausage, a generous gulp of cider will help get it down. Pork and cider, on the other hand, is one of the classic combinations of Norman cooking. Opt for some pork chops to follow and they come drowned in a thick, deliciously satisfying sauce with as much cream in it as cider. At this point, you may be offered the trou normand: a shot of Calvados apple brandy that helps digestion, apparently by lighting a fire in the pit of your stomach that burns through even the toughest andouilles' intestines. The trou clears just enough room for a slice of Camembert or Pont-l'Evêque, two of the famous cheeses produced in the Pays d'Auge, before you can finally leave the table, full and just a bit wobbly.

105 ASSEMBLING A PICNIC FROM SARLAT MARKET

FRANCE Ready for lunch? Given the range and quality of foodstuffs available from small producers in France, there's nothing better than to buy your own picnic at a local market – and no better place to do it than Sarlat. This medieval town tucked in a fold of hills on the edge of the Dordogne valley hosts one of the biggest and best markets in southwest France.

For centuries people have been flocking to Sarlat market, where the banter is just as likely to be in local dialect as in French. The stalls under their jaunty parasols groan with local produce, from a rainbow array of seasonal fruit and vegetables to home-baked cakes and the famous pâté de foie gras, the fattened liver of goose or duck.

Let your nose guide you first to the charcuterie van selling aromatic pork or venison sausage and locally cured ham. There are terrines of rillettes, a coarse duck or goose pâté, and melt-in-the-mouth foie gras, sometimes laced with truffles, the "black diamonds of Périgord". Next up is the farmer tempting customers with slivers of cheese. The regional speciality is cabécou, a small, flat medallion of goats' cheese, but you'll also find creamy ewes'-milk cheese from the Pyrenees and Salers and Bleu d'Auvergne from the Massif Central.

A few tomatoes – still sun-warm and packed with flavour – and a cucumber make a quick salad. Then you need bread. Traditionalists will opt for a crusty pain de campagne, but wholemeal baguettes and rye or seed-speckled granary breads are just as prevalent. While you're at it, ask for some wedges of walnut cake or pastis, a lip-smacking apple tart topped with crinkled pastry and more than a hint of armagnac.

Last stop is the fruit stall, groaning with the season's bounty, from the first cherries of spring through summer strawberries to autumn's apples, pears and fat chasselas grapes. Now tear yourself away to find a sunny spot on the banks of the Dordogne – not forgetting the wine and corkscrew of course. Bon appétit!

AUSTRIA With its deep valleys and craggy peaks, there can be no better way to see the Zillertal than from a paraglide, with the grandiose scenery unfolding below you. Just a few steps take you off the hill – usually the Zillertaler Höhenstraße or the steep grassy slopes of Penkenjoch – and before you know it you are gliding calmly above a landscape so outstanding that your fears are forgotten. Snow-topped mountains glint in the sun. Verdant green meadows, dotted with wooden chalets, roll out before you. Add the exhilarating rush of flying, and seeing this dramatic region from the ground can never be quite the same again.

107 GORGING ON CHOCOLATES IN BRUSSELS

BELGIUM The Mayans may have invented chocolate long ago, but Belgium is today its world headquarters, and nowhere more so than Brussels, whose temples to the art of the brown stuff are second to none. It's not just a tourist thing, although within the vicinity of the Grande-Place you could be forgiven for thinking so. Chocolate is massively popular in Belgium, and even the smallest town has at least a couple of chocolate shops; in fact, the country has two thousand all told, and produces 172,000 tonnes of chocolate every year. You may think that this would make for a nation of obese lardcakes, especially as Belgium's other favourite thing is beer (not even mentioning the country's obsession with pommes frites). However, whatever your doctor may tell you, chocolate in moderation is quite healthy. It reduces cholesterol and is easily digested; some claim it's an aphrodisiac as well.

So what are you waiting for? Everyone has their favourite chocolatier – some swear by Neuhaus, while others rely on good old Leonidas, which has a shop on every corner in Brussels – but Godiva is perhaps the best-known Belgian name, formed in the early 1900s by Joseph Draps, one of whose descendants now runs a chocolate museum on the Grande-Place. Once you've checked that out (and gobbled down a few free samples), make for the elegant Place du Grand Sablon, with not only a Godiva outlet, but also the stylish shop of Pierre Marcolini, who produces some of best chocs in the city, if not the world. *Wittamer*, also on Place du Grand Sablon, doesn't just do chocolates, and in fact you can sip coffee and munch on a chocolate-covered choux pastry at its rather nice café; you're probably best off saving that big box of Wittamer's delicious pralines for later … though trying just a few now surely can't hurt. If you're not feeling queasy by this point, stop at *Planète Chocolate*, on rue du Lombard, where you can find the city's most exotic and adventurous flavours – pepper, rose, various kinds of tea – as well as watch the chocolate-making process in action, followed by (what else?) the obligatory tasting. Moderation be damned.

SCHLOSS NEUSCHWANSTEIN:
the ultimate fairytale castle

GERMANY If you could only visit one castle in the world, then Schloss Neuschwanstein must be it. Boldly perched on a rocky outcrop high above the Bavarian village of Hohenschwangau, the schloss lords it over some of the most spectacular countryside in the country. It looks every bit the storybook castle, a forest of capped grey granite turrets rising from a monumental edifice. And the all-important intriguing background? Built in 1869 as a refuge from reality by King Ludwig II, a crazed monarch who compared himself to the mythical medieval "Grail King" Parzival, Neuschwanstein ticks that box, too.

109 SKATING THE SUPERHUMAN RACE

THE NETHERLANDS The Dutch Eleven Towns Race or Elfstedentocht is the most famous and most gruelling long-distance ice-skating race in the world. It's an amazing spectacle, much like the big city road marathons that take place around the world, only this time on ice skates, with around 17,000 participants, only a few hundred of whom – the skating elite – are actually racing; the rest are there for the thrill of taking part, and the race is many times over-subscribed every year. It's an incredible spectacle, but sadly can only happen when the weather is super-cold, and the ice has frozen to a depth of 15cm for most of the 200km route. Inspectors are out checking the ice every day leading up to the event, which normally takes place in February, and if it goes ahead then it's broadcast live on Dutch TV. However, the competition has only been staged fifteen times since its inception in 1909 and the last time it happened was in 1997 – and with the weather getting warmer no one's holding their breath for the next one. In the meantime, you'll have to make do with inline skating tours that follows the same route (but by road) every summer between May and September. The trip can take anything from four to seven days depending on how quickly you want to go and how good a skater you are – though even the fastest are quite a contrast to the six hours or so it took the last winner of Elfstedentocht to cover the same route.

110 SPENDING THE DAY IN AMSTERDAM'S MUSEUM QUARTER

THE NETHERLANDS If you crave a cultural day out, then look no further than Amsterdam's Museum Quarter. For those who have always been intrigued by those black-hatted burghers who stare at us out of the gloom, the Rijksmuseum is the perfect place to get in touch with the achievements of the country's seventeenth-century Golden Age – the works of Rembrandt, Hals and Vermeer and the other great artists of the era have extraordinary power up-close. The quarter is well named, and afterwards you can continue by strolling across Museumplein to the Van Gogh Museum, whose superb Rietveld-designed building is home to a fabulous collection of the artist's work – the world's best. Finish up at the Stedelijk Museum, which from 2009 will be back in its original home next door to the Van Gogh, and displaying its collection of the more wacko works from the world of twentieth century and contemporary art, before repairing for drinks at the nearby *CoBrA Café*, whose walls are homage to the funky, trans-national post-war art movement that was in part based here.

111 PARTYING THE NIGHT AWAY AT A SUMMER FÊTE

FRANCE Catching a village fête is more down to serendipity than planning. A tiny poster in the local boulangerie or boucherie might be the only sign that something's afoot, but don't let rural France's publicity deficiencies put you off. All and sundry are welcome at the annual alfresco parties hosted by each commune; just turn up, dust off your beginners' French and prepare for something infinitely more absorbing than the minor soiree suggested by the posters. Returning to the village on fête night is often like being transported to a different planet: market stalls are packed away, and people from neighbouring towns spill out of once-sleepy bars whose evening clientele usually only numbers the barman and a sole farmer nursing a cognac.

Trestle tables groaning with delicacies are set up around the square, jealously presided over by the village grand-mères. Faddy eaters would be advised to ensure that their personal bête-noire foodstuff doesn't coincide with the local specialities that inevitably dominate the menu: intestine-filled andouillette sausages in the north, perhaps, or salads sprinkled with gésiers (goose gizzards), and tripoux – sheep's stomach stuffed with tripe, trotters, pork and garlic – in the Dordogne and Lot. Most offerings are delicious, but if you do encounter something that offends your palate, it can at least be washed down with a couple of glasses of vin de table – which tastes a whole lot better in the open air than it should, particularly when drunk from plastic pint glasses.

Later in the evening, "le rock" bands pour their music into the darkening air and the strings of lights decorating the trees provide a sparkly, festive air. Street performers wander and, as the sun finally sets, everyone gets down to some serious wine consumption and dancing. The sight of the village elders and teenagers dancing together to slightly dubious French bands on hastily erected stages may seem incongruous, but only serves to reinforce the nagging feeling that everything is somehow more civilized in France.

112 KAYAKING ACROSS BORDERS ON LAKE CONSTANCE

GERMANY, SWITZERLAND & AUSTRIA Germany drifted behind me and I could spy Switzerland ahead – their red-and-white flag fluttering in the breeze. Like whales in a fish pond, approaching ferries created tidal waves that thrashed both sides of my kayak and rocked it so hard that I thought the dreaded Eskimo Roll was imminent. Still, I was loving every minute of it. But then it's hard not to love Lake Constance, Europe's third largest lake; where you can wake up on the beach in Germany, cool off with a swim in Switzerland and still make it to Austria in time for a schnitzel dinner with alpine views.

Ahhh, this was the life – summer on the turquoise lake, rotating my paddle, stabbing the rippling water with a double-edged blade and pulling back with the strength of bionic woman. A floating speck on this mother of a lake, I felt as inconspicuous as a fly on the wall (albeit one in a dazzling red life jacket); passing sailing boats full of – surely not! – nude Germans sunbathing on deck, swanky yachts where über-cool Zurich day-trippers in designer shades popped corks, and families frolicking in the water and grilling bratwurst in horseshoe-shaped bays.

Allensbach's onion-domed church faded and I was heading for the fruit-growing island of Reichenau: a World Heritage site famed for its twin-towered Benedictine abbey. Too attached to my kayak to get out and explore, I skirted around the marshes and propelled the craft towards Mannenbach in Switzerland, to dive into the deliciously cold water and picnic on the shore. Just across the way, I reached the fringes of Wollmatinger Ried nature reserve, as the late afternoon sun glinted on my kayak's name – Wolke Sieben (Cloud Number Nine). Well it's not far off, I thought. Nearer than Austria, anyway.

113 WINE-TASTING IN BORDEAUX

FRANCE Margaux, Pauillac, Sauternes, St-Emilion – some of the world's most famous wines come from the vineyards encircling Bordeaux. So famous, in fact, that until recently, most châteaux didn't bother about marketing their wares. But times are changing: faced with greater competition and falling demand, more and more are opening their doors to the public. It's never been easier to visit these châteaux and sample the wines aptly described as "bottled sunlight".

Ranging from top-rank names such as Mouton-Rothschild and Palmer to small, family-run concerns, there are plenty to choose from. Some make their wine according to time-honoured techniques; others are ultra high-tech, with gleaming, computer-controlled vats and automated bottling lines – and there are a growing number of organic producers, too. All are equally rewarding. During the visit you'll learn about soil types and grape varieties, about fermentation, clarification and the long, complicated process which transforms grapes into wine.

Though you rarely get to see inside the châteaux themselves, several offer other attractions to draw in the punters, from wine or wine-related museums to introductory wine-tasting classes (this being France, you can sometimes sign up children for the latter, too). And because not everyone is just here for the wine, there are also art galleries, sculpture parks, hot-air balloon trips and, around St-Emilion, underground quarries to explore.

All visits, nevertheless, end in the tasting room. In top-rank châteaux, an almost reverential hush descends as the bottles are lovingly poured out. The aficionados swirl glasses and sniff the aromas, take a sip, savour it and then spit it out. If you feel like it, an appreciative nod always goes down well. And often, you will feel like it – because despite all the detailed scientific explanations of how they're produced, the taste of these wines suggests that magic still plays a part.

114

PLAYBOYS AND PETROLHEADS: THE MONACO GRAND PRIX

MONACO From the hotel-sized yachts in the harbour to the celebrity-filled Casino, the Grand Prix in Monaco is more than a motor race – it's a three day playboy paradise. The Monaco crown is still the most sought after in motor-racing circles, although today's event is as much a showcase for the richest men and women on the planet as it is for the drivers.

Set amongst the winding streets of the world's second smallest and most densely populated principality, this is the most glamorous and high-profile date on the Formula One calendar. Attracting a global television audience of millions, the cars roar their way around the city centre at four-times the speed the streets were designed for. The circuit is blessed with some of the most historic and memorable corners in motor racing: St Devote, Mirabeau, La Rascasse, Casino and, of course, the Tunnel. Part of Monaco's appeal is its renowned difficulty. Three-times Formula One World Champion Nelson Piquet once described the tackling the circuit as like, "riding a bicycle around your living room."

Watching this gladiatorial spectacle around the Portier corner is particularly thrilling – one of the few possible, if unlikely, overtaking points on the course – seeing the cars' flaming exhausts before they disappear into the Tunnel, the deafening roar of the engines echoing behind. But one of the best and cheapest places to watch the race is the standing-only Secteur Rocher, a grassy area on a hill above the last corner – Rascasse – at the circuit's western end, which offers fine views and attracts the most passionate F1 supporters. The cars look pretty small from up here, but watching them sweep past is incredible. And afterwards you can climb down for a stroll or drive around the circuit, which is reopened to traffic every evening: just don't imagine you're Michael Schumacher – the normal speed limit still applies.

HIKING CORSICA'S
GR20

115

FRANCE We'd set out in pre-dawn darkness to ascend the spectacular head of the Vallée d'Asco, ringed by peaks nudging 3000m. High above, an enfolding wall of snow-streaked granite glowed crimson in the first rays of daylight. Small flocks of mouflon sheep were already grazing overhead, sending small pebbles spiralling down the cliffs as we began the first pass of the day.

The view from the col was astounding. Looking northwards along the serrated ridge-tops of the watershed, tiers of shadowy summits receded to a sea the colour of lapis. The light was exceptionally vivid all the way to the horizon, where a front of white cloud was floating above the French Riviera.

Except it wasn't cloud. As a glance through the binoculars confirmed, the white apparition in the distance was in fact the southern reaches of the Alps – a staggering 250km away. What we'd assumed was a small yacht on its way to St Tropez or Toulon

was in fact a massive car ferry the size of a block of flats. The realization was overwhelming, completely overturning our sense of space and scale.

Seeing the Alps from such a distance may have been a one off, but every day on the GR20 – France's famous haute route across the Mediterranean island of Corsica – brings astonishing moments. The ingenious red-and-white waymarks lead you across terrain of incredible variety. On a typical étape you could climb passes nearly two-and-a-half kilometres high, picnic by frozen glacial lakes, skinny dip in mountain streams, skid down eternal snow patches and come face to face at the bottom with a wild boar.

Best of all, at the end of it, having hauled yourself through all fifteen étapes, you can rest your aching bones in some of the most translucent turquoise waters in the entire Mediterranean.

116 EXPLORING THE PREHISTORIC CAVE ART OF PECH-MERLE

FRANCE Imagine a cave in total darkness. Then a tiny flame from a tar torch appears, piercing the blackness, and a small party of men carrying ochre pigment and charcoal crawl through the labyrinth. They select a spot on the cold, damp walls and start to paint, using nothing but their hands and a vivid imagination. Finished, they gather their torches and leave their work to the dark.

Until now. A mind-blowing 25,000 years later, you can stand in the Grotte de Pech-Merle and admire this same astonishing painting: two horses, the right-hand figure with a bold, naturalistic outline that contrasts with the decidedly abstract black dots – 200 of them – that fill up its body and surround the head. The whole thing is circled, enigmatically, by six handprints, while a red fish positioned above its back adds to the sense of the surreal.

Short of inventing a time machine, this is the closest you'll get to the mind of Stone Age man. And it's this intimacy, enhanced by the cool dimness of the cave, that makes a visit here so overwhelming. Unlike Lascaux in the Dordogne, Pech-Merle allows visitors to view the original art, and the so-called dotted horses are just the best-known of the cave's mesmerizing ensemble of 700 paintings, finger drawings and engravings of bison, mammoths and horses.

It was once common to think of prehistoric peoples as brutish, shaggy-haired cavemen waving clubs, but some 30,000 years ago here in France, they were busy creating the world's first naturalistic and abstract art. No one's sure just why they made these paintings, but it's possible that the tranquil, womb-like caves were sacred places linked to fertility cults, the drawings divided into male and female symbols suffused with Paleolithic mythology. But new theories suggest something far more prosaic: that the paintings were made primarily by teenage boys who had the subjects of hunting and women foremost on their minds. Perhaps Pech-Merle's most poignant treasure backs this up – the foot print of an adolescent boy, captured in clay as he left the cave one evening, some 25,000 years ago.

117 HAVING A BEER IN BRUSSELS

BELGIUM Don't just ask for a beer in Belgium – your request will be met with a blank stare. Because no one produces such a wide range of beers as they do here: there are lagers, wheat beers, dark amber ales, strong beers brewed by Trappist monks, beers with fruit added, even beers mixed with grapes. Some beers are fermented in the cask, others in the bottle and corked champagne-like. And each beer has its own glass, specifically developed to enhance the enjoyment of that particular brew.

Brussels is the best place to try all of them, including its own beery speciality, Lambic, a flattish concoction that is brewed in open barrels and fermented with the naturally occurring yeasts in the air of the Payottenland (the area around Brussels). It's not much changed from the stuff they drank in Bruegel's time, and a few glasses is enough to have you behaving like one of the peasants in his paintings – something you can do to your heart's content at *La Becasse*, down an alley not far from the Grande-Place, or at the *Cantillon Brewery* in the Anderlecht district, where they still brew beer using these old methods, and which you can visit on regular tours.

You can taste another potent brew, Gueuze, a sparkling, cidery affair, at *La Mort Subite*, a dodgy-sounding name for a comfortable fin-de-siècle café; your ale will be served with brisk efficiency by one of the ancient staff, and while you sip it you can munch on cubes of cheese with celery salt or cold meats like jellied pigs cheeks. After this aperitif, make your way to *'t Spinnekopke*, a restaurant that cooks everything in beer, and has lots to drink as well, or just head for *Delirium*, a quarter of whose 2000-strong beer menu is Belgian. Finish up with a glass of Westvleteren brown ale, a Trappist brew that was recently voted the best beer in the world – and at 10.3 percent it's also one of the strongest.

118 PAYING YOUR RESPECTS IN NORMANDY

FRANCE Apart from the German stronghold of Pointe du Hoc, where gleeful kids take time out from building sandcastles to clamber over the rubble of battered bunkers, the D-Day landing beaches – Sword, Juno, Gold, Omaha and Utah – contain few physical traces of their bloody past. It's almost as though the cheery banality of summertime in the seaside towns along this stretch of the Norman coast has grown like poppies over the painful memories of June 6, 1944. The beaches are dotted with gaily painted wooden bathing huts; the odd windsurfer braves the choppy grey-green waters; walkers ramble along the dunes; families up from Paris eat moules frites at beachside terraces – all a far cry from those horrible events as re-enacted in the shocking opening scene of *Saving Private Ryan*.

But while the sands are consumed by summer's frivolity, the cemeteries built to bury the D-Day dead serve as sanctuaries for those who don't want to forget. People shuffle in silence across the well-manicured lawns of the American burial ground on a cliff overlooking Omaha, where rows of perfectly aligned white crosses sweep down to the cliff's edge and appear to continue for miles into the sea. In the church-like peace and tranquillity, broken only by the sharp cries of seagulls, uniformed veterans remember fallen comrades and families lost husbands and fathers. Even the children, too young to even understand the sacrifices made, are humbled by the solemnity of their surroundings, affording only glancing and indifferent looks at the kites swirling in the breeze before returning to the poignantly simple white crosses that have made the grown-ups so quiet.

119 SNOW WONDER: PODDING IT UP IN THE SWISS ALPS

SWITZERLAND You can barely see *Whitepod*, a zero-impact, luxury "camp" until you're almost on it, so well is it camouflaged against the deep snows of this tranquil forest setting, high in the Alps and far from any roads.

Each pod – eight of them comprise the camp – is a mini geodesic dome sheathed in white canvas, a sturdy, igloo-shaped construction set on a raised wooden platform. But this is no wilderness campsite: the emphasis is squarely on modern, five-star comforts. Inside each pod – heated by its own wood-burning stove – you get a proper king-size bed with multiple fluffy down covers and comfortable armchairs, along with an iPod and designer toiletries.

So far, so typical of the ski industry – hardly the world's most environmentally sound, with all those snow cannon and piste-grooming machines, not to mention traffic jams on Alpine roads. But *Whitepod*, the idea of a Swiss entrepreneur, is different: no concrete is used in the pods, so there is no impact on the ground beneath, and everything is sourced locally, from the logs to the solar power to the organic food.

For showers, meals and relaxing with other guests, you cross to the wooden chalet in the centre of the site, which has been updated inside – all soft lighting, comfortable lounging and chic designer touches. The atmosphere is great – out in the wild woods, boasting spectacular views of the mountains, yet with every comfort taken care of in an understated, very Swiss way.

And *Whitepod*'s impeccable credentials don't get in the way of a good time: you can indulge in all sorts of Alpine activities up here, including dog-sledding with huskies, parahiking (hike to the top of a summit and then paraglide down), horse-riding and more. This far from the resorts, the only skiing on offer is testing off-piste stuff – with the prospect of a relaxing massage and a spectacular sunset when you get back to your pod.

120 MACAROONS FOR HER MAJESTY

FRANCE It's 5.30pm on a Friday, and a queue stretches out through the door of Ladurée, on rue Royale near the place de la Madeleine. If you're wondering what the fuss is about, just take one look at the display of fabulous cakes and pastries inside – so renowned are Ladurée's confections that foodies will cross Paris for them and patiently wait their turn to have their purchases packed into elegant boxes.

If you feel you've earned yourself a sightseeing break, you could bypass the queue and head for the adjoining salon de thé or tea room, though the English translation hardly does justice to this luxurious parlour dating from 1862, decorated with gilt-edged mirrors, marble-topped tables and ceiling frescoes.

Once you're installed at your table, surrounded by elegantly coiffed grandes dames sporting Hermès scarves and fashionistas flanked by designer bags, a waitress in a long polka-dotted apron will take your order and flash you a complicitous look as you name your desired confection. You could let yourself be tempted by any number of heavenly gateaux, but if you've never tasted them, it's Ladurée's famous macarons (macaroons) that you should try. Nothing like the stodgy coconut-heavy cookies that you may know from back home, these are delicate almondy biscuits with a delicious ganache filling – at once crunchy and gooey. They come in a variety of flavours and pastel colours – the chocolate and blackcurrant are the best – and, like designer fashion collections, new flavours are launched each season.

More extravagant creations are also available, such as the saint-honoré rose-framboise; made of choux pastry, Chantilly, raspberry compote and raspberries, and topped off with a rose petal, it has all the flouncy froufrou of a dress from the court of Versailles. Perhaps unsurprising, then, that Ladurée was appointed the official patissier for Sofia Coppola's film, *Marie Antoinette*. "Let them eat cake!", the French queen was supposed to have said. And when the cakes are this good, it's hard to imagine why you'd want to eat anything else.

121 CATHAR CASTLES OF LANGUEDOC-ROUSSILLON

FRANCE It's hard to forget the first time you catch a glimpse of the Château de Peyrepertuse. In fact, it takes a while before you realize that this really is a castle, not just some fantastic rock formation sprouting from the mountain top. But it's no mirage – 800 years ago, men really did haul slabs of stone up here to build one of the most hauntingly beautiful fortresses in Europe.

In medieval France, war was frequent, life often violent – the point of castles, obviously enough, was to provide a degree of protection from all of that. Location was all-important –and the Cathar lords of Languedoc-Roussillon took this to ludicrous extremes, building them in seemingly impossible places. How they even laid foundations boggles the mind. Approach Peyrepertuse on foot, from the village of Duilhac, and you'll soon see why. Improbably perched on the edge of long, rocky ridge, it's surrounded by a sheer drop of several hundred metres, and its outer walls cleverly follow the contours of the mountain, snaking around the summit like a stone viper.

Inside, at the lower end, is the main keep, a solid grey cube of rock that looks like it could withstand a battering from smart bombs, never mind medieval cannon. But to really appreciate the fortress, you have to get closer.

It's a sweaty hour-long hike to the top, but when you clamber through the main entrance and onto the upper keep, the views from the battlements are stupendous: here, where the mountain ends in a vast, jagged stub of granite, there are no walls – you'd need wings to attack from this side.

Ironically, even castles like this couldn't protect the Cathars. In the early thirteenth century, this Christian cult was virtually exterminated after forty years of war and a series of massacres that were brutal even by medieval standards. Peyrepertuse was surrendered in 1240, but the fact that it still survives, as impressive now as it must have been centuries ago, is testament both to the Cathars' ingenious building skills and their passionate struggle for freedom.

122 CRANKING UP THE VOLUME ON QUEEN'S DAY

THE NETHERLANDS Every April 30, Amsterdam, a city famed for its easy-going, fun-loving population, manages to crank the party volume a few notches higher in a street party that blasts away for a full 24 hours. Held to celebrate the official birthday of the Dutch monarch, Queen's Day is traditionally the one time each year when the police are forbidden from interfering with any activity, no matter how outrageous; and, of course, it's always a challenge to see where they really draw the line.

Stages piled high with huge sound systems take over every available open space, blasting out the beats all day and night – the main stages are on Rembrandtplein and particularly Thorbeckplein, Leidseplein, Nieuwmarkt and Museumplein – and whatever your inclination, you'll find enough beer-chugging, pill-popping and red-hot partying to satisfy the most voracious of appetites. There are only two rules: you must dress as ridiculously as possible, preferably in orange, the Dutch national colour, which adorns virtually every building, boat and body on the day; and you must drink enough beer not to care.

The extensive and picturesque canals are one of the best things about Amsterdam, and Queen's Day makes the most of them, as boating restrictions are lifted (or perhaps just ignored) and everyone goes bananas on the water – rowboats, barges and old fishing vessels crammed with people, crates of beer and sound systems, pound their way along the canals like entrants in some particularly disorganized aquatic carnival. Your mission is to get on board, as they're a great way to get around – pick one with good tunes and people you like the look of. Or just hang out with everyone else and watch the boats come and go: crowds gather on the larger bridges and canal junctions to cheer on each bizarre vessel – Prinsengracht is a good canal for this, with Reguliersgracht and Prinsengracht a particularly chaotic and enjoyable intersection.

THE CRESTA RUN:

SLEDGING WITH A DIFFERENCE

123

SWITZERLAND Are you man enough for this challenge? Requiring great upper body strength and stamina, the Cresta Run in St Moritz is strictly only for those with the XY chromosome – women have been banned since 1929. Oh, and you also have to be fearless, a bit of a thrill-seeker and slightly crazy.

Positioned on a skeleton toboggan, hurtling headfirst down a sheet-hard ice track at speeds of up to a terrifying 145kph, you will probably wonder, hysterically, if you'll ever see your loved ones again. Shoulders braced – for the very natural fear of being propelled skywards at every perilous twist and turn – you'd be hard pushed to find a more adrenalin-filled ride.

Unbelievably, the majority of racers make it down in one piece. But even so, the sane amongst us will be content just to watch.

124 BERLIN BY NIGHT

GERMANY Every bit as compelling as the daytime city, night-time Berlin is offbeat, makeshift and restlessly inventive: nothing seems to last forever, and that's part of the thrill, because the joy of finding some new one-nighter in a freaky and obscure venue triumphs over the disappointment when some long-established favourite is suddenly shuttered, dark and abandoned.

Berlin at night has a spectral landscape of its own: over the years, club promoters have reworked the spaces left forgotten and unloved by the city's tortured history to create some of Europe's most memorable venues, from the undercrofts of railway stations to the old Friedrichstrasse Tränenpalast, where East and West Berliners said their farewells during the Cold War, and from the outwardly average street-corner kneipen to the extraordinary communist swank of Café Moskau on the Karl Marx Allee.

Pounding dance rhythms rule: techno may have been invented in Detroit, but it came alive at Tresor, the legendary (and recently resurrected) club that was the standard bearer of Berlin's dance scene throughout the Nineties. But it's not just about the dancing – multimedia shows, live performance and even literary readings have their place – nor is it just about the mindless partying: live performance might mean ponderous electronic soundscapes at SO36; a reading is highly likely to be an excerpt from Kafka; and the celebrated Russendisko does more for German-Russian understanding than a month of Merkel-Putin summits. Berlin is also famously libertine in matters of sex, from housewives in rubber at the KitKat Club to gay men cruising in the dark at Tom's.

What Berlin's nightlife mostly lacks is the haughtiness and status-consciousness of wealthier cities like London or New York – the tyranny of the velvet rope. You can sip cocktails in chichi surroundings at Newton or the Bar am Lützowplatz if that's what you want, but the truth is that Berlin is flat broke – poor but sexy, as Mayor Wowereit put it – and it just doesn't have the spending power for such airs and graces. Still, with the spirit of make-do-and-mend serving it so well, money is the last thing to worry about. At least until the morning comes.

125 DELUXE DINING IN PARIS

FRANCE Sumptuous decor, exquisite food, service that purrs along like a Rolls Royce and a hint of the theatrical – Lasserre has all the ingredients of a classic haute cuisine restaurant, and is almost a parody of classic French dining as it used to be. The drama starts as soon as you arrive, a lift lined with deep-purple velvet delivers you into an opulent Neoclassical-style salon. Pillars and balustrades festooned with flowers form the backdrop to elegant tables laid with antique silver cruets and Meissen porcelain. The walls and drapes are decorated in rich reds and golds and the ceiling is painted with a whirl of sylphlike dancing women; a chandelier provides the central flourish. Diners are greeted by the charming Monsieur Louis, who has been at the restaurant for nearly forty years; very soon you're in the hands of a highly efficient and discreet corps of waiters in tails, anticipating your every need and unfailingly attentive – monsieur has spilt a little potage on his silk tie? Not to worry, a deft hand is soon dabbing it away.

But it's the food that really takes centre stage. This is cuisine of the hautest kind, traditional rather than modern: rich sauces, foie gras, caviar and truffles. Each dish is prepared with consummate artistry, each mouthful exquisitely intense. You might start with the artichokes in a wine sauce with courgette flowers and broad beans in argan oil, while for mains you could plump for one of the restaurant's classic dishes, such as canard á l'orange or pigeon André Malraux, the latter named after the Resistance hero and writer who once lunched here almost daily.

Save room for the signature dessert, timbale Elysée-Lasserre, a sublime creation of ice-cream, strawberries and chantilly cream canopied with a lattice of caramelized sugar. And it goes without saying that the wine list is exceptional – Lasserre's cellar holds some 200,000 bottles, mostly from Burgundy and Bordeaux, and there are fifty champagnes to choose from.

126 BIG FOOT: SNOWSHOEING THROUGH THE BLACK FOREST

GERMANY There's nothing more satisfying than being the first person to step on deep virgin snow. Except, perhaps, being able to step on it without sinking to your thighs. The solution? Snowshoes: clumsy tennis-racket contraptions that have morphed into lighter, high-tech models with snazzy spikes and the power to glide. Forget the adrenaline rush of bombing down the Alps; snowshoeing offers silent winter thrills in frozen forests and the chance to see a country's wild side. I'd picked the Black Forest in Germany, a winter wonderland of fir-clad hills custom-made for this low-impact sport.

Just for the "wow factor", I decided to hike the forest's highest peak, 1493-metre Feldberg, geared up for snowshoers like me, with mile upon mile of well-marked trails. Leaving civilization behind, I took my first giant steps through layers of crunchy powder, little by little adapting to the shuffle and swoosh of my snowshoes in quiet exhilaration. More confident now, I tried a few Bambi-style leaps and bounces down a smooth white slope. Heart racing and cheeks glowing, it dawned on me that I'd have to climb back up that hill. Damn.

I've seen some big trees in my time, but Black Forest firs beat them all – Goliaths standing to attention, their branches thick with gloopy snow as though someone got a bit carried away with the icing sugar. I flopped beneath one of them, slurping hot tea and enjoying the isolation of being out of my depth in snow and surrounded by utter silence. Taking long, rhythmic strides past fox prints, deer poo and stacks of fresh-cut timber, I finally emerged at Feldberg's summit. Ahead, the panorama opened up to reveal glacier-carved valleys framed by the pointy Alps and Vosges. Behind me, a solitary set of footprints twinkled in the midday sun.

MISCELLANY

HIGHLIGHTS

The highest point in Western Europe is Mont Blanc, in the French–Italian Alps, at 4807m above sea level. Europe's highest permanently occupied settlement is Juf, a hamlet near St Moritz in Switzerland, at 2126m above sea level.

HAUTE CUISINE

France is synonymous with gastronomic perfection, though some historians (and most Italians) claim that **haute cuisine** was introduced to the nation in the 1540s by Florence native Catherine de Medici, who brought a team of skilled chefs to Paris when she married Henri II. Whatever the truth, France had developed its own rich culinary tradition by the eighteenth century, blending regional styles with the lavish cuisine served at the royal court.

Today, gastronomic excellence is rewarded by **Michelin stars** (three being the highest), which were introduced in 1926 by way of the French tyre manufacturer's travel guides. According to *Restaurant* magazine, the country's top restaurants of 2006 are as follows:

Alain Ducasse at Plaza Athénée Paris. Modern French cooking from the only chef in the world with three Michelin stars in three different countries (France, the USA and Monaco).

L'Astrance Paris. Intimate split-level restaurant, serving contemporary, creative menus from chef Pascal Barbot.

Le Cinq Paris. Domain of chef Philippe Legendre, who creates sumptuous haute cuisine in the opulent surroundings of the Four Seasons George V hotel.

Michel Bras Laguiole. Deep in the Auvergne, blending minimalist Japanese presentation with traditional local specialities.

Pierre Gagnaire Paris. Modern and sophisticated decor to match modern, innovative (and very expensive) French cuisine.

FROMAGE FORMIDABLE

Cheese is a French obsession. More fromage is consumed here than in any other European nation, at 23kg per person per year, while France produces over 500 types of highly prized regional varieties, from Normandy's soft, creamy Camembert and Brie to Vieux Boulogne, an unpasteurized, beer-washed concoction that's widely held to be one of the smelliest in the world. The most expensive French cheese is truffle-stuffed Brie, which sells at around £45/US$85 per kilo, while the hardest is reputed to be -Mimolette -Extra Vielle, with an outer shell as solid as a coconut. France is also the world's top producer of **goat's cheese**, with over 100 varieties, many of them sold in bizarre and highly memorable forms: Pouligny Saint Pierre comes in pyramids, while Sainte Maure de Touraine is sold in cylinders, each with a straw running through the middle as proof of authenticity.

"How can anyone govern a nation that has 246 different kinds of cheese?"

Charles de Gaulle. There are now between 350 and 400 French cheeses

MAKING A PIG OF YOURSELF

Held every August at Trie-sur-Baise in the Midi-Pyrénées and drawing a loyal cult following, the **French Pig-Squealing Championships** are one of France's most bizarre "fêtes folles", and sees participants act like pigs, competing on the basis of oinks, grunts and even, disturbingly, simulated suckling and mating.

DUTCH WONDER

According to the American Society of Civil Engineers, the **North Sea Protection Works** in the Netherlands is one of the Seven Modern Wonders of the World. This unique and complex system of dams, floodgates and storm surge barriers protects the Netherlands from the North Sea. The main features are a nineteen-mile-long dam to block the Zuider Zee, and the Eastern Schelde Barrier, two miles of gates between huge concrete piers.

NO BEER PLEASE, WE'RE GERMAN

There are a record 1270 breweries in Germany, producing over 5000 different brews, but despite these impressive figures, the nation's beer consumption is steadily dwindling, down from 133 litres in 1994 to 114 in 2007. It would seem that Germans are looking elsewhere for their bubbles as mineral water has become the tipple of choice; in fact, the country consumes the most mineral water in the world, at around 130 litres a year.

SWEET SUITES

According to Forbes magazine, the **world's most expensive hotel suite** is the Penthouse Suite at the Hotel Martinez in Cannes, France. It comes with four bedrooms, a private Jacuzzi and a huge terrace with views of the Mediterranean, but it'll set you back €28,000. Bargain hunters can save fifteen hundred or so euros by checking in to the President Wilson Hotel in Geneva, Switzerland, whose Royal Penthouse Suite comes second on Forbes' list. Here, €26,500 gets you a private elevator, bulletproof doors and windows, plus panoramas over Lake Geneva.

WESTERN EUROPE'S GREAT RIVERS

River	Rises in...	Drains into...	Length
Danube	Germany	Black Sea	2850km
Rhine	Switzerland	North Sea	1320km
Loire	France	Atlantic Ocean	1012km
Rhône	Switzerland	Mediterranean Sea	800km

SPORTS TO TRY

Sport	Played mostly in	What happens
Boules	France	The best-known type of boules is pétanque; played on a gravel surface, players toss metal balls to land as close as possible to a target wooden ball.
Hornussen	Switzerland	An outlandish mixture of golf and baseball: one player launches a puck along a curved track with a long cane; the others try to hit it with large wooden bats before it touches the ground.
Korfball	Belgium, The Netherlands	Like egalitarian netball: two teams (of 4 men and 4 women each) try to score baskets against each other.

NOW THERE'S A THOUGHT...

France has produced some of the greatest thinkers in the history of philosophy, from Descartes and his seminal work on natural philosophy and geometry or Jean-Paul Sartre and the great existentialist thinkers of the Left Bank to post-modernists such as Michel Foucault.

GREAT FRENCH
PHILOSOPHERS

René Descartes (1596–1650) Best known for claiming "I think therefore I am", Descartes was a leading proponent of rationalism – using the rational mind rather than the unreliable senses to deduct scientific truth, as the empiricists advocated.

Blaise Pascal (1623–1662) Starting his career as a scientist, Pascal began the *Pensées* ("Thoughts"), after a religious epiphany in 1654, attacking Descartes' rationalism with Pascal's Wager – the concept that it is always better to believe in God, as the expected benefit from that belief is always greater than atheism.

Voltaire (1694–1778) Leading light of the French Enlightenment, and author of satires such as Candide, Voltaire is best known for his defence of religious freedom.

Jean-Paul Sarte (1905–1980) One of the founders of existentialism, but also lauded for his works of fiction and political activism, he refused the Nobel Prize for Literature in 1964 on the grounds that he had never accepted honours before, and did not want to be associated with establishment institutions.

Jacques Derrida (1930–2004) The founder of "deconstruction", a new insight into the meaning (or lack thereof) of words and texts, and regarded as one of the world's foremost modern philosophers.

GREAT COUNTRYSIDE RESTAURANTS

Olivier Roellinger Cancale, France. Sensational cooking in a small Brittany harbour town, featuring local fish and seafood enhanced with exotic spices.

Oud Sluis Sluis, the Netherlands. This sleepy seaside village near the Belgian border hosts a young, innovative chef quietly working culinary magic.

Schwarzwaldstube Baiersbronn, Germany. Sublime French cuisine in a sturdily traditional setting, with panoramic views over the Black Forest.

"Never interrupt your enemy when he is making a mistake"

Napoleon Bonaparte

WINE AND BEER

France is the largest wine-producing country in the world, exporting 22 percent of the world's wine sales and producing 5,329,449 tonnes annually. It also is typically said to have the best, holding the renowned regions of Bordeaux, Burgundy and Champagne.

Essen, Germany, has the highest beer consumption of any city in the world with an astonishing 230 litres drunk per person per year. **Belgium** has the greatest number of beer varieties, the strongest of which is the Trappist ale Westvleteren, which weighs in at around 12%, although Samichlaus, a brew produced each year in Austria for Christmas is more alcoholic, at 14%.

FIVE FAMOUS BELGIANS

Plastic Bertrand (1954–) Who can forget Plastic's one-hit wonder *Ca Plane Pour Moi*, which was Belgium's biggest punk hit in 1977. After nearly twenty years in the Walloon wilderness he made a comeback in the late-1990s and is now a presenter on French telly and has recently released his eighth album.

Jacques Brel (1929–1978) The legendary singer, songwriter and actor, whose work has recently been revived by Scott Walker, is one of the greatest exponents of the French chanson – though ironically he was of Flemish descent. You can visit his house in Brussels, which is now a museum.

Eddy Merckx (1945–) Regularly voted the greatest ever Belgian by both Flemish- and French-speakers, Merckx is perhaps the greatest competitive cyclist of all time. He won both the Tour de France and Giro d'Italia five times and is still involved in the sport, as a race commentator and bike manufacturer.

Adolphe Sax (1814–1894) Soul and jazz music would have been much the poorer without the contribution of Adolphe Sax, who invented the saxophone in Dinant in 1846. You can pay homage at his house – now a museum – in the sleepy Ardennes town.

Georges Simenon (1903–1989) Famous philanderer (he apparently slept with 10,000 women) and creator of the the classically deadpan European detective in Maigret, Simeon hailed from Liege but spent most of his adult life in Paris, where he set most of his books.

PLAYING WITH FIRE AT LAS FALLAS • SKIING UNDER A SPANISH SUN • PULPO ADDICTION: GOING GASTRO IN GALICIA • LA RIOJA: LAND OF THE RISING VINE • GAWPING AT THE GUGGENHEIM • CASTLE IN THE SKY: OVER THE MESETA TO MORELLA • THE LOST STREETS OF RIO HONOR DE CASTILLA • TAPAS CRAWLING IN MADRID • PORTRAITS AND PURGATORY AT THE PRADO • PRAY MACARENA! EASTER IN SEVILLE • SURFING THE COAST OF LIGHT FROM TARIFA TO TANGIER • HIKING IN THE PYRENEES • A DROP OF THE BARD'S STUFF: DRINKING SHERRY SPANISH STYLE • ROAMING LAS RAMBLAS • HIKING IN THE PYRENEES • LEARNING TO SURF ON THE ATLANTIC COAST • FLAMENCO: BACKSTREETS AND GYPSY BEATS • SEEING STARS IN SAN SEBASTIÁN • COUNTING DOLPHINS IN THE MEDITERRANEAN • MODERNISME AND MAÑANA: GAUDÍ'S SAGRADA FAMILIA • HEADING FOR THE HEIGHTS IN THE PICOS DE EUROPA • MARVELLING INSIDE THE MEZQUITA • CLEARING YOUR CALENDAR FOR BACALHAU • GOING FOR YOUR GUNS AT ALMERÍA • POETIC LICENSE IN DEIA • SEEING SUMMER OFF IN STYLE: IBIZA'S CLOSING PARTIES • TAKING TO THE STREETS OF TENERIFE • GETTING LOST AT THE PILGRIM'S PALACE • DROPPING IN AT MUNDAKA • ALPARGATAS: THE SOUL IS IN THE SOLE • PAINTING THE TOWN RED AT LA TOMATINA • SURREAL LIFE AT THE DALÍ MUSEUM • IN SEARCH OF THE PERFECT TART • WATCHING REAL MADRID AT THE BERNABÉU • LIVING WITHOUT SLEEP IN VALENCIA • CRUISING THROUGH THE COTO DE DOÑANA • TRAM 28: TAKING A RIDE THROUGH LISBON'S HISTORIC QUARTERS • HIKING THE ANCIENT FORESTS OF LA GOMERA • EXPLORING MYSTICAL SINTRA • CYCLING FOR THE SOUL: EL CAMINO DE SANTIAGO • MOORISH GRANADA: EXPLORING THE ALHAMBRA • DISCOVERING CONQUISTADORS' SPOILS • RUNNING WITH THE BULLS • STOP! IT'S HAMMER TIME AT THE FESTA DE SÃO JOÃO • PLAYING WITH FIRE AT LAS FALLAS • SKIING UNDER A SPANISH SUN • PULPO ADDICTION: GOING GASTRO IN GALICIA • LA RIOJA: LAND OF THE RISING VINE • SURREAL LIFE AT THE DALÍ MUSEUM • GAWPING AT THE GUGGENHEIM • CASTLE IN THE SKY: OVER THE MESETA TO MORELLA • THE LOST STREETS OF RIO HONOR DE CASTILLA • TAPAS CRAWLING IN MADRID • PORTRAITS AND PURGATORY AT THE PRADO • PRAY MACARENA! EASTER IN SEVILLE • SURFING THE COAST OF LIGHT FROM TARIFA TO TANGIER • HIKING IN THE PYRENEES • A DROP OF THE BARD'S STUFF: DRINKING SHERRY SPANISH STYLE • ROAMING LAS RAMBLAS • HIKING IN THE PYRENEES • LEARNING TO SURF ON THE ATLANTIC COAST • FLAMENCO: BACKSTREETS AND GYPSY BEATS • COUNTING DOLPHINS IN THE MEDITERRANEAN • SEEING STARS IN SAN SEBASTIÁN • MODERNISME AND MAÑANA: GAUDÍ'S SAGRADA FAMILIA • HEADING FOR THE HEIGHTS IN THE PICOS DE EUROPA • MARVELLING INSIDE THE MEZQUITA • CLEARING YOUR CALENDAR FOR BACALHAU • GOING FOR YOUR GUNS AT ALMERÍA • POETIC LICENSE IN DEIA • SEEING SUMMER OFF IN STYLE: IBIZA'S CLOSING PARTIES • TAKING TO THE STREETS OF TENERIFE • GETTING LOST AT THE PILGRIM'S PALACE • DROPPING IN AT MUNDAKA • PAINTING THE TOWN RED AT LA TOMATINA • IN SEARCH OF THE PERFECT TART • WATCHING REAL MADRID AT THE BERNABÉU • LIVING WITHOUT SLEEP IN VALENCIA • TRAM 28: TAKING A RIDE THROUGH LISBON'S HISTORIC QUARTERS • CRUISING THROUGH THE COTO DE DOÑANA • HIKING THE ANCIENT FORESTS OF LA GOMERA • EXPLORING MYSTICAL SINTRA • MOORISH GRANADA: EXPLORING THE ALHAMBRA • CYCLING FOR THE SOUL: EL CAMINO DE SANTIAGO • DISCOVERING CONQUISTADORS' SPOILS • STOP! IT'S HAMMER TIME AT THE FESTA DE SÃO JOÃO • PLAYING WITH FIRE AT LAS FALLAS • SKIING UNDER A SPANISH SUN • PULPO ADDICTION: GOING GASTRO IN GALICIA • LA RIOJA: LAND OF THE RISING VINE • SURREAL LIFE AT THE DALÍ MUSEUM • GAWPING AT THE GUGGENHEIM • CASTLE IN THE SKY: OVER THE MESETA TO MORELLA • THE LOST STREETS OF RIO HONOR

THE IBERIAN PENINSULA

127–178

CYCLING FOR THE SOUL:
EL CAMINO DE SANTIAGO **173**

GAWPING AT
THE GUGGENHEIM **131**

SURREAL LIFE
AT THE DALÍ MUSEUM **165**

STOP! IT'S HAMMER TIME
AT THE FESTA DO SÃO JOÃO

146

PORTUGAL

SPAIN

COUNTING DOLPHINS
IN THE MEDITERRANEAN

143

TRAM #28: A RIDE THROUGH
LISBON'S HISTORIC QUARTERS **170**

PLAYING WITH FIRE
AT LAS FALLAS **127**

BALEARIC
ISLANDS

MARVELLING INSIDE
THE MESQUITA **151**

MOORISH GRANADA:
EXPLORING THE ALHAMBRA **174**

CLEARING **150**
YOUR CALENDAR
FOR BACALHAU

MADEIRA

CANARY ISLANDS

AZORES

PLAYING WITH FIRE AT LAS FALLAS

127

SPAIN While Wicker Man fever has only crept back into Britain over the last decade or so, Catholic Spain has traditionally held faster to old habits, synchronising Saints' days with ancient seasonal rites.

The most famous – and noisiest – festival of all is Las Fallas: in mid-March Valencia's streets combust in a riot of flame and firecrackers, ostensibly in celebration of St Joseph. As a recent local article put it: "Gunpowder is like blood for any Valencian Festival", and that goes double for Las Fallas; it's (barely) controlled pyromania on a scale unrivalled anywhere in Europe, a festival where the neighbourhood firemen are on overtime and beauty sleep is in short supply.

If you're not still partying from the night before, a typical Fallas day will see you rudely awakened at 7am by the galumphing cacophony of a brass band (perhaps it's no coincidence that the shawm – an ancestor of the oboe – was originally employed by Arab armies as an early form of psychological warfare).

By 2pm sharp, you'll be part of the baying mob in the Plaza Ayuntamiento, standing gape-mouthed in anticipation of the Mascletà, a daily round of colour and seismic blasts. The fallas themselves are huge satirical tableaux peopled by ninots, or allegorical figures – everyone from voluptuous harlots to George W. Bush – painstakingly crafted out of wood, wax, papiermâché and cardboard. They're exhibited by their respective *Casals* Faller – the grass-roots community houses which run the festival – during nightly street parties, before all 500 of them literally go up in smoke; the Cremà (the burning) represents the festival's climax, kicking off at midnight on March 19.

If the heady aroma of cordite, wood-fired paella, buñuelos (pumpkin fritters) and industrial-strength drinking chocolate is all too much for you, you can always view the fallas that got away (one gets a reprieve each year) in the quieter – and saner – environs of the city's Museu Faller.

128 SKIING UNDER A SPANISH SUN

SPAIN Sun, sea and ski: it just doesn't sound right. Yet Spain is the second highest landmass in Europe after Switzerland, boasting more than five times as many resorts as Scotland. The most southerly ski area in Europe, the Sierra Nevada warily eyes Africa across the Mediterranean. Its often erratic snow conditions aren't the greatest, but the T-shirt temperatures and dearth of attitude are a breath of fresh mountain air.

More than anything, though, the lure of Andalucían skiing lies in its location, in the glorious novelty of sunning yourself on the Cabo de Gata in the morning and going on the piste in the afternoon. Its height – the towering Mulhacén stands at well over 3500 metres – is another factor: as late as May, when resorts further north are covered in Alpine grass and trekkers, skiing is still an option.

At heart, the resort is a beginner's playground, with miles of gentle piste and special "magic carpet" conveyor lifts. If you've ever squinted through a howling wall of Glenshee sleet, or had your legs embarassingly part company with your tow at a 45-degree angle, you'll appreciate Sierra Nevada's undulating rhythm and sapphire skies.

If such wimpish gradients are anathema, or you like your snow a little more stylish, head for the swanky, relatively remote resort of Baqueira-Beret in Catalunya's Vall d'Aran. A morning dip on the Costa Brava will mean getting up a hell of a lot earlier, but as a haunt of Spain's great and good, the place boasts the Catalan Pyrenees' best facilities and most challenging pick of pine-dotted pistes.

Intermediates with a taste for Atlantic weather should seek out the modern Cantabrian resort of Alto Campoo. The number of lifts and tows barely makes it into double figures but the area's tranquillity and unassuming beauty has made it increasingly popular. Whichever resort you choose, enjoy it while it lasts – global warming looks likely to hit the industry hard.

129 SEEING STARS IN SAN SEBASTIÁN

SPAIN Many who make their way to the genteel resort of San Sebastián, in Spain's Basque region, have one thing on their mind: food. Within the country, Pais Vasco – as the Basque area is known – has always been recognized as serving Spain's finest cuisine, but it's only relatively recently that word has got beyond its borders. The city in fact boasts the most impressive per capita concentration of Michelin stars in the world, a recognition that its deep-rooted gastronomic tradition has finally come of age. And while feisty newcomers like *Mugaritz* make international headlines, Juan Mari Arzak is widely regarded as the one who kicked it all off back in the 1970s.

Long the holder of three of those cherished stars, his *Arzak* restaurant remains the parlour-informal, family-friendly temple of audacious yet almost always recognizably Basque food; a meal here is a thrilling affair. Deftly incorporating line-caught fruits of the Cantabrian sea, the flora and fauna of the Basque countryside and flavours from further afield (a sister branch operates in Mexico City), Arzak and his daughter Elena are as likely to cook with smoked chocolate, cardamom, dry ice-assisted sauces and ash-charred vinaigrette as the signature truffles and foie gras. Bold, subversive takes on Spanish classics – strawberry gazpacho anyone? – confound and exhilarate while longstanding favourites like truffle-distilled poached egg are so flawlessly presented you'll hesitate to slice into them. And despite the gourmet prices, the ratio of gregarious locals to foodie pilgrims means there's little scope for snobbery.

Still, if cost is an issue, you can experience San Sebastián's epicurean passions by way of a txikiteo, the Basque version of a tapas crawl. You can taste your way through a succession of tempting pintxos – their name for the baroque miniatures on offer – at hearteningly unpretentious bars such as *Txepetxa*, *Ganbara* and *La Cuchara de San Telmo*, in the parte vieja (old town). Marinated anchovies with sea urchin roe, papaya or spider crab salad, tumblers of viscous garlic broth and earthy wild mushroom confit come with a tiny price tag – just a few euros – but with lasting reward.

130 LA RIOJA: LAND OF THE RISING VINE

SPAIN It's a tipple that the Castillian court appreciated sufficiently to issue quasi-protectionist decrees as early as the twelfth century, but, with French know-how, only really began assuming its contemporary character in the 1850s. Having retreated to Bordeaux to escape political unrest at home, one Camilo Hurtado de Amézaga, otherwise known as Marqués de Riscal, returned to northern Spain armed with vines, oak casks and an amateur's enthusiasm, and pioneered classic, oak-aged Rioja from his own bodega in the town of Elciego.

More than a century and a half later, the Marqués de Riscal dynasty is pioneering another seismic shift, and precipitating mass enotourism with a Frank O. Gehry-designed City Of Wine. Topped by leaves of lilac- and gold-tinted steel, transposing vines into modern art, the complex incorporates a hotel, restaurant, museum and even a trendy spa. Not that they're the first bodega to hire a hip architect: the strikingly situated and designed Bodegas Ysios, near the hill town of Laguardia, is the work of Santiago Calatrava. It is an aluminium Mexican wave of a building housing a wine acclaimed for its fruit-driven complexity.

Other bodegas have invested the shock of the new solely in their finished product – places like Roda in Haro, the slightly dowdy but charming viticultural hub in the region's far northwest. Strategically planned and purpose-built, Roda painstakingly fine-tunes its winemaking process, selecting old-vine grapes for its celebrated, tannin-rich Cirsión range. Still dedicated to traditional oak fermentation, Haro's Muga is a wonderful old bodega down by the town's train station, where they crack open eggs by the hundred, using the white to filter the wine, and you can watch reticent-looking artisans crafting in-house barrels.

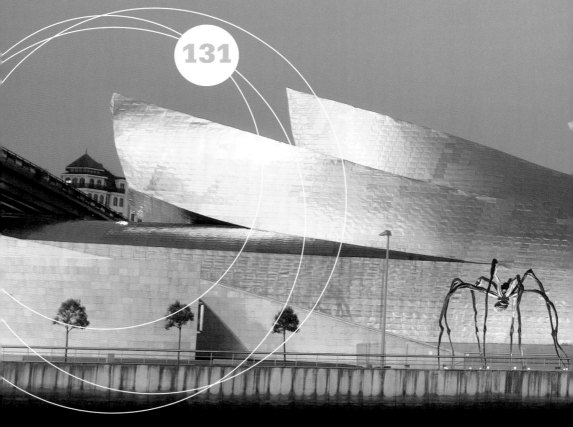

GAWPING
AT THE
GUGGENHEIM

131

SPAIN In the same way Glasgow outlived a grimy past to become the darling of America's travel media, Bilbao gambled on the cultural dollar and won. By becoming the first European city to fully embrace New York's Guggenheim franchise, it transformed itself from a briny, rusting behemoth into a modern art mecca. Frank O. Gehry's brief was to draw the gaze of the world; his response was an audacious, ingenious conflation of Bilbao's past and future, a riverine citadel moulded from titanium and limestone, steel and glass. Up close it appears as an urban planner's daydream gone delightfully wrong; viewed from the opposite bank of the river it assumes the guise of a gilded, glittering ark. But it all depends on your mood and the notoriously unpredictable Basque weather: on other days it broods like a computer-generated *Marie Celeste*, or glints rudely like a capricious cross between Monty Python and El Dorado. Gehry extends the aquatic theme by subsuming Bilbao's historic waterway into his design, so you can also take its measure by means of the nifty raised walkway and the connecting bridge, Puente de la Salve.

By the main entrance sits Jeff Koons' *Puppy*, an oversized, overstuffed floral statue, lost in an eternal siesta. Even the entrance is surreal, descending into the museum's huge atrium and voluminous galleries where, inevitably, the contents are rarely afforded quite as much attention as the surroundings. In amidst the rotated collections of Abstract Expressionism and Pop Art, interactive installations and excitable knots of foreign students, the powers that be continue to envisage the wordless horror of Picasso's *Guernica* as a centrepiece, even if it still languishes in Madrid. *Guernica* or no, every city and its satellite is now clamouring for a piece of the Guggenheim action – stand up Guadalajara, sit down Rio – but Spain remains the titanium template, proof that Bilbao's ship has finally come in.

132 CASTLE IN THE SKY: OVER THE MESETA TO MORELLA

SPAIN When you finally tire of sand, sea and mullets, the great thing about Spain is how easy it is to jump centuries in a few hours. Currently petitioning UNESCO for World Heritage status, Morella is the kind of living Knights Templar fantasy you're more likely to find in Castille or northern Portugal, yet it's located a mere 62km from the Mediterranean. Half the fun is actually getting there; after ascending from the anonymous sprawl of Castellón via plunging forests and queasy gradients, breaching the snow line and emerging into the liberating vastness of the meseta (plateau), you'll find Morella hunched inside beautifully preserved medieval walls, in the lee of a formidable castle, itself perched on a sheer, almost biblical outcrop of rock.

Even with the spring sunshine penetrating the town's precipitous, arcaded shadows, it's not too difficult to imagine how harsh and poverty-stricken the Franco-era winters were. Yet the locals are among the friendliest and most hospitable in Spain – the merest hint of political sympathies will likely inspire an endless supply of insight and gratis Gran Reserva. Talk with them for any length of time, and you'll soon get a sense of how fiercely proud the town is of its regional identity, to the extent that Spanish nationality itself is amorphous.

Nowadays the place thrives on a steady trickle of – largely Spanish – tourists, roaming narrow streets studded with gothic mansions (you can even lodge in one – the famous *Hotel Cardenal Ram* – for ridiculously reasonable rates), wooden balconies and restaurants serving the mouthwatering local speciality, *trufas negras* (black truffles). All roads ultimately lead to the castle, a truly magical site where crimson poppies and luminous butterflies adorn dusty, serpentine paths and stupendous views, and the spiritual strata of past occupants – Ibero-Celts, Romans and Moors among them – lingers in every crumbling wall and cul-de-sac.

133 EXPLORING MYSTICAL SINTRA

PORTUGAL Inspiration for a host of writers – including Lord Byron and William Beckford – Sintra, the former summer retreat of Portuguese monarchs, is a town dotted with palaces and mansions, and surrounded by a series of wooded ravines. Now one of Europe's finest UNESCO World Heritage sites, Sintra has been a centre for cult worship for centuries: the early Celts named it Mountain of the Moon after one of their gods, and the hills are scattered with ley lines and mysterious tombs. Locals say batteries drain noticeably faster here and light bulbs pop with monotonous regularity.

Some claim it is because of the angle of iron in the rocks, others that it is all part of the mystical powers that lurk in Sintra's hills and valleys. There are certainly plenty of geographical and meteorological quirks: house-sized boulders litter the landscape as if thrown by giants, while a white cloud – affectionately known as "the queen's fart" – regularly hovers over Sintra's palaces even on the clearest summer day.

The fairytale palace of Palácio da Pena on the heights above town, with its dizzy views over the surrounding woodlands, looks like something from *Shrek*, complete with elaborate walkways, domes and drawbridges. Inside, its kitsch decor is kept just as it was when Portugal's last monarch, Manuel, fled at the birth of the republic. Quinta da Regaleira, a private estate from the turn of the twentieth century, is no less extraordinary. The gardens of this landowner's mansion hide the Initiation Well, entered via a revolving stone door. Inside, a moss-covered spiral staircase leads to a subterranean tunnel that resurfaces by a lake – a bizarre and mysterious place, which, like all of Sintra, shelters tales as fantastical as the buildings.

134 TAPAS CRAWLING IN MADRID

SPAIN Tapas crawling is to the Spaniard what pub crawling is to the northern European, with the added bonus that you're not literally crawling by the end of the night, or at least you shouldn't be if you've faithfully scoffed a titbit with each drink.

In Granada and assorted hinterlands they're still a complimentary courtesy; in the rest of the country a free lunch has gone the way of the siesta and the peseta. But if you're going to pay for your nibbles, Madrid offers one of the meanest tapas crawls in the land, starting from the central Puerta del Sol. In and around the narrow streets between Sol and Plaza Santa Ana you can tuck into fluffy fried prawns and erm...more prawns *(al ajillo,* in garlic), washed down by heady house wine at the Lilliputian *Casa del Abuelo* (c/Victoria 12). Unpretentious, atmospheric bars also serving authentic bites are *Las Bravas* (c/Alvarez Gato 3), a former barbers turned fried-potato-in-spicy-sauce specialist with a closely guarded recipe, and *La Oreja de Oro* (c/Victoria 9), which translates as "The Golden Ear", but in fact serves ears of the conspicuously edible variety. The fried pigs' parts are a concession to local tastes, but the rest of the menu – including Ribeiro wine served in bowls and pimientos de Padrón (unpredictably hot fried peppers) – wears its Galician colours proudly. If cartilage doesn't tickle your tastebuds, it's probably worth taking a little detour back to the western edge of the Plaza Mayor for *Mesón del Champiñones* (Cava de San Miguel 17), an earthy *taberna* that's been doling out mouthwatering pan-fried mushrooms and sangria for longer than most Madrileños can remember. Even older is *Taberna de Antonio Sanchez* (c/Mesón de Paredes 13) in nearby Lavapiés, a bullfighters' den dating from 1830, where the dark wood walls are heavy with scarred taurine trophies from long-forgotten duels. For something less queasy to finish up, cut back east to *Taberna de Dolores* (Plaza de Jesús 4), where the slender Roquefort and anchovy canapés will ensure you wake up with fearsome breath, if not a hangover.

135 PORTRAITS AND PURGATORY AT THE PRADO

SPAIN Opened in 1819 at the behest of Ferdinand VII, Madrid's El Prado has long been one of the world's premier art galleries, with a collection so vast only a fraction of its paintings can be exhibited at any one time. Among those treasures – gleaned largely from the salons of the Spanish nobility – are half of the complete works of Diego Velázquez, virtuoso court painter to Felipe IV. Such was the clamour surrounding a 1990 exhibition that half-a-million people filed through the turnstiles; those locked out clashed with civil guards. What Velázquez himself would've made of it all is hard to say; in his celebrated masterpiece *Las Meninas*, he peers out inscrutably from behind his own canvas, dissolving the boundaries between viewer and viewed, superimposing scene upon reflected scene.

Strung out over two floors, the works of Francisco de Goya are equally revolutionary, ranging from sensous portraiture to piercing documents of personal and political trauma. It's difficult to imagine public disorder over his infamous *Pinturas Negras*, nor do they attract the spectatorial logjams of *Las Meninas*, yet they're not works you'll forget in a hurry. The terrible magnetism of paintings like *The Colossus* and *Saturn Devouring One of His Sons* is easier to comprehend in the context of their creation, as the last will and testament of a deaf and disillusioned old man, fearful of his own flight into madness. Originally daubed on the walls of his farmhouse, the black paintings take to extremes motifs that Goya had pioneered: *Tres de Mayo* is unflinching in depicting the tawdry horror of war, its faceless Napoleonic executioners firing a fusillade that echoes into the twenty-first century.

136 PRAY MACARENA! EASTER IN SEVILLE

SPAIN The Spanish flock may be wavering but, being Catholic and proud, they take their religious festivals as seriously as they did in the days when a pointy hat meant the Inquisition. Semana Santa (or Holy Week) is the most spectacular of all the Catholic celebrations, and Seville carries it off with an unrivalled pomp and ceremony. Conceived as an extravagant antidote to Protestant asceticism, the festivities were designed to steep the common man in Christ's Passion, and it's the same today – the dazzling climax to months of preparation. You don't need to be a Christian to appreciate the outlandish spectacle or the exquisitely choreographed attention to detail. Granted, if you're not expecting it, the sight of massed hooded penitents can be disorientating and not a little disturbing – rows of eyes opaque with concentration, feet stepping slavishly in time with brass and percussion. But Holy Week is also about the pasos, or floats, elaborate slow-motion platforms graced with piercing, tottering images of Jesus and the Virgin Mary, swathed in Sevillano finery. All across Seville, crowds hold their collective breath as they anticipate the moment when their local church doors are thrown back and the paso commences its unsteady journey, the costaleros (or bearers) sweating underneath, hidden from view. With almost sixty cofradías, or brotherhoods, all mounting their own processions between Palm Sunday and Good Friday, the city assumes the guise of a sacred snakes-and-ladders board, criss-crossed by caped, candle-lit columns at all hours of the day and night, heavy with the ambrosial scent of incense and orange blossom, and pierced by the plaintive lament of the saetas, unaccompanied flights of religious song sung by locals on their balconies. Regardless of where the processions start they all converge on c/Sierpes, the commercial thoroughfare jammed with families who've paid for a front-seat view. From here they proceed to the cathedral, where on Good Friday morning the whole thing reaches an ecstatic climax with the appearance of La Macarena, the protector of Seville's bullfighters long before she graced the pop charts.

137 SURFING THE COAST OF LIGHT: FROM TARIFA TO TANGIER

SPAIN No Spanish town is more synonymous with wind than Tarifa. Facing down Morocco across the Gibraltar Straits, it's both a windsurfing magnet and a suicide blackspot where the relentless gusting can literally drive people mad. But don't let that put you off; you're more likely to be driven to distraction in the concrete inferno of Costas Brava, Blanca or Sol, an orgy of development from which the Costa de la Luz has thus far abstained.

In contrast, Tarifa is a whitewashed rendezvous, a chimerical canvas where the Med meets the Atlantic, the Poniente wind meets the Levante and Africa meets Europe. Even as muscled windsurfers ride the tide and live large, the Rif Mountains of kif farms and Paul Bowles-imagined Gothic loom across the waves like emissaries of another, darker star.

Climatic conditions for wind- and kitesurfing are optimal in the afternoon and early evening once the Levante hits its stride, although beginners are usually schooled in the morning. There are several rental places in Tarifa itself, and other facilities farther up the crescent of bleached-sand beach. When the sun goes down, Tangier's lights start beckoning, and it is possible (just) to get your afternoon's surfing fix before heading to Morocco for the evening, avoiding the daytime scrum of quayside touts, and arriving just as sunset breathes new energy into the city's pavement cafés.

Stumbling into a harshly day-lit street from a hotel you entered in darkness, the culture shock hits hard. Despite its seedy reputation, Tangier is a fascinating place, where you can meditate over William Burroughs and mint tea, take an incorrigibly polite tour of an Anglican church, zone out on gnawa music and make the medina muezzin your dawn alarm. And once you've experienced Morocco, the sight of Tarifa's harbour walls and bulging sails on your return seems even more illusory, more a continuation of North Africa than an outpost of Europe.

138 ROAMING LAS RAMBLAS

SPAIN A life-sized silver statue of a winged woman glints in the noonday sun. You walk by – and then turn back to look. A crowd is gathering around her. "Holaaa!" screams out a little boy, advancing bravely. The statue's eyebrow twitches. More people stop. A gust of wind catches the statue's wings, but otherwise she's still as stone. A few onlookers shift uneasily. And then the statue cocks her silver head, bows grandly and rattles a tin cup for change. Just another performer in the daily spectacle of Las Ramblas, Barcelona's thronged pedestrian promenade.

There may be no better place in the country to partake in the ritual of a paseo (stroll) than Las Ramblas, which cuts a wide swath through the old town, from Plaça Catalunya to the Mediterranean Sea. While charged with a carnivalesque energy – jugglers toss batons into the air, buskers strum wistful tunes, mimers funny-walk behind people – at its core Las Ramblas is a thriving commercial strip. Bird vendors hawk cages of screeching parakeets; streetside florists do a brisk trade in fragrant bouquets; newsstands sell everything from the Herald Tribune to porno magazines; caricaturists sketch their way through reams of paper; and waiters in shiny black vests coax you to "tomar una copa!" and come over for a drink. You finally accept, and settle at an outdoor table, sipping a tart sangria floating with orange slices, as the late-afternoon sun splinters through the trees and warms the top of your head. You muse about something you read, that Federico Garcia Lorca once called Las Ramblas "the very spirit of the city". It's true, you think, Las Ramblas is Barcelona; it's hard to imagine one without the other. A couple of pitchers later – and a sweet glass of sherry, on the house – you wander again up this celebrated street. You pass an old man plucking soulfully at his Spanish guitar. Then you spot a flash of silver. It's the winged statue, back on her pedestal. A crowd is gathering. The show must go on.

139 HIKING IN THE PYRENEES

SPAIN When is a national park not a national park? Catalunya's Parc Nacional d'Aigüestortes i Estany de Sant Maurici doesn't make the grade internationally yet under any other definition it fits the bill spectacularly. Soaring and plunging amidst a rarefied conclave of snow-veined peaks near the French border, it's one of the most bracingly handsome stretches of the Pyrenean range. Apart from the hydroelectric works that preclude wider official status, the park remains unspoilt habitat for such singular fauna as the Alpine marmot and the Pyrenean desman, an aquatic mole which forages in glacial streams. The entire 140-square-kilometre reach is studded with high-altitude lakes, fir and pine trees blanketing the lower slopes, beneath barbarous granite pinnacles reaching 2400 metres.

If, as likely, you approach from the east at Espot, you'll save yourself blistered feet by negotiating the lengthy paved road into the park by 4WD-taxi. Once the road ends, a warren of trails fans out from the cobalt waters of the Estany de Sant Maurici, with conveniently sited refuges at several of the intersections. Bisected by a main road and tunnel, the range then lunges westwards towards the equally impressive Parque Nacional de Ordesa y Monte Perdido. Inaugurated in 1918, it gets the nod from UNESCO and the attention of climbers looking to tackle its vertigo-stricken, Wild West-gone-alpine canyons, which thunder with glacial meltwater in late spring. Those with a less adventurous head for heights can admire the limestone strangeness from the depths of the Ordesa gorge, where an unusual east–west orientation funnels in damp Atlantic air and supports unexpectedly lush vegetation; access is most common from the west, via the village of Torla. Some 10km further south, Añisclo, an equally breathtaking and far less tourist-trodden canyon, can be accessed via a minor road turning off at Sarvisé. Sequestered in its hulking gorge wall is the hermitage of San Urbez, bearing witness to the days when the park was an untrammelled wilderness, home to mystics rather than wardens.

140 LEARNING TO SURF ON THE ATLANTIC COAST

PORTUGAL Ask friends who surf about their hobby and you'll hear tales of razor-sharp reefs, territorial warfare and a task of almost Zen-like difficulty, in which years of backbreaking effort are required to attain anything approaching competence. But while gung-ho mythology is part of the sport, you shouldn't take their tales too seriously.

The Algarve's dusty, undeveloped southwestern edge feels a million miles from the apartments and resorts of the west, but thanks to big waves and an unspoilt coastline, it's a fine place to learn to surf. Week-long courses start with a spot of board-less wave-catching, in which you throw yourselves shorewards, getting a handle on the sea's momentum. The next step is on the beach, practising the lift in which you straighten your arms and arch your back, ready to smoothly spring to your feet.

Inevitably, it's hard once you hit the water – it's not even that easy on the sand – and there's so much to remember that falling off sometimes comes as a blessed relief. The instructors, meanwhile, seem to consider balancing on your knees to be a surfing sin that's somewhere above manslaughter in the grand scheme of things. But, like anything, you pick it up. That precious moment when you stand, knees bent and mind humming, the horizon to your back, the sea flexing beneath your feet, and your board turning – actually turning! – when you shift your weight is worth all the aches and pratfalls. When it clicks, you bound back into the water, pulling away at the sea with your arms in a merry rush to get "outside", to the point where whitewater begins life as swelling waves and the experts sit, slowly bobbing on their boards and waiting for the perfect ride. At which point, flustered by your sudden confidence, it's all too easy to fall off again.

A DROP OF THE BARD'S STUFF: DRINKING SHERRY SPANISH STYLE

SPAIN Sixteenth-century England mightn't have been so green and pleasant for Spain's Armada but at least Shakespeare was busy lauding its wine. Falstaff's avowal of the properties of "sherris-sack" should probably be taken with a pincho of salt, but there's nothing quite like a chilled glass of fino in the Andalucían shade. The vineyards from which it derives are among the oldest on earth, surviving the disapproval of Moorish rulers, the ravages of civil war and a phylloxera epidemic, only to face a twenty-first-century market saturated with trendy New World competition. Downsized but unbowed, they still occupy the famous sherry triangle bounded by the southwestern towns of Jerez de la Frontera, San Lúcar de Barrameda and El Puerto de Santa María, intent on attracting a younger, hipper market. And why

not; the sickly cream sherries mouldering in British cupboards are a world away from the lithe tang of a fino or bleached-dry manzanilla, which dance on the palette and flirt coquettishly with tapas. In terms of sprucing up sherry's rather fusty image (at least outside Spain), González Byass have been leading the way with their rebranding of the famed Tio Pepe. Their cobbled lanes and dim, vaulted cellars are among the oldest in Jerez, one of the most atmospheric – if touristy – places to sample a fino or an almond-nutty amontillada straight from the bota (sherry cask); you can even anoint your soles with some of their hallowed grapes during the September harvest. And if you're still hankering after the kind of tipple granny used to pour, nose out the chocolatey bitter-richness of a dry oloroso instead. Falstaff would approve.

142 FLAMENCO: BACKSTREETS AND GYPSY BEATS

SPAIN With Diego El Cigala cleaning up at the Grammys, Catalan gypsy-punks Ojos de Brujo scooping a BBC Radio 3 World Music Award and Enrique Morente jamming with Sonic Youth in Valencia, the socio-musico-cultural phenomenon that is Spanish flamenco has never been hotter. Like any improvisational art form (particularly jazz, with which it often shares a platform), it's most effective in the raw, on stage, as hands and heels thwack in virile syncopation, a guitar bleeds unfathomable flurries of notes and the dancer flaunts her disdain with a flourish of ruffled silk.

Those in serious search of the elusive duende may find themselves faced with a surfeit of touristy options, but genuine flamenco is almost always out there if you look hard enough. Madrid is home to producer extrodinaire Javier Limón and his new *Casa Limón* label, and boasts such famous tablaos as *Casa Patas*, *Corral de la Morería* and *El Corral de la Pacheca*, where Hollywood actors are as ubiquitous as the tiles and white linen. *Calle 54* is another

Madrid institution, a latin jazz venue that often plays host to flamenco-centric artists: ace pianist Chano Domínguez is a regular and Cuba's Son De La Frontera appeared in 2005. Less pricey and more accommodating to the spirit of the juerga (spontaneous session) is the wonderful *La Soleá*, where both local and out-of-town enthusiasts test their mettle. Festivals include the annual Flamenco Pa'Tos charity bash and the new Suma Flamenca event that farms out shows to Madrid's wider communidad.

One of Spain's biggest festivals is Seville's La Bienal de Flamenco, an award-winning event held from mid-September to mid-October. In the city itself, *Los Gallos* is one of the oldest tablaos, but it's worth scouring the cobbled backstreets for *La Carbonería*, a former coal merchants where free flamenco pulls in a volubly appreciative scrum of locals and tourists, or heading to the old gyspy quarter of Triana where barrio hangouts like *Casa Anselma* exult in Seville's homegrown form, the Sevillana.

143 COUNTING DOLPHINS IN THE MEDITERRANEAN

SPAIN "Sighting!" shouts Captain Ricardo Sagarminaga, as the dorsal fins flicker into view. Moments later, a hundred striped dolphins are speeding alongside the boat, leaping out of the waves and riding the wake of the bow. On board *Toftevaag*, our antique wooden sailboat, a very international crew of volunteers and scientists springs into action. The Dane grabs the sonar reader, the American opens the behaviour log, the Spaniard sets up her SLR, and the Brit slaps on the factor 40. It's going to be a long, hot afternoon of serious dolphin counting.

The volunteers, mostly office workers in need of some sea air, have set sail off the southern coast of Spain with the international environmental charity Earthwatch to play at being marine biologists for a dozen days. On board, we help scientists to monitor dolphin populations, pollution levels and the impact of over-fishing. Photo-identifications, behavioural notes, skin swabs, environmental data and oceanographic readings are all gathered during the frequent sightings, and are transformed into impressive graphs and reports by the captain's wife, marine biologist Dr. Ana Cañadas. In 2000, Ana and Ricardo's research into a decline in dolphin populations persuaded the Spanish government to create a Marine Protected Area in this region. Today, the couple continue to monitor and manage the area, working alongside visiting scientists, volunteers and local fishing communities.

For us volunteers, working on the boat is no easy ride – assisting the scientists during sightings, cooking and cleaning for the whole crew – in a sweltering galley – sleeping onboard in cramped bunks and setting sail at 7am. But awe-inspiring encounters are practically guaranteed. Common, bottlenose and striped dolphins, pilot whales, sperm whales and loggerhead turtles are all regularly sighted from the boat, and we leave the *Toftevaag* with a greater understanding of marine conservation issues, and with memories of wild dolphins leaping from the open sea.

144 MODERNISME AND MAÑANA: GAUDÍ'S SAGRADA FAMILIA

SPAIN If you've ever been at the mercy of a Spanish tradesman, or merely tried to buy a litre of milk after midday, you'll know that the Iberian concept of time is not just slightly elastic but positively twangy. The master of twang, however, has to be Antoni Gaudí i Cornet, the Catalan architect whose pièce de résistance is famously still under construction more than a century after he took the project on: "My client is not in a hurry" was his jocular riposte to the epic timescale.

Conceived as a riposte to secular radicalism, the Temple Expiatiori de la Sagrada Família consumed the final decade and a half of a life that had become increasingly reclusive. Gaudí couldn't have imagined that a new millennium would find his creation feted as a wonder of the post-modern world, symbolic of a Barcelona reborn and the single most popular tourist attraction in Spain. Craning your neck up to the totemic, honeycomb-gothic meltdown of the Sagrada Família's towers today, it's perhaps not so difficult to believe that he was a nature-loving vegetarian as well as an ardent Catholic and nationalist. By subsuming the organic intricacy of cellular life, his off-kilter modernisme wields a hypnotic, outlandish power, a complexity of design that entwines itself around your grey matter in a single glance. Which is half its charm; if you don't fancy dodging sweaty tourists and piles of mosaics in progress, simply take a constitutional around the exterior. Personally masterminded by Gaudí before his death, the Nativity facade garlands its virgin birth with microcosmic stone flora, a stark contrast to the Cubist austerity of the recently completed Passion façade.

The main reward for venturing inside is an elevator ride up one of the towers, a less tiring, crowded and claustrophobic experience than taking the stairs (hundreds of them!), leaving you with sufficient energy to goggle at the city through a prism of threaded stone and ceramics.

145 PULPO ADDICTION: GOING GASTRO IN GALICIA

SPAIN Given that Galicia's patron saint was originally a fisherman, it's only right that the place serves up some of the best seafood in the world. Its rias (inlets), are filled with the kind of fishy abundance that Steve Zissou would trade his red beanie for; a life aquatic numbering gourmet varieties of scallops, eel, clams, mussels, prawns, lobster and crabs, many of which end up in local restaurant windows. The rugged, world's end coast further north, meanwhile, nurtures such outlandish delicacies as the digit-like percebes, or goose-barnacle. Like a modern-day equivalent to the St Kilda egg collectors, percebeiros gather these obscene-looking creatures from wave-lashed rocks, risking life and limb for what the Spanish – and clued-up foreign foodies – consider manna from the ocean. If you sample them amidst the chandeliers and sharp suits of a Madrid institution like *Casa Rafa*,

you'll pay two or three times what you would for freshly gathered specimens in Galicia itself (you might even get a free tasting at O Grove's shellfish festival in mid-October); either way they're boiled and eaten as they are, so not a single molecule of luscious, gulf stream-pure flavour is lost.

Cheaper and much more abundant is pulpo a la gallega, a characteristically simple yet ravishing dish of boiled, chopped octopus dressed with olive oil, crusty sea salt and sweet, pungent pimentón (paprika), served at earthy specialist eateries called pulperías. As pulpo á feira, it's usually the dish of choice at the region's many festivals and is the sole focus of a summer bash in Carballiño, near Ourense, where hefty, flame-haired Galician matriarchs man copper urns and serve their wares on wooden platters on the second Sunday in August.

146 STOP! IT'S HAMMER TIME AT THE FESTA DE SÃO JOÃO

PORTUGAL The old cliché that Porto works while Lisbon plays is redundant on June 24, when Portugal's second city teaches the capital a thing or two about having fun. The Festa de São João is a magnificent display of midsummer madness – one giant street party, where bands of hammer-wielding lunatics roam the town, and every available outdoor space in Porto is given over to a full night of eating, drinking and dancing to welcome in the city's saint's day.

By the evening of June 23, the tripeiros, as the residents of Porto are known, are already in the party mood. A tide of whistle-blowing, hammer-wielding people begins to seep down the steep streets towards the river. No one seems to know the origin of the tradition of hitting people on the head on this day, but what was traditionally a rather harmless pat with a leek has evolved into a somewhat firmer clout with a plastic hammer. You should know that everyone has a plastic hammer, and everyone wants to hit someone else with it.

People begin dancing to the live music by the Rio Douro while it's still light, banging their hammers on metal café tables to the rhythm of the Latin and African sounds. Elsewhere, live music performances vary from pop and rock to traditional folk music and choral singing, and as darkness falls, exploding fireworks thunder through the night sky above the glowing neon of the port-wine lodges over the Douro.

Midnight sees the inevitable climax of fireworks, but the night is far from over. As dawn approaches, the emphasis shifts west to the beach of Praia dos Ingleses in the suburb of Foz do Douro. Here, there's space to participate in the tradition of lighting bonfires for São João, with youths challenging each other to jump over the largest flames. As the beach party rumbles on, pace yourself and before you know it the crowds will start to thin slightly and the first signs of daylight will appear on the horizon. Congratulations. You've made it through to the day of São João itself.

147 BROWSING LA BOQUERIA

SPAIN It happens to most newcomers: noses flare, eyes widen and pulses quicken upon entering La Boqueria, Barcelona's cathedral to comida fresca (fresh food). Pass through the handsome Modernista cast-iron gateway and you're rapidly sucked in by the raw, noisy energy of the cavernous hall, the air dense with the salty tang of the sea and freshly spilled blood. As they say in these parts, if you can't find it in La Boqueria, you can't find it anywhere: pyramids of downy peaches face whole cow heads – their eyes rolled back – and hairy curls of rabo de toro (bulls' tails). Pale-pink piglets are strung up by their hind legs, snouts pointing south, while dorada (sea bream) twitch on beds of ice next to a tangle of black eels.

The Mercat de Sant Josep, as it's officially called, was built in 1836 on the site of a former convent, though records show that there had been a market here since the thirteenth century. Its devotees are as diverse as the offerings: bargain-hunting grandmas rooting through dusty bins; gran cocineros (master chefs) from around Europe palming eggplants and holding persimmons up to the light; and droves of wide-eyed visitors weaving through the hubbub. At its core, though, La Boqueria is a family affair. Ask for directions and you might be told to turn right at Pili's place, then left at the Oliveros brothers. More than half of the stalls – and attendant professions – have been passed down through generations for over a century.

When it comes time to eat, do it here. The small bar-restaurants tucked away in La Boqueria may be low on frills, but they serve some of the finest market-fresh Catalan fare in the city. Flames lick over the dozens of orders crammed onto the tiny grill at Pinotxo, a bustling bar that has been around since 1940. Pull up a stool, and choose from the day's specials that are rattled off by various members of the extended family, like the affable, seventy-something Juanito. Tuck into bubbling samfaina, a Catalan ratatouille, or try cap i pota, stewed head and hoof of pig. As the afternoon meal winds down, Juanito walks the bar, topping up glasses from a jug of red wine. There's a toast – "Salud!" – and then everyone takes long, warming swallows, as all around the shuttered market sighs to a close.

148 DANCING TILL DAWN AT BENICÀSSIM

SPAIN One thing it isn't is peaceful. The music goes on till 8am, and by 10am most tents are too hot to sleep in, sweat dripping from skin to sleeping mat and back. By day, you eat tapas in bars and snooze in precious patches of shade at the nearby beach. But the awesomely entertaining four-day Festival International de Benicàssim is really about the night-time, about strolling, Spanish-style, between Anglo-American rock bands (the Pixies, Radiohead and the Arctic Monkeys have starred in recent years) and local musicians, flexing your limbs in the numerous dance tents and drinking with strangers under the bright lights of stalls. You'll regret it in the morning, of course – but morning has probably already arrived.

149 BIG-GAME FISHING IN THE MID-ATLANTIC

THE AZORES Way out in the Atlantic, a thousand miles off the coast of Portugal, the string of volcanic islands that make up the Azores is probably the only part of the European Union in which you can go big-game fishing – and for blue marlin, too, the mother of all large fish, weighing in at 150 kilos or more. The islands regularly host the European and World Big Game Championships if you want to see how it's done. Alternatively, you can hire a boat and a skipper and try your own luck; the abundance of marlin in summer and bluefin tuna in spring – as well as shark and swordfish year round – make the Azores a game-fishers' paradise. And while you're waiting for them to bite, keep an eye out for the dolphins and whales that frolic just offshore.

150 CLEARING YOUR CALENDAR FOR BACALHAU

PORTUGAL On Lisbon's Rua do Arsenal, whole window displays are lined with what looks like crinkly grey cardboard. The smell is far from alluring, but from these humble slabs of cod the Portuguese are able to conjure up an alleged 365 different recipes for bacalhau, one for each day of the year. Reassuringly, none of this mummified fish dates back to when it first became popular in the 1500s, when the Corte Real brothers sailed as far as Newfoundland for its rich cod banks. To preserve the fish for the journey back, the brothers salted and dried it – the result was an instant hit both with Portuguese landlubbers and navigators, who could safely store it for their long explorations of the new world.

Nowadays, bacalhau is the national dish, served in just about every restaurant in the country and every family home on Christmas Day. Even in Setúbal – where harbour restaurants are stacked with the fresh variety – salted cod appears on most menus, bathed in water for up to two days, and then its skin and bones pulled away from the swelled and softened flesh, before being boiled and strained into a fishy goo.

Some bacalhau dishes can be an acquired taste. My first experience was in a restaurant on the mosaic-paved old town of Cascais, where my stolid bacalhau com grau (boiled with chick peas) nearly put me off for life. But start with rissóis de bacalhau (cod rissoles), commonly served as a bar snack, and you'll soon be hooked. Then move on to bacalhau com natas (baked with cream) or bacalhau a brás (with fried potatos, olives and egg) and there's no looking back.

With fourteen bacalhau options on its menu, *Sabores a Bacalhau*, in Lisbon's Parque das Nações, is a good place to start. In a restaurant swathed in decorative azulejos tiles appropriately showing sea creatures, a waiter tells me, "Bacalhau is like the Kama Sutra. There may be hundreds of different variations, but you get to know the two or three types that are enjoyable!". Only the Portuguese could compare bacalhau with sex, but you can't argue that it is good.

SPAIN La Mezquita: a name that evokes the mystery and grace of Córdoba's famous monument so much more seductively than the English translation. It's been a while since the Great Mosque was used as such (1236 to be exact), but at one time it was not only the largest in the city – dwarfing a thousand others – but in all al-Andalus and nigh on the entire world.

Almost a millennium later, its hallucinatory interior still hushes the garrulous into silence and the jaded into awe, a dreamscape of candy-striped arches piled upon arches, sifting light from shadow. Since the Christians took over it's been mostly shadow, yet at one time the Mezquita's dense grove of recycled Roman columns was open to the sunlight, creating a generous, arboreal harmony with its courtyard and wider social environment. Today's visitors still enter through that same orange blossom compound, the Patio de los Naranjos, proceeding through the Puerta de las Palmas where they doff their cap rather than removing their shoes. As your eyes adjust to the gloom, you're confronted with a jasper and marble forest, so constant, fluid and deceptively symmetrical in design that its ingenious system of secondary supporting arches barely registers. Gradually, the resourcefulness of the Muslim architects sinks in, the way they improvised on the inadequacy of their salvaged pillars, inversely propping up the great weight of the roof arches and ceiling.

That first flush of wonder ebbs slightly once you stumble upon an edifice clearly out of step with the Moorish scheme of things, if gracious enough in its own right. In 1523, despite fierce local opposition, the more zealous Christians finally got their revenge by tearing out the Mosque's heart and erecting a Renaissance cathedral. Carlos V's verdict was damning: "you have destroyed something that was unique in the world". Thankfully they left intact the famous Mihrab, a prayer niche of sublime perfection braided by Byzantine mosaics and roofed with a single block of marble. Like the Mezquita itself, its beauty transcends religious difference.

151

the Mezquita **Marvelling** inside the Mezquita Marvelling inside the Mez
Mezquita Marvelling **inside the** Mezquita Marvelling inside the Mezquita M
uita Marvelling inside the **Mezquita** Marvelling inside the Mezquita Marve

152 RUNNING WITH THE BULLS

SPAIN For one week each year the Spanish town of Pamplona parties so hard that the foothills of the nearby Pyrenees start shaking. The scariest, loudest and most raucous party you'll ever come across, the Fiesta de San Fermín, held in honour of Pamplona's patron saint, has been celebrated since the early sixteenth century. But it's the daily ritual of the notoriously dangerous encierro (bull run) – the most prominent feature of the event for at least two hundred years and something of a rite of passage for young men of the region – that gets all the attention. Nothing can prepare you for your first Pamplona experience: the constant flow of beer and sangria, the outrageous drunken partying, the hordes of excited people in the streets, and, most

of all, the early morning terror of the bull run. It only lasts about three-and-a-half minutes but is pure adrenaline all the way, with half-a-dozen bulls running 800m or so to the town's main bullring behind several thousand would-be heroes. The first bull run is held on the morning of July 7, after which the ritual of all-night partying followed by a morning bull run followed by a few hours sleep is repeated until July 14, when there's a solemn closing ceremony. There are also bullfights every evening, a naked procession to protest at the cruelty of the whole event and regular drunken diving from one of the statues in the main square. You've got to hand it to the Spanish – they certainly know how to host a phenomenal party.

153 DROPPING IN AT MUNDAKA

SPAIN At first sight, the weather-beaten surfers wandering the narrow alleyways of Mundaka, a picturesque port clinging to the northern coast of Spain, seem a little out of place. This is deep Basque country – a quiet, traditional area where the locals gather under the fluttering Basque flag to play pelota, drink cider and talk politics.

But then you walk out onto the pretty little town's harbour walls, and there she is, the object of their undying affection: a beautiful, glassy, rolling barrel of a wave that peels off into the distance, dumping white water – and exhilarated surfers – onto the golden sands of Laida, far away on the other side of the estuary. This, the longest left-hand wave in Europe, could just be the ride of your life.

154 FAIR PLAY AT THE FERIA

SPAIN The Feria de Abril, or Spring Fair, is the kind of big, raunchy party that the Spanish do so well – a heady mix of tradition, drinking and dancing that takes place two weeks after the country's more solemn Semana Santa (Easter Week) activities. Similar spring festivals are held around Andalucía, but none match Seville's for the intensity of colour, pageant and sheer party energy. Held in the city's vast feria grounds on the west bank of the Guadalquivir river, it runs all week from midnight on Monday. Sevillanos don traditional Andalucían finery and parade around the fairground on horseback or in elegant horse-drawn carriages, there are daily bullfights, and there's lots of all-night eating, drinking and dancing, Saucy couples frolic in the shadows, and you can stagger from one party to another until dawn. Things reach a crescendo on Friday and Saturday nights, when the grounds are full to bursting, and the whole thing comes to an end on Sunday night with a deafening fireworks display.

155 GETTING LOST IN THE PILGRIM'S PALACE

SPAIN Though you may well get lost in the sprawling *Parador de Santiago de Compostela*, you certainly won't mind if you do. This is medieval Spain in all its gold-flecked grandeur – a post-sherry saunter from the echoing banquet hall has you padding down crimson-carpeted hallways lined with heavy tapestries and presided over by stern-faced busts of a veritable who's who of Spanish history. And that's just one wing.

The golden-granite parador was built in 1499 for Queen Isabella and King Ferdinand as the Hostal dos Reis Católicos, a royal hospital that provided refuge and relief to all the foot-blistered pilgrims who streamed into this damp northwestern corner of Spain. Five centuries on, travellers still seek shelter here – though now high-thread-count sheets and heated towel racks are part of the package.

This hospice-turned-haute hotel is the grande dame of Spain's paradores, a chain of government-run hotels – now numbering nearly 100 – established in the 1920s. The aim was both to provide accommodation in Spain's more remote, pastoral areas, and to revive and maintain ancient edifices, from castles and convents to

monasteries and manor houses, that might otherwise fall into ruin. Today, staying in a parador not only offers the chance to bed down in a historical monument, but also helps ensure its survival.

Suites here are fit for a king – literally: kick back on canopied, four-poster beds like those once warmed by Spanish monarchs, tug on a tassel to turn on the light, catch your reflection in an antique mirror. Having catered to devout pilgrims, the parador is awash in spiritual nooks: leafy, hushed cloisters offer moments of absolute stillness in the late afternoon, as shadows fall across the stone pillars, one by one.

The parador shares the Praza do Obradoiro with the city's splendid cathedral. All roads to Santiago lead to this Baroque behemoth, where the mortal remains of St James are supposedly buried. Roam the Romanesque interior – all the more memorable when the massive botafumeiro (incense burner) is being used: hung on ropes as thick as well-fed pythons, it's swung in a wide arc across the transept, a rite originally performed to perfume the disheveled, pungent pilgrims as they filed into the cathedral. These days, a scented bath at the parador should suffice.

156 TAKING TO THE STREETS OF TENERIFE

CANARY ISLANDS A small island two hundred miles off the African coast, Tenerife seems an unlikely spot for one of the world's largest carnival parties. Yet festivals are in Tenerife's blood – it hosts over three hundred of them – and in the run-up to Lent, over a quarter of a million revellers converge on the capital, Santa Cruz, dressed in costumes so elaborate and cumbersome that they often need trolleys to hold them up.

Absorbed by their quest for winter sun, most tourists are oblivious to the goings-on in Santa Cruz. Those who do make the trip to the capital for carnival usually leave after the formal events finish – certainly before the night really gets going, when stages along the Plaza de España pump out vibrant salsa rhythms, and street kiosks play dance music until dawn. The gregarious locals will be more than happy to party with you, though, as long as you're in fancy dress: you'll be well provided for by the stores along Santa Cruz's main pedestrian drag, Calle del Castillo.

Carnival doesn't really kick off until the Friday before Shrove Tuesday, with an opening parade of bands and floats. After everyone's recovered from the weekend, the flagship event of the official carnival is the Coso or "Grand Procession", a lively five-hour cavalcade of floats, bands, dancing troupes and entertainers that dances its way along the dockside road on the afternoon of Shrove Tuesday itself. The following night's Burial of the Sardine is a tongue-in-cheek event centred on a huge wood-and-paper fish and its cortege of wailing priests and "widows" – mostly moustachioed men in drag. Failing to bow to the onset of Lent, the carnival doesn't reach its climactic end until the following weekend, when some of the festival's most intense partying follows a kids' parade on the Saturday and a seniors' parade on the Sunday.

157 WASHING AWAY THE CIDER HOUSE BLUES

SPAIN The Basques are a proud people. And boy do they take pride in their regional produce. Which is why they have the finest fish on the Spanish coast, the tastiest tapas across Iberia – and some of the most scrumptious cider in all of Europe. Prohibited under the Franco regime, cider is back with a bang – or, at least, with a sharp, mouth-watering fizz. The beauty of Basque cider is that it's succulently simple. There are no must or extracts here, no gas or sweeteners added. Just a blend of three types of apple: bitter, sour and sweet, all lovingly combined in the perfect proportions.

The best cider is drunk on site: head out to the orchards of Astigarraga and spend the day at one of the area's many sagardotegiak, or cider houses, drinking the golden liquor straight from kupelas (large barrels). Empty the glass each time with one quick gulp – it preserves the cider's txinparta: its colour, bouquet and that tangy, tantalizing taste.

158 DANCING IN THE STREETS OF GRACIA

SPAIN Barcelonans are notoriously passionate about their all-night revelries, most exuberantly in autumn during the week-long La Mercè. However, for serious aficionados of Catalan fun, it's the Gracia festival that stirs the soul.

Now a district of Barcelona, this formerly autonomous town still clings fervently to its roots, and every year for two weeks starting 15 August, Gracia's neighbourhoods shift into high gear, laying on everything from cutting-edge alternative rock to folk-dancing, along with traditional human castles and fireworks. Sidestreets host ethnic eateries and gaudy makeshift theatres, staging plays, parodies, satires, and comic sketches, and the whole place throbs with activity until at least 3am, depending these days on the tender mercies of the noise police.

159 MEDITERRANEAN HIGHS: PUIG DE MARIA

BALEARIC ISLANDS I flung open the green shutters and took a deep breath: honeysuckle and pine. And another: incense, zesty lemons and the smell of the sea. The early Mallorcan sun bathed the bricks of Puig de Maria monastery in gold light, and the sense of calm was overwhelming: only the clang of goat bells broke the morning silence. Sipping my cafecito on the terrace, I could pick out the half-moon Bay of Pollença, Alcúdia, and the Formentor penin-sula, flicking out into Mediterranean like a knobbly dragon's tail.

Rising three hundred metres above Pollença, this hilltop retreat in Mallorca's northeast corner has done well to keep a low profile: it's blissfully quiet, barely touched by tourism and has arguably the best 360-degree panoramas on the island. As I slipped into a hermit's shoes for a few days, my life took on a different rhythm. Once I'd explored the secluded courtyards, the beamed fifteenth-century refectory and the silent gothic chapel, there was little left to see. And the feeling was liberating. Those lazy days spilled into lazy nights on the cobbled patio – eating paella, drinking Rioja and watching the stars twinkle above and the bays twinkle below.

At Puig de Maria, solitude is real and your senses become more alert – from the rustle of the trees and the crackling of an open fire to the feeling of stones slipping underfoot on the steep trail that weaves down to the valley. The buzz of the coast seems a million miles away and you're more likely to encounter buzzards than Brits abroad. The only way to reach the peak is to brave the hairpin bends zigzagging up to monastery's car park, then walk the rest on foot, or take the pilgrim's way – an hour's hot hike through pine forest. But it's worth every bit to experience the Mallorca that once was and, far from Magaluf's madding crowd, thankfully still is.

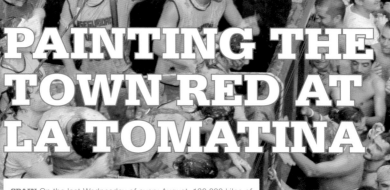

PAINTING THE TOWN RED AT LA TOMATINA

SPAIN On the last Wednesday of every August, 130,000 kilos of over-ripe tomatoes are hurled around the alleyways of Buñol until the tiny town's streets are ankle deep in squelching fruit. What started in the 1940s as an impromptu food fight between friends has turned into one of the most bizarre and downright infantile fiestas on earth, a world-famous summer spectacular in which thirty thousand or so finger-twitching participants try to dispose of the entire EU tomato mountain by way of a massive hour-long food fight.

Locals, young and old, spend the morning attaching protective plastic sheeting to their house fronts, draping them over the balconies and bolting closed the shutters. By midday, the town's plaza and surrounding streets are brimming to the edges with a mass of overheated humans, and the chant of "To-ma-te, To-ma-te" begins to ring out across the town.

As the church clock chimes noon, dozens of trucks rumble into the plaza, disgorging their messy ammunition onto the dusty streets. And then all hell breaks. There are no allies, no protection, nowhere to hide; everyone – man or woman, young or old – is out for themselves. The first five minutes is tough going: the tomatoes are surprisingly hard and they actually hurt until they have been thrown a few times. Some are fired head-on at point-blank range, others sneakily aimed from behind, and the skilled lobber might get one to splat straight onto the top of your head. After what seems like an eternity, the battle dies down as the tomatoes disintegrate into an unthrowable mush. The combatants slump exhausted into a dazed ecstasy, grinning inanely at one another and basking in the glory of the battle. But the armistice is short-lived as another truck rumbles into the square to deposit its load. Battle commences once more, until the next load of ammunition is exhausted. Six trucks come and go before the final ceasefire. All in all, it only lasts about an hour, but it's probably the most stupidly childish hour you'll ever enjoy as an adult.

160

161 GOING FOR YOUR GUNS IN ALMERÍA

SPAIN The only genuine desert in Europe, Almería's merciless canyons and moonscape gulches did, once upon a time in the Spanish Wild West, play host to Hollywood. Back in the Sixties, Spaghetti Western don Sergio Leone shot his landmark trilogy here, climaxing with *The Good, The Bad & The Ugly*. Since this golden era, the place has had the occasional flash of former glories: in the mid-Eighties Alex Cox revisited the terrain with his all-star spaghetti parody *Straight To Hell*, and Sean Connery pitched up for *Indiana Jones and the Last Crusade*.

As recently as 2002, Spanish director Alex de la Iglesia's critically acclaimed *800 Bullets* actually subsumed Almerían cinema's rise and fall into its plot, centring on the Fort Bravo studios/Texas Hollywood, where the most authentic film-set experience is still to be had. It's a gloriously eerie, down at heel place, which, likely as not, you'll have to yourself. Unfortunately, there's no explanation as to which sets were used in which films, but the splintered wood, fading paintwork and general dilapidation certainly feels genuine. A wholesale Mexican compound complete with a blinding white mission chapel is the atmospheric centrepiece; close your eyes and you can just about smell the gunpowder. The saloon is the very same one that David Beckham stalked through in a 2003 TV ad, where the cream of Real Madrid fortified themselves on Pepsi before a showdown with the Manchester United squad.

A couple of kilometres down the road is Mini-Hollywood, the sanitized big daddy of the region's three film-set theme parks, with a must-see museum of original poster art. And Leone diehards will want to complete the tour with a visit to nearby Western Leone, which houses the extant debris of the man's masterpiece, *Once Upon A Time In The West*. Hopeless cowboys (and girls) can even take a four–day horse-riding tour into the desert, scouting various locations amid breathtakingly desolate scenery.

162 WAGING WINE WAR IN LA RIOJA

SPAIN For grape gourmets, it might seem a terrible waste of wine, but each year several villages in Rioja spend an entire day soaking each other in the stuff. One of the truly great events of the Spanish summer, the Wine War (Batallo de Vino) is the modern-day remnant of ancient feuds between the wine town of Haro and its Riojan neighbours. A wine-fight of epic – and historic – proportions.

The festival begins with what must be one of the most bizarre religious processions anywhere: the congregation – as many as five thousand people, mostly dressed in white – comes armed not with Bibles, crucifixes and rosary beads but with an ingenious array of wine-weapons, ranging from buckets, water pistols and bota bags (wine-skin bottles) to agricultural spraying equipment.

The battle is thick and fast, with warring factions drenching each other with medium-bodied Rioja. In theory, the townsfolk of Haro are battling it out with those of neighbouring Miranda de Ebro, but in the good-humoured but frantic battle that rages, there are no obvious sides, and no winners or losers. Instead, the object is perfectly straightforward: to squirt, hose, blast or throw some 25,000 litres of what is presumably not vintage vino tinto over as many people as possible.

You won't be spared as a spectator, so you may as well join in. At the very least, come armed with a water pistol, though be warned that the locals have perfected the art of the portable water cannon, and can practically blast you off your feet from five metres. But what a way to go.

163 POETIC LICENSE IN DEIÀ

SPAIN When it comes to artists and their muses, Henry Miller had Anaïs Nin, Scott Fitzgerald had Zelda, Picasso had too many to list, and novelist and poet Robert Graves had Deià – an ancient village perched high in the Sierra de Tramuntana, a mighty range that marches across the northwest coast of Mallorca. Graves first alighted here in the 1930s and stayed on throughout much of his life, banging out historical novels and introducing many of his literary brethren to Deià's rustic folds.

You're here, like many of the bohemian sorts before you, because Deià is everything that the thong-thronged, disco-revved Balearic beaches are not. The only sounds on a summer morning are the church bells pealing through the narrow cobbled streets, and the rustle of olive trees on the terraced hills. You've come up from Palma for the day, to lose yourself in the mountain stillness, to roam past the stone houses and perhaps close your eyes for a moment in the coolness of the country church. You'll probably pass the afternoon in *Cafe Sa*

Fonda, along with most of the village, at the outdoor terrace, under aging trees and flitting birds, with just a cafe con leche and your thoughts, until an impromptu group of musicians pull out their instruments, accompanying the sinking sun with the strains of jazz.

Graves once said, "If there's no money in poetry, neither is there poetry in money". But he did find poetry in the hills of Deià, where he chose to be buried. Behind the church, the small village cemetery tumbles down the mountainside. Here, you can sit on the sun-warmed grass, fat flies buzzing amid the wildflowers and gravestones. Your sense of isolation is made complete when you catch a glimpse of the rocky coves far below, which give way to the wide, blue Mediterranean Sea. The pleasant reminder washes over you that you're on an island, separated from the rest of the world by a voluminous body of water. Maybe you'll stay another day. Or a week. Or even longer. Graves, it seems, had the right idea.

164 SEEING SUMMER OFF IN STYLE: IBIZA'S CLOSING PARTIES

BALEARIC ISLANDS Ibiza's summer clubbing season is an orgy of hedonism, full of beats, late nights and frazzled young things. It reaches a messy climax in September, when the main club promoters and venues host a series of seratonin-sapping parties to round things off and extract a few final euros from their battered punters. These end-of-season events tend to attract an older clubbing crowd, who prefer to hop over to Ibiza for a long weekend (a "cheeky one" in clubber speak), avoiding the gangs of teenage pill-monsters that descend on the island in late July and August. The British rave dinosaurs join a resident hardcore of Ibizan clubbers and an international cast of party freaks and techno geeks, all brought together by a common appetite for dance music.

Where you go depends on your tastes. In San Antonio, the young crowd gathers at *Eden* and *Es Paradis*, whose entire dancefloor is flooded just before sunrise, while in the village of San Rafel *Amnesia*'s essential closing party usually throws open its doors

for free after 4am – the last worn-out dancers are often still there come mid-afternoon. At *Privilege*, across the road, *Manumission* is legendary for its closing party – in a laudable attempt to inject fresh energy into the scene, it has also recently added guitar bands, including the Arctic Monkeys and The Fratellis, to its summer lineup. In Ibiza Town, the elegant *Pacha* is unmissable, with the cream of the world's best DJs, including Erick Morillo and Roger Sanchez, cranking up the pressure to delirious levels. Four kilometres south of Ibiza Town, *Space* usually opens at 8am, with punters donning shades and getting down on the legendary terrace before moving inside, where the walls quiver to pounding progressive techno. The *Space* closing party was once the event in the Ibiza club calendar but, for many, the hardcore action has shifted a couple of kilometres south to *DC10*, a no-frills, always packed-out club in rustic no-man's land, with a dancefloor surrounded by reeds and bullrushes. The scene here has exploded in popularity, and now draws the hippest crowd (and the most outrageous mullets) in Ibiza.

SPAIN Nothing can ready you for the sheer volume of outwardly respectable, smart-casual tourists crowding desperately around the unwholesome creations of Catalonia's most eccentric, outrageous and egotistical son. Within a salmon pink, egg-topped palace ("like Elton John's holiday home", quipped one visitor) in the heart of Figueres, class and generation gaps dissolve as young and old strain to aim their cameras at a siren-like Queen of Persia riding barefoot atop an Al Capone car. In the back seat, wet and hollow-chested passengers look like they have tussled with *Day Of The Triffids* just one time too many. As the irreverence of the exhibits triggers an irreverence of the spirit, standard gallery politesse goes out the window. A funhouse-like frisson takes its place as frumpy pensioners queue to climb a staircase and gape at a distorted approximation of Mae West's face; gangling students make what they will of an incongruous Duke Ellington album sleeve, an Alice Cooper

hologram and a gilded monkey skeleton; and designer-tagged señoritas jostle for a good position to crane their necks, point and click at a kitschy, fleshy footed self-portrait reaching for the heavens. Even if you're only dimly aware of Dalí's liquefied Surrealism, an hour in the man's domain will convince you that queasy paintings like the candle-faced *Cosmic Athletes* were dredged from one of the most singular subconscious minds of the twentieth century, one unhitched from the Surrealist vanguard in favour of his own, brilliantly christened "paranoiac-critical" method.

Like Gaudí before him, Salvador Dalí's monument was also his last, reclusive refuge. The man is actually buried in the crypt, right below your feet, and it's easy to imagine his moustachioed ghost prowling the half-moon corridors, bug-eyed and impish, revelling in the knowledge that his lurid mausoleum is Spain's most sought-after art spectacular after the Prado.

165

SURREAL LIFE
AT THE
DALÍ MUSEUM

Surreal Life at
Surreal Life at
Surreal

Surreal
Life at
Dali
museum

166 IN SEARCH OF THE PERFECT TART

PORTUGAL I like to ensure I have a tart in every port of call when I visit Portugal. It is a surprise, however, to see these very same tarts making an appearance near my UK home. For pastéis de nata – custard cream tarts to you and me – are becoming Portugal's hottest export since Ronaldo. To have them at their best, though, means seeking out their ancestral home in Portugal.

The Portuguese lay claim to introducing the British to tea and cakes after Catherine of Bragança showed the English court how to do it in the seventeenth century. But Portuguese pastries are more akin to those in North Africa, largely based around almonds and very sweet egg-based toppings. Despite their often risqué names – such as Papas de Anjo (Angel's Breasts) – many recipes were honed in convent kitchens, including pastéis de nata, which are made with sweet, egg-based custard, best served slightly warm, lightly caramelized, in a crispy pastry casing.

In Porto's Belle Époque *Café Majestic*, pastéis de nata arrive on silver trays borne by bow-tied waiters, fresh from glass counters stashed with row upon row of comforting bolos (cakes). Another good spot for pastéis is *Café Aliança* near Faro's harbour, now slightly down at heel but little changed from when Simone de Beauvoir and Fernando Pessoa used to hang out here in the 1930s.

But to find the best pastéis of all means following in the footsteps of the great Portuguese navigators, to their famous departure point at Belém in Lisbon's western suburbs. Here, the *Antiga Confeitaria de Belém* has been serving pastéis – here called pastéis de Belém – since 1837, using their own secret recipe acquired from a nearby monastery. Come on a Sunday and it feels as if the whole of Lisbon has descended for their small and sublimely crisp tarts, served on marble table tops, each with their own shakers – one for cinnamon and one for icing sugar. Somehow, the cavernous warren of tiled rooms seems to absorb the throngs with ease, despite the queues for takeaway pasties, lovingly dispensed in cardboard tubes.

167 LIVING WITHOUT SLEEP IN VALENCIA

SPAIN *Vivir Sin Dormir* (Live Without Sleep) is the name of Valencia's most famous seafront club; it's also a time-honoured fallback for travel writers in pursuit of a pithy maxim. Valencianos really do seem to survive on a minimum of shut-eye, and who can blame them? They enjoy one of the most vibrant bar and club scenes in mainland Spain, its reputation forged back in the 1980s when the phrase first came into circulation; clubbers drove from Barcelona, Madrid and even Bilbao to lose themselves in the pioneering techno soundtrack and all-night – and usually well into the next day – opening hours. This so-called Ruta del Bacalao may be superannuated cliché but Valencia still parties hard and long.

These days you don't even have to leave the cosseting antiquity of the Barrio del Carmen, the hugely atmospheric old town where vintage tapas joints rub shoulders with postmodern tea shops, live jazz locks horns with BPMs and each dimly lit lane holds the promise of something funky. Once the domain of the infamous Borgia clan, the central Calle Caballeros now plays host to a boisterous cross section of mullet-headed locals, fur-lined theatre-goers, fresh-faced Erasmus students and guiris (foreign tourists) of every stripe. Many of their paths cross at *Radio City*, a bohemian cauldron of live theatre and dance. Flamenco and world music fans can indulge in the village-hall-style intimacy of *Café Del Duende* and *La Bodegueta*, a haunt of legends like Paco de Lucia. Valencia also boasts Spain's biggest salsa scene, situated to the south of Carmen around Plaza de España, where clubs such as *Gran Caimán* and *Glamour de Bachata* are within swinging distance of each other. *Bounty* and *Pinball* are both excellent boltholes for funk-soul luddites, and when the Barrio does eventually wind down around 4am, hardened clubbers need only nip across town to *Latex*, *Piccadilly* or the Valencian branch of superclub *Pacha*, all of which will shake your booty till breakfast time.

168 WATCHING REAL MADRID AT THE BERNABÉU

SPAIN Picture the Queen schmoozing Tony Blair at Old Trafford; difficult, isn't it? In Spain, politics, royalty and football have always mixed more freely. Not only did General Franco infamously adopt Real Madrid as the de facto sporting wing of his regime, but King Juan Carlos counselled Spain's first post-Franco prime minister during a game with Zaragoza. These days, it's the players who get the red carpet treatment, and Real Madrid – now a billion-dollar brand and one of the biggest franchises in sport – can boast the bluest blooded line-up of all. Real's underperforming Galácticos may have been royally humbled in recent times, but on a good day they can still dribble, shoot and shimmy like the fantasy football team they are. You can see them up close at the Bernabéu, Real's majestic – Fifa describe it as "mythical" – 80,000 capacity stadium named after the president who masterminded it, which has witnessed such grand sporting occasions as the Euro 1964 final (when Franco's Spain snatched victory from the USSR) and the 1982 World Cup final.

It's an imposing place, one where you can sense history seeping through the concrete, right to your seemingly vertically tiered plastic seat. Don't be surprised if many of them remain empty as kick-off draws near: the legendary Spanish tardiness means no one likes to turn up too soon. Besides, you wouldn't want to miss the pre-match atmosphere in the surrounding bars – even the obligatory Irish pub is ablaze with Real colours. Fans may not make as much noise as you'd expect, but – if their team isn't cutting it – they'll soon whip out their famous white hankies. Real Madrid's superstar cachet and the huge number of season ticket holders means most matches are sell-outs – Champions League Group Stage games are your best bet – but you can always console yourself with a tour of their bulging trophy cabinets.

169 CRUISING THROUGH THE COTO DE DOÑANA

SPAIN The supposed site of the lost city of Atlantis, the preserve of the Duchess of Alba, Goya's muse, and a favourite hunting haunt of seventeenth-century monarchs Felipe IV and Felipe V, Andalucía's Coto de Doñana was also, up until recently, the infamous domain of malaria-carrying mosquitos.

While many of Spain's wetland areas were drained in the fight against the disease, which put paid to many a royal and was only eradicated in1964, the swampy triangle that is the Rio Guadalquivir delta escaped with its water and wildlife intact. Five years after the area was declared disease-free, almost 350 square kilometres came under the aegis of the Parque Nacional de Doñana, Spain's largest national park. Today, the area is both a UNESCO World Heritage Site and Biosphere Reserve, and encompasses more than 770 square kilometres. Illuminated by the hallucinatory glare of the Costa de la Luz sun, it's a place of tart air and buckled horizons, with that almost mystical lure encountered in unbroken landscapes.

Bordered by the urban centres of Seville, Huelva and Cádiz, it suffers the kind of man-made encroachments from which remoter parks are immune, so it's likely your visit will be confined to a guided tour in an incongruously militaristic 4WD bus. Yet as your driver barrels past sand dunes, sun-blind lagoons and pine stands with typically brusque abandon, you can rest easy in the knowledge that the flamingos, wild boar, tortoise, red deer, mongoose and vultures that reside here are otherwise left in peace. Eking out a living alongside them are small, endangered populations of imperial eagles and Iberian lynx, as well as a rude array of migratory birds that alight in flooded marshes on their way back from West Africa in winter and spring. How many of them you actually see will depend on luck, season and a good pair of binoculars; just remember to pack that repellent.

TRAM 28:
taking a ride
through Lisbon's
historic quarters

PORTUGAL Just as you should arrive in Venice on a boat, it is best to arrive in Lisbon on a tram, from the point where many people leave it for good: at Prazeres, by the city's picturesque main cemetery. Get a taxi to the suburban terminus of tram 28 for one of the most atmospheric public-transport rides in the world: a slow-motion roller coaster into the city's historic heart.

Electric trams first served Lisbon in 1901, though the route 28 fleet are remodelled 1930s versions. The polished wood interiors are gems of craftsmanship, from the grooved wooden floors to the shiny seats and sliding window panels. And the operators don't so much drive the trams as handle them like ancient caravels, adjusting pulleys and levers as the streetcar pitches and rolls across Lisbon's wavy terrain. As tram 28 rumbles past the towering dome of the Estrela Basilica, remember the famous bottoms that have probably sat exactly where you are: the writers Pessoa and Saramago, the singer Mariza, footballers Figo and Eusebio.

You reach central Lisbon at the smart Chiado district, glimpses of the steely Tagus flashing into view between the terracotta roof tiles and church spires. Suddenly you pitch steeply downhill, the tram hissing and straining against the gradients of Rua Vitor Cordon, before veering into the historic downtown Baixa district. Shoppers pile in and it's standing room only for newcomers, but those already seated can admire the row of traditional shops selling sequins and beads along Rua da Conceição through the open windows.

Now you climb past Lisbon's ancient cathedral and skirt the hilltop castle, the vistas across the Tagus estuary below truly dazzling. The best bit of the ride is yet to come though, a weaving, grinding climb through the Alfama district, Lisbon's village-within-a-city where most roads are too narrow for cars. Entering Rua das Escolas Gerais, the street is just over tram width, its shopfronts so close that you can almost lean out and take a tin of sardines off the shelves.

171 HIKING THE ANCIENT FORESTS OF LA GOMERA

CANARY ISLANDS Though an easy ferry ride from Tenerife, La Gomera, the smallest of Spain's Canary Islands, is one of Europe's most remote corners. Indeed, this is where a number of 1960s American draft dodgers sought refuge, and it remains a perfect place to get away from it all. In its centre the ancient forests of the Parque Nacional De Garajonay unfold, a tangled mass of moss-cloaked laurel trees thriving among swirling mists to produce an eerie landscape straight out of a Tolkien novel.

The park is best explored along the rough paths that twist between the many labyrinthine root systems. Embark on its finest hike, a 9km trek that's manageable in about four hours if you use a bus or taxi to access the start (a road intersection called Pajarito) and finish points. The lush route takes in the island's central peak, Garajonay; from its summit, you can enjoy immense views looking out over dense tree canopy to neighbouring islands,

including Tenerife's towering volcano Mount Teide – at 3718m, Spain's highest point. From Garajonay's peak, follow a crystal-clear stream through thick, dark forest to the cultivated terraces around the hamlet of El Cedro.

Here you can camp, get a basic room or even rent a no-frills cottage – but be sure to at least pause at its rustic bar. Settled on a wooden bench, try some thick watercress soup sprinkled with the traditional bread-substitute gofio, a flour made from roasted grains.

Beyond El Cedro the valley opens up to the craggy and precipitous landscape that surrounds the town of Hermigua. The terrain around here is so difficult that for centuries a whistling language thrived as a means of communication, but today catching a bus back to your base – via dizzyingly steep hillside roads – is an easy matter.

172 THE LOST STREETS OF RIO HONOR DE CASTILLA

SPAIN Long before Spanish–Portuguese borders were abandoned to EU integration and the elements, the good folk of Rio Honor de Castilla/Rio de Onor lived as though they'd never existed. Isolated at the tip of Spain's Old Castille and Portugal's Trás-Os-Montes regions, these two villages-in-one effectively ignored political frontiers while the rest of Europe tore itself apart. Nowadays any lawbreaking that goes on is subject to respective national laws rather than the traditional fines in wine, but the unique egalitarian systems and language (Rionorês, a hybrid of Portuguese and the Castillian dialect of Leonese) stand as a testament to the absurdity of arbitrary division.

Though the young people have long departed, the old ways survive and there's a tangible sense that things have always been done differently: in contrast to neighbouring villages, the leathery, black-clad elders are garrulous and inquisitive. They still tend a

central plot of land and lead their animals through dung-clotted streets, stabling them below their sagging schist houses. The few narrow streets on either side of the settlement are among the most haunting in the whole of the Iberian peninsula; untold years of cross-cultural birth, life, work and death linger in the mountain air, even as the population peters out.

If you're linguistically equipped, you can savour the novelty of speaking Portuguese in the tiny, ancient bar and Castillian in the grocery store where, true to type, the owner – not so used to the company of guiris – can talk for Spain (or Portugal). A stone bridge is all that separates the two villages; how long they can work together to stave off the ravages of depopulation is another question. For now at least, though, Rio Honor de Castilla/Rio de Onor is a fascinating, hugely atmospheric step back in time.

173 CYCLING FOR THE SOUL: EL CAMINO DE SANTIAGO

SPAIN Traditionally, pilgrimage meant hoofing it, wayfaring the hard way. Yet most Catholic authorities will tell you there's nothing particularly sinful about making it easier on yourself. You could roughly trace Spain's Camino de Santiago, or Way of St James, by car … but then taking full advantage of the fringe benefits – discount accommodation and gorgeous red wine – would prove difficult. The answer? Get on your bike.

With reasonable fitness and not a little tenacity, the mantra of two wheels good four wheels bad can take you far, on a religious pilgrimage route that pretty much patented European tourism back in the Middle Ages. The most popular section begins at the Pyrenean Monastery of Roncesvalles, rolling right across northwestern Spain to the stunning (and stunningly wet) Galician city of Santiago de Compostela, where the presence of St James' mortal remains defines the whole exercise. Pack your mac, but spare a thought for the pre-Gortex, pre-Penny Farthing millions who tramped through history, walking 500 miles to lay down at Santiago's door.

Bikers can expect a slight spiritual snag: 200km to qualify for a

purgatorial reprieve (twice the minimum for walkers – allow two to three weeks), but by the time you're hurtling down to Pamplona with a woody, moist Basque wind in your hair, purgatory will be the last thing on your mind. Granted, the vast, windswept plains between Burgos and León have greater potential for torment, but by then you'll have crossed the Ebro and perhaps taken a little detour to linger amongst the vineyards of La Rioja, fortifying your weary pins with Spain's most acclaimed wine.

The Camino was in fact responsible for spreading Rioja's reputation, as pilgrims used to slake their thirst at the monastery of Santo Domingo de la Calzada. The medieval grapevine likewise popularized the Romanesque architecture for which the route is celebrated; today many of the monasteries, convents and churches house walkers and cyclists. Once you're past the Cebreiro pass and into Celtic-green Galicia, rolling past hand-ploughed plots and slate-roofed villages, even a bike will seem new-fangled amidst rhythms that have scarcely changed since St James's remains first turned up in 813.

174 MOORISH GRANADA: EXPLORING THE ALHAMBRA

SPAIN Towering out of an elm-wooded hillside above Granada, a snowy Sierra Nevada behind, there are few more iconic images of Spain than the ochre-tinted enclave of the Alhambra. By the time the last Moorish prince, Boabdil, was scolded (by his mother) with the immortal line "Do not weep like a woman for what you could not defend like a man", a succession of Nasrid rulers had expanded upon the bare bones of the Alcazaba (or citadel). In doing so they created an exalted wonder of the world, elevating its inhabitants with voluptuous waterways and liberating inscriptions.

Yet its current status as the country's most revered monument is due at least in part to Washington Irving, a sometime American diplomat in Madrid better known for writing *The Legend Of Sleepy Hollow*. In the mid-nineteenth century, at a time when no one gave the place a second glance, Irving recognized its faded glamour, completing his *Tales of the Alhambra* in the abandoned palace.

Now over five thousand visitors wander through the restored complex every day, its chambers and gardens once again alive with cosmopolitan chatter if not free-flowing verse. No amount of words, however, can approximate the sensual charge of seeing the Palacios Nazaries, the best preserved palace of the Nasrid dynasty, for the first time. As a building, the palace's function was to concentrate the mind on the oneness of God, and nowhere is this more apparent than the Patio de los Leones courtyard. Here Arabic calligraphy sweeps across the stucco with unparalleled grace, stalactite vaulting dazzles in its intricate irregularity and white marble lions guard a symbolic representation of paradise. The sweet irony is that none of it was built to last; its simple adobe and wood in harmony with the elements and in stark contrast to the Alcazaba fortress opposite, the impregnable looking towers of which have defined the Granada skyline for centuries.

175 DISCOVERING THE CONQUISTADORS' SPOILS

SPAIN In any account of Extremadura's history, a neat parallel is usually drawn between the austerity of the landscape and the savagery of the conquistadors born and raised there. The alternately broiling and bitterly cold plains hold an allure that's hard to shake off, and the contrast with the towns is striking. Both Trujillo and Cáceres remain synonymous with conquistador plunder, rich in lavish solares (mansions) built by New World returnees. Cáceres is UNESCO-protected, but Trujillo is even prettier, and its sons more infamous. This was the birthplace of Francisco Pizarro, illiterate conqueror of Peru and scourge of the Incas.

While a bronze likeness coolly surveys the Plaza Mayor, the legacy of his less bloodthirsty half-brother bother, Hernando, is more imposing: the Palacio de la Conquista lords it over the square, its richly ornamented facade adorned with a doomed Atahualpa (the last Inca ruler) and spuriously sage-like busts of both Pizarro siblings – the ultimate expression of local hombres made good.

Nearby is the Palacio de Orellana-Pizarro, transformed from a fortress into a conquistador's des res by Francisco's cousin Juan, and crowned by an exquisite Renaissance balcony.

Keeping it in the family was important in Cáceres: the town's most impressive mansion, the Casa de Toledo-Moctezuma, is a work of mannerist indulgence and august grandeur, a place with royal Aztec connections where the son of conquistador Juan Cano (an acolyte of Hernán Cortés) and Doña Isabel (daughter of the Mexican emperor) settled down with his Spanish bride. Across the old town, the gorgeous honeyed-gothic facade of the Casa de los Golfines de Abajo dates back to the years immediately prior to the New World voyages.

These days, the wealth of the Indies arrives in the form of sweet music: the world music jamboree that is WOMAD flings open its doors in Cáceres for four days each May. With consummate irony, it's possible to bask in balmy Latin American sounds, surrounded by mansions financed by Latin American gold.

176 ABOVE THE CLOUDS ON PICO RUIVO

MADEIRA A local challenge is to build a snowman on your bonnet, then drive to the beach for a swim before it melts. There are not many places where you can be in the mountains at ten in the morning and bathing in the sea by 11, but such is the height of Madeira's peaks that in winter this is often possible.

More often associated with its dazzling flora and year-round sunshine, Madeira also boasts some of Europe's most dramatic mountain ranges. Long extinct volcanic peaks jut to nearly 2000 metres above the warm Atlantic waters, and one of the island's greatest walks is a dizzy footpath linking its highest points.

The walk to the island's highest peak, Pico Ruivo, is well signed and immediately dramatic, following a high ridge across a volcanic landscape. Skeletal bones of basalt columns and sills jut out of the soft, reddish ferrous soil, but as you climb, the scenery is far from barren. In summer, the path is lined with miniature pink geraniums, weird interlocking leaves of house leeks and the contorted trunks of ancient heather trees.

The eleven-kilometre path is endlessly varied, sometimes following steps up steep inclines, or skirting cliffs along terrifyingly narrow (but thankfully fenced) ledges. Despite the cool mountain air, you soon feel the heat of the high sun and it can be thirsty work, though you can shelter in caves, once used by shepherds. At times, the track passes through rock tunnels hewn through dramatic outcrops.

After some five hours, you reach a government rest house just below the final ascent to Pico Ruivo. At 1862 metres, this is the highest point on Madeira, and on clear days you can see both the north and south coasts of the Portuguese island from here, though more often the view is over a fluffy landscape of billowing clouds.

177 ALPARGATAS: THE SOUL IS IN THE SOLE

SPAIN Barcelona's Carrer Avinyó, once a steamy, brothel-studded street specializing in debauchery, unfolds amid the Barri Gòtic's chaotic warren of cobblestone alleys and gloomy medieval portals. It was the prostitutes of Avinyó – dark eyes flashing invitation from behind crimson curtains – who supposedly inspired Picasso to paint his seminal cubist work, Les Demoiselles d'Avignon. These days, what draws the customers isn't the sex but the shoes. Head to La Manual Alpargatera, Barcelona's oldest alpargatas store, to peruse the city's finest selection of the popular rope-soled canvas shoes, best known internationally by their French name, "espadrille".

This old-time cobbler haven, which opened in 1941, offers a glimpse into the living history of the Barri Gòtic. Beyond the white-washed facade, wrought-iron lamps hang from beamed ceilings. Wooden benches ring the main room, and an enormous floor-to-ceiling shelf crammed with alpargatas dwarfs everyone who passes under it. The alpargata's soul is in its sole, which is made from tough hemp fibres that are stripped from the cannabis bush, and then braided and woven. In the back workshop, the dry, crackly smell of fresh-cut rope and hot-ironed fabric fills the air, while assistants pull on spools of bright ribbons, creating made-to-order shoes in a skilful blur of the fingers.

Sophia Loren glamourized the alpargata in the 1960s, parading the pages of glossy fashion mags in high-heeled espadrilles with boldly coloured ribbons criss-crossing her calves. But alpargatas are of humble origins, shoes of the paisanos, simple country folk who lived off the land. The ribbons that Sophia Loren strutted to stardom were born out of the most practical of necessities: to keep the alpargata snugly on as the farmer sloughed through the manure of his field. In staying true to their roots, alpargatas are still remarkably cheap. You can saunter out with a basic pair for as little as five euros – which leaves plenty left over for a pitcher or three of sangria at the nearby bars.

178 HEADING FOR THE HEIGHTS IN THE PICOS DE EUROPA

SPAIN Defining the topography of Asturias and Cantabria, and even nudging into neighbouring León, the Parque Nacional Picos de Europa throws a lot of limestone weight around for a comparatively compact range.

It's also stubbornly diverse and disarmingly magnificent, long the destination of choice for not only discerning European trekkers and climbers but also cavers, who are drawn to the 1km-plus depths of its tentacle-like drainage system. Much like the parks of northern Portugal, the Picos shelter countless stone-clad villages and hamlets which the land has sustained for centuries and where the trekking industry is comparatively recent. But the layered vista of beech-forested valleys, flinty summer pasture and incongruous lunar peaks makes the range particularly alluring and deceptively deep.

The history likewise generates its own mystique, literally enshrined in stone at the pilgrimage site of Covadonga on the park's far western fringe. This was where, in the early eighth century, the beleaguered Christians allegedly took their first Moorish scalp and kick-started the Reconquista.

You don't have to be a believer to wonder at the beauty of the Picos, although a sense of divine presence might help, especially in negotiating the forbidding, 1.5km-deep chasm that is the Cares Gorge. It remains the definitive Picos experience, usually accessed from the village of Caín, from whence the most impressive bridges and tunnels are in easy reach. As griffon vultures tailspin high overhead, well-fed day-trippers and the occasional heavily laden hiker pick their way along a path audaciously gouged out of the cliff face. The gorge forms a natural boundary between the less visited western mountains and the central massif, where the official daddy of the Picos, Torre Cerredo, is outclassed by its rakish, orange-bronzed rival, the Naranjo de Bulnes. The Naranjo is a perennial favourite with climbers, although even they have been known to succumb to the less arduous thrill of the teleférico, which shudders up more than 750 metres of sheer cliff.

MISCELLANY

DUENDE

Duende is a quintessentially Spanish, supposedly **untranslatable** concept, originally referring to a supernatural fairy or spirit and still widely used in this sense in Latin America. In Spain, the term has come to signify a moment of cathartic ecstasy in art, particularly flamenco and bullfighting (if bullfighting can be called art), when the artist or performer, and by extension the audience, is consumed with the raw, volatile energy of pure creation in the face of death.

"Better a red face than a black heart"

Portuguese proverb

FIVE TOP TAPAS BARS

Barbiana c/Albareda 11, Seville. Thunderous conversation and flaky-fresh Costa de la Luz fish.
Cal Pep Plaça de les Olles 8, Barcelona. Seafood landmark with queues of loyal Catalans.
La Casa Del Abuelo c/Victoria 12, Madrid. Forget the mantra of consumer choice; this place only serves one dish – prawns – and they've spent 100 years doing so.
La Cuchara de San Telmo c/31 de Agosto 28, San Sebastian. Pintxo-sized portions of trendy Basque gastronomy for a few euros and no fuss.
La Taberna Del Gourmet, Alicante. Pricey but immaculate food, organic wine and Spanish tradition without the brusqueness.

SPORT

Spain and Portugal are nations of **fútbol** obsessives, and while the latter has top teams in Benfica and Porto, Spain is home to a league that has long been the envy of Europe. Barcelona and Real Madrid remain two of the biggest names in world football, yet – with

typical contrariness – the Spanish national team are perennial underachievers; their best showing to date was fourth place in the 1950 World Cup.

A 2003 survey by the University of Navarra ranked Spain as the **third most sedentary nation** in the EU, and Portugal as the second; only Belgium does less exercise.

FIVE BEAUTIFUL BEACHES

Bolonia Costa de la Luz, Tarifa, Spain Relentless wind keeps the crowds away at this remote, very low-key quasi-resort, flanked by the Roman ruins of Baelo Claudia.
Playa de Oyambre Comillas, Cantabria, Spain A great white escape from Santander, popular with surfers.
Praia de São Rafael, Albufeira, Portugal Stunning cove beach a couple of kilometres west of town, dotted with wave-etched sandstone pillars.
Ponta da Calheta–Penado do Sono, Porto Santo, Madeira A six-kilometre stretch of golden sand fringes the southeast coast of this little island, 75km off Madeira.
Xilloi O Vecedo, Lugo, Spain Crystal clear, blue-flag bay buffered by emerald cliffs.

THE SPANISH CIVIL WAR

A bloody prelude to World War II, the Spanish Civil War broke out in July 1936 and lasted for almost three years, until beleaguered Republican forces surrendered on April 1, 1939. An uneasy coalition of liberals, socialists, Communists and anarchists had fought alongside the army, loyal to the leftist Popular Front government, against a Nationalist uprising by **General Francisco Franco**. He was supported by the landed gentry, Carlist monarchists, fascists and the majority of Catholic priests. The fact that the Nationalists were aided by Italy, Germany and Portugal (albeit strategically), and the Republicans by the USSR, also made it a prelude to the Cold War, while the

International Brigades (foreign volunteers fighting on the Republican side) demonstrated the passions aroused by the conflict worldwide. Franco's victory inaugurated almost four decades of dictatorship, isolation and repression, shaping modern Spanish life and politics.

MADEIRA WINE

The **fortified wine** Madeira was discovered after table wine bound for the East Indies was "cooked" in the extreme heat onboard ship. Surprisingly, the wine improved with the heat, and until the end of the nineteenth century, Madeira was made by transporting wine to Indonesia and back to achieve the right temperature.

THE BASQUES

The Basques are widely recognized as being the oldest ethnic group in Europe, with archaeological findings suggesting a continuous presence for more than 30,000 years. Known as **Euskal Herria** to the Basque people, the Basque region covers the three Basque provinces in Spain: Gipuzkoa, Bizkaia and Alava, together with Navarra and part of southwestern France. Their language, Euskarra, bears no relation to the Indo-European languages that spawned Latin, Castilian, Catalan and French, and some linguists have claimed to show an even older genesis by highlighting vocabulary relating to the stone age, a theory seemingly backed up by homogenous blood type.

The Spanish state's battle with paramilitary Basque nationalist group ETA, or **Euskadi Ta Askatasuna** (Euskadi and Freedom), has been going on since the early 1960s. Initially formed out of resistance to the cultural repression and brutality of the Franco regime, the group went on to target academics, businessmen, journalists and tourists. After an earlier ceasefire in 1998, the group finally declared a "permanent ceasefire" in March 2006, before announcing six months later that they would continue with armed struggle until Basque independence. Negotiations with José Luis Rodríguez Zapatero's government are nevertheless ongoing.

FIVE FOODS TO TRY

Churros Spain Strips of fried dough dunked in viscous chocolate.
Pasteidas Natas Portugal Sweet custard tarts with a caramelized topping
Jamón serrano Spain Cured ham, perfected in Extremadura.
Caldeirada de Lulas Madeira Local take on the Portuguese stew, with squid instead of fish, and added ginger.
Bacalhau Portugal Salted cod, cooked in hundreds of mouthwatering ways.

WILDLIFE

The **Iberian Lynx**, one of the region's most graceful wild animals, is the most endangered big cat in the world as well as the most endangered carnivorous species in Europe. Just over a hundred adults survive, largely in two pockets of Andalucía, one near Andujar in the north of the province, and one on the fringes of the Coto de Doñana national park, though there are also a number in Portugal's Serra da Malcata. Hunting, disease-ravaged rabbit populations and road traffic have all contributed to the dwindling numbers, although a lynx reserve is planned in the hills of the Algarve and a captive breeding programme in Spain may yet prevent extinction.

THE SIESTA

Contrary to popular belief, the Spanish siesta, or early afternoon nap, originated in the Alentejo region of Portugal. Although the practice is being eroded due to economic demands, in most of Spain you'll still find **nothing doing** between 2 and 5pm. The shutdown is generally spent over a long lunch rather than in the sack, but a recent national commission blamed the lengthy lunch hour for sleep deprivation (due to working later at night and going to bed later), attendant low productivity and even increased physical and mental illness. It looks unlikely, however, that leisurely afternoons will be abandoned with any great enthusiasm, and the Portuguese have even formed a pressure group to defend them.

IBERIAN INGENUITY

Perhaps the most famous of Spanish inventions is the **six-string guitar**, although they've also brought us the submarine, graded lenses for glasses and the humble lollipop. Portugal's finest invention is the **caravel**, a small, nimble vessel that was the preferred ship of the early explorers.

"Waking up earlier won't make the sun rise faster"
Spanish proverb

FIVE OF THE BEST BOOKS ON SPAIN

Homage to Catalonia George Orwell Gripping first-person account of the Spanish Civil War, unflinching in its portrayal of internecine conflict.
The New Spaniards John Hooper Exhaustive and perceptive analysis of pretty much every facet of life in post-Franco Spain, though badly in need of updating.
Our Lady of the Sewers Paul Richardson With a brief "to sieve out the ancient, perverse and eccentric from the new, nice and normal" how could he fail? Engrossing, casually hilarious and outrageously well informed.
Sacred Roads Nicholas Shrady A book on global pilgrimages rather than Spain, but Shrady's winter journey along the camino francés remains one of the most lucid contemporary accounts in print.
Voices of the Old Sea Norman Lewis With tender humour and pristine prose, Lewis recreates the lost world of post-war peasant and fishing communities soon to be eclipsed by tourism.

BIGGEST REGIONS

Region	Population	Languages Spoken
Andalucía (Spain)	7.85 million	Castilian
Catalunya (Spain)	6.99 million	Catalan, Castilian, Aranese
Madrid (Spain)	5.96 million	Castilian
Valencia (Spain)	4.69 million	Valencian, Castilian
Costa Verde (Portugal)	3.69 million	Portuguese

A TOAST TO VIKINGS IN BORNHOLM • CHRISTMAS IN THE HAPPIEST PLACE IN THE WORLD • DANISH DELIGHTS: TIVOLI'S FAIRGROUND ATTRACTIONS • GOING GASTRO AT NORDIC NOMA • SEEING THE LIGHT AT JUTLAND'S EDGE • **WATCHING HAMLET IN KRONBORG SLOT** • PUFFIN AND PANTIN' • FEELING THE HEAT IN A FINNISH SAUNA • GOING TO THE DOGS IN FINNISH LAPLAND • DEBUNKING MYTHS IN KVERKFJÖLL • TREKKING TO DOOR MOUNTAIN • PARTYING ALL NIGHT IN REYKJAVÍK • TESTING YOUR TASTEBUDS IN ICELAND • SELJALANDSFOSS: BEHIND THE GLASS CURTAIN • SNORKELLING "THE RIFT" • SOAKING IN LAKE MYVTAN'S HOT SPRINGS • DRESSING UP FOR THE WESTMANN ISLANDS FESTIVAL • A TO B BY CROSS-COUNTRY SKI • CRUISING THE COOLEST COAST IN EUROPE • FJORD FOCUS: TOURING THE WESTERN WATERWAYS • LIVING THE QUIET LIFE IN LOFOTEN • HIKING THE BESSEGGEN RIDGE • BREAKFASTING WITH THE STARS AT THE GRAND HOTEL • CHILLING OUT IN THE ICEHOTEL • NAVIGATING A SWEDISH SMÖRGÅSBORD • LAPPING UP LIFE IN LAPLAND • SUMMER SAILING IN THE STOCKHOLM ARCHIPELAGO • VISTING THE VIKINGS OF VISBY • A TOAST TO VIKINGS IN BORNHOLM • CHRISTMAS IN THE HAPPIEST PLACE IN THE WORLD • DANISH DELIGHTS: TIVOLI'S FAIRGROUND ATTRACTIONS • GOING GASTRO AT NORDIC NOMA • SEEING THE LIGHT AT JUTLAND'S EDGE • WATCHING *HAMLET* IN KRONBORG SLOT • PUFFIN AND PANTIN' • FEELING THE HEAT IN A FINNISH SAUNA • GOING TO THE DOGS IN FINNISH LAPLAND • DEBUNKING MYTHS IN KVERKFJÖLL • TREKKING TO DOOR MOUNTAIN • **PARTYING ALL NIGHT IN REYKJAVÍK** • TESTING YOUR TASTEBUDS IN ICELAND • SELJALANDSFOSS: BEHIND THE GLASS CURTAIN • SNORKELLING "THE RIFT" • SOAKING IN LAKE MYVTAN'S HOT SPRINGS • DRESSING UP FOR THE WESTMANN ISLANDS FESTIVAL • A TO B BY CROSS-COUNTRY SKI • CRUISING THE COOLEST COAST IN EUROPE • **FJORD FOCUS: TOURING THE WESTERN WATERWAYS** • LIVING THE QUIET LIFE IN LOFOTEN • HIKING THE BESSEGGEN RIDGE • BREAKFASTING WITH THE STARS AT THE GRAND HOTEL • CHILLING OUT IN THE ICEHOTEL • NAVIGATING A SWEDISH SMÖRGÅSBORD • LAPPING UP LIFE IN LAPLAND • SUMMER SAILING IN THE STOCKHOLM ARCHIPELAGO • VISTING THE VIKINGS OF VISBY • A TOAST TO VIKINGS IN BORNHOLM • CHRISTMAS IN THE HAPPIEST PLACE IN THE WORLD • DANISH DELIGHTS: TIVOLI'S FAIRGROUND ATTRACTIONS • GOING GASTRO AT NORDIC NOMA • SEEING THE LIGHT AT JUTLAND'S EDGE • WATCHING *HAMLET* IN KRONBORG SLOT • PUFFIN AND PANTIN' • **FEELING THE HEAT IN A FINNISH SAUNA** • GOING TO THE DOGS IN FINNISH LAPLAND • DEBUNKING MYTHS IN KVERKFJÖLL • TREKKING TO DOOR MOUNTAIN • PARTYING ALL NIGHT IN REYKJAVÍK • TESTING YOUR TASTEBUDS IN ICELAND • SELJALANDSFOSS: BEHIND THE GLASS CURTAIN • SNORKELLING "THE RIFT" • SOAKING IN LAKE MYVTAN'S HOT SPRINGS • DRESSING UP FOR THE WESTMANN ISLANDS FESTIVAL • A TO B BY CROSS-COUNTRY SKI • CRUISING THE COOLEST COAST IN EUROPE • FJORD FOCUS: TOURING THE WESTERN WATERWAYS • LIVING THE QUIET LIFE IN LOFOTEN • HIKING THE BESSEGGEN RIDGE • BREAKFASTING WITH THE STARS AT THE GRAND HOTEL • **CHILLING OUT IN THE ICEHOTEL** • NAVIGATING A SWEDISH SMÖRGÅSBORD • SEEING THE NORTHERN LIGHTS • LAPPING UP LIFE IN LAPLAND • SUMMER SAILING IN THE STOCKHOLM ARCHIPELAGO • VISTING THE VIKINGS OF VISBY • A TOAST TO VIKINGS IN BORNHOLM • CHRISTMAS IN THE HAPPIEST PLACE IN THE WORLD • DANISH DELIGHTS: TIVOLI'S FAIRGROUND ATTRACTIONS • GOING GASTRO AT NORDIC NOMA • SEEING THE LIGHT AT JUTLAND'S EDGE • WATCHING HAMLET IN KRONBORG SLOT • PUFFIN AND PANTIN' • FEELING THE HEAT IN A FINNISH SAUNA • GOING TO THE DOGS IN FINNISH LAPLAND • DEBUNKING MYTHS IN KVERKFJÖLL • TREKKING TO DOOR MOUNTAIN • PARTYING ALL NIGHT IN REYKJAVÍK •

SCANDINAVIA

179–208

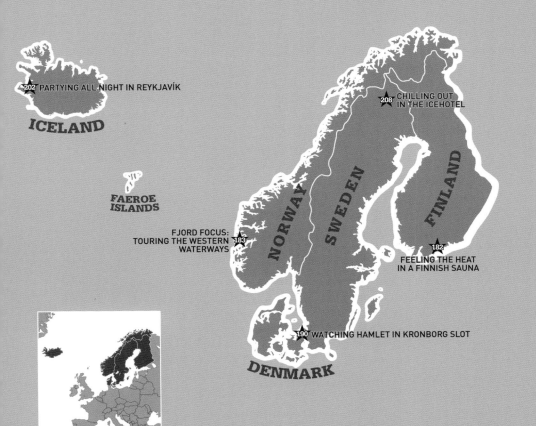

202 PARTYING ALL NIGHT IN REYKJAVÍK

ICELAND

208 CHILLING OUT IN THE ICEHOTEL

FAEROE ISLANDS

NORWAY

SWEDEN

FINLAND

FJORD FOCUS: TOURING THE WESTERN WATERWAYS 183

182 FEELING THE HEAT IN A FINNISH SAUNA

190 WATCHING HAMLET IN KRONBORG SLOT

DENMARK

179 LAPPING UP LIFE IN LAPLAND

SWEDEN The last great wilderness in Europe, Swedish Lapland is void of human habitation and unblemished by development bar a few idle roads. Here in the Arctic north, the landscape has an elemental beauty: sweeping plains of tundra are punctuated by herds of grazing reindeer and hundreds of sparkling mountain tarns, edged by forests of dwarf birch and craggy peaks. This is nature in the raw.

The best way to explore Lapland is on foot along the Kungsleden trail. Sweden's longest and best-known hiking route stretches 500km from Abisko in the north to Hemavan, passing the country's highest peak, Kebnekaise (2114m), and the enigmatic mountaintops of Lapporten, which the local indigenous people, the Sámi, use to guide their reindeer between summer and winter grazing pastures. Hiking the whole of it would take you about a month, but there's no shame in tackling just one of the segments; the stretch between Kvikkjokk and Ammarnäs is probably the most rugged and the most isolated.

In the wild, remote section from Jäkkvik to Adolfström, you snake steeply up the valley side through mountain birch forest, and are treated to awe-inspiring views of the double jagged forms of Mount Pieljekaise, the Sámi name for an ear, which the peak resembles in shape, and carpets of the bright yellow globeflower, which grows extensively in this part of the Swedish Arctic. Keep your eyes peeled, too, for eagles and gyrfalcons, which breed in the national park here, and for bears and arctic foxes. The best time to hike the Kungsleden is between late June, when the last of the snow has melted and the terrain has dried out a little, and mid-September, when the deep golden autumn colours of the leaves and mosses are quite spectacular.

180 DEBUNKING MYTHS IN KVERKFJÖLL

ICELAND As you approach the entrance to the Kverkfjöll Glacier Caves, in Iceland's stark interior, you may begin to understand why local myths of trolls and mystical beings are given a surprising amount of credence. Beneath a drooping archway of ice, a shadowy cavern is partly obscured by wisps of sulphurous steam – an eerie, almost magical scene, but one entirely of nature's doing. Lurking deep beneath is a frighteningly active volcano whose intense heat melts ice from the base of the glacier, creating rivers of warm water that burrow through the ice as easily as a hot knife through butter. The tunnels and caverns etched by the rivers are enthralling frozen palaces that stretch for over 2km into the glacier.

The caves, situated along the northern edge of the Vatnajökull Glacier at the end of a rough track that passes barren lava fields and volcanic badlands, are not to be taken lightly. Falling ice, swollen rivers and toxic gases can make the caves dangerous, and it is best to explore them with an experienced guide.

Inside the cave the air feels muggy and slightly intoxicating; given the heat, it's surprising to touch the cave walls and find them numbingly cold. Every surface is dimpled like a choppy sea, sculpted by heat and steam, but as smooth as glass. Slowly your eyes adjust to the light, and you are struck by dazzling shades of blue, from ultramarine to the deepest blue-black. As you make your way deeper into the cave, following tunnels that twist and turn, filtered light gives the ice an unnatural glow. Above the noise of crampons and the echo of running water you can hear the groans of the ice as it is slowly moulded by pressure and geothermal heat – the elements, not trolls, hard at work.

181 NAVIGATING A SWEDISH SMÖRGÅSBORD

SWEDEN Offhand, how many different ways can you think of to prepare herring or salmon? The two fish are staples of the smörgåsbord and, at last count, there were well over 120 varieties being used in restaurants and kitchens across Sweden.

The Swedish smörgåsbord (literally "buttered table") is a massive all-you-can-eat buffet where you can sample almost anything under the midnight sun, from heaving plates of fish and seafood – pickled, curried, fried or cured – to a dizzying assortment of eggs, breads, cheeses, salads, pâtés, terrines and cold cuts, and even delicacies such as smoked reindeer and caviar.

You're best off arriving early and on an empty stomach. Just don't pile everything high onto your plate at once – remember that the tradition is as much celebratory social ritual as it is one of consumption. That means cleansing your palate first with a shot of ice-cold aquavit (caraway-flavoured schnapps), then drinking beer throughout – which as it happens goes especially well with herring, no matter the preparation.

Plan to attack your food in three separate stages – cold fish, cold meats and warm dishes – as it's generally not kosher to mix fish and meat dishes on the same plate. Layer some slices of herring onto a bit of rye bread, and side it with a boiled potato, before moving on to smoked or roasted salmon, jellied eel or roe. Follow this with any number of cold meats such as liver pâté, cured ham and oven-baked chicken. Then try a hot item or two – Swedish meatballs, wild mushroom soup, perhaps Janssons frestelse ("Jansson's temptation"), a rich casserole of crispy matchstick potatoes, anchovies and onion baked in a sweet cream. Wind down with a plate of cheese, crackers and crisp Wasa bread and, if you can still move, fruit salad, pastries or berry-filled pies for dessert, capped by a cup of piping hot coffee. Then feel free to pass out.

FINLAND There are over half a million saunas in Finland – that's one for every ten Finns – and they have played an integral part in Finnish life for centuries. Finns believe the sauna to be an exorcism of all ills, and there's certainly nothing quite like it for inducing a feeling of serenity.

Always a single-sex affair, the sauna is a wonderfully levelling experience since everybody is naked (it's insisted upon for hygiene reasons). After first showering, take a paper towel or a small wooden tray and place this on one of the benches inside, arranged in the form of a gallery, before you sit down. This stops the benches from burning your skin. Traditionally a sauna is heated by a wood-burning stove which fills the room with a rich smell of wood smoke. However, more often than not, modern saunas are electrically heated, typically at around 80–90°C, a claustrophobic, lung-filling heat. Every so often, when the air gets too dry, water is thrown onto the hot stones that sit on top of the stove, which then hiss furiously and cause a blast of steam.

By this point you'll be sweating profusely, streams pouring off you and pooling on the ground, prompting the next stage in your sauna experience – lashing yourself with birch twigs. The best saunas provide bathers with small birch branches, with leaves still on, with which you gently strike yourself to increase blood circulation. The fresh smell of the birch in the hot air, coupled with the tingling feeling on the skin, is wondrously sensual. Traditionally, Finns end their sauna by mercilessly plunging straight into the nearest lake or, in winter, by rolling in the icy snow outside – the intense searing cold that follows the sweltering heat creating a compelling, addictive rush at the boundary of pleasure and pain.

FEELING THE HEAT IN A FINNISH SAUNA

182

NORWAY Everything about the Geirangerfjord is dramatic, even the approach: zigzagging up through the mountains from Åndalsnes before throwing yourself round a series of hair-raising bends as you descend the aptly named Ørnevegen, or Eagle's Highway, the fjord glittering like a precious gem below.

The Geirangerfjord, a great slice of deep blue carved into the crystalline rock walls and snaking out an "S" shape as it weaves west, is one of the region's smallest fjords, and one of its most beautiful. From the pretty little village that marks its eastern end, ferries set out on the sixteen-kilometre trip along the fjord west to Hellesylt. On a summer's day, as the ferry eases away from the wooden pier and chugs off slowly through the passage, waterfalls cascading down the sheer walls on either side and dolphins playing in the bow waves – as they have done since the first cruise ship found its way up here in 1869 – it's easy to see why UNESCO considered this to be the archetypal fjord, recently awarding it World Heritage status.

As beautiful as it is, Geirangerfjord is just one sliver of water in a network of stunning strands, and you need to see a few fjords to appreciate their magnificence as a whole. Head south for Naerøyfjord, the narrowest fjord in the world, where you can savour the emerald-green waters close up, in a kayak. Or hop in the car and glide across on a tiny ferry, over nearby Norddalsfjord, or – to the south – glass-like Lustrafjord, the wind whipping off the water as you stand at the very mouth of the boat, the imposing silhouette of Urnes' Viking stave church looming ever closer.

183 FJORD FOCUS: TOURING THE WESTERN WATERWAYS

184 LIVING THE QUIET LIFE IN LOFOTEN

NORWAY Draped across the turbulent waters of the Norwegian Sea, far above the Arctic Circle, Norway's Lofoten Islands are, by any standard, staggeringly beautiful.

In a largely tamed and heavily populated continent, the Lofoten are a rare wilderness outpost, an untrammelled landscape of rearing mountains, deep fjords, squawking seabird colonies and long, surf-swept beaches. This was never a land for the faint-hearted, but, since Viking times, a few hundred islanders have always managed to hang on here, eking out a tough existence from the thin soils and cod-rich waters. Many emigrated – and those who stayed came to think they were unlucky: unlucky with the price of the fish on which they were dependent, unlucky to be so isolated and unlucky when the storms rolled in to lash their tiny villages.

Then Norway found tourism. The first boatloads turned out to be English missionaries bent on saving souls, but subsequent contacts proved more financially rewarding. Even better, the Norwegians found oil in the 1960s, lots and lots of oil, quite enough to extend the road network to the smallest village – the end of rural isolation at a stroke.The islands' villages have benefited from this road-building bonanza and yet kept their erstwhile charm, from the remote Å i Lofoten in the south through to the beguiling headland hamlet of Henningsvaer, extravagantly picturesque Nusfjord and solitary Stamsund.

Today, the Lofoten have their own relaxed pace and, for somewhere so far north, the weather can be exceptionally mild: you can spend summer days sunbathing on the rocks or hiking around the superb coastline. When it rains, as it does frequently, life focuses on the rorbuer (fishermen's huts), where freshly caught fish are cooked over wood-burning stoves, tales are told and time gently wasted. If that sounds contrived, in a sense it is – the way of life here is to some extent preserved for the tourists. But it's rare to find anyone who isn't less than enthralled by it all.

185 DRESSING UP FOR THE WESTMANN ISLANDS FESTIVAL

ICELAND Held on a five-kilometre wide volcanic outcrop off the south coast of Iceland, this music fest has it all: smoking volcanoes, immense bonfires and great music – even though, hailing as it does mainly from Iceland, Greenland and the Faroes, you won't necessarily be familiar with much of it. The festival commemorates the signing of Iceland's first constitution on July 1, 1874, which granted it semi-independence from Denmark. The story goes that foul weather prevented the Westmann Islanders from reaching the celebrations on the mainland, so they held their own a few weeks later, on the island of Heimaey.

The location remains unchanged, and most Icelandic partygoers now turn up in very un-waterproof fancy dress – as Hawaiian hula dancers, snowmen, superheroes and the like. But it's likely to be cold, wet and miserable, and you're better off with plenty of warm clothes, booze and, if you run out of booze, money – in 2006, Iceland was voted the world's most expensive country. The entertainment starts on the Friday afternoon, but things only really get going from midnight onwards, when a huge bonfire is lit on a small hill at the edge of the camp. Saturday night also gets going at midnight, with a pretty awesome fireworks display followed by the headline bands. Sunday night is more communal, the whole crowd joining in with traditional Icelandic songs, sitting around small bonfires and finishing off the last of the booze until 6am.

Throughout the weekend, festival-goers run from bar to volcanic hot-pool to freezing sea and back to the bar again. By the time the hour of darkness arrives that marks night – due to the extreme northern setting, the weekend passes in almost perpetual daylight – everyone is very, very drunk, and jumping around the pools with complete abandon, usually naked, and usually still necking vodka shots. It's a sight that will stay with you for a very long time.

186 GOING TO THE DOGS IN FINNISH LAPLAND

FINLAND Huskies love to run. When our team was being made up at the farm they were all barking, and jumping in the air seemingly shouting, "Take me! Take me!" They ran all day yesterday and this morning they're off again. We actually have a snow anchor on the sled that you dig in whenever the driver calls a break, or else they'd be off without us.

Yesterday, I was the driver standing on the back of the sled, pushing it up hills and applying the brake as our doggy team hurtled down the other side. It was exhilarating and beautiful, too: we seemed to speed through permanent twilight. But after our night in a purpose-built igloo drinking vodka, telling stories and sleeping under smelly skins, it's my turn to be the passenger.

It's certainly a different perspective. You're well wrapped up and skimming through forests and fells at a rate of knots, but the view is dominated by six dogs, tails in the air – there are many ways to see Finland but I hadn't expected to spend so much time gazing at a pooch's posterior.

My colleague, an investment analyst from Boston, quickly picked up the essentials. The forest trails are narrow and practical but you have to lean into a turn, like a motorcyclist, otherwise the driver can easily be thrown off on a sharp bend.

As passenger, you're pretty much level with the ground. All you hear is the swish of the sled as it slices through snow, plus the occasional bark of dogs and the cries of the drivers: "Mene! Mene!" ("Go! Go!") Brightly coloured ski jackets aside, it's a way of travelling that has hardly changed in thousands of years.

187 CREATIVE CUISINE AT NORDIC NOMA

DENMARK Copenhagen is an unlikely city to produce one of the world's most exciting restaurants, but *Noma* is drawing the same jet-set pilgrims who might've gone to the *Fat Duck* five years ago, or *El Bulli* ten years before that. It's only just appeared on the radar – in 2007, *Noma* earned a second star from the *Guide Michelin* and was named one of the fifty best restaurants in the world by *Restaurant* magazine – but being tucked away in a fashionably derelict corner of a sleepy capital has its advantages, and during a quiet lunch you could walk in, take your pick of tables, and enjoy a meal more sophisticated, delicate, inspired and, ultimately, delicious, than anything you could find in Milan, Marseille or Madrid.

"Noma" is an abbreviation for Nordisk mad, or Nordic food, and those two words are restaurant dogma: every single ingredient, from the familiar (salt and butter) to the foraged (skærtoftmølle barley and sea buckthorn), comes from the region. So, musk ox appears with caramelized apples and woodruff, turbot comes with mead reduction, and instead of olive oil, chef René Redzepi infuses rapeseed oil with herbs and drizzles it over salads.

Noma's style of cooking could be called molecular gastronomy, that culinary sleight-of-hand where sauces are solids and everything is foamed, but the toys in its kitchen are used judiciously, to expand the possibilities of food. Take the beef neck seared to a perfectly bloody rare: it shouldn't be possible – neck is one of the toughest cuts of meat, and should never see a sauté pan – but Redzepi simmers it sous vide at 58 degrees for 36 hours with Gammel Dansk, the bitter digestif, then finishes it over a high flame, and it has the deep flavour of an all-day stew but the texture of a fillet.

As the meal unfolds, Scandinavia seems as bountiful as Tuscany. There are bright sorrel leaves the size of clovers, raw shrimps in cucumber water, impossibly sweet Faroe Island langoustines, and wild mushrooms shaved paper-thin. Then caramels appear on a bentwood tray, and an elderberry cake might be accompanied by tarragon ice cream in a heavy a copper bowl; when nobody was looking, Danish cuisine caught up with Danish design.

188 CRUISING THE COOLEST COAST IN EUROPE

NORWAY For over a hundred years, the *Hurtigrute* boat service has made the dramatic voyage from Bergen in the western fjords of Norway to Kirkenes, deep within the Arctic Circle and hard up against the Russian border. It's a beautiful trawl up the coast, past towering peaks and deep-blue fjords, the views growing more spectacular with every passing knot.

This is far from your average cruise. Quoits are distinctly absent from the upper deck and there are no afternoon salsa classes with the crew; entertainment comes instead in the form of the pounding ocean and some truly staggering scenery. The Hurtigrute calls in at 35 ports on the way – some thriving cities steeped in maritime history, others little more than a jetty and a cluster of uniform wooden houses painted in the ubiquitous red. Joining the boat at Bodø in the far north of Norway you're ensured a spectacular start.

Easing gently out of Bodø and into the Norwegian Sea, the boat turns starboard for the Lofoten Islands, the soaring crags of the Lofotenveggen – a jagged wall of mountains that stretches 160km along the shore – looming ever closer. Hopping in and out of a couple of rustic fishing villages along the coast, it then squeezes through the Vesterålen Islands, almost rubbing its bows along the sheer cliff-faces that line the Trollfjord, before pushing on to Tromsø, a teeming metropolis compared with the sparse settlements left behind. From here, the *Hurtigrute* sets off on its final leg, stopping for a couple of hours at Nordkaap, a desolate spot that marks the northernmost point in mainland Europe, before traversing the Barents Sea. Finally, six days after leaving Bergen and 67 hours from Bodø, it triumphantly chugs into the uniformly lacklustre town of Kirkenes, concrete proof – after such a journey – that it is often better to travel than to arrive.

189 TREKKING TO DOOR MOUNTAIN

ICELAND At the wild and sparsely inhabited eastern edge of Iceland, the granite crag of Dyrfjöll towers above the natural amphitheatre known as Stórurð (the Elves' Bowl). One edge is sharp and steep, the other a flattened tabletop, and in between, the giant square gap that earns the whole its name: Door Mountain. Hewn by a glacier millions of years ago, the gap is two hundred metres lower than the surrounding cliffs. Heather crowned with blueberries lines the route to Door Mountain and there are sweeping views across the Héradsflói valley, a vast moorland plain where strands of meltwater from Europe's largest glacier shine like silver threads on a brown blanket. Few roads cross this landscape, and it remains the last great wilderness in Europe.

190 WATCHING HAMLET IN KRONBORG SLOT

DENMARK "To be or not to be: that is the question." Walking through the hallowed halls of the sixteenth-century Kronborg Slot in northeast Denmark you're likely to hear that famous phrase time and again. For it was here that Shakespeare's *Hamlet* was purportedly set; scores of visitors now come to marvel at this UNESCO World Heritage Site, and few can resist citing the tragic prince's most famous line. Even better, though, is if you time your visit to catch one of the annual performances of the play in the dramatically sited castle grounds, overlooking the sea – the spine-tingling authenticity of the Bard's characters coming to life in their original setting is theatre at its finest.

ICELAND Few places on earth can match Silfra for snorkelling. The setting is unique, a fissure crack running between the American and Eurasian continents, its precise location changing with the shifting of the plates each year. But it's the water – or more accurately, the stunning clarity of the water – that makes this site remarkable.

Silfra has arguably the finest visibility anywhere in the world. Crystal is cloudy in comparison. The temperature helps, hovering at around 3°C, as does the water's glacial purity – it takes 2000 years to get here, drip-feeding its way through fields of lava. In fact, the combination creates a clarity so intense that people have been known to experience vertigo on entering the water, suspended like astronauts over a gully that seemingly drops away into the very centre of the earth.

191
SNORKELLING
"THE RIFT"

192 A TO B BY CROSS-COUNTRY SKI

NORWAY With 30,000km of marked trails, Norway is the true home of cross-country skiing, the original and most effective means of getting yourself across snowbound winter landscapes. And it's easier and less daunting to learn than the more popular downhill variety (well, more popular outside Scandinavia – here, everyone is a cross-country skier from the age of two).

As your skills quickly develop, you'll soon want to take on more challenging hills (both up and down) and to test yourself a little more – there are different techniques for using cross-country skis on the flat, downhill and uphill.

And once you've mastered the basics, a truly beautiful winter world will open up. Popular ski resorts such as Voss, to the east of Bergen, offer a plethora of cross-country tracks, which snake their way under snow-shrouded forests and round lowland hills, whilst the Peer Gynt Ski Region, north of Lillehammer, has over 600km of marked trails winding through pine-scented forests, alongside frozen lakes and over huge whaleback mountains.

It may sound blindingly obvious, but try to go in the depths of winter, for in this season the low angle of the midwinter sun creates beautiful pastel shades of lilac, mauve and purple on the deep, expansive folds of hard-packed powder, especially at the beginning and end of the day.

Ski trails are graded for difficulty and length so you won't bite off more than you can chew, and you'll usually find various ski hütte (huts) along the way where you can stop for a warming loganberry juice. As your skills develop, you may even want to take on a multiday tour, staying overnight at cosy mountain lodges and discovering the high country of Scandinavia in marvellously traditional fashion.

193 HIKING THE BESSEGGEN RIDGE

NORWAY As trekking goes, the beginning of the Besseggen Ridge is a breeze: sitting on the bow of a little tug as it chugs along picturesque Lake Gjende in central Norway's Jotunheimen Nasjonalpark, you'd be forgiven for wondering what all the fuss is about – this is, after all, Norway's best-known day hike, in the country's most illustrious national park. But then the boat drops you off at a tiny jetty, and is quickly gone, and you start the hike up the hill, knowing that each step takes you closer to the crest – a threadline precipice that'll turn even the toughest mountaineer's legs to jelly.

You'll need a good head for heights but it's not a technically difficult walk: the path is generally wide, and well marked by intermittent cairns, splashed with fading red "T"s. After the initial climb away from the jetty, the route levels out before ascending again across boulder-strewn terrain until – some two and a half hours into the trek – you arrive at the base of the ridge itself.

The actual clamber up the ridge takes about half an hour, though the Norwegian youngsters who stride past, frighteningly upright, seem to do it much more quickly. It's incredibly steep and requires a lot of heaving yourself up and over chest-high ledges; in places, the rock just drops away into thin air. But the views are some of the finest in Norway: a wide sweep of jagged peaks and rolling glaciers, and, far, far below, Lake Gjende, glinting green on sunny days but more often – thanks to the unpredictably moody weather up here – resembling a menacing pool of cold, hard steel.

From there on, the going is comparatively easy, and you'll probably scamper the remaining few kilometres back to Gjendesheim, your energy bolstered by the biggest adrenaline boost you have had in a very long time.

194 SUMMER SAILING IN THE STOCKHOLM ARCHIPELAGO

SWEDEN The truly amazing thing about the Vikings was that they ever decided to leave home. With warm sunshine, cool breezes and the smell of fresh pine drifting across verdant landscapes of hillocks and heather, Scandinavia boasts some of Europe's most alluring summers. Few experiences can top a week spent exploring the nooks and crannies of the Baltic, ending each day on the stern of a ship against a jaw-dropping sunset.

Splayed out across 25,000 islands, islets and skerries – only 150 of which are inhabited – the Stockholm archipelago is made up of thickly wooded inner islands and more rugged, bare and windblown atolls further out. During the day, you'll ply the waters in ferries, sailboats or kayaks, while at night you can either take to your berth or hop ashore to spend the night in a rustic inn, cottage or campsite.

Depart from Stockholm's marina and follow the day-trippers to Vaxholm, just an hour away, where an imposing sixteenth-century fortress citadel towers over a charming wharf loaded with art galleries, shops and several excellent restaurants. Another 10km on is Grinda, less crowded and great for swimming, and just next door, Viggsö, a tiny green islet where the members of ABBA penned many of their hit songs. Sail east to Sandhamn, a paradise for the yachting fraternity and home to sandy beaches that rival those of the Med. Wend your way south of here to Fjärdlång, a 3.5-kilometre pine-filled nature reserve ideal for bird-watchers, kayakers and hikers, before heading just inland to Kymmendö, a tiny outcrop of fifteen residents that Strindberg called "paradise on earth"; you can hire a cycle and pedal to his tiny cottage. Or push on further out into the sparkling waters for Björnö, where small sandy cove beaches, dense reed beds, lush hillocks and undiscovered oak forests await.

DENMARK The fishing town of Skagen could have been torn from the pages of a Hans Christian Andersen fairy tale: half-timbered houses line the cobblestone streets and lemon-yellow daffodils bob behind white picket fences. Wander beyond the tidy hamlet, though, and the wilder side of northern Jutland reveals itself: here, the icy Baltic Sea pounds the shore, whipped up by powerful gales. At Grenen point, you can saunter along a pale finger of sand and plant your feet in the frothy coupling of two seas, the Skagerrak and Kattegat. And just south of Skagen lies the largest migrating sand dune in Northern Europe. Thanks to the strong winds, the Råbjerg Mile moves eastward at the rate of about fifteen metres a year, collecting loose debris in its path, like a giant mop.

But it's the region's luminous skies that have long seduced artists, starting with the Skagen painters – or Danish Impressionists – who arrived in the late 1800s. Viggo Johansen, Anna and Michael Ancher, and P.S. Krøyer all immortalized the remote seaside village, capturing its everyday coastal existence – burly fishermen unloading the daily catch, women in high-necked gowns with parasols strolling the beach – amid milky-white sand dunes glowing under a radiant light.

You can view their paintings at the Skagens Museum, founded in 1908, which features the world's largest collection of works by these great Danes. The beautifully designed space abounds with windows and skylights to maximize the natural sunlight, so you can admire their portrayals of Skagen's ethereal glow in a room that's bathed in it, and then gaze out of the window to see the real thing.

Next to the museum sits the whitewashed, country-style *Brøndum's Hotel*, a favourite hangout of the bohemian artists – who enjoyed long, loose luncheons here – and still the social heart of town. Settle at one of the outdoor tables, and after a couple of Tuborgs you may also be inspired to pull out the paintbrushes and capture the bright northern skies yawning above you.

195 SEEING THE LIGHT AT JUTLAND'S EDGE

196 VISITING VISBY'S VIKINGS

SWEDEN Gotland is the Sweden of the imagination: old fishing villages, hearty country food and unspoilt countryside. It has great beaches, towering limestone stacks and some of Europe's richest fossil-hunting areas but it is also, more importantly, the archaic home of the Vikings – around eighty percent of all Viking treasure ever discovered has come from Gotland, and the countryside is home to dozens of mysterious Bronze Age sites, notably rings in the shape of longships made of stone.

At the island's heart is the well-preserved medieval walled town of Visby, a World Heritage Site, which comes alive each August, when Gotland Medieval Week sees the city's cobbled streets festooned with banners, and there is jousting and archery beside the ancient castle walls.

197 WHITE-WATER RAFTING WITH A DIFFERENCE

FINLAND You've got to hand it to those alternative-thinking Finns. Never ones to go with the flow, they've taken the sport of white-water rafting and given it their own special twist – by getting rid of the rafts. Instead, kitted out in layers of thermal underwear and wrapped inside a bright orange drysuit, "rapid swimmers" hurl themselves into the freezing waters of Eastern Finland and float off downstream, feet-first, over the bubbling Kuhmo Pajakkakoski rapids. If the idea of bobbing down a river looking like a DayGlo Michelin Man seems a little odd, then the reality is even more bizarre: the most exotic time to go rapid swimming is in the deep mid-winter, when you tumble downstream surrounded on all sides by frost-covered trees and a sparkling blanket of snow.

198 DANISH DELIGHTS: TIVOLI'S FAIRGROUND ATTRACTIONS

DENMARK Not many cities have a rollercoaster, a pirate ship and an eighty-metre-high carousel slap bang in their centre, but Copenhagen is home to Tivoli – probably the best fairground in the world. The famous pleasure gardens have dished out fun and thrills to a bewitched public since 1843 – to the deeply patriotic Danes they're a national treasure, while most foreign visitors are lured through the gates by the charming mix of old and new: pretty landscaped gardens, fairground stalls, pantomime theatres and old-fashioned rickety rides rub shoulders with brash, high-octane newcomers such as the Golden Tower, which will have you plunging vertically from a height of sixty metres, and the Demon – a stomach-churning three-loop rollercoaster.

But the rides are just the icing on the cake – whether you're grabbing a hot dog or candy floss from the fast-food stands or splashing out in one of the thirty or so restaurants, eating is also part of the Tivoli experience. Music plays a big role, too, be it jazz and blues in the bandstands, Friday night rock on the open-air stage or the more stellar offerings of Tivoli Koncertshal, with its big-name international acts – anyone from Anne-Sophie Mutter to Beck. In October, the whole place is festooned with pumpkins, ghouls and witches for a Halloween-themed extravaganza, and in the weeks around Christmas, the festive spirit is cranked up with spectacular lighting displays, a "Christmas Market", a skating rink by the Chinese pagoda and all sorts of tasty Christmas nibbles and warming glögg, while the braziers and torches help keep the worst of the Danish winter at bay.

Even if fairs usually leave you cold, you can't fail to be won over by the innocent pleasures of Tivoli. On a fine summer's night, with the twinkling illuminations, music drifting across the flowerbeds and fireworks exploding overhead, it's nothing short of magical.

199 A TOAST TO VIKINGS IN BORNHOLM

DENMARK Thick smoke wafts over the rows of slender herring, as their silvery scales warm into a golden-red. The flushed Dane, in coveralls and clogs, prods the alderwood embers with a long pole swathed in rags at one end. Inside the smokehouse, it's damp and dark, not much larger than a garden shed – and just as basic. Then again, so is the herring preparation – here on the wave-lashed Danish island of Bornholm, this tradition of fish meeting fire owes a debt to the island's first Viking inhabitants, who pulled up in their longboats a millennium ago.

The petite kingdom has come a long way. These days, bright ferries filled with sun-seekers pull up to an island that embodies Denmark's penchant for all things hygellig, or "cosy and warm": brick-tiled roofs top custard-yellow half-timbered houses, lace curtains frame doll's-house windows and, in the quiet harbour, fishing boats bob to the squawks of gulls circling lazily above. Off in the distance, slender smokehouse chimneys punctuate the low-rise landscape, snorting smoke into the bright northern sky.

Emerge from the tangled Almindingen forest and you'll come across places like Gudhjem, or "God's Home" – just what you might expect if the Man Upstairs were to design his perfect village, especially when the last gasp of sunlight strikes the cobblestone streets. The island's twelfth-century round churches (rundkirke) – whitewashed fortresses capped with ink-black conical roofs – lend a stylized, medieval splendour to the otherwise tidy pastureland.

While the Vikings' table manners likely raised a few eyebrows – they didn't use plates or utensils except for the knives they pulled from their sheaths – today, or so the saying goes, the only time you'll see a Dane with a knife in hand is when he has a fork in the other. Still, as you feast on "Sun over Gudjhem" (smoked herring on dark bread, topped with a quivering egg and raw onions), washed down with glass after glass of chilled Tuborg, you may feel some distant connection to those helmet-wearing voyagers. They did know a thing or two about having a good time.

200 SELJALANDSFOSS: BEHIND THE GLASS CURTAIN

ICELAND It's not as if there's any shortage of gorgeous natural attractions in Iceland, but there's something about its waterfalls – dotted throughout the country, endlessly varied in character and all truly spectacular.

The bus taking me to Seljalandsfoss (foss is Icelandic for "waterfall"), in south central Iceland, contained twenty-odd passengers, mostly chattering away in various European languages. But I was oblivious to their presence, keeping to myself as I tried to connect with my inner Nordic spirit. Seljalandsfoss was to be my last stop before heading back to the city, and the place that would leave the sharpest impression of Iceland on my brain.

Sixty-five-metre Seljalandsfoss is the fourth highest falls in the country, but it offers something most others don't – the chance to get inside the thing, not just peer over the top behind a guardrail. Following a set of slatted stairs that led up the side of the hill cradling the thin cascade, I scrambled up the rest of the impossibly green outcrop to a path midway up, a trail that snaked behind the falling water. Leaving the grass behind, it narrowed and took me along the slippery, rock-strewn hollow. The falls' backspray clouded my glasses, and threatened the life of my camera.

The relative quiet I had found at the base disappeared, replaced with the growl of the water as it slammed into a shallow pool below. And yet for all its inhospitable elements, there was a cool tranquillity behind the sheet of water, sheltered from the high sun. I propped myself there for a good half hour, enjoying the white noise until I was motioned to return to the other visitors. As I made my way down the somewhat steeper set of stairs on the other side, I felt as if I'd passed through a mental carwash, and was now clean and ready to roll.

201 CHRISTMAS IN THE HAPPIEST PLACE IN THE WORLD

DENMARK What is happiness? It depends on whom you ask, of course, but the Danes seem to have it figured out. According to yearly surveys, petite Denmark consistently emerges as the happiest place in the world. It makes sense, really. This is the country that invented Lego, after all. Danes enjoy free healthcare and education, and punctual, spotless public transport. They make good beer, and better smoked herring. No wonder all those apple-cheeked blondes cycling the cobblestone streets of Copenhagen are beaming.

And then there's the Danish Christmas, or Jul, which ties it all together with a fat red bow. If happiness starts with the slow warmth of anticipation, then December's the month to be here. Meander through any town, large or small, and the holiday fervour is palpable: wreaths heavy with berries hang on front doors; delicate paper cutouts of snowflakes dangle from ceilings; and fragrant Christmas trees are bedecked in wooden angels and white candles. In these northern reaches of the globe, frigid temperatures are a given. But in Denmark, a dusting of snow on the thatched roofs and bright-red mailboxes only adds to the allure.

Mischief is also in the air: as any Danish kid knows, when a sock goes missing, or when the milk suddenly spills as if an invisible hand has pushed it, then the nimble *nisser* (elves) are up to their tricks again – and will be unless you leave a bowl of porridge out before going to bed.

Christmas is celebrated on the evening of December 24, with a feast of roast duck stuffed with oranges or prunes, followed by creamy rice pudding. Then, everyone rises from the table and, in the Danish tradition, forms a ring around the Christmas tree. The singing begins, softly at first, as young and old start to dance, circling the tree and swaying together, small hands in big ones – a moment of sharing that is happiness, no matter whom you ask.

202 PARTYING ALL NIGHT IN REYKJAVÍK

ICELAND In recent years Reykjavík has earned a reputation for wild revelry that's totally disproportionate to its diminutive size. Spend a summer Friday or Saturday night out here, when there's virtually 24 hours of daylight, and it's easy to see why getting wrecked in Reykjavík has become a rite of passage for Europe's most dedicated hedonists.

Known as the rúntur, a Reykjavík pub crawl is precisely what its Icelandic name implies, a "round tour" of the city's drinking establishments. However, a serious night out actually starts at home to help reduce the punitive cost of drinking in Iceland. After several generous vodkas, Reykjavík's well-dressed, well-heeled and well-tipsy take to the streets, albeit somewhat unsteadily, to hit the scene.

As a new face in town, expect to be accosted by revellers dying to know what you think of the local nightlife – they may even invite you to join them. Things change fast on the Reykjavík club scene, but currently the place with the hottest action is *Oliver*, Laugavegur 20a, whose dancefloor is full of strutting twenty-somethings. Two other favourites are *Hverfisbarinn*, Hverfisgata 20, a buzzy glass-fronted bar that's always packed with beautiful people, and *Sirkus*, Klapparstígur 31, a bohemian club where Björk sometimes DJs.

When the clubs empty at around 3 or 4am, the party continues in central Lækjartorg square, where those still standing swap notes on how many beers they downed and the night's gossip. Reykjavík is probably the only place in the world where you can go into a club at midnight, just as it's getting dark, party amongst some of Europe's most stylish and fashionable people, and emerge barely a few hours later in broad daylight, wrecked, maybe, but having had a night to remember.

203 BREAKFASTING WITH THE STARS AT THE GRAND HOTEL

SWEDEN Ever since the Nobel Prizes were first awarded in 1901, the winners have stayed at Stockholm's *Grand Hotel*. And for good reason. Set on the waterfront at Blasieholmshamnen, the hotel has one of the most spectacular city views in the world. Straight ahead is the Swedish Royal Palace, the parliament building and the small island of Gamla Stan, Stockholm's old town with its narrow lanes and cobbled alleys. From the large picture windows of its fine dining room, the Veranda, you can watch the bustle of the promenade and the small boats ferrying people out to the islands of the archipelago.

No one of consequence visits Stockholm without staying at the *Grand*, and the signatures in the guest book read like an almanac of twentieth-century life. There is music: Leonard Bernstein, Herbert von Karajan, Bruce Springsteen, Elton John, Michael Jackson, Tina Turner and Bono. There is literature: Hemingway, Steinbeck, Beckett and Camus. And there is global politics: Mandela, Churchill, Thatcher, Chirac and the Dalai Lama. But, for me, it is the Hollywood connection

that makes the location special: Charlie Chaplin, Grace Kelly, Marlene Dietrich, Alfred Hitchcock, Ingrid Bergman and, of course, Greta Garbo, just a few of the great stars that have stayed here.

As if the guest book wasn't enough to tempt you with delusions of celebrity, the *Grand* has another secret. It serves what is probably the best breakfast in all of Europe. Naturally you can order the usual things: eggs coddled, fried, poached, boiled and served with bacon, ham, toast, muffins, crumpets, waffles and mushrooms. There are crunchy Swedish crispbreads, fresh croissants, rigorously wholesome mueslis and regularizing porridge. Home-made pâtés, marmalades and jams moisten the palate. And then there is herring – pickled or curried in a mouth-watering number of ways – as well as cold cuts and terrines. The choice seems endless, with more than 120 hot and cold dishes to sample. Sitting at a table by the window in the glass-walled *Veranda*, you begin your day with an infusion of fine tea, crisp white linen and that subtle Scandinavian light.

204 TESTING YOUR TASTEBUDS IN REYKJAVÍK

ICELAND "Icelandic cuisine" promised the menu outside *Laekjarbrekka*, a Reykjavík institution for over thirty years, and while I didn't exactly know what that meant, the opportunity, for an adventurous eater like myself, was too good to pass up.

I ordered the house appetizer, which the cheerful waitress promptly delivered – a dubious-looking platter of reindeer carpaccio, marinated trout and smoked puffin. I stepped up to the plate, as it were, and found three piles: greyish flaked fish (obviously the trout), some thin red disks with a dark outline, and a few short black strips that looked as if they came from the dark, bruised sections of a beet. The trout was very tasty, but truth be told, a bit common. I guessed the circular option was the reindeer. It was actually quite good, with a rich, outdoorsy flavour that lingered after I swallowed it.

I stabbed a piece of must-be-the-puffin with my fork. A bit more sturdy than I'd expected. It didn't have a smell, so I wasn't prepared for what my mouth told me it tasted like. It had the consistency of well-done steak, and a strong, oily-fishy flavour, a combination that could politely be described as "conflicting". And yet, I kept eating it, certain that the taste would change, or that I could at least deem it "not bad" in a quirky culinary sort of way. It didn't.

Delighting in my expression, the waitress happily informed me that puffin paled in comparison to some of the country's other "delicacies". Real daredevil diners, it seems, skip the orange-beaked bird and tuck straight into hakarl (rotten shark meat that's buried for six months) or pickled ram's testicles. Those, I promised my stomach, would have to wait for the next trip.

205 PUFFIN AND PANTIN'

FAROE ISLANDS It is mating season on the unspoilt Faroe Islands, about 300km north of Scotland in the windswept, weather-tossed North Atlantic. Heavy waves batter tall, chalky cliffs. Clouds of seagulls sweep through the skies, touching down on fields of purple orchids, flanked by traditional, brightly coloured houses with roofs of turf. Pairs of puffins, their feathers ruffled from the raging sea, wash up on the island, standing proud and rubbing their beaks together in displays of matrimony. The show has just begun. For the next four months, these curious seabirds will mate, nest and raise their offspring on the towering Vestmanna cliffs. They will spend their days diving in and out of the sea, digging burrows, bringing home fish suppers and preparing for migration in late August. All of which makes for great viewing. Boats chug out here from Tórshavn, so you can gaze up at the thousands of nesting birds, hanging on to the crags of the 450-metre-high cliffs far above.

206 SLEEPING WITH THE FISHES AT UTTER INN

SWEDEN In many ways, the *Utter Inn* is your archetypal Swedish house: its walls are wood-panelled and painted red, there's a white gabled roof, and the location – propped on a little island in the middle of Lake Malaren – is classic Scandinavia.

But things get slightly surreal once you look out the window of the hotel's solitary room. A large Baltic salmon glides past, followed by a huge shoal of smelt. The orange soles of ducks' feet wheel through the water above. These are not your average lakeside views, but then you're not actually lakeside. The island is a pontoon, the red house just the tip of the architectural iceberg: *Utter Inn* lies three metres below the surface of the lake. A night spent here is literally like living life in a goldfish bowl.

207 SOAKING IN LAKE MÝVATN'S HOT SPRINGS

ICELAND Most people visit Iceland in summer, when once or twice a week it actually stops raining and the sun shines in a way that makes you think, briefly, about taking off your sweater. The hills show off their green, yellow and red gravel faces to best effect, and you can even get around easily without a snowplough. But if you really want to see what makes this odd country tick, consider a winter visit. True, you'll find many places cut off from the outside world until Easter, people drinking themselves into oblivion to make those endless nocturnal stretches race by (though they do the same thing in summer, filled with joy at the endless daylight) and tourist information booths boarded up until the thaw. On the other hand, you can do some things in winter that you will never forget.

Up in the northeast, Lake Mývatn is surrounded by craters, boiling mud pools and other evidence of Iceland's unstable tectonics. Near its northeast shore lie crevasses, flooded by thermal springs welling up out of the earth. They are too hot for summer bathing, but in winter the water temperature drops to just within human tolerance, and the springs are best visited in a blizzard, when you'll need to be well rugged up against the bitter, driving wind and swirling snow. Clamber up the steep slope and look down over the edge: rising steam from the narrow, flooded fissure five metres below has built up a thick ice coating, so it's out with the ice axes to cut footholds for the climb down to a narrow ledge, where you undress in the cold and, shivering, ease yourself into the pale-blue water. And then... heaven! You tread water and look up into the falling snow and weird half-light, your damp hair nearly frozen but your body flooded with heat. Five minutes later, you can't take any more and clamber out, face red as a lobster and your body feeling so hot you're surprised that the overhanging ice sheets haven't started to melt.

208 CHILLING OUT IN THE ICEHOTEL

SWEDEN The *Icehotel* is the only upmarket establishment in the world where you're guaranteed a frosty reception. Every October, huge chunks of crystal-clear ice are cut from Sweden's River Torne and pieced together, jigsaw style, in the village of Jukkasjärvi, on the river's northern bank. From December through to late spring, when the ice melts back into the river, the designer igloo opens its frozen doors to intrepid visitors, who travel deep inside the Swedish Arctic Circle for a night in this exceptionally cool hotel.

Pretty much everything in the entire complex, from the sculpted beds to the hotel's own chapel, is made out of ice; even the lights – intricately carved chandeliers – were once flowing water. While the overall effect is undoubtedly stunning, such sub-zero surroundings are hardly conducive to kicking back and relaxing, and there are plenty of (expensive) activities to keep your circulation going.

By day, you can scoot off across the powder behind a pack of exuberant huskies, with only the sound of your sledge's runners gliding through the soft snow for company. By night, you can hop on your own snowmobile and head out into the inky blackness in search of the Northern Lights, their technicolour brushstrokes delivered with an artist's flick across the pristine sky.

Back at the hotel, there's just enough time to hit the *Absolut Bar* for a zingy Wolf's Paw cocktail, served in glasses carved – you guessed it – out of ice, before turning in for the night. With room temperatures hovering at a balmy -5°C, the interior designers have wisely gone for reindeer pelts and expedition-strength sleeping bags instead of crisp linen and home-brand hand lotions. You won't get a wink of sleep, of course, but then if it's a cosy night's kip you're after you've definitely come to the wrong place.

MISCELLANY

FIVE GREAT BEACHES

Gudminderup Lyng Strand, Denmark Regularly heralded as the best beach in Denmark, this lengthy strand makes a great place to go for a late-afternoon swim.

Hvide Sande, Denmark This popular beach boasts excellent facilities, and is one of the best places in the country for windsurfing.

Seurasaari, Finland This small wooded island, delightfully set in a sheltered bay, is a popular stop for Helsinki residents, and there's a separate nudist beach lining the western shore.

Solastranden, Norway Located outside the city of Stavanger, Solastranden's pure white sands are great for sunbathing and sunset walks.

Halland, Sweden The entire Baltic coast of this region, the so-called Swedish Riviera, gets more sunshine than anywhere else in the country and has dozens of great stretches of "strand" (beach).

SCANDINAVIAN OR NORDIC?

In linguistic terms, "Skandinavien" is an Old Norse term describing the ancient territories of the Norsemen – that is, the Danes, Swedes and Norwegians. Technically, however, Iceland and the Faroe Islands are also included in this, and Greenland, Shetland and Orkney also share some cultural affinities. "Scanvinavica" is the Latin word for the peninsula shared by Norway, Sweden and northern Finland. "The Nordic Countries" came into being as a term with the creation of the Nordic Council in the 1950s. It includes Finland and Iceland and is the most politically correct and accepted term to include the five main countries of the region. "Scandinavia", however, still trumps other descriptions of the region when it comes to conjuring up romantic notions of cold, mountainous landscapes of forests, fjords and glaciers.

WILD MEALS

With nearly 30,000km of coastline, 500,000 islands and 750,000 lakes, it should come as little surprise that seafood predominates in Norwegian kitchens. But why not splurge on something a bit more unusual. Reindeer, a tender venison, is frequently served as fillets or thinly sliced in a thick cream sauce, and can be found in all four countries, even (on occasion) Denmark. A much more exotic meat is whale, a real delicacy in Norway, often served as fillets fried with boiled beans and potato scallops. Seal, generally available in spring, towards the end of the hunting season, has a more oily consistency to it, and often comes boiled or roasted; the most tender meat is the flipper.

LANGUAGES

Norwegian, Danish and **Swedish** are mutually intelligible Germanic languages with a strong kinship to English, but **Finnish** is grammatically eons away from the others. One of the most complicated languages in the world to learn, it is easily recognisable from the other three for its frequent double consonants and vowels – most evident in "epäjärjestelmällistyttämättömyydellänsäkään", which roughly translates as "even with its quality of not being possible to be made irrational". Related to Finnish is the Sámi language, whose dozen or so dialects are spoken across the region from the coast of western Norway to the Barents Sea.

WHAT DAY IS IT?

English derives four of its days of the week from the names of Norse gods: Tiu (Tuesday), Odin (Wednesday), Thor (Thursday) and Freya (Friday).

LITERATURE

FIVE GREAT CLASSIC READS

The Unknown Soldier, Vainö Linna
The Fairy Tale of My Life, Hans Christian Andersen
Hunger, Knut Hamsun
Pippi Longstocking, Astrid Lindgren
The Kalevala, Elias Lonnröt

FIVE GREAT MODERN READS

Borderliners, Peter Høeg
Sophie's World, Jostein Gaarder
Under the Snow, Kerstin Ekman
The Year of Hare, Arto Paasilinna
The Sun, My Father, Nils-Aslak Valkeapää

FINE DESIGN

Scandinavian design seeks to meld organic forms and materials with a minimalist, utilitarian sensibility. Danes have long held the torch for the most renowned designs in the world: **Arne Jacobsen**, whose cradle-like Egg Chair put Scandinavian design on the global map in the 1950s, leads the pack, while the architectural works of **Jørn Utzon** (Sydney Opera House) and **Henning Larsen** (Copenhagen Opera House) make striking statements on modern life amidst their urban landscapes.

The oh-so-practical aesthetic of long-standing Swedish brand **IKEA** is now firmly planted in the bedrooms and living-rooms of millions of people around the world, although the bold, exuberant designs of Finnish textile and clothier **Marimekko** are fast becoming sought-after objects for the high-class home owner.

THE END OF THE WORLD AS THEY KNOW IT

The mythological Old Norse accounts of the beginning and end of the world are described in the Völuspá ("The Seeress's Prophecy"), the first and best-known poem in the sensational *Poetic Edda*, a defining sixty-five-stanza verse history of Norse mythological civilization. The text exists as a de facto sacred book of the Scandinavian religion, composed in the late tenth century at a time when Scandinavia's pagan practices were being thwarted by the onset of Christianity. The *Völuspá* is recounted by a seeress so old she remembers the beginning of the world and so wise that she can see forth to its demise, Ragnarök ("Doom of the Gods"), the prophesied battle at the end of the world.

WHO'S YOUR DADDY?

Like many places in Western Europe, patronymics (last names derived from the father's name) were widely employed in the Scandinavian countries for hundreds of years. Fathers would pass on their first names to their sons, to which -sen in Denmark and Norway and -son in Sweden were added, while women used the suffix -datter, -dottir or -dotter in Denmark, Norway and Sweden, respectively, to indicate who their father was. Family names became a legal necessity in the nineteenth century, and only in Iceland and the Faroe Islands has the age-old means of naming been kept alive.

TOP VIKING SITES

Denmark, Norway and Sweden were the centres of Viking rule and strategic strongholds for the regulation of shipping and piracy, and there are traces of Viking societies and communities all over the place. The following are the region's best-preserved and most notable sites:

Jelling Stones, Denmark Large runic stone erected more than 1000 years ago by King Gorm the Old, and featuring the first written mention of the nation called "Danmark".
Ladby Skibet, Denmark Underground tenth-century tomb – the only Viking ship burial mound ever to be discovered in Denmark – containing the remains of a Viking chieftain and his longboat.
Trelleborg, Denmark Preserved ring fortress, noted for the mathematical precision of its construction, dating back to 980 AD and the reign of Harald Bluetooth.
Birka, Sweden The oldest town in Sweden and an important early Viking trade centre. Nearby Hovgarden contains the remains of thousands of Viking burial mounds.
Vikingeskibsmuseet, Norway Spectacular museum in Oslo housing near-complete reconstructions from several buried Viking ships recovered from Tune, Gokstad, Oseberg and Borre.

THE FIVE BEST SCANDINAVIAN FILMS YOU'VE NEVER SEEN

Änglagård (*House of Angels*; 1992). A touching film about two hard rockers who inherit a farm in rural Gotland and the effect their move has on the town's residents.
Kauas pilvet karkaavat (*Drifting Clouds*; 1996). One of acclaimed director Aki Kaurismäki's most beloved films, this slow-paced, melancholic story follows a Helsinki couple straightening out their lives after losing their jobs in a recession.
Veiviseren (*Pathfinder*; 1987). Outstanding Oscar-nominated Sámi film about the revenge a boy takes against the gang of killers who murdered his family.
Babettes gæstebud (*Babette's Feast*; 1987). Simple, touching story about a French woman in eighteenth-century rural Denmark and her relationship with the pair of religious sisters who take her in.
Kristin Lavransdatter (1995). Liv Ullman's gorgeous interpretation of the first volume of Sigrid Unset's medieval trilogy about Kristin's stormy encounter with love.

FAMOUS SCANDINAVIANS

Björn Borg Charismatic, handsome Swedish tennis player who made tennis a sexy sport for much of the world.
Harald Bluetooth Named for his dark hair – though legend has it he loved eating blueberries – it was because of him that Christianity became the state religion of Denmark, even if his reasons for doing so (to stave off imminent invasion by French and Germans) weren't entirely spiritual.
Leif Ericsson Norwegian who travelled to Greenland and North America in 1000 AD, marking him as the first European on record to set foot in the Americas.
Ingvar Kamprad Originally from a small rural town in Sweden, this entrepreneur founded IKEA in 1943 when he was just 17; the company initially sold nylon stockings.
Alfred Nobel Immensely successful Swedish inventor and businessman who invented dynamite and bequeathed his massive fortune for an annual prize awarded to citizens who advance humanity in the field of physics, chemistry, physiology or medicine, literature and peace.

SOCIAL WELFARE

The Scandinavian welfare model refers to the way in which the Nordic countries organize and finance their social security systems, public health services and high-quality education. The principle is based on the Lutheran ideal that benefits should be given universally to all citizens, which are supported by a taxation system that has both a broad basis of taxation and a high taxation burden – around 46 percent for most workers – ultimately bringing about a greater redistribution of wealth.

FIVE HOT SUMMER MUSIC FESTIVALS

Roskilde Festival, Demark Early July. A four-day party for nearly 100,000 people with some of the biggest music groups in the world, plus plenty of newcomers. Ⓦ www.roskilde-festival.com.
Copenhagen Jazz Festival, Denmark Mid-July. The capital's largest festival, showcasing everything from live bebop to spoken-word poetry. Ⓦ www.festival.jazz.dk.
Savonlinna Opera Festival, Finland July. One of Europe's liveliest and most prestigious opera festivals, with many of the classics of European opera performed within the walls of a fifteenth-century castle. Ⓦ www.operafestival.fi.
Malmö Festival, Sweden Mid-August. Features over 250 live music concerts and somewhere around 1.5 million visitors over eight days, but best of all, it's free. Ⓦ www.malmofestivalen.se
Telemark Folk Music Festival, Norway Mid-July. Folk enthusiasts from all over the country converge to catch several dozen concerts of authentic world folk music, with a focus on the rich tradition of Nordic folk dancing. Ⓦ www.telemarkfestivalen.no.

BEARS AND BOARS: TREKKING IN THE ABRUZZO NATIONAL PARK • FINDING YOURSELF ON CAPRI • THE ZAGÓRI AND VIKOS GORGE • **TREADING THE BOARDWALKS AT THE PLITVICE LAKES** • ALL YOU CAN EAT – WITH MUSIC! • BALKAN BRASS MADNESS IN GUČA • ON THE TRAIL OF CARAVAGGIO • GETTING LOST IN DIOCLETIAN'S PALACE • DIVINE MADNESS IN CALABRIA • HAVING A BLAST IN BELGRADE • GOING WITH THE FLOW IN NAPLES • SOLVING THE MYSTERIES OF POMPEII • **BACK FROM THE BRINK: THE BRIDGE OF MOSTAR** • STALAGMITES, STALACTITES AND A HUMAN FISH • PARADISE REGAINED: ITALY'S OLDEST NATIONAL PARK • WALKING DUBROVNIK'S WALLS • THIS IS THE LIGHT: EASTER CELEBRATIONS IN LOUTRÓ • SHARING THE LOVES OF THE GODS AT THE PALAZZO FARNESE • THE COLOSSEUM IN WINTER • TACKLING OLD MR THREE HEADS • SOMETHING FISHY IN MARSAXLOKK • WORKING UP A LAVA ON STROMBOLI'S SLOPES • CHEWING THE FAT: A GLUTTON'S TOUR OF BOLOGNA • PLAYING FOR HIGH STAKES AT SIENA'S PALIO • COMINO'S BLUE LAGOON • WATCHING WORLDS COLLIDE IN SICILY • LISTENING FOR NIGHTINGALES ON SAMOS • **LOCKED UP IN LJUBLJANA: HOSTEL CELICA** • JOINING THE TRUFFLE TRAIN IN BUZET • MUSIC, DANCE AND DRAMA IN ANCIENT ASPENDOS • CLASSICAL STUDIES IN SICILY • BEANS AND ORANGES IN IVREA • LOSE YOURSELF AT MYSTRA • GREEK ISLAND HOPPING • VISITING FEDERICO'S PALACE IN URBINO • A NIGHT OUT ON INDEPENDENCE STREET • SHOPPING WITH STYLE IN MILAN • ENJOYING DA VINCI'S LAST SUPPER • **BUNKERING DOWN IN DURRES** • GETTING THE MEASURE OF THE MEDICIS: THE UFFIZI • EUROPE'S MOST ANCIENT TEMPLES • MONASTIC MOUNT ÁTHOS • CARNIVAL IN VENICE • LIVING IT UP ON THE AMALFI COAST • THE PEACE OF PAESTUM • GETTING YOUR KIT OFF IN FLORENCE • FEASTING IN BERGAMO • RING OF FIRE: WALKING ON HOT COALS • OSTIA ANTICA • CLASSICAL DRAMA AT EPIDAVROS • **MONASTERIES SUSPENDED IN THE AIR** • CELEBRATING THE BIENNALE • IN THE FOOTSTEPS OF ODYSSEUS ON ITHACA • CLIMB EVERY MOUNTAIN: REINHOLD MESSNER • CAPPADOCIA: LAND OF THE FAIRY CHIMNEYS • CALLED BY RUMI: DERVISHES IN ISTANBUL • **DOING PENANCE IN THE SISTINE CHAPEL** • WALKING THE CINQUE TERRE • BRAVING THE MIDDAY SUN IN LECCE • SNUFFLING FOR TRUFFLES IN PIEMONTE • GETTING DOWN AND DIRTY IN DALYAN • MAKING THE PARTY LAST ALL NIGHT IN TIRANA • HIKING THE VIA FERRATA • LOOKING FOR PASTA HEAVEN • NAVIGATING THE NOCTURNAL UNDERWORLD IN ZAGREB • SEEING LEGENDS COME ALIVE IN CRETE • **SHOP TILL YOU DROP IN ISTANBUL** • INSIDE A METAPHOR: TROY • SPOTTING GIOTTO IN PADUA • VENICE: EUROPE'S FIRST MODERN CITY? • LIVE LIKE A DOGE: ONE NIGHT AT THE DANIELI • STUDENICA AND THE MAGICAL MONASTERIES • **GRAND MASTER FLASH** • CHILLING OUT ON THE MONTENEGRIN COAST • VISITING THE HOME OF PIZZA • STRIKING OIL IN EDIRNE • SAMPLING THE GRILLED TROUT OF LAKE OHRID • TOURING THE TUSCAN HILLTOWNS • BEARS AND BOARS: TREKKING IN THE ABRUZZO NATIONAL PARK • FINDING YOURSELF ON CAPRI • THE ZAGÓRI AND VIKOS GORGE • ALL YOU CAN EAT – WITH MUSIC! • TREADING THE BOARDWALKS AT THE PLITVICE LAKES • BALKAN BRASS MADNESS IN GUČA • ON THE TRAIL OF CARAVAGGIO • GETTING LOST IN DIOCLETIAN'S PALACE • DIVINE MADNESS IN CALABRIA • **HAVING A BLAST IN BELGRADE** • GOING WITH THE FLOW IN NAPLES • SOLVING THE MYSTERIES OF POMPEII • **RAFTING THE TARA CANYON** • STALAGMITES, STALACTITES AND A HUMAN FISH • PARADISE REGAINED: ITALY'S OLDEST NATIONAL PARK • WALKING DUBROVNIK'S WALLS • THIS IS THE LIGHT: EASTER CELEBRATIONS IN LOUTRÓ • SHARING THE LOVES OF THE GODS AT THE PALAZZO FARNESE • THE COLOSSEUM IN WINTER • TACKLING OLD MR THREE HEADS • SOMETHING FISHY IN MARSAXLOKK • WORKING UP A LAVA ON STROMBOLI'S SLOPES • CHEWING THE FAT: A GLUTTON'S TOUR OF BOLOGNA • PLAYING FOR HIGH STAKES AT SIENA'S PALIO • COMINO'S

SOUTHEAST EUROPE

209–288

LOCKED UP IN LJUBLJANA: **236** HOSTEL CELICA

ITALY

SLOVENIA

CROATIA

TREADING THE BOARDWALKS **213** AT THE PLITVICE LAKES

BOSNIA HERZEGOVINA

HAVING A BLAST **218** IN BELGRADE

SERBIA

BACK FROM THE BRINK: **221** THE BRIDGE OF MOSTAR

RAFTING THE TARA CANYON **268**

MONTENEGRO

ALBANIA

DOING PENANCE IN **265** THE SISTINE CHAPEL

BUNKERING DOWN IN DURRES **247**

SHOP TILL YOU DROP **282** IN İSTANBUL

TURKEY

MONASTERIES **259** SUSPENDED IN THE AIR

GREECE

MALTA **283** GRAND MASTER FLASH

209 BEARS AND BOARS: TREKKING IN THE ABRUZZO NATIONAL PARK

ITALY The Apennines stretch for some thirteen hundred kilometres down the very spine of Italy. They are Italy at its roughest and least showy. But these mountains are far from dull. In their loftiest and most rugged stretch, in the central region of Abruzzo, two hours from Rome, you'll find peaks rising up from gentle pastures, and swathes of beech woodland that roll up from deep valleys before petering out just short of the steepest ridges.

Such is the landscape of the Parco Nazionale d'Abruzzo. Romans come here to walk, climb and enjoy rustic foods like wild boar prosciutto and local sheep's cheese, washed down by the hearty Montepulciano d'Abruzzo wine. Foreign visitors are rare, and you can walk for hours without seeing another person. This tranquillity isn't lost on the park's wildlife. Chamois, roe deer, martens and even wolves have found a haven here, and the park is also one of the last refuges in Western Europe of the Marsican brown bear. They haven't survived by being easy to spot. After the furtive lynx – an animal which stalks its prey by night before launching an attack that can only be described as explosive – bears are among the park's most elusive creatures. You may be lucky enough to see one briefly, tantalizingly exposed while crossing an open mountain ridge. You're more likely, however, to find just paw prints or rocks overturned in the hunt for moths.

The best base is Pescasseroli, a ridge-top village with a cluster of homely hotels and a park visitor centre. From here, you can hike straight into the forest and up along the long ridge that crests and falls from Monte Petroso (2247m) to the aptly named Monte Tranquillo (1830m) and on to Monte Cornacchia (2003m). Or you can take a bicycle on hundreds of kilometres of rough roads that thread through the area. By the time you've done this, you will have earned your plate of wild boar.

210 FINDING YOURSELF ON CAPRI

ITALY Falling in love with Capri came quickly and easily. I was living in Rome, and some friends had a historic family villa in the heart of the island. Going down for long weekends soon became a regular ritual.

The enigma of the place is that there are really two Capris: the stunning, magical island gulped down all in one mad dash by day-trippers; and the unassuming yet more captivating Capri, privy only to those who decide to spend the night. Day visits mean barely enough time to hike up to Villa Jovis or over to the Arco Naturale, to wander a bit through the chic shops of Capri town and have a bite to eat, to take the harrowing bus-ride up to Anacapri and from there the chairlift up to Monte Solaro. Trying to fit in the Blue Grotto requires foregoing at least one of the other major attractions. The experience is satisfying enough but it means never getting away from the crowds.

A stay, however, means savouring the glow of dusk on the sea, with the distant lights of Naples twinkling under the Milky Way, later sipping limoncello in a restaurant where Capri resident Graham Greene might have dined. Then rising early to see the sun come up over the Bay of Naples, perhaps from atop a sheer cliff, at which point you will understand why everyone from Roman emperors to writers have found solace and inspiration here – even Lenin reportedly said that "Capri makes you forget everything." Maybe what he really meant was that it makes you remember yourself. Get to know it even a little, and Capri can feel like your true, timeless home. Take your time to seek out the breathtaking lookout points, the secret grottoes and silent groves and you will find a serene world that's yours, and yours alone.

211 THE ZAGÓRI AND VIKOS GORGE

GREECE The Zagóri region in Greece is one of southern Europe's least discovered corners – a beautifully rugged region of limestone mountains, fast-flowing rivers crossed by rustic stone bridges and oddly monumental villages full of ancient mansions in various states of disrepair. At its heart, the Vikos Gorge is perhaps the most stunning spot – just under 16km long, and in fact the world's deepest gorge in proportion to its width, with walls as high as 1000m in places. It's easily the match of the more famous Samarian Gorge in Crete, and, although it's by no means undiscovered, much quieter too. You can hike through it in a day, but spend longer if you can, holing up at one of the various inns and tavernas in Vikos village at the northern end of the gorge before exploring further.

212 ALL YOU CAN EAT – WITH MUSIC!

ITALY There's no better way to unwind after the Uffizi than by eating the food of one of Italy's top chefs, Fabio Picchi, whose restaurant has been feeding hungry Florentines for years. There's a posh restaurant and a much cheaper trattoria at the same location, both serving delicious takes on traditional Tuscan cuisine (no pasta), but the place you might prefer to try is his latest venture, the *Teatro del Sale*, where you can scoff as much as you like for just €25 and be entertained at the same time. You can order wine, but otherwise the food is just brought to you course by course – pasta or risotto to start, followed by a meat dish and then dessert, after which you're treated to a programme of music, poetry or Italian drama.

CROATIA The area is by no means unvisited, but Croatia's Plitvice Lakes National Park, some 80km from the coast, is deservedly the country's most enticing natural attraction. Like a colossal water garden, this eight-kilometre string of sixteen crystal-clear, turquoise lakes descends through some of Europe's most primeval forests (complete with brown bears, if you know where to look), connected by rushing waterfalls and linked by footpaths, wooden bridges and walkways (kids love it). Plitvice's limestone geology makes it unique, and has brought it UNESCO World Heritage site status. As such, visiting is a well-organized affair, with big crowds in the summer. But the lakes have a minor-key majesty that makes the crowds bearable, and out of season they can be relatively quiet. By using the shuttle buses and boats, you can see much of the park in a day, taking the bus to the upper lakes and walking down. Better still, spend a few days here: there's a cluster of hotels near the middle, and private rooms in nearby villages, meaning you can get up early to enjoy the lakes in all their pristine, untouched glory.

213

TREADING THE BOARDWALKS AT THE
PLITVICE LAKES

BALKAN
BRASS MADNESS
IN GUČA

SERBIA Bars, restaurants and tents blast out hard Romani funk, punters slap Serbian dinar notes on to the heads of sweat-soaked musicians, and men and women of all ages and dispositions form a kolo – a joyous, fast-paced circular formation dance. For one week each summer, the otherwise tranquil village of Guča (pronounced goo-chah), located some 250km south of the Serbian capital Belgrade, is transformed into the undisputed party capital of the Balkans. Guča is home to the Dragačevo Trumpet Festival, the largest, loudest – and quite possibly, craziest – event of its kind anywhere in the world. Essentially a celebration of folk and brass music from across the Balkans, principally Serbia, it stars dozens of bands competing for the coveted Golden Trumpet.

The king of Guča, and the finest trumpet player of his generation, is Boban Markovič who, with his fabulous twelve-piece orchestra – which includes his teenage son Marko – has scooped the Golden Trumpet several times. Such has been their dominance that they no longer bother competing for the big prize, though they do still make the occasional feted appearance. Markovič is typical of the large number of Roma, or Gypsy, musicians that attend Guča, and who make this event the rocking spectacle that it is. With their ecstatic, turbo-charged sounds, these outrageously talented and charismatic performers provide a potent sonic odyssey – indeed, in what is an oft-repeated quote, Miles Davis was once moved to remark "I never knew a trumpet could be played like that". Welcome to Guča, welcome to brass madness.

215 ON THE TRAIL OF CARAVAGGIO

ITALY With his dark, dramatic paintings and violent, hell-raising private life, no other Italian artist captures the modern imagination quite as much as Michelangelo Merisi da Caravaggio. Perhaps it was his rock-and-roll lifestyle, or maybe it's the sheer narrative force of his paintings – which were considered at the time as at best unseemly, at worst downright sacrilegious. Viewed now, his work still packs quite a punch; so it's no surprise to learn that Caravaggio's reputation at the time was that of a maverick.

There's no better place to track down some of Caravaggio's best works than in his adopted home town of Rome. And what's more, many of the paintings you can see here are still in the churches for which they were commissioned. The trail starts bang in the centre of the city, where the church of San Luigi dei Francesi is home to *The Calling of St Matthew*, a typically dramatic piece of work, depicting the tax collector Matthew in the sort of rough-and-ready tavern environment that Caravaggio would have understood well – counting money, and looking up in surprise as he is called away from his companions. Ten minutes' walk north from here, the church of Santa Maria del Popolo has two paintings hung side by side, one showing *The Conversion of St Paul* – bathed in beatific light under his horse on the road to Damascus – and the other *The Crucifixion of St Peter*, with muscular henchmen hauling the elderly but clearly weighty bulk of St Peter onto his upside-down cross. These are powerful paintings, and looking at them up close like this you almost feel that you are intruding into a private moment. Indeed, it's maybe no surprise that they have been dubbed the most revolutionary works in the whole history of sacred art – a tag that could also be applied to the *Madonna of the Pilgrims* in the church of Sant'Agostino, which shows the Virgin as an ordinary Roman woman, standing in a typically shabby doorway, adored by dirty pilgrims in tattered clothes.

Caravaggio's work peppers Roman galleries too, and you should stop by the Galleria Borghese, where a small collection of his paintings includes his last work, *David with the Head of Goliath*, painted while on the run from Rome for murder, and oddly prescient of the artist's own death. It's not a joyful painting: David holds the head of Goliath away from him in disgust, and the scene is one of sorrow rather than triumph. Most tellingly, it's believed that the bloody, severed head is a self-portrait of Caravaggio himself; and gazing at the anguished, bearded face feels like staring across the centuries into the artist's soul.

216 GETTING LOST IN DIOCLETIAN'S PALACE

CROATIA Try imagining Pompeii still existing as a functioning twenty-first-century city, and you'll probably get a good idea of what the Croatian port of Split looks like. At its heart lies a confusing warren of narrow streets, crooked alleys and Corinthian-style colonnades that looks like a computer-generated reconstruction of an archeological dig. High-street shops, banks, restaurants and bars seem stuffed into this structure like incongruous afterthoughts.

Split began life as the purpose-built palace of Roman Emperor Diocletian, who retired here after his abdication in 305 AD. When marauding Avars sacked the nearby city of Salona in 615, fleeing inhabitants sought refuge within the palace walls, improvising a home in what must have been the most grandiose squat of all time. Diocletian's mausoleum was turned into a cathedral, the Temple of Jupiter became a baptistery, and medieval tenement blocks were built into the palace walls.

Nowadays the palace's crumbling courtyards provide the perfect setting for some of the best bars in the Mediterranean. The only problem is that Split's maze-like street plan makes it head-scratchingly difficult to navigate your way back to the welcoming drinking hole you discovered the previous night. Split folk themselves possess a highly developed system of nocturnal radar, flitting from one place to the next without ever staying anywhere long enough to make it look as if they haven't got a better party to go to.

The best way not to get disoriented is to locate Dosud, a split-level zigzag of an alley in the southwestern corner of the palace. Here you'll find ultra-trendy *Puls*, which, with its post-industrial interior and cushion-splashed stone-stepped terrace, is an essential stop on any bar crawl; and its polar opposite, *Tri Volta*, a resolutely old-fashioned local that has long catered to neighbourhood bohemians. In between the two is *Ghetto*, a temple to graffiti art with a beautiful flower-filled courtyard which occasionally hosts al fresco gigs. History doesn't record whether Diocletian was much of a drinker, but this proudly pagan emperor would surely have approved of Split's enduring appetite for Bacchic indulgence.

217 DIVINE MADNESS IN CALABRIA

ITALY Ecstasies of the cult of Dionysus, the god of divine madness, flourish still in the fishing hamlet of Gioiosa Ionica, which hugs the Ionian Sea on the instep of Italy's boot. A legacy of the ancient Greeks, the wholly incongruous excuse for this pre-Christian bacchanal is the festival of the fourteenth-century Saint Roch, who with his dog ministered to plague victims. Every August, in the crushing summer light and heat, skimpily clad devotees throng the tiny hilltown's cobbled lanes, packing around the church at the top. When his life-size effigy breaches the portal, snare drums pound a tattoo and participants roar "Roccu, Roccu, Roccu, viva Santu Roccu! Non mi toccare che non ti toccu!" ("Roc, Roc, Roc, long live Saint Roc! Don't touch me and I won't touch you!"). Suddenly everyone leaps into a frenzied tarantella, an ancient fertility dance officially banned by the Church, which imitates the mating ritual of the partridge, once considered the most lascivious of creatures.

218 HAVING A BLAST IN BELGRADE

SERBIA It is the quintessential Balkan city, a noisy, vigorous metropolis, whose nightlife is as varied as it is exciting, and whose sophisticated citizens really know how to party hard. For these reasons, Belgrade has every right to proclaim itself the good-time capital of Eastern Europe. As good a place as any to start is Strahinjića bana, otherwise known as Silicone Valley owing to the number of surgically enhanced women who parade up and down here. You can get the evening going with a glass of hoppy Nikšićko beer or shot of Šlivjovica (a ferocious plum brandy) in one of the many über-hip bars packed cheek-by-jowl along this fantastically lively street. From here it's time to hit *Andergraund*, a venerable techno joint located in the vast catacombs beneath the Kalemegdan citadel. Complete with a funky chill-out zone, this vibrant and popular place is typical of the city's clubs, and though the scene is in a constant state of flux, good dance venues are the rule rather than the exception.

To experience a different side to Belgrade's nightlife, head down to the banks of the Danube and Sava rivers which, during the summer months, are lined with a multitude of river rafts (splavovi), variously housing restaurants, bars and discos, or a combination of all three. These places can get seriously boisterous, but are popular with devotees of Serbia's infamous turbo-folk music, a brilliantly kitsch hybrid of traditional folk and electronic pop. If this type of music presses your buttons – and it is worth experiencing at least once – you can also check out one of the city's several Folkotekes, discos specializing in turbo-folk. Another quirky, yet somewhat more restrained, Belgrade institution is the hobby bar; these are small, privately owned cafés or bars, run by young entrepreneurs ostensibly for the entertainment of their pals, though anyone is welcome to visit. The next morning the chances are that you'll be good for nothing more than a cup of strong Turkish coffee in one of the many cafés sprawled across Trg Republike – before doing it all over again in the evening.

219 GOING WITH THE FLOW IN NAPLES

ITALY The capital of the Italian South, Naples is quite unlike anywhere else in Italy. It's a city of extremes, fiercely Catholic, its streets punctuated by bright neon Madonnas cut into niches and its miraculous cults regulating the lives of people here almost much as they always did. None more so than the cult of San Gennaro, Naples' patron saint, whose dried blood, kept in a vial in the cathedral, spontaneously liquefies three times a year, thereby ensuring the city's safety for the months to come. It is supposed to take place on the first Saturday in May, on September 19 – San Gennaro's feast day – and also on December 16, and the liquefaction (or otherwise) of San Gennaro's blood is the biggest annual event in the city's calendar by far, attended by the great and the good of the city, not to mention a huge press corps.

The blood is supposed to liquefy during a Mass, which you can attend if you get to the Duomo early enough (ie the middle of the night). The doors open at 9am, when a huge crowd will have gathered, and you're ushered into the church by armed carabinieri, who then stand guard at the high altar while the service goes on, the priest placing the vial containing the saint's blood on a stand and occasionally taking it down to see if anything has happened, while the faithful, led by a group of devout women called the "parenti di San Gennaro", chant prayers for deliverance. The longer it takes, the worse the portents for the city are. And if it doesn't liquefy at all... well, you will know all about it. It didn't happen in 1944, the last time Vesuvius erupted, and in 1980, when a huge earthquake struck the city, so people are understandably jumpy. Luckily, the blood has been behaving itself for the past couple of decades, a period which has coincided to some extent with the city's resurgence. As the mayor of Naples commented the last time it liquefied: "it's a sign that San Gennaro is still protecting our city, a strong sign of hope and an encouragement for everyone to work for the common good". You may not believe in any of it, of course, but being here while it is all going on is an experience like no other.

220 SOLVING THE MYSTERIES OF POMPEII

ITALY Pity the poor folk picking through the rubble of the Forum in Rome. To make the most of the ruins there you have to use your imagination. In the ancient Roman resort town of Pompeii, however, it's a little easier. Pompeii was famously buried by Vesuvius in 79 AD, and the result is perhaps the best-preserved Roman town anywhere, with a street plan that is easy to discern – not to mention wander – and a number of palatial villas that are still largely intact. It's crowded, not surprisingly, but is a large site, and it's quite possible to escape the hordes and experience the strangely still quality of Pompeii, sitting around ancient swimming pools, peering at frescoes and mosaics still standing behind the counters of ancient shops.

Finish up your visit at the incredible Villa of Mysteries, a suburban dwelling just outside the ancient city. Its layout is much the same as the other villas of the city, but its walls are decorated with a cycle of frescoes that give a unique insight into the ancient world – and most importantly they are viewable in situ, unlike most of the rest of Pompeii's mosaics and frescoes, which have found their way to Naples' archeological museum. No one can be sure what these pictures represent, but it's thought that they show the initiation rites of a young woman preparing for marriage. Set against deep ruby-red backgrounds, and full of marvellously preserved detail, they are dramatic and universal works, showing the initiate's progress from naïve young girl to eligible young woman. But above all they tell a story – one that speaks to us loud and clear from 79 AD.

BACK FROM THE BRINK:
THE BRIDGE OF MOSTAR

BOSNIA Above the teal-green waters of the Neretva River, the single arch of Mostar's bridge is the colour of toasted almonds. It's unfeasibly clean, untainted yet by the streaky grey of time, and with good reason: Mostar's historic bridge is only three years old. The original Stari Most had both literally and symbolically linked the Muslim-inhabited east and Croat-dominated west banks of Mostar for more than four hundred years. In November 1993, however, it was decimated by the shells and grenades of the Croatian forces that occupied the surrounding hills. Built by the Ottomans in 1566, the town had grown up around it, indeed it was named after the bridge-keepers or mostari who looked after it. Mostar was known for its tolerance and ethnic diversity; interfaith marriages were common. But by the time of the bridge's destruction, the people of Mostar had borne many months of violence. They'd seen thousands killed. Thousands more had fled the town as its eastern bank was reduced virtually to rubble. When those who remained watched the centuries-old stonework of the Stari Most tumble into the river, they felt their own last hopes sink with it. A fragile peace was brokered in March 1994, and the new "old bridge" was completed ten years later. An exact replica of the original construction, the new bridge holds a special significance in this beautiful but war-scarred town. Among a population still ravaged by ethnic divisions, it's seen now, more than ever, as a symbol of unity. And when, in the summer, young men of all religions flaunt their virility by diving from the arch's peak as they have done for centuries, a glimmer of optimism resurfaces from the cold, green depths once more.

SLOVENIA Of Slovenia's many show caves, none has quite the pulling power of Postojna, located in the heart of the country's beguiling Karst region. And, at more than 20km long, it is Europe's most expansive cave system. Writing about Postojna in the seventeenth century, the great Slovene polymath Janez Vajkard Valvasor remarked: "in some places you see terrifying heights, elsewhere everything is in columns so strangely shaped as to seem like some creepy-crawly, snake or other animal in front of one", an apt description for this immense grotto – a jungle of impossibly shaped stalactites and stalagmites, Gothic columns and translucent stone draperies, all of which are the result of millions of years of erosion and corrosion of the permeable limestone surface by rainwater. Postojna has been Slovenia's most emblematic tourist draw ever since Emperor Franz Josef I set foot here in 1819, though the smudged signatures etched into the craggy walls would indicate an earlier human presence in the caves, possibly as far back as the thirteenth century.

Visiting the cave first entails a two-kilometre-long ride through narrow tunnels on the open-topped cave train – a somewhat more sophisticated version compared to the hand-pushed wagons used in the nineteenth century – before you emerge into the vast chambers of formations and colours. Among them there's the Beautiful Cave, which takes its name from the many lustrous features on display; the Spaghetti Hall, so-called because of its thousands of dripping, needle-like formations; and the Winter Chamber, which is home to a beast of a stalagmite called "Brilliant", on account of its dazzling snow-white colour.

Despite all this, Postojna's most prized asset, and most famous resident, is Proteus anguinus, aka the Human Fish. This enigmatic 25-centimetre-long, pigmentless amphibian has a peculiar snake-like appearance, with two tiny pairs of legs – hence the name – and a flat, pointed fin to propel itself through water. Almost totally blind, and with a lifespan approaching one hundred years, it can also go years without food, though it's been known to dabble in a spot of cannibalism. Indeed, the abiding memory for many visitors to Postojna is of this most bizarre and reclusive of creatures slinking about its dimly lit tank.

222
STALAGMITES,
STALACTITES AND A
HUMAN FISH

223 PARADISE REGAINED: ITALY'S OLDEST NATIONAL PARK

ITALY Treading where once only royals and aristos held sway is an everyday occurrence in Italy: once-forbidding palaces, castles and gardens are now open to all. One of the most exhilarating former royal enclaves is a celebration of the sheer wonder of nature, the Parco del Gran Paradiso – a pristine alpine wilderness that lies within yodelling distance of the Swiss Alps and Mont Blanc.

King Vittorio Emanuele II donated what had been the private hunting grounds of the House of Savoy to the Italian state in 1922. The rapacious royals had managed to see off the entire population of bears and wolves, but the scimitar-horned ibex – now the majestic symbol of the park – and the park's other native mountain goat species, the chamois, survived, and now thrive in the protected environment. Even the golden eagle has been reintroduced, and currently numbers about ten pairs, while the other animals of size that you may encounter are cuddly-looking marmots, which, along with perky martens, are the preferred quarry of the major birds of prey.

In winter, the park is paradise indeed for skiers, particularly those of the cross-country variety, who embark from the enticing village of Cogne. However, most visitors come to the park in the warmer months, when the rocky heights are spectacularly pure and the hundreds of species of vibrant wildflowers dazzle the eye – and when you're also more likely to spot wildlife. The verdant valley slopes and vertiginous ridges are all traversable by kilometres of walking and hiking trails of all degrees of difficulty, which in turn link any number of refuges where you can spend the night. There's climbing, too, throughout all of the ten valleys. You could try an assault on the 4000-metre-high summit of Gran Paradiso itself – not a particularly difficult ascent if you have the right equipment, and guides – or the more gentle trek up to the sanctuary of San Besso, a two-hour hike to over 2000m, where the church and refuge nestle under a primeval overhanging massif.

224 WALKING DUBROVNIK'S WALLS

CROATIA "If you want to see heaven on earth, come to Dubrovnik", George Bernard Shaw once opined. And it's possible he'd still feel the same, even after the influx of tourists. And the best way to appreciate the old city is by walking around it. Encircling the old town are some 2km of ramparts, originally constructed between the twelfth and thirteenth centuries, with subsequent reinforcements in the fifteenth century, ostensibly to keep the Ottomans at bay. And for as long as the walls have been here, people have walked them.

Standing some 25m high and, in parts, measuring more than 6m thick, this ancient battlement looks remarkable, thanks mainly to its formidable array of turrets and bastions. The best place to start – and go first thing in the morning to avoid the inevitable crush – is the Pile Gate, which is actually the main entrance into the old town. Thereafter, you walk clockwise along a narrow, inclining path up towards the imposing Minčeta Fortress – one of five almost completely intact towers

strategically spotted along the walls – before progressing towards the sea-facing section. Meanwhile, contained within the walls, there are endless reminders of the city's past, as yet another Baroque palace, medieval church or monastery passes beneath your feet.

Most reckon on completing the walk in a leisurely hour or so, though, given the magnificent vistas – both inwards towards the flutter of red-tiled roofs and impossibly narrow cobbled streets, and outwards towards the cool, blue Adriatic sea – don't be surprised if it takes double that time. Having completed the walk, head down to the evening korzo on Stradun, the old town's main thoroughfare, whose limestone surface has been polished to a dazzling sheen thanks to centuries of tramping pedestrians. Indulge in a plate of girice (tiny deep-fried fish), wash it down with a glass of Dingač, the local headache-inducing red wine, and kick back just in time to watch the sun go down.

225 THIS IS THE LIGHT: EASTER CELEBRATIONS IN LOUTRÓ

GREECE A faint glimmer of flame behind the altar of the darkened church and the black-clad papás appears, holding aloft a lighted taper and chanting "Avto to Fos" – This is the Light of the World. Thus Easter Sunday begins at the stroke of midnight in a tiny chapel in the small seaside village of Loutró, southern Crete. Minutes earlier, the congregation and entire village had been plunged into darkness. Now, as the priest ignites the first candle and the flame is passed from neighbour to neighbour, light spreads again throughout the church. As the congregation pours out into the street the candlelight is distributed to every home along with the cry of "Christos Anesti" (Christ is Risen). It's an extraordinary experience – a symbolic reawakening of brightness and hope

with clear echoes of more ancient rites of spring – and within minutes wilder celebrations begin; firecrackers are thrown and traditional dishes devoured to break the week-long fast that the more devout have observed.

The rituals of the Greek Orthodox Church permeate every aspect of Greek society, but never so clearly as at Easter. As a visitor you are inevitably drawn in, especially in a place as small as Loutró – accessible only by boat or on foot – where the locals go out of their way to include you.

After a few hours' sleep you wake to the smell of lambs and goats roasting on spits. As they cook, the wine and beer flow freely until the whole village, locals and visitors alike, join the great feasts to mark the end of Lent.

226

SHARING THE LOVES OF THE GODS AT THE PALAZZO FARNESE

ITALY One of the greatest art experiences in Italy is also one of its best-kept secrets. And for that you have to thank not the Italians, but the French, whose embassy has occupied Rome's Palazzo Farnese for the past century or so.

Inside, Annibale Carracci's remarkable ceiling fresco, *The Loves of the Gods*, was until relatively recently almost entirely off-limits, open only to scholars, VIPs and those with a proven interest in Renaissance art. Now, with a little planning, it's possible to see it for yourself, and it's perhaps one of the most extraordinary pieces of work you'll see in Rome apart from the Sistine Chapel; plus you get to view it with a small group of art lovers rather than a huge scrum of other tourists.

The work was commissioned from the then unknown Bolognese painter, Annibale Carracci, by Odoardo Farnese at the turn of the sixteenth century to decorate one of the rooms of the palace. It's a work of magnificent vitality, and seems almost impossible that it could be the work of just one man. In fact, it wasn't. Annibale devised the scheme and did the main ceiling, but the rest was finished by his brother and cousin, Agostino and Lodovico, and assistants like Guido Reni and Guercino, who went on to become some of the most sought-after artists of the seventeenth century. The central painting, with its complex and dramatically arranged figures, great swathes of naked flesh, and vivid colours, is often seen as the first great work of the Baroque era, a fantastic, fleshy spectacle of virtuoso technique – and perfect anatomy. The main painting, centring on the marriage of Bacchus and Ariadne, which is supposed to represent the binding of the Aldobrandini and Farnese families, leaps out of its frame in an erotic hotchpotch of cavorting, surrounded by similarly fervent works illustrating various classical themes. Between and below them, nude figures peer out – amazing exercises in perspective that almost seem to be alongside you in the room. Carracci was paid a pittance for the work, and died a penniless drunk shortly after finishing it, but the triumph of its design, and the amazing technical accomplishment of its painting, shines brighter than ever.

227 THE COLOSSEUM IN WINTER

ITALY Is there a more recognizable architectural profile in existence? Featured on everything from Olympic medals to Italy's five-euro coin, the Colosseum has been the model for just about every stadium built since. Even our word "arena" derives from the Latin word for sand, which was used to soak up the blood of the unfortunate gladiators and various beasts who died here.

The Colosseum wasn't good enough for the film director Ridley Scott, who regarded it as too small for the film *Gladiator* and had a larger replica mocked up in Malta instead. But for the rest of the world it does nicely as a reminder of the cruelty and brutality of the Roman world, home as it was to its gladiatorial games and the ritual slaughter of exotic animals by the ton; the emperor Trajan was perhaps the most bloodthirsty ruler to raise his thumb here: his games of 108–109 AD consumed around 11,000 animals and involved 10,000 gladiators. The blood baths may have gone out of fashion, but the Colosseum's magnificent architecture is timeless. The Romans were not known for their diminutive constructions, but this is by far the largest building they produced – and probably the cleverest too, ingeniously designed so that its 60,000 spectators could exit in around twenty minutes.

Nowadays it's a bit of a Disneyland of kiss-me-quick gladiators and long queues, so it's better to visit out of season, preferably on a weekday as soon as it opens, when there's no one around. Coming here on a gloomy January morning may not have quite the same appeal as a sunny day in spring or summer, but wandering alone through the Colosseum's grand corridors and gazing down into its perfectly proportioned arena gives you the chance to appreciate this seminal building at its best.

228 TACKLING OLD MR THREE HEADS

SLOVENIA It's said that every Slovene has to climb Mount Triglav, the country's highest (2864m) and most exalted peak, at least once in their lifetime. They're joined by hikers and climbers from many nations, who arrive in droves each summer. The mountain's nickname, Old Mr Three Heads (Triglav means "Three Heads"), originated with the early Slavs, who believed that it accommodated a three-headed deity who watched over the earth, sky and underworld.

The most difficult approach is via the indomitable north face, a stark 1200-metre-high rock wall, certainly not for the faint-hearted. Most hikers opt for the route from Lake Bohinj further south; watched over by steeply pitched mountain faces, this brooding body of water is the perfect place to relax before embarking on the mountain trail ahead.

Starting at the lake's western shore, you pass the spectacular Savica Waterfall, before a stiff climb over the formidable Komarča

cliff, and then a more welcome ramble through meadows and pastureland. Beyond here lies the highlight of this route: rich in alpine and karstic flora, the Valley of the Seven Lakes is a series of beautiful tarns surrounded by majestic limestone cliffs. The views are glorious, though by this stage most hikers are hankering after the simple comforts of a mountain hut.

Not only is Triglav a tough nut to crack in one day, but these convivial refuges are great places to catch up with fellow hikers as well as refuel with a steaming goulash and a mug of sweet lemon-infused tea. Most people push on at the crack of dawn, eager to tackle the toughest part of the ascent, entailing tricky scrambles, before the triple-crested peak of Triglav looms into view. Once completed, according to tradition, there's just one final act for first-timers, namely to be "birched" – in other words, soundly thrashed across the buttocks with a birch branch.

229 SOMETHING FISHY IN MARSAXLOKK

MALTA Bobbing in the sea, staring at passers-by, the eyes of a luzzu appear to follow you as you walk along the promenade in Marsaxlokk – Malta's premier fishing port. Traditionally painted in red, blue, yellow and occasionally green, boats line the waterfront of this otherwise small village on Malta's southeast coast. The luzzu is one of Malta's national symbols and features on a series of the country's lira coins. Originally equipped with sails, today the boats are motorized and some double as transport for tourists. Said to be the eye of Osiris, the Phoenician god of protection from evil, the luzzu's eye is thought to save the boat's owners from the dangers of the sea. A natural harbour, Marsaxlokk is home to over 250 registered fishing vessels, from the traditional luzzu, to larger skunas and smaller fregatinas (rowing boats), in which you'll see men sitting, close to shore, handreels dangling over the side, hoping to take a catch in the pristine water. Marsaxlokk is perhaps the most picturesque seaside locality in Malta and surely the most photographed; on a bright day, the sun dances off the water, drawing out the colours in the luzzus and reflecting off the fishing nets splayed out to dry. If you wish to escape the glare of the luzzus' eyes, head towards the local market for a spot of shopping. Once purely a fish market where local fishermen sell their daily catch, Sunday is now the best day to purchase all types of aquatic fare, with other days of the week perfect for stocking up on souvenirs including handmade bags constructed from recycled fishing nets and dyed a rainbow of colours. Once you're done strolling along the promenade, duck into one of the many restaurants along the waterfront – this is, unsurprisingly, the perfect town in which to eat fish – under the watchful eye of a luzzu.

230 WORKING UP A LAVA ON STROMBOLI'S SLOPES

ITALY For years, I had watched Stromboli from my house on the island of Salina. It's the most active volcano in Europe, and on clear nights, even from a distance of 40km, I would see its worms of red lava glowing in the dark. If there was any place on earth where mankind was not meant to go, surely it was the crater of an active volcano. And yet the lure was irresistible.

The steady, three-hour climb to the top proved not to be difficult. We passed through the rich aromas of the maquis that emanated from the wild roses, fig trees, prickly pears and clumps of capers all around us. The sky was clear, the sea blue and the breathtaking view spanned from Mount Etna to Calabria. I was wondering what I'd been scared of, when a resounding clash, like an iron door slamming shut, reminded me. I jumped. Mario the guide turned round: "Don't worry, it's normal". I tried to look as though walking up an erupting volcano were the most natural thing in the world.

Abruptly, the vegetation ended. The ground beneath our feet turned to sand, strewn with small jagged boulders spewed out by the volcano. We stopped to don heavy clothes and helmets, and follow the final ridge to the top. There was a freezing northern wind.

At the top, all I could see were clouds of white steam. Then, suddenly, they glowed a fierce, translucent red as four spouts of fire threw up a fountain of glowing boulders that drew tracks of red light across the night sky. Mario chose that moment to start talking on the radio. A sudden, panicked thought: we were in danger. But no, this was Stromboli, and things were normal – he was discussing dinner.

231 CHEWING THE FAT: A GLUTTON'S TOUR OF BOLOGNA

ITALY Bologna has more nicknames than Sean "P. Diddy" Combs. It's "La Dotta" or "The Learned", for its ages-old university, one of the first in Europe; "La Rossa" or "The Red", for the colour of its politics. But its most deserving nickname is "La Grassa" or "The Fat" for the richness of its food. After all, even fiercely proud fellow Italians will acknowledge, when pressed, that Bologna's cooking is the best in the country.

This gourmet-leaning university city doesn't expect starving students to shell out a month's rent for a fine meal, either. It's the last major Italian centre where lunch with wine barely breaks €10 a head, and €25 will buy a de luxe, multi-course dinner. The only people who should be wary are vegetarians and calorie counters: dishes here are meaty and diet-busting – the Bolognese traditionally chow down on cured hams, game and creamy pasta sauces. Smells of smoked meat waft onto the sidewalk from the old-fashioned grocery-cum-canteen, *Tamburini*, off the main square; it's staffed with old, white-uniformed men, brandishing hocks of ready-to-slice prosciutto amid a clatter of dishes at lunchtime as dozens of locals jostle around the dining room. The via delle Pescherie Vecchie nearby is still jammed with traditional market stalls, fallen produce squishing on the street and sharp-voiced women heckling the stall holders over prices.

But Bologna's love of food is clearest through its drinks: specifically, at cocktail hour, when in bars you can load up for free on stuzzichini, Italy's hefty answer to tapas, for as long as you nurse that G&T. With its cream sofas, sparkly chandelier and thirty-something crowd, the *Café de Paris* serves a buffet of watermelon slices and tortilla wraps; and the minimalist *Nu Lounge* nearby, on the colonnaded gallery known as the Buca San Petronio, has fancier nibbles, such as dates wrapped in ham or Martini glasses full of fresh chopped steak tartare.

ITALY Siena's famous bareback horserace – Il Palio – is a highly charged, death-defying dash around the boundary of the city's majestic Piazza del Campo. It's also likely to be the most rabidly partisan event you'll ever witness. Twice every summer riders elected by each of the city's ancient districts – the contrade – compete in a bid to win the much prized "Palio" or banner. Sounds like fun? It is. But the Palio is not just a bit of tourist fluff. On the two days that the race takes place – as well as throughout the exacting year-long preparations – the Sienese are playing for very high stakes indeed, and the air positively crackles with the seriousness of it all.

There's a parade around the piazza at 5pm, with banner hurlers – bandierati – from each contrada, accompanied by the chimes of the bell-tower, after which the square is a riot of colour until the "War Chariot", drawn by two pairs of white oxen, displays the prize for the coming contest. The race itself takes only ninety seconds to complete, and the only rule is that there are no rules: practically any sort of violence toward rival riders or animals is permitted, and anything short of directly interfering with another jockey's reins or flinging a rider to the ground is seen as fair game. Each jockey carries a special whip or nerbo – by tradition fashioned from the skin of a bull's penis and thus thought to give a particularly deep sting, not to mention conferring super-potency on its wielder. The course is so treacherous, with its sharp turns and sloping, slippery surfaces that often fewer than half of the participants finish. But in any case it's only the horse that matters – the beast that crosses the line first (even without its rider), is the winner, after which the residents of the victorious district sing, dance and celebrate their victory into the small hours.

PLAYING FOR HIGH STAKES AT

SIENA'S PALIO

232

233 COMINO'S BLUE LAGOON

MALTA Sparkling in the sun, Comino's Blue Lagoon is a glorious azure. It's early afternoon as our gullet anchors itself amongst the flotilla of other boats, emptied of their passengers who are gliding through crystal waters with an effortless kick of their flippered feet. Already, some of our group have leapt overboard, immersing themselves in the refreshing sea, their bodies visible through the transparent waters.

Sheltered between the islands of Comino and Cominotto, framed by rocky cliffs, open sea and white sandy beaches, this area is astonishing even to a hardened traveller. Its natural beauty makes it a favourite with locals – speak to one of the four permanent residents of Comino or one of their neighbours from Gozo, and they'll tell you the lagoon is at its most idyllic in the morning, before the tourists and boats arrive, when the water is like still gossamer covering the pure snow-white sand on the sea bed below. Year-round, the lagoon is popular with divers and snorkellers, exploring the rich marine life easily visible in the cobalt hue of water. The island of Comino also offers hiking, cycling and great windsurfing, but most people are interested in the blue water, which is used increasingly as a film location by Hollywood's big studios.

It's not a pristine place, and most people arrive at the lagoon by tour boat, but despite the people the richness of colour is transfixing. White sands and turquoise waters mix with the sun-bleached landscape, brightly reflecting the sun. And there's a tranquillity in the beauty, unbroken by nearby boats sounding their horns, beckoning passengers back on board for departure, which is impossible to capture in photographs. As our boat, the last to leave, hoists its sails, I turn back to savour the view of the still, crystal waters. The purity of the Blue Lagoon, untainted by resort developments or garish hotels, etches itself into the memory.

234 WATCHING WORLDS COLLIDE IN SICILY

ITALY Dangling off Italy's toe at the centre of the Mediterranean, Sicily is a rich minestrone of ingredients – from smoking volcanoes to celeb-studded resorts, from screeching scooter boys and clamorous street markets to intense and emotional Catholic ceremonies.

The Med's largest island can boast vestiges of most of Europe's great civilizations, including majestic Greek temples and resplendent Norman mosaics. Sicily's capital, Palermo, is a distillation of the entire island, and in many ways the most idiosyncratic of Italy's regional capitals. In this full-on city set against a jagged mountain backdrop, you can experience the exotic, chaotic interface of Europe and North Africa.

The Arab flavour lingers on in such quarters as La Kalsa, in the dusty red cupolas of palm-encircled churches and in street markets that pulsate with energy, where you can pick up anything from a brace of still-flapping mullet to Rococo statuary. Religious fervour manifests itself throughout the city in such raucous festivals as July's Santa Rosalia, while the churches offer extraordinary beauty, as in the glittering mosaics of Monreale or the swirling curlicues of the omnipresent Baroque. You can also experience the flamboyant flights of the Baroque imagination in the hundreds of elegantly crumbling palazzi, more often than not concealed behind stout walls, and sometimes – as in Bagheria – with dark, grotesque embellishments. And of course, you can eat royally in this most sensuous of cities: tuck into pasta con sarde, the local speciality, in boisterous restaurants, and then gorge on cassata ice cream cake crammed with candied fruit.

If you're feeling stifled by the noise and confusion, escape is simple: sunbathe by day and jive by night at Palermo's seaside resort of Mondello; explore wooded Monte Pellegrino on a rented Vespa; or jump on a ferry to the offshore isle of Ustica, a marine reserve and diving paradise. Then, once revived, immerse yourself all over again.

235 LISTENING FOR NIGHTINGALES ON SAMOS

GREECE I closed my eyes and concentrated. Nothing. A burly six-foot Dutch guy stood beside me, glued to his high-tech binoculars. "It's a small brown bird. You must keep very still and listen," he whispered. Hmmm…my eyes combed the hazy plane and cypress trees studding Aïdhónia, Valley of the Nightingales, an Eden-like pocket in northern Samos. After what seemed an eternity, a crescendo whistling pierced the silence, rising from the scrub and filling the valley with rich song. "That's it," he enthused. "That's a nightingale!" I could barely breathe.

The nightingale usually turns up unannounced, so catching it involves luck and timing. Spring is a pretty safe bet. And this is also the season to experience the island in bloom and relatively tourist-free. A drop in the cobalt blue Aegean, just over 1km from Turkey, there are few Greek Islands that can match Samos for sheer stop-in-your-tracks beauty. It's as though someone plucked all the best bits and threw them together: a vineyard here, a steep gorge there, mix in some olive groves, add a pinch of 1000-metre-plus mountains. OK, so the beaches are pebbly, but if you just want to flop and sizzle, you're in the wrong place.

Phew, this was hot work. The cobbled trail wove uphill past citrus groves, vineyards and sculpted terraces. I gathered some purple flowers en route and, soon after, a toothless old lady stopped me dead in my tracks. "Thymari!" she exclaimed. I later discovered I'd picked a huge bunch of wild thyme. But as I had nothing to cook it with, I settled for mezze with a glass of sweet Samos wine in a taverna in Manolátes. As the sun set over the village's jumble of neat whitewashed houses, I listened out for a last song from the nightingales …

236 LOCKED UP IN LJUBLJANA: HOSTEL CELICA

SLOVENIA Fancy being banged up for the night? Well, be Celica's guest. Born from the gutted remains of a former military prison, Ljubljana's *Hostel Celica* (meaning "cell") possesses a dozen or so conventional dorms, but it's the twenty two- and three-bed rooms, or, more precisely, cells, that makes it so unique.

A range of designers was assigned to come up with themes for each one, resulting in a series of funky and brilliantly original sleeping spaces – one room features a circular bunk bed, for example, and in another a bunk is perched high above the door. That's to say nothing of the wonderfully artistic flourishes, such as the colourful murals and smart wooden furnishings, that illuminate many of the rooms. Surprisingly, the cells are not at all claustrophobic, though some authentic touches, such as the thick window bars and metal, cage-like doors, remain – there's little chance of being robbed here.

The hostel stands at the heart of a complex of buildings originally commissioned by Vienna for the evening Austro-Hungarian army and which later served as the barracks of the former Yugoslav People's Army. Following Slovenia's declaration of independence in 1991, this complex was taken over by a number of student and cultural movements, evolving into a chaotic and cosmopolitan cluster of bars, clubs and NGOs collectively entitled Metelkova.

Despite repeated attempts by authorities to legalize, and even demolish, the site, the community has stood firm as the city's alternative cultural hub, with club nights, live music (punk, metal, dub/techno, lo-fi) and performance art all part of its fantastically diverse programme. Indeed, if you don't fancy the short stroll into Ljubljana's lovely old town centre for a few drinks, this makes a lively place to hang out before stumbling back to your cell. Just don't throw away the key.

237 JOINING THE TRUFFLE TRAIN IN BUZET

CROATIA Even the most committed of culinary explorers often find the truffle to be something of an acquired taste. Part nutty, part mushroomy, part sweaty sock, the subtle but insistent flavour of this subterranean fungus nevertheless inspires something approaching gastronomic hysteria among its army of admirers.

Nowhere is truffle worship more fervent than in the Croatian province of Istria, a beautiful region where medieval hill towns sit above bottle-green forests. Summer is the season for the delicately flavoured white truffle, although it's the more pungent autumnal black truffle that will really bring out the gourmet in you. A few shavings of the stuff delicately sprinkled over pasta has an overpowering, lingering effect on your tastebuds.

The fungus-hunting season is marked by a plethora of animated rural festivals. Biggest of the lot is held in the normally sleepy town of Buzet, where virtually everyone who is anyone in Istria gathers on a mid-September weekend to celebrate the Buzetska Subotina, or "Buzet Saturday". As evening

approaches, thousands of locals queue for a slice of the world's biggest truffle omelette, fried up in a mind-bogglingly large pan on the town's main square. With the evening rounded out with folk dancing, fireworks, al-fresco pop concerts and large quantities of biska – the local mistletoe-flavoured brandy – this is one small-town knees-up that no one forgets in a hurry.

Buzet's reputation as Istria's truffle capital has made this otherwise bland provincial town a magnet for in-the-know foodie travellers. The revered fungus plays a starring role in the dishes at *Toklarija*, a converted oil-pressing shed in the nearby hilltop settlement of Sovinjsko polje, whose head chef changes the menu nightly in accordance with what's fresh in the village. One of the best meals you're likely to eat is in the neighbouring hamlet of Vrh, where the family-run *Vrh Inn* serves fat rolls of home-made pasta stuffed with truffles, mushrooms, asparagus and other locally gathered goodies. With the ubiquitous mistletoe brandy also on the menu, a warm glow of satisfaction is guaranteed.

238 MUSIC, DANCE AND DRAMA IN ANCIENT ASPENDOS

TURKEY It's a hot summer's evening; overhead is a soft, purple-black and star-strewn sky. There's the incessant chirrup of cicadas, mingled with the murmur of thousands of voices – Turkish, German, English, Russian – and the popping of corks, as the 15,000-strong audience settles down, passes round wine and olives and eagerly awaits the entertainment ahead. All are perched on hard, solid marble, still warm from the heat of the day, but the discomfort is a small price to pay to experience what a Roman citizen would have 1800 years ago, when this theatre, the largest and best preserved in Asia Minor, was built.

The views from the semicircular auditorium, comprising forty tiers cut into the hillside, are magnificent. At sunset, the fading light on the remains of this once wealthy and powerful city and the Pamphylian plain beyond shows it at its best. There's a faint taste of the nearby Mediterranean on the breeze and the Taurus range in splendid silhouette to the north.

The stage lights play across the facade of the multi-level stage building, ornamented with Ionic and Corinthian columns, niches that once sported marble statues and elaborate friezes and pediments. The lights dim and the massed ranks of spectators fall silent. Slowly the intensity of the lights increases and the show begins. Maybe it's Verdi's *Aida*, set in ancient Egypt, whose pomp and splendour match the setting perfectly.

Afterwards, close to midnight, throngs of people – having suspended disbelief for a few memorable hours – disgorge into the night, scrambling not for their chariots but for cars and buses as reality sets in and the ancient entertainments are left behind.

239 CLASSICAL STUDIES IN SICILY

ITALY Gorgeous bays and smouldering volcanoes, boisterous markets and fabulous food, Sicily has the lot. But what is less well-known is the fact that, amid the energy and chaos of the contemporary island, it is also home to some of Italy's oldest and most perfectly preserved classical sites. What's more, the most historic places on Sicily are usually the most sublimely located – isolated specimens of classical civilization where you come face to face with a distant era of heroism, hedonism and unforgiving gods. Joining their dots is a fun and evocative way to explore the island.

Starting in the far west of Sicily, the fifth-century BC Greek temple of Segesta, secluded on a hilltop west of Palermo, enjoys perhaps the most magnificent location of all, the skeletal symmetry of its Doric temple and brilliantly sited theatre giving views right across the bay – not to mention the autostrada snaking far below. Further east, just outside the south coast town of Agrigento, there are more Doric temples, this time from a century earlier and dramatically arrayed along a ridge overlooking the sea. They would have been the imposing setting for inscrutable and often blood-curdling ceremonies – and yet you can walk a bit further and you're back in the Catholic present (at the tiny Norman church of San Biagio). Inland from here, leap forward almost 1000 years and you're still only in the Roman era, viewing the vivid mosaics of the Villa Romana just outside Piazza Armerina – sumptuous works that date from the fourth century AD and show manly Romans snaring tigers, ostriches and elephants, and a delightful children's hunt with the kids being chased by their prey (don't worry – they're only hares and peacocks).

Then, on the east coast, there are the marvellous theatres of Taormina and Siracusa. The former once staged gladiatorial combats and is now the scene of perhaps the most stirringly sited arts performances in the world, with views that encompass sparkling seas and Europe's friskiest volcano, Mount Etna – usually topped by a menacing plume of smoke. Siracusa's Greek Theatre is one of the biggest and best preserved of all classical auditoriums, and although it lacks the panoramic panache of Taormina, its grander scale more than makes up for it. It's used every summer for concerts and Greek drama, and a starlit evening at either theatre is the perfect way to round off your classical tour.

240 BEANS AND ORANGES IN IVREA

ITALY One of Italy's biggest and most peculiar carnival celebrations takes place in Ivrea, not far from Turin, when on the Sunday before Shrove Tuesday the town fills with revellers who tuck into bowls of beans ladled out from giant cauldrons in the main square before taking part in a humongous orange fight, which starts at the same time each afternoon for the next three days. Anyone and anything is fair game here, and by the end of each day everyone is covered in pulp and drenched in freshly squeezed juice; there's nowhere to walk that's not swimming in vitamin C, and the air is full of the bitter smell of oranges. On Shrove Tuesday it finishes with a huge procession and a celebratory bonfire in the square.

241 LOSE YOURSELF AT MYSTRA

GREECE The Peloponnese is littered with ancient sites, but arguably none is quite as evocative as Mystra, a ruined Byzantine city that dates back to the mid-thirteenth century. It's an intriguing place to explore, strung down a steep hillside and extraordinarily intact, with crumbling mansions and tiny churches that sport monumental frescoes, as well as an ancient convent at its heart that is still inhabited by half a dozen nuns. It's not over-crowded, and you can lose yourself in its alleys and arches – which is just what you should do, maybe combining a visit with some hiking in the nearby beautiful and remote Langhada Pass between Kalamata and Sparta, said to be a route taken by Telemachus in *The Odyssey*.

GREEK ISLAND HOPPING 242

GREECE There's an indefinable scent that, in an instant, brings the Greek islands vividly to mind. A mixture, perhaps, of thyme-covered slopes cooling overnight and the more prosaic smells of the port, of fish and octopus, overlaid with the diesel exhaust of the ferry that's carrying you there. A moment at night when you can sense approaching land but not yet see it, just moonlight reflecting off the black Aegean and sparkling in the churning wake.

Travelling between the islands by boat, it feels like little has changed in hundreds of years. Dolphins really do still leap around the prow, days are stiflingly hot, nights starlit and glassy. The ferries may be modern but the old adventure stubbornly refuses to die.

There are well over 1000 Greek islands, perhaps a tenth of them inhabited. Almost all of those have some kind of ferry connection, and no two are the same. From party islands like Íos or Mýkonos to the sober, monastic atmosphere of Pátmos, from tiny rocks to the vastness of Crete, there's an island for every mood. And there's a visceral thrill in travelling by sea that no plane or coach or car can ever match. Sleeping on deck under the stars; arriving in a rock-girt island port at dawn; chaos as cars and trucks and human cargo spill off the ship; black-clad old ladies competing to extol the virtues of their rooms. Clichéd images perhaps, but clichés for a reason – this is still one of the essentials of world travel, uniquely Greek, hopelessly romantic.

243 VISITING FEDERICO'S PALACE IN URBINO

ITALY Having evolved from a patchwork of city-states, Italy is littered with amazing palaces raised by local rulers, but none is more stunning than the Palazzo Ducale in Urbino. Baldassarre Castiglione, whose sixteenth-century handbook of courtly etiquette, *Il Cortegiane* (The Courtier), is set in the palace, reckoned it to be the most beautiful in all Italy, and few would disagree with that verdict.

Dominating this attractive little university town in the heart of the rural province of Marche, the Palazzo Ducale was commissioned in 1468 by Federico da Montefeltro, one of the most remarkable men of his era. A brilliant soldier, Federico kept the coffers of Urbino full by selling his military services, but he was also a man of genuine learning and a great patron of the arts. A friend of the great architect and theorist Leon Battista Alberti, he regarded architecture as the highest form of aesthetic activity, and studied the subject so thoroughly that it was written of him that "no lord or gentleman of his own day knew as much about it as he did." His residence – designed primarily by the otherwise obscure Luciano Laurana – is unforgettable testimony to his discernment.

From the street it's not an especially handsome building, but once you step into the Cortile d'Onore you'll see what this place is all about: elegant, exquisitely crafted yet unostentatious, it's the perfect blend of practicality and discreet grandeur. Inside, many of the rooms are occupied by the Galleria Nazionale delle Marche, where one of the prize exhibits is a portrait of Federico by Pedro Berruguete – he's painted, as always, in profile, having lost his right eye in battle. In Federico's private suite of rooms you'll see paintings by the finest of all the artists he sponsored, Piero della Francesca, including the enigmatic *Flagellation*. Two adjoining chapels – one dedicated to Apollo and the Muses, the other to the Christian God – are indicative of the complexity of the duke's world-view, as is the astounding Studiolo, where wall panels of inlaid wood create some startling illusory perspectives – you'll see some delicately hued landscapes of Urbino here, and portraits of great men ranging from Homer and Petrarch to Solomon and St Ambrose.

244 A NIGHT OUT ON INDEPENDENCE STREET

TURKEY You've had a day or two's heavy sightseeing in Istanbul's Sultanahmet. You're culturally replete – but have a nagging feeling that you've missed something: the locals – just what the hell do they do in this metropolis of fifteen million souls? To find out, head across the Golden Horn to Independence Street (Istiklal Caddesi), the nation's liveliest thoroughfare. Lined with nineteenth-century apartment blocks and churches, and with a cute red turn-of-the-twentieth-century tramway, it was the fashionable centre of Istanbul's European quarter before independence, and it is now where young Istanbulites (it has the youngest population of any European city) come to shop, eat, drink, take in a film, club, gig and gawk, 24/7.

By day, bare-shouldered girls in Benetton vests, miniskirts and Converse Allstars mingle with Armani-clad businessmen

riding the city's financial boom, and music stores and fashion boutiques blare out the latest club sounds onto the shopper-thronged street. At night the alleyways off the main drag come to life. Cheerful tavernas serve noisy diners (the Turks are great talkers) wonderful mezze, fish and lethal raki. Later, blues, jazz and rock venues, pubs and trendy clubs burst into life – with the streets even busier than in daylight hours. You won't see many head-scarved women here, and the call to prayer will be drowned by thumping Western sounds. But though Islam may have lost its grip on Istanbul's westernized youth, traditional Turkish hospitality survives even on Independence Street, and you may find yourself being offered a free beer or two. This is Istanbul's happening European heart; no wonder it has been heralded as "Europe's Hippest City".

245 SHOPPING WITH STYLE IN MILAN

ITALY Milan is synonymous with shopping: boutiques from all the world's top clothes and accessory designers are within a hop, skip and a high-heeled teeter from each other. The atmosphere is snooty, the labels elitist and the experience priceless.

The city has been associated with top-end fashion since the 1970s, when local designers broke with the staid atmosphere of Italy's traditional fashion home, the Palazzo Pitti in Florence. It was during the 1980s, however, that the worldwide thirst for designer labels consolidated the international reputation of home-grown talent such as Armani, Gucci, Prada, Versace and Dolce & Gabbana.

You don't need to be rich to feel part of it. These days the stores themselves make almost as important a statement as the clothes. In-house cafés are springing up, as are exhibition spaces, even

barbers and spas. Even if you're not in the market for splashing out, you can still indulge yourself without breaking the bank: for a handful of euros you can sip a cocktail at *Bar Martini*, in the Dolce & Gabbana flagship store at Corso Venezia 15; enjoy an espresso and a monogrammed chocolate at the *Gucci Café* inside Milan's famous nineteenth-century Galleria Vittorio Emanuele II; or, perhaps, drink prosecco at the tables outside the *Armani Café*, at Via Manzoni 31, part of the four-storey temple to all things Giorgio. And, as you're here for the experience, why not head for the ultimate in bling at *Just Cavalli Food*, in Via della Spiga, where the leopardskin-clad clientele floats down in a cloud-lift to the boutique's café, which is lined with a saltwater aquarium swimming with brightly coloured tropical fish.

246 ENJOYING DA VINCI'S LAST SUPPER

ITALY It has always been busy, and boisterous crowds still line up around the Santa Maria delle Grazie convent in Milan, sometimes for hours in the summer. But these days viewing Leonardo Da Vinci's *Last Supper* has been imbued with a renewed sense of wonder, mystery and, above all, conspiracy. Worn, heavily thumbed copies of Dan Brown's bestseller give some indication of what's on their minds: does the image of John really look like a woman? Is there a triangle (the symbol for "holy grail") between Jesus and John? Put such burning questions aside for a moment, and use your precious fifteen minutes to focus on the real wonder inside – Da Vinci's exquisite artistry.

The Renaissance master was in his forties when he painted his depiction of Christ and the twelve disciples, a mural that also served as an experiment with oil paints, a decision that led to its decay in Da Vinci's own lifetime. A shadow of its former self, the epic 21-year restoration, completed in 1999, has nevertheless revealed some of the original colours, and Da Vinci's skills as a painter; his technique is flawless, the painting loaded with meaning and symbolism. Light draws attention to Jesus who sits at the centre, having just informed his disciples that one of them will betray him. The genius of the painting is the realism with which Da Vinci shows the reaction of each: Andrew on the left, his hands held up in utter disbelief; Judas, half in shadow, clutching his bag of silver; Peter next to him, full of rage; and James the Greater on the right, his hands thrown into the air.

Housed in the sealed and climate-controlled refectory of the convent, the focus on just one great work, combined with the laborious process of booking a slot and lining up to get in (25 at a time), heightens the sense of expectation. Once inside, there's usually a dramatic change in atmosphere – viewers become subdued, often overwhelmed by the majesty of the painting, and just for a second they stop looking for that elusive grail.

247 BUNKERING DOWN IN DURRES

ALBANIA A small, rickety Ferris wheel now turns on the spot in Skanderbeg Square where Enver Hoxha's colossal gilded statue once stood. After his death in 1985, Hoxha's busts were gradually removed from public view and the National Historical Museum in Tirana was "ideologically renovated". However, despite the cosmetic surgery, Albania just can't seem to shrug off one legacy of Hoxha's brutal brand of Stalinism.

The ultra-paranoid dictator covered Albania's pretty rural landscape with over 700,000 bunkers – one for every four citizens – to protect his people from invading hordes of imperialists, fascists and counter-revolutionaries. The enemy tanks never arrived, but the bunkers were built so strongly that to this day few have been removed. These small concrete domes occupy every possible vantage point in the rolling countryside that flanks the road between the capital and the port city of Durres on the Adriatic coast: gloomy relics of the old regime that have been reinvented to represent the spirit of the new Albania.

The rusty ledge of one bunker's entrance is lined with pretty potted flowers, while rows of tomatoes grow defiantly around it. Inside, candles struggle to stay alight in the stale air, scarcely lighting the table around which a family of five, who have chosen to call this suffocating box home, are eating dinner. Other bunkers are painted with jaunty murals or emblazoned with the colours of football teams or lovers' names: unambiguous expressions of the new priorities in Albanians' lives. A young couple emerges from a solitary bunker on the brow of a hill, walk down to a beaten-up Mercedes parked by the roadside and stop for a lingering kiss before driving back to Tirana.

And at Durres, the odd imperialist tourist freshly arrived on the ferry from Italy sips beer and listens to one ABBA hit after another in the dark, slightly dank surroundings of a beachside bunker bar, as Hoxha turns lividly in his grave.

248 GETTING THE MEASURE OF THE MEDICIS: THE UFFIZI

ITALY It's a simple equation: Florence was the centre of the Italian Renaissance; the Medici were the greatest art patrons of Renaissance Florence; their collection was bequeathed to the city by the last Medici, Anna Maria Lodovica; therefore the Uffizi Gallery – which occupies offices (uffizi) built for the Medici in 1560 – is the greatest display of Renaissance painting in the world. Which is why the Uffizi attracts more visitors than any other building in Italy – more than one and a half million of them every year.

The key to enjoying the Uffizi is to book your ticket in advance and to ration yourself; if you try to see everything you'll barely be able to skate over the surface. For your first visit, limit yourself to the first eighteen rooms or so – this will take you as far as the Bronzino portraits in the octagonal Tribuna. Arranged more or less chronologically, the Uffizi encapsulates the genesis of the Renaissance in a room of three altarpieces of the Maestà (Madonna Enthroned) by Duccio, Cimabue and Giotto. After a diversion through the exquisite late Gothic art of Simone Martini and Gentile da Fabriano the narrative of the Renaissance resumes with Paolo Uccello's *The Battle of San Romano* and continues with Piero della Francesca, Filippo Lippi (and his son Filippino), and of course Botticelli: it doesn't matter how many times you've seen photos of them, the *Primavera* and the *Birth of Venus* will stop you in your tracks. And there's still Leonardo da Vinci to come before you reach the halfway point.

Should you decide to make a dash to the end, you'll see a remarkable collection of Venetian painting (Giorgione, Giovanni Bellini, Paolo Veronese, Tintoretto and no fewer than nine Titians), a clutch of fabulous Mantegnas and Raphaels, and the extraordinary Doni Tondo, the only easel painting Michelangelo ever came close to completing. Ahead of you are fabulous pieces by Dürer, Holbein and Cranach, del Sarto and Parmigianino, Caravaggio and Rembrandt, Goya and Chardin. Wherever you stop in the Uffizi, there's a masterpiece staring you in the face.

249 EUROPE'S MOST ANCIENT TEMPLES

MALTA Ggantija, Hagar Qim, Mnajdra, Ta' Hagrat, Ta' Skorba and Tarxien. Not the most recognizable names, but these Maltese locations host some of the most ancient buildings in the world. Better known by their official title of the Megalithic Temples of Malta, the seven sites (two are at Ggantija) are listed as a UNESCO World Heritage Site, and most of them date back to around 3600 BC, before even the more famous Pyramids at Giza and Stonehenge in England.

On the main island of Malta, Tarxien is the most popularly visited site of the seven, considered by some to be the cathedral of European megalithic culture. Discovered in 1914 by a farmer who had grown increasingly curious about the rocks that kept ruining his plough, the temple held a wealth of prehistoric artefacts, including the Magna Mater (or the Fat Lady as she's lovingly referred to by the locals). Estimated to have stood more than 2.5m tall when complete, only the lower half of the statue was found during excavations. The original is now housed in the archeology museum in Valletta, with a replica standing on the site of its discovery, but a visit to Tarxien will capture your imagination. The mystery of why the temples were built – and how – continues to baffle experts worldwide, but the beauty of the spiral and dotted motifs that are carved into the stones, and the simple yet structurally sound building methods and intricately interwoven passageways, somehow make you not really care.

250 MONASTIC MOUNT ÁTHOS

GREECE Leaving the boat I'd caught in Ouranoúpoli, the last Greek-Macedonian village before the border with the monastic republic of Áthos, I disembark at a small harbour. I toil uphill onto the peninsula's endangered cobbled-trail system, and find myself deep in broad-leafed forest – without mobile reception. An anxious hour ensues before a signal reappears; it's essential to reserve a bed in advance at most of the mountain's twenty fortified monasteries.

Lunch, four hours later, is at Hilandharíou. The young monks at this thirteenth-century Serbian monastery are amazingly courteous considering that NATO has just flattened their country. Despite losing my way on overgrown paths, I reach shipshape Stavronikíta on the north coast by nightfall, where I am offered a frugal meal of soup, salad, bread and an apple – typical fast-day fare.

My room comes complete with snoring roommate; seeing my hesitation, the guest-master takes pity and lodges me in private quarters – until 3.30am, when a símandro (hammered-plank-bell) announces obligatory matins. After a 6am coffee and biscuit, I'm sent on my way – hospitality is for one night only – munching on the nuts and sesame cake Áthos trekkers use to keep their strength up.

Father Iakovos, the kindly, multilingual librarian at tenth-century Iviron, greets me. I mention the disgraceful state of Áthonite paths, and he offers me Philip Sherrard's monograph on their spiritual meaning. After lunch, a monastic jeep gives me a lift to Áthos's spectacularly rugged, roadless tip, where I stay at a primitive kellí (agricultural colony).

Next morning, in the echoing corridors of Ayíou Pávlou monastery, a small boy, brought along by his father, cries inconsolably for his mum – unluckily for him, the only woman allowed on the Holy Mountain is the Holy Virgin.

Dawn after my last overnight at Grigoríou, on the fourth day of July trekking, finds me filthy; Áthonite guest quarters have no bathing facilities. (A particularly ripe medieval Orthodox monk, challenged about his hygiene, retorted, "I am washed once in the blood of Christ. Why wash again?")

Below the trail that takes me back to the boat, I find a secluded cove, strip naked, and plunge into the satiny Aegean. Miraculously, the Virgin does not strike me dead.

CARNIVAL IN VENICE

251

ITALY As a setting for a carnival, Venice is unique. The city's location, built across several islands of a lagoon bordering the Adriatic Sea, means that here carnival floats are literally that, gliding along on the water itself rather than chugging down the road on the back of a truck. The maze of narrow pedestrian streets and interlaced canals is a source of discovery at every turn – all the more so if you're kitted out in a fancy costume or, at the very least, a mask – and Venice is an authentic backdrop for the theatrical celebrations that form the basis of the festival. Ultimately, the sheer visual delight of the city, and the tangible feeling that somehow you are adrift on an island in some parallel universe, are what make Carnival an experience like no other. Apart from the two weekends of Carnival, there are two particularly frenetic evenings, those of the second Thursday, Giovedi Grasso (Fat Thursday), and the last day, Martedi Grasso (Shrove Tuesday), when there are live-music spectaculars in Piazza San Marco, with Tuesday's always being the Notte de la Taranta, the wild, intoxicated dance of those bitten, as the legend goes, by the tarantula; a cavorting shared by thousands and topped off with massive fireworks at the tolling of midnight. Also on the piazza, the first Sunday sees an "angel" in white flowing robes (usually a famous Italian athlete) descending from the heights of the San Marco bell tower to land at the feet of a host of historically attired dignitaries. Away from here, carnival disperses itself among the labyrinthine streets and small, atmospheric squares. Piazzetta San Marco is home to performances of Baroque music and Commedia dell'Arte, while little Campo San Luca offers edgier live music and maybe some over-confident natives climbing flagpoles, or a spontaneous DJ set near the Ponte Rialto. Larger squares are other focal points: Campo Santa Margherita is the setting for live music stages, the Stazione Marittima forms the venue for dance-orientated diversions; and Campo San Polo has plenty on offer for young children during the day – play areas, music, and small theatre productions. On the water itself, small flotillas of decorated gondolas periodically sweep through the canals, to the cheers of revellers who crowd the bridges for a spectacular "aerial" view.

252 LIVING IT UP ON THE AMALFI COAST

ITALY The Amalfi Coast, playground of the rich and famous, exudes Italian chic. The landscape is breathtakingly dramatic: sheer, craggy cliffs plunge down to meet the water which is a shimmering, cerulean blue, and tiny secluded coves dot the coastline, accessible only by very expensive yacht. Setting off down the coastal road, you can't help but fancy yourself a bit of a jetsetter.

The drive itself deserves celebrity status; you may think you've seen coastal roads, but this one's in a class of its own, hewn into the sides of the mountain and barely wide enough for two large cars to pass comfortably, let alone the gargantuan buses that whiz between the main towns. On one side rises an impenetrable wall of mountain, while on the other there's nothing but a sheer, unforgiving drop to the sea. Overcome the instinct to hide your head in your hands, and embrace the

exhilaration – this is not a ride to miss. The road snakes its way along the side of the mountain, plunging headlong into dark, roughly-hewn tunnels, curving sharply around headlands, and traversing the odd crevice on the way. Every hair-raising bend presents you with yet another sweeping vista.

Don't get so caught up in the drive that you forget to stop and enjoy the calm beauty of the effortlessly exclusive coastal towns. Explore the posh cliffside town of Positano or stroll the peaceful promenades and piazzas of elegant hilltop Ravello. And in more down-to-earth Amalfi, just below, readjust to the languorous pace of resort-town life at a café before heading off to enjoy the town's sandy beach. Presided over by a towering cathedral adorned with glittering gold tiles and a lush and peaceful cloister, it's the perfect antidote to the adrenaline rush of the Amalfi Drive.

253 THE PEACE OF PAESTUM

ITALY The travel writer Norman Lewis called it a "scene of unearthly enchantment", and Paestum is still one of southern Italy's most haunting ancient sites. Its three Greek temples brood magnificently over their marshy location just south of Naples, where, despite the proximity of the city, there are relatively few visitors. Perhaps everyone goes to Pompeii? Whatever the reason, the site is an overgrown and romantic joy, only partially excavated and still the domain of snakes, lizards and other wildlife rather than large numbers of visitors. The splendid museum holds some fantastic finds from the site, including a marvellous mosaic of a diver in mid-plunge that is worth the price of entry alone. Afterwards you can fumble your way back through the undergrowth for a lounge and a swim on some nice nearby beaches lined by scruffy campsites.

254 GETTING YOUR KIT OFF IN FLORENCE

ITALY If the idea of a weekend in Florence bores the pants off you, then you might just consider taking your turn as a life model, posing for some of the city's numerous aspirant painters and sculptors in the home of the Renaissance. Florence is host to a number of brave folk willing to strip off, but there's always room for a few more, and it's easy to join them and take your place in your very own work of art. Posing as a life model might not be your idea of fun, but there is something appropriate about going starkers in a city where the nude is king. Whether it's Botticelli's *Venus*, Michelangelo's *David* or Masaccio's *Adam and Eve*, there's certainly no shortage of homespun inspiration.

255 FEASTING IN BERGAMO

ITALY Hiking through the steep hills north of Bergamo, not far from Milan, you'll notice an eerie silence. After a while it dawns on you that there is no birdsong. People around here traditionally love to hunt, and until recently one of the staples of the local cuisine was polenta e osei – or polenta with small birds: traditionally larks or thrushes skewered whole and roasted and served over cornmeal that is slow-cooked to a creamy mash. This dish is considered a cruel affair nowadays, not least because the birds were often roasted while still alive, so it's rare that you'll get the opportunity to taste it outside someone's home; and in any case you might not relish scoffing the birds whole, beak and all, as you are supposed to. But Bergamo remains one of Italy's great food cities, and you can still find osei scapai, literally "birds that got away", served with the same yellow polenta – which is a staple of the town to the extent that its inhabitants are known to the rest of Italy as polentoni. The "birds", though, are nowadays a mixed grill of veal, bacon and chicken livers cooked up with fresh sage and then roasted in the oven. Just as delicious, and a lot easier to eat!

Bergamo is perfect for a foodie weekend. Rambling up narrow, cobbled Via Gombito, the pedestrianized main street of Bergamo's Upper Town, you're drawn in by the profusion of greengrocers, cavernous salumerie festooned with all kinds of cured meats and mustily fragrant cheese shops. Sit under the streetside loggia at *Donizetti* and have a degustazione platter of prosciutto, bresaola (wafer-thin slices of air-dried beef) and goose sausage, along with gorgonzola and spicy bagoss cheese, washed down with sparkling Franciacorta wine. Take in an evening meal at *Da Mimmo*, a family-run restaurant where you can opt for casoncelli, ravioli stuffed with sausagemeat, sage and butter, or flavourful rabbit stew, served with – what else? – polenta. Don't miss dessert either, especially as it gives you the chance to savour more fake birds in another version of polenta e osei – basically sponge cake topped with tiny marzipan larks. Round things off with a post-prandial coffee at the *Caffè Funicolare*, at the top of the funicular station that links the upper and lower town. From here the view over Bergamo is stupendous, looking south towards Milan. But with food this good, who needs Milan?

256 RING OF FIRE: WALKING ON HOT COALS

GREECE In a handful of sleepy farming villages in northern Greece, the fire-walking ritual is an annual celebration of a thirteenth-century miracle, when locals rescued icons from a burning church – without being burned themselves. By nightfall, the towering bonfire in the main square has dwindled to glowing embers. Every light is put out and all eyes are on the white-hot coals – and the cluster of people about to make the barefoot dash across them. Fire-walkers limber up for the main event with rhythmic dancing, which escalates into frenzied writhing as they channel the spirit of St Constantine, believed to shield them from harm. Clutching icons for further protection, the fire-walkers step out onto the coals, stomping on the smouldering embers with gusto, as though kicking up autumn leaves. An inspection of feet after the rite reveals miraculously unmarked soles, a sign of St Constantine's divine protection – and an excuse for a slap-up feast.

257 OSTIA ANTICA

ITALY Rome's best ancient Roman sight isn't in fact in the city, but a half-hour train ride away at Ostia, where the ruins of the ancient city's port (Ostia was formerly on the coast) are fantastically well-preserved. Ostia was the beating heart of Rome's trading empire, but it is relatively free of the bustle of tourists you find in the city proper. There are marvellously preserved streets, with shops and upstairs apartments, evocative arcaded passages and floor mosaics, and even an old café with outside seats, an original counter and wall paintings displaying of parts of the menu. There's a small theatre and a main square that would have been full of traders from all over the ancient world, with mosaics of boats, ropes, fish and suchlike denoting their trade. Afterwards you should climb up on to the roofs of some of the more sumptuous houses and enjoy the views that once would have looked out over Ostia's busy harbour.

258 CLASSICAL DRAMA AT EPIDAVROS

GREECE There's no better place to experience classical drama than the ancient theatre at Epidavros, just outside the pretty harbour town of Nafplio in the Greek Peloponnese. Dating back to the fourth century BC, it seats 14,000 people and is known above all for its extraordinary acoustics – as guides regular demonstrate, you can literally hear a pin drop in its circular orchestra (the most complete in existence) even if you're sitting on the highest of the theatre's 54 tiers. It's a venue for regular performances of the plays of Sophocles and Euripedes between June and September every year. Occasionally these are in English, but whether you understand the modern Greek in which they are usually performed or not, the setting is utterly unforgettable, carved into the hill behind and with the brooding mountains beyond.

259 MONASTERIES SUSPENDED IN THE AIR

GREECE When scouting around for a secluded refuge from the cares of the world, it's perhaps not surprising that a group of eleventh-century Greek monks should have hit upon Meteora (literally, "suspended in the air"). These otherworldly, towering sandstone pinnacles, jutting upwards from the plains of Thessaly, take the notion of remoteness to another level. In those days, access to the monasteries was by way of nets hoisted heavenwards by hand-cranked windlasses; nowadays, hard-core climbers get their kicks by making the same journey up nigh-on vertical pillars of rock with names like the Corner of Madness. For those who prefer to take the stairs, the six monasteries are also accessible by steps hewn into the rock in the 1920s. Well-worn trails zigzag between monasteries, their rust-coloured roof tiles in cheery contrast to the desolate greyness of the wind-blasted rock. Inside, you'll find superb frescoes and late Byzantine art. Outside, top-of-the-world views.

260 CELEBRATING THE BIENNALE

ITALY Several European cities hold major contemporary art fairs, but the leader of the pack is the Venice Biennale, an event that has more glamour, prestige and news value than any other cultural jamboree. Nowadays it's associated with the cutting edge, but it hasn't always been that way. First held in 1895 as the city's contribution to the celebrations for the silver wedding anniversary of King Umberto I and Margherita of Savoy, in its early years it was essentially a showcase for salon painting.

Since World War II, however, the Biennale has become a self-consciously avant-garde event, a transformation symbolized by the award of the major Biennale prize in 1964 to Robert Rauschenberg, one of the enfants terribles of the American art scene. The French contingent campaigned vigorously against the nomination of this New World upstart, and virtually every Biennale since then has been characterized by controversy of some sort.

After decades of occurring in even-numbered years, the Biennale shifted back to being held every odd-numbered year from June to November so that the centenary show could be held in 1995. The main site is in the Giardini Pubblici, where there are permanent pavilions for about forty countries that participate every time, plus space for a thematic international exhibition. The pavilions are a show in themselves, forming a unique colony that features work by some of the great names of modern architecture and design: the Austrian pavilion, for example, was built by the Secession architect Josef Hoffmann in the 1930s, and the Finnish pavilion was created by Alvar Aalto in the 1950s. Naturally enough, the biggest pavilion is the Italian one – it's five times larger than the next largest.

The central part of the Biennale is supplemented by exhibitions in venues that are normally closed to the public. This is another big attraction of the event – only during the Biennale are you likely to see the colossal Corderie in the Arsenale (the former rope-factory) or the huge salt warehouses over on the Záttere. In addition, various sites throughout the city (including the streets) host fringe exhibitions, installations and performances, particularly in the opening weeks. And with artists, critics and collectors swarming around the bars and restaurants, the artworld buzz of the Biennale penetrates every corner of Venice.

261 IN THE FOOTSTEPS OF ODYSSEUS ON ITHACA

GREECE In Homer's epic poem, the hero Odysseus needs ten years to return home to Ithaca after the Trojan War. I needed just over an hour on the early-morning ferry from Lefkas. But from the moment I set foot in the harbour of Frikes, I felt there was something special about this sleepy, rugged island. The craggy coast zigzagged south to Kiuni, an amphitheatric bay lined with swanky yachts and smart tavernas. It was pleasant enough, but I knew I'd have to embark on a little adventure of my own to really slip under Ithaca's skin.

Homer describes Ithaca as a "rocky severe island good for goats." The reason why became clear as I climbed the wildly overgrown donkey trail weaving uphill from Kiuni, where oak and pine canopies provided shade from the blistering sun. I cut a path through the thicket, keeping track of the faded blue-and-yellow signs to Anoyi and listening to the out-of-tune toll of hundreds of goat bells. Locked in a time warp, these forgotten woods were marvellously eerie and evocative of Odysseus' island. Before the main coastal road sprang up in the nineteenth century, the island had been combed by mule trails like this, the definition of a road then being a path wide enough for two laden donkeys to pass.

Mount Niritos loomed large, but my eyes were drawn to bizarre rock formations studding the boulder-strewn plateau, in particular Heracles, a striking eight-metre megalith. Arriving in Anoyi, a near ghost town, I was forced to look up again – this time at a free-standing Venetian campanile that dwarfed the deserted square. Further north, Stavros' shady square was far from deserted. Better still, it was the perfect spot to sip a glass of local white and rest my weary feet. The bougainvillea-clad houses blushed pink as the sun set over the glassy Ionian Sea. It was poetic stuff and Homer's mythical verses had never seemed so appropriate:

I am Odysseus, Laertes' son, world-famed
For stratagems: my name has reached the heavens.
Bright Ithaca is my home: it has a mountain,
Leaf-quivering Neriton, far visible.

262 CLIMB EVERY MOUNTAIN: REINHOLD MESSNER

ITALY As one of the world's greatest ever mountaineers, the first person to climb Everest without oxygen, and the first to conquer all fourteen of the world's highest peaks (over 8000m), Reinhold Messner hardly needs to leave any other legacy. But for the past ten years or so he has been busy creating a network of "mountain museums" in the Sud-Tyrol region of Italy that make the most of some amazing locations. Some are housed in ancient castles, and the centrepiece, Firmian, which opened in 2006, enjoys a spectacular location south of the town of Bolzano, that has to be seen to be believed. Like the others, its courtyards and halls are filled with artefacts picked up by Messner during his time in the Himalayas – sculptures and textiles and beautiful objects that sit evocatively in the alpine landscape, but also junk from the mountains: oxygen masks and climbing accessories that are a chilling reminder of the human traffic that is threatening to overwhelm the place. All in all, this is a magical spot, and a fittingly epic testimony to the extraordinary man who created it.

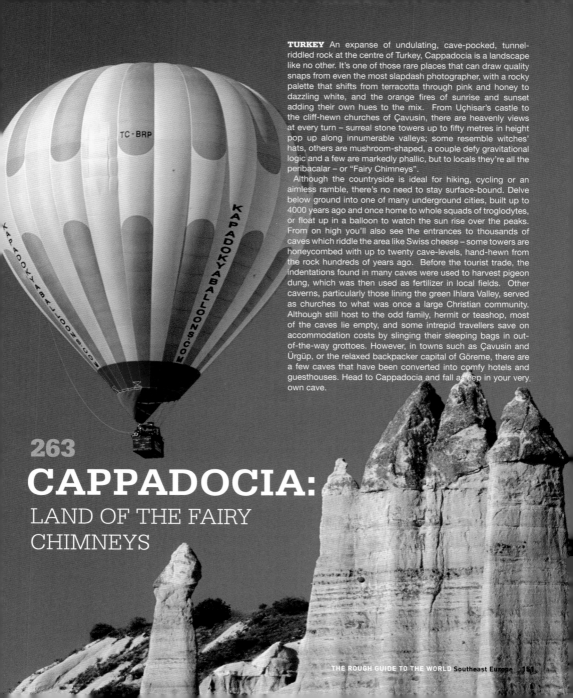

TURKEY An expanse of undulating, cave-pocked, tunnel-riddled rock at the centre of Turkey, Cappadocia is a landscape like no other. It's one of those rare places that can draw quality snaps from even the most slapdash photographer, with a rocky palette that shifts from terracotta through pink and honey to dazzling white, and the orange fires of sunrise and sunset adding their own hues to the mix. From Uçhisar's castle to the cliff-hewn churches of Çavusin, there are heavenly views at every turn – surreal stone towers up to fifty metres in height pop up along innumerable valleys; some resemble witches' hats, others are mushroom-shaped, a couple defy gravitational logic and a few are markedly phallic, but to locals they're all the peribacalar – or "Fairy Chimneys".

Although the countryside is ideal for hiking, cycling or an aimless ramble, there's no need to stay surface-bound. Delve below ground into one of many underground cities, built up to 4000 years ago and once home to whole squads of troglodytes, or float up in a balloon to watch the sun rise over the peaks. From on high you'll also see the entrances to thousands of caves which riddle the area like Swiss cheese – some towers are honeycombed with up to twenty cave-levels, hand-hewn from the rock hundreds of years ago. Before the tourist trade, the indentations found in many caves were used to harvest pigeon dung, which was then used as fertilizer in local fields. Other caverns, particularly those lining the green Ihlara Valley, served as churches to what was once a large Christian community. Although still host to the odd family, hermit or teashop, most of the caves lie empty, and some intrepid travellers save on accommodation costs by slinging their sleeping bags in out-of-the-way grottoes. However, in towns such as Çavusin and Ürgüp, or the relaxed backpacker capital of Göreme, there are a few caves that have been converted into comfy hotels and guesthouses. Head to Cappadocia and fall asleep in your very own cave.

263
CAPPADOCIA:
LAND OF THE FAIRY CHIMNEYS

CALLED BY RUMI: DERVISHES IN ISTANBUL

264

TURKEY A few years ago my wife and I had borrowed an old wooden house in Istanbul from a carpet-dealing friend. It was beloved by cats, and at dawn it echoed to the call of half a dozen minarets. There was a salon at the top of the narrow house with a tiny balcony where we could bathe our baby daughter in a washing-up basin filled with mineral water. This was necessary as the builders had walked out without plumbing the sink, which drained out over your lap and onto the floor if used, and Istanbul's tap water is lethal. Although there was a historic mosque on the edge of the neighbourhood, it was otherwise undisturbed by visitors, a quiet little residential enclave where the women would let down baskets from their apartment windows to be filled up by the grocer's boy. In the evening you could wander out through a hole in the walls and watch the long line of ships that were anchored off the Marmara shore, awaiting crews, cargoes and their chance to sail up the narrow straits of the Bosphorus. We were adopted by the local taverna, where white rice was served free of charge to our daughter and the young waiters bossed us

around shamelessly about proper child-care. One evening for a change in mood we were walking down the Istiklal Caddesi, Istanbul's main shopping street in the dusky gloom. Above the bustle of the shop-keepers and drinkers we caught the haunting sound of a single flute. Drawn by this music, we passed through a gate in the high stone walls and, feeling increasingly nervous, walked through a garden of eighteenth century turbaned tombs towards the source of the sound. As if in a dream, rather than being expelled by a security guard we were welcomed and shown into a seat into a beautiful octagonal hall. It was the founder of the dervish order Rumi's birthday, and on this day the Mevlevi Dervishes are allowed to celebrate with their music and whirling dances. I have been back many times since, but nothing can equal that first mysterious beckoning and the almost illicit celebration of the unworldly beauty of the mystical poet. It is said that the sound of the flute always transmits a hidden desire to be returned to the reed bed, which Rumi likened to the soul searching for its home.

265 DOING PENANCE IN THE SISTINE CHAPEL

ITALY You've seen them a thousand times before you even get there. Michelangelo's ceiling and wall frescoes of the Sistine Chapel are perhaps the most recognizable pieces of art in the world, reproduced so much that they've become part of the visual furniture of our lives. Getting to this enormous work isn't easy; indeed, it's almost an act of penance in itself, waiting in endless queues and battling flag-following tour groups. But none of that, nor the simple entrance to the chapel, can prepare you for the magnificence of what lies beyond.

Despite the crowds, the noise and the periodic chiding of the guards, seeing these luminous paintings in the flesh for the first time is a moving experience. The ceiling frescoes get the most attention, although staring at them for long in the high, barrel-vaulted chapel isn't great for the neck muscles. Commissioned by Pope Julius II in 1508, they depict scenes from the Old Testament, from the Creation of Light at the altar end to the Drunkenness of Noah at the other, interspersed with pagan sybils and biblical prophets, who peer out spookily from between the vivid main scenes. Look out for the hag-like Cumean sybil, and the prophet Jeremiah, a self-portrait of an exhausted-looking Michelangelo. Or just gaze in wonder at the whole decorative scheme – not bad for someone who considered himself a sculptor rather than a painter.

Once you've feasted on the ceiling, turn your attention to the altar wall, which was decorated by Michelangelo, by now an elderly man, over twenty years later, depicting in graphic and vivid detail the Last Judgement. The painting took him five years, a single-handed effort that is probably the most inspired large-scale work that you're ever likely to see. Its depiction of Christ, turning angrily as he condemns the damned to hell, while, above, the blessed levitate to heaven, might strike you as familiar. But standing in front of it, even surrounded by crocodiles of people, still feels like an enormous privilege.

266 WALKING THE CINQUE TERRE

ITALY Walking the coastal path that links the five spectacularly sited fishing villages of the Cinque Terre is one of Italy's finest hikes - and, what's more, it can be done in a day. In fact, walking is the only real way to see the Cinque Terre; you can't access the villages by car, and although trains call at each, the views can't compare with what you will see if you do it under your own steam. There are a number of paths to choose from, crisscrossing the hillsides above the houses, but the most direct route from Riomaggiore to Montorosso is the blue trail. The path takes you through a delightful array of scenery, from the wide, paved Via dell'Amore (Lovers' Way) meandering along the coast between Riomaggiore and Manorola, to gentle uphill climbs through olive groves and vineyards, and some rather more strenuous tracks wending their rocky way along the steep mountainsides, with sheer drops to the sea below. Each of the five villages has its own distinctive character: the first two, Riomaggiore and Manorola, are the most similar, with cobbled streets and brightly coloured fishing boats, not to mention the obligatory pottery shops, filled to bursting with Italian ceramics. Beyond here the trail clings to the shoreline, and reaches its lowest point before climbing up a long, zigzagging flight of steps to Corniglia, the highest of the five villages, charmingly situated amongst vineyards and olive groves. The seemingly endless climb makes Corniglia the least busy of the villages, and a good place to escape the crowds. In the spring the square here is a mass of colour with pots everywhere overflowing with fresh blooms. The fourth village, Vernazza, is perhaps the most picturesque, with a lovely sheltered bay and small sandy beach. If you have the energy to complete the journey on foot (a strenuous climb up scrub and light bush) your efforts will be rewarded with wonderful views down over the last village, Montorosso, not to mention the view back over the rugged coastline. Spectacular.

267 BRAVING THE MIDDAY SUN IN LECCE

ITALY In a mid-August heatwave, the heel of Italy is not a place many people would choose to be. Still less standing in the centre of Lecce's Piazza del Duomo, a heatsink square paved with burning stone flags, surrounded by burning stone buildings and overlooked by a sun that seems as hard and unrelenting as the stone itself. In such conditions the day begins at thirty degrees, and rises smoothly through the forties before topping out at a temperature that should be measured in gas marks, you feel, not degrees centigrade.

Squinting up at the towering stone facade of the Duomo and the adjacent bishop's palace, however, it all starts to make sense. Here, and on the surfaces of churches and palaces all over the city, the stone breaks out in exuberant encrustations, as if the very heat had caused the underlying architecture to boil over into fantastical shapes and accretions.

In fact, it wasn't the heat that caused Lecce's stone to crawl with decoration. It was a rare combination of time and place. The city lies beside a unique outcrop of soft sandstone in the razor-hard limestone that forms the tip of the heel of the Italian boot – and stonemasons' chisels take to this pietra Leccese like hot knives to butter. And at the very time the masons were setting to work, in the early sixteenth century, the flamboyant ornamentation of the Baroque style was taking hold in Italy. Lecce, the city they call the Florence of the South, was the fervid, sun-struck result.

262

RAFTING THE
TARA CANYON

MONTENEGRO Eighty kilometres long, and with an average depth of 1100m, the Tara river gorge is Europe's largest canyon, not to mention one of its most spectacular natural wonders; and slicing a course through the immense vertical cliffs is the eponymous Tara River. By far the most exhilarating way to get up close and personal with the Tara is to raft it, the most popular excursion being the three-hour trip between Splavište and Šćepan Polje, some 18km distant. Once you've been kitted out in boots, life vest and helmet, and then clambered aboard the sturdy rubber boat with around ten other equally mad souls (thankfully, a steersman is included), the thrills and spills get under way – well, sort of. The early stages of the river are characterized by a series of soft rapids and languid, almost still waters, the silence broken only by the occasional rumble of a waterfall spilling from the steeply pitched canyon walls. But after passing beneath the magnificent Tara Bridge – a 165-metre high, 365-metre long, five-arched structure built in 1940 – things take a dramatic turn. The sudden increase in gradient means faster currents, which in turn means more powerful rapids. Approaching Miševo vrelo, the deepest section of the canyon at some 1300m, your skills as an oarsman are put to a severe test, as the foaming waters toss the raft every which way and you struggle to keep balance. For those feeling vulnerable, straps on the side of the raft – somewhat unflatteringly termed "chicken lines" – are there to assist. The river eventually relents, just in time for the home stretch. Exhausted and hungry, it's time for some Durmitor lamb, cooked in milk and prepared "ispod sača" – the traditional Montenegrin way meaning "under the coals". Served with potatoes and kajmak (sour cream cheese), and washed down with a glass of local rich-red Vranac wine, it's the perfect way to round off a day on the river.

269 SNUFFLING FOR TRUFFLES IN PIEMONTE

ITALY One of Italy's great seasonal events is the autumn truffle season, when Italian gastronomes descend upon the historic town of Alba in search of the white Piemontese tartufo or truffle. The tuber magnatum pico, as it's known, develops in cool damp chalky soil 10–15cm underground, and is only found in this part of Piemonte. Local farmers use specially trained dogs or tabui (literally "bastards") to sniff them out in the oak and hazelnut forests near Alba, usually at night – not only because the whole thing is tremendously secretive but also because fully mature truffles are said to emit a stronger perfume after dark.

On the final weekend in October, the market for truffles in Alba's old centre is at its peak. Once inside the covered venue, the experience is a sensory overload. Never again will you whiff so many truffles – or truffle products – in such a confined space. However, buying one of these little gastronomic gems can be stressful. Prices are steep – €3000–4000 a kilo – and the market traders as sharp as they come. They'll happily let you pick up and smell as many truffles as you wish, but learning how to discern a decent truffle's characteristics isn't easy.

Observe the locals. Truffles must be consumed within ten days of their discovery: they should be brownish-white in colour and clean of dirt – greyish truffles are old truffles. They should be firm to the touch and knobbly in texture; a spongy truffle must be eaten that day or not at all. Look out also for any holes which might have been filled with dirt to increase the weight. Above all, be sure to smell the truffle thoroughly: a mature specimen will possess a strong and nutty bouquet. If you feel the need for a second opinion, the "Quality Commission" in the centre of the market will take a look for you. You might think they would shave off a small piece. But that's not needed. All they do is remove the truffle from the paper towel, place it on the scales, test the firmness between the thumb and index finger, and, finally, put it as close to the nose as physically possible and SNIFF. Once authenticated, the truffle is placed in a numbered paper bag. Is it really worth all the hype? Well, the taste is sensual, earthy and curiously moreish, whether it's shaved thinly over pasta, or as the basis of various oils, cream sauces and butters. And where else could you get to eat something quite so expensive?

270 GETTING DOWN AND DIRTY IN DALYAN

TURKEY Stepping off the boat at Dalyan's mud baths, you'll be forgiven for wishing you hadn't. But don't be put off by the revolting rotten egg stench of the sulphur pools – after a revitalizing day here, you'll be gagging for more. The instructions are simple – roll in the mud, bake yourself in the sun till your mud cast cracks, shower off and then dunk yourself in the warm, therapeutic waters of the sulphur pool. Not only will your skin be baby-soft and deliciously tingly, you will also revert to behaving like a big kid: a huge mud bath can mean only one thing – a giant mud fight.

271 MAKING THE PARTY LAST ALL NIGHT IN TIRANA

ALBANIA Reinvented and energized by its youth, Tirana is finally emerging from its communist past to reclaim the present. Not without irony, the centre of things is the Blloku quarter, once only accessible by the communist elite but now reclaimed and transformed, and buzzing with cafés, bars and clubs. An evening here begins with a typically Mediterranean xhiro (evening stroll) through newly restored streets and parks, before lingering over an espresso at the rooftop *Sky Club Café*. The pace may be mellow but the evenings are long, stretching on to clubs where local DJs spin sounds that exemplify the city's new-found exuberance.

272 HIKING THE VIA FERRATA

ITALY An exhilarating sense of triumph overtakes you as you climb the crest of a jagged, snow-laced limestone peak. From your roost above the valley floor, Cortina's campanile and the hotel where you had breakfast this morning are barely visible. The most spectacular climbing routes in the Dolomites are now within your grasp. You've suddenly joined the ranks of the world's elite alpine climbers – or so you would like to think. Actually, most of the credit goes to the cleverly placed system of cables, ladders, rungs and bridges known as Via Ferrata, or "Iron Way".

These fixed-protection climbing paths were first created by alpine guides to give clients access to more challenging routes. During World War I, existing routes were extended and used to aid troop movements and secure high mountain positions. But today, hundreds of Via Ferrata routes enable enthusiasts to climb steep rock faces, traverse narrow ledges and cross gaping chasms that

would otherwise be accessible only to experienced rock jocks.

With the protective hardware already cemented into the rock, you can climb most Via Ferrata routes without a rope, climbing shoes or the rack of expensive hardware used by traditional rock climbers. With just a helmet, harness and clipping system, you fix your karabiner into the fixed cable, find your feet on one of the iron rungs and start climbing. It's an amazingly fun way to conquer some stunning vertical terrain and quickly ascend to airy alpine paths.

Via Ferrata climbing doesn't require polished technique, exceptional strength, balance or even prior rock climbing experience. It does demand decent aerobic conditioning for a sustained ascent of several hundred vertical metres. Once you put aside any fear of heights, you'll find a secure and surefooted excitement in this aerial playground.

273 LOOKING FOR PASTA HEAVEN

ITALY It may be just a simple combination of basic ingredients – flour, water and sometimes eggs – but pasta is the food that most defines Italy. It's one of the most versatile foods you could imagine, and is eaten all over the country – although it is in fact the basic staple of the South. There are hundreds of pasta shapes and sizes, each designed for a certain kind of sauce, and it's testimony to its importance in the Italian diet that each shape is identified according to a nationally recognized numbering system. Spaghetti is the best-known and most versatile; tubular rigatoni and shell-like conchiglie are great vehicles for ragù or meat sauce, as are Bolognese tagliatelle noodles, while thick papardelle are perfect foils for porcini mushrooms and thick, gamey sauces. Like most Italian cooking, pasta is best at its simplest, cooked with lots of liberally salted water and taken out at precisely the right moment and served al dente – ie not soft, but with a bite – and then combined with the freshest possible ingredients.

What you eat depends – as ever in Italy – on where you are in the country. Everything is regional. It's hard to find a restaurant in Liguria that doesn't serve pasta al pesto, usually with trofie – short, fat pellets of pasta and potato – and with a few green beans and boiled potatoes. Most eateries in Rome serve spaghetti al carbonara – with raw eggs and bacon; bucatini cacio e pepe – thick hollow noodles with pepper and lots of pecorino cheese; or all'amatriciana – with tomatoes and smoked bacon. In Bologna you will usually find lots of filled pasta alternatives like agnolotti, tortellini and ravioli. But the city that is renowned for the best pasta is Naples, and it's here that you'll get the closest to pasta heaven. They claim the water down here improves the quality of the pasta, and the sauces are simple yet hearty: spaghetti alle vongole, with tomatoes, lots of garlic and baby clams – and, perhaps the simplest and most ubiquitous Italian dish of them all, spaghetti al pomodoro, with tomatoes, garlic and a little fresh basil. "The angels in paradise", once opined the mayor of Naples, "eat nothing but pasta al pomodoro". And after eating spaghetti in Naples, you might be forced to agree.

274 NAVIGATING THE NOCTURNAL UNDERWORLD IN ZAGREB

CROATIA For anyone with more than a passing interest in the far frontiers of amplified music, Zagreb is not so much a city break as an addiction. Even the habitually staid local tourist office has realized that there is more to life than galleries and opera. Their monthly Events and Performances booklet dutifully details upcoming events in the National Theatre before energetically moving on to page after page of mind-bogglingly varied gigs and club nights in the strangest of places.

Out-of-town gig-hoppers should beware, however, that Zagreb is an insider's city that requires bat-like navigational instincts. You could waste an entire evening searching for KSET, a legendary black box of a bar hidden behind grey university buildings. Virtually everyone who is anyone in the experimental-jazz-noise-dub-punk-ska world has played here, usually to a gleeful, packed-to-the-rafters public.

Still more legwork is required to reach the riverside Močvara ("Swamp"), a former factory building splashed with the sci-fi comic-book murals of deranged artist Igor Hofbauer. Not so much a club as the cultural embassy of a hitherto unmapped country, Močvara offers a seven-days-a-week programme of audacious events.

Spend enough time in Mo˘cvara and KSET and you'll probably find out what's going on in an anarcho-punk squat called *Villa Kiseljak*, whose interior-design amalgam of graffiti art and bits of an old washing machine probably deserves a lifestyle article all to itself. One of the most bizarre fixtures in Zagreb's club calendar is Tuesday nights at Gjuro II, when media professionals and arty 20-to-40-somethings frug to a fiendishly effective cocktail of indie and retro sounds. So popular that it's impossible to breathe, never mind get served at the bar, it's the kind of event that would descend into madness, paranoia and violence if it were held in any other European country. In Zagreb, such a squeeze is just another excuse for good-natured flirting. Never will the idea of being crushed to death seem so full of possibilities.

275 CONQUERING MOUNT OLYMPUS

GREECE Work off that moussaka with a hike up the most monumental of the Greek mountains – Mount Olympus. Soaring to 2920m, the mountain is swathed in mysticism and majesty, mainly due to its reputation as the home of the Ancient Greek gods. Reaching the peak isn't something you can achieve in an afternoon – you'll need at least two days' trekking, staying overnight in refuges or tents. You don't need to be climber but you do need to be prepared: it's a tough climb to the summit, and requires a lot of stamina – and some degree of caution; the weather may be stiflingly hot at the bottom, but there could still be a blizzard blowing halfway up. Passing sumptuous wild flowers and dense forests on the lower slopes, the rocky, boulder-strewn terrain and hair-raisingly sheer drops of the summit are well worth the struggle. Just watch out for Zeus's thunderbolt on the way up.

276 SEEING LEGENDS COME ALIVE IN CRETE

GREECE Crete has never been just another Greek island. True, it has everything you could ask for – crystalline waters, sunwashed beaches, isolated villages and hospitable people. But it is also much more than that.

On Crete, legends come alive. Here, Homer's stories of King Minos emerged from myth and were proven to be fact; Zeus was born here (and died here too, some Cretans claim); and four thousand years ago the first civilization in Europe flourished on this island, while the rest of Greece was just learning to speak Greek.

Crete's size and position – as close to Africa as to Athens, a meeting point of east and west – has meant a history of exceptional richness, a history that has moulded the islanders and forged a spirit of indomitable resistance. There are mountain villages where you can see the traces of all those 4000 years of continuous human occupation, and the many invaders and locals who have left their mark.

If you want, you can swim and lie by the beach and know nothing of any of this. But even so, it's hard to ignore Crete's bold physical presence – its great mountain ranges, snow-capped well into the summer, dominate the inland landscape. Cutting through them are impressive gorges, most famously at Samariá, that offer fabulous opportunities for walkers. At the mountains' feet lie the great Minoan palaces, but also lesser-known relics: Roman cities; frescoed Byzantine churches; Venetian and Turkish fortresses.

Even the food is redolent of tradition, the wines, olive oil and simple fare tasting of the Mediterranean sun and Cretan soil – linking you closer to this fertile land of legends.

277 INSIDE A METAPHOR: TROY

TURKEY Zeki, the Canakkale taxi driver, sighed when I said our destination was Truva, but he was still willing to take our fare. Later, careening along in his battered Fiat, he asked why Westerners seemed compelled to visit the desolate plateau overlooking the Dardanelles.

"Rage," said my wife, separating our fighting boys. "It's all about rage," she emphasized as our two warriors lapsed into sullen silence. The answer was ingenious. Rage is mentioned in the first sentence of the *Iliad* and is the dominant emotion throughout. It's the abstract power of la force that makes the story of the ancient city so compelling and still so relevant. Look from Troy out towards the distant sea and you realize the importance of this strategic position between Europe and Asia. Whether the city burned for a sea tax or "possession of a charming whore", there can be little doubt it would have been passionately fought over.

Yet, my wife missed Zeki's point. Turkey contains remains of scores of civilizations and empires stretching from prehistory to the twentieth century. When compared to Ayia Sophia or the ruins at Ephesus, the broken walls protruding from sunburnt Hissarlik Hill seem unspectacular. Still, a century of excavation has breathed life back into the ruins. Walking around the site with Dr Manfred Korfmann's *A Tour of Troia* is insightful, but it is the fierce glory of Troy that captures the imagination. Considered the first and possibly greatest literary work about war, Homer's tale is the prototype of human conflict. The epic has supplied the themes of literature, art and cinema ranging from Euripides to Shakespeare, and from Eugene O'Neill to Wolfgang Peterson. Stand upon the sloped ramparts, look down upon the broad Troad plain, and it is easy to imagine a besieging army gathering below. And for kids, there is the wooden horse to clamber inside, inspiring curiosity in the story in another generation.

278 SPOTTING GIOTTO IN PADUA

ITALY It could be argued that the frescoes in Padua's Cappella degli Scrovegni are the single most significant sequence of paintings in all of Italy. The masterpiece of Giotto, these pictures mark the point at which the spirit of humanism began to subvert the stylized, icon-like conventions of medieval art – Giotto's figures are living, breathing people who inhabit a three-dimensional world, and for many subsequent artists, such as Masaccio and Michelangelo, the study of Giotto was fundamental to their work. But in addition to being of supreme importance, the frescoes are immensely fragile, having been infiltrated by damp rising from the swampy ground on which the chapel is built, and by moisture exhaled by millions of admiring tourists. Extraordinary measures have been taken to save the chapel from further damage: only 25 visitors at a time are allowed in, for just a quarter of an hour, and entrance is via an elaborate airlock.

The chapel was commissioned in 1303 by Enrico Scrovegni in atonement for the usury of his father, who died screaming "give me the keys to my strong box" and was denied a Christian burial. As soon as the walls were built, Giotto was commissioned to cover every inch of the interior with illustrations of the lives of Jesus, Mary and Joachim (Mary's father), and the story of the Passion, arranged in three tightly knit tiers and painted against a backdrop of saturated blue. There's little precedent in Western art for the psychological tension of these scenes – the exchange of glances between the two shepherds in *The Arrival of Joachim* is particularly powerful, as are the tender gestures of *Joachim and Anna at the Golden Gate* and *The Visit of Mary to Elizabeth*. And look out for what's said to be Giotto's self-portrait in the fresco of the *Last Judgement* – he's among the redeemed, fourth from the left at the bottom.

279 VENICE: EUROPE'S FIRST MODERN CITY?

ITALY In Venice you are constantly coming upon something that amazes: a magnificent and dilapidated palace, a lurching church tower, an impossibly narrow alleyway that ends in the water. The coffee-table books don't lie – this really is the most beautiful city in the world. The thing is, it's so beautiful that you might not see just how remarkable it is.

Weaving your way through the city, you have to remind yourself that every single building is a miracle of ingenuity; the urban fabric of Venice is extraordinarily dense, but the walls have been raised on nothing more than mudflats. The canalscapes are picturesque, undeniably, but they're an extremely efficient circulatory system as well – freight in Venice goes by water, leaving pedestrians in complete control of the land. Venice was also a pioneer of industrial technologies; the glass factories of Murano were one of the continent's earliest manufacturing zones, while the dockyards of the Arsenale were Europe's first production line, operating so smoothly that a functioning battleship could be assembled in the course of a day. Socially

and politically, too, Venice was in the vanguard. At a time when most other European states were ruled by monarchs and hoodlums, Venice was a republic, and it lasted for a thousand years.

At its zenith, Venice was a metropolis of some 250,000 people (about four times the present population), with an empire that extended from the Dolomites to Cyprus, and trading networks that spread right across Asia. And trade was what made this one of Europe's great multicultural cities: the main post office was once the HQ of the German merchants; the natural history museum occupies the premises of the Turkish traders; and all over the city you'll find traces of its Greek, Albanian, Slavic, Armenian and Jewish communities.

Of course, the monuments of Venice attract tourists in their millions. Most, however, see nothing more than St Mark's Square. To escape the crowds, and see the place clearly, you just have to stroll for ten minutes in any direction and lose yourself in the world's most remarkable labyrinth.

280 LIVE LIKE A DOGE: ONE NIGHT AT THE DANIELI

ITALY Venice has more hotels per square kilometre than any other city in Europe, and for more than 150 years one particular hotel has maintained its status as the most charismatic of them all – the *Danieli*. Founded in 1822 by Giuseppe Dal Niel, it began as a simple guesthouse on one floor of the Palazzo Dandolo, but within twenty years it became so popular that Dal Niel was able to buy the whole building. Rechristened with an anagram of his own name, the hotel established itself as the Venetian address of choice for visiting luminaries: Balzac, Wagner, Dickens, John Ruskin and Proust all stayed here, and nowadays it's a favourite with the Film Festival crowd and the bigwigs of the art world who assemble for the Biennale.

So what makes the *Danieli* special? Well, for a start there's the beauty of the Palazzo Dandolo. Built at the end of the fourteenth century for a family that produced four of the doges of Venice, the palazzo is a fine example of Venetian Gothic architecture, and its entrance hall, with its amazing arched staircase, is the

most spectacular hotel interior in the city. The rooms in this part of the *Danieli* are furnished with fine antiques, with the best of them looking out over the lagoon towards the magnificent church of San Giorgio Maggiore. This is the other crucial factor in the *Danieli's* success – location. It stands in the very heart of Venice, right next to the Doge's Palace, on the waterfront promenade called the Riva degli Schiavoni, and in the evening you can eat at the rooftop *La Terrazza* restaurant, admiring a view that no other tables in town can equal.

All this comes at a price, of course; the *Danieli* is one of the most expensive places to stay in this most expensive of cities. There are three parts to the hotel: the old Palazzo Dandolo, known as the Casa Vecchia; an adjoining palazzo; and a block built in 1948. The best rooms, with lagoon views, are in the Casa Vecchia. If your Lottery ticket has come up, however, you might want to consider the delirious gilt and marble extravagance of the Doge's Suite – yours for around €4000 per night.

281 STUDENICA AND THE MAGICAL MONASTERIES

SERBIA For obvious reasons Serbia hasn't been Europe's most popular destination over recent years. But it is surely ready for rediscovery. The steep wooded hills of the countryside south of Belgrade are beautiful and host a network of medieval monasteries located in deliberately out-of-the-way spots. Most boast well-preserved frescoes that the Serbs keenly tout as examples of their superior civilization before the Ottomans. But the real allure is in the locations – magical spots where the peace is disturbed only by the clinking of goat bells. Studenica is perhaps the greatest of

them all, sitting in a gorgeous location 12km from the nearest town – Uscé – in the high alpine pastures of central Serbia; there's a hotel up there too so you can experience the location at its most exquisitely peaceful. Other monasteries include Ravanica, easily accessible on a day-trip from the capital, and Kalenić (though the latter is especially difficult to get to); Sopoćani, whose frescoes are especially fine, and Mileševa, southwest towards the Bosnian border, which was the last resting place of St Sava, founder of the Serbian Orthodox Church.

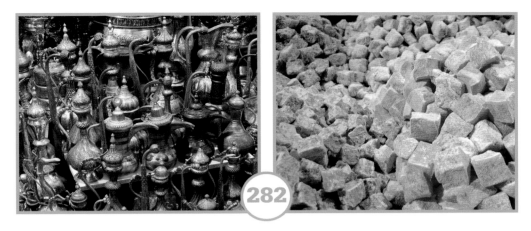

282

SHOP TILL YOU DROP IN İSTANBUL

TURKEY The phrase "shop till you drop" might have been invented by a Turk, and he or she might have had Istanbul's Kapali Çarşi or "covered market" in mind, for this Ottoman-era labyrinth of shops, stalls and alleys is truly is the prototype for all shopping centres worldwide – a humming magnet for consumers that boasts as many as 4000 outlets selling everything from carpets, tiles and pots to mundane household items, food, antiques – you name it. Unlike shopping centres in the west there are no prices but instead pazarlik (haggling) is the norm, deals being done over long sessions fuelled by tea and mock horror at insulting offers. Visit here not hoping to snag a bargain, nor necessarily even to buy anything at all – a lack of self-induced pressure will mean you're more like to find something you like. You will certainly have a much better time.

283 GRAND MASTER FLASH

MALTA The interior of Valetta's St John's Co-Cathedral is sculpted in Baroque motifs in such florid detail that the walls seem ablaze, as though rippling. The floor is a screaming patchwork of tombstones, all uniquely rendered in dense inlaid marble; and the nave's ceiling holds exulted vignettes depicting the life of St John the Baptist. It took Mattia Preti five years to paint the vignettes, but after five minutes of looking up my neck began to ache with the strain. I walked around the Co-Cathedral, taking in its many features; then I walked a second and third time and spotted things I had missed in my previous rounds. There was nowhere my eyes could rest and pause.

The Knights of Malta didn't set out to create Christianity's most ornate building, yet their former convent church has become their defining legacy. The transformation from austere shrine to grand Baroque monument took place in the seventeenth century when Malta's military defences were complete, and the Knights – the cream of Europe's aristocrats – embraced the exuberant style that was sweeping Catholic Europe. They didn't hold back, and courted some of the best artists to work on their church, enticing Preti and, more famously, Caravaggio, whose *Beheading of St John the Baptist* is now considered one of the finest paintings of the seventeenth century.

More money was poured into the artistic makeover by regional groupings of Knights, called langues, and by individual Knights whose personal wealth matched their boundless vanity. Each side-chapel was assigned to a different langue – and each competed to out-perform the others in flamboyance. The design-scheme differs from one chapel to the next, but all have grand mausoleums that commemorate the Grand Masters elected from each langue. Busts of Grand Masters are mounted among objects that signify power and glory – lions, angels, lances, trumpets and so on – in an orgy of pompous and chivalrous self-aggrandizement that is so overwhelming that stepping outdoors into the bright Maltese light leaves you giddy and disoriented.

284 CHILLING OUT ON THE MONTENEGRIN COAST

MONTENEGRO "At the moment of the birth of our planet, the most beautiful meeting of land and sea was on the Montenegrin coast," gushed Lord Byron back in the nineteenth century. Since then, much has happened to this tiny and outrageously beautiful country, most importantly in 2006 when it became the last of the ex-Yugoslav republics to gain independence. Sprinkled along its short-but-sweet 300-kilometre-long coastline is a multiplicity of comely fishing villages, ancient stone walled towns and energetic beach resorts.

Should you be thirsting for a drop of culture, make a beeline for breathtaking Kotor, a UNESCO-protected, medieval-walled town huddled under the gaze of Mount Lovćen, Montenegro's holiest mountain, and framed by a series of spectacular inland fjords. For more razzle-dazzle, head to the lively resort of Budva, a short drive or ferry trip south. Its long, curving pebble

beach is packed with young sun-worshippers, while the many vine-covered restaurants stretched along the esplanade do a roaring trade serving up enormous plates of kačamak (white flour, potato and melted kajmak, a creamy cheese) and raštan (dried smoked ribs with cabbage). Later on, as the sun dips, bars and cafés dispense glasses of Vranac, the local red wine, and Loza, a fiery, throat-tingling grape brandy.

Sveti Stefan is the coast's most iconic site. Linked to the mainland by a taper-thin concrete causeway, this magnificent-walled island – complete with luxurious hotel – was once a popular retreat for Tito, who also entertained superstar celebrities such as Elizabeth Taylor and Richard Burton here. With its laid-back charm and lack of pretence, the Montenegrin coast is a cracking place to be right now, before the crowds return.

285 VISITING THE HOME OF PIZZA

ITALY A simple dish of bread dough spread with tomatoes and mozzarella cheese cooked in the hottest oven you can muster, pizza is probably the most widespread – and most misunderstood – fast food in the world. Given that they serve it just about everywhere, it's also the least exotic, and certainly one of the most variable. Some say that pizza is like sex: even when it's bad it's still pretty good. Truth is, it can be terrible. But in Italy, the home of pizza, it can be sublime.

Making something this elemental is a precise art, and it's all in the base – toppings are kept plain in Italy, especially in Naples, where pizza was invented. Here even cheese is sometimes considered a luxury. The base must be thrown around within an inch of its life by the pizza-maker or piazzaiolo, until it is light and airy, rolled thin, spread with its topping, and then thrown into a wood-fired brick oven until it just begins to burn and blister – a pizza that doesn't have at least a few traces of carbon just isn't worth eating.

Neapolitan pizzas, thin-based but typically with a thick, chewy crust, are unusually venerated; even northern Italians, who hate everything from the South, acknowledge that these are the best. Roman pizzas are no slouch either, always served crispy-thin, and, as in Naples, with the simplest of toppings – although specifically Roman ingredients like zucchini flowers may be added. Rome is also the home of pizza bianca – no topping really, just sprinkled with herbs and drizzled with oil – and fantastic by the slice (al taglio).

You can of course get versions of the above from your supermarket, or perhaps order up a pie from the nearest delivery spot and never leave the comfort of your own home. But without making the trip to Italy you won't know what it's like to eat the real thing – and there are so many great places to do it: some of the country's best pizzerias are the most basic, with limited menus and rough-and-ready service. One thing to remember: although you can of course get pizza any time, proper pizzerias only open in the evening. Expecting to have one for lunch will mark you out as a hopeless tourist!

286 STRIKING OIL IN EDIRNE

TURKEY If you enjoy watching grown men dressed in leather and doused in oil grappling with each other, the Kirkpinar oil wrestling championships, held just outside Edirne every July since 1924, are definitely for you. Competitors are smeared all over with a special variety of olive oil before each bout, and the object is to pin your opponent's shoulders to the ground or prise out a verbal submission. Over a thousand wrestlers take part in the tournament, and you can either watch the 45-minute bouts as they happen, or just enjoy the fairground atmosphere that prevails, with gypsy bands, dancing bears and lots and lots of kebabs.

287 SAMPLING THE GRILLED TROUT OF LAKE OHRID

MACEDONIA Lake Ohrid is the oldest and perhaps the deepest lake in Europe. Yet nobody knows about it, which is just as well as it is truly one of the most alluring corners of the Balkans. It's home also to its own species of trout, delicious served stuffed with herbs and charcoal grilled, as well as an eponymously named and extremely pretty lakeside town, where a number of orthodox churches point to Ohrid's status as a religious centre of some repute.

TOURING THE TUSCAN HILLTOWNS

288

ITALY The ancient hilltown, with its crumbling houses and belltowers rising above a landscape of vineyards and olive groves, is one of the quintessential images of Italy, and nowhere in the country provides more photogenic examples than the area around Siena.

The Chianti region, immediately to the north of Siena, has numerous pretty little hilltowns, with Castellina in Chianti making the obvious target for a half-day trip. Equally close is Colle di Val d'Elsa – the industrial zone of the lower town mars the view a little, but the upper town is a real gem. The most famous of all the Sienese satellites, however, is San Gimignano, whose tower-filled skyline is one of Europe's great medieval urban landscapes. On the downside, in high season the narrow lanes of San Gimignano get as busy as London's Oxford Street, so if you're touring in summer and don't relish the crowds, head instead to windswept Volterra, a dramatically situated place whose Etruscan origins are never far from the surface. Like Pitigliano, in the far south of Tuscany, Volterra is more a clifftop settlement than a hilltown – walk just a few minutes from the cathedral and you'll come upon the Balze, a sheer wall of rock down which a fair chunk of Volterra has tumbled over the centuries.

Some 40km south of Siena lies Montalcino, as handsome a hilltown as you could hope to find; famed for the mighty red wines produced in the surrounding vineyards, it's also very close to the ancient abbey of Sant'Antimo, one of Tuscany's most beautiful churches. From Montalcino you could loop to the even more handsome Montelpulciano, which is ranged along a narrow ridge and strewn with Renaissance palaces – and is the home of another renowned wine, the Vino Nobile di Montepulciano. East of here, on the other side of the river plain known as the Valdichiana, lofty Cortona is reached by a five-kilometre road that winds up from the valley floor through terraces of vines and olives. Clinging so closely to the slopes that there's barely a horizontal street in the centre, Cortona commands a gorgeous panorama; climb to the summit of the town at night and you'll see the villages of southern Tuscany twinkling like ships' lights on a dark sea.

MISCELLANY

TOP TEN TUCK-INS

Gorgonzola One of the great Italian cheeses, hailing from Lombardy, blue-veined and either creamy (dolce) or sharp (piccante).

Lahmacun Street vendors in Turkey hawk these delicious small "pizzas" with meat-based toppings.

Mezes An extensive array of cold appetizers in all shapes and sizes, the most common being dolma (peppers or vine leaves stuffed with rice), patlican salata (aubergine in tomato sauce), and acili (a mixture of tomato paste, onion, chilli and parsley), which, along with sebze turlu (vegetable stew), and nohut (chickpeas), are the few dishes available for vegetarians.

Pesto alla Genovese The Ligurian pasta sauce, made from basil, olive oil, garlic, parmesan and pine nuts.

Porchetta Basically roast pork, with lots of stuffing and crackling, and sold from open-air stalls in Umbria, Tuscany and Lazio.

Prosciutto di San Daniele The greatest of the great cured hams from Parma and around.

Tiramisù Treviso's scrumptious coffee dessert.

Truffles Italy produces twenty percent of all black truffles, a delicacy of Umbria, and virtually all white truffles (from Piedmont).

Turkish delight Solidified sugar and pectin, flavoured with rosewater or pistachios, and sprinkled with powdered sugar.

Tyrópites and spanakópites Cheese and spinach pies respectively, on sale everywhere in Greece.

Flower power The Turkish drink of salep is derived from the tubers of various orchid varieties; its popularity has led to the decline of Turkey's wild orchid population, and exporting salep is now illegal.

ITALIAN FOOTBALL

English workers brought football to Italy in the 1890s, with James Richardson Spensley establishing Genoa in 1896, and Alfred Edwards AC Milan three years later; both clubs still incorporate the cross of St George in their team badges. Italy's national team (known as the "Azzurri" for their dark blue shirts) went on to win the World Cup four times (1934, 1938, 1982 and 2006). Italy's clubs have won 27 major European trophies, more than any other nation. Their Serie A is one of the best leagues in the world, despite being rocked by a match-fixing scandal in 2006. The league is traditionally dominated by AC Milan and Internazionale (also from Milan), and Juventus from Turin (historically Italy's most successful team), although the two principal Rome teams, Roma and Lazio, are also among the biggies these days.

AT THE MOVIES

Bicycle Thieves (1948) This neo-realist Italian classic is many people's favourite film of all time.

La Dolce Vita (1960) Federico Fellini's most celebrated film, satirizing the vacuity of the Sixties era in Rome.

Z (1969) Banned in Greece during the dictatorship, this tense political thriller about the assassination of a left-wing politician won an Oscar for Best Foreign Language Film.

Death in Venice (1971) Luchino Visconti's film of the Thomas Mann book goes for the jugular in this Mahler-drenched emotional epic.

Room with a View (1984) Merchant & Ivory classic of E M Forster's novel, half set in early twentieth-century Florence.

Time of the Gypsies (1989) Ethereal, compassionate and witty film about this most marginalized of races by Bosnian director Emir Kusturica, featuring a sublime soundtrack.

Hamam (1996). A lyrical feature about a man who escapes a troubled marriage to run a Turkish bath in Istanbul.

The Talented Mr Ripley (1999). A disturbing tale of deception, obsession and murder, set in Venice, Rome and along the coast near Naples.

No Man's Land (2001). Deeply affecting and darkly comic Oscar-winning movie about a Bosnian and a Serb trapped together in a trench.

INVENTIONS

No invention has had a greater impact on man's ability to conquer distance than the wheel, which came into use in Mesopotamia during the Neolithic Age. Galileo Galilei (1564–1642) was born in Pisa and is regarded as the father of modern astronomy and science, making major breakthroughs in scientific method and theory, improving the telescope and discovering several of Jupiter's moons.

BEST HOTELS

Ajia Hotel, Istanbul, Turkey A Bosphorus palace with an elegant modern interior.

Bauer il Palazzo, Venice, Italy This boutique hotel in Venice enjoys an unbeatable location in a grand palazzo on the Grand Canal.

Grand Hotel a Villa Feltrinelli, Gargnano, Italy A sumptuous palace dating from 1892 and beautifully restored, right on the shore of Lake Garda.

Hotel de Russie, Rome, Italy This could just be the capital's best-located and most luxurious hotel, with a fantastic courtyard garden in which to sip cocktails, and a gorgeous terraced garden full of butterflies.

Marmara Bodrum, Bodrum, Turkey A dazzling retreat with all the luxuries you could ask for, including, of course, a Turkish bath.

Melenos Lindos Hotel, Rhodes, Greece A boutique hotel featuring impressive antiques and beautiful gardens.

Punta Tragara, Capri, Italy Where better to stay on Capri, high above the Faraglioni rocks, and with a stunning poolside restaurant.

Sea Captain's House, Santorini, Greece. Set on pumice cliffs overlooking the Aegean, this soothing whitewashed paradise offers all modern luxuries.

Riva Hotel, Hvar, Croatia. A lovely and luxurious harbourside hotel located on a stunning Adriatic island.

Villa San Michele, Fiesole, Italy. Set in a fifteenth-century monastery, this small luxury hotel just outside Florence is pure class.

HISTORY

Ancient Greece was the crucible for much of what endures in European politics, social institutions and culture. The glories of its Classical civilization came to an end with the Peloponnesian War in the fifth century BC between Athens and Sparta.

According to legend, Rome was founded by **Romulus and Remus** in 753 BC. At its peak, the Roman Empire covered much of Europe, North Africa and the Middle East, and its eastern offshoot, the Byzantine Empire, endured until 1453.

The Romans inspired many imitators: The Holy Roman Empire was founded when **Charlemagne** was crowned by Pope Leo III in Rome in 800, and only dissolved in 1806; the titles Kaiser (Germany) and Tsar (Russia) stem from "**Caesar**".

Benito Mussolini (1883–1945) ruled Italy 1922–1945, the world's first fascist dictator. The word fascio was first used in the 1870s in Italy, giving way to "**fascism**" in the 1920s.

Malta was granted independence from Britain in 1964, becoming a republic in 1974.

The bloody **Balkan Conflict** raged between 1991 and 2001, affecting the **six former Yugoslav republics**. The region was ripped apart by ethnic and religious conflict, in the main between Serbs and Croats. The UN's International Criminal Tribunal was set up to bring charges of genocide against the participants.

> *"The Balkans produce more history than they can consume"*
>
> **Winston Churchill**

GREAT FESTIVALS

- **Anastenariá,** Serres and Thessaloníki, Greece. May.
- **Apokriatiká,** Patras, Greece. February.
- **Corsa dei Ceri,** Gubbio, Italy. May.
- **Dubrovnik Summer Festival,** Dubrovnik, Croatia. July & August.
- **Exit Festival,** Serbia and Montenegro. July
- **Festa del Redentore,** Venice, Italy. July.
- **Il Palio,** Siena, Italy. July & September.
- **Oil wrestling festival,** Kırkpınar, Turkey. End of June.
- **Venice Carnival,** Venice, Italy. February/March.

ATLANTIS

The Atlantis myth is one of the most famous of all "lost world" legends, an island state first mentioned by **Plato**. According to him Atlantis lay "beyond the pillars of Hercules", and eventually sank into the ocean around 9000 years before his birth. Speculation on its location has focused on numerous places, including **Crete, Sardinia** and **Santorini** in the Mediterranean.

A GOOD READ

The Betrothed Alessandro Manzoni The great Italian nineteenth-century novel.

Divine Comedy Dante Aligheri A journey through Heaven and Hell – the greatest literary work of medieval Europe.

Epic poems. The most famous epic poems of antiquity are Homer's *Odyssey*, relating the ten-year journey of Odysseus back to his native Ithaca and his wife Penelope after the fall of Troy, and Virgil's *Aeneid*, following Aeneas in his wanderings from Troy to the shores of Italy. A hallmark of both works is the tenaciousness of their main protagonists, who overcome all obstacles – from the wrath of the gods to attacks by terrifying beasts such as the Cyclops – to achieve their goals.

My Name is Red Orhan Pamuk An exotic murder mystery located in sixteenth-century Istanbul.

Name of the Rose Umberto Eco This tightly plotted monastic detective story was one of the great Italian literary successes of the modern era.

ICONIC BUILDINGS

- **Aya Sofya** Istanbul, Turkey A stunning sixth-century cathedral which provides a fascinating glimpse into the city's Byzantine past.
- **The Pantheon** Rome, Italy The most complete ancient Roman structure in the city, with an imposing poured-concrete dome.
- **The Parthenon** Athens, Greece One of the archetypal images of Western culture.

> *"The marbles were born and created in Athens and belong to the Parthenon"*
>
> **Nana Mouskouri**

DO ITALIANS DO IT BETTER?

Giacomo Casanova (1725–1798), a Venetian, claimed in his autobiography to have slept with 122 women, and Italians are often stereotyped as the world's greatest lovers. However, the Durex Sex Survey (2005) placed Italy **twentieth** in terms of frequency of sex (106 times per year compared to the winner, **Greece**, at 138 times).

STAYING WITH A REAL-LIFE TRANSYLVANIAN COUNT • BURROWING FOR BARGAINS IN KRAKÓW • TRIAL BY TROLLEYBUS: SIMFEROPOL TO YALTA • **ON THE DRACULA TRAIL IN TRANSYLVANIA** • TAKING A TRIP ON THE MOSCOW METRO • SOVIET EXHIBITIONISM IN MOSCOW • BEAVERING AWAY IN LAHEMAA NATIONAL PARK • DISCOVERING JEWISH VILNIUS • HIGH ON A HILL WITH A LONELY GOATHERD • A GOLDEN MOULDIE: DRINKING TOKAJ IN ANCIENT CELLARS • THE TALE AND THE TONGUE OF ST JOHN OF NEPOMUK • HIKING IN THE TATRAS • ST PETERSBURG'S WILD WHITE NIGHTS • **ECCENTRIC ARCHITECTURE: WANDERING THE STREETS OF RĪGA** • MILLS AND MALLS: ON THE INDUSTRIAL HERITAGE TRAIL IN ŁÓDŹ • COUNTING COLOURS IN KIEV • TRACKING CARNIVORES IN THE CARPATHIAN MOUNTAINS • NIGHT-CLUBBING BACK IN THE (OLD) USSR • HORRORS OF THE HOLOCAUST: VISITING AUSCHWITZ • SPENDING A NIGHT IN EUROPE'S TWILIGHT ZONE • VULTURE-WATCHING IN THE MADZHAROVO NATURE RESERVE • **WOODEN CHURCHES: "MASS" TOURISM WITH A TWIST** • SOOTHE YOUR TROUBLES AT THE HOTEL GELLERT • MOUNT ELBRUS: CLIMBING EUROPE'S MIGHTIEST PEAK • DRINKING PILSENER FROM ITS HOME-TOWN TAPS • PONDERING ARMAGEDDON AT THE PLOKŠTINE MISSILE BASE • **TAKING A TRIP ON THE MOSCOW METRO** • A MINDBLOWING MUSEUM: ST PETERSBURG'S HERMITAGE • SUPPING A REAL BUD IN ČESKÉ BUDĚJOVICE • STANDING AT THE HEART OF MOTHER RUSSIA • STAYING WITH A REAL-LIFE TRANSYLVANIAN COUNT • BURROWING FOR BARGAINS IN KRAKÓW • TRIAL BY TROLLEYBUS: SIMFEROPOL TO YALTA • ON THE DRACULA TRAIL IN TRANSYLVANIA • SOVIET EXHIBITIONISM IN MOSCOW • BEAVERING AWAY IN LAHEMAA NATIONAL PARK • DISCOVERING JEWISH VILNIUS • HIGH ON A HILL WITH A LONELY GOATHERD • A GOLDEN MOULDIE: DRINKING TOKAJ IN ANCIENT CELLARS • THE TALE AND THE TONGUE OF ST JOHN OF NEPOMUK • **HIKING IN THE TATRAS** • ECCENTRIC ARCHITECTURE: WANDERING THE STREETS OF RĪGA • ST PETERSBURG'S WILD WHITE NIGHTS • MILLS AND MALLS: ON THE INDUSTRIAL HERITAGE TRAIL IN ŁÓDŹ • TRACKING CARNIVORES IN THE CARPATHIAN MOUNTAINS • **COUNTING COLOURS IN KIEV** • NIGHT-CLUBBING BACK IN THE (OLD) USSR • HORRORS OF THE HOLOCAUST: VISITING AUSCHWITZ • SPENDING A NIGHT IN EUROPE'S TWILIGHT ZONE • VULTURE-WATCHING IN THE MADZHAROVO NATURE RESERVE • **SOOTHE YOUR TROUBLES AT THE HOTEL GELLERT** • WOODEN CHURCHES: "MASS" TOURISM WITH A TWIST • MOUNT ELBRUS: CLIMBING EUROPE'S MIGHTIEST PEAK • DRINKING PILSENER FROM ITS HOME-TOWN TAPS • PONDERING ARMAGEDDON AT THE PLOKŠTINE MISSILE BASE • A MINDBLOWING MUSEUM: ST PETERSBURG'S HERMITAGE • **SUPPING A REAL BUD IN ČESKÉ BUDĚJOVICE** • STANDING AT THE HEART OF MOTHER RUSSIA • STAYING WITH A REAL-LIFE TRANSYLVANIAN COUNT • BURROWING FOR BARGAINS IN KRAKÓW • TRIAL BY TROLLEYBUS: SIMFEROPOL TO YALTA • ON THE DRACULA TRAIL IN TRANSYLVANIA • TAKING A TRIP ON THE MOSCOW METRO • SOVIET EXHIBITIONISM IN MOSCOW • DISCOVERING JEWISH VILNIUS • **BEAVERING AWAY IN LAHEMAA NATIONAL PARK** • HIGH ON A HILL WITH A LONELY GOATHERD • A GOLDEN MOULDIE: DRINKING TOKAJ IN ANCIENT CELLARS • THE TALE AND THE TONGUE OF ST JOHN OF NEPOMUK • HIKING IN THE TATRAS • ECCENTRIC ARCHITECTURE: WANDERING THE STREETS OF RĪGA • ST PETERSBURG'S WILD WHITE NIGHTS • MILLS AND MALLS: ON THE INDUSTRIAL HERITAGE TRAIL IN ŁÓDŹ • COUNTING COLOURS IN KIEV • TRACKING CARNIVORES IN THE CARPATHIAN MOUNTAINS • NIGHT-CLUBBING BACK IN THE (OLD) USSR • HORRORS OF THE HOLOCAUST: VISITING AUSCHWITZ • SPENDING A NIGHT IN EUROPE'S TWILIGHT ZONE • **VULTURE-WATCHING IN THE MADZHAROVO NATURE RESERVE** • SOOTHE YOUR TROUBLES AT THE HOTEL GELLERT • WOODEN CHURCHES: "MASS" TOURISM WITH A TWIST

EASTERN EUROPE

289–319

BEAVERING AWAY IN
LAHEMAA NATIONAL PARK — 315

ESTONIA

RUSSIA

LATVIA

ECCENTRIC ARCHITECTURE:
WANDERING THE STREETS OF RIGA — 297

TAKING A TRIP
ON THE MOSCOW METRO — 313

LITHUANIA

RUSSIA

POLAND

BELARUS

HIKING IN
THE TATRAS

UKRAINE

COUNTING COLOURS
300 — IN KIEV

CZECH REP.
307

SUPPING A REAL BUD
IN ČESKÉ BUDĚJOVICE

304

WOODEN CHURCHES:
"MASS" TOURISM WITH A TWIST

SLOVAKIA 290

SOOTHE YOUR TROUBLES
AT THE HOTEL GELLERT — 289

HUNGARY

MOLDOVA

ON THE DRACULA TRAIL
IN TRANSYLVANIA — 296

ROMANIA

BULGARIA

VULTURE-WATCHING
319 — IN THE MADZHAROVO NATURE RESERVE

SOOTHE YOUR TROUBLES AT THE

HOTEL GELLERT

HUNGARY You might be impressed by the stately location of the *Hotel Gellert*, just over the "Liberty Bridge" on the western bank of the Danube, anchoring the old section of Buda. You might enjoy this picturesque scene especially after dark (and you'll certainly feel compelled to take pictures) on your way back across the bridge from a night out in Pest: the entire, rambling building, frontlit, glows like some giant Art Nouveau birthday cake at the base of craggy Gellert-hegy cliff. You might be awed by the grand staircases leading from the lobby; charmed by the cosy, hideaway bar and its array of Hungarian liquors; spun around by the long corridors and various turns getting to and from your room (especially after a drink or two of Unicum at the aforementioned bar); satisfied by the size of the room – better still if it comes with a view of the river in front or hills behind. But none of this is by itself necessarily a reason to stay. There's a greater motivation for that.

Wake up early to find out, and pull on the robe that hangs in the closet. Go to the excruciatingly slow, caged elevator on your floor. Tip the lift operator as you reach the bottom, exit and pick your way through the milling crowd to see what they're all waiting for. Don't be embarrassed about your state of relative undress – soon you'll all be in the same boat. Then – behold the glory of the Gellert baths.

The grandeur of the vaulted entry hall, its tiling, statuary and skylit ceiling, is a worthy precursor to the pools themselves. First, the segregated areas: a dip in the 34°C waters, while admiring the magnificent mosaics and ornamental spouts; a sit-down in the aromatic sauna; a bracing splash in a tiny, freezing cold bath; a plunge into another pool, this one 38° . . . Repeat the ritual again, then finish with some invigorating laps in the colonnaded central pool, the one place where the sexes intermingle. Consider doing the backstroke to enjoy best the light streaming through the retractable stained-glass roof above. And think about extending your stay another day or two.

290 WOODEN CHURCHES: "MASS" TOURISM WITH A TWIST

SLOVAKIA You have to see the task of finding the all-important kľúč (key) as part of the experience when visiting the wooden churches of Slovakia's Carpathian foothills. Sure enough, there's nearly always a little sign (in Slovak) pinned to the wooden door, telling you which house harbours it, but finding the right one in a village without street names and only (often fairly random) house numbers, is a feat in itself. It's a sure way to get to meet the local head-scarved babičky (grannies), but don't expect to get to see too many churches in one day.

The churches look like something straight out of an East European fairy tale, or a Chagall painting: perched on slight hillocks by the edge of the woods, looking down on their villages, their dark-brown shingled exterior sprouting a trio of onion domes. Most were built in the eighteenth century when the influence of Baroque was making itself felt even among the carpenter architects of the Carpathians. Once inside, you can't help but be struck by the musty murkiness of the dark wooden interiors. At one end a vast and vibrantly decorated iconostasis reaches from the floor to the ceiling, its niches filled with saints. Elsewhere, a local folk artist allows his imagination to go wild in a gory depiction of the *Last Judgement*, with the damned being burned, boiled and decapitated with macabre abandon.

Despite the fact that the churches are more often than not locked, they're still very much in use, mostly (but not exclusively) by the Greek Catholic church, a unique strand of Roman Catholicism. Should you happen upon one when there's a service, note that Mass is celebrated in Old Slavonic.

291 DRINKING PILSNER FROM ITS HOME-TOWN TAPS

CZECH REPUBLIC On initial scrutiny, the town of Plzeň has little to commend it – save for the country's tallest steeple atop St Bartholomew's Church (338 steps, if you're climbing). Yet, to beer cognoscenti, it's a place of pilgrimage. The clue is in the name, for this is the birthplace of Pilsner – the fine, golden liquid that English speakers call "lager".

In 1842, all beer was dark, but then somebody invented beer glasses and from the breweries of Plzeň emerged a golden beer, created by Bavarian Josef Groll and known today as Pilsner Urquell (German for "Pilsner from the Original Source"), or Plzeňsky Prazdroj in Czech. It took the world by storm, and lager is now the most popular style of beer on the planet.

Prague may be an architectural gem and Český Krumlov might be the most stunning medieval town in Eastern Europe, but the true beauty of the Czech Republic is that it still produces "real" draught lager, an increasingly rare beer. Those who know only the bland fizz that passes for lager in Britain or the US should prepare themselves for one almighty taste shock. The bubbles in a fresh pint of Czech beer is the natural product of fermentation, not some falsely manufactured CO_2 that's pumped into the beer as it emerges from the tap – which is what you get elsewhere. If you're still not outraged, consider this. How would you feel if you were offered a glass of stale house white with gas squirted into it and told it was champagne? Exactly.

Naturally, there are many places to sample Urquell in its hometown, but you should start off at *Na Spilce*. It's the largest beer hall in the country, and is in the brewery yard itself, so you'll be right on hand to pay homage. Standing at the arched gates that commemorate Urquell's fiftieth birthday in 1892, you can almost hear the springs gurgling beneath the brewery. It's allegedly the softness of this water that provides Urquell's distinctive taste, along with its own malted Moravian barley, Žatec hops, and a house yeast that is – understandably – a very well-kept secret.

292 PONDERING ARMAGEDDON AT THE PLOKŠTINE MISSILE BASE

LITHUANIA It's not often you're invited to join a guided tour of a nuclear missile base, especially when you're in the middle of one of northeastern Europe's most idyllic areas of unspoiled wilderness. However, this is exactly what's on offer at the friendly tourist information centre at Plateliai, the rustic, timber-built village in the centre of western Lithuania's Zemaitija National Park.

Long popular with a happy-go-lucky bunch of Lithuanian hostellers, campers and canoeists, the park is famous for its emblematic Baltic landscape. Calm grey lakes are fringed by squelchy bogs, forests of silver birch, and intricately carved wooden crosses which sprout from farmhouse gardens like totem poles. It's perversely appropriate that Soviet military planners chose this tranquil spot as the perfect place to hide a rocket base. Located at the end of a harmless-looking gravel track, the Plokštine base is virtually invisible at ground level, its low-lying grey-green domes blending sympathetically with the local landscape of stubby coniferous shrubs. There's no front door: an innocuous-looking metal panel opens to reveal a staircase, descending into an abandoned world of concrete-floored, metal-doored rooms, linked by passageways which bring to mind the galleries of an underground cave system.

Built in 1962, the installation at Plokštine was one of the first such sites in the then Soviet Union, housing four nuclear missiles capable of hitting targets throughout Western and southern Europe. Closed down in 1978 and left to rot, it's now eerily empty of any signs, panels or technical equipment that would indicate its previous purpose.

Until, that is, you come to one of the silos themselves – a vast, metal-lined cylindrical pit deep enough to accommodate twenty-two metres of slender, warhead-tipped rocket. The missile itself was evacuated long ago, but peering into the abyss from the maintenance gallery can still be a heart-stopping experience. Especially when you consider that similar silos, from North America to North Korea, are still very much in working order.

293 SOVIET EXHIBITIONISM IN MOSCOW

RUSSIA For a taste of all the Soviet Union once promised and an illustration of what it has come to, there's nowhere better than the all-Russian Exhibition centre, known by its acronym VDNKh. This enormous park in northeast Moscow is a glorious illustration of Soviet hubris, an exuberant cultural mix 'n' match vision of a world where sixteen republics join hand in socialist hand to present a cornucopia of human achievement, ranging from agricultural tools and farm animals to atomic energy.

Opened in 1939 as the All-Union Agricultural Exhibition, the grounds were extended in the 1950s to include culture, science and technology, and continued to expand till 1989. Nevertheless, the overall atmosphere is of prewar optimism, when all progress was good and man was master of the world, living in a kind of mechanized agricultural paradise where even the streetlights were shaped like ears of corn.

Set around the gaudy gold fountain of the Friendship of Nations, pavilions for the former Soviet socialist republics and areas of economic achievement make a gesture towards national building styles while remaining unmistakably Stalinist. Particularly striking are the Ukraine Pavilion, a sparkling mosaic and majolica jewelbox; the Uzbekistan Pavilion, patterned with interlocking geometric designs; and the stylish, Art-Deco-influenced Grain Pavilion. Beyond, a copy of the rocket which took Yuri Gagarin into space points skywards in front of the Aerospace Pavilion. Built in 1966, the pavilion's railway-station-like hangar and glass dome are still breathtaking in their vastness.

It's a little disappointing to find the working models of hydroelectric power stations and the herds of prize cattle long gone, and even the famous Soviet worker and collective farm girl monument vanished recently amid rumours that it's been melted down for scrap metal. But the casual traders and cheap beer stands that now fill VDNKh lend the place a certain raffish charm. Perhaps it's fitting that the monumental worker and farm girl have been replaced by a succinct image of today's Russia: rows of salesmen from the Caucasus selling everything from Belarusian bras to cheap Chinese trainers under the Aerospace Pavilion's thousand unlit light bulbs.

294 BURROWING FOR BARGAINS IN KRAKÓW

POLAND One of the hazards of hitting Kraków on a Saturday night is that you usually have to spend the next day in bed recovering from the experience. If you're a fan of Sunday-morning flea markets, however, then this is one place where it's well worth dragging yourself out from under the duvet.

Prime target for the city's jumble junkies is Hala Targowa, a semi-covered fruit-and-veg market which is taken over one day a week by stall after stall of old furniture, domestic knick-knacks, objets d'art and – just occasionally – the odd genuine antique. Obsessive collectors can sort through everything from old postcards to used phonecards, or try their luck with the militaria man who carefully lays out his collection on a trestle table and then barks, "That's not for sale!" whenever anyone takes an interest.

Bargain hunters also abound at the city's other favourite Sunday-morning hangout, the second-hand clothes market on Plac Nowy in the bohemian suburb of Kazimierz. It's a great place to browse, meet friends and tuck into the fat grilled sausages that are permanently on the menu at Poland's markets.

Kraków has a huge student population, always on the lookout for all sorts of bargains. The narrow streets of the city's historic centre are crammed with second-hand bookshops, and not everything they sell is in Polish – Kraków's burgeoning expat population ensures that there's a lot of English-language tomes changing hands as well.

One bookshop that has become a cult location in recent years is Massolit, housed in a rambling, creaky-floored apartment whose floor-to-ceiling shelves are stuffed with books in English on every aspect of central and eastern European history and culture. Named after the chaotic writers' union described in Russian writer Mikhail Bulgakov's novel *The Master and Margarita*, Massolit also serves Kraków's most delicious home-baked cakes. For anyone weary after a day's bargain hunting, Massolit offers the ideal escape.

295 TRIAL BY TROLLEYBUS: SIMFEROPOL TO YALTA

UKRAINE Bounce, bounce. Squeak, squeak. I've got an elbow in my ear, an unknown child on my lap and the cardboard box wedged under my seat, taking up all my legroom, is making strange cheeping noises. Of course there are easier ways of getting to the seaside. On the other hand, the Simferopol–Yalta trolleybus route in Crimea, at 86km and 742m – over the Angarskiy pass – is the world's longest and highest trolleybus line, so this journey is an event in itself. I wonder if the rest of the jam-packed passengers, clinging on for dear life round hair-raising bends, are also consoling themselves with that fact.

The line was completed in 1961 to ferry Soviet holidaymakers from the rail terminal at Simferopol to the Black Sea coast. I'm lucky enough to ride in a pleasingly rotund Skoda 9Tr, one of the original trolleybus fleet. There are bizarre, yet characterful moments when the trolleybus poles become detached from the overhead electric wires and the driver has to get out and haul them back into place using ropes, a process not unlike a kind of upside-down fishing.

We squeak and bounce through vine-covered villages and slow up for the long climb to the Angarskiy pass, where the silvery Crimean mountains open out on either side. Then there's the exhilarating cruise down, down, down – enough to make your ears pop – to the coast. After more than two hours of extreme discomfort in the close proximity of bossy fat grandmothers, wriggling children, and men who clearly breakfasted on vodka and garlic, the final appearance of the satiny blue Black Sea is nothing short of miraculous. Salty breezes blow in through the windows, and I find I'm almost sorry to reach Yalta. I give up the child – to whom I've become rather attached – and can't resist asking the owner of the squeaking box under my seat what on earth is in there. It's full of cheeping fluffy yellow chicks. I'm still wondering why he was taking them to the seaside.

ROMANIA Few figures capture the imagination as dramatically as Dracula, the bloodthirsty vampire count from deepest, darkest Transylvania – at least that's how Bram Stoker portrayed the mythical version in his 1897 novel. The real Dracula was in fact the fifteenth-century Wallachian prince Vlad Ţepeş, better known as Vlad the Impaler. Although he was never accused of vampirism, his methods of execution – spread-eagled victims were bound and a stake hammered up their rectum, then raised aloft and left to die in agony – earned him a certain notoriety, especially amongst his long-time adversaries, the anti-crusading Turks, who pathologically feared him.

Inevitably, the legend of Dracula is touted for all it's worth, but finding anything meaningful associated with Vlad is tricky. Aside from his birthplace in the delightful town of Sighişoara – now a high-class if kitschy restaurant – the most played-up Dracula connection is in the small southern Transylvanian town of Bran. Looking every inch like a vampire count's residence, the splendidly sited Bran Castle is hyped as Dracula's haunt and encompassed by an army of souvenir stalls flogging vampire tack. The more mundane reality, however, is that Vlad may have laid siege to it once.

Dracula's real castle lies in the foothills of the stunning Făgăraş mountains in northern Wallachia. Located just north of the village of Arefu, a steep hillside path – an exacting climb up 1400 steps – brings you to Poienari Castle, one of Vlad's key fortresses and where, allegedly, his wife flung herself out of a window, exclaiming that she "would rather have her body rot and be eaten by the fish of the Argeş" than be captured by the Turks. Aside from some reasonably intact towers, this surprisingly small citadel is now little more than a jumble of ruins. However, its dramatic setting ensures an authentically spooky atmosphere, no doubt the sort that Bram Stoker had in mind when penning his masterpiece about the ultimate horror icon.

ECCENTRIC ARCHITECTURE: WANDERING THE STREETS OF RĪGA

LATVIA Walking along Alberta iela in Rīga is a bit like visiting an abandoned film studio where a biblical epic, a gothic gore-fest and a children's fairy tale were being filmed at the same time. Imperious stone sphinxes stand guard outside no. 2, while malevolent gape-mouthed satyrs gaze down from the facade across the street. Further down at no. 11, a grey apartment block with steep-pitched roofs and asymmetrical windows looks like an oversized farmhouse squatted by a community of Transylvanian counts.

Alberta iela is the most spectacular street in a city that is famous for its eccentric buildings – products of a pre-World War I construction boom that saw architects indulge in all manner of decorative obsessions. Many of the structures dating from this period are described in the guidebooks as Art Nouveau, although the sheer range of eye-catching embellishments suggests a much wider palette of influences. Most influential of the local architects was Mikhail Eisenstein, father of Soviet film director Sergei. Responsible for the sphinx-house at Alberta iela 2, Eisenstein filled his designs with Egyptian- Greek- and Roman-inspired details, producing buildings that looked like extravagantly iced cakes adorning the party-table of a deranged emperor. The most famous of his creations is just around the corner from Alberta iela at Elizabetes 10, a purple and cream confection with a scarily huge pair of female heads staring impassively from the pediment.

An imprint of equal substance was left on the city by Latvian architect Eižens Laube, who brought the folk architecture of the Baltic country cottage into the heart of the city. The apartment block at Alberta iela 11 is very much his trademark, employing shingled roofs and soaring, pointy gables to produce a disconcerting half-breed borne of gingerbread house and Gotham City. Something of an architectural equivalent to the Brothers Grimm, Laube's creations add a compellingly moody character to the bustling boulevards of Rīga's main shopping and business districts.

Rīga's Art Nouveau-period apartment blocks seem all the more incongruous when you consider that they were built to house the stolid middle-class citizens of a down-to-earth mercantile city. Judging by the sheer number of stuccoed sprites, mythical animals and come-hither mermaids staring out from the city's facades, psychoanalysts would have had a field day analyzing the architectural tastes of Rīga's pre-World War I bourgeoisie.

298 ST PETERSBURG'S WILD WHITE NIGHTS

RUSSIA Imagine spending all day sightseeing, taking a shower and a nap, and then looking out of the window to see the sky as bright as midday. Your body kicks into overdrive, and the whole day seems to lie ahead of you. The streets throng with people toting guitars and bottles of champagne or vodka; naval cadets and their girlfriends walking arm in arm, and pensioners performing impromptu tea-dances on the riverbank. The smell of black tobacco mingles with the perfume of lilac in parks full of sunbathers. It's eight o'clock in the evening, and St Petersburg is gearing up for another of its wild White Nights.

Freezing cold and dark three months of the year, St Petersburg enjoys six weeks of sweltering heat when the sun barely dips below the horizon – its famous White Nights or Byele Nochy. Children are banished to dachas in the countryside with grandparents, leaving parents free to enjoy themselves. Life becomes a sequence of tsusovki (gatherings), as people encounter long-lost friends strolling on Nevsky prospekt or feasting in the Summer Garden at midnight.

To avoid disrupting the daytime flow of traffic, the city's bridges are raised from 2am onwards to allow a stream of ships to sail upriver into Russia's vast interior. Although normally not a spectacle, during White Nights everyone converges on the River Neva embankments to watch, while bottles are passed from person to person, and strangers join impromptu singsongs around anyone with a guitar or harmonium – chorusing folk ballads or "thieves' songs" from the Gulag. Those with money often hire a boat to cruise the canals that wend through the heart of the city.

The bridges are briefly lowered during the middle of the night, allowing queues of traffic fifteen minutes to race across. Keeping in lane is entirely ignored, with drivers jockeying for position as if it was a chariot race. By this time, people are stripping off and jumping into the Neva – those too prodigiously drunk to realize go swimming fully clothed.

299 MILLS AND MALLS: ON THE INDUSTRIAL HERITAGE TRAIL OF ŁÓDZ

POLAND I'd never seen an Art Nouveau power station until I went to Łódź. I found it while strolling through the south-central district of Księży Młyn, an enormous complex of red-brick mill buildings and workers' tenements built by Karl Scheibler, a nineteenth-century textile magnate of megalomaniacal ambition. Seduced by the seemingly derelict building's sensuously curvy facade, I advanced through a half-open door to be greeted by an enthusiastic group of trainee rock-climbers dangling on ropes from the wall of the main turbine hall. Below them, antiquated generators and instrument panels stood on parade like exhibits in an art gallery. It was a suitably bizarre introduction to the most unexpectedly absorbing of Polish cities.

If Florence is a must-visit for anyone keen to get to grips with the Renaissance, then Łódź should be an essential stop-off for those interested in the Industrial Revolution. Once dubbed the "Polish Manchester" on account of its thriving textile industry, the city still throngs with soaring chimneys and fortress-like mill buildings of extraordinary, temple-like beauty. Many of the mills went bankrupt after the collapse of communism in 1989, and economically depressed Łódź became as unfashionable as it is unpronounceable

("Woodge", by the way, is how you actually say it).

Like the original Manchester, however, Łódź is in the throes of reinventing itself as a Mecca for modish lifestyles rather than manufacturing might. Central to the city's rebranding is the Manufaktura, a revitalization project of gargantuan proportions which has taken a post-industrial graveyard of abandoned warehouses on the fringes of the centre, and stuffed it with shopping malls, cinemas and coffee bars. Running along the southern flanks of the Manufaktura complex is the erstwhile Poznański Factory, whose castellated facade stands in eloquent testimony to the self-aggrandizing tastes of nineteenth-century Łódź's mercantile elite. Textile pharaoh Izrael Poznański lived next door to his factory in the Poznański Palace (now the town museum), whose rooms are opulently decorated with flamboyant woodcarving, stuccoed nymphs and stained glass. Rumour has it that Poznański didn't quite understand what his architect meant by terms such as Neo-classical, Neo-renaissance and Neo-baroque, and so enthusiastically ordered all three. With a shopping list such as this, Łódź's new mall-cruising culture couldn't have wished for a more appropriate forefather.

300 COUNTING COLOURS IN KIEV

UKRAINE In the shade of a hundred chestnut trees, we wander through the cobbled streets of Kiev's old quarter. We pass Soviet statues, golden domed churches and ageing apartment blocks painted in cornflower-blue and dandelion. It's said that you can walk from one side of the Ukrainian capital to the other without once stepping out of the dappled shadows of the trees. Following the trail of the chestnut flowers is better than any guidebook; the pyramids of tiny blooms – in white and pink – are prettier than any map.

As we near Independence Square, white and pink give way to thoughts of orange. On a spring day much like today, hundreds of thousands of protesters massed here during the Orange

Revolution, demonstrating against the 2004 presidential election campaign. A nod to the gilded statue of Archangel Michael, the patron and guardian of Kiev, and we're off.

Next stop is St Sophia. Kiev's oldest standing church and a UNESCO World Heritage Site, it resembles a fairy-tale cathedral, with its green and white turrets. As we cross into the modern quarter, luxury stores, sushi bars and traditional Ukrainian watering holes line the boulevards. We sit down at a riverside café and order salo, a local delicacy that can best be described as salted pig fat. It's surprisingly good. Above us, a canopy of white candles flickers in the breeze and we realize that we have not stepped out of the shade of the chestnut trees all day.

301 NIGHTCLUBBING BACK IN THE (OLD) USSR

MOLDOVA Hemmed in between Romania and Ukraine, tiny Moldova has not gained a great reputation as an oasis of hedonism over the years. And arriving in temperatures of -20°C in Chisinau, the capital city of this landlocked nation, it appeared from the miles of unspeakably bleak Soviet-era tenement buildings, driving snow and belching car exhausts, that the closest I was going to get to excess was necking vodka from under my hotel bed sheets.

This fear was only confirmed when my cab driver told me that the best place in town on a Monday was the *Military Pub*. The thought of a spartan, female-free basement full of inebriated and underpaid soldiers was hardly appealing, but when your hotel room is so cold that the bedding is dusted with a layer of frost – as I found mine was – then you haven't really got an option. At least, not in Chisinau.

The first inkling that my night in the "Pub" was going to be an interesting one was the huge Soviet-era army tank slap-bang in the middle of the dancefloor. The DJ, complete with his decks, was hidden inside it blasting out some deep House, which was being lapped up by the hordes of sultry, beautiful, smiling women and their slightly more bashful, chain-smoking boyfriends. A giant portrait of Lenin hung above the DJ-booth tank. Sandbags were lying everywhere. The atmosphere was raucous but friendly – and there wasn't an army uniform in sight.

Every few minutes, a huge bell hanging above the bar would be rung vigorously by one of the grinning staff, the signal for an urgently frugging dancer to be dragged off the floor and plonked on top of the bar where he or she would be forced to down a dark green-coloured shot of a local spirit that seemed to give everyone who drank it the sudden urge to take all their clothes off and run outside. By my reckoning, it was now down to -25°C. Strange behaviour maybe, but it somehow seemed so in keeping with this utterly unnoticed corner of Eastern Europe.

302 GOLDEN MOULDIE: DRINKING TOKAJ IN ANCIENT CELLARS

HUNGARY Eastern European wine receives few accolades. Apart from one, that is: the "wine of kings, the king of wines", was how Louis XVI described Tokaj, Hungary's most celebrated drink – indeed, so important is it to Hungarians that it's even cited in the national anthem.

Harvested amongst the rolling green hills of the Tokaj-Hegyalja region in northeast Hungary, the most famous variety of Tokaj is Aszú, a devilishly sweet dessert wine that owes its distinctive character to the region's volcanic loess soil and the prolonged sunlight that prevails here. More importantly, though, it's down to the winemaking techniques employed, whereby the grapes are left to become overripe, leading to botrytization – in layman's terms, attacked by rot (grandly termed the "noble rot" in these parts). This shrivels the grapes to raisin-sized proportions and gives them their concentrated sweetness. Otherwise, nothing beats a few hours in one of the cosy cellars lining the town's narrow streets, the most venerable of which is the Rákóczi cellar, named after the seventeenth-century prince, Ferenc Rákóczi. Reposed in 24 eerily cobwebbed, chandelier-lit passages are thousands upon thousands of bottles of the region's choicest wines. No less esteemed is the cellar of the same name located in the town of Sárospatak; it was here that Rákóczi would come to smoke his pipe, indulge in his favourite tipple, and plot the downfall of the Habsburgs. Hewn out by prisoners from the castle dungeons, the kilometre-long cellar, chock-full of handsome oak barrels, is thickly coated with penész, the "noble mould" – everything's noble where Tokaj is concerned – whose presence is integral to the wine's flavour. Whether quaffing this most regal of wines in the open air, down a cellar, or on a boat, the taste of Tokaj is something you won't forget in a hurry.

303 STANDING AT THE HEART OF MOTHER RUSSIA

RUSSIA Stand in the middle of Moscow's Red Square and in a 360-degree turn, the turbulent past and present of Russia is encapsulated in one fell swoop: flagships of Orthodox Christianity, Tsarist autocracy, communist dictatorship and rampant consumerism confront each other before your eyes.

Red Square, is, well, red-ish, but its name actually derives from an old Russian word for "beautiful". It might no longer be undeniably so – its sometime bloody history has put paid to that – but it continues to be Moscow's main draw. In summer, postcard sellers jostle with photographers, keen to capture your image in front of one of the many iconic buildings; but in winter, you step back in time a few decades as Muscovites, in their ubiquitous shapki fur hats, negotiate their way through piles of snow, while the factory chimneys behind St Basil's Cathedral churn out copious amounts of smoke.

It's hard to avoid being drawn immediately to St Basil's, its magnificent Mr Whippy domes the fitting final resting place of the eponymous holy fool. Should retail, rather than spiritual, therapy, be more your bag, try GUM, the elegant nineteenth-century shopping arcade, which now houses mainly western boutiques, way out of the pocket of the average Russian, but very decent for a spot of window shopping or a coffee, or just to shelter from the elements outside. If you think that the presence of Versace and other beacons of capitalism would have Lenin spinning in his grave, you can check for yourself at the mausoleum opposite, where his wax-like torso still lies in state. Despite the overthrow of communism, surly guards are on hand to ensure proper respect is shown: no cameras or bags, no hands in pockets and certainly no laughing. Putin's police officers are never far away, casting a wary eye over it all – perhaps having learned a thing or two from Lenin's bedfellows and disciples (including Uncle Joe), who are lined up behind the mausoleum under the imposing walls of the Kremlin.

304

HIKING IN THE TATRAS

POLAND The country's traditional attractions – Warsaw's lively old town and Kraków's gorgeous squares – are worthwhile stops, but it's easy to forget that there is another Poland, a genuine wilderness of high (and often snowbound) peaks, populated by lynx and bears. The Tatras Mountains are as beautiful as any national park in Europe, and their numerous trails – from vertiginous ridge-walks to forested rambles – are enormously popular with the locals, who troop here in their thousands in summer. The hamlet of Kuźnice, just south of the resort of Zakopane, has a cable car that climbs to almost 2000m above sea level (it feels a lot higher); from here, the very heart of the Tatras, marked trails for walkers of all abilities pick their way amongst the pinnacles.

305

A MINDBLOWING MUSEUM:
ST PETERSBURG'S
HERMITAGE

RUSSIA The Hermitage's collections run the gamut of the ancient world and European art. Where else could you find Rubens, Matisse, prehistoric dope-smoking gear and the world's largest vase under one roof?

The museum occupies the Imperial Winter Palace and the Old and New Hermitages, added by successive tsars. To avoid the crowds, start by checking out the little-visited ancient Siberian artefacts in the palace's dingy ground-floor west wing. The permafrost preserved burial mounds that contained mummified humans and horses, and chariots – all discovered by Soviet archeologists 2500 years later. They even found a brazier encrusted with marijuana – Altai nomads used to inhale it inside miniature tents – which was still potent.

Next, luxuriate in the State Rooms, glittering with gold leaf and semi-precious stones. The Malachite Drawing Room has an underwater feel, being awash with the eponymous green stone. The Provisional Government met there until their arrest by the Bolsheviks. On certain days, the English Peacock Clock spreads its bejewelled tail in the Pavilion Hall, whose decor fuses Islamic, Roman and Renaissance motifs. By this time the tour groups are thinking of lunch, making it a good time to investigate the art collection.

The adjacent Old and New Hermitages are stuffed with antiquities and artworks and it's difficult knowing where to turn. Old Masters are on the first floor – Botticelli, Van Dyck and twenty paintings by Rembrandt (including *Danaë*, restored after a deranged visitor slashed it) – plus works by Velázquez and Goya. If you prefer more modern art, be overwhelmed by Renoirs, Van Goghs, and Gauguins – all "trophy art" taken from Nazi Germany in 1945. The Post-Impressionist collection on the top floor has a superb array of Matisses and Picassos, acquired by two Muscovite philanthropists in the 1900s. Matisse's *Music* and *Dance* were commissioned for his patron's mansion, whose owner feared that the nude flautist might offend guests, and painted out his genitals – which the Hermitage's restorers have carefully restored.

Merely glancing at each item in the collection, it would still take nine years to see the whole lot. With not quite so much time on your hands, you may prefer to browse what you missed in one of the many catalogues, from the comfort of a nearby café.

306 DISCOVERING JEWISH VILNIUS

LITHUANIA For a city that suffered countless occupations in the twentieth century, and has been renamed at least three times, Vilnius – Wilno (Polish) or Vilna (Russian) as was – is a surprisingly self-confident place. Compact and attractive, it has an active café scene and a vibrant, not-too-boisterous nightlife. On its streets of well-dressed inhabitants chatting amiably on mobile phones and head-scarved old women selling icons, it's possible to find vestiges of its previous incarnations, from Polish statues to Russian Orthodox churches. But with the destruction wrought during World War II and subsequent Soviet control over the city's reconstruction, it is its unofficial name, "the Jerusalem of the North" – allegedly conferred by Napoleon – that leaves you wondering what is left today of one of Europe's most significant Jewish communities, devastated by the Nazis.

Vilnius's Jewish quarter centres around the aptly named Žydu gatve – "Jews' Street". As interest is rekindled in the city's Jewish past, old Yiddish shop signs are being uncovered and restored and it's possible, through photos at the Jewish Museum, to see what a vigorous mass of kosher butchers, matzoh makers and tailors vying for business this once was. From a prewar tally of more than a hundred synagogues, Vilnius now has only one, but many religious items were saved from destruction, including Torah scrolls and menorah, and are now displayed at the museum. The lively secular life of the Jewish population is well represented, too, with a fascinating collection of Yiddish theatre posters and sports club memorabilia.

In contrast, the showcases at the museum in Paneriai, the forest where most of Vilnius's Jews were killed, hold only a few stark items taken from the pits in which people were shot: rusty keys, an engraved comb, a pair of spectacles, a child's ragged toy – these few personal belongings representing the thousands who were murdered here.

Lithuania lost nearly 95 percent of its Jewish population in the Holocaust. At an exhibition about people who risked their lives to hide Jews during the war, I stop in front of a photograph of a couple with a baby. A woman approaches. "That's me," she smiles, pointing at the baby. "I was born in hiding." A group of Lithuanian schoolchildren stare in fascination and immediately crowd around her; she patiently answers their eager questions.

307 SUPPING A REAL BUD IN ČESKÉ BUDĚJOVICE

CZECH REPUBLIC The best Czech pubs are straightforward places: tables, benches, beer mats and an endless supply of the best beer in the world. And there are few more atmospheric venues for drinking the stuff in than Masné kramy, the complex of medieval butchers' stalls in the southern Bohemian town of České Budějovice (Budweis in German).

Walk into the long central hall, sit down and place a beer mat in front of you. Soon enough a waiter will walk round with a large tray of frothing beer mugs and slap one down on your table. As you near the end of the glass, before you've even begun to worry about catching the waiter's eye, you'll have been served another. At which point it becomes clear why the Czechs don't go in for pub crawls. With table service the norm, you need a serious strength of will (and a clear head) to get up and leave. Little surprise then that the Czechs top the world beer consumption league, downing approximately a pint a day for every man, woman and child in the country.

There's another reason why Masné kramy is a great place in which to quaff the amber nectar – they serve Budvar, produced by the only major Czech brewery not owned by a multinational. Instead, the brewery still belongs to the Czech state, primarily to stave off a takeover bid by Anheuser-Busch, the world's largest beer producer, responsible for the hugely inferior American Budweiser, or Bud as it's universally known. Litigation over the shared name has been going on for nearly a century, and looks set to continue well into the future. For the moment, however, Budvar is in safe hands and continues to be brewed according to traditional techniques. So enjoy the taste – smooth, hoppy, slightly bitter, with an undercurrent of vanilla – while the going's good.

308 HIGH ON A HILL WITH A LONELY GOATHERD

BULGARIA Most people tend to use an alarm clock, but in rural Bulgaria you can rely on the goats to get you out of bed. In the east Bulgarian village of Zheravna, an age-old Balkan ritual is enacted daily between 6 and 7am, when the local goatherd takes the beasts to pasture, collecting them one by one from the individual households where they spend the night. Bells clanging raucously as they pass, it makes for a novel dawn chorus.

With tumbledown stone houses leaning over crooked cobbled alleyways, Zheravna is a perfect example of a village whose rustic character has remained largely unchanged since the nineteenth century. Goat farming is no longer the most lucrative of industries, however, and rural depopulation has all but emptied the place of its young. Nowadays, the renovation of old houses and the development of rustic B&Bs points at a tourist-friendly future.

Zheravna is far from being the only remote community whose combination of highland scenery, historic architecture and hospitable landladies has made it a crucial stopoff on any village-hopping itinerary. Lying at the end of a potholed mountain road in Bulgaria's rugged southwest, Kovachevitsa is a bewitching knot of half-timbered houses and full of no-frills accommodation: just don't expect to see "vacancy" signs hanging outside gateways or tourist offices taking reservations. Instead, Kovachevitsa's mayoress hangs around at the village tavern keeping an eye open for any approaching cars bearing registration plates she doesn't immediately recognize. She then, goat-herding instincts intact, guides the newcomers to the house of a granny she knows who has a double bed made up and ready. Breakfast will include locally made herbal teas, and yoghurt so healthy it could add years to your life.

There's not a great deal to do when you get here, although that is undoubtedly part of the attraction. Lolling around in wildflower-carpeted meadows and meditating in the middle of a pine forest are just two of the activities on offer. If stuck for ideas you could always follow the goats, whose taste for invigorating air and gourmet grasses will lead you up into some of the most exhilarating wilderness areas in Europe.

309 MOUNT ELBRUS: CLIMBING EUROPE'S MIGHTIEST PEAK

RUSSIA "Are you ready?" my guide says to me as we clamber off the snowmobile at Pastuckhov Rocks. I'm not sure if I am. I'm on Mount Elbrus – at 5642m, Europe's highest mountain. It's snowing. I've been training for the climb for weeks, but now it's actually happening I freeze. "Come on," he laughs, chucking a snowball at me.

The peak of Mount Elbrus towers over the western Caucasus, close to the border with Georgia. The mountain's icecap feeds over twenty glaciers, serving the chilly Baksan, Kuban and Malka rivers. You can travel by cable car or snowmobile to a height of around 3000m, from where the summit is fairly accessible.

Or so my guide says. Even though it is not unusual for up to one hundred climbers to be on the mountain at any one time, I'm rather glad I trained for this. At 3000m, I'm already breathless – though this is thanks to the incredible view as much as the altitude. Risking a rare glance down, I catch a glimpse of vertiginous mountain passes shingled with rocks and camping stations.

We pass clean white meadows, black rock and glacial valleys. Freezing fog gives way to a fat blue sky. Later, as I throw my crampons down on the summit of Europe's highest peak, I reach down to make a snowball to throw back at my guide and suddenly realize we are standing on a grassy plain. The sun is shining down on us and there's not a jot of snow in sight.

310 TRACKING CARNIVORES IN THE CARPATHIAN MOUNTAINS

ROMANIA Bloodthirsty vampires, howling werewolves and medieval hamlets lashed by vicious storms – welcome to the popular, and mostly mythical, image of Transylvania. This beautiful and ancient region (from the Latin for "Beyond the forest"), nestled in the breathtakingly dramatic horseshoe curve of the Carpathian Mountains, is the location for the greatest reservoir of large-carnivore species outside Russia. It's home to Europe's biggest refuge for grey wolves, of which there are now an estimated two thousand, while more than five thousand brown bear roam the wooded slopes. It's all a far cry from the time when Nicolae Ceauşescu, a fanatical hunter, offered bounties equivalent to half a month's salary to anyone who managed to kill a wolf. Once the mad, megalomaniac president realized that Romanian bears were actually quite valuable, though, he afforded them protected status – albeit so that he could shoot them himself.

Amongst the many fascinating wildlife programmes on offer in Romania, few are as popular or capture the imagination quite as much as wolf- and bear-tracking. The creatures are initially tracked by following prints in the soft mud or snow, and, when caught, are tagged with a small radio transmitter that enables their behaviour and movement to be closely monitored. Occasionally, scats (droppings) can be found, which are collected and analyzed in order to determine what these intelligent and adaptable predators have been feasting on for lunch. Other telltale signs might include a flattened patch of grass where a bear has had an afternoon snooze, a log overturned in the frantic search for food, or a tree stump that has been scratched for ants. However, due to the vastness of the terrain and the highly elusive nature of these animals, there's certainly no guarantee of a sighting, but it's the tantalizing prospect of a brief encounter that makes the exhaustive search so worthwhile.

311 CROSSING CULTURAL BOUNDARIES IN KRAKÓW

POLAND It's May 2005 and Poland's oldest football team, Cracovia Kraków, are playing a crucial end-of-season fixture against second-division promotion rivals Pogon Szeczecin. Cracovia's stadium, an old-fashioned arena of banked-earthed terraces, is besieged by what seems to be the biggest horde of skinheads ever assembled in one place. The only adult male present with any hair, I pass gingerly through the turnstiles and try to blend in by joining the queue at the sausage stand. In the event the crowd is as good-tempered as they come: Cracovia secure the point they need, and the orc-like army depart in a happy mood.

Cracovia's supporters weren't always such a uniform bunch. In fact the club serves as a metaphor for the multicultural history of the city. During the interwar years, Cracovia were nicknamed the "Yids" because significant members of Kraków's Jewish community could be found on both the terraces and the team sheet. They also happened to be the favourite team of local boy Karol Wojtyła, the future Pope John Paul II.

Before World War II, many of Cracovia's supporters came from Kazimierz, the inner-city suburb where Poles and Jews had lived cheek-by-jowl for centuries. Most of Kazimierz's Jews perished in the nearby camps of Płaszów and Auschwitz, but their synagogues and tenement houses remain, providing a walk-round history lesson in Jewish heritage and culture. Kazimierz's complex identity is underlined by the presence of some of Kraków's most revered medieval churches. The weekend after the Cracovia match, I watch the suburb's narrow streets swell with the solemn, banner-bearing Corpus Christi processions that are among the best-attended events in the Polish Catholic calendar.

Today Kazimierz's Jewish population is a tiny fraction of what it was in the 1930s, but the district retains a vibrant melting-pot atmosphere – thanks in large part to its varied population of working-class Poles, impoverished artists, and inner-city-lifestyle-addicted yuppies. The most dramatic change of recent years has been its reinvention as a bohemian nightlife district, full of zanily decorated cellar bars, pubs that look like antique shops, and cafés that double as art galleries. With the area's non-conformist, anything-goes atmosphere drawing increasing numbers of the open-minded, tolerant and curious, Kazimierz is emerging once more as a unique incubator of cultural exchange.

312 HORRORS OF THE HOLOCAUST: VISITING AUSCHWITZ

POLAND What I remember most is the hair. Mousy, dark clumps of it and even a child's pigtail still wound like a piece of rope, all piled together like the relics from an ancient crypt. But there are no bones here. The hair in this room was deliberately, carefully, shaved from the heads of men, women and children, ready for transportation to factories where it would be turned into haircloth and socks. This is Auschwitz, the most notorious extermination camp operated by the Nazis.

No one knows how many people died here: estimates range from 1.1million to 1.6 million, mostly Jews. They starved to death, died of dysentery, were shot or beaten. And then from 1941, the Final Solution, death by cyanide gas ("Zyklon-B"): 20,000 people could be gassed and cremated each day.

Auschwitz still has a chilling, raw atmosphere, as if the Nazis had simply walked away the day before. You'd think the gas chambers would be the worst place – imagining the ashy smoke billowing from the chimneys, and inside, the agonizing struggles of the naked prisoners as the gas poisoned their blood. But the horror of Auschwitz doesn't hit you at once, it spreads over you slowly, like an infection, so that the more you see, the sicker you feel, until you can't take any more. The camp video is loaded with images too horrible to take in: plastic-like bodies being bulldozed into pits, bags of bones with faces.

As I left, I saw an old Polish woman on her knees, near the sign that says "Arbeit Macht Frei" ("Work Will Make You Free"), trembling but silent. It's a terrible place, full of terrible, haunting memories. But everyone should go – so that no one will forget.

313 TAKING A TRIP ON THE MOSCOW METRO

RUSSIA After a few vodkas my Russian neighbour unfailingly produces the two English phrases he learned in his Soviet childhood. One concerns friendship between nations, the other, that the Moscow metro is the greatest in the world.

This second assertion isn't far from the truth. The Moscow metro was designed as an eighth wonder of the world, a great egalitarian art gallery for the proletariat, combining utility and beauty as it ferried workers around the city, beguiled them with sculpture and chandeliers and indoctrinated them with Soviet propaganda. Even now, it's hard not to believe, just a little bit, in the Soviet dream when you step out of a clean, quick underground train (one every two minutes) into the fabulously ornate stations. Perhaps that's why hard-bitten Muscovites never seem to raise their eyes from their hurrying feet, and it's easy to spot the tourists.

With twelve lines and over 170 stations, the problem is where to start exploring. The Koltsevaya, or ring, is the most distinctive and navigable metro line. Built in the 1950s, its twelve stops include some of the finest stations, and as it's a circular line, it's hard to get lost. Park Kultury was the first station to be built on the line, and is decorated with bas-reliefs of workers enjoying sports and dancing. Travelling anti-clockwise, pretty, white and sky-blue Taganskaya is a mere prelude to Komsomolskaya, one of the most awesome stations on the whole system. Komsomolskaya connects to railway terminals for St Petersburg and Siberia, and the vast chandeliers suspended from an opulent baroque ceiling are designed to impress newly arrived travellers.

Towards the end of the circuit, Novoslobodskaya is the loveliest station of all. In the light of its jewel-bright stained-glass panels, even infamously surly Muscovites seem to smile and, recalling my Russian neighbour's English phrases, you may even start believing in friendship between nations. Which takes us neatly to Kievskaya, adorned with mosaic depictions of historical events uniting Russia and Ukraine, and the last stop on your circular journey.

314 STAYING WITH A REAL-LIFE TRANSYLVANIAN COUNT

ROMANIA Driving to the remote Romanian village of Miklósvár to stay in the guesthouse of Count Tibar Kalnoky, I started to feel like Jonathan Harker – the unsuspecting young lawyer in Bram Stoker's *Dracula* – who made a similar journey on such terrain to meet a different Transylvanian count. Even by car, rather than horse and carriage, the road had a nineteenth-century feel to it, being littered with potholes and random home-bound livestock. Since my pleas for directions were answered with nothing more than indecipherable mumbles and sympathetic shrugs, I began to question the wisdom of my journey.

On my eventual arrival I was met, not by the count, but by his mysterious housekeeper (OK, actually a glamorous Scottish guide) and shown to my room, or rather house, all done up with beautifully restored Szekely antique furniture, and complete with a welcoming decanter of home-made plum brandy.

Heading into the candlelit wine cellar for dinner, I wondered whether, since it was now dark, we might clap eyes on the elusive count. But, after supping on delicious vegetarian goulash

(carnivores had their own version), there was still no sign. Following a restful night under the downiest duvet imaginable, and a filling breakfast which included, of all things, muesli (a rare treat in Transylvania), we finally got a glimpse of him, looking more as if he had stepped out of a Ralph Lauren catalogue than a Hammer movie and sporting a suntan that would seem to belie a fear of daylight. I fell immediately under his spell.

Speaking with an alluring aristocratic lilt – part Mitteleuropa, part transatlantic – and sounding nothing like Christopher Lee, the count explained that while not immortal himself, his family has been in Miklósvár for centuries. Barred by the communists until 1989, he was later able to reclaim the family's former hunting lodge, previously a socialist "cultural" centre; he now uses the profits made from renting out the beautifully decorated guesthouses to restore it. When completed, it will become an upmarket hotel in stunning grounds, with the family crest intact – rejuvenated here by tourists' interest and cash, rather than by their blood.

315 BEAVERING AWAY IN LAHEMAA NATIONAL PARK

ESTONIA Visitors to Lahemaa National Park, a 725-square-kilometre area of pastureland and wilderness that runs along Estonia's northern seaboard, are often frustrated by never setting eyes on the forest-roaming bears, moose and lynx that guidebooks promise. The best they can hope for is the fleeting glimpse of a deer or rabbit – hardly the thing of which travellers' tales are made. Beavers, however, are a different matter. Although they're just as elusive as many of their peers (you'd probably need infra-red vision and the patience of an Easter Island statue to see one in action), evidence of their activity is everywhere.

My own induction into beaver-world occurred at the Oandu beaver trail, a well-marked nature walk that begins on the eastern fringes of the park. Embracing dense forest, desolate bogs, coastal wetlands and archaic fishing villages, Lahemaa is the best possible introduction to this Baltic country's unspoiled rural character.

Leading through thick woodland, the trail crosses several streams where log-built dams and freshly gnawed tree trunks indicate the presence of a highly industrious animal. Beavers

are the architects of the animal world, endlessly redesigning their environment until it meets their bark- and twig-munching requirements. The main mission of a beaver's life is to carve out a feeding area by felling trees, building a dam, and flooding an area of forest that other herbivores are loath to enter. Free of competition, it can then merrily stuff its face with all the vegetal matter trapped within its semi-sunken realm.

These beaver-created landscapes can be found throughout the Baltic States. The Pedvale open-air sculpture park in Latvia even includes a "Mr Beaver" in its list of featured artists – a real-life furry prankster who mischievously flooded part of the grounds.

Despite two years of trawling through the protected areas of the Baltics, the only beaver I set eyes on was the tombstone-toothed cartoon character who appeared nightly to advertise toothpaste on Lithuanian television. When I finally came face to face with one, it was basking in Mediterranean sunshine in the middle of a Croatian zoo. It would be nice to think that, somewhere in a dank Baltic forest, there's a birch tree with his name on it.

316 THE TALE AND THE TONGUE OF ST JOHN OF NEPOMUK

CZECH REPUBLIC As you shuffle along with your fellow tourists round the chancel of Prague's main cathedral, there's not a lot to see beyond the remains of a few medieval Czech kings with unpronounceable names – Břetislav, Spytihněv, Bořivoj. That is, until you find your way virtually barred by a giant silver tomb, which looks for all the world as if it has been abandoned by a bunch of Baroque builders upon discovering it was too big to fit into one of the side chapels. Turning your attention to the tomb itself, you're faced with one of the most gobsmackingly kitsch mausoleums imaginable – sculpted in solid silver, with airborne angels holding up the heavy drapery of the baldachin; and you notice the saint's rather fetching five-star sunburst halo, and back to back with him, a cherub proudly pointing to a glass case. On closer inspection, you realize the case contains a severed tongue.

Jesuits were nothing if not theatrical, and here, in the tomb of their favourite martyr, St John of Nepomuk, the severed tongue adds that extra bit of macabre intrigue. Arrested, tortured and then thrown – bound and gagged – off the Charles Bridge, John was martyred in 1393 for refusing to divulge the secrets of the queen's confession to the king. A cluster of stars appeared above the spot where he was drowned – or so the story goes – and are depicted on all his statues, including the one on the Charles Bridge. The gruesome twist was added when the Jesuits had his corpse exhumed in 1715 and produced what they claimed was the martyr's tongue – alive and licking so to speak – and stuck it in the glass case. Unfortunately, science had the last say, and in 1973 tests proved that the tongue was in fact part of his decomposed brain. Sadly, the object you now see on his tomb is a tongue-shaped replica.

317 SPENDING A NIGHT IN EUROPE'S TWILIGHT ZONE

TRANSDNIESTR Our bus now within sight of the "border", a youngish man sitting one seat ahead chooses this moment to break the silence. "Are you foreign?" he asks. A nod is the only possible response. "Welcome… to the Twilight Zone." His mysterious greeting delivered, the man returns to face the front, but then swings back for an equally deadpan punchline: "…and I'm not joking."

Transdniestr is a self-declared republic on the eastern flank of Moldova, and modern Europe's closest approximation to the former Soviet Union. Though once Soviet, Moldova's people and language have always been far more proximate to those of neighbouring Romania, but this skinny sliver of land east of the Dniestr River is largely made up of Russians and Ukrainians. Following the Soviet collapse, Moldova's subsequent independence and a minor war, Transdniestr chose to go it alone, but even though it now has its own leader, currency, anthem and flag, it remains unrecognized by the outside world. For this reason, most governments advise against entry, for which the border police – possessing no real authority but some very real weapons – may choose to charge you anything from one to one hundred dollars, depending on their mood. A few words of Russian will go down very nicely, as will a bottle of whisky.

After squeezing through Bendery, a city just over the border, the bus dives into the capital, Tiraspol, at one point passing a gleaming football stadium – conspicuous by its presence in Europe's poorest corner, it's the most visible example of misused government funds. Tiraspol itself is remarkably laid-back, though it thankfully fulfils a few of those Soviet-era stereotypes: a wartime tank is the city's focal point; red stars and nationalist slogans are everywhere you look; and you'll probably see the odd civilian sporting a Kalashnikov, or a fleet of missiles on their way to the Ukraine. When you've wandered its wide boulevards enough for one day, head for the *Hotel Druzhba*, the town's most atmospheric place to stay (think of a Soviet version of *The Shining*). Follow the gaze of the Lenin statue and you won't miss it. It's unlikely that you'll forget it either.

318 RECLAIMING THE STREETS AT THE PAGEANT OF THE JUNI

ROMANIA Lacking the Dracula connections of its near neighbours, Brašov, an atmospheric medieval town in deepest Transylvania, has to rely on more accurate historical events for its folklore traditions. One such festival is the colourful Pageant of Juni, a horseback parade that celebrates the only day of the year – the first Sunday in May – on which, traditionally, Romanians could freely enter the Saxon city. Dressing up in elaborate costumes, young townsfolk ride through the streets of the historic quarter – with the married men, or "Old Juni" trailing behind – before heading out into the surrounding hills. Here they break off into groups to perform the rhythmic horaş (round dances), a stamina-sapping danceathon that's almost as tiring to watch as it is to perform.

VULTURE-WATCHING
IN THE MADZHAROVO
NATURE RESERVE

319

BULGARIA You are crouched in juniper bushes exuding the smell of gin when suddenly the wind shifts and a foul odour sweeps through the gorge. From their perch halfway up the cliffs, three vultures launch themselves onto the thermals before plunging into the thickets of Salix trees, emerging with their talons and beaks laden with rotting flesh. Refocusing your binoculars, you track them back to their nests, where they start to feed a ravenous brood of chicks.

Vulture-watching at Bulgaria's Madzharovo nature reserve isn't your standard ornithological experience. Vultures are ugly, vicious creatures that feed on carrion; their intestinal systems have evolved to handle any microbe nature can throw at them. The Arda Gorge is one of the few breeding grounds in Europe for Egyptian, Griffon and black vultures; here twitchers can also spot eight kinds of falcons and nine kinds of woodpecker as well as black storks, bee-eaters, olive-tree warblers, and several species of bats.

All this wildlife is right on the doorstep of an ex-mining town of crumbling concrete low-rises – a juxtaposition of magnificent nature and man-made stagnation that's all too common in the Rhodope Mountains.

With its forests of pine and spruce, alpine meadows, crags and gorges, this is one of the wildest and most beautiful regions of Bulgaria. Travelling to the reserve through its villages, you're struck by the degrees of separation between its Christian and Pomak (Slav Muslim) inhabitants, with some villages exclusively one, others a mixture of both – signified by churches and mosques, miniskirts and veils. With villages half-depopulated by the flight of able-bodied adults to richer nations of the European Union, and remaining subsistence farmers too poor to afford pesticides or herbicides, the land is as ecologically rich as it is economically blighted.

MISCELLANY

MEAT AND TWO VEG

Eastern European food is generally heavy on animal flesh, beetroot and cabbage. Vegetarians take note: ham and salami are not considered to be meat in this part of the world and come under veggie sections on the menu. The northern nations' cuisine is influenced by Germany and Scandinavia, whereas southern countries take their cues from Greece, Turkey and Georgia. Some national dishes to consider are:

"Ukrainian Snickers" Raw pig fat with rye bread.
Fried potatoes and onions A dish so hallowed in Slovenia that it has its own festival.
Kukurec Albanian speciality of stuffed sheep's intestines.
Verivorst and mulgikkapsad Estonian blood sausage with sauerkraut.
Kavarma Stew of pork, tomatoes, lard and leeks, beloved in Bulgaria.

COOL AS A CUCUMBER

If a Czech thinks he's been asked an obvious question he may reply "I'm not here for the blueberries", whereas if involved in a boring activity may claim, "it's like throwing peas at a wall". A Bulgarian might warn you not to carry two melons under the same armpit. If a Russian tells you that you look like a cucumber, say thank you, but be upset if you are called an old horseradish. A pointless activity may be compared to "knocking pears out of a tree with your dick".

WHEN IN...
Five must reads

• **Transylvania, Romania**
Bram Stoker's *Dracula*
• **St Petersburg, Russia** Fyodor Dostoevsky's *Crime and Punishment*
• **Sofia, Bulgaria**
Georgi Gospodinov's *Natural Novel*
• **Odessa, Ukraine**
Isaac Babel's *Odessa Tales*
• **Gdansk, Poland**
Günter Grass's *The Tin Drum*

TOP TIPPLES

Calling someone a teetotaller in Eastern Europe usually just means that they don't drink spirits – every day. As well as the usual selection, each country has its own particular liquor, made with local fruit or herbs; if you are (un)lucky you may get to down a homemade version.

BEST DRINKS TO TRY

Vodka Drunk throughout the region, it's warming and supposedly aids digestion.
Beer Poles and Balts make lovely malty dark versions, but Czechs, since they invented it, have the best lager.
Brandy Moldovans modestly claim theirs is the finest in Europe.
Champagne Crimean, though no rival to French, is perfectly palatable – and far cheaper.
Wine Bulgarian, Hungarian and Romanian vintages are very decent; best of all is Tokaj, the world-renowned Hungarian dessert wine.
Borovička A gorgeous Slovak sloe spirit, similar to, yet more fiery than gin.

"Don't walk around hot porridge!"

Czech saying

Balaclava-wearing robots

The **robot** (Czech) in a **balaclava** (Ukrainian) sat in a **coach** (Hungarian), using a **biro** (Hungarian) to tot up his **bridge** (Russian) score while the **sleazy** (Latvian) **Cossack** (Ukrainian) waved his **sabre** (Hungarian) at the **cosmonaut** (Russian); he then shot a **horde** (Polish) of **mammoths** (Russian) with a **pistol** (Czech). They all retired to a **bistro** (Russian) to **talk** (Lithuanian) and eat some **pastrami** (Romanian).

REVOLUTIONS
Match the revolutions with the countries:

A Orange		**1** Poland
B Velvet		**2** Estonia
C Singing		**3** Czechoslovakia
D Solidarity		**4** Ukraine

(answers: A/4, B/3, C/2, D/1).

"A man goes into his local garage and asks, 'Do you have a windscreen wiper for my Škoda?' 'Sounds like a fair swap', replies the man in the garage"

One of many jokes about the Czech car, whose name unfortunately means "pity" or "shame" in Czech

EUROVISION
SONG CONTEST

No current Eastern European nation had managed to capture this most dubious of titles until Estonia emerged victorious in 2001. This kick-started an impressive run of success, with Latvia, in 2002, and the Ukraine, in 2004, both coming first. One of the contest's more controversial acts in recent times were the Russian female duo **T.a.T.u**, who caused a bit of a storm thanks to marketing themselves as a (faux) lesbian couple.

TOP FIVE DISCOVERIES AND INVENTIONS	COUNTRY
The helicopter Igor Sikorsky	(Ukraine)
The periodic table Dimitri Mendeleyev	(Russia)
Modern astronomy Copernicus	(Poland)
Radium Marie Curie	(Poland)
The parachute Štefan Banič	(Slovakia)

Did you know…?

The geographical centre of Europe is located 25km north of Vilnius.

SPORTING STARS

Eastern European nations have a fantastically rich sporting heritage, and the following individuals have attained sporting immortality:

Hungarian fencer **Aladár Gerevich** who racked up an incredible six Olympic titles between 1932 and 1960. Czech long-distance runner **Emil Zátopek** who won three gold medals at the 1952 Olympic games, in the 5000m, 10000m and marathon races.

Romanian gymnast **Nadia Comaneci** who, at the 1976 Montreal Olympics, aged just 14, won three gold medals and became the first gymnast in Olympic history to achieve a perfect 10 score.

Fantasy football
all-time East European 11

The region has given us some pretty decent footballers, too:

1 Lev Yashin (USSR)
2 József Bozsik (Hungary)
3 Nándor Hidegkuti (Hungary)
4 Anatoli Demianeko (Ukraine)
5 Josef Masopust (Czechoslovakia)
6 Pavel Nedvéd (Czech Republic)
7 Andriy Shevchenko (Ukraine)
8 Hristo Stoichkov (Bulgaria)
9 Ferenc Puskás (Hungary)
10 Gheorghe Hagi (Romania)
11 Oleg Blokhin (USSR)

"We are the winners of Eurovision

We are, we are! We are, we are!

We are the winners of Eurovision

We are, we are! We are, we are!"

Lithuanian entry 2006 by LT United. Lithuania remains the only Baltic state yet to win the Eurovision Song Contest.

Five largest Eastern European cities

• Moscow	(pop. 10.5m)
• St Petersburg	(pop. 4.7m)
• Kiev	(pop. 2.7m)
• Bucharest	(pop. 2m)
• Minsk	(pop. 1.8m)

EAST EUROPEAN JEWS

Before World War II, Eastern Europe had the largest Jewish population in the world. Historically, Jews had suffered exclusion from many parts of Europe, but since 1791 had been allowed to live in the Pale of Settlement – an area established by Catherine the Great, which covered much of Eastern Poland and Russia. In the twentieth century, this is where the majority of Europe's Jews still remained, many of them in shtetls – predominantly Jewish small towns – where they had been forced to live having been previously excluded from cities. With the Nazi takeover of Eastern Europe, aided by strong feelings of local anti-Semitism, all but a remnant of the Jewish population was murdered. Of the fraction who remained, many fought as partisans, or were able to hide undiscovered. Since the demise of communism there has been a rekindling of interest in Jewish life evident in the emergence of new cultural centres, renovated synagogues and theatres in many of the places where their loss was felt so strongly, in particular in the cities of Vilnius and Kraków.

FIVE OUTSTANDING NATURAL ATTRACTIONS

Carpathian Mountains, Romania/ Ukraine Stunning hiking terrain - sheltering quaint villages and home to some fabulous wildlife, including wolves and brown bears.

High Tatras, Slovakia Jagged granite peaks rising spectacularly from the Poprad Plain.

Couronian Spit, Lithuania Dramatic landscape of pine forests, pristine sands and calm lagoons.

The Danube River from the Black Forest to the Black Sea, this majestic waterway is Europe's second longest (2857km) after the Volga in Russia.

Puszcza Białowieska, Poland A national park containing the last major tract of primeval forest left in Europe

ETIQUETTE

Bulgarians shake their heads when they mean "yes" and nod when they mean "no". In a Czech pub, never top up a new glass of beer with the remains of the previous one.

When a Russian lights a cigarette, wish him good health, however ironic it seems.

OLD MR CHLAPITSKY
HAD A FARM

Many East European expressions seem to revolve around the farmyard:

I'll slap you so hard you'll see green horses (a Romanian threat).
You're as fat as a sheep's knees (Romanian for "slim").
You're like a cow with a new gate in front of her (Romanian for "you look lost").
I'll do it when it's the horse's Easter (Romanian for "never").
A steel mare goes barefoot (Czech saying).
You ox! (A Czech insult – though friendly too, like "mate").
You can't get bacon from a dog (Hungarian for "a leopard can't change its spots").
A hungry pig always thinks about acorns ("you can't teach an old dog new tricks" in Hungarian).
The owl shouldn't tell the sparrow he has a big head (Hungarian for "the pot calling the kettle black").
Don't go into the forest if you don't like wolves (Russian saying).
God's cow, fly away to heaven, where your children are eating cutlets (Russian equivalent to "Ladybird, ladybird, fly away home").

"It is better to have ten friends than one enemy"
Polish saying

INTERESTING
PLACES TO STAY

Do time in Vaclav Havel's cell at the **Unitas Hotel**, Prague, a former prison.

Feel like you're in a John le Carré novel at the **Palace Athena Hotel**, Bucharest – a hive of espionage activity during the Cold War.

Bed down in a monk's bunk in the stunning but spartan **Rila monastery**, Bulgaria.

Sleep in the communist police force's former HQ in Budapest – now, snubbingly, transformed into the luxury **Le Meridien** hotel.

THE PYRAMIDS OF GIZA • CAMEL TREKKING IN THE SAHARA • HIKING IN THE HOGGAR • LEARNING THE ART OF TRAVEL WRITING IN MARRAKESH • DISCOVERING ROCK ART ON THE TASSILI N'AJJER PLATEAU • **STROLLING THROUGH THE RUINS OF LEPTIS MAGNA** • TOURING TROGLODYTE VILLAGES • HANGING OUT IN THE JEMAA EL FNA • GREETING THE PHARAOHS IN THE VALLEY OF THE KINGS • DRIFTING DOWN THE NILE • RAMADAN NIGHTS • HITTING THE ROAD ACROSS THE SAHARA • DIVING IN THE RED SEA CORAL GARDENS • MOUNTAINS AND MIRAGES IN JEBEL ACACUS • A WALK OF REPENTANCE: CLIMBING MOUNT SINAI • LOSING YOURSELF IN A GOOD BOOK AT THE BIBLIOTHECA ALEXANDRINA • GOING OVER THE TOP IN THE ATLAS MOUNTAINS • EXPLORING THE ROMAN RUINS AT DOUGGA • KEEPING COOL IN THE OLD TOWN OF GHADAMES • HAGGLING IN THE SOUKS OF FES • MOPPING UP A MOROCCAN TAJINE • TRANS-SAHARA BY MOTORBIKE • **CAMEL FIGHTING AT THE FESTIVAL OF THE SAHARA** • DRIVING THE ROUTE OF A THOUSAND KASBAHS • STAYING WITH A FAMILY IN MERZOUGA • IDLING THE DAY AWAY IN ESSAOUIRA • ENJOYING THE VIEW FROM THE FISHAWI CAFÉ • EXPLORING THE DUNE LAKES OF UBARI • GILF KEBIR: THE LAND OF THE ENGLISH PATIENT • AROUND THE WORLD AT THE FESTIVAL OF SACRED MUSIC • THE MOULID OF SAYYID AHMAD AL-BADAWI • **THE PYRAMIDS OF GIZA** • CAMEL TREKKING IN THE SAHARA • HIKING IN THE HOGGAR • LEARNING THE ART OF TRAVEL WRITING IN MARRAKESH • DISCOVERING ROCK ART ON THE TASSILI N'AJJER PLATEAU • TOURING TROGLODYTE VILLAGES • STROLLING THROUGH THE RUINS OF LEPTIS MAGNA • HANGING OUT IN THE JEMAA EL FNA • GREETING THE PHARAOHS IN THE VALLEY OF THE KINGS • DRIFTING DOWN THE NILE • RAMADAN NIGHTS • HITTING THE ROAD ACROSS THE SAHARA • DIVING IN THE RED SEA CORAL GARDENS • MOUNTAINS AND MIRAGES IN JEBEL ACACUS • A WALK OF REPENTANCE: CLIMBING MOUNT SINAI • LOSING YOURSELF IN A GOOD BOOK AT THE BIBLIOTHECA ALEXANDRINA • GOING OVER THE TOP IN THE ATLAS MOUNTAINS • EXPLORING THE ROMAN RUINS AT DOUGGA • KEEPING COOL IN THE OLD TOWN OF GHADAMES • **HAGGLING IN THE SOUKS OF FES** • MOPPING UP A MOROCCAN TAJINE • TRANS-SAHARA BY MOTORBIKE • CAMEL FIGHTING AT THE FESTIVAL OF THE SAHARA • DRIVING THE ROUTE OF A THOUSAND KASBAHS • STAYING WITH A FAMILY IN MERZOUGA • IDLING THE DAY AWAY IN ESSAOUIRA • ENJOYING THE VIEW FROM THE FISHAWI CAFÉ • EXPLORING THE DUNE LAKES OF UBARI • GILF KEBIR: THE LAND OF THE ENGLISH PATIENT • AROUND THE WORLD AT THE FESTIVAL OF SACRED MUSIC • THE MOULID OF SAYYID AHMAD AL-BADAWI • THE PYRAMIDS OF GIZA • CAMEL TREKKING IN THE SAHARA • HIKING IN THE HOGGAR • LEARNING THE ART OF TRAVEL WRITING IN MARRAKESH • DISCOVERING ROCK ART ON THE TASSILI N'AJJER PLATEAU • TOURING TROGLODYTE VILLAGES • STROLLING THROUGH THE RUINS OF LEPTIS MAGNA • HANGING OUT IN THE JEMAA EL FNA • GREETING THE PHARAOHS IN THE VALLEY OF THE KINGS • DRIFTING DOWN THE NILE • RAMADAN NIGHTS • HITTING THE ROAD ACROSS THE SAHARA • DIVING IN THE RED SEA CORAL GARDENS • MOUNTAINS AND MIRAGES IN JEBEL ACACUS • A WALK OF REPENTANCE: CLIMBING MOUNT SINAI • LOSING YOURSELF IN A GOOD BOOK AT THE BIBLIOTHECA ALEXANDRINA • **TRANS-SAHARA BY MOTORBIKE** • GOING OVER THE TOP IN THE ATLAS MOUNTAINS • EXPLORING THE ROMAN RUINS AT DOUGGA • KEEPING COOL IN THE OLD TOWN OF GHADAMES • HAGGLING IN THE SOUKS OF FES • MOPPING UP A MOROCCAN TAJINE • CAMEL FIGHTING AT THE FESTIVAL OF THE SAHARA • DRIVING THE ROUTE OF A THOUSAND KASBAHS • STAYING WITH A FAMILY IN MERZOUGA • IDLING THE DAY AWAY IN ESSAOUIRA • ENJOYING THE VIEW FROM THE FISHAWI CAFÉ • EXPLORING THE DUNE LAKES OF UBARI • GILF KEBIR: THE LAND OF THE ENGLISH PATIENT • AROUND THE WORLD AT THE FESTIVAL OF SACRED MUSIC

NORTH AFRICA

320–354

HAGGLING IN
THE SOUKS OF FES ★ 340

CAMEL FIGHTING AT THE
FESTIVAL OF THE SAHARA ★ 343

TUNISIA

STROLLING THROUGH THE RUINS ★ 326
OF LEPTIS MAGNA

MOROCCO

ALGERIA

LIBYA

THE PYRAMIDS OF GIZA ★ 320

EGYPT

TRANS-SAHARA BY MOTORBIKE ★ 351

THE
PYRAMIDS
OF
GIZA

320

EGYPT The Pyramids at Giza were built at the very beginning of recorded human history, and for nearly five millennia they have stood on the edge of the desert plateau in magnificent communion with the sky.

Today they sit on the edge of the city, and it must be a strange experience indeed to look out of the windows of the nearby tower blocks to a view like this. The closest, the Great Pyramid, contains the tomb of Cheops, the Fourth Dynasty pharaoh who ruled Egypt during the Old Kingdom. This is the oldest of the group, built around 2570 BC, and the largest – in fact it's the most massive single monument on the face of the earth today. The others, built by Cheops' son Chephren and his grandson Mycerinus, stand in descending order of age and size along a southwest axis; when built they were probably aligned precisely with the North Star, with their entrance corridors pointing straight at it.

You enter the Great Pyramid through a hole hacked into its north face in the ninth century AD by the caliph Mamun who was hunting for buried treasure. Crouching along narrow passages you arrive at the Great Gallery which ascends through the heart of the pyramid to Chephren's burial chamber. Chances are you'll have the chamber to yourself, as claustrophobia and inadequate oxygen mean that few people venture this far. Occasionally visitors are accidentally locked in overnight.

The overwhelming impression made by the pyramids is due not only to the magnitude of their age and size, but also to their elemental form, their simple but compelling triangular silhouettes against the sky. The best way to enjoy this is to hire a horse or camel and ride about the desert, observing them from different angles, close up and looming, or far off and standing lonely but defiantly on the open sands. Seen at prime times – dawn, sunset and night – they form as much a part of the natural order as the sun, the moon and the stars.

321 CAMEL TREKKING IN THE SAHARA

TUNISIA I had to insist on having control of my own camel. Too many of these treks resemble a ride at the zoo with a minder walking alongside holding the bridle. Hamid saw the advantage, though. If I went solo, he could send one of his sons home and I'd stop moaning that Lawrence of Arabia drove his own beastie.

The Grinch and I have been companions for four days now. I call him Grinch because he's forever grumbling. Camels gripe a lot, a deep basso mutter whatever you ask them to do. When I enquired about his name, Hamid looked at me in surprise. Camels are for work. They don't have names any more than computers have names in my country. I must have seemed very twee. However, if I'm going to be rocking up and down on somebody's shoulders for seven days, I like to know whose they are.

The Grinch and I have come a long way since Douz, the trekking

Mecca of the Sahara. We're averaging five hours a day, which is a lot of time up top if you sit "properly", ankles crossed round the hump. It's also a long time if your camel quickly deduces that you're a soft touch and that he can keep lunging down to nibble on any scrubby bit of plant that pokes up through the dunes. At first I was indulgent, but after a morning falling behind the main caravan, I toughened up. They say there are a thousand words for camel in Arabic – not all of them are pleasant.

Still, there is something wonderfully timeless about this kind of transport and a real thrill in knowing that the only way to reach our destination, the former Roman garrison of Ksar Ghilane, is on the back of The Grinch, or by far less romantic 4WD. Roads, such as they were, ran out days ago. Best of all are the evenings sitting round the fire while Hamid's family cook, and more stars than I ever thought possible twinkle down at us.

322 HIKING IN THE HOGGAR

ALGERIA Rising from the very centre of the Sahara, on a vast, brooding plateau, the peaks of the Hoggar spire towards a shimmering blue dome of sky. The heat is relentless – turbocharged – and yet the arid air removes every trace of perspiration as soon as it forms on your brow. Keep your cheche (headscarf) wrapped across your mouth and you can breathe moist air: it's a good trick. This is a waterless, inhospitable environment – a surreal, otherworldly landscape of volcanic plugs rearing vertically for hundreds of metres – and silent: when you stop, you can hear the blood coursing past your ears.

In the Hoggar, you can explore, or climb, in some of the most remote peaks and wadis (dry water courses) in the world, and find examples of the rock art left here thousands of years ago when the region was fertile, hunter-gatherer country.

Today, the solitude leaves the Hoggar largely uninhabited, save for the nomadic Tuareg, reliant entirely on their herds and

their ability to endure hardships that would destroy most people in a couple of days. It was a fascination with the Tuareg that drew Père Charles de Foucauld, a French priest, to a remote vantage point on the high col at Assekrem in the central Hoggar – the small stone chapel where he lived as a hermit for sixteen years at the beginning of the twentieth century is the best-known target for hikers.

"The view is more beautiful than can be conveyed or imagined", de Foucauld wrote of his isolated home. "The very sight of it makes you think of God, and I can scarcely take my eyes from a sight whose beauty and impression of infinitude are so reminiscent of the Creator of all; and at the same time its loneliness and wildness remind me that I am alone with Him".

A hundred years later, you stand and stare, from the lonely col, gazing at the infinite geological wonders across your field of view. The great outdoors doesn't get much greater.

323 AROUND THE WORLD AT THE FESTIVAL OF SACRED MUSIC

MOROCCO Rabat may be the political capital of Morocco, but Fes el Bali – old Fes, the most complete living medieval city in the world – is the nation's beating heart; and the World Sacred Music Festival offers visitors the opportunity to tap straight into its rich, multilayered cultural and spiritual life.

The festival styles itself as "a beacon of peace from the Islamic world" and deliberately draws performers from many different faiths and traditions. Alongside internationally acclaimed world-music stars such as master sitar player Ravi Shankar and Malian superstar Salif Keita, both of whom have headlined in recent

years, are offerings as diverse as African-American gospel choirs, English chamber singers, Japanese court musicians and Spanish flamenco artists.

The ticketed concerts, held in the palace courtyard of Bab Makina or the wonderful, cedar-scented gardens of the Musée Bathar, are glamorous, high-society events, attended by well-groomed locals keen to see and be seen. There's a daily programme of free events, too, held at dusk in Bab Boujloud, one of the city's main squares. Late in the evening, people move on to the Dar Tazi Gardens, to sway to hypnotic hadras, traditional Sufi chants.

324

DISCOVERING ROCK ART ON THE TASSILI N'AJJER PLATEAU

ALGERIA The world's biggest open-air art gallery lurks in the heart of the Sahara, among the wind-carved ramparts of southeastern Algeria's Tassili n'Ajjer plateau.

Its caves and overhangs shelter countless prehistoric images, customarily termed frescoes, laboriously engraved or painted onto the rock in shades of ochre, white and charcoal black. When discovered in the 1930s, these images – including elephants, hippos and rhinos – helped illustrate the dramatic influence climate change has had on human development.

The most impressive concentration of rock-art sites is on the plateau above the remote oasis of Djanet. When, after an hour's steep hike, you finally encounter the frescoes for the first time, it's a humbling experience, heightened by the arid desolation. Was the Sahara once so green that right where you stand, women would grind corn or milk cows alongside flowing rivers, as some frescoes depict?

These scenes, some as fine as on any Greek vase, reflect the main theme of the rock paintings, that of the Neolithic Revolution, when humans progressed from eons of hunter-gathering to a settled lifestyle tending crops and domesticating animals. Not all such endeavours were ultimately successful, though – look out for engravings of giraffes on leads.

Elsewhere, figures with large round heads don't depict spacemen, as once theorized, but arcane gods, presaging the dawn of religious consciousness. Subsequently, the descendants of the ancient hunters are shown turning their bows and spears on each other as horse-drawn charioteers invade from the north. The story ends as the current arid phase takes hold, driving the people of the Tassili towards the Mediterranean and the Nile Valley. The rest, as they say, is history.

325 TOURING TROGLODYTE VILLAGES

TUNISIA When Tunisia gained its independence in 1956, its then president, Habib Bourguiba, proclaimed a new nation in which "people will no longer live in caves, like animals". He was addressing the reality that across the arid far south of the country, people did live in caves, not uncommonly with their livestock. Gradually, these people were moved into new houses put up by the government, and most of the cave dwellings were abandoned.

Visit the troglodyte villages today, however, and you'll see they're enjoying a new lease of life – some even offer tourist accommodation. Many are stunningly sited. At Chenini, Douiret and Guermessa, set in a jagged prehistoric landscape, you're confronted by mountainsides riddled with cave dwellings and guarded by rugged stone forts. At nearby Ghoumrassen, three folds of a rocky spur are studded with caves, under the gaze of a whitewashed mosque. Yet more scenic is Toujane, built on two sides of a gorge, with breathtaking views. Anywhere you spot oil stains down the hillside signifies caves housing ancient olive presses; visit after the olive harvest and you may well see some of these being powered by donkeys.

But the big centre for troglodyte homes is Matmata, whose people live, to this day, in pit dwellings. Signs outside some invite you to visit, and for a few dinars you can descend into a central courtyard dug deep into soft sandstone, which serves to keep the rooms – excavated into the sides – comfortably cool in summer and warm in winter. Better still, Matmata has three hotels in converted pit dwellings, including the *Sidi Driss*, which was used as one of the locations in *Star Wars* – here you can dine where Luke Skywalker once did.

326 STROLLING THROUGH THE RUINS OF LEPTIS MAGNA

LIBYA North Africa is dotted with Roman remains, but the one that beats them all is Leptis Magna, arguably the most impressive Roman site outside Pompeii.

Leptis Magna reached its zenith under local boy Septimius Severus, who rose to become emperor in 193 AD, and died in battle eighteen years later in a far-flung province called Britain. Fittingly, if there's one superlative edifice at Leptis Magna, it's the amazing four-way arch Septimius commissioned. One of the first monuments you encounter, it is nearly forty metres tall, and bears a plethora of superb, recently restored marble reliefs. Septimius also endowed the city with the more imposing of its two forums, squares where people met to socialize and conduct business. Strewn though it now is with fallen columns, you can stand in the middle and still feel awed by its size and grandeur.

So well preserved is the city's luxurious bathhouse, endowed by Septimius's predecessor, Hadrian, that it's easily recognizable as a direct ancestor of the hammams found across North Africa. Walking through, you follow the route that bathers took, from the frigidarium (cold room) through the tepidarium (warm room, but actually more like an open-air swimming pool) to the caldarium (hot room), where they would sweat out the grime and scrub it off – just as in a today's hammams.

Elsewhere, there's an enormous amphitheatre (for gladiatorial and other sporting events, more likely than not involving Christians and lions), a hippodrome (for horse races) and a substantial, well-preserved theatre to take in, among other remains. There's also a good museum with commentaries in English. But one of the very best things to do at Leptis Magna is simply to wander the maze of colonnaded streets, so intact that you can imagine toga-clad Romans approaching at every corner.

327 HANGING OUT IN THE JEMAA EL FNA

MOROCCO There's nowhere on earth like the Jemaa el Fna, the square at the heart of old Marrakesh. The focus of the evening promenade for Marrakehis, the Jemaa is a heady blend of alfresco food bazaar and street theatre: for as long as you're in town, you'll want to come back here again and again.

Goings-on in the square by day merely hint at the evening's spectacle. Breeze through and you'll stumble upon a few snake charmers, tooth pullers and medicine men plying their trade, while henna tattooists offer to paint your hands with a traditional design. In case you're thirsty, water sellers dressed in gaudy costumes – complete with enormous bright red hats – vie for your custom alongside a line of stalls offering orange and grapefruit juice, pressed on the spot. Around dusk, however, you'll find yourself swept up in a pulsating circus of performers.

There are acrobats from the Atlas Mountains, dancers in drag, and musicians from a religious brotherhood called the Gnaoua, chanting and beating out rhythms late into the night with their clanging iron castanets. Other groups play Moroccan folk music, while storytellers, heirs to an ancient tradition, draw raucous crowds to hear their tales.

In their midst dozens of food stalls are set up, lit by gas lanterns and surrounded by delicious-smelling plumes of cooking smoke. Here you can partake of spicy harira soup, try charcoal-roasted kebabs or merguez sausage, or, if you're really adventurous (and hungry), a whole sheep's head, including the eyes – all beneath the looming presence of the floodlit, perfectly proportioned Koutoubia minaret to the west, making a backdrop without compare.

328 LEARNING THE ART OF TRAVEL WRITING IN MARRAKESH

MOROCCO Ever wondered what goes into writing for the Sunday newspaper travel section? Thought about trying your hand at travel guidebooks or magazine feature articles? How about spending a week in one of the world's most romantic, bewitching cities, honing your creative skills and learning the fine art of travel writing?

Every year in the spring, aspiring journalists decamp to North Africa for a week-long crash course in the fundamentals of writing about travel, geared as much towards amateurs as well as seasoned professionals. Taught by editors and senior writers from some of the most well-known travel magazines and broadsheets in the business, you'll have no want for expert tuition. The course is held in Marrakesh, an enchanting, ancient city boasting an alluring medina, serpentine alleyways and a vibrant market square alive with snake charmers, street performers and traditional storytellers. And accommodated in an atmospheric Moroccan riad – a classic estate of the Arab elite – you'll hardly be at a loss for creative inspiration.

To start off, instructors walk you through a comprehensive overview of the basics of travel writing – hook, story, style and narrative – using the city as a muse. Once you're comfortable with the fundamentals of producing a travel article, you'll drive out to the Atlas Mountains and the Dades Valley for a change of scene and mood, where you can try your hand at describing dramatic sierra landscapes, historic castle ruins and ancient desert oases, experiencing the challenges and excitement of conjuring up that perfect portrayal. Throughout the course, your tutors hold a series of private, one-on-one tutorial sessions, providing you with the opportunity to hone and polish your writing skills and giving you the inside scoop on what top travel editors look for in a story. In short: how to go from being a traveller who writes to a writer who travels.

329 HITTING THE ROAD ACROSS THE SAHARA

MOROCCO–MAURITANIA It didn't make the headlines but a couple of years ago a significant event occurred in the Sahara: a 3200-kilometre all-weather road was completed linking Morocco to Senegal. For the first time in two thousand years of trans-Saharan trade you no longer need a camel caravan or an all-terrain vehicle to cross the desert with ease.

This new road won't last; the desert has a habit of suffocating tarmac with dunes or ripping it out during flash floods, but for the moment any old car can make the journey, so get there while the going is good.

Arriving in Tangier from Spain gives you your first dose of culture shock. Moneychangers, scammers and beggars come at you from all directions. Northern Morocco can be a rough introduction to the continent, but once south of the imposing Atlas Mountains the atmosphere becomes decidedly more relaxed.

As you continue south the fertile Mediterranean countryside gradually becomes more desiccated. Trees thin out and eventu-ally disappear as the desert pushes through right to the Atlantic shore. The people look different, too, as the angular Arabic features of the fierce Reguibat and Moorish nomads become more prevalent. Once you reach the port of Tan Tan the famous camel arch, the "Gateway to the Sahara", confirms that you've entered a new land.

For much of this portion of the journey, the coast is cliff-bound and windy so it's better to camp under the stars on the desert floor, beneath low dunes and limestone escarpments. At the Mauritanian border there's no turning back. The new road runs inland, passing huge dune fields dotted with nomadic encampments; forty years ago nearly all Mauritanians were tent-dwelling nomads. Trepidation turns to fascination as you acclimatize to the adventure and the warmer weather. Within a couple of days of the border you roll into the capital, Nouakchott, and suddenly it's all over. After the solitude of the desert, the big-city commotion can be hard to deal with. You've crossed the Sahara and now you're really in Africa.

330 THE MOULID OF SAYYID AHMAD AL-BADAWI

EGYPT The Egyptian year is awash with moulids (festivals honouring local saints), but they don't come much bigger than the Moulid of Sayyid Ahmad al-Badawi, when the otherwise nondescript Nile Delta city of Tanta is besieged by some two million pilgrims, who converge on the triple-domed mosque where al-Badawi is buried.

Moulids are especially associated with Sufis – Islamic mystics, who use singing, chanting and dancing to bring themselves closer to God. Some fifty Sufi brotherhoods put up their tents around Tanta and set to work chanting and beating out a rhythm on drums or tambourines, as devotees perform their zikrs (ritual dances). In the less frenetic tents, you can relax with a sheesha (water-pipe) or a cup of tea, while scoffing festive treats such as roasted chickpeas and sugared nuts. The atmosphere is intense, the crowds dense, and pickpocketing rife (so leave your valuables at home).

Tanta doesn't have much in the way of accommodation, and most people just bunk down in the tents, but if that doesn't appeal and you can't get a room, it's near enough to Cairo to take in on a day-trip. Wherever you stay, make sure that you're here for the spectacular last-night parade, when the Ahmediya, the Sufi brotherhood founded by al-Badawi himself, take to the streets in a colourful blur of banners.

331 DRIFTING DOWN THE NILE

EGYPT Often called "the gift of the Nile", Egypt has always depended on the river as a life source. Without the Nile, the country could not survive, and would not have nurtured the great civilizations of its pharaonic past.

Snaking the full length of the country, the Nile flows from south to north and boats of all varieties ply it day and night. For an authentic – and uniquely Egyptian – taste of river life, opt for a voyage on a felucca.

These traditional, lateen rigged wooden vessels – used on the Nile since antiquity – are small: our group of six fitted comfortably. We'd negotiated in Aswan, Egypt's southernmost city, for a two-night trip downriver; bargaining and gathering supplies was frenetic, but as soon as the captain guided the boat out onto open water, the bustle faded away. There was nothing to do but lie back and soak up the atmosphere.

Our stately progress and the drowsy heat during the day were countered by the cooler evenings, with the boat moored in the shallows and the captain cooking up a simple meal on board.

It felt timeless. Drifting gently down the Nile in a traditional wooden boat, shaded from the African sun by a square of colourful cloth, watching the fields and palm groves slide past, kids waving from the banks. Nothing could be more seductive.

It wasn't timeless, of course: the cloth was polyester, the kids had trinkets to sell and there were Japanese pickups parked in the shoreside villages – but one can dream…

332 DIVING IN THE RED SEA CORAL GARDENS

EGYPT Mask on and regulator in place, I'm clinging onto a rail at the stern of the boat, waiting for the signal to step out over the swelling water. It's my first drift dive in what could be a very fast current, fairly daunting for a newly qualified diver who hasn't quite mastered neutral buoyancy. But this is one of the top ten dives in the world, and I'm going to do it, however anxious I feel.

The waves rocking the boat make up part of the Ras Mohammed National Park, one of the Red Sea's prime diving areas. Of a variety of starting points, the dive instructor chooses Anemone City, a sloping underwater plateau covered with sea anemones hosting cute but ferocious pairs of clownfish. Once we've descended to 20m, we swim through the blue toward Shark Reef. There's no frame of reference now except my buddy: up, down, left and right become meaningless – but for a cloud of silvery jacks and tangle of barracuda circling overhead, there'd be nothing to see at all.

Reaching the 700m vertical wall of Shark Reef, we're suddenly on a virtual conveyor belt, drifting past a kaleidoscopic natural aquarium. Home to countless species, from gaudily striped butterflyfish to long-horned unicornfish, the wall is also a nursery for baby fishes, flapping their fins madly just to remain stationary. The current sweeps us on and we enter the coral garden at Yolanda Reef. Huge Gorgonian fans wave as though wafting in the wind, while bunches of broccoli sprout up alongside giant mushroom shapes. My buddy prods me and I turn to see a turtle chomping steadily on the coral; as I move a little closer, I can hear the crunch over my own Darth Vader breathing. We drift along, joined now by a metre-long Napoleon wrasse, with its comical, humped head and sad, swivelling eye that follows us closely.

Around the corner is the wreck of the *Yolanda* itself, which sank carrying bathroom supplies, now assimilated by the sea and encrusted with coral layers camouflaging crocodile- and scorpionfish, its cargo of toilets adorned with stinging green fire corals. A blue-spotted ray rises from the sandy bottom and flaps gracefully away. Looking at my gauge, I realize my air's nearly finished; time to re-enter the world above.

MOUNTAINS AND MIRAGES IN
JEBEL ACACUS

333

LIBYA The prehistoric rock art in Libya's Jebel Acacus depicts a world that no longer exists. It's found only in the under-hangs and caves, where the inhabitants lived and painted the world around them thousands of years ago: elephants, giraffes, ostriches, lions, deer, buffalo, as well as hunting scenes, human rituals, and epic battles. What a contrast today; the vistas now are of a silent, empty land of extraordinary beauty – bare mountains, rocky pinnacles, vast gorges, sand dunes – all radiant with vibrant colours, shades of orange, black, brown, azure (and not a wisp of cloud).

The lush landscape of forests and big game vanished 5000 years ago when the Sahara Desert dramatically dried up. I could feel the dryness in my cracked lips, in the dust that stung my eyes. The only stirrings were the hum of the wind, and the mirages, which are intensely all-consuming, like tongues of flames skidding across the surface, giving the land a rarefied, uncertain quality, as if everything is morphing into something else.

In three days at Jebel Acacus, clocking 370km in a Land Cruiser, camping outdoors under a million stars, I found much to fire the imagination: the ever-changing perspective of the landscape; the sparse flora and fauna, which exists in some valleys despite the four-hundred-metre-deep water table. The plants, looking monstrous and weird, were well adapted; no camel could munch on the thorny acacias, or the bitter desert melons, or the hallucinogenic plant known as felesles.

The herds of wild camels gawked at us as if we were aliens from another world. And if my untrustworthy perceptions were a reality test, then maybe we were – how many times did I see a black smudge on the horizon and wonder if it was a man, or a rock, or something else, for it to be nothing, just another illusion in a landscape so surreal that imagination and reality become one?

334 A WALK OF REPENTANCE: CLIMBING MOUNT SINAI

EGYPT Irrespective of your religious views, the trek up to the summit of Mount Sinai, also known as Mount Horeb and Jabel Musa (literally the "Mountain of Moses") is an inspiring one. Famous for being the supposed location of the Burning Bush and where Moses received the Ten Commandments, Sinai also features in Islamic lore as the place where Mohammed's horse, Boraq, rose into heaven. The landscape is awesome – not in the way the word is bandied about today, but literally, in that it inspires awe in the beholder – a dry, barren vista of craggy peaks, scattered with various chapels, churches and mosques.

There are two possible routes to the summit: the Steps of Repentance, 3750 steps carved out of the rock by monks that lived in St Catherine's Monastery at the mountain's base; and the longer but less steep "Siket el Bashait" – a path that can be tackled either on foot or on camel.

Only the Siket el Bashait can be ascended safely at night, and I was hell-bent on seeing the sun rise over the mountain, so we walked in darkness along the dusty trail, finally climbing the last 750 steps to the summit as the first light of dawn approached. There was no noise save our heavy panting as we made our way up the final stairs. And at the top, only silence – and the sunrise.

335 EXPLORING THE ROMAN RUINS AT DOUGGA

TUNISIA The columns and arches of the crumbling Roman city loomed above us, its winding passages hinting at secret spaces. Below stretched the countryside, the slopes patterned with olive trees and dotted with the occasional dwelling. But this is North Africa, not northern Italy, and in a country more renowned for beach holidays and desert safaris.

Modern Tunisia is unmistakably Arab, but two millennia ago it was the heart of the Romans' North African empire. Just one hundred and forty kilometres from Sicily, the region grew rich selling grain and olive oil to its Mediterranean neighbours, and the cities were large and lavish. Dougga, a couple of hours south of the modern-day capital of Tunis, was one of the biggest. The Romans usually built on flat terrain but here they took a pre-existing Carthaginian township perched on a hilltop and made it their own. The citizens built their homes in the lower reaches, saving the higher regions for the municipal goods: the peak features a cluster of public buildings made of golden stone,

including a theatre, a market, and several temples, the biggest of which is dedicated to Jupiter, the king of the gods. The only clue of an earlier age is a mausoleum tower dating from the ancient African Numidian civilization.

On a bleak January day, we had the place mostly to ourselves, save the odd donkey. We took shelter from the stinging wind and rain in an ancient bathhouse, tiptoeing around the edges to avoid damaging the still-vivid floor mosaic. It is – like everything else here – in remarkably good repair, considering that the local people lived among the ruins until the early twentieth century. They now live a few miles away in Nouvelle Dougga, but many remain connected to the site through work. As the rain cleared, we saw a dozen men in Berber cloaks emerge from the stones and resume repairing the wall of the amphitheatre.

Some Roman ruins are one part scattered stones, nine parts imagination; Dougga is not one of them.

336 GOING OVER THE TOP IN THE ATLAS MOUNTAINS

MOROCCO In the cold early-morning sun, Midelt was a huddle of bright ochre buildings with the mountains of the High Atlas rising pink and huge to the south. But I pressed on, passing just one settlement, the mud-baked village of Aït Balasane, on the way to the top of Col Talghomt, a wide, empty plateau between peaks.

Balasane looked positively biblical bar the solar panels fitted to its houses and mosque. A woman who had been carrying a bundle of rushes home on her back came running towards me, as did her son. They saw my camera and demanded dirhams for photos (I took two). Then they wanted "stylos". Very soon I was swamped with more mothers and children. I picked up my pace before they picked me clean.

It took me an hour to get to the Ziz Valley. Now this is a scary sight. It's difficult to imagine the ferocity with which the Wadi Ziz has cut through the strata thrown up when the Atlas range was being built. Wrenched and folded beyond belief, the rock collapses in shards either side of the river – and yet, to my amazement, lines of sheep calmly traverse the near-vertical slopes. They seemed wholly unaware of the torrent – and the drop – below. Just watching them made me feel dizzy.

Clutching my water bottle, I continued down the road, which seemed to drop forever. Passing the town of Rich, I headed north in the hope of a quiet hotel. I found one, *Kasbah Dounia*, a modern building in the old fortified style, opposite a small oasis. The manager, Abdul, was pleased to see me and we sat drinking tea as huge storks rose out of palm trees on the opposite side of the road. Abdul receives few guests and was clearly delighted to have me in his hotel. But not half as delighted as I was to be there.

337 LOSING YOURSELF IN A GOOD BOOK AT THE BIBLIOTHECA ALEXANDRINA

EGYPT A hallmark of modern architecture, the Bibliotheca Alexandrina is a superb addition to Alexandria's cityscape. A stunning work of stone and metal, the central library features a huge, tilted glass roof reminiscent of a sundial, and the walls are carved with text from over 120 languages, ancient and modern. Its location beside the Mediterranean only emphasizes its sophisticated lines of construction. Everything is created to inspire admiration and to remind the visitor of the importance of the library's role in the past.

The Bibliotheca, which opened in 2003, harks back to Alexandria's role as a prominent seat of learning in ancient times. Ptolemy II of Egypt opened the original Library of Alexandria in the third century BC, from which point it grew into the largest library in the world. Whilst the modern incarnation does not have such high aspirations – it is still relatively small when compared with other international libraries – it is well on its way to establishing itself on the academic circuit, and will continue to do so as the collection grows.

But this is much more than a library. In addition to the central collection there are museums of antiquities, manuscripts and the history of science; galleries for temporary art displays; a planetarium; special sections for children with special workshops; and rare books available nowhere else in the world. You can wander around the permanent collection of Egyptian filmmaker, writer and artist Shadi Abdel Salam. Or take a seat in front of a cultural film relating the history of Egypt. And once you've done all that, it's not a bad place to find a quiet corner and settle down with a good book or two.

338 SLOGGING OVER SAND DUNES IN THE MARATHON DES SABLES

MOROCCO Eating tajine at the Jemaa el Fna. Listening to Berber storytelling under a star-lit sky. Staying in a converted kasbah. These are all great North African experiences you would want to do again. The Marathon des Sables is not.

"The Toughest Footrace on Earth". "The Ultimate Endurance Event". Call it what you like but at the end of the day – at the end of six long, gruelling days to be precise – it's still the hardest, most ridiculous thing you will probably ever do.

Running a marathon in the 120-degree heat of the Sahara is courageous. Running six, back to back, is downright crazy, but that's exactly what's required if you want to call yourself a finisher in this 254-kilometre-long footslog. And it's what eight hundred competitors manage to do each year – and all of them carrying everything they think they'll need for the duration of the race (food, clothes, sleeping bag and so on) in a rucksack on their back.

Most runners complete the course in around six days, although the record is an incredible 19 hours. Poor old Mauro Prosperi, on the other hand, came home in closer to two weeks, after losing his way in a sandstorm and wandering lost in the desert for more than nine days. Just make sure you pack a compass in your rucksack as well.

339 KEEPING COOL IN THE OLD TOWN OF GHADAMES

LIBYA I stumble in the darkness of the covered walkways of Ghadames, feeling giddy as though an intruder in a forbidden town. The alleys have many branches; I follow the pools of light streaming in from the scattering of high skylights. The design of covered walkways certainly works; it's chilly and musty, and I forget that I'm in the Sahara Desert until I reach an open square. Its pastel colours are romantic: yellow-orange sand on the ground, radiant-white gypsum walls, green palm-trunk doorways and an azure cloudless sky.

The houses in Ghadames are as dense as honeycomb – it's possible for the women to travel about town by walking on the rooftops (keeping separate from the men) – and its covered alleys like an underground maze. I imagine the inhabitants milling about in dark corners, but now Ghadames belongs to ghosts: government handouts have enticed its former 6000 Berber inhabitants to modern houses outside the old town. The desolation is part of the allure; I only occasionally meet other tourists.

So I wander aimlessly and marvel at the old town's intelligent design; the way, for example, water was tapped from aquifers and channelled to the inhabitants in stringent allocations. There is much to see – public baths, old mosques, groves of date palms – and there are birds everywhere, hoopoes and doves and other colourful desert species. Then I find an open house, and the decor inside is so intense – geometric designs blooming across the walls, trunks and rugs covering the rest of the interior, and many, many mirrors, strategically placed to amplify light from the skylight – that for a moment I suspect that it is overdone for tourists' awe. No, the owner says, this is typical, and the inhabitants still maintain the houses as summer retreats. The air-con in their modern abodes can't cope with the fifty-degree heat, and only Ghadames's natural-cooling design offers a reprieve. The old town continues to endure, as it has done for hundreds of years.

340
HAGGLING IN THE SOUKS OF FES

MOROCCO Everywhere you look in Fes's Medina – the ancient walled part of the city – there are alleys bedecked with exquisite handmade crafts. Here the city's distinctive ceramics jostle for space with rich fabrics, musical instruments and red tasselled fezzes (which take their name from the city). Most of these items are made in the medina itself, in areas such as the carpenters' souk, redolent of cedarwood, or in the rather less aromatic tanneries, where leather is cured in stinky vats of cow's urine and pigeon poo, among other substances. In the dyers' souk, the cobbles run with multicoloured pigments used to tint gaudy hanks of wool, while nearby Place Seffarine, by the tenth-century Kairaouine Mosque, reverberates to the sound of metalworkers hammering intricate designs into brass.

Should you wish to buy, however, it's not a matter of "how much?", "here you go", "bye". Love it or hate it, haggling is de rigueur. These crafts are made with love and patience, and should not be bought in a rush. Rather, the shopkeeper will expect you to dally awhile, perhaps enjoy a cup of tea – sweet, green and flavoured with Moroccan mint – and come to an agreement on a price. This is both a commercial transaction and a game, and skilled hagglers are adept at theatrics – "How much? Are you crazy?" "For this fine piece of art? Don't insult me!"

Know how much you are prepared to pay, offer something less, and let the seller argue you up. If you don't agree a price, nothing is lost, and you've spent a pleasant time conversing with the shopkeeper. And you can always go back the next day and reopen discussions.

341 MOPPING UP A MOROCCAN TAJINE

MOROCCO Robert Carrier, one of the twentieth century's most influential food writers, rated Moroccan cuisine as second only to that of France. Which is perhaps a little hyperbolic, for, outside the grandest kitchens, Moroccan cooking is decidedly simple, with only a half dozen or so dishes popping up on most local menus. But no matter where you are in the country, from a top restaurant to the humblest roadside stall, there is one dish you can depend upon: the tajine.

A tajine is basically a stew. It is steam-cooked in an earthenware dish (also called a tajine) with a fancifully conical lid, and most often prepared over a charcoal fire. That means slow-cooking, with flavours locked in and meat that falls from the bone.

What goes in depends on what's available, but a number of combinations have achieved classic and ubiquitous status: mrouzia (lamb or mutton with prunes and almonds – and lots of honey) and mqualli (chicken with olives and pickled lemons), for example. On the coast, you might be offered a fish tajine, too, frequently red snapper or swordfish. And tajines can taste almost as good with just vegetables: artichokes, tomatoes, potatoes, peppers, olives, and again those pickled lemons, which you see in tall jars in every shop and market stall. The herbs and spices, too, are crucial: cinnamon, ginger, garlic and a pinch of the mysterious ras al-hanut, the "best in shop" spice selection any Moroccan stall can prepare for you.

There's no need for a knife or fork. Tajines are served in the dish in which they are cooked, and then scooped and mopped up – using your right hand, of course – with delicious Moroccan flat bread. Perfect for sharing.

And when you're through, don't forget to sit back and enjoy the customary three tiny glasses of super-sweet mint tea.

342 RAMADAN NIGHTS

EGYPT Dusk is falling and everyone is out on the street. After a day spent under the burning sun, with reserves of patience and blood-sugar at zero, Cairo's fasting millions all seem intent on letting their hair down.

You might think visiting Cairo during Ramadan is a bit perverse. This ninth month of the Muslim calendar was when Prophet Mohammed received his first revelation and is, consequently, holy: Muslims abstain from eating, drinking and smoking during daylight hours. But while the days are tough, with tempers on a short fuse, after dark you get to join in with what feels like a citywide carnival.

As sunset approaches, Cairenes move at a blistering pace, scampering to catch buses and weaving heedlessly through the traffic. Everyone is rushing to be in place at the table when the mosques sound the call to prayer – the sign that the day's fasting is over. Many restaurants open for iftar (the sunset meal): take your place at a communal bench and wait until the mosques sound the call. Traditionally, you break the fast with dates, and then everyone tucks into fuul (beans) whether you are in a simple café or a lavish buffet in the poshest eateries – always in a welcoming spirit of shared endeavour. Restaurants overflow with people, scoffing happily together under traditional decorative Ramadan lanterns.

As the evening rolls on, the party spirit takes hold. Dressed-up Cairenes pack the streets. Lights blaze. Traffic toots. Firecrackers explode. All the souks – including the famous Khan el-Khalili bazaar – do a roaring trade. Whirling dervishes perform in the squares and live music concerts take place across the city. Full-scale partying continues into the small hours – whereupon suhour, the dawn meal, marks the start of another day's fasting.

343 CAMEL FIGHTING AT THE FESTIVAL OF THE SAHARA

TUNISIA If the landscape of Douz seems familiar, it's because the town was used as the backdrop for *Star Wars*. But this desert settlement, known as the "Gateway of the Sahara", isn't just for Jedi pilgrimages. At the end of each year, the locals make the most of the fantastic desert location for a four-day knees-up, the aptly named Festival of the Sahara. Over the course of a long weekend, thousands of people gather to smoke hookahs, take in displays of traditional craft, music and dance, and watch a huge variety of events and spectacles, from juggling and belly dancing to the incredible sport of camel fighting. A bizarre but fascinating spectacle, camel fights entail all the pomp of a big-name boxing match, and almost as much betting. After being paraded around in front of their enthusiastic followers, the camels circle each other cautiously, looking for an opening before locking themselves into combat – a good fighter has a repertoire of dexterous moves, including tripping, throwing (by pushing their head between their rival's legs) and forcing a submission through sheer neck power. And you thought they could only spit.

344 GREETING THE PHARAOHS IN THE VALLEY OF THE KINGS

EGYPT They're badly lit, hot and claustrophobic. They're packed with sweating, camera-toting tour groups. But nowhere else can you get so vivid a glimpse of ancient Egypt than in the 3000-year-old tombs where the ancient dynasties of Thebes laid their rulers to rest – in the Valley of the Kings.

Thebes' temples were built on the east bank of the Nile, to greet the rising sun and celebrate life. But where the sun set was a place of death. Here, the pharaohs sank tombs into the rock to hide their embalmed bodies, decorating the subterranean passageways with images of the gods they would meet after death on their journey to immortality.

The Valley of the Kings is huge, located across the river from the busy town of Luxor and hemmed between crags in an arid desertscape under the scorching sun. Its light is glaring, the heat exhausting, the air dry as dust. There are dozens of tombs, so you need to choose judiciously: Tutankhamun is an obvious draw, but Tut was a minor pharaoh and his tomb is relatively small (and commands a hefty surcharge).

Instead, go for Ramses III – one of the grandest and longest tombs, running for almost 200m under the rubbly hills. As you descend narrow steps to the tomb entrance, the walls close in. Pass through the dim gateway and the floor drops further: you're in a narrow, gloomy shaft, with images of scarabs, crocodiles and dog-headed gods for company. Further down into the musty depths, you come face to face with the garishly colourful wall-paintings for which these tombs are famous: the sun god Ra journeys through the twelve gates of the underworld, harpists sing to the god of the air and pictorial spells weave magic to protect the dead pharaoh in the afterlife.

345 DRIVING THE ROUTE OF A THOUSAND KASBAHS

MOROCCO East of Marrakesh, up over the dizzying Tizi n'Tichka pass, runs one of the oldest trading routes in history, snaking out across the Sahara and linking the Berber heartland with Timbuktu, Niger and old Sudan.

The gold and slaves that once financed the southern oases are long gone, but the road is still peppered with the remains of their fabulous kasbahs – fortified dwellings of baked mud and straw – and as it sprints out into the Sahara, it passes great sweeping palmeries of dates, olives and almonds, their lush greens a vivid contrast to the barren desert.

The cream of the architectural crop is at Aït Benhaddou, near the start of the route. Although most of the inhabitants have moved to the modern village across the river, it's a magical place, its stunning collection of crenellated kasbahs, their crumbling clay walls glowing orange in the soft light of late afternoon, among the most intricately decorated of the deep south.

STAYING WITH A FAMILY IN MERZOUGA

346

MOROCCO Waking up in a nomad's black-wool tent, surrounded by mile upon mile of ochre-coloured sand dunes, the first thing that struck me was the silence: a deep, muffled nothing. The second was the cold. Even beneath a stack of blankets, it was chilly enough to numb the end of my nose. Only after three glasses of mint tea by the fireside were my fingers warm enough to tackle the zip on my puffa jacket and help saddle up the camels for the day's trek.

Despite the chilly mornings, January is the best month to visit southern Morocco's Erg Chebbi dunes. The skies are big and blue, the horizons crisp and, best of all, the hordes who descend here later in the year blissfully absent. Back at our guesthouse, *Chez Tihri*, at the end of our morning's ride, we could enjoy the wondrous spectacle of the sand hills in peace and quiet.

Chez Tihri is a rarity in a corner of the country notorious for its highly commoditized versions of the desert and its people: an auberge run by a Tamasheq-speaking Amazigh (Tuareg) where you actually feel a genuine sense of place. Built in old-school kasbah style, its crenellated pisé walls, adorned with bold geometric patterns in patriotic reds and greens, shelter a warren of cosy rooms, each decorated with rugs, pottery and lanterns, and interconnected by dark, earthy corridors.

As well as being a congenial host, Omar Tihri, dressed in imposing white turban and flowing robe, is a passionate advocate for Amazigh traditions and culture, and living proof that tourism can be a force for good in this region. A slice of the profits from *Chez Tihri* go towards funding a women's weaving co-op, in addition to a small school where Tamasheq-speaking children, who are poorly catered for by the mainstream state education in the area, can learn French and Arabic.

347 IDLING THE DAY AWAY IN ESSAOUIRA

MOROCCO Few things can match the maritime thrill of snacking on freshly grilled fish while ambling over an active harbour's sun-bleached planks, seagulls circling above ancient stone ramparts. Such is life in the laid-back Moroccan beach town of Essaouira.

The leafy, cobblestone boulevards and the soft, salt-steeped air of Essaouira (or Mogador) are a world away from bustling Marrakesh. After a stroll around the blue and white ribs of partially built boats, head down past the ruffled pines to the windswept beach below. Instead of caving in to the insistent offers of camel rides on some seriously rough-looking dromedaries, you'd do better to venture south along the shore. Even those sceptical of local lore will want to cut inland at the estuary to visit the small Berber town of Diabat, where Jimi Hendrix allegedly hung out during his 1969 trip to Morocco, – it's worth it if only for the fun of scrambling over a bridge made of stone chunks from a fallen rampart.

You should cover up on the more popular stretch of beach near town, but it's fine to strip off for a bikini-clad swim in the less crowded waters further along the coast, where wild, pastel-green waves break in tiers like some kinetic layer cake. Behind you, silky dunes erode and re-form before your eyes under the fierce North African wind.

Once you've cooled off, head back to the harbour to cap your beach wanderings with just-caught sardines, the country's main export, grilled to sizzling perfection in front of you. Walk beyond the fish stands to pick up a whipped fruit juice drink at one of the many seaside cafés and rest your legs while watching the sea darken to a deep Mogador blue, a shade named specially for the town.

348 ENJOYING THE VIEW FROM THE FISHAWI CAFÉ

EGYPT In a small alley in the heart of medieval Cairo is the famous *Fishawi Café*, where you sit on cane chairs at marble-topped tables in the narrow mirror-lined passage. Waiters carrying brass trays dart from table to table, weaving in and out among the street hawkers who offer you everything from a shoeshine to a woman's song accompanied by a tambourine to necklaces of jasmine flowers.

Fishawi has been open every day and night for over two hundred years, and here as you sip a thick black coffee or a sweet tea and perhaps enjoy the gentle smoke of a narghile, the Egyptian water pipe, you can immerse your senses in the atmosphere of the Thousand and One Nights, for all around you is Khan al-Khalili, a vast bazaar dating back to the fourteenth century, its shaded streets as intricate as inlay work, its shops and stalls sharp with spices, sweet with perfumes and dazzling with brass and gold and silver. This is exotic pandemonium, lively throughout the day and well into the night.

Fishawi is within hearing of the calls to prayer rising from the minarets of the Sayyidna al-Hussein, the principal congregational mosque of the city, and of the popular nightly celebrations that take place in the square outside throughout the month of Ramadan. Opposite the square, and far older, is the mosque of al-Azhar, the oldest university in the world and the foremost centre or Islamic theology. Naguib Mahfouz, Egypt's Nobel Prize-winning novelist, was born and raised in the neighbourhood, and it provided him with the setting of many of his novels. For Mahfouz, the streets and alleyways around the *Fishawi Café* were a timeless world, which, as he wrote of Midaq Alley, a five-minute walk from the cafe, "connects with life as a whole and yet at the same time retains a number of the secrets of a world now past".

Fishawi is on the corner of Sikket al-Bedestan, the main street through Khan al-Khalili, on which the classy *Naguib Mahfouz Café* takes the novelist's name but otherwise has nothing to do with him. For atmosphere and mystery, take one of those little tables at the *Fishawi Café*.

349 EXPLORING THE DUNE LAKES OF UBARI

LIBYA One of the Sahara's many natural wonders lies west of Sebha in southwestern Libya. The vast Idhan Ubari or Ubari Sand Sea spills out in all directions like a vast barrier but exploring the interior in a 4WD leads to the unexpected sight of half a dozen palm-rimmed lakes twinkling at the feet of immense dunes. Where the water comes from is still unknown – some lakes are warm, others cold, and once a long-gone tribe survived here off lake shrimps mashed with dates. The best known is Lake Gabroun, but the prettiest is Um el Ma (Mother of the Waters), many people's idealized image of a Saharan oasis.

350 SEEING THE OLD CITY OF TLEMCEN

ALGERIA The mountain vastness of Tlemcen is one of northern Algeria's pre-eminent cities, and one of the Islamic world's great centres, stuffed with mosques (with visiting hours for non-Muslims), its architecture redolent of the Andalusian period, centuries before the European carve-up of North Africa. Inside the city walls, the visually arresting interior of the eleventhth-century Grand Mosquée, inspired by the Mezquita in Cordoba, Spain, includes multiple rows of columns and arches. Tlemcen's old centre is a warren of narrow alleys, strictly explorable on foot only, and seething with commercial energy – cabinet-making, embroidery, jewellery-making and leather-working.

351

TRANS-SAHARA

BY MOTORBIKE

ALGERIA–NIGER Riding across Africa, two stages stand out: the clammy, bug-ridden byways of the Congo Basin – where "infrastructure" is just a good score in Scrabble – and the Sahara. The latter's appeal is uncomplicated: the stark purity of landforms stirred by dawn winds; the simplicity of your daily mission – survival; and the brief serenity of hushed, starlit evenings. It's just you, your bike and the desert.

Disembarking at Algiers is chaos, but muddle through and by nightfall you'll emerge in the ravines of the Atlas, where the desert unrolls before you. By Ghardaia things are warming up and near El Meniaa breathtaking dunes begin spilling over the road. Settlements now appear maybe only once a day and so become vital staging posts. Other travellers, too, acquire a hallowed status: fellow pilgrims on the desert highway.

Some days the road is washed away, submerged in sand or lost in a dust storm, but you soldier on. You pass through the Arak Gorge, a portal to the white sands and granite domes of the haunting Immidir plateau. By now your apprehension has subsided and you dare to relax. Within days the volcanic peaks of the Hoggar rise and you roll into Tamanrasset; chugging down the main street you look at the locals and they look back, at a dusty wanderer on a horse with no name.

It's time to focus on the final leg – four days across the long-dreaded piste to Agadez. Those first few moments riding the loaded machine on the sands will be a shock but you must be assertive, gunning the throttle across soft patches, resting where you can.

The Niger border is a crossroads: monochrome sobriety meets the colourful exuberance of sub-Saharan Africa. Brightly clothed women mix with mysterious nomads and, for you, an ice-cold beer in the shabby *Hotel Sahara* washes away the desert dust.

352 EXPLORING BENI-ABBÈS AND TIMIMOUN

ALGERIA As you race along the strip of road south of the Atlas Mountains, the presence of the Sahara in all its vastness begins to dawn on you. It's almost comforting to reach the Arabian Nights oasis of Beni-Abbès, where you can camp in the endless, swaying groves of date palms near the water, or stay in town beneath the colossal dunes. Further south, and almost impossibly exotic in its high red walls, the remote outpost of Timimoun, deep in the desert away from the main trans-Sahara route, exerts a more severe appeal, but it is a fabulous and little-visited destination, with a wonderful old centre of shady alleys full of crafts workers. To the north of town, irrigated palm groves and gardens stretch over a dry salt lake, with more villages to explore, many with inhabitants of West African ancestry.

353 GETTING TO KNOW THE SOUKS OF TRIPOLI

LIBYA Tripoli is one of the world's safest big cities, and has excellent souks: a fine combination that encourages you to wander freely. Most of the souks, or market quarters, are located in the arched alleys of the Medina – the walled old city of Tripoli right by the port – and each has its own speciality and character, from the noisy clamour of the copper-smiths' souk to the colour and commerce of tailors' and shoe shops and the aroma of vegetable, fish, spice and meat stalls along Souk al-Turk. When it comes to buying, there's refreshingly little hard sell, and no need to haggle like crazy. Gold and silver, sold by weight, are good purchases, as are Berber wool rugs in geometric patterns, and more utilitarian domestic items that often make the best souvenirs, like baskets and leather, local robes (galabeyas), pottery and metal utensils, and charms and folk medicine from across the Sahara.

354 GILF KEBIR: THE LAND OF THE ENGLISH PATIENT

EGYPT The Cave of the Swimmers depicted in the film *The English Patient* exists, in the far southwest of Egypt, the most arid corner of the Sahara, and an area even nomads avoid. Discovered by Count Laszlo de Almasy, the real "English Patient" in 1933, a couple of "swimming" figures survive on the flaking walls and today rock art sites depicting long extinct animals and abstruse rituals are still being discovered. This is the Gilf Kebir, unoccupied since Neolithic times. Legends abound of lost oases and invading armies swallowed by the sands. On the desert floor, World War II fuel cans mingle with the earliest pottery and Paleolithic stone axes, from a time when humans first took to their feet.

MISCELLANY

UNESCO WORLD HERITAGE SITES

ALGERIA

Al Qal'a of Beni Hammad
Djémila
M'zab Valley
Tassili n'Ajjer Mountains
Timgad
Tipasa
Algiers Kasbah

EGYPT

Abu Mena
Ancient Thebes
Memphis
The Pyramids of Giza
Abu Simbel
St Catherine's Monastery, Sinai
Wadi Al-Hitan

LIBYA

Cyrene
Leptis Magna
Sabratha
Rock-art sites of Jebel Acacus
Ghadamès old town

MOROCCO

Fes medina
Marrakesh medina
Ksar of Aït Benhaddou
Meknes
Volubilis
Tétouan medina
Essaouira medina
El Jadida Portuguese town

TUNISIA

Amphitheatre of El Jem
Tunis medina
Carthage
Ichkeul National Park
Kerkuane
Kairouan
Sousse medina
Dougga

AFRICAN EXPLORERS

The colourful exploits of European adventurers such as David Livingstone, Mungo Park and Richard Burton are well known, but arguably the world's greatest explorer is actually from Africa. In the fourteenth century, Morocco's **Ibn Battuta** travelled over 100,000km over a thirty-year period. In addition to much of Africa, Battuta's claim to have been all over the Middle East, Central and Southeast Asia and China, far outstripped the travelling credentials of his near-contemporary, Marco Polo.

RETURN OF THE MUMMY

Egyptologist Zahi Hawass is a leading voice in the archaeological **repatriation** movement – the campaign to get artefacts, many looted in colonial times, returned to their places of origin. The Rosetta Stone at the British Museum is perhaps the most significant, but it may only be a matter of time before the increasing sophistication of DNA testing and genealogical techniques lead to demands for the return of many of the embalmed nobles and dignitaries – mummies – whose haunting faces can be seen in museums around the world.

MOROCCAN, NOT

Africa is all in African hands these days, isn't it? Not quite. The first landfall for many European visitors to Africa is another part of Europe, the tiny **Spanish enclave** of Ceuta, facing another strange colonial outpost, Gibraltar, across the famous Strait. Ceuta is an integral part of Spain, complete with euros, churros and toros. The similar Spanish enclave of Melilla, a little further east along the Moroccan coast, is even smaller. Both territories are now defended by huge fences to prevent African refugees from disappearing into the EU.

BERBERS

Dialects of Arabic are spoken throughout the countries of North Africa. The people, however, have more diverse **ethnic origins** than you might imagine. The original inhabitants of the region were the **Berbers**, whose adoption of Arabic and Islam came through conquest and migration from the east. Berber languages are still spoken in the highlands of Morocco and Algeria and by the Tuareg nomads whose heartland was Libya but who move with their camels (and occasionally 4WDs) all over the Sahara, the men (but rarely women) often veiled in indigo-dyed headscarves.

"A stone from the hand of a friend is an apple"

Moroccan proverb

SAHARA SCALE

The biggest desert in the world (or, to geographers who insist on including Antarctica, the second biggest), the **Sahara** defies imagination in its scale. At nearly ten million square kilometres, it would easily swallow the USA. Crossing the middle, from north to south, takes a good four days of steady driving, over largely trackless wastes: even today, there's no continuous tarmac. By the time you reach the outpost of Tamanrasset, halfway across, you're further from Algiers than Algiers is from London. Big dunes (known as barkans) are comparatively rare, but there are some monsters in southern Algeria, where they can reach more than 450m high – taller than New York's Empire State Building.

HOT SPOT

The highest **temperature** ever recorded was in the Libyan town of Al 'Aziziyah on September 13, 1922, when the mercury reached 57.7°C (135.9°F) – in the shade.

POT SPOT

"Wanna buy hashish? Very nice. Cool, my friend. Have a little piece." You can't visit Morocco and escape at least one **drugs** offer, often hundreds (it seems to depend on your look more than your age). Most of the hash – resin rubbed from marijuana plants grown on Rif mountain cannabis farms – is filched surplus from the huge quantities destined to be smuggled to Europe and beyond.

SENSITIVE CARTOGRAPHY

In 1975, King Hassan II of Morocco organized a mass, popular march into the phosphate-rich region of **Western Sahara**, nominally a Spanish colony at the time, to claim it for Greater Morocco. More than a quarter of a million Moroccans joined the procession, and, despite international protests and UN resolutions, tens of thousands of Moroccans have since emigrated into the Sahrawis' homeland. The Polisario armed resistance movement, with its sprawling refugee capital at Tindouf, deep in the desert, has repeatedly struck back, usually with Algerian assistance, to little avail. A UN-sponsored autonomy referendum, long overdue, is still supposed to be held, one day, but as the years go by, the question of who is and who isn't a Sahrawi gets harder to ascertain. Meanwhile, Moroccan security police still examine the maps and guides of travellers to check they're not carrying any misleading information.

TANGIER: HOME OF THE BEATS

The year Jack Kerouac's *On The Road* was first published, 1957, coincided with a wave of interest from writers and artists in the bohemian lifestyle supposedly on offer in the international port city of **Tangier**. Kerouac and Allen Ginsberg stayed at the *Hôtel el Muniria*, where William Burroughs wrote *The Naked Lunch* in room 9.

GO ON A DATE

Large and squishy, chewy like toffee, hard as wood, weevily – the **date** is the quintessential Saharan food. Since the earliest camel caravans, it was the dry-skinned, sugary fruit like a small turd that supported human endeavours where no other food could cope. Dates originated, like so much else, in the land of two rivers, present-day Iraq, and date palms are today grown in orchards throughout North Africa, and in oasis settlements in the deepest parts of the Sahara.

ISABELLE EBERHARDT

Nineteenth-century European society threw up some extraordinary individuals, few more so than **Isabelle Eberhardt**. Born into a radical family in Geneva in 1877, she went to Algeria when she was 20 to start a new life with her widowed mother, who died soon after they arrived, leaving Isabelle to fend for herself. She soon spoke fluent Arabic and travelled widely in the desert, dressed as a man, and, eschewing her European anarchist background, following the pious code of Wahhabist Islam. At the same time, she continued to pursue a passionate and uninhibited lifestyle that recklessly toyed with the mores of her adopted home. The fascinating and inspiring *Diaries of Isabelle Eberhardt* are a highly recommended read if you're travelling in North Africa. Eberhardt was killed in a flash flood in the Sahara in 1904.

"The whole world is in revolt. Soon there will be only five kings left: the King of England, the King of Spades, the King of Clubs, the King of Hearts, and the King of Diamonds"

King Farouk, Egypt's last reigning monarch

THE BATTLE OF ALGIERS

If there's one film you must see before visiting Algeria, it's Gillo Pontecorvo's multi-Oscar-nominated 1966 masterpiece, **The Battle of Algiers**. Shot in black and white, in a neo-realist documentary style, it follows the radicalization of anti-colonial sentiment in the capital's old city, the Kasbah, in the early 1950s, as the war with the French was raging. Sounds like a hard viewing experience? Well, it's not Tom Cruise and Tom Hanks, but the movie's honesty about atrocities on both sides, its use of location and non-professional actors, and its superb score by Ennio Morricone make for a compelling two hours.

SACRED SERPENTS

The **asp**, also known as the Egyptian cobra, was worshipped in ancient Egypt. The snake was seen as a symbol of power, and its image adorned the crown of the pharaohs.

NILE FEVER

The dancing known in the west as belly dance is an Egyptian form known as **raks sharki**. A long-established solo performance repertoire it holds a major place in the hearts of millions of Egyptians and is often performed at weddings and other family occasions.

THE ELEPHANTS OF CARTHAGE

Carthage was a Phoenician city near Tunis, founded by migrants from present-day Lebanon, which became a civilization to rival Rome in the second and third centuries BC. The state wielded formidable military might, and included specialist divisions, one of which was a mounted army of war-elephants. These, the jumbos that Hannibal led over the Alps to take Rome by surprise, were a hardy and tractable desert subspecies, Loxodonta Africana pharaoensis, that became extinct in the early Christian era.

CLUBBING IN DAKAR • **SOAKING IN WIKKI WARM SPRINGS** • PARTYING WITH THE TUAREG AT THE FESTIVAL IN THE DESERT • THE GOLD COAST: SUN, SEA AND SLAVE FORTS • TAKE A WALK IN THE RAINFOREST • ISLAND-HOPPING OFF THE AFRICAN COAST • TWITCHERS' DELIGHT: WATCHING HORNBILLS • PEAKING ON FOGO • GETTING BACK TO BASICS WITH THE PEOPLE OF THE VEIL • SEEING THE JUNGLE THROUGH THE EYES OF THE BAKA • DESTINATION TIMBUKTU • TREKKING IN DOGON COUNTRY • DEMYSTIFYING VOODOO IN OUIDAH • CYCLING A RING ROAD WITH A DIFFERENCE • ADMIRING THE CATCH ON SANYANG BEACH • BIRD-WATCHING IN THE BANC D'ARGUIN • RIDING THE WAGONS ON THE WORLD'S LONGEST TRAIN • IN SEARCH OF THE BEST CHOCOLATE IN THE WORLD • RUNNING AGROUND IN THE BIJAGÓS ISLANDS • SACRED SPACE: THE GRAND MOSQUE IN DJENNÉ • JOURNEYING UP THE RIVER NIGER • **CONQUERING MOUNT CAMEROON** • THE MYSTERIOUS RUINS OF DJADO • VISITING THE ANCIENT LIBRARIES OF CHINGUETTI • CLUBBING IN DAKAR • SOAKING IN WIKKI WARM SPRINGS • PARTYING WITH THE TUAREG AT THE FESTIVAL IN THE DESERT • THE GOLD COAST: SUN, SEA AND SLAVE FORTS • TAKE A WALK IN THE RAINFOREST • ISLAND-HOPPING OFF THE AFRICAN COAST • TWITCHERS' DELIGHT: WATCHING HORNBILLS • PEAKING ON FOGO • SEEING THE JUNGLE THROUGH THE EYES OF THE BAKA • GETTING BACK TO BASICS WITH THE PEOPLE OF THE VEIL • DESTINATION TIMBUKTU • TREKKING IN DOGON COUNTRY • DEMYSTIFYING VOODOO IN OUIDAH • CYCLING A RING ROAD WITH A DIFFERENCE • ADMIRING THE CATCH ON SANYANG BEACH • **BIRD-WATCHING IN THE BANC D'ARGUIN** • RIDING THE WAGONS ON THE WORLD'S LONGEST TRAIN • IN SEARCH OF THE BEST CHOCOLATE IN THE WORLD • RUNNING AGROUND IN THE BIJAGÓS ISLANDS • SACRED SPACE: THE GRAND MOSQUE IN DJENNÉ • JOURNEYING UP THE RIVER NIGER • CONQUERING MOUNT CAMEROON • THE MYSTERIOUS RUINS OF DJADO • VISITING THE ANCIENT LIBRARIES OF CHINGUETTI • **CLUBBING IN DAKAR** • SOAKING IN WIKKI WARM SPRINGS • PARTYING WITH THE TUAREG AT THE FESTIVAL IN THE DESERT • THE GOLD COAST: SUN, SEA AND SLAVE FORTS • TAKE A WALK IN THE RAINFOREST • ISLAND-HOPPING OFF THE AFRICAN COAST • TWITCHERS' DELIGHT: WATCHING HORNBILLS • PEAKING ON FOGO • SEEING THE JUNGLE THROUGH THE EYES OF THE BAKA • GETTING BACK TO BASICS WITH THE PEOPLE OF THE VEIL • DESTINATION TIMBUKTU • TREKKING IN DOGON COUNTRY • DEMYSTIFYING VOODOO IN OUIDAH • CYCLING A RING ROAD WITH A DIFFERENCE • ADMIRING THE CATCH ON SANYANG BEACH • BIRD-WATCHING IN THE BANC D'ARGUIN • RIDING THE WAGONS ON THE WORLD'S LONGEST TRAIN • IN SEARCH OF THE BEST CHOCOLATE IN THE WORLD • RUNNING AGROUND IN THE BIJAGÓS ISLANDS • JOURNEYING UP THE RIVER NIGER • **SACRED SPACE: THE GRAND MOSQUE IN DJENNÉ** • CONQUERING MOUNT CAMEROON • THE MYSTERIOUS RUINS OF DJADO • VISITING THE ANCIENT LIBRARIES OF CHINGUETTI • CLUBBING IN DAKAR • SOAKING IN WIKKI WARM SPRINGS • PARTYING WITH THE TUAREG AT THE FESTIVAL IN THE DESERT • THE GOLD COAST: SUN, SEA AND SLAVE FORTS • TAKE A WALK IN THE RAINFOREST • ISLAND-HOPPING OFF THE AFRICAN COAST • TWITCHERS' DELIGHT: WATCHING HORNBILLS • PEAKING ON FOGO • SEEING THE JUNGLE THROUGH THE EYES OF THE BAKA • GETTING BACK TO BASICS WITH THE PEOPLE OF THE VEIL • DESTINATION TIMBUKTU • TREKKING IN DOGON COUNTRY • DEMYSTIFYING VOODOO IN OUIDAH • CYCLING A RING ROAD WITH A DIFFERENCE • ADMIRING THE CATCH ON SANYANG BEACH • BIRD-WATCHING IN THE BANC D'ARGUIN • RIDING THE WAGONS ON THE WORLD'S LONGEST TRAIN • IN SEARCH OF THE BEST CHOCOLATE IN THE WORLD • RUNNING AGROUND IN THE BIJAGÓS ISLANDS • SACRED SPACE: THE GRAND MOSQUE IN DJENNÉ • JOURNEYING UP THE RIVER

WEST AFRICA

355–378

CAPE
VERDE
ISLANDS

BIRD-WATCHING
IN THE BANC D'ARGUIN

MAURITANIA

MALI

NIGER

CLUBBING IN DAKAR 355

SENEGAL

THE GAMBIA

GUINEA-BISSAU

GUINEA

SACRED SPACE:
THE GRAND MOSQUE IN DJENNÉ

BURKINA
FASO

CÔTE
D'IVOIRE

GHANA

SOAKING IN
WIKKI WARM SPRINGS 362

SIERRA
LEONE

NIGERIA

LIBERIA

TOGO
BENIN

CAMEROON

CONQUERING
MOUNT CAMEROON

355 CLUBBING IN DAKAR

SENEGAL "Nanga def?" "Jama rek." The throaty greeting and response of the Wolof language is all around us as we hustle to get into a soiree at one of the busy clubs in Dakar, Senegal's dusty capital. Under the orange glow of street lamps, some outrageously upfront flirting is going on and pervades the warm, perfume-laden air like static.

Inside, the lights swirl; the simple stage fills; the clear, high tones of the lead vocals surge through a battering of drums; and the floor becomes a mass of shaking hips, bellies, arms and legs. It's no place to be shy – but there's no better place in Africa to get over shyness quickly.

Nightlife in Dakar is dominated by big-name musicians and their clubs. The city, staunchly Muslim (most Senegalese are devoted followers of Sufi saints) yet keenly fun-loving, is a magnet for musicians from across West Africa, drawn by a thriving CD market, famous venues and the best recording facilities in the region. The principal sounds are mbalax – the frenetic, drum-driven style popularized by Youssou N'Dour and his Super Etoile band – and hip-hop, whose ambassadors Daara J introduced the Senegalese streets to the world.

Going out in Dakar is not only about music and mating: clued-up Dakarois are obsessed with the mercurial fashion scene. However you wear it, your look is very important; go for bold and shiny and you won't fail to impress. Recently girls have all been adopting singer Viviane N'Dour's cut-offs-and-skimpy-top style, which is a daring innovation in a country where yards of beaten damask cloth is still a byword for glamour.

356 DESTINATION TIMBUKTU

MALI The medieval city of Timbuktu, clinging to life between Saharan dunes and an ancient loop of the Niger River, has always held a certain mystique. The name alone conjures resonant images of the camel caravans and gold merchants of its heyday. Yet even now, its glory days long faded, Timbuktu still retains its appeal as a destination, largely because of its physical isolation – getting here is always a challenge.

Taking the easiest approach via Mali's main road – a narrow strip of tarmac that runs across the plains – we halt at the truck-stop at Douentza. Here, over a bowl of rice and sauce, we ask everyone we see about "transport à Tombouctou". In fine West African style, something is bound to turn up.

The next day, at sunrise, the hotel night watch raps on our door to tell us we have a lift, and within minutes we're in a Land Rover, driven by a former Tuareg rebel commander, thrashing up the gravel road north in the coolness of dawn. The day unfolds in a blur of dust, bouncing suspension and shuddering halts as the "road" dissolves periodically into a plait of sandy tracks. We pass Tuareg encampments and groups of camels, hobbled to stop them straying. Near a Fula shepherd camp, we stop to make tea in the roasting, silent noontime, breaking twigs from the acacia giving us shade to coax a tiny fire. A girl brings us a calabash of goat's milk – traditional rules of hospitality still apply.

Early in the afternoon, we pitch over a gentle rise, and there is the Niger, fronted by a great flat apron of dried mud beach to cross before we fetch up by the ferry embarkation point. Ten minutes up the avenue, on the other side, we reach the entrance to the city. While the mosques, sandy streets and markets are beguiling, it's the sense of achievement we feel at simply getting here, and having our passports stamped at the tourist office – where they welcome each visitor with a warm handshake – that really leaves an impression.

357 THE GOLD COAST: SUN, SEA AND SLAVE FORTS

GHANA In 1471, the Portuguese merchant seamen arrived on the palm-lined shore of the Gold Coast and bought a fort at Elmina. Over the next four hundred years they were followed by the British, Dutch, Swedes, Danes and Baltic adventurers. Gold was their first desire, but the slave trade soon became the dominant activity, and more than three dozen forts were established here, largely to run the exchange of human cargo for cloth, liquor and guns. Today, thirty forts still stand, several in dramatic locations and offering atmospheric tours and accommodation. Here you can combine poignant historical discovery with time on the beach – a rare blend in this part of the world.

One of the biggest forts is the seventeenth-century Cape Coast castle, which dominates the lively town of the same name. Just walking through its claustrophobic dungeons, where slaves were held before being shipped across the Atlantic, moves some visitors to tears with the incomprehensible scale of the cruelties that took place here. A particularly good time to visit the town is September, when the huge harvest festival, the Oguaa Fetu, takes over a noisy, palm-wine-lubricated parade of chiefs, fetish priests and queen mothers. If you want to be made particularly welcome, bring along some schnapps, the customary gift for traditional rulers, with whom you may well be granted an audience.

Elmina, now a bustling fishing port, is home to the photogenically sited St George's Castle and Fort St Jago, eyeballing each other across the lagoon. St George's offers a worthwhile historical and cultural exhibition, and in the town itself you can ogle several intricate traditional shrines – pastel-coloured edifices of platforms, arches and militaristic figurines.

Some of the best beaches are at Busua, which has a low-key resort an easy walk from the cutely perched Fort Metal Cross. A day-trip to the far western coast, between Princestown and Axim, brings you to an even finer stretch of beaches and sandy coves punctuated with jungle-swathed headlands.

CONQUERING MOUNT CAMEROON

CAMEROON Slowly regaining consciousness, I realized I was cold – an odd feeling when you're in Africa. But then it dawned on me. I was halfway up Mount Cameroon – at 4095m, West Africa's highest mountain – and had been unconscious, rather than sleeping, because the day before's trekking had been so utterly exhausting that I had collapsed in a pile as soon as we reached camp. Tough going doesn't begin to describe it.

Rising directly from sea level, Mount Cameroon is a highly active volcano – it last erupted in May 2000 – its flanks littered with craters and lava streams. Walking on solidified lava isn't easy. It's like walking on a pebble beach, only on a steep slope, meaning that for every two steps up, you go one step back down again. Sisyphus springs to mind. And lava clumps have jagged edges, so every time your hand touches the ground for support, the lava cuts into your fingers.

But there's no gain without pain and the reward on Mount Cameroon is the breathtaking scenery en route. Lava might not be pleasing to walk on, but it looks pretty damn spectacular. And the hardy plants that manage to set root into its inhospitable surface – many of them endemic to the area – seem only to blossom in the brightest of colours.

Conquering Mount Cameroon isn't all about the lava, though. Over three days, we passed through village plantations, primary and montane rainforest, and open savannah, the climate getting gradually cooler as we progressed ever upwards until we finally reached the summit.

For a moment, we were on top of the world, knowing that the leg-dissolving descent would take little more than a day. And not knowing that it would take two weeks to recover fully.

359 IN SEARCH OF THE BEST CHOCOLATE IN THE WORLD

SÃO TOMÉ & PRINCIPE You know you're in a country far from modernity when one of the main problems facing landowners is re-forestation. São Tomé, the smallest nation in Africa, has largely been forgotten by the outside world since Portuguese colonizers packed up and left in the mid-1970s.

Away from São Tomé town – where the faded colonial-era buildings try their best to decay with elegiac ease, despite the occasional tree bursting out of a rooftop – and into the awesomely lush interior, the occasional remain of a long-abandoned train track is the only clue that you are about to stumble upon one of the many old plantation or roca buildings. Built by Angolan and Portuguese slaves, these grandiose structures helped make São Tomé one of the world's leading coca and coffee producers at the turn of the twentieth century. The owner's residence of the large Augustino Neto plantation looks something like a minor Inca fortress but, like most others on the island, it is derelict – independence and subsequent Marxist governments have brought coca production to its knees.

There are, however, smaller signs of life elsewhere. Individual entrepreneurs are slowly arriving at this tiny island, drawn to try and work with São Tomé's exceptionally fertile soil. Italian Claudio Corrallo has started a tiny coca plantation on the even smaller neighbouring island of Principe, where his chocolate is so luxurious that it is bought by Fortnum and Mason in London. He'll tell you how his cottage industry has cultivated coca species that many thought extinct, and ask him nicely, as I did one sweltering afternoon, and he might even give you some coca powder. A tiny teaspoon mixed with boiling water sipped on his rotting veranda in a chipped and battered mug is an explosion of rich and sumptuous flavour. This is sweetness taken straight from the raw coalface of chocolate production, and as Claudio reminds me, though he really doesn't need to, "the taste is out of this world."

360 TWITCHERS' DELIGHT: WATCHING HORNBILLS

THE GAMBIA Just like its people, the avian population of this small West African nation are a welcoming lot. There's a remarkable abundance and variety of birds to be found, and a great many are colourful, conspicuous individuals with a "look at me!" attitude – it's bird-nerd heaven. Spotting them is as easy as stepping out onto your veranda, as every hotel garden is alive with jaunty little finches, doves, sunbirds and glossy starlings, all far more colourful and alluring than their European counterparts. But the adventurous will want to hire a guide and head off on the kind of walk where you get burrs in your socks and need frequent swigs from your water bottle. In some areas, you can clock up a hundred or more species in a few hours: common wetland birds such as kingfishers, pelicans, herons and egrets, and savannah-dwellers such as vultures and rollers are practically guaranteed – as are many twitcher's favourites: the hornbills.

As endearing as they are faintly ridiculous, hornbills' beaks seem too large for their bodies, and their flapping, gliding flight looks nothing short of haphazard. What's more, they take parental paranoia to grand extremes: if it's breeding season (July and August), you may see a male incarcerating his female and her brood in a nest sealed with mud, high up in a tree, where they'll stay until the young are strong enough to survive on their own.

The most lugubrious fellow of all is the Abyssinian ground hornbill. Nearly a metre tall, cloaked in black and with a beak of gothic proportions, it strides through the open grassland with the undignified haste of an undertaker who's late for an urgent appointment. It's by far the largest – and the most impressive – of the hornbills, so if you manage to spot one, you've really scored. And before you know it, you'll be posting gloating field notes on the Internet like a true convert.

361 ISLAND-HOPPING OFF THE AFRICAN COAST

CAPE VERDE Follow the pointing finger of Senegal westwards and, 400km off the African coast, you reach the archipelago of Cape Verde, home of soulful world-music superstar Cesaria Evora. This nation of nine small islands remained uninhabited until 1462 when it was colonized by the Portuguese. The new arrivals brought in slaves from the mainland to work their sugar-cane fields. Not quite African and not quite European, Cape Verde today is almost Brazilian in feel.

Start in Praia, the capital, dramatically sited on a plateau on the largest and greenest island, Santiago, and offering relaxed street life, a small museum and a scattering of restaurants and clubs. From here, take the thirty-minute flight to Fogo ("Fire") island, dominated by a vast volcanic crater, where Cape Verde's only vineyards flourish. It's surmounted by the cone of a more recent volcano, steep but climbable, with sweeping views across the Atlantic from the summit that fully justify the effort.

The flat, desert islands of the east – Sal, Maio, Boa Vista – have the best beaches, azure seas and windsurfing schools. On Boa Vista you can rent a jeep and drive to the uninhabited south coast, where turtle tracks are almost the only sign of life, and images of Robinson Crusoe spring irresistibly to mind.

Out on the northwest fringe of the archipelago lies the canyon-grooved mass of Santo Antão, where local buses cut precipitous routes along nineteenth-century cobbled roads overlooking the ocean. It's one of the more fertile islands, and you can enjoy superb hikes along rural farmers' paths. Nearby is São Vicente, most noteworthy for playing host to an exuberant Carnaval every February, and the international Baia das Gatas music festival every August. So what would you eat and drink in Cape Verde? Typical is pork or tuna, in a hybrid of Portuguese and African styles, washed down with shots of grogue, a powerful, aromatic sugar-cane rum.

362 SOAKING IN WIKKI WARM SPRINGS

NIGERIA Bathing in the near-perfect natural pool at Wikki Warm Springs, part of Nigeria's remote Yankari National Park, is simply one of West Africa's most gratifying experiences. Below the park lodge, down a steep path, the upper Gaji stream bubbles up from a deep cleft beneath a rose-coloured, sandstone cliff. Twelve million litres a day, at a constant 31°C, flood out over sparkling sand between a dense bank of overhanging tropical foliage on one side, and the concrete apron that serves as a beach on the other – the one dud note in an otherwise picture-perfect environment, though the concrete helps keep the crystal-clear water clean. Floodlighting makes the springs equally idyllic at night, giving them a satisfyingly theatrical appearance, like an elaborate New Age interior design piece. A good deal larger than most swimming pools, the springs are the ideal place to wash away the frustrations of travelling in Nigeria. But should you tire of simply drifting on your back above the gentle current, you can explore the woods around the lodge for their abundant birdlife. It's also possible to go on a guided game drive with Yankari's rangers, bringing you into close contact with the park's savannah mammals, including several species of antelope, a variable population of elephant and, it's said, even lions. If, as occasionally happens, the viewing isn't up to much, returning to Wikki Warm Springs, and that delightful initial immersion, is more than ample compensation.

363 TREKKING IN DOGON COUNTRY

MALI When the research of French anthropologist Marcel Griaule first shed some light on the mysterious lives of Mali's Dogon people back in the 1930s, no one could have predicted that barely a generation later backpackers would be trudging along the Bandiagara escarpment, drinking Coke with village elders and filling their stomachs with the slimy green gumbo that Griaule had no doubt laboured over during his field trips. But a trek through Dogon country, exploring the spectacular villages built precariously on the rise of the escarpment, has become a highlight of any trip to West Africa. It's not necessarily an extreme activity, nor does it involve overly difficult tramping, but there's plenty of intrigue and adventure nonetheless. Just as the villages themselves have an enchanted air about them, hanging for dear life to the cliff-face, so the ways of the Dogon seem imbued with a near-magical quality.

The services of a good guide are indispensable in a land where simple mounds of earth are in fact sacred altars and random markings in the sand are really questions to the gods. As you wander from one village to the next under a hot sun that beats down on the escarpment and warms the sandy plain that stretches towards Burkina Faso, a palpable energy follows you. It seeps through the mud pillbox granaries, their thatched roofs peaked like witches' hats; it hovers over the togu na ("House of Words") during a village council meeting; and it makes you feel that you are in a strange place indeed. As darkness falls over the escarpment, this energy is sucked up by the caves overhanging the cliff-face to sleep with the skeletons of the Dogon who are buried there, and when morning comes it swoops back down on the village just as you are contemplating your first spoonful of yet another steaming gumbo breakfast.

364 SEEING THE JUNGLE THROUGH THE EYES OF THE BAKA

CAMEROON Hot and sticky, with impenetrable green stretching as far as the eye could see. If first impressions really do count, then our relationship with the equatorial rainforest, in the extreme southeastern corner of Cameroon, looked like it wasn't going to last. But then our Baka guide led us into the jungle – and we immediately knew that this was the start of something beautiful.

The Baka are one of the many bands of so-called Pygmies that inhabit the forests of southern Cameroon. These "people of small stature", believed to be the original inhabitants of the equatorial rainforest, have for centuries lived as nomadic hunter-gatherers in perfect harmony with their surroundings. Sadly, European ivory traders, loggers, and the introduction of a Western market economy have gradually made it impossible for the Baka to maintain their traditional lifestyle, and they now find financial solace in guiding clumsy tourists like ourselves through the rainforest.

We were heading for a clearing – bais in Baka – where a stilt-ed platform had been erected to watch safely wildlife pass underneath, following our guide in awe as he moved quickly and stealthily through the forest, stopping mid-stride whenever something caught his attention. Then, standing completely motionless, one foot still dangling in the air, he would crane his neck and track the sounds – the crack of a breaking branch or the shuffling of leaves – as they came ever closer. Even with the smallest noise, he would turn around, smile at us and mouth, "colobus", or "snake", and we'd go "huh?", not realizing it was anything more than a leaf turning in the wind or a seed falling from a tree.

Watching our guide in his element was highlight enough, but then halfway to the bais he suddenly froze and whispered "gorilla", following up with an unmistakable hand gesture to make it clear he wanted us to stay absolutely still. Right in front of us, bushes were shaking, and as the noise became louder, so did the thumping of our hearts. In an instant, a beautiful silverback exploded from the undergrowth, rushing past. And then, just as quickly, he was gone. And we headed deeper into the jungle.

365 ADMIRING THE CATCH ON SANYANG BEACH

THE GAMBIA With pockets full of treasure – a sand dollar, a cowrie, a piece of wave-bitten wood – we're padding along off Sanyang Beach. It's late in the day, and we hardly recognize the place, even though we were here just a few hours ago, strolling in the opposite direction. In the monochrome midday heat, the shoreline had been near-deserted. It's since become a boat park, a fish market, a playground for bright-eyed kids, and a scavenging site for squabbling seabirds. The whole scene is a riot of colour.

A few brightly painted pirogues are still heading home on the incoming tide, their twelve-metre lengths dipping into the water, heavy with the day's haul. It takes strength to manhandle them onto logs and roll them up the beach. Once ashore, prize catches such as small sharks or whip-tailed rays are held up and admired, and quick deals are struck as the quarry is divided among the crew members or offloaded to traders.

The fishermen's wives and daughters, their heads wrapped in vivid cotton tikos, squat beside buckets of greasy-skinned bonga fish, scraping scales onto the sand or slicing open sea snails to reveal oozing grey innards. The metallic tang of salt and blood mingles with the eye-wateringly pungent dried fish aroma wafting across from the smokehouses.

We're only a few kilometres from the busiest Gambian resorts. Fifteen minutes' drive and we'd be hearing a different kaleidoscope of sounds – the snap and sigh of beer bottles opening, the hairdryer-whirr of tourists getting ready for the evening ahead. But, right now, there's nothing I'd rather be listening to than these fishermen shouting good-natured jokes while the gulls wheel and call overhead.

366 PARTYING WITH THE TUAREG AT THE FESTIVAL IN THE DESERT

MALI Way back in pre-Islamic times, Tuareg nomads would have gathered in the desert to settle disputes, race camels and entertain one another with displays of swordsmanship, music and dance. Today, Mali's Festival in the Desert combines these traditions with the chance to hear a dazzling range of African sounds under the clear desert sky. The music and the setting among the rolling white dunes of the southern Sahara are hard to beat, but it's the people – men in richly coloured robes perched on camels bedecked with tassels; women in black, their faces stained with indigo – and the sea of white tents where families have set up camp with their livestock that make the event so unforgettable.

By day most of the action takes place in and around a shallow natural amphitheatre where women drum, clap and sing and tribesmen dance, swiping swords through the air as they skip and sway to the hypnotic rhythms. Stalls nearby sell metal and leatherwork, beads of glass and amber and moon-faced fertility dolls. Here you can have a cloth-seller tie you a turban against the burning sun, or learn about nomadic life as you bargain over glasses of bittersweet Tuareg tea.

After nightfall, as temperatures plummet, you'll be wrapping up warm and planting yourself close to one of the charcoal braziers among the dunes. From the one proper stage, the festival's main acts pump out an astonishing range of music, from the pure, limpid tones of the harp-like kora to timeless desert blues of the kind made famous by the late, great Ali Farka Touré.

367 CYCLING A RING ROAD WITH A DIFFERENCE

CAMEROON The green, hilly Western Region, straddling the fault line between English- and French-speaking Cameroon, is one of Africa's most verdant corners, a spectacularly beautiful, bubble-wrap landscape of grass-swathed volcanic hills, rivers, lakes and forests. The single "main road" that circles round the region in a two-hundred-kilometre red-earth loop, like a cicatrization through the jungle, makes a perfect route for a superb week of cycling.

Start from the cacophonous, English-speaking town of Bamenda, then pedal north for an hour or two to Bafut, of naturalist Gerald Durrell's *Bafut Beagles* fame – his book recounts his visit collecting zoo animals here in the 1950s, when he stayed with the traditional ruler, the Fon of Bafut. His son, the present Fon (chief), encourages visits to the thatched-roofed palace complex and, if you're here at the end of the dry season, you can participate in the riotous, palm wine-lubricated grass-cutting ceremony.

Further north, one or more wooden bridges on the Ring Road are often down – usually busted by heavy lorries – so your much laughed-at mode of transport (locals think it hilarious for tourists to cycle) will prove a wise, as well as fun, choice. In the village markets, look out for fantastic arrays of fruit and veg – the best, intensely flavoured, green-skinned, orange-fleshed mangoes to be had anywhere, and avocados the size of boats. Less blithe is the experience of passing Lake Nyos, where, in 1986, a freak cloud of naturally occurring carbon dioxide belched from the lake one night and asphyxiated thousands of people and animals.

At Dumbo, past the lush pastures of the Grassfields, you have the option of completing the Ring Road round to Bamenda or setting off north to Nigeria, down a vertiginous escarpment of boulders, tree roots and twisting paths. If the latter takes your fancy, you can hire a porter in Dumbo for the two-day hike – he'll even carry your bike, padded and trussed up and balanced on his head.

GETTING BACK TO
BASICS

WITH THE PEOPLE OF THE VEIL

NIGER The Sahara is the world's largest desert – and arguably the most desolate, inhospitable place on earth. It's roughly the size of the USA, yet has a population of less than a million people, and its vast expanse divides North Africa from so-called sub-Saharan Africa in a great swath of dunes, sand seas, mountains and plateaus.

How do you get to experience this natural wonder? Well, not surprisingly the traditional caravan routes in northern Africa have long since been supplanted by more modern modes of transport. But a camel journey across the Sahara is not just a retro-chic way of "doing the desert"; it adds up to an authentic and intimate experience that gets to the core of the desert's appeal. You become immersed in the landscape at a natural pace, savouring the simplicity, space and silence.

Your journey begins a day's drive from Agadez in northern Niger. Camels grumble as loads are lashed to their backs, but saddles are mostly unoccupied. Forget the romantic image of the dromedary's lolling gait transporting you effortlessly over the sands. A camel is more mule than horse so you'll be on foot most of the time. Your Tuareg guide will show you how to put on the traditional turban or tagelmoust worn by all desert men, and soon you'll adapt to their pace, rising at dawn, strolling towards a shady noontime rest, and camping again around mid-afternoon when the camels are unloaded to forage for food. You cover around 15km a day, stopping for mint tea at scruffy encampments where half-naked kids chase the goats and girls giggle shyly from behind their indigo shawls. The landscape is more diverse than you might expect, with the 2000-metre-high blue-grey peaks of Niger's Aïr Mountains merging with the amber-pink sand sheet of the Ténéré Desert far beyond the eastern horizon – the classic Saharan combination.

Tuareg nomad culture is alive and well in the Aïr despite a hostile government in the distant capital, Niamey. But "Tuareg" is in fact a derogatory Arabic term. From southwest Libya to Timbuktu in Mali these proud nomads describe themselves collectively as Kel Tagelmoust: "the People of the Veil".

BIRD-WATCHING
IN THE BANC D'ARGUIN

369

MAURITANIA Once known to French colonialists as Le Grande Vide ("The Great Void"), Mauritania covers more than one million square kilometres of Saharan dunes – nearly a third of the entire country is desert. Brush the sand aside, however, and you'll discover that Mauritania's national parks – set about verdant coastal wetlands – make for some of the most spectacular bird-watching in the world, with opportunities for sighting more than 500 individual species, many of them endangered or threatened.

Parc National du Banc d'Arguin, located on the western fringes of the Sahara, comprises thousands of acres of shallow seagrass bed and intertidal flats and creeks. Together, these grounds are home to millions of families of migrating birds who nest and raise their chicks in these areas from April to July and again between October and January. Thirty percent of all waders using the East Atlantic flyway winter here. Birds to watch out for include flamingoes, pelicans, herons and cormorants, as well as European spoonbills, godwits and terns. Particularly numerous are the many small shorebirds that gather in large flocks around coastal settlements – keep an eye out especially for the sanderling and ruddy turnstone. The environs are complemented by a unique ecosystem of marine and animal life that includes seals, tortoises, dolphins and crabs, as well as jackals and gazelles.

The prodigious flocks of birds scatter across the vast 290km-long coastline during the day, so it's best to head out at dawn to catch them before they make for the offshore islets. For the most intimate viewing, visit one of several native Imragen villages, where an early-morning guided boat trip lets you get up close to immense flocks flying low over the water on their way to feeding grounds.

370 RIDING THE WAGONS ON THE WORLD'S LONGEST TRAIN

MAURITANIA Waiting beside the track in the dead of night, we are offered tea and encouraged to huddle round a small fire. Somewhere, out across the emptiness, our train is rattling towards us, an endless chain of wagons that cuts its way through the Sahara Desert, transporting iron-ore from the Adrar to the Atlantic port of Nouadhibou.

We've been straining our eyes and ears since 6pm, but delays are frequent and tonight the thunder of wagons is not heard until 1am. The locals rush to hoist us on top of the cargo – iron is the real business here and paying passengers fare little better than the rooftop stowaways – and someone starts laying down a bed of blankets for everyone. We bless their kindness, as the crushed ore looks far from comfortable and the desert night is far from warm. But despite our being wrapped in headscarves and countless layers of clothing, the cold soon works its way into the soul. The black soot that clouds the train is no less persistent.

We are soon rocked to sleep beneath the star-lit sky by the rhythm of the carriages until the sun rises and the desert stretches out on either side. The morning quickly warms and the remaining journey seems as infinite as the Sahara. Hours are whiled away, sharing tea, trying to speak French and staring into a sandy horizon. Finally, we roll into Nouadhibou, and start the long walk to the front of the train – and town.

371 PEAKING ON FOGO

CAPE VERDE First impressions of Fogo, rising in a cone 2800m above the ocean, are of its forbidding mass, the steep, dark slopes looming above the clouds. The small plane is buffeted on Atlantic winds as you dip onto the runway, perched high on dun-coloured cliffs above a thin strip of black beach and ultramarine sea.

Fogo ("Fire" in Portuguese) is the most captivating of the Cape Verde Islands, with its dramatic caldera and peak, its fearsomely robust red wine, its traditional music and the hospitable Fogo islanders themselves.

Up in the weird moonscape of the caldera, after a slow, shared taxi ride from the picturesque capital, São Filipe, you'll be dropped on the rocky plain at a straggle of houses made of grey volcanic tufa. One of a handful of charmingly rakish-looking guides will greet you, host you in his own home and, early next morning, take you up the steep path to the summit, Pico de Fogo, with its extraordinary panorama. The descent is better than any theme-park ride as both guide and guided leap and tumble through the scree in an entertaining, inelegant freestyle.

Shaking out the dust and volcanic gravel at the bottom, you'll fetch up at the local social club where an impromptu band – guitar, violin, keyboard, scraper and cavaquinho (four-stringed mini-guitar) – emboldened by the consumption of much vinho and local hooch or grogue, often strikes up around the bar. Wind down your evening listening to Fogo's beautiful mornas – mournful laments of loss and longing that hark back to the archipelago's whaling past and to families far away.

372 RUNNING AGROUND IN THE BIJAGÓS ISLANDS

GUINEA-BISSAU With only two trips a week, it was important that every last bit of cargo was crammed into the pirogue's damp, cavernous hull. The boat listed slightly as it lurched out of Bissau, a few over-ripe tomatoes rolling off the tarpaulin roof and into the harbour, but gained an even keel in open water. The blue expanse of sea was utterly flat and so shallow that mounds of sand poked above the surface like dunes. Off the port side, the distant mangrove swamps of Bolama could have been an oasis. A bottle of palm wine on board was doing a wonderful job deflecting attention away from the cramped legroom and oily stench of fish – until the captain appropriated it for himself and his rudder-man. Moments later, a few more tomatoes rolled off the roof as the pirogue ran aground. A chorus of Bijagó expletives caught the attention of flamingoes sunning themselves on a nearby sandbar…and then silence, the boat rocking gently in the rising tides that would eventually set it free.

Bathed in the golden light of the sinking sun, Bubaque felt like the undiscovered fantasy island of a wisened explorer. Wispy plumes of smoke rose from the wooded interior and cries of "branco, branco" greeted the pirogue at the small jetty – the arrival of a white man is still an event worthy of exclamation in this little-visited corner of West Africa. The cargo was unloaded onto the island's two cars, which then bumped along tracks through the bush to deliver bottles of Coke to the few hotels and a new generator for the hospital. Their raspy engines reverberated across the island and reached back down to the jetty, where the captain was snoring peacefully in his simple vessel under thousands of stars.

373

SACRED SPACE: THE GRAND MOSQUE IN DJENNÉ

MALI is a treasure box of a country, where fishermen ply the River Niger in brightly painted pirogues, kora-playing jalis sing songs written for the rulers of an ancient, glittering empire and the faithful worship in spectacular mosques made of timber and mud.

Djenné's Grande Mosquée is the most famous of all. Beautifully simple but with a potent presence, it exudes the kind of gravitas shared by all the world's great sacred buildings. But there's also something gloriously organic – sensuous, even – about its Soudanic curves and crenellations; and it's a fitting focal point for a community which guards its traditions fiercely while embracing a brand of Islam that is neither repressive nor restrictive. Djenné itself is steeped in history, and works hard to maintain its meticulously preserved state. Mud-built houses need regular attention, and at the end of each rainy season the whole town pitches in to make good the building's russet facades. Several hundred workers scale the walls of the Grande Mosquée with the help of the timber struts that sprout from the minarets like bristles.

Visit the Grande Mosquée on any Monday and it's abuzz with activity of a different sort. In the large, dusty marketplace in front of the mosque, traders preside over pyramids of knobbly bitter tomatoes or sacks of pungent dried fish, Fula women with heavy gold earrings pore over brightly patterned cotton fabrics and rickety donkey carts weave through the crowds. The market is thoroughly absorbing. But to appreciate Djenné more deeply, you'll need to stay on after the hubbub has dispersed, and savour that last, golden hour of the day when the call of the muezzin wafts over the city, just as it has every evening for seven hundred years.

MALI The shore was awash with colours and voices. People clambered aboard like pirates, vaulting over barriers and passing down goods and livestock in exchange for wardrobes and other essential items. Just time to get a few more sheep stowed and we were off.

The "big" boats have been ferrying people up and down the River Niger since 1964, playing a vital role in Malian society by providing the only form of access to some villages and transporting traders to sell their wares. In their heyday, the boats were packed with a thousand passengers; floating villages with people marooned in their cabins or sleeping amongst the cargo below. These days you are more likely to find three hundred more goats than people on board.

It takes a six-day journey to drift from Koulikoro, near the capital Bamako, to Gao, a Sahelian city 1300km to the north, stopping along the way to explore the bustling market towns of Mopti and Niafunké, home of the late, great Malian musician, Ali Farka Touré. When it's not possible to go ashore, boys pull up in dug-out canoes to sell provisions to passengers – the warm aroma of exotic food wafts across deck from their small charcoal stoves.

The richness of the experience of travelling on the "big" boat is spending time with the locals, sharing stories and exchanging views. And there's no better way to get close to Malian life, as you slip through the scenery. Villages clinging to the cliff side, sand dunes reaching down to the water's edge. Fishermen on pirogues, camels on the bank, hippopotamus in the shallows: it all passes slowly by.

JOURNEYING UP THE RIVER NIGER

218 MAKE THE MOST OF YOUR TIME ON EARTH

375 DEMYSTIFYING VOODOO IN OUIDAH

BENIN Despite the fact that Ouidah boasts one of West Africa's most beautiful beaches, the Atlantic walkway is not its main attraction. Situated 40km west of Cotonou, Benin's defacto capital, this former centre of West Africa's slave trade is the home of voodoo's eleventh supreme chief, the Daagbo (His Majesty) Tomadjlehoukpon II Metogbokandji. For visitors and locals alike, Ouidah is one of the region's most important centres of this oft-misunderstood belief.

Voodoo, Benin's official religion, isn't about sticking pins in dolls fashioned in the form of your mother-in-law or ex-boyfriend. Nor is it about the evil spells or devil worship that Hollywood makes it out to be. It's actually a faith with over fifty million followers worldwide, all worshipping a Supreme Being and hundreds of lesser gods and spirits.

In Ouidah, the cityscape is detailed with evidence of its influence. Fetishes – any man-made object that has been occupied by a spirit – lurk among the faded Portuguese-style buildings and along the grassy road to the beach. You may notice them because they look out of place in their environment, or are covered in the bloody, waxy remains of a recent animal sacrifice.

About a kilometre down a dirt track from town lies the Sacred Forest of Kpassé, guarded by a dozen or so statues honouring the various divinities of the gods. Several are made from old motorcycle parts, but the most striking lies near the entrance, a roughly one-metre-high horned creature with an enormous phallus, symbolizing strength and fertility. When ceremonies to the snake god Dangbé (also known as Dan) are not underway in Ouidah's Temple of the Python, opposite the Ouidah Basilica, visitors can creep inside its cement walls to have their photos taken with sleepy and harmless pythons slung around their necks.

The town also hosts a voodoo festival each January, and various ceremonies are held throughout the year, when costumed dancers and those "fortunate" enough to be temporarily possessed by spirits sway to the beat of drums, summoning the gods. And, if you're really lucky, you might get invited in for an audience with the Supreme Chief himself, regally perched in an imitation La-Z-Boy and sipping a Fanta. Imagine the Pope being so hospitable.

376 TAKE A WALK IN THE RAINFOREST

SIERRA LEONE Deep in the maze of waterways, woodland and farm plots of southeast Sierra Leone lies Tiwai Island Wildlife Sanctuary, sheltering an extraordinarily rich fauna.

Tiwai means literally 'Big Island' in the local language, and this truly is the Africa of the imagination, the air saturated with the incessant chirrups, squawks and yelps of birds, chimpanzees, tree hyraxes, assorted insects and hundreds of other creatures, all doing their thing in twelve square kilometres of rainforest. In the background, you can hear the dim rush of the Moa River where it splits to roar around Tiwai through channels and over rocks.

As you weave along paths between the giant buttress roots of the trees, park guides will track troops of colobus and diana monkeys and should know where to find the chimps. The rarest

and most secretive of Tiwai's denizens is the hog-sized pygmy hippo, which you're not likely to see unless you go jungle walking at night, when they traipse their habitual solitary paths through the undergrowth.

Exploring after dark with a guide is, in fact, highly recommended – take a lamp with plenty of kerosene, and a good torch. By night, the forest is a powerful presence, with an immense, consuming vigour: every rotten branch teems with termites, and all around you sense the organs of detection of a million unseen creatures waving at your illuminated figure as you stumble over the roots. You can also take a boat tour of the Moa river in a canoe or motorboat, watching out for rare birds and butterflies and looking for turtles below the surface.

377 VISITING THE ANCIENT LIBRARIES OF CHINGUETTI

MAURITANIA Al-Habot's house is a house like any other in the warren of lanes that makes up the old mud-walled desert town of Chinguetti. A heavy wooden door creaks open onto a courtyard and your guide reaches for a foot-long key carved from tamarisk to unlock a smaller portal. Inside the dimly lit cavern are piles of boxes containing manuscripts dating back to the twelfth century when Islam first reached this region. Finely penned Arabic scripts, still readable today, offer guidance on grammar or etiquette. Other parchments record civil disputes or manifests, for Chinguetti has been a key staging post on trans-Sahara trade routes for over a thousand years.

378 THE MYSTERIOUS RUINS OF DJADO

NIGER Timbuktu? Forget it. A far more intriguing mystery lies hidden on the far side of Niger's Ténéré Desert; here, the mud-brick citadel of Djado rises from palm-fringed pools crammed with bright-green reeds, like some unworldly goblin's castle from a Tolkien yarn. Explore the honeycomb of sand-chocked passages inside, there's no one around. Eventually, you'll emerge atop the crumbling ramparts and comprehend the isolation: a barren plateau to the east; infinite sand sheets unrolling westwards. When was Djado built? Why was it abandoned? The hot wind stirs the palms but keeps its secrets.

MISCELLANY

TRADING PLACES

One of the main factors that shaped the history of West Africa between the eleventh and seventeenth centuries was trans-Saharan trade. **Gold** from Buré (in modern-day Guinea), Bambouk (in modern-day Senegal) and Akan (in modern-day Ghana) was transported across the desert to North Africa, as were **slaves**, while **salt** from mines in the Sahara went south. Powerful desert trading outposts were created, such as Oualata and Aoudaghost (both in modern-day Mauritania) and, most famously, Timbuktu in Mali – once so wealthy that its streets were said to be lined with gold. Huge camel caravans, known as azalaïs, still transport salt mined in Taoudenni, in northern Mali, across the Sahara, though trucks and 4x4s increasingly supplant these ships of the desert.

GO IN STYLE

Ever felt the Western way of death was a little too. . .solemn? The Ga people from the Accra area in Ghana came to that conclusion some time ago, and for those who can afford it, several famous **coffin** makers construct elaborate, glossily painted caskets in any design you like. Fish? Lion? Mercedes? A little too traditional perhaps, or a mobile phone, or a mouse?

What's in a name?

Most West African countries retain the names by which they were known in colonial times, or earlier, such as the Ivory Coast, Guinea and Nigeria. But certain nations chose names at independence that would give their new nationhood an extra shine. Ghana is named after the huge medieval empire of the same name, whose capital was in the southeast of present-day Mauritania; the French colony of Dahomey selected the name Benin, after the wealthy city state of that name in southern Nigeria, famed for its bronzes;

and as recently as 1983, the revolutionary government in Upper Volta threw out the old descriptive moniker referring to the country's main river and came up with Burkina Faso, an altogether more challenging epithet that means "Land of Honourable Men".

> *"If you are in hiding, don't light a fire"*
> **Ghanaian proverb**

DOGON STARSTRUCK

When, in the late 1930s, the reclusive **Dogon people** of Mali gave French anthropologist Marcel Griaule an insight into their customs and beliefs, it was apparent that they had a considerable knowledge of the heavens. They knew about Saturn's rings and four of Jupiter's moons, and claimed that Sirius, the brightest star as seen from Earth, was orbited by two other stars, one of which was extremely dense. Modern astronomers only identified this dense companion, Sirius B, in 1970, so how was it that this remote African tribe had known of it? The puzzle prompted Robert Temple to speculate in his book *The Sirius Mystery*, that the Dogon must have been visited by extraterrestrials from Sirius.

African birdwings

Africa's biggest butterfly, the **giant swallowtail** (Papilio antimachus), lives in the great rainforests of Guinea, Sierra Leone, Liberia and the Ivory Coast. You can occasionally see the splendid orange males – with their twenty-centimetre wingspan and long, narrow wings – on forest paths, where they suck moisture and minerals from the mud. The slightly smaller females are rarely spotted, as they prefer to stay in the treetop canopy.

Senegal's holy beggars

Senegal is unique in West Africa in the degree of its attachment to **Sufi Muslim brotherhoods**, originally introduced by North African prophet-nomads between the twelfth and nineteenth centuries. Holy beggars, the dreadlocked Baye Fall (followers of one of the biggest sects, the Mourides), traipse around in noisy gangs, swirling their multi-coloured robes, drumming and singing, and living from charity. This is somewhat at variance with their roots: the Mourides' leader, Amadou Bamba, is supposed to have advised an illiterate follower that studying the Koran was only one route to paradise and that God would look equally favourably on him if he laboured hard in the groundnut (peanut) fields. Despite the paradoxical imagery, Senegal's secular governments, both colonial French and democratic independent, have chosen to exploit this part of the Mouride philososphy and ally themselves with the brotherhood for the purposes of economic and political stability. As it says on the buses in Dakar, "Ligey si top, yala la bok" – "Work is part of religion".

THE PLYMOUTH-BANJUL RALLY

Forget the Paris-Dakar, that's a big commercial event for men who wanna kick up dust, get lost and blow away a few villagers. No, if you're a petrolhead with a conscience, you should check out the Plymouth-Banjul Rally, which takes place every February. The rules are simple: you have to acquire your car for £100 or less, you have to drive it from the UK to The Gambia, and then you have to auction it and give away the proceeds to a local development charity.

> *"When an old man dies,
> it is as if a library burns
> down"*
>
> **Amadou Hampaté Bâ (Malian writer)**

LARGER
THAN LIFE

The largest Christian church in the world, at 30,000 square metres, is the Basilica of Our Lady of Peace in the Ivory Coast. It was built by the diminutive long-time ruler of the country, Félix Houphouët-Boigny, in the insignificant village of Yamoussoukro where he was born, and which is now the country's capital. Asked whether a colossal cathedral was precisely what a developing country dependent on one commodity – cocoa – needed, Houphouët would have none of it: "I did a deal with God", he sniffed. "You would not expect me to discuss God's business in public, would you?".

USING A LITTLE IMRAGENATION

The **Imragen tribe** of Mauritania's remote coastal desert region between Nouakchott and Nouadhibou have devised a cunning way of teaming up with dolphins, to their mutual advantage. By banging drums in the shallows they alert the dolphins, which swim to the shore, herding fish into the shallows where they're clubbed and netted. The fishermen take their pick and the dolphins get an easy snack.

DR. PRESIDENT

The Gambia's president, soldier-out-of-uniform **Yahya Jammeh**, discovered in 2007 that he possessed special gifts. To the bemusement of local doctors – and foreign journalists – he followed his latest rigged election triumph with a series of visits to hospitals where he dispensed herbal medicines to AIDS patients, saying he had a guaranteed cure. Patients were told to trust the big man and give up their anti-retroviral drugs. It was yet another respectability set back for a government that has stunned African observers with its poor record on human rights and democratic accountability. But at least the little Banjul diplomatic community had something to laugh about.

BELIEFS

A wide range of **indigenous beliefs** co-exist with Africa's two main faiths, Christianity and Islam. Traditionally, for example, the Igbo of southeast Nigeria believe that every man has two souls. Upon death, the life force perishes with the body, but the eternal ego survives in the form of a ghost, a shadow or a reflection. The spirit of a good Igbo will come back as a vigorous animal, such as a cow, leopard or elephant; a bad person might return as some kind of plant.

THE SLAVE
TRADE

West Africa was one of the main regions from where captive slaves were deported to the Americas and Caribbean. The shape of the trade varied from district to district, but at its heart – powered by insatiable appetites for wealth on all sides – lay the almost mechanical cycle of exports and imports: traders from African states bought firearms, cloth and other imported goods and sold slaves to be shipped out on the infamous **Middle Passage**; sugar, cotton and other raw materials produced with slave labour in the New World colonies were shipped back to Europe; and manufactured goods from the weapons factories, textile mills and refineries of Europe were exported to West Africa. Each link in the chain pulled the others harder until, by the mid-eighteenth century, when Charleston in South Carolina began importing slaves in large numbers, as many as 100,000 captives a year were being herded between the decks in shackles to endure the six-week crossing. Most slaves were enemy prisoners or luckless refugees fleeing wars in the interior fuelled by the flood of firearms. A few were hapless child servants, pawned by their families in times of hardship and then sold on to dealers, contrary to the terms of traditional agreements.

> *"Wisdom is like a baobab
> tree; no one individual can
> embrace it"*
>
> **West African saying**

BATTLE
OF THE SEXES

In 2005, Liberia's Ellen Johnson-Sirleaf became Africa's first elected **female president**, defeating football legend George Weah in the vote.

HOT-AIR BALLOONING OVER THE MAASAI MARA • CAMPING WITH HIPPOS IN MURCHISON FALLS • THE REAL BAT CAVE • CRUISING THE CONGO • MOUNTAIN-BIKING WITH THE HERDS • WANDERING LAMU ISLAND • REEF ENCOUNTER: ECO-LIVING ON CHUMBE ISLAND • THE GREAT AFRICAN MEAT FEAST • FOLLOWING THE GREATEST SHOW ON EARTH • TOURING THE SPICE ISLAND • **WILDLIFE-SPOTTING IN THE NGORONGORO CRATER** • SUSTAINABLE SAFARIS WITH THE MAASAI • PLAYING TARZAN ON CHOLE ISLAND • TREKKING IN THE SIMIEN MOUNTAINS • CLIMBING KILIMANJARO • UNWINDING AT MAIA RESORT AND SPA • MEETING THE CHEEKY MONKEYS OF KIBALE • LOSING THE CROWDS AT KATAVI NATIONAL PARK • THAT'S MAGIC: PEMBA'S DJINN • **THE GORILLAS OF KAHUZI-BIEGA** • SHARE AND SHARE ALIKE: MAKING A MEAL OF INJERA • SWIMMING WITH TURTLES IN THE INDIAN OCEAN • A NIGHT ON THE EQUATOR WITH KENYA RAILWAYS • DROPPING IN ON THE CHURCHES OF LALIBELA • LANGOUÉ BAI: THE LAST PLACE ON EARTH • MOUNT ELGON: THE ELEPHANTS OF KITUM CAVE • DINNER AT MOSES' PLACE • FULFILLING FANTASIES ON FRÉGATE ISLAND • GETTING UP CLOSE AND PERSONAL WITH A GIRAFFE • STORYTELLING ON THE SSESE ISLANDS • SURF'S UP: WATCHING HIPPOS HIT THE WAVES • **EXPLORING THE PYRAMIDS OF MEROË** • WHITE-WATER RAFTING AT THE SOURCE OF THE NILE • HOT-AIR BALLOONING OVER THE MAASAI MARA • CAMPING WITH HIPPOS IN MURCHISON FALLS • THE REAL BAT CAVE • **CRUISING THE CONGO** • MOUNTAIN-BIKING WITH THE HERDS • WANDERING LAMU ISLAND • REEF ENCOUNTER: ECO-LIVING ON CHUMBE ISLAND • THE GREAT AFRICAN MEAT FEAST • FOLLOWING THE GREATEST SHOW ON EARTH • TOURING THE SPICE ISLAND • WILDLIFE-SPOTTING IN THE NGORONGORO CRATER • SUSTAINABLE SAFARIS WITH THE MAASAI • PLAYING TARZAN ON CHOLE ISLAND • TREKKING IN THE SIMIEN MOUNTAINS • CLIMBING KILIMANJARO • UNWINDING AT MAIA RESORT AND SPA • MEETING THE CHEEKY MONKEYS OF KIBALE • LOSING THE CROWDS AT KATAVI NATIONAL PARK • THAT'S MAGIC: PEMBA'S DJINN • THE GORILLAS OF KAHUZI-BIEGA • **SHARE AND SHARE ALIKE: MAKING A MEAL OF INJERA** • SWIMMING WITH TURTLES IN THE INDIAN OCEAN • A NIGHT ON THE EQUATOR WITH KENYA RAILWAYS • DROPPING IN ON THE CHURCHES OF LALIBELA • **LANGOUÉ BAI: THE LAST PLACE ON EARTH** • MOUNT ELGON: THE ELEPHANTS OF KITUM CAVE • DINNER AT MOSES' PLACE • FULFILLING FANTASIES ON FRÉGATE ISLAND • GETTING UP CLOSE AND PERSONAL WITH A GIRAFFE • STORYTELLING ON THE SSESE ISLANDS • SURF'S UP: WATCHING HIPPOS HIT THE WAVES • EXPLORING THE PYRAMIDS OF MEROË • WHITE-WATER RAFTING AT THE SOURCE OF THE NILE • HOT-AIR BALLOONING OVER THE MAASAI MARA • **CAMPING WITH HIPPOS IN MURCHISON FALLS** • THE REAL BAT CAVE • CRUISING THE CONGO • MOUNTAIN-BIKING WITH THE HERDS • WANDERING LAMU ISLAND • REEF ENCOUNTER: ECO-LIVING ON CHUMBE ISLAND • THE GREAT AFRICAN MEAT FEAST • FOLLOWING THE GREATEST SHOW ON EARTH • **TOURING THE SPICE ISLAND** • WILDLIFE-SPOTTING IN THE NGORONGORO CRATER • SUSTAINABLE SAFARIS WITH THE MAASAI • PLAYING TARZAN ON CHOLE ISLAND • TREKKING IN THE SIMIEN MOUNTAINS • CLIMBING KILIMANJARO • UNWINDING AT MAIA RESORT AND SPA • MEETING THE CHEEKY MONKEYS OF KIBALE • LOSING THE CROWDS AT KATAVI NATIONAL PARK • THAT'S MAGIC: PEMBA'S DJINN • **FULFILLING FANTASIES ON FRÉGATE ISLAND** • THE GORILLAS OF KAHUZI-BIEGA • SHARE AND SHARE ALIKE: MAKING A MEAL OF INJERA • SWIMMING WITH TURTLES IN THE INDIAN OCEAN • A NIGHT ON THE EQUATOR WITH KENYA RAILWAYS • DROPPING IN ON THE CHURCHES OF LALIBELA • LANGOUÉ BAI: THE LAST PLACE ON EARTH • MOUNT ELGON: THE ELEPHANTS OF KITUM CAVE • DINNER AT MOSES' PLACE • GET UP CLOSE AND PERSONAL WITH A GIRAFFE •

CENTRAL & EAST AFRICA

379–411

EXPLORING THE PYRAMIDS OF MEROË ★ 402

SUDAN

SHARE AND SHARE ALIKE:
★ 388 MAKING A MEAL OF INJERA

ETHIOPIA

CAMPING WITH HIPPOS
IN MURCHISON FALLS ★ 379

LANGOUÉ BAI:
★ 391 THE LAST PLACE
ON EARTH

UGANDA

RWANDA

KENYA

HOT-AIR BALLOONING
★ 408 OVER THE MAASAI MARA

GABON

THE GORILLAS
OF KAHUZI-BIEGA ★ 387

WILDLIFE-SPOTTING
★ 403 IN THE NGORONGORO CRATER

CONGO

★ 381

DR CONGO

BURUNDI

FULFILLING FANTASIES
ON FRÉGATE ISLAND ★ 396

CRUISING
THE CONGO

TOURING
THE SPICE ISLAND ★ 395

TANZANIA

SEYCHELLES

CAMPING WITH
HIPPOS
IN MURCHISON
FALLS

379

UGANDA A faint rustling woke me up. Had I just rolled onto the canvas floor of my tent? Or was it a nearby camper? No, there it was again. A sound of an animal, a quiet animal. Silence. And then stepping – or tugging? – on the grass. I wouldn't have heard it an hour earlier, when the Red Chilli Rest Camp's generators had been humming. Even now, it was hardly distinguishable from the frogs and insects.

Could it be a lion? During the morning driving safari, the park rangers had said that the lions lived on the other side of the Nile, that the lions can't swim and that they certainly can't take the ferry that connects the two halves of Murchison Falls National Park here in northwestern Uganda. But later, at the open-air dining section of the rest camp, the bartender had mentioned that a female lived on our side, near the famous waterfalls.

"But we're camping outside!" I'd cried. "We're a lion lunch in a canvas wrapper!"

"Lions don't like tents," he'd said. But now there was another rustle – right in front of my tent. Crocodiles were on both sides of the Nile, I realized. The boat safari had taken us past a half-dozen sneering crocs earlier in the day.

The rustling ballooned into a fully-fledged racket. Surely the crocodile was ready to pounce. The leopard was going to take my carcass up a tree. The lion could smell me. Why hadn't I showered?

"If I'm going to be eaten by a wild animal, I want to know what's eating me," I thought. I zipped open the tent fly and shined my torch right onto a giant pink-and-grey...

Hippo bum... I pulled the zip down fast, and quaked silently. The hippo ignored me, kept munching grass, and then slowly moved off into the bush, following his nightly feeding trail that would take him back down the hill to the safety of the Nile.

380 THE REAL BAT CAVE

UGANDA Five enormous pythons setting up house with a giant monitor lizard doesn't sound like a marriage made in heaven. But, odd bedfellows as they may be, they're quiet content to share their cave, tucked away in a corner of Queen Elizabeth National Park. The reason they're so content is simple: food. And lots of it.

The cave mouth is as wide as a pair of Chingford semis, not quite as high but definitely with more residents. Home to around a million fruit bats, this is the real bat cave, where what seems like rock is actually a mass of writhing and chattering flesh. It's also a one-stop hypermarket for the corpulent reptiles.

Mountains of guano, an incredible stench and astonishing body heat are the backdrop to the most impressive case of over-crowding on the planet.

381 CRUISING THE CONGO

DEMOCRATIC REPUBLIC OF CONGO For decades, drifting down the Congo River was one of the classic African adventures. But the journey on its longest navigable part, between Kinshasa and Kisangani, was all but impossible to undertake during the country's civil war from 1996 to 2006. Now, with peace reigning in this part of the country – relatively – once more, the barges are making the journey more regularly, and tour operators are beginning to offer the trip on their own vessels.

If you want to try it, get to one of the ports along the Congo and ask about boats leaving: you'll need to be fully self-sufficient, proofed against mosquitoes, happy to munch on manioc sticks and bush meat, and, just in case, a good swimmer. The rewards are remarkable river scenes that few foreigners have ever witnessed, and the joyous welcome of locals on the river just glad to know you want to be there.

382 MOUNTAIN-BIKING WITH THE HERDS

KENYA How about a cool, low-key private game sanctuary, with delightfully eccentric lodgings built from mud, thatch, reclaimed timber and recycled ranch fencing? How about staying in your own cottage shaded by superb acacia trees, fronted by sloping lawns, close to a rushing river and not far from the Happy Valley of colonial days? *Malewa River Lodge*, set in Kenya's Kigio Conservancy, is such a place.

A recent, private venture that has converted a cattle ranch on the banks of the Malewa River into a thriving sanctuary for the kind of wildlife you can mingle with in relative safety, the Kigio Conservancy harbours a breeding herd of rare Rothschild's giraffe, good numbers of zebra, impala and waterbuck, and several charmingly inquisitive ostriches.

Staying at the lodge, you can rent mountain bikes, or take horses, and head off through the bush for a few hours, following an easy network of tracks and landmarks. In 2004 the BBC filmed the high-stakes translocation of a pair of white rhinos into Kigio, and you can track the docile couple, alone or with a

guide. There are no large predators in the conservancy, which is fenced on three sides and bounded to the north by the river. The brown and churning Malewa itself wows kids, and young-at-heart adults.

The forest-swathed riverbank near the lodge harbours troupes of monkeys and dozens of species of birds, while a mini suspension bridge gives access to the foothills of the Aberdares, from where you can look out for the local pod of hippos. Head downstream and you come to a weir and waterfall and cliffs ideal for river-jumping.

The adventure doesn't end as night falls. Grab a torch to make your way through the bush to the dining room. The *Malewa River Lodge* chef conjures excellent meals from fresh, local food, and they serve the best coffee in the Rift Valley. After dinner, you'll gather with the other guests to share animal stories by a huge fire. They have electricity at the office, but mostly your nights will be lit by the flicker of candles and kerosene lamps.

383 WANDERING LAMU ISLAND

KENYA At the northern end of the Kenyan coast lies the magical Lamu archipelago. Fringed by sandy beaches and mangrove forests, this clutch of islands is the northern centre of Swahili civilization, the blend of African and Persian Gulf cultures that formed a thousand years ago as traders from the Middle East settled among Bantu-speaking farmers and fishers.

Visit the town of Lamu, on the island of the same name, and you'll discover an endlessly diverting warren of alleys and multi-storeyed stone houses, some dating back hundreds of years, all built around an interior courtyard. Devoid of cars, and full of quiet corners and arresting street scenes – donkeys bearing TVs, a turbaned man with a swordfish – the town is best appreciated by serendipity, and there is plenty to chance upon, including

two dozen old mosques and various colonial-style waterfront buildings. And as you explore, you'll encounter women in black cover-all buibuis, and swarthy sailors wearing the sarong known as a kikoi; you might even meet one of the area's traditional transvestite community. Once you've exhausted the town's nooks and crannies, at low tide you can simply walk south along the waterfront to reach the charming village of Shela, and Lamu's enticing ten-kilometre-long beach.

The most enthralling time to visit Lamu is during Maulidi (starting on March 20 in 2008), the week-long celebration of Muhammad's birth, when the entire town is swept up in processions and dances, cafés and restaurants are buzzing and locals are likely to invite you to dine with them.

384 A NIGHT ON THE EQUATOR WITH KENYA RAILWAYS

KENYA Constructed in the 1890s, Kenya's "Lunatic Line" (so named by the British press for the folly of building a line into the unexplored interior of Africa) has come to be one of Africa's best-loved train journeys.

Your London-style cab pulls into the forecourt of Nairobi's scruffy but civilized railway station and an elderly porter beats his colleagues to the door. Minutes later, installed in your compartment, you feel the train pull out – 7pm sharp; outside it is pitch dark.

Just after departure, a steward in a shiny-buttoned, frayed, white tunic strides through the carriages ringing a bell – time for dinner: a kind of do-it-yourself version of silver service accompanied by waiters leaning with wobbling plates of tomato soup, tilapia fish and curry. So begins your 526km overnight journey across the savannah to the island city of Mombasa.

Every evening one diesel train pulls out of the capital bound for the coast and another leaves in the opposite direction. Give or take five minutes – and a suitably synchronized passing at the only stretch of double line in the middle – each train arrives

at the other end at 9am.

Outside, with Nairobi's shanties left behind, the big, dark spaces begin. You peer into the nocturnal emptiness of the plains, where Maasai and Akamba herders traipse by day, tending their cattle among zebra, wildebeest, giraffe and ostrich, and you make a mental note to keep your eyes peeled over breakfast on the return journey. Back at your compartment, beds have been made up and sleep, with the incessant rocking of the carriage, comes quickly.

In the mild, grey light of pre-dawn, you awake to an awareness that the climate has changed: you're out of the 5000-foot highlands and dropping to the Indian Ocean coast. As you twist on your bunk to stare out of the window, tropical odours and humidity percolate through the carriages, together with a fresh brew of coffee. The equatorial sun rises as fast as it set as the train jolts at walking speed through the suburbs of Mombasa. With prayer calls in the air and Indian sweet shops on the streets, you disembark, already seduced by the coast's beguiling combination of Asia, Africa and Arabia.

385 PLAYING TARZAN ON CHOLE ISLAND

TANZANIA Remember that incredible tree house you always dreamed of as a kid? The one hidden away in a jungle, set high up in the branches with a cool breeze rustling through the rooms and, in particularly inventive moments, surrounded by ancient ruins? The one that, despite your dad's best efforts with a hammer and a few pieces of plywood, never got any further than your imagination?

Well, that tree house exists. It might not be at the bottom of your garden, but it is on a paradise island marooned in the Indian Ocean, which comes a pretty close second. Tiny Chole Island, one of a cluster of reef-ringed islets that make up Tanzania's Mafia archipelago, is a place where you can swim alongside turtles and go to sleep at night thirty feet off the ground. Think Swiss Family Robinson with a little luxury. Hidden among a string

of ruins – the crumbling, root-tangled legacy of a once-thriving trading centre – and set amid the upper boughs of immense baobab trees, these wooden wonders are the epitome of high-level living. The work of local dhow-builders, each one has a regal four-poster bed – some hanging from ropes, hammock style – on its top deck, just a few lazy steps from an elevated platform offering superb views over the mangroves and out into the sapphire sea beyond.

And after a hard day doing nothing, there can be few finer ways to end an evening than by gently swinging yourself to sleep, a dinner of fresh fish, octopus and lobster – cooked to perfection in rich Swahili sauces and served either up in your tree house or at lantern-lit tables dotted amongst the ruins – helping you on your way.

386 UNWINDING AT MAIA RESORT AND SPA

SEYCHELLES "Can we make this one just half an hour?" I said to the massage therapist. "I don't have much time before lunch, and straight after that I'm…"

It would have been daft to keep talking. Why book yourself into one of the world's most luxurious island spas if you're not prepared to let go of your city habits? Why fill your day with appointments and then cut each one short just to fit them all in? Why not make the most of now?

So I settled for the full session. And when the therapist started drawing to a close after what felt like forty minutes (but was actually well over sixty) I was ready to float back to my villa and spend the rest of the afternoon doing nothing more taxing than enjoying the sparkling ocean view.

Maia's gorgeous thatched villas nestle among tropical foliage on a rocky hillside high above Anse Louis, a dreamy curve of pale sand washed by the sapphire-coloured Indian Ocean.

Some villas have glamorous outdoor bathtubs, others have dramatic clifftop infinity pools; each has a private butler for whom nothing is too much trouble.

This is a resort that takes relaxation very seriously. *Maia*'s ongoing staff-training programme includes an "EQ" (Emotional Quotient) test to measure emotional maturity and attitude, and everyone, from the therapists to the kitchen porters, jump-starts their morning with a group yoga session led by the general manager.

Maia takes indulgence seriously, too. One look at the seven-page spa menu and you can guess what kind of guests it tends to attract. On offer are caviar facials that promise to "transform even the dullest complexions" and hand-drawn herb-scented baths "served with champagne".

If you decide to take the plunge, then just don't book too many massage treatments, or before you know it, your all-too-short visit may have melted away.

THE GORILLAS OF KAHUZI-BIEGA

DEMOCRATIC REPUBLIC OF CONGO We set out on foot from the park headquarters at Tsivanga, and spent the next two hours following a wildly gushing watercourse upstream, climbing steeply all the time. The trackers were somewhere up ahead of us, and messages were passed regularly on the radio. After a particularly strenuous uphill stretch, clutching at roots and branches to drag ourselves up a near-vertical slope, we heard a sudden stentorian roar as a fully grown male gorilla (known to the guides as Chimanuka) burst out of the undergrowth. I knew what I was meant to do. The park's chief guide had briefed us: "If a gorilla charges, stand still," he said. "Lower your head. Look submissive." He stared pointedly at me. "Better wear a hat. If they see your fair hair, they may think you're another silverback."

Yes, I knew what to do all right. But when Chimanuka sprang from the bush in all his glory, his solid muscle rippling in the dappled sunlight, I didn't stand my ground and lower my head. I jumped behind our pygmy tracker and held my breath. This was a huge and magnificent animal, weighing two hundred kilograms and, when standing upright, getting on for two-metres tall – I had never seen anything like it before.

Chimanuka must have charged us at least half a dozen times that morning. He seemed to enjoy it. The pattern went as follows: a charge would be followed by a period of chewing the cud. He would sit on his haunches, rolling his eyes and swiping the available vegetation with his long prehensile arms so as to grab any accessible fruits or succulent stalks. After ten minutes or so, he would rise and turn away from us to show off his magnificent coat (it really is silver), before crashing off again through the undergrowth. Shock and awe. That's what you feel when you first see a gorilla in the wild.

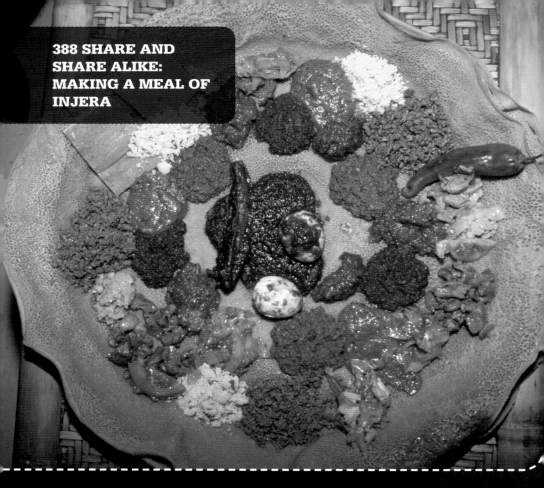

388 SHARE AND SHARE ALIKE: MAKING A MEAL OF INJERA

ETHIOPIA Crunch! A grain of sand slipped between my teeth as I bit into my spongy injera dipped in spicy pureed chickpeas. The Ethiopian grandmother sitting across from me smiled at my surprise, perhaps assuming I was taken aback by the strong spiciness of the shiro wat. She teased me in Amharic, then tore off a piece of injera – using her freshly washed right hand – and deftly scooped up a pile of mushy lentils from her side of our shared platter.

This was the Horn of Africa, where the staple grain is teff, ground on the spot and turned into a soft, yeast-free sour pancake-like bread that becomes both fork and plate. Sand is not a usual feature of Ethiopian cuisine, but this was a hut, a rural home – the owner's lounge doubling as a restaurant – near the Sudanese border. The grain had been fermenting in a pot in the unscreened home, in a town where goats, donkeys, and buses travelled the central dirt road. A little sand was to be expected.

"Can we have doro wat?" I had a craving for a spicy chicken dish. The grandmother shook her head. "It's Wednesday," explained her son in English. A fasting day. "Fasting" in Ethiopia means eating only vegetarian food, and this happens every Wednesday and Friday as well as during Lent.

Tearing a spoon-sized piece of injera off of a separate folded pancake, I used it to scoop up a dark red stew from one of five puddles of coloured wat on the flattened bread. I popped the stew into my mouth and my eyeballs nearly blew.

"Berbere," chuckled the grandmother. Red pepper spice.

Never mind, I thought. It was still an exquisite experience. How often do you get to eat your plate?

389 SWIMMING WITH TURTLES IN THE INDIAN OCEAN

SEYCHELLES A cluster of granite islands enveloped in deep-green tropical vegetation and edged with beaches of blindingly white sand that's so fine it squeaks when you walk across it, the Seychelles are the nearest thing on earth to the Garden of Eden. The turquoise waters of the surrounding Indian Ocean are also one of the best places in the world to see marine turtles, especially the hawksbill; once severely endangered by the trade in its beautifully patterned shells, which were used to make combs, spectacle frames and the like. With most of the Seychelles' waters now a marine reserve, hawksbill numbers have bounced back locally, though the species is still threatened worldwide.

The best place to see them is on their home turf, so don mask, snorkel and fins – or full scuba gear – and get into the sea. Watching them flapping effortlessly past you into the blue is an incredible spectacle; they're sometimes curious, sometimes indifferent, but usually wary of letting you get too close – best to catch them asleep under coral overhangs or in shallow caves, where they can spend up to an hour dozing. If you're not prepared to get wet, try to time your visit during the October–February nesting season when, just after dark, you'll find females heaving themselves up the beaches to just above the high-tide line before using their hind flippers to scoop out a deep pit. They then lay about fifty round, parchment-shelled eggs before shovelling all the sand back on top of them and making their way back down to the water. The eggs incubate in the sand (the sex of the entire clutch is determined by the surrounding temperature) until the young hatch around ten weeks later. Perfect hawksbills in miniature, they dig themselves out of the nest after dark and, using the moon as a guide, scuttle frenetically down the beach toward the sea like an army of wind-up bath toys.

390 DROPPING IN ON THE CHURCHES OF LALIBELA

ETHIOPIA Lalibela, in Ethiopia's highlands, is so rural that it doesn't even have a bank. Yet in the thirteenth century it was capital of the Zagwe dynasty, one of whose last rulers, King Lalibela, embarked on a quest to build a Holy Land on Ethiopian soil.

Historians say he was inspired to build the town's famous rock-hewn churches after a pilgrimage to Jerusalem, while the devout claim that he was instructed by angels during a poison-induced sleep. Whatever the real reason, the town of Lalibela, built as a "new Jerusalem", leaves pilgrims and visitors alike humbled by the elegance of its churches. Gracing a rocky plateau and intricately carved, they mostly lie in two interconnected groups scattered along the "Jordan River", another biblical landscape feature that King Lalibela designed.

This major UNESCO World Heritage Site is hidden from view until you are literally upon it – a strategic choice, offering protection from marauders. All the churches are monolithic structures, dug deep down into the rock. As you pass through carved gullies leading from one church to the next, you can look in on caves containing the skeletons of monks, or gaze up to cubby holes in the red rock face to see yellow-robed pilgrims reciting the Bible in Ge'ez, an archaic form of Amharic.

The churches remain vibrant centres of worship, their monks, nuns and priests fervently engaged with the Ethiopian Orthodox Church's demanding calendar of events. Every church has a hereditary guardian priest dedicated to this medieval world of incense, beeswax candles and ritual – though, incongruously, they all seem to keep a pair of sunglasses handy should you try a photograph using a flash.

391 LANGOUÉ BAI: THE LAST PLACE ON EARTH

GABON The pygmy tribes of the Central African rainforest gave Langoué Bai its name, but it was Mike Fay who put it on the map. When, in 1999, the American ecologist set himself the task of walking from Bomassa in Congo to Loango in Gabon, a project he called the Megatransect Expedition, he already knew that the natural riches of this challenging wilderness were diminishing fast. Together with National Geographic photographer Michael Nichols, his mission was to monitor the impact of human activity on this beautiful but fragile environment.

Their work revealed a hidden world where forest elephants are glimpsed, fleetingly, through thick foliage, western lowland gorillas bathe waist-deep in the cool water of marshy clearings, and chimpanzees stare in astonishment at a primate they rarely see – man. Their data inspired the government of Gabon to protect a significant proportion of this, the second largest rainforest in the world, through the creation of thirteen new national parks.

Langoué Bai, a large natural clearing surrounded by dense vegetation, is a jewel in the heart of one of these parks: Ivindo. Well-watered and remote, the bai attracts a host of wildlife – not just forest elephants and endangered gorillas but also forest buffalo, antelopes (small, shy duikers and marsh-loving sitatungas) and red river hogs, whose tufty ears give them a comical, gremlin-like look. Hidden in the trees, viewing platforms built by Fay's colleagues at the Wildlife Conservation Society provide the perfect vantage point. It's a sweaty hour or two's trek from camp, but it's worth every step just to witness the spectacle of so many highly elusive species gathered together in one arena. No wonder Nichols and Fay dubbed this forest "The Last Place on Earth".

392 MOUNT ELGON: THE ELEPHANTS OF KITUM CAVE

KENYA The volcanic mass of Mount Elgon straddles the border of Kenya and Uganda like a great, pockmarked fried egg, sunny side up. The biggest freestanding volcano in the world, Elgon's lower slopes are riddled with ancient caves and tunnels. Kitum Cave, on the Kenyan side, is famous for its tusk-mining elephants, who plod here from their daytime grazing areas to gouge tasty minerals from its deeply scarred walls at night.

Accompanied by a suitably armed and experienced ranger, you can camp out nearby to await their arrival. They don't visit every night, but when they do, they forage around for hours, their language of stomach rumbles, snorts and sniffs and occasional squeals and trumpets reverberating around the huge cave.

393 WHITEWATER RAFTING AT THE SOURCE OF THE NILE

UGANDA A nearby memorial celebrates Gandhi – some of his ashes were placed here – but even with him present, peace isn't assured. At Jinja, minutes after it calmly ebbs from Lake Victoria, the world's longest river roars into life as the White Nile.

After basic whitewater training, our instructor describes rapids ranging in strength from grade 1 (gentle) to grade 5 (life threatening). Hair of the Dog, Overtime, The Bad Place – they'll all be ridden. The grade 2 rapids are a livid, turbulent stream. It's only a taster for the next set – a granddaddy grade 5. A rush of adrenaline revved by fear precedes the spectacular frothing outrage. The elements are unleashed, magnificent super-nature lets rip and a deafening roar magnifies the strange euphoria of being eaten alive by the Nile.

394 FOLLOWING THE GREATEST SHOW ON EARTH

TANZANIA & KENYA Imagine squinting into the shimmering Serengeti horizon and seeing a herd of wildebeest trundle into view. They're moving slowly, stopping every now and then to graze on what's left of the parched savannah. At first, they number a couple of dozen, but as you watch, tens become hundreds, and hundreds become thousands. And still they come – a snorting, braying mass, relentlessly marching north in search of food. This is the wildebeest migration, and watching it play out on the sweeping plains of Tanzania's Serengeti National Park is unforgettable.

The statistics are staggering: in May each year, over 2.5 million animals, mostly wildebeest but also several hundred thousand zebra and antelope, set out on a three-month journey from the short-grass plains of the southern Serengeti to Kenya's Maasai Mara Game Reserve. On the way, they'll cover some 800km of open plains and croc-infested rivers, running the gauntlet of predators such as lions, cheetahs, hyenas and hunting dogs.

By June, the herds have passed deep into the park's Western Corridor and are nervously starting to cross the Grumeti River. This is the migration at its most savage – and the defining moment of countless wildlife documentaries – as the reluctant wildebeest gather at the riverbank, too scared to go any further, until the mass behind them is so intense that they spill down into the water and are suddenly swimming, scraping and fighting in a desperate attempt to get across. Many are injured or drowned in the mayhem, while huge Nile crocodiles pick off the weak and unwary.

Those that do make it are still some 65km from the Mara River, the last and brutal barrier between them and the rain-ripened grasses of the Masaai Mara. Once there, they'll have three months to eat their fill before going through it all over again on the return journey south.

395 TOURING THE SPICE ISLAND

ZANZIBAR Caressed by the warm waters of the Indian Ocean and cleansed by its monsoon, Zanzibar – East Africa's "Spice Island" – feels worlds apart from the Tanzanian mainland just 40km away. A millennia of trade with lateen-rigged dhows (sailing vessels) introduced numerous peoples from faraway climes, all of whom contributed to the Swahili culture and language and also brought most of the ingredients that infuse one of Africa's most distinctive, and delicious, cuisines.

There's nutmeg and cloves from the Moluccas; cardamom, rice and pepper corns from India; aromatic Sri Lankan cinnamon; and sweet basil (and hookah pipes) from Persia. Portuguese caravels carried chili, vanilla and cassava from the Americas; Indonesians arrived with bananas, turmeric and coconuts; the Arabs introduced coriander and cumin; and Chinese fleets unloaded ginger, along with porcelain and silks for the wealthy.

A spice tour is de rigueur for visitors, but it's on the plate that Zanzibar's fragrant culinary marriage really shines. At nightfall in Stone Town's waterfront Forodhani Gardens, dozens of cooks set up trestle tables and charcoal stoves to prepare nightly banquets that would please any sultan, all in the flickering light of oil lanterns, and at bargain prices. Feast on octopus stewed in coconut sauce, along with fresh lobster, shrimp, prawns, king fish (diced and grilled), whole snappers and even shark. Cool your throat with tropical juices like coconut straight from the shell, tangy tamarind, mango, papaya, pineapple, banana and sugar cane – though you'll have to bear the banshee-like wails of an ancient iron press to sample that one.

Top off your meal with a tiny cup of Omani-style coffee laced with cardamom, and a glob of halua, a sticky, gooey confection made from wheat, pistachios, saffron and cardamom, and unbelievable amounts of sugar – the perfect sweet finale to a spicy feast.

FULFILLING FANTASIES ON
396 FRÉGATE ISLAND

SEYCHELLES They say there is pirate's treasure buried here. Pure white fairy terns nest in the branches of the tangled banyan trees. Fruit bats with metre-wide wings wide emerge from the forest at sunset, chattering like schoolchildren as they feast on papaya and custard apples. Giant tortoises creep among the pandanus palms, and bright green geckos perch on the trunks of the swaying bamboo. Seven beaches of purest white sand are lapped by the turquoise Indian Ocean, and just fourteen villas perch on the granite rocks that make Frégate one of the most beautiful islands in all of Seychelles.

The island is private with a capital "P". Bill Gates stayed here, and Liz Hurley jetted in to Frégate for her honeymoon. Pierce Brosnan once hired the entire island after finishing a Bond film. Every villa has its own outdoor Jacuzzi, an outdoor shower, two marble bathrooms, and bedrooms where rich teak woodwork, tropical daybeds and swathes of silk and muslin create a luxurious cocoon where anyone can hide from the real world. Sleek motor yachts are on hand ready to take the guests out on diving excursions or to try their hand at deep-sea fishing in search of wahoo and kingfish.

Frégate Island is not your typical hotel. Privately owned, and conserved, it is home to one of the world's rarest birds: the magpie robin, rescued from the brink of extinction when there were less than thirty individuals. Now, the little black and white birds are breeding successfully, and mating pairs have been transported to nearby islands to help increase their chances. There are turtles, too, nesting on the soft moonlit beaches at high tide.

Neither is it your typically flat coral island. At sunset, the pink granite boulders catch the light and from the top of the island's own miniature peak, Mount Signal, the Indian Ocean is an endless expanse of blue.

397
CLIMBING KILIMANJARO

TANZANIA The statistics are impressive. Measuring some forty kilometres across and rising 5895m above sea level, Kilimanjaro is easily Africa's highest mountain.

But such bald facts fail to capture the thrill of actually climbing it: the days spent tramping from muggy montane forest to snowy summit, pausing occasionally to admire the views over the lush lower slopes and beyond to the dusty plains, or scrutinize the unique mountain flora; the blissful evenings gazing at the panoply of stars with fellow trekkers; and the wonderful esprit de corps that builds between yourself and your crew, a camaraderie that grows with every step until, exhausted, you stand together at the highest point in Africa.

Beguiling though the mountain may be, those contemplating an assault on Kili should consider its hazards and hardships. For one thing, though it's possible to walk to the summit, it's not easy. An iron will and calves of steel are both essential, for this is a mountain that really tests your mettle. Then there are the extreme discomforts on the slopes, from sweat-drenched shirts in the sweltering forest to frozen water bottles and wind-blasted faces at the summit. And there's the altitude itself, inducing headaches and nausea for those who ascend too fast.

Such privations, however, are totally eclipsed by the exhilaration of watching the sunrise from the Roof of Africa, with an entire continent seemingly spread out beneath you. The sense of fulfilment that courses through you on the mountaintop will stay with you, long after you've finally said goodbye to Kili.

398 REEF ENCOUNTER: ECO-LIVING ON CHUMBE ISLAND

ZANZIBAR It's difficult to know which way to look, snorkelling in the turquoise waters off Chumbe Island: at the oriental sweetlips, bobbing in unison around a huge coral fan? At the blue-spotted stingrays, shuffling under the sand along the bottom? Or at any one of the other four hundred or so species of fish that help make the island's reef, Tanzania's first marine protected area, one of the finest coral gardens in the world?

Overlooking the reef at Chumbe's western edge are seven palm-thatched eco-lodges; the rest of the island is a designated nature reserve of creeping mangroves and coral rag forest, left to the local wildlife – including the rare Ader's duiker and the endangered coconut crab, the largest land crab in the world. Everything about the lodges shouts "green": their roofs are designed to collect rainwater, which is then filtered before running through to the shower; hot water and electricity are provided by solar power; toilets are of the composting variety; and the air-conditioning system is probably the most efficient you'll ever see – a pulley lowers the bedroom's tree-top front wall, cooling the room with a fresh sea breeze.

With a maximum of twelve guests at any one time, Chumbe is a real honeymoon hideaway – indeed, it's often used to round off a once-in-a-lifetime safari, maybe as an ecological appeasement for all those internal flights spent whizzing from one park to another on the African mainland. The only other visitors are school children from nearby Zanzibar, who visit the island on educational snorkelling trips. Watching them come back in off the reef, chatting excitedly about following a hawksbill turtle along the outer shelf or trying to outdo each other with the size of the groupers they've just seen, is almost as much fun as drifting above the coral yourself.

399 MEETING THE CHEEKY MONKEYS OF KIBALE

UGANDA It's unnerving to hear a bass drum being thumped when a) you're deep in a tropical forest and b) there is no one present to beat it. But exciting things happen in Kibale Forest National Park. And there's nothing more thrilling than when you find who it is that's responsible for the noise: wild chimpanzees. Kibale contains the highest concentration of primates in the world; there are twelve species in total but it is the chimps that enchant the most. After beating on flying-buttress roots with their feet, they decide on other scare tactics. Unsettling screams echo through the forest canopy – it's an exhilarating din. But the acoustics have got nothing on their terrific aerial acrobatics and displays of great ape machismo. But then they're off, moving through the branches at high speed, and it's impossible to keep up.

400 GETTING CLOSE UP AND PERSONAL WITH A GIRAFFE

KENYA *Giraffe Manor* is an exquisite country house on the outskirts of Nairobi with magnificent views southwards to Mount Kilimanjaro. Roaming the grounds – and peering through the windows – is a breeding herd of rare Rothschild's giraffe, rescued from the brink of extinction by Jock and Betty Leslie-Melville in the 1970s. Guests at the antique-filled manor get a taste of the lifestyle made famous by Karen Blixen in *Out of Africa*.

Next door, the Giraffe Centre raises funds for environmental education among African schools; climb onto a wooden platform at giraffe height and, if you're brave enough, place a food pellet between your lips – one of the centre's giraffes, its lovely long eyelashes undoubtedly flickering, will "kiss" you with its long purple tongue.

401 THE GREAT AFRICAN MEAT FEAST

KENYA Ask any expat East African what food they miss most and they'll tell you nyama choma. In The Gambia, it's known as afra; and in South Africa it's what you have at a braai. All over the continent, roast or grilled meat is the heart of any big meal and, whenever possible, it is the meal. A meat feast is also the only occasion in Africa when you'll find men doing the cooking – charring hunks of bloody flesh clearly answering a visceral male need that every king of the cookout would admit.

Most people don't eat meat often, subsisting on a simple starch dish for their regular meal of the day, so it's perhaps not surprising that when the occasion demands or provides a banquet, meat is the main fare. In Kenya or Tanzania, unless you happen to be invited to a wedding or funeral, you'll go to a purpose-built nyama choma bar, where flowing beer and loud music are the standard accompaniments, with greens and ugali (a stiff, corn porridge, like grits) optional. The choice is usually between goat and beef, with game meat such as impala, zebra or ostrich available at fancier places. If you select one of these, usually with an all-you-can-eat price tag equivalent to about a week's average wages, you should cannily resist the early offerings of soup, bread and sausages, leaving space for the main events.

After roasting, your meat is brought to your table on a wooden platter, chopped up to bite-size with a sharp knife, and served with a small pile of spiced salt and a hot sauce of tomato, onion, lime and chilies. You eat with your fingers, of course. You'll need a good appetite, strong jaws and plenty of time – to wait for your chosen roast, to chew and digest, to pick your teeth while downing a few more beers and to honour the dance requests that inevitably come your way, no matter how full you might feel.

SUDAN Egypt is famed for its great pyramids, but Sudan has many more. The most striking examples make up the ancient ruined city of Meroë. For nearly a thousand years from 600 BC, the little-known Kingdom of Kush prospered here alongside the Nile, once successfully repelling an attack by Alexander the Great and for centuries interring its rulers in the small but distinctively slender pyramids. Some thirty survive today, while all around small dunes in turn entomb the rubble. Meroë gets few visitors, so chances are you'll have this incredible site all to yourself.

EXPLORING THE PYRAMIDS OF MEROË
402

WILDLIFE-SPOTTING IN THE
NGORONGORO CRATER

TANZANIA The tectonic forces that created East Africa's Great Rift Valley also threw up a rash of volcanoes, one of which blew itself to smithereens 2.5 million years ago. Its legacy, the nineteen-kilometre-wide Ngorongoro Crater, is a place that holiday brochures like to call "the eighth wonder of the world". They're not far wrong. Ngorongoro's natural amphitheatre is home to virtually every emblematic animal species you might want to see in Africa, and the crater's deep, bluish-purple sides provide spectacular backdrops to any photograph.

The magic begins long before you reach the crater. As you ascend from the Rift Valley along a series of hairpins, the extent of the region's geological tumult becomes breathtakingly apparent. Continuing up through liana-draped forest, you're suddenly at the crater's edge, surveying an ever-changing patchwork of green and yellow hues streaked with shadows and mist.

Living in the crater's grasslands, swamps, glades and lakes is Africa's highest density of predators – lions and leopards, hyenas and jackals among them – for whom a sumptuous banquet of antelope and other delicacies awaits. Glimpsing lions is an unforgettable thrill; just as memorable but far more unsettling is the macabre excitement of witnessing a kill. You'll also see elephants and black rhino, the latter poached to the brink of extinction. Twitchers have plenty to go for, too, including swashes of pink flamingoes adorning the alkaline Lake Magadi in the Crater's heart. If ogling wildlife from a vehicle doesn't do it for you, stretch your legs – and escape the crowds – on a hike through the Crater Highlands, in the company of an armed ranger and a Maasai guide.

404 SUSTAINABLE SAFARIS WITH THE MAASAI

KENYA North of Mount Kenya, the Laikipia region, a vast sweep of rangelands, ridges and seasonal rivers, stretches out towards the northern deserts. Here, former ranches are converting to eco-tourism and conservation, and pastoral communities are setting up innovative experiments in tourist development.

Many places in Laikipia make efforts to limit their environmental footprint and Il Ngwesi – owned and run by the six-thousand-strong Il Ngwesi Laikipiak Maasai community – has taken the lead.

The lodge, located on a remote, bush-covered ridge, is delightful. It's a bird-watcher's paradise: you awake to a jaw-dropping dawn chorus, and birds – from drongos to hornbills – fill the air all day long, crowding the footpaths and branches, and often appearing in the rooms themselves. Six huge bandas (artfully rustic, thatch and tree-trunk cottages) are spaced out along the west-facing slope, their open-sided fronts graced with magnificent decks and chunky furniture made of polished branches. Banda number one has amazing good views of the elephants that congregate around Il Ngwesi's magical waterhole, and, like number five, features a giant mosquito-netted four-poster bed that you can pull out onto the deck.

There's no wood burning or fossil fuel use at Il Ngwesi – all electricity is supplied by solar power – and the community has a water-use association to monitor consumption and pollution, ensuring the local herds have plenty to drink and leaving enough for the lodge's beautiful infinity pool. Although strictly a private conservancy, the area swarms with wildlife, and game walks with Maasai guides and armed rangers are the norm. It's especially satisfying that all the money goes back into the community, which – among other things – has enabled them to bring back rhinos, formerly hunted out of the area, and to track and monitor at least one pack of highly endangered African wild dogs.

405 TREKKING IN THE SIMIEN MOUNTAINS

ETHIOPIA The great mass of the Simien range – formed from one of Africa's ancient super-volcanoes – rears up in Ethiopia's remote, northern hinterland, broken into towering plateaux and peaks by a slew of rushing rivers and trailing waterfalls. In the heart of the mountains, the UNESCO Natural Heritage site of Simien National Park is a spellbinding wilderness of fertile valleys and grassy moors, the jewel in Ethiopia's crown of natural attractions, offering one of Africa's, if not the world's, most spectacular hikes – an eight-day return trek to the snow-capped peak of Ras Dashen (4620m).

Once the fortified home of Ethiopia's Jewish community, the Simiens remain largely roadless, but are still traced by footpaths and scattered with Amhara villages. On the misty heights within the pristine national park live three large mammals unique to the region: the impressively-horned and vulnerable Walia ibex (a nimble, shaggy goat that you only ever see hundreds of metres away on a sheer, high cliff-face); the critically rare and beautiful red-coated Simien wolf; and the remarkable, grass-eating Gelada baboon, which you are very likely to see grazing on the steep, Alpine meadows, sometimes in parties numbering hundreds.

Foot-slogging and mules are the usual transport in the Simiens, and you'll soon get used to the steady pace and moderate height gains required at these altitudes, with stunning birdlife, such as the huge lammergeyer vulture, and giant African Alpine vegetation to distract you from your heaving chest and throbbing legs.

406 LOSING THE CROWDS AT KATAVI NATIONAL PARK

TANZANIA Unlike the parks of northern Tanzania, where increasingly one of the most common species is *Homo sapiens touristicus*, the remoter west of the country, close to Lake Tanganyika, feels more like central Africa, and is little visited. The rich concentrations of wildlife in Katavi, which only gets a hundred or so visitors a month, include big herds of magnificent roan and sable antelopes, some 4000 elephants and as many as 60,000 buffalo, among dozens of other species, supported by seasonally flooded grasslands. With stunning flocks of waterbirds at the right time of year, and reliable numbers of hippos snorting and crocs sunning around palm-fringed Lake Katavi, it's a wonderful environment – best explored on foot, with an armed ranger you can hire on the spot.

407 THAT'S MAGIC: PEMBA'S DJINN

ZANZIBAR There's no better place to seek help from the potent East African spirits than Pemba Island. The place quietly reeks with the supernatural and is home to the area's djinn: form-changing spirits.

Popo Bawa – half bat and half man, but without any Hollywood blockbusters to his name – is an infamous resident. He flies into homes late at night and does, ahem, dastardly things to men as they slumber in their beds; look out for groups of men sleeping outside in their porches or on the streets – a tell-tale sign of a recent "attack".

A charm placed at the base of fig tree or the sacrifice of a goat are usually enough to keep Popo Bawa away. Respect the culture and tradition and, if lucky, an invitation to a sacrificial ceremony might just come your way.

KENYA The Maasai Mara is Kenya's slab of the Serengeti, a succulent, acacia-dotted grassland that's home to some of the densest concentrations of wildlife in Africa. This is where the BBC films "Big Cat Diary", and where wildebeest by the thousand swarm across the crocodile-jammed Mara river. Animals hold such dazzling sway here you feel as if you've landed in the natural world's equivalent of New York.

But if you need to get away from even this, take a balloon flight over the reserve: every vivid second will stay with you for the rest of your life. You'll be woken at 5am, in the pitch-dark chill of the savannah pre-dawn, and driven to the riverbank, where a boat takes you across to the launching site. As the doves start their dawn chorus and the sun's rays sneak through the woods, the huge Mongolfier is inflated. With little ceremony, you climb in and, a few hot blasts later, begin to rise through the trees. There's almost no sound apart from that occasional whoosh, and nothing to detract from the exquisite sensation of floating in space, the soft brush of the breeze on your cheek, and animals in every direction.

Just below, vultures wheel from treetop roosts. The chocolate-brown river reveals stirring hippos. Hyenas might be scrapping over a buffalo carcass, and you might notice jackals bravely rushing in for a nip of their share. An invisible lion vents a guttural roar, more like a huge belch. Zebra and wildebeest canter away from the balloon's advancing shadow. And a line of elephants emerges from the trees, adults ear-flapping, youngsters fooling at the sides. After it's all over, the slap-up breakfast and chilled sparkling wine you're served upon returning to terra firma almost seem unnecessary fripperies.

HOT-AIR BALLOONING OVER THE
MAASAI
MARA 408

409 STORYTELLING ON THE SSESE ISLANDS

UGANDA The Ssese Islands of Lake Victoria are a sleepy, sibilant archipelago, yet slumber doesn't do them justice. "Ssese" is a corruption of "tsetse", the fly that carried the disease that at one point devastated the entire region.

Kalangala, the main town on Buggala Island, still snoozes even though it is repopulated now. But there's action at the local beer stall; Kasiim, a small righteous man, will be telling fearful stories loaded with folklore and superstition to a credible audience. Join his enraptured audience gathered around the beer-crate table, charmed by tales of magic, gravely nodding and eyes popping to the fabulous night-time entertainment.

410 DINNER AT MOSES' PLACE

ZANZIBAR There's no shortage of beautiful beachfront restaurants in Jambiani on Zanzibar's east coast but for something just that little bit different, why not drop in on the locals?

Little Moses, no more than 12 years old, had ran up to us on the beach earlier in the day to invite us round for a bargain-priced, home-cooked meal. Arriving at his basic stone house, we caught our young host running off to his neighbours in search of a few more chairs. Seated in the roofless dining area – now complete with borrowed stools – we waited eagerly as a huge pot of octopus curry was laid on the table by Moses' mother, dished up with platefuls of piping hot chapati-style bread. "I caught the octopus this morning," Moses told us proudly. No frills, no fancy trimmings, just fresh, simple and delicious food. And certainly the most memorable of the trip.

411 SURF'S UP: WATCHING HIPPOS HIT THE WAVES

GABON Barely touched by tourism, and with a small and localized population leaving much of it as virgin rainforest, Gabon's lagoon-broken coast is one of the few places in the world where you can watch hippos in the sea – and not simply swimming from island to island, as they do in Guinea-Bissau. These hippos are surfers.

In the stunning Loango National Park, in order to get from one river mouth to another, the hippos swim out far enough to ride in again on the breaking waves – a remarkable adaptation that's safer, quicker and much more fun – and far cooler – than plodding along the shore or breaking through the jungle. And if the hippos don't fancy the conditions on any particular day, then there's always the elephants on the beach, the whales offshore, or the gorillas and chimps inland – all of which help make Loango unique in Africa.

MISCELLANY

SWAHILI TIME

Time calculations in Swahili are made from dawn to dusk (which, with minor variations east and west, are pretty close to 6am and 6pm throughout the Swahili-speaking region of Kenya, Tanzania, Uganda and eastern Congo. So, saa moja ("one o'clock") is seven o'clock and saa nane ("four o'clock") is ten o'clock. You add asubuhi (morning), jioni (evening) and usiku (night) to be more precise. It sounds confusing, but once you've learnt your Swahili numbers, it soon becomes automatic to subtract six for Swahili time. Watch out, however, for Swahili-speakers practising their English and forgetting to add six when they arrange an appointment.

OUT OF AFRICA

Most anthropologists believe that humankind is of African descent. Genetic analysis indicates that modern humans share a common matrilineal ancestor, nicknamed **African Eve**, who lived in what is now Ethiopia, Kenya or Tanzania about 150,000 years ago and whose descendents subsequently migrated to every corner of the world. However, almost every year brings fresh fossil discoveries. The complexity of the picture, and particularly the view of how many early proto-human species may have shared time together in Africa, changes constantly, but some of the putative ancestors of Homo sapiens are indicated in the table below.

WAR AND PEACE

Few countries in the region have escaped some sort of **violent internal strife** since winning their independence. The fighting in the Democratic Republic of Congo (the former Zaire) claimed more than four million lives, making it the deadliest conflict since World War II. In 1994, over a three-month period, nearly one million, largely Tutsi, civilians were slaughtered during the Rwandan genocide. Hundreds of thousands have been killed and two million people displaced by the various conflicts in Sudan. And Africa's longest civil war, in Angola, lasted 27 years, from the overthrow of the Portuguese dictatorship in 1975 until 2002. Today, Rwanda is counting on building an economy based on tourism and IT; the Democratic Republic of Congo's war is stuttering to an end; and in Angola, security has finally returned, and with it food production and dreams of investment and tourism. Meanwhile, the countries in the region that currently receive nearly all the tourists – Uganda, Kenya and Tanzania – are, if not evenly prosperous, democratic and respectful of human rights, then at least generally moving in the right direction.

LAKE VICTORIA

Africa's largest lake, **Victoria Nyanza**, spreads across approximately 69,000 square kilometres – approximately, because the surface area varies seasonally and the fringes are so choked with water hyacinth that it can be hard to determine the shoreline – making it the largest lake in Africa and the second largest freshwater lake in the world, equivalent an area the size of Ireland.

TALLNESS, IN SHORT

The Central and East African region is home to a great variety of ethnic groups, including some of the shortest and tallest people in the world. The so-called **Pygmies**, who live all over Central Africa and speak a multitude of languages, measure on average 1.37m (4ft 6in). In contrast, the average height of the **Tutsi** (or Watusi) of Rwanda and Burundi is just over 1.83m (6ft).

RUNNING HIGH

Although athletes from North Africa are rapidly gaining ground, it is still the East Africans who dominate middle- and long-distance running. Academics have long tried to explain the endurance of athletes from countries such as Ethiopia and Kenya. Some researchers believe that living and training at high altitudes produces great athletes. For others, it's all a matter of genetics: in the late 1980s, for example, the Nandi people comprised less than two percent of Kenya's population, but made up two-fifths of the nation's elite runners.

"I am the hero of Africa"

Idi Amin (Ugandan dictator)

CONGO TO CONGO

The world's shortest international flight links the Congolese capital, Brazzaville, with Kinshasa, the capital of the Democratic Republic of Congo, formerly Zaire. The cities are just 4km apart, on opposite banks of the Congo River, and the flight, which takes less than fifteen minutes, gives pilots just time to get into position for a landing on the other side.

MONKEY BUSINESS

Dame Jane Goodall, a British primatologist, almost single-handedly changed the way scientists view the ape world. Famous for her studies of **chimpanzees** on the shores of Tanzania's

THE FOUR OLDEST HOMINID FOSSILS DISCOVERIES

SPECIES	LOCATION DISCOVERED	DATE DISCOVERED	ESTIMATED AGE
Sahelanthropus tchadensis	Southern Sahara, Chad	2001	6 to 7 million years
Ardipithecus ramidus	Aramis, Ethiopia	1992–93	4.4 million years
Australopithecus anamensis	Kanapoi, Kenya	1965	4 million years
Australopithecus afarensis	Laetoli, Tanzania	1978	3.7 million years

Lake Tanganyika, Goodall was the first person to prove that animals had distinct personalities; she also discovered that chimps fashioned tools and fought long-term wars with rival groups. In 1965, she established the **Gombe Stream Research Centre** in Tanzania, and in 1977 founded the **Jane Goodall Institute** (wwww.janegoodall.org) to provide support for field research into wild chimpanzees. American conservationist **Dian Fossey** spent nearly twenty years living among the **mountain gorillas** of the Virunga volcanoes region. In 1967, she established the world's first mountain gorilla research institute – the **Karisoke Research Centre** in Rwanda – but it was her autobiographical novel **Gorillas in the Mist**, published in 1983 and subsequently transferred to film in 1987, that brought their plight to a global audience. Fossey spent the latter part of her life waging war on illegal poaching; she was murdered – probably by a poacher – in December 1985 and lies buried in the cemetery close to her beloved gorillas. The **Gorilla Organization** (®www.gorillas.org) was set up to continue her work.

INDEBTED

Although some countries in East and Central Africa have been given debt relief, several, including Kenya and the Democratic Republic of Congo, are still among the continent's most heavily indebted. The region's countries have **national debts** of between $400 million and $30 billion, totalling nearly $90 billion between them – burdens that mire them in the deepest poverty.

SOUKOUS

The variety of **Congolese music** called **soukous**, with its high-tempo beat, thumping bass lines and ringing guitars, is among the most popular – and sexy – of Africa's many musical styles. **Soukous** has its roots in Cuban music, particularly rumba, which became popular in the booming cities of Leopoldville (now Kinshasa) and Brazzaville during the early 1940s. For a time, the indigenous music industry boomed, but these days, with the average Congolese income at less than US$1 a day and music often being sold on bootlegged CDs, the stars of **soukous** are making most of their money in the West.

FIVE LEGENDARY CONGOLESE MUSICIANS

Papa Wendo The first star of African rumba.
Joseph Kabasele Leader of African Jazz, one of the big bands that transformed the African take on Cuban rumba into soukous.
Franco Luambo Nicknamed the "Sorcerer of the Guitar", Franco was the front man of OK Jazz, African Jazz's big rival during the 1950s.
Tabu Ley Rochereau Tabu Ley's band African Fiesta dominated Congolese music in the 1960s.
Papa Wemba The best-known soukous musician around today, with a stunningly pure, high voice.

"He who waits until the whole animal is visible spears its tail"

Swahili proverb

CONFINEMENT, EURO-STYLE

The **Maasai** term for the first white people who visited their districts spoke directly of the Victorian obsession with modesty. Unlike the Maasai, who rarely wore much at all, and never more than a simple cloth or blanket, the Europeans went by the colourful appellation *iloridaa enjekat* – "those who confine their farts".

FRONTLINE

The tiny nation of Djibouti, independent from France only since 1977, was formerly one of the French Foreign Legion's biggest bases in Africa. Today, it's one of the USA's biggest bases in Africa, on the frontline in Washington's so-called War on Terror.

THE LAKE THAT WAS

Lake Chad, after which the republic of Chad is named, used to extend to nearly 30,000 square kilometres. Millions of Chadians, Cameroonians, Nigerians and Nigériens (citizens of Niger) depended on its shallow waters for fish, drinking water and transport. But over-use and **climate change** had shrunk it, by the millennium, to less than 2000 square kilometres, and the governments of all four countries are resigned to the view that it will dry out completely by 2020.

THE BIG FIVE IN THE TWENTY-FIRST CENTURY

"Safari" is Swahili for "journey" (kusafiri meaning "to travel"); it entered the English language in the nineteenth century, when Europeans first visited Africa on game-hunting expeditions. Today, the lion, elephant, rhino, leopard and buffalo are still known as the "**big five**" – a phrase originally coined in recognition of their trophy value, but one which has somehow outlived the rifle into the digital camera age (don't forget your battery charger and spare memory cards).

LAND OF THREE COUNTRIES

Somalia has had no recognized central government since 1991. The capital Mogadishu is a hornet's nest of warring clan militias – you go there at your peril. In the north of the country, **Puntland** (capital Bosaso) is a self-declared autonomous federal region of Somalia, while in the northwest, **Somaliland** (capital Hargeisa) has declared outright independence.

OMAR BONGO

The longest ruling African president, **El Hadj Omar Bongo Ondimba**, has run the republic of Gabon (which has close political and business ties with France) since 1967. Bongo is married to the daughter of the president of Congo, another French ally. Benefiting from his country's oil reserves, he's reputed to be one of the richest heads of state in the world.

REDISCOVERING THE FORGOTTEN COAST • TRACKING RHINO IN DAMARALAND • EXPLORING THE SKELETON COAST • **JUNGLE OPERATICS: THE LEMURS OF ANDASIBE-MANTADIA** • GOING BUSH IN ONGAVA GAME RESERVE • ACROSS THE GREAT KAROO • DIGGING AND DANCING ON A PIONEER PROGRAMME • **GIVING SOMETHING BACK AT GULUDO BEACH LODGE** • TRACING MANDELA'S ROOTS IN THE EASTERN CAPE • LIVING WITH THE KUNDA • CROSSING THE MAKGADIKGADI PANS • ON A SWING AND A PRAYER: FLYING THROUGH THE TSITSIKAMMA FOREST CANOPY • LEARNING ABOUT ELEPHANTS IN THE BOTSWANAN BUSH • THE EARTH MUSIC OF TSIMANIN DROA • EATING THE FAT OF THE LAND IN KLEIN KAROO • LOOKING FOR LIONS IN MADIKWE • VAMIZI ISLAND: PARADISE WITH PRINCIPLES • TSINGY: A FOREST OF LIMESTONE PEAKS • **SAMPLING WINES IN THE WESTERN CAPE** • SWIGGING THE MOST REMOTE BEER ON EARTH • IN AT THE DEEP END: WHITE-WATER RAFTING ON THE ZAMBEZI • UP THE TSIRIBIHINA IN A DUGOUT CANOE • **COUNTING FISH IN LAKE MALAWI** • ON YOUR BIKE: CYCLING THROUGH THE NYIKA PLATEAU • THE SMOKE THAT THUNDERS AT VICTORIA FALLS • TOURING A TOWNSHIP • MALALOTJA: A BIG PLACE IN A SMALL COUNTRY • CLIMBING TABLE MOUNTAIN • GETTING HOT AND BOTHERED ON THE DRAKENSBERG • ENJOYING THE SHOW IN ETOSHA NATIONAL PARK • DANCING WITH THE KING AT BIG NCWALA • **PONY-TREKKING IN THE MOUNTAIN KINGDOM** • TAKING A WALK ON THE WILD SIDE • RUSTIC ROCKING AT RUSTLER'S VALLEY FESTIVALS • GETTING OUT OF YOUR TREE AT THE WORLD'S SMALLEST PUB • WATCHING THE DESERT BLOOM IN NAMAQUALAND • **TRICKY TOPOGRAPHY: THE OKAVANGO DELTA** • HIKING THROUGH THE FISH RIVER CANYON • A TASTE OF THE SWEET LIFE AT KANDE BEACH BAR • TROU AUX CERFS: INSIDE THE CRATER • DREAMING IN COLOUR: BALLOONING OVER THE NAMIB • CAPE CROSS COLONY: THE SEAL DEAL • REDISCOVERING THE FORGOTTEN COAST • JUNGLE OPERATICS: THE LEMURS OF ANDASIBE-MANTADIA • EXPLORING THE SKELETON COAST • GOING BUSH IN ONGAVA GAME RESERVE • GIVING SOMETHING BACK AT GULUDO BEACH LODGE • ACROSS THE GREAT KAROO • **TRACKING RHINO IN DAMARALAND** • DIGGING AND DANCING ON A PIONEER PROGRAMME • TRACING MANDELA'S ROOTS IN THE EASTERN CAPE • LIVING WITH THE KUNDA • CROSSING THE MAKGADIKGADI PANS • ON A SWING AND A PRAYER: FLYING THROUGH THE TSITSIKAMMA FOREST CANOPY • LEARNING ABOUT ELEPHANTS IN THE BOTSWANAN BUSH • **IN AT THE DEEP END: WHITE-WATER RAFTING ON THE ZAMBEZI** • THE EARTH MUSIC OF TSIMANIN DROA • EATING THE FAT OF THE LAND IN KLEIN KAROO • LOOKING FOR LIONS IN MADIKWE • VAMIZI ISLAND: PARADISE WITH PRINCIPLES • TSINGY: A FOREST OF LIMESTONE PEAKS • SAMPLING WINES IN THE WESTERN CAPE • SWIGGING THE MOST REMOTE BEER ON EARTH • COUNTING FISH IN LAKE MALAWI • **THE SMOKE THAT THUNDERS AT VICTORIA FALLS** • UP THE TSIRIBIHINA IN A DUGOUT CANOE • ON YOUR BIKE: CYCLING THROUGH THE NYIKA PLATEAU • TOURING A TOWNSHIP • MALALOTJA: A BIG PLACE IN A SMALL COUNTRY • CLIMBING TABLE MOUNTAIN • GETTING HOT AND BOTHERED ON THE DRAKENSBERG • ENJOYING THE SHOW IN ETOSHA NATIONAL PARK • DANCING WITH THE KING AT BIG NCWALA • PONY-TREKKING IN THE MOUNTAIN KINGDOM • TAKING A WALK ON THE WILD SIDE • RUSTIC ROCKING AT RUSTLER'S VALLEY FESTIVALS • GETTING OUT OF YOUR TREE AT THE WORLD'S SMALLEST PUB • WATCHING THE DESERT BLOOM IN NAMAQUALAND • TRICKY TOPOGRAPHY: THE OKAVANGO DELTA • HIKING THROUGH THE FISH RIVER CANYON • A TASTE OF THE SWEET LIFE AT KANDE BEACH BAR • **TROU AUX CERFS: INSIDE THE CRATER** • DREAMING IN COLOUR: BALLOONING OVER THE NAMIB • CAPE CROSS COLONY: THE SEAL DEAL • REDISCOVERING THE FORGOTTEN COAST • TRACKING RHINO IN DAMARALAND • JUNGLE OPERATICS: THE LEMURS

SOUTHERN AFRICA
412–455

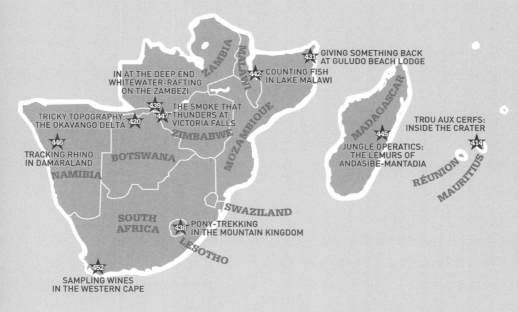

GIVING SOMETHING BACK
AT GULUDO BEACH LODGE — 431

COUNTING FISH
IN LAKE MALAWI — 442

IN AT THE DEEP END:
WHITEWATER-RAFTING
ON THE ZAMBEZI

THE SMOKE THAT
THUNDERS AT
VICTORIA FALLS — 447

TRICKY TOPOGRAPHY:
THE OKAVANGO DELTA — 420

439

TRACKING RHINO
IN DAMARALAND — 446

TROU AUX CERFS:
INSIDE THE CRATER — 414

JUNGLE OPERATICS:
THE LEMURS OF
ANDASIBE-MANTADIA — 445

PONY-TREKKING
IN THE MOUNTAIN KINGDOM — 438

SAMPLING WINES
IN THE WESTERN CAPE — 452

ZAMBIA

MALAWI

MOZAMBIQUE

ZIMBABWE

BOTSWANA

NAMIBIA

SOUTH
AFRICA

SWAZILAND

LESOTHO

MADAGASCAR

RÉUNION

MAURITIUS

SOUTH AFRICA An indistinct crackle on the ranger's radio broke the peace of our unhurried journey back to the lodge.

Danie translated over his shoulder, ear straining for more reports as he cajoled the Land Rover into picking up a bit more speed. "Two of the unattached young lions are on the move. This is their territory and we've had an idea for a few days that there was another male trying to move in. There's a bit of light from the moon tonight. There could be a rumble." The radio crackled again and we took a sharp turning. "Hold on," said Danie. "They're heading for the waterhole."

We drove hard for a few minutes. The sunset had all but drained from our surroundings, twilight dimming to evening monochrome. At the waterhole there was another vehicle. We drew alongside softly. A ranger in the same uniform as Danie shook his head quickly, then motioned with his hands that we take different routes.

Every movement in the bush made us twitch. The Land Rover bumped slowly over the rutted track.

We came round a corner and stopped suddenly. Danie flicked off his headlights, and with his foot on the clutch slid the gearstick into reverse. The lions were thirty metres away.

They sat on their haunches, peering into the bush away from us, their dark manes bristling. By comparison, the pride we'd seen earlier that day seemed lethargic and uninterested.

No one dared breathe. One of the lions lifted his head and, starting from somewhere around the end of his tail, let out a grumbling, tumbling growl which built into a massive, full-throated primal roar. The sound left the air around us shaking.

A reply rose from further away. Our pair pushed up onto all fours, then moved off purposefully. In seconds they had slipped into the dark shadows of the bush.

"Good luck, guys," said Danie. He flicked on the lights. "I think we'd best leave them to it."

LOOKING FOR LIONS IN MADIKWE

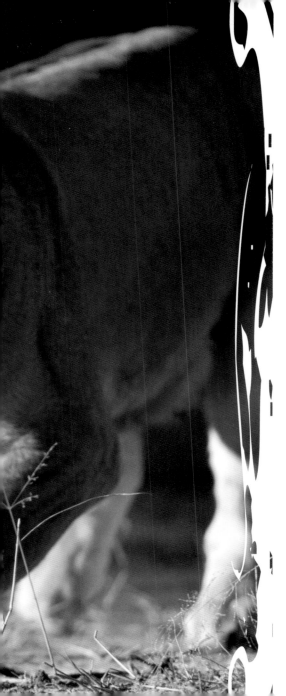

413 BIRDING IN THE GREATER ST LUCIA WETLANDS

SOUTH AFRICA Safari in South Africa is not all about lions, leopards and laughing hyenas. The Greater St Lucia Wetlands has its hippos and its crocs, but it's the staggering number of birds that makes this northeastern corner of KwaZulu Natal so special.

Over 500 species pass through the wetlands each year, drawn by the park's unique confluence of world-class wilderness: dune-backed beaches, tidal estuaries, coastal forest, swamps, saltwater marshes and dry thornveld, all bordering the 360-square-kilometre Lake St Lucia, one of South Africa's most important water-bird breeding areas.

On the lake's western shore, a number of self-guided trails lead off through the vegetation. African broadbills chase butterflies through the forest, southern banded snake eagles circle overhead, and Neergaard's sunbirds flit between succulent bunches of weeping boer-beans. In the Greater St Lucia Wetlands, small really is beautiful.

414 TROU AUX CERFS: INSIDE THE CRATER

MAURITIUS Up in the hilly heartland plateau of Mauritius, the extinct volcanic crater of Trou aux Cerfs ("Stag Crater") rises incongruously from the centre of the Indian Ocean island's highest town, Curepipe. A superb escape from urban life (and the heat at sea level), there's a road to the rim, and around it, from where you get stunning panoramas of the island, including the sheer peaks of the Trois Mamelles ("Three Breasts") rising to the west. The inner slopes are thickly wooded, and there's a good chance you'll see some of Mauritius's unique birdlife, including the endangered pink pigeon. Down on the crater floor, the lake varies seasonally from pristine to weed-choked, but it's deep, so watch your step.

415 TSINGY: A FOREST OF LIMESTONE PEAKS

MADAGASCAR Some of the butterflies are so large they hardly look able to get off the ground. But the lemurs and hairy crabs aren't interested in them, nor are the lime green parrots. They're too busy fussing through the tsingy.

These serrated limestone rock formations, sharp as bread-knives, cut up through the landscape of western Madagascar, creating baroque grottos and pinnacles. Dry and seemingly inhospitable, they are home to extraordinary wildlife. Even fat baobabs manage to grab hold in this alien environment. But extraordinary beauty is also found in the detail: miniature red ants and tiny jewelled orchids dazzle against jagged bone-coloured stone.

416 GETTING OUT OF YOUR TREE AT THE WORLD'S SMALLEST PUB

SOUTH AFRICA They call them upside down trees around here. Baobabs are a common sight in the parched scrubland that dominates remote Limpopo Province in the far north of South Africa. Solitary, and often visible from the side of the freeway that wiggles down towards the Zimbabwe border, these trees look like the work of some deranged abstract sculptor whose marbles have gone slightly awry in the searing bush heat, their roots snarling, twirling, and twisting like a hundred fossilized snakes, splayed and pointing almost accusingly, into the ground. Indeed, the indigenous tribes of centuries past believed that baobabs had offended God and that he had planted them upside down to exact revenge.

The Sunland Baobab is the oldest in existence, thought to be anything from 2000 to 6000 years old. At a scarcely believable forty-seven metres in circumference, it's also far and away the biggest baobab in the world. It's so large, in fact, that I've been able to have a game of darts, put a couple of tunes on the jukebox and sink a couple of beers inside its trunk.

Trees of this size suck moisture out of the earth and store it for so long that, after a few centuries, the insides start to hollow out. The Van Heerdren family who own the land made quite a discovery when they started clearing compost out of its hollow nineteen years ago – there are many baobabs with insides that you can crawl into for the night, but none so large that it can hold a full bar, a wine cellar and room for fifty people to drink the night away.

The Sunland is still alive, and still growing. Apparently, there are plans for an extension about 2000 years from now.

417 DREAMING IN COLOUR: BALLOONING OVER THE NAMIB

NAMIBIA Yellow ochre, burnt sienna, raw umber, salmon pink. The early morning landscape that's unfolding beneath us summons a litany of colour-names remembered from old paintboxes. Spice colours, too - cinnamon, turmeric, nutmeg, powdered ginger – and palest blond, the colour of bone, straw or freshly-cut wood.

If you picture the desert as a stark, monochrome place, you couldn't be further from the truth. As our balloon floats over crumpled hills, powdery dunes and saltpans dotted with skeleton trees, the rich, complex subtlety of the desert palette is so beautiful that I'm determined to imprint it on my memory. I feel like an Inuit searching for new words to describe the colour of snow.

Here, nature is sculptor. The Namib, considered the world's most ancient desert, was carved by water and wind. From the air, your eye can trace the rhythmic alignment of the eighty-million-year-old dunes, like ripples in a storm-blown sea.

Incredibly, a few species manage to survive in this near-barren environment. We drift over a towering dune the colour of clotted cream and peer down to watch a long-shadowed oryx climbing the ridge on slow, stiff legs. It's the kind of antelope that Picasso might have dreamed up – its facial markings bold, its horns strikingly graphic. On the plain at the foot of the dune, a male ostrich races across the sand, its feathers fluffed up like a bustle. Beyond, a small herd of mountain zebra mill about under heat-wizened camelthorn trees.

"I'm taking her higher", says our pilot. There's a roar from the burner and the balloon begins to ascend. The scene below softens and recedes, and the luminous African sky grows larger and larger. And I turn my gaze to the endless horizon.

418 A TASTE OF THE SWEET LIFE AT KANDE BEACH BAR

MALAWI Kande Beach – such an apt name for this little piece of backpacker paradise in northern Malawi. For life is sweet here, whether you're partaking in some of the many waterbound activities the lake affords or just snoozing on a beachfront hammock. But perhaps the sweetest pleasure of all is to be had at the famed *Kande Beach Bar*. Grab a cold one and settle in under the shade of the open wood-framed bar – lake shimmering just beyond, music softly playing in the background. As the sun sets and the revelling steps up a notch, the only sour note is knowing you can't stay forever.

419 CAPE CROSS COLONY: THE SEAL DEAL

NAMIBIA You'll smell them before you hear them: a pungent oily aroma wafting off the Atlantic Ocean. You'll hear them before you see them: a chorus of grunts and snorts carried on the breeze. And then you finally clap eyes on them – a writhing mass of spray-shrouded seals stretching far along the Skeleton Coast. The colony at Cape Cross is overcrowding in action, with up to 100,000 cape fur seals gathering here at any one time. Word has it that this is actually a beach, but you'd never know it underneath all that blubber. Large bulls fight for territory; pups fight just to stay alive. And just offshore, the breaking waves bubble with hundreds more seals, waiting for a scrap of sandy space on which to wedge themselves

420 TRICKY TOPOGRAPHY: THE OKAVANGO DELTA

BOTSWANA The Okavango Delta is unique. It is formed where the waters of the Okavango river flow into the vast ultra-flat plain of arid nothingness that constitutes northern Botswana. It's like a strange contest – desert versus river – and here the desert wins. With no gradient to guide it, the water spreads out over 15,000 square kilometres, then gives up and seeps away or evaporates in the heat. Nothing like it happens anywhere else on earth. The river disappears.

The area is a birder's paradise and a cartographer's nightmare. No one seems able to decide if it should be green or blue on a map. The waters rise and fall in tune with distant rainfall patterns, creating a bewildering maze of islands, waterways and lagoons, much of which disappears underwater during floods, only to reappear in a quite different arrangement when the waters recede.

The best way to see the delta is in a mokoro, the local variety of canoe; a poler will guide you, often along waterways that are precisely the width of a hippo's body, for the simple reason that they have been formed by the daily migration of hippos from the lagoons, where they bask during the day, through the reeds to the shore, where they graze all night.

The water is utterly clear, with hundreds of tiny fish darting just below the surface. The hippo-made waterways snake and curve through the tall reeds, which seem to glow in the low, bright African sun, occasionally opening out into wide lagoons, each of which is only the most minuscule fraction of this endless, mysterious landscape of not-quite-land, not-exactly-water. The only sound is the swish of the pole in the water, and the croak of frogs, happily proclaiming that they have found themselves in frog heaven.

HIKING THROUGH THE
FISH RIVER CANYON

NAMIBIA Africa's biggest ravine and one of southern Africa's great hiking trails, the Fish River Canyon is a mega-rent in the earth's crust more than half a kilometre deep, twenty kilometres wide and one hundred and fifty kilometres long, snaking south to vent its river into the mighty Orange. Although the Grand Canyon is a good deal bigger, Fish River, ranked second in the world, is still unfathomably vast, the result of tens of millions of years of erosion, yet on a scale that is more accessible. The area's astounding natural beauty and the ease with which you can walk – it takes five days to traverse the canyon – and camp here, together with the bird-watching opportunities, have made it one of Namibia's greatest outdoor attractions.

422 GETTING HOT AND BOTHERED ON THE DRAKENSBERG

SOUTH AFRICA It's hot and it's dry and the mountains are huge. They just hang there – craggy, grey and wholly unsympathetic. We've been heading up towards the Amphitheatre for an hour or so and the damn thing hardly seems any closer. The Afrikaaners called this range the Dragon Mountains. In Zulu, they are ukhahlamba, "the Barrier of Spears", hundreds of kilometres of flat-topped peaks that are the remnants of a once vast South African plateau. As soon as you see them, you know you've got to climb. It's a guy thing.

You can get up and down in a day; that's what Witness, our chef at *Tendele Camp*, said. We've already given him our supplies and by the time we get back tonight he'll have prepared supper and have it set out beside the bungalow. I'm already looking forward to that meal. For the moment, though, I chew on a piece of biltong and realize that I'm getting through my water bottles too fast. This is an epic struggle between mountain and man and the man is very hot indeed.

Fortunately, as we stumble through a wooded section of the Tugela Gorge, there's a stream cascading over huge basalt boulders. I don't just drink. I fill my hat and upend it over my head. Fifteen minutes later, we're ready to start again.

I know what lies ahead: the notorious chain ladder up the last section of the Amphitheatre. Rusty and dented from thousands of sweaty bodies, it's the only way to get on top of Mont aux Sources. Lesser men have baulked at its hundred rungs up a near vertical rock face.

Still, the view from the top is breathtaking; that's what Witness claims and he's been doing this route since childhood. Wringing out my damp headgear, I follow the rest of our small band of brothers. We've still to reach Tugela Falls, the second highest waterfall in the world, plunging down 948m in five dramatic leaps. Only we'll be going up, not down. Tonight, we will have such stories to tell Witness.

423 ENJOYING THE SHOW IN ETOSHA NATIONAL PARK

NAMIBIA Just this morning, through the dust and glare, eighty nodding zebra had filed out of the thorn scrub, the leaders forced belly-deep into the waterhole by the jostling ranks behind. Now, darkness assembles a new cast. The first player enters stage right: a black rhino, huffing from the shadows, calf at her heels. She pauses at the moan of a distant lion – radar ears rotating and nostrils scouring the breeze. Then, with a stamp and a snort, she steps up to drink.

It's a safari truism that the real thing is not like the TV version: the animals don't simply queue for your viewing pleasure. Except, perhaps, at Etosha. Namibia's premier national park is endowed with a string of spring-fed waterholes that, in the dry season, suck the wildlife from the surrounding bush. And with floodlights at each of the three main camps, you get to see the nocturnal action, too. You'll have to share it with others, mind:

Etosha is safari central. But the wildlife is unbeatable.

On this September night at Halali Camp, black rhino is just for starters. Next, a herd of forty elephants arrives, taking over the waterhole with their lumbering frolics. Then, as the jumbos ghost away into the night, a single male lion pads in from stage left. He drinks long and deep before departing purposefully – on a mission. Four hyenas soon follow, giggling in some edgy dispute. Meanwhile, hares, eagle owls and other night creatures come and go, while a honey badger sniffs around the rocks where I perch.

Next morning, out on the road, Etosha is all horizons: dusty plains, blinding saltpan, bleached skies. The place has none of Okavango's lushness or Serengeti's grandeur. It's just huge and harsh, with herds – everywhere – trudging across its flat immensities. No point trying to follow them. Just pack your sandwiches, pick a waterhole and wait: they'll come to you.

424 LIVING WITH THE KUNDA

ZAMBIA Waking up in a comfortable and traditional African hut in the early light of dawn, children and animals rousing around you, the sounds of women preparing the first meal of the day carried on the still morning air – such is the experience of living with the Kunda.

The villagers of Kawaza, a small hamlet on the fringes of Zambia's South Luangwa National Park, earned their livings from subsistence agriculture and working in safari lodges until they started offering tourists the chance to experience village life by spending a night or two with them. From the income this generates, the villagers – the village guides, the traditional healer I visited, and the drummers and dancers who performed a spectacular evening display for us under the moonlight – are paid. The remaining balance goes into a central fund, which the community allocates to projects such as Kawaza's village school. Six years ago the school had 327 pupils and four

teachers – now there are 551 pupils and sixteen teachers.

Kawaza village consists of immaculate thatched huts or bandas surrounded by patchwork fields of crops. It's a happy place full of playful children, women going about their daily work and men discussing the issues of the day. You can't help but feel incredibly "grounded" in the village – maybe because somewhere in our ancient past our relatives lived in a similar way. I spent two nights there, and it's the most positive – not to mention authentic – travel experience I've had.

I spent the days in the village playing football with the kids – using a ball made out of crushed paper tied up with string – and simply sitting and talking with the locals, including an old lady from the village called Elimina Banda, who says she is happy to see whites in the village and would like to spend all day with them. "There was a time when I was scared of them," she says, "but not now."

425 CROSSING THE MAKGADIKGADI PANS

BOTSWANA We stand at the edge of a sea of grass looking out onto the salt pan. "A flat and featureless expanse of sun-baked clay," says our guidebook. It's not far wrong. We can see our route ahead of us: twin tyre tracks meandering sketchily towards the horizon, disappearing into the blinding heat-haze. But this is where we stop. Going onward requires expedition-style gear: winch, GPS, satellite phone, the works. One wrong turn and you're through the crust, axle-deep in treacherous silt. The next vehicle might be days. Weeks, even.

This was once a lake. On Kubu Island, a baobab-studded granite outcrop to the south, ancient beaches record the lapping waves of another era. Fossilised aquatic creatures are strewn among the shingle – as are Stone Age arrowheads, relics of a people who once called this desolation home. But during the subsequent millennia, geology intervened: seismic forces tilted the centre of Botswana, diverting its rivers and cutting off the lake from its supply. Today, the pans receive an annual trickle – the overspill from the Okavango. Briefly, they become glassy sheets of shallow, salty water.

Wildlife here is nomadic. Hit the right season, and you'll find springbok and zebra massing on the grasslands, pans washed pink with flamingos, and wandering lions adding their throaty voice to the nocturnal soundtrack. At other times, the plains seem empty – just the odd ostrich stalking the horizon, dodging the dust devils. But tracks and signs tell of meerkats, springhares and other permanent residents that quietly eke out a precarious living.

Other parts of Botswana may have bigger game, but if it's wilderness, isolation and sheer space you crave, then the Makgadikgadi Pans are hard to beat. Here, on the northern frontier of the Kalahari, it's a big place for feeling small.

426 ON YOUR BIKE: CYCLING THROUGH THE NYIKA PLATEAU

MALAWI Now the going gets tougher. The red dirt track has narrowed, and your wheels crunch leaf litter as you enter the dense miombo woodland of the Rukuru Valley. Splintered branches strewn across the track tell of recent elephants. You eye the undergrowth apprehensively, but daren't risk your balance by looking up too often. At least it's downhill. The Chisanga Falls are somewhere below: a chance to dismount and wash the dust off jolted limbs. But beyond them lies a climb of 40km, back onto the western escarpment where camp awaits.

Just thirty minutes earlier you had been on top of the world – or at least on top of the Nyika Plateau, which must feel pretty similar. Grazing zebra had lifted their heads to stare, as you'd passed them on your two-wheeled steed. Eland, ever cautious, had filed away along the distant ridge. They're still filing now, five kilometres behind you, silhouetted against a towering cloudscape.

"It doesn't look like Africa" comes the refrain from first-timers to the Nyika. Laurens Van der Post made the same point, albeit more poetically, in his classic *Venture to the Interior*. Certainly, the undulating treeless terrain up top can be more suggestive of the moors than the tropics. But what do you expect at 2500m? The logbook at *Chelinda Lodge* tells of a young couple who, only last week, cycled around a corner to find a leopard lying on the track. That was certainly enough "Africa" for them.

There's a final day's hard pedalling ahead, but tonight the reward for your exertions will be a campfire beneath the stars with a continent laid out below you: Zambia to the west, Tanzania to the north and, lying far below like a darkened pool, Lake Malawi to the east.

427 GOING BUSH IN ONGAVA GAME RESERVE

NAMIBIA Dinner in *Ongava Tented Camp* is always a memorable occasion: an open-air fireplace, a dozen or so guests, and, milling around the floodlit waterhole a few feet away, the evening's entertainment – an ageing bull elephant, maybe a rhino and her calf, or, on a lucky night, a pair of lionesses, returning from a hunt. Nestled at the foot of the tongue-twisting Ondundozonanandana Range, in Ongava Game Reserve, one of Namibia's largest private concessions, the intimate camp is everything you could ask for in an African safari experience: small and sumptuous – with just six tastefully furnished tents, each with an open-air bathroom for showering under the stars – and exhilaratingly wild.

The 75,000 acres of scrubby bush that surround the camp are prime territory for spotting both African species of rhino, as well as zebra, cheetah and a whole host of other smaller residents, including the rare black-faced impala. And once you've ticked those off your list, it's just a fifteen-minute drive to Etosha National Park, a salt pan the size of Switzerland, and one of Africa's truly great game parks, where you can add giraffe, kudu, leopard and ostrich to the roll call.

It's at night though, when the immense African sun has melted behind the hills and the sky is a thick, star-studded blanket of black, that *Ongava Tented Camp* really casts its spell. The campfire embers are slowly cooling and you're tucked up in a bed that wouldn't look out of place in a five-star hotel when the deep roar of a large male lion comes rumbling across the plains, washing over the canvas like a thunder clap. You're safe, of course, but the effect is still electrifying. That sound, that feeling, is one that you won't forget in a very long time.

428 TRACING MANDELA'S ROOTS IN THE EASTERN CAPE

SOUTH AFRICA True to its name, South Africa's Wild Coast is one of the country's most unspoilt areas – a vast stretch of undulating hills dotted with traditional African villages, lush forest and kilometres of undeveloped beaches punctuated by rivers. Arguably the best place to taste the Wild Coast is at *Bulungula Lodge*, a joint enterprise between the people of Nqileni Village and seasoned traveller and development worker, Dave Martin.

Idyllically sited along the mouth of the Bulungula River, Nqileni and the lodge lie in a remote region of the former Transkei, the notionally "independent homeland" to which Xhosa-speaking black South Africans were relegated under apartheid. One consequence of South Africa's racial policies was the neglect suffered by the Wild Coast, but this also meant it escaped the intense coastal development that has ravaged many former whites-only coastal areas.

With a dearth of formal jobs, people in the Transkei still live rural lives in thatched adobe huts, growing maize, fishing and cooking on wood fires, while young lads still herd cattle, pretty much as Nelson Mandela did when he was a boy some seventy years ago. Wander around Nqileni and chances are you'll be invited into someone's house for a slug of traditional beer or you can take part in everyday business, such as mud-brick making or maize stamping.

Bulungula also gives a livelihood to members of the community, who take visitors exploring on horseback or canoeing up the Xhora River to look for malachite kingfishers, or teach them how to fish with a throw net. You can meander along the beach to watch whales and dolphins or have one of the villagers take you out on an all-day expedition to beautiful Coffee Bay. At night, the skies are so clear and the shooting stars so plentiful that, according to the lodge's owner, "if you look at the sky for half an hour without seeing one, you can stay the night for free."

429 DIGGING AND DANCING ON A PIONEER PROGRAMME

MADAGASCAR As someone who'd never wielded a shovel in her life, I was pretty pleased with my first day's efforts on the Azafady Pioneer programme. Azafady makes a point of pitching its volunteers into the thick of things, which in my case meant digging a well in a remote Malagasy village, bounded on one side by forested hillsides and on the other by the most idyllic beaches I'd ever set eyes on. Not that we had much chance to gaze at the scenery. Half buried in red dust and mud, most of the day was spent digging and slapping on trowels of cement under the watchful eye of our local project coordinator.

Sometimes, volunteering initiatives seem geared more towards benefiting the volunteers themselves than the communities they are ostensibly there to help. But this isn't the case with Azafady, where the work carried out – supporting NGOs on a range of health, sanitation and environmental schemes – really does make a positive impact on the environment and lives of local people. It's an award-winning project that provides a very special way to get under the surface of life on La Grande Île. Moreover, all the profits are ploughed back into sustainable development.

After an intensive seven-day orientation course, where you're taught the basics of local Malagasi dialects, the volunteer work proper begins. Ours involved planting fruit trees, making puppets and writing songs to help teach children about the importance of washing their hands before eating. Out in the forest, we spent days collecting rare seeds, surveying the impact of logging and assisting with studies of birds, plants and lemurs.

The hands-on nature of the work means it can be physically demanding at times, but Azafady make sure there's enough downtime for its volunteers to surf and, more importantly, hang out with the local people they work with. There were some amazing parties on the beach outside Ambinanibe, the village where we dug the well. Fuelled by bottles of warm Three Horses beer, we were shown how to drum, sing bawdy songs in the local lingo and, best of all, do the mangaliba – the sexiest dance in all the Indian Ocean.

430 ACROSS THE GREAT KAROO

SOUTH AFRICA Take on the 1400-kilometre drive between Cape Town and Johannesburg and you'll discover there's an awful lot of nothing in South Africa's interior. This vast, semi-desert is called the Great Karoo, meaning "place of thirst", and it stretches from the southwestern Cape Mountains northeast to the Orange River. The name is apt: summer heat is fierce here, and the winter cold is biting; rain is elusive and the soil is all but barren. Slow creaking windmills struggle to bring water to the surface and the baked, red-brown earth is roamed only by skittish knots of springbok or small merino sheep. Few are the human inhabitants and those that do brave the desolation live on remote farms or are huddled in squat, whitewashed settlements which seem to drift like rafts in an arid ocean.

You can – as most do – speed along the straight, featureless N1 highway at a steady 120 km/h. Every few hours you'll come upon a sterile service station offering some shade, a refrigerated drink and the chance to scrape the accumulated layers of insects from your front windscreen.

Alternatively, you could stop off for a while: the total emptiness is quite awe-inspiring. Sitting in the shade of their verandahs, locals will tell you that after a few days, or maybe weeks, you'll come to relish the crispness of the air, the orange and ochre colours of the rocks on the flat-topped hills at sunset and the tenacious succulents and desert flowers that defy the heat and drought. There are few places on earth where you can see so much sky; at night, there are so many stars that even the familiar constellations get lost in the crowded galaxies. The water-starved Karoo is called Great for a reason.

431 GIVING SOMETHING BACK AT GULUDO BEACH LODGE

MOZAMBIQUE Translucent turquoise water swarming with rainbow-coloured fish; sand the colour and consistency of finely ground pearls; a hinterland of irrepressible tropical greenery . . . it sounds like paradise. But for the inhabitants of this remote stretch of the Mozambique coast, still licking its wounds after four decades of civil war, life isn't a beach. Infant mortality runs at one in three, and – thanks to rampant malaria, a shortage of clean water and poor sanitation – average life expectancy struggles to exceed forty years.

It was exactly this glaring juxtaposition of beach idyll and grinding poverty that inspired a team of young British entrepreneurs to establish a tourist resort with a difference on the deserted seashore near Guludo village, just north of the Quirimbas National Park. But instead of carving out an exclusive enclave, the primary aim of the project was to provide a sustainable means of alleviating hardship in the neighbourhood: 55 local people have been trained to work in the tourist lodge, and one day they'll run the place entirely.

Guludo Beach Lodge was designed to have minimal impact on the environment. Its nine "rooms" are thatched, tented shelters, or, with raised inner platforms – private, but open to the sea breezes and views, and equipped with luxurious beds, mozzie nets and al fresco marble bathrooms. All the wonderful food is sourced locally, and all waste is recycled.

Far from being screened from local conditions, guests are actively encouraged to visit Guludo village, patronize handicraft businesses there, play in the weekly locals-versus-staff football match, and generally get involved in the development projects financed by the resort. Five percent of the lodge's profits are channelled directly into schemes such as well excavation, health and sanitation workshops, support and training for midwives and – most ambitiously – the construction of a new school for the village.

LEARNING ABOUT
ELEPHANTS
IN THE BOTSWANAN BUSH

BOTSWANA Elephant lesson number one: the world's mightiest land mammals are chatty creatures, but they keep their gossip amongst themselves. Many of the sounds they make, though audible by other elephants up to ten kilometres away, are far too low-pitched for the human ear to detect.

I learnt this from the man sharing my saddle: the elephant handler who's my guide for the afternoon. Apparently, there's much, much more to an elephant's vocal range than the ear-splitting trumpeting we all remember from *The Jungle Book*. I particularly like the peculiar noise that sounds like a stomach-rumble, but is actually voiced – that's an elephant expressing blissful contentment.

You get a whole new perspective on elephants from the back of one – and a whole new perspective on the bush, too. You're higher than you would be in the back of a Jeep and,

with no rattling engine or grinding gears to distract you, you can concentrate on elephant noises, along with bird calls, the screeching of insects and even the snorting of zebras and gazelles. Most grazing herbivores turn tail and flee at the sight of humans on foot, but the elephant-plus-human combo doesn't seem to faze them: they stay put, and chew on.

In many ways, an elephant makes the perfect alternative to a 4WD. Eco-friendly and even-tempered, they tackle the terrain with ease, only pausing in their stride when a particularly tasty looking tree catches their eye.

Which leads nicely on to elephant lesson number ninety-nine. Elephants love their snack breaks, and safari elephants are no exception. After all, what to you is a thrilling ride in pristine bush is, to them, a pleasant amble through an open-air salad bar.

SOUTH AFRICA Skip back a few millennia and we were all arboreal primates. We'll never know for sure what those ancestors of ours looked like. But in Tsitsikamma National Park, you can discover the primate within by swinging through the canopy – thirty metres up.

I say swinging, but whizzing is a better word, for instead of bombing through the forest on the end of a vine, Tarzan-style, you're strapped into a high-tech harness and sent careering along a steel cable that's strung between two trees. But you can yodel as much as you want.

Each cable slide – there's a circuit of eleven – leads to a timber platform high up in a mighty outeniqua forest. Here, as you catch your breath, a guide sorts out your karabiner clips, gives you a few nature notes and gets you ready for the next slide.

The platforms and slides may stir up childhood memories of monkeying around in tree houses, but in fact they're state-of-the-art. Cleverly engineered using tensile forces, leverage and rubber blocks instead of bolts to keep the trees as pristine as possible, the whole circuit is based on a system designed by ecologists working in the Costa Rican rainforest. They used their cables to collect specimens and data. Trust the adventure-mad South Africans to use theirs just for fun.

The longest and steepest slides are the best: with a good shove, you can hurtle along at up to 50kmph, hyped with excitement. But on the gentler ones, there's more time to enjoy the scenery: the light and shade playing on the foliage above, the intricate forms of the giant ferns below, the passing birds and staring monkeys. Or you can just soak up the rich, unfamiliar smells – the musty whiff of decaying vegetation mixed with the damp freshness of new growth – and the heart-pounding sensation of exploring a new domain.

ON A SWING AND A PRAYER:
FLYING THROUGH THE TSITSIKAMMA FOREST CANOPY

433

434 WATCHING THE DESERT BLOOM IN NAMAQUALAND

NAMIBIA & SOUTH AFRICA Spring in Namaqualand brings the kind of miracle for which time-lapse photography was invented. After the brief winter rains, mile after mile of barren-looking semi-desert is transformed, within days, into a sea of flowers – a dazzling display that sends butterflies, bees and long-tongued flies into a frenzy.

Namaqualand, a thirsty, rocky region encompassing South Africa's northwestern corner and Namibia's extreme south, supports over 4000 wild floral species, a quarter of them endemic. It's this diversity that gives the annual display so much charm. The key lies below the surface: seeds and bulbs can lie dormant through many years of drought, and when conditions suddenly improve, the plants grow roots of differing length, so numerous species can exploit relatively small stretches of terrain.

The least showy of the plants are the succulents, some shaped like fingers, others (such as lithops) like pebbles. These cling to life on the ground, where the colour of the gravel can mean the difference between extinction and survival – a few chips of white quartz may be sufficient to lower the local air temperature by a degree or so, just enough for a plant to cope.

Intriguing though the succulents are, it's the colourful blooms that draw the crowds. Visit on a sunny day in a good year and you'll see meadow after meadow sprinkled with aloes and lilies, daisies and gladioli, purple ruschias, golden ursinias and gaudy vermillion gazanias, as bright as hundreds and thousands on a fairy cake.

It's a photographer's dream – and a heaven for painters, too. If Claude Monet had set up his easel near Springbok instead of Argenteuil, the Namaqualand daisy would by now be every bit as famous as the Val d'Oise poppy.

435 VAMIZI ISLAND: PARADISE WITH PRINCIPLES

MOZAMBIQUE Twenty-five metres below the sparkling waters of the Indian Ocean, the rock pinnacle sticks out from the reef like a talon. Behind me, a coral wall stretches north and south as far as the eye can see, its sheer face plummeting into an underwater chasm five hundred metres deep. Hanging above the dark space, I am concentrating on the biggest creatures in the vicinity: twenty-three grey reef sharks that circle the pinnacle but retreat into the deep when I approach too close. Like divers, the sharks congregate here because the fish life is extremely rich – yellow snappers, kingfish, sweetlips and glittering shoals of anthias swirl above the reef.

Vamizi is just twelve kilometres long, one of dozens of islands in the Quirimbas archipelago at the northern tip of Mozambique's 3000-kilometre long coastline. At *Vamizi Lodge*, the island's only upscale accommodation, ten luxurious palm-thatched villas have their own private views of the glittering ocean edged with blindingly white sand. The enormous villas deliver a sumptuous holiday experience complete with giant four-poster beds swathed in billowing muslin. There are antique Zanzibari lamps, and showers made of marble, seductive day beds festooned in plump cushions, and beautifully carved wooden shutters that allow the trade winds to cool the rooms without the need for air-con. At least once a week, dinner is served beside a beach bonfire under the stars, and fresh, locally caught fish is available at every meal. Game fishing and diving are the main activities, but the island is rich in birdlife – and one morning I was awoken by a pair of chattering Samango monkeys sitting in a tree outside my room.

But this isn't just about bagging a bit of barefoot luxury. Vamizi is part of the Maluane conservation project, where scientific research is undertaken in collaboration with the Zoological Society of London. Nesting turtles are protected and the local African community benefits from tourism revenues being used to build a clinic and a schoolhouse, and to train local fishermen as reef monitors to help map the fisheries resources around this very special island paradise.

436 THE EARTH MUSIC OF TSIMANIN DROA

MADAGASCAR Near the village where locals paint their noses white is a place where the earth makes music. You can't help but buy into its mystery. Tsimanin Droa, 120km north of Majunga on the Madagascan west coast, means "There's No Other One". Which is true – there isn't another hill for miles around. The cave that plunges deep inside it could also bear the name quite happily, too.

After acclimatizing to the dark in the eerie depths, stalactites and stalagmites appear like a winter wonderland of frozen pipe-bursts. With a little practise, they can be played like a giant marimba, making an evocative sound that's as old as the hills.

437 EATING THE FAT OF THE LAND IN KLEIN KAROO

SOUTH AFRICA Oenophiles and gluttons beware. There's a hidden gem in the Klein Karoo that'll have you salivating.

Jan Harmsgat is a name more suited to a Muppet chef rather than a rural guesthouse, but don't be deceived. Their tiny kitchen produces first-rate gastronomy; the cellar startlingly good wine. But then they are in the heart of the Robertson Winelands, after all. Exceptional local produce is served in an intimate dining room, but be sure to book as it has an equally tiny capacity.

And it gets better: this is food with morals. Being part of the Fair Trade in South African Tourism initiative, you can feel like you're feasting with a conscience.

438

PONY-TREKKING IN THE MOUNTAIN KINGDOM

LESOTHO Landlocked within South Africa, the mountain kingdom of Lesotho is a poor but magical place.

A lot of the magic is encapsulated in those two words – mountain kingdom. Lesotho is one of Africa's few surviving monarchies, proud of its distinctive history, and the whole country lies above an altitude of 1000 metres, its highest peaks soaring into a distinctly un-African realm of mists and dank cloud. Back in the nineteenth century, the dominant figure in the country's history, King Moshoeshoe (pronounced Mo-shweh-shweh) acquired a pony stolen from a farm in the Cape. Its suitability for Lesotho's hilly terrain was soon clear, and the people, the Basotho, quickly became a nation of horse riders. They remain so today. Few of the scattered villages of the mountains are reached by any road, tarred or otherwise. Everywhere is connected by paths, and to get anywhere you need to walk or ride.

Pony trekking isn't really an "activity", something to do instead of canoeing or bird-watching; get atop a horse here and you're participating in Basotho life. There's nothing prim about it either; no one will comment on your posture or how you hold the reins, and given that the paths only go uphill or downhill, you'll do a lot more plodding than prancing. You'll greet passing locals, breathe mountain air, village woodsmoke and the scent of clammy horse sweat, and hear the ringing shouts of barefoot children rounding up goats on the hillside – accompanied, all the while, by the steady clip-clop of your sure-footed pony picking its way along the path.

IN AT THE DEEP END:
WHITE-WATER RAFTING
ON THE ZAMBEZI

ZAMBIA Ever thought it might be fun to be trapped inside a giant washing machine as it switches from rinse to spin? No, nor had I, until, after a dozen drenchings and umpteen mouthfuls of river water, I found myself tumbling headlong down the Stairway to Heaven, yelling like a maniac, high on the thrill of just staying alive.

Dropping eight metres over a ten-metre-long distance, the Stairway is one of the steepest of the world-class rapids that churn up the mighty Zambezi just below Victoria Falls. But it's by no means the scariest. The names the rafters give the toughest runs – Gnashing Jaws of Death, Overland Truck Eater, Double Trouble, Oblivion - say it all.

The Lower Zambezi rafting route begins in one of the most dramatic mid-river locations on earth. You paddle across the foam-marbled water of the Batoka Gorge – the steep-sided ravine that receives the full fury of the fifteen-hundred-metre-wide, one-hundred-metre-high falls. Behind you, water crashes against water and hurtles into the heavens as spray. It's a nerve-jangling display of natural energy.

The first three rapids come hard and fast, then there's a sharp left turn as the gorge zigzags downhill. Before you know it, you're tackling Morning Glory, the first big challenge, where a "hole" that's almost as wide as the river threatens to swallow you in one gulp.

Survive this and, thanking the river gods for their kindness, you can prepare for the Stairway. But you'll never be truly ready for Rapid 18: Oblivion. This one eats rafts for breakfast – the chances of making it through its three monster-sized waves without your raft being flipped are only one in four. They say that a baptism in the Zambezi purifies the soul: one tussle with Oblivion and you'll be praying for mercy.

440 MALALOTJA: A BIG PLACE IN A SMALL COUNTRY

SWAZILAND Another false summit. Defeated, you lever the pack from your back and slump into the shade of a sugar bush, porcupine quills strewn at your feet like some primitive offering. Bird calls drift up from the canopy below: the chirrup of bulbuls, the growling of a turaco. Down in the forest, the trail had been all cool, green filtered light. Up here on the shattered slopes, the sun has you pinioned to the hillside like a beetle on a sand dune. An unseen baboon barks its alarm from the ridge-top. But the rush of the falls is a siren call. One more push?

The grandeur of Malolotja belies the bijou dimensions of Swaziland. This, the biggest park in southern Africa's tiniest nation, protects a muscular wilderness of peaks, grasslands and gorges, with vistas that stretch far beyond the country's borders. Highlights include the world's oldest iron-ore mine, and the ninety-metre bridal veil cascade of Malolotja falls, and the "potholes" – a terraced series of circular plunge pools that lure footsore hikers deep into an echoing ravine. Hiking trails embroider the wild ridges and forested clefts. And every stream swells the exuberant Malolotja river, which carves its way downwards and northwards until it hits the Komati and turns east for the Indian Ocean.

For birders, Malolotja means the blue swallow – southern Africa's rarest bird and just one of a fine cast of avian A-listers. Other wildlife is rich, but elusive: alert hikers might meet mountain reedbuck skittering across the rocky slopes, an otter lolloping along the riverbank, or maybe a shy serval stalking the marsh. Plants, too, are prolific: orchids in the grasslands, cycads in the forests, aloes and coral trees spotting the hillsides with scarlet. It's not "Big Five country", give or take the occasional leopard print. But whatever you find, you'll have it all to yourself.

441 RUSTIC ROCKING AT RUSTLER'S VALLEY FESTIVALS

SOUTH AFRICA Renowned even in South Africa for its small-town conservatism, the province of Free State rarely lives up to its enticing name, but the excellent Rustler's Valley Festivals are a notable exception – the parties feel and operate like true celebrations, and the revellers are experts at getting down to fine music in a stunning location. Held on a spacious farm in Rustler's Valley, at the foot of the majestic Maluti mountains, the festivals span the summer, offering mainly DJ'd sounds interspersed with live music, a muddy dam to cool off in, tepees and sweat lodges, plus accompanying devotees, good food and even stuff for the kids to do (not to mention babysitting) – all good, New Agey fun. The parties are just big enough to make you feel you're part of a scene, but just small enough to keep it a family affair.

The focus of the Rustler's Valley Festivals is the centrepiece World Stage, which has hosted a mixture of chart-topping headline acts, a bit of rock, and, most recently, a uniquely southern African blend of experimental jazz and folk. Whatever the tunes, there is always a heavy percussion element in the music. In the early 2000s, live music was ditched at Rustler's because the organizers felt the same old bands were doing the rounds, and line-ups had become far too predictable. DJ sounds now dominate, but as a new wave of local musos emerges, live bands, mostly from Cape Town, are gradually being reintroduced into the festivals' programmes. For a break from the 24-hour-a-day musical action at the World Stage, the *Saucery Restaurant* doubles up as a chill space dishing up mellower sounds that include large dollops of music from across the continent.

Part of the Rustler's scene is the veritable New Age checklist of tepees, eclectically inspired shamanic ceremonies, healers, astrologers and crystals. In keeping with the eco spirit of the place, energy is provided by windmills and solar panels. At some stage during the parties, a lot of people take to the surrounding hills to chill out, and from the festival site you can see dozens of small convoys traipsing over the beautiful Maluti sandstone.

442 COUNTING FISH IN LAKE MALAWI

MALAWI On satellite images of the Rift Valley, Africa's third largest lake looks like a long, dark gash in a crumpled curtain. But visit Lake Malawi on a bright day, and it's luminous. The turquoise waters stretch way beyond the horizon. It's as vast as a sea but benign, its sandy shore lapped by the gentlest of waves.

Explore beneath the surface and you'll soon be drifting through granite archways among clouds of brilliantly coloured cichlids. These small fish, prized by aquarium-keepers, are abundant in Lake Malawi. Scientists have counted over 1500 endemic species; as evolutionary hotspots go, the lake is almost as fascinating as Madagascar or the Galapagos.

If you're new to diving, it's a dream. It's far more fun to work through your drills on the sandy bottom of a warm lake than on the cold, hard tiles of a swimming pool. As you practise flooding your mask and clearing it again, the fresh, clear, chlorine-free water won't sting. And the lake has advantages over the ocean, too. There are no awkward currents or underwater menaces to spook you, no moray eels, jellyfish or sharks. You'll need less weight on your belt to help you sink. And once you're back on dry land, there's no salt to rinse off your gear – just head down to the campfire where, after dark, you can swap stories under the stars.

443 CLIMBING TABLE MOUNTAIN

SOUTH AFRICA If the skies are clear on your first day in Cape Town, drop everything and head straight for Table Mountain. It's an ecological marvel, and a powerful icon for the entire African continent. What's more, the views from the top are unmissable – as long as the celebrated "tablecloth" of cloud stays away.

For Capetonians, Table Mountain is a backdrop and an anchor, both physically and spiritually. Close to the South African coast, it was one of the beacons that Nelson Mandela and his fellow inmates fixed upon during their incarceration on Robben Island, just offshore.

The mountain's famous plateau is part of a short upland chain that stretches from Signal Hill, just west of the city centre, to Cape Point, where a lighthouse marks the meeting of the Indian Ocean and the Atlantic. The obvious, and most popular, route to the top is to take the aerial cableway – a sizeable cable car that, thrillingly, gently rotates on the ascent. But if you'd rather work a little harder, you can tackle one of the hiking trails that snake their way up the cliffs.

Visit in the South African spring or summer and the fynbos vegetation, unique to the Cape, will be in full bloom. You'll see plenty of pretty daisies and ericas in the tussocky wilderness, while proteas, sundews and watsonias add splashes of red, white and pink. Botanists have identified over 1470 plant species on the mountain – there's more floral diversity here than in the entire United Kingdom. The wildlife scores top marks for entertainment value, too. Stars of the show are the dassies, placid creatures that look a bit like monster guinea pigs and are more than happy to pose for photos.

And then there's that view. You may only be a thousand metres up, but gaze out over the city to the ocean beyond and you'll feel on top of the world.

444 REDISCOVERING THE FORGOTTEN COAST

MOZAMBIQUE It seems inconceivable that a country that was embroiled in one of Africa's bloodiest civil wars less than fifteen years ago might become one of the continent's most popular beach destinations. Yet before the bombs and bloodshed redefined Mozambique, there was nowhere better in the whole of southern Africa to spend a few lazy days by the beach, with endless stretches of gorgeous sand bathed by the enticing waters of the Indian Ocean.

South Africans are rediscovering the beaches of southern Mozambique, but once you head north past the popular resort town of Vilankulo, the seaside paradise takes on a hint of the Twilight Zone. Some 250km due north lies energetic Beira, Mozambique's second city, where you can tuck into gigantic prawns at quiet beach bars backed by bombed-out buildings. Much further north is the otherworldly island of Ilha do Moçambique, the oldest European settlement in East Africa, full of enchanting fortresses, palaces and churches – but still with hardly a tourist in sight. The northernmost province of Cabo Delgado is even quieter. Grand sweeps of beach are strung along its coastline all the way to Tanzania; get out on the water in these parts, and you'll be swimming with whale sharks rather than riding on an inflated banana.

For the quintessential beach getaway, head to the Bazaruto Archipelago, a string of islands endowed with luxury lodges, just north of Vilankulo. Here honeymooning couples swing languorously in hammocks in between five-course meals, and burnt-out stockbrokers re-energize by fishing for marlin – a throwback to the pre-civil war days, and no doubt a harbinger of things to come.

445 JUNGLE OPERATICS: THE LEMURS OF ANDASIBE-MANTADIA

MADAGASCAR Close your eyes and imagine the haunting song of a humpback whale; add heat, humidity and air infused with damp vegetation and moss that tingles your nasal passages. Sounds improbable, doesn't it? Now open your eyes: you're in a Madagascan rainforest listening to a group of indri, the largest of the island's lemurs, proclaiming rights to their territories like arboreal opera singers.

This is the sound of Madagascar. In the early mornings, the forests of Andasibe-Mantadia National Park ring out with the indri's eerie, wailing chorus. It wafts through the canopy in wave after glorious wave, sending shivers down your spine and making every nerve-end jangle.

A number of Indri family groups here have become thoroughly accustomed to people. With the help of a local guide, they're easily seen, and their cute teddy bear looks, striking black-and-white coats and comically inquisitive manner make them hugely endearing – most people fall for them immediately. When you first come upon them, the indri are likely to be high in the canopy, shrouded by a veil of foliage, but it pays to be patient and wait (something many people don't do), as they regularly descend to lower levels and are quite happy to sit and munch their leafy breakfasts while you watch in wonder from close by.

Eleven other lemur species live in the national park, and there's a good chance of seeing several of these, too. One of the most remarkable is the diademed sifaka, its orange and silver fur contrasting vividly with the dark recesses of the forest. I've seen both indri and diademed sifakas many, many times, but it's impossible to tire of what I think are the most beautiful primates on the planet: on each occasion, the intense thrill of tracking them down has always lived up to the excitement of my initial sighting.

TRACKING RHINO IN DAMARALAND

NAMIBIA Did you know that the footprint of a black rhino can measure a full 30cm from toe to hefty heel? Nor did I until I found myself standing in the middle of one in northern Namibia's Damaraland, my size nines dwarfed by the dusty imprint. A big male had passed here in the night, maybe as little as two hours previously. Our guide finished inspecting the considerable pile of dung teetering on the trail a few metres up ahead, slung his high-calibre rifle onto his shoulder and gestured for us to move on. We were heading east, in the direction of the tracks, for a rendezvous with a BMW-sized beast.

Damaraland is the only place in the world where you can find free-roaming black rhino. But you've got to know where to look. And the trackers from *Palmwag* – a mobile tented camp set amidst the grassy plains and light scrub of a million-acre private reserve – know exactly where to look. Noticing a stack of steaming spores is easy enough; spotting an acacia bush that's been crumpled by the hooked lips of a browsing black rhino isn't – and it's that sort of proficiency that pretty much guarantees you sneaking up on one just a few hours after leaving camp.

Rhinos have terrible eyesight, but their hearing and sense of smell are acute. As we approach a mother and her calf from downwind, the previously innocuous dry scrub suddenly becomes one giant, crackling boobytrap. We inch ourselves closer and closer, until we can make out oxpecker birds picking insects off the mother's back. She's immense, yet beautiful – 900 kilos of rippling muscle, ribs shifting as she digests the shrubbery. No one talks. I don't breathe. And then they have moved on, and we start talking – and breathing – again.

447

THE SMOKE THAT THUNDERS AT VICTORIA FALLS

ZIMBABWE You know that a place is special when it can inspire true love. Victoria Falls is just such a spot. Over 500 million litres of water crashing every minute from heights of up to 450 metres is a pretty powerful phenomenon; it creates an intangible but nonetheless potent magic in the air. Looking around, you'll see it in the eyes of vacationing couples, or in that young pair who have met on their travels, now locked together, a fine spray of warm mist shrouding them as they succumb to the irresistible power of the Falls' charms.

And for the non-romantics? Well, there's plenty to do other than gaze into someone's eyes. Vic Falls is a huge draw for adventure sport addicts – the mighty Zambezi river, from which the Falls flow, offers up white-water rafting that is widely thought to be second-to-none. Or you could try plunging by bungy 110m from the bridge between Zambia and Zimbabwe – the roar of the falls, and likely your screams, ringing in your ears. For a different perspective, book a hot air balloon, microlight or helicopter ride and marvel at the bird's-eye view of what the locals call Mosi-oa-Tunya – "The Smoke That Thunders".

High-octane madness aside, your experience would be equally as spectacular just ambling along the network of marked paths in the surrounding rainforest, sharing the trail with a baboon or two before the lush, dense foliage opens up to vistas of the world's most incredible curtain of ever-flowing water.

448 TOURING A TOWNSHIP

SOUTH AFRICA I'm listening to a group of children singing folk songs in a timber-shack assembly hall. It's tiny – far too small for a school of this size – and very basic. But compared to the old shipping containers that serve as classrooms, it's generous.

When the kids segue into *Nkosi Sikelel 'i Afrika*, I feel a lump rise in my throat. Who could fail to be moved by these earnest young voices singing South Africa's unmistakably poignant anthem? Blinking hard, I gulp back my emotions and know, without looking round, that my companions are doing the same.

Some of us had misgivings about joining a guided tour of Langa and Khayelitsha. We'd be travelling around the oldest and largest of the black townships in Cape Town's poverty-stricken Cape Flats. Would we feel like voyeurs, intruders, or cultural imperialists? By just dipping in for a day, would we be reinforcing the outdated social and spatial divisions that first brought the townships into existence?

The reality turns out to be more complicated. Brian, our guide, himself a township resident, doesn't shield us from the difficulties that the communities face: overpopulation, unemployment, inadequate health care. As we drive past Guguletu cemetery, fresh graves bear testament to one of the bitterest problems – it's believed that eight out of ten residents may be HIV positive.

But there's another message. Our itinerary is all about meeting people – albeit in rather contrived circumstances. We visit places and projects where motivated individuals are chipping away at the heavy burden of deprivation that keeps the townships on their knees. There's Maureen Jacobs, the head teacher who's giving kids from the informal settlements a start in life; Rosie Gwadiso, founder of a community kitchen, who sends children to school nourished instead of hungry; and Golden Nongawuza, who runs a workshop making ornamental flowers out of recycled tin cans. "This gives you an introduction", says Brian. "Come back in a year or so and you'll see how much more will have changed for the better".

449 TAKING A WALK ON THE WILD SIDE

ZAMBIA Call me a safari snob, but to my mind the Big Five are seriously over-rated. Leopards may be gorgeous, but they're maddeningly elusive – set your heart on finding one and you're heading for disappointment. Elephants are entertaining, but if you've seen them pull a forest to pieces you'll know how thuggish they can be. Lions are forever grumbling at each other, rhinos are miserably shy, and buffalo are just bulky, belligerent cows.

But show me a trap set by an antlion and talk me through the way this crafty little larva nabs its prey, and I'm all ears. Stop beneath a fig tree, break open one of its fruit and explain the intricate symbiotic relationship it enjoys with a fig-wasp, and I'll listen intently. Crouch beside a fallen branch to point out a chameleon, its eyes swivelling madly, its tail perfectly coiled, and I'm enthralled.

One of the very best ways to enjoy the African wilderness is to forget about the Big Five and go out walking with somebody who knows his quails from his queleas and his munga from his mutemwa. Africa has plenty of first-rate guides, but Zambia's walking-safari guides are the crème de la crème. Find one you click with and he'll turn everything, from the commonest shrub to the tiniest bug, into a discovery worth pages of your travel journal.

Exploring on foot is a much more subtle experience than charging around in a vehicle. While you probably won't get close to the kind of wildlife that considers humans a threat, your ears, nose and eyes will tune in to every rustle, whiff and movement, just in case. And if you do spot something larger than a squirrel, it's a heart-thumping experience.

It's almost as thrilling, though, to examine signs of animal activity – spoor, dung, flattened vegetation – and work out what happened next. Any guide worth the name can read tracks in the dust as clearly as a morning newspaper.

Let the canopy-topped Land Rovers and zebra-striped minibuses charge off in search of marauding lions and stampeding buffalo – I'd rather keep my feet firmly on the ground, and walk.

450 LEARNING THE WAYS OF A WILDLIFE RANGER

SOUTH AFRICA Two weeks ago, it would have been just another pile of poo. But now, a fortnight into your ranger-training course, this tower of dung is so much more than that. Now, it means that elephants have passed through here recently, maybe within the last few hours. It means that the herd is heading west, looking for fresh foliage. And it means that if you swing your Land Rover around and take the dusty track behind you, you'll have a good chance of beating them to the waterhole. And the guests in the back of your 4WD will have yet another great tale to tell the folks back home.

The wildlife ranger-training course in Kruger National Park is the epitome of "hands-on" learning. You'll spend eight hours a day out in the bush – on foot and in a 4WD – discovering how to take a game drive effectively, understanding animal behaviour, brushing up your tracking skills, and getting used to handling a high-calibre rifle. You'll drive a heavy-duty Land Rover along rutted roads, you'll sit up-font in the tracking seat to scan the undergrowth for antelope, and you'll probably have one of the most incredible months of your life.

451 SWIGGING THE MOST REMOTE BEER ON EARTH

TRISTAN DA CUNHA The *Albatross Inn* does a rather decent lobster quiche as a bar snack. The lager isn't bad either. It's a good job really, because there's no alternative place to get a drink or a bite to eat for 2815 kilometres. This is the only pub on the most remote inhabited island on earth.

Tristan da Cunha is one of the far-flung hotch potch of islands that make up what's left of the British Empire. None, however, are as isolated. Situated in the middle of the notoriously rough patch of the South Atlantic Ocean known as the Roaring Forties, its closest landmass is southern Africa, some 540km nearer than South America. The island has no airport and can only be reached by fishing vessel from Cape Town; a trip that can take upwards of six days with no guarantee of being able to dock in the island's tiny harbour because of the often torrid weather.

The sole settlement is the evocatively named "Edinburgh of the Seven Seas" which is where, in a motley collection of tin-roofed bungalows, the 272 islanders live and work, mainly as fishermen of Tristan's number one export: crayfish. Everything is dwarfed by the volcano that rises over 1700m above sea level. It is rarely climbed by locals, and there are signs everywhere of the 1962 eruption, not least the huge pile of volcanic debris that still lies just outside the village. In the wake of the eruption, the islanders were evacuated to the UK, where they spent two unhappy years before being allowed to return.

With no mobile phones, one shop, one school, one policeman and one available TV channel many things about Tristan remain unchanged by the twenty-first century. The accent spoken is a curious, and almost incomprehensible, dialect of early eighteenth-century seafaring English; everyone's birthday is celebrated by a party in the Prince Phillip Hall next to the Albatross; and absolutely nobody seems to have any desire to leave their epically remote home. "People think we're stranded here", the barman tells me over yet another slice of quiche. "But it's not true. We're happy, and we're here because we want to be".

452 SAMPLING WINES IN THE WESTERN CAPE

SOUTH AFRICA We're sitting around the elegant dining table of a 200-year-old Cape Dutch manor house, set in beautiful countryside near Paarl. Our host, effusive wine expert Katinka van Niekerk, has us under strict instructions to sample the heavenly wines before us in a pre-planned order. Before each mouthful, we must eat something of a particular flavour or texture – curry for spice, cheese for sweetness, bread to neutralize the palate once again – and note the effects. It's fascinating stuff.

When we're asked to wash down a piece of bread and Marmite with a mouthful of vintage Pinotage, master winemaker Razvan Macici, who has joined us for this session, grimaces. The Marmite represents the flavour known as umami, also found in soy sauce, Parmesan and certain mushrooms. It wrecks Pinotage, the signature Cape red. But the same wine with a chunk of roast lamb tastes like a dream.

Earlier in the day we toured the massive Nederburg estate, admiring the ranks of vines which stretch away to the purple-tinged Drakenstein Mountains, sniffing the heady, oaky aromas of the barrel rooms and marvelling at the cellars' hi-tech temperature-controlled steel tanks. Then it was time for our first tasting. We all eyed the spitoons rather squeamishly and went for what seemed, at the time, the more decorous option – raising each glass to our noses to inhale the bouquet and then taking delicate sips.

It's amazing how quickly all those sips add up. So it is that when, replete from our wine-and-food-pairing lunch, we stagger out onto the lawn to enjoy the sunshine and spring flowers, we're all merrily speaking double Dutch.

453 DANCING WITH THE KING AT BIG NCWALA

SWAZILAND It's difficult to imagine the Queen of England boogeying away on the balcony of Buckingham Palace in celebration of Coronation Day. But the King of Swaziland is a little less restrained in commemorating his own festival. The Ncwala, or "First Fruits", festival is a raucous thanksgiving celebration, offering the Swazi people a chance to honour the royal family as a source of fertility for the country – duties that the late King Sobhuza took seriously, fathering over six hundred children with one hundred wives in his mission to populate his homeland.

Starting on a date decided upon by Swaziland's royal astrologers, the first days of the festival see the Bemanti or "Water People" travelling to the coast to capture foam from the waves (believed to have healing powers) and celebrating what is known as "Little Ncwala". But it's the main event, Big Ncwala, that's really worth travelling to this pocket of Southern Africa for.

On the day of the full moon, warriors assemble in the royal compound kitted out in traditional dress – animal skins and grass skirts – waiting for the king to emerge in full regalia, his face painted, his hair plumed in preparation for his sacred dance. It's not everyday you get to see royalty doing the rumba – and the Swazi seem just as excited, throwing themselves into a frenzy of all-night dancing and drinking that rocks this tiny nation to its roots.

454 EXPLORING THE SKELETON COAST

NAMIBIA Namibia's extreme northwest is called the Skeleton Coast, with good reason. Its treacherous conditions have scuppered ships – the beach is littered with rusting iron and weathered timbers from long-abandoned wrecks – and whales, too, have met their end here, their massive vertebrae bleaching on the shore, lapped by the tides.

As a visitor, you'll need an eye for detail to appreciate the allure of this bleak and barren place, where the chilly Atlantic meets mountainous dunes and endless, grey-white gravel plains, and distant wind-sculpted rocks cast unearthly shadows. Look carefully and you'll begin to realize that the desert is not as devoid of life as it might seem. Walking through the rugged landscapes with a guide, you'll learn how beetles, lizards and sidewinder adders survive on the moisture brought by the early morning mists. You may begin to distinguish the different lichens – delicate smudges of black, white and ginger which decorate slabs of quartz and basalt. Drought-resistant succulents like the bizarre, pebble-like lithops and the ragged, ancient-looking Welwitschia mirabilis cling to life in the gravel. Among the few mammals hardy enough to survive in this environment are black-backed jackals and noisy, malodorous colonies of Cape fur seals, the latter a potential target for hungry lions, which very occasionally can be seen prowling the shoreline. Perhaps the best way to enjoy the desert's strange beauty is from the air. Soar over the landscape in a light aircraft and you feel like an astronaut over an alien world, the scene below mottled and textured like a vast abstract painting.

455 UP THE TSIRIBIHINA IN A DUGOUT CANOE

MADAGASCAR The early morning daylight filters through the tent and slowly warms your aching body. You awaken to the muffled sounds of roosters crowing and the echo of beating drums from a neighboring village. A faint whiff of smoke entices you out of your slumber and onto the sandy riverbank to join the guides and a few curious onlookers around a crackling campfire. Together, you share fried eggs, fresh fruit, stale baguettes and a cup of strongly brewed coffee. Another day on the Tsiribihina River has begun.

After breakfast, the guides pack camp and load the wooden pirogues. Within minutes, you're drifting down the muddy waters and into the heartland of Madagascar. Exploring this fascinating country is not complete until you've experienced a few days on this remote waterway: meeting local villagers, paddling alongside impressive landscapes, and discovering Malagasy folklore.

The scorching sun shines brightly overhead as you glide past thatched-hut villages where scores of excited children run into the shallow waters waving and screaming 'bon voyage'. Gradually, the landscape transforms from low-lying flood plains lined with lush green rice paddies to sparsely covered rolling hills and impenetrable forests, the river slicing through deep gorges before widening once more as it drains into the Mozambique Channel. Along the way, you make chance encounters with wildlife: Verreaux's sifaka forage high in the canopies and enormous flying foxes flutter by while river crocodiles lurk in the murky waters below. Hundreds of exotic birds vie for your attention: metallic-coloured kingfishers dart along the shoreline, white egrets hitch a ride on floating mats of hyacinths and a lone majestic harrier hawk wheels on the horizon.

At the end of a long day's journey, you reach camp on the shores of yet another sandbank, arriving just in time to witness a spectacular sunset framed against a rugged mountainous backdrop. While dinner is prepared, you set up the tents and begin to wind down for the evening. Dancing fireflies and singing katydids give way to a night sky filled with flickering stars.

MISCELLANY

SNOW IN AFRICA

Lesotho is one of the few parts of Southern Africa that regularly gets serious **snowfalls**, especially in the highlands between May and July, when even main roads can be blocked for days. There's some informal skiing in the kingdom near the 3220-metre Mahlasela Pass, but for a proper ski resort, albeit a small one, head to Tiffendell in South Africa's Eastern Cape Drakensberg, where artificial snow makes up for unreliable cover, despite freezing-cold conditions.

ORIGINAL PEOPLES

The original inhabitants of Southern Africa were speakers of ancient **Khoi-San** languages incorporating various unusual click sounds now found in the languages of several South African peoples who arrived later, such as the Zulu and Xhosa. The San hunter-gatherers, formerly known as Bushmen, and the herding Khoi or Khoikhoi, once known as Hottentots (both names are now considered offensive) are believed to be among the world's most ancient cultures.

FOREVER?

Botswana is widely seen as one of Africa's great success stories, on account of one, precious export – gem-quality **diamonds**, of which it's the world's leading producer.

PLACE OF GOLD

South Africa's largest city, **Johannesburg**, is the capital of the country's smallest province, **Gauteng**, meaning Place of Gold in the Sotho language. It dates back only to 1886 when gold was discovered, and has remained a tough city of business and pleasure rather than government, and the touchstone of South Africa's national psyche.

STATE OF MULTI-CULTURALISM

Zambia has **78 different language groups,** or tribes as they're unselfconsciously referred to in the country, most of them speaking Bantu languages, with the Bemba and Tonga together forming about a third of the population. There are small communities of Zambians of European and Asian descent and the country has welcomed dispossessed white farmers fleeing Zimbawe.

REAL AND FAKE HEALING

Traditional medicine is widely used all over Africa, often in preference to Western forms of treatment, and can comprise anything from prayers and incantations to administering remedies derived from almost any plant or animal you can think of. Some such medicines are useful in treatment, but much to the dismay of sexual health campaigners, at the 2006 International AIDS Conference in Toronto, South Africa's health minister recommended a mixture of garlic, beetroot, lemon and potatoes as an alternative to anti-retroviral drugs in the fight against HIV.

POOR ZIMBABWE

Potentially one of Africa's richest countries, Zimbabwe's government under independence-leader-turned-mad-dictator **Robert Mugabe** has thrown it all away. A programme of "land reforms" saw rich, white farmers flung off their properties, which, with no planning, then failed to produce the maize Zimbabweans relied upon; vindictive politics denied a voice to the opposition while the government, running scared, failed the most basic tests of competency in running the country; tourism and investment dried up; and the inflation rate by mid-2007 was running at more than 100 percent a month – in other words, a monthly doubling of prices – making the vast majority of the population destitute.

GREAT ZIMBABWE

Despite the gloom about its current predicament, the ruins of Zimbabwe's Great Zimbabwe, with its haunting, curved walls and pillars built of carefully interlocked dry stones, are a magnificent reminder of the depth of African history and the complicated context on which today's countries were overlaid. There were in fact hundreds of zimbabwes (the word means "stone house towns" in Shona) built during the slow advance of Bantu-speaking peoples across southern Africa between the eleventh and fifteenth centuries AD. Great Zimbabwe was just one of the biggest, symbolising the dominance of the Monomotapa state that constructed it.

"If you want to make peace with your enemy, you have to work with your enemy. Then he becomes your partner"

Nelson Mandela

KEEPING THE WORLD'S BIGGEST AQUARIUM FIT FOR TOURISTS

Lake Malawi's famous tropical fish – the **cichlids** – are one of Malawi's most popular sights – and one of the country's biggest exports. Ranging from tiny slivers a few centimetres long to the predatory and torpedo-like **Champsochromis caeruleus** that's as big as your forearm, the rarer varieties can sell to fish fanciers for hundreds of dollars. In certain parts of the lake, over-fishing has resulted in an increase in the population of snails carrying the disease **bilharzia**, so there are now sound economic as well as environmental reasons to conserve fish stocks.

THREE KINGS
OF AFRICA

The powers of the kings of Morocco and Lesotho are limited by their country's constitutions, but no such check seems to be placed on Africa's last absolute monarch, **King Mswati III of Swaziland**, who has ruled in an authoritarian – and eccentric – style since 1986. In 2001, he signed a decree banning newspapers, stating afterwards: "I must admit that when I signed this decree, I did not read it at all. I just signed it." Another decree banned women under 18 from having sex, in an attempt to combat the country's massive HIV problem (around forty percent of Swaziland's population is HIV-positive), but just two months after imposing the ban the king himself broke it in marrying his ninth wife, who was just 16 – for which he fined himself a cow.

PARK OF PEACE

Stretching across the borders of Mozambique, Zimbabwe and South Africa, the **Great Limpopo Transfrontier Park** is a gigantic new conservation area incorporating South Africa's Kruger, Mozambique's Limpopo and Zimbabwe's Gonarezhou national parks that will eventually enable visitors to travel freely throughout 100,000 square kilometres of wildlife-rich bush. For the moment, circumstances in Zimbabwe are hindering progress. Sponsored by the Peace Parks foundation, established to rectify some of the damage done to Africa by the carve-up of the 1885 Berlin Conference, the dream is to enable animals – and people – to move more freely across ancestral lands.

"A baby that does not cry out, dies on its mother's back"

Xhosa saying

HOLY JOURNEY

Each January, the mountain of **Nhlangakazi**, in South Africa's KwaZulu-Natal province, is the scene for ritual dances by thousands of members of the Shembe church, which preaches a hybrid of Christian and Zulu traditional beliefs.

SOUTHERN SANDS

The **Namib Desert** in Namibia has existed for at least 80 million years, making it the world's oldest desert, and the one with the world's highest dunes, some of which have drifted to more than 300m in height. The region's other desert, the **Kalahari** in southern Botswana, is better vegetated, thanks to occasional rainfall, and supports the traditional hunter-gatherer lifestyle of the San.

KUNG FU
ISLAND

You might expect Madagascar, a former French colony, to be largely Roman Catholic. In fact, decades of British involvement (an "arms in exchange for anti-slavery" agreement from their base on neighbouring Mauritius) led finally to the Protestant baptism of the Queen of the dominant Merina people and much of her royal court in 1869, and there's been a strong Anglican presence ever since. On an island of multiple surprises, it seems unpredictably fitting that a century after the Queen's baptism not only was the government Marxist, but the opposition coalition rallied under the banner of Kung Fu clubs with tens of thousands of Bruce Lee-mad members demonstrating on the streets.

STILL UNITED

The island of **Réunion**, east of Madagascar, is one of the four overseas regions of France, the others being French Guyana in South America, and Martinique and Guadéloupe, in the Caribbean. Like Burgundy or Brittany, all of them are treated as fully participating constituents of the French republic. Réunion is thus a part of Africa that's also in the **EU**, elects an MEP and has the Euro as its currency. **Mayotte**, in the Comoros archipelago, also uses the Euro and is a special French overseas **département** (a status that 99 percent of its inhabitants voted to retain).

SAMORA MACHEL

The charismatic first president of an independent **Mozambique** was killed when his plane crashed on the South African border in 1986, a crash that has never been satisfactorily explained and remains the subject of widespread conspiracy theories about South African sabotage. His widow, **Graça Machel,** went on to marry the first president of post-apartheid South Africa, Nelson Mandela, and continues to demand a full enquiry.

DUTY-FREE AND ONLINE

The cosmopolitan Indian Ocean island of **Mauritius**, much beloved of South African tourists, boasts one of Africa's most successful economies. Although built on the slave trade and sugar plantations, the country zoomed into the twenty-first century with ambitious plans to go entirely **duty-free** and to make the whole island a free **WiFi** access point, already largely achieved.

THE RIGHT TIMING

Come to the magical wilderness of De Hoop Nature Reserve in South Africa's Western Cape province at the right time of year – July to December – and you can see sometimes dozens of female **Southern Right Whales** lounging in the bay with their newly born calves. It's reckoned to be the best place in the world. And why are they called Right Whales? Because whalers considered them the right whales to harpoon for the best yield of oil.

SHOPPING IN THE CITY OF GOLD • CHRISTMAS AT THE CHURCH OF THE NATIVITY IN BETHLEHEM • WALKING AROUND THE OLD CITY OF JERUSALEM • WANDERING OLD SANA'A • FLOATING ON THE DEAD SEA • MUD-BRICK MARVELS: EXPERIENCING THE ARCHITECTURE OF SANA'A, TARIM AND SHIBAM • DISCOVERING MADA'IN SALEH • DIVING THE GULF OF AQABA • SAND-SKIING IN THE DUNES • **FROLICKING WITH DOLPHINS OFF MUSCAT** • SEARCHING FOR DRAGON'S BLOOD • ON THE INCENSE TRAIL IN ARABIA FELIX • CARVING A PATH THROUGH PERSEPOLIS • SUNSET OVER PALMYRA • RELAXING IN A DAMASCUS HAMMAM • CHECKING OUT THE BAUHAUS ARCHITECTURE IN TEL AVIV • BARGAINING IN THE ALEPPO SOUK • BLAZING A TRAIL AT DANA NATURE RESERVE • **KRAK DES CHEVALIERS: THE FINEST CASTLE IN THE WORLD** • GETTING ACQUAINTED WITH ARABIC SWEETS • PEARL DIVING IN THE PERSIAN GULF • FEASTING ON LEBANESE MEZZE • THE BURJ AL ARAB SHOWS OFF IN DUBAI • THE ARAB ORGANIZATIONS BUILDING: AN OFFICE WITH ATTITUDE • **MASADA: CONQUERING HEROD'S HILLTOP PALACE** • BEDOUIN CAMPING AT WADI RUM • FEELING DWARFED BY BAALBEK • CAMEL RACING IN THE WAHIBA SANDS • TAWI ATTAIR: THE "SINGING" SINKHOLE • FIGHTING OFF THE CATS IN ACRE • HEARING THE GROANS IN HAMA • **VISITING THE "HANGING VILLAGE" OF HABALAH** • SWIMMING THE WADI SHAB • FLAUNTING IT AT THE EMIRATES PALACE • TAKING TEA IN ISFAHAN • WALKING THE SIQ TO PETRA • ROBOT CAMEL-BACK RACING • HAUNTING THE DEAD CITIES • TAKING A DIP IN THE RIVER JORDAN • OFF-ROADING FOR REAL: ACROSS THE DUNES TO KHOR AL-ADAID • SHOPPING IN THE CITY OF GOLD • **SOAKING UP THE MASJID I-IMAM** • CHRISTMAS AT THE CHURCH OF THE NATIVITY IN BETHLEHEM • WALKING AROUND THE OLD CITY OF JERUSALEM • WANDERING OLD SANA'A • FLOATING ON THE DEAD SEA • MUD-BRICK MARVELS: EXPERIENCING THE ARCHITECTURE OF SANA'A, TARIM AND SHIBAM • DISCOVERING MADA'IN SALEH • DIVING THE GULF OF AQABA • SAND-SKIING IN THE DUNES • **SEARCHING FOR DRAGON'S BLOOD** • ON THE INCENSE TRAIL IN ARABIA FELIX • CARVING A PATH THROUGH PERSEPOLIS • SUNSET OVER PALMYRA • FROLICKING WITH DOLPHINS OFF MUSCAT • RELAXING IN A DAMASCUS HAMMAM • CHECKING OUT THE BAUHAUS ARCHITECTURE IN TEL AVIV • BARGAINING IN THE ALEPPO SOUK • BLAZING A TRAIL AT DANA NATURE RESERVE • KRAK DES CHEVALIERS: THE FINEST CASTLE IN THE WORLD • GETTING ACQUAINTED WITH ARABIC SWEETS • PEARL DIVING IN THE PERSIAN GULF • **FEASTING ON LEBANESE MEZZE** • THE ARAB ORGANIZATIONS BUILDING: AN OFFICE WITH ATTITUDE • BEDOUIN CAMPING AT WADI RUM • FEELING DWARFED BY BAALBEK • CAMEL RACING IN THE WAHIBA SANDS • TAWI ATTAIR: THE "SINGING" SINKHOLE • MASADA: CONQUERING HEROD'S HILLTOP PALACE • FIGHTING OFF THE CATS IN ACRE • HEARING THE GROANS IN HAMA • **THE BURJ AL ARAB SHOWS OFF IN DUBAI** • SWIMMING THE WADI SHAB • VISITING THE "HANGING VILLAGE" OF HABALAH • FLAUNTING IT AT THE EMIRATES PALACE • SOAKING UP THE MASJID I-IMAM • TAKING TEA IN ISFAHAN • **WALKING THE SIQ TO PETRA** • ROBOT CAMEL-BACK RACING • HAUNTING THE DEAD CITIES • TAKING A DIP IN THE RIVER JORDAN • OFF-ROADING FOR REAL: ACROSS THE DUNES TO KHOR AL-ADAID • SHOPPING IN THE CITY OF GOLD • CHRISTMAS AT THE CHURCH OF THE NATIVITY IN BETHLEHEM • WALKING AROUND THE OLD CITY OF JERUSALEM • WANDERING OLD SANA'A • FLOATING ON THE DEAD SEA • MUD-BRICK MARVELS: EXPERIENCING THE ARCHITECTURE OF SANA'A, TARIM AND SHIBAM • DISCOVERING MADA'IN SALEH • DIVING THE GULF OF AQABA • **SAND-SKIING IN THE DUNES** • SEARCHING FOR DRAGON'S BLOOD • ON THE INCENSE TRAIL IN ARABIA FELIX • CARVING A PATH THROUGH PERSEPOLIS • SUNSET OVER PALMYRA • FROLICKING WITH DOLPHINS OFF MUSCAT • RELAXING IN A DAMASCUS HAMMAM • CHECKING OUT THE BAUHAUS

THE MIDDLE EAST

456–498

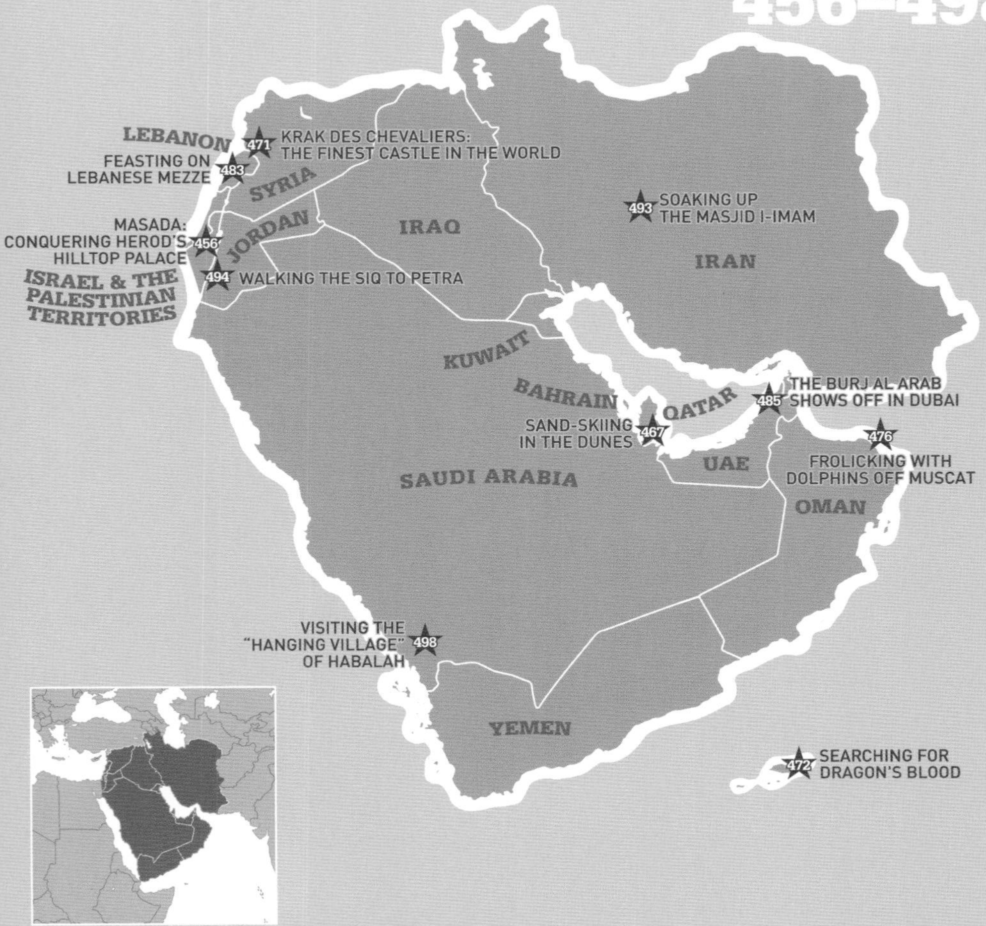

LEBANON
471 KRAK DES CHEVALIERS:
THE FINEST CASTLE IN THE WORLD

FEASTING ON
LEBANESE MEZZE **483**

SYRIA

493 SOAKING UP
THE MASJID I-IMAM

MASADA:
CONQUERING HEROD'S
HILLTOP PALACE **456**

JORDAN

IRAQ

IRAN

ISRAEL & THE
PALESTINIAN
TERRITORIES

494 WALKING THE SIQ TO PETRA

KUWAIT

BAHRAIN

THE BURJ AL-ARAB
485 SHOWS OFF IN DUBAI

SAND-SKIING
IN THE DUNES **467**

QATAR

476 FROLICKING WITH
DOLPHINS OFF MUSCAT

SAUDI ARABIA

UAE

OMAN

VISITING THE
"HANGING VILLAGE"
OF HABALAH **498**

YEMEN

472 SEARCHING FOR
DRAGON'S BLOOD

MASADA: CONQUERING HEROD'S HILLTOP PALACE

456

ISRAEL & THE PALESTINIAN TERRITORIES The steep cliffs rising out of the Judean desert look like an unlikely place for a fortress, but there, four hundred metres up, overlooking the Dead Sea, sits the legendary stronghold of Masada. Masada was first fortified by Herod the Great in the late first century BC, who was apparently so scared his people would revolt that he built this virtually impenetrable fortress.

The setting is indeed off-putting. Despite such history and legend, it's easy to baulk at the thought of trying to reach it

yourself. There's a cable car for those who don't fancy taking one of the various different paths that lead up the hill, but to get the feeling that you really conquered Masada, opt for the ancient snake path, which winds its unsheltered way up the eastern side. It's not an easy walk, but it only takes forty minutes and the hard toil is well worth the effort: the reward, an archeological site, including the Northern Palace, which appears to dangle over the edge of the precipice, and tremendous views across the desert and the Dead Sea.

457 BARGAINING IN THE ALEPPO SOUK

SYRIA "Best price to you, my friend!" are familiar words to anyone who's tried to strike a deal in a Middle Eastern souk. To buy here you have to bargain – prices are always open to discussion.

Shopping in these bazaars is, for many visitors, the epitome of the Middle Eastern experience. With busy, narrow, shop-lined lanes crowded with people, souks are always redolent with the aroma of food and spices mingling with the stink of animals; they're packed with sights and sounds and full of atmosphere.

Aleppo's souk is one of the best. You can get lost here time and time again, roaming the dimly lit lanes past windows full of gold jewellery and stalls piled high with rope or soap or ice cream. Hit the wall as donkey-carts and minivans force a path through the shoppers; linger among the perfume shops, sample fresh almonds and finger exquisite silks.

If you're after a particular item, play it cool. Work out the most you would be prepared to pay – then take the time to chat. In the souk, shopkeepers are never in hurry; they want to talk, pass the time of day, offer you a glass of tea and a sit-down – whether you're a customer or not.

Eventually you can casually enquire how much the item costs. The first price quoted will be twice, perhaps three or four times, as much as the shopkeeper would be prepared to accept, so counter it with a low offer of your own. In response he'll tut, knit his brows, perhaps wag a finger at you – it's all part of the game.

There are only two rules to bargaining: never lose your temper, and never let a price pass your lips that you're not prepared to pay. And don't forget: the "best price" never is. In the souk, everyone's a sucker.

458 WALKING AROUND THE OLD CITY OF JERUSALEM

ISRAEL & THE PALESTINIAN TERRITORIES For a place so dear to so many hearts, and so violently fought over, the walled Old City of Jerusalem is not as grandiose as you might imagine; it's compact and easy to find your way around, though you'll stumble at almost every turn over holy or historic sites. The streets hum with activity: handcarts, sellers of religious artefacts, Jews scurrying through the Muslim quarter to pray at the Wailing Wall, and Palestinian youths trying to avoid the attentions of Israeli soldiers patrolling the streets.

The three biggest attractions are the major religious sites. The Church of the Holy Sepulchre is a dark, musty, cavernous old building, reeking of incense, and home to the site of the crucifixion. Pilgrims approach the church by the Via Dolorosa, the path that Jesus took to his execution, observing each Station of the Cross and not infrequently dragging large wooden crosses through the narrow streets, where local residents pay them scant attention.

Heading through the heart of the Old City, past a meat market, piled high with offal and sheep's heads, you emerge blinking into the sun-drenched esplanade that fronts Judaism's holiest site, the Western ("Wailing") Wall, last remnant of the ancient Jewish Temple that was originally built by King Solomon and later rebuilt by Herod. From here, you can nip into the Western Wall Tunnels that run under the city's Muslim Quarter; with subterranean synagogues, underground gateways and ancient aqueducts, they're fascinating to explore.

Around the side of the Wailing Wall, up on Temple Mount, is the Dome of the Rock, Islam's third-holiest site. This is the spot where Abraham offered to sacrifice his son to God, and where Mohammed later ascended to Heaven upon a winged steed. The perfect blue octagon topped with a golden dome is a fabulous gem of Ummayad architecture, immediately recognizable as the symbol of Jerusalem.

The wealth of sights in this ancient, entrancing city is overwhelming, so don't forget to make time on your wanderings for more mundane pleasures: a cardamom-scented Turkish coffee at the café just inside the Damascus Gate, or hummus at *Abu Shukri's*, arguably more divine than anything religious.

459 BOBBING ABOUT ON THE MUSANDAM FJORDS

OMAN The scenery is majestic: towering mountains plunge like runaway rock into the turquoise water two thousand metres below, and crystal-clear waterways knife their way through craggy cliffs.

These are fjords alright, but not as I know them. There are no snow-capped peaks around here, no gushing waterfalls or fertile slopes. Instead, a heat-haze hangs over the Hajar, and the waters are plied not by 3000-ton ferries but by the odd fishing dhow, bobbing its way towards Khasab harbour with a bounty of grouper and spiny lobster. Welcome to the Musandam Peninsula, an isolated entity, cut off from the rest of Oman by the United Arab Emirates and jutting out into the Strait of Hormouz. It's a strikingly rugged region, dominated by the Hajar Mountains, which, having snaked across the UAE, topple off into the Gulf of Oman.

Such grandeur is best appreciated from below, from one of the sheltered fjords, or khors, that riddle the peninsula. What better way to start the day than by setting sail from Khasab in a traditional wooden dhow, maybe a landj, a batil or the larger mashuwwah? And what more relaxing way to spend it than by propping yourself up amongst the Persian carpets and thick, lolling cushions, and gazing out at the tiny villages that somewhere cling to the cliff face, and at the humpback dolphins that cavort alongside your boat..

460 FLOATING ON THE DEAD SEA

JORDAN I peered past my toes at the burning sun, framed between craggy mountains opposite. Bobbing gently, outstretched and motionless on the surface of the sea, I felt like a human cork. I tried to swim, but my body rode too high in the water and I ended up splashing ineffectually; droplets on my lips tasted horribly bitter, and the water in my eyes stung like mad.

At 400m below sea level, the Dead Sea – hot, hazy and the deepest blue – is the lowest point on Earth and is named for its uniquely salty water, which kills off virtually all marine life. Normal seawater is three or four percent salt, but Dead Sea water measures over thirty percent. The lake is fed mainly by the River Jordan, but due to geological upheavals it has no outflow; instead, the sun evaporates water off the surface at the rate of millions of litres a day, leading to salt and minerals – washed down from the hills by the river – crystallizing onto the beach in a fringe of white.

The high salt content makes the water so buoyant that it's literally impossible to sink. As you walk in from the beach you'll find your feet are forced up from under you – you couldn't touch the bottom if you tried – and the water supports you like a cradle. Floating is effortless.

The heat was oppressive and the air, with an unmistakeable whiff of sulphur, lay heavy in my nostrils. All sound was dampened by a thick atmospheric haze of evaporation and the near silence was eerie. As I lay, taking in the entire surreal experience, I realized just how aptly named this place is: the Dead Sea really feels dead.

461 MUD-BRICK MARVELS: EXPERIENCING THE ARCHITECTURE OF SANA'A, TARIM AND SHIBAM

YEMEN Arriving in Yemen and plunging straight into the old quarter of the capital, Sana'a, is a surreal experience. All the bustle, familiar from Arab cities across the Middle East, is there with craft-sellers, textile merchants and all the smells – but instead of the backdrop being modern breezeblock or brutalist concrete, you're surrounded by perfectly preserved traditional Yemeni architecture. This ornate style, found nowhere else, is at its best in Sana'a and makes you feel as if you've been transported to another world: forests of tower-houses, built on ancient stone foundations and rising to six or eight storeys, their intricate facades and mud-brick material giving them a striking, gingerbread-house look that is unique to Yemen.

East of the capital, in the Hadhramaut Valley, lies Tarim, a settlement famous for its elaborate mud-brick mosques and palaces – at 53 metres, the minaret of the Al Muhdhar mosque is the tallest earth structure in the world. Tarim's links with the Indian Ocean are evident in its architecture: Hadhrami craftsmen incorporated Neoclassicism, Rococo, Mughal, Art Nuevo and Art Deco styles into their tradition of mud-brick construction.

Just west of here, in the ancient desert town of Shibam, still enclosed by its fortified wall, the trademark traditional architecture predominates. Here the concentration of tower-houses is so dense that the British explorer Freya Stark dubbed it "the Manhattan of the Desert". Down at dust level amidst a looming thicket of ancient, organic buildings, Shibam is not so much claustrophobic as all-enveloping: sandy tones and mud-and-lime gingerbread decoration fill the eye, from ground level virtually to the sky – a shelter from the harshness of the sun and the desert.

462 HEARING THE GROANS IN HAMA

SYRIA As we came into the centre of Hama, a pleasant city in an idyllic location on the Orontes river south of Aleppo, the sound of groaning filled our ears. In 1982, an Islamist uprising here was brutally suppressed by the Syrian army; the medieval old quarter was bombed and tens of thousands died. It felt to us like the city hadn't really recovered. A generation on, people were still treading gingerly.

And always the sound of groaning. All along the riverbank stand giant wooden waterwheels, or norias, seventeen of them, up to twenty metres high – relics of an Ottoman irrigation system. They are elegant examples of early technology, but as they turn, the grinding of wood on wood produces a hair-raisingly mournful sound. Hama is filled with groans.

463 FLAUNTING IT AT THE EMIRATES PALACE

UNITED ARAB EMIRATES Once upon a time, if you wanted the biggest, the richest, the fanciest, you went to New York. Nowadays, you go to the Gulf. Alongside all the mega-projects of Dubai up the coast, Abu Dhabi – the capital of the UAE – is staking some claims of its own. Topping the pile is the jaw-dropping Emirates Palace, reputedly the most expensive hotel ever built, at a cool US$3 billion. Most of the interior is in gold and marble, reflecting the light from more than a thousand crystal chandeliers. The largest of 114 domes spans 42 metres, while taking a stroll around the building involves a leg-stretching hike of 2.5km. And the rooms are opulent in the extreme. Fancy a suite for the night? That'll be US$15,000.

464 ON THE INCENSE TRAIL IN ARABIA FELIX

OMAN In antiquity, the Romans knew southern Arabia – the area of modern Yemen and the far southwestern tip of Oman – as Arabia Felix, meaning fortunate. This rugged land was so named for its fabulous wealth, derived from trade in exotic goods such as spices, perfumes, ivory and alabaster (most of which were brought from India) and, above all, locally cultivated frankincense and myrrh.

The incense trail was followed, in ancient times, by camel caravan from Salalah, regional capital of Oman's Dhofar region and traditionally regarded as the source of the world's finest frankincense, to Petra in Jordan.

Plunging into the alleys of Salalah's souk is a heady experience. Here, hemmed in by coconut groves, stalls and shops are crammed tightly together, offering everything from snack foods to textiles and jewellery. The air is filled with the cries of hawkers, the sweet smell of perfumes and the rich, lemony scents of frankincense and myrrh.

Prohibitively expensive commodities in the ancient world, frankincense and myrrh were offered by two of the wise men as gifts to the newborn Jesus Christ. They were also essential to religious ritual in every temple in every town. Buying them today is a fascinating business: shopkeepers will show you crystals of varying purity, sold by grade and by weight; sniff each before choosing. Coals and an ornate little pottery burner complete the purchase.

After Salalah, you can follow your own incense trail and, if spending several months on a camel to Petra doesn't appeal, try driving west towards the Yemeni border on a spectacular coast road that skirts undeveloped beaches before climbing into mountains lush with frankincense trees – or head for the lost city of Ubar, legendary centre of Arabia's frankincense trade, reputed to lie near Shisr, the location of Oman's most highly prized groves.

465 PEARL DIVING IN THE PERSIAN GULF

BAHRAIN The largest of their kind in the world, Bahrain's 650 square kilometres of oyster beds have attracted divers since ancient times. Before oil was discovered, the country's economy was dependent upon these little sea treasures, which provided riches where the desert landscape could not. Pearl diving was done without equipment – divers descended on a weighted rope and spent only one minute underwater at a time. Though no longer the industry it was, visitors can now experience this tradition for themselves – unlike the divers of long ago, those lucky enough to find a pearl today are allowed to keep it for themselves.

466 FIGHTING OFF THE CATS IN ACRE

ISRAEL & THE PALESTINIAN TERRITORIES The Middle East isn't all desert, desert, desert. Take a break from sand and head for the water: stand on the walls of Acre and watch the sun sink into the Mediterranean.

Acre is one of the most evocative Palestinian towns inside Israel, an old Crusader stronghold that has survived as a fabulous skein of tight alleyways and atmospheric markets, wreathed around – of course – by the fragrance of fresh-caught fish, for sale in the souk and offered at a dozen restaurants down by the old port. Fight off the cats to get your share.

467 SAND-SKIING IN THE DUNES

QATAR Skiing in the desert? You don't have to go to Dubai's super-cooled ski dome to experience it.

Launching yourself down the slopes under a scorching desert sun is possible in Qatar (pronounced something like cutter), a small Gulf country midway between Kuwait and Dubai – but forget about snow machines and fake icicles. Here, the ski slopes are all natural.

Jaded ski bums looking for a new thrill should take a 4WD trip to Khor al-Adaid – known as Qatar's Inland Sea. This is a salt-water inlet from the blue waters of the Gulf which penetrates far into the desert interior and is surrounded on all sides by monumental formations of giant, silvery sand dunes.

These are almost all crescent-shaped barchan dunes. Both points of the crescent face downwind; between them is a steep slip face of loose sand, while the back of the dune, facing into the breeze, is a shallow, hard slope of wind-packed grains.

This formation lends itself particularly well to sand-skiing or, perhaps more commonly, sand-boarding, both of which are identical to their more familiar snow-based cousins – except offering a softer landing for novices. The 4WD delivers you to the top of the dune, whereupon you set off down the loose slip face, carving through the soft sand to the desert floor; friction is minimal, and this kind of dry, powdery sand lets you glide like a dream.

And Khor al-Adaid comes into its own as sunset approaches. With low sunshine illuminating the creamy-smooth slopes and glittering light reflected up off the calm surface of the khor's blue waters, a surreal, almost mystical quality settles on the dunes. Après-ski with a difference.

468 CAMEL RACING IN THE WAHIBA SANDS

OMAN Every year following the lively date harvest festivals, Bedouin families decamp to the oasis trading town of Ibra, the nucleus of camel racing in Oman. Ibra is set in the middle of the great Wahiba desert, a jigsaw of amber, ochre, and copper-coloured dunes that reach heights of 150m. In this oasis of prosopis and acacia plants, camels are thoroughbred for the track by the Bedouins, and a winning racer can fetch over US$100,000. Races are generally held on Fridays, and while betting is not officially legal in Oman, a blind eye is usually turned when it comes to betting on the humps.

Arrive at the track early – around 6am – to catch the preliminary hubbub as the jockeys prepare themselves for the twenty-kilometre race. The riders are made up almost exclusively of local boys – some as young as five years old – and those weighing the least are often fastened to the camel saddles with Velcro. Once the whistle is blown, the camels race out of the gates, reaching speeds of up to 60kmph, and their owners can often be seen driving alongside them in 4WD vehicles, tracking their progress.

469 FEELING DWARFED BY BAALBEK

LEBANON One of the wonders of the ancient world and easily the most ambitious construction project known to man, the unparalleled Roman archaeological site of Baalbek – a place that, in the words of Robert Byron, "dwarfs New York into a home of ants" – holds awe-inspiring temples, porticoes, courtyards and palatial stone stairways, all of which took some two hundred years to complete.

Avoid the midday heat and crowds by arriving late in the afternoon, when you're likely to catch the sky as it turns a purplish orange, flanked by Mount Lebanon and the colossal Temple of Jupiter. Ascend the temple's restored steps – which long ago stretched to twenty times their current breadth – to the chiseled portico, once covered in cedar and supported by twelve massive Corinthian columns. The central door gives to a hexagonal courtyard encircled with exedrae, small, carved recesses in the walls where Romans would come to ponder the world. Further on, past the inner sanctum, the main court is overshadowed by six elephantine stone columns – the largest in

the world – below which two large open basins served to bathe bovines for sacrificial rites and above which once towered a massive Roman basilica.

Even more striking is the towering Temple of Bacchus just next door – larger than the Parthenon and once a Mecca for decadent orgies and pagan sacrifice rituals. Dozens of engraved, fluted columns shoot up off the podium into the sky, while the portico above is adorned with colonnades, friezes of lions and bulls and ornately carved grapes and poppies; the temple is appropriately attributed to the god of wine and pleasure. Looking on, the sacred cella is impeccably decorated with an assortment of windows, columns and niches.

Exit though a tunnel below the acropolis for Baalbek's other sites: the Temple of Venus; the Ummayad Grand Mosque; and the Hajar al-Hubla, the largest cut block of stone known to man. Forged from local crystalline limestone, it supposedly took 40,000 men to move and its power has been known to render barren women fertile.

470 TAWI ATTAIR: THE "SINGING" SINKHOLE

OMAN At the edge of an emerald highland plain patrolled by Jabali tribesmen and their herds of camels and cattle lies the opening to Tawi Attair ("the Well of Birds"), one of the largest sinkholes in the world. A massive, gaping limestone cavity 150m in diameter and 211m deep, the well was formed eons ago when a cave roof collapsed into itself; today, it could house half the Empire State Building. Thousands of visitors come here each year to witness numerous bird species swooping in and out once the torrential khaleef (monsoon) has drenched the Omani plains.

Ply through the marshy grasses towards the edge of the pit and gaze down: bedecked with specks of green foliage amidst crumbling mounds of dirt and the occasional falling rock, the craggy walls are swimming with hundreds of birds

– raptors, swifts and rock doves – their warbles and chirps welling up in a harmonious flurry of sound. From the side of the opening, carefully follow the stony path down to the small platform for better views of the deep abyss eighty metres below – you'll need a powerful torch, though, to see all the way down to the bottom, where an aquamarine pool funnels into a complex, intertwined system of subaquatic caves. The platform is the best vantage point to hear the famed birdcalls of the well's diverse residents – exotic, isolated species such as the Yemen serin, Bonelli's eagle and African rock bunting, among many, many others. Once the birds embark on their flight towards the sky, their coos hushed, the silence down here is uncanny, trumping even that of that the vast desert above.

471 KRAK DE CHEVALIERS:
THE FINEST CASTLE IN THE WORLD

SYRIA When T E Lawrence was not yet "of Arabia' but merely of Oxford and still only 20, he went on a summer's walking tour of Crusader castles. Writing home after spending three days at Krak des Chevaliers, he described it as, "the finest castle in the world: certainly the most picturesque I have seen – quite marvellous". What immediately struck him was that it was "neither a ruin nor a show place", and that it had remained "as formidable as of old". The wonderful impression that Krak made on Lawrence early in the twentieth century, the genius and the grace of its construction, strikes the visitor as much as ever today.

As you approach along the Homs-Tartus highway, you notice the trees bent eastwards, forever blown by draughts of Mediterranean air sucked through the Homs Gap by the rising heat of the interior. This is the only point between Turkey and Israel at which the otherwise unbroken line of coastal mountains allows access between the deserts and plains of Syria and the sea. Where the gap narrows and the mountains press against you like a wall, you see Krak riding aloft on a spur of the Jebel al-Sariya, like a vast battleship on station, forever cresting a giant wave.

The standard of the Knights Hospitaller fluttered from the top of the Warden's Tower, where a spiral staircase rises to a voluminous chamber, the Grand Master's apartment, dating from the mid-thirteenth century and decorated with delicate pilasters, Gothic ribbed vaulting and a frieze of five-petalled flowers carved in stone. From here there is a splendid view of the concentric circles of Krak's defences spiralling around you, an encircling curtain wall with a line of round towers, then within this and rising higher, a tighter ring of protective walls and towers surrounding a central court.

In the end, Krak was not taken; it was given away. During the last years of the Frankish states the Hospitallers could not raise sufficient manpower and the castle was reduced to a lonely outpost facing a still-gathering enemy. Finally, after Krak had been in Christian hands for 161 years, and after a month's siege by the Egyptian Mameluke sultan Baybars, the remaining knights accepted his offer of safe conduct and, in 1271, rode to Tartus and the sea for the last time.

SEARCHING FOR
DRAGON'S
BLOOD

YEMEN The island of Socotra – Yemeni territory, though it lies closer to Somalia than Arabia – is the most far-flung and unique destination in the Middle East. Cut off from the mainland for half the year by monsoon winds and high seas, Socotra has developed a unique ecosystem. Much of its flora is endemic to the island – odd flowers, strange plants, weirdly shaped trees. Add in the misty mountains and sense of isolation, and Socotra looks and feels like a prehistoric world.

Coming into the capital, Hadibo, you'll be struck first by the mountains – sheer pinnacles of granite soaring into the clouds behind the town. Next you'll squint sceptically at the bizarre bottle-shaped trunks of the cucumber trees in the foothills, as the feeling of entering a bizarre parallel universe heightens. But the real curiosity here, perching on the crags of the mountains,

are the outlandish Dracaena cinnabari, or dragon's blood trees – Socotra's most famous residents.

Also called "inside-out umbrella" trees, they resemble giant mushrooms in silhouette, with a thick trunk sweeping up to a broad cap of dense foliage, supported by spoke-like branches. They look like something out of Alice in Wonderland – or one of Willy Wonka's absurd creations. Blink hard, but they're really there.

Socotrans still gather the reddish dragon's blood tree sap, known as cinnabar – once used as a cure-all by the Romans. It was employed in alchemy and witchcraft in medieval times; Europeans believed that this mysterious crimson resin was the authentic dried blood of dragons and it's considered a magical ingredient in Caribbean voodoo. Hold a piece up to the sun – when it begins to glow blood-red, you'll understand why.

473 CHRISTMAS AT THE CHURCH OF THE NATIVITY IN BETHLEHEM

ISRAEL & THE PALESTINIAN TERRITORIES Everyone has an image of Bethlehem in their minds: a quaint, humble town where Christ was born in a stable and attended by shepherds, while wise magi followed his star from the east; the reality won't disillusion you. Though battered by the strife of occupation and intifada, Bethlehem remains a friendly and unassuming little town. At its heart lies the Church of the Nativity, a sanctuary which might not be quite as holy as Jerusalem's Holy Sepulchre, but surely holds a fonder place in Christian hearts.

One of the oldest in the world, the church was first erected by the Roman emperor Hadrian as a shrine to Adonis to prevent Christian worship at the place where Jesus was born; ironically, that is how we know where it was. In 339 AD, Helena, mother of the Christian emperor Constantine, had the church put up to replace the shrine. From the outside, it looks more like a fortress, and it actually performed that function in 2002 when a mixture of militants, civilians and peace activists were kept under siege for five weeks by Israeli troops.

Queues of devotees wait patiently to pass through the hallowed precincts. Most are elderly, brought in by the coachload for the pilgrimage of a lifetime. Many clutch crucifixes or rosaries, some praying fervently, some weeping in awe. Inside, the church is sombre and dark: a big, cold space, broken by pillars that seem only to deepen the gloom. But the real attraction lies beneath in the Grotto of the Nativity, into which you descend by one set of stairs, coming back up by another. In the grotto, a star, like the "X" on a treasure map, marks the exact spot where Jesus was born, and altars mark the location of the manger and the place where the magi knelt in adoration. And if it appears rather unlike a stable to you, don't forget that in first-century BC Palestine, people usually kept their animals in caves.

For a Christian, the greatest time to visit the Church of the Nativity is of course Christmas Eve, when a midnight mass is held and candle-waving crowds brave the cold to gather outside in Manger Square. Here, in the magic of the moment, you can truly feel the spirit of Christmas, right where it all began.

474 DISCOVERING MADA'IN SALEH

SAUDI ARABIA Remote and isolated in the Arabian desert, Mada'in Saleh is the location of the magnificent Nabatean city known in ancient times as Hegra. With its great, rock-cut facades carved from warm golden sandstone, this city was once an important stop on the powerful Arabian tribe's incense trail.

Built in the first century AD on the fringes of Nabatean territory, Hegra lay at a junction of trade routes. Camel caravans travelling north from the incense towns of Arabia would stop here; animals would be rested, merchants would do business, taxes would be collected. With the constant traffic and trade,

Hegra prospered, and the ruins here are suitably grand.

Roaming Mada'in Saleh you'll see all the styles typical of Nabatean architecture, set against breathtaking desert landscapes. Ornate, classically influenced tombs are carved into the cliffs, displaying impressively intricate workmanship; their detailing, preserved in the dry desert air, remains crisp and sharp. Standing beneath these towering funerary edifices, you'll feel the heavy, silent heat pressing down upon you and sense that Mada'in Saleh, while devoid of tourists, is full of Nabatean ghosts.

475 SUNSET OVER PALMYRA

SYRIA Sunsets make the desert come alive. The low, rich light brings out textures and colours that are lost in the bleached-out glare of noon. It had been a hot, dusty day, but now, perched on a summit high above the desert floor, with the sun at our backs, the views made it all worthwhile.

Spread out below us was the ruined city of Palmyra. For most of the second and third centuries AD, this was one of the wealthiest and most important trading centres in the eastern Roman Empire, perfectly positioned at the fulcrum of trade between Persia and Rome.

We'd spent the day exploring its fabulously romantic array of semi-ruined temples and tombs, their honey-coloured stonework bronzed by the desert sun.Inside the huge Temple of Bel, we'd stood where the Palmyrenes' chief deity was worshipped alongside the gods of the moon and the sun. And

then walked the length of Palmyra's Great Colonnade, an ancient street more than a kilometre long, flanked by tall columns and set amidst the sandy ruins of temples, marketplaces, a theatre and other buildings which once formed the core of the city.

Overlooking us from the west were the ramparts of a ruined, seventeenth-century Arab castle. As sunset approached, we'd ventured up here. It was then that Palmyra's most evocative tale hit home.

At the height of the city's wealth and influence, in 267 AD, Queen Zenobia led her army against the might of Rome, rapidly seizing the whole of Syria and Egypt. Rome hit back, sacking Palmyra in 273 and parading Zenobia in chains through the streets of Rome – but those few short years of rebellion created a legend: Zenobia as the most powerful of Arab queens, Palmyra as her desert citadel.

476 FROLICKING WITH DOLPHINS OFF MUSCAT

OMAN Lightly wedged along a coastal strip between the Hajar mountains and the blue waters of the Gulf, Muscat in Oman has been called the Arabian Peninsula's most enigmatic capital for its bewildering mixture of conservative tradition and contemporary style. Muscat itself – the walled, seafront quarter that hosts the Sultan's Palace – is one of three towns comprising the city. Inland lies the busy, modern area of Ruwi, while a short walk along the coast from Muscat is Mutrah, site of the souk and daily fish market – but the city's unmissable attraction is the astonishing display of marine acrobatics to be seen daily just offshore.

Dolphins are the star performers, dancing and pirouetting on the water in the sparkling sunlight. From various points along the coast near Muscat, tour operators run dolphin-watching trips, departing around 6.30 or 7am. The early start is worth it, as each morning numerous pods of dolphins congregate beside the little boats including common, bottlenose and the aptly named spinner dolphins, which delight in somersaulting out of the water with eye-popping virtuosity, directly under your gaze. Adults and youngsters alike take part, seemingly showing off to each other as well as the goggling humans; nobody knows why they spin, but they do it every morning, before sliding off into deeper waters. Whales have also been sighted close to shore in the winter months (Oct–May), amongst them humpbacks and even killer whales.

And if that's not enough, you can return at sunset for more dolphin-watching, or alternatively even take to the water yourself for a closer look: kayaking with the dolphins, morning or evening, is a real treat. Paddling a short distance into the midst of the frolicking beasts brings you close enough to interact with them, their squeaks and clicks filling the air as they come and investigate who or what you might be.

477 DIVING IN THE GULF OF AQABA

JORDAN Tucked between the arid lands of northern Africa and the Arabian Peninsula, the Red Sea is one of the world's premier diving destinations, and leading off from its northern tip the Gulf of Aqaba boasts some of its best and least damaged stretches of coral. The long Egyptian coastline is filled with brash, bustling and rather commercial resorts, and Israel's slender coast around Eilat can get uncomfortably crowded, but the unsung Jordanian resort of Aqaba offers a tranquility and lack of hustle that, for many, makes it top choice in these parts.

Diving from Aqaba is simple and rewarding: the reef begins directly from the shallows and shore dives are the norm; only one hundred metres offshore, you can explore coral walls and canyons, shipwrecks and ethereal undersea gardens.

The water here is nearly always warm and the reefs exquisite. Wide fields of soft corals stretch off into the startlingly clear blue gulf, schools of anthias shimmering over the various fans, sea fingers and sea whips. Huge heads of stony, hard corals grow literally as big as a house, their limestone skeletons supporting an abundance of marine life, including turtles, rays and moray eels. Endless species of multicoloured fish goggle back at you from all sides: seabass, lionfish and groupers patrol the fringing reef of First Bay; shoals of barracuda circle the sunken Lebanese freighter *Cedar Pride*; while the views along the sheer wall of the Power Station are worth the dive alone – though, if the fates are really smiling on you, you might be lucky enough to spot a shark circling in the depths below.

478 RELAXING IN A DAMASCUS HAMMAM

SYRIA Hammams – or "Turkish" steam baths – are often inconspicuous from the street, with nondescript, run-down facades. Inside though, the best of them – like the Hammam Nur ad-Din in Damascus – are architecturally splendid, with fountains, grand, tiled halls and coloured glass set into domed roofs to admit shafts of sunlight. Gloomy warrens of passages snake off from the entrance into the steamy distance, flanked by sweatrooms and plunge pools. The Nur ad-Din has been in operation since the twelfth century and the sense of history here is every bit as powerful as it is in the ruins and museums outside.

After depositing your clothes in a locker and donning a towel-cum-loincloth – modesty is always preserved for men, although women can strip off completely – head first for a scaldingly hot sauna, your body stewing in its own juices as you lie on a marble slab working up the mother of all sweats. Public hammams are always single-sex: some admit only men, while others may publicize set hours for women (and children), when male staff are replaced by female counterparts.

An ice-cold shower follows, after which you can expect to be approached by a heavily built, no-nonsense attendant bearing a rough-textured glove, used to scrub every inch of your body and loosen layers of dirt and dead skin you didn't even know you had.

You may then be offered a massage, which often involves much pummelling and joint-cracking. With your circulation restored to maximum and every sinew tingling, seemingly endless rounds of soaping, steaming, splashing and cold plunging follow, for as long as you like, at the end of which you'll be swaddled in towels and brought a refreshing glass of sweet tea to aid recovery. Sheer heaven.

WANDERING OLD SANA'A

YEMEN Nestled between Yemen's al-Surated mountain range, the timeless city of Sana'a is said to have been built by Noah's son. Modernity has since thankfully stayed well away from the city's old quarter, where traditional architecture has endured for over a thousand years.

Begin your day at the medina's southeastern portico, the Bab al-Yaman, which still welcomes local traders on their way to Turkish coffee-houses for a strong shot of local brew. From here, head north to marvel at the Grand Mosque (al-Jama'a al-Kabir), just one of fifty city mosques, and the home of the largest collection of Islamic manuscripts in Yemen. Non-Muslims aren't allowed in, but admiring the beautifully constructed minarets and domes all over the city won't cost you a thing. Continue on to the Souk al-Milh (salt market), where you'll be confronted with a beguiling collection of stalls purveying coffee, incense, spices and cloth.

From here, notch your head back to take in a vista of the nearly 15,000 ancient tower-houses of Old Sana'a. You can amble about the old city for hours without seeing a single "new" structure. The buildings range in height from six to eight stories and are made of locally quarried dark basalt stone with whitewashed facades of chalk and limestone, which protects against rain. The exteriors display a gorgeous mélange of traditional Yemeni and Islamic styles, with windows done in artful friezes. At the very top of each building, framing the manzar (attic), are the rooms that look out across the city, windowed with moon-shaped stained glass. Some call them the world's first skyscrapers, and Yemeni families still live in them today as they have for centuries. Once you've had your fill of traditional architecture, rest yourself in a resplendent evening bath at the Hammam Abhar, Sana'a's finest. But after the sun has set, return once more for a walk through Old Sana'a: at nighttime, the entire medina is bathed in gorgeous, golden hues emanating from the weathered stained-glass windows.

480 SHOPPING IN THE CITY OF GOLD

UNITED ARAB EMIRATES Dubai's nickname, the "City of Gold", is well earned: gold jewellery is sold here at some of the world's most competitive prices and shopping among the constant flow of customers, many here for their marriage dowries, is an exceptional experience.

The Gold Souk is a fascinating warren of tiny shops and stalls clustered together in the old quarter of Deira. Visit in the cool of early evening when the souk is at its best, with lights blazing and window-shoppers out in force. Every corner is crammed with jewellery of every style and variety; spotlights pick out choice pieces and racks holding dozens of sparkling gold bangles and chains dazzle the eye.

Buying is a cagey but always good-natured process: treat it as the chance to have a friendly chat with the shopkeeper, talking about family, work, life – anything but the item you've got your eye on. Then ask to see a few pieces, while surreptitiously assessing quality and sizing up your adversary, before lighting on the piece you knew you wanted from the start.

When the time comes to discuss money, bear in mind that the gold price fluctuates daily – and every shopkeeper in the souk knows the current price to several decimal places. Whereas in the West gold jewellery is sold at a fixed price, in Dubai the cost of each item has two separate components: the weight of the gold and the quality of craftsmanship involved in creating it. The former is fixed, according to the daily price-per-gramme (listed in the newspaper) set against the item's purity; the latter is where bargaining comes into play, with you and the shopkeeper trading prices – always with a smile – until you reach agreement.

It takes a cool head, amidst all that glittering gold, not to be dazzled into paying over the odds, but the experience is more than worth it.

481 CARVING A PATH THROUGH PERSEPOLIS

IRAN You begin to feel the historical weight of Persepolis as you drive down the tree-lined approach, long before reaching the actual site. Here, on the dusty plain of Marvdasht at the foot of the Zagros mountains, the heat is ferocious, but nothing can detract from the sight before you: a once-magnificent city, looming high above the plain on a series of terraces.

Enter through the massive, crumbling stone Gate of All Nations, adorned with cuneiform inscriptions that laud the mighty Persian emperor whose father built the city across a gap of 2500 years, "I am Xerxes, king of kings, son of Darius...". Walking between great carved guardian bulls standing to attention on either side of the gate, you come out on a vast terrace, stretching almost 500 metres along each side.

It's not the scale though, but the details – specifically the carvings – that make Persepolis special. Wherever you look, they indicate what went on in each area: in private quarters, bas-reliefs show servants carrying platters of food; in the Hall of Audience, Darius is being borne aloft by representatives of 28 nations, their arms interlinked. Everywhere you can trace the intricately worked details of curly beards and the even more impressive expressions of body language that show the skill of the ancient artists.

The centrepiece is the ruined Apadana Palace, where you come nose-to-nose with elaborately carved depictions of the splendours of Darius the Great's empire – royal processions, horse-drawn chariots and massed ranks of armed soldiers. Look closer and you'll spot human-headed winged lions, carved alongside esoteric symbols of the deity Ahura Mazda. Begun around 518 BC by Darius to be the centrepiece of his vast empire, Persepolis was a demonstration of Persian wealth and sophistication – and it shows.

482 CHECKING OUT THE BAUHAUS ARCHITECTURE IN TEL AVIV

ISRAEL & THE PALESTINIAN TERRITORIES Tel Aviv is a city with chutzpah, a loud, gesticulating expression of urban Jewish culture; revelling in a Mediterranean-style café culture, it has dozens of bars and clubs – all aimed squarely at the under-30s. Founded in 1909, it's not likely to have much in the way of architectural interest, or so you'd think. Take a closer look and Tel Aviv reveals a wealth of buildings constructed in the International Style, inspired by the German Bauhaus school. Not as grandiose as its predecessor, Art Deco – indeed, deliberately understated in contrast – this style has its own charm, and abounds in Tel Aviv as nowhere else in the world.

Wandering the streets, you don't at first see the architecture, but then you start to notice it, and suddenly you'll see it everywhere – it really is a signature of the city. The International Style's beauty lies not in ornamentation or grand gestures, but in its no-nonsense crispness: lines are clean, with lots of right-angles; decoration is minimal, consisting only of protruding balconies and occasionally flanged edges, designed to cast sharp shadows in the harsh Mediterranean sunlight; and it wears whitewash especially well, giving the whole of Tel Aviv an almost Hockneyesque feel with its straight white lines and hard edges, as if someone had turned up the contrast button just a mite too high.

Check it out on Rehov Bialik, a small residential street in the very centre of town. Take a stroll on Sederot Rothschild, a fine 1930s avenue with some very classic Bauhaus buildings. A further wander around the streets in between Bialik and Rothschild yields still more examples of the genre, as does a visit to the more workaday district of Florentin.

Cool and stylish as its cafés, Tel Aviv's architecture reflects the attitude of the city itself – young, brash and straightforward. Like the city, it may not impress at first, but it definitely grows on you.

483 FEASTING ON LEBANESE MEZZE

LEBANON Lebanese food is one of the great pleasures of travel in the Middle East, and the mainstay of this cuisine is mezze. Meaning an array of appetizers, mezze is served simultaneously on small plates and can form the extended hors d'oeuvres of a larger meal or, often, a full meal in itself.

The concept extends far back into history: the ancient Greeks and Persians both served small dishes of nuts and dried fruits with wine as an appetizer, a tradition which continued (with a non-alcoholic beverage) throughout the medieval Arab period.

Today, good restaurants might have thirty or forty choices of mezze on the menu, ranging from simple dishes of herbs, olives and pickled vegetables, labneh (tart yoghurt), and dips such as hummus (chickpea) and baba ghanouj (aubergine), up to grander creations like kibbeh – the national dish of Lebanon, a mixture of cracked wheat, grated onion and minced lamb pounded to a paste, shaped into oval torpedoes and deep-fried, tabbouleh (another Lebanese speciality: parsley and tomato salad with cracked wheat), shanklish (spiced goat's cheese), warag aynab (stuffed vine leaves) and so on. Kibbeh nayeh (lamb's meat pounded smooth and served raw) is perhaps the most celebrated of all mezze, while mini-mains such as lamb or chicken shish kebabs, charcoal-roasted larks and even seafood are also common. Everything is always accompanied by unlimited quantities of hot, fresh-baked flat bread, used for scooping and dipping.

Mezze exist to slow down the process of eating, turning a solitary refuelling into a convivial celebration of good food and good company. Sitting at a table swamped in colours and aromas, and eating a meal of myriad different flavours and textures, is nothing short of sensuous delight – as, indeed, it's intended to be.

Bedouin camping at Wadi Rum

JORDAN My Bedouin guide settled forward over his ribaba, a simple traditional stringed instrument. As he drew the bow to and fro, the mournful, reedy music seemed to fill the cool night air, echoing back off the cliff soaring above us. The fire threw dancing shadows across the sand. A billion stars looked down.

"Bedouin" means desert-dweller. It's a cultural term: Bedouin today, whether they live in the desert or not (many are settled urban professionals), retain a strong sense of identity with their ancestral tribe. You'll find this desert culture across the Middle East, but to get a feel for its origins you need to travel into its homeland – which is why I'd come to southern Jordan, specifically Wadi Rum.

Here, the dunes and desert vistas form one of the classic landscapes of the Middle East – the backdrop for the movie Lawrence of Arabia. Granite and sandstone mountains rise up to 800m sheer from the desert floor. The heat during the day is intense: with no shade, temperatures down on the shimmering sand soar. Views stretch for tens of kilometres; the silence and sense of limitless space are awe-inspiring.

I'd come to spend a night camping. Camels were available as transport, but I'd opted instead for a jeep ride. Bumping out into the deep desert, we headed for camp: a distinctive Bedouin "house of hair" – a long, low tent hand-woven from dark goat's hair and pitched in the sands – would serve as quarters for the night.

As blissful evening coolness descended, the sun set over the desert in a spectacular show of light and colour, and the clarity of the unpolluted air produced a starry sky of stunning beauty.

The Burj Al Arab shows off in Dubai

485

UNITED ARAB EMIRATES Dubai is a desert turned Disney. What was once a sleepy fishing village is now a futuristic cyber city, with sparkling skyscrapers, shopping malls, water parks, golf courses, and hotels so flashy that Elton John would be proud to call them home. Top of the lot is the iconic Burj Al Arab, a striking 28-storey symbol of new-world bling. The gleaming building, the tallest hotel in the world, is shaped like a billowing sail – and to say it dominates the skyline is an understatement. At night, surrounded by choreographed fountains of water and fire, it is truly spectacular.

Start as you mean to go on with a Rolls Royce pick-up from the airport and you will swiftly get the picture. Huge tropical aquariums and backlit waterfalls dominate the lobby, the carpets are a whirl of lurid reds, greens and blues, and on-site stores glitter with diamonds and emeralds. Modestly marketed as "the world's first seven-star hotel", it has a helipad on the roof (where Federer and Agassi played out that tennis match) and more than 1200 staff poised to satisfy your every whim.

The bedrooms are all gigantic suites, their decor the epitome of Arabian kitsch. We're talking mirrors above the beds, leopard-print chairs and gold-tapped Jacuzzis in every bathroom. The 42-inch TV screens are framed in gold and the curtains and doors can be operated electronically. If all this doesn't quite cut it for you, the two show-stopping Royal Suites come with their own private elevators, cinemas and rotating beds. A bargain at $28,000 per night.

When it comes to food, naturally your personal butler can rustle up anything you desire, or you might prefer to take a three minute-trip in a simulated submarine to the underwater restaurant. Oh, and don't miss a drink in Burj Al Arab's famous bar, situated on the 27th floor, 200m above sea level. From here you can gaze across at The Palm and The World – extraordinary manmade islands shaped like their namesakes and prime real estate to some of the wealthiest people on the planet.

The Burj Al Arab is the ultimate in ostentatious opulence. Embrace the excess and smile.

486 THE ARAB ORGANIZATIONS BUILDING: AN OFFICE WITH ATTITUDE

KUWAIT The Arab Organizations Headquarters is an office building like no other. Just over ten years old, its grey granite exterior hides a superior craftsmanship and attention to detail that only money can buy – so it's no surprise that the building is home to a number of Arabian petroleum organizations, who kindly regularly open it up to the public on tours. No expense was spared on the Moroccan waterwall in the lobby, the huge hand-painted doors, or the country-themed meeting rooms furnished with the finest indigenous materials, and the building as a whole deliberately emobodies common Arab themes and culture. Focal point is the atrium: an Egyptian *mashrabiya*

(a twelfth-century-style lattice screen work) covers the full nine storeys on one side – neatly hiding the lift shaft – while opposite a huge wall of glass on the eastern face lets in the light. In the centre, forty-year-old Syrian Ficus trees grow in large pots on rollers that are rotated every day so they don't have to bend towards the light, and the cavernous building is filled with sweet bird song courtesy of the caged birds hanging under their branches. It's an incredible space, and overall an unforgettable building that is a curious mixture of old and new, an office environment in contemporary style that is at the same time a homage to traditional Arab crafts.

487 GETTING ACQUAINTED WITH ARABIC SWEETS

JORDAN Whenever I go back to Jordan (which is often), my first appointment is in downtown Amman. There, up an un-promising-looking alleyway alongside a bank building, is a hole-in-the-wall outlet of Habiba, a citywide chain devoted to halawiyyat (literally "sweets", or sweet pastries and desserts). I join a line – there's always a line – and, for the equivalent of a few cents, I get a square of kunafeh, hot and dripping with syrup, handed to me on a paper plate with a plastic fork. It is a joyous experience: for the Ammanis hanging out and wolf-ing down the stuff, it's everyday; for me, it's like coming home. Habiba's kunafeh is worth crossing continents for.

Kunafeh is the king of Arabic sweets. Originating from the Palestinian city of Nablus, it comprises buttery shredded filo pastry layered over melted goat's cheese, baked in large, round trays, doused liberally with syrup and cut up into squares for serving. It is cousin to the better-known baklawa, layered flaky pastry filled with pistachios, cashews or other nuts, also available widely.

However, you're rarely served such treats in Arabic restaurants: there's not a strong tradition of post-prandial desserts. Instead, you'll need to head to one of the larger outlets of Habiba, or their competitors Jabri or Zalatimo, patisseries with a café section.

Glass-fronted fridges hold individual portions of Umm Ali, an Egyptian milk-and-coconut speciality, sprinkled with nuts and cinnamon, and muhallabiyyeh, a semi-set almond cream pudding, enhanced with rosewater: comfort food, Arab-style. Choose one to go with a coffee and perhaps a water-pipe of flavoured tobacco.

Or get a box of assorted sweets – baklawa, maamoul (buttery, crumbly, rose-scented cookie-style biscuits), burma (nut pastries baked golden brown), basma (delicate lacy pastries also filled with cashews) and other delectably sticky and aromatic varieties – the perfect gift if you're lucky enough to be invited to someone's home. Forget, too, about Western-bred inhibitions: in the Arab world, as far as halawiyyat are concerned, consumption is guilt-free!

488 BLAZING A TRAIL AT DANA NATURE RESERVE

JORDAN When you think of eco-friendly travel, you don't immediately think of the Middle East. In environmental terms, the region is a disaster, characterized by a general lack of awareness of the issues and poor – if any – legislative safeguards. But Jordan is quietly working wonders and the impact in the last few years of the country's Royal Society for the Conservation of Nature (RSCN) has been striking: areas of outstanding natural beauty are now under legal protection and sustainable development is squarely on the political agenda.

The RSCN's flagship project is the Dana Nature Reserve, the Middle East's only successful example of sustainable tourism. Up until 1993, Dana was dying: the stone-built mountain village was crumbling, its hinterland suffering from hunting and overgrazing, while local people were abandoning their homes in search of better opportunities in the towns.

Then the RSCN stepped in and set up the Dana Nature Reserve, drawing up zoning plans to establish wilderness regions and

semi-intensive use areas where tourism could be introduced, building a guesthouse and founding a scientific research station. Virtually all the jobs – tour guides, rangers, cooks, receptionists, scientists and more – were taken by villagers.

Today, over eight hundred local people benefit from the success of Dana, and the reserve's running costs are covered almost entirely from tourism revenues. The Guesthouse continues to thrive, with its spectacular views out over the V-shaped Dana valley, while a three-hour walk away in the hills lies the idyllic Rummana campsite, from where you can embark on dawn excursions to watch ibex and eagles.

But the reserve also stretches down the valley towards the Dead Sea Rift – and here, a memorable five-hour walk from the Guesthouse, stands the *Feinan Wilderness Lodge*, set amidst an arid sandy landscape quite different from Dana village. The lodge is powered by solar energy and lit by candles; with no road access at all, it's a bewitchingly calm and contemplative desert retreat.

489 SWIMMING THE WADI SHAB

OMANI If Adam and Eve had carried Omani passports, they'd probably have bitten into their poison apple somewhere in the waters of Wadi Shab. Arguably the country's most enchanting destination, the edenic Wadi Shab ("Gorge of Cliffs" in Arabic) runs full of water for much of the year thanks to a series of flash floods and torrential rains. Here, the region's barren rocky desert plains give way to a heavenly oasis ornamented with natural, shallow pools of aquamarine water, verdurous plantations and cascading waterfalls, with caverns, grottoes, crevices and sheer rock faces providing a haven from the beating sun.

From the fishing village of Quriyat, follow the bumpy coastal track alongside stretches of white beach to arrive at the wadi, bordering a lake. Hop in one of the small rope-pulled ferries to traverse the lagoon, plying your way through the oleander and brush, from where you'll enter a steep, rifted valley, overgrown and shaded with trees, grasses and date palms. Lazily wade through the azure waters – it should only come up to your knees – before making your way up for a hike along the craggy, winding hills, during which you might even come upon an Omani family, ready to offer traditional dates and coffee. After a good two hours of medium-intensity trekking, you'll arrive at a cave that drops down to a shimmering pool of water. Perch yourself on the ladder and climb down for a well-earned swim along schools of iridescent kingfishers. Now the tricky part: you'll need to swim through a small keyhole opening in the cavern rock to access a small subaquatic channel. But it's a worthy endeavour, as the channel leads to a second cavernous pool that empties into the mouth of the wadi itself, where the idyllic, sandy Fins Beach is adorned with fishing boats and makes a perfect spot for a picnic – assuming you've remembered to waterproof your packed lunch.

490 TAKING A DIP IN THE RIVER JORDAN

JORDAN I could scarcely believe my eyes. Since 1948, the River Jordan had fallen within a restricted military zone; never once had I even got close to it. Now, with the peace treaty between Jordan and Israel, civilians could once again visit – and I took the chance to stand on the reedy banks and dip my toe in the narrow, slow-flowing river.

That was a few years ago; now the Baptism Site, on the Jordanian east bank, is a world-famous archeological site, authenticated by historians and the Vatican alike as the most probable location where John the Baptist baptized Jesus Christ. There are ancient churches, medieval pilgrim hostels, communal baptismal pools – but the star attraction is the Jordan itself, full of silt, pollution and unequalled biblical resonance.

491 BEIRUT'S BUNKER BAR

LEBANON Beirut is a city that takes pride in its edgy nightlife. Head east towards the Forum de Beirut and you'll find out why. Dug into an industrial lot is *B018*, a steel-roofed bunker of a bar submerged under what looks like an overblown helipad. It's the embodiment of a Bond villain's lair – except that the patrons are hell-bent on dancing rather than domination.

B018 lies at the heart of La Quarantine, an area that was virtually destroyed by the Phalangist militia in 1976. The club doesn't shy away from tackling these ghosts – the back wall has a slit cut into it like a sniper's window – but it's the way the structure plays with its environment that makes this a night out to remember. The entire roof slides back, one giant flap raised at an angle to reflect the scenes above: the sweep of approaching headlights, the Mediterranean sky glowing orange to red to star-studded black.

492 TAKING TEA IN ISFAHAN

IRAN You could easily devote a day to exploring Isfahan's great Maydan Naqsh-i Jahan, a vast rectangular space dotted with gardens, pools and fountains and ringed by arcades, above which rise the domes of the adjacent mosques. Separate from the bustle of this cultured city, it has even managed to cling onto its original polo goals, though the game hasn't been played here for centuries.

The square is always busy with people. It spreads south from the sprawling Bazar-e Bozorg, packed with shops offering Isfahan's most famous export – hand-woven Persian carpets. As you stroll the square you may well find yourself engaged in conversation by an eminently courteous Iranian with impeccable English, who turns out to have a brother/uncle/cousin with a carpet shop – where, of course, there's no charge for looking…

Even if you're able to resist the charms of the carpet bazaar, you won't be able to ignore the square's exquisite seventeenth-century Islamic architecture. To the south is the Masjid i-Imam mosque, its portal and towering dome sheathed in glittering tiles of turquoise and blue, while to one side, the smaller Sheikh Lotfollah Mosque – marked by a dome of cream-coloured tiles which glow rosy pink in the afternoon sun – is, if anything, even more stunning, with fine mosaics and a dizzyingly decorated interior. Opposite, the Ali Qapu Palace – an ex-royal residence – boasts a sensational view over the square from its high terrace.

Either way, be back at one of the terrace teashops as sunset approaches. The square fills with Isfahani families strolling or picnicking on the grass and you get a grandstand view over the scene, sipping chay (tea) as floodlights turn the arcades, domes and minarets to gold.

493

SOAKING UP THE

MASJID I-IMAM

IRAN Known to the Persians as Nisf-e-Jahan ("Half the World"), Isfahan – a two-time capital of the Persian Empire – is home to the crowning jewel of Islamic architecture, the stunning Masjid i-Imam mosque. It is said that if you must visit all the mosques in Iran, visit this one last, as its beauty will supplant your memory of all others.

Built over 26 years, the Safavid-era mosque sits on the southern edge of the Maydan Naqsh i-Jahan, a massive fountained square in central Isfahan where royal equestrian arts and polo games were once put on for the shah and his court. Stroll around the outside of the mosque to take in the wild collection of diverse motifs, colors and calligraphic designs that adorn the various portals, walls and vaults. In the centre of it all is a beguiling, 54-metre-high bulbous dome. On either side of the main prayer hall courtyard are the halls of a medrese, an important Islamic school in use until the nineteenth century.

Enter the mosque through its enveloping front portal, its foundation of white marble supporting a facade of rich floral calligraphy, moulded niches, gorgeous azure tilework and slender, rocket-like patterned minarets that shoot up forty-eight metres towards the heavens, their balconies still reverberating with the trebly calls to prayer of Isfahan's muezzins. Follow the corridor through to the inner courtyard, where a reflective washing pool is encircled by four porched, blue-and-yellow walls, each leading to its own iwan (vaulted space). The southern entrance gives way to a central sanctuary, whose domed ceiling – the same dome you just saw from the outside – is bedecked with golden rose floral designs surrounded by breathtaking mosaics. The usual silence of Islamic holy places is likely to be broken here by the clapping hands and giggles of children testing out the dome's renowned echo. To capture a memorable photograph of the whole thing, visit the Ali Qapu pavilion just across the square for the most impressive vistas.

494

JORDAN Tucked away between parallel rocky ranges in southern Jordan, Petra is awe-inspiring. Popular but rarely crowded, this fabled site could keep you occupied for half a day or half a year: you can roam its dusty tracks and byways for miles in every direction.

Petra was the capital of the Nabateans, a tribe originally from Arabia who traded with, and were eventually taken over by, the Romans. Grand temples and even Christian-era church mosaics survive, but Petra is known for the hundreds of ornate classical-style facades carved into its red sandstone cliffs, the grandest of which mark the tombs of the Nabatean kings.

As you approach, modern urban civilization falls away and you are enveloped by the arid desert hills; the texture and colouring of the sandstone, along with the stillness, heat and clarity of light bombard your senses. But it's the lingering, under-the-skin quality of supernatural power that seems to seep out of the

As in antiquity, the Siq, meaning "gorge", is still the main entrance into Petra – and its most dramatic natural feature. The Siq path twists and turns between bizarrely eroded cliffs for over a kilometre, sometimes widening to form sunlit piazzas in the echoing heart of the mountain; in other places, the looming walls (150m high) close in to little more than a couple of metres apart, blocking out sound, warmth and even daylight.

When you think the gorge can't go on any longer, you enter a dark, narrow defile, opening at its end on to a strip of extraordinary classical architecture. As you step out into the sunlight, the famous facade of Petra's Treasury looms before you. Carved directly into the cliff face and standing forty metres tall, it's no wonder this edifice starred in Indiana Jones and the Last Crusade as the repository to the Holy Grail – the magnificent portico is nothing short of divine.

495 ROBOT CAMEL-BACK RACING

KUWAIT A stampede of two-year-old camels tore down the racetrack, their sinewy tan bodies stirring up brown dust as they speed along, trying to outpace the other camels nearby. A flurry of crops flicked across their backsides – but this was not the work of an overzealous jockey. Instead, strapped across the back of each camel rode remote-controlled robots, limbless mechanical boy-sized torsos bucking with every stride.

Keeping pace in the Kuwaiti desert just beyond the track railing, a fleet of modern "ships of the desert" – SUVs and minivans – pursued the dromedaries, chase vehicles from which the camels' owners expertly maneuvered the whips by remote control.

Radio-controlled jockeys are new, having spread across Kuwait and several other Arabian countries after laws banning child jockeys were passed. The substitute? Strapped-on whipping machines, wrapped cylinders with faceless sock monkey-heads here in Kuwait. In some countries, plastic human-shaped heads adorn the robots.

Camel racing is part of Kuwait's cultural heritage, though the robots and chase cars are all products of the modern world. But the audience, sitting atop overstuffed, black leather armchairs and comfortably ensconced in an air-conditioned glass pavilion, is still full of men dressed in traditional Kuwaiti robes and white headdresses. Children of businessmen and sheikhs frolic on the maroon carpets. Strangers are offered tea – "One hump or two?" – or even camel's milk.

A distant pounding echoes and the crowd quiets down. The camels are coming. Teacups are set aside as attention shifts from the flat-screen television monitors showing distant action to the finish line right in front of the clubhouse. It's a close call, but the jockeys seem far from fazed.

496 OFF-ROADING FOR REAL: ACROSS THE SAND DUNES TO KHOR AL-ADAID

QATAR In southern Qatar, the roads simply stop, swallowed by fuming waves of sand. Every weekend, countless Qatari 4WD enthusiasts make the pilgrimage to the desert to push their vehicles to the limit and find solitude in a shifting world of shimmering heat and rolling dunes.

Moussad introduced himself with a beaming smile, which matched his white thobe (floor-length white robe), and headscarf. He ushered the four of us – all excited Westerners – into his latest-model Toyota Landcruiser and took off for the dunes.

Moussad is one of many four drivers who whisk tourists out of Doha, Qatar's main city, down to the desert for a day of adventure. After an hour's drive south on a pot-holed freeway, huge sand dunes loomed on the horizon marking the end of the road. Numerous 4WDs were parked up in the shadows, their drivers scurrying from tyre to tyre letting out air for better traction on the slippery sand.

Loud hip-hop and techno blared from the assembled entourage of expensive cars, Qatar's modern day equivalent of the camel – gone are the their plodding steeds of yesteryear, exchanged for faster, gruntier and air-conditioned contemporaries that are thirstier and also tend to roll more often.

Moussad cranked the volume up and charged into the desert, roaring up near-vertical walls of sand and carving down steep slopes sideways, skilfully riding the dunes in his 4WD like a surfer riding a wave or snowboarder riding a mountain, but with added horsepower.

As the day came to an end, deep shadows accentuated the desert's sensuous curves. The sun hung low in the sky like a red orb, and reflected across Khor al-Adaid, the inland sea bordering Saudi Arabia.

497 HAUNTING THE DEAD CITIES

SYRIA I was half expecting some toga'd Roman character to pop his head out of a side window and ask me what the heck I thought I was doing, trespassing on his land. This was Serjilla, one of the best preserved and most complete of the "Dead Cities", a network of Roman-Byzantine towns that once thrived in the fertile plains of northern Syria. Serjilla, like its neighbours, has been abandoned for more than a millennium – but it didn't feel that way: I explored Roman houses that were virtually complete, popped into church, visited the baths and the temple, while all those Roman ghosts looked on with disdain.

498 VISITING THE "HANGING VILLAGE" OF HABALAH

SAUDI ARABIA Appearing to hang from a 250-metre cliffface over a deep valley, the deserted village of Habalah is a truly unique settlement. The village name comes from "habl", meaning "rope" – a reference to the rope ladders that the long-gone inhabitants used to descend to their dwellings. These days, a cable car runs visitors down to the village, offering outstanding views over the dramatic Arabian landscape along the way. Built out of the rock on which they stand, the houses offer a fascinating insight into traditional Saudi life, and give a whole new meaning to the phrase "living on the edge".

MISCELLANY

FIVE GREAT RESTAURANTS

Arabi, Zahlé, Lebanon Lining the Bardouni river in the mountain town of Zahlé are dozens of terrace restaurants serving superb Lebanese mezze. *Arabi* is the top choice, a great place to relax over an all-day lunch.

Burj al-Hamam, Kuwait City Jutting out into the Arabian Gulf, this restaurant is famous not only for its food, but also for its sea views, and those of the iconic Kuwait Towers. Join the locals smoking sheesha late into the evening, or dine on traditional Lebanese cuisine, in chic understated modern surroundings.

Khayyam, Tehran, Iran One of Tehran's best-known restaurants, set in a 300-year-old building that was once part of a mosque and is now beautifully restored. The menu of classic Persian dishes is unsurpassed, and there's the added attraction of traditional music, played live nightly.

Sissi House, Aleppo, Syria A charming restaurant occupying a splendid seventeenth-century townhouse on a quiet alley in the Armenian quarter of Aleppo. The ambience is sophisticated, with candlelit tables filling an open courtyard, and the food is nothing short of exquisite.

Tannoureen, Amman, Jordan For the discerning Middle Eastern gourmet, Amman stands second only to Beirut in terms of quality of food and standards of service – and *Tannoureen* is its finest Lebanese restaurant, with sensational cuisine served in a cultured, atmospheric setting.

DRINK

The Middle East's best-known alcoholic tipple is **arak**, an aniseed spirit most famously distilled in Lebanon, which – like Israel – also has a thriving wine industry.

Shiraz once stood at the centre of a renowned wine region. Its name lives on as one of the world's most famous grapes (aka Syrah), though the city itself now lies in Iran, where the production of alcohol is effectively banned.

The Middle East's only microbrewery, producing **Taybeh** beer, is located near the Palestinian city of Ramallah.

KABBALAH

Kabbalah is not a religion, but a branch of Jewish mysticism established in the sixteenth century in the town of Safed (or Tzfat), in modern Israel, which uses devotional and esoteric practices to unlock the hidden meanings of the Torah (the Jewish holy book). It has become a fashion among celebrities like Madonna, who mix it with gnosticism, humanism and elements of the occult in a heady but – some say – insubstantial New Age brew.

MOUNTAINS

At 5671m, **Mount Damavand**, in Iran, is higher than any European peak. The summit is reachable in three days of steep walking. **Mount Sinai** (2285m), in Egypt, is venerated by Jews, Christians and Muslims as the place where God revealed the Ten Commandments to Moses. It's a popular spot from which to watch the sun rise. Near Bcharré, on the slopes of **Qornet as-Sawda**, the highest mountain in Lebanon (3090m), stands the last surviving forest of Lebanese cedar trees.

A TRUE DIVA

The Egyptian diva Umm Kalthoum (also spelled in a number of other ways, including Oum Kalsoum and Om Kolsum; 1904–75) remains the best-loved singer in the Arab world, outselling many contemporary stars. At her peak – the 1950s to 1970s – she was able to empty the streets of Cairo and other Arab cities, as people stopped everything to listen to her monthly radio concerts. These were nothing short of epic, often consisting of a four- or five-hour performance of a single song – generally on the themes of love, loss and yearning – to an orchestral accompaniment. An estimated four million mourners attended her funeral.

"Squeeze the past like a sponge, smell the present like a rose and send a kiss to the future"

Arab proverb

FIVE GREAT HOTELS

• **American Colony Hotel, Jerusalem** This is the holy city's most famous hotel, more than 120 years old – genteel, sophisticated and tasteful, set in tranquil grounds.

• **Baron Hotel, Aleppo, Syria** Once the luxurious choice of Agatha Christie and Lawrence of Arabia, the Baron has fallen on hard times: it's got bags of character, if you can overlook deficiencies in the ancient plumbing and bedsprings.

• **Burj al-Arab, Dubai, UAE** Perhaps the most famous luxury hotel in the Middle East, an iconic 321m tower in the shape of a billowing sail that dominates the Dubai waterfront.

• **Dead Sea Mövenpick, Jordan** An innovative, superbly designed five-star hotel and spa resort, looking west over the Dead Sea.

• **Old Cataract Hotel, Aswan** This splendid Edwardian-Moorish relic on the banks of the Nile dates from 1902 and has been tastefully renovated to luxurious standards.

INVENTIONS

The Sumerians, an ancient people from southeastern Iraq, developed a network of city-states well before 3000 BC – the world's first civilization. Sumerian inventions include the wheel, writing and agriculture. The Sumerian clock, based on a sexagesimal system (60 seconds, 60 minutes, 12 hours), is still in use today.

Around the fifth century BC, mathematicians at Babylon, in Iraq, invented zero.

Byblos (or Jbeil, in Lebanon) was the source of the world's first alphabet, developed around 1200 BC.

"A book is a garden that you carry in your pocket"

Saadi, thirteenth-century Persian Sufi poet

LITERATURE

Naguib Mahfouz is the only writer in Arabic to win the Nobel Prize for Literature, in 1988. His most famous works, including *Midaq Alley* (1947) and *Children of Gebelawi* (1959), evoke Cairo's street life amidst a cast of colourful characters.

S.Y. Agnon is the only writer in Hebrew to win the Nobel Prize for Literature, in 1966. *The Bridal Canopy* (1931) and *Only Yesterday* (1945), two of Agnon's best-known books, use a surreal style to explore conflicts between Jewish tradition and modernity.

Simin Daneshvar's *Suvashun* (1969) explores themes of modernity in her home town of Shiraz, and is the highest-selling novel ever written in Persian.

CALENDARS

Where Western or Christian cultures use "BC" (Before Christ) and "AD" (Anno Domini; the Year of Our Lord), the accepted terms in Jewish and Islamic contexts are "BCE" (Before the Common Era) and "CE" (Common Era).Many different calendars are used in the Middle East. The most important are:

Calendar	Dated from...	Type	2007 equates to...
Islamic	Muhammad's emigration to Medina	Lunar	1427–1428 AH
Jewish	The Creation	Lunisolar	5767–5768 AM
Persian	Muhammad's emigration to Medina	Solar	1385–1386 AP
Western (Gregorian)	Birth of Jesus	Solar	2007 AD/2007 CE

WILDLIFE PRESERVATION

The Arabian oryx is a beautiful, long-horned white antelope that is indigenous to the Middle East. Throughout the twentieth century hunting drastically reduced its numbers, until the last wild oryx was shot in Oman in 1972. Captive breeding programmes in the USA, Jordan, Qatar and Oman ensured the survival of the species and oryx have now been reintroduced to the wild in Israel, Jordan, Oman and Saudi Arabia, all of which – along with Qatar and the UAE – maintain herds in wildlife reserves.

DERIVATIONS

The primary language in the Middle East is Arabic, from which many English words are derived.

• **admiral** from **ami:r-al/ -bahr** "ruler of the seas"
• **checkmate** from **sha:h ma:t** "the king is dead"
• **mattress** from **matrah** "place where something is thrown"
• **zero** from **s,ifr** "empty"

HUBBLY BUBBLY

Water-pipes are common across the Middle East, known variously as a **nargila, argila, sheesha, qalyan** or **"hubbly bubbly"**. They stand on the floor, reaching to table-top height.As you suck on the mouthpiece, smoke is drawn down into the water chamber with a distinctive bubbling sound. It is cool and tastes silky smooth – utterly unlike cigarette smoke. Contrary to myth, all the sweet smells drifting around Arab cafés are flavoured tobacco (honey and apple are popular): cannabis is never smoked in public.

THE CALIPHS OF ISLAM

For centuries following the death of the Prophet Muhammad, the head of the worldwide community of Islam was termed a caliph. Unity was rare: a group of Muslims soon disputed the succession and split away, becoming the Shia branch of Islam (standing in opposition to more mainstream Sunni Islam), and dynasties in various parts of the Muslim world often set up their own short-lived caliphates to rival the central authority. The caliphate was abolished by the secular Turkish parliament in 1924.

FESTIVALS

Lebanon's **Baalbek Festival**, held amid vast Roman temples, features world-class performers in classical music, opera and jazz, while the **Beiteddine Festival**, staged at a magnificent eighteenth-century mountain palace, concentrates on Arab music and performers. Both are held in July and August. Jordan's **Jerash Festival**, which presents both Western and Arab music alongside dance and drama in an equally impressive Roman setting, also takes place in July.

ENCHANTING OASES

• **Israel**
South of Beersheva in the Negev desert is the extraordinary **Ein Avdat** – a spring and waterfall of cold water, concealed in a lush canyon.

• **Jordan**
The string of "desert castles" (actually, Islamic-era lodges) east of Amman leads to **Azraq Oasis**, desert hideout of Lawrence of Arabia.

• **Saudia Arabia**
In the desert south of Dhahran lies Hofuf, a town located within the vast date-palm oasis of **Al-Hasa**.

• **UAE**
The romantic oasis of **Liwa**, south of Abu Dhabi, is set amidst the dunes on the edge of the famous Empty Quarter of Saudi Arabia.

CATCHING A BASEBALL GAME AT WRIGLEY FIELD • SCOPING OUT THE SCENE ON MIAMI'S OCEAN DRIVE • MAKING LIKE KING KONG AT THE EMPIRE STATE BUILDING • FINDING PARADISE ON KAUAI'S NORTH SHORE • WITNESSING POWER IN ACTION ON CAPITOL HILL • HIKING HALF DOME IN YOSEMITE • CHASING STORMS IN TORNADO ALLEY • EATING BARBECUE IN TEXAS HILL COUNTRY • GOING TO THE SUN IN GLACIER NATIONAL PARK • ATTENDING A CEREMONIAL DANCE AT TAOS PUEBLO • WATCHING THE FISH FLY AT PIKE PLACE MARKET • STROLLING THROUGH DOWNTOWN SAVANNAH • HIT THE HUT: ATTENDING NATURE'S BOOT CAMP • IN HIGH SPIRITS ON THE BOURBON TRAIL • THE QUINTESSENTIAL SNACK IN AMERICA'S FOOD CAPITAL GETTING IN LINE AT MARDI GRAS • SPENDING A WEEKEND IN WINE COUNTRY • RIDING HIGH ON THE BLUE RIDGE PARKWAY • BIKING THE GOLDEN GATE BRIDGE • RIDING THE SLICKROCK IN MOAB • MIGHTY REAL IN LAS VEGAS • A NIGHT AT THE LOBSTER POUND • RECONSIDERING THE WILD WEST IN MONUMENT VALLEY • LEAVING IT ALL BEHIND ON THE APPALACHIAN TRAIL SEA KAYAKING IN PRINCE WILLIAM SOUND • CRUISING THE INSIDE PASSAGE • CEDAR POINT: THE ROLLER COASTER CAPITAL OF THE WORLD • HIKING THE CHILKOOT TRAIL • CHECKING THE PROGRESS OF THE CRAZY HORSE MEMORIAL • CHOOSING THE RIGHT PHILLY CHEESESTEAK MAKING A MESS WITH MARYLAND CRABS • LEAF-PEEPING ALONG ROUTE 100 • SIDESTEPPING ASH AND LAVA ON KILAUEA • BURNING MAN FESTIVAL • GAZING AT A NANTUCKET SUNSET CALIFORNIA IN A CONVERTIBLE: DRIVING THE LENGTH OF HIGHWAY 1 • ON THE ROAD WITH THE GREEN TORTOISE • PLAYING BALL AT THE FIELD OF DREAMS • UP CLOSE WITH ALLIGATORS ON THE ANHINGA TRAIL • ANGLING FOR BROWN BEARS AT BROOKS FALLS • RUNNING THE NEW YORK CITY MARATHON • HALLOWEEN IN NEW YORK • BED, BARRACUDA AND BREAKFAST: JULES' UNDERSEA LODGE • LUNCHING ON CREOLE CUISINE • CELEBRATING FANTASY FEST IN KEY WEST • TRACING CIVIL RIGHTS HISTORY IN MONTGOMERY • SLEEPING NEAR THE CORNER IN WINSLOW • TAKING THE A-TRAIN THROUGH MANHATTAN • SKIING AT ALTA AND SNOWBIRD WOLF-WATCHING IN YELLOWSTONE NATIONAL PARK • TOURING GRACELAND • HITTING THE TRACK AT THE INDIANAPOLIS 500 • LOST FOR WORDS AT THE GRAND CANYON • PRIMAL POINT REYES • SPOOKED IN THE OLD SOUTH • TRAVEL THE TURQUOISE TRAIL • TOURING ALASKA BY RV • GOING BATTY IN AUSTIN • PAYING HOMAGE TO COUNTRY MUSIC • HANG-GLIDING IN THE OUTER BANKS • MAKING LIKE KING KONG AT THE EMPIRE STATE BUILDING • SETTING UP CAMP IN THE ADIRONDACKS • BIKING THE SAN ANTONIO MISSION TRAIL • HARVARD YARD: VISITING AMERICA'S SEAT OF LEARNING • SCOPING OUT THE SCENE ON MIAMI'S OCEAN DRIVE CATCHING A BASEBALL GAME AT WRIGLEY FIELD • CHASING STORMS IN TORNADO ALLEY FINDING PARADISE ON KAUAI'S NORTH SHORE • HIKING HALF DOME IN YOSEMITE • GOING TO THE SUN IN GLACIER NATIONAL PARK • ATTENDING A CEREMONIAL DANCE AT TAOS PUEBLO • WATCHING THE FISH FLY AT PIKE PLACE MARKET • STROLLING THROUGH DOWNTOWN SAVANNAH • HIT THE HUT: ATTENDING NATURE'S BOOT CAMP • IN HIGH SPIRITS ON THE BOURBON TRAIL • THE QUINTESSENTIAL SNACK IN AMERICA'S FOOD CAPITAL • GETTING IN LINE AT MARDI GRAS • SPENDING A WEEKEND IN WINE COUNTRY • RIDING HIGH ON THE BLUE RIDGE PARKWAY • BIKING THE GOLDEN GATE BRIDGE • EATING BARBECUE IN TEXAS HILL COUNTRY • RIDING THE SLICKROCK IN MOAB • MIGHTY REAL IN LAS VEGAS • A NIGHT AT THE LOBSTER POUND • RECONSIDERING THE WILD WEST IN MONUMENT VALLEY • LEAVING IT ALL BEHIND ON THE APPALACHIAN TRAIL • WITNESSING POWER IN ACTION ON CAPITOL HILL • SEA KAYAKING IN PRINCE WILLIAM SOUND • CRUISING THE INSIDE PASSAGE • CEDAR POINT: THE ROLLER COASTER CAPITAL OF THE WORLD • HIKING THE CHILKOOT TRAIL • CHECKING THE PROGRESS

USA
499–565

WOLF-WATCHING IN
YELLOWSTONE NATIONAL PARK ★ 561

MAKING LIKE KING KONG
AT THE EMPIRE STATE BUILDING ★ 501

CATCHING A BASEBALL GAME
AT WRIGLEY FIELD ★ 500

WITNESSING
POWER IN ACTION
ON CAPITOL HILL ★ 509

UNITED STATES OF AMERICA

CALIFORNIA IN
A CONVERTIBLE:
DRIVING THE LENGTH ★ 542
OF HIGHWAY 1

★ 502 CHASING STORMS
IN TORNADO ALLEY

GETTING IN LINE
AT MARDI GRAS

EATING BARBECUE ★ 547
IN TEXAS HILL COUNTRY

★ 504

ALASKA

★ 564 ANGLING FOR BROWN BEARS
AT BROOKS FALLS

★ 508 FINDING PARADISE
ON KAUAI'S NORTH SHORE

HAWAII

499 SCOPING OUT THE SCENE ON MIAMI'S OCEAN DRIVE

FLORIDA At sundown, the main promenade of Miami's hedonistic South Beach was like a gigantic movie set, where several different films were being shot simultaneously.

A 1978 Mustang pulled up outside the *Kent Hotel* and three Latino men, designer shirts unbuttoned almost down to the navel and sporting heavy gold chains, stepped out in what could have been a scene from *Scarface*. A bronzed male rollerblader in a "Gold's Gym" tank-top weaved between the pedestrian traffic that crept past the thoroughfare's swanky cocktail lounges, thrusting his hips from left to right, a gasping Pomeranian struggling to keep up. Cheesy gay porn sprang to mind. Crossing the road in the direction of the beach brought the area's famed Art Deco buildings perfectly into view – a strip of pastel yellows, blues and oranges bathed so dramatically in the fading sunlight that you could have been standing in the middle of a Disney cartoon.

As sunbathers gradually left the beach, a couple of real-life Barbie dolls with tiny waists and enormous chests lingered on the sand to be filmed for some dubious Internet site. The poolside at the *Clevelander* began to fill up with Spring Break schmoozers and girls with plenty of potential for going wild. Electronic music that earlier had drifted gently from hotel lobbies was now being pumped out in energetic beats, heralding the transformation of twilight's languorous Ocean Drive into night-time's frenetic strip of revelry – clubbers flashed synthetically manufactured smiles as they hurried to the latest place to be seen. Pretty hostesses talked to you when you stopped to have a look at the expensive restaurant menu they were touting, and the waitress at the *Kent* scribbled her number on a napkin when the three Latinos from the Mustang slapped down a generous tip.

Just another day in the neighbourhood.

500 CATCHING A BASEBALL GAME AT WRIGLEY FIELD

ILLINOIS Home to an iconic, ivy-covered outfield wall, Chicago's Wrigley Field is where America's pastime reaches its apotheosis. Though it dates to 1914, it's neither the oldest nor the smallest ballpark in the major leagues (both honours go to Boston's equally famed Fenway Park, opened two years earlier). And as for team play... well, the kindest thing to say is that the stadium and the fans that fill it have borne witness to some hard times: the home-team Chicago Cubs haven't won a World Series since 1908, the longest such streak by four decades. But for baseball purists, there's no better place to properly enjoy a game.

Nicknamed "The Friendly Confines" by Cubs' legend Ernie Banks, the idiosyncratic park anchors the buzzing neighbourhood of Wrigleyville. The stadium melds perfectly with its surroundings: along Waveland Avenue, fans wait just outside the low outfield wall hoping to catch a stray home-run (and throw it back on the field, if it's hit by the opposing

team), and the views from adjacent apartment rooftops – some sporting grandstands – are better than from the faraway seats in mega-parks elsewhere. If you can't get a ticket, pull up a stool at *Murphy's Bleachers* or *Sheffield's*, two of Wrigleyville's finer watering holes – you'll be surrounded by fans decked out in Cubs' colours.

Inside the park, the game feels more like a mammoth picnic than a high-stakes competition, particularly during summer afternoon contests. (The park didn't add lights until 1988, and the majority of Cubs' home games are still played during the day.) It's no stretch to say that fans expect to have fun rather than win: after all, why should things change now? So get a cheap seat with the so-called "Bleacher Bums" and join in the raucous sing-along of *Take Me Out to the Ball Game* during the seventh-inning stretch. If the Cubs don't win, it's really not such a shame.

501 MAKING LIKE KING KONG AT THE EMPIRE STATE BUILDING

NEW YORK The Empire State Building has been lauded as the pinnacle of Art Deco style in the 1930s, hit by an American bomber during World War II and used as a staging point for failed parachutists, aerial suiciders and, of course, an oversized Hollywood simian. However, you don't have to have a flair for drama to visit – just a taste for glorious views and a clear lack of acrophobia.

Provided you can endure the tedious queues at the base, when visiting you'll have two choices: take the conventional route to the 86th-floor observatory, or pay a few dollars more and add another sixteen storeys to your ascent. The pinnacle of the latter is the 102nd-storey observatory, sitting just below the building's spire and near its T-shaped mooring units: it was built for the structure's short-lived use as a blimp dock.

While its height is certainly impressive, the top observatory's glass-enclosed views and cramped confines don't do justice to the stunning panorama of New York laid out before your eyes. For a 200-mile view of the terrain – both leafy green and steely modern – save your money and choose the 86th-floor option. Exposed to the biting wind in the cooler months and always crowded with onlookers, this storey's observatory is nevertheless hard to beat for a visual spectacle. Aside from trying to figure out what Connecticut looks like in the distance or identifying Manhattan's many steel and mirror-glass boxes, you can also take a big gulp and look straight down to see the building's magisterial facade dropping a thousand feet below you. You can't stray too far up here, but you can peer out just enough to get an unobstructed view of the skyline of one of the world's great cities.

TORNADO ALLEY

KANSAS, NEBRASKA & OKLAHOMA The central plains may not seem the likeliest of places to find a weather wonder, but every long, hot summer these cornfield-flat states play witness to some of the most powerful storms on earth. In fact, Mother Nature gets so aggressive around here, and with such consistency, that the area – along with Texas – has been dubbed "Tornado Alley" thanks to the record number of funnel and wedge tornadoes that batter its turf each year.

This is ideal twister-tracking territory. Behind every great storm is an even greater equipped team of daredevil stormchasers who specialize in stalking tornados across the central plains from vans loaded with the latest in GPS systems, Doppler radars, satellites and lightening-detector sensors. You can join these professionals on the hunt, keeping an eye on the skies as they try to anticipate growing storms. With every cloud-gathering there is a tingle of expectation, and the hope that this is the one they're looking for: a supercell. The Holy Grail of high winds – spreading as far as a mile wide and reaching up to 300mph – this is the biggest and baddest of them all.

RECONSIDERING THE
WILD WEST
IN MONUMENT VALLEY

503

ARIZONA When you think of the American West, it's hard to conjure a more iconic image than Monument Valley, with its awesome mesas, spires of jagged sandstone and arid, desert-like plains. This is the Wild West of popular culture – a vast, empty landscape that dates back to antiquity and can make you feel at once tiny and insignificant and completely free and uninhibited. These qualities have made it the perfect location for Westerns, which is perhaps why it seems so familiar: *Stagecoach*, *The Searchers* and *How the West Was Won* are among the numerous movies that have been filmed here.

But while Hollywood favours heroic cowboys on stallions, you won't be restaging the gunfight at the OK Corral while here (head south to Tombstone, Arizona for that). Instead, this is sacred Indian country managed by the Navajo Nation, and to visit the area today is to experience the West through their eyes. From the Anasazi petroglyphs in Mystery Valley to the traditional hogans still inhabited by local Navajo, every rock here tells a story. The valley's most famous formations – like the twin buttes of the Mittens, with their skinny "thumbs" of sandstone, and the giant bulk of Hunt's Mesa – can be seen from the circular, seventeen-mile track (starting at the Visitors' Center) that's usually smothered in red dust. Navajo guides, who fill you in on local history and culture, lead 4WD rides around the track, as well as longer, usually overnight, expeditions by foot. These may start before dawn, allowing you to reach the top of a mesa before it gets too hot and watch the sunrise across a land where sand and rock stretch endlessly before you to the horizon.

THE ROUGH GUIDE TO THE WORLD USA 297

504 GETTING IN LINE AT MARDI GRAS

LOUISIANA America's most over-the-top and hedonistic spectacle, Mardi Gras (Fat Tuesday, the night before Ash Wednesday) in New Orleans reflects as much a medieval, European carnival as it does a drunken Spring Break ritual. Behind the scenes, the official celebration revolves around exclusive, invitation-only balls; for such an astonishingly big event, it can seem put on more for locals than the revellers who descend on the town, but you'll hardly be wanting for entertainment or feeling left out.

Following routes of up to seven miles long, more than sixty parades wind their way through the city's historic French Quarter. Multi-tiered floats snake along the cobblestone streets, flanked by masked horsemen, stilt-walking curiosities and, of course, second liners – dancers and passersby who informally join the procession. There's equal fun in participating as there is in looking on.

Whichever way you choose to see it, you'll probably vie at some point to catch one of the famous "throws" (strings of beads, knickers, fluffy toys – whatever is hurled by the towering float-riders into the crowd); the competition can be fierce. Float-riders, milking it for all it's worth, taunt and jeer the crowd endlessly, while along storied Bourbon Street, women bare their breasts and men drop their trousers in return for some baubles and beads.

As accompaniment, the whole celebration is set to one of the greatest soundtracks in the world: strains of funk, R&B, New Orleans Dixie and more stream out of every bar and blare off rooftops – no surprise, of course, considering the city's status as the birthplace of jazz.

You might have thought that all of this madness would have been curtailed in the wake of Hurricane Katrina, but like New Orleans, the party carries on in the face of long odds; indeed, the year following, many of the weird and wonderful costumes were made from the bright blue tarps that have swathed so much of the city since the storm.

505 THE QUINTESSENTIAL SNACK IN AMERICA'S FOOD CAPITAL

NEW YORK The long list of things to try is staring you in the face. Overstuffed pastrami sandwich at *Katz's Deli*. Foot-long hot dog out at *Nathan's* at Coney Island. Eight-course tasting menu costing a couple of hundred of dollars at *Jean Georges*, or *Per Se* or *Gramercy Tavern*. Soup dumplings costing next to nothing at any number of Chinatown holes-in-the-wall. Brunch at an impossibly cute West Village café. The bistro burger, washed down with a $2 McSorley's, at *Corner Bistro*. Then again, this is why you came to New York.

But there's one grave omission, one that may well be the most "New York" dish of all. And it's got everything to do with the water. At least that's what they say: a crusty yet chewy New York bagel, first boiled in that water before being baked, is just better because of it. Whether that comes near to the truth, no snack is more symbolic of the city than a bagel with cream cheese, piled high with lox (smoked salmon), a few slices of tomato and red onion and perhaps some capers for effect. You can find bagels nearly everywhere, of course, and many claim to be the best, but no one does it quite like *Russ and Daughters*.

It's not a restaurant or diner but an "appetizing" store, family-owned to boot, that has spent four generations brining, baking, whipping and generally perfecting the art of righteous Jewish food. It's mostly known for its smoked fish, and you can't go wrong with any of their salmon offerings (or their whitefish or sable, for that matter). But the salty belly lox, cured rather than smoked, may be most toothsome of all. Lay it over their own home-made, soul-satisfying cream cheese, smeared on a garlic bagel, also made in-house, and you've got the best accompaniment to a cup of coffee and the *New York Times* known to man.

506 SPENDING A WEEKEND IN WINE COUNTRY

CALIFORNIA With its rolling green hills, bucolic landscapes and small towns heavy on antique charm, California's Wine Country, centring on Napa and Sonoma valleys, is one of the most beautiful places in the West. Beyond touring the wineries – Beringer, Silver Oak, Stag's Leap, Robert Mondavi and many more, all of which allow you to sample the goods – there's no shortage of things to see and do. Come here for a weekend retreat (preferably not at the peak of summer, when the hordes descend), and your first instinct might be to pack in as much as possible. But in a place where the main point is to relax, indulge and melt away the stresses of modern life, that's the last thing you should do.

Instead, aim for just a few choice tastes of the good life. Start with a spot of nature, either driving the Silverado Trail (parallel to Hwy-29), taking in the mountains and vineyards along the way, or enjoying a peaceful walk through the woods in Jack London State Historic Park, once ranchland owned by the famed naturalist writer. Next, rest your aching bones and revitalize your senses by checking into one of the resort spas near Calistoga. At Dr Wilkinson's Hot Springs, dip yourself in a mix of heated mineral water and volcanic ash, or at Mount View Spa, enjoy the mud baths and herbal applications, as well as aromatherapy, hydrotherapy and other refined New Age treatments that pamper both the body and soul.

Round out your experience with a great, even legendary, meal at one of the region's many gourmet restaurants; these days the area is known as much for food as the vino. Foremost among these is Thomas Keller's *French Laundry*, an icon of California Cuisine known for its blend of fresh local ingredients and creative, spellbinding presentation. It won't come cheap and you'll have to reserve months in advance, but it's reason enough to visit.

507 RIDING HIGH ON THE BLUE RIDGE PARKWAY

VIRGINIA & NORTH CAROLINA Slicing through some of the most stunning scenery in the country, the Blue Ridge Parkway winds its way along the crest of the Appalachian Mountains, from Shenandoah National Park in Virginia to Great Smoky Mountains National Park between North Carolina and Tennessee. Once dotted with isolated frontier communities where bluegrass was born, today you'll find traces of the region's history – like old gristmills, abandoned wooden barns and ramshackle diners – scattered along the road, but in truth much of what has been preserved is aimed squarely at the tourist trade. What the parkway is best for is simply a heavy dose of nature at its finest.

The first part of the drive cuts through northern Virginia, and here the ridge is very apparent, sometimes narrowing to a ledge not much wider than the road. The central section is much less dramatic – the land is heavily farmed and the road busier with local traffic, especially around Roanoke. But the lower highway, which snakes through North Carolina, is the most spectacular part. There's plenty of kitschy development here (the town of Blowing Rock is a full-scale resort, with shopping malls and themed motels), but the views are astonishing – at nearby Grandfather Mountain, on Hwy-221 one mile south of the parkway, a mile-high swinging bridge hangs over an 80ft chasm with 360° views.

Further south, near Mount Pisgah, the road reaches its highest point. As you ascend toward it you'll have numerous chances to stop at overlooks, or just pull onto the shoulder, for breathtaking vistas: hazy blue ridges, smothered in vast swathes of hickory, dogwood and birch and groves of mountain ash bursting with orange berries.

508
FINDING PARADISE ON KAUAI'S NORTH SHORE

HAWAII Kauai is the Hawaii you dream about. Spectacular South Seas scenery, white-sand beaches, pounding surf, laid-back island life – it's all here. While the other Hawaiian islands have the above to varying degrees, none has quite the breath-taking beauty nor sheer variety of beguiling landscapes of Kauai. And none has a shoreline as magnificent as the Na Pali Coast ("the cliffs" in Hawaiian), where lush valleys are separated by staggering knife-edge ridges of rock, some towering almost 3000ft tall and all clad in glowing green vegetation that makes them resemble vast pleated velvet curtains.

The one road that circles Kauai peters out on the North Shore. Shrinking ever narrower to cross a series of one-lane wooden bridges, it finally gives up where lovely Ke'e Beach nestles at the foot of a mighty mountain. Swim out a short distance here, and you'll glimpse the mysterious, shadowy cliffs in the distance, dropping into the ocean.

Now deserted, the remote valleys beyond the end of the road once supported large Hawaiian populations, who navigated the fearsome waves between them in canoes. The only way to reach the valleys these days is on foot. One of the world's great hikes, the eleven-mile Kalalau Trail is a long, muddy scramble: one moment you're perched high above the Pacific on an exposed ledge, and the next you're wading a fast-flowing mountain stream. Your reward at the far end – an irresistible campsite on a long golden beach, where you can breathe the purest air on Earth, explore the tumbling waterfalls of Kalalau Valley and then gaze at the star-filled sky into the night – is a little slice of heaven.

509 WITNESSING POWER IN ACTION ON CAPITOL HILL

WASHINGTON DC Dominated by massive monuments, museums, war memorials and statues, Washington DC represents the purest expression of political might. But the seat of government of the world's only superpower is a surprisingly accessible place – it's by the people, for the people, after all – and though certain security measures may seem an obstacle, you shouldn't miss the chance to see the corridors of power, and maybe even catch a glimpse of the action.

Wherever you go in DC, it'll be hard to avoid the looming, cast-iron dome of the US Capitol building. From its marvellous Rotunda (styled after Rome's Pantheon) to the stately figures of National Statuary Hall, you won't be disappointed (and may be slightly awed) by the country's centre of legislative power – pick up a ticket for a free tour at the kiosk on the building's southwest side. For an upclose look at the angry speech-making and partisan posturing of Congress, however, you'll need to get a special pass in advance of your trip.

Although "Dubya" and his advisors stay well out of the public eye, you can still tour the seat of the executive branch, aka the White House. The Georgian Revival home of the president is full of historical furnishings and rooms decked out in various styles; if you make reservations months in advance you can check out sights like the richly draped, chandeliered East Room, the silk-trimmed and portrait-heavy Green Room, the oval, French-decorated Blue Room and a glittery display of presidential china.

Perhaps the most rewarding spot for actually seeing the American government at work is the US Supreme Court. The building itself is stately enough, with its grand Greek Revival columns and pediment, but the real sight is all nine justices arrayed behind their bench, meticulously probing the lawyers making their arguments. From these arguments the Court writes its opinions, affirming or striking down existing laws and at times making history before your very eyes.

510 HIKING HALF DOME IN YOSEMITE

CALIFORNIA Even if you start out at dawn from Yosemite Valley, after five hours you're still not at the top of Half Dome, whose looming, truncated form ("like it had been sliced with a knife") makes it one of the most iconic mountains in North America. The sun is beating down, you're dehydrated and the most challenging section is still ahead. In front of you, rearing up at an impossibly steep angle, lies a vast curving sheet of virtually smooth gray granite. There's no way you'd get a grip in even the best sticky-rubber hiking boots but, fortunately, some determined souls have forged the way, drilling holes in the ancient rock and attaching a series of cables and wooden steps. Help yourself to a pair of leather gloves stashed at the base of the "staircase", grab the cables and haul your way up the final 400ft to the 320-acre summit plateau. It's an exhilarating finish to a superb hike.

From the top, nearly 9000ft up, the dramatic views will render you speechless. Those who dare can edge toward Half Dome's lip and dangle their feet over the side, while the very brave (or very foolish) may inch out along a projecting finger of rock for a vertiginous look straight down the near-vertical face. But neither is necessary to appreciate how far you've come – just turn to gaze back at your route along a section of the famed 212-mile John Muir Trail; even the two magnificent waterfalls you passed – the Vernal and Nevada falls – look puny from this height. Then take in the snowy spine of the Sierra Nevada mountains, the rippling granite sheets that run up to the summit of Cloud's Rest and the wonderland of forests and alpine meadows that comprise Yosemite National Park. Sit back, take a deep breath and enjoy the view

511 STROLLING THROUGH DOWNTOWN SAVANNAH

GEORGIA When an intrepid British Utopian named James Oglethorpe founded Savannah in 1733, he thought he could tame the local marshes and alligators without the aid of slaves or – more preposterous – hard liquor. The latter ban fell by the wayside less than twenty years later, and Savannahians have been devoted to immoderation ever since. Any walking tour of the three-square-mile downtown historic district should, for tradition's sake, be accompanied by a cold beer in a perfectly legal "to-go cup". (The traditional local tipple, Chatham Artillery Punch, is more safely appreciated sitting down, however.)

One element of Oglethorpe's vision that did stick was the city's layout – a repetition of grids and squares that have become 21 miniature parks, each offering a different proportion of dappled shade, fountains and monuments. The squares are most alluring in the spring, when the azalea, dogwood and honey-rich magnolia trees are in full bloom. But even in the thick of an August heat wave, when the air is like a sauna

and the greenery is growing wildly up the cast-iron balconies, the squares offer a respite from the untamed mugginess. The sunlight shimmers through craggy oak boughs and Spanish moss, the cicadas drone and cars motor laconically around the cobblestone streets. The stately homes that face each square represent all of the most decadent styles of the eighteenth and nineteenth centuries: Neoclassical, Federal, Regency, Georgian, French Second Empire and Italianate.

"The Belle of Georgia", as the city is known, hasn't always been so; for much of the twentieth century, decadence had slipped into outright decay. But in 1955, seven elderly ladies banded together against developers to prevent the 1821 Davenport House from being turned into a parking lot, and the Historic Savannah Foundation was born. Fortunately, no such effort is required of today's casual visitor – you can just stroll, sip your drink and watch the centuries roll by.

512 GOING TO THE SUN IN GLACIER NATIONAL PARK

MONTANA Sitting at the northern edge of America's Rocky Mountains, magnificent Glacier National Park's craggy cliffs, awe-inspiring peaks and beautiful deep-blue lakes are, true to the park's name, a result of massive tongues of ice invading the land from the north some 20,000 years ago. While the trails through this magical terrain are stunning – leading you past colourful mountain meadows, towering columns of rock up to 1.6 billion years old and all manner of elk, bighorn sheep and mountain goats, as well as grizzly and black bears – you can also gaze at some of the park's best, and most harrowing, views along the Going-to-the-Sun Road.

Cutting across the middle of the park, connecting the wooded groves of Montana's Rockies with the sprawling dry expanse of the Great Plains, the road offers an eye-popping jaunt over the Continental Divide, where at Logan Pass (6680ft) there's a Visitors' Center and a chance to stretch your legs in the shadow of the park's mighty peaks. By the time you get there, you'll have ascended through gently rolling foothills from charming, low-lying Lake MacDonald to a sudden series of switchbacks that rise ever higher with each mile.

The stunning views from the road as it contours along the jagged face of the Rockies feature sheer precipices that drop far down into shadowy forests, frozen rivers of ice framed by stark canyon walls and splashing waterfalls fed by snowmelt. While the road can be perilous at times, its narrow width straining to accommodate passing cars and its sheer-edged drop-offs not allowing much room for driving error, a white-knuckle ride is simply not possible, due to the slow speed of traffic during the peak summer season and most drivers being so overcome by the visual splendour that they forget about things like speed, direction or destination.

513 ATTENDING A CEREMONIAL DANCE AT TAOS PUEBLO

NEW MEXICO The sun shines down from the cloudless turquoise sky, but your feet are cold. You stamp them impatiently, squint your eyes against the glare and tuck your mitten-swaddled hands under your armpits. The rest of the crowd seems unconcerned, even though the scheduled starting time was surely hours ago, so you continue breathing in the freezing air, fragrant with wood smoke, and watching your breath cloud in front of you. Inside the adobe church Christmas Mass has come and gone, and people mill around the open plaza greeting friends and chatting quietly, the elders and women settling into folding chairs with blankets over their laps or wrapped around their shoulders. Some begin to pay holiday visits inside the mud buildings that rise up, in haphazard stacks, three or four storeys high.

And then, from the direction of Taos Mountain, which stands beyond the soft edges of the ancient pueblo, you hear a distant drone. The murmuring crowd goes quiet. The muffled drumbeats grow clearer, now accompanied by the rhythmic shimmer of bells, and you forget about your feet. The waiting throng forms a border around the pueblo's sacred dance space, instinctively giving prime spots to residents of this thousand-year-old settlement. The crowd parts easily as a procession of men arrives – they are no longer men but deer, their antlers swinging, their dainty hooves picking at the earth. The drums boom, the chanting swells and the transformation is complete – the circle is a forest glade, and hunters trace the edges, taking aim with their symbolic arrows.

Hours pass, or perhaps only minutes, and then the drums stop. The illusion lifts: these are mere men, some boys, labouring under slippery elk hides, many of which look as though they were butchered only this morning. Shirtless, the men are breathing hard from the rigour of the hunt, giddy and sombre at the same time. The women now take their place in the circle, making delicate hand motions with switches of piñon tree, and you stamp your feet again, tuck your hands tighter and surrender once more to the heart-pounding drums.

514 RIDING THE SLICKROCK IN MOAB

UTAH The allure of the small town of Moab, 238 miles southeast of Salt Lake City and 325 miles from Denver, lies not in the inspiring desert landscape that surrounds it, nor the stunning moonscape of ochre rocks, deep folded canyons, mesas or spires. Nor is it the spectacular landforms in nearby Arches National Park, the gurgling Colorado River, which swoops past town, or the landscape of mesas and buttes that stretch out before a backdrop of the snow-capped La Sal Mountains. No, what makes the place really remarkable is the incredible grip offered by the sandpapery surfaces of a group of contorted sandstone rocks near town – the location of the exceptional Slickrock mountain-bike trail.

From a distance these rocks look smooth, their neat shapes resembling a giant basket of eggs, but up close they offer bikers traction that's positively unreal, and with it a sense of possessing superhuman skills. You'll be able to glide across areas where you'd expect the bike to slip out from under you and astonish yourself with the grades you can climb and descend – all adding up to a mind-blowing roller-coaster ride in wonderful desert surroundings. It's all so extraordinary that the trail – little more than a series of dots daubed on the rock to form a 10-mile loop – has become the most famous ride in the mountain-biking world. But perhaps best of all, it doesn't really matter how experienced a mountain biker you are: the Slickrock experience is accessible to anyone who can ride a bike, thanks to a 2.5 mile practice loop that never strays more than a half-hour's walk from the parking lot.

515 HALLOWEEN IN NYC

NEW YORK Halloween is a big event in America, and nowhere more so than in New York, where a massive parade takes over much of downtown Manhattan – from the bottom of SoHo to the top of Chelsea – making it the biggest Halloween celebration on the planet and the only major night parade in the US. It's a totally over-the-top, costumed street party, at which it's impossible not to have a good time. New York's Halloween has become something of a gay event in recent years, although everyone, gay or straight, young or old, uses it as the last pre-winter excuse to go nuts in the streets while wearing just about anything from a Frankenstein mask to a clingfilm wrap bridal gown – maybe at the same time.

The Halloween Parade runs up Sixth Avenue from just south of Spring Street in SoHo to 23rd Street in Chelsea. Nearly two million spectators descend on downtown Manhattan to check out the costumed proceedings each year, so head to the route well in advance of the 7pm starting time if you want to be able to see anything. It's worth it though, as there's nothing that beats the views of the parade's tremendous skeletal puppets, unique features of New York's celebrations, that loom overhead, pointing their bony fingers towards the crowds. The parade usually runs two to three hours from start to finish; if you stay in one spot, you can see the whole thing pass in around an hour.

Watching the parade is all very well, but if you're really going to do Halloween in New York, you need to put on a costume. You could opt for the classic scary – witches, vampires, devils – and non-scary – French maid, King Arthur, Winnie the Pooh – looks, or dress up as an "overnight wonder" from recent popular movies or current events. You could go down the conceptual-costume route (don a pig-nose mask and wave a Canadian flag and you're Canadian Bacon) or raise the oufit ante with a really scary number, the kind that's done so convincingly that no one's even sure it's a costume at all. And then there's always the option of going in drag – scary in a whole other way and not really a costume for some. But whatever you choose to go as, go the whole hog, and remember that, above all, it's the costume that will determine what sort of night you have – and who you end up spending it with.

516 TRAVEL THE TURQUOISE TRAIL

NEW MEXICO A stunning 52-mile stretch of Highway 14 – known as the Turquoise Trail – links Santa Fe and Albuquerque. It's a day-tripper's delight: start with a bit of ghost town charm in Cerrillos, where you'll be greeted by little more than tumbleweed, dirt roads and empty western storefronts complete with hitching posts. Continue south, taking in golden hills, desert meadows and swaths of startling blue sky, and head to the mining town-cum-artist enclave Madrid. Here you can shop for turquoise jewellery, check out local art and visit the Old Coal Mine Museum. Top off your trip with a beer at the *Mine Shaft Tavern*, an old roadhouse-style saloon that boasts the longest bar in New Mexico.

517 AURA CLEANSING IN OLD FLORIDA

FLORIDA Back in the day, when Florida was still Edenic wilderness, the state lured many varieties of eccentrics and freethinkers, and the Cassadaga spiritualist community of latter-day sibyls, founded in 1895, is one such transplantation that thrived. It's actually the oldest practicing religious society in the Southeast, and the quaint village today is a harmonic convergence of psychics, mediums, healers and clairvoyants, espousing self-realization classes, guided meditations, private readings and personal messages from the Other Side. New Agers, nosy Parkers, and dyed-in-the-wool nay-sayers, all are welcome.

518 BIKING THE GOLDEN GATE BRIDGE

CALIFORNIA Like a bright-orange necklace draped across the neck of San Francisco Bay, the Golden Gate Bridge is said to be the most photographed man-made structure in the world, and no wonder: you can snap a postcard-worthy picture of it from almost any hilltop in the city. But to really experience the span, you need to get close. You need to feel it. And the best way to do that is by biking it. The eight-mile trip from Fisherman's Wharf over the bridge to Sausalito is truly spectacular and, just as important, truly flat.

Rent some wheels at the base of Hyde Street Pier, then cruise through manicured Aquatic Park. It's a short climb to Fort Mason Park, where you can catch eerie glimpses of Alcatraz through the thick cypress trees. Swoop down to Marina Green, past the legions of kite flyers and the small harbour, and you'll soon be gliding past Crissy Field, replete with newly planted sea grasses, sand dunes and the occasional great blue heron. Grab a grass-fed beef hot dog from the popular *Let's Be Frank* cart, then press on to the end of the path, where at historic Fort Point you can peer up into the bridge's awesome latticework underbelly.

You'll have to double back a few hundred yards to the road leading up to the bridge approach. But the steep ascent is worth it as you serenely pedal past the mobs of tourists and onto the bike and pedestrian path. As the crowds thin out, you can contemplate the bridge's stunning Art Deco lines and mind-boggling scale. The towers rise 65 stories and contain 600,000 rivets apiece. The three-foot-wide suspension cables comprise 80,000 miles of pencil-thin steel wire. More darkly, over a thousand people have jumped to their deaths from this very trail.

There's one last viewing platform on the Marin County anchorage, after which it's time to drift downhill along the twisting road to the quaint town of Sausalito, where you can catch the ferry back to San Francisco. Though it hardly seems possible, the view from the ferry landing may be the most magnificent of the whole journey, especially at sunset, when the white lights of the city glow against the darkening bay.

519 MAKING A MESS WITH MARYLAND CRABS

MARYLAND Hands stained red with Old Bay seasoning, fingers so slick with crab fat you can hardly clutch your beer, maybe a few stray bits of shell stuck in your hair or to your cheek – that's the sort of dishevelled look you should be aiming for at a Maryland crab feast.

"Picking" hard-shell steamed blue crabs is a sport Marylanders attack with gusto from May to October – though anyone will tell you that the heaviest, juiciest number-one "jimmies" are available only near the end of the summer. That's when the most popular crab restaurants up and down the bay have lines out the door, and every other backyard in Baltimore seems to ring with the sound of wood mallets smacking on crab legs.

It's simplicity itself: a bushel or two of crabs in the steamer with some beer and lashings of spicy Old Bay, and yesterday's newspaper laid out on a big picnic table, along with a few rolls of paper towels. What else? Only more beer (cold this time), some corn on the cob, a hot dish or two ... nothing to distract from the main attraction.

Then it's down to business. The process starts with yanking what can only be described as an easy-open pull tab on the crab's under-shell. From there, dig out the yellowish fat called "mustard", as well as the gills, then snap the hard-back shell in half and proceed to scoop out the sweet, succulent flesh. Soon you'll be whacking the claws just so with a wooden mallet and gouging the meat out with a knife.

It's easier than it sounds, and the crabmeat is certainly a powerful motivator for thorough picking (and fast learning). In the process, you can't help but marvel at man's cleverness when it comes to eating critters with the prickliest of defences. But maybe that's just the beer talking.

520 MIGHTY REAL IN LAS VEGAS

NEVADA New York City has its skyscrapers, Cairo its pyramids, Paris the Eiffel Tower, Venice its canals. Las Vegas? It's got all the above, and then some.

People travel round the globe in search of the authentic. But you won't find this in Vegas. In its place are simulacra, kitschy homage and pure, unadulterated spectacle. Here, in the middle of the Nevada desert, hotel entrepreneurs play an ever-higher-stakes game of "Can you top this?", and everything has to be newer, bigger, and brighter than before. In fact, the newness of everything is a fake, too. What's new really means what's been done before and re-imagined. The Forum Shops at *Caesars Palace*? A cunningly themed shopping mall that's an indoor re-creation of Rome's open-air bazaar, where the "sky" (well, the ceiling) changes as the day goes on. Nobu Matsuhisa's inviting namesake restaurant in the *Hard Rock Hotel*? A splashier replica of his original, internationally acclaimed raw-fish emporium in Manhattan. It's no wonder that so much of the big-ticket night-time entertainment is centred around magicians and gravity-defying acts like Cirque du Soleil. The whole of Las Vegas is an illusion, and one that to most people is utterly irresistible – and, just as importantly, unabashedly, trashily American. Who needs the whiff of authenticity when you've got all this in one place? The smoky glass pyramid of the *Luxor*, from which emanates the world's most powerful beam of light, is heralded by an enormous sphinx. The choreographed fountains at the giant lake in front of the *Bellagio* can't help but thrill. You can ride on a gondola at *The Venetian* – inside the hotel – or a roller-coaster at *New York-New York*. Most importantly, you can sustain the illusion for as long as you want – or can afford. No wonder no one ever wants to leave.

521 A NIGHT AT THE LOBSTER POUND

MAINE You're seated at a picnic table at *Two Lights Lobster Shack*, which has be one of the most picturesque spots in the country: an unassuming, clapboard restaurant with a storybook lighthouse to the left and craggy cliffs pummelled by an unruly sea to the right. Maine's slogan is "The Way Life Should Be", and here, along its gorgeous, corrugated coastline, you can't help but agree. That is, of course, if you're able to think of anything other than the red, hot challenge in front of you – one freshly steamed Maine lobster, waiting to be cracked open.

Eating Maine lobster is a culinary rite of passage for visitors to the state. It requires tools (nutcracker, teeny-tiny fork), patience and enough hubris to believe that you can look cool even while wearing a disposable bib. It's smart to bring along an experienced lobster slayer; your first lobster can be intimidating, and it's nice to have a bit of guidance (as well as someone to take that requisite embarrassing photograph).

When you're ready to begin, crack the claws in half, pull out the meat with your little fork and dip it in the melted butter. Lobster meat comes well-defended, so be wary of sharp points along the shell. The tail follows the claws: tear it from the body, pushing the meat from the end. Finally (if you're feeling emboldened), pull off the legs to suck out the last bit of flesh. There is no other meat like lobster – tender, sweet, elusive – and in Maine, where lobster is king, the crimson crustacean is celebrated with parades, festivals and an energetic devotion that's shared by everyone

At its best, a lobster dinner should be an all-around sensory experience. Breathe in the salty ocean breezes. Listen for the booms coming from the lighthouse. Finally, lick the butter off your fingers, remove the bib and give your dining partner a high five – you've just taken part in a Maine institution.

522 CASTLES MADE OF SAND: ACTING LIKE A KID AT CANNON BEACH

OREGON Dreaming of a forum for your long-repressed artistic abilities? Hoping to construct a life-size sand-version of Elvis, Jesus or someone else close to your heart, then have it washed away with the afternoon tide?

Sandcastle Day in Cannon Beach offers just the opportunity – along with the chance to have your creation gawked at by thousands of onlookers, in America's oldest sandcastle-building competition. Others may have surpassed it in size since its debut in 1964, but there's something to be said for taking part in the original. The field is limited to 150 entrants, so you may have some qualms about taking some expert's place, but don't worry too much; unless you've won in a comp before, you won't be eligible for the "masters" competition – where the architects gets serious with their sand.

523 JUMPING THROUGH HOOPS TO SEE THE HULA

HAWAII In a state filled with some of the country's most lavish resorts, where you generally go to sleep late and relax on the beach, it's well-nigh perverse to camp in a park, rise before sunset and head on a bus to the top of a mountain – meant to be off-limits to the general public – for the ceremonial beginning of a hula festival. Of course, coming to Molokai in the first place, the Hawaiian island best known for its leper colony, seems somewhat perverse, too. But everything here is so refreshingly unpretentious and uncommercialized that the appeal soon becomes obvious. As does that of the hula festival, Ka Hula Piko; this is, after all, where the art purportedly began. The sound of the conch shell signals the start. The dancers' movements steadily increase in intensity. The celebration continues down under the trees at Papohaku Beach Park, not far from a blindingly beautiful strand of golden sand abutting crashing crystal-blue waters. The pre-dawn wakeup call becomes a distant memory.

524 SEA KAYAKING IN PRINCE WILLIAM SOUND

ALASKA As you manoeuvre your way towards the towering face of one of Alaska's many tidewater glaciers, the gentle crunch of ice against the fibreglass hull of your kayak sounds faintly ominous. It's nothing, though, compared to the thunderclap that echoes across the water when a great wall of ice peels away from the glacier and sends waves surging toward you. Your first reaction is quite naturally a jolt of fear, but no need to panic: if you're at least 500 yards away from the glacier face (as any sensible paddler is), the danger will have dissipated by the time whatever's left of the waves reaches you.

Watching glaciers calve while paddling round a frozen margarita of opaque blue water and brash ice is an undoubted highlight of sea kayaking in Prince William Sound. Perhaps better still are the opportunities for viewing marine life here. Seals often loll around on icebergs close to glaciers, while sea otters swim in the frigid waters, protected by the wonderfully thick fur that made them prized by the eighteenth-century Russian traders who partly colonized Alaska. In deeper water, look for pods of orca, which cruise the waterways searching for their favourite food, seals (no wonder they hang back on the icebergs). You might even spot a few humpback whales, which congregate in small groups and breach spectacularly on occasion. Keep a splash-proof camera handy at all times.

Even if you miss out on a great action photo, there is considerable pleasure in just gliding around the generally calm waters of the fjords, where cliffs clad in Sitka spruce and Douglas fir rise steeply from the depths. For full atmospheric effect, stay in a simple Forest Service cabin or camp out on a small beach or at a designated campsite in one of the state marine parks; it's a wonderfully relaxing way to while away a few days – falling sheets of ice aside, of course.

525 LEAVING IT ALL BEHIND ON THE APPALACHIAN TRAIL

GEORGIA–MAINE Hiking the Appalachian Trail, the epic trek that stretches 2186 miles from the peak of Springer Mountain in Georgia to the top of Mount Katahdin in Maine, changes your perspective on life, whether you want it to or not. When your house weighs a pound, your job involves walking from sunrise to sunset and your nights are filled with strangers' stories round roaring campfires, the mundane routines of the modern world are replaced with the realities of survival: water, gear, aching joints and the insatiable rumbling in your stomach.

A popular saying on the AT is that the only thing that separates a hiker from a hobo is a thin layer of Gore-Tex. So why do so many choose to spend upwards of four months walking a distance that could be covered by a car in two days? As you plan your route across the snowcapped peaks of the Smokies at the end of winter, then the indigo waves of the Blue Ridge Mountains in early spring, the grassy green mounds of the Shenandoahs in the heat of mosquito season and finally the striking profiles of the Presidentials in early fall, you find there's a sublime satisfaction in mapping out your future, one mountain at a time. (Most thru-hikers walk from south to north, to catch the best weather.)

But the trail is really about those countless days when you walk twenty-five miles through three thunderstorms and over six mountains, and arrive at your campsite feeling exhausted yet triumphantly alive. That and the sleepy towns to which you hitchhike for supplies, where welcoming locals ply you with pitchers of beer at the local bar and blueberry pancakes for breakfast and offer lifts to buy new shoes for the next leg of your trip.

526 CRUISING THE INSIDE PASSAGE

ALASKA There's little better than sitting on deck and nursing a warm nightcap sometime around 11pm, as the sun slowly dips towards the horizon and you cruise past mile after gorgeous mile of spruce- and hemlock-choked shoreline. If you're lucky, whales will make an appearance; perhaps just a fluke or a tail but maybe a full-body breach. This is Alaska's Inside Passage, flanked by impenetrable snow-capped coastal mountains and incised by hairline fjords that create an interlocking archipelago of over a thousand densely forested islands.

Gliding into port at successive small settlements, you can't help but think these towns insignificant after the large-scale drama of the surrounding landscape. They cling to the few tiny patches of flat land, their streets spilling out onto a network of boardwalks over the sea. Shops, streets and even large salmon canneries are perched picturesquely along the waterside on spruce poles.

Everything is green, courtesy of the low clouds which cloak the surrounding hills and offer frequent rain. The dripping leaves, sodden mosses and wispy mist seem to suit ravens and bald eagles. You'll see them everywhere: ravens line up along the railings overlooking the small boat harbours while bald eagles perch, solitary and regal, in the trees above.

The next stop is Glacier Bay National Park, a vast wonderland of ice and barren rock where massive tidewater glaciers push right into the ocean. The ship lingers a few hours here as everyone trains their eyes on the three-mile-wide face where walls of ice periodically crumble away and crash into the iceberg-flecked sea. The schedule is pressing and it is time to move on, and the moment you turn away, the loudest rumble of the day tells you you've just missed the big one.

527

OHIO The air of anticipation on the platform is palpable, but you're trying not to think about what comes next. You scan the crowd for a sympathetic face, but to no avail; everyone is feverish with excitement. Are they all mad? The train rounds the corner suddenly, its brakes exhaling along with its passengers. It comes to a rest alongside you, bringing into sharp relief your seat and its present occupant, a girl who is sobbing. Your knees buckle slightly and you step in. The safety bar locks over your lap: there is no going back. Above the rallying cries of your fellow riders, one question screams inside your head: "Why am I here?"

"Here" is Cedar Point, the Roller Coaster Capital of the World, which sits on the shores of Lake Erie in Sandusky, Ohio, seventy miles west of Cleveland. Though the carnival atmosphere, corn dogs and freedom to act like a five-year-old are all compelling reasons to spend a day at this massive amusement park, the real draw is the profusion of rides. From antique cars and bucking horse carousels to a giant swing set and the sinister Demon Drop – an experience not unlike a ten-storey freefall – nearly seventy rides stand ready to spin you, soak you, flip you upside down and heave you to and fro. None, however, manages to do so quite so frighteningly as the undisputed headliners, the roller coasters. Seventeen dot the park – more than anywhere else on the planet – including a fair share of the fastest, steepest and longest thrill rides ever designed, like the perennial favourite, the Magnum XL-200.

The train climbs the Magnum's first hill with a cold determination. You can see nothing but the blue sky above. Now is not the time to steal a glance over the side, but you can't help it and so you do and immediately wish you hadn't. For far longer than seems sensible, the train presses up the hopelessly narrow track. Abruptly the screams begin in earnest, portents of the 60-degree descent. On cloudless days like this one it's possible to see Canada from the ride's zenith 205ft off the ground, but it's hard to focus when your life is passing before your eyes. Ninety heart-pounding seconds later it's all over and you're still in one piece. There's only one place to go: back in line.

CEDAR POINT:

THE ROLLER COASTER CAPITAL OF THE WORLD

528 HIKING THE CHILKOOT TRAIL

ALASKA The long, steep, hand-over-hand slog up The Scales on the Chilkoot Trail somehow connects you to the Gold Rush hopefuls who made the same journey over a century ago. Even though it is a pleasant summer day and your pack only weighs thirty pounds, you can begin to get a sense of the exhaustion felt by those bound for the Klondike, who hauled a ton of goods over this pass in winter. Thousands of miners came this way, and industries developed to serve them. When the rush was over everything was left where it stood, and today hiking the 33-mile Chilkoot Trail from Skagway to Lake Bennett, British Columbia, is like walking though a giant wilderness museum.

Entrepreneurs built an aerial tramway to carry all their gear, and you can still see coils of heavy wire, twisted metal fittings and the hollow ruin of an old steam boiler. Glass bottles and collapsed huts recall the winter of 1897–98 when the route was a series of boisterous camps. And right at the top of the pass keen fossickers will find a stash of rolled up canvas boats which were never used. The idea was to carry them to the Yukon River then float down to the goldfields. For reasons unknown, they were discarded along the way.

Artefacts aside, it is gorgeous country, initially among tall forests of spruce and hemlock. As you climb, these fall away to reveal long views of turquoise sub-Arctic lakes backed by the snow-capped mountains that mark the US–Canada border. There is no accommodation and nowhere to buy food along the way, but campsites are well spaced. The trail finishes at Lake Bennett, where several days a week you can board the wonderful White Pass and Yukon Route railway for the winding journey back to Skagway.

529 CHECKING THE PROGRESS OF THE CRAZY HORSE MEMORIAL

SOUTH DAKOTA Angered by the completion of Mount Rushmore in 1941, a group of Lakota Sioux chiefs led by Henry Standing Bear asked sculptor Korczak Ziolkowski to build a monument to the Native American legend known as Crazy Horse: victor of The Battle of the Little Big Horn; a leader who never signed a treaty; and a warrior who never surrendered. Mount Rushmore, just seventeen miles down the road, was big – this had to be bigger. As Henry Standing Bear put it, "we want to let the white man know we have heroes too".

The first thing that hits you when you gaze upon the memorial, deep in the Black Hills of South Dakota, is actually its enormity. While the images of Mount Rushmore were carved onto existing rockface, Ziolkowski reshaped an entire mountain, blasting, drilling and carving, slab by slab, an image of the revered warrior atop his horse, his arm stretched over the land he fought to defend in the 1870s. The modern Orientation Center is over a mile from the 563ft peak, so initially you won't even grasp the memorial's true dimensions, but take a bus to its base and you'll be utterly mesmerized.

It's not just the proportions that are overwhelming. The audacious, seemingly hopeless, timescale of the project makes the great Gothic cathedrals of Europe seem like prefabs. When Ziolkowski died in 1982, his family continued the work he had begun 34 years earlier; Crazy Horse's face, with its finely shaped nose and eyes, measures 87ft tall and was completed as recently as 1998. Today, his horse is gradually taking shape through a series of blasted-out ridges, but it's impossible to estimate when everything will be finished. No matter though: time seems to have little significance here, as the construction work – careful, reverential – has become almost as sacred as the monument itself.

530 CHOOSING THE RIGHT PHILLY CHEESESTEAK

PENNSYLVANIA Ask a native Philadelphian where to go for a proper steak in the City of Brotherly Love, and chances are you won't be shown to the local branch of *Ruth's Chris*. No, in Philadelphia, where the art museum is best known for a sweaty (and fictional) southpaw fighter lumbering up its steps, it's only fitting that you'll be sent to Ninth and Passyunk. At this hardscrabble south Philly corner, *Pat's King of Steaks* and archrival *Geno's* have been grilling Hatfield-and-McCoy-style for the past forty years for the honour of the city's best cheesesteak. It's no small prize – indeed, perhaps no dish in America is as closely tied to a city's mojo.

Join one of the two lines that spill out into the intersection at which these two institutions reside and prepare for fast food nirvana. Ordering requires adhering to a certain local etiquette, specifying first the cheese of your choice – provolone, American or dayglo Cheez Whiz – and then "wit" or "wit-out" to indicate your feelings about grilled onions. It's tough not to be a little nervous once you find yourself at the front of the snaking line and a Balboa-esque baritone booms "Next!" from a shroud of billowing steam, before the guy in front of you has even finished his order. But $7 and a "whizwit" later, you've got your hands on a national treasure – finely sliced ribeye grilled hibachi style, layered in gooey cheese and slipped into a crusty roll that's fluffy but firm.

Seventy years after hotdog vendor Pat Olivieri first slapped a slab of grilled steak on a bun, Philly has become something of a rising star on the nation's gourmet scene. Local restaurant guru Stephen Starr has opened a dozen spots to set the Zagat crowd abuzz – even one that hawks a $100 Kobe cheesesteak. But it's the thousands of street carts and unpretentious restaurants vying for bragging rights to the city's finest greasebomb that make Philly's wheels turn. And you won't know the soul of this town until you stand on a street corner, tear off the paper wrapper and feel the molten cheese drip through your fingertips. It's a rite of passage.

531 WATCHING THE FISH FLY AT PIKE PLACE MARKET

WASHINGTON It's not often that you see a twenty-pound King salmon being heaved through the air. At the bustling agora of Seattle's Pike Place Market, though, it's a daily activity. Large men in butcher smocks bellow each time they toss of one of the aquatic beasts. Occasionally the intended target (the open arms of other large men in butcher smocks) is missed, and the finned projectile ends up bouncing across the concrete or, even better, into the lap of a gaping tourist.

This crazy, sometimes violent, seafood spectacle is far from the market's only emblematic sight, however. There's the charming plump figure of the brass pig, an oversized piggy bank at the market's entrance that draws money for charity; the very first *Starbucks*, dating from 1971, with its original racy, bare-chested mermaid logo intact; and the grand neon letters of the market sign itself, whose soft red glow has popped up in a handful of movies, *Sleepless in Seattle* being the most famous.

As the signature market in the Pacific Northwest, Pike Place is anything but a simple array of agricultural stands: it's a virtual rabbit warren of stairways, corridors and cantilevered storeys built into the hillside of the Seattle waterfront, a teeming mass of clubs, bars, restaurants and shops. The market has been here for a century, but only since it was almost demolished in the 1970s has it gone on to become the signature attraction of the Emerald City to visitors and locals alike – everyone from upscale yuppies to old-timers to down-and-dirty punk rockers. Its array of eclectic vendors includes the Sub Pop Megamart for indie rock, Left Bank Books for radical reads, *Three Girls Bakery* for delectable pastries and more java joints, ethnic diners and cherry, berry and apple dealers than you can imagine. And if all else fails, there's always the fishmongers, who can get you anything from salmon and trout to marlin and halibut – just be sure to duck.

532 VISITING HARVARD YARD

MASSACHUSETTS Leafy and shaded during Cambridge's oppressively humid summers, littered with flaming orange foliage in the autumn, cloaked in a blanket of snow during winter and buzzing with Frisbee-tossing students in spring, Harvard Yard is captivating at any time of year. The centre of Harvard University's campus life and its oldest section, this grassy expanse is crisscrossed by walkways and while you won't be able to "pahk the cah in Hahvahd Yahd" (a sentence often used to illustrate the distinctive accent of true Bostonians), you can certainly go for an amble, taking in the impressive pomp of America's most prestigious place of higher learning. The student-led tours are great but you may want to think twice before you follow in the footsteps of most tourists and rub the foot of the John Harvard Statue for good luck – it's a frequent target of student pranks, not least of which involves a competition to urinate on it before graduation.

533 SEEING THE BAY AREA FROM ATOP MOUNT TAM

CALIFORNIA Marin County's emblematic peak, Mount Tamalpais (Miwok for "coast mountain") promises limitless prospects for hiking and hang-gliding. The winding ascent towards the crowning state park reveals at each switchback more exhilarating views of the steep, grassy slopes of the headlands and the wind-driven Pacific beyond. A stony hike leads to the summit, a lofty eyrie above San Francisco Bay. Perched on a boulder beside the lookout tower, take in the soaring panorama that stretches some thirty miles and more in all directions: the bridges, the City and the Bay, the Santa Cruz range and the beaches to the south. Watch the coastal fog below unroll like a fleece blanket, and catch the rainbows as wispy mists waft up against the overhanging crags.

534 SIDESTEPPING ASH AND LAVA ON KILAUEA

HAWAII The Hawaiian islands are the summits of volcanoes rooted 20,000 feet below the Pacific. Kilauea, on the Big Island, is the youngest of these volcanoes, and it's been erupting continuously ever since 1983. Mark Twain described its crater as a dazzling lake of fire, but the action these days is lower down its flanks, where molten lava explodes directly into the ocean.

I parked my car where the Chain of Craters Road, which winds from the crater down to the sea, was abruptly blocked by fresh black lava. No path set off beyond; instead I picked my way through broken slabs, and stepped across mysterious cracks, dodging the vapours that hissed from gashes in the rock. I finally found myself ten feet above the crashing waves, on a precarious "bench" of lava. Down at sea level, a sluggish river of incandescent rock churned into the water, amid plumes of steam and evil-smelling gases. Other hikers prodded at the eggshell crust with sticks, to see if they could break through to the river beneath their feet and set the wood ablaze.

I stayed until the sun went down, and the molten glow of the lava was the only light. A small cone of fine ash had formed at the seafront. As I climbed it, my feet sank deep with every step, and sent a fine powder slithering around me. From the top I looked down into a fiery orange pool that gently bubbled and popped, sending up phlegmy strings of rock.

There were three or four people nearby, silhouetted against the orange clouds. A sudden thud from below, solid as a hammer stroke, made my knees buckle. As I turned, the volcano nonchalantly spewed a shower of rocks high into the air. Now I felt entitled to run, through wading through thick volcanic ash felt more like a slow-motion nightmare. I struggled to speed up, all too aware that it was a matter of pure luck whether any of the lumps overhead would hit me.

As it turned out, a glowing boulder larger than my head thumped down six feet away. I crept back to examine it, bright orange on the black moonscape, then stumbled away through the night.

BURNING MAN
FESTIVAL

NEVADA Picture a nudist miniature golf course, an advanced pole-dancing workshop and a bunch of neon-painted bodies glowing in the night, and you may be getting close to imagining what Burning Man is all about. Every year during the last week of August, several thousand digerati geeks, pyrotechnic maniacs, death-guild Goths, crusty hippies and too-hip yuppies descend on a prehistoric dry lakebed in the Nevada desert to build a temporary autonomous "city" – one that rivals some of Nevada's largest in size and leaves no trace when it disbands. Known as Black Rock City, it's not the ideal place to consume a heady cocktail of alcohol and drugs – temperatures are scorching – but the thousands of anarchists, deviants, techno-heads, trance-dancers and freakish performance artists that arrive here from all over the world give it their best shot.

Art and interactivity are at the very core of the Burning Man ethos. Basically, this is the most survivalist, futuristic and utterly surreal show on earth, where the strangest part of your alter ego reigns supreme. Leashed slaves with foot fetishes wander around offering footbaths, faceless Pythia give advice in oracle booths, flying zebras circle, caged men in ape suits pounce and motorized lobster cars tool about. Some of Burning Man's participants see the event as a social experiment and others a total free-for-all. But the main goal is the same: you're there to participate, not observe. Burning Man allows all the black sheep of the world to graze together, so the more experiential art you share, gifts you give, bizarre costumes you wear, or free services you provide, the better.

The highlight of the week is the burning of a fifty-foot-tall effigy of a man, built from wood and neon and stuffed with fireworks. After all the laser-filled skies, electroluminscent wired bodysuits and fire-breathing mecahnical dragons that illuminate the skies every evening for the rest of the week, it's almost an anticlimax, but it's still certainly a sight to behold. If you fancy making a smaller-scale statement, you can choose whatever alter ego or fantasy you desire. Just pack your politically correct non-feathered boas, body paint and imagination, and you're all set.

536 LEAF-PEEPING ALONG ROUTE 100

VERMONT Route 100 is beautiful year-round – winding its way through quintessential New England scenery, it skirts tidy chocolate-box villages dotted with white-steepled churches, clapboard houses and home-made sweet shops, all nestled beneath the Green Mountains. But from late-September to early October, when the leaves start to change colour, the road is transformed into a two-hundred-mile, skin-prickling display of arboreal pyrotechnics; it's as if the entire state has been set ablaze. Even the most die-hard cosmopolitan will find it hard not to be seduced by the spectacular scenery, as dizzying peaks give way to a conflagration of vermillion sugar maples, buttery aspens, scarlet sourwoods and acid-yellow ashes.

This yearly riot of colour can be appreciated whether you choose to ever leave your car or not. Gliding along a winding stretch of open road, crawling through an impossibly picturesque nineteenth-century town, or off-roading along serpentine country lanes, the explosion of unreal-looking leaves is inescapable – and unadulterated (no billboards or malls are allowed along the route). For an up-close look, pull off Route 100 and head into Green Mountain National Forest to walk along part of the 265-mile Long Trail, which has countless leaf-peeping opportunities alongside rugged, mountainous terrain, flowing streams and placid ponds.

537 ON THE ROAD WITH THE GREEN TORTOISE

NEW YORK–CALIFORNIA For two weeks we travelled, on a unique version of the Great American Road Trip. We didn't go like Sal and Dean did, in Jack Kerouac's *On the Road*, balling that jack hard along Route 66; rather we rambled in style – keep in mind that there's no accounting for taste – on the Green Tortoise, a green-painted, ramshackle and raucous "sleeper bus" that makes the trip several times a year (along with its turtle brethren) from the East Coast to the West Coast.

We loaded up our colourful packs in NYC; and as we rolled out of Manhattan across the George Washington Bridge, a swelling rose within our breasts. As Simon and Garfunkel sang, "We've all come to look for America".

And what'd ya know – we found it. From the Big Apple it was down the Eastern Seaboard, to Cape Hatteras and Okefenokee, where the gators lurked in the swamps. Thence we turned right and started that long crossing. We partied all night in New Orleans, where one of us, we thought, had got pinched by the cops. We had a big party down by a Louisiana river, spanned by one of the last elevator bridges in the country. The morning

after, our campsite looked like the scene of some mad war. We blew through the rest of the South and right by Houston, which loomed up on the left, an alien planet silver and shining.

Out west, though, where we began to meander and linger, was where things got really interesting. We smoked a joint among the prickly pears and wandered stoned through the cool Carlsbad Caverns. We gambled in Vegas, the Great Unwashed at Caesar's blackjack tables. One early morning after a hard rain we coasted calmly into the soaked, red Valley of the Gods – and, after a hike as we drank "cowboy coffee" on a hill, the strains of Van Morrison's *And It Stoned Me* reached our ears for the first time ever and, well, stoned us.

After that was denouement. We pulled, ragged and ravished, into San Francisco and the *Green Tortoise Hostel* in North Beach, just up from where Ginsberg published *Howl*. Fog-wracked and fresh, San Fran felt like a city with no memory – but memories, of a whole continent behind us, were all we had left.

538 GAZING AT A NANTUCKET SUNSET

MASSACHUSETTS You spent the morning beside a pep-permint-striped lighthouse, and then meandered past shin-gled, rose-covered cottages. For lunch, you feasted on freshly steamed lobster and sweet corn on the cob. But in truth, you only really feel like you've arrived in Nantucket once you've sauntered along one of its long stretches of sugary white sand, with the moorlands and breezy dunes to your back, and to the west, a gorgeous, swirly pink sun slipping into a glowing sea. Sunset in Nantucket is a near-spiritual affair, and here, sur-rounded by sky and sea, you remember again why you have journeyed so far to a place that's so small.

Difficult to access – it's a two-hour, no-land-in-sight boat ride south from mainland Cape Cod – and primarily a summertime destination, the tiny island is imbued with a catch-it-while-you-can ambience. It's as if the sun and surf have filtered out the details of life on the mainland, shaping the island into a quiet, sandy idyll. There's not really much "to do" in Nantucket, but

that's where its charm lies – content yourself with ice cream cones and seashells, salty sea air and bike rides to the beach.

As the evening fog rolls in – the island is famous for it, even owing its nickname, "the Grey Lady", to the mist–beach-weary folk head for Nantucket Town, packing into the drugstore for creamy milkshakes from its time-worn soda fountain where the stools still spin.

Nantucket wasn't always a land of leisure. During the eighteenth and nineteenth centuries, it served as a hub for the whaling trade, a dangerous industry marked by meager pay and gruelling years at sea. Evidence of this hard-working heritage is well preserved in the pretty sea captains' homes and cobblestones that line Main Street, restorative efforts largely funded by the island's well-heeled summer residents.

More than anything, windswept Nantucket is a wistful sort of place. As you board the ferry to go home, you'll long not only for simpler days, but also for the chance to come back again.

539 SETTING UP CAMP IN THE ADIRONDACKS

NEW YORK In the Adirondacks, going to a rustic camp can mean two very different things. Pick almost any majestic lake or forest in the region and you'll find a campground to pitch your tent and wallow in the beautiful scenery; wake up early to put your canoe out on the reflective waters or to take a mountain hike. Better still, merely pretend you're roughing it and head to the historic *Wawbeek*, one of the timber-and-stone "Great Camps" that served as mountain lodge retreats for the well-to-do in the late-nineteenth and early twentieth centuries. Note the finely hewn Adirondack-style architecture and furnishings, have dinner on the outside terrace while the sun sinks over Upper Saranac Lake and finish with a drink in the bar under a giant moose head, before retiring to your cabin. Camp never seemed so inviting.

540 PAYING HOMAGE TO COUNTRY MUSIC

VIRGINIA Along a highway disguised as a country road in the town of Hiltons, the Carter Family Fold showcases acoustic mountain music in a place where time stands still. Here it might as well be 1927, the year of the "Big Bang" in country music, when the original Carter Family sang about hard times and wildwood flowers. The children of Sara and A.P. Carter constructed and nurtured this unique structure, built right into the hillside. An on-site museum in A.P.'s old grocery store contains snapshots of "Mother Maybelle", a lock of Sara's hair and the clothes June Carter Cash and Johnny Cash wore when they entertained at the Nixon White House. And during the weekly concerts, the site still evokes a direct connection to them, to their famous forebears who are honoured here, and to all of the music that came from these mountains.

541 GOING BATTY IN AUSTIN

TEXAS Every evening from mid-March to early November Austin plays host to one of urban America's most entertaining natural spectacles, as Mexican free-tailed bats perform at the city's Congress Avenue Bridge. They emerge from the bridge's deep crevices just after sunset, flapping and squeaking in a long ribbon across the sky. An eclectic mix of townies and tourists watches from the south bank of Town Lake, from boats, from blankets at the *Austin American-Statesman*'s observation centre and from the bridge itself. Picturesque from any spot, the bats' game of follow-the-leader is most impressive when you stand beneath the ribbon and look up – that's when the sheer number of these creatures hits home. During the summer, the best viewing season, more than 1.5 million bats reside here, making it the largest urban bat colony in North America. Caves elsewhere in Texas host larger colonies, but in Austin there is a certain wonder in watching natural and man-made worlds collide harmoniously.

CALIFORNIA IN A CONVERTIBLE:
driving the length of
HIGHWAY 1

CALIFORNIA Highway 1 starts in little Leggett, but most people pick it up in San Francisco, just after it has raced US-101 across the Golden Gate Bridge and wiggled its way through the city. Roll down the rooftop on your convertible – this is California, after all – and chase the horizon south, through Santa Cruz and misty Monterey and then on to Big Sur, one of the most dramatic stretches of coastline in the world, where the forest-clad foothills of the Santa Lucia Mountains ripple down to a ninety-mile zigzag of deeply rugged shore.

You could easily spend a week in one of the mountain lodges here, hiking in the region's two superb state parks or watching grey whales gliding through the surf, but SoCal's sands are calling. Gun the gas down through San Luis Obispo and swanky Santa Barbara until you hit Malibu, from where – as the Pacific Coast Highway – the road tiptoes around Los Angeles, dipping in and out of the beachside suburbs of Santa Monica, Venice and Long Beach.

Highway 1 eventually peters out at San Juan Capistrano, but most people pull off a few miles shy, finishing their journey in Los Angeles. Leaving Malibu's multi-million-dollar condos behind and easing gently into the downtown LA traffic, it'll suddenly dawn on you that the hardest part of the journey is still to come – at some point soon, you're going to have to say goodbye to the convertible.

UP CLOSE WITH
alligators
on the
ANHINGA TRAIL
543

FLORIDA Stepping onto the concrete Anhinga Trail, you can't help but doubt its reputation as serious gator territory. Leading straight from a car park and with a friendly little visitor centre at its head, the half-mile circular pathway smacks of the type of "nature trail" on which you'd be lucky to catch sight of a sparrow. But don't judge it hastily – the Everglades is full of surprises.

Located way down in Florida's tropical south, the Everglades National Park covers 1.5 million acres of sawgrass-covered marshland and swamp, the largest subtropical wilderness in the United States and the perfect home for the American alligator. So as you stroll along admiring the exotic birdlife, don't let your guard down: all around you, massive carnivorous reptiles are lurking in the shallows, blending effortlessly into their surroundings. Almost comically prehistoric-looking, they sunbathe inches from the path or sometimes even stretched across it, motionless and slit-eyed, with seemingly hundreds of long, pointed teeth glinting in the hot Florida sun.

The sheer number of lazing alligators is remarkable, but your effortless proximity to them is even more incredible. In fact, you nearly forget you're in the wild – it all seems far too zoo-like (or even museum-esque, since the animals don't stir); and then, almost before you realize it, and with truly incredible speed, an alligator moves – and the enjoyable awe and excitement you were feeling morphs into sheer terror. When they take to the water and adopt that classic alligator pose – only eyes, teeth and powerful, ridged tail visible as they glide quietly and quickly towards their prey – it's nigh-on impossible to stop yourself from leaping away down the path, burning to tell someone of your near-death experience.

544 BIKING THE SAN ANTONIO MISSION TRAIL

TEXAS Any old sap can take a tour bus to the Alamo, but insiders know that the best way to check out San Antonio's mission history starts with a visit to the Blue Star Brewing Company. Here the owners have combined their two passions – cycling and drinking – into one cool business. Outfitted with a tuned-up cruiser and a map of the twenty-mile trek, you start out pedalling through the historic King William District, with its impressive mansions shaded by giant pecan and cypress trees. Next you head for the official mission trail, which wends its way along the San Antonio River. You encounter four major missions along this bucolic journey, all built in the early eighteenth century by Spanish friars with the goal of converting the local natives and securing a claim to the land. The fascinating medieval peasant societies have been carefully preserved, and in fact, the missions still operate as Catholic parishes, lending to the sense of witnessing history in action. And as the Texas sun heats up and you find yourself fading, don't forget there's a nice cold pint waiting for you at the end of your ride.

545 HANG-GLIDING IN THE OUTER BANKS

NORTH CAROLINA There are few coastal spots in America – maybe some of the wilder places on Cape Cod – as magnificent as Carolina's Outer Banks. Your main goal here should be contemplating the fragility of the shifting sands and unique ecosystems, hitting as many deserted beaches as you can along the southern portions of the barrier islands, in Cape Hatteras, Ocracoke Island and largely undeveloped Cape Lookout. But getting off – and above – beach level is an experience not to be missed either: there's a hang-gliding school in Jockey Ridge State Park where you can soon be soaring over the largest sand dunes in the eastern US, in Nags Head. Once airborne you may well consider what fired the imagination of Orville and Wilbur Wright, who launched their historic flight just a few miles north.

546 TOURING ALASKA BY RV

ALASKA Navigating curves and windy back roads behind the wheel of a vehicle only marginally shorter than your average eighteen-wheeler might seem an ungainly way to travel, but in a land as enormous as Alaska the size of an RV (recreational vehicle) makes perfect sense. With vast distances often separating one town from the next and from the state's many spectacular natural wonders, the appeal of taking your kitchen, bathroom, living room and bedroom with you is obvious. Free from the worries of finding where you'll eat your next meal or rest after a long day of outdoor adventures, you'll find that just about any itinerary you can conceive is possible. And with so many options – from bear watching at McNeil River and hiking the Chilkoot Trail to driving the Denali Highway and seeing the aurora borealis – you'll soon be singing the praises of the lumbering leviathan that you call home.

547 EATING BARBECUE IN TEXAS HILL COUNTRY

TEXAS If you think barbecue is a sloppy pulled-pork sandwich or a platter of ribs drowned in a sticky, sweet sauce, a Texan will happily correct you. In the rolling hills around Austin – where pecan trees provide shade, pickup trucks rule the road and the radio is devoted to Waylon, Willie and Merle – you'll find barbecue as it should be: nothing but pure, succulent, unadulterated meat, smoked for hours over a low wood fire. In fact, at one veteran vendor in Lockhart, *Kreuz Market*, the management maintains a strict no-sauce policy, so as not to distract from the perfectly tender slabs of brisket. Your meat, ordered by weight, comes on butcher paper with just crackers to dress it up.

Thankfully, this austerity applies only to the substance – not the quantity – of the meat. Gut-busting excess is what makes barbecue truly American, after all, especially at places like the legendary *Salt Lick*, southwest of Austin near the town of Driftwood. The all-you-can-eat spread here includes heaps of beef brisket, pork ribs and sausage, all bearing the signature smoke-stained pink outer layer that signifies authentic barbecue. On the side, you get the traditional fixin's: German-style coleslaw and potato salad, soupy pinto beans, sour pickles, plain old white bread and thick slices of onion.

So whether you visit *The Salt Lick*, *Kreuz Market* (those anti-sauce hardliners in Lockhart), *Black's* (another Lockhart gem, which has conceded to a light sauce), *Louie Mueller BBQ* (in an old wood-floor gymnasium in Taylor), *City Market* (in Luling) or any of the other esteemed purveyors a local barbecue fetishist points you to, don't ever forget: it's all about the meat.

548 HIT THE HUT: ATTENDING NATURE'S BOOT CAMP

COLORADO A far cry from glamorous Aspen and Vail, yet close to both, the basic cabins of the 10th Mountain Division Hut System – named in honour of the US Army ski corps that trained here during World War II – offer a unique look at Colorado's backcountry, and an atmospheric alternative to a typical alpine vacation. A stay in any one of them (there are 29 in total) grants you access to the pristine Sawatch Mountains and some 350 miles of underused cross-country skiing, snowshoeing, hiking and mountain-biking trails within central Colorado's national forest.

Although you probably won't be using hickory-board skis and striking out with ninety pounds of gear on your back like the soldiers did, the hut system is still about simplicity and making your way in the wild. Accommodation is basic, equipped only with mattresses, wood-burning stoves and rudimentary cooking facilities. Your water will come from melting snow, and you'll be bunking down with sixteen or so strangers who typically share a hut. A normal day might be spent very unassumingly – taking a few runs on nearby slopes, heading back to your hut to warm up by the fire, then venturing out again to build a snowman or go sledding before settling in to cook a simple dinner, perhaps making some new friends while you're at it.

While it's the self-sufficient, back-to-nature aspect of this experience that makes it so memorable, the other side is that you're at nature's mercy. You'll need to be fit, have great gear and adequate wilderness skills: in the event of an emergency, it can take a good six hours for help to arrive. It's easy to tire quickly at the high altitudes and become confused by whiteouts in the fading light of winter as you search for elusive way-markers. But once you pass muster at nature's boot camp, stylish ski resorts may never hold the same appeal.

549 IN HIGH SPIRITS ON THE BOURBON TRAIL

KENTUCKY What is the spirit of the United States? Ask an average citizen or, worse, a politician, and you may get a rambling metaphysical reply longer than the Bill of Rights. Ask a seasoned bartender, however, and you'll get that rarest of responses, the one-word answer: bourbon.

The country's sole native spirit and, thanks to a congressional declaration, its official one as well, bourbon is a form of whiskey. Technically speaking, the grain used to make bourbon must be at least 51 percent corn, and it must be aged a minimum of two years inside charred, white-oak barrels – though both the percentage and years are typically much greater. And while bourbon can be produced elsewhere, the spirit of the spirit resides in Kentucky, home to the finest distilleries as well as, according to local legend, its birthplace, where late eighteenth-century settlers in Bourbon County combined their extra corn harvests with local iron-free water to make the fabled whiskey.

The best place to find out more is along the Bourbon Trail, a meandering route through the rolling hills of central Kentucky that links several distilleries and historic towns. Must-sees include Loretto, where you can watch the deliciously smooth Maker's Mark being produced in a picture-perfect setting laced with green pastures and well-preserved nineteenth-century buildings like the Master Distiller's House, and the Jim Beam Distillery an hour's drive away in Clermont, whose pedestrian main brand is augmented by several "small batch" potions, like the fiery Knob Greek and silky Basil Hayden's, that can be sampled on-site.

Tucked in between the two is friendly Bardstown, the state's second-oldest city and best base along the Bourbon Trail, home to the Oscar Getz Museum of Whiskey History and September's lively Bourbon Festival. Book a bed at the *Old Talbott Tavern*, whose guests have included Abraham Lincoln and Daniel Boone, and you'll only have a few steps to walk after an evening spent using your newfound knowledge comparing local bourbons at the bar.

RUNNING THE NEW YORK CITY MARATHON

550

NEW YORK The best way to experience New York is by running through it on marathon day.

At 6am, along Avenue of Americas in near dark, lone figures emerge from side streets, with marathon bags like mine flung over their shoulders, their walk brisk, determined. In the lobby of the *Sheraton Hotel*, athletes drink water or tea, devour one last banana, nibble on bagels, stretch, pace, wait.

On the bus to the starting line, a hedge–fund executive offers a sip of his soy latte; I repay with a vanilla protein bar. The executive will run with mementos in his fanny pack. "This was my grandmother's favorite Psalm – Number 23", he says, revealing a folded piece of paper on which is written the complete verse, beginning with, "The Lord is my Shepherd".

At the start area, runners pee into empty Poland Spring bottles before jockeying for footing as the starting "gun" blasts. It's impossible not to feel adrenalin, even after twenty prior marathons, shoulder to shoulder with the world's runners, sun sneaking through fog as I traverse the majestic Verrazano-Narrows Bridge, music blaring from ghetto blasters or live bands, the massive block party only just begun.

By mile two, I'm running with new friends Ray, of the New York Police Department, and Tommy, as his T-shirt reads, of the Staten Island Sanitation Department. Just after the five-mile mark, Tommy plants a kiss on an attractive female spectator's lips; he will deliver many a kiss to many an eager Brooklyn woman. His antics keep me smiling through the pain.

As we trudge up the gruelling incline of Queensboro Bridge, near the sixteen-mile mark, the reward is Manhattan's romantic skyline. Just as spirits dampen, a call from behind, "Are we having fun yet?" In unison, hundreds of runners intone, "Yes!"

At twenty-five miles, right thigh cramps. A woman at a first-aid stand massages it with "Icy Hot" and I cautiously continue, animated spectators' faces and cheers a lovely blur as my mind carries my body through the finish chute. The clock shows a personal worst time, but, hobbling off, there's still the raw joy of achievement.

Later, over a beer at a swank West Side restaurant, a young Dutch woman, her first marathon behind her, says, "I was crying so often out of happiness. Every time people would call out my name, again the tears". Like nowhere else, this marathon recharges the spirit, makes everyone a New Yorker for a day.

551 BED, BARRACUDA AND BREAKFAST: JULES' UNDERSEA LODGE

FLORIDA *Jules' Undersea Lodge* – named after intrepid aqua-explorer Jules Verne – began life as a research lab off the coast of Puerto Rico in the 1970s; it was moved to the Florida Keys and converted to its current use in 1986 by a pair of diving buffs and budding hoteliers.

A pod that sits a few feet above the lagoon floor, the lodge has just two smallish guest bedrooms, fitted out with TVs, VCRs, phones and hot showers, plus a fully equipped kitchen and common room. All very ordinary – except, of course, that you are 21 feet below the sea. Expert scuba divers can spend up to 22 hours exploring the marine habitat each day – safety regulations permit no longer than that; first-timers, meanwhile, need only take a three-hour tutorial on the basics of underwater swimming and survival before they can duck down for check-in.

(Fitful types will sleep with the fishes far more restfully knowing that there's 24-hour safety monitoring from land nearby.)

Guests – or "aquanauts" as the lodge-owners call them – must swim down to reach the lodge, which, shaped like a figure of eight, has a small opening on the base in the centre. Your first point of arrival is into a wet room; the disconcerting sensation is much like surfacing from a swimming pool, except, of course, that you're still underwater. Compressed air keeps the sea from flooding in.

Once ensconced in this enclave, most guests spend their time gazing out of the enormous, 42-inch windows in the lodge's hull: these vast portholes make a spectacular spot to spy on its surroundings. *Jules' Undersea Lodge* is anchored in the heart of a mangrove habitat, the ideal nursery for scores of marine animals, including angelfish, parrotfish and snapper; meanwhile, anemones and sponges stud the sea floor. Anyone too busy fish-spotting to whip up a spot of dinner needn't worry, as there's a chef on hand who can scuba down to prepare meals; or, for late night munchies, a local take-out joint offers a unique delivery service – perfectly crisp, underwater pizza.

552 PLAYING BALL AT THE FIELD OF DREAMS

IOWA "If you build it, they will come". So runs the memorable line from the movie Field of Dreams, an idealized ode to America's national pastime in which an Iowa farmer is inspired to construct a baseball diamond slap bang in the middle of his cornfield. And ever since the movie's set was carved across a pretty little family farm at Dyersville in Iowa, that's exactly what they've done. Within a few weeks of its release in 1989, and with the diamond still in place from filming, the first visitor arrived, travelling over 1000 miles from his home in New York just to sit in the bleachers behind right field.

Since then, over a million people have come to this tiny corner of the rural Midwest, drawn by some strange compulsion to bat a few balls, play a little catch and fulfil a dream or two. In the late summer of 1997, I was one of them, stashing my weathered but trusty mitt into the glove compartment and driving north with a college friend in search of our own piece of baseball mythology. It was early September, the corn surrounding the field was high and green – just as it is in the movie – and as we pulled into the bijou car park, a pick-up game was just getting going. A family from California was manning the bases, and a kid from nearby Indiana was practicing his curveballs from the mound, so we took our places in the outfield. After fielding a couple of grounders (my friend) and dropping a fly ball (me – I still blame the glare of the sun), we retired to the bleachers as the young pitcher moved onto his frighteningly quick fastballs.

Is this heaven? No, it's Iowa, a place where, for a few hours on a soft summer's day, you can enjoy the simple pleasures of a little make-believe.

553 LUNCHING ON CREOLE CUISINE IN NEW ORLEANS

LOUISIANA New Orleans is a gourmand's town, and its restaurants are far more than places to eat. These are social hubs and ports in a storm – sometimes literally, in the case of the French Quarter kitchens that stayed open post-Katrina, dishing out red beans and rice to the stubborn souls who refused to abandon their beloved city. Above all, they are where New Orleans comes to celebrate itself, in all its quirky, battered beauty. And no restaurant is more quintessentially New Orleans than *Galatoire's*, the grande dame of local Creole cuisine.

Lunch, particularly on Friday and Sunday, is the meal of choice; set aside an entire afternoon. Reservations aren't taken for the downstairs room (the place to be), so you'll need to come early and wait in line. In true New Orleans fashion, this bastion of haute Creole style sits on the city's bawdiest stretch, Bourbon Street. Picking your way through the morning-after remnants of a Bourbon Saturday night – plastic cups floating in pools of fetid liquid, a distinctive miasma of drains and stale booze and

rotting magnolias – brings you to a display worthy of a Tennessee Williams play. Seersucker-clad powerbrokers puff on fat cigars, dangling dainty Southern belles on their arms; immaculately coiffured women greet each other with loud cries of "dawlin'!" Inside – or downstairs at least – it's like time has stood still: brass ceiling fans whir overhead, giant old mirrors reflect the lights cast by Art Nouveau lamps, and black-jacketed waiters, who have worked here forever, crack wise with their favourite diners.

It's the same century-old menu, too: basically French, pepped up with the herbs and spices of Spain, Africa and the West Indies. Lump crabmeat and plump oysters come with creamy French sauces or a piquant rémoulade, a blend of tomato, onion, Creole mustard, horseradish and herbs; side dishes might be featherlight soufflé potatoes or fried eggplant. To end with a kick, order a steaming tureen of potent *café brûlot* – jet-black java heated with brandy, orange peel and spices – prepared tableside with all the ceremony of a religious ritual.

554 TRACING CIVIL RIGHTS HISTORY IN MONTGOMERY

ALABAMA The struggle for African-American civil rights – one of the great social causes of American history – played out all across the South in the 1950s and 60s. To try to gain a grasp on its legacy, and a sense of how the fabric of the country has still in a way never quite healed, make your way to Montgomery, Alabama, the culmination of the so-called Selma-to-Montgomery National History Trail.

Start at the state capitol building (which looks like a cross between the US Capitol and a plantation manor), where you can almost hear Dr Martin Luther King Jr in 1963 declaring at the end of the four-day Selma-to-Montgomery civil rights march, "however difficult the moment, however frustrating the hour, it will not be long, because truth pressed to earth will rise again". To experience more of King's spirit, take in a passionate Sunday service at the Dexter Avenue King Memorial Baptist

Church, where today's ministers use King's example to inspire both parishioners and casual visitors. The church's basement holds a mural depicting scenes from King's life, as well as his preserved desk, office and pulpit. His birthplace, for those interested, is in the Sweet Auburn district of Atlanta, Georgia.

The Rosa Parks Museum honours the Montgomery event that started it all. Parks's refusal in 1955 to accept a seat at the back of a Montgomery bus in essence sparked the civil rights movement; her inspiring story is told through photographs and dioramas, and you can step onto a replica of that city bus. Most poignant, though, is the civil rights memorial, centred on a black-granite table designed by Maya Lin and inscribed with the names of forty activists killed by racist violence from 1954 to 1968. The events described on the table are as good an overview of the era as you're likely to find.

555 TAKING THE A-TRAIN THROUGH MANHATTAN

NEW YORK It may be just a dirty, run-of-the-mill inner-city commuter train, but ever since 1941 when Duke Ellington's band immortalized the A-train – the subway from Brooklyn up through the heart of Manhattan and into Harlem – the route's been associated with jazz, the Harlem Renaissance and the gritty glamour of travelling through New York. The iconic tin-can carriages – long a favourite location for television cop dramas – rattle along on this express route, taking you to some of Manhattan's most varied neighbourhoods.

Wherever you choose to board the train, getting out at Jay Street in Brooklyn Heights, and stopping at one of the cafés on leafy Montague Street for a long, lazy brunch starts the day in true New York style. From here, the Brooklyn Bridge beckons; cross on foot and enter downtown Manhattan, taking in the spectacular views of the skyline as you traverse the sparkling East River, the Statue of Liberty just visible to your left.

Rejoin the A-train at Park Place and head up the line. Jump off at West 4th Street and browse the boutiques alongside funky West Villagers; stop at Columbus Circle, emerging at the southwest corner of Central Park for a leafy stroll. From here it's a non-stop express trip whizzing under the Upper West Side – sit in the front carriage for a driver's eye view of the glinting tracks as they disappear beneath the train.

Your final stop is Duke Ellington's own journey's end: 145th Street for Harlem's Sugar Hill. High above the city, with hazy views back along Manhattan's straight avenues, this was the more upmarket part of the neighbourhood during the Jazz Age. Today, well into its second renaissance, the area's art and music scenes thrive, nowhere so much as in its classic jazz clubs. Stick your head into *St Nick's Pub*, known to the greats as *Lucky's Rendezvous*, and catch some improv – Duke would definitely approve.

556 SLEEPING NEAR THE CORNER IN WINSLOW

ARIZONA The Eagles may have sung about "standin' on the corner in Winslow, Arizona" – Standin' on the Corner Park supposedly marks the spot – but things at this desert outpost have been pretty sleepy since interstate I-40 supplanted Route 66.

Strange place, then, to find the most magical hotel in America. *La Posada* is the masterpiece of pioneering Southwestern architect Mary Jane Colter. For the last and greatest of the Fred Harvey company's railroad hotels, she was given the opportunity to create a showpiece property from the ground up, with complete control over everything from the overall design to the interior decor.

Although in reality the whole place was built in 1929, Colter gave it an intricate backstory, a romantic previous life as a Spanish-style hacienda – laid out by a Hispanic cattle baron in the 1860s, it was expanded as he grew rich, and finally "converted" into a hotel. The sprawling complex combined Mexican antiques and local craftsmanship with the Art Deco trimmings and fancy innovations expected by 1930s travellers. With the decline of the railroads, *La Posada* closed in 1957; Colter herself died a year later, after sadly observing "There's such a thing as living too long".

Forty years later, however, *La Posada* reopened, restored by enthusiasts who proclaim "we are not hoteliers – for us this is about art". This is no lifeless museum, however; it's bursting with earthy Southwestern style and imaginative adornments, not least the dazzling modernist canvases by co-owner Tina Mion that bedeck the public spaces. Each guest room is individually furnished – fittings range from hand-carved four-poster beds and inlaid wooden floors to deeply luxurious Jacuzzis – and named after illustrious former guests from John Wayne to Shirley Temple.

A fabulous restaurant, designed to mimic the dining car of the Santa Fe Railroad's Super Chief, and using Colter's original Pueblo-influenced tableware, serves contemporary Southwestern cuisine, using ingredients like Navajo-raised lamb and wild turkey. And irresistibly, this is still a train station, even if the former ticketing area and waiting rooms now serve as cosy public lounges; doors from the lobby lead straight to the platform, and the distant sound of train whistles provide a haunting backdrop to your slumbers.

557 CELEBRATING FANTASY FEST IN KEY WEST

FLORIDA The saucy climax of Key West's calendar, capping the end of hurricane season in October, is a week-long party known as Fantasy Fest. The old town is transformed into an outdoor costume bash, somewhat tenuously pegged to Halloween; really, it's a gay-heavy take on Mardi Gras, with campy themes (past ones have included "Freaks, Geeks and Goddesses" and "TV Jeebies") and flesh-flashing costumes.

The week is punctuated with offbeat events, like the pet costume contest where dogs and their owners dress the same, and a sequin-spangled satire of a high school prom. On Saturday, the final parade slinks down the main drag, Duval Street, on a well-lubricated, booze-fuelled route.

It's not surprising that such an irresistibly kitschy shindig should have emerged and endured in Key West. Save San Francisco, there's nowhere in America more synonymous with out and proud gay life than this final, isolated, all-but-

an-island in the Florida Keys – the town's been a byword for homocentric hedonism since the sexually liberated 1970s. But in many ways, Key West's queer reputation is misleading. Sure, it's still a gay hotspot, as the thong-sporting go-go boys, who wield their crotches like weapons in bars along Duval Street, attest. But what drew the gay community here in the first place was the town's liberal, all-inclusiveness; be who you want to be, the locals say, whatever that is. It's all summed up by the town's official motto: "One Human Family". Indeed, Key West welcomes everyone, from President Truman, who holed up in the so-called Little White House here in the 1940s to an oddball bar owner like "Buddy" today, who built his ramshackle café-cum-pub, *B.O.'s Fish Wagon*, out of piles of junk. After a few days, these kind of visual quirks seem quite standard – except maybe that pet costume contest.

558 SPOOKED IN THE OLD SOUTH

SOUTH CAROLINA By day, a meander through Charleston takes you past stately homes, leafy patios and romantic bougainvillea. Embark on the eerie "Ghosts of Charleston" tour under a Carolina moon, though, and a pervasive air of mystery seems to lurk around every street corner. Perhaps it's the spirits of Blackbeard's pirates, who were imprisoned and hanged in the mouldy Provost Dungeon for terrorizing the town years ago. Or maybe it's the sad, ghostly soul of a former church deacon's assistant-turned-prostitute roaming the old *Planter's Inn*. Nah, surely it's just your imagination playing tricks on you … right?

559 PRIMAL POINT REYES

CALIFORNIA A slender peninsula jutting from California's northern coast, Point Reyes National Seashore is all about what happens when the ocean meets the land – but don't expect beach chairs. Out here the cold surf pounds the rocks, marine fog courses over the hills, and the wind ruffles the fur, fins and feathers of an astonishing number of creatures, including whales, elk, bobcats and 490 species of birds. Take a strenuous hike, join one of the expert-led birdspotting walks or just loaf about. But don't forget to sample the delectable oysters and local cheese.

SKIING AT
SNOWBIRD and ALTA
560

UTAH Although the 2002 Winter Olympics skipped Alta and Snowbird, downhillers searching for bottomless powder know better than to follow suit. Squeezed side-by-side at the upper end of Little Cottonwood Canyon, the resorts first linked their lifts the same winter the games kicked off in nearby Salt Lake City; ever since, their nearly 5000 combined acres have added up to the finest downhill skiing experience in North America. Like two brothers forced to share a bedroom, the resorts have learned to co-exist while maintaining their distinctive characters. Alta, the little resort that could – or, better yet, wouldn't – opened in 1939. Not much has changed since then, and therein lies Alta's charm: while other resorts loudly embrace all thing modern, anachronistic Alta tenaciously holds onto its old-world lodges, creaky double-chair lifts and ban on snowboarding, prizing tradition over convenience at nearly ever turn. Opened forty years later, brash Snowbird next door welcomes boarders and any other daredevils willing to ride the thrilling aerial tram zipping nearly 3000 vertical feet up to the crest of hidden peak. Steep-and-deep is the quickest way to describe the riding here, where a ski-it-if-you-can ethos prevails.

Granted, you won't find a hip village like nearby Park City, or the glitzy crowds that flock to Aspen and Vail in Colorado at either resort. Instead you'll encounter laid-back downhillers happy to spend their time exploring a spine-tingling collection of chutes, cirques, cliffs and knee-knocking steeps that can leave even the most hardcore enthusiast humbled. Softening the inevitable spills, an epic 500 inches of yearly snowfall forms light, fluffy pillows. So much snow can dump at once, in fact, that breakfast is often accompanied by the deep, pleasing boom of World War II-era howitzers blasting away at fresh drifts, readying the slopes for a morning filled with first tracks through deep powder.

561 WOLF-WATCHING IN YELLOWSTONE NATIONAL PARK

WYOMING Waking at ink-black 4am to groggily don layers of long-underwear is an inauspicious start to a day. And huddling with strangers on a roadside turnout a half-hour later, shivering against the well-below freezing temperature, hardly sounds better. But as a crack of light on the horizon grows and an eerie chorus of hair-raising howls rises from the gloom ahead, your discomfort is soon forgotten. The morning's wolf-watch is already a success. When it was founded in 1872, Yellowstone was celebrated as a wonderland of gushing geysers, where elk and bison roamed freely. But while visitors flocked to the world's first national park to glory in the steady steam of Old Faithful, indigenous animals believed to be a danger to man were trapped and killed at virtually every opportunity. Gray wolves were particularly feared, and the last pack was exterminated in 1926. For nearly seventy years, wolves, once the continent's most abundant predator, were absent from the country's most prized ecosystem.

It took until the winter of 1995 for the first group of Canadian gray wolves to be trucked in under the Roosevelt Arch. The reintroduction program has been a runaway success and, at the time of writing, about 150 wolves roam here. Thanks to the high density of prey, a single pack in Yellowstone can live within less than fifty square miles, making the park the world's most reliable place in the wild for watching wolves. The Lamar Valley, where the wolves were all originally released, remains the best spot to catch a glimpse of these complex and social creatures, who rely on teamwork to take down prey in bloody battles but also to raise new pups each spring. Even if you're not fortunate enough to see a wolf, you'll get to interact with the omnipresent wolf-watching parties clustered along the park's highways, exchanging stories of favorite wolves and dramatic hunts between peeks through a line of spotting scopes.

562 TOURING GRACELAND

TENNESSEE As pilgrimages go, touring Graceland isn't the most obvious religious experience. The Memphis home of legendary rock-and-roll star Elvis Presley doesn't promise miraculous healing or other spiritual rewards. But for those who perceive truth in timeless popular music – as well as in touchingly bad taste – a visit to the home of "the king" is more illuminating than Lourdes.

From Elvis's first flush of success (he bought the house in 1957 with the profits from his first hit, *Heartbreak Hotel*) to his ignominious death twenty years later, Graceland witnessed the bloom and eventual bloat of one of America's biggest legends. Just as he mixed country, gospel and rhythm and blues to concoct the new sound of rock-and-roll, Presley had an "anything goes" attitude toward decorating. The tiki splendour of the jungle room, which has green shag carpeting on the floor and the ceiling, is only steps from the billiards room, where the couch and the walls are covered in matching quilt-print upholstery. In the living room, a fifteen-foot-long white sofa sets off a glistening black grand piano. (The audio tour commentary, from Lisa Marie Presley, is understandably preoccupied with her father's impetuous shopping habits.)

Amid all the glitz, though, you can still glimpse an underlying humility. A modest, windowless kitchen was one of the King's favourite rooms, and the blocky, colonial-style house itself is nothing compared to today's mega-mansions, especially considering he shared the place with his extended family for decades. The quiet, green grounds are a respite from the less-than-attractive patch of Memphis outside. And even after passing through a monumental trophy room and a display of Elvis's finest jewel-encrusted jumpsuits, you can't help but think that this was a man who hadn't strayed too far from his rural Mississippi roots.

Serious pilgrims pay their respects at Elvis's grave, set in the garden at the side of the house. Around the mid-August anniversary of the singer's death, tens of thousands flock here to deposit flowers, notes and gifts – an homage to a uniquely American sort of saint.

563 HITTING THE TRACK AT THE INDIANAPOLIS 500

INDIANA "Gentlemen, start your engines!" With that, the crowd noise crescendos to a deafening roar and 33 cars line up to await the start of the most thrilling speedway race in the world. The numbers boggle the mind: five hundred tension-filled laps, speeds topping off around 230mph, more than half-a-million spectators, $10 million-plus in prize money. The Indy 500 is an electrifying experience, not to mention the event that best embodies the American obsession with getting somewhere FAST – in this case, right back where you started.

Visitors come for the glitz and glamour as well as the star-power of legends like Mario Andretti, hailed as the greatest driver of all time, who conquered Indy in 1969 and now watches his sons, grandson and nephew compete. But the race is not without its homespun midwestern charm: rather than a champagne spray, the winner's celebratory libation is … milk, a tradition since 1937, after three-time winner Louis Meyer chugged a glass of buttermilk in Victory Lane the year before. The garage area is still referred to as Gasoline Alley, even though the cars run on methanol, and the final practice race is known as "Carb day," despite the switch to fuel-injection systems.

If the earsplitting noise and heart-stopping speeds don't provide enough of a rush, pivoting your foot on the accelerator of a real 600 horsepower V-8 Nascar certainly will. The BePetty School of Racing allows you to experience first-hand the thrill of Indy-car racing on the actual Indy track. After being kitted out in racing suits, each class of around twenty aspiring Andrettis is given a crash course in safety, driving instructions and an introduction to the philosophy of "trust the car" before competing for the fastest average lap speed. If your blood's not racing when you step out of the car, you must be made of stone.

ANGLING FOR BROWN BEARS AT BROOKS FALLS

564

ALASKA If you've ever seen a photo of a huge brown bear standing knee-deep in rushing water, poised to catch a leaping salmon in its mouth, there's a 95 percent chance it was taken at Brooks Falls, a stalling point for the millions of sockeye salmon that make their annual spawning run up the Brooks River. Each July, at the height of the migration, bears flock in to exploit the excellent feeding possibilities, and with viewing platforms set up a few feet from the action, watching them is both exhilarating and slightly nerve-racking. It's easy to feel as though you're right in the middle of a wildlife documentary.

At any one time, you might see a dozen or more jockeying for position. Such proximity causes considerable friction among these naturally solitary animals, but size, age and experience define a hierarchy that allows posturing and roaring to take the place of genuine battles. Fluffy and defenceless babies are highly vulnerable to fatal attacks from adult males, so the mothers go to great lengths to ensure they're secure, sending their cubs to the topmost branches of nearby trees and then fishing warily close by. Daring juveniles like to grab the prime fishing spot atop the falls, but become very nervous if bears higher up the pecking order come close – successfully holding pole position might mean moving up the rankings, but the youngster risks a severe beating. Some older and wiser bears prefer wallowing in the pool below the falls: one regular visitor dives down every few minutes and always seems to come up with flapping sockeye in his mouth. Come the end of the salmon run, the bears head for the hills, only to return in September for a final pre-hibernation gorge on the carcasses of the spent fish as they drift downstream.

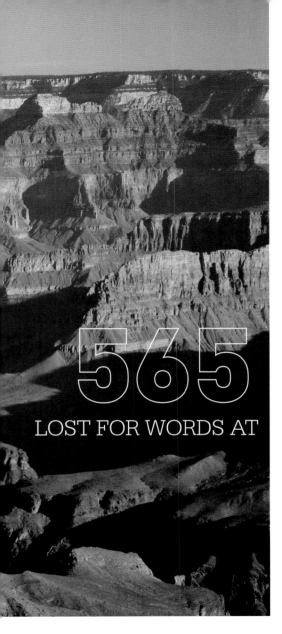

565

LOST FOR WORDS AT

ARIZONA If a guidebook tells you that something is "impossible to describe", it usually means the writer can't be bothered to describe it – with one exception. After pondering the views of the Grand Canyon for the first time, the most spectacular natural wonder on earth, most visitors are stunned into silence. Committed travellers hike down to the canyon floor on foot or by mule, spending a night at *Phantom Ranch*, or hover above in a helicopter to get a better feeling for its dimensions. But it is still hard to grasp. The problem isn't lack of words. It's just that the canyon is so vast and so deep, that the vista stretches so far across your line of vision, up, down and across, giving the impression of hundreds of miles of space, that it's a bit like looking at one of those puzzles in reverse – the more you stare, the more it becomes harder to work out what it is or where you are. Distance becomes meaningless, depth blurs, and your sense of time and space withers away.

The facts are similarly mind-boggling: the Grand Canyon is around 277 miles long and one mile deep. The South Rim, where most of the tourists go, averages 7000 feet, while the North Rim is over 8000 feet high – its alpine landscape only adding to the sense of the surreal. On the canyon floor flows the Colorado River, its waters carving out the gorge over five to six million years and exposing rocks that are up to two billion years old through vividly coloured strata. It's this incredible chromatic element that stays with you almost as much as the canyon's size, with the various layers of reds, ochres and yellows seemingly painted over the strangely shaped tower formations and broken cliffs. Think of it this way: the Grand Canyon is like a mountain range upside down. The country around the top is basically flat and all the rugged, craggy elements are below you. The abruptness of the drop is bizarre and, for some, unnerving. But the Grand Canyon is like that: it picks you up and takes you out of your comfort zone, dropping you back just that little bit changed.

THE GRAND CANYON

MISCELLANY

CITIES

The most populous US cities are New York City (8.1 million people), Los Angeles (3.8 million), Chicago (2.8 million) and Houston (2 million), followed by a close race between Philadelphia and Phoenix (both around 1.5 million); the latter is also the country's fastest-growing major city. Among the fastest-shrinking major cities are Detroit, Boston, Cincinnati and St Louis; New Orleans, which lost a great deal of its population after Hurricane Katrina, has started to see growth again, and recent estimates put the population at around 250,000, or a bit more than half its pre-Katrina levels.

FIVE STYLISH HOTELS

Hotel Bel-Air Los Angeles, CA Set in a lush, isolated canyon in the elite confines of Bel Air. The most luxurious hotel on the West Coast.
The Carlyle New York, NY A grand Upper East Side landmark with a fine view of Central Park, genteel service and classically styled rooms and suites.
The Hay-Adams Washington DC Elegant Renaissance Revival icon overlooking the White House since the 1920s.
The Phoenician Scottsdale, AZ Among the country's best resorts, in the shadow of Camelback Mountain.
The Peabody Memphis, TN Luxurious downtown hotel, famous for the resident ducks that parade to and from the lobby every day.

EXTREME CLIMATE

The lowest, hottest and driest points in the US are all in **Death Valley**. Badwater basin is 282 feet below sea level, while the ironically named Greenland Ranch reached 135°F in 2001 (the highest temperature ever recorded in the US and the second-highest in the world). Death Valley's overall average precipitation is less than two inches per year.

ELVIS IS EVERYWHERE

Elvis Presley had 31 #1 songs between Billboard's US charts and the UK top 40, the first of which was the bluesy **Heartbreak Hotel**, in 1956; the most recent was a remix of **A Little Less Conversation**, in 2002 (which only hit #50 in the US). Coincidentally, Elvis made 31 movies during his lifetime, sharing the screen with everyone from Walter Matthau and Bill Bixby to Barbara Stanwyck and Mary Tyler Moore. More than 600,000 visitors make the pilgrimage each year to visit the King's home, Graceland, in Memphis, Tennessee.

"Whoever wants to know America had better learn baseball"

Jacques Barzun

CHEERS

Far and away the American drink of choice is carbonated soda; it's consumed in quantities more than twice as great as its nearest competitors (coffee, bottled water, tap water and beer, not necessarily in that order). Bottled water is the beverage growing fastest in market share; meanwhile, Americans consume four times as much beer as they do wine, not taking into account the difference in serving size (12oz vs 5oz).

FIVE UNUSUAL FESTIVALS

World Grits Festival, St George, SC (mid-April). Consuming corn porridge in the grits-eating capital of the world.
Solstice Parade, Seattle, WA (mid-June). Nude bike-riding.
Redneck Games, East Dublin, GA (early July). Hillbilly Olympics, featuring seed spitting and bobbing for pig's feet.
Lumberjack World Championships, Hayward, WI (late July). Climbing, sawing and rolling logs.
Punkin' Chuckin', Millsboro, DE (early Nov). Hurling pumpkins by catapult.

CUISINE

One of the more refined American cooking styles, **California Cuisine** was pioneered in the 1970s by Alice Waters of *Chez Panisse* in Berkeley and Michael McCarty of *Michael's* in Santa Monica; both restaurants, and restaurateurs, are still going strong. Borrowing from French *nouvelle cuisine*, the California variant emphasizes fresh, local ingredients, creative presentation and novel combinations. California Cuisine predates New American Cuisine, which brought these notions to a wider national audience starting in the 1980s. Other – and typically heartier – regional American cuisines include:

INDIGENOUS CUISINE	SIGNATURE DISH	CULINARY CAPITAL
Barbecue	ribs/brisket	Texas
Cajun	jambalaya	New Orleans, LA
Creole	gumbo	New Orleans, LA
Southern	grits (boiled milled corn)	Atlanta, GA/Charleston, SC
Southwestern	chili con carne	Arizona/New Mexico
Tex-Mex	fajitas	South Texas

STATE MOTTOES

STATE	MOTTTO
California	Eureka
Kansas	To the stars through difficulties
Maine	I direct
Maryland	Manly deeds, womanly words
Massachusetts	By the sword we seek peace, but peace only under liberty
Michigan	If you seek a pleasant peninsula, look around you
Montana	Gold and silver
New Hampshire	Live free or die
New Mexico	It grows as it goes
New York	Excelsior!
Oregon	She flies with her own wings
Texas	Friendship
Utah	Industry
Virginia	Thus always to tyrants
West Virginia	Mountaineers are always free

MOVIES

Citizen Kane, Orson Welles' groundbreaking tale of power and corruption, is generally considered the greatest American film ever made, though *Casablanca, The Godfather* and *Raging Bull*, among others, tend to figure in the debate.

The worst American film ever made is generally acknowledged to be *Plan 9 from Outer Space* (1959), Ed Wood's classic sci-fi schlock-fest that, perversely, also has fans claiming it among the best – or at least most fun – films ever made.

On a less subjective note, the five highest grossing American films of all time (US box office only; figures not adjusted for inflation) are *Titanic* (1997), *Star Wars* (1977), *Shrek 2* (2004), *ET: the Extra Terrestrial* (1982), and *Star Wars: Episode I – The Phantom Menace* (1999).

THANKSGIVING

Thanksgiving has been officially observed in the US since the Civil War, though its legend dates back to 1621 as part of a goodwill ceremony between English Pilgrims and Wampanoag Indians in Plymouth Plantation. These days a traditional menu includes:

One large turkey
Bread or mushroom stuffing
Mashed potatoes with gravy
Sweet potatoes/yams
Cranberry sauce
Creamed onions
Green beans or Brussels sprouts
Waldorf or other salad (Waldorf salad is typically apples, celery, walnuts and mayonnaise)
Rolls or biscuits
Pumpkin/pecan/apple pie(s)

PRESIDENTS

There have been 42 US presidents but since one, Grover Cleveland, was elected twice (non-consecutively), George W. Bush is considered the 43rd president. Presidents serve four years in a term and have a two-term limit.

Gerald Ford is the only person in US history to have served as vice president and president without having been elected to either position; he was appointed to both positions after the resignations of Spiro Agnew and Richard Nixon, respectively.

Because US presidents are elected by electoral votes and not popular votes, four men have become president without receiving the most votes from the people: John Quincy Adams (1824), Rutherford B. Hayes (1876), Benjamin Harrison (1888) and George W. Bush (2000).

"In America, anyone can become president. That's one of the risks you take"

Adlai Stevenson

POLITICS

Two parties dominate politics in America. The Democratic Party is the world's second-oldest still-functional political party, dating from 1792 when it was known as the Democratic-Republican Party. Today's Republican Party was formed in 1854, largely from anti-slavery factions. Once prominent political parties that no longer exist include the Federalist, Anti-Federalist, Anti-Masonic, Whig, Know-Nothing, Free Soil, Populist and Progressive.

TELEVISION

According to *TV Guide*, the greatest American television shows in history are, in order, *Seinfeld*, *I Love Lucy*, *The Honeymooners*, *All In the Family*, and *The Sopranos*. The worst, in reverse order, are *Hogan's Heroes*, *The Brady Bunch Hour* (variety show), *XFL Football*, *My Mother the Car* and *The Jerry Springer Show*.

The two most watched American primetime telecasts of all time were the finale of *M*A*S*H* (more than 100 million viewers; February 28, 1983) and the episode of *Dallas* known as "Who Shot J.R?" (more than 90 million viewers; November 21, 1980). According to recent A.C. Nielsen figures, the average American watches 4 hours and 32 minutes of TV per day – equivalent to fourteen years of viewing for the average lifespan.

A DOG'S LIFE

Americans' favorite pets are dogs (36 percent of households have at least one), cats (32 percent), birds (5 percent), and horses (2 percent). Dogs are favoured by all income groups and households – except those living alone, who favour cats.

GREAT AMERICAN NOVELS

Invisible Man, Ralph Ellison. The greatest, and most depressing, portrait of race relations in mid-twentieth-century America.
The Sound and the Fury, William Faulkner. The quintessential Southern writer's masterwork, told from four different perspectives in four wildly different styles.
Moby Dick, Herman Melville. A regular contender for *the* greatest American novel, tells a gripping tale of survival, salvation and society on the high seas.
The Adventures of Huckleberry Finn, Mark Twain. Still complex and challenging after 120 years, the signature tale of life on the Mississippi River in antebellum America.
Slaughterhouse Five, Kurt Vonnegut. The most experimental of the country's greatest novels, blending a brutal wartime saga with time travel and a fractured narrative.

CYCLING AROUND STANLEY PARK • CRUISING GEORGIAN BAY • THE THRILL OF BACK COUNTRY SKIING • BEACHING IT WITH A LITERARY CLASSIC • CAMPING BENEATH HEAD-SMASHED-IN BUFFALO JUMP • CATCHING A WAVE ON VANCOUVER ISLAND • COASTING ON THE P'TIT TRAIN DU NORD • CROSSING THE PRAIRIES BY TRAIN • THE ICE ROAD FROM INUVIK TO TUKTOYAKTUK • EATING YOUR WAY AROUND THE WORLD IN TORONTO • EXPLORING ANCIENT CULTURE ON HAIDA GWAII • GETTING LOST WITHIN THE WALLS OF VIEUX-QUEBEC • LIGHTING UP THE SKY IN MONTREAL • DRIVING THE ICEFIELDS PARKWAY • PADDLING YOUR WAY THROUGH ALGONQUIN PROVINCIAL PARK • SPYING WHALES AND SPOTTING PUFFINS IN THE ATLANTIC • REDEFINING REMOTE ON THE HUDSON BAY TRAIN • RELIVING THE WILD WEST AT THE CALGARY STAMPEDE • SEA KAYAKING IN THE MINGAM ARCHIPELAGO • SEEING OLD RIVALS IN AN ICE HOCKEY GAME • SKI FROM THE SKY IN THE ROCKIES • STAYING AFLOAT ON LITTLE MANITOU LAKE • STRIKING IT LUCKY IN DAWSON CITY • TAKING AFTERNOON TEA IN VICTORIA • FOLLOWING THE YUKON QUEST TRAIL • IN AWE OF THE AURORA BOREALIS IN YELLOWKNIFE • WATCHING THE TIDE ROLL AWAY IN THE BAY OF FUNDY • CRUISING GEORGIAN BAY • THE THRILL OF BACK COUNTRY SKIING • BEACHING IT WITH A LITERARY CLASSIC • CATCHING A WAVE ON VANCOUVER ISLAND • COASTING ON THE P'TIT TRAIN DU NORD • CROSSING THE PRAIRIES BY TRAIN • CYCLING AROUND STANLEY PARK • DRIVING THE ICEFIELDS PARKWAY • THE ICE ROAD FROM INUVIK TO TUKTOYAKTUK • EATING YOUR WAY AROUND THE WORLD IN TORONTO • EXPLORING ANCIENT CULTURE ON HAIDA GWAII • FORM A LASTING IMPRESSION AT NIAGARA FALLS • TRACKING DOWN POLAR BEARS IN CHURCHILL • GETTING LOST WITHIN THE WALLS OF VIEUX-QUEBEC • HIKING AROUND LAKE LOUISE • LIGHTING UP THE SKY IN MONTREAL • PADDLING YOUR WAY THROUGH ALGONQUIN PROVINCIAL PARK • TRACKING DOWN POLAR BEARS IN CHURCHILL • SEEING OLD RIVALS IN AN ICE HOCKEY GAME • REDEFINING REMOTE ON THE HUDSON BAY TRAIN • RELIVING THE WILD WEST AT THE CALGARY STAMPEDE • SEA KAYAKING IN THE MINGAM ARCHIPELAGO • SKI FROM THE SKY IN THE ROCKIES • SPYING WHALES AND SPOTTING PUFFINS IN THE ATLANTIC • STAYING AFLOAT ON LITTLE MANITOU LAKE • STRIKING IT LUCKY IN DAWSON CITY • TAKING AFTERNOON TEA IN VICTORIA • FOLLOWING THE YUKON QUEST TRAIL • IN AWE OF THE AURORA BOREALIS IN YELLOWKNIFE • FORM A LASTING IMPRESSION AT NIAGARA FALLS • WATCHING THE TIDE ROLL AWAY IN THE BAY OF FUNDY • CRUISING GEORGIAN BAY • THE THRILL OF BACK COUNTRY SKIING • BEACHING IT WITH A LITERARY CLASSIC • CAMPING BENEATH HEAD-SMASHED-IN BUFFALO JUMP • CATCHING A WAVE ON VANCOUVER ISLAND • COASTING ON THE P'TIT TRAIN DU NORD • CROSSING THE PRAIRIES BY TRAIN • CYCLING AROUND STANLEY PARK • DRIVING THE ICEFIELDS PARKWAY • THE ICE ROAD FROM INUVIK TO TUKTOYAKTUK • EATING YOUR WAY AROUND THE WORLD IN TORONTO • EXPLORING ANCIENT CULTURE ON HAIDA GWAII • FORM A LASTING IMPRESSION AT NIAGARA FALLS • GETTING LOST WITHIN THE WALLS OF VIEUX-QUEBEC • HIKING AROUND LAKE LOUISE • LIGHTING UP THE SKY IN MONTREAL • PADDLING YOUR WAY THROUGH ALGONQUIN PROVINCIAL PARK • TRACKING DOWN POLAR BEARS IN CHURCHILL • CAMPING BENEATH HEAD-SMASHED-IN BUFFALO JUMP • REDEFINING REMOTE ON THE HUDSON BAY TRAIN • RELIVING THE WILD WEST AT THE CALGARY STAMPEDE • SEA KAYAKING IN THE MINGAM ARCHIPELAGO • SEEING OLD RIVALS IN AN ICE HOCKEY GAME • SKI FROM THE SKY IN THE ROCKIES • SPYING WHALES AND SPOTTING PUFFINS IN THE ATLANTIC • STAYING AFLOAT ON LITTLE MANITOU LAKE • HIKING AROUND LAKE LOUISE • CRUISING GEORGIAN BAY • THE THRILL OF BACK COUNTRY SKIING • BEACHING IT WITH A LITERARY

CANADA

566–596

STRIKING IT LUCKY
IN DAWSON CITY — 579

IN AWE OF THE
AURORA BOREALIS — 569

TRACKING DOWN POLAR BEARS
IN CHURCHILL — 587

SPYING WHALES AND
SPOTTING PUFFINS
IN THE ATLANTIC — 580

CANADA

CYCLING AROUND
STANLEY PARK — 589

CROSSING THE PRAIRIES
BY TRAIN — 571

GETTING LOST
WITHIN THE WALLS
OF VIEUX-QUÉBEC — 567

CAMPING BENEATH
HEAD-SMASHED-IN
BUFFALO JUMP — 574

SEEING OLD RIVALS
IN AN ICE-HOCKEY GAME — 592

FORM A LASTING IMPRESSION
AT NIAGARA FALLS — 593

ALBERTA It's the kind of place you have to see to believe: an impossibly turquoise lake backed by forested slopes, snow-clad mountains and an imposing white glacier. Once this perfect vision is in view, your first instinct will be to take photograph after photograph, as if frightened that the place might suddenly, inexplicably, disappear. Your next instinct should be to strike out into the wilderness that surrounds resplendent Lake Louise, jewel of Banff National Park – not just to see the lake from a few more angles, but to conquer some of the most astonishing day-hiking territory in the world.

The immediate area has hours of well-maintained trails. Some are flat and follow the lake's edge, offering images of towering white peaks reflected in serene, crystal clear water; others climb up, deep into the forest, to rustic teahouses and smaller shimmering lakes cradled in the mountains. Dazzling views unfold at every switchback. The most strenuous hike takes you on a twenty-kilometre odyssey to Louise's smaller, scenic rival (hard as that may be to believe), Moraine Lake. Another trail brings you face-to-face with the icy, crevassed Victoria Glacier which, every spring, melts and flows into Lake Louise, carrying with it the finely ground glacial silt which gives the lake its emerald hue. Here, you can also watch massive chunks of snow crash from mountainsides, creating almighty booms that reverberate throughout the valley.

HIKING AROUND
LAKE LOUISE

566

Getting lost within the
walls of Vieux-Québec

QUÉBEC You'd be forgiven for mistaking Canada's most graceful downtown for somewhere in the middle of Europe. As you amble the cobbled streets of a centuries-old walled city, where the views encompass castle turrets and battlefields – and the main language spoken is French – it's easy to feel you've left North America behind. Founded by the French in 1608, Québec City was taken by the English in a 1759 battle just outside the city walls; the victory also won them control of all Canada. The fortifications survive today, making it North America's only walled city; they mark the boundaries of the old town, or Vieux-Québec. Its lovingly maintained chaotic tangle of streets holds a treasury of historic architecture, fine restaurants and tiny museums. Puttering around its pedestrianized precincts – which are virtually untouched by minimarts, chain stores and fast-food restaurants – is the chief pleasure of a visit here.

The lower town, particularly the Quartier Petit-Champlain – a beautiful warren of narrow lanes and hidden staircases lined by carefully restored limestone buildings – is a good place to begin an aimless wander. It's easy to idle away hours soaking up the historic charm, listening to buskers and browsing refined boutiques, antique shops and studio-galleries where artists are often at work, before being tempted by the aromas that drift from the doorways of the many old-fashioned restaurants.

Luckily the climbs up and down the steeply sloping streets and staircases around the town help justify indulging in rich, multicourse meals. After some Québecois foie gras, local duck, rabbit or wild game, and creamy local cheeses, you'll need to hit the streets again to walk it all off.

568 EXPLORING ANCIENT CULTURE ON HAIDA GWAII

BRITISH COLUMBIA Soaking in natural hot springs on a rainforest island while a pod of humpback whales swims past . . . suddenly the "Canadian Galápagos" moniker, occasionally used to describe the remote archipelago of Haida Gwaii, doesn't seem so far-fetched.

Cast some 150km off the west coast of British Columbia, Haida Gwaii (formerly the Queen Charlotte Islands) is a place where the world's largest black bears forage on deserted beaches, black-footed albatross show off their enormous wingspan, and sea stars the size of coffee tables and the shades of disco lights sprawl languidly on rocks.

Only two thousand people a year make the journey to the pristine national park in the southern portion of the islands. Here, it takes eight people to hug a thousand-year-old cedar tree, months to kayak around the 1750km of coastline and a lifetime for an archaeologist to uncover artefacts left untouched by a 10,000-year-old civilization. There is an underlying eeriness to this place that was, until recently, home to thousands of Haida – the most sophisticated and artistically prolific of British Columbia's indigenous people.

These days, moss-covered beams of long houses and decaying totem poles are the lingering remains of the ancient Haida villages, whose populations left after being drastically reduced in an 1880s smallpox epidemic. The most haunting and remote of the deserted villages is SGang Gwaay (Ninstints), a mist-shrouded UNESCO World Heritage Site on the southernmost tip of the park, where the world's largest collection of Haida mortuary poles stare defiantly out to sea.

Looking up at this forest of tree trunks – expertly carved with the wide-eyed features of bears, frogs, beavers, eagles, ravens and whales – is to gaze into the weather-beaten face of history. However, as is the wish of the Haida, there is little attempt at preserving the totems. Some day soon the poles will lean, fall, rot, and – like everything else here – return to nature.

569 IN AWE OF THE AURORA BOREALIS

NORTHWEST TERRITORIES Both a natural wonder and altogether otherworldly, the stunning aurora borealis (northern lights) are every bit worth travelling to the far reaches of Canada's Great North to see – and in sub-zero temperatures, no less. Some Inuit peoples believed they were the spirits of animals or ancestors, while others thought they represented wicked forces. Today, science explains the phenomenon as the result of "solar wind" – charged particles hurled from the sun and drawn into the earth's atmosphere by the magnetism of the poles – and the solar wind's interaction with the earth's magnetic field. Some of this energy is released as visible light, offering an extraordinary chance to observe the upper limits of the atmosphere.

The ethereal display can be seen over large areas of northern Canada, but nowhere better than between December and March in Yellowknife, the capital of the Northwest Territories. Just 400 kilometres south of the Arctic Circle, Yellowknife's northerly location combined with the surrounding flat terrain offers the perfect vantage point.

A faint glow on the northeastern horizon after dusk signals that it's time to swaddle in parkas, ski pants, thick-soled boots, woolly headgear and gauntlet-sized gloves, and head out to watch the full show as night deepens. Eventually the sky will appear to shimmer with dancing curtains of colour, ranging from luminescent monotones – most commonly fantastic green or a dark red veil. Soon their movement becomes more animated, sometimes building up into a finale, in which rays seem to flare in all directions from a central point, slowly waving and swirling like incandescent tassels.

570 SKI FROM THE SKY IN THE ROCKIES

BRITISH COLUMBIA The small town of Golden, between Glacier and Revelstoke national parks near the BC-Alberta border, doesn't seem like much as you pass through. But descend on a snowy peak in the area from a helicopter, skis in tow, and you're likely to form a totally different opinion.

Heliskiing got its start here, and the Rocky Mountains of British Columbia are still one of the best places on earth to do this terrifically expensive, fairly dangerous and undeniably thrilling activity. It's a pristine mountain wonderland filled with open bowls and endless tree runs, all coated in a layer of light and powdery snow. Accessing these stashes by helicopter, with its odd mix of mobility and avian fragility, only intensifies the feeling of exploration and isolation. From the air, you'll eagerly envision making your signature squiggles in the untouched powder fields. And once the helicopter leaves you alone and recedes into the distance, you'll feel every inch the pioneer.

After you've adjusted to the rhythm and bounce of skiing or riding this light powder, you might find yourself on a good day descending twice the typical distance as at a top ski resort.

You're also likely to discover that the deeper the snow and steeper the grade, the more exhilarating the run. Cornices and drop-offs that seemed foreboding from the helicopter will be a daring enticement; trees that from a distance looked impossibly dense reveal tempting paths; you'll drop into pitches that would have been unthinkable on harder snow, plunging in and out of chest-deep powder again and again. But be warned: all this may be enough to transform you into one of the many die hards who sign up for their next heliskiing adventure the moment they reach base.

571 EATING YOUR WAY AROUND THE WORLD IN TORONTO

ONTARIO Walking around Toronto's main Chinatown, you may find resistance futile: the smells of spicy black bean sauce, Peking duck and fried noodles hit you from every direction. Besides the restaurants – not all Chinese of course, with plenty of Vietnamese, Thai and Japanese eateries as well – street grocers vend everything from stinky durian fruit to delightful pork-stuffed buns. However, eating in Chinatown – like the rest of Toronto – is not just about the food: choose a restaurant busy with locals, order a cup of green or bubble tea, then sit back and be transported to the country of your choice.

Near Chinatown is Kensington Market, an ethnically diverse area crowded with street stalls. Dodge the clothing sellers and let your nose lead you to the food section, where you'll find a selection of crêpe and poutine vendors. A nod to early French and British influences, poutine is as close to a national dish as

you'll get in a country this immense. Gloriously golden fries drip with melted cheese, capped by a pool of gravy; it's a simple pleasure that's actually quite hard to get right, as they do here.

The suburbs of Toronto also resemble hamlets of faraway lands. Little India is the spot for your favourite spicy vindaloos and Little Portugal where to get a bowl of caldo verde, while in Greektown you'll find the perfect strong mid-afternoon cup of coffee alongside divine Greek pastries – a little pick-me-up before contemplating your next culinary stop.

For that, go back downtown; while others line up for dinner at the rotating restaurant in the CN Tower, you might consider somewhere like *Canoe*, up on the 54th floor of the Dominion Tower. You still get great views, but in a less touristy venue that happens to serve up some of the best Canadian food (and wines) in the country.

572 TAKING AFTERNOON TEA IN VICTORIA

BRITISH COLUMBIA Silver cutlery tinkles against Royal Doulton china as piano music wafts over idle chatter. "Would you like one lump or two?" enquires the waitress politely as she pours the piping hot tea. You'll take two, you say, and sink back into the floral sofa, taking in this most splendid view of Victoria's Inner Harbour from the *Tea Lobby* in the *Empress Hotel*. Rudyard Kipling once took afternoon tea in this very room and described Victoria as "Brighton Pavilion with the Himalayas for a backdrop". You can't help but agree with him.

Indeed, this provincial capital on the southern tip of wild and windy Vancouver Island is doing its bit to keep the "British" in British Columbia. Vancouver may have embraced lofty glass condominiums and coffee, but across the Georgia Strait, Victoria has clung steadfastly to its English heritage, preserving its turn-of-the-twentieth-century architecture and keeping alive the age-old tradition of afternoon tea.

There are many quaint places in Victoria to indulge this whim – small, suburban teahouses surrounded by royal family memorabilia, or amidst the floral finery of the Butchart Gardens – but none can match the palatial *Empress Hotel* for grandiosity or price. Shirley Temple, John Travolta and Queen Elizabeth II have all been spotted here piling on the pounds.

The multicourse ritual starts off innocently enough, with seasonal fruit topped with Chantilly cream along with a choice of eight tea blends. Then a three-tiered plate arrives, heaving with cucumber and smoked salmon sandwiches, raisin scones slathered with jam and clotted cream and, on top, a glorious selection of pastries oozing with chocolate. If you're too self-conscious to indulge in the very un-English practice of stuffing yourself silly, you could always fall back on the distinctly North American custom of asking for a doggie bag.

573 SEA KAYAKING IN THE MINGAN ARCHIPELAGO

QUÉBEC On the map, the Mingan Archipelago, stretching 150km from Longue-Pointe-de-Mingan to Aguanish, looks like a trail of biscuit crumbs scattered in the Gulf of St Lawrence. From the vantage point of your sea kayak, cruising through the channels that separate this collection of forty uninhabited islands and nearly a thousand islets and reefs, it's a much different story. For one, it's impossible to miss the tall rock monoliths that guard the bays. The sea has worn the rock into smooth curves, and the monoliths look very much like people from a distance, like towers of abandoned flying saucers placed one on top of the other from closer to shore. For another, much of what you're paddling around to see actually lurks beneath the surface. The waters are a feeding ground for the largest mammal on earth, the blue whale, as well as minke, fin, beluga and humpback whales. Keep your eyes trained on the horizon

looking for the telltale puff of water vapour blown by a whale as it surfaces. But don't ignore what's right around you: seals pop their heads through the waves, like periscopes, no more than a few strokes away. As if curious, they stare at you with their moustachioed faces and big brown eyes, before disappearing with a flash of silver underbelly.

Beneath your paddles the water is so clear that it magnifies the seabed. Bright orange sea stars, deep red urchins and lime green kelp crust the sea floor, the rock worn into underwater monoliths or crazy paved ledges. As sunset stains the sea pink and purple, you'll need to pick an island and a beachside campsite. Civilization feels a galaxy away as you laze around the campfire or scramble up a clifftop for a last gaze out at sea, hopeful of spotting the silhouette of a whale against the sinking sun.

574 CAMPING BENEATH HEAD-SMASHED-IN BUFFALO JUMP

ALBERTA Long ago, our ancestors subsisted on berries, roots, birds and small animals. Buffalo herds roamed the grasslands of the Great Plains, but they weren't hunted, as these enormous, horned mammals attacked humans. Then one day, Napi, the Blackfoot Supreme Being, visited his people, and saw scattered bodies that had been partly devoured by buffalo. Napi declared, "This will not do, I will change this. My people shall eat the buffalo".

This was one of several stories told to us by our host, a young member of the Blackfoot's Peigan tribe, around the campfire of the tepee site beneath poetically named Head-Smashed-In Buffalo Jump. Here, in southern Alberta, Napi supposedly led a buffalo herd to the rugged Porcupine Hills and unveiled the pis'kun – buffalo jump – method of killing the animal. Whatever credence the myth has, Head-Smashed-In was used as a staging ground for killing great numbers of bison for over 10,000 years, up until around 150 years ago.

Earlier that day, our host had shown us V-shaped lanes along which buffalo, stalked by hundreds of Blackfoot braves wrapped in buffalo or coyote robes, were stampeded in a tight herd, led over the dust-obscured cliff to fall to their deaths. Cunningly built into the cliff now is an impressive interpretive centre, which further explains the custom and offers excellent insight into the old Blackfoot way of life. But so did our guide, who stressed how the Blackfoot let nothing go to waste. Objects fashioned from a bewildering array of buffalo parts got passed around; for the Blackfoot, a herd resembled "a walking department store", providing for their every need.

In this remote provincial corner, the beast remains a powerful cultural symbol, and a night's camping the chance to commune with a disappearing way of life. As midnight struck and the fire burned its last, we entered our tepee. The moon and stars illuminated the vast prairie, the still night interrupted only by the occasional mooing of cattle grazing on the range beyond the campsite.

575 THE ICE ROAD FROM INUVIK TO TUKTOYAKTUK

NORTHWEST TERRITORIES Tuktoyaktuk is an Inuit community on the shores of the Beaufort Sea. In the summer, its thousand inhabitants can access the outside world only by air or water. During the dark Arctic winter, though, one aspect of life is easier for the people of Tuk. They can drive to their nearest town, Inuvik in Canada's Northwest Territories, on the 194-kilometre ice road that's carved into the surface of the Mackenzie River and across the frozen ocean itself – and visitors can rent a jeep to visit them.

"You've gotta go slow", the manager of the car rental firm advises first-timers. "Remember, it's all white out there". The cautious visitor chugs tentatively onto the ice. The road is wide, smooth and gleams like a figure-skating rink. Its route weaves with the meanderings of this waterway that has featured in the writings of explorers such as Mackenzie, Franklin and Stefansson for centuries.

Early in the journey, spindly trees poke out from the land to either side of the river's banks. Then the tree line is passed and they vanish. It's utterly silent – just the occasional thrum of a passing car resonates through the still air – but it's not entirely white. As the eye adjusts to its surroundings it picks out the buttery yellow of low sunlight on ice; the inky-blue shadows thrown by mounds of snow; the pink tinge in the sky as the weak sun dips. It's not all flat, either. Pingos – mounds of earth pushed up by frozen water trapped beneath the permafrost – loom like giant molehills and, as the road leaves the river and strikes out across the ice of the Beaufort Sea, the landscape is detailed in tiny, icy peaks and troughs coloured palest violet and washed-out denim blue.

At last, the lone driver sees dark specks on the horizon: this is the settlement of Tuk, but even though it's visible to the eye, the traveller still has some way to go. This is a vast canvas and perspective has been sucked away into the white, icy air at the very top of the world.

576 THE THRILL OF BACK-COUNTRY SKIING

BRITISH COLUMBIA For back-country skiers the world over British Columbia is something of a holy grail. Mountain ranges with splendid monikers such as the Chilcotins and the Valhallas offer the textbook landscapes you'd expect of this wild province, with ice-blue glaciers clinging to high alpine peaks beneath which lie open powder fields, deep forests and white frozen lakes and rivers – scenery unchanged since humankind first moved into the area over ten thousand years ago.

A back-country ski trip offers the finest and most soulful way to explore these inspiring winter landscapes. And it's easy to give it a go since most mountain towns in British Columbia are surrounded by pristine high country. Start off on a day-trip with your mountain guide, which will have you "skinning up" gently angled slopes on your skis. This refers to the use of "skins" which are attached to the bottom of your skis and allow you to walk uphill in conjunction with special bindings that can be released at the heel.

You'll eventually emerge from pine forests into a high alpine bowl, continuing upwards to a point where, after a couple of hours, you can stop for a well-earned rest, enjoy some lunch and drink in the views.

And the best bit still awaits – remove your skins, fasten your bindings and ride all the way back down through untracked, boot-deep powder glistening in the afternoon sun.

577 CROSSING THE PRAIRIES BY TRAIN

SASKATCHEWAN & MANITOBA The prairie provinces have a somewhat unfair reputation for being uninspiring and dreary. There's no denying the winters are bitingly cold – temperatures regularly sit below -40°C and residents of Winnipeg have been known to break out the shorts when it climbs to 10°C – and perhaps the area lacks any dynamic, must-see cities. But the prairies are also the heartland of Canada, a wide-open landscape untainted by glittering skyscrapers and traffic congestion, seen to best advantage on a coast-to-coast train ride.

The train originates in Vancouver, but it's not until it heads east from Edmonton that the prairie landscape begins. From there a blanket of darkness, decorated only by stars, engulfs you. When the train pulls into Saskatchewan's capital, Saskatoon, around 2am, you're fast asleep, lulled by the train's movement, surrounded by the same darkened sky and glistening stars.

Rise in the morning and head to the viewing dome car for a panoramic view of the countryside. Snowcapped mountains and towering trees are a distant memory, replaced by seemingly endless fields of wheat and grassland. There are no houses, no signs of life except for the occasional view of elk or deer grazing trackside.

The hypnotic monotony of the journey is broken by a brief stop in Winnipeg. Canada's coldest city, "Winterpeg" is home to the windiest intersection in the country and a heated labyrinth weaving its way under the central shopping arcade. Leaving the city, you see proof of population – grain elevators and wheat silos dot the horizon, most approaching ruin; battered by the elements, they now provide a perch for the large number of bird species who feed off the fields of grain.

When you finally step off the train at its ultimate destination, bustling Toronto, the serenity of the prairies becomes a distant, lovely memory.

578 COASTING ON THE P'TIT TRAIN DU NORD

QUÉBEC After a day of pedalling, a long downhill coast is a moment to be savoured. On either side the forest is a blur of green tinged with gold and the breeze ruffling your hair smells faintly of pine and earth. The treetops almost form a tunnel around the trail but in the glimpses of sky loom crinkled mountains, and off to the right, screened by foliage, roars the frothing fury of the Rivière Rouge, the Red River.

In the silence of the forest it's hard to imagine that fume-belching locomotives once thundered along the same route as your bicycle tyres. The P'tit Train du Nord was a busy railroad for eighty years, eventually closing in 1989. Instead of abandoning the route to the forest, the rail bed was transformed into a magnificent cycle trail that winds for 200km through the splendour of the Laurentian region of southwest Québec. Many of the original railroad station houses have been converted into cafés, information booths and facilities for cyclists, their decorative wooden gables and shady terraces restored with vibrant paint and blooming baskets.

The northern half of the trail is wild and remote, crossing numerous rivers dyed chestnut-brown by minerals and passing blue-black lakes close enough to wet your wheels. Small villages full of silver-steepled churches and impossibly cosy cottages cluster around the southern half of the trail. But whichever part you choose to ride (if not the whole course), nearly every bend holds an inviting picnic spot to laze in or a shady pool to revive sore feet and aching muscles.

579 STRIKING IT LUCKY IN DAWSON CITY

YUKON In the 1890s, rumour spread that the streets of Dawson City were paved with gold. In the most hysterical gold rush stampede the world has ever known, tens of thousands of fortune-seekers packed their bags and headed north for this former patch of moose pasture just below the Arctic Circle. By the time they arrived, most of the claims had been staked, and the brothels, dance halls and theatres of this burgeoning city were busy mining every last cent from the dejected prospectors.

More than a hundred years on, the streets of Dawson City are still not paved with gold. In fact, they're not paved at all, and you need not bother panning for the few flakes of gold left in the creeks just outside town. Instead, make the trek to appreciate the rough-and-tumble feel and gold-rush-era charm, of which Dawson City still has plenty.

With its historic wooden false-fronted buildings, dirt streets, creaking boardwalks and midnight sun, it's easy to see how Dawson City inspired literary titans such as Jack London and Robert Service – not just to write about the place but to live here too.

As for striking it lucky, your best chance is at Diamond Tooth Gertie's Gambling Hall, Canada's oldest legal casino, where women in breathtaking corsets and ruffle skirts hustle up drinks while you bet your way to boom or bust. Having doubled your chips at the roulette table, it's customary to celebrate at the *Sourdough Saloon*, in the *Downtown Hotel*, where the house tipple is the sour-toe cocktail – a drink that includes a real pickled human toe in a shot of alcohol (local charitable frostbite victims keep the bar well-stocked). As the rule goes: you can drink it fast or drink it slow, but your lips must touch the toe.

SPYING **WHALES** AND SPOTTING **PUFFINS** IN THE **ATLANTIC** 580

NEWFOUNDLAND & LABRADOR Every spring and summer the waters off the coasts of Newfoundland and Labrador play host to the largest concentration of nesting seabirds and migrating humpback whales anywhere in the world. This spectacle unfolds just a few kilometres off shore, at the confluence of the warm Gulf Stream and the frigid Labrador Current. Here, where cod has been overfished to the point of near-elimination, nature enthusiasts come to experience the thrill of seeing hundreds of thousands of nesting seabirds, the feeding frenzy of 40-tonne whales and the occasional sighting of a 10,000-year-old iceberg drifting southwards from its Arctic home.

The way to observe this is on board one of the many passenger ferries that operate from Bay Bulls Harbour, bound for the Witless Bay Ecological Reserve. As your boat chugs towards the mist-shrouded islands, the patter of your guides and the jovial folk singing recede in deference to a loud hum, accompanied by an overpowering stench – its origin apparent only when the fog lifts. All of a sudden you're surrounded by what seems like millions of clown-faced puffins, penguin-like murres and black-legged kittiwakes diving in and out of the waters, delivering beakloads of capelin to their young.

The flurry of activity overhead nearly distracts you from seeing the tell-tale spray of a giant humpback in the distance. A short while later a guide announces that a small pod of minke whales has been spotted near the stern. Soon more dorsal fins slice through the gentle swells and the characteristic forked tails slap the seas as the whales submerge to feed. It's only now that you appreciate the immense size of these cetaceans as they follow alongside your boat.

The three-hour cruise is over far too quickly. Before you know it your guide asks, "Are you ready to become an honorary Newfoundlander?" Your intentions seem obvious as you quickly down a shot of Screech (the local rum) and kiss a stuffed puffin in front of a rowdy group of fellow passengers.

RELIVING THE WILD WEST AT THE CALGARY STAMPEDE

581

ALBERTA For ten days each year, during the middle of July, the usually conservative city of Calgary loses its collective head (or finds a new cover for it, at least). Virtually everyone turns out in white Stetsons, bolo ties, blue jeans and hand-tooled boots, while addressing one another in bastardized cowboy slang. Rather than a new trend in fashion, it's a signal that it's time for the Calgary Stampede.

For Canada's rural folk – who often live on isolated farms or in tiny communities – this is the opportunity to bring their culture into the big city and really let rip. For the half-million visitors from elsewhere, it's a chance to witness the ultimate Wild West carnival, said to be North America's roughest rodeo.

Many activities, both kitschy and quite serious, vie for your attention. The main event is the daily rodeo competition, featuring the likes of bronco riding, native-buffalo riding, calf-roping, steer-wrestling, barrel-racing and wild-cow milking. But what sets the stampede apart from other rodeos is the presence of the ludicrously dangerous, hugely exciting, chuck-wagon races: a team of horsemen pack a stove and tent into a chuckwagon, then rush around the track at breakneck speeds.

The non-rodeo action takes place at the festival's focal point, Stampede Park. Top attractions include a First Nations tepee village where you can try traditional foods; the satisfyingly obscure World Blacksmith Competition; and an Agricultural Building that's home to many a handsome cow and bull.

Finish each day with a dash of stampede nightlife, yet another world unto itself. The drinking, gambling and partying at various bars and mega-cabarets goes on into the small hours, sustained by a seemingly endless supply of barbecued meat and baked beans.

582 LIGHTING UP THE SKY IN MONTRÉAL

QUÉBEC Summer is a celebratory time in Montréal. After the hibernation of winter, Montréalers spill on to the street terraces and fill the parks at the first sign of fine weather. Keen to milk it for all it's worth, the city lays on all sorts of colourful outdoor parties – such as the calypso-tinged Cariefiesta and the world's pre-eminent jazz festival – that keep you tapping your feet. But the constant crowd-pleaser just requires you look up: the twice-weekly spectacular fireworks display, from mid-June to late July, which pays tribute to balmy nights in a normally frigid city.

OK, so the Montréal International Fireworks Competition was not created back in 1985 simply to fête summer, but it has become so synonymous with Montréal's best months that it could well have been. Instead, the idea is to synchronize music and pyrotechnics in order to tell some kind of a story, to create

an ephemeral fantasy world above the skies of this atmospheric town. Fireworks companies representing different countries let off their considerable arsenals at La Ronde – an amusement park on an island in the middle of the St Lawrence River – and the shows are stunningly artistic.

The thousands upon thousands of wheels, candles, fountains and rockets that light the night sky are intended to be viewed with the accompanying musical score (broadcast live on local radio). From there it's not too far a leap to imagine Evita disappearing in smoke over the river to the strains of *Don't Cry For Me Argentina* or to take a profusion of red stars and comets set to the soundtrack of *Born Free* to be the rising African sun. Then again, you could just turn off the radio, tilt your head skyward and be thankful that summertime has come.

583 WATCHING THE TIDE ROLL AWAY IN THE BAY OF FUNDY

NOVA SCOTIA & NEW BRUNSWICK There's an eeriness to the Bay of Fundy, never more so than when the banking fogs that sweep in off the Atlantic shroud its churning waters, rendering its sea cliffs and coves barely visible in an all-pervasive gloom. Tourist brochures would lovingly call this "atmospheric", which it is. But what they tend to play up more are the bay's impressive stats: this is where the highest tides in the world come crashing in – there is up to 16m difference between high tide and low tide; in some places, the tide retreats four to five kilometres (2.5 to 3 miles) as it ebbs.

You don't need numbers, just your own eyes. Stand on the steps at Evangeline Beach in Grand-Pré, and see young boys pedaling bicycles across far-reaching mud flats, then return a few hours later to find the beach deserted, the water three metres high and rising. You could build a giant IMAX movie

screen on the mud flats at low tide and it would be completely submerged at high tide, just six hours later.

The effect comes in part from the bay's shape. At its mouth it is 100km wide, but it gradually narrows and shallows, producing a funnelling effect when the water comes in. Many of the rivers that lead off the upper bay are sites of tidal bores – basically the name for what occurs when the water rushes against the current. This is what people come to see.

When you first spot it from a distance, it may be subtle: just a faint line across a wide section of water. But as the river narrows and the water closes in, seeming to pick up speed, it's more like a moving wall – one that submerges islets, rides up high on floating docks and provides plenty of challenge for those fool enough to break out surfboards or inflatable Zodiac boats.

584 STAYING AFLOAT ON LITTLE MANITOU LAKE

SASKATCHEWAN In the minds of most Canadians, Saskatchewan is the heart of the rather plain prairies: a land of vast skies and dull Trans-Canada Highway drives. But within easy reach of the highway lies a lake with world-class therapeutic waters that must rank as the province's, if not the country's, best-kept secret. Little Manitou Lake and the adjacent basic Manitou Springs resort offer a no-frills spa experience where you come out heavily coated with minerals and feeling much the better for it.

The lake's waters contain high levels of magnesium – good for the skin – iodine, good for the glands and joints, and overall a dip in the water promotes healing and is effective against dermatological problems. But reasons to soak here go well beyond skin therapy, the relief of aches and pains, or even the many claimed cures attributed to the waters: in short, it's just a

whole lot of fun. With the water three times saltier than seawater and denser than that of the Dead Sea, you'll find yourself floating on the surface, feet up. This unique sensation of floating effortlessly is as close as you'll likely get to the weightlessness of space; it brings with it all sorts of acrobatic possibilities, or just the chance to bob on your back and comfortably read a newspaper.

The waters have long been celebrated, first by the Native Americans who camped on its shores and named it for its healing properties, later by homesteaders who spread the news of the mineral-rich lake, and of course by the Manitou Mineral Water Company, which shipped it as a product all across North America. But things have quietened down from its height as a spa town, so for once there are few to rebuke you for time spent aimlessly adrift.

585 REDEFINING REMOTE ON THE HUDSON BAY TRAIN

MANITOBA There's something deeply alluring about travelling somewhere you can't reach by car – a truly remote place, far from anywhere. The tiny settlement of Churchill, shivering by the shores of the great Hudson Bay in Canada's far north, is just such a place; its only connection to the rest of the world is a 1600km railway that begins in the prairie town of Winnipeg. You start your journey in the agricultural heartland of Canada and end it in a frozen wasteland where only arctic mosses and lichen can grow. It's a startling transformation – a real journey to the edge of the world.

The train itself – the Hudson Bay – oozes character with its 1950s stainless steel carriages, polished chrome fixtures and an old-fashioned dining car. This is the place to get chatting to your fellow travellers, among them gnarled fishermen and trappers, Cree and Chipewyan natives and even a few Inuit. Most of them know this land like the back of their hands, and will readily tell you the names of the flora and fauna passing by. They'll also fill you in on the minor scandals attached to the various communities along the line: the embezzling mayor who ended his days trapping furs to earn his crusts; the village where a Mountie was shot dead by a Cree outlaw a hundred years ago.

The journey includes two nights on the train; waking up from your second night, pull open the blind and you'll feel as if you're on another planet: gone are the verdant forests of yesterday, replaced by stunted, shrivelled stumps which peter out altogether as you enter the Barren Lands – a region of fierce winds, bitter cold and permanently frozen soil. And then you pull into Churchill and the phrase "end of the line" takes on a whole new meaning. Way up here, in Canada's sub-Arctic, you'll feel farther from civilization than you ever thought possible.

586 PADDLING YOUR WAY THROUGH ALGONQUIN PROVINCIAL PARK

ONTARIO The day may start like this: the rain eases and the mist on the lake begins to dissipate as the early sun breaks through the trees, onto your secluded campsite. You awaken to the melodious songs of warblers overhead, to the unspoiled wilderness of Algonquin Provincial Park.

After breakfast you put your canoe in the water and ponder your route. This dense, forested park has an extensive network of interconnected lakes, rivers and overland portages, some 1500km of paddling circuits; exploring by canoe is almost essential to understanding Algonquin. As you slide along you begin to get a truer sense of the dramatic landscape: thick stands of maples, towering red pines, black spruce bogs. There are granite ridges and sandy beaches and everywhere there is water, from ephemeral ponds to bottomless lakes.

You make chance acquaintances with wildlife. The canoe drifts by a lone moose foraging chest-deep in a marshy wetland; a black bear appears along the shore – the distance between the two of you feels close enough. A beaver quietly constructs his lodge in a transparent pond, and a family of newly emerged mergansers swims alongside your small craft, like non-paying passengers on your voyage.

At the end of a long day's paddle the blue skies give way to a star-filled night and you settle around the crackling campfire to a plate of freshly caught fish. A new cast of characters croon their forest tunes: the haunted calls of loons ricochet off the lakeshores, wolves howl in distant highlands. A barred owl hoots, and you think you might be hearing things. In a place where you could easily go for days on end without human contact, you may swear it said, "Who cooks for you? Who cooks for you all?"

587 TRACKING DOWN POLAR BEARS IN CHURCHILL

MANITOBA Signs boldly reading "Polar Bear Alert – Stop, don't walk in this area" dot the city limits of Churchill, Manitoba. Beyond them lie wide expanses of the bleak and often frozen Hudson Bay or the treeless, endlessly flat tundra. It's this location – on the threshold of the two environments – that makes the town the unchallenged "polar bear capital of the world".

Local polar bears spend most of their lives roaming the platform of ice covering the Hudson Bay to hunt seals. But by July the ice melt forces the bears ashore to subsist on berries, lichen, seaweed, mosses and grasses. This brings the animals close to your doorstep; indeed, during the summer Churchill's Polar Bear Police typically remove over a hundred bears from the town. While this might sound like fun, the reality is quite different: these cuddly-looking bears are the largest land carnivores in existence. They can run at 50kph, and kill with a single whack of their foot-wide, clawed paws. And, unaccustomed to humans, they'll quickly size you up as potential prey.

Better to wait until later in the year, from the relative comfort of a tundra buggy – a converted bus that rides high above the ground on giant balloon tyres – to do your bear-watching. At the beginning of October, around two hundred polar bears gather near town to wait for the bay to freeze. With temperatures beginning to drop below zero and winds gusting up to 60kph, the prime viewing season begins.

Lean and mean from the meagre summer diet, male polar bears spend the autumn sparring with one another for hours on end – standing on their hind legs to throw gentlemanly chest-punches. Females steer well clear of these shenanigans, particularly when with cubs, and spotting a mother lying back on a snowbank nursing her offspring – making tenderness and brute force temporary bedfellows – is a surprisingly touching scene.

588 CATCHING A WAVE ON VANCOUVER ISLAND

BRITISH COLUMBIA For some of the wildest surfing in the world, head to the shipwreck-strewn west coast of Vancouver Island, also known as "the graveyard of the Pacific". Flanked by the lush temperate rainforest of the 130-kilometre-long Pacific Rim National Park, the waters here are ferocious. Swells reach up to six metres, and epic storms uproot trees, sending drifting logs down the face of waves. Whales have been known to sneak up on unsuspecting surfers, diving under their boards and lifting them clean out of the water. And barking territorial sea lions will chase surfers from the ocean back to shore. On land, it's just as wild – bald eagles soar between giant trees, and wolves and black bears fossick for food amid piles of sun-bleached driftwood.

Even in summer, when swells ease to a gentle one to two metres, the water remains bone-chillingly cold, hovering around 13°C/55°F. Plenty of wannabe surfies flock to the chilled-out surf centre of Tofino to practise their "pop-ups", but a thick skin – or a thick wetsuit – is required.

Come winter, the waves start pummelling in from the Pacific like a boxer laying a victory blow. The wind whips off the snow-capped mountains, the ocean cools down to a shocking 8°C/46°F and hardy surfers hit the waves wearing five-millimetre-thick wetsuits as well as boots, gloves and protective hoods. For the novice, it's time to peel off the wetsuit and watch the waves roll in from the blissful confines of a seaside hot tub.

CYCLING AROUND

STANLEY PARK

589

BRITISH COLUMBIA More so than any other Canadian city, nature-loving Vancouver embraces the ethos "two wheels good, four wheels bad". And cycling around Stanley Park's breathtaking shoreline, you're bound to start invoking it yourself. It could be as Mount Baker comes into view, rearing up from the horizon like a glaciated castle. Or as a lone raccoon scampers across the bicycle path, seducing you with its big guilty eyes before darting into the rainforest. Or as you spot a couple sharing an ice cream while watching the sunset from a beachside log.

Whatever the case, it might be the best place to discover what the city is all about: the cycle path that goes along the sea wall sketches the great green heart of Vancouver. Jutting out into the ocean from just beyond the shimmering glass skyscrapers of downtown, Stanley Park is the largest urban park in North America, a 14-square-kilometre oasis of towering forests, lakes, manicured gardens, marshland and beaches.

Come winter, when Vancouver's outdoor types relocate to the ski slopes of Grouse, Cyprus and Whistler, cyclists can enjoy this natural splendour in relative solitude. On a scorching summer Sunday, however, the sea wall is chock-full of children whizzing past on training wheels, students trying to balance on roller blades and fitness fanatics pedaling their way to an invisible finishing line.

On such days, it is wise to leave the path most travelled to cycle deep into the park's shaded interior, past lofty hemlock, Douglas fir and cedar trees, past colourful totem poles and out to serene and secluded Beaver Lake. Here – surrounded by water lilies – you'll declare your undying love for the city, and the two good wheels you rode in on.

590 GETTING WET ON THE WEST COAST TRAIL

BRITISH COLUMBIA Between raging Pacific gales and steady rainforest downpours, chances are you're going to get wet. Very wet. But it's the rain that has made the primordial landscape of the West Coast Trail, a 77-kilometre hike along a remote and rugged stretch of western Vancouver Island, almost magical for its lushness of life. Deep shades of green colour much of what grows here, from thick stands of evergreen trees and giant ageless cedars to the smooth rocks dappled with emerald moss and billowing kelp strands floating just beneath the water's surface.

Though only 52 people each day are permitted to embark on the trail, you won't be alone as you wade across rivers, negotiate log bridges and climb up and down ladders. Expect to catch glimpses of seals, sea lions, great blue herons, bald eagles and migrating grey whales. Just don't expect to stay dry.

591 CRUISING GEORGIAN BAY

ONTARIO The rocky little islets and crystal-blue waters of Georgian Bay, a long and wide appendage to Lake Huron, are the best parts of the wild and wonderful landscape that begins not far north of Toronto. Set sail, catch a water taxi or join a day-trip cruise from Honey Harbour to see what inspired the "Group of Seven" artists, who declared this true "painter's country", the lone pine set against the sky their favourite motif. Beausoleil Island, at the centre of Georgian Bay Islands National Park, makes for scenic hiking back on dry land, with thick maple stands in the south and glacier-scraped rock in the north.

592 SEEING OLD RIVALS IN AN ICE-HOCKEY GAME

ONTARIO & QUÉBEC Saturday is known, on TV at least, as "Hockey Night in Canada" – pretty much all you need to know in terms of the country's fanaticism for its national game. Actually, lacrosse is the official national game, but it doesn't arouse nearly the same passions.

Perhaps it's the nature of the game itself. You'll have to focus hard to track the movement of the puck and the hurried but fluid way the teams shift players – frequently – in the middle of it all. And with those skaters hurtling around at 50kph and pucks clocking speeds above 160kph, this would be a high-adrenaline sport even without its relaxed attitude to combat on the rink. As an old Canadian adage has it, "I went to see a fight and an ice-hockey game broke out".

To maximize your exposure to the madness, get a seat near the rink for a game matching old rivals. Any of the six Canada-based teams will do, but when the Montréal Canadiens, the most successful team in hockey history, and the Toronto Maple Leafs, part of the National Hockey League since 1927, meet – mirroring the country's Francophone and Anglophone divisions – you'll get a real feel for the electricity a match can generate. You may even see a hockey game break out.

ONTARIO In 1860, thousands watched as Charles Blondin walked a tightrope across Niagara Falls for the third time. Midway, he paused to cook an omelette on a portable grill and then had a marksman shoot a hole through his hat from the *Maid of the Mist* tugboat, 50m below. Suffice to say, the falls simply can't be beat as a theatrical setting.

Like much good theatre, Niagara makes a stupendous first impression, as it crashes over a 52-metre cliff shrouded in oceans of mist. It's actually two cataracts: tiny Goat Island, which must be one of the wettest places on earth, divides the accelerating water into two channels on either side of the US-Canadian border. The spectacle is, if anything, even more extraordinary in winter, when snow-bent trees edge a jagged armoury of freezing mist and heaped ice blocks.

You won't just be choosing sides – note that the American Falls are but half the width of Canada's Horseshoe Falls – but also how best to see the falls beyond that first impression. A bevy of boats, viewing towers, helicopters, cable cars and even tunnels in the rock-face behind the cascade ensure that every angle is covered.

Two methods are especially thrilling and get you quite near the action: the *Maid of the Mist* boats, which struggle against the cauldron to get as close to the Falls as they dare; and the tunnels of the "Journey Behind the Falls", which lead to points directly behind the waterfall. Either way guarantees that your first impression won't be the last one to register.

593

FORM A LASTING IMPRESSION AT
NIAGARA FALLS

594 BEACHING IT WITH A LITERARY CLASSIC

PRINCE EDWARD ISLAND It may be Canada's smallest province, but Prince Edward Island has produced an enduring classic of children's literature. Lucy Maud Montgomery, the creator of pigtailed orphan girl Anne of Green Gables, loved the place, describing it as floating "on the waves of the blue gulf, a green seclusion and haunt of ancient peace". Much of the peace went with the arrival of the motor car, but the island is still delightfully rural, its rolling fields studded with timber farmsteads and its coasts with inviting coves and bays.

Montgomery spent much of her youth in the tiny hamlet of Cavendish and her childhood home – Green Gables House – attracts visitors by the busload. It's a short stroll from the seashore, where a narrow band of low red cliff and marram-covered sand dunes flanks a gorgeous beach, extending as far as the eye can see. With the odd interruption for a cove here and an inlet there, it stretches along the island's north shore for some 40km, dotted with campsites and easy hiking trails. Now protected as the Prince Edward Island National Park, the beach is a beautiful place for long, blustery walks in winter and swimming and sunbathing in the summer, and a narrow road running just inland provides easy access by car or bike.

Locals usually take a picnic when they head off to the beach, but in the summertime it's always worth looking out for the island's famous lobster suppers. All along the coast, especially in and around the village of New Glasgow, churches and community halls compete – in a thoroughly neighbourly manner – to lay on the island's best seafood. Montgomery, you sense, would feel right at home.

595 FOLLOWING THE YUKON QUEST

YUKON At the start of the Yukon Quest dogsledding race, a din has broken out. Dogs are barking, whining and caterwauling as they're hooked up to their lines. They leap high in the air. They haul forwards with all their might, trying to shift the truck that anchors them. Their ears are pricked, their tails wave, their tongues loll, their wide mouths grin. Anyone who suggests that sled dogs run against their will has never witnessed this. These dogs can't wait to start.

The course of the Yukon Quest crosses a 1600km of inhospitable winter wilderness between Fairbanks, Alaska and Whitehorse in Canada's Yukon Territory. In temperatures that can drop into the minus 40°C, mushers and their dogs negotiate blizzards and white-outs, sheer mountains and frozen rivers and overflow ice that snaps and cracks under paws and sled. Checkpoints are far apart (while the more famous Iditarod has twenty-five checkpoints, the Yukon Quest has just ten); with more than 300 kilometres between some of them, teams have to camp beside the trail. Mushers must be able to care for themselves and their dogs no matter what the elements throw at them – and, except at the race's halfway point in Dawson City, they're allowed to accept no outside help.

As the days progress, spectators following the race observe the mushers' eyes go bloodshot and rheumy. Their hair becomes matted; their posture stoops. These men and women are enjoying little sleep. They may stop to rest their dogs for six hours in every twelve but by the time they've massaged ointment into their team's feet, melted snow for water and fed both the dogs – who burn ten thousand calories a day when racing – and themselves, only a couple of hours remain. The curious spectator wonders, what could motivate these people to endure such hardship? Then darkness falls, the moon rises and the northern lights weave green and red against the cold night sky.

596 DRIVING THE ICEFIELDS PARKWAY

ALBERTA "This wondertrail will be world renowned", predicted a 1920s surveyor when Highway 93 North – now better known as the Icefields Parkway – was only a fanciful idea. And sure enough, when it opened twenty years later, built as a Depression-era public works programme, the 230-kilometre road between Lake Louise and Jasper immediately became one of the world's ultimate drives.

It still is. The highway snakes through the cornucopia of snowcapped peaks that crown the Continental Divide, running right down the heart of the Rockies. Between the peaks lies an almost overwhelming combination of natural splendour: immense glaciers, blue-green iridescent lakes, foaming waterfalls, wild-flower meadows, forests and wildlife from elk and moose to brown bears and grizzly bears.

You could drive the whole highway in about four hours, but to do so would be to miss out on the many trails and viewpoints along the way, as well as the chance to appreciate properly all the subtle shifts in scenery and mood: rivers broaden or narrow, move from churning to sluggish; light changes according to the fickle mountain weather, sometimes producing a rosy pink reflection on a distant peak.

Several points along the route outstrip any superlatives. Bow Pass, at 2070m the road's highest point, is spectacular not only for the views but the delicate sub-alpine ecosystem that ekes out its existence at these windy, snowy heights. Here moss-lined paths lead between dark stands of towering fir and spruce while mountain heather and alpine forget-me-nots provide splashes of pink, yellow and white.

Far bleaker is the 325-square-kilometre Columbia Icefield itself – one of the largest accumulations of ice south of the Arctic Circle. Its rock-strewn moonscape has remained virtually unchanged since the last ice age, and at its edge you can watch 200-year-old snow slowly melting.

MISCELLANY

PEOPLE

Canada has 33 million people, of whom some 86 percent are white. Around 10 percent are Asian; 2 percent are black, mostly from the Caribbean; and around 3 percent are native or aboriginal peoples.

The native peoples of Canada number fewer than a million, and have been categorized in three distinct groups: the **Metis**, largely in the western provinces, whose mixed heritage derives from aboriginal peoples and British and French-Canadian settlers; the **Inuit**, formerly called Eskimos, living in the far north of the country; and the **First Nations**, who have a wide variety of languages and ethnic backgrounds, and are broadly defined by geography.

FIVE UNUSUAL HOTELS

Chateau Montebello, Montebello, Québec. Once known as the world's largest log cabin, this classic 1930s resort still has a rough-hewn charm amid the modern luxury.
Fantasy Land, Edmonton, Alberta. The ultimate in kid-friendly theme accommodation, with the rooms decked out in 120 different styles, from ancient Roman to Polynesian.
Ice Hotel, Québec City, Québec. Constructed entirely of ice, this deep-frozen luxury item is open only three months of the year, so book a igloo-style room before the place melts.
Sentry Mountain Lodge, Golden, British Columbia. Poised at 2000 metres on a snowy peak, this elegant retreat is accessible only by helicopter.
West Point Lighthouse, O'Leary, Prince Edward Island. Rugged 1875 lighthouse tower that holds a romantic, windswept B&B.

CITIES, PROVINCES AND TERRITORIES

Canada comprises ten provinces, which have some autonomy within the federation, and three territories, which are more dependent on the federal government and have only one third of one percent of the country's people. The most populous province is Ontario, which not only contains Toronto, the biggest Canadian city (2.6 million people), but Ottawa, the nation's capital and its fourth largest city (just under a million people). The least populous province or territory is Nunavut, in the far north, which is also the newest territory – officially formed in 1999.

LISTEN TO THESE

Music from Big Pink (1968) The Band. Folk-flavoured roots rock that turned the flower-power era on its ear, with some help from Bob Dylan.
Songs of Leonard Cohen (1968) Leonard Cohen. Gloomy introspection and a true poetic flair are the hallmarks of this legendary troubadour.
After the Gold Rush (1970) Neil Young. A lovely song cycle that defined his early blend of folk and hippie rock.
Blue (1971) Joni Mitchell. There's nary a false note on this shimmering folk-rock milestone.
Funeral (2004) Arcade Fire. The brightest current hope for Canadian – or maybe any – indie rock, with a huge cast of musicians and a cache of infectious melodies.

PRIME MINISTERS

There have been 22 Canadian prime ministers in 140 years, starting with Sir John A. Macdonald in 1867 and leading up to Stephen Harper today. Perhaps the most dominant recent PM was **Pierre Trudeau**, who, except for one year in 1979–80, led the Liberal majority in Parliament from 1968 to 1984.

The prime minister, of course, is not the official head of state – that crown belongs to the **reigning monarch of the United Kingdom**. Although Elizabeth II has been Canada's head of state since 1952, the country has had only one woman prime minister – Kim Campbell, who served just over four months in 1993.

SCTV CAST

Famous comedian	Typical character	Most famous character
John Candy	jovial fat man	Yosh Schmenge
Joe Flahert	neurotic bigshot	Guy Caballero
Eugene Levy	sleazy nerd	Bobby Bittman
Andrea Martin	annoying eccentric	Edith Prickley
Rick Moranis	antic short fellow	Bob Mackenzie
Catherine O'Hara	ditzy blonde	Lola Heatherton
Harold Ramis	sneaky oddball	Moe Green
Martin Short	excitable freak	Ed Grimley
Dave Thomas	suspicious lunkhead	Doug Mackenzie

TALL BUILDINGS

Canada boasts the tallest freestanding structure in the world, the CN Tower (553m). It's in Toronto, as are the country's five tallest buildings; of these, First Canadian Place, which was built in in 1975, tops the list at 298m.

> *"I don't even know what street Canada is on"*
> **Al Capone**

ROCKS AND LAKES

Canada is built on some of the oldest rocks in the world. The **Canadian Shield**, a huge swath of terrain roughly stretching around Hudson Bay, is made up of a good amount of Precambrian metamorphic rock, some of it 4.5 billion years old – or as old as the earth itself.

Most of Canada's **lakes** derive from the effects of the Ice Age, when huge retreating **glaciers** cut deep crevasses across the landscape or, in the case of the largest, Hudson Bay, depressed the land enough to allow it to fill with water. Not counting the Great Lakes (of which Superior and Huron would be the nation's biggest), the two largest lakes fully within Canada are both in the Northwest Territories: Great Bear (31,328 sq km) and Great Slave (28,568 sq km).

CANADA AT THE MOVIES

The Barbarian Invasions (2003). Québec's leading director Denys Arcand applies his dialogue-heavy realism to Montréal intellectuals and their politics, sexuality and mortality.

Exotica (1994). Perhaps the most existential film ever set in a strip club (in Toronto), imagined by Atom Egoyan in dramatic and eye-opening detail.

Mon Oncle Antoine (1972). Claude Jutra's bracing, realist classic of a young boy growing up in a mining town in Québec still resonates after more than thirty years.

Neighbours (1952). Norman McLaren did pioneering work for the National Film Board of Canada, but may be most known for this short, scathing satire about two men going to war over possession of a flower.

Videodrome (1983). One of the creepiest films ever, David Cronenberg's opus filmed in Toronto has much in common with the rest of his work – sex, obsession, decay, violence and an odd sort of humour.

WINE AND CHEESE CURDS

Canada doesn't have one overriding cuisine, but all sorts of regional differences, from the heavily French-influenced fare of Québec to the seafood of the coastal provinces to the Western-style steaks and hearty eats of the prairies and Rocky Mountain region. Signature dishes include the likes of poutine (French fries with cheese curds and gravy, found mainly in Québec) and butter tarts (small sugar pies, popular all around).

Though Canada is by no means a winemaking powerhouse – the cold has much do with that – it is the world's leading producer of ice wines, or wines made from pressed frozen grapes; these are most frequently served with, or as, dessert.

"Canada is a country whose main exports are hockey players and cold fronts. Our main imports are baseball players and acid rain" **Pierre Trudeau**

FAR AND WIDE

The **second biggest country** in the world, Canada is huge: almost 10 million sq km in area, with a top distance of 5700km between the edges of Newfoundland and the Yukon Territory – or the same distance from Toronto to London. The most extreme points of all are:

Point	Name	Location	Feature
NORTHERNMOST	Cape Columbia	Ellesmere Island, Nunavut	world's northernmost after Greenland
SOUTHERNMOST	Middle Island	near Pelee Island, Ontario	bird sanctuary
WESTERNMOST	Beaver Creek	western Yukon Territory	Alaska border town
EASTERNMOST	Cape Spear	near St John's, Newfoundland	lighthouse site

FRENCH CANADA

By the mid-eighteenth-century France controlled a huge swath of territory from what's now Canada down to the Mississippi River and Gulf Coast to the Caribbean. That reign ended with the country's loss in the Seven Years' War to Britain in 1763.

Although Britain expelled the **Acadians** of Nova Scotia (to Louisiana, where they became "Cajuns"), most French speakers remained, and today form a **Francophone belt** that includes all of Québec and parts of Ontario and New Brunswick.

Québec is Canada's only **majority-French-speaking province**, where 82 percent of the population speaks the language – more than six times the amount of English speakers.

PROVINCIAL MOTTOS

Alberta Strong and free
British Columbia Splendour without diminishment
Manitoba Glorious and free
New Brunswick Hope was restored
Newfoundland Seek ye first the kingdom of God
Nova Scotia One defends and the other conquers
Nunavut (territory) Our land, our strength
Ontario Loyal she began, loyal she remains
Prince Edward Island The strong under the protection of the great
Québec I remember
Saskatchewan From many peoples, strength

GREAT BOOKS

Margaret Atwood The Handmaid's Tale. Terrifying tale of a misogynist dystopia, rendered with the same dark colours as Orwell's Nineteen Eighty-Four.
Robertson Davies The Deptford Trilogy. Davies memorably spins picaresque tales of mystery and magic in the early twentieth century.
Alice Munro The Love of a Good Woman. A selection by Canada's most renowned short-story author, mainly set in the West.
Michael Ondaatje The English Patient. Complex, multilayered narrative of love, loss and mystery at the end of World War II. Much better than the Hollywood version.
Mordecai Richler The Apprenticeship of Duddy Kravitz. Early novel by the comic master, detailing the obsessive rise of a young man out of working–class Montréal.

RELIGION Canadians affiliated by religion are 77 percent Christian, 2 percent Muslim, and 1 percent each Buddhist, Hindu, Sikh and Jewish, while 17 percent claim no affiliation. The largest denominations are Catholic (43 percent), Protestant (29 percent), and Eastern Orthodox (2 percent). Half of all Catholics reside in Québec (which is 83 percent Catholic); indeed, the tallest church in Canada is St Joseph's Oratory, in Montréal (129m), which is Roman Catholic. Its dome is the second largest in the world.

SEA KAYAKING IN THE EXUMAS • FINDING INSPIRATION AT GOLDENEYE • SNIFFING SULPHUR AT BOILING LAKE • KITEBOARDING IN CABARETE • SHRIMP BBQ AND RUM PUNCH ON THE BEACH • EXPERIENCING THE EXTREMES OF PORT-AU-PRINCE • SUGAR AND SPICE: TOURING RUM-MAKERS • GOING UNDERGROUND IN SANTO DOMINGO • SUN-WORSHIP LIKE A CELEBRITY IN ST BARTS • CELEBRATING CROP OVER • LIVING IT UP AT FIESTA DE MERENGUE • DOING JUNKANOO • GROOVING AT REGGAE SUMFEST • THE CAVE OF INDESCRIBABLE HORRORS • GET ON BAD IN TRINIDAD • DISCOVERING TREASURE ON JAMAICA'S COAST • WHALE-WATCHING IN SAMANÁ • CLASSIC CARS & CUISINE • MEET THE PEOPLE: FAIR TRADE AND FRUIT PASSION • DEEPEST BLUE: DIVING BLOODY BAY WALL • LAND OF THE MIDNIGHT *SON* • FEASTING YOUR WAY THROUGH OLD SAN JUAN • HIGH ADVENTURE IN THE WEST INDIES • EXPLORING ARUBA'S OUTBACK • SNORKELLING WITH TURTLES • IN SEARCH OF THE CITADELLE • FINDING INSPIRATION AT GOLDENEYE • SHRIMP BBQ AND RUM PUNCH ON THE BEACH • EXPERIENCING THE EXTREMES OF PORT-AU-PRINCE • GET ON BAD IN TRINIDAD • SUGAR AND SPICE: TOURING RUM-MAKERS • GOING UNDERGROUND IN SANTO DOMINGO • SUN-WORSHIP LIKE A CELEBRITY IN ST BARTS • CELEBRATING CROP OVER • LIVING IT UP AT FIESTA DE MERENGUE • DOING JUNKANOO • GROOVING AT REGGAE SUMFEST • THE CAVE OF INDESCRIBABLE HORRORS • SEA KAYAKING IN THE EXUMAS • FINDING INSPIRATION AT GOLDENEYE • SNIFFING SULPHUR AT BOILING LAKE • KITEBOARDING IN CABARETE • SHRIMP BBQ AND RUM PUNCH ON THE BEACH • EXPERIENCING THE EXTREMES OF PORT-AU-PRINCE • SUGAR AND SPICE: TOURING RUM-MAKERS • GOING UNDERGROUND IN SANTO DOMINGO • SUN-WORSHIP LIKE A CELEBRITY IN ST BARTS • CELEBRATING CROP OVER • LIVING IT UP AT FIESTA DE MERENGUE • DOING JUNKANOO • THE NOCTURNAL SYMPHONY OF EL YUNQUE • GROOVING AT REGGAE SUMFEST • THE CAVE OF INDESCRIBABLE HORRORS • GET ON BAD IN TRINIDAD • DISCOVERING TREASURE ON JAMAICA'S COAST • WHALE-WATCHING IN SAMANÁ • CLASSIC CARS & CUISINE • MEET THE PEOPLE: FAIR TRADE AND FRUIT PASSION • DEEPEST BLUE: DIVING BLOODY BAY WALL • LAND OF THE MIDNIGHT *SON* • FEASTING YOUR WAY THROUGH OLD SAN JUAN • HIGH ADVENTURE IN THE WEST INDIES • IN SEARCH OF THE CITADELLE • EXPLORING ARUBA'S OUTBACK • SNORKELLING WITH TURTLES • FINDING INSPIRATION AT GOLDENEYE • SHRIMP BBQ AND RUM PUNCH ON THE BEACH • EXPERIENCING THE EXTREMES OF PORT-AU-PRINCE • SUGAR AND SPICE: TOURING RUM-MAKERS • GOING UNDERGROUND IN SANTO DOMINGO • CELEBRATING CROP OVER • LIVING IT UP AT FIESTA DE MERENGUE • DOING JUNKANOO • GROOVING AT REGGAE SUMFEST • THE CAVE OF INDESCRIBABLE HORRORS • GET ON BAD IN TRINIDAD • SEA KAYAKING IN THE EXUMAS • SUN-WORSHIP LIKE A CELEBRITY IN ST BARTS • FINDING INSPIRATION AT GOLDENEYE • SNIFFING SULPHUR AT BOILING LAKE • KITEBOARDING IN CABARETE • SAVOURING THE FAMILIAR AT CRESCENT MOON • SHRIMP BBQ AND RUM PUNCH ON THE BEACH • EXPERIENCING THE EXTREMES OF PORT-AU-PRINCE • SUGAR AND SPICE: TOURING RUM-MAKERS • GOING UNDERGROUND IN SANTO DOMINGO • SUN-WORSHIP LIKE A CELEBRITY IN ST BARTS • CELEBRATING CROP OVER • LIVING IT UP AT FIESTA DE MERENGUE • DOING JUNKANOO • THE CAVE OF INDESCRIBABLE HORRORS • GET ON BAD IN TRINIDAD • DISCOVERING TREASURE ON JAMAICA'S COAST • GROOVING AT REGGAE SUMFEST • WHALE-WATCHING IN SAMANÁ • CLASSIC CARS & CUISINE • MEET THE PEOPLE: FAIR TRADE AND FRUIT PASSION • DEEPEST BLUE: DIVING BLOODY BAY WALL • LAND OF THE MIDNIGHT *SON* • FEASTING YOUR WAY THROUGH OLD SAN JUAN • HIGH ADVENTURE IN THE WEST INDIES • EXPLORING ARUBA'S OUTBACK • SNORKELLING WITH TURTLES • IN SEARCH OF THE CITADELLE • FINDING INSPIRATION AT

BAHAMAS

SEA KAYAKING IN THE EXUMAS 619

CUBA

LAND OF THE MIDNIGHT *SON* 613

TURKS & CAICOS IS.

KITEBOARDING IN CABARETE 611

CAYMAN IS.

IN SEARCH OF THE CITADELLE 622

GROOVING AT REGGAE SUMFEST 614

JAMAICA

HAITI

DOMINICAN REPUBLIC

THE NOCTURNAL SYMPHONY OF EL YUNQUE

PUERTO RICO 620

BRITISH VIRGIN IS.

ANGUILLA

ST BARTS

SUN-WORSHIP LIKE A CELEBRITY IN ST BARTS 626

US VIRGIN IS.

ST MARTIN/SINT MAARTEN

ST KITTS & NEVIS

MONTSERRAT

BARBUDA

ANTIGUA

GUADELOUPE

DOMINICA

MARTINIQUE

HIGH ADVENTURE IN THE WEST INDIES 606

ST LUCIA

ARUBA

BONAIRE

CURAÇAO

ST VINCENT

GRENADA

BARBADOS 597

CELEBRATING CROP OVER

"GET ON BAD" IN TRINIDAD 603

TRINIDAD & TOBAGO

CELEBRATING CROP OVER

597

BARBADOS The yell of "Crop Over!", traditionally marking the end of the island's back-breaking sugar harvest, is the gleeful signal for the start of one of the Caribbean's most extravagant summer carnivals. For most of its history, sugar cane has pretty much defined Barbados and, although it's not as important as it once was, the delivery of the last crop still prompts a prolonged party. During the carnival, the whole of this beautiful Caribbean island explodes into a festival of parades, calypso concerts and jump-ups – rum-fuelled block parties, which shake the entire place. Colourful costumes are brought out of storage, a legion of musical instruments gets dusted off and the rum starts to flow more liberally than ever.

The three weeks at the end of July leading up to Grand Kadooment is a mellow time in Barbados, with a cool, laid-back party atmosphere that, as the day approaches, slowly cranks up to the max. The ceremonial delivery of the last canes

of the harvest sparks an all-night party, with competing stages hosting a variety of events, and dozens of stalls selling food and drink to keep you energized into the early hours.

Don't miss the best party of all – Monday's Grand Kadooment (from the Bajan vernacular "to-do-ment" or "Big Fuss"). Starting around 9am, dozens of bands, some of them with hundreds of colourfully dressed groupies, parade around the National Stadium before embarking on a long road march to the capital that ends up in a drunken spree along the Spring Garden highway, which runs parallel to the beach just north of Bridgetown. Crowd participation is encouraged (at times, it's insisted on), and you'd be well advised to join the throng as they snake their way around the streets of the capital. Make an effort with your costume and whistle and you'll be invited to top up your glass from the iced rum punch generously hosed out of the nearest float.

598 DOING JUNKANOO

BAHAMAS The country's most important and spectacular party, Junkanoo is a blast to the senses. It's organized pandemonium, held in the pre-dawn hours on two days each year – December 26 and New Year's Day. It has its roots in Africa, and is reminiscent of New Orleans' Mardi Gras and Rio's Carnival, but really, Junkanoo is distinctively Bahamian. There is no other festival like it – not in the Caribbean, not anywhere.

Parades flood the streets of Nassau in a whirling, reeling mass of singing and dancing chaos, as competing groups or "crews" rush out to meet the dawn, moving toward one another from all directions rather than following each other in the semi-organized fashion of the modern parade. Various groups and societies compete to have the biggest and loudest floats, which means you'll see stilt-dancers, clowns, acrobats, go-go girls, goatskin drummers and conch and cowbell players, all blaring out their tunes in an awesome celebration of life that can only have originated in the Caribbean.

The distant beats of Goombay drums indicate that the paraders are shifting into formation, and this is your cue to join the spectators jockeying for the best views, climbing trees and spilling onto balconies and the verandas of stores, hotels and houses. Under the Christmas lights, the crowds reach a frenzy of anticipation. The first cowbells are heard soon after, everyone swigs from bottles of rum and fireworks crackle in the background. Behind, in Nassau harbour, the looming cruise ships form almost a surreal counterpoint to the phantasmagoric crowds, who are now stamping and clamouring in time to the music. Then, as if from everywhere and nowhere, Junkanoo crews – some numbering a thousand – flood the streets in a swirling, kaleidoscopic mass of singing and dancing.

599 EXPERIENCING THE EXTREMES OF PORT-AU-PRINCE

HAITI It's as though you've been plunged into deepest Africa in the middle of the Caribbean. Arriving in Port-au-Prince, the dichotomy of Haiti is immediately obvious. The world's first black republic reverberates to the beat of Creole music while the colours and culture of voodoo fill the air.

A small boy leads his tiny brother by the hand along a dusty path. They are naked apart from their ragged underwear. Nearby, a pig rummages in a pile of litter on the edge of the azure Caribbean. Rainbow-coloured buses rattle past. They are stuffed with people and daubed with messages such as "Everything is just vanity" and "Love Baby". Little girls in immaculate school uniforms appear not to notice the open trucks charging by that carry men in army fatigues with guns. Above their heads, blood-red voodoo flags flutter next to banners warning about the danger of AIDS.

In the hills above the slums of the capital sit beautiful French-style houses with manicured gardens. The restaurants here in Petionville wouldn't be out of place in Paris – apart from the prices they charge.

Because of its climate, geography and location, Haiti was one of the Caribbean's earliest holiday destinations. But political and civil unrest have long since robbed it of its place on the traditional tourist circuit, and the scourges of intense deforestation and overpopulation have stripped away its once lush vegetation. Don't let that put you off; the capital city just sets the tone for the rough-edged beauty and vibrant culture to be found elsewhere on the island.

600 BATHTIME IN VIRGIN GORDA

BRITISH VIRGIN ISLANDS In the extreme southwest of Virgin Gorda, a bizarre landscape/seascape of volcanic boulders known as The Baths offer a prehistoric twist on the archetypal Caribbean beach. These granite rocks, some the size of houses, stretch from the wooded slopes behind the sands right on into the clear aquamarine sea, forming a series of striking grottoes, pools and underwater caves through which you can swim, snorkel or just bob around in. The usually calm waters and sun-streaked private nooks can help make a day at the beach seem like a visit to the largest, most outlandish bathtub imaginable.

601 SPICE SHOPPING IN ST GEORGE'S

GRENADA Nutmeg, mace, cinnamon and ginger. It doesn't quite ring like parsley, sage, rosemary and thyme, but the island of Grenada – one of a few worldwide to lay claim to the moniker "Spice Island" – might still be glad to adopt it as its theme song. And Grenada produces thyme as well, come to think of it. Though Hurricane Ivan knocked out much of the island's agriculture industry a few years ago, the recovery effort has been great and the central market in the capital, St George's, once again bristles with activity. It's a riot of sounds and smells: this is the place to get sacks of exotic spices, bottles of local rum, cacao, tropical fruits and vegetables, perhaps even a nutmeg-infused medicinal ointment.

602 CLASSIC CUBAN CARS & CUISINE

CUBA There's no more striking reminder of the relationship, once a tempestuous love affair but long since turned rancorous, between Cuba and the US than at the Parque de la Fraternidad on the edge of Habana Vieja. The Capitolio – the Cuban replica of Washington's Capitol Building – dwarfs the surrounding nineteenth- and early twentieth-century balconied buildings, many faded and crumbling under the weight of the sheer number of families living inside them.

On the park roads, you'll see lines of Buicks and Chevrolets, Oldsmobiles and Chryslers, some apparently still in their heyday fifty years on, most looking more their age. They're all taxis – and their numerous ranks are one of the more prominent examples of the market flexing its muscle in this Communist stronghold.

Your destination is *La Guarida* – and the journey is a short one. Once you've negotiated a price, the taxi driver negotiates the streets, clattering over potholes on a ride that takes you from colonial Habana Vieja to neocolonial Centro Habana, a dusty mass of apartment buildings enclosing shadowy streets, where kids play bottle-cap baseball amid the chatter of doorstep politics.

La Guarida is one of the capital's best paladares, the family restaurants allowed to compete with the state-run monopoly. As the taxi pulls up, you may first think there has been some mistake. All that's visible is a dingy hallway and a dirty marble staircase that winds away out of sight. Even after scaling the first flight of steps, which lead to a semi-derelict first floor, you may still be in doubt. Then, on the third floor, a door opens onto a small cloakroom that gives way to what was clearly once someone's home. The owners have gotten away with providing more than twelve chairs for their diners, usually the legal limit for a private eatery, which is just as well, as the popularity far outstrips the capacity. And for good reason: tucking into some of the finest Habana cuisine at the top of a crowded decrepit apartment building offers an unforgettable glimpse into today's Cuba.

603 "GET ON BAD" IN TRINIDAD

TRINIDAD & TOBAGO Trinidadians are famed for their legendary party stamina, and nowhere is this dedication to good times more evident than in their annual Carnival, a huge, joyful, all-encompassing event that's the biggest festival in the Caribbean, and one which quite possibly delivers the most fun you'll ever have – period. And as Carnival here is all about participation – rather than watching from the sidelines à la Rio – anyone with a willingness to "get on bad" is welcome to sign up with a masquerade band, which gets you a costume and the chance to dance through the streets alongside tens of thousands of your fellow revellers.

Preceded by weeks of all-night outdoor fetes, as parties here are known, as well as competitions for the best steel bands and calypso and soca singers, the main event starts at 1am on Carnival Sunday with Jouvert. This anarchic and raunchy street party is pure, unadulterated bacchanalia, with generous coatings of mud, chocolate, oil or body paint – and libations of kick-ass local rum, of course – helping you lose all inhibitions and slip and slide through the streets until dawn in an anonymous mass of dirty, drunken, happy humanity, accompanied by music from steel bands, sound-system trucks or the traditional "rhythm section" band of percussionists. Once the sun is fully up, and a quick dip in the Caribbean has dispensed with the worst of the mud, the masquerade bands hit the streets, their followers dancing along in the wake of the pounding soca. This is a mere warm-up for the main parade the following day, however, when full costumes are worn and the streets are awash with colour. The music trucks are back in earnest and the city reverberates with music, becoming one giant street party until "las lap" and total exhaustion closes proceedings for another year.

604 THE CAVE OF INDESCRIBABLE HORRORS

BAHAMAS The remote island of San Salvador in the eastern Bahamas has a little something for everyone – sun, sand, scuba and a dank hole in the ground some call the "Cave of Indescribable Horrors". Formally known as the Lighthouse Cave, locals will smile nervously and maybe wag a finger at the notion of leading you through its watery belly. You'll have better luck bribing the American students from the nearby marine science lab to take you.

From the antique, hand-cranked, kerosene-fuelled lighthouse perched atop Dixon Hill, an overgrown trail snakes down to an ominous gap in the ground with an unsteady rusty ladder poking out of the darkness. The entry chamber may seem a little spooky with its swooping bats, pungent guano and piercing stalactites, but it pales in comparison to what lurks ahead.

Wielding your waterproof flashlight like a gun, you muster up enough courage to enter a cool pool of chest-deep water and meander down a passageway that narrows to a dead end. To proceed you must hold your breath and duck underwater, passing beneath a narrow but psychologically terrorizing lip of limestone to pop out the other side into a pitch-black room. This is a perfect place to gather the troops, shut off all flashlights and either fabricate a tale about human sacrifices, or just contemplate that you are wet, cold and muddy and somewhere inside a fossilized sand dune when you could be at the beach with a good book and a fruity drink.

Exit through a crack in the rock, wade through more water, clamber up some caved-in ceiling and crawl on your belly through a three-metre tube and plop a few metres down into another pool of water. Just when you thought you were hopelessly lost you'll wind up back near the entrance with a few rays of sunlight beckoning escape.

605 WHALE-WATCHING IN SAMANÁ

DOMINICAN REPUBLIC There's no Caribbean island experience that tops sitting on a seaside veranda in the sleepy town of Samaná, on the Dominican Republic's northeast coast, and sipping a cuba libre servicio – two Cokes, a bottle of aged rum and a bucket of ice – as you watch a series of massive humpback whales dive just offshore. Thousands of whales – the entire Atlantic population – flock to the Samaná waters each winter to breed and give birth. And no matter how long you relax there, looking out at the swaying palms backed by a long strand of bone-white sand, you never cease to be surprised as one whale after another sidles up the coastline and emerges from the tepid depths of the Samaná Bay before coming back down with a crowd-pleasing crash.

Sleepy Samaná is refreshingly free from package tourists. The modest expat community is almost all French, and they've set up a series of laid-back outdoor eateries along the main road. A lot of the native Dominicans are from the United States originally – free blacks from the time of slavery who moved here in the early nineteenth century when it was a part of Haiti, the world's first black republic.

Samaná also once held an allure for the Emperor Napoleon, who envisioned making its natural harbour the capital of his New World empire. While he never carried out his grand plans, look out over Samaná today and you can still imagine the great Napoleonic city destined to remain an Emperor's dream: a flotilla of sailboats stands to attention behind the palm-ridged island chain, and in place of the impenetrable French fortress that was to jut atop the western promontory is a small, whitewashed hotel.

For now, though, Samaná remains passed over, which means you can have its natural beauty, tree-lined streets and, above all, its spectacular whale population, pretty much all to yourself.

HIGH ADVENTURE IN THE WEST INDIES 606

ST LUCIA High adventure in the Caribbean usually comes in the form of charter flights between islands, but not so on St Lucia. Standing sentinel on the southwestern coast are the twin peaks of the Pitons, two of the tallest and most striking mountains in the West Indies. Gros Piton, at 798m, is the taller of the two and makes for a challenging and dramatic day-hike, with its steep trail that winds past a former cave hideout of slave freedom fighters and through a dense tropical landscape home to several colourful bird and butterfly species. Set out early to avoid climbing in the stifling midday heat, and at the summit you'll be rewarded with breathtaking views of Petit Piton and the azure Caribbean below.

607 SNIFFING SULPHUR AT BOILING LAKE

DOMINICA Reggae pumped from the speakers and lush foliage blurred through the windows of a Chinese-made minibus recklessly winding into the mountains at six in the morning. "Make sure you have enough water". "Dem shoes look like dey could melt". "Watch out your silver don't turn black". This sage advice came from Seacat, a Rastafarian guide to a small group of groggy but ambitious hikers about to trek to Dominica's famous Boiling Lake.

He grinned as he led them atop an elevated wooden water pipe that snaked through groves of the sweetest grapefruit on earth and clusters of familiar-looking office plants growing berserk in their native habitat. A trail shot uphill into the rainforest, a dense canopy of plants growing over plants that created a dark yet serene environment for the next two hours of climbing. Nearing the peak, the dense flora thinned into elfin trees and shrubs stunted by the powerful winds.

"Getting close," said the guide upon the first whiffs of sulphur, a reminder that an active volcano lurked nearby. The group clambered down into the caldera, appropriately named the Valley of Desolation for its scorched rock landscape. Mineral-encrusted fumaroles spewed boiling multi-hued gasses, sounding remarkably like a fleet of small jet engines. The group instinctively gathered together, some held hands, and everyone followed the guide's footsteps across this freakish landscape in which pterodactyls and dinosaurs would not appear out of place.

As the group inched toward a precipice overlooking a cauldron of bubbling muddy water nearly 70 metres across, they were enshrouded in steam and fog. Sulphurous gasses, reeking more powerfully than ever, had turned any silver jewellery to black. The guide climbed down to the edge of the water to boil a few eggs, proving a point.

On the return, hikers took a refreshing swim through a steep, dark gorge to a small waterfall to rinse off the day's mud, soak weary muscles and postpone the white-knuckle ride out of the mountains and back to civilization.

608 FINDING INSPIRATION AT GOLDENEYE

JAMAICA It has been the scene of many an iconic James Bond moment, from the London double-decker bus chase through the palms to Ursula Andress emerging goddess-like from the sea. And though the island doesn't make a huge deal of its connection with Bond's creator Ian Fleming, who wrote most of his infamous novels on Jamaican soil, there are a few places where you can pick up on the 007 trail. Named by the Spanish for the golden light that bathes the area, the sleepy village of Oracabessa was chosen by Fleming as the site for his Jamaican home, Goldeneye.

These days, though, his classy bungalow by the sea forms the centrepiece of one of Jamaica's most beautiful hotels, a homage to all things chic and a far cry from the bowing obsequiousness of the all-inclusive "tourist prisons". Swathed in lush greenery, the property sits atop a bluff overlooking the Caribbean, with its own private beach and a teeming reef within paddling distance. And whether you bed down in Fleming's old pad, with its luxurious outdoor bathroom and his old Remington typewriter still on his desk, or go for seclusion at Naomi Campbell's fabulous cottage right on the water, it's pretty much guaranteed that as you sip a sundowner, you'll find the same inspiration as Fleming himself: "would these books have been born if I hadn't been living in the gorgeous vacuum of a Jamaican holiday? I doubt it".

609 SUGAR AND SPICE: TOURING RUM-MAKERS

PUERTO RICO Rum is history on this island. Track down its greatest rum-making dynasties and you might meet Fernando Fernandez, heir to the family that has been making Ron de Barrilito since 1880. His office lies inside the shell of a graceful windmill built in 1827, surrounded by aged photographs of his grandfather and dusty bottles of what many believe to be the finest rum in the world. The rambling hacienda outside contains cellars crammed with white-oak barrels of rum, once used to mature Spanish sherry, the air thick with the burnt, sweet aroma of sugar molasses. Workers bottle the rum by hand, slap on the labels and then pile them, delicately, onto trucks for distribution.

Real connoisseurs drink Barrilito on ice – a spicy, rich spirit that goes down like fine Cognac – but the top rum-maker in Puerto Rico is Don Q. The brand was created by the Serrallés family, who started selling rum in 1865 in the southern coastal city of Ponce. Casa Don Q is their San Juan outpost, housing a small exhibition about the company, and a bar where you can sample fine Don Q rum for free.

Then there's Casa Bacardí. Visit this slick tourist centre inside the "cathedral of rum", the vast Bacardí distillery across San Juan Bay, and you'll enter another world – Cuba, to be precise. The Bacardí family started making rum in Santiago de Cuba in 1862, and now utterly dominate the world market. Hand-held audio devices and enthusiastic human guides – who pass you from on to the other – help you navigate the seven sections of the centre. Special barrels allow you to "nose" the effects of wood barrelling, ageing and finishing, as well as the various Bacardí brands on offer: sweetly scented apple and melon flavours and the rich, addictive aroma of coconut-laced rum – piña colada in a bottle. Mercifully, there are two free drinks waiting for you at the end of the tour. Bacardí abandoned Cuba in 1960 and now has headquarters in Bermuda, but while you can argue about where it came from or who made it first, there's no doubt that today the home of rum is Puerto Rico.

610 MEET THE PEOPLE: FAIR TRADE AND FRUIT PASSION

CUBA With his sticking-out ears and Groucho Marx moustache, Lucio Parada Camenate makes an unlikely revolutionary hero, but as the face of Fruit Passion, his mugshot appears on juice cartons across the world, wherever Fair Trade products are marketed – much to the evident amusement of his colleagues, who tease him mercilessly for being famoso.

Lucio is one of several guest-star guides featured on Fair Trade's "Meet the People" tour of Cuba – part holiday, part crash course on the culture and society of Fidel Castro's economically disadvantaged island. Visiting coffee plantations, citrus orchards and juice factories – not to mention primary schools and maternity wards – may not sound as alluring as slurping mojitos by the poolside in Fuerteventura, but the reality turns out to be just as much fun as it is instructive.

Being pitched into the middle of ordinary people's lives lets you experience first hand the pervasive impact of the US trade embargo, and the ways in which Fair Trade initiatives have been able to circumvent it. Holiday pleasures of a more conventional kind are also included in the packed itinerary – from visiting salsa bars in Havana to trekking across mountains draped in rainforest – but it's the encounters with Cubans themselves that stand out.

One evening, we were trundled on an ox cart down five kilometres of bumpy track to a small wooden farm house for a typically Cuban family hog roast. Everyone from the 96-year-old patriarch, Clemente, to his great-grandchildren scampering around after the chickens, was delighted to share a meal with visitors from Canada and Europe. Afterwards, while the women were given an impromptu salsa lesson indoors, the rum and guitars appeared on the verandah, and glasses were raised in a toast to "¡Libertad, Independencia y Comercio Justo!" – "Freedom, Independence and Fair Trade!".

611 KITEBOARDING IN CABARETE

DOMINICAN REPUBLIC Kiters from around the world come in droves to the broad, archetypically Caribbean cove of Cabarete off the north coast on the Dominican Republic. Some never leave, hanging out on the beach in a state of perpetual kite-slacker bliss, like lotus-eaters from Homer's Odyssey. Others shuttle in on weekends between stints at investment banking firms and crash at the high-end condos on the edge of town. All seem perpetually chilled, except for those moments when they're riding the Caribbean trade winds like a hundred little neon-coloured insects trained to do circus tricks for the nearby beach loungers. Life is good here.

And why not? Cabarete's bay seems engineered by a benevolent God of Kiteboarding. Steady trade winds blow east to west, allowing easy passage out to the bay's offshore reefs and then back to the sand. Downwind, the waters lap onto the sardonically named Bozo Beach, which catches anybody unfortunate enough to have a mishap. The offshore reef provides plenty of surf for the experts who ride the waves here, performing tricks and some incredibly spectacular jumps. The reef also shelters the inshore waters so that on all but the roughest of winter days the waters remain calm. During the morning the winds are little more than a gentle breeze, and this, coupled with the flat water, makes the bay ideal for beginners, especially in summer when the surface can resemble a mirror. Then, as the temperature rises, the trades kick in big-time and the real show starts.

Increasingly, the kiteboarding community has left the built-up main village to the windsurfers and retreated west to the newly dubbed Kite Beach. Here you can experience Cabarete as it was ten years ago, a kiteboarder's paradise filled solely with fellow wind worshippers and a lively outdoor nightlife scene, including bonfires along the beach into the wee hours.

612 ARIKOK NATIONAL PARK: THE CARIBBEAN OUTBACK

ARUBA Massive boulders, towering cacti, ancient petroglyphs, abandoned gold mines and secluded limestone grottoes dotting a hilly interior await as you set out on the dirt trail. Playing the part of the Australian Outback is Arikok National Park, a bizarre desert-like landscape in the northeastern corner of Aruba sharing little in common with the rest of the island, save for the blazing tropical sun above.

As you traverse some of the 34km of self-guided trails you gain a truer sense of the untamed beauty: patches of reddish-orange rocky outcrops interspersed with gnarled divi-divi trees and herds of wandering goats give way to gently rolling sand dunes and a rugged shoreline sprinkled with sheltered white sandy coves ideal for a picnic retreat from the midday desert heat. Nearby, limestone caves are adorned with Arawak Indian rock drawings and beautiful flowstone formations, while burrowing owls, rattlesnakes and lizards guard the ruins at the Miralamar gold mine.

In the stifling afternoon heat you find yourself at the base of Cerro Arikok (176m), the second-highest peak on the island. A 1.5-kilometre pathway guides you through an example of what the typical Aruban countryside would have looked like in the nineteenth century. Along the way, you'll pass aloe plants growing alongside other endemic thorny shrubs, large diorite boulders and a petroglyph of an ancient bird left behind by the Amerindians. Halfway through your trek you come across a partially restored casa di torta farmhouse, a small traditional country home constructed with dried cactus husks and glued together with layers of mud and grass. A short stroll uphill brings you to the peak and a stunning panoramic view of the surrounding park and its unique natural treasures.

LAND of the MIDNIGHT SON

613

CUBA It's a sweltering Saturday night in Santiago de Cuba, and the entire barrio seems to be packed into the well-loved nightclub *La Casa de las Tradiciones*. A mist of rum, beer and sweat permeates the air while dozens of pairs of feet pound the flexing plywood floors. The wail of a trumpet rides above the locomotive percussion – maracas, congas and guiros all chugging along in rhythmic, rumba unison.

The cajón player raises his hand, instantly silencing the band and the room. From somewhere among the revellers, a reed-thin voice salvages the melody, this time with less urgency but more emotion. The aged cantor takes the stage, his voice bolstered by an upright bass, violin and tres. Momentary transfixion melts into sinuous shuffle-steps as the audience swoons to his rousing *son*. The rest of the band joins in again, and soon the crowd is echoing the singer's refrains as his voice soars with the vigor and vibrato of someone half his age.

As dawn steadily approaches and the performance winds down, word arrives of a nearby wedding reception. Eager celebrants spill outside and navigate the barely lit streets between tiny houses, cement bunkers with corrugated tin roofs and the flickering eyes of stray dogs. Along the way, party-goers rush into their homes and emerge with bottles of bootlegged ron and a cornucopia of musical instruments.

Arriving at the scene, they're welcomed with cheers and the neighbourhood fiesta surges with renewed energy. One man hammers away at a bata drum while a teenage girl plonks a pair of wooden claves. An older fellow raises an ancient trumpet to his lips; it's dented, with only the memory of a sheen left, but sits in his hands as if he's held it since birth. Then he wades into the roiling descarga, horn crowing wildly as morning begins to glow at the edges of the sky.

614 GROOVING AT REGGAE SUMFEST

JAMAICA As you might expect from what has become Jamaica's flagship music festival, Sumfest is one of the best reggae shows in the world. If you're expecting a bacchanalian free-for-all of campfires on the sand, you'll be sorely disappointed – it's a four-day series of concerts and sound-system jams. But if you're interested in seeing the hottest names in Jamaican music past and present, with a few international R&B or hip-hop acts thrown in for good measure, then you're in for a serious treat. It's best to arrive in Montego Bay a week or so before the event – held in late July or early August – and head for the beach to rid yourself of that fresh-off-the-plane pallor, and to attend pre-festival events: the Blast-Off beach party on the Sunday before the festival starts, and the Monday street Party with DJs and outdoor jams. Once the festival is underway, the island's stage shows start late, carry on until dawn and involve some serious audience participation – or lack of it, if a performer fails to please the famously fickle local crowd. And it's doubtful you'll find a better high than standing under the stars in a grassy bowl by the Caribbean with the music echoing out over the bay.

615 SNORKELLING WITH TURTLES

BONAIRE After months of planning and years of dreaming you've finally arrived at a small, uninhabited cay off the coast of Bonaire. A final equipment check and a few parting words from the boat captain are all that remain before you embark on an unforgettable snorkelling adventure. Beneath the crystal-blue waters awaits a spectacle unparalleled in the marine world. Immense schools of tropical fish in every conceivable shape, size and colour swim alongside sea turtles and dolphins in and around the most impressive coral and sponge gardens in the Caribbean.

Located 80km north of Venezuela and south of the hurricane belt, the waters surrounding this tiny boomerang-shaped island have been designated as a marine park since 1979. Here, deep ocean currents carry nutrient-rich waters to the surface, nourishing the magnificent reef communities. These same currents bring minimal rainfall to Bonaire, which in turn reduces surface runoff to create the clearest waters imaginable.

Once underwater you immediately hear the continuous grinding of parrotfish grazing on the algae that grows on top of coral heads. Within seconds, a dazzling spectrum of reef fish comes out of hiding from the delicate stands of soft and hard corals. Schools of brightly coloured butterfly fish, angle fish and damselfish swim in and out of the crevices and between colonies of elkhorn and staghorn corals. Several metres below, purple sea fans and the tentacles of anemones sway back and forth as the swift current pushes you along. You take a deep breath through your snorkel and submerge to the seafloor where you peek into nooks and crannies to spy on wrasse, tangs and other fish. You spot the slender body of a trunkfish carefully hidden amidst the branches of sea rods patiently waiting for its prey to drift by. A lunging moray eel emerges out of hiding, warning you not to get too close, while a triangular-shaped boxfish hovers nearby.

Before you realize it the captain signals it's time to return on board. As you prepare to board the craft you take one final glance at your underworld surroundings just in time to spot two Hawksbill turtles cruising by.

616 FEASTING YOUR WAY THROUGH OLD SAN JUAN

PUERTO RICO Forget diets: trawl the narrow streets of Old San Juan for a day, and you'll see why Puerto Ricans are passionate about food. Get going with breakfast at the 1960s diner *Cafeteria Mallorca*, where nonchalant baristas pour steaming hot coffee from aged steel machines, and toast mallorcas, delicious pastries filled with ham and cheese, dusted with sugared icing. Around midday the side streets waft with the rich aromas of cocina criolla, the eclectic blend of Caribbean and Spanish influences at the heart of Puerto Rican food. Cosy cafés such as *El Jibarito* knock out hearty potions of mofongo, a blend of mashed plantains, garlic, herbs and chicken, served with rice and beans. As the heat rises, quench your thirst with a piragua, a mound of flavoured ice, or gorge on deep-fried bacalaitos, cod fritters, as you lounge on a shady bench overlooking the marina. When night falls, get dressed up and join the crowds in SoFo, where hip restaurants offer artsy decor and good food to San Juan's beautiful people.

617 SHRIMP BBQ AND RUM PUNCH ON THE BEACH

NEVIS *Sunshine's Bar and BBQ* is a ramshackle hut with just a couple of picnic tables on Pinney's Beach, but once you've tasted the signature rum drinks and burned your lips on the spicy charred shrimp you won't care what it looks like. The owner himself serves up the sweet syrupy "killer bee", a special rum punch made from a secret and lethal recipe (though its name hints at the inclusion of honey among the closely guarded ingredient list) – sip it slowly while you wait for the food. Then, sitting under the shade of a palm-frond umbrella or in the steeply shelving sand, take your first, delicious bite. In the heavy, humid air of the West Indies the sharp heat of the shrimp, straight from the fire pit, hits you first and then intensifies as the insanely hot spices sear your taste buds. Cool your toes in the gently lapping water and soothe your burning mouth with a long gulp of ice-cold rum punch – now you're living like an islander.

618 LIVING IT UP AT FIESTA DE MERENGUE

DOMINICAN REPUBLIC The last week of July every summer since 1967, the three-million-plus denizens of Santo Domingo have converged on the Malecón, a seven-kilometre strand of palm-lined Caribbean boulevard that runs along the southern side of the Zona Colonial, for the Dominican Republic's biggest event of the year. The Fiesta de Merengue is the ultimate rum-drenched tropical blast-out, with twenty different bandstands belting out live music from local stars past, present and future – including the city's former mayor, hip-swivelling singing legend Johnny Ventura. The atmosphere and location are unbeatable – an expansive ribbon of turquoise sea stretches out into the distance, and headline acts play under the spectacular limestone palace of Christopher Columbus and the ruins of the walled city he built five centuries ago.

The Fiesta fills the beachfront Malecón, a labyrinth of jam-packed venues that has been dubbed the world's largest disco. As always at such events, the crowd is more than half the fun. Phalanxes of drunken youths bump up against white-haired old folks cutting quick, graceful moves across the asphalt; beaming teenage girls in formal, powder-pink dresses couple off together at the fringes and giggle in rhythm as they bob up and down; candy-striped vendors weave through the masses hawking everything from sugar cane and boiled corn to condoms and Clorets; and Mayor Ventura ploughs across the promenade at midnight in a horse-and-carriage, shaking his thang in a tailored three-piece suit as he waves to his fans. Local politicians get in on the act, too, as pickup trucks driven by blatantly tipsy party members slowly cruise the major city streets, blaring out merengue jingles as they go.

619 SEA KAYAKING IN THE EXUMAS

BAHAMAS "Wilderness" is not the first word that springs to mind when someone mentions the Bahamas; rum cocktails, high-rise hotels and limbo contests are the ready images. Yet a short hop from the wall-to-wall cruise ship carnival in Nassau lie the Exuma Cays, a chain of a couple of hundred mainly uninhabited islands stretching for more than 65km along the edge of the Great Bahama Bank. Separated by a tranquil sea, the low-lying chunks of honeycombed limestone rimmed by powdery white sand and covered in dense vegetation have seemingly been designed with one mode of exploration in mind: the sea kayak.

The Exuma Land and Sea Park, in the middle section of the cays, makes for an excellent starting point, though this could be said of almost anywhere in the chain. Your ride begins at dawn, when the mirror-smooth sea takes on a delicate shade of pink. The languid morning hours are spent blissfully dipping your paddle into turquoise waters lit from beneath by sunlight

reflected off a brilliant white sandy bottom and brimming with lush undersea gardens, coral reefs and a profusion of tropical fish. At midday, beach your kayak on an inviting swath of sand and picnic under a palm tree. Snorkel over bright-hued clumps of coral, marvelling at the dazzling colours and patterns of the fish as they dart among the waving purple sea fans. Visit the colonies of metre-long iguanas sunning themselves on beaches scattered throughout the islands. Hike the footpath to the summit of Boo Boo Hill on Warderick Wells Cay and enjoy a commanding view down the length of the island chain as it trails off over the horizon. Watch the sunset through its operatic gradations of red, pink and purple.

At night, a bright moon looms overhead and an opulent canopy of stars appears close enough to pluck. Lying on the sand, you'll fall asleep to nothing – aside from the periodic muffled thump of a coconut falling from a tree – but the gentle lapping of the waves.

620 THE NOCTURNAL SYMPHONY OF EL YUNQUE

PUERTO RICO "Ko-kee!, ko-kee!" As the moon climbs over mist-cloaked El Yunque Rainforest, the shrill symphony of tiny voices swells – "ko-kee, ko-kee, ko-keeeeee!" – echoing through the tropical tangle of dewy palms, orchids and feathery ferns. Stand still on the damp trail, and the whistling chorus rises all around you. The din is the mating call of the petite coqui frog, which is endemic to Puerto Rico. Even though you could fit several in the palm of your hand, the noise they make is incredible, and El Yunque, with its tumbling waterfalls and mossy pools, is their concert hall. As the sun dips, the frogs climb to the tops of trees, where they begin their nocturnal ensemble. The males belt out "ko" to scare off rivals from their territory, followed by the proud, piercing "kee" to attract the ladies. As day breaks, they leap off the branches, spreading their arms and legs so that they float, parachute-like, to the ground, where they land with a quiet plop.

621 SAVOURING THE FAMILIAR AT CRESCENT MOON

DOMINICA If when you arrive at *Crescent Moon Cabins*, nestled high in lush Morne Trois Pitons National Park, you find it has a familiar feel, it should: this is the Caribbean retreat you've always dreamed of. Blissfully secluded and smartly incorporated into the surrounding rainforest, this ecological gem features spring water pumped daily, an ever-expanding organic garden and cabins beautifully designed from local wood – all powered by wind generators. After a day spent hiking to the nearby volcanic crater and serene mountain lakes, and cooling off in the soothing pools of a sixty-metre-high waterfall, you can follow the winding footpath back to your cabin and admire the sweeping vistas of the ocean and jungle valley from the verandah. You could linger here until the day's end, were it not for the sweet aromas that signal dinner is about to be served. In fact, it's quite possible your dreams didn't do this place justice.

IN SEARCH OF THE
CITADELLE

HAITI High in the hills above the northern plains sits an imposing fortress, an architectural marvel really, that would undoubtedly be among the Caribbean's top destinations were it not for the grave lack of tourists in Haiti. Constructed in the early 1800s following the successful revolt of Haiti's massive and angry slave population, the Citadelle La Ferriere was designed to house and protect the new black royal family of Henri Christophe and 5000 soldiers for up to one year, in the event of a French retaliatory attack, which never came.

Travelling to the Citadelle is an adventure in itself, taking nearly an hour to traverse 20km of motorway riddled with craterous pot-holes, pedestrians and roadside repais. In the peaceful town of Milot visitors can expect to be descended upon by a horde of would-be guides. Although the Citadelle is easy enough to get to, guiding is important to the local economy and each visitor will end up with one, like it or not. Some offer sad horses that look as though they should be carried up the hill, not vice versa.

During the two-hour ascent you'll be immersed in a day in the life of Haitian rural poverty – families living in one-room shacks without running water yet boasting proud smiles. A lively entrepreneurial spirit thrives along this cobblestone trail, with vendors and kids selling fresh fruit, handmade dolls and artefacts. There is even a small vodou peristyle, or temple, along the way and anybody hanging about would be happy to show you the sacred space for a small donation.

Entering the Citadelle via massive doors through nearly ten-metre-thick walls, the massive interior reveals moss-covered staircases, chambers and cisterns, topped by panoramic views of Haiti's sadly deforested yet strikingly beautiful landscape. Hundreds of cannons of all shapes, sizes and nationalities, salvaged from shipwrecks off the treacherous coast, are aimed toward unseen enemies, while thousands of unused, rusting cannonballs remain stacked into pyramids, a testament to the ultimate success of the revolution.

623 DISCOVERING TREASURE ON JAMAICA'S COAST

JAMAICA In countries whose main income is from tourism, holidaying can be a somewhat surreal experience – and Jamaica is no exception. The big resorts are dominated by fenced-off all-inclusive hotels, the best bits of beach are pay-to-enter and most visitors' only interaction with Jamaicans is when ordering a beer or a burger. It's easy to see why savvier tourists have begun to forego resorts entirely in favour of something more authentic, heading away from the white sand and gin-clear waters of the north to the black sand and breakers of the south.

In Treasure Beach, sustainable, community-based tourism is the order of the day. Locals have taken control of development, opening low-key hotels and guesthouses instead of selling up to the multinational chains, ensuring that the tourist dollar goes straight into the community and not some corporate US bank account. Rather than themed restaurants and bars selling flavoured margaritas and bongs of beer, you'll find laid-back,

locally run outfits where you can feast on Jamaican home-cooking, learn the art of dominoes Caribbean-style or sip a white rum while the regulars teach you the latest dancehall moves. And thanks mostly to community group BREDS – named after "bredrin", the patois term for friend – tourism has had a tangibly positive effect: funds raised by visitor donations and an annual triathlon and fishing tournament have, among many other achievements, bought an ambulance (essential in a place where few have a car and the nearest hospital is 24km away), upgraded the local school and given financial aid to low-income families whose lives were ripped apart by Hurricane Ivan. A cheering thought as you hop in a fishing pirogue-cum-tour boat to head up the coast to the *Pelican Bar*, a rickety shack built on a sandbar a mile out to sea – easily the coolest drinking spot in Jamaica, with not a flavoured margarita in sight.

624 DEEPEST BLUE: DIVING BLOODY BAY WALL

LITTLE CAYMAN The reeftop is fairly flat and relatively shallow – around 8m deep – but when you swim to the edge you are looking into the abyss, 2000m straight down a vertical wall of coral. Bloody Bay Wall is over 3km long and dotted with coral arches, chimneys and sand chutes. Giant barrel sponges as tall as a man cling to the wall, while barracuda, Nassau groupers and turtles patrol the wall. The waters around Little Cayman are among the clearest in the Caribbean, let alone the world, and floating over the drop-off is a unique experience – as close to skydiving underwater as you can get.

625 GOING UNDERGROUND IN SANTO DOMINGO

DOMINICAN REPUBLIC Originally used by the indigenous Taino people for religious ceremonies, this massive, multi-level underground cave now attracts those who worship a different type of deity – the DJ. In a city full of hot clubs, *La Guacara Taina*, or simply "The Cave", is Santo Domingo's best, attracting world-class musicians and hordes of ravers. Decadence awaits as you descend into the club, passing bars, stalactites and scantily clad, well-to-do locals. If the intricate lightshow and three throbbing dance floors don't pull you out into the crowd, you can pass the evening sipping your Presidente in one of the smooth rock alcoves in the back.

626 SUN-WORSHIP LIKE A CELEBRITY ON ST BARTS

ST BARTHÉLEMY There are plenty of ways to do the Caribbean on a budget, but why suffer through the concrete package hotels with their nasty food and Hawaiian shirt-wearing hordes when you could blow the nest egg on a once-in-a-lifetime experience in St Barts? This little gem of a desert island isn't exactly splashy, though – celebrities like Nicole Kidman and Uma Thurman make it out here for its understated elegance and the privacy that such a high price-tag can afford them.

The atmosphere here is decidedly low-key, and local zoning laws make sure it stays that way, forbidding big resort development along the main beaches and ensuring that buildings in the small capital town of Gustavia are a height shorter than the highest palm trees. While there is a handful of nice hotels sprinkled about, the way to do St Barths is to rent your own red-roofed villa in one of the many isolated nooks and crannies along the shore of this boomerang-shaped oasis.

The local population consists mostly of descendants of the original French settlers to St Barts, who led a hard-scrabble

existence during the first centuries of its colonization, as the sandy soil didn't do much in the way of large-scale agriculture. The high-end tourism industry has therefore been something of a diamond-encrusted life preserver to the locals, who operate a mix of excellent boulangeries, creperies and restaurants that help make the St Barts experience exquisite. Dinner options range from super-hip, ambient Indian couch lounges to unpretentious beachfront diners with tasty Creole seafood.

You'll find a slew of archetypally pristine, white-sand beaches throughout the island, some of them accessible only by sea, which lends a sense of Robinson Crusoe seclusion that's hard to come by elsewhere in the Caribbean these days. And there's a Zarathustrian view from above on the west end of the island at Anse des Flamands that's about as majestic as you can get. Those seeking a bit of civilization can hop on over to dollhouse-quaint Gustavia, its U-shaped harbour lined with designer boutiques from Gucci and Hermes to Louis Vuitton and Lacoste – a veritable Champs Élysées on the sand.

MISCELLANY

CELEBRITY ISLES

ISLAND	OWNER(S)
Bonds Cay, Bahamas (700 acres)	Roger Waters and pop singer Shakira (joint business venture) in 2006 for a reported US$16m
Leaf Cay, Bahamas (25 acres)	Nicolas Cage in 2006 for a reputed US$3m
Little Hall's Pond Cay, Bahamas (45 acres)	Johnny Depp in 2004 for US$3.2m
Necker Island, British Virgin Islands (74 acres)	Richard Branson in 1978 for US$303,000 (currently valued at around US$106m)

PIRATES & PLUNDERERS

Welsh-born, Jamaica-based privateer **Sir Henry Morgan** was the terror of the Spanish fleet in the latter half of the seventeenth century, routinely undermining their attempts to control the region by destroying their ships and plundering their treasure. Today his malevolent grin graces every bottle of Captain Morgan rum.

Legendary pirate **Anne Bonny** was born in Ireland in the early 1700s and later moved with her husband to the Bahamas. Soon after, she eloped with "Calico Jack" Rackham, who introduced her to the seafaring life. Female pirates were not unheard of – there may even have been another on Rackham's ship – and some historians contest the popular belief that Bonny concealed her gender, showing just how formidable she was.

"At sunset Martin Alonzo called out with great joy from his vessel that he saw land, and demanded of the Admiral a reward for his intelligence"

Christopher Columbus on the discovery of San Salvador, Bahamas

FIVE GREAT FESTIVALS

Crop Over – Bridgetown, Barbados, July/Aug. Historic carnival celebrating the end of the sugar-cane harvest.

Fiesta de Merengue – Santo Domingo, Dominican Republic, late July. Honours the country's musical obsession.

Junkanoo – Nassau, New Providence Island, Bahamas, Dec 26/New Year's Day. Bacchanal recalling vacation days granted by slave-owners.

Trinidad Carnival – Port of Spain, Trinidad and Tobago, Feb/March. The Caribbean's biggest, craziest Carnival.

Shakespeare Mas' – Carriacou, Grenadines, Feb/March. A Shakespeare-reciting competition in which losers are punished with a whack to the (helmeted) head.

MIGHTY WINDS

Caribbean islands are frequently visited – and ravaged – by hurricanes. The Great Hurricane of 1780 killed over 22,000 people in Barbados, Martinique and Sint Eustatius. Abaco, in the Bahamas, is considered the Caribbean's historic **hurricane capital**, having withstood eighteen big ones since 1851. Since 1944, however, it's received fewer than **Grand Bahama**, which sees one roughly every four years; also since 1944, **Nevis** has taken the brunt of the Caribbean's heaviest storms, with Hurricane Lenny severely depressing the island's economy in 1999. In general, the eastern Caribbean sees fewer hurricanes than the rest of the region – and **Bonaire** and **Curaçao** get the fewest, with only eleven named storms passing through in the last 150 years.

TREASURE ISLAND

Robert Louis Stevenson's *Treasure Island* is one of the world's best-loved stories, with pirates, parrots and buried chests of gold. Though Stevenson's Skeleton Island may have been based on several real-world locales, he once wrote that tiny Dead Man's Chest Island, in the British Virgin Islands, provided the "seed" for his classic book.

"Fifteen men on the dead man's chest – Yo-ho-ho, and a bottle of rum!"

Robert Louis Stevenson, *Treasure Island*

THE PRICE OF PARADISE

Musha Cay in the Bahamas is the world's most expensive private resort island; it's a whopping US$3m per weekend to rent the whole thing. The celebrity hangout of Mustique is a comparative bargain, with its 85 luxury villas in the Grenadines for US$4000–35,000 each per week, depending on the season.

ISLAND PEAKS

Pico Duarte, in the Dominican Republic, is the Caribbean's tallest mountain at 3087m. The island of St Lucia is well known for its twin mountains (once active volcanoes), **Petit Piton** and **Gros Piton**, rising 734m and 798m above sea level.

JAMAICAN FAITH

Jamaica is purported to have the highest number of churches per capita in the world. Many are Anglican, given the island's history of British rule, but others are Moravian, Baptist, Methodist, Adventist and Pentecostal.

PARLEZ VOUS CREOLE?

In addition to the European languages imported by the Caribbean's major colonizers – French, Spanish and English – many islanders also speak variations of these, called **patois** or **Creole**. Often mistaken for mere "simplifications" of European languages, they are distinct dialects with their own grammatical and syntactical rules. While French is the official language of Haiti, kreyol is what Haitians really speak. Papiamento, from the Dutch Leeward Islands, comes primarily from Portuguese, but is influenced by Spanish, Dutch, West African dialects and Arawak, an indigenous language of the region.

CARIBBEAN AUTHORS

Born on St Lucia, Nobel-prize winner **Derek Walcott** is best known for his epic poem *Omeros*, which charts a fictional journey through the Caribbean, while **V.S. Naipaul**, another Nobel winner, hails from Trinidad. **Aimé Césaire**, the iconic poet and author of *Return to My Native Land*, about Africans' place in the New World, is a native of Martinique. **Edwidge Danticat** grew up in Haiti and relates the challenges of life there in *The Farming of Bones*.

RUM

Since Europeans first colonized the Caribbean with West African slaves, **rum** has been one of the region's most important exports. Sugar cane grows abundantly in the hot climes, and molasses, a by-product of sugar refinement, was collected by British ships for distillation into rum. Ships would cross the Atlantic to deliver rum to Europe, and then, on their way back to the Americas, swing by West Africa to pick up more slaves to work in the cane fields.

On British Admiral **Horatio Nelson**'s journey back to England from Antigua, where he'd been an administrator, a barrel of rum was on hand to preserve his body in case he died of fever.

Since 1862, the black bat has been the mascot of **Bacardi**, Puerto Rico's famous rum. The logo honours the fruit bats that roosted in the first Bacardi distillery.

THE BERMUDA TRIANGLE

Despite its name (Bermuda is technically not part of the Caribbean), this notorious area includes parts of the Bahamas. Famous in popular culture as a focus of supernatural powers that turn ships and airplanes off course and lead their crews to watery deaths, there are several scientific explanations for the number of wrecks here (which some scholars argue is no higher than anywhere else). Hurricanes, methane hydrates released from the sea floor that reduce the buoyancy of ships and fluctuations in magnetic declination, which can affect compass readings, are just a few.

FIVE ISLAND FILMS

Club Paradise (1986) Robin Williams and reggae icon Jimmy Cliff star in this comedy about an off-the-wall Caribbean resort development.

Dr Doolittle (1967) The beloved, double Oscar-winning story of a veterinarian who can speak to his patients was filmed in Marigot Bay on the island of St Lucia.

Dr No (1962) In the first 007 flick, Bond is sent to steamy Jamaica to investigate the death of a fellow operative, which leads him to the shadowy Dr. No on Crab Key.

Pirates of the Caribbean (2003, 2006 & 2007) Disney ride-turned-movie featuring pirates and rum-soaked islands in the sun.

Buena Vista Social Club (1999) Critically acclaimed documentary that propelled a group of nearly forgotten Cuban son musicians from obscurity to immortality.

TROPICAL EATS

Acra – Fish fritter made with saltfish, eggs and a combination of vegetables, popular in Martinique.

Lambi – Ubiquitous Caribbean stew made with the flesh of the conch, a large marine gastropod.

Saltfish – Salted and dried fish, usually mackerel or cod, used in a variety of Caribbean (particularly Jamaican) dishes.

Soursop – Related to the cherimoya, this large fruit is said to combine the flavours and textures of strawberry, coconut, banana and pineapple.

Stinking toe – Sweet-tasting but foul-smelling (hence the name), toe-shaped fruit used in Caribbean (especially Jamaican and Antiguan) cooking. Also an ingredient in folk medicines.

"Reason, I sacrifice you to the evening breeze"
Aimé Césaire

NATURE UNDER FIRE

The Puerto Rican island of **Culebra**, a National Wildlife Refuge, has been protected since US President Theodore Roosevelt established a bird refuge there in 1909. Today it's still home to a huge variety of birds and other animal and plant life. However, between World War II and 1975, the US Navy used it for bombing and gunning practice. Another Puerto Rican island, **Vieques**, is now used for similar purposes by the US military.

On **Bequia**, in the Grenadines, the long-standing tradition of harpooning **whales** is still legal. Natives are permitted by the International Whaling Commission to take four whales per year using traditional methods and weapons.

Guana Island, in the British Virgin Islands, on the other hand, is said to be the Caribbean locale least disturbed by humans.

SAMPLING FISH TACOS IN ENSENADA • TURTLE-WATCHING IN TORTUGUERO • TOURING THE ZAPATISTA HEARTLAND • HOPPING ABOARD THE COPPER CANYON RAILWAY • SURFING NEAR LA LIBERTAD • FLOATING THROUGH XOCHIMILCO • CHASING WHALE SHARKS NEAR UTILA • MARKET DAY IN OAXACA • A GLIMPSE OF THE MURALS AT BONAMPAK • WANDERING THE BACK ALLEYS OF ZACATECAS • GALLOPING THROUGH GUANACASTE • MAKING PEACE WITH TEQUILA IN TEQUILA • CLIMBING EL CASTILLO AT CHICHÉN ITZÁ • HONOURING THE DEAD IN JANITZIO • REVEL IN ECO-LUXURY AT MORGAN'S ROCK • RUSTIC LUXURY IN THE BELIZEAN FOREST • WHALE-WATCHING IN BAJA CALIFORNIA • VACATION LIKE A DRUG LORD IN TULUM • TREKKING IN CORCOVADO NATIONAL PARK • BIKING THE BAJA PENINSULA • ISLA BARRO COLORADO: THE APPLIANCE OF SCIENCE • PADDLING GLOVER'S REEF • CIRCLING LAGO ATITLÁN • HEADING TO MARKET IN THE GUATEMALAN HIGHLANDS • A COSTA RICA FAMILY ADVENTURE • MEETING THE MONARCHS IN MICHOACÁN • DAWN AT TIKAL • ALL ABOARD THE CHICKEN BUSES • OBSERVING SEMANA SANTA IN ANTIGUA • FLOATING DOWN THE NEW RIVER TO LAMANAI • ENCOUNTERING KUNA CULTURE • RIDING DOWN THE RÍO SAN JUAN • A TASTE OF MOLE POBLANO IN PUEBLA • BEING SERENADED BY MARIACHIS IN GUADALAJARA • DIVING AT PALANCAR REEF • STELAE STORIES OF COPÁN • SEARCHING FOR JAGUARS IN COCKSCOMB BASIN WILDLIFE SANCTUARY • ISLA DE OMETEPE BY MOTORCYCLE • BIRD-WATCHING ON THE PIPELINE ROAD • TAKING A DIP IN THE YUCATÁN'S CENOTES • FAMILY SAILING ACROSS THE PACIFIC • EASING INTO THE NEW YEAR ON CAYE CAULKER • TURTLE-WATCHING IN TORTUGUERO • TOURING THE ZAPATISTA HEARTLAND • HOPPING ABOARD THE COPPER CANYON RAILWAY • SURFING NEAR LA LIBERTAD • SAMPLING FISH TACOS IN ENSENADA • FLOATING THROUGH XOCHIMILCO • CHASING WHALE SHARKS NEAR UTILA • MARKET DAY IN OAXACA • A GLIMPSE OF THE MURALS AT BONAMPAK • WANDERING THE BACK ALLEYS OF ZACATECAS • KAYAKING IN THE SEA OF CORTÉS • REVEL IN ECO-LUXURY AT MORGAN'S ROCK • MAKING PEACE WITH TEQUILA IN TEQUILA • CLIMBING EL CASTILLO AT CHICHÉN ITZÁ • HONOURING THE DEAD IN JANITZIO • RUSTIC LUXURY IN THE BELIZEAN FOREST • GALLOPING THROUGH GUANACASTE • WHALE-WATCHING IN BAJA CALIFORNIA • VACATION LIKE A DRUG LORD IN TULUM • TREKKING IN CORCOVADO NATIONAL PARK • BIKING THE BAJA PENINSULA • FROM SEA TO SHINING SEA: CRUISING THE PANAMA CANAL • ISLA BARRO COLORADO: THE APPLIANCE OF SCIENCE • PADDLING GLOVER'S REEF • CIRCLING LAGO ATITLÁN • HEADING TO MARKET IN THE GUATEMALAN HIGHLANDS • A COSTA RICA FAMILY ADVENTURE • MEETING THE MONARCHS IN MICHOACÁN • DAWN AT TIKAL • ALL ABOARD THE CHICKEN BUSES • OBSERVING SEMANA SANTA IN ANTIGUA • FLOATING DOWN THE NEW RIVER TO LAMANAI • ENCOUNTERING KUNA CULTURE • KAYAKING IN THE SEA OF CORTÉS • RIDING DOWN THE RÍO SAN JUAN • A TASTE OF MOLE POBLANO IN PUEBLA • DIVING AT PALANCAR REEF • STELAE STORIES OF COPÁN • BEING SERENADED BY MARIACHIS IN GUADALAJARA • SEARCHING FOR JAGUARS IN COCKSCOMB BASIN WILDLIFE SANCTUARY • ISLA DE OMETEPE BY MOTORCYCLE • INDULGING IN THE JUNGLE • HANDMADE HAMMOCKS IN MASAYA • MEXICO CITY'S MURALS • BIRD-WATCHING ON THE PIPELINE ROAD • TAKING A DIP IN THE YUCATÁN'S CENOTES • FAMILY SAILING ACROSS THE PACIFIC • EASING INTO THE NEW YEAR ON CAYE CAULKER • TURTLE-WATCHING IN TORTUGUERO • TOURING THE ZAPATISTA HEARTLAND • FROM SEA TO SHINING SEA: CRUISING THE PANAMA CANAL • HOPPING ABOARD THE COPPER CANYON RAILWAY • SURFING NEAR LA LIBERTAD • SAMPLING FISH TACOS IN ENSENADA • FLOATING THROUGH XOCHIMILCO • CHASING WHALE SHARKS NEAR UTILA • MARKET DAY IN OAXACA • A GLIMPSE OF THE MURALS AT BONAMPAK • WANDERING THE BACK ALLEYS OF

MEXICO & CENTRAL AMERICA

627–673

652 SAMPLING FISH TACOS IN ENSENADA

651 KAYAKING IN THE SEA OF CORTÉS

MEXICO

665 BEING SERENADED BY MARIACHIS IN GUADALAJARA

635 MARKET DAY IN OAXACA

657 DAWN AT TIKAL

BELIZE

644 PADDLING GLOVER'S REEF

HONDURAS

GUATEMALA

630 SURFING NEAR LA LIBERTAD

EL SALVADOR

NICARAGUA

638 REVEL IN ECO-LUXURY AT MORGAN'S ROCK

639 GALLOPING THROUGH GUANACASTE

COSTA RICA

PANAMA

669 FROM SEA TO SHINING SEA: CRUISING THE PANAMA CANAL

627 TURTLE-WATCHING IN TORTUGUERO

COSTA RICA It's a clear, moonless night when we assemble for our pilgrimage to the beach. I can't understand how we are going to see anything in the blackness, but the guide's eyes seem to penetrate even the darkest shadows. We begin walking, our vision adjusting slowly.

We've come to Tortuguero National Park, in northeast Costa Rica, to witness sea turtles nesting. Once the domain of only biologists and locals, turtle-watching is now one of the more popular activities in ecotourism-friendly Costa Rica. As the most important nesting site in the western Caribbean, Tortuguero sees more than its fair share of visitors – since 1980, the annual number of observers has gone from 240 to 50,000.

The guide stops, points out two deep furrows in the sand – the sign of a turtle's presence – and places a finger to his lips, making the "shhh" gesture. The nesting females can be spooked by the slightest noise or light. He gathers us around a crater in the beach; inside it is an enormous creature. We hear her rasp and sigh as she brushes aside sand for her nest.

In whispers, we comment on her plight: the solitude of her task, the low survival rate of her hatchlings – only one of every 5000 will make it past the birds, crabs, sharks, seaweed and human pollution to adulthood.

We are all mesmerized by the turtle's bulk. Though we are not allowed to get too close, we can catch the glint of her eyes. She doesn't seem to register our presence at all. The whirring sound of discharged sand continues. After a bit the guide moves us away. My eyes have adapted to the darkness now, and I can make out other gigantic oblong forms labouring slowly up the beach – a silent, purposeful armada.

628 TOURING THE ZAPATISTA HEARTLAND

MEXICO As the chanting reached a crescendo and the incense thickened to a fog, the chicken's neck snapped like a pencil. The seemingly ageless executioner sat on a carpet of pine needles, surrounded by hundreds of candles, his eyes fixed upon a brightly painted saintly icon. The man took a swig from a Coca-Cola bottle, a sign not of globalization, but of the expurgating power of soda – the Tzotzil people believe that evil spirits can be expulsed through a robust burp. Here, inside the church of San Juan de Chamula, such faith doesn't seem all that far-fetched.

This is the Zapatista heartland of Chiapas, a lost world of dense jungle and indigenous villages where descendants of the Maya cling to the rituals of their ancestors. Throughout the region, the iconography of Subcomandante Marcos, guerrilla leader and poster child of the struggle for indigenous rights, reveals a continuing undercurrent of rebellion – San Cristóbal de las Casas, one of Mexico's most alluring towns, was the site of an armed Zapatista revolt in 1994.

Outside San Cristóbal, the village of San Juan de Chamula is literally a law unto itself, with its own judges, jail and council. Timeless rituals are revealed: women sell brightly coloured, hand-woven garments in the main square, returning home at midday to prepare a meal for their husbands, many of whom are shared (men can have up to three wives at a time). Every year during the pre-Lenten festival, perhaps the most exciting time to visit, the village's men run barefoot through blazing wheat.

Four kilometres from Chamula, San Lorenzo Zinacantán is equally fascinating. Here, the men, in red-and-white ponchos and flat hats strewn with ribbons (tied if they are married, loose if not), launch rockets skyward to stir the gods into sending rain. The women pummel tortillas and weave textiles, always with a watchful eye on the sky – many houses have gone up in smoke as a result of rogue fireworks.

629 HOPPING ABOARD THE COPPER CANYON RAILWAY

MEXICO As the countryside – by turns savage, pristine, lush – flashes past the windows of the Chihuahua-Pacific Express, Mexico reveals a side of itself that is both spectacular and unexpected.

"El Chepe", as the train is known, traverses the country's most remote landscape, a region of rugged splendour called the Copper Canyon. Spanning six prodigious canyons and a labyrinth of some two hundred gorges, this natural wonder is four times the size of the Grand Canyon. Harsh, inaccessible and thoroughly untamed, the canyons are sparsely populated only by the Rarámuri, an indigenous agrarian people.

El Chepe's journey commences on Mexico's Pacific coast, in Los Mochis, then trundles through 75km of arid, cactus-strewn wasteland past placid El Fuerte, the gateway to the canyons. From here, the track climbs, the air cools and the scenery shifts: for the next six hours you roll past one incredible vista after another. In a continual skyward ascent, El Chepe plunges in and out of tunnels, rattles over bridges and makes hair-pin turns.

Colossal stone cliffs, folds of rock and serpentine rivers flicker by. Above you, mountains rise like fortified cities, while gaping chasms open on either side. Then, all at once, the stone corridor yields to a sweeping plateau of pine-scattered towers and stratified monoliths.

At Divisadero, 300km from Los Mochis and 2000m above sea level, three canyons converge to form an astonishing panorama. The train makes a brief stop here, giving you time to snap some pictures and breathe in the ozone and pine. Creel, another 60km along, is the place to stop for extended excursions – forests, gorges, waterfalls and hot springs all lie within easy reach.

The 655-kilometre expedition concludes on the desert plains of Chihuahua, though it feels as if you've travelled further. Stepping off the train, you're as likely to feel humbled as you are exhilarated.

630 SURFING AT LA LIBERTAD

EL SALVADOR It's not surprising that the beach in La Libertad is packed on Sundays. The port town is less than an hour's drive from the choked capital of San Salvador, its oceanfront restaurants serve the finest mariscada (creamy seafood soup) in the country and, of course, there's el surf.

The western end of the beach here has one of the longest right point breaks, prosaically called punta roca (rocky point), in the world. On a good day – and with year-round warm water and consistent and uncrowded waves there are plenty of those – skilled surfistas can ride a thousand yards from the head of the point into the beach. Amateur surfers, meanwhile, opt for the section of gentler waves, known as La Paz, that roll into the mid-shore.

It's rare to walk through the town without seeing one of the local boys running barefoot, board under arm, down to the sea or hanging outside the Hospital de las Tablas while a dent or tear is repaired. Some, like Jimmy Rottingham, whose American father kick-started the expat surf scene when he arrived in the 1970s (witness the psychedelic surfboards on the walls of *Punta Roca* restaurant), have become semi-professional.

If you're looking for quieter, cleaner breaks, join the foreign surfers who head west of La Libertad to beaches such as El Zonte. These days it's a backpacker heaven, but until 1998 the point break here was secret among locals and students from Santa Tecla. The village's best surfer, El Teco, was inspired to jump on a board after watching Hawaii Five-O, later polishing his technique by observing pelicans surfing the waves. Even if you miss out on "olas de mantequilla" (waves like butter) or suffer too many "wipeadas" there's always the Zonte scene: at weekends the capital's hip kids come down to party amid bonfires, fire dancers and all-night drumming.

631 CHASING WHALE SHARKS NEAR UTILA

HONDURAS The island of Utila, off the coast of Honduras, isn't your ordinary scuba-diving base. Sure, there's plenty of stunningly beautiful marine life to be seen. It isn't the beautiful, though, that draws many diving enthusiasts here. Rather, it's the exotically monstrous – Utila is one of the few places on Earth that the whale shark, the world's largest fish, can be spotted year-round.

Whale sharks, which are harmless to humans, remain elusive creatures – relatively little is known about them, and their scientific name (rhincodon typhus) wasn't even established until 1984. Measuring up to an estimated fifteen metres (and twenty tonnes), they are filter feeders, sieving tropical seas for nutrients and migrating across oceans and up and down the coast of Central America. Oceanic upswells close to Utila consistently sweep together a rich soup of plankton and krill, making them a prime feeding ground for the immense creatures.

Most mornings, dive boats scour the seas north of Utila between reef dives looking for "boils": feeding frenzies created by bonito tuna rounding up huge schools of baitfish, or krill. Hungry sharks home in on the boils, gliding just below the surface, mouths agape as they scythe through the sea. Their blue-grey upper bodies are sprinkled with intricate patterns of white spots (which appear electric blue from a distance in the sunlight), interspersed with chessboard-style markings.

Often, they feed upright, an astonishing sight – watch as the great fish manoeuvre themselves into a vertical position, bobbing up and down and gulping sea water into two-metre-wide mouths. If you'd like, you can slip into the water with them. But do it while you can – the chance to swim among them is usually fleeting, as the boils disintegrate rapidly and the sharks disappear as quickly as they came.

632

FLOATING THROUGH **XOCHIMILCO**

MEXICO Spend a few days in the intoxicating, maddening centro histórico of Mexico City, and you'll understand why thousands of Mexicans make the journey each Sunday to the "floating gardens" of Xochimilco, the country's very own Venice.

Built by the Aztecs to grow food, this network of meandering waterways and man-made islands, or chinampas, is an important gardening centre for the city, and where families living in and around the capital come to spend their day of rest. Many start their trip with a visit to the beautiful sixteenth-century church of San Bernadino in the suburb's main plaza, lighting candles and giving thanks for the day's outing. Duty done, they head down to one of several docks, or embarcaderos, on the water to hire out a trajinera for a few hours. These flat, brightly painted gondolas – with names such as *Viva Lupita*, *Adios Miriam*, *El Truinfo* and *Titanic* – come fitted with table and chairs, perfect for a picnic.

The colourful boats shunt their way out along the canals, provoking lots of good-natured shouting from the men wielding the poles. As the silky green waters, overhung with trees, wind past flower-filled meadows, the cacophony and congestion of the city are forgotten. Mothers and grannies unwrap copious parcels and pots of food, men open bottles of beer and aged tequila; someone starts to sing. By midday, Xochimilco is full of carefree holidaymakers.

Don't worry if you haven't come with provisions – the trajineras are routinely hunted down by vendors selling snacks, drinks and even lavish meals from small wooden canoes. Others flog trinkets, sweets and souvenirs. And if you've left your guitar at home, no problem: boatloads of musicians – mariachis in full costume, marimba bands and wailing ranchera singers – will cruise alongside or climb aboard and knock out as many tunes as you've money to pay for.

633 CIRCLING LAGO ATITLÁN

GUATEMALA Ever since Aldous Huxley passed this way in the 1930s, writers have lauded the natural beauty of Lago Atitlán. Ringed by three volcanoes, the lake is also surrounded by a series of Maya villages, each with its own appeal and some still quite traditional, despite the influx of visitors. A week spent circumnavigating Atitlán is the ideal way to experience its unique blend of Maya tradition and bohemian counterculture.

Start at the main entry point, Panajachel, which was "discovered" by beatniks in the 1950s and remains the most popular lakeside settlement. The hotels and shopping (especially for textiles) are excellent, even if the place has become something approaching a resort.

By contrast, Santiago Atitlán remains close to one hundred percent Tz'utujil Maya and has a frenetic and non-touristy market that fires up early each Friday morning. It's a riot of colour and commerce as a tide of highlanders overloaded with vegetables and weavings struggles between dock and plaza. Elsewhere, drop by the textile museum, the parish church and the shrine of the Maya pagan saint Maximón, where you can pay your respects with offerings of liquor and tobacco.

Neighbouring San Pedro is another Tz'utujil village, but in the last decade or so has become Guatemala's countercultural centre, with a plethora of language schools and cheapo digs for backpacking bong-puffers and bongo drummers. Even if this puts you off, you can content yourself with the village's great restaurants and a hike up nearby San Pedro volcano.

It's a short hop on to San Marcos, for some New Age vibes at the renowned *Las Pirámides* meditation-cum-yoga retreat. Last stop is Santa Cruz, where a few wonderful guesthouses make the ideal base for days spent idling in a hammock and admiring the perfect lake views.

634 RUSTIC LUXURY IN THE BELIZEAN FOREST

BELIZE The story goes that Francis Ford Coppola built *Blancaneaux* as a place to write, and it's hard to imagine a more inspiring base than this luxuriously rustic resort in Belize's Mountain Pine Ridge Forest Reserve. Just two or three hours' drive from the airport – or a short hop in your private plane – and you're poised for an idyllic few days where nature comes with all mod cons. Everything here seems designed to showcase the natural environment. Thatched cabanas scattered through the lush gardens, furnished with Central American textiles and artworks, feature decks and bathrooms half-open to the elements; thankfully, bedrooms are secured against mosquitoes and other nasties.

Twice a day, honeymooners and hikers alike troop up to the restaurant for tasty American breakfasts and Italian dinners, cooked using ingredients from the on-site organic garden. Staff will happily make you a packed lunch to enjoy while out exploring. Several of Belize's sights are within easy reach by 4WD, chief among them the ancient Maya city of Caracol – still under excavation – where you might find yourself wandering the overgrown ruins alone but for your driver-guide. Armed with every fact there is to know about Belizean history and wildlife, he'll regularly stop the car en route to point out a king vulture, perhaps, or to let you sniff the fragrant bark of a tree used in traditional medicines.

With so many activities to choose from, you'll need to set aside time to enjoy *Blancaneaux* for its own sake: lazing in a hammock overlooking the jungle, taking a dip in the natural pools formed by the Privassion Creek as it runs through the grounds, or hanging out in the bar, chatting with the guides about whether to go horse-riding, hiking or mountain-biking tomorrow.

However you spend your days, be sure to get up one morning while it's still dark. As the sky lightens and a misty scene comes into focus, parrots fly past, screeching an alarm over the sound of the rushing river. Sitting snuggled in a fleece on your deck, watching the jungle awaken before you in all its cawing, chirruping and whirring glory, is worth getting out of bed for.

635 MARKET DAY IN OAXACA

MEXICO Oaxaca is pure magical realism – an elegant fusion of colonial grandeur and indigenous mysticism. From the zócalo, the city's main square, streets unfold in a patchwork of belle époque theatres, romantic courtyards and sublime churches.

While the city's colonial history reaches its zenith in the breathtaking Iglesia de Santo Domingo, pre-Hispanic traditions ignite in its kaleidoscopic markets. The largest of these is the bustling Mercado de Abastos, which bombards the senses with riotous colours, intoxicating aromas and exotic tastes.

Indigenous women dressed in embroidered huipiles, or tunics, squat amidst baskets overflowing with red chillis and chapulines (baked grasshoppers), weaving pozahuancos, wrap-around skirts dyed with secretions from snails. Stalls are piled with artesanía from across the region. Leather sandals, or huaraches, are the speciality of Tlacolula; made from recycled tyres, they guarantee even the most intrepid backpacker a lifetime of mileage.

Hand-woven rugs from Teotitlán del Valle, coloured using century-old recipes including pomegranate and cochineal beetles, are the most prized. The shiny black finish on the pottery from San Bartolo Coyotepec gives it an ornamental function – a promotion from the days when it was used to carry mescal to market.

Street-smart vendors meander the labyrinthine alleyways, offering up the panaceas of ancient deities – tejate, the "Drink of the Gods", is a cacao-based beverage with a curd consistency and muddy hue. (A more guaranteed elixir is a mug of hot chocolate, laced with cinnamon and chilli, from Mayordormo, the Willy Wonka of Oaxaca.) The stalls around the outer edges of the market sell shots of mescal; distilled from the sugary heart of the cactus-like maguey plant and mixed with local herbs, it promises a cure to all ailments. With a dead worm at the bottom as proof of authenticity, it's an appropriately mind-bending libation for watching civilization and supernaturalism merge on a grand scale.

636 WANDERING THE BACK ALLEYS OF ZACATECAS

MEXICO Zacatecas is a sophisticated little city, so I was a bit surprised to see a donkey amble past the café window where I sat, its ears poking through a straw sombrero. Only when I saw that its panniers were full of tequila, and that it was being followed by a dozen hombres in gaudy ponchos blasting away on brass instruments, did things begin to make sense.

I was seeing a callejóneada (from callejón, or alley). I had heard of these, but had never witnessed one before. I nipped outside, just catching the tail end of the procession as it snaked away down the city's narrow alleys – a throng of maybe a hundred people slowly meandered through the streets behind the donkey. Though we effectively blocked traffic, no one seemed much concerned – callejóneadas are a way of life in Zacatecas, and people in the historic centre know to expect a little donkey congestion. Drivers just cranked up their stereos and waited for us to turn down another alley.

Callejóneadas are usually organized to celebrate a special event, such as a birthday or a wedding. Someone hires a band and a donkey, then buys enough tequila and small ceramic cups for everyone in the party. Periodically the donkey driver (or one of his enthusiastic assistants) makes the rounds, pouring everyone a shot.

I felt out of place, not having a cup of my own (it is courteous to bring your own refreshments), but I soon made friends and was given one, the tequila purveyor dutifully summoned. Though downing the alcohol in one swift gulp is obligatory, callejóneadas aren't about excessive consumption. Rather, they are an excuse to enjoy time with friends (and any strangers who happen along), meander through alleys in the balmy night air, listen to the band and occasionally even dance.

After a while, the band exhausted its repertoire and my companions began to disperse, some going home for a late dinner, others heading straight to the city's bars and clubs, leaving the alleys quiet for another evening.

637 CLIMBING EL CASTILLO AT CHICHÉN ITZÁ

MEXICO Clambering up the impossibly steep face of the central pyramid of Chichén Itzá, nicknamed "the castle" by the Spaniards, you can't help but count your steps. And that's exactly what the ancient Maya wanted you to do.

By the time you reach the platform at the top (25m above the grassy lawn at the base), you should have counted to 91. After you've caught your breath and got your vertigo under control, do a little maths: 91 steps up each of the four sides of the structure totals 364. Add the step you're standing on, and you get, not coincidentally, the number of days in a year.

The Maya were obsessed with the passage of time. Their complex calendar system completed a full cycle every 52 years, and with that came certain rituals. The seemingly solid pyramid you're standing on encases a second, smaller one. According to the glyphs on the buildings, the castillo was built 52 years after its miniature core.

The pyramid is dedicated to Kukulcán, the feathered serpent who headed the Maya pantheon. His gaping mouth adorns either side of the main set of stairs, but his full image emerges only at the spring and fall equinoxes, when the sun creates a long, snaking shadow up the staircase.

But given how little archeologists have been able to discern about Maya culture after centuries of study, how true is this interpretation of the monument? What seem like resonant facts to us – the number of steps, the shadow – may have meant next to nothing to the Maya, and the real object of their fascination could still lie well beyond our reach.

At the base of El Castillo, the scene is one of modern tourist mayhem, with guides spinning tales about the people who once inhabited the place. From your perch far above the fray, however, you get the feeling that many of the Maya's secrets are still locked in these stones.

638 REVEL IN ECO-LUXURY AT MORGAN'S ROCK

NICARAGUA The largest area of virgin rainforest north of the Amazon, endless miles of pristine coastline, 76 national parks brimming with wildlife, six active volcanoes – Nicaragua is an ecotourist's fantasy. After decades of political turbulence, the largest country in Central America is set to become the buzz word for adventurous travellers with a conscience – like Costa Rica before the swarm.

Leading the way in terms of environmentally friendly accommodation is the country's first five-star resort, *Morgan's Rock Hacienda and Ecolodge*. The hacienda's fifteen chalets are built like stupendous treehouses, with open sides offering gorgeous views onto a private beach where giant leatherback turtles lay their eggs; wake in the night to witness hundreds of flapping babies (Aug–Jan). Simple furniture is handmade by regional artisans, the friendly staff are locals and the open-air showers are heated by solar panels.

This is a hotel that takes the "eco" part of its billing incredibly seriously. Behind the scenes, *Morgan's* is a clean dream of organic living. The owners of the hacienda have planted almost 1.5 million trees and have set aside 8 square kilometres of primary forest for conservation – home to spider monkeys, armadillos and sloths, as well as dozens of exotic birds, and brought alive on awesome wildlife tours by trained biologists. Endangered animal species are being reintroduced, whilst existing animals are protected from hunters. Then there is the restaurant, which offers some of the freshest, purest food you will ever taste – including organic algae-fed shrimp, cheese made from the hacienda's cows and sweet home-made rum.

Luxurious ethical travel doesn't come better than this. Enjoy moonlit walks on the beach or wallow in the salt-water pool, happy in the knowledge that what's good for you is also good for the planet. It's back-to-nature bliss.

COSTA RICA This is not the Costa Rica you may have imagined: one glance at the wide-open spaces, the legions of heat-stunned cattle or the mounted sabaneros (cowboys) trotting alongside the Pan-American Highway reveals that Guanacaste has little in common with the rest of the country. Often called "the Texas of Costa Rica", this is ranching territory: the lush, humid rainforest that blankets most of the country is notably absent here, replaced by a swath of tropical dry forest. It's one of the last significant patches of such land in Central America.

Given the region's livelihood, it's only fitting that the best way to tour Guanacaste is astride a horse. Don't be shy about scrambling into the saddle – many of the working ranches in the province double as hotels, and almost all of them offer horseback tours, giving you a chance to participate in the region's sabanero culture. From your perch high above the ground, the strange, silvery beauty of the dry forest appears to much greater advantage – in the dry season, the trees shed their leaves in an effort to conserve water, leaving the landscape eerily bare and melancholy. You'll be able to spot all kinds of wildlife, from monkeys and pot-bellied iguanas to birds and even the odd boa constrictor (though the horses may not be impressed by this one).

For a different sort of scenery, head to the area around still-active Rincón de la Vieja, where you can ride around bubbling mud pots (pilas de barro) and puffing steam vents, all under the shadow of the towering, mist-shrouded volcano.

Some of the region's ranches-cum-hotels even let guests put in a day's work riding out with their hands, provided fence-mending and cattle-herding skills are up to scratch. Regardless of your level of equestrian expertise, once you've had a gallop through Guanacaste, you'll never look at sightseeing on foot the same way again.

GALLOPING THROUGH

639

GUANACASTE

640 TREKKING IN CORCOVADO NATIONAL PARK

COSTA RICA The road to Corcovado National Park was once paved with gold – lots of gold – and although most of it was carried off by the Diqui Indians, miners still pan here illegally. These days, though, it's just an unpaved track that fords half a dozen rivers during the bone-rattling two-hour ride from the nearest town, Puerto Jiménez, and which runs out at Carate, the southern gateway to the park and a one-horse "town" that comprises just a single store.

The journey in doesn't make an auspicious start to a hike in Corcovado – and it gets worse. Trekking here is not for the faint-hearted: the humidity is 100 percent, there are fast-flowing rivers to cross and the beach-walking that makes up many of the hikes can only be done at low tide. Cantankerous peccaries roam the woods, and deadly fer-de-lance and bushmaster snakes slip through the shrub.

But you're here because Corcovado is among the most biologically abundant places on earth, encompassing thirteen eco-systems, including lowland rainforests, highland cloudforests, mangrove swamps, lagoons and coastal and marine habitats. And it's all spectacularly beautiful, even by the high standards of Costa Rica.

Streams trickle down over beaches pounded by Pacific waves, where turtles (hawksbill, leatherback and Olive Ridley) lay their eggs in the sand and where the shore is dotted with footprints – not human, but tapir, or possibly jaguar. Palm trees hang in bent clumps, and behind them the forest rises up in a sixty-metre wall of dense vegetation.

Corcovado has the largest scarlet macaw population in Central America, and the trees flash with bursts of their showy red, blue and yellow plumage. One hotel in the area offers free accommodation if visitors don't see one during their stay – it's never happened. And after the first sighting of the birds flying out from the trees in perfectly coordinated pairs, the long journey to reach Corcovado seems a short way to come.

641 HONOURING THE DEAD IN JANITZIO

MEXICO Mexicans believe that the thin veil between the land of the living and the world of the spirits is at its most permeable on the night of November 1, as All Saints' Day slips silently into All Souls' Day. This is the one time each year, it is said, when the dead can visit the relatives they have left behind. Mexicans all over the country aim to make them feel welcome when they do, though nowhere are the preparations as elaborate as on the island of Janitzio in Lago Pátzcuaro.

Market stalls laden with papier-mâché skeletons and sugar skulls appear weeks in advance; the decorations and sweets go on shrines set up in people's homes. Dedicated to the departed, the shrines come complete with a photo of the deceased and an array of their favourite treats – perhaps some cigarettes, a few tamales and, of course, preferred brands of tequila and beer.

When the big day comes, you don't want to arrive too early at the cemetery – it isn't until around 11pm, as the witching hour approaches, that the island's indigenous Purhépecha people start filtering into the graveyard. They come equipped with candles, incense and wooden frames draped in a riot of puffy orange marigolds. Pretty soon the entire site is aglow with candles, the abundantly adorned graves slightly eerie in the flickering light. So begins the all-night vigil: some observers doze silently, others reminisce with friends seated at nearby graves. It is a solemn, though by no means sombre, occasion. Indeed, unlike most cultures, Mexicans live with death and celebrate it.

By early morning the cemetery is peaceful, and in the pre-dawn chill, as sleep threatens to overtake you, it is easier to see how the dead could be tempted back for a brief visit, and why people return year after year to commune with the departed.

642 ALL ABOARD THE CHICKEN BUSES

GUATEMALA Camionetas ("chicken buses") start their lives as North American school buses, Bluebirds built to ferry under-eights from casa to classroom. Once they move down to these parts, they're decked out with gaudy "go-faster" stripes and windshield stickers bearing religious mantras ("Jesús es el Señor"). Comfort, however, is not customizable: bench seat legroom is so limited that gringo knees are guaranteed a bruise or two, and the roads have enough crater-sized potholes to ensure that your gluteus maximus will take a serious pounding. But you choose to hop aboard in Antigua just the same, to say you've ridden one if for no other reason.

Pre-departure rituals must be observed. Street vendors stream down the aisles, offering everything from chuchitos (mini tamales) to bibles. Expect a travelling salesman-cum-quack to appear and utter a heartfelt monologue testifying how his elixir will boost libido, cure piles and insomnia (which won't be a problem on the journey ahead). Don't be surprised to find an indigenous family of delightful but snotty-nosed, taco-munching kids on your lap and a basket of dried shrimp under your feet; on the chicken bus, there's no such thing as "maximum capacity".

A moustachioed driver jumps aboard, plugs in a tape of the cheesiest merengue the marketplace has to offer, and you're off. The exhaust smoke is so dense even the street dogs run for cover. A wiry teenage conductor, the ayudante, extracts your fare; he's strong enough to carry sacks of beans up to the roof rack but lithe enough to squeeze through the packed aisles.

Antigua to Nebaj doesn't look much on a map – around 165 kilometres or so – but the route passes through four distinct Maya regions, so you look out for the tightly woven zig-zag shawls typical of Chichicastengo and the scarlet turban-like headdresses worn by the women of the Ixil. Considering the way the bus negotiates the blind bends of the Pan-American Highway, you'll take anything to divert your attention.

With some luck, after five hours you arrive in Nebaj, a little shaken, slightly bruised, but with a story to tell.

643 WHALE–WATCHING IN BAJA CALIFORNIA

MEXICO Whale shapes are picked out in fairy lights; whalebones are hung on restaurant walls and garden fences; posters, flyers and sandwich boards depict whales outside every shop and bar – even the name of the supermarket here, La Ballena, means whale.

If you didn't already know, you might guess that Guerrero Negro, a flyblown pit stop halfway down the long, spindly peninsula of Baja California, is the main base for whale-watching in Mexico. Every November, California grey whales leave Alaska en masse and migrate south to calve, arriving in the warm waters of Mexico in January and February.

The lagoon close to Guerrero Negro is where most fetch up – and the tour to see them, with a guaranteed sighting at close quarters, is one of Mexico's most unforgettable experiences.

And it goes like this. By the time the small boat reaches the middle of the glassy-smooth lagoon and the captain switches

off the engine, all its excitable passengers have been silenced. Someone spots a distant, cloudy spray – then a great grey body, studded white with barnacles, rises out of the water and curves back in with a deep, resounding splash, leaving a trail of smooth rings across the surface of the water. The little boat rocks and shakes, and curious whales come closer.

Round and round they swim, nine metres of pure elegance twisting, flipping, rolling and spouting, their brand-new offspring gliding alongside – the boat's passengers can almost touch them. And the whales are often joined by dolphins, aquatic bodyguards swimming in perfectly synchronized pairs to protect the whale calves, and by sea lions, their cheeky whiskered faces nearly stealing the show. Then just as suddenly as the mammals arrived, they disappear back into the deep. The lagoon settles and, moved to silence or even tears, a boatload of awestruck tourists motors back to shore.

644 PADDLING GLOVER'S REEF

BELIZE The Caribbean coastline of Belize is something of a paradise cliché. The second largest coral reef in the world, all 320km of it, runs the length of the country, sheltering around 1200 small islands, or "cayes", in its calm inshore waters – some are developed tourist resorts, others low-key backpacker haunts and uninhabited, palm-shaded sandbanks. As if this wasn't enough, three of the Caribbean's four coral atolls (extinct volcanoes) are close offshore, providing stupendous diving. Cliché, indeed.

The Blue Hole may be the most famous of these atolls, but the best developed is Glover's Reef. About 50km off Dangriga, it spans 35km from north to south, and is encircled by deep, stunning walls of coral. A handful of cayes pepper the central lagoon; underwater, they're surrounded by several hundred colourful patch reefs.

To explore Glover's by sea kayak couldn't be more perfect.

The cayes in the central lagoon are a good place to start out – each has a white-coral beach, and all are easy to reach. Many visitors elect to go as part of a guided tour, but it's also possible to spend a few days on your own, meandering from caye to caye, camping and living on barbecued grouper and lobster. More adventurous kayakers can head miles out to sea through calm swells, where, although you leave your human companions behind, you're never alone – pelicans, nesting ospreys and other seabirds are always close by. Snorkelling straight off the kayak reveals staggering underwater biodiversity – sea turtles, parrotfish, rays and dolphins all make frequent appearances, and whale sharks haunt the waters around Glover's in the spring. If laid-back Belize has really got under your skin, opt for a kayak with a kite sail, which allows you to sit back and follow the trade winds through the cayes. Bliss.

645 ISLA BARRO COLORADO: THE APPLIANCE OF SCIENCE

PANAMA Semi-hidden in the thick forest floor, a nervy agouti is on the forage for food. It stops to nibble on some spiny palm fruit, sandwiching each bite with anxious glances into the surrounding undergrowth. Less than five metres away from the unsuspecting rodent, and closing the gap with every stealthy stride, an ocelot moves in for the kill. The agouti enjoys its last few drips of sweet palm juice, and then...BANG. The cat gets the cream.

In the surrounding rainforest, several scientists from the Smithsonian Tropical Research Institute (STRI) monitor the moment, another important step in piecing together the relationship between ocelot and agouti, predator and prey. Further south, more scientists observe the family behaviour of white-faced capuchins; to the west, the evolution of Baird's tapirs is the focus. Welcome to Isla Barro Colorado, the most intensely studied tropical island on earth.

Sitting plum in the middle of man-made Lago Gatún, roughly halfway along the Panama Canal, Barro Colorado is a living

laboratory, fifteen square kilometres of abundant biodiversity – more than a thousand plant species, nearly four hundred types of bird and over a hundred species of mammals – that the island owes to the canal itself. Flooding the area to facilitate its construction chased much of the wildlife in the surrounding forests on to higher ground. The one-time plateau became an island, and the island became a modern-day Noah's Ark, the animals coming in two by two dozen to seek refuge in its dense rainforest covering.

The Smithsonian has run a research station on Barro Colorado for over eighty years, but only fairly recently have they opened their doors to tourists. It's been worth the wait, though – hiking through the rainforest in the company of expert guides, the jungle canopy abuzz with screeching howler monkeys and ablaze with red-billed toucans, is an incredible experience, even if the Hoffman's two-toed sloths, hanging lazily from the trees, seem distinctly underwhelmed by it all.

646 MAKING PEACE WITH TEQUILA IN TEQUILA

MEXICO My first taste of tequila in Tequila was terrible – rough as guts and horribly strong. We were on a tour of one of the area's many distilleries, and the sample had been extracted straight from the production line. My stomach swooped uncomfortably as I looked at the steaming piles of blue agave cactus pulp. Definitely not going back for seconds.

Things began to look up when we entered the distillery's ancient storage sheds: this was where they kept the good stuff as it aged. As yet another round of samples went around, the guide explained the subtleties of the various styles and how best to appreciate them (no, the gringo accompaniments of salt, lime and bare skin are not obligatory). A few sips and my stomach, still nervous about receiving more of the fresh stuff, began to settle down – my conversion was underway.

Light-headed but not entirely sated, we headed back to

Guadalajara, where we repaired to La Maestranza, a dimly lit bar festooned with old bullfight memorabilia: half a dozen stuffed bulls' heads were arranged above the row of tequila bottles on the top shelf of the bar, as if to drive the point home. Someone ordered us a round of banderas, a trio of hefty tumblers that together form the green, white and red of the Mexican flag – the first is half-filled with fresh lime juice, the second with tequila, and the third with sangrita, a slightly sweet combination of spicy tomato juice and orange juice. Some chose to savour theirs, conforming to the recommended sequence (the sweetness of the sangrita settles the astringency of the tequila), others knocked them back without a second thought, then rapidly ordered another round. And another. All in all, I think that first taste was deceiving.

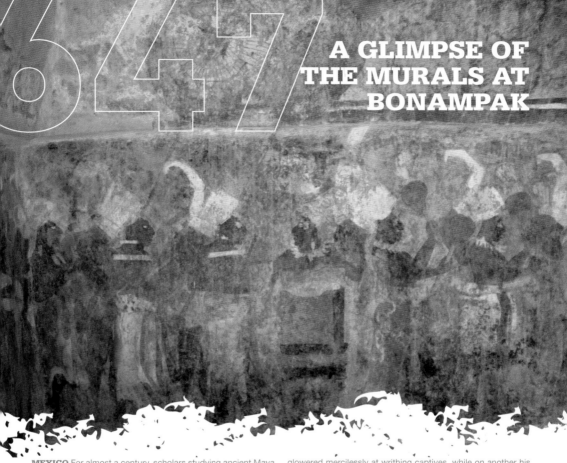

A GLIMPSE OF THE MURALS AT BONAMPAK

MEXICO For almost a century, scholars studying ancient Maya culture believed the Maya to be pacifists, devoted to their arcane calendar and other harmless pursuits. It wasn't until 1946, when a few Lacandón Maya led an American photographer to a ruined temple at Bonampak, deep in the Chiapas jungle, that they had any reason to think differently.

As the party entered the narrow building perched at the top of the temple and torchlight played across its interior, the ancient Maya flickered into living colour. A series of murals covered the walls and ceilings of three rooms, depicting the Maya in fascinating detail. Lords paraded in yellow-spotted jaguar pelts and elaborate headdresses, while attendants sported blue-green jade jewellery.

More remarkable was the quantity of bright-red gore splashed on scenes throughout the rooms: severed heads rolled, prisoners oozed blood from mangled fingers, sacrifice victims littered the ground. On one wall, the eighth-century king Chan Muan glowered mercilessly at writhing captives, while on another his soldiers engaged in a frenzied battle.

The artistry of the murals was undeniable: even the most gruesome images – such as the king's wife threading a thorn-studded rope through her tongue – were balanced by lush colours and captivating precision. But the discovery, while offering unparalleled insight for anthropologists and Maya experts, must have been somewhat unsettling, too: to see Chan Muan poised to lop the head off a prisoner was astounding.

Visiting the Bonampak murals is slightly easier now than it was when they were found sixty years ago, but only just. They remain buried far enough in the humid Lacandón forest that you can still feel – when you step into the dimly lit rooms – a sense of drama and revelation. If you can't make it out to Chiapas, there are also reproductions in the National Museum of Anthropology in Mexico City, where the colours are brighter but the ambience lacking.

Observing SEMANA SANTA in Antigua

GUATEMALA Combining solemn Catholic ritual and a distinctly Latin American passion for colour and clamour, the Easter week processions in Antigua, Guatemala, are a spectacular affair. By far the largest such processions in the Western hemisphere, the annual event involves virtually the entire population of the city and its surrounding villages, and draws in tens of thousands of visitors from all over the globe.

Preparations begin far in advance, with residents spending hours creating dazzling alfombras (carpets) using coloured sawdust, flower petals and pine needles; the intricate displays often cover several blocks of the city's streets. Then, beginning the weekend before Easter, colossal wooden floats known as andas (some weigh over three tonnes), each topped with an image of Christ or another biblical figure, are carried through the streets. Step by step, the bearers shuffle towards the city's churches, their laborious progress grinding the meticulously assembled carpets into the dirt. Accompanying the processions

are trumpeters playing funeral elegies, while clouds of thick copal incense hang over the streets. Many Antigueños wear period costume for the processions, albeit with a slightly modern flare: look closely and you'll see that the Roman centurions' helmet plumes are actually upended broom heads, and the Arabs are wearing Nike sports shoes beneath their purple robes.

The processions gain in intensity and fervour throughout the week, with Good Friday witnessing the most dramatic events. Starting at 3am, as Christ's death sentence is announced and the symbolic search for him begins, the cobbled lanes reverberate with the pounding of horses' hooves – the Roman cavalry. Massive, intricate andas emerge from the city's main churches later in the morning, toiling along carpet after carpet, while smaller ones, borne by women with statues of the Virgin Mary, follow close behind. Events culminate two days later, on Easter Sunday, as Christ comes forward from the church of San Pedro to shouts of "Que viva el Rey" ("Long live the King").

649 FLOATING DOWN THE NEW RIVER TO LAMANAI

BELIZE "It looks fake", says the Canadian, peering through his sunglasses at a reptilian hump in the distance. Our paint-flecked boat – *Mrs Cristina* – glides closer, nosing marshy reeds. Captain Ignacio cuts the engine, and water ripples gently over the ridged torso, which remains motionless.

"Yeah, it's just a piece of driftwood", says the New Yorker, handing the binoculars over.

And with that, the baby crocodile pushes off with a muscular thrust of its tail, leaving a solitary, expanding water ring in its wake. A prescient sign – we're floating down the New River to the Maya site of Lamanai, whose name comes from "submerged crocodile".

Like many of Belize's splendid Maya ruins, Lamanai lies deep in the jungle – but it also overlooks the New River Lagoon, so most visitors journey here on a riverboat from Orange Walk, just as we were doing.

And getting here really is half the fun. Though the river waters are eerily placid, the steamy jungle along its banks are not: howler monkeys scamper overhead, emitting guttural howls, while a great blue heron extends its long neck, and flaps regally into the sky. As we float near a strange black cluster quivering on a tree branch, the swarm disbands, and hundreds of bats fly off every which way.

An old barge, heavy in the water with its load of molasses, slowly drifts past us. On the deck sit three sun-browned beefy locals in sunglasses who raise their hands in unison. Around a bend, in the distance, lies the Mennonite settlement of Shipyard – the men in wide-brimmed hats and women in ankle-length dresses an arresting image, particularly against the tropical backdrop of Belize.

Our boat pulls up to the wooden dock at the Lamanai entrance, and it begins to rain – fat, heavy drops as we clomp single-file, stumbling over muddy roots. We're sweating in our windbreakers, mosquitoes are biting and it all seems like a lot of effort – and then the first majestic temple looms into view.

Once the sun comes out, we start on the thigh-aching slog up the thirty-five-metre "High Temple", which was the largest structure in the Maya world when it was first constructed in 100 BC. We pull on a slippery rope, heaving up one massive step, then another. At the top, panting, we gaze out at the jungle canopy, a magnificent 360-degree panorama of dewy, tangled green stretching into the horizon. From up here, anything seems possible. Until you look at the climb down.

650 BIKING THE BAJA PENINSULA

MEXICO With its record-breaking heat, long stretches of barren desert, crazed feral dogs and frantic Mexican truck drivers, the pothole-riddled Transpeninsular Highway that runs a thousand miles through Mexico's Baja California is one of the greatest pedal-powered road trips in the world.

Turning your back on the skyscrapers of San Diego and cycling across the heavily guarded no-man's-land into the dusty, litter-strewn streets of Tijuana, you may as well be entering a new world. New smells, new language, new rules – your Mexican cycling adventure is underway.

Leaving Tijuana, the highway begins along the Pacific coast with its crashing waves and perfect sunsets, but it soon leads inland to the dry heat of the unforgiving Desierto de Vizcaíno. Here, days of gruelling climbs in sun-baked surrounds and nights camped amongst the cactus and coyotes are eventually rewarded with the mirage-like vision of San Ignacio. This sixteenth-century Jesuit Mission, built around the cool, palm-lined waters of a natural oasis, is a perfect rest stop for lounging in the shade of the bougainvillea and refuelling on sticky, energy-packed local dates. Back in the saddle, you re-enter the desert, riding through the forests of giant Cardon cacti and Boojum trees that stretch endlessly towards the distant blue mountains beyond. Limping into La Paz, after the best part of a month on the road, your journey through Baja is almost complete. All that remains is to grab a couple of fish tacos and a cold bottle of Pacifico and head to the waterfront malecón to watch your last spectacular Baja sunset.

651 KAYAKING IN THE SEA OF CORTÉS

MEXICO Standing on the east coast of Baja California, surveying the peninsula's near-lifeless ochre landscape, it's hard to imagine that a frenzy of nature lies just steps away. But launch a sea kayak into the glistening surf of the Sea of Cortés and you'll find yourself surrounded by rich and varied wildlife – a veritable natural aquarium.

The remote and ruggedly beautiful Baja coastline has become a favourite destination for sea kayakers – and for good reason. The calm waters of the Sea of Cortés make for easy surf launches and smooth paddling. Hundreds of unexplored coves, uninhabited islands and miles of mangrove-lined estuaries play host to sea lions, turtles and nesting birds. Just the shell of your kayak separates you from dolphins, grey whales, coral reefs and over 600 species of fish as you glide through placid lagoons, volcanic caves and natural arches.

It's a good idea to keep your snorkelling gear handy – should you ever tire of the topside scenery, you can make a quick escape to an even more spectacular underwater world. Rookeries of sea lions dot island coasts, and if you approach them slowly, the pups can be especially playful, even mimicking your underwater movements before performing a ballet of their own.

Back on land, as you camp on white-sand beaches and feast on freshly made ceviche under the glow of a glorious sunset, you'll have time to enjoy some peace and quiet before pondering your next launch.

652 SAMPLING FISH TACOS IN ENSENADA

MEXICO The taco de pescado – Baja California's gift to locals, dust-caked off-road explorers and cruise-boat day-trippers alike – exemplifies the simple pleasures that make the peninsula so appealing.

Constructed by piling freshly fried pieces of white fish on two warm corn tortillas and topping with shredded cabbage, a little light mayo, a splash of hot sauce and a squirt of lime, the taco de pescado is Mexican food at its most basic and delicious. Like all great street food, fish tacos taste better when served somewhere devoid of any atmosphere – most choice locations lack a proper floor, ceiling, walls or any combination thereof. The quality of the tacos corresponds directly to the length of time it takes for the cook to get them to you, then for you to get them into your mouth.

Ensenada, a large fishing centre on the peninsula's northwest coast, is one of the best places to sample the taco de pescado – it's said that the dish was first concocted here by Japanese fishermen. Fifteen minutes inland from the port and the Mercado Negro fish market lies a well-established street vendor, Tacos Fenix. The three-person outfit operates from the sidewalk: one person preps the ingredients, a second mans the frying pan and the third handles the money and drinks. You don't have to know much Spanish (beyond "por favor" and "gracias") to order; just listen and watch the people in front of you. And don't worry about the juices running down your hand after the first bite – getting dirty is part of the fun.

653 HEADING TO MARKET IN THE GUATEMALAN HIGHLANDS

GUATEMALA The market town of San Francisco el Alto adopts its suffix for good reason. Perched at 2610m atop a rocky escarpment, it looks down over the plain of Quetzaltenango to the perfect volcanic cone of Santa María that pierces the horizon to the southwest.

But on Friday mornings, few of the thousands that gather here linger to take in the view; instead, the largest market in Guatemala's western highlands commands their attention. Things start early, as traders arrive in the dead of night to assemble their stalls by candlelight and lanterns, stopping periodically to slurp from a bowl of steaming caldo or for a slug of chicha liquor to ward off the chilly night air.

By dawn a convoy of pick-ups, chicken buses and microbuses struggle up the vertiginous access road, and by sunrise the streets are thick with action as blanket vendors and tomato seekers elbow their way through lanes lined with shacks. There's virtually nothing geared at the tourist dollar, unless you're in desperate need of a Chinese-made alarm clock or a sack of beans, but it's a terrific opportunity to experience Guatemala's indigenous way of life – all business is conducted in hushed, considered tones using ritualistic politeness that's uniquely Maya.

Above the plaza is the fascinating animal market, where goats, sheep, turkeys, chickens and pigs are inspected as if contestants at an agricultural show. Vendors probe screeching porkers' mouths to check out teeth, tongues and gums, and the whole event can descend into chaos as man and beast wrestle around in the dirt before a deal can be struck.

654 A COSTA RICA FAMILY ADVENTURE

COSTA RICA The best thing about a family adventure trip is that kids are up for anything "if everyone else is doing it". In Costa Rica, this means a full turnout not just to go whitewater rafting, but for a 5am glide down the jungle waterways of Tortuguero – a huge swath of mangrove swamps and lagoons, where howler monkeys and spider monkeys cavort in the canopy, and river otters and caiman dip into the riverbanks. In summer you can also go down to the beach at night to see green sea turtles hauling themselves up to lay their eggs on the Caribbean beach.

What kid could resist that? And who could fail to be excited by Arenal, Costa Rica's most active volcano, best observed floating on your back in a swimming pool, watching puffs of smoke emerge, like some home science kit?

From one wonder to another: the Monteverde Cloud Forest Reserve. This is the country's most famous ecosystem, where cloud rather than rain nurtures a huge diversity of wildlife, including most of the iconic tree frogs. They, and indeed the cloudforest itself, are under threat from climate change, but the protection of this reserve – and Costa Rica's acknowledgement of its wildlife as a national resource – is an inspiration. And the frogs, which you can see most easily in the village's well-designed Ranario, are a phenomenon, every possible colour and size, from fingernail-miniature to something as big as a rabbit.

Monteverde is also ingeniously making its forest into a resource by creating a knock-out experience for kids – canopy zipwire tours. If you think you've done zipwires, think again: these are vast, climaxing in a six-hundred-metre ride, strung out across a whole valley.

After all the action, and the travelling, you're more than ready for seaside. Which for our group meant the coastal park of Manuel Antonio – perfect white sandy Pacific beach, where we gazed up from the water to see capuchin monkeys descending on our sandwiches.

655 MEETING THE MONARCHS IN MICHOACÁN

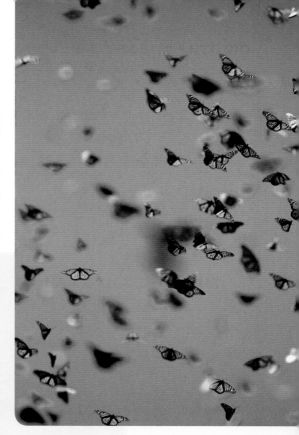

MEXICO Early morning in the mountains of Michoacán. There's a stillness in the wooded glades and a delicate scent of piny resin in the air. Mostly oyamel firs, the trees are oddly coated in a scrunched orange blanket – some kind of fungus? Diseased bark? Then the sun breaks through the mist and thousands of butterflies swoop from the branches to bathe in the sunlight, their patterned orange and black wings looking like stained-glass windows or Turkish rugs – the original Mexican wave. The forest floor is carpeted with them. Branches buckle and snap under their weight. And there's a faint noise, a pitter-patter like gentle rain – the rarely heard sound of massed butterflies flapping their wings.

The annual migration of hundreds of millions of monarch butterflies from North America to this small area of central Mexico – no more than 96 square kilometres – is one of the last mysteries of the scientific world. For years, their winter home was known only to the locals, but in 1975, two determined American biologists finally pinpointed the location, and now visitors (mainly Mexican) flock in during the season to witness one of nature's most impressive spectacles. In the silence of the forest sanctuary, people stand stock-still for hours at a time, almost afraid to breathe as millions of butterflies fill the air, brushing delicately against faces and alighting briefly on hands.

No one is entirely clear why the butterflies have chosen this area. Some say it's the oyamel's needle-like leaves, ideal for the monarch's hooked legs to cling onto; or that the cool highland climate slows down their metabolism and allows them to rest and lay down fat before their arduous mating season. The Aztecs, however, had other ideas, believing that the butterflies – which arrive in Mexico shortly after the Day of the Dead on November 1 – were the returning souls of their fallen warriors, clad in the bright colours of battle.

656 INDULGING IN THE JUNGLE

BELIZE It's all in the mud. Plumbed from the earth and brimming with minerals, this is the kind of rich goop that you'll happily smear on your body parts, then submit to its rejuvenating tingle while reclining in a breezy cabana, eyes closed against the warm sun, and hold on – is that a howler monkey? The Maruba Resort and Jungle Spa sits amid the dewy tropical foliage of Belize, where it offers pampering with a primal edge: retreat into a palm-shaded hideaway for the signature "mood mud" body scrub rooted in ancient Maya customs, then zone out to the low thrum of piped-in drumbeats mingled with the rustling of wild critters foraging in the undergrowth. At Maruba – as in much of Belize – it's the lush outdoors that makes all the difference. And let's face it – there's something especially hedonistic about a pedicure in the jungle.

The splendid Maya site of Altun Ha lies near Maruba, so you can trek up giant stone temples in the early light of day, then wind down with a scalp massage and an African Honey Bee scrub. As night falls, sip rum punch from a hairy coconut with the top lopped off. As you might expect, the primitive-meets-posh Maruba is all very decadent – think gleaming mahogany ceilings, billowing silks, feather beds, wafting incense and hibiscus-strewn, mosaic bathrooms – but it's done with a wink. Quirky, jungle-chic details abound: a carved penis as a toilet paper holder in the lobby bathroom; palm fronds as placemats; rough-hewn walls studded with recycled glass bottles of Belikin beer and Fanta. In the ecological spirit of Belize, little goes to waste at this largely self-sustaining resort, where the natural surroundings are respectfully incorporated at every turn. So, not only will you emerge with your pores clean and glowing, but your conscience too.

Dawn at 657
TIKAL

GUATEMALA The dense jungles of northern Guatemala, once the heartland of the Maya civilization, were home to dozens of thriving cities during Classic Maya times (250–909 AD). Tikal was arguably the greatest of them all, controlling an empire of vassal states and trade routes between the southern highlands and the Caribbean. The symbols of its dominance – six great temples – still stand.

Impressive at any time of day, Tikal shows itself to full advantage in the hours around sunrise. Because of the nature of the terrain – the extreme humidity of the forest usually shrouds the sun's early rays – it's rare actually to see the sun come up over the jungle. But even without a perfect sunrise, as the ruins of this Maya city come to life around you, dawn is still a magical time.

As day breaks, head for the top of Temple IV or Temple V. An ocean of green unfurls before you, the jungle canopy broken only by the chalk-white roofcombs of the other pyramids, soaring over the giant ceiba and zapote trees. The forest's denizens gradually begin to appear, emerging from their night-time resting places. Flocks of green parakeets career over the temple tops and keel-billed toucans hop along bromeliad-rich branches. Howler monkeys are at their most vociferous at dawn, their roars echoing around the graceful plazas and towering temples. Many of the animals that live in Tikal have become accustomed to seeing humans, so you're virtually guaranteed to come across packs of playful racoon-like coati snuffling through the undergrowth or the startling blue-chested ocellated turkey strutting around in search of its first feed of the day. As the sun climbs higher in the sky and the heat of the day increases, things begin to calm down. By 9am, when the large tour groups roll in, nature's activity has all but faded away, until the jungle awakes the next morning.

658 ENCOUNTERING KUNA CULTURE

PANAMA It's often said that there's an island for every day of the year in the San Blas archipelago. In fact, there are slightly more than that in this chain of coral atolls that stretches for 375km along the Caribbean coast of Panama. This is Kuna Yala, the autonomous homeland of the Kuna Indians, one of the most independent indigenous cultures in Central America. Even if you haven't heard of the Kuna before, you've probably seen them: the women, wearing piratical headscarves, gold nose rings and colourful traditional costumes are the pin-ups of the indigenous world. With palm-fringed beaches and coral reefs, Kuna Yala is the stuff of Caribbean dreams, but it is the Kuna themselves, with their rich cultural traditions, that most people come here to see.

In some ways, visiting Kuna Yala gives a feel of what the Caribbean must have been like before European colonists arrived. No outside development is allowed – non-Kuna cannot own land or property. You'll need to ask permission of a community's headman, or sahila, if you wish to visit a particular town or island, and you must be accompanied by a Kuna guide. Around forty of the islands are inhabited; some are home to several thousand people, while others are narrow sandbanks sheltering only a few families.

Despite the regulations, you can still explore Kuna culture and your natural surroundings pretty widely. Travelling by motorized dugout canoe, your guide will take you to pristine beaches and reefs where you can swim and snorkel, as well as to other island communities. You may even be lucky enough to witness a traditional religious ceremony or join a fiesta in a communal hall (casa de congreso), where poet-historians sing myths and legends from hammocks, leaving you with a lasting impression of the Kuna heritage.

659 RIDING DOWN THE RÍO SAN JUAN

NICARAGUA It was the end of a hot day in earthquake-flattened Managua. "There," I hissed in frustration, pointing at a poster on the wall, "that is where I want to go."

I had seen the photograph before, slapped up on café, bar and shop walls all over Nicaragua. The prize-winning photo, chosen by the tourist board to promote the country's pristine beauty, does not show the colonial streets of Granada. Nor does it illustrate the volcanoes of Ometepe or the cayes off the Caribbean coast.

Instead, it depicts a bend in a wide river, fringed by green meadows and dotted with small boats. The waterway is the 170-kilometre-long Río San Juan, which starts at vast Lago Nicaragua, runs along the country's border with Costa Rica and finally spills into the Caribbean Sea.

The river has a rich – if tumultuous – history: it once carried supplies from Spain to its new colony and was besieged by pirates who came to sack Granada. Now better known for its ecotourism opportunities, the Río San Juan is surrounded by some of the most peaceful wilderness in Central America. Hundreds of species of wildlife live along its banks, from caymans, herons, manatees and jaguars to howler monkeys, sloths and flocks of rainbow-coloured parrots – don't forget your camera.

Remote as the river is, carved into dense rainforest, there is one notable pocket of civilization. In contrast to the small collection of ramshackle fishing villages along its banks, and sleazy San Carlos at its head, the old Spanish fort of El Castillo, two and a half hours downstream, shimmers like a mirage. Its waterfront is lined with wooden homes on stilts, their porches covered in carefully tended plants and connected by a meandering lane. The lovely setting is framed with a ruined castle atop a grassy knoll. And at the end of the village, as it seeps gently back into the forest, is the bend in the river in the photograph.

660 A TASTE OF MOLE POBLANO IN PUEBLA

MEXICO Visitors to Mexico may find some of the country's culinary offerings a bit odd – not only do fried grasshoppers, baked maggots and raw ant eggs occasionally appear, but the national dish, mole poblano, combines two flavours, chilli and chocolate, that would seem to have little use for each other. Mole (or mólli), a Nahuatl word, means "mixture", of which there are actually dozens in Mexico; mole poblano, the most revered, comes from Puebla.

A rich sauce normally served with turkey or chicken, mole poblano can boast upwards of thirty ingredients; the most cherished recipes are guarded like state secrets. Fruits, nuts and spices are toasted over a fire, ground by hand and mixed into a paste. The chocolate, added at the last minute, is in its traditional unsweetened form, powdered cacao seeds.

The dish was created in the seventeenth century in the kitchens of the Convento de Santa Rosa for a banquet. It's still made for special occasions: no wedding in Puebla is complete without the women spending days preparing their mole poblano in huge black cauldrons. Among Cholulteca families, a live turkey is considered the guest of honour at wedding receptions; the bird is slaughtered the next day to serve as the base for the newlyweds' first mole.

A prime time to sample the sauce is during the Festival of Mole Poblano, held on three consecutive Sundays each July, when local restaurants compete to have their mole judged the city's best. The dish also stars on menus across the city on the fifth of May, or Cinco de Mayo, a national holiday that celebrates the defeat of Napoleon's invading army in Puebla in 1872. After the festivities, join the crowds and top off the night by feasting on the city's savoury speciality.

PALANCAR REEF

377

MEXICO The view from the boat is beautiful, with the variegated blues and greens of the Caribbean stretching toward the Yucatán coast on one side, and palm trees bowing over Cozumel's pearly-white beach on the other.

From the surface, though, you'd never know that the most stunning sight of all is directly beneath you: Palancar Reef, a 5-kilometre stretch of some of the globe's richest coral beds, and the kind of vivid world people tend to imagine only with the aid of hallucinogens. Teeming with marine life, Palancar is just one small part of the Mesoamerican Barrier Reef, which stretches from Mexico to Honduras, but it is in a prime position to flourish. Just off the southwest corner of the island of Cozumel, and part of a larger ring of coral around much of the island, it is washed by slow, steady currents that keep the water clear and bear nutrients from nearby mangrove swamps.

Bumped by clumsy snorkellers, battered by hurricanes and boiled by freakish spikes in water temperature, Palancar not only survives but prospers as a fascinating and complex ecosystem. Any diver, novice or expert, could explore this reef for hours – or, if you're Jacques Cousteau, who put this place on divers' maps in the 1960s, years. Lobsters pick their way delicately along outcrops, feelers blown by the current, while blue-green parrotfish gnaw at the coral with their beaky mouths. (Their digestive system produces the powdery sand that slopes away into the deep-blue distance.) Striped clownfish hide in the protective tentacles of an anemone, immune to its toxic sting; mellow turtles graze on algae; a graceful ray glides by. All this happens as if in a dream, in near-complete silence – the only audible sound is the rush of your own breath. Lovely as the surface world is, when you come up for air, it will all seem impossibly drab.

662 VACATION LIKE A DRUG LORD IN TULUM

MEXICO Even drug kingpins – perhaps especially drug kingpins – need a little time away from it all. The late Pablo Escobar, the Colombian drug lord once ranked by *Forbes* as the seventh richest man in the world, favoured beach getaways. In the 1980s, he built an airy, eight-bedroom mansion just footsteps away from the ocean in the one-street town of Tulum, about 100km south of Cancún on Mexico's Caribbean coast.

In 1993, after Colombian police killed Escobar in a shootout in Medellín, his Tulum mansion, nicknamed *Casa Magna*, became the property of the Mexican government. Over the next decade, as the town around it evolved into an ecofriendly, yoga-centric beach paradise, *Casa Magna* fell into disrepair. Finally, in 2005, Mexico leased the house to the owners of *Amansala*, a Tulum resort best-known for its yoga-and-fruit shake bikini bootcamps. *Amansala*'s owners – Americans Melissa Perlman and Erica Gragg – painstakingly renovated the villa, replacing its rustic drug-dealer style with minimalist Asian beach-chic.

Ironically, the former kingpin's party house has become perhaps the quietest, most understated resort in what's now known as the "Mayan Riviera". This is the place to sit back and enjoy the white sand, gentle waves and warm water of the Caribbean – and a wide array of the most comfortable beach furniture on earth.

Take care when choosing a bedroom, however, as *Casa Magna*'s rooms are numbered, essentially in order of desirability, from one to eight. The secluded room one must have been Pablo's – its two private decks offer views of both the ocean and the sunset. The dark, viewless room eight, on the other hand, was surely the domain of tag-alongs and lowly members of his extended posse. If the room available is numbered higher than six, you may want to seek alternative accommodation – luckily, the equally stunning *Casa Magna Two*, Pablo's second vacation home, is just down the road.

663 EASING INTO THE NEW YEAR ON CAYE CAULKER

BELIZE Forget the beer-soaked hordes in party hats and the sloppy midnight renditions of *Auld Lang Syne*. And forget the high-minded resolutions that you're going to break anyway. You've rung in the New Year every which way – watching the ball drop in Times Square, and defiantly alone with a jug of cheap wine and Aretha's *Respect* on the stereo. But this year you've picked a wave-licked little island in the Caribbean, and it's the best move you've made in a long time.

"Go slow" is the motto on Caye Caulker, which is pretty much the only speed your golf cart will travel, barring the occasional burst to avoid an iguana crossing the sandy lane. Here, chilling out is a way of life, reggae the music and ten languorous paces the distance from your beach shack to the Caribbean Sea. Decisions are similarly weighty: snorkel or sunbathe? Hairbraiding or henna tattoo? It's this sun-warmed simplicity that shapes your last day of the year: you spend the morning floating on your back, then munching on shrimp kebabs from a beach grill, licking the tart juices from your fingers. After this, you gel into a hammock for a foot massage, followed by a siesta under the rustling leaves of a fan palm. As night falls, you saunter to the split at the north end of the caye. Somewhere, the midnight countdown is being chanted by thousands, but here your only companions are the bright moon, the rhythmic whoosh of the waves, and a chilled Belikin beer – and the New Year's resolution to do this every year.

664 FAMILY SAILING ACROSS THE PACIFIC

PANAMA TO THE SOUTH PACIFIC A sailboat crossing the Pacific from Australasia to the Americas is no place for an eleven-year-old and a rebellious teen. The other direction is another story. Wind and ocean currents, beholden to Coriolis forces, make sailors the following offer: "Go west," they say, "and the breeze will be steady, the sun will shine and you will visit places most only imagine." Near but not on the equator, in the trade winds and out of the doldrums, travelling from island to island offers smooth sailing and plenty of adventure.

A little over a week after leaving Panama you drop anchor in the Galápagos Islands. International law grants a stopover to restock, take on water and stretch your legs. Three days of volcanic rock inhabited by cacti that look like trees, birds that act like conga dancers, tortoises like nothing else and equatorial penguins is the only reality check you get, however, before another month out of sight of land.

Life is simple at sea. Hours can be passed with Tolstoy, algebra and whist. Parents are unlikely to permit a dip overboard, but a toe extended past the leeward gunwhales will just reach the water below. Dolphins and pilot whales share your wake, and an adventurous seabird might drop in to rest. Flying fish run afoul of the deck and make tasty snacks, and every now and then you feast on very fresh tuna salad.

The clear horizon gives a new perspective on weather. As you glide beneath blue sky and wispy clouds, dark cumulous clumps of rain and stronger winds loom in the distance. Approaching one of these head-on calls for shortening sails, rigging water catchments and then standing ready with a bottle of shampoo.

After thirty days you arrive in the Marquesas Islands and passages never again exceed two weeks as you hop between colonial outposts and independent kingdoms, each with their own cultural offerings, natural beauty and warm welcome for strangers from the sea.

A trip like this instills an understanding of freedom and the size and diversity of the world that will shape a life. And every night, there are the stars.

MEXICO Saturday night in downtown Guadalajara, Mexico's second city: the Plazuela de los Mariachis, squeezed into a corner of the colonial heart of the city, reverberates with the sounds of instruments being tuned. You'll no doubt recognize the violins, trumpets and guitars; more exotic to the ear – and unique to the music you're about to hear – are the vihuela, a small plinky guitar with a bowed back, and the guitarron, a large bass guitar. For time-honoured tunes, you're in the right spot: Guadalajara, also the most traditional of Mexico's cities, is also the birthplace of mariachi, the country's famous musical export.

A smartly dressed couple – he with hair slicked back and she in her best dress – start the festivities with a request for an old love song. The mariachis line up around their table, forming a wall of charro (nineteenth-century cowboy) outfits: large bow ties, gleaming belt buckles, jackets and trousers decorated with embroidery and silver fastenings. A trumpeter raises his instrument to his lips, and the first familiar notes of *Cielito Lindo* ("Ay, ay, ay, ay, canta y no llores") float over the square. Another song follows, then another. The couple get to their feet and begin to waltz slowly between the packed café tables. Several troupes join the fray, serenading elderly couples, students, young lovers, fascinated travellers. Each group competes to be louder and more flamboyant than the next, and the noise – a melodious cacophony – is ear-splitting.

Fittingly, the evening winds down with several howled rounds of one of the most popular mariachi tunes: "Guadalajara, Guadalajara, tienes el alma de provinciana, hueles a limpia rosa temprana" ("you have the soul of the provinces, you smell of fresh early roses").

BEING SERENADED BY MARIACHIS IN GUADALAJARA

665

SEARCHING FOR JAGUARS IN COCKSCOMB BASIN WILDLIFE SANCTUARY

BELIZE Looking for tigers? Head to India. Lions or cheetahs? You'll want to be in southern Africa. If it's jaguars you're after, though, few places are more spectacular than the rainforests of Belize.

Here, in the Cockscomb Basin Wildlife Sanctuary, the world's only jaguar reserve, the enormous, elusive wildcats roam freely through forty thousand hectares of pristine jungle.

According to local guides, sunrise is the best time to glimpse jaguars. Almost every day, eager cat-spotters set out in the small hours from Maya Centre, an indigenous Mopan Maya community and the hub for trips into the reserve. In the half-light, the rainforest teems with wildlife. The trees form a cavernous canopy above your head; in combination with the thick undergrowth, the vegetation can overwhelm – and the atmosphere is intensified by sightings of red-eyed tree frogs, tarantulas, bats and iguanas. Gibnuts – small, rat-like creatures – rustle through the scrub. Keep an eye out for the four other species of wildcats that also call the reserve home, including margay, who favour the canopy, and pumas, who slink through the surrounding mountains. As the forest warms up, 4000 species of flowering plants spring into bloom, and toucans, king vultures and scarlet macaws flit through the trees.

You've come for the jaguars, though, and as the sun climbs in the sky, you still haven't seen one. Let's be honest – you're far more likely to see the eyes of a gibnut shining from the undergrowth than you are the glamorous yet camera-shy felines. It's the hunt that makes Cockscomb so special. You know they're there, and they know you know it – if your wits happen to collide you'll be rewarded with a sight very few people are lucky enough to witness. In the meantime, don't forget to enjoy the natural wonderland around you.

667 BIRD-WATCHING ON THE PIPELINE ROAD

PANAMA The logbook at Parque Nacional Soberanía's headquarters reads like a "who's who" of exotic bird species. There are mealy Amazons, purple-throated fruitcrows, shining honeycreepers and red-capped manakins; ocellated antbirds make a regular appearance, alongside grey-headed chachalacas, thick-billed motmots and the diminutive tropical pewee. Each entry is more gushing than the last – someone had almost torn through the page describing their chance encounter with a rufous-vented ground cuckoo – but if there's one place on earth that's guaranteed to send twitchers into a feathery frenzy, it's the seventeen-kilometre-long trail at the heart of Soberanía: a dirt track they call the Pipeline Road.

During World War II, the US government built a pipeline along the Panama Canal to transport fuel from the Pacific to the Atlantic in the event the waterway was attacked. The backup was never needed and the "road" constructed to maintain the pipeline barely used. Over time, it was swallowed by the rainforest. But nature's gain was also man's, and the thin stretch of track now provides some of the finest bird-spotting on the planet; in 1996, the Audubon Society counted an incredible 360 different specimens, a world record for the highest number of bird species identified in a 24-hour period.

The Pipeline Road, or Camino del Oleoducto, runs through a range of habitats, from second-growth woodland to mature rainforest. A network of side tracks, creeks and rivers can be followed into the surrounding forest, but the road itself is a rich hunting ground, especially in the soft light of dawn or the cool hours around dusk, when activity is at its greatest. Army ant swarms attract birds by the hundred, while the trail is a popular location for leks – an incredible avian dance-off where males gather at the same spot each season for the purposes of elaborate (and very competitive) courtship displays. Just don't be surprised if you find yourself rushing back to HQ, pen at the ready.

668 ISLA DE OMETEPE BY MOTORCYCLE

NICARAGUA When it comes to getting around Central America with speed and ease, there are two extremes: a luxury coach and a motorcycle. The former option allows tourists to turn off their minds as they and fifty others ride across the land in supreme comfort. The latter option involves a little effort, a lot of wind in one's face and journeys quite unlike any other.

On Nicaragua's Isla de Ometepe, the largest of 400 islands sprinkled across Lago de Nicaragua, there are no luxury coaches disembarking from the island's ferry port. Which begs the question, how will you navigate around this 250-square-kilometre, hourglass-shaped island? With only one mostly unpaved and bumpy road that circles the island, the choices are limited: one of the overcrowded and unreliable modified school buses that serve as public transport, the only Jeep for lease on the island for $60 a day, or for one-tenth as much you can rent a 125cc dirt bike from an enterprising Ometepean. The choice is an easy one.

As you loop around the island, you'll pass plantain plantations and several small villages, giving you a chance to see rural Nicaraguan life up-close. Two towering volcanoes – Concepción at 1640m and Madera at 1340m – dominate the landscape, and a hike up to Madera's crater makes for an excellent and challenging break from the road. Riding a dirt bike also gives easy access to pre-Columbian petroglyphs and stone statues, made by the indigenous Chorotega people, the San Ramon waterfalls on the southern slope of Madera, and prime swimming spots at Ojo de Agua spring and Charco Verde Beach, the latter tucked majestically between the two volcanoes. So hit the road, easy rider, but mind the stray dogs, wandering pigs and sharp turns.

669 FROM SEA TO SHINING SEA: CRUISING THE PANAMA CANAL

PANAMA The Panama Canal, a narrow channel surrounded by virgin jungles teeming with toucans and white-faced capuchin monkeys, takes only a day to traverse. But during that day you'll experience an amazing feat of engineering and cross the Continental Divide. Politically fraught from its inception and burdened by the death of nearly thirty thousand workers during its construction, the eighty-kilometre canal, opened in 1914, is a controversial yet fascinating waterway which offers safe passage to over 14,000 vessels per year.

Your trip begins in the Caribbean near the rough-and-tumble town of Colón, which prospered during the canal's construction but has since declined, its ramshackle colonial buildings and hand-painted signs frozen in time. Once on board, ships enter the narrow Gatún locks; the canal rises over 25 metres above sea level as it crosses the Panamanian isthmus, so you start and end your journey in a series of locks which elevate and then lower you from the ocean on either end.

On the far side, the enormous, sparkling Gatún Lake was formed by a flooded jungle valley and serves as an intersection for shipping freighters, cruise ships, local pleasure boaters and environmentalists, drawn by the lake's isolated islands – basically the tops of mountains that remained above water level. They and the surrounding rainforest are home to thousands of species of wildlife, including monkeys, sloths, lizards and a variety of tropical birds, all of which you'll see from the boat.

With the lake behind you, you enter the narrowest part of the canal – the Gaillard Cut. Blasted out of solid rock and shale mountainside, this channel is so perilously close that it's impossible for two large ships to pass; as you enter, your clothes stick to your skin in the hot, heavy equatorial air, the rainforest feels very close by. Listen for the calls of the myriad birds, loud and distinct above the engine's low-speed hum, and scan the banks, where you'll pick out crocodiles floating menacingly in the shallows.

After nearly 14km of slow, careful progress, you emerge at the Miraflores Locks, beyond which lies the Pacific. As you exit the final chamber and pass under the Bridge of the Americas at Balboa, the bright lights and skyscrapers of Panama City appear on your left. From the timeworn streets of Colón to the bustling metropolis ahead, you have truly travelled from one side of the world to the other.

670 STELAE STORIES OF COPAN

HONDURAS It's hot, the air is thick with fragrant tropical aromas and the undergrowth is wrapping its verdant claws around everything in sight. It's a wonder, then, that Copan's 700-year-old stelae are still standing and that the tangled jungle hasn't completely taken over these intricately carved stone slabs that line the processional walkways between Copan's decaying pyramids.

The carvings on the stelae may at first simply look like big-beaked birds and stylized plants amid swirls and scrolls, but a closer investigation reveals these to be Maya hieroglyphs that tell the detailed stories of this long-gone civilisation. Each depicts the illustrious King Waxak Lahun Ubah K'awil (also known as Eighteen Rabbit), the most powerful of Copan's leaders, in a variety of guises including his apotheosis as several Mayan gods. He is remembered for his patronage of the arts and for sourcing some of the best craftsmen the Mayan world had ever seen.

671 HANDMADE HAMMOCKS IN MASAYA

NICARAGUA Masaya is the centre of Nicaragua's artesania production and home to a couple of lively craft markets: the main market near the bus terminal and the Mercado Nacional de Artesanía. These are the easiest places to buy excellent-quality handmade souvenirs, masks, leather products and jewellery, though they can seem perhaps a tad tourist-friendly; if you can swing it, make your way to the Monimbó barrio a little west towards the stadium and lagoon, where you can watch hammocks being made by hand and buy them directly from the producers. They're far more intricate and detailed items than you might imagine, with colourful cottons and trademark fringes; considering the patience you'll occasionally need to travel around Central America, there may be no better keepsake to have handy than your own personal relaxation device.

672 MEXICO CITY'S MURALS

MEXICO Nothing prepares you for Mexico City. This sprawling, chaotic, ancient, beautiful, congested powerhouse buzzes like New York or Paris. In the central square, the zócalo, they fly an enormous national flag which it takes ten soldiers to carry from the Palacio National each day.

Understanding the history of this seven-hundred-year-old capital isn't easy. But one Mexican artist holds the clue. Stepping inside the cool central arcade of the Palacio Nacional, you are confronted by Mexican history laid out in the giant murals of Diego Rivera. Above the main staircase the leaders of Mexican independence are all there: Father Hidalgo, Salvador Allende and later revolutionaries including Emiliano Zapata and Pancho Villa. It is an overwhelmingly bold piece of art, full of encyclopaedic detail, representing everyone from the ancient Maya to the rapacious conquistadors. Eagles, plumed serpents and raging volcanoes compete with peasants grinding maize, picking tropical fruit and holding hairless dogs.

673 TAKING A DIP IN THE YUCATÁN'S CENOTES

MEXICO The Yucatán Peninsula can be unpleasantly muggy in the summer. At the same time, the low-lying region's unique geography holds the perfect antidote to hot afternoons: the limestone shelf that forms the peninsula is riddled with underground rivers, accessible at sinkholes called cenotes – a geological phenomenon found only here.

Nature's perfect swimming spots, cenotes are filled with cool fresh water year-round, and they're so plentiful that you're bound to find one nearby when you need a refreshing dip. Some are unremarkable holes in the middle of a farmer's field, while others, like Cenote Azul near Laguna Bacalar, are enormous, deep wells complete with diving platforms and on-site restaurants.

The most visited and photographed cenotes are set in dramatic caverns in and around the old colonial city of Valladolid. Cenote Zací, in the centre of town, occupies a full city block. Half-covered by a shell of rock, the pool exudes a chill that becomes downright cold as you descend the access stairs. Just outside town, Dzitnup and neighbouring Samula are almost completely underground. Shinny down some rickety stairs, and you'll find yourself in cathedral-like spaces, where sound and light bounce off the walls. Both cenotes are beautifully illuminated by the sun, which shines through a hole in the ceiling, forming a glowing spotlight on the turquoise water.

Even more remarkable, however, is that these caverns extend underwater. Strap on a snorkel or scuba gear, and drop below the surface to spy a still world of delicate stalagmites. Exploring these ghostly spaces, it's easy to see why the Maya considered cenotes gateways to the underworld. The liminal sensation is heightened by the clarity of the water, which makes you feel as if you're suspended in air.

MISCELLANY

RING OF FIRE

Mexico and Central America are home to almost one hundred volcanoes (most are found in Mexico, Costa Rica, El Salvador, Guatemala and Nicaragua) – the region is part of the "ring of fire", a zone of frequent volcanic eruptions and earthquakes that encircles the Pacific Basin. A handful of these volcanoes are still considered active, and it's possible to see spectacular light shows of molten lava at Arenal in Costa Rica and Picaya in Guatemala. Most, however, have long been dormant, leaving their slopes open to hikers.

WATERWAYS

Central America is laced with lakes (several of them vast), rivers and canals. The longest rivers flow into the Caribbean Sea, while many smaller waterways drain into the Pacific Ocean. Travelling by boat in these areas is a fascinating though uncomfortable experience (be prepared to get wet).

FIVE GREAT READS

One Day of Life **Manlio Argueta**. A day in the life of one fictional El Salvadoran family caught up in their country's civil war.
Men of Maize **Miguel Angel Asturias**. Experimental novel dealing with the desecration of indigenous Maya culture in Guatemala.
The Country Under My Skin **Gioconda Belli**. Nicaraguan poet's memoir of her evolution from traditional upper-class wife to Sandinista revolutionary and government minister.
The Death of Artemio Cruz **Carlos Fuentes**. A wealthy, dying businessman reflects on his life, focusing on the Mexican Revolution and the post-war years.
Labyrinth of Solitude **Octavio Paz**. Originally published in 1950, poet Paz's influential study of Mexican character and thought.

"Love is blind. But not the neighbours"
Mexican proverb

THE MAYA

One of the western hemisphere's most sophisticated pre-Columbian civilizations, the Maya flourished in Mexico and northern Central America between 300 and 900 AD. An intricate calendar based on the solar year, an advanced form of hieroglyphics and enormous temples are just a few elements of the Maya legacy.

COCKS AND BULLS

Cockfighting is a popular backwoods sport in Mexico (where it is legal and official arenas – plazas de gallos – exist). Birds are specially trained for months, substantial bets are laid and fights go on until one of two cocks is killed by the other (metal spurs are attached to their legs). Bullfighting is also still popular in Mexico; the world's largest bullfighting ring, Plaza México, is in Mexico City. Neither of these are spectator sports for the squeamish.

LANGUAGE

Spanish is the official language of Mexico and the countries of Central America, with the exception of Belize, where people speak a type of patois – English with a lilting accent, simplified grammar and phonetic spelling. The Amerindians of Mexico and Guatemala also have their own dialects. Mexican Spanish is very distinct, with drawn-out nasal cadences and lots of expression. Guatemalans tend to speak very slowly and clearly. Hondurans and El Salvadorans have strong regional accents, while Nicaraguans are known for the variety and richness of their slang. Panamanians speak a kind of Caribbean Spanish, similar to Cubans or Puerto Ricans.

ZÓCALO

The centre of every Mexican town, big or small, is its zócalo (main square). Evenings see food vendors wheeling their carts into the streets, balloon-sellers touting their wares, café tables filled with patrons and roving musicians breaking into their repertoires. Three of the most distinctive zócalos in Mexico are in Mexico City, Oaxaca and Veracruz.

THINK GREEN

Ecotourism was practically invented in Central America. Costa Rica has the region's most organized network of national parks and reserves; 27 percent of the country's territory is protected. The interior of Belize is largely undamaged, and boasts Central America's highest waterfall, Thousand-Foot Falls and the world's only jaguar reserve, Cockscomb Basin Wildlife Sanctuary. Panama's great biodiversity is showcased in two enormous wildlife havens, Parque Nacional Darién, where over five hundred species of birds have been spotted, and Parque Internacional La Amistad, which encompasses nine life zones, or vegetative communities.

MEXICO AT THE MOVIES

Mexico has a thriving film industry, one of the world's oldest. The home-grown film business saw its golden age during the 1940s, with stars such as Cantiflas (the Mexican Charlie Chaplin) and Dolores del Rio. In the 1950s and 60s the country became known for its cult horror flicks, but recent dramas like *Amores Perros* and *Y Tu Mama Tambien* have once again brought Mexico to the forefront of the international film scene.

"There's more time than life"
Nicaraguan proverb

POLITICAL MURALS

Wall paintings were made popular shortly after the Mexican Revolution by three artists: Diego Rivera, David Siqueiros and José Clemente Orozco. Their enormous, vibrant murals can still be seen today in government buildings – Rivera's *History of Mexico* in Mexico City's National Palace and Orozco's frescoes in the Hospicio Cabañas in Guadalajara are particularly memorable. In Central America, the civil wars of the 1970s and 80s spawned a number of naïve paintings depicting revolutionaries and their tormenters. To this day, official political campaigns are hand-painted on the sides of buildings, walls and even telegraph poles throughout the region.

"It's better to be a living chicken than a dead cockerel"

Mexican proverb

FIVE FAVOURITE DISHES

Chiles en nogada, Mexico. Stuffed green peppers covered in a white sauce (walnuts and either cream cheese or sour cream) and pomegranate.

Pupusas, El Salvador. Small tortillas filled with cheese, beans, and pork crackling, and served piping hot with tomato juice, hot sauce and curtido (pickled cabbage, beetroot and carrots).

Sancocho, Panama. A hearty chicken soup with yucca, plantains and other root vegetables and flavoured with coriander.

Anafre, Honduras. A fondue-like dish of cheese, beans or meat, or some combination of all three.

Ron don, Nicaragua. "To cook", in local parlance – a stew of yucca, chayote and other vegetables, and some kind of meat; it's simmered for at least a day and traditionally eaten at weekends.

CORAL REEFS

The world's second largest coral reef, the Mesoamerican Barrier Reef, lies off the Caribbean coast of Mexico, Belize, Guatemala and Honduras, making the region a magnificent aquatic playground. Hot spots for scuba diving and snorkelling, the two most popular pursuits, include the Mexican island of Cozumel, Belize's cayes (tiny islands; home to three atolls and the Blue Hole, a collapsed cave made famous by Jacques Cousteau) and the Bay Islands of Honduras.

LONGEST RIVERS OF CENTRAL AMERICA

COUNTRY	RIVER	LENGTH
Honduras	Coco	800km
Nicaragua	Grande	430km
Guatemala	Motagua	400km
El Salvador	Lempa	320km
Belize	Belize River	290km
Costa Rica	Grande de Terraba	198km
Panama	Tuira	170km

BIRDS

There are over a thousand species of birds in Mexico and Central America. The most sought-after by birders are the quetzal, with its shimmering green and red feathers; the scarlet macaw (lapa); and the toucan. Some places to look include:

Quetzal	Cloudforests of Guatemala, Nicaragua and Costa Rica
Scarlet macaws	Parque Nacional Corcovado, Costa Rica, and Parque Nacional Darién, Panama
Toucans	Along the Pacific coast; especially in Parque Nacional Soberania, Panama

LIQUID REFRESHMENT

Delicious non-alcoholic drinks include freshly made fruit juices (jugos and licuados), flavoured waters (aguas frescas – the most popular are jamaica, made from hibiscus flowers, and tamarindo) and horchata (milk made from rice and almonds, served chilled). Beer, usually lager-style cerveza clara, is available everywhere. Spirits include Mexican tequila and less well-known mescal (made from maguey cactus and like a rough, woody tequila), and in Central America, aguardiente (aniseed-flavoured and translucent).

RICE & BEANS

Food in Central America is fairly basic – the standard diet is rice and beans accompanied by chunks of meat, fried fish or eggs – though most every country has at least one specialty dish. Mexican fare is more sophisticated, with complicated moles (sauces), stews and lime-flavoured seafood cocktails.

SURF'S UP

The Pacific coast of Mexico and Central America has a long-established reputation among surfers for consistent waves and uncrowded waters. Top spots in Mexico include most of the Baja peninsula, particularly Punta el Conejo and Todos Santos; Puerto Escondido, on the Oaxaca coast; and around Lázaro Cárdenas in Michoacan. There are very good point breaks in El Salvador, with several surfing beaches along the coast west of La Libertad. San Juan del Sur in Nicaragua has a large expat surfing community. Costa Rica actually has breaks on its Caribbean coast – the salsa brava at Puerto Viejo is the country's biggest wave.

FIVE UNIQUE DRINKS

Seaweed, Belize. A blend of seaweed, milk, cinnamon, sugar and cream; strangely delicious.
Guifiti, Honduras. A distilled moonshine flavoured with cloves and tasting a bit like toothache medication, available in the north coast Garífuna villages.
Pitahaya juice, Nicaragua. Made from the fruit of a cactus, it's a virulent purple in colour – it'll probably stain your tongue.
Guaro, Costa Rica. An indigenous sugarcane-based spirit; Cacique is the most popular brand.
Hot chocolate, Mexico. Not the drink of your childhood – here it's spicy and semi-bitter, often flavoured with chilli powder.

WAKE UP AND SMELL THE COFFEE: THE ZONA CAFETERA • WATCHING WILDLIFE IN THE CHACO • NATURAL REJECTION IN THE GALÁPAGOS ISLANDS • WINE TASTING IN MENDOZA • TAPATI: FUN AND GAMES ON EASTER ISLAND • SEEING THE SUN RISE FROM VOLCÁN COTOPAXI • EXPERIENCING THE TWO SIDES OF PUNTA DEL ESTE • HONOURING THE ORIXÁS IN SALVADOR • CELEBRATE QOYLLUR RITI • SWEPT OFF YOUR FEET IN BUENOS AIRES • NAVIGATING THE NARROW STREETS OF CARTAGENA • RETAIL THERAPY AT OTAVALO CRAFTS MARKET • BRAVING THE WIND IN TORRES DEL PAINE • RAFTING ON SACRED WATERS IN URUBAMBA VALLEY • GOING DOWNHILL IN THE ANDES • MAKING A PILGRIMAGE TO THE ISLA DEL SOL • LOOKING DOWN ON KAIETEUR FALLS • CATCHING A LAUNCH AT THE CENTRE SPATIAL GUYANAIS • FOLLOWING ANCIENT FOOTSTEPS ON THE INCA TRAIL • STAR-GAZING ON CERRO MAMALLUCA • GOING TO THE OPERA AT TEATRO AMAZONAS • THE SECRET SENSATION OF POUSADA MARAVILHA • ENJOYING ISOLATION AT THE TERMAS DE PUYUHUAPI • DRIFTING DOWN THE AMAZON • PUTTING THE BOOT IN ON THE FALKLAND ISLANDS • ITAIPÚ: PLUGGING THE WORLD'S BIGGEST DAM • LIFE ON THE QUIET SIDE: HOMESTAYS ON LAGO TITICACA • DOWNING CAIPIRINHAS IN RIO DE JANEIRO • DRIVING THROUGH THE ALTIPLANO • BEEFEATER'S PARADISE – THE ARGENTINE PARRILLA • FLY-FISHING IN TIERRA DEL FUEGO • LOST IN TIME ON BRAZIL'S ROYAL ROAD • FROLICKING WITH FUR SEALS • SIZE MATTERS: IN SEARCH OF THE WORLD'S LONGEST SNAKE • TREKKING THROUGH THE PANTANAL WETLANDS • WINE AND HORSES AT ESTANCIA COLOMÉ • SEARCHING FOR THE PERFECT OYSTER ON ISLA MARGARITA • GOING TO CHURCH IN CHILOÉ • DRIVING THE CARRETERA AUSTRAL • MOUNTAIN-BIKING THE WORLD'S MOST DANGEROUS ROAD • MACHU PICHHU: THE ROAD TO THE RUINS • EQUITORIAL DIFFERENCES IN QUITO • WATCHING A FOOTBALL MATCH • THE GIANTS OF RAPA NUI • THE FRENZY OF BOI BUMBA • EXPLORING FERNANDO DE NORONHA • BOATING TO THE ANGEL FALLS • TAKING A RING-SIDE SEAT AT THE PENÍNSULA VALDÉS • ON THE TRAIL OF BUTCH CASSIDY AND THE SUNDANCE KID • CHASING CONDORS IN COLCA CANYON • SHOW NO RESTRAINT IN RIO • SAVOURING CEVICHE IN LIMA • COMMUNING WITH A SHAMAN • WALKING ON ICE: THE PERITO MORENO GLACIER • THE HOTEL TERMALES DE RUIZ • TREKKING AT THE END OF THE WORLD • PIRANHA-FISHING IN THE JUNGLE • GETTING SOAKED AT IGUAZÚ • TRAVERSING THE SALAR DE UYUNI • GETTING HIGH IN CARACAS • EXPLORING COLONIA DEL SACRAMENTO BY SCOOTER • ICE CLIMBING IN THE CORDILLERA REAL • CRASHING OUT BY LAGO CHUNGARÁ • A ROYAL WELCOME AT HOTEL CENTINELA • RETAIL THERAPY AT OTAVALO CRAFTS MARKET • SANDBOARDING AT HUACACHINA • EXPLORING SILVER MINES IN THE ANDES • SEEKING HEAT IN THE CHAPADA DIAMANTIA • VISITING THE LAST PANAMA HAT-WEAVERS • WATCHING WILDLIFE IN THE CHACO • NATURAL REJECTION IN THE GALÁPAGOS ISLANDS • WINE TASTING IN MENDOZA • TAPATI: FUN AND GAMES ON EASTER ISLAND • SEEING THE SUN RISE FROM VOLCÁN COTOPAXI • EXPERIENCING THE TWO SIDES OF PUNTA DEL ESTE • HONOURING THE ORIXÁS IN SALVADOR • CELEBRATE QOYLLUR RITI • NAVIGATING THE NARROW STREETS OF CARTAGENA • BRAVING THE WIND IN TORRES DEL PAINE • RAFTING ON SACRED WATERS IN URUBAMBA VALLEY • GOING DOWNHILL IN THE ANDES • SWEPT OFF YOUR FEET IN BUENOS AIRES • MAKING A PILGRIMAGE TO THE ISLA DEL SOL • CATCHING A LAUNCH AT THE CENTRE SPATIAL GUYANAIS • LOOKING DOWN ON KAIETEUR FALLS • FOLLOWING ANCIENT FOOTSTEPS ON THE INCA TRAIL • STAR-GAZING ON CERRO MAMALLUCA • GOING TO THE OPERA AT TEATRO AMAZONAS • THE SECRET SENSATION OF POUSADA MARAVILHA • ENJOYING ISOLATION AT THE TERMAS DE PUYUHUAPI • DRIFTING DOWN THE AMAZON • PUTTING THE BOOT IN ON THE FALKLAND ISLANDS • ITAIPÚ: PLUGGING

SOUTH AMERICA

SEARCHING FOR
THE PERFECT OYSTER
ON ISLA MARGARITA

WAKE UP AND
SMELL THE COFFEE:
THE ZONA CAFETERA

VENEZUELA

GUYANA

SURINAME

FRENCH GUIANA

COLOMBIA

CATCHING A LAUNCH
AT THE CENTRE SPATIAL GUYANAIS

RETAIL THERAPY AT
OTAVALO CRAFTS MARKET

ECUADOR

PERU

DRIFTING DOWN THE AMAZON

BRAZIL

THE ROAD TO RUINS:
MACHU PICCHU

BOLIVIA

TRAVERSING THE SALAR DE UYUNI

PARAGUAY

SHOW NO RESTRAINT
IN RIO

CHILE

ARGENTINA

URUGUAY

SWEPT OFF YOUR FEET
IN BUENOS AIRES

FROLICKING
WITH FUR SEALS

674 WATCHING WILDLIFE IN THE CHACO

PARAGUAY All the faces in our safari party wear the same expression of awe as we stare at the jaguar lazily strolling down the dusty track. This one looks a lot bigger than its TV counterparts, and we feel a healthy sense of respect now that there's nothing but a clear path separating it from us. With paws the size of dinner-plates and a head as big as a sack of potatoes, there is no doubt that he rules here, and we are tolerated by him just as we tolerate the gnats that buzz around our ears.

The scene plays out not in the lush, virgin Amazonia, or in the verdant, marshy Pantanal, but in the Paraguayan Chaco – one of the hottest, driest and most inhospitable environments on Earth. However, in spite of its image as a thorny, dusty wilderness, the unspoilt splendour of the High Chaco is one of the best places in South America for wildlife-watching. Here big mammals still roam about in large numbers and encounter humans so infrequently that they show no fear toward us. In fact, so few people visit that in 1976 the discovery of the pig-like Chaco peccary, or tagua, shook the zoological world – until then it was known only from fossils.

From November to March the Chaco defies its popular arid image as heavy rains stimulate plant growth, converting dry grasslands to lush wetlands – a haven for waterbirds such as the enormous jabiru and flocks of snow-white egrets. Cayman sun themselves on sandbanks and herds of capybara take advantage of the season of plenty to raise their young.

As we watch, the jaguar moves off into the distance. Our driver restarts the engine to approach him. The jaguar turns abruptly, flashes us a look of contempt and disappears into the bush.

675 NATURAL REJECTION IN THE GALÁPAGOS ISLANDS

ECUADOR The utter indifference (some call it fearlessness) that most of the animals of the Galápagos Islands show humans is as if they knew all along they'd be the ones to change humanity's perception of itself forever. It was, after all, this famous menagerie of accidental inmates, washed or blown from the mainland across a thousand kilometres of ocean and cut off from the rest of their kind, that started the cogs turning in Charles Darwin's mind. His theory of natural selection changed humankind's understanding of its place in the world, and by extension, some might say, its place in the universe.

Peering out to shore from your cabin, you little suspect that the neon sea and coral beaches mark not the fringes of paradise, but of hell solidified – a ferocious wasteland of petrified lava lakes, ash-striped cliffs, serrated clinker tracts and smouldering volcanoes. Even so, as you walk through this scarred landscape, you find that life abounds, albeit peculiar life, the product of many generations of adaptation to a comfortless home. A marine iguana flashes an impish grin at you and, unlike its more familiar ancestors on the continent, scuttles into the sea to feed. On a rocky spur nearby, another one-of-a-kind, a flightless cormorant, which long ago abandoned its aerial talents for ones nautical, hangs its useless wing-stumps out to dry. With each island, new animal oddities reveal themselves to you – giant tortoises, canoodling waved albatrosses, lumbering land iguanas and Darwin's finches to name but a few – each a key player in the world's most celebrated workshop of evolution. And except for the friendly mockingbirds that pick at your shoelaces, most life on Galápagos is blank to your existence, making you feel like a most privileged kind of gatecrasher, one who's allowed an up-close look at a long-kept secret: the mechanics of life on Earth.

676 WINE-TASTING IN MENDOZA

ARGENTINA Recently named the eighth "Great Wine Capital", putting it alongside more famous regions like Napa and Bordeaux, Mendoza is the main reason Argentina has become one of the best wine-producing countries. The area attracts top-flight vintners from around the world, though arguably the finest wines in the region are those of Argentine Nicolás Catena. Even if you've already had the bacchanalian pleasure of uncorking one of his US$100 bottles, nothing can match the excitement of visiting his otherworldly winery, Bodega Catena Zapata, where the grapes are harvested from February to April.

Rising like a Maya pyramid from the dusty flatlands that surround Mendoza, the adobe and glass structure stands against the breathtaking backdrop of the 6962m Aconcagua, the highest peak in the Americas. Descend through a pathway of stone arches into the building's cool, dimly lit sarcophagus, where the wine barrels are stored, and a long oak table is set with a sampler to quicken your pulse. It's the perfect setting for a taste of Mendoza's signature red grape, Malbec, which has prospered like no other in this dry, high desert terroir. For decades after being brought over from Europe by Italian immigrants like Catena's grandfather, the ruby-coloured grape was deemed too robust for all but the unfussy Argentine palate accustomed to a beef-heavy diet. Now widening curiosity among wine consumers and more consistent growing techniques have made this fruity and full-bodied nectar the latest toast of the wine world.

With hundreds of tasting rooms within reach – many in the traditional bodegas are still free – there's no shortage of places to visit. So get an early start, and unless you want to topple over in a sun-kissed, drunken haze, abide by the sommelier's golden rule: swirl 'n' spit.

HONOURING THE ORIXÁS
IN SALVADOR

677

BRAZIL Along the "Red Beach" of Salvador da Bahia, worshippers dressed in ethereal white robes gather around sand altars festooned with gardenias. Some may fall into trances, writhing on the beach, screaming so intensely you'd think they were being torn limb from limb. Perhaps in more familiar settings you'd be calling an ambulance, but this is Salvador, the epicentre of the syncretic, African-based religion known as candomblé, in which worshippers take part in toques, a ritual that involves becoming possessed by the spirit of their Orixá.

A composite of Portuguese Catholicism and African paganism, candomblé is most fervently practised in Salvador, but it defines the piquancy and raw sensuality of Brazilian soul throughout the entire country. In this pagan religion, each person has an Orixá, or protector god, from birth. This Orixá personifies a natural force, such as fire or water, and is allied to an animal, colour, day of the week, food, music and dance. The ceremonies are performed on sacred ground called terreiros and typically feature animal sacrifices, hypnotic drumming, chanting and convulsing. Props and paraphernalia are themed accordingly; the house is decorated with the colour of the honorary Orixá, and usually the god's favourite African dish is served.

Ceremonies are specialized for each god, but no matter which Orixá you are celebrating, you can be sure that the experience will rank among the most bizarre of your life. If you attend a ritual for Ossaim, the Orixá of leaves, for example, chances are that you will be swept from head to foot in foliage. If pyrotechnics are your thing, better pay homage to Xango, god of fire, whose ceremony reaches a rather hazardous climax as bowls of fire are passed, head to head, among the participants. While animal sacrifice, one central aspect of the ceremony, may not be for the faint-hearted, music and feasting provide a more universally palatable denouement to the public "mass". After you enter the realm of candomblé, you may view Salvador, and indeed Brazil, through an ethereal prism that challenges your accepted reason.

CELEBRATE
QOYLLUR RITI

PERU Most visitors to the ancient Inca capital of Cusco in southern Peru are drawn by the extraordinary ruined temples and palaces and the dramatic scenery of the high Andes. But the only true way to get to the heart of the indigenous Andean culture is to join a traditional fiesta. Nearly every town and village in the region engages in these raucous and chaotic celebrations, a window on a secret world that has survived centuries of oppression.

Of all the fiestas, the most extraordinary and spectacular is Qoyllur Riti, held at an extremely high altitude in a remote Andean valley to the south of Cusco. Here you can join tens of thousands of indigenous pilgrims as they trek up to a campsite at the foot of a glacier to celebrate the reappearance of the

Pleiades constellation in the southern sky – a phenomenon that has long been used to predict when crops should be planted. At the heart of the fiesta are young men dressed in ritual costumes of the Ukuku, a half-man, half-bear trickster hero from Andean mythology, and if you're hardy enough, you can join them as they climb even higher to spend the night singing, dancing and engaging in ritual combat on the glacier itself. Be warned, though, that this is an extreme celebration. When the pilgrim-celebrants descend from the mountain at first light, waving flags and toting blocks of ice on their backs, they also carry the bodies of those who've died during the night, frozen or fallen into crevasses, their blood sacrifice at once mourned and celebrated as vital to the success of the agricultural year ahead.

679 TREKKING AT THE END OF THE WORLD

CHILE You've really got to appreciate hiking to tackle the Circuito de los Dientes. The seventy-kilometre trail is fairly demanding in itself, a tough trek through a spectacular wilderness studded with barren peaks and isolated valleys. But getting here is something else. Isla Navarino, across which the circuito wanders, is the southernmost inhabited part of Chilean Tierra del Fuego. Antarctica is far closer than the country's capital. What's more, Navarino's main town, Puerto Williams, from where the trail starts, is the most southerly in the world – despite what they may say in Ushuaia, an Argentine city that is ever so slightly but oh so importantly north of Williams.

Remote is not the word. But fulfilling a desire to come this far south and this far away from "civilization" is part of the appeal. The other part is that it happens to mean spending five days hiking through some of the most desolately beautiful terrain in Patagonia. The only blots on the otherwise pristine landscape are the flooded bogs caused by the dams of feral beavers, originally introduced from Canada for fur farming. But the rest of the island is stunning, and there's an abundance of birdlife to enjoy, including the red-headed Magellanic woodpecker and the flightless steamer duck, which uses its wings in comic paddle-steamer fashion to hurry itself away from danger.

Los Dientes del Navarino, the dramatic range of peaks through which the trail weaves, affords superb views north across the Beagle Channel, and south, over the misty islands of Cape Horn and into the Atlantic Ocean beyond. And when these have all been soaked up, and you're safely back in Puerto Williams, there's no better way to celebrate than by gorging your tired body on castor (beaver), a rich, pungent red meat. Protecting the environment never tasted so good.

680 NAVIGATING THE NARROW STREETS OF CARTAGENA

COLOMBIA You can bet that the great riches that flowed through Cartagena during colonial times proved an irresistible attraction to the pirates and privateers that roamed the Caribbean. Founded nearly five centuries ago as Cartagena de Indias – the Carthage of the Indies – this was one of the most strategically vital points in the Spanish empire. It was here that the galleon fleets would gather before making the perilous return journey to Spain, their holds laden with the gold and silver looted from the great indigenous civilizations of the Americas. Here, too, was the empire's main slave market, a clearing-house for the ill-fated Africans whose blood and sweat underwrote the entire colonial venture.

Though the Spanish have long since departed, Cartagena's colonial heritage is inescapable. The narrow, winding streets of the old walled city are still lined with grand mansions painted in the vibrant pastel hues of the Caribbean, with overhanging balconies draped in flowers and arched doorways that lead into cool courtyard gardens. Its nightclubs and rum shops pulsate with salsa, cumbia and reggaeton – African rhythms little changed from those brought over in the first slave ships. As you wander down these almost fantastical, decaying streets, it's easy to understand how this city inspired Colombia's greatest author, Gabriel García Márquez, to create his masterpieces of magical realism.

Stop for a coffee in the run-down artisans' neighbourhood of Getsemaní, or cool off with a freshly blended tropical fruit juice by the docks, and you could be rubbing shoulders with Marxist guerrillas plotting against the government, cocaine traffickers planning their next shipment, emerald smugglers cutting a deal or just a local hustler cooking up his latest scam. In the country of dreams, as the locals call it, anything is possible.

681 RETAIL THERAPY AT OTAVALO CRAFTS MARKET

ECUADOR Just about every traveller is struck at some point by the panic-inducing realization that there are people back home expecting to be lavished with exotic gifts from faraway lands. If you happen to find yourself in Ecuador at this anxiety-ridden moment you're in luck: Otavalo's spectacular indigenous artesanías market is one of the largest crafts fairs on the continent and one of the most enjoyable alfresco retail experiences to be had anywhere.

Up for grabs are handicrafts of every description – ceramics, jewellery, paintings, musical instruments, carvings and above all a dazzling array of weavings and textiles, for which the Otavalo Valley has long been famous. Looms in back rooms across the countryside clatter away to produce chunky sweaters, hats, gloves, trousers and tablecloths, while weavings of the highest quality, indigenous ponchos, blouses, belts and tapestries, are still made by master-craftsmen using traditional means in tiny village workshops. Come Saturday, when the crafts market combines with a general produce, hardware and animal market to create a megabazaar that engulfs much of the town, people stream in from miles around for a day of frenzied trading.

The Plaza de Ponchos is the epicentre of the crafts melee, a blazing labyrinth of makeshift passageways and endless ranks of tapestries, jumpers, hammocks, cloths and shawls, amid which Otavaleños dressed in all their finery lurk at strategic points to tempt potential customers. But hard sell isn't their style; gentle, good-natured coaxing is far more effective at weakening the customer's resolve. Even the most hardened skinflints will soon be stuffing their bags with everything they never knew they needed and plenty else besides. The only tricky part is deciding who back home should get the two-metre rain-stick and who should get the sheepskin chaps.

682 BRAVING THE WIND IN TORRES DEL PAINE

CHILE You have to keep your head down. Despite the spray-laden wind, it's tempting to lift it above the rim of the boat and look ahead, so you can see the foam-capped waves racing past as the Zodiac inflatable roars upstream. Soon, in the distance, a towering peak of rock rises up. As you get closer you see shattering precipices and giant towers dusted with snow.

This is Torres del Paine, the citadel in Chile's epic south and one of the wildest national parks in the world. When the inboard of the Zodiac inflatable is finally switched off, all you can hear is the fury of the wind. The waves die down and the water reflects the massif in a pool as perfect as you could imagine, fringed by gnarled trees and blasted by bitter winds. Close by is a huge glacier, an offshoot of one of the largest ice fields in the world.

Then you set off walking, shifting the weight of your pack to get comfortable. There are other hikers around you, too – this isn't deserted wilderness by any means – but the largeness of the landscape can more than accommodate everyone. High up to the east, and overlooking the scrub and blasted forest, are the unnaturally sculpted Paine Towers themselves, and in front of you, dark-capped, are weird sculptures of the peaks of the Cuernos del Paine. If you're lucky you'll stumble across some guanacos, wild relations of the llama, or even a shy ñandú, the South American ostrich. But perhaps the best experience to be had here is simply to inhale the air, which is so crisp and thin that breathing is like drinking iced water.

683 SIZE MATTERS: IN SEARCH OF THE WORLD'S LONGEST SNAKE

VENEZUELA At an average of 7m long and weighing up to 250kg, you'd think it'd be impossible for the green anaconda to find somewhere to hide. But gazing out over Venezuela's Los Llanos floodplain, probably the best place in the world to find these super-sized serpents, all I can see are a couple of scarlet ibis and a herd of capybara. But Felipe, my guide, assures me that they are out there, and we set off into the wetlands.

Anacondas entwine their prey in a horrific hug, unhinging their jaws and swallowing it whole; digesting their meal headfirst is easier for them, Felipe tells me, as their prey's limbs tend to fold this way. With this nugget of gratuitously detailed information fresh in my mind, I follow him closely, keeping a comforting rodent shield of capybaras – the anaconda's snack of choice – between myself and the water. Fed by the Orinoco River, Los Llanos spills across 300,000 square kilometres of flooded savannah – almost a third of the country – but Felipe seems to know exactly which patch of indiscriminate reeds to head for. His expertise is complemented by the very latest in anaconda detection tools – a stick – and he sets to work, prodding the swampy foliage in front of him at regular (and cautious) intervals.

It seems to work – after half an hour, Felipe strikes ophidian oil. Quick as a flash, he grabs the tail; Carlos, his assistant, grabs the head, and the battle begins. The beast is big: a good 3.5m long, I estimate (from a good 4m away). I pluck up enough courage to inch closer until I can reach out and touch it. It's like patting a wet tyre: cold, damp and dense. After a few more minutes of sizing it up, the two men let it go, and it ripples off into the water. And then it's just Felipe, Carlos and me, and the seemingly endless watery horizon of Los Llanos.

684 RAFTING ON SACRED WATERS IN THE URUBAMBA VALLEY

PERU Snaking along from the Andes out to the Apurímac in the Amazon basin, the mighty Urubamba is the main fluvial artery pulsing through the Inca heartland, winding between many of their most revered sites, making the river itself sacred. Not all the Urubamba is negotiable by craft, but one section, not far from the start of the Inca Trail, is perfect for a bit of gentle white-water rafting.

On the first stretch, a serene meander through the Urubamba Valley, novice rafters will have the chance to get used to the feeling of having nothing but inflated plastic between them and some fairly sharp rocks. This is a chance to enjoy the superb views of the snowy peaks of the Andes in the distance on one side, and the wooded slopes of the valley stretching up hundreds of metres on the other, where Quechua-speaking llama herders ply the steep trails of their ancestors and the distinctive black and white forms of condors can be seen wheeling far above. Blink and you'll miss the rows of ancient Inca grain stores, carved from rock and piled impossibly high on the emerald-green banks.

Don't be lulled into thinking this is naught but a pleasure boat, though. The roar of the rapids quickly gets louder as the raft moves faster. Following the instructor's command, you'll row harder and duck lower as the raft shoots down increasingly larger and faster falls. However secular you are, you may find yourself praying to the ancient spirits of the Incas as you go rushing down the final and biggest drop along this beginner's stretch. There are scarier, more dangerous river rapids in Peru for experienced rafters – the excellent class V rapids of the Colca Canyon, for instance – but none can rival the beauty and majesty of the sacred river of the Incas.

ARGENTINA Argentines rich and poor tend to base their high-protein diets around beef; they eat more of it per capita than any other people on earth. Who can blame them? Succulent, juicy and flavourful, Argentine beef has a distinct, refined taste, redolent of the perfect pastures that the cattle graze upon – the incredibly fertile pampa, an emerald green carpet radiating out for hundreds of kilometres around Buenos Aires.

The beef's flavour is expertly brought out in its preparation. The traditional – in fact, practically the only – method is on a parrilla, a barbecue using wood (or occasionally charcoal, but certainly never gas). Almost sacred to Argentines, the parrilla is a custom that has its roots in gaucho (cowboy) culture: the fire is lit on Sundays, holidays, after football matches, pretty much at any excuse. In the countryside, ranch hands spread the embers along the ground; in the town, chefs use a metal pit. A grill is hung above and the food lined up – fat chorizo sausages and rounds of melting provolone cheese to start, followed by tasty asado ribs and, finally, huge slabs of steak.

The meat is of such quality that there's no need to drown it in sauces – the parrillero (cook) will lightly season it and offer up some chimichurri to add zip. Made of herbs, garlic and peppers in oil, chimichurri was purportedly invented by a Scottish (or Irish) gaucho named Jimmy McCurry (or Curry), who mixed the only ingredients he had to hand to spice up his diet. Vegetables are an afterthought, mostly restricted to fries and salad – the only essential accompaniments to a parrilla are bread and a bottle of rich, red Argentine Malbec.

The best parrillas are found outside Buenos Aires, closer to the source. Stay on an estancia (ranch), such as El Ombú, to enjoy beef reared on site, or seek out family-run parrillas found in pretty much every countryside town. Alternatively, upmarket city restaurants like *Cabaña Las Lilas*, in the capital's converted docks area, offer premium cuts of meat in more sophisticated surroundings.

BEEFEATER'S PARADISE: 685
THE ARGENTINE PARRILLA

PERU Huacachina appears like a mirage. In the northern stretches of the Atacama – the driest desert on earth – the oasis is a precious sapphire in an unrelenting world of sand. As you drive from the dusty town of Ica, there is no hint of what is to come until your taxi reaches the crest of a hill, when suddenly the glory of the place is revealed. Your eyes are drawn to the water, palm trees and crumbling grandeur of the promenade, a reminder of the days when Huacachina was a secluded retreat for only the very wealthiest Peruvians. But once you've descended into the town huddled around the lake, your perspective changes entirely. The dunes, not the water, take centre stage: viewed from the oasis, they ascend dramatically in steep mountains of sand, some of them 300m high. From up there, all you wanted to do was be by the cool of the water. From down here, all you can think about is scaling an enormous dune and sliding down again.

Sandboarding sounds glamorous, but it's really pretty low-tech. You need to embark as early as possible to avoid being cooked by the sun. At a house where guinea pigs, chickens and children run free in the back room, a grinning, toothless woman will rent you a board and a candle. If someone in a dune buggy offers to take you up the hill, accept. Otherwise you have to climb: there is no ski-lift. Every step up is a heroic effort, immediately deflated by a half-a-step slide down again. Progress is slow. The sandboarding, however, is not: a well-waxed board will fly down the slope. Whether you're experienced enough to stand up and catch the dune or just sit down and cling to the board for dear life, it's an exhilarating ride. It's also exhausting. After an hour or two your perspective changes again, and you'll want to recuperate at a bar by the oasis – where you can start removing the sand that coats your body.

SANDBOARDING AT
HUACACHINA

686

687 TREKKING THROUGH THE PANTANAL

BRAZIL Weary travellers twist in their hammocks as the sun rises; few have slept. All night long, the small campsite glade has resounded with the noise of snuffling, snorting and bashing through the undergrowth, broken only by a hideous high-pitched yelling and the sound of thrashing water. And then, the deafening squawking of the dawn chorus.

"The snuffling?" says one of the gaucho-cum-guides over cafezinho coffees and toast. "That's the peccaries. It's normal." And the thrashing water? "Ah, you were lucky. That was an anaconda killing a cow in the stream over there." The stream we waded through last night on a so-called torchlit adventure? "Yes." And the birds? "Parrots – possibly. Parakeets. Or toucans. Storks. Roseate spoonbills. Kingfishers. Snowy egrets. Red-crested cardinals . . ."

Some 650 species of bird inhabit the Pantanal, the world's largest freshwater wetland, alongside 3500 plant species, 250 types of fish, 110 kinds of mammal and 50 different reptiles.

And when the waters of the Paraguay River recede in April, its grassy plains resemble nothing other than a vast, cageless zoo. Caymans, capybaras and giant otters wallow in the murky lagoons and rivers, jaguars and ocelots prowl the long grass, armadillos and anteaters forage for insects. And eight million cows graze.

The gauchos who roam the Pantanal on horseback comprise most of its human population, and they make the most knowledgeable guides. They'll track down flocks of magnificent hyacinth macaws, roosting in trees and preening their violet feathers. They'll wrestle a crocodile out of the water for close-up viewing, or point out the jabiru stork, as tall as a man, picking its way delicately around the edge of a lily-choked pond. And in the evening they'll invite their visitors to sit round a blazing fire while they play accordions, pass round yerba mate tea and tell derring-do stories of life in the plains of the Pantanal.

688 FOLLOWING ANCIENT FOOTSTEPS ON THE INCA TRAIL

PERU Once the stomping ground for colourfully dressed Incas paying homage to the mountain gods, after five hundred years the Inca Trail still wends its way between towering glaciated peaks, and local Indians still follow the same route, albeit these days carrying tents and food for tourists.

Leaving the Cusco train at Km88, where the trail begins, hikers make first contact with their porters. Underpaid and barefoot (or in recycled tyre sandals), these are the trek's true heroes. With their help, you don't have to be marathon-fit to climb the Inca Trail, and once you conquer its most difficult stretch, Dead Woman's Pass (Abra de Huarmihuañusca) on the second morning, the next few days are relatively easy – just make sure you've acclimatized to the altitude before climbing.

Slow and steady is the best strategy for tackling the steep

gradients, ancient stone steps and tunnels carved through sheer rock; along the way you'll be able to glimpse the remains of several finely built Inca palaces and temples that punctuate the trail. Even though you'll be travelling and camping with a lot of other hikers in an organized group, it's still possible to wander alone at times and soak up the stunning landscape.

Seeking sunrise at Machu Picchu, most people set off from Wiñay Wayna (the last campsite) for the final leg around 4am. After two hours through languid cloudforest the trail finishes at Intipunku, the magnificent stone entrance to Machu Picchu. This impressive gateway offers the first views across one of the greatest wonders of the world – a magical citadel of vast proportions, surrounded by impossibly precipitous terraces and perched high up above the Urubamba Valley.

689 DOWNING CAIPIRINHAS IN RIO DE JANIERO

BRAZIL What could be simpler than a caipirinha? Made with just cachaça (a rum-like spirit distilled from fermented sugarcane juice), fresh lime, sugar and ice, the caipirinha (literally "little peasant girl") is served at nearly every bar and restaurant in Brazil. Neither insipidly sweet nor jarringly alcoholic, it's one of the easiest and most pleasant cocktails to drink.

Therein lies the problem: because it's so smooth-drinking, it's all too common to lose count of just how many you've imbibed. And as lots of bars mix the cocktail with the cheapest available cachaça, chances are that the next day you'll have to deal with a thumping headache, scarcely a just reward after a hard day at the beach. So a true aficionado will only accept the cocktail made with cachaça that's good enough to sip neat.

There's no better place to find this than at Rio de Janeiro's *Academia da Cachaça*. Opened in 1985, when Brazil's aspirant whisky-drinking middle class tended to dismiss cachaça as the

drink of the poor, the *Academia* has about a hundred varieties on offer, and the bar's friendly owners and staff enjoy nothing more than offering tasting hints to their customers.

As you enter you may well wonder what all the fuss is about. The green and yellow Brazilian-flag themed decor is utterly unremarkable and the music inaudible. But the shelves on the walls of the tiny bar, lined with a bewildering selection of bottles, remind you why you've come.

The caipirinhas are everything one might hope for, with just the right balance of alcohol, tang and sweetness. After one or two, you may even feel ready to forego the sugar, lime and ice and start downing shots. Choosing a label is easy: if you don't listen to the house recommendations, the regulars around you will intervene to suggest their personal favourites. The spirit inspires debates, not unlike those over the finest single malt whiskies. The perfection of the caipirinha, on the other hand, is undebatable.

690 GOING TO THE OPERA AT TEATRO AMAZONAS

BRAZIL A noisy concrete forest of tower blocks and brightly lit malls, the remote Amazonian capital and duty-free zone of Manaus throngs with shoppers braving the hot, humid streets to buy cheap electronic goods. Glittering in the twilight and visible above the chaos and heat of downtown is a large dome whose 36,000 ceramic tiles are painted gold, green and blue, the colours of the Brazilian flag. The palatial building it presides over is a grand pink and white confection of belle époque architecture, the Teatro Amazonas.

Nothing could seem more out of place. Built in the late nineteenth century during the height of Brazil's rubber boom, the lavish opera house was designed by Italians to look Parisian (indeed, almost all the materials were brought over from Europe). Abandoned for many years when the rubber industry died and Manaus could scarcely afford its electricity bill, the theatre is now funded by a large state budget and hosts regular performances of jazz and ballet, though nothing is quite so singular as its staging of top-quality opera in the middle of the jungle.

The surreal experience begins the moment you enter the foyer and step onto a floor covered in gleaming hardwood; walls are lined with columns made from the finest Carrara marble and ornate Italian frescoes decorate the ceiling. Hundreds of chandeliers hang in falling crystal formations. It's as if you've been transported to a European capital. You're ushered through red velvet curtains by men dressed in tailcoats and top hats. The orchestra, the Amazonas Philharmonic, pick up instruments that have been specially treated to cope with the humidity of the jungle, and the chatter dissipates abruptly. The conductor raises his baton, and the first familiar notes of Wagner's *Ring Cycle* fill the auditorium, then seep out languidly into the steamy night.

691 LOOKING DOWN ON KAIETEUR FALLS

GUYANA From the vantage point of a Cessna, the great expanse of Guyana's rainforest interior looks like billows of green cloud. The little plane drones over the soft canopy, almost low enough that the passengers could blow and the trees would disperse like smoke, revealing whatever mysteries lie hidden beneath. About an hour out of Georgetown, just as the unbroken jungle scenery starts to get monotonous, the plane banks sharply to the right, losing roughly half of its altitude in a couple of seconds, and heads down towards a gorge bordered by thick forest. As the plane descends farther, a waterfall soon comes into view, cascading down the middle of the gorge, not in tumultuous rumbles of white foam, but in a single, rapier-like gush of water that seems to come from nowhere.

Enjoying the kind of splendid isolation that Niagara Falls can only dream of, Kaieteur Falls is five times as high as Niagara and infinitely more enigmatic. The narrow band of water that runs off the side of the Kaieteur Gorge plunges 226m to the bottom, making the falls here the highest single-drop waterfall in the world. Flying close enough to hear the water's roar blend menacingly with the sound of whirring propellers, it all seems dark and forbidding down below. The plane's passengers may start to worry about those hardy souls who opted to walk through the rainforest for several days in order to reach the falls, getting their first glimpse of Kaieteur dropping on top of them – a somewhat intimidating experience when compared with the exhilaration of flying in, but no less awesome.

692 TAPATI: FUN AND GAMES ON EASTER ISLAND

CHILE Rapa Nui – Easter Island – is shrouded in mystery. How did its people get there? Where did they come from? How did they move those gigantic statues? Some of that enigma comes to life during January's fortnight-long Tapati, a festival that combines ancient customs, such as carving and canoeing, with modern sports, such as the triathlon and horse racing.

First, the islanders form two competing teams, representing the age-old clans, so if you want to participate, it's best to get to know one of the captains. The opening ceremony kicks off with Umu Tahu, a massive barbecue, followed by a parade of would-be carnival queens wearing traditional grass skirts.

Most of the sports events are for men only: one breathtaking highlight is the bareback horse race along Vaihu Beach. If you fancy your chances against the proud locals, be prepared to wear little more than a bandana, a skimpy sarong and copious body paint. Another event, staged in the majestic crater at

Rano Raraku, has contestants – including the odd tourist – paddling across the lake in reed canoes, running round the muddy banks carrying two handfuls of bananas and finally swimming across, with huge crowds cheering them on.

Meanwhile, the womenfolk compete to weave the best basket, craft the most elegant shell necklace or produce the finest grass skirt; visitors are welcome to participate. Little girls and venerable matriarchs alike play leading roles in the after-dark singing and dancing contests. They croon and sway through the night until the judges declare the winning team, usually around daybreak.

But the true climax is Haka Pei: three-dozen foolhardy athletes slide down the steep slopes of Maunga Pu'i Hill – lying on banana trunks. Top speeds reach 80kph, total chaos reigns and usually a limb or two is broken, but the crowds love it. Should they ask you to take part, learn two vital Rapa Nui words: "mauru uru", "no thanks".

693 MOUNTAIN-BIKING THE WORLD'S MOST DANGEROUS ROAD

BOLIVIA The reputation of the road linking La Paz with the tropical lowlands of Bolivia is enough to put most travellers off. But for downhill mountain-bikers and all-round adrenaline junkies, it's an irresistible challenge. The World's Most Dangerous Road, as this byway is colloquially known, is a stunning ride through some of the most dramatic scenery South America has to offer, and with a vertical descent of around 3500m over just 64km, it's one of the longest continuous downhill rides on earth.

Starting amid the icebound peaks of the Andes at over 4000m above sea level, the road plunges through the clouds into the humid valleys of the Upper Amazon basin, winding along deep, narrow gorges where dense cloudforest clings to even the steepest of slopes. The descent is an intense, white-knuckle experience, not made easier by the sight of so many stone crosses marking where buses and trucks have left the road.

The surface is so bad that in most countries it wouldn't even be classified as a road. On one side, dizzying precipices drop down hundreds of metres to the thin, silver ribbon of a river below; on the other, a sheer rock wall rises into the clouds. In the rainy season, waterfalls cascade across the road, making its broken surface even more treacherous. At every hairpin bend, there's a risk a heavy lorry may lurch round the corner, leaving very little room for manoeuvre on a track only 3m wide.

On a mountain bike at least you have some control over your own destiny, instead of depending on the skills of a Bolivian bus driver, the efficacy of his brakes and the dubious impact of the offerings he makes to the earth goddess Pachamama to secure safe passage. By the time you're sipping beer and resting aching limbs by the pool in the tropical heat of Coroico, the resort town at the end of the ride, your only fear will be that bus ride back up to La Paz.

694 SEEING THE SUN RISE IN THE VALLEY OF THE MOON

CHILE The bracing early morning air of the Atacama Desert rouses you out of your slumber as you leave behind the comfy confines of your adobe residencial. Gradually your eyes adjust to a darkness illuminated softly by a crescent moon, and you make out the well-trodden dirt road just ahead. Leading out from the village of San Pedro, the track wends its way 14km to your destination, the surreal Valle de la Luna – the Valley of the Moon. It's about 90min before sunrise and time to get moving, which is just as good – your chattering teeth are doing little to warm you. Driven in equal measure by a need to generate body heat and the joy of embarking on an otherworldly mountain bike ride, you start pedaling west.

Though the prospect of seeing the sun rise in the Valle de la Luna is what lured you out of bed, there is more than a bit of truth

in saying that the journey is the destination. Enveloped in silence and without another soul in sight, you ride across the Atacama with a stunning panorama for a backdrop – flat arid fields punctuated by jagged age-old boulders give way to red crested dunes and valleys layered in a thin orange and white crust. It's easy to see why NASA chose here to field test their Martian rover, but surely they didn't have as much fun as you are with your two knobby tires and a suspension that is thankfully forgiving.

When dawn breaks, the sky springs to life in fiery hues, from blood-red to burnt amber. Taking it in from the perch of one of the higher crests, you gaze upon the lunar landscape that surrounds you – a perfect vantage point to see how far you've come and to plot your course back to the earthy comforts of sleepy San Pedro.

695 PUTTING THE BOOT IN ON THE FALKLAND ISLANDS

ARGENTINA There are only four pubs in Stanley, which is four more smiles than I saw as I staggered in and out of them. The capital of the Falkland Islands is barely more than a village and as the skies darken at 3.30 in the afternoon over the frozen tundra's cement-grey moors and landmine-strewn beaches, the impulse to drink heavily from the stocks of cheap imported Heineken is a hard one to refuse.

"They've got it even worse up on that fucking hill, though," says one grizzled farmer, visiting Stanley from "camp" – what the 2300 islanders call anywhere outside the capital. He refers to the extra 2000 or so inhabitants of the island: British soldiers, based in an echoing warren of corridors and prefabs called "Mount Pleasant", 56km away. It was built after Argentina invaded a quarter of a century ago in a short but bloody war that killed nearly a thousand soldiers. Conditions are anything but pleasant for the soldiers there, with many claiming it to be the worst posting on earth.

Tensions are still very strained between the Falklands and Argentina, and despite being 8000 miles away from the UK, there is a defiant Britishness about the place evident from the immaculate Victorian-era terraced houses on the seafront to the huge Sunday roasts on offer in the pubs. A group of soldiers enters the *Upland Goose* hotel for their Yorkshire puddings, all sporting black eyes from fighting locals the night before. They call the Falklanders "bennys" (after a yokel character from an ancient British soap opera). The locals call the army "when I's" because, they claim, every sentence they utter begins with "When I was in…"

As stubbornly loyal as many Falklanders are, many leave each year for better work prospects, education and weather. Everyone who does must, by tradition, leave a single piece of footwear behind at Boot Hill. The hill is actually a roadside clearing near the airport where a motley collection of trainers, stilettos and Wellingtons are left to be slowly worn away by the relentless howling winds. Locals are reminded that they can come and collect their footwear should they ever return. More often than not, though, the boots remain there forever.

696 EXPERIENCING THE TWO SIDES OF PUNTA DEL ESTE

URUGUAY The continent's most exclusive beach resort by far, Punta del Este is Uruguay's answer to St Tropez. There's a certain level of celebrity that's achieved simply by being here: if you don that outrageously expensive Sauvage swimsuit, act like you belong and hit the beach, chances are you may end up in the pages of a South American glossy mag. Punta is largely about glitzy casinos, all-night parties, designer sushi and fashionistas sipping frozen mojitos. It's the kind of place where you might spot Naomi Campbell and Prince Albert of Monaco on the same evening – though probably not in the same Ferrari convertible. Every January half a million visitors – mostly Argentines and Brazilians – cram themselves in between surfers' paradise Playa Brava and family-friendly Playa Mansa, so you can easily lose yourself in the crowds.

But there's another side to Punta. Leave the Quiksilver-clad funboarders and world beach-volly tournaments behind and head for one of the infinite golden playas way beyond Punta Ballena, on the River Plate side of things. Explore Chihuahua, where you can sunbathe among the enormous straw-hued dunes, take cover in the secluded pine groves and even venture into the tepid waters. At night, drive across the landmark rollercoaster bridge to La Barra – ignore the bronzed beauties queuing for flambéed lobster along the main drag – and race past the windswept ocean strands to José Ignacio. Dine in discreet style right on the seafront. Enjoy your simply barbecued squid and chilled sauvignon blanc, listen to the breakers crashing onto the sand, feel the Atlantic breeze in your hair. And rest assured that the shutterbugs are all busy snapping the heir to the Spanish throne at some heaving cocktail bar in Punta.

697 ITAIPÚ: PLUGGING THE WORLD'S BIGGEST DAM

PARAGUAY Colossal, gargantuan, mammoth, gigantic – it's difficult to find the right adjective to capture the sheer magnitude of the Itaipú dam. The joint property of Paraguay and Brazil, it has been voted one of the seven wonders of the modern world by the American Society of Civil Engineers (who should know what they're talking about), and is arguably man's greatest ever feat of practical engineering, virtually meeting the energy needs of the whole of Paraguay as well as a large chunk of southern Brazil. You don't need to be mechanically minded to appreciate it, however: the introductory video about the finer details of electricity generation might not hold your attention, but the sheer awe-inspiring scale of the structure certainly will.

It took sixteen years to build the dam, a project that was begun in the dark days of Stroessner's dictatorship and finally completed in the early years of democracy; its inception created a reservoir so deep and wide that it completely flooded the Sete Quedas, a set of waterfalls comparable in size to those at nearby Iguazú. At 8km long and 195m high, standing next to it and looking up is as dizzying as you might expect. But to really feel insignificant, make a visit to the inside of the dam and the extraordinary one-kilometre-long machine room. It's like the inside of an anthill, with workers scurrying around, dwarfed by the sheer scale of their surroundings. The dam is at its most impressive when water levels are at their peak during the rainy season, when torrents of water rush down the chutes and the roar can be deafening. Whenever you're here, though, it's an amazing sight – and one that for once does justice to even the highest expectations.

698 LOST IN TIME ON THE ROYAL ROAD

BRAZIL To travel along the Estrada Real feels like taking a step back in time. This "Royal Road", commissioned by the Portuguese Crown in 1697 to provide access to the gold- and gem-rich mountains, stretches 1000km through Brazil's interior. Wending its way from the small colonial-era port of Paraty in the south through former mining outposts all the way to Diamantina, a town deep in the Brazilian highlands, the road fell into disuse after the end of the Gold Rush a century or so later; in recent years, however, the route has experienced something of a renaissance, with visitors drawn by the fine colonial architecture and old-world feel of its communities as well as the unspoiled, bucolic scenery it takes in.

With time and determination, you can walk the length of the Estrada Real, but most just choose a small section for leisurely exploration. Hiking up the steep and often slippery twelve-kilometre stretch of the original cobblestone surface from Paraty, you'll enter the Serra do Mar, the rainforest-covered mountain range separating the coast from the interior. Here hummingbirds hover at brightly coloured flowers and monkeys swing from branches overhead. As you trudge deeper into the forest, sharing the road with pack mules headed for isolated farmsteads, you can stop for a refreshing dip in a series of cascading waterfalls. Further on, you'll be rewarded by a sign pointing towards a simple pousada – a country inn – with spectacular views of Paraty and the ocean beyond.

The further north one travels along the Estrada Real the more parched the landscape becomes. The sixty-kilometre stretch linking Diamantina and Serro, for example, appears positively lunar; yet even in its most abandoned sections the road shelters oasis-like hamlets whose enterprising locals have caught on to the benefits of tourism. Stop off at a roadside stall for a bottle of home-produced cachaça (a sugar-based firewater) or to sample fresh Minas cheese. If you're not in a hurry, stay over in a pousada and feast on the local cuisine: rich, greasy and incredibly tasty pork, jerked-beef, beans and rice, all cooked in traditional fashion, on wood-burning stoves.

699 FROLICKING WITH FUR SEALS

CHILE Reaching the Juan Fernández archipelago – three volcanic crags way out in the Pacific – is an adventure in itself: three hours from Santiago de Chile in a juddering twin-propeller plane, a half-hour trudge down a dusty track and a two-hour ride in a leaky fishing-boat just get to the midget capital of Juan Bautista. The first inhabitants you see are a small welcoming party of endemic Juan Fernández fur seals, which wait faithfully for each planeload of visitors in the rocky cove below the airstrip. Wildlife certainly knows how to forgive – until the early twentieth century, islanders slaughtered the seals for their prized pelts, butchering hundreds of thousands and bringing the species to the brink of extinction, but since hunting became illegal, careful conservation has brought the numbers of these photogenic little mammals to over 10,000.

Reassured that accustoming the seals to human contact doesn't threaten their survival, we donned wetsuits, clambered into another fishing smack and headed for one of the biggest colonies. As we floundered around in our fins and snorkels, our hosts – especially the endearing pups, with their wide-eyed, innocent looks – showed us just why the water is their kingdom. It was a truly hands-on exercise – body contact is definitely encouraged and the seals somehow manage to be slippery and cuddly at the same time. While they performed endless somersaults, pikes, tucks and twists around, below and over us, we simultaneously tried to float, signal to the fishermen to take our photo and stay away from the huge grandfather bull. His blustering snorts suggested that his grandchildren were getting too familiar with us, but guide Marcelo said it was just his way of saying hello. And as we chugged away into the sunset it also seemed to be his way of saying goodbye – but not, we hoped, good riddance.

700 ENJOYING ISOLATION AT THE TERMAS DE PUYUHUAPI

CHILE It can take you days to reach the *Termas de Puyuhuapi* – but then getting there is all part of the fun. One of the remotest hideaways in the world, the luxurious lodge-cum-spa sits halfway down Chile's Carretera Austral, or "Southern Highway", a thousand-kilometre, mostly unpaved road that threads its way through a pristine wilderness of soaring mountains, Ice Age glaciers, turquoise fjords and lush temperate rainforest. The most exciting way to travel down it is to rent a 4WD – you'll rarely get above 30kph per hour, but with scenery like this, who cares?

Separated from the carretera by a shimmering fjord, the lodge is unreachable by land. Instead, a little motor launch will whisk you across in ten minutes. It's hard to imagine a more romantic way to arrive, especially during one of the frequent downpours that plague the region, when guests are met off the boat by dapper young porters carrying enormous white umbrellas.

The hotel is made up of a series of beautifully designed low-lying buildings, constructed from local timber with lots of glass, that blend in handsomely with their surroundings. Having come quite so far to get here it would be a shame not to splash out on one of the eight shoreside rooms, with their mesmerizing views across the fjord. Inside, it's all understated luxury: flickering log fires, bare wooden floors, sofas to sink into, light streaming in from all directions.

You can take to the wilderness in a number of ways: go sea-kayaking (with dolphins, if you're lucky); learn to fly-fish in secret rivers packed with trout and salmon; take a hike through the rainforest to a nearby glacier. And afterwards soak your bones in the hotel's raison d'être, its steaming hot springs, channelled into three fabulous outdoor pools – two of them right on the edge of the fjord, the other (the hottest of all) enclosed by overhanging ferns. Lying here at night, gazing at the millions of stars above, you'd think you were in heaven. And really, you'd be right.

701 SEEING THE SUN RISE FROM VOLCÁN COTOPAXI

ECUADOR A shard of sunlight cracks open the horizon, spilling crimson into the sky and across the last icy crest, glittering like a crown of diamonds above you. Your exhausted legs can barely lift your snow-encrusted boots and the crampons that stubbornly grip the ice, but you're almost at the top. Gasping in the thin air, you haul yourself from the chilly shadow of night into the daylight. As the sun bursts across your face, the most spectacular dawn you've ever seen spreads out before you.

The perfect cone of Volcán Cotopaxi, regarded by early explorer Alexander von Humboldt as "the most beautiful and regular of all the colossal peaks in the high Andes", at 5897m is one of the highest and most magnificent active volcanoes in the world. From the refuge at 4800m, tucked just below a girdle of ice and snow encircling the peak, it's around six to eight gruelling hours to the summit on a route that picks its way between gaping crevasses and fragile seracs, over ladders and up vertical ice. For some it's just as well that much of this steep climb is done unseen at night; hopefuls must rouse themselves from a fitful and breathless slumber at midnight to climb before the heat of the day makes the glacier unstable. The payback is arriving at the summit just as the sun rises, when you're treated to mind-blowing views of Cotopaxi's yawning crater, the giant peaks of the Andes in the distance, and through the clouds, glimpses of Quito sleeping far below.

702 BIRD-WATCH AND BE WATCHED

SURINAME The strap of your binoculars chafes the back of your neck and the mosquitoes, constant companions in this nature reserve, form a pesky aura around your head. Yet you can't tear yourself away from what's locked in your sight: a flock of bright orange cocks-of-the-rock stripping a tree of Suriname cherries. A flurry of feathers to your left signals the arrival of a pair of sparrow-sized antbirds. They peer intently at your hiking boots, which are parked right in the marching path of their black, crawling prey. Leaving the little feasters to their work, you press deeper into the jungle until you're stopped dead by the piercing whee-oo! of an ornate hawk-eagle. With the discreetness of an Apache helicopter it lands on a branch and seizes you in its fierce glower – you must have ventured too near its nest. It's a funny thing they call bird-watching, when you're so often the one being watched.

703 SOARING OVER THE NAZCA LINES

PERU Buzzing at a few hundred feet over the desert in a paper-thin Cessna, my breakfast is starting to feel a little too familiar. But as soon as I spot the first of the gargantuan figures, a fanged spider, etched into the dry earth below, I forget about airsickness. One of the most compelling sights in a country full of wonders, Peru's Nazca Lines still baffle scholars and travellers alike: no one can agree on exactly how, and more to the point, why, the ancient Nazca people created these huge zoomorphic and geometrical shapes. A form coalesces out of the haze and becomes a monkey with a spiral tail; next we bank right and cruise over a huge hummingbird and a psychedelic shaman. If, as some experts suggest, the Lines pointed the way to water, I hope they still work; these dusty plains inspire quite a thirst.

Drifting down the Amazon

BRAZIL Of all the wonders of South America, none captures the imagination perhaps as much as the Amazon rainforest. Covering an area almost as large as the continental United States, and extending from Brazil into seven other countries, the Amazon basin is by far the most biologically diverse region on earth, home to an astonishing variety of plant and animal life – rare birds and mammals, extraordinary insects and reptiles and literally millions of plant species – all woven together into a rich and complex natural tapestry.

Despite its immense size, the forest is disappearing at an alarming rate, and if you want to see the fabulous wildlife close up you need to head upstream by boat, taking either one of the many excursion boats or – better – a motorized dugout canoe. As you chug into the remote backwaters of the Amazon, every twist and turn offers the prospect of something to see: turtles or cayman crocodiles basking in the sun; pink river dolphins playing in the brown waters; flocks of brightly coloured macaws or toucans flying overhead; monkeys cavorting in the treetops on either side; and perhaps even a giant anteater drinking along the river bank.

For accommodation, you can camp out on the riverbank, with the nocturnal noise of the forest all around, or stay at one of a growing number of eco-lodges. Some of these are run by indigenous tribes, built in traditional style from natural materials harvested from the forest but with modern additions, such as solar-powered lighting. Staying with indigenous hosts gives an insight into cultures that have developed over many centuries of living in close harmony with the rainforest. You'll get a chance to sample traditional Amazonian food – minus the endangered animal species that are now hunted for photographs rather than food – and learn how people survive in a natural environment that to outsiders can seem extremely hostile. Best of all, you'll get to walk forest trails with an indigenous guide, and tap in to their encyclopedic knowledge of the rainforest ecosystem. The guides may not know the scientific name of every species you encounter, but they can usually explain its behaviour, uses and place in local legend. In fact, many visitors find the lifestyle and culture of their Amazonian hosts as fascinating as any of the plants or animals they see in the rainforest.

MAKING A PILGRIMAGE
TO THE ISLA DEL SOL

BOLIVIA Set against the parched grasslands of the Altiplano, the deep, sapphire-blue waters of the world's highest navigable lake, Titicaca, offer the promise of life and fertility in this arid region, where all agriculture is dependent on irrigation or capricious rainfall. The Incas believed the creator god Viracocha rose from the waters of this lake, calling forth the sun and the moon to light up the world, from an island in its centre now called the Isla del Sol – the Island of the Sun.

Claiming their own dynasty also originated there, they built a complex of shrines and temples on the island, transforming it into a religious centre of enormous importance, a pan-Andean pilgrimage destination once visited by thousands of worshippers annually from across their vast empire.

Modern visitors can follow the same route as the pilgrims of Inca times, travelling by boat from the port town of Copacabana – itself a pilgrimage centre for the now nominally Christian population of the Bolivian highlands.

With no roads or cars on the island, the only way to visit the Inca ruins is on foot, trekking through the tranquil villages of the indigenous Aymara who raise crops on the intricate agricultural terraces left by the Incas, and who still regard Lago Titicaca as a powerful female deity capable of regulating climate and rainfall.

The ruined temples themselves are small in comparison with Inca sites elsewhere in the Andes, but the setting more than makes up for this. The great rock where the sun and moon were created looks out on all sides across the tranquil expanse of the lake, which is in turn surrounded by mighty, snowcapped mountains, each of which is still worshipped as a deity in its own right. The serene beauty of this sacred Andean geography imparts a powerful spiritual energy, which makes it easy to believe this could indeed be the centre of the universe.

706 TACKLING THE FITZ ROY MASSIF

ARGENTINA From the sandstone canyons of La Rioja to the granite peaks of Patagonia, Argentina's superb network of national parks form the backdrop to some of the continent's most diverse trekking. Most visitors, however, head south to the Andes, and the legendary Parque Nacional Los Glaciares, the northernmost section of which – the Fitz Roy massif – contains some of the most breathtakingly beautiful mountains on the planet.

At the centre of the massif, puncturing the wide Patagonian sky, is the 3405-metre incisor of Monte Fitz Roy, known to the native Tehuelche as El Chaltén, "The Mountain that Smokes", in reference to the whisps of cloud that almost continually drape from its summit. Alongside Fitz Roy rise Cerro Poincenot and Aguja Saint-Exupéry, whilst set back from them is the forbidding needle of Cerro Torre, a crooked finger standing in bold defiance of all the elements that the Hielo Continental Sur, the immense icecap that lurks behind the massif, can hurl at it. A series of excellent trails crisscross the massif, several of which can be combined into the Monte Fitz Roy/Cerro Torre Loop, a three-day jaunt done under the perpetual shadow of these imposing peaks.

707 WAKE UP AND SMELL THE COFFEE: THE ZONA CAFETERA

COLOMBIA You've probably got an image of Colombia, even if you've been nowhere near it. More likely than not it's one of two things: that of shadowy, menacing drug cartels or of the proud, smiling face of coffee grower Juan Valdez. They're both a bit outdated, and the latter was in any case a fiction – a marketing tool used to promote Colombian coffee, which is the nation's biggest export, and second only to Brazilian coffee in worldwide production. However, you can get close to that homespun image of Colombia by going to stay at a coffee farm (finca) in the country's Tierra Paisa (also known as the zona cafetera, or Tierra Templada region). Plenty of these are still run by single families, looking for ways to supplement their modest incomes, and you'll spend much of your time learning about the history of the area and wandering around, perhaps on horseback, drinking in the atmosphere and mountain scenery.

708 LIGHT SHOW IN LA PAZ

BOLIVIA At an elevation of 3600 metres, La Paz is the highest capital city in the world. You can quickly lose yourself here, either walking through the winding, steeply pitched streets or gazing at the unbelievable hugeness of distant Mount Illimani. Come nightfall, climb a hill at the edge of town for some of the most dazzling pyrotechnics on the continent: as darkness descends on the city, thousands of tiny electric lights blink on and wrap it in a starry blanket. If your breath hasn't already been taken away by the altitude, it surely will be now.

Going to church in Chiloé

CHILE Never mind that just a thirty-minute ferry ride separates the main island in the Chiloé archipelago and the second largest in South America from mainland Chile. You sense it with your first step on Isla Grande: this is a land wholly unto its own. Though centuries-old legends of trolls and witches haunting the archipelago's forests and secluded coves still linger, there's more to Chiloé's identity than mythical underpinnings. With its rural way of life and sleepy fishing villages of palafitos – wooden houses built on stilts above the sea – it's often regarded as a curiosity even among Chileans, but there's no better way to get to know Chiloé than by going to church.

Over 150 reverently maintained eighteenth- and nineteenth-century timber churches dot the islands, with the greatest concentration on Isla Grande. Start your journey in the north at Ancud, where the red- and orange-tiled Iglesia Pio X makes for an excellent introduction to the distinctive style – bold colours, arched porticoes and striking hexagonal bell towers – first created by Jesuit missionaries and the local indigenous population and later enhanced by Franciscan monks. As you make your way south, you'll pass delicate roadside shrines and quiet side roads that lead to solitary churches standing in an open field or presiding over breezy plazas. Though few of these aspire to the grandiose design of the yellow and eggshell blue of Iglesia San Francisco in Castro, the island's capital, they each shed light on the essence of Chiloé in their own way. The trick is to take your time exploring, and when you're done gazing upon the churches, be sure to turn around and take in what lies before them. Chances are it's the sea.

710 EXPLORING SILVER MINES IN THE ANDES

BOLIVIA Dried goats'-blood framed the small hole in the side of the mountain. Peering into the darkness with a lantern, my bravado faltered. I took one last look at the rustic city spread out in the valley below before bending in half and descending into the blackness.

Cerro Rico crouches like a red demon above the city of Potosi. Known for being the highest city in the world, Potosi was also once the richest thanks to the silver mines burrowing beneath the nearby peak. Its streets are lined with grandiose colonial architecture harking back to a time when the city's silver bankrolled the entire Spanish empire – built on the backs of millions of Indian and African slaves who died working the mines during Spanish rule. The mining carries on – still a hazardous proposition – ten hours a day, six days a week.

I thought of the workers' ghosts as my lantern caught two eyes glittering in the darkness; we were heading deeper and deeper into the twisting tunnels. Terror rose in my gut as a horned man materialized in the gloom, adorned with coca leaves and cigarettes. It was an altar to pagan god El Tio, whom the miners beseech to spare their lives.

My Bolivian guide promised we would be back outside before the blasting started at 1pm, but a loud explosion reverberated through the darkness at eleven, shattering our already taut nerves. It seemed like it took forever negotiating the slippery narrow shafts before we resurfaced. I have never been so glad to see the sky.

711 SEARCHING FOR THE PERFECT OYSTER ON ISLA MARGARITA

VENEZUELA Oysters provide a great source of inspiration for a food-driven odyssey. You can travel far and wide looking for the freshest, finest specimen; once discovered, you might consume it on the half-shell, or fried up in a po-boy sandwich, or perhaps as part of a shrimp and oyster omelette – a South Korean favourite.

Consider first what they are: sensitive little creatures that thrive in unpolluted areas, where fresh water and sea water mix and where temperatures aren't too hot in summer or too freezing in winter. In short, relatively unspoilt and often unusually attractive coastal spots. So you'll not only enjoy the goods when you arrive, you may find a picture-perfect setting too.

These spots lie in a band across the globe, taking in wild oysters from the fjords of Norway and South Africa lagoon oysters, as well as European oyster plantations in Loch Fynne (Scotland), Whitstable (England) and the 350-plus oyster farms on the Arcachon basin, in France. But for our money, there's no cooler crustacean than mangrove oysters, and no more inspiring location in which to consume them than the coconut grove-lined beaches of Isla Margarita, Venezuela.

These bivalves, who call the roots of the red mangrove home are much smaller than other oysters – typically measuring no more than 4cm across – so knocking back a couple dozen briny salty-sweet ones for lunch (raw, of course, with a dash of citrus – the purist's choice), mandatory frosty Polar beer in hand, is no problem at all. While you're lazing on the beach, you only need to corral a vendor: armed with just a small blunt knife, a bag full of limes, a jar of fiery cocktail sauce and a plastic bucket full of lagoon water and mangrove oysters, these traders dispense a little bit of paradise.

712 EQUITORIAL DIFFERENCES IN QUITO

ECUADOR If you find yourself in Quito, a visit to the equator is more or less obligatory – the middle of the earth is only about a thirty-minute drive north from the Ecuadorean capital. As you get closer, the highland vegetation gives way to sandy plains punctuated by uninspiring brown hills. The "Mitad del Mundo" monument itself is even less exciting: a low-level metal-and-stone affair, it sits at the point determined by a French scientific expedition in 1736 to be latitude 0° 0′ 0″. The real treat here is to stand on the red-painted equator line, with one foot in each hemisphere. Doing so is more than just an unmissable photo opportunity: you can't help but be struck by a sense of reverence.

It all seems a bit unreal – and it may be: about 150m north, a short walk up the highway, is a rival museum, Inti Ñan, which claims that it sits on the location of the real equator line, a point well known to mystics from Ecuador's indigenous Quichua peoples since pre-Columbian times. There's no monument and everything has a very home-made feel, but you do get to interact with the magnetic forces at work here. A sink is produced, filled and then emptied of water to show you that instead of swirling water at the equator runs straight down the plug. You can also balance an egg on a nail, since the forces of gravity are weaker. The passion of the guides involves more than the position of the equator line: Inti Ñan is about honouring traditional knowledge as much as scientific accuracy.

Ultimately, a visit to the equator would be incomplete if you didn't go to each of the museums, tipping your hat to the achievements of both early modern science and ancient heritage. Rather than transcendental cosmic awe, you're more likely to be somewhat comforted by the kitschy, understatedness of it all, as if the Earth is having the last laugh.

713 SEEKING HEAT IN THE CHAPADA DIAMANTIA

BRAZIL If it weren't for the forró band playing in its tiny plaza, Lençois, at the heart of Brazil's vast Parque Nacional da Chapada Diamantina, could be an outpost in the American Southwest. Then again, a cold caipirinha and a crispy chicken picadinho aren't so easily found in Arizona. The dry, rugged sertão of northeastern Brazil offers something unique: a Martian landscape of rifts and ridges, ideal for hiking or bouldering and dotted with modest but vibrant villages still scraping by since the days this area was mined for diamonds. Climb the 300-metre-high, vaguely camel-shaped mesa called Morro do Pai Inácio – named for a legendary lover who threw himself from its edge – or watch a stream make a similar plunge from the top of Cachoeira Glass, the country's tallest waterfall. When the sun reaches its apex, take cover in any of several grottoes that puncture the plain. Whatever you do, bring plenty of liquids, for the heat – like the otherworldy terrain – is mind-altering.

714 FLY-FISHING IN TIERRA DEL FUEGO

ARGENTINA It may seem a long way to come to cast your line, but down in the toe of Argentina's boot the rivers run with gold. Well, with brown and rainbow.

The waters of the Río Grande literally boil with trout. Back, flick, cast, catch. Back, flick, cast, catch. It's like taking candy from a baby. And some fairly hefty candy at that, as the Río Grande is home to some of the most super-sized sea-running brown trout in the world, whose forays into the nutrient-rich ocean help them swell to weights in excess of 14kg.

Back, flick, cast, catch. The fly barely has time to settle on the surface before another monster gobbles it up and is triumphantly reeled up onto the bank.

715 EXPLORING COLONIA DEL SACRAMENTO BY SCOOTER

URUGUAY Perched on a peninsula at the confluence of the Río Uruguay and Río del Plata, Colonia del Sacramento is perhaps the most picturesque town in all of Uruguay. One of the best ways to explore it is by scooter, zipping past the brightly coloured homes, tiny bars and craft stores that line the perfectly preserved maze of cobblestone streets in the Barrio Histórico. Cut through the lovely Plaza Mayor, where parakeets screech in the trees, and head for the town's lighthouse, El Faro, which sits next to the ruins of a former convent. Take a break from your scooter here, and ascend the top of this still-operating beacon to see a stunning panorama of the surrounding city and shoreline. Be sure to make it down before dusk, though, as you'll want to head to the sloping Calle de los Suspeiros (Street of Sighs) to watch the sun sink slowly into the silver water of the rivers – the street has some of the best views of sunset in the city.

716

THE ROAD TO RUINS: MACHU PICCHU

PERU There's a point on the Inca Trail when you suddenly forget all the accumulated aches and pains of four days' hard slog across the Andes. You're standing at Inti Punku, the Sun Gate, the first golden rays of dawn slowly bringing the jungle to life. Down below, revealing itself in tantalizing glimpses as the early-morning mist burns gradually away, are the distinctive ruins of Machu Picchu, looking every bit the lost Inca citadel it was until less than a century ago.

The hordes of visitors that will arrive by mid-morning are still tucked up in bed; for the next couple of hours or so, it's just you, your group and a small herd of llamas, grazing indifferently on the terraced slopes. That first unforgettable sunrise view from Inti Punku is just the start: thanks to its remote location – hugging the peaks at 2500m and hidden in the mountains some 120km from Cusco – Machu Picchu escaped the ravages of the Spanish conquistadores and remained semi-buried in the Peruvian jungle until Hiram Bingham, an American explorer, "rediscovered" them in 1911. Which means that, descending onto the terraces and working your way through the stonework labyrinth, you'll discover some of the best-preserved Inca remains in the world.

Sites such as the Temple of the Sun and the Intihuatana appear exactly as they did some six hundred years ago. The insight they give us into the cultures and customs of the Inca is still as rewarding – the former's window frames the constellation of Pleiades, an important symbol of crop fertility – and their structural design, pieced together like an ancient architectural jigsaw, just as incredible.

717 COMMUNING WITH A SHAMAN

PERU The moto taxis and smog begin to disappear as you venture deeper into the jungle, leaving behind you a series of log-choked Amazonian ports. Canoes transport families across the deep, wide river. Tree trunks bob downstream past villages hidden behind towering banana trees. Your shallow wooden boat splutters along, full of people laden with wares from the market, pink dolphins popping up alongside and parrots flapping overhead. And then your destination comes into sight: the shaman's house.

In Peru, the Amazonian shaman is no Hollywood witch doctor – the popular images of wild eyes, wilder hair, flailing arms and mysterious bones are patently false. Instead, the shaman wears a cayman's tooth strung on a necklace of huayruro seeds, which are said to promote fertility. At his side are plastic bottles filled with his special brew, ayahuasca, and a machete. Ayahuasca is a potent, earthy-smelling liquid, terracotta in colour and made from the macerated vine of the ayahuasca plant and other jungle leaves. The hallucinogenic drink is used to rid villagers of ailments they believe are caused by bad spirits. The shaman says drinking it allows him to travel into the spirit world, where he sees what is afflicting his patients and how he can cure them. Sometimes the treatment involves giving them ayahuasca, but this can produce occasionally dangerous side effects, such as serious vomiting and diarrhoea. Most authentic shamans deter visitors from taking ayahuasca and allow participation in such ceremonies only after adequate preparation, which may take several days.

As you sit cross-legged in the shaman's wooden house, below a ceiling of dried palm fronds and under a sky sparkling with a million celestial diamonds, you know this is one doctor's appointment where you don't need medicine to feel better. With the night sky chiming with crickets and monkeys, parrots and bats, you feel ready to commune with the spirits.

718 LIFE ON THE QUIET SIDE: HOMESTAYS ON LAGO TITICACA

PERU Set against a backdrop of desert mountains, the shimmering waters of Lago Titicaca have formed the heart of Peru's highland altiplano civilizations since ancient times, nourishing the Pukara, Tiawanaku and Colla peoples, whose enigmatic ruins still dot the shoreline. More than seventy of Titicaca's scattered islands remain inhabited, among them the famous islas flotantes, floating islands created centuries ago from compacted reed beds by the Uros Indians.

In recent decades, such attractions have made the lake one of Peru's top visitor destinations; as a consequence, only in the most remote corners can you still encounter traditional settlements that aren't overrun with camera-toting outsiders.

Yet merely by visiting such isolated places, aren't travellers running the risk of eroding the very ways of life they've come to see? Not in distant Anapia, a cluster of five tiny islets near the border with Bolivia, whose ethnic Aymara residents – descendants of the altiplano's original inhabitants – make a living from subsistence agriculture and fishing, maintaining their own music, dance, costume and weaving traditions.

Fifteen Anapian families have got together to create their own homestay scheme. Each takes it in turn to host visitors, in the same way they've traditionally rotated grazing rights. Accommodation is simple, but clean and warm: you get your own room and bathroom but share meals with the host family on tables spread with brightly coloured homespun cloth. Potatoes are the main staple, and if you're lucky they'll be prepared huatia-style, baked in an earth oven with fresh fish and herbs from the lake shore.

Walking, fishing, sailing and rowing trips fill your time. A guided excursion also takes you to the uninhabited island of Vipisque, where the Aymara rear vicuñas – small, cinnamon-coloured cousins of the alpaca, prized for their fine wool. From the hilltop at the centre of the island, the view extends all the way across Lago Titicaca to the ice peaks of Bolivia's Cordillera Real – one of South America's most magnificent panoramas.

719 CRASHING OUT BY LAGO CHUNGARÁ

CHILE The drive up from the grubby seaside city of Arica into Lauca National Park takes you along modern motorways to a place of dusty hamlets, whitewashed churches and eerie silence. This is where the Atacama – the world's driest desert – hits the Andes, and it feels like a spectacularly pure landscape. At 4500m, Chungará is one of the world's highest lakes, inhabited by flamingoes and ducks. We spent our evening here drinking Pisco, the local brandy, and the night shivering outdoors under a poncho, stalactites of ice forming from our condensed sweat. The nearby refugio might be a better way to enjoy the morning – when the sky is a piercing blue, alpacas hop along the stony slopes and, on a still day, you can see a stunning reflection of the nearby peaks in the lake's chilly waters.

720 ICE CLIMBING IN THE CORDILLERA REAL

BOLIVIA You're halfway up a sheer ice wall in the high Andes, with crampons on your feet, an ice axe in each hand and your stomach quavering somewhere around knee level, when you sense that there are some things humans were not really meant to do. Yet if you don't mind the odd moment of panic and pain, the Cordillera Real, strung across Bolivia between the barren altiplano and the Amazon basin, is a wonderful place to begin mountaineering. For one thing, it's substantially cheaper than Europe or the US. More importantly, this harsh landscape, with its thin air, intimidating peaks and snow-covered ridges, is an unforgettable one, a world away from hectic La Paz and another planet from the one most of us live on.

ARGENTINA & BRAZIL Few sporting events rival the raucous spectacle of a football match in South America. From a small, local but enthusiastically supported game in the Andes to a clash of the titans in one of the great cathedrals of the sport in Brazil or Argentina, even those who can't tell a goal kick from a penalty kick won't fail to be impressed by the colour and passion – both on the pitch and in the stands.

Fans of the sport can look forward to fast, attacking football, individual star turns, lots of goals (0-0 draws are practically unheard of, as is defensive play), red cards aplenty and quite possibly a pitch invasion.

The bigger the team, the bigger the stadium, and the louder the roar of the crowd. Choose Rio's Maracanã, one the world's largest, São Paulo's Art Deco Pacaembú, or Buenos Aires's Bombonera ("chocolate box", for its shape) for a full-on assault of the senses – particularly if you time your visit for a local derby such as São Paulo v Corinthians or Boca Juniors v River Plate.

As well as their teams' jersey, fans will go armed with ticker tape, flags, flares, horns and drums. Don't be surprised if you can hardly see the players through the resulting clouds of red, blue or yellow. You certainly won't be able to miss the supporters' loud and, ahem, colourful singing before, during and after the match, whether their team wins or loses, accompanied by entire brass bands and battalions of drummers. The frenetic, all-standing terraces (popular in Argentina, "geral" in Brazil) are the noisiest part of the stands, but first-time attendees are advised to head to the relative calm of the seating area (platea or arquibancada respectively). After a big game, follow the (winning) crowds to the boisterous after-match street parties.

WATCHING A
FOOTBALL 721
MATCH

CHILE An insignificant speck in the South Pacific, Easter Island, or Rapa Nui in Polynesian, is one of the most isolated islands in the world. South America lies 3600km to the east, and with the vast expanse of the Pacific never far from view, the sense of utter isolation can be unnerving. Yet despite its location, Easter Island is famous, thanks to its enigmatic *moai*, whose squat torsos and long, brooding heads loom sombrely over the island's coastline, their mysterious existence making them symbols of a lost civilization, crackpot Atlantis theories, alien intelligence or, more plausibly, ecological disaster.

The moai might look familiar, but it's only when you visit the island that the overwhelming scale of their construction sinks in – it's littered with hundreds of them, most toppled over, face down in the tussock grass. The carvings, many 30m tall, have a majestic, serene quality that is certainly captivating, and it helps that many have been raised and restored, top knots and coral eyes included. They are thought to represent the ancestors of a Polynesian tribe that settled on the island some time before the eleventh century, and it's easy to see why their obsessive production intensified the drift towards catastrophe. No one knows why the carvers dropped their tools and abandoned their work so suddenly, or what caused this highly organized society to self-destruct, descending into anarchy, but by the time the first European ships arrived here in the eighteenth century, only a few impoverished villages remained. Today, the sleepy settlement of Hanga Roa exists only for tourists and virtually every morsel of food is imported on weekly flights from Chile.

So how did the Polynesians even find this place, never mind survive? The longer you stay, the more impossible it seems that people travelling thousands of kilometres in canoes could ever get here. By the time you leave, Easter Island's secrets will seem more unfathomable than ever, and those theories of alien intervention and lost Atlantis less cranky after all.

722

THE GIANTS
OF RAPA NUI

723 WINE AND HORSES AT ESTANCIA COLOMÉ

ARGENTINA Estancias are Argentina's proud answer to haciendas: working ranches with prize land stretching to the horizon, a stable full of thoroughbred horses and a distinctly noble flavour. Recently, a number of estancias have allowed guests to share their comforts while enjoying a back-to-nature experience. One such, the luxurious *Colomé*, is unusual in that it's also a winery. Not just any winery, but one of the world's highest, more than 2300m above sea level. The first grapevines, planted by the conquistadores in the sixteenth century, flourished thanks to the region's cool nights, warm, sunny days, and just the right amount of rain. Argentina's last remaining Spanish aristocrats ran the place in the nineteenth century. And then, as the world entered the new millennium, an ecologically minded Swiss entrepreneur turned *Colomé* into a luxury resort.

Nine modern suites form a neo-colonial quadrangle around a galleried patio and a gently gurgling fountain. Most afford sweeping views across to the snowcapped Andes, best enjoyed from a private veranda that looks directly onto a garden of native plants. *Colomé* manages to be spacious yet cosy – when the outdoor temperature drops, under-floor heating allows you to pad around barefoot. In any case, if you so wish, the butler will come with his bellows and light a fire in your very own hearth.

To discover the wild surroundings at a leisurely pace, tie on some chaps, mount a criollo steed and let Ernesto, a taciturn horse-whisperer from Chile, lead the way. Rides take you along dried-up riverbeds past thorny scrub with magnificent sierras as a backdrop. Flocks of parrots screech overhead. Gaudy butterflies sip at cactus blooms. Back at the ranch, you can meditate in the Zen room, take a dip in the turquoise pool, or admire the soothing works of avant-garde artist James Turrell. And, most important of all, lose yourself in a ruby glass of 2004 Colomé malbec, while lounging in the gaucho bar. Then dinner is served…

724 THE SECRET SENSATION OF POUSADA MARAVILHA

BRAZIL Fernando de Noronha is an impossibly beautiful secret island just an hour's flight from Recife in northern Brazil. A pristine National Marine Park, it was once visited by Charles Darwin and is so eco-orientated that on some beaches no sun cream or flip-flops are allowed. It has long been a hideaway for the Brazilian jet set, and is all the more alluring because the number of visitors permitted entry is limited to just 400 a day. Mention the island to any Brazilian and they will sigh with longing. UNESCO has measured the air as the second purest in the world after the Arctic.

Until recently, the island's only weakness was the lack of a decent hotel. Thus the *Pousada Maravilha*, owned by the scions of some of Brazil's wealthiest families, is reason to rejoice. There are just eight white, bright rooms, very contemporary, and all with billowy curtains and bouncy beds. Views stretch out onto a brilliant peacock-green ocean, and you can enjoy outdoor jungle showers, a private Japanese hot tub and lazy-time hammocks. If you can bear to leave your room, the sleek infinity-edged pool is rock-star cool, with funky low-level day beds and more of those awesome views.

During the day your best bet is to hire a beach buggy, bomb around on roads blissfully free of traffic lights and discover the most breathtaking deserted beaches – many of them lurking at the end of bumpy, dusty tracks, and some with cavorting dolphins. Divers will delight in the gin-clear water – visibility up to 50m – and ridiculously rich marine life; those who prefer to stay on shore can watch Green Sea baby turtles hatch on the beach in the dead of night. Showtime runs from December to May.

Returning to the hotel is the ultimate treat. Candlelit massages are knock-out; suppers waist-expanding. The staff are so accommodating that they even check you in for your flight out, so you have to face the airport only minutes before departure. Heaven.

725 GETTING HIGH IN CARACAS

VENEZUELA After a day or two spent amidst the chaos of Caracas, you'll most likely be looking to escape from the city. But before you leave, don't miss the teleférico cable-car ride up El Avila mountain, one of the few places you can enjoy the Venezuelan capital's best offerings: beautiful Caribbean weather in a spectacular setting. The ride up is not for those with vertigo: it's an eighteen-minute journey, one of the longest such trips in the Americas, and it takes you hundreds of metres above breathtaking cloudforest scenery, where trees and plants vie for limited space. As soon as you get over the first ridge, the noise around you abruptly quietens. With every passing minute you journey further from the city's relentless mass of concrete and glass. Caracas shrinks below you, and nature gradually vanquishes the urban sprawl.

At the top, you emerge in a different world. Seen in its geographical context, with a backdrop of tropical mountains, Caracas is deceptively attractive. On the other side, sharp slopes lead down to red-roofed cottages perched on the side of mountains and fields of flowers. Beyond them you can see the Caribbean Sea. The altitude makes the top sunny yet cool, and nature seems more vivid in comparison with the noisy capital. Birds are all around you, flying daringly close. Even the plants are different: highland varieties grow well here, 2100m above sea level. The attraction is not free from tat – there are several overpriced souvenir shops and, bizarrely, an ice rink – but it doesn't spoil the beauty of the place. Most locals head up here for sunset, choosing to spurn the view of twinkling hills opposite and snog furiously instead. A better option is the late morning on a weekday, when El Avila is just beginning to heat up at the top and the path is blissfully deserted.

726 TAKING A RING-SIDE SEAT AT THE PENÍNSULA VALDÉS

ARGENTINA "SHWOCK!" Or should that be "SHWAP!"?

It's difficult to pin down precisely the slapping sound that emanates when six tonnes of blubbery wet flesh collides, but while I was still working out if it actually wasn't more of a "SHWACK!" than either, the two huge bull elephant seals thundered together again, sending gallons of sea water flying in their titanic battle.

The object of their affection, a fertile female with a twinkle in her coal-black eyes, had spent the last twenty minutes preening her coat to the height of seductive softness but was now far more concerned with keeping her month-old pup well clear of the thriving mass.

This is October on the Península Valdés, a scrubby blob of land clinging to the side of Argentina's Atlantic coast that, other than being the only continental breeding ground for southern elephant seals, also happens to be one of the world's most significant marine reserves. The strip of sand on which the seals try proving their prowess is also crammed with some of the area's 20,000-strong sea-lion population.

Along the coast, a colony of Magellanic penguins have pocked the rugged hillside with their burrows, coming ashore each afternoon to make their comical but arduous waddle up the hill and home, while up to half of the world's southern right whales frolic in the peninsula's sheltered waters.

At the shingle spits of Caleta Valdés, and around wild Punta Norte, further up the coast, the sight of ominous black dorsal fins cruising just offshore is the precursor for one of nature's most incredible sights: killer whales storming the shingle banks, beaching themselves at up to 50kph in an attempt to snap up a baby sea lion or young elephant seal.

Back at the beach, though, mother and pup are still dodging the fighting fatties. Behind them both – and as equally impressed with her perfect pelt – two more gigantic males square up, clashing with such force that the sand shakes. And this time, there's no doubt that it's a "SHWACK!"…

727 ACROSS THE ALTIPLANO

CHILE For those unfazed by appalling dirt roads, stray llamas and a singular lack of road signs, a drive through the Chilean altiplano makes for an unforgettable trip. A high plateau connecting the eastern and western ranges of the Andes, the altiplano is shared by several neighbouring countries – but nowhere is the getting there more dramatic than in Chile, where your journey starts right by the ocean, passes through a desert and winds up 4500m above sea level.

Starting in the coastal town of Iquique in Chile's far north, the first leg of the journey takes you through the flat, scorched pampa of the Atacama Desert – a seemingly endless expanse of dull yellow and brown. Just when you think you'll never get out of this flat wasteland, you'll start climbing, gently at first, into the foothills of the Andes. A few hours later you're high in the mountains, in a world of turquoise lakes, snowcapped volcanoes and thin, freezing air. Beautiful and desolate in equal measure, the altiplano is sparsely populated by dwindling numbers of indigenous Aymara people, who've herded llamas up here for centuries; their semi-abandoned villages (most people now make their living in Iquique, returning to their home villages only for festivals and funerals), with whitewashed churches, make a striking sight.

For the ultimate altiplano experience, turn off the main road just before you hit the Bolivian border and take a bumpy ride north through Parque Nacional Isluga and onto Parque Nacional Lauca – your reward will be an extravaganza of salt flats, hot springs, volcanoes and wildlife. From Lauca you can head back down to civilization, ending your epic journey back by the ocean at the lively beach resort city of Arica, near the Peruvian border.

728 THE FRENZY OF BOI BUMBA

BRAZIL One of South America's greatest parties, Boi Bumba is a riot of colour, dancing, pageantry and parades on Parintins Island, deep in the Amazonian jungle, and as remote as any major festival, even in Brazil, gets – it's a two-day boat journey from "nearby" Manaus. Surrounded by more than 1000km of rainforest on all sides, the isolated location is key to making the festival special. Whereas partygoers in Rio or Salvador gather for the parades and disperse anonymously into the city afterwards, in Parintins the sixty-thousand-plus crowd is contained by the Amazon itself – over the three-day frenzy, the festival becomes a private party of familiar faces and dancing bodies.

The origins of the event, which takes place every June, lie in the northeastern Bumba Meu Boi festival (it was introduced to Parintins by emigrants from the state of Maranhão), telling the story of Pai Francisco, his wife Mae Catarina and their theft of a prize bull from a wealthy landowner. But it tells it on a huge scale, in a purpose-built forty-thousand-seat stadium called the Bumbódromo. Here, two competing teams, Caprichoso and Garantido, parade a series of vast floats made up of thirty-metre-tall serpent heads, jaguars, macaws and other rainforrest creatures, which change like scenes from a play, wheeled on by troupes dressed in Indian costumes and surrounded by one-hundred-strong drum orchestras and scores of scantily clad dancers. Against this spectacular backdrop, a whole host of characters tell the story, led by the beautiful feminine spirit of the rainforest, the Cunhã-Poranga, and an Indian shaman, both of whom emerge in a burst of fireworks from the mouth of a serpent or jaguar on the most extravagant and dramatic of the floats. Fans of each group are fiercely partisan, and roar their encouragement from the stadium stands throughout.

729 CHASING CONDORS
IN COLCA CANYON

PERU The rays of the morning sun begin to evaporate the mist that shrouds the depths of Peru's Colca Canyon. You've come out in the early hours to see the condor, or Andean vulture, in action, and as the mist dissipates, you can see hundreds of others have done the same. Many cluster at the mirador, or Cruz del Condor. Others perch above pre-Inca terraces embedded into walls twice as deep as the Grand Canyon. Audacious visitors clamber to the rocks below to see the condor, but a short hike along the rim of the canyon allows for a viewpoint that is less precarious and just as private.

Wrapped up against the cold, you whisper excitedly and wait for the show to begin. Suddenly, a condor rises on the morning thermals, soaring like an acrobat – so close you think you could reach out and touch its giant charcoal wings. It scours the surroundings, swooping lower and then higher, then lower again, in a rollercoaster pursuit of food. Soon it is joined by another bird, and another, in a graceful airborne ballet.

Eventually, the birds abandon the audience in their hunt for sustenance, and the mirador becomes home to a less elusive species. Peruvian women, brightly dressed in multilayered skirts, squat on their haunches, hawking food, drinks and souvenirs – everything from woolly Andean hats to purses embroidered with the condor.

The panpipe sounds of El Condor Pasa are played so often in Peru that they become the theme tune for many trips. Simon and Garfunkel might have made the song famous with their cover version, but its the eponymous bird that deserves a place in your Peruvian holiday.

730

BRAZIL has a monopoly on exhibitionism. There's no other country on the planet where the unbridled pursuit of pleasure is such a national obsession, transcending race, class and religion. Brazilian bacchanal reaches its apogee during Carnaval, when the entire country enters a collective state of alcohol-fuelled frenzy. Rio is home to the most glitzy and outrageous celebration of them all, an X-rated theatre of the absurd and the greatest spectacle of flesh, fetish and fantasy you are ever likely to see. For this four-day blowout before Lent the streets of the Cidade Maravilhosa are overrun with Amazonian-sized plumed headdresses, enormous floppy carrots, cavorting frogs, drag queens and head-to-toe gilded supermodels clad in impossibly tiny tassels, sequins and strategically applied body paint, challenging the ban on complete nudity.

The centrepiece of Carnaval is the parade of the sixteen samba schools (a neighbourhood association, there's nothing academic about it) down the kilometre-long parade strip of the colossal Sambódromo (a specially constructed parade stadium). Samba schools often hail from the poorest communities and spend nearly the entire year preparing a flamboyant allegory of their chosen theme, which is dramatized through a highly choreographed display of impassioned songs, wild dances, gigantic papier-mâché figures, lavish costumes and pulsating percussion.

It doesn't take long for such organized celebrations to erupt with infectious delirium as the whole city voraciously indulges in sensual pleasure at every turn – Rio's denizens, also known as cariocas, have never been known for their temperance. The neighbourhood blocos, or parades, are the most accessible, authentic and impromptu way to immerse yourself in the city's sexually charged atmosphere. In this freewheeling fantasy land – trucks are converted to moving stage sets with bands and loudspeakers – truly anything goes. Even the most rigid of hips will gyrate freely, and as the night unravels, the more you'll have to try to forget in the manhã.

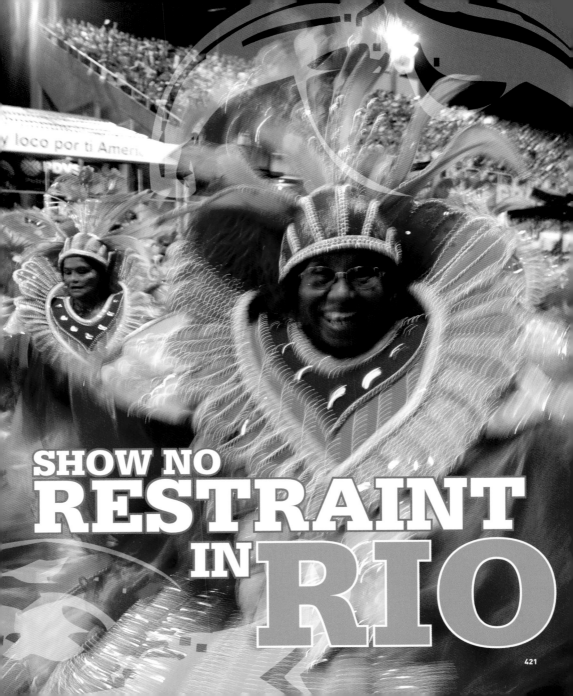

y loco por ti Americ

SHOW NO
RESTRAINT
IN RIO

731 TRAVERSING THE SALAR DE UYUNI

BOLIVIA Driving across the immaculate white expanse of the Salar de Uyuni, you'd think you were on another planet, so alien and inhospitable is the terrain. Some 3650m above sea level in the remote Andes of southwest Bolivia, the Salar is the largest salt flat in the world, a brilliant white and perfectly flat desert that stretches over 10,000 square kilometres.

In some places the salt is over 120m deep, saturated with water but with a thick surface crust patterned with strange polygonal lines of raised salt crystals that add to the unearthly feel. When dry, the salt shines with such intensity you'll find yourself reaching down to check that it's not ice or snow. After a heavy rainfall, the Salar transforms into an immense mirror, reflecting the sky and the surrounding snowcapped peaks so pristinely that at times the horizon disappears and the mountains

seem like islands floating in the sky. The best views are from Isla del Pescado, a rocky island at the centre of the Salar that's home to an extraordinary array of giant cactuses that somehow manage to thrive in this harsh saline environment.

To appreciate the sheer scale and surreal beauty of the landscape, it's worth taking the full four-day tour, travelling right across the Salar in a 4WD and sleeping in rudimentary huts and shelters on the shores of the lake; you can even stay in a hotel made entirely from salt. These trips also take in the Eduardo Abaroa Andean Fauna National Reserve, south of the Salar, a windswept region of high-altitude deserts, icebound volcanoes and mineral-stained lakes where you can see an unlikely variety of wildlife, including flocks of flamingoes and herds of vicuña, the delicate and extremely rare wild relative of the llama.

732 DRIVING THE CARRETERA AUSTRAL

CHILE The Carretera Austral – Chile's Southern Highway – begins nowhere and leads nowhere. Over 1000km in length, it was hewn and blasted through the wettest, greenest and narrowest part of the country. This sliver of Patagonia is a majestic land of snowcapped volcanoes, Ice Age glaciers, emerald fjords, turquoise lakes and jade-coloured rivers, set among lush temperate forest where giant trees seem to drip with rain the whole year long. The Carretera was built with the very purpose of settling this damp, secluded sliver of territory, but the only way to reach it from the rest of Chile is by boat or plane or overland from Argentina. Few roads can feel more remote.

Although some picturesquely rickety buses ply the route, they are irregular, unreliable and can't take you everywhere you'll want to go. It's far more rewarding, though not much quicker, to rent a 4WD pickup truck, pack a can of fuel and plentiful supplies and drive yourself. The slippery, loose-gravel surface demands the utmost respect, so don't expect to average more

than 50kph. As the locals will tell you: hereabouts, if you hurry, you never arrive! Lashing rain, gales, and passing vehicles – albeit few and far between – are the only likely hazards. The pleasures, however, are many and varied: make pit stops to wallow in the thermal springs at Cahuelmó after the bone-rattling ride, enjoy the warm hospitality and delicious cakes at *Casa Ludwig* in Puyuhuapi, or feast on roast Patagonian lamb by the fireside at *El Reloj* in Coyhaique. Most of the route affords incredible views of the Andean cordillera, and along the way you'll see dense groves of southern beech and immense lakes like miniature seas, the amazing "hanging glacier" in the Parque Nacional Queulat – or the Capilla de Mármol, a magical grotto carved into the blue and white limestone cliffs looming from Lago Carrera. But the best bit is the feeling of driving through utterly virgin lands – especially the southernmost stretch that leads to pioneering Villa O'Higgins, completed only in 2002. The road seems to fly over the barren crags to the place where, according to local legend, the Devil left his poncho.

733 SAVOURING CEVICHE IN LIMA

PERU On the edge of one of the world's least rained-upon deserts, Lima is among the driest cities on the planet, with miles of hot, red rocks stretching inland beyond its limits. You'd be forgiven for assuming its residents eke out a scorched, *Road Warrior*-style existence, but, as descendants of the Inca, innovators of irrigation systems and aqueducts, Peruvians have made their capital surprisingly verdant.

Lima's foliage finds sanctuary in manicured parks, as should you: they're perfect venues for picnicking with old travelling friends or new limeño acquaintances. Savoury anticuchos and spicy papas a la huancaína make a marvellous menu, but if you can pull together a few kitchen utensils and an ice-filled cooler, nothing completes the feast better than a freshly made ceviche.

Something like fish salad, ceviche is "cooked" in an acidic bath of lemon and lime juice and diced onion, tomato, cilantro and ají pepper, leaving the fish soft, moist and cool. Peruvians are proud of their national dish, and its preparation is a familiar ritual. Though other countries have tried to claim it, peruanos know it's as unique to their heritage as Machu Picchu and the Nazca lines. They've even mythologized it: leche de tigre, the bracingly sour "tiger's milk" that remains after the fish has been devoured, is a potent aphrodisiac.

So find a shady spot – one with a picnic table is best – and don't forget the choclo (boiled, large-kernel corn cobs) and sweet yams, ceviche's traditional accompaniments. Once the work's been divvied up and completed, sit back for a couple hours while the fish marinates. Savour the afternoon light, the warm chatter of nearby families, perhaps a slight breeze off a man-made pond. Take an icy sip of a pisco sour, and try to remember those desert dunes you heard about, now so very far from this lush oasis.

734 CATCHING A LAUNCH AT THE CENTRE SPATIAL GUYANAIS

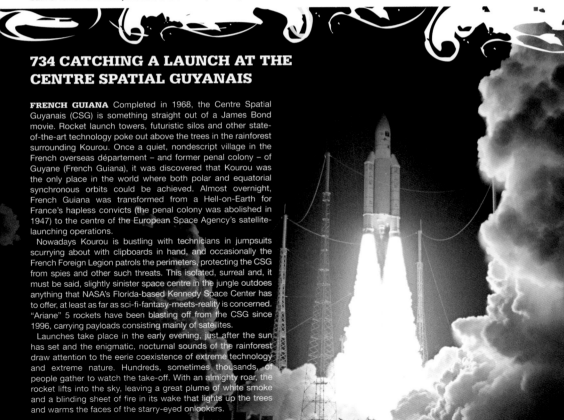

FRENCH GUIANA Completed in 1968, the Centre Spatial Guyanais (CSG) is something straight out of a James Bond movie. Rocket launch towers, futuristic silos and other state-of-the-art technology poke out above the trees in the rainforest surrounding Kourou. Once a quiet, nondescript village in the French overseas département – and former penal colony – of Guyane (French Guiana), it was discovered that Kourou was the only place in the world where both polar and equatorial synchronous orbits could be achieved. Almost overnight, French Guiana was transformed from a Hell-on-Earth for France's hapless convicts (the penal colony was abolished in 1947) to the centre of the European Space Agency's satellite-launching operations.

Nowadays Kourou is bustling with technicians in jumpsuits scurrying about with clipboards in hand, and occasionally the French Foreign Legion patrols the perimeters, protecting the CSG from spies and other such threats. This isolated, surreal and, it must be said, slightly sinister space centre in the jungle outdoes anything that NASA's Florida-based Kennedy Space Center has to offer, at least as far as sci-fi-fantasy-meets-reality is concerned. "Ariane" 5 rockets have been blasting off from the CSG since 1996, carrying payloads consisting mainly of satellites.

Launches take place in the early evening, just after the sun has set and the enigmatic, nocturnal sounds of the rainforest draw attention to the eerie coexistence of extreme technology and extreme nature. Hundreds, sometimes thousands, of people gather to watch the take-off. With an almighty roar, the rocket lifts into the sky, leaving a great plume of white smoke and a blinding sheet of fire in its wake that lights up the trees and warms the faces of the starry-eyed onlookers.

WALKING ON ICE: THE
PERITO
MORENO
GLACIER

735

ARGENTINA Fed by one of the planet's largest freshwater reserves – the Southern Patagonian Icecap – the Perito Moreno Glacier is the world's biggest ice-cube dispenser. It could also be described as a gigantic frozen Blue Lady, thanks to centuries of compression which has turned the deepest ice a deep shade of curaçao, whose sapphire veins can be tantalizingly glimpsed through plunging fissures. This icy leviathan of a cocktail is one to linger over, gradually letting it intoxicate you, as you survey its infiniteness from the viewing platform across the Lago Argentino. One of the few advancing glaciers in the world, it does move, but, well, at glacial speed. It's noisy, too, squeaking and whining and occasionally even exploding, as every few minutes a wardrobe-sized chunk splashes into the lake's chilly waters and bobs away as an iceberg. But the spectacular event you'll be hoping to see, the "ruptura", when Perito Moreno lunges forward, relatively speaking, forms a dam of ice and

then violently breaks, happens only every four to five years. And throughout the 1990s it didn't happen at all...

A great way of getting to know this icy beast is to go for a walk on it. Standing on the glacier, you can see every crack and crevice, every tiny pinnacle. Even on a warm summer's day, the glacier, unsurprisingly, remains chilly, so wrap up well. Protect your eyes and exposed skin from the immense white glare with sunglasses and a high-factor sunscreen. The ice can be slippery, but it's not dangerous as long as you stick to sensible footwear and snap on the crampons issued by all the tour companies offering glacier-treks. They're a bit like soccer boots, but the spikes are adapted to snow and ice. And when you've walked far enough, you'll be glad to know that most treks end up with a tumbler of whisky on the rocks, made with ice-cubes chipped out of the glacier, of course.

736 GOING DOWNHILL IN THE ANDES

ARGENTINA Skip the beach this year. Instead, embrace winter in July and get a tan on the sunny slopes of the Andes in the middle of Argentina's Lake District at Bariloche, a laconic town turned major South American skiing destination. Surrounded by spectacular forests, pristine rivers and lakes, rifted valleys and towering alpine peaks, and with average seasonal temperatures around 4ºC, it's no wonder that this is prime ski country for South Americans. Luckily, since the rest of the world hasn't quite caught on, you won't spend a fortune on rentals and lift tickets, or wait a lifetime in line.

Start by hitting the slopes at Cerro Catedral, the oldest, largest and most developed ski resort in South America, which features a new gondola, a vertical drop of 1070m and over 75km of marked trails, gullies and chutes – the longest run is 4km long – to say nothing of the off-piste possibilities, with back-country riding that rivals anything in the French Alps or Colorado. Skiing is a lot less common in South America than elsewhere in the world, and mid-level skiers will find themselves in plenty of good company here. On the other hand, if you're a superstar on the snow, the more challenging pistes are much less crowded and yours for the shredding.

Unlike the massive resorts of US and European ski centres, Argentina's mountain destinations are decidedly more low-key in terms of their sprawl, though don't think for a moment that this means there is less going on. Argentines are well known for their indulgence in the refined institution of après-ski, and Bariloche's off-slope adventures include dozens of discos, casinos and wine bars, with ample restaurants for savouring Argentina's scrumptious cuisine. After all, what would a week (a month? an entire season?) on the slopes be without exploring the excellent winter nightlife?

737 A ROYAL WELCOME AT HOTEL CENTINELA

CHILE As daylight fades, the snow on the cone of the volcano across the lake turns pink, and the shards of light that dance on the water's surface disappear. The clear blue sky changes to pastel orange, then darkens, filling with stars. The day's warmth dissipates with the sunlight, and you and your fellow guests turn away from the view to enjoy the other amenities *Hotel Centinela* has to offer – a home-cooked dinner and delicious local wines await.

At the end of a peninsula and within a nature reserve, *Hotel Centinela* provides a peaceful retreat from modern life. When it was first built in 1914, the hotel served as a summer house for wealthy Chilean families and the only access was via Lake Llanquihue. Today there is a boat for trips on the lake, but the hotel is reached by a rugged road from neighbouring Puerto Octay.

Time continues to go slowly here, though, and it seems like little has changed since those early years. You'll find beautiful period furniture and polished wooden walls and floors in the twelve bedrooms within the main building. Outside, a handful of lakeside cabins provide romantic privacy or a good base for families. With such a glorious setting and beautiful facilities, the place seems fit for royalty.

In fact, it has been: in 1931, the Prince of Wales visited with his brother Albert. Five years later, the Prince of Wales became King Edward VIII, but abdicated shortly after ascending the throne in order to marry American divorcée Wallis Simpson. Albert became King George VI. Although the details of their stay are somewhat murky, the hotel owner proudly shows off the suite where Edward stayed. His younger brother had less salubrious digs – who could have guessed he would become king?

After dinner, as you huddle by the open fire, sharing stories beneath the high wooden ceiling of the great hall, you can almost feel the echoes of the past.

738 PIRANHA-FISHING IN THE JUNGLE

ECUADOR Halfway through a five-day trip in the Amazon the crew, having returned from voting for their next president, declared the afternoon be spent hunting for the Amazon's most notorious predators. This tag might be applied to logging crews, missionaries or mosquitoes; that day, it was the piranha.

Feared by many for their flesh-stripping teeth and frenzied mob attacks, piranha are surrounded by no shortage of myths – many of which Romero, the guide, was quick to dispel. Scrambling into the motorized dugout canoe the group headed upriver to find some still water – classic piranha territory. Romero handed out the rather primitive bait and tackle: a large stick, a piece of twine, a very large metal hook and a chunk of somewhat ripe chicken. An hour later, and there hadn't been as much as a nibble. Enthusiasm was on the wane, and the ranks began discussing a return to comfortable hammocks and warm cans of flat Venezuelan beer. Then a cry from the back signalled that all was not in vain – a line had found its target.

Unhooking the fish proved a challenge, Romero dropping it to the bottom of the crowded canoe instead of the bottom of the ocean. Faces instantly turned from surprise to blind panic, which increased when the murky water in the boat proved a good hiding place. Only when the canoe was free of passengers could the fish finally be retrieved.

739 VISITING THE LAST PANAMA-HAT WEAVERS

ECUADOR If you're going to make the mistake of thinking a Panama hat comes from Panama, don't do so in Ecuador. Authentic Panamas – or sombreros de paja toquilla, as they call them locally – are only woven in the Andean country, from the straw of the toquilla plant, which grows in the swamps near Ecuador's central coast. The origin of the misnomer comes from the hat's widespread use by the workers who built the Panama Canal from 1904 to 1914. Toquilla hats have been woven in Ecuador for at least five hundred years, but in the face of cheap Chinese competition, lower demand and the massive emigration of young Ecuadoreans, the traditionally woven Panama hat is now an endangered species.

It's well worth seeking out the last few artisans who create the very best superfinos. Most tourists on the trail go to Cuenca, a weaving centre in the southern highlands. A better option is to head west to Montecristi, which is to Panama-hat lovers what Havana is to cigar aficionados. It's no tourist Mecca: the dust-and-concrete town is an inauspicious centre for the production of some of the most expensive headgear in the world. But ask around for a local comisionista (middlemen who travel around villages and buy hats from weavers) and arrange a trip to meet the weavers in nearby villages such as Pile.

The time to arrive is just after dawn, when the light is atmospheric and the heat and humidity are perfect for weaving. The contrast between the beautiful hats – the finest of which are woven so tightly they look like off-white cotton – and the conditions in which they are produced is stark. The weavers, who spend up to four months weaving each hat, live in ragged redbrick dwellings with rusting corrugated-iron roofs, linked by degraded dirt streets patrolled by strutting chickens and shuffling pigs. Be sure to visit the straw-cutters, too, and accompany them on a hike to see the plants growing. The more you see of the hats and the weavers, the better equipped you'll be to buy your own.

740 STAR-GAZING ON CERRO MAMALLUCA

CHILE In the northern half of Chile, the driest place on Earth, clouds are virtually unknown and the skies are of the brightest blue. At night, far away from the lights of major settlements, you can look up at a dark vault simply shimmering with stars. The near-perfect visibility almost every night of the year makes the region ideal for observing the universe – indeed, there are more astronomical observatories here than anywhere else on Earth – but you don't need to be an astronomer to get a great view.

Some of the world's most powerful computerized telescopes reside here, but you can also catch sight of constellations such as the Southern Cross and familiar heavenly bodies like Jupiter or Mars at more modest observatories, such as Mamalluca. Set aside one evening, resist that extra pisco sour and book one of the regular stargazing tours that depart in the wee hours. These take you high up on Cerro Mamalluca, where the darkness is absolute and the air is crisp. There's the classic visit – a short talk giving you a grounding in basic astronomy, followed by a few minutes looking through a telescope – or the Andean Cosmovision tour, in which guides explain how the pre-Columbian peoples interpreted the night sky, and perform native songs, with flutes and drums accompanying mystic verses, speaking of a local cosmology dating back thousands of years.

741 SWEPT OFF YOUR FEET IN BUENOS AIRES

ARGENTINA When it first emerged in the city's brothels and slums sometime in the 1890s, the world's sexiest ballroom dance, the tango, horrified the genteel residents of Buenos Aires. Some of the city's more liberal-minded upper-class youths fell in love with tango, though, and brought it to Paris, where the dance's characteristic haunting melodies, seductive gazes and prostitute-inspired split skirts took the capital of passion by storm. By the 1910s tango's popularity had gone global, but Buenos Aires was and remains the spiritual and professional home of both the music form and dance.

If you want to keep a low profile, head to a tango show – aimed squarely at tourists, these are glitzy, polished, expensive affairs where the dance is performed on stage by professionals. More earthy and authentic – and worth seeking out – are the milongas, or tango gatherings, where everyone takes part. These range from stately mid-afternoon affairs in the city's exquisite Art Deco tea salons to smoky, late-night events behind unmarked doors deep in the suburbs, and to youthful tango-meets-techno milongas in the city's trendy districts. Long-running milongas include the traditional Tango Ideal at the Confitería Ideal and the hip Parakultural events in Palermo.

For those who want to take part, some milongas are preceded by a tango lesson – you'll need several of these, and, if you're a woman, a killer pair of heels – before you can master the basics of the fairly complex dance. It's also perfectly acceptable to turn up, albeit smartly dressed, and simply enjoy the music while watching the dancers glide with apparent ease across the floor. Beware, though: the music and the locals may have you under their spell – and in their arms – faster than you may have anticipated.

742

GETTING SOAKED AT IGUAZÚ

ARGENTINA Upon first seeing Iguazú Falls, all Eleanor Roosevelt could manage was "Poor Niagara". Every year, tens of thousands of visitors from around the world try to evaluate the sheer dimension of this natural miracle – a collection of more than two-hundred cascades thundering over an eighty-metre cliff – and usually fail. However you spell it – Iguazú, Iguaçu or Iguassu – the Guaraní name, translating as "Big Water", is something of an understatement. Situated on the border of Brazil, Argentina and Paraguay, the falls are surrounded by lush tropical forest that's home to more than 2000 species of flora, over 500 bird species and approximately 80 different mammals.

Many marvel at these massive falls from the relative dryness of the Brazilian side, but you are advised against looking down at them from a Brazilian helicopter, for ecological reasons. You can even watch these gushing waterfalls rival Robert De Niro and Jeremy Irons for the leading role in the 1986 epic film *The Mission*. But the true way to experience the rapids, or cataratas, as the locals call them, is to land right in the action and get soaked to the skin. Leave your state-of-the-art digital camera and your iPod in your hotel room; think twice before wearing that new crimson top that might run or the T-shirt that becomes transparent when wet; don't even bother with the waterproof gear the guidebooks tell you to bring. Just give the boat crew the kick they never tire of: take a soothingly tepid bath in the world's biggest open-air shower, the ominously named Devil's Throat, the most majestic of Iguazú's numerous cascades.

743

BRAZIL A tentative peek from the ramp reveals treetops far below and the beachfront high-rises of São Conrado in the distance. A safety briefing follows, and then, strapped side-by-side with your instructor, you charge down the ramp. After the initial pleasant surprise of realizing that you haven't plummeted to your death, you can start to enjoy the flight. Soaring past a sheer cliff face, feeling the lift as the sea breeze takes you vertically up, is an experience you will never forget. Then finally, cruising in over backyard swimming pools, you come in to land on the beach, which twenty minutes ago was about five kilometres away and five hundred metres below.

FLYING DOWN TO
RIO

744 ON THE TRAIL OF BUTCH CASSIDY AND THE SUNDANCE KID

BOLIVIA No one really knows how Butch Cassidy and the Sundance Kid spent their final days. Ruours still abound, enhanced by the classic 1969 Hollywood film starring Paul Newman and Robert Redford. But this much is true: the outlaws pulled their last heist – stealing the $90,000 payroll of a mine company – in Bolivia.

To pick up their trail, start in the easygoing southern Altiplano town of Tupiza, set in a lush valley that slices through striking desert landscape. It was in the leafy main square that the gunslingers devised their plan to overtake the payroll transport, and locals can show you where they lived – in a house just behind the mansion of the mining family they were to rob. From there, take a scenic jeep tour 100km northwest to the dusty village of San Vicente, where Butch and Sundance, with the military hot on their heels, sought shelter for the night. It is here, according to the prevailing belief, that the pair met their end inside a simple adobe home after a gunfight with a small military patrol. But will a close inspection of the hut and a visit to their unmarked grave in the cemetery be enough to convince you?

745 CAPOEIRA UP CLOSE

BRAZIL There's not meant to be any physical contact in this age-old, ritualistic melding of martial arts and breakdancing. Your instructor probably explained that, though unless you happen to speak Portuguese you probably didn't understand (and if you did, would you trust it to be true?). But you're ready to give it a whirl; who knows, you may even get to sing or play an instrument to help keep the beat – tambourine, drum, some kind of gourd with strung beads. Probably not the berimbau, a stringed bow struck while positioned against your stomach; that looks more difficult. In fact, it all looks difficult: how can the dancer-combatants fly and spin with such grace, spending as much time on their hands and airborne as on their feet? Maybe you should just passively observe, or head back to any number of street corners in Salvador, where capoeiristas cartwheel and kick encircled by onlookers. And save your own handstand prowess for another day.

746 TAKING TIME OVER MATÉ

URUGUAY The process is long, the preparation meticulous. The matecito, a wooden, hollowed-out gourd, is stuffed with yerba herb. A bombilla, a straw-shaped tube of silver, thrust into the leaves, then water – very hot but not boiling – trickled down its side, slowly, carefully, wetting the yerba from below.

"¿Como lo tomás?" the cebador, the maté-maker, asks you. "Amargo", you reply. Without sugar. The connoisseur's choice. You take a suck. Long and smooth. And bitter – a shock to first-timers, who are far better off taking it dulce (sweet). You pass it on, with your right hand, and clockwise, as tradition dictates.

A little more yerba, a little more water. The matecito is emptied, the process started afresh.

MISCELLANY

FIVE FAMOUS FIESTAS

Virgen de la Candelaria (February 2)

Saint's Day of a particular representation of the Virgin Mary revered in many South American cities.

Carnaval (late February or early March)

The pre-Lenten carnival celebrated all over South America. The most extravagant is of course in Rio, but other cities such as Salvador de Bahia in Brazil and Oruro in Bolivia also hold massive celebrations.

Semana Santa (March or April)

The Easter Holy Week is marked throughout the region with colourful religious processions.

Corpus Christi (June)

Another major Catholic religious festival celebrated with processions and costumed dancers, most notably in Peru and Venezuela.

Todos Santos/ Dia de los Muertos (November 1 and 2)

On All Saint's Day people in Peru and Bolivia go to the cemetery to commemorate their dead relatives, bringing them food and drink and sometimes taking them out of their tombs.

EL DORADO

Despite centuries of exploration, legends persist of fabulous cities of gold, known as Paititi or El Dorado, hidden deep in the Amazon rainforest or the remote Andes. And substantial new ruins are still being discovered every few years. **Machu Picchu** is the most famous of these, but others include **Ciudad Perdida**, in Colombia, and **Vilcabamba**, **Kuelap**, **Choquequirau** and **Gran Pajaten**, all in Peru.

SOUTH AMERICA ON FILM

Blood of the Condor (Yawar mallku), 1968. Scathing attack on the impact of US imperialism on the indigenous people of the Bolivian Andes.

Central Station, 1998. Heart-rending story of a Brazilian woman who abandons her cynicism to help a homeless boy search for the father he's never known.

City of God, 2002. Gripping portrayal of life and death among the teenage drug gangs in the slums of Rio de Janeiro.

The Motorcycle Diaries, 2004. Delightful adaptation of Che Guevara's diary, in which the future revolutionary and a friend travel across South America by motorbike in search of adventure.

The Official Story, 1985. Harrowing tale of an Argentine woman who has to face up to the truth about military rule as she discovers her adopted daughter was stolen from one of the "disappeared".

CAFÉ

The plant may have originated in Africa, but South America has a strong claim to producing the best coffee in the world. The largest producers, Brazil and Colombia, are also the most passionate consumers, and both tend to keep the best of their coffee crop to themselves. In Colombia, mild black coffee known as tinto is sold from Thermoses on every street corner, while in Brazil, small, strong cups of cafezinho are seen as an essential accompaniment to almost every activity.

HAMMOCK SIESTAS

Of all the inventions of the indigenous peoples of South America, the hammock is one the greatest contributions to world civilization. Strung up in an instant anywhere there are trees, roof beams or upright poles, the hammock is both a perfect place to adjust to the local pace of life and a cool and comfortable alternative to a bed.

"God is big, but the forest is bigger"

Brazilian proverb

CUISINE

With its mixture of European, African, Asian and indigenous influences, South America boasts some fantastic food. The finest national cuisines are considered to be those of Peru, Argentina and Brazil, in that order. Don't miss Argentine **beef**, **ceviche** in Peru or **fejoada**, a classic Brazilian stew of black beans and meat. For the more adventurous, there's **cuy** (roast guinea pig) in Peru and Ecuador, and **hormiga culona** (big-butt queen ants with a nutty flavour) in northern Colombia.

DANCE THE NIGHT AWAY

Wherever you go in South America you'll be surrounded by music that encapsulates the majesty of the landscape and the idiosyncrasy of the people – and makes you want to head for the dancefloor. Try **salsa** moves in Cali, **tango** in Buenos Aires, **samba** in Rio de Janeiro or **merengue** in Caracas.

HIGHEST ANDEAN PEAKS

Aconcagua	6962m Argentina
Ojos del Salado	6893m Chile (world's highest volcano)
Monte Pissis	6795m Argentina
Bonete	6759m Argentina
Tres Cruces Sur	6748m Argentina/Chile

FOOTBALL

It's often said that the unofficial religion of South America is football (futbol in Spanish, futebol in Portuguese). Everywhere you go you'll find people watching, talking about and playing what's known as the beautiful game. Almost every village has a football pitch, and it's not unusual to come across South Americans who are the proud owners of a pair of football boots but have no other shoes. Uruguay, Argentina and Brazil have produced a series of World Cup-winning teams, and the continent has also produced the two greatest footballers ever: Argentine Diego Maradona and Brazilian Edson Nascimiento da Silva, better known as **Pelé**.

"Those who serve a revolution plough the sea"

Simón Bolívar

LIBERATORS

In most South American countries the wars of independence from Spain in the early nineteenth century are seen as national epics of sacrifice and heroism, and the leaders of that struggle are lionized as near-godlike figures. None is more revered than **Simón Bolívar**, known as the Liberator, whose armies drove the Spanish out of Venezuela, Colombia, Ecuador, Peru and finally Bolivia, which was named in his honour. You'll find statues of Bolívar throughout South America, above all in his native Venezuela, where any disrespect to his image can still get you in serious trouble. Ernesto "**Che**" Guevara, who died in 1967 trying to start a continent-wide revolution, is accorded similar reverence.

COCA

Demonized in Europe and the United States as the raw material for the production of cocaine, the small green coca-leaf has been used for thousands of years by the indigenous people of the Andes as both a mild stimulant and a key ingredient in traditional rituals and medicine. In Peru and Bolivia, where it's still legal, it's considered an important symbol of indigenous identity. When made into a herbal tea, it's also a useful treatment for altitude sickness.

LANGUAGE

South America is dominated by two main languages brought over by European conquerors in the sixteenth century: **Portuguese** in Brazil, and **Spanish** almost everywhere else. The exceptions are the small countries of Guyana, French Guyana (technically part of France) and Suriname, which are English, French and Dutch-speaking respectively. Throughout the continent, hundreds of indigenous languages are still spoken, some by only a few hundred people, others by nations of millions. These are particularly concentrated in the Andean regions of Peru, Bolivia and Ecuador and in Paraguay, which has the highest level of bilingualism in the world.

CHOICE SOUVENIRS

Hammocks from Colombia.

Panama hats from Ecuador (despite the name).

Ponchos and other weavings from the indigenous markets of the Andes.

Magical Candomblé beads from Brazil.

Yerba mate cups and drinking straws from Argentina.

"If you don't have a solution, you don't have a problem"

South American proverb

RELIGION

The vast majority of people in South America are Roman Catholics, following the religion brought over by the Spanish and Portuguese conquerors in the sixteenth century. However, many combine their Catholicism with animist religious beliefs inherited from their indigenous ancestors, often involving the worship of natural features such as mountains and rivers. African beliefs brought over by slaves in the colonial period also remain strong in regions with large black populations, particularly Brazil. And recent decades have seen a surge in the number of people turning to Evangelical Protestant sects, many of them funded from the United States.

FIVE GREAT READS

Of Love and Shadows **Isabel Allende** Powerful love story set in an imaginary country of arbitrary arrests, sudden disappearances and executions that closely resembles the author's Chilean homeland in the 1970s and 1980s.

Dona Flor and Her Two Husbands **Jorge Amado** Supernatural romance set in the Brazilian state of Bahia. When Flor's first husband comes back from the dead, how can she resist his advances?

Labyrinths **Jorge Luis Borges** Collection of essays and short stories that encapsulate the unique style and approach of Argentina's greatest writer.

One Hundred Years of Solitude **Gabriel García Márquez** Epic tale of a Colombian family in love and war that defined magical realism.

Conversation in the Cathedral **Mario Vargas Llosa** A labyrinth of power, corruption and the search for identity in Peru.

UNFORGETTABLE HOTELS

Albergue Ecologico Chalalá, Parque Nacional Madidi, Bolivia. Traditionally built eco-lodge run by the indigenous Quechua-Tacana people in the Amazon rainforest.

Alvear Palace Hotel, Buenos Aires, Argentina. Exquisite 1930s hotel in the heart of the country's capital, oozing old-world charm.

Hacienda Los Lingues, San Fernando, Chile. Beautifully preserved colonial hacienda converted into a luxury hotel but still inhabited and operated as a ranch by one of Chile's aristocratic families.

Hotel Glória, Rio de Janeiro, Brazil. A palatial 1920s hotel with an unrivalled setting near the centre of Rio, offering spectacular views of the city.

Hotel Monasterio, Cusco, Peru. Luxurious establishment set in a beautifully restored sixteenth-century Spanish monastery.

VISITING THE PITS OF HELL • SHOPPING AT THE MOTHER OF ALL MARKETS • LOSING YOUR SHIRT IN MACAU • PEAKING EARLY IN HONG KONG • JOINING THE PILGRIM'S TRAIL AT EMEI SHAN • STALKING CRANES AT CAOHAI • GETTING LOST IN THE FORBIDDEN CITY • CRUISING THE THREE GORGES • FACES FROM THE PAST: XI'AN'S TERRACOTTA ARMY • THEY EAT SHOOTS AND LEAVES: PANDA CUBS IN CHENGDU • GETTING BEATEN AT WUDANG SHAN • QUALITY SPACE: ADMIRING SUZHOU'S GARDENS • GETTING SOUSED AT SISTERS' MEAL FESTIVAL • CRACKING THE ICE FESTIVAL • HORSING ABOUT WITH THE MONGOLS • GORGING ON DIM SUM IN GUANGZHOU • ON FOOT THROUGH TIGER LEAPING GORGE • BLOWN AWAY BY THE GREAT WALL • TAKING TEA IN CHENGDU • RELAXING IN TROPICAL TAKETOMI-JIMA • UNSCROLLING THE LI RIVER • DWARFED BY HONG KONG'S SKYSCRAPERS • STEP AEROBICS: CLIMBING HUANG SHAN • CIRCUITING THE JOKHANG, LHASA • VIEWING THE ARIRANG MASS GYMNASTICS FESTIVAL • BEACH LOUNGING AT BEIDAIHE • SWEET DREAMS JAPANESE-STYLE • JOUSTING FOR A TASTE OF BEIJING DUCK • CLIMBING FUJI • TREKKING THROUGH THE VALLEY OF THE GEYSERS • LOSING TRACK OF TIME: BEIJING TO MOSCOW ON THE TRANS-SIBERIAN • SUSHI AT 300KPH: RIDING THE SHINKANSEN • FILLING UP ON LITTLE EATS • VISITING HENAN'S MONA LISA • STROLLING THE SHANGHAI BUND • BUDDHIST BOOT CAMP AT HAEINSA TEMPLE • A FLORAL WAVE OF CHERRY BLOSSOMS • TSUKIJI: WHERE THE SEAFOOD GETS SERIOUS • GETTING NAKED IN RURAL JAPAN • SHOOTING TO THE TOP OF THE WORLD'S TALLEST BUILDING • WALKING WITH THE QUEEN OF HEAVEN • EYEBALLING SOLDIERS IN THE "SCARIEST PLACE ON EARTH" • CHASING TEMPLES IN SHIKOKU • SKIING IN THE LAND OF FIRE AND ICE • TREKKING ANCIENT PATHS IN BHUTAN • SLEEPING IN A YURT • SITTING RINGSIDE AT A SUMO TOURNAMENT • BATHING WITH SNOW MONKEYS • LIVING THE NOMADIC LIFE • SAUNTERING THROUGH SEOUL • GETTING STEAMY IN A JJIMJILBANG • WALKING AMONG SILLA ROYALTY • CELEBRATING THE DRAGON BOAT RACES • NAADAM: THE MANLY GAMES • MORNING PRAYERS AT DISKIT MONASTERY • A LITTLE LOCAL FLAVOUR IN PYONGYANG • PAST MEETS PRESENT AT GION MATSURI • TWO WHEELS GOOD: BIKING AROUND RURAL YANGSHUO • RIDING BY BUS TO DÊGÊ • SHOPPING AT THE MOTHER OF ALL MARKETS • LOSING YOUR SHIRT IN MACAU • PEAKING EARLY IN HONG KONG • JOINING THE PILGRIM'S TRAIL AT EMEI SHAN • STALKING CRANES AT CAOHAI • GETTING LOST IN THE FORBIDDEN CITY • CRUISING THE THREE GORGES • FACES FROM THE PAST: XI'AN'S TERRACOTTA ARMY • THEY EAT SHOOTS AND LEAVES: PANDA CUBS IN CHENGDU • GETTING BEATEN AT WUDANG SHAN • QUALITY SPACE: ADMIRING SUZHOU'S GARDENS • CRACKING THE ICE FESTIVAL • GETTING SOUSED AT SISTERS' MEAL FESTIVAL • HORSING ABOUT WITH THE MONGOLS • GORGING ON DIM SUM IN GUANGZHOU • ON FOOT THROUGH TIGER LEAPING GORGE • BLOWN AWAY BY THE GREAT WALL • TAKING TEA IN CHENGDU • RELAXING IN TROPICAL TAKETOMI-JIMA • UNSCROLLING THE LI RIVER • DWARFED BY HONG KONG'S SKYSCRAPERS • STEP AEROBICS: CLIMBING HUANG SHAN • BEACH LOUNGING AT BEIDAIHE • SWEET DREAMS JAPANESE-STYLE • JOUSTING FOR A TASTE OF BEIJING DUCK • CIRCUITING THE JOKHANG • CLIMBING FUJI • TREKKING THROUGH THE VALLEY OF THE GEYSERS • LOSING TRACK OF TIME: BEIJING TO MOSCOW ON THE TRANS-SIBERIAN • SUSHI AT 300KPH: RIDING THE SHINKANSEN • FILLING UP ON LITTLE EATS • VISITING HENAN'S MONA LISA • STROLLING THE SHANGHAI BUND • A FLORAL WAVE OF CHERRY BLOSSOMS • TSUKIJI: WHERE THE SEAFOOD GETS SERIOUS • GETTING NAKED IN RURAL JAPAN • SHOOTING TO THE TOP OF THE WORLD'S TALLEST BUILDING • WALKING WITH THE QUEEN OF HEAVEN • BUDDHIST BOOT CAMP AT HAEINSA TEMPLE • EYEBALLING SOLDIERS IN THE

CENTRAL & NORTHERN ASIA

747–808

RUSSIA

KAZAKHSTAN

MONGOLIA

CRACKING THE
ICE FESTIVAL
751

SKIING IN
THE LAND OF
FIRE AND ICE
804

SHOPPING AT
THE MOTHER OF
ALL MARKETS

NORTH
KOREA

VIEWING THE ARIRANG
MASS GYMNASTICS FESTIVAL

VISITING THE
PITS OF HELL
792

782

BLOWN AWAY BY
THE GREAT WALL
770

789

BATHING WITH SNOW MONKEYS
777

BUDDHIST BOOT CAMP
AT HAEINSA TEMPLE
769

TURKMENISTAN

UZBEKISTAN

CIRCUITING
THE JOKHANG
767

CHINA

SOUTH
KOREA

JAPAN

BHUTAN

SHOOTING TO THE TOP OF
THE WORLD'S TALLEST BUILDING
797

TAIWAN

747 STALKING CRANES AT CAOHAI

CHINA If it's beauty you're after, the small town of Weining in Guizhou province's far western reaches will certainly disappoint. Impoverished, shabby and built up in charmless grey concrete, it is even less appealing than usual if you arrive one frigid night after a shocking six-hour bus ride to find the only hotel's facilities don't include hot water or heating. Or food, for that matter. You'll probably wind up eating grilled potato slices at a roadside barbeque run by women of the Muslim Hui nationality, one of China's many ethnic minority groups. As your mouth buzzes from the amount of chilli they've powdered your dinner with, you'll be relieved to find the journey here hasn't been wasted.

Caohai, the "Grass Sea", is a reed-fringed lake on Weining's outskirts which goes a long way towards making up for the town. A placid spread of water reflecting cloudless skies, it's also the winter residence of four hundred rare black-necked cranes. Seeing these is as easy as renting a punt and poling up to them, an extraordinary liberty in a country where human population pressure makes it unusual (except in markets and on menus) to get on familiar terms with wildlife.

So hire a punt and get out into the maze of channels cut through Caohai's reedy shallows. Weining's traffic, crowds and coal dust will be forgotten in a light breeze, the whisper of the punt pushing through reeds, and small flocks of geese and ducks bobbing on the lake. With luck, you should be able to corner a group or two of cranes, stately creatures stalking through the water, their black heads held high. Considerately, they'll let you get within telephoto range before flapping lazily away to join another distant group. Weining turns out to be not so disappointing after all.

748 TSUKIJI: WHERE SEAFOOD GETS SERIOUS

JAPAN Tsukiji does fish in the way that DeBeers dabbles in diamonds. Over four hundred different types of seafood – from mussels to marlin – wash up here every day, from sixty countries on six continents.

At 5am, when the surrounding streets of Chuo-ku are dark and deserted, the 56 acres of reclaimed land that make up the Tokyo Metropolitan Central Wholesale Market, or Tsukiji Fish Market as it's more commonly known, are a hive of activity. Small, motorized carts nip about the network of wholesalers' stalls, dodging the throngs of people who are washing, weighing, slicing, and selling. Stern-looking vendors specialize in scallops, clams and curious-looking crustaceans, while others do a swift trade in pickled octopus and bottles of thick black squid ink. Elsewhere, huge torpedoes of tuna are skilfully prepared for the kitchen – they're so big it takes three people to filet them, carefully running an oroshi hocho, a five-foot curved blade, through the chunky flesh.

Every day, nearly 2300 tonnes of fish – most of it still very much alive – passes through Tsukiji. Working your way around the stalls involves negotiating crates of ice-packed pufferfish; red snapper; and giant, round opah, their wet scales shining like silver under the glare of a dozen bare light bulbs. You'll need to slip past polystyrene boxes bubbling with squid, urchins, sea cucumbers and spider crabs. There are tubs of squelchy seaweed; large white blobs that look like dumplings but are decidedly not; and a rainbow of red, yellow, pink and green fish, their names – scribbled in kanji symbols – a mystery to most. Roe comes in all shades of rouge, giant clams are translucent white, while the deep-golden pellets selling for ¥165,000 a kilo are actually dried sea-slug caviar. And at the very centre of the market are the biggest blue-fin tunas you will ever see, their steaming, ice-frosted carcasses – tagged with their weight and country of origin – laid out in formation, ready for auction.

749 CRUISING THE THREE GORGES

CHINA There's something about China that's constantly cutting you down to size: the density of the crowds, the five thousand years of history, the complexity of the language, the awkwardness of chopsticks… But often it's the scenery alone, no more so than at Qutang Gorge, the first and most ferocious of the famous Three Gorges that together flank a 300-kilometre-long stretch of the Yangzi. "A thousand seas poured into one teacup" was how the poet Su Dongpo described this narrow, steep-sided canyon – though that was before the river had been domesticated by the dynamite and dams that have cleared hidden shoals, raised water levels and slowed the flow. Yet it's not to be scoffed at even today, and you won't find much excuse to hide in your cabin for the duration of the three-day cruise between Chongqing and Hubei provinces (not that a spartan four square metres of lumpy mattress and blocked toilet costing the price of a three-star hotel room is any competition). The landscape might be humbling but it also demands to be admired. The best of it isn't on the Yangzi but the offshoot Daning River, through the Little Three Gorges – a cool stretch of lime-blue water with monkeys and prehistoric coffins hanging from perpendicular cliffs. But where to attach superlatives? The Wu Gorge, framed by mountains which drop sheer from their peaks to the water? Or Xiling Gorge, seventy-six kilometres of cliffs with names like Ox Liver or Horse Lung? Or the final, man-made obstruction, the 1983-metre-long, 185-metre-high Three Gorges Dam – which, this being China, is naturally the largest in the world.

FACES FROM THE PAST:
XI'AN'S
TERRACOTTA
ARMY

750

CHINA Qin Shihuang, China's first emperor, never did anything by halves. Not content with building the Great Wall, he spent his last years roaming the fringes of his empire, seeking a key to immortality. When (with inevitable irony) he died on his quest, his entourage returned to the capital near modern-day Xi'an and buried his corpse in a subterranean, city-sized mausoleum whose ceiling was studded with precious stones and where lakes and rivers were represented by mercury.

Or so wrote the historian Sima Qian a century after a popular uprising had overthrown Qin Shihuang's grandson and established the Han dynasty in 206 BC. Nobody knows for sure how true the account is – the tomb remains unexcavated – but in 1974 peasants digging a well nearby found Qin Shihuang's guardians in the afterlife: an army of over ten thousand life-sized terracotta troops arranged in battle formation, filling three huge rectangular vaults.

Make no mistake, the Terracotta Army is not like some giant schoolboy's collection of clay soldiers lined up in ranks under a protective modern hangar. The figures are shockingly human, in a way that makes your skin crawl: each and every one is different, from their facial features to their hands, hairstyles, postures and clothing. They are so individual that you can't help feel that these are real people, tragically fossilized by some natural disaster – more so in places where excavations are incomplete, leaving their half-buried busts gripped by the earth. Even their horses, tethered to the remains of wooden chariots, are so faithfully sculpted that the very breed has been established, as well as – yes, by, examining their teeth – their age.

At the end, there's just one burning question: have they found a statue of Qin Shihuang leading them all? A realistic statue over two thousand years old of China's first emperor – now that surely would be immortality.

CRACKING THE
ICE FESTIVAL

CHINA Getting out and about when the temperature dips to forty below may seem a little crazy, but that doesn't stop the thousands of visitors who every January don thick coats, hats and gloves and head to Harbin, capital of the wintery, northeastern province of Heilongjiang. That's when an army of builders from China, Russia, Europe, Asia and even Australia descend on the city, fire up their chainsaws, axes and chisels and kick off Harbin's month-long Winter Ice Festival by carving out all sorts of extraordinary sculptures in the city's parks from ice blocks cut from the Songhua River.

A surreal cityscape of cathedrals, pyramids, Thai palaces and Chinese temples rises in Zhaolin Park, most of the replicas built to scale but so large you can actually wander through them, though some – including a section of the Great Wall, which inevitably puts in an appearance – are life-sized. And as if a parkful of transparent, fairytale castles wasn't enough, at night everything is lit up splendidly in lurid colours by light bulbs embedded in the ice, drawing huge crowds despite the intense cold. Across the Songhua River, Sun Island is another park populated, this time, by snow sculptures. A few of these follow traditional Chinese themes (you'll usually find a giant Guanyin, the Buddhist incarnation of mercy), but most are more contemporary cartoon characters, overblown mythical creatures or fantastical inhabitants of the sculptor's mind. And then amongst these are straightforward busts of famous Americans, or just a life-sized sculpture of a horse, which – amongst such bizarre companions – pull you up by their very ordinariness.

752 NAADAM: THE MANLY GAMES

MONGOLIA Enin Gurvan Naadam – Naadam, for short (literally, "Manly Games") – is one of the world's oldest and most spectacular annual events. After seeing it, you'll understand how the Mongols once conquered half the planet. Basically a sporting contest, the festival pits the nation's best athletes against each other in tests of skill in the "manly sports" of archery, horse racing and wrestling – the very talents with which Genghis Khan forged an empire. It's an experience you won't forget easily: you know you've done Naadam when you're squeezed into a nomad's tent, swilling Genghis Khan vodka with a pair of 300-pound wrestlers in their bikini briefs while a women in traditional silk robes sets before you a platter full of sheep parts.

Held every July on Mongolia's vast grassy steppes, Naadam brings the country to a standstill. It's a time of rest as well as a celebration of sport and manly virtues. Life is hard on the steppes – herding livestock and moving encampments – and the festival offers Mongolians a chance to visit friends, discuss current events and enjoy life before the winter sets in.

753 TAKING TEA IN CHENGDU

CHINA It is a busy place and the Chinese are a busy people, not overly given to spending time that could be spent on making money sitting idly around in public. Which is why many Chinese from other provinces consider the Sichuanese – particularly those from Chengdu – inherently lazy. They're not, they just like their local culture, and have filled just about every available public space, from temple gardens to pavements alongside busy roads, with teahouses. Actually, calling most of these places "teahouses" is a bit grand: they can be just a humble cluster of plastic tables and chairs, though the best look like something from a Chinese film set, all medieval curly roofs, wooden screens and wobbly bamboo furniture around which waiters navigate with stacks of porcelain cups and kettles of hot water.

All around are comfortably sociable groups reading newspapers, playing mahjong, staring off into space with cheroots between their teeth or chatting to friends. Really ambitious establishments even offer light meals, though it's not really what people are here for – in a country where it's usually so hard to relax in public, teahouses are a welcome escape.

754 TWO WHEELS GOOD: BIKING AROUND RURAL YANGSHUO

CHINA For once, not being able to read the road signs or ask for directions in Chinese doesn't really matter, because in the lush rural landscape around Yangshuo you simply hop on your rented bicycle and follow the course of your chosen river. Stony tracks wind through the karst-spiked landscape along the Li and Yulong rivers, leading you into mud-brick villages and past sweet-scented orange and pomelo orchards and great stands of golden bamboo. You'll barely see a car the entire day, just cycles, carts and the occasional lumbering water buffalo. Stop for a pot of invigorating ginger tea at a teashop jutting out over the water and then decide whether you've got the energy to cycle all the way home again; if not, simply haul your bike onto a bamboo raft and get ferried back downriver in relative style.

CELEBRATING THE
DRAGON
BOAT
RACES

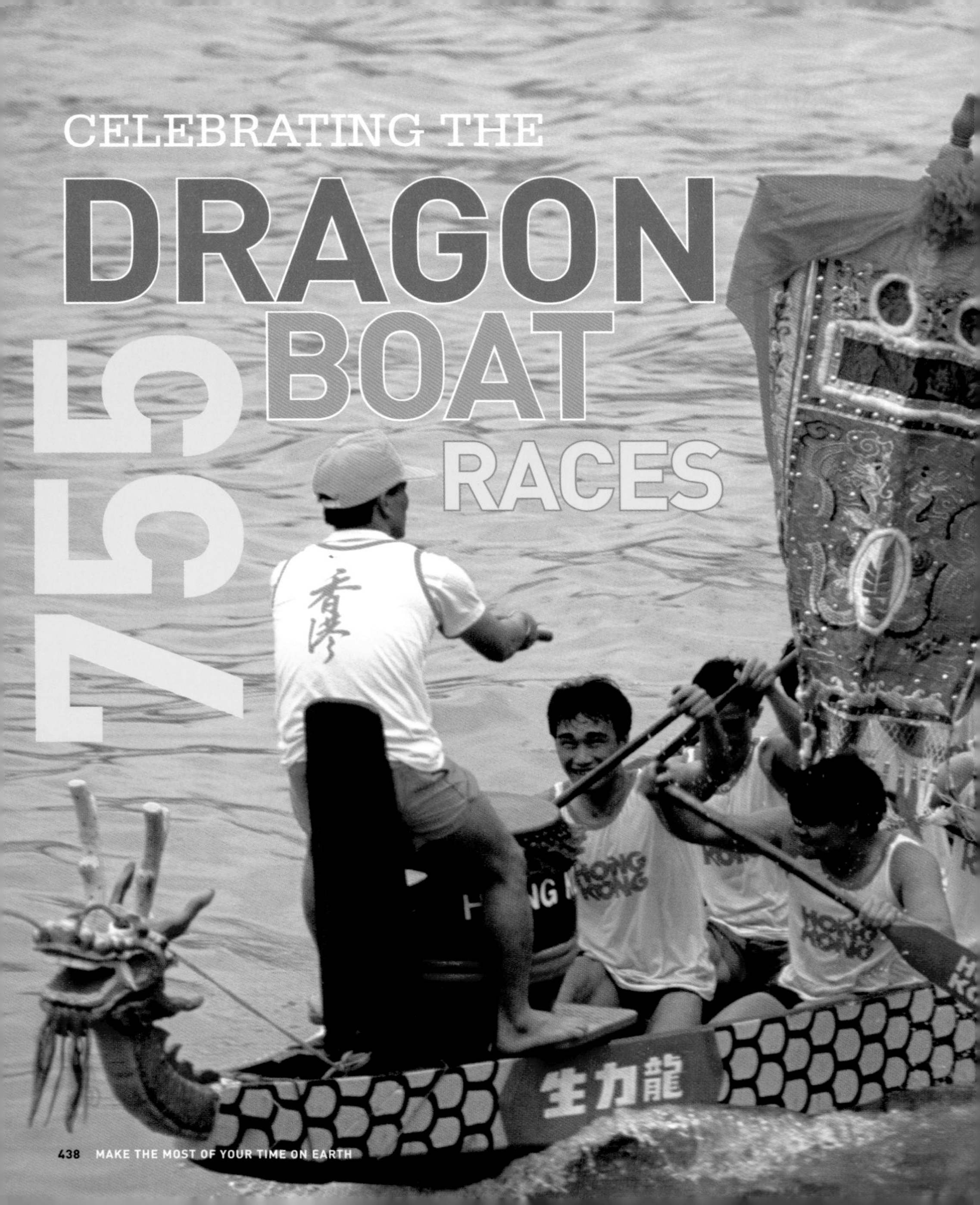

755

生力龍

CHINA Hong Kong's dragon boat races commemorate the aquatic suicide of an upright regional governor, Qu Yuan, who jumped into a river in central China in 278 BC rather than live to see his home state invaded by a neighbouring province's army. Distraught locals raced to save him in their boats, but were too late; later on, they threw packets of sticky rice into the river as an offering to his ghost.

There are festivities all over China on May 31 remembering the uncompromising Qu Yuan, but the race in Hong Kong's Stanley Harbour is one of the best, with huge quantities of sticky rice consumed and some fierce competition between the dragon-boat teams, who speed their narrow vessels across the harbour to the steady boom of pacing drums. To soak up the best of the buzz, go down to the waterside with a cold beer and take in the festive atmosphere, though you'll need to get up early to catch the dedication ceremonies of the dragon-head prows. The celebrations carry on through the evening, with firecrackers and traditional dragon dances.

756 UNSCROLLING THE LI RIVER

CHINA You know that Chinese scroll painting on the wall of your local takeaway, the one where a river with tiny boats winds between jutting, strangely shaped peaks, their tips blurred by clouds? Well, that could be a scene from along the Li River between Guilin city and the market town of Yangshuo in northern Guangxi province, an eighty-kilometre-long stretch that has provided inspiration to painters and poets for at least the last thousand years.

Today it also inspires the tourist industry, but despite the river being almost clogged with armadas of cruise boats, the journey still allows a look at the timeless Chinese countryside.

As is often the case in China, however, those expecting a peaceful commune with nature will be disappointed. But get into the cheerful, noisy Chinese way of enjoying a day out, and it's great fun: loaded with food and drink, head up to the cruise boat's observation deck and watch while the scenery unrolls itself for your pleasure. At first it's all green paddy-fields and buffaloes wallowing in the shallows, then the peaks begin to spring up – isolated at first, and none of them much over 200 metres tall, but weathered into fantastic shapes. They all have names too, and legends: this is Waiting-for-Husband Hill, where a wife turned to stone waiting for her travelling husband to come home; over there is Fish-Tail Peak and the Penholder; that rockface is Nine-Horses Fresco Hill. Tall bamboo screens the bank, source of the rafts which are poled fearlessly over the Li's shoals where cruise boats – flat-bottomed though they are – would founder. Cormorants sit on each raft, trained to retrieve fish for their owners; they get to eat every sixth one or refuse to work. And then, around a bend, is Yangshuo and the end of the trip; cameras are bagged and jaws are tightened at the sight of souvenir touts lined up along the pier.

757 WALKING WITH THE QUEEN OF HEAVEN

TAIWAN First come the police cars and media vans, followed by a series of flag-waving and drum-beating teams, along with musicians and performers dressed as legendary Chinese folk heroes, their faces painted red, black and blue, with fierce eyes and pointed teeth. Finally, carried by a special team of bearers, comes the ornate palanquin housing the sacred image of the Queen of Heaven. The whole thing looks as heavy as a small car: the men carrying her are wet with perspiration, stripped down to T-shirts with towels wrapped around their necks. Ordinary pilgrims – people like us – follow up behind.

Every year, tens of thousands of people participate in a 300km, eight-day pilgrimage between revered temples in the centre of Taiwan, in a tradition that goes back hundreds of years. The procession honours one of the most popular Taoist deities, a sort of patron saint of the island: the Queen of Heaven, Tianhou, also known as Mazu or Goddess of the Sea. In true Taiwanese style, the pilgrimage is as much media circus as fervent religious experience, with the parade attracting ambitious politicians and even street gangs who in the past have ended up fighting over who "protects" the Goddess during the procession.

Becoming a pilgrim for the day provides an illuminating insight into Taiwanese culture – you'll also make lots of friends, walk around 20km and eat like a horse. The streets are lined with locals paying respects and handing out free drinks and snacks, from peanuts to steaming meat buns and fried dumplings. At lunch, you'll get a huge bowl of sumptuous noodles from a gargantuan, bubbling vat managed by a team of sprightly old ladies. As well as a constant cacophony of music and drums, great heaps of firecrackers are set off every few metres. Whole boxes seem to disintegrate into clouds of smoke and everyone goes deaf and is dusted with ashy debris. No one cares – the noise drives off ghosts and evil spirits, ensuring that the Queen can pass in spiritual safety, and in any case, it's all part of the fun.

758 GORGING ON DIM SUM IN GUANGZHOU

CHINA The Chinese don't look for a quiet, romantic, candle-lit ambience in their restaurants. No, for them the hallmark of a great eating experience is bright lights, the happy chatter of satisfied customers stuffing their faces, and an atmosphere best described as renao – "hot and noisy" – and it would be hard to imagine a hotter, noisier restaurant than *Liwan Mingshijia* at 99 Dishifu Lu, Guangzhou (aka Canton). It's small – just a single room – but the benches and heavy wood-and-marble tables are so closely packed that the waitresses have a tough time getting close enough to deliver your meal, which only adds to the chaotic environment. No chance of getting a table to yourself either; you're forced to cheerfully jog elbows and spill tea over your neighbours, who will probably be curious to find out whether, as a foreigner, you can use chopsticks and what you've ordered

to eat. This is, crudely speaking, a traditional-style dim sum house, serving lots of little dishes of dumplings, soups, cakes and savouries to be eaten with tea. The menu is hand-written item-by-item on scores of small wooden boards hung around the walls, which you have to decipher before pushing your way to the rear counter, placing your order, and getting back to your seat. The crowds here speak for the food being fantastic, and it is: highlights are sheung fan, paper-thin steamed rice-noodle sheets scattered with prawns and rolled up; cones of sticky rice wrapped in lotus leaves and stuffed with chicken and bamboo; and unusual tang yuan (rice-flour balls), filled with red bean paste and served in a sweet soup flavoured with medicinal lily bulbs. And the cost of a meal for four, including excellent tie guanyin tea – just twelve yuan (around £1) a head.

759 EYEBALLING SOLDIERS IN THE "SCARIEST PLACE ON EARTH"

NORTH & SOUTH KOREA Your bus leaves central Seoul. After awhile, the buildings start to decrease in size, before disappearing completely. Then, just ninety minutes from the capital, you see it – a barbed wire fence that runs, in parallel to its spiky northern twin, from sea to sea across the Korean peninsula, separating South Korea from the hermit-like North, capitalism from communism, green from red. Between these jagged frontiers stretches a 4km-wide demilitarized zone (DMZ), across which the two countries aim undefined weapons at each other; bang in the middle of this is the village of Panmunjeom, where it's possible, under the escort of American infantry, to see now-nuclear North Korea at first-hand, and even take a few precious steps inside it.

This is the most heavily fortified border in the world, a fact that prompted a visiting Bill Clinton to describe it as "the scariest place on Earth." While he had the advantage of knowing the full scope and power of the surrounding weaponry, as well as what might

happen should the fuses be lit, many visitors are surprised by the tranquility of the place – there's birdsong among the barbed wire, and the DMZ is home to two small farming communities, one on each side of the Military Demarcation Line.

Your soldier-guide will take you by bus from Camp Bonifas – home to 5000 troops, and a single par-3 golf hole – to the DMZ itself, and before long you'll be in the Joint Security Area, where the two sets of soldiers stand almost eyeball-to-eyeball. Three small, sky-blue buildings here are shared by both sides, and by entering one and circumnavigating its central table you'll technically be able to straddle, walk across and take pictures of the border. The microphones on the table are left on, so whatever you say can be heard by the North Korean military; but there's no need to guard your words, as your guide himself will be a young pup, full of stories and propaganda – don't hesitate to ask questions. The scariest place on earth? Visit and see for yourself.

760 THE RITUAL OF A KAISEKI MEAL

JAPAN Kaiseki-ryori, Japanese haute-cuisine, was developed as an accompaniment to the tea ceremony; it has the same sense of ritual, meticulous attention to detail and exquisite artistry, all of which combine for a sublime sensory – if rather pricey – experience.

At a kaiseki restaurant the atmosphere is just as important as the food. Ideally, it will be in a traditional, wood-framed building. Kimono-clad waiting staff show you to a table set out on rice-straw tatami mats. A hanging scroll and a perfectly balanced flower arrangement, both chosen to reflect the season, enhance the air of cultural refinement. You look out on one of those wonderful Japanese gardens with not a leaf or pebble out of place.

The food fits the occasion and setting. A full kaiseki meal usually consists of ten to twenty small dishes, perhaps succulent slivers of raw fish with fiery wasabi relish, a few simmered vegetables, silky smooth tofu, toothsome pickled items, tempura as light as

air. Only the freshest ingredients are used to create a flawless array of seasonal delicacies designed to complement each other in every way – taste, aroma, texture, visual appeal.

No less care goes into selecting the serving dishes. Lacquerware, hand-painted ceramics, natural bamboo and rustic earthenware both offset their contents and present a harmonious whole. It's all exceedingly subtle and full of cultural references, but don't worry – anyone can appreciate the sheer craftsmanship and the hours of preparation that have gone into the feast before you.

It seems almost a crime to disturb the dramatic effect, but it would be an equal crime not to taste as much as possible. There isn't any particular order to diving in, just try to savour each delectable mouthful. The only firm rule is that rice and soup come last, as a filler – should you have any room to spare. And even in these august surroundings, it's perfectly acceptable to slurp your noodles.

761 A TREK BACK IN TIME IN RURAL YUNNAN

CHINA In Xishuangbanna, in the far south of Yunnan province, the earth is a rich, rust-red and the foliage an intense, glowing green. This area of China, just a few kilometres from the Burmese border, is about as rural as you can get, and a far cry from the hurly-burly of the urban boom. Here, there is no machinery and no roads, and the people tend their crops with rudimentary tools, just as they have for centuries.

I was trekking through this overgrowth with my guide. We were heading for a village inhabited by the Hani tribe, whose ancestors migrated south from the Tibetan plateau thousands of years ago. Every couple of hours we came upon a different village tucked away in a clearing between the trees: first an Akha settlement, then one belonging to the Bulang tribe. Near the Hani village, we found a white waterfall tumbling into a clear, icy pool that we jumped into to wash off the coating of red dust acquired on our long humid hike.

Later in the evening, we met our hosts at the Hani village. The houses here are topped with decorative horns. The story goes that more than two thousand years ago, during the Warring States period, a general helped the Hani people and they've honoured him ever since by decorating their houses with the horns from his helmet. The eldest son of the family in whose hut we were staying was out helping a neighbour build his home. There are customs to observe: no modern tools are used and the house's construction is measured out precisely into nine days. On the evening of the ninth day, the new homeowner threw a party to thank his neighbours for their help. Later we cooked meat, vegetables and rice and ate on low stools seated around the family's fire. Looking out from our perch in the lush, leafy jungle, modern China was nowhere to be seen.

762 HORSING ABOUT WITH THE MONGOLS

MONGOLIA For Mongols, life has always been portable – homes, families, and livelihoods are all carried on horseback. There's no better conveyance for this rolling grassy terrain than their well-trained steeds, and certainly no other way to immerse yourself in this last great nomadic culture. To enlist in this itinerant life you'll saddle up for the grassy steppe of the Darhat Valley, where horsemen and herders find prime summer pastures.

From an encampment on the shores of Lake Khovsgol, a day's horse trek across the Jigleg Pass leads through forests of Siberian larch trees laced with magenta fireweed before descending into the Darhat Valley – but this is just the beginning. Throughout your days on horseback you will come upon isolated encampments dotting the grassy expanse, each with several gers, the traditional lattice-framed, felt-covered home of nomadic herders. Mongols are quick to invite you inside where you'll witness their shamanistic rituals as they call for rain or predict the future from the shoulder bone of a sheep. As you sit on the felt-lined ger floor, they'll reach for a leather bag and pour you a bowl of airag, a fermented horse milk beverage – think fizzy sour milk with a kick. It's an acquired taste, but it quenches thirst and a swig will help wash down that morsel of roasted marmot you've been gnawing. Evenings will be spent in comfortable ger camps and in tents with all the accoutrements of catered camping.

As you approach the southern skirt of the valley you can expect to encounter the Tsaatan, a tribe that both rides and herds reindeer. The Darhat Valley is their favoured home for summer grazing before they retreat to the more protective forest highlands in the winter.

With fresh horses, you'll leave the Darhat through mountainous birch woods, bringing you back to Lake Khovsgol – the conclusion of your passage into a vanishing, but still vigorous, way of life.

763 GETTING NAKED IN INAZAWA

JAPAN Old men start to scream as the crush of naked flesh becomes so intense that steam is rising from the enormous crowd. It's only lunchtime and everyone's liver is saturated with sake. The chants of "Washyoi! Washyoi"! ("enhance yourself") rises to an ear-rupturing crescendo from the 9000 men, all dressed in giant nappies, or fundoshis. Finally, just when it seems that the entire town of Inazawa is about to be ransacked by the baying mob, the Naked Man appears.

Dating back 1200 years, the Naked Man festival was originally a call to prayer, decreed by Emperor Shotoku in order to dispel a plague that was sweeping the region. The plan worked, so at a date determined by the lunar calendar each year (usually around February or March) men of all ages, though particularly those who are 25 and 42, which are considered yakudoshi or unlucky ages, gather in the narrow lane that leads up to the town's Shinto temple in order to touch the Naked Man and get rid of their own personal curses.

On the day of the festival, the volunteer Naked Man, minus even a fundoshi, must run through the crowd, all of whom are hoping to touch him in order to transfer all their bad fortune and calamity. The ordeal is terrifying. The crowds punch, kick, drag and crush anyone in sight in order to get near. The Naked Man himself disappears under the tidal wave of nakedness. It is only around twenty minutes later that he emerges at the end of the temple lane: his hair ripped out, nose broken and with scars all over his body.

The spectacle is intense, frightening and utterly unique. Only a handful of Westerners have ever been brave enough to compete. It's strongly suggested that you watch from the sidelines – an exhilarating enough experience, and one that is more likely to leave you in full possession of your hair, teeth and sanity.

A FLORAL WAVE OF CHERRY BLOSSOMS

764

JAPAN The arrival of the sakura, or cherry blossom, has long been a profound yet simple Japanese lesson about the nature of human existence. For centuries, poets have fired off reams of haiku comparing the brief but blazing lives of the flowers to those of our own – a tragically fragile beauty to be treasured and contemplated.

In Japan, spring sees the country gradually coated in a light pink shade, soft petals slowly clustering on their branches as if puffed through by some benevolent underground spirit. The sakura-zensen, or cherry blossom front, flushes like a floral wave that laps the country from south to north; this is followed ardently by the Japanese, who know that when the advancing flowers hit their locality, they'll only have a week or so to enjoy the annual gift to its fullest. This desire is most commonly expressed in the centuries-old form of countless hanami parties – the word literally means "flower viewing" in Japanese – which take place in the rosy shade of the sakura-zensen throughout

the entire duration of its course. The existential contemplation is often over in seconds, before the party's real raison d'etre: consumption. Female members of the group are expected to provide the food, and then, of course, there's alcohol - hanami are often convenient ways for grievances to be aired in highly conservative Japan.

Hanami are typically friends-and-family affairs taking place in the most convenient location to the partygoers – often a park or river bank. Some of the most popular places are illuminated at night, and many are decorated with red-and-white paper lanterns. Of course, the coming of the blossom can be enjoyed in any way you see fit; among the best places to go are Kiyomizu-tera, a gorgeous temple in Kyoto, Tokyo's Ueno Park or the castles in Osaka or Himeji, all of which are lent a dreamlike air by puffs of flower each spring. A hanami party may even be possible in your own country – hunt down some sake, roll up some rice balls and become one with the nearest flowering cherry tree.

CHINA The term "Buddhist cave art" sounds worthy and dull, conjuring an image of a bald, bearded recluse brightening up his lonely mountain retreat with some crude daubings. Actually, that wouldn't be bad, but the reality is even better. Though the medium here is sculpture, Chinese cave art is closer to the illuminated manuscripts of medieval Christian Europe: holy images in a cartoon format which manage to be comic, exciting and – occasionally – even realistic, without losing the importance of an "inner message".

In China, the idea of carving rockfaces with religious scenes seems to have arrived with the Tobas, one of several regional dynasties who shared power between the break-up of the Han empire in 220 AD and the country's reunification four centuries later under the Tang. They injected central Asian, Indian and Greek influences into Chinese art, while their Buddhist fervour

and that their Tang successors inspired a trail of rock art sites stretching from northwestern Silk Road oases to the central Chinese heartlands in Henan, where the art form reached a peak at Longmen Caves.

There are over a hundred thousand figures chiselled into a honeycomb of grottoes at Longmen, a task that took even the industrious Chinese four hundred years to complete. Most of the figures are life-sized or smaller, but the biggest and best is a seventeen-metre-high Buddhist trinity whose main figure's ears alone (at over two metres long) humble you into insignificance, whilst almost making you laugh at the proportions. But the Buddha's expression – of calm, powerful insight – is, like the Mona Lisa's smile, full of unselfconscious spirit, a trait which later seeped out of Chinese art, leaving only an institutionalized woodenness.

VISITING
HENAN'S
MONA LISA
765

766 GETTING STEAMY IN A JJIMJILBANG

SOUTH KOREA Although the word "sauna" may have certain connotations, the family-oriented Korean subspecies represents one of the most distinctive ways – and certainly the cheapest – to spend a night in the country, as almost all are open 24 hours a day.

Your *jjimjilbang* journey starts at the reception desk. After handing over some cash, you'll receive nightclothes and a locker key, then be directed to the single-sex changing areas; these are commonly accessed by lift and on separate floors, populated by Koreans in varying states of relaxation and undress. Your own clothing sacrificed and locked away, you're free to head to the pool area; here you'll find several pools and steam rooms, but it's incredibly bad form to jump into either without a preliminary shower – free soap is provided. After this, it's up to you: there are usually several pools, ranging from icy to skin-boiling, and some are even infused with giant tea-bags.

On exiting the pool area you'll find a towel to dry off with, and a free-to-use array of hairdryers, cotton buds and scents on the way back to your locker. Don the kindergarten-style t-shirt and shorts given to you earlier (often pink for females and baby blue for the gents) and head to the large, unisex common area; these usually contain televisions, Internet terminals, water dispensers, massage rooms and snack bars. A cushioned mat will be your bed for the night, and though you're free to sleep pretty much wherever you want – like cats, the Koreans can nod off anywhere, in any position – you'll usually be able to track down a sensible little corner, and can doze off with the knowledge that you've just enjoyed a quintessentially Korean experience.

767 CIRCUITING THE JOKHANG

TIBET The Jokhang is the holiest temple in Tibetan Buddhism, and what it lacks in appearance – a very shabby facade compared with the nearby Potala Palace – it makes up in atmosphere. Sited in the cobbled lanes of the Barkhor district, Lhasa's sole surviving traditional quarter, there's an excited air of reverence as you approach, with a continuous throng of Tibetan pilgrims circuiting the complex anti-clockwise, spinning hand-held prayer wheels and sticking out their tongues at each other in greeting. A good many prostrate themselves at every step, their knees and hands protected from the accumulated battering by wooden pads, which set up irregular clacking noises. Most of the pilgrims are wild-haired Tibetan peasants reeking of yak butter and dressed in thick, shabby layers against the cold; especially tough-looking are the Khampas from eastern Tibet, who almost always have one arm exposed to the shoulder, whatever the weather.

Devout they may be, but there's absolutely nothing precious about their actions, no air of hushed, respectful reverence – stand still for a second and you'll be knocked aside in the rush to get around. Inside, the various halls are lit by butter lamps, leaving much of the wooden halls rather gloomy and adding a spooky edge to the close-packed saintly statues clothed in multicoloured flags, brocade banners hanging from the ceiling, and especially gory murals of demons draped in skulls and peeling skin off sinners – a far less forgiving picture of Buddhism than the version practised elsewhere in China. The bustle is even more overwhelming here, the crowds increased by red-robed monks, busy topping up the lamps or tidying altars. Make sure you catch the Chapel of Jowo Sakyamuni at the rear of the complex, which sports a beautiful statue of the twelve-year-old Buddha; and the Jokhang's flat roof, where you can look out over the rest of the city.

768 FILLING UP ON LITTLE EATS

TAIWAN Crowded alleyways, blaring scooter horns and a mix of Mandopop and Nokia tunes may not sound like an appealing night out, but there's a reason why Taiwan's night markets pack people in – some of the best food in Asia.

The Taiwanese love food so much, they've perfected what's known in Chinese as "little eats" (xiaochi), tasty snacks served in small portions – think Chinese take-out meets tapas. The places most associated with xiaochi are night markets held all over the island; most get going in the evening and don't typically close till after midnight. Each stall has a speciality, a "little eat" it likes to promote as food fit for an emperor. But royal lineage is unimportant, as is language: just point, pay and stuff it down.

At Shilin, Taipei's best and biggest night market, a typical evening starts with a few warm-up laps, perhaps grabbing a couple of appetizers along the way: a sugar-glazed strawberry, fried pancake with egg, or succulent Shilin sausage served with raw garlic and eaten with a cocktail stick. Suitably inspired, it's time for a little more chopstick work: many stalls own a cluster of plastic tables and chairs where you can slurp and munch while seated. Classic dishes include slippery oyster omelettes covered in luscious red sauce, and addictive lu rou fan, juicy stewed pork on rice. Still hungry? Try some celebrated regional specialties: danzi mian from Tainan (noodles with pork, egg and shrimp), or deep-fried meatballs from Changhua.

Serious connoisseurs – or more likely those with adventurous palates – can opt for the really scary stuff. Most infamous are chou doufu, cooked in pig fat and better known as stinky tofu, the smell of which sickens newcomers but the taste of which is sublime (the fried, crispy outer layer perfectly balances the fluffy tofu underneath), and lu wei, a savoury blend of animal guts, simmered in broth, and often eaten cold. Try this, washed down with a cold Taiwan beer, and you're certain to win the respect of the incredulous Taiwanese sitting next to you.

SOUTH KOREA It's 2.30am on Sunday. Your head is spinning, and you feel like you might fall over, or even throw up. No, this is not another night out in one of Seoul's rowdy bars – it's an ordinary evening at Haeinsa, one of South Korea's most beautiful and famous Buddhist temples. Unlike other temples, where foreigners are introduced to "Buddhism lite", Haeinsa – meaning Temple of Reflection on a Smooth Sea – is not for the faint-hearted. It is a kind of Buddhist university, or rather Buddhist boot camp, for trainee monks and game foreigners.

On a typical weekend trip, you arrive on Saturday afternoon and immediately cast off your worldly attire – and all your worldly cares – in favour of baggy, unflattering grey monk pyjamas. Then it's straight into temple etiquette and meditation practice. No unnecessary talking, no unnecessary touching, no unnecessary thinking – just clear your mind and adhere to the rules. Bedtime is at 9pm. That's for a good reason, as you have to get up at

2.30 in the morning. After waking up and donning your grey outfit in a daze, it's out into the cold night for a monk's ritual.

First you head to the main dharma hall, where you're expected to perform 108 bowing moves, an effort that takes almost an hour. That's a lot of kneeling, standing, kneeling and standing, in the middle of the night – not easy for unpractised backs and heads. Then, at 4am it's time to walk down a quiet mountain path to a specially built, round marble meditation area. Here, you sit on the edge of what looks like it should be a pond, legs crossed. Clearing your mind is much easier in this environment. Staying awake is not. But luckily there are monks on hand to prod slumping backs.

After what seems like hours spent in meditation, you head back to the dharma hall for a simple breakfast before watching the sun rise around this beautiful temple. Despite feeling battered and exhausted, your soul definitely feels lighter.

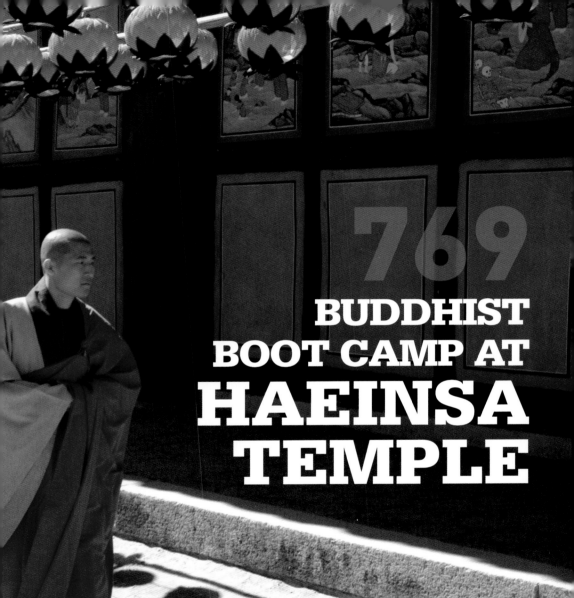

769

BUDDHIST BOOT CAMP AT HAEINSA TEMPLE

BLOWN AWAY BY THE
GREAT WALL 770

CHINA The Great Wall is one of those sights that you've seen and heard so much about that you know reality is going to have a tough time living up to the hype. But having made it all the way to Beijing, it seems perverse to ignore this overblown landmark, so arm yourself with a thermos of tea and catch a bus north from the capital to Simatai, one of several sections of this 4800-kilometre-long structure which has been restored.

It's easy to find bad things to say about the Great Wall. The work of China's megalomaniac first emperor Qin Shi Huang, over a million forced labourers are said to have died building the original around 250 BC, and the simple truth is that this seven-metre-high, seven-metre-thick barrier didn't even work. History is littered with "barbarian" invaders who proved sophisticated enough to fight or bribe their way around the wall's 25,000 watch-towers, most notably the Mongols in the thirteenth century, and

the Manchus – who went on to become China's final dynasty – in 1644. Indeed, the Manchus were so unimpressed with the wall that they let the entire thing fall into ruin.

And yet, you'll be blown away. Not even swarms of hawkers and other tourists can ruin the sight of this blue-grey ribbon snaking across the dusty, shattered hills into the hazy distance, beyond which one end finally runs into the sea, while the other simply stops in northwestern China's deserts. You can spend hours walking between battlements along the top – in places, following the contours of the hills up amazingly steep inclines – until restorations give way to rubble, and even then you can't quite believe that such a solid, organic part of the scenery is only an artefact, built by simple human endeavour. If ever proof were needed of Chinese determination, this is it.

771 RELAXING IN TROPICAL TAKETOMI-JIMA

JAPAN On tiny Taketomi-jima the traditional bungalow homes are ringed by rocky walls draped with hibiscus and bougainvillea. From the low-slung terracotta-tiled roofs glare shiisa, ferocious, bug-eyed lion figures. The only traffic is cyclists on rickety bikes negotiating the sandy lanes, and buffalo-drawn carts, hauling visitors to the beaches in search of minuscule star-shaped shells.

This is Japan – but not as you might know it. Taketomi-jima is one of the hundred-plus sub-tropical islands of Okinawa that trail, like scattered grains of rice, some 700km across the South China Sea. Cultural influences from China, Southeast Asia and the US, who occupied Okinawa until 1972 following WWII, have all seeped into the local way of life, providing a fascinating counterpoint to the conformity and fast-paced modernity of mainland Japan.

Fringed by soft, golden beaches, the islands are popular with Japanese looking for some R & R. Taketomi-jima especially is often besieged with daytrippers, as it's just a short ferry ride from the mountainous Ishigaki-jima, the main island of the Okinawan sub-collection known as the Yaeyamas. The trick is to stay on after the masses have left. Take up residence in one of the many family-run *minshuku* – small guesthouses with tatami mat floors, futons and rice-paper shoji screens. After a refreshing bath, slip into the provided *yukata* (cotton robe) and dig into a tasty dinner of local delicacies, including tender pork and fresh seafood, and then wander down to the beach to watch the glorious sunset.

On returning to the *minshuku*, it's not unusual for a bottle or two of Okinawa's pungent rice liquor awamori to appear. Locals strum on a *sanshin* (three-stringed lute) and lead guests in a gentle sing-along of Okinawan folk favourites. As the awamori takes effect, don't be surprised if you also learn a few local dance moves.

772 SUSHI AT 300KPH: RIDING THE SHINKANSEN

JAPAN A sleek, space-age train glides into the station precisely on time. When it pulls to a stop the doors align exactly in front of each orderly queue of passengers. The guard, wearing immaculate white gloves and a very natty peaked cap, bows as you climb aboard. Where but Japan could a train journey start in such style?

Japan's high-speed Shinkansen, popularly known as the bullet train, is the envy of the world, and while it's not cheap, it's something you just have to do once. The Tokaido-Sanyo line runs from Tokyo west to Kyoto and Hiroshima – 900km – and the fastest "Nozomi" trains cover this in just four hours. In places, they reach 300km per hour, yet the ride is as smooth as silk.

It's only by looking out of the window that you get a sense of speed; neat rows of houses flicker by, gradually giving way to rice fields, woods and the occasional temple, as you leave Tokyo's sprawling metropolis behind. If the weather's clear, you'll catch Mount Fuji's iconic, snow-capped cone.

Meanwhile, inside the train all is hushed calm. People sleep, punch messages into mobile phones (calls are forbidden), or tuck into eki-ben, take-away station meals that are an art form in themselves.

Before you know it, you're pulling in to Kyoto's monumental new station – eyesore or emblem, depending on whom you ask. No time for the city's myriad temples now, though. The doors swoosh shut and you're off again. Osaka brings yet more urban sprawl, but after Kobe the tracks run along the coast, offering tantalizing glimpses of the island-speckled Inland Sea as you near Hiroshima, journey's end.

In a country where cutting-edge design coexists alongside ancient traditions and courtesies, the bullet train is a shining example of the extraordinary attention to detail and awesome teamwork that lies at the heart of Japanese society. Far more than a mere journey, riding the Shinkansen provides a glimpse into what makes Japan tick.

773 LIVING THE NOMADIC LIFE

KYRGYZSTAN Sleeping in a yurt is akin to sleeping in a sheep's stomach. It's warm but damp, smelling of wool and filled with strange gurgling noises. In a lush Kyrgyz pasture at 3000m, I joined Noorgul and her family at their lakeside summer residence – a row of round woollen tents, an open cauldron for cooking, a pen for the goats, a well-used long drop-off to one side and nothing to do but enjoy the Nomadic style of life.

In this jailoo (pasture) in Son Kul, a bone-jarring eight-hour drive in an old Soviet truck from the capital Bishkek into the centre of Kyrgyzstan, I stepped back in time to the days when life was simple, as long as Genghis Khan wasn't around.

Kyrgyz families have been moving around these sweeping pastures with their yurt tents for centuries, folding up the rugs and the walls and carting the huge circular roof frame from meadow to meadow, taking their animals to greener fields or simply opting for a change in summer scenery.

Inside the yurt, traditional Krygyz shyrdak rugs hung from the walls as colourful insulation. The wooden wheel-like roof had spokes ascending to the apex of the cone, while a little hat sat on the cone on the outside, flung on or off for ventilation or to keep in the heat.

We arrived at night and settled on the hand-made felt rugs of the central yurt and enjoyed a magnificent feast of flat Kyrgyz bread, chunky soup, plov (rice and meat), laghman (noodles) and endless glasses of questionable vodka, each one preceded by an elaborate toast.

The next morning I was saddled up on an awaiting pony. From there we explored the hills beyond the camp, riding up through the hushed valleys to imposing peaks overlooking the glacial lakes, as we galloped across the wide pastures back to the yurts. Along the way we bought kymys, fermented mare's milk, from a farmer sporting a high, peaked traditional woolen hat. The fizzy beverage nipped the back of my throat – the perfect way to quench a Kyrgyz pasture thirst.

774 A LITTLE LOCAL FLAVOUR IN PYONGYANG

NORTH KOREA Nuclear threats, espionage and famine under the shadowy rule of a President long deceased... you've heard it all before, but North Korea's dubious charms make it the Holy Grail for hard-bitten travellers. A trip to this tightly-controlled Communist society is only possible as part of an expensive package, but a high proportion of those fortunate and intrepid enough to visit end up deeming it their most interesting travel experience.

Pyongyang, the capital, is an empty and rather eerie concrete-and-marble experiment in socialist realism, studded with bronze statues and huge murals in honour of Kim Il-song: father of Kim Jong-il and the country itself, he remains its official President despite the traditional drawback of being dead. Every single local wears a badge depicting one of the Kims – generally revered as the greatest examples of humanity ever to walk the Earth – but their lapses in judgement are all too apparent, exemplified by the *Ryugyong Hotel*, a colossal 105-floor pyramidal shell that has never been blessed with carpets, electricity or visitors.

For all the faults of Kim Jong-il and his cohorts, the locals are a friendly bunch, and more relaxed than you might expect. Much is also made of the fact that tourists are in the near-constant presence of local guides, but these are usually amiable people, and those that form a good relationship with them from the start are likely to be let off the leash occasionally – it's not beyond the realms of possibility to find yourself sharing a picnic with a local family, dancing with a North Korean grandmother, or walking half-a-mile down a Pyongyang street, surrounded by curious citizens.

Meeting North Koreans will confirm some of the things you've heard about the country, while destroying other preconceptions. One guarantee is that you'll leave with more questions than answers.

775 STEP AEROBICS: CLIMBING HUANG SHAN

CHINA The Chinese would say that "where there is yin, there is yang"; Westerners would more prosaically opine "no gain without pain". At Huang Shan, Anhui province's Yellow Mountains, this means ravishing scenery tempered by steps, steps and more steps. All fifteen kilometres of the path to the top of Huang Shan are cut into steps and paved in stone, which has been quarried, carried up here and laid by hand in an amazing human endeavour. Incidentally, it has also made the mountain accessible to generations of the country's greatest painters and poets, whose impressions have turned Huang Shan into a national icon of natural beauty, today drawing the inevitable cartloads of footstepping tourists. The mountain's procession of clouds, soaring granite monoliths and wind-contorted pine trees at first give the impression of being in a Chinese garden writ large. You soon realize, however, that the experience of being here is what those gardens' designers were trying to capture and fit into some rich patron's backyard, where it could be appreciated without the need for having to do eight hours of step aerobics.

Unsurprisingly, the reality is not quite the same. You can come in winter, when there are very few people and the mountain is overlaid with another layer of grandeur, but it's far easier to enjoy spring or autumn – colourful times when nature is in transition. The crowds are worse (though not as bad as they are during summer), but at least you have someone to share your pain with while gasping ever upwards. Yet the toughest moment of all is on reaching the "top", only to find there's no real summit to stand on, rather a plateau ringed in little peaks which bring Huang Shan's height to within a whisker of 1900m. The finest sight here is watching as the sun rises from or sets into a cloud sea, while sharing the experience with hundreds of other onlookers, all momentarily hushed by the spectacle.

776 ON FOOT THROUGH TIGER LEAPING GORGE

CHINA "A stony path winds up to cool hills", or so goes a Chinese poem. Well, it was never truer than where a youthful Yangzi channels violently through Tiger Leaping Gorge in Yunnan province, the stony path in question winding up to the foothills of an ash-grey, spiky range – though the peaks, at over 5000m high, spoil the comparison by actually being mountains. Of course, poetry also doesn't mention anything as mundane as what it's like to lug a backpack around for three days at this altitude: rather tiring. Nor does it explain the 100-metre-wide gorge's name. After asking a handful of villagers, you'll suspect that you might not be the first idiot who has quizzed them about it: "A tiger was being chased, and it leaped across the river to escape" is their well-rehearsed answer.

Altitude and names aside though, trekking through the gorge is fantastic. The Chinese don't usually have a romantic view of nature, rather they see the Great Outdoors as being frighteningly empty, unless livened up by tour groups, cable cars, stone staircases, strategically placed pavilions, souvenir hawkers and noodle stands. But here there is nothing – just the mountains, the path, the gorge and a huge, blue sky. Occasionally you'll see a farmer or some goats; every few hours' walking throws up a couple of houses. You sleep along the way at small villages, and can sit outside under a gloriously luminous Milky Way while an unlikely number of satellites race in straight lines across the night.

JAPAN Should you choose to imagine a monkey, for whatever reason, it's likely to be surrounded in your mind's eye by tropical vines or thick jungle, trading screams with the parrots or chowing down a banana. Snowy peaks would not usually be on the agenda, but Japan is home to a particular breed of macaque that positively revels in the stuff. These clever monkeys share a number of common bonds with human beings – they're one of the only two animals known to wash their food before eating it, and no other primates live further north. Also, like their occasionally more intelligent two-legged cousins, many macaques counter the winter cold by hunting down a source of warmth; in Japan, you're never far from a hot spring, and one of the country's most magical winter sights is the view of a horde of apes silhouetted in the mist of an outdoor pool.

With a number of hot springs and other hydrothermal features – though most have been straddled by resorts and cut off from the outside world by a ticket booth – Japan offers its snow-loving macaques a place to escape the freezing temperatures. The winter coincides with the mating season, and it's hard to say what's more amusing – monkeys engaging in poolside trysts, or the Japanese pretending not to notice.

Tourists head to the relevant resorts to catch glimpses of the bathing apes, especially the loveable baby macaques. Given their schedules, the monkeys are usually the first to arrive, their faces standing out against the snow – pink Easter Island statues in balaclavas of fur. Bear in mind that though their eyes may appear dispassionate, it's unwise to look directly into them for too long, lest it be taken as a sign of aggression. In contrast, their postures can sometimes be eerily human as they plonk themselves into the water, slouched over the poolside in contented silence, and then perch on an outer stone to cool off.

BATHING WITH
SNOW MONKEYS
777

778 RIDING BY BUS TO DÊGÊ

CHINA Bored with western Sichuan's pandas, pristine blue lakes, raw mountain scenery and Tibetan monasteries? Well then, for what is likely to prove one of the most adrenaline-packed eight hours of your life, ride the public bus from Ganzi to Dêgê. You start already 3500 metres up in a river valley at the foot of the Que'er Shan range, Ganzi's dusty sprawl of tiled concrete buildings disappearing abruptly around a corner behind you, the bus packed to capacity with raucous crowds of Tibetans. The road – like all roads here if you're riding west towards the Himalayan Plateau – heads ever upwards, crossing a wide pass festooned with bright prayer flags at the head of the valley, at which point the Tibetans all cheer and hurl handfuls of paper prayers out the windows like clouds of confetti. Beyond is the halfway town of Manigange, where the passengers get out and (despite their Buddhist leanings) consume vast quantities of meat dumplings and butter tea

– the latter revolting as tea but satisfying if thought of as soup. Back into the bus, past brown glaciers hemming in the holy lake of Yilhun Lhatso and boulders carved in Tibetan script with "Om Mani Padme Hum", and the valley reaches a rounded conclusion beneath some particularly wicked-looking, spiky, snow-bound peaks. Unfortunately, the road goes on, winding back on itself as it climbs up... and up... and up. The Tibetans are no longer so boisterous; several are blatantly chanting prayers, thumbing rosaries with their eyes screwed up tight. Up amongst the peaks now, and the bus is suddenly rocked by winds as the road wobbles through the narrow, 5050-metre-high pass and around a corner so tight that at night you'd be over the edge before you even knew that there was a corner to turn. On the far side, the road slaloms down a virtually vertical rockface to the valley far below, and then it's an unadventurous run to Dêgê, just an hour away.

779 STROLLING THE SHANGHAI BUND

CHINA If Europeans ever made a real impact on China it was in the part they played in turning interwar Shanghai into one of the busiest, raciest cities in the world. Haunt of aristocrats, businessmen, gangsters and untold millions of beggars, prostitutes and day-labourers who barely managed to scrape together their daily bowl of rice, Shanghai through the 1920s and 30s was almost a caricature of itself – and also why the city was deliberately run down by the Chinese Communist government that took over in 1949. Today, however, Shanghai is booming again, with a growth in hyper-modern architecture and commercial dealings which is beginning to offer serious competition to its long-term rival and fellow former colonial construction, Hong Kong.

And yet it's still one of old Shanghai's landmarks that is used as a benchmark of how the city is changing. Running south along the west bank of the Huangpu River for a couple of kilometres, the road known as the Bund was once Shanghai's docks and commercial heart in one, lined with European neo-classical

warehouses, banks and expensive hotels, some of which survive amongst the modern cityscape. Walking south, you pass the former British and Russian consulates and waterside Huangpu Park, infamous for signs once allegedly barring "dogs or Chinese" and now one of the best places to promenade and watch the latest high-tech developments springing up over the river at Pudong district. Further on are the one-time headquarters of Jardine Matheson (which made its original fortune in the opium trade) and the art-deco Peace Hotel, known as the Cathay Hotel through the 1930s when its jazz band was the talk of the town. Incredibly, some of the musicians' descendants still provide a nightly show. Beyond here are the Bank of China, Customs House (still functioning), the Hong Kong and Shanghai Bank (HSBC), and Dongfeng Hotel, once the men-only Shanghai Club whose 33-metre-long mahogany bar is sadly no more. Wind up your walk nearby with a meal at *M On The Bund*, where the views (if not the Mediterranean-style food) are outstanding.

780 SHARING ANCIENT ROADS WITH YAK HERDERS

BHUTAN To trek in Bhutan is to visit not only another land but also another time – a rare privilege. Buffering China to the north and India to the south, the terrain ranges from the 7000m peaks of the Himalayas through high-altitude meadows and forests to the jungle-covered foothills in the south. Bhutan has no illusions about its preciousness, having guarded its borders for centuries and now restricting access to only a few thousand visitors annually and charging US$200 a day per visitor. As a result of this exclusivity, many Bhutanese villagers living high in the mountains have never seen Westerners before.

While the urban centres of this mountainous Himalayan country are modernized, many Bhutanese living in remote areas

lead an ancient way of life where walking is the vital mode of transport and shipments of school supplies and general goods from the major towns are delivered by horse and cart, taking several days to arrive. Visitors trekking in Bhutan use ancient pathways to access these remote areas and to witness a way of life that has remained unchanged for generations. You can embark on hikes of any length and all levels of difficulty from easy day walks stopping at temples along the glorious but flat Bumthang Valley, to the gruelling 24-day Snowman trek across the far North. Along the way, you'll share the road with nomadic yak herders and processions of maroon-clad monks.

SITTING RINGSIDE AT A SUMO TOURNAMENT

JAPAN Forget the comical western stereotype of gargantuan men in nappies slapping each other around – sumo is serious business. Few sports have as long a pedigree, and sumo has been around for a millennium. The basic object of the fighters is to force their opponent out of the ring, or get them to touch the ground with any part of their body other than their feet. The enormous body mass involved ensures that fights are brief but blazing, though these guys are no mere spheres of flesh – to see a rikishi hoist up to 200kg of squirming human by the belt and carry it out of the ring is nothing short of astonishing.

Six tournaments, or basho, take place across the year – one every odd month – and last for fifteen days. Good rikishi progress though the ranks to makuuichi, the highest level; here, the top 42 wrestlers fight once per day, their main aim the posting of a positive tournament record of at least eight wins. The very best rise to yokozuna level and national superstardom, before a ceremonial cutting of their top-knotted hair on retirement.

Your ticket entitles you to nine hours of fight-time and hundreds of bouts; since many spectators only come for the makuuichi fights at the end, it's often possible to pinch a first-class seat for much of the day. Keep in mind that ringside seats come with an element of risk. Arriving early also increases the chances of sharing your train journey in with a wrestler or two; many are more than willing to chat, though the super-formal dialect drilled into them at their training "stable" can be impenetrable even for Japanese-speakers. One certainty is that you won't be able to miss them.

782 SHOPPING AT THE MOTHER OF ALL MARKETS

CHINA They call it the "Mother of all Markets", and so they should: every week, one hundred thousand nomads, villagers and traders from all over central Asia converge on Kashgar, the last sizeable place you'll come to in China if you're heading northwest along the ancient Silk Road. They're here to take part in the Yekshenba Bazaar, the Sunday Market, which fills the teahouses and dusty lanes of this Muslim city with a blur of noise and smells that went out of fashion elsewhere in the world after the Middle Ages. Ground zero is a trampled area to the east of the city, where customers and traders haggle with melodramatic flair over the merits of horses, sheep, camels and donkeys. Just when it seems as if someone is about to get a knife in the ribs, the shouting and fist-shaking gives way to satisfied nods, money changes hands, an d the new owner leads his purchases

away. Beyond all this horse-trading is the covered market, a maze of shaded stalls better-stocked than a Western shopping mall, whose owners sip tea, chat with their friends, and do their best to catch your eye so that they can beckon you over. They are masters of soft-sell; each in their friendly, persuasive way makes it hard to escape without buying something. "Need some kitchenware – a new cleaver, some pots and pans? No problem, I have these. How about a carpet? This one, from Khotan, perhaps – or how about a fine kilim, handmade by nomads? Some Iranian saffron then; yes, more expensive than gold. A pity to come so far and leave empty-handed." But where to start – over here are musical instruments, wooden chests inlaid with tin (used for carrying gifts to prospective brides), and enough food to last a lifetime – where to start?

783 LOSING YOUR SHIRT IN MACAU

CHINA There are few impediments to entry into Macau's best and brightest form of entertainment: if you're over eighteen, are not wearing sandals, shorts or slippers, and you're carrying a passport and are happy to check bags and cameras in at reception, then the management of any one of the territory's seventeen-odd casinos will welcome you in to fritter your hard-earned cash away. Actually, even if you don't gamble, it's worth a look, if only to hang out with the local Macanese and Hong Kongers who come here to play the weekend away, or the gambling-starved hopefuls who flood over from mainland China. The main hotspot is over on the eastern side of town along kilometre-long Avenida da Amizade, where rival establishments rub elbows within sight of the Outer Port. Each casino has its own atmosphere: notable venues include the legendary Hotel Lisboa, with four heavily packed floors decked out in mock 1930s mirrors, light fittings and wood panelling; the uniquely foreign-owned Sands, whose gold-plated glass exterior makes it resemble a pile of bullion; the Floating Casino, full of gilded dragon carvings and red wallpaper; and the Jai-Alai, an old sports stadium full of hard-faced, downmarket Chinese punters. Most of these seem to have a fairly reckless attitude towards games of chance. One reason for this might be because (rumour has it) some are party bigwigs busy squandering public funds, though none has ever actually been caught in a casino here. If you've been rash enough to ignore the tiny notices at the door ("Betting for fun only, not to get rich") and find funds in short supply, there's a score of pawnbrokers within stumbling distance – their signs look like a bat roosting upside down.

784 WALKING AMONG SILLA ROYALTY

SOUTH KOREA In the centre of Gyeongju lies a gently undulating series of mysterious, grass-covered bumps. Though smaller and much softer to the eye, these mounds serve a similar purpose to the great Egyptian pyramids: tombs for great leaders from an ancient civilization, the great Silla dynasty, that ruled southeastern Korea for nearly a millennium, more than a millennium ago.

For some, the feeling of ancient power becomes quite palpable when walking through Tumuli Park, Gyeongju's district of burial mounds. Though close to the city centre, there's surprisingly little intrusion from the modern world – Gyeongju's more recent rulers chose to impose a cap on the height of buildings and encouraged the use of traditional roofing, all of which fosters a natural, relaxed feeling hard to come by in other Korean cities. As you walk around the park, you'll pass gentle green humps on your left and right – the larger the bump, the more important the occupant. The largest is a double-humped mound belonging to a King and Queen, and it's even possible to enter a slightly smaller one to see a cross-sectioned display of the surroundings of deceased Sillan nobility. These tombs have yielded wonderful treasures from the period, most notably an elaborate golden crown, once worn like rabbit ears on the head of a now unknown King.

Gyeongju's pleasures do not start and finish with its tombs. Bulguksa, a temple dating from 528 and viewed by many as the most beautiful in the country, lies near to the east. It exudes vitality, and is surrounded by some staggering mountain scenery. Delving into said scenery on a meandering uphill path you'll eventually come across a grotto known as Seokguram. Here you'll see a stone Buddha that has long fixed his gaze over the East Sea – a perfect place to catch the sunset at day's end.

785 JOINING THE PILGRIMS' TRAIL AT EMEI SHAN

CHINA To start with, Emei is a holy Buddhist site associated with Puxian, the incarnation of Truth, and the mountain's slopes are studded with temples dating back in part to Tang times, which offer travellers wonderfully atmospheric accommodation. And the mountain is also overwhelmingly picturesque, the lower two-thirds covered in thick forests whose plants range from tropical species to high-altitude rhododendrons and camellias – most temples sit immersed in greenery, with wild monkeys and birds roaming about at will.

While many mountains in China are far tougher in terms of gradient, few can rival Emei in terms of distance – the shorter of the two trails to the summit is forty kilometres long, meaning a two-day slog to the top. Dropping into temples along the way breaks the journey: Wannian Si packs the biggest punch, with its life-sized enamelled statue of Puxian riding a six-tusked elephant, but Xianfeng Si and Xixiang Chi – though rather weatherbeaten – are more atmospheric. Your fellow pilgrims are also like to be of interest: either groups of blocky businessmen smoking as they puff along behind their tour guides, or youngsters dressed in blatant disregard of the conditions (men in jackets and leather brogues, women wearing high heels). But you occasionally meet wandering monks too, chanting prayers or thumbing rosaries as they walk, or even locals trying to coax teams of exhausted, heavily-laden horses along the steep paths. Sadly, the forests fade out during the last third of the hike, leaving open moorland and tangled undergrowth, and Emei's top temple is vulgarly over-decorated. But there's a soft touch even here in the dense clumps of padlocks clipped onto the protective railings, left by couples to symbolize their love for each other.

786 DWARFED BY HONG KONG'S SKYSCRAPERS

CHINA If there's anywhere in the world that can cut you down to size it's Central district, on the north shore of Hong Kong Island. Walking around here you're humbled by just about everything – the crowds, the incomprehensible language which eveyone else seems to have mastered, the heat, the superbly enticing smells of Chinese cooking and the dazzling beauty of Hong Kong harbour, dotted with ferries and tankers. More than anything, though, it feels like being at the bottom of a well: this is Asia's financial hub, and Hong Kong is a place where size really does matter, so building a one-story, local branch-style financial institution is simply not an option. Skyscrapers rear up all around, so closely packed that their lower stories have been linked by a network of pedestrian walkways.

The tallest building here, Tower Two of the International Finance Centre, literally touches the clouds at 420m high. Nonetheless, local boys Bank of China (BOC) and the Hong Kong and Shanghai Banking Corporation (HSBC) have been slugging it out for decades over who can build the most auspicious building. And here it's not just size alone that counts, but the Chinese belief in feng shui, or how the different parts of a landscape influence each other. HSBC is built off the ground – you can walk right underneath it and look up at the offices surrounding the hollow central well – because otherwise it would have blocked the flow of "good luck" between Government House (further uphill behind it) and the waterfront. Built in the 1980s, it's gargantuan next to the BOC of the time, but the Chinese picked up their act and in the 1990s built a new bank headquarters which is not only so high that the head of the BOC can look down on his competitor, but also puts feng shui to some nasty use – the new BOC tower points skywards like a knife, stabbing the heavens and pulling out its good luck.

787 SWEET DREAMS JAPANESE-STYLE

JAPAN From the discreet entrance way to the tatami-mat guestroom, everything about a ryokan, a traditional Japanese inn, oozes understated elegance. You'll need a little knowledge of etiquette – and a few yen – to stay in one, but both are amply rewarded.

Sliding open the wooden front door, identified by a modest sign if at all, you enter a world of tinkling shamisen music and kimono-clad staff. Exquisite hanging scrolls and painted screens contrast with rustic woodwork and a seemingly casual arrangement of seasonal flowers soft-lit through shoji paper screens. It's an artful, quintessentially Japanese blend of refinement and simplicity.

Your shoes replaced with simple slippers, you'll be led along hushed corridors to your individually styled guestroom. It's stockinged feet only now on the rice-straw tatami mats. There's no sign of bedding, just a low table in an almost bare room. Attention is focused on the alcove, with its wall hanging and minimalist flower arrangement, and on the garden. For the full-blown ryokan experience, it's essential for the guestroom to look out on a traditional garden, no matter how small. Again it contains nothing flamboyant – no garish flowers, but a harmonious arrangement of moss, stone and neatly trimmed trees and bushes. If you are lucky, the forms and colours will be intensified by a recent rain shower: nature idealized.

The same attention to detail and sense of aesthetics is apparent in the food served. You'll be brought trays overflowing with meticulously balanced and presented seasonal delicacies. With its array of serving dishes and its delicate aromas a ryokan meal is as much a feast for the eyes and nose as for the taste buds. Don't just tuck in; savour the moment.

And the senses are in for one last treat before bedtime. The traditional Japanese bath is a ritual in itself. The basic rule is to scrub down thoroughly at the taps, then ease yourself into the cypress-wood tub full of piping hot water. Then simply soak. It's absolute bliss.

Returning to your room you'll find your futon has been laid out for you. Sleep comes in an instant, soothed by the gentle beat of the bamboo water-dripper nodding back and forth in the garden.

788 GETTING LOST IN THE FORBIDDEN CITY

CHINA At Beijing's heart is Gugong, literally the "Imperial Palace" but more evocatively known as the Forbidden City. For hundreds of years this was China's psychic centre despite being barred to all but the emperor and his colossal retinue of advisors, wives, and eunuchs. Even today, almost a century after the last emperor was deposed, there's nowhere else in China that leaves such a lasting impression of just how wealthy the emperors were compared with their subjects, nor how lonely and isolated they must have been here, their lives regulated to an extraordinary degree by official and religious ceremony.

The Forbidden City's boundaries are marked by a tall red wall, with guard-towers at the corners; red is a lucky colour in China, but the overall effect is austere and, well, forbidding. But nothing prepares you for the awe-inspiring, bleak splendour of the first courtyard, a vast, alienating space paved in grey slabs within which the entire imperial court – one hundred thousand people – could assemble at once. Marble bridges cross a ceremonial "stream" here to a succession of red-pillared halls, each housing increasingly gaudy thrones where the emperor would fulfil ceremonial functions (Hall of Supreme Harmony), receive visitors (Hall of Protective Harmony) or spend his wedding nights (Palace of Earthly Peace). At the end are the Imperial Gardens with their gnarled trees, golden lions and pavilions, but even here the beauty is artificial and structured, and there's no relief from the notion of splendid order and routine – in the middle is the wooded Hill of Accumulated Elegance, which the emperor and consort were required to climb every ninth day of the ninth lunar month to admire the scenery.

789

VIEWING THE ARIRANG
MASS GYMNASTICS FESTIVAL

NORTH KOREA When it comes to collective displays, North Korea is in a league of its own. And there is nothing more collective than the Arirang festival – a jaw-dropping mass gymnastics display performed in Pyongyang, the capital of the world's most isolated, tightly controlled state.

Walking into the huge, May Day Stadium in Pyongyang, you are first confronted with a giant human billboard. In the bleachers opposite the main entrance sit about 20,000 school children holding books with 170 colourful flip-pages, which they open in perfect unison throughout the ninety-minute performance, to provide a backdrop to the gymnastics display.

Through this performance, Kim Jong-il's regime is able to create the socialist paradise it has not been able to produce in reality. Into the arena march literally tens of thousands of performers – elaborately dressed female dancers, soldiers

doing tae kwon do, labourers and cows and six-year-old children bouncing around in swimming costumes. There are even motorbikes riding across high wires above the stadium.

The performers swirl, leap, sashay, march, jump and shout around the stadium, enacting the traditional Korean "Arirang" love story interwoven with motifs of hardship under Japanese colonialism, the tragedy of the separation of the Korean peninsula, but mainly the prowess of the North Korean state, which George W Bush once labeled part of the "axis of evil".

Sitting among crowds of North Korean families, you'll be caught up in the incredible spectacle. It's hard to believe that so many performers could move in such precise unison, so many spectators could cheer at exactly the right time and a country would spend so much money on gymnastics rather than rice.

790

THEY EAT SHOOTS AND LEAVES:
MEETING PANDAS IN CHENGDU

CHINA There's only one thing cuter than a giant panda: its cuddly, bumbling baby, the closest animal equivalent to a real live teddy. But these loveable black-and-white bears are one of the most reproductively challenged species on the planet, with exceptionally low birth rates; it's thought that there are fewer than two thousand of them left worldwide. The Giant Panda Breeding Research Base, just outside Chengdu in Sichuan, was established to preserve this cherished emblem of China, and has become a magnet for panda fans worldwide. It's extremely rare to see a cub in zoos, and it's virtually impossible to see any pandas at all in the wild – but come to the research base and you'll see plenty. And as over eighty cubs have been successfully bred here since 1987, you're almost guaranteed to see youngsters as well as adult bears. Most of the centre is covered in forest to replicate the mountain habitat of the bears, with naturalistic, spacious enclosures replete with trees and pools, and sleeping quarters designed to resemble caves.

There are no bars or railings here; instead, each enclosure is separated from the public pathways by a deep trench – come at feeding time and you can gaze unobstructed as mummy panda languidly chews her way through several heaps of bamboo shoots and leaves, slumped nonchalantly on the floor and occasionally throwing a bemused glance at her adoring admirers.

But there's no doubt who steals the show. Panda cubs come charging out of the compounds with surprising energy, romping over the grass and scrambling up the trees, invariably tumbling to the ground again and again as they make hilariously slapstick attempts to reach the top. While the adults like to lounge, babies love to play – and it simply doesn't get any cuter than this.

791 BEATEN AND BRUISED AT WUDANG SHAN

CHINA If in travels around China you hope to find a place where bearded mystics totter around mountain temples in between performing amazing feats of martial prowess, then head for Wudang Shan (the Martial Mountain) in Hubei province. Mythologized versions of this place can be seen in big-screen martial arts epics such as *Crouching Tiger, Hidden Dragon*, which made such a big impression in the West; if domestic critical response was more muted, it's only because people here were already used to this sort of thing. But there's no doubt that kungfu is a growth industry in modern China, not least because of the need for security: crime rates have mirrored the explosion in personal wealth with today's more capitalist-driven, free-market society, and the demand for bodyguards has increased alongside. Students can study kungfu privately, at martial art academies (where many hope to become film stars), and even at Wudang Shan, which is one of the homes of traditional Chinese kungfu.

There is a catch, however. Firstly, to study full-time at one of Wudang's temples you have to become a Taoist monk, which – what with the accompanying sexual abstinence, spartan living conditions and religious doctrine – might not appeal. Secondly, these people are serious. Not necessarily vicious, but you'll have to get used to being hit with fists, fingers, palms, feet, sticks and and an escalating number of weapons. Turn up casually, however, and you'll probably find people willing to spend an hour or two teaching you some basics of their systems without involving too much hand-to-hand combat. And even if you're not in the slightest bit interested in getting into a scrap, the mountain and its temples are a rare treat, with stone paths rising through thin woodland to the magnificent sight of the mountain's summit completely ringed by a fortress-like stone wall, a group of gold- and green-tiled temples rising within.

792 VISITING THE PITS OF HELL

TURKMENISTAN I felt like I was standing on the edge of Hell. Huge flames leapt out from the massive crater and fire balls exploded, sending rocks cascading down the sides to the unseen pit, the jagged edges threatening to give way and send me there too.

Here, in the middle of the desert in northern Turkmenistan, lay nine craters created when the Soviet gas explorers came searching for energy. Some bright spark had the idea of setting one alight, and for the last two decades it has burned continuously, creating an orange glow that can be seen for miles at night and smelt from just slightly closer. There can be few attractions stranger than these Darvaza gas craters, and that's saying something considering the idiosyncracies of this

country, home to one of the world's most bizarre personality cults (second only to North Korea).

We set up camp in the desert, looking out for giant zemzen desert lizards, and waiting for night to fall. After the sky was inky, Oleg, our guide, revved his Niva 4WD, ready to crash through the dunes. Banging into sand walls and dropping into sand holes, we careered though the emptiness towards the craters.

As we got closer, the glow became brighter and the heat and smell hit us as soon as we got out of the car. And once I beheld this burning, furious pit in the middle of all the nothingness, I had a more vivid understanding of the saying "a snowball's chance in hell".

793 GETTING SOUSED AT SISTERS' MEAL FESTIVAL

CHINA "Make him do it again!" This from a young policeman who had just missed his chance to photograph me spilling about a pint of home-made rice wine down my front. For the second time. Well, it's not every day that you get carjacked by a score of beautiful girls dressed in exquisitely embroidered silk jackets and enough silverware to sink a battleship, and forced to quaff from a buffalo-horn's worth of raw spirit if you want to carry on your way. "Don't touch the horn" warned a friend, "or you'll have to drain it!" So I stood with my hands behind my back while one of the girls held up the wine and tried to get me to sip. But buffalo-horn goblets are obviously not designed for Westerners – a mouthful went in, but my big nose bumped the edge, and my shirt got the rest. The crowd loved it.

Such are the hazards of attending the Miao people's Sisters'

Meal Festival at Shidong, Guizhou province, the time of the year when all marriageable girls from the local villages pick a husband. This was the third and final day, by which time I'd already got involved in vigorous group dances, had fireworks thrown at me (nothing personal – just part of the action) during a riotous late-night dragon-lantern competition, and narrowly missed being trampled by the loser at a buffalo-wrestling contest. Now all twenty thousand participants were heading to a nearby river to wind the festival up with some dragon-boat races. The roadblock was passed at last, but not before the policeman had got his photos, I'd sunk a skinful, and the world had become decidedly fuzzy around the edges. All I can remember is that after the boat races, all twenty thousand of us formed rings and danced and sang until dawn. At least, that's what my head felt like I'd done the next morning.

794 QUALITY SPACE: ADMIRING SUZHOU'S GARDENS

CHINA Since the thirteenth century, even Westerners have known about the cultured city of Suzhou, after Marco Polo wrote of its skilful artisans and sages in his book of travels. Incredibly, it still occupies an elevated position in the modern Chinese psyche: a popular saying lists Suzhou's virtues as its beautiful women, silk, and – especially – gardens, the design of which dates back over a thousand years to the Song dynasty. Polo probably never saw one, however; far from being for the enjoyment of the masses, gardens were attached to family mansions, designed by wealthy merchants and scholars as private, contemplative retreats. Most pack a lot of detail into a very small space, and their construction was a genuine art, using carefully positioned rocks, pools, walls, windows and trees to create a sense of balance, harmony and proportion, where literature could be studied or a friend entertained over a cup of wine.

Well, that was the original idea, but holding on to any such lofty notions today is asking to be crushingly disappointed by the daily hordes of tourists that pack out these delicate, interlinked courtyards. Get around a few, however – about ten are open to the public – and you'll still pick up on echoes of what they were originally planned for, though the famous and complementary Wangshi Yuan (best viewed in moonlight), Shizi Lin with its naturally shaped rocks, and watery Zhuozheng Yuan are constantly seething with people. If you're lucky and get in first thing in the morning before others arrive, however, you might even find a few minutes to yourself at the relatively unknown Canglang Ting and Ou Yuan gardens, and maybe catch just a glimpse of a more refined time.

795 SAUNTERING THROUGH SEOUL

SOUTH KOREA One of the most densely populated and digitized metropolises on the planet, Seoul is not usually the ideal place for a quiet, meditative walk. But stumble around Insadong-gil, a road surrounded by innumerable tearooms and art galleries, and take in the regal splendour of a couple of the nearby palaces, and you have the perfect recipe for a day's ambling.

Start at Gyeongbokgung, the most impressive of the palaces and home to the country's kings for 200 years prior to the 1592 Japanese invasion. Set against the jagged, pine-encrusted backdrop of the Bukhansan mountain range, traditional wooden buildings dot the complex; even the largest – the throne hall – manages to look delicate despite supporting tons of traditional roofing. Yet more charming, but still colossal, is an island pavilion in a tranquil lotus pond.

When you've had your fill of all things regal, head for the northern end of Insadong-gil. On the way here you'll pass umpteen art galleries, and there are even more on the road itself, a delightful mix of the traditional and the trendy. Should this bring your muse out to play, shops selling paints, brushes and handmade paper will be able to sate your desires. The less arty can relax in one of many excellent tearooms, which sell high-quality teas such as ginger, cinnamon and quince, though racier sorts may want to try the shocking pink "five flavours" tea (omija-cha). The lovely Yetchatjip tearoom even has a tiny army of amiable finches fluttering around the room,

Locally made trinkets are on sale all the way down Insadong-gil, and the many tiny alleyways that zigzag off the main road are crammed to bursting point with restaurants. Here you can sample Korean cuisine such as bibimbap, a mix of vegetables on rice, or galbi, pork or beef barbequed on your table. The road terminates at Tapgol, a small park full of old men playing cards, and the perfect place to reflect on your day.

796 PEAKING EARLY IN HONG KONG

CHINA If you like to get on top of everything in your travels, then Hong Kong's summit to conquer is the 552-metre-high Victoria Peak, about the only thing in Hong Kong island that outstrips the eighty-eight-storey IFC2 Tower. And unlike everything else to do in the downtown area, not only is the Peak (as locals call it) not man-made, but you don't need a wad of cash to enjoy it, at least if you walk up – though then you'll lose in sweat what you save in money.

It is, however, a great walk through a cross-section of the city, taking you from the harbour, underneath the HSBC Tower and along elevated walkways, around the knife-like Bank of China Tower, into Hong Kong Park. Continue uphill and exit the park near the jaguar cage, then follow ever-steeper inclines between high-rise apartments until the pavement turns into a concrete path and winds up into shady rainforest. Here you'll be overtaken by joggers gasping themselves into an early grave, while the path climbs for another forty minutes past some exclusive, isolated houses (Hong Kong's costliest real estate), and then you're there.

If this all sounds a bit much, then the Peak Tram is a more stylish, faster and less exhausting way to ascend the Peak. In use since the 1880s, the Tram sidesteps the legwork but still gives the feel of the Peak's severe gradients in the way you sink back into your wooden seat as the carriage is hauled upwards. Whichever method you use to conquer the Peak, however, you'll find that reaching the summit brings a sense of let-down in a horrible concrete viewing platform, despite which you'd have to be very hardened not to find the views down on Hong Kong's towering architecture and splendid harbour inspiring.

SHOOTING TO THE TOP OF THE
WORLD'S TALLEST BUILDING

TAIWAN Shooting up to the observation deck of Taipei 101, the world's tallest building, in the world's fastest elevators, it's easy to lose all sense of perspective. To start with, the lift you're in is moving at over 60km per hour. Pressurized like an aircraft cabin, it takes just 37 seconds to travel the 382.2m from the 5th floor entrance to the 89th floor observatory. Once you've arrived, the disorientation is compounded by a mind-blowing mismatch of scale: looming over the modern heart of Taipei, the tower dwarves everything around it. You'll feel far closer to the jagged mountains to the south, and to the thick clouds that frequently collect over the Taipei Basin – half the tower is often shrouded within one.

Taipei 101 became the world's tallest building in 2003, when it topped out at 508m. But what makes it truly unique is its location. Taiwan experiences a vicious typhoon season and is one of the most seismically active parts of the planet. For anyone who has experienced an apartment block shaking like a pile of jelly, mixing earthquakes with tall buildings might seem a touch insane. Yet the designers of Taipei 101 managed to come up with a solution: their main innovation was to hang a 660-tonne steel pendulum, known as a tuned mass damper, from the 89th floor to offset strong winds and tremors. The damper is also the world's largest – surprise, surprise – and can be viewed from the observation deck. Don't worry though: if all else fails remember that the building is divided into eight canted sections, considered a lucky number in Chinese tradition, and that the whole project was approved by a Feng Shui master.

LOSING TRACK OF TIME:
BEIJING TO MOSCOW ON THE TRANS-SIBERIAN

CHINA TO RUSSIA On the fourth day I stopped caring about time. I thought it was the fourth day, in fact it was the third. Beijing was a receding memory, Moscow impossibly distant. I had slipped into the habit of sleeping for four hours and then getting up for four hours, it didn't matter whether it was light or dark. Life inside the train bore no relation to the outside world – Siberia – which barreled past, cold, unwelcoming and as predictable as wallpaper: birch trees, hills, birch trees, plains, birch trees.

"I hate those trees", said the elderly German in my compartment. "I want to cut them all down".

Occasionally we passed an untidy village of wooden cabins but mostly the only human touch to the epic landscape was the telegraph poles at the side of the track.

My first Russian was a young guy in a shell suit with a moustache and an anarchy tattoo. "The Beatles", he said, on hearing I was British.

"The Rolling Stones", I countered.

He nodded "The Doors".

"Pearl Jam?" I inquired.

"Nirvana", he asserted. "Napalm Death".

Once or twice a day the train stopped and I'd emerge for fresh air, dizzy and blinking, onto a platform swarming with frenzied shoppers. Traders stood in the carriage door and the townsfolk, who had waited all week for two minutes of consumerism, rioted to get to them. To save time the traders threw money over their shoulders into the corridor to be collected by colleagues. They sold World Cup t-shirts, plastic jewellery and Mickey Mouse umbrellas. Even the man from the dining car had a cupboard of trainers, which was perhaps why he could only offer gherkins and soup in his official capacity.

I played cards then slept, battleships, slept, charades, slept. It was an invalid's life – a long slow delirium in comfortable confinement. But on the seventh day, or perhaps the sixth, when grey housing blocks started appearing and Moscow was imminent, I suddenly felt nostalgic for that easy sloth. When I finally got off, something felt terribly wrong; it took me a while to figure it out – oh yes, the ground wasn't moving.

799 TEA IN THE LAND OF FIRE

AZERBAIJAN The teashop was unexceptional in almost every respect. It was a long, single-storey building with a rudimentary toilet at one end and a couple of tables standing outdoors at the other. The setup was like hundreds of cafés all across the Muslim world, except that this teashop just happened to be situated next to a hillside that was on fire.

The tables were covered in brightly coloured plastic veneer. An elderly man was sitting at one with two children. The man was sipping from a glass of black tea, the kids had cherry juice. These were his grandchildren, he told us as we took seats at the other table.

Khasay, my interpreter, ordered for us as I took in the view. The tables overlooked the hill. It wasn't a very impressive hill, more like a ridge, less than ten metres in height. The unusual thing about it was the fire burning at its base. I don't mean a bonfire or a barbecue, I mean the lower part of the incline was alight. But it wasn't a bushfire either. There was nothing obviously combustible in view. Large, bright orange flames just leapt out of the rocks. It was the slope itself that was ablaze.

Or, I suppose more strictly speaking, the natural gas that was seeping through fissures in the rock. The fire had been alight for nearly 50 years, the old man told us.

Here you could sip your tea outside all through the winter, he said, gesturing with his glass towards the flames. As the temperature dropped, all you had to do was move your table closer to the blazing incline. It was a bizarre spectacle, like drinking tea beside a trapdoor to Hades. I shouldn't have been surprised – "Azerbaijan" means Land of Fire. I just hadn't expected it literally.

800 JOUSTING FOR A TASTE OF BEIJING DUCK

CHINA Beijing 1985: Mao has been dead for nine years but China is still reeling from the effects of his restrictive policies, which have held the country's economy back at almost pre-industrial levels. People shuffle around dispiritedly in blue Mao suits, bicycles outnumber cars about a thousand to one, the air is heavy with the smell of charcoal burning in braziers and the most modern buildings are functional, grey, communist-inspired concrete blocks. The only shops selling anything other than daily necessities are the "Friendship Stores", full of imported luxuries such as televisions and the locals that dream about earning enough money to own one. Restaurants serving anything other than bland, uninspiring food are extremely thin on the ground. With one very notable exception: the *Quanjude Roast Duck* restaurant, founded in 1864 and recently resurrected after being closed down during the Maoist era. Enter most restaurants in China and you're herded into a special "foreigners' only" section out of sight of indigenous diners (for whose benefit it isn't clear), but not here: for Chinese and foreigners alike it's a free-for-all, where only the quick and strong get fed. The dining hall is so crammed with tables that there's barely room to fit the chairs in, and that's a big problem because all available room – absolutely every inch – is occupied by salivating customers hovering like vultures beside each chair, waiting for the person sitting down to finish their meal and begin to get up. The ensuing moments of hand-to-hand combat, as three people try to occupy the half-empty seat, end with the victor knowing that they are about to enjoy a cholesterol-laden feast. First comes the duck's skin, crispy brown and aromatic; next the juicy meat, carefully sliced and eaten with spring onion slivers, all wrapped inside a thin pancake; and lastly, a soup made from duck bones and innards. And all for ¥12 – less than two dollars for a night's entertainment.

801 CHASING TEMPLES IN SHIKOKU

JAPAN Japanese temples have a faint air of magic about them. Though somewhat austere in comparison to those of other Asian nations, less has long been more in Japan. A good sunset can haul simmering shades of gold from the bareness, while dusk can make white flashes of paint seem to hover against dark, brooding backgrounds – an anime come to life. Occasional paper doors and windows play similar optical tricks within the buildings, filtering the light of the outside world into a soft, mind-cleansing cream.

While the former capital of Kyoto is arguably home to the most ornate temples in the country, some of the more atmospheric are in the nooks and crannies of small towns or farming communities. Those truly in the know head to Shikoku – this smallest and most bucolic of Japan's four main islands is home to a mammoth 88-temple pilgrimage, which takes around three months to complete on foot. The overwhelming majority follow the route in a car or on a bus tour, but in warmer months you're sure to see staff-wielding pilgrims, or henro-san, pacing the route, as well as hikers who don traditional white costumes along with their backpacks.

Few will have the time or inclination necessary to complete the whole pilgrimage, but the number of temples on it – only a fraction of the total number on the island – means that opportunities for shorter treks are plentiful. Though each temple has its merits, one of the most commonly visited is Zentsu-ji, the birthplace of Kobo Daishi, in whose memory the pilgrimage is made. Despite its official status as number seventy-five on the clockwise course, the temple is one of the first you'll come upon after crossing the Seto Ohashi, a series of bridges slung across the spectacular island-peppered sea between Shikoku and the main Japanese island of Honshu. From there, green Shikoku and its temples are yours to discover.

802 SHOPPING FOR A NATIONAL TREASURE AT TOLKUCHKA MARKET

TURKMENISTAN "Water is a Turkmen's life, a horse is his wings, and a carpet is his soul". A proverb from days of yore it may be, but it's difficult to over-egg the role that carpets play in modern-day Turkmenistan. The national flag features the carpet guls (rug designs) of the country's five major tribes. Ashgabat's most popular cultural centre is the Carpet Museum. And on the last Sunday in May, the whole country grinds to a halt to celebrate Carpet Day. In short, nothing gets a Turkmen going like the perfect weave.

The museum shop is a good place to start your browsing, but for the finest designs, join the locals at Ashgabat's Tolkuchka Market, a sprawling bazaar on the outskirts of town at the edge of the Karakum Desert. Soft kilims lie alongside beshirs and kerkis, huge yomuds are splayed across the floor (the more knots in their finely trimmed ends, the pricier the pile), and Teke rugs tower in neat, folded rolls. But the finest of all, the carpet of connoisseurs, are the stunning Akhal-Teke, intricately designed wefts that dazzle in their symmetry. Mostly woven with a red background, the rarer blue designs can sell for several thousand dollars.

You won't be the first to leave Turkmenistan wishing that you'd left more rug room in your suitcase. Marco Polo came here in the thirteenth century and was sufficiently moved to declare that Turkmen carpets were the most beautiful in the world – seven hundred years later, and the quality of the craftsmanship is still beyond compare.

803 DOUBLE HAPPINESS AT THE TIANYUANKI GUESTHOUSE

CHINA The historic walled town of Pingyao is UNESCO-listed for its graceful temples and grand nineteenth-century mansions, so you'll want to stay in a hotel that doesn't break the spell.

The *Tianyuankui Guesthouse*, dating back to 1791, fits the bill perfectly, tastefully invoking its earlier incarnation as a courtyard home during the Qing Dynasty. Rooms open onto courtyards hung with large red lanterns and dotted with stone guardian lions, eaves are flamboyantly coloured in kingfisher blues and greens and gold-painted lintels depict exquisite scenes from literature and folklore.

Every room displays an intricate, red-paper cut-out on its window: if you're a newlywed you'll be given the one with lovebirds encircling the character for "double happiness". Entering your room through a lattice-wood door, you find miniature red lanterns suspended above an enormous platform bed, or kang, wide enough to sleep four and with space underneath for a toe-warming brazier.

RUSSIA An average ski run in Kamchatka is not like that of your regular ski resort; it's not unusual to get in more than 10,000m of "vertical" in a single day. You're pumped full of adrenalin before you even start, thanks to the half-hour ride to your first run in a huge, ramshackle Russian-built MI-8 helicopter.

Your guide will head down an enormous, open powder field running 180m or more down the flanks of a volcano and you're then free to follow, with almost infinite space in which to lay down your own tracks. You may pass beside hissing volcanic vents (one of which last erupted in 2001) or alongside glinting blue glaciers or just bliss out on endless turns in shin-deep fluff. You may even end up on a Pacific beach where you can take a frigid skinny dip. And then you'll clamber back into the helicopter to do it all over again – and again, and again.

804
SKIING IN THE LAND OF
FIRE AND ICE

805

PAST MEETS PRESENT AT

GION MATSURI

JAPAN It can be a weird place, at least to the uninitiated. Sometimes, Japan is the epitome of modern, urban life; at others, it's as if the country is stuck in the Middle Ages. Nowhere is this more evident, or perhaps more jarring, than in Kyoto, and there's no better time to be here than during the annual ten-day Gion Matsuri every July – a series of events dating back over a thousand years that culminates in a massive, full-on procession through the modern main streets of the old capital. Thousands of people of all ages line the route: youngsters in colourful summer kimonos, wobbling precariously on wooden sandals while they pose for pictures or chat on mobile phones, and tour buses full of middle-aged country folk, videocams out waiting to capture the moment when the floats – some of them two storeys high, and dragged by locals in loincloths – come by in a compelling drone of drums, bells, voices and flute.

806 CLIMBING FUJI

JAPAN The Japanese call it Fuji-san, as if they're politely addressing a neighbour. Most famously glimpsed on winter days when the clouds clear and the symmetrical snow-capped cone is etched against a brilliant blue sky, Mount Fuji is the site of an annual pilgrimage. During the climbing season from July to September tens of thousands take on the dormant volcano's crumbling black ash slopes and trudge through the night to the summit of Japan's highest mountain (3776m).

Fuji is divided into ten stations, with the first being at sea level and the tenth the summit. A paved road runs to Kawaguchi-ko, the fifth station, a Swiss chalet-style giftshop about halfway up the volcano. This is where many people begin the ascent on foot, and at a steady pace it's a six-hour climb from here to the top. However, there's no rush: the true Fuji experience is more about the shared camaraderie of the climb rather than setting speed records.

The common approach is to start climbing in the afternoon aiming for one of the mountain huts at the seventh or eighth station levels. Here you can get dinner, meet fellow climbers and rest, waking in the dead of night to complete the final stages of the climb before dawn, which can be as early as 4.30am. The tiny lights of climbers' torches, like a line of fireflies trailing up the volcanic scree, will guide you to the summit.

Having witnessed the goraiko (Buddha's Halo) sunrise, you'll then have an opportunity to take part in the time-honoured tradition of making a phone call or mailing a letter from the post office. A circuit of the crater is also in order, keeping your fingers crossed that this is not the day that Fuji decides to reawake.

807 TREKKING THROUGH THE VALLEY OF THE GEYSERS

RUSSIA Penetrating Kamchatka's remote and rugged terrain to discover one of the world's most restless regions of seismic hyperactivity has never been easy. With no roads or nearby settlements, the spectacular Valley of the Geysers wasn't discovered until 1941. Not even Russians were permitted to travel to this far-eastern peninsula until after the fall of communism. Today, a trek through the Kronotsky Reserve on the peninsula's eastern edge leads you into this land of fire and ice, and brings you face to face with the full range of Kamchatka's volcanic phenomena.

You'll be dropped into the heart of the million-hectare bioreserve by helicopter, cruising over several of Kamchatka's 29 active volcanoes along the way. Your trek involves ten days and 130km of moderately strenuous hiking through coastal mountains, forests, bush thickets and some forest-less highlands. As you navigate this landscape down to the Pacific shore you'll ring active glacier-flanked volcanoes and encounter piping fumaroles, belching mudpots and bubbling cauldrons.

Through forests of Siberian pine you'll descend into the Uzon Caldera, a marshy depression scattered with scalding lakes, warm streams and over a thousand hot springs. Steaming waterfalls cascade into rivers running with red salmon, migratory birds find green vegetation in April and bears coming out of hibernation warm themselves by simmering mud cauldrons.

From a forested ridge you descend into the Valley of the Geysers along the steamy banks of the River Geyzernaya, one of dozens of rivers that bisect the reserve en route to the Pacific shore. You don't immediately sense what's going on underfoot, as dozens of tributaries feed a concentration of hot springs below the surface.

Over twenty major geysers fill the narrow valley, each performing on its own timetable: some erupt every ten minutes, while others take 4–5 hours between show times. Some pulse in an erect column while others surprise you with a side shot – stick to the boardwalk or you might be nailed by an unexpected burst of scalding water.

Your onward descent to the Pacific shore leads through bushy and mossy tundras to an abandoned fur-trading outpost where, if all goes according to plan, your helicopter awaits for the return ride. Kamchatka's never-ending volcanic display is a reminder that earth's creation is a work in progress.

808 BEACH LOUNGING AT BEIDAIHE

CHINA With its faintly Mediterranean atmosphere, what better place to while away a warm summer day than Beidaihe, on the coast just a few hours fom Beijing?

There was once a time when foreigners in China were the only people with a handle on beach life, and the Chinese would sit in uncomfortable family groups, ill at ease in their bathing gear, clearly worried about wading out of their depth in the water, and looking as if they knew that it should all be fun, but wondering how to go about it. China's non-steroid-enhanced swim team's performance at the 2004 Olympic Games in Athens swept all that away. Now, fired by national pride, the water beckons the athletic, while the less-competitive remainder parade in their surprisingly skimpy swimsuits, lounge on the sand, or play beachball between the huge granite statues of heroic workers which once set the political tone. Most people here are ordinary, aspiring youngsters and nouveaux riches from Beijing, though the occasional cruising black Audi with dark windows harks back to a time when the sand and surf were reserved for the sole enjoyment of the party elite. Back along the promenade, shops sell exactly the sort of seaside kitsch you'd expect from the setting (fluorescent swimsuits, animal sculptures made of seashells), while private villas of the rich sport ludicrously overblown architectural flourishes. The best places to hang out, once you've had enough of the beach, are the many excellent restaurants, where you can down a cold beer and make your choice from seafood so fresh that it's still flapping around in a bucket.

MISCELLANY

HORSEPLAY

Kumis, or fermented mare's milk, is an important beverage to Mongols and the people of the Central Asian steppes. Kumis production requires great skill – it's tricky to milk a horse – and the beverage is traditionally fermented in a horsehide pouch.

AGE-OLD ACCOMMODATION

Hoshi Ryokan, a traditional Japanese establishment in the heart of Ishikawa Prefecture, Japan, is the **world's oldest hotel**; it has been receiving guests since AD 717.

SERVICE WITH A SMILE

Nyotaimori, the art of eating sushi off of a naked woman, is a Japanese practice dating back to the late nineteenth century. Before their shift, servers bathe in fragrance-free soap and splash themselves with cold water to keep body temperature down for the food.

"Great souls have wills; feeble ones have only wishes"

Chinese proverb

FROM TERRORISM TO TOURISM

If the underground dwellings in Spain and Turkey leave you cold, then perhaps the mountains of east Afghanistan will be more up your street: a former mujahaddin warlord is investing $10 million in a new hotel complex overlooking the Tora Bora caves, where Al-Qaeda leader **Osama Bin Laden** hid out to avoid US forces in December 2001.

TABLE MANNERS

In **Afghanistan**, if bread is dropped on the floor while eating at a table, it should picked up, kissed and put to one's forehead before it is returned to the table-top; in **Russia** it is considered rude to look into someone else's plate or cup; while in **China** you should never stick chopsticks into a bowl of rice, leaving them standing upwards, as this resembles the incense sticks that some Asians use as offerings to deceased family members.

DANGEROUS FOOD

Takifugu (or, colloquially, **fugu**) is a highly toxic pufferfish served as a delicacy in Japan. Because of its poisonous nature, only specially licensed chefs can prepare and sell it to the public, and would-be fugu chefs have to apprentice for two to three years before taking an official fugu-preparation test. Even then, only about one-third of applicants pass the rigorous examination. Ironically, many actually find the fish to be flavourless, eating it solely for the allure of cheating death.

Japanese poet Yosa Buson (1716–83) summed it up with a haiku:

I cannot see her tonight.
I have to give her up
So I will eat fugu

TEA

Tea has been drunk in China for at least three thousand years and was introduced to Japan in the ninth century. There are three main types, depending on how the leaves are processed: green tea, where the leaves are picked and dried directly; black tea, where the leaves are fermented before being dried; and oolong tea, which is semi-fermented.

GOING, GOING....

Despite some improvements in the last two years, the **Aral Sea** in Central Asia is surely the world's largest man-made disaster: a once vast natural lake, it has not only been heavily polluted from weapons testing and industry, but it has also been reduced in size by sixty percent over the last forty years (mainly as a result of river diversion), and whole villages and fleets of ships lie stranded in the sand, hundreds of miles from water.

CHINESE HOROSCOPES

Animal	Date of birth	Characteristics
Rat	1936, 1948, 1960, 1972, 1984, 1996	generous, intelligent, insecure
Ox	1937, 1949, 1961, 1973, 1985, 1997	obstinate, independent, conservative
Tiger	1938, 1950, 1962, 1974, 1986, 1998	adventurous; creative, fearless
Rabbit	1939, 1951, 1963, 1975, 1987, 1999	peace-loving, timid, long-lived
Dragon	1940, 1952, 1964, 1976, 1988, 2000	commanding, popular, athletic
Snake	1941, 1953, 1965, 1977, 1989, 2001	charming, selfish, secretive
Horse	1942, 1954, 1966, 1978, 1990, 2002	ambitious, popular, fickle
Goat	1943, 1955, 1967, 1979, 1991, 2003	charming, lucky, unpunctual
Monkey	1944, 1956, 1968, 1980, 1992, 2004	intelligent, egoistic, entertaining
Rooster	1945, 1957, 1969, 1981, 1993, 2005	reckless, tactless; imaginative
Dog	1946, 1958, 1970, 1982, 1994, 2006	watchful, responsible, home-loving
Pig	1947, 1959, 1971, 1983, 1995, 2007	honest, naïve, kind

HIGHEST PEAKS IN CHINA

Rank in world	Mountain	Metres
1	Everest	8848m
2	K2	8611m
4	Makalu	8463m
5	Cho Oyu	8210m
11	Gasherbrum I	8068m

CHINA'S TOP NATURAL
ATTRACTIONS

- **Jiuzhaigou, Sichuan** One of China's most spectacular landscapes.
- **Flaming Mountains, Xinjiang** Stunning red sandstone hillsides.
- **Changbai Shan, Heilongjiang** The northeast's loveliest nature reserve.
- **Huang Shan, Anhui** Arguably China's most scenic mountain.
- **Zhangjiajie, Hunan** Mystical landscape of limestone towers.

CHINA ON FILM

A Chinese Ghost Story (1987). One of the seminal Hong Kong films of the 1980s – part horror film, part love story, part martial-arts blockbuster.

Beijing Bastards (1993). One of the best of China's "underground movies".

Crouching Tiger, Hidden Dragon (2000) Epic martial arts film that was a massive hit in the West.

Blind Shaft (2003). Deemed too controversial for domestic release – a telling indictment of runaway capitalism and a great piece of film noir.

Kung Fu Hustle (2004). A melange of surreal comedy, pastiche, slapstick and kung fu.

BUDDHISM IN BHUTAN

Buddhism in **Bhutan** originated in neighbouring Tibet, and today most Bhutanese follow either the Drukpa Kagyu or the Nyingmapa school of Tibetan Buddhism. The **Bhutan** government closely regulates outside influences and tourism in part to preserve its traditional Buddhist culture, making the Himalayan nation one of the least-visited and most isolated countries in the world.

GETTING TO KNOW THE
DALAI LAMA

- "Dalai" means "ocean" in Mongolian, while "Lama" is Tibetan for "spiritual teacher".
- The Dalai Lama is believed to be the incarnation of the Bodhisattva Avalokiteshvara
- Familiarity with the possessions of the previous Dalai Lama is regarded as the main sign of the reincarnation.
- The first Dalai Lama was born in 1391.
- The current Dalai Lama – the 14th – won the Nobel Peace prize in 1989.

"In a mad world, only the mad are sane"

Akira Kurosawa, Japanese film director

THE TWO KOREAS

The two states on the Korean Peninsula – **North Korea and South Korea** – are technically still at war with each other, and have been since 1953. Separated arbitrarily along the 38th Parallel into two spheres of ideological influence by invading US and Soviet troops in 1945, the peninsula saw intense ground and air fighting during the hostilities of the Korean Conflict (1950–53). Though a cease-fire was ultimately established, a peace treaty was never signed, and to this day a demilitarized zone – guarded to the north by North Korean troops, and to the south by South Korean and American troops – sits between the two countries, along the 38th Parallel.

FESTIVALS

Country	Festival	When and where
Bhutan	Paro Tshechu Crowds in the thousands, masked dancers and an enormous tapestry	March/April; temples countrywide
China	Sisters' Meal Festival Dragon-lantern dances and buffalo fights	April/May; Kaili, Guizhou Province
Mongolia	Naadam Three-day festival that celebrates horseracing, archery and wrestling	July; countrywide
Taiwan	Dragon-boat festival Day-long festival of stunningly designed boats racing in commemoration of the suicide of the poet Chu Yuan.	July; countrywide
Japan	Kodo Drummers' Earth Celebration Enormous drums, dynamic drummers, and plenty of dancing	August; Sado-ga-shima Island
Uzbekistan	Uzbek Tubeteika Folk Festival Dedicated to the artistry of Uzbek national skull-caps	September; Shakhrisabz
South Korea	Chungju World Martial Arts Festival Seven-day martial arts extravaganza in the spiritual home of tae kwon do.	October; Chungju

BRIGHT LIGHTS, BIG CITIES

The **most populated city** in the world is Seoul, South Korea, while ten of the world's fifty most populated cities are in China. **Beihai**, in southern China, is forecast be the fastest growing city in the world, with a projected annual growth rate of over 10 percent – over twice that of the next highest city on the list.

FIVE BIGGEST CITIES

City	Population
Seoul, South Korea	10, 231,000
Shanghai, China	8,214,000
Tokyo, Japan	8,130,000
Beijing, China	7,362,000
Hong Kong, China	6,843,000

WHERE IS EVERYBODY?

Mongolia has the lowest population density of any country in the world – just two people per square kilometre.

NOT ACCORDING TO BORAT

Though Borat has some people believing otherwise, **Kazakhstan** is not the world's number one exporter of potassium – oil is the country's chief economic resource, while the traditional Kazakh greeting is "**Salamatsyz ba**" (good afternoon) – not "**jagshemash**".

SLIDING ALONG THE HIMALAYAN ICE HIGHWAY • RHYTHM MADNESS AT THE THRISSUR PURAM • BOLLYWOOD GLITZ AT THE MUMBAI METRO • TREKKING TO THE SOURCE OF THE GANGES • **THE DANCING GODDESS OF KERALA** • TRACKING THE TURTLE ARRIBADA AT ORISSA • WATCHING THE SUN RISE OVER ACHYUTARAYA TEMPLE • **VISITING THE TAJ BY MOONLIGHT** • BIRDING BY RICKSHAW AT KEOLADEO • EXPLORING THE THAR DESERT BY CAMEL • WALKING TO "PARADISE" AT GOKARNA • DRIVING OVER THE ROOF OF THE WORLD • ENVISIONING A LOST CIVILIZATION AT AJANTA • **EATING A BANANA-LEAF LUNCH IN CHIDAMBARAM** • ON THE EDGE IN THE ANDAMANS • SUFI GROOVES: QAWWALI AT NIZZAMUDDIN • TRACKING TIGERS IN BANDHAVGARH • CRUISING THE KERALAN BACKWATERS • SEEING RED DURING HOLI • CRICKET MAYHEM AT EDEN GARDENS • CATCHING THE SEA BREEZE AT ELSEWHERE • STAYING WITH A FAMILY IN THE HIMALAYAS • BEATING THE DROUGHT IN THE THAR • SADHU-SPOTTING AT THE KUMBH MELA • CHRISTMAS SHOPPING IN KUTCH • HOPPING ON BOARD FOR A KERALAN SADYA • GETTING SWEPT AWAY AT DURGA PUJA • TAKING TEA IN DHARAMSALA • **HIGH IN HAPUTALE** • LOWERING THE FLAG AT THE INDIA–PAKISTAN BORDER • SACRED PEAKS: TREKKING IN THE HIMALAYAS • **BAREFOOT BLISS AT SONEVA GILI** • RIDING WAVES IN THE INDIAN OCEAN • LAKESIDE ROMANCE IN RAJASTHAN • CATCHING THE PERFECT WAVE IN THE MALDIVES • **WATCHING THE PONIES AT THE WORLD'S HIGHEST POLO TOURNAMENT** • INDIA'S ACROPOLIS: A SHRINE TO THE FISH-EYED GODDESS • EMBARKING ON AN ELEPHANT SAFARI AT KAZIRANGA • RIDING THE ROCKET ACROSS THE GANGES DELTA • CLIMBING ADAM'S PEAK • CROWD-WATCHING AT KARTIK PURNIMA • CYCLING THE KARAKORAM HIGHWAY • PARIKRAMA AT THE GOLDEN TEMPLE • TRIPPING THROUGH THE PHALGUN FESTIVALS • ELBOWING THROUGH THE CROWDS FOR ESALA PERAHERA • SNOWBOARDING IN KASHMIR • CITY OF LIGHT: BOATING DOWN THE GANGES AT VARANASI • **BOLLYWOOD GLITZ AT THE MUMBAI METRO** • HAULING IN DINNER IN GOA • WATCHING A KATHAKALI PERFORMANCE IN KOCHI • WATCHING ELEPHANTS BATHE AT PINNAWALA • SLIDING ALONG THE HIMALAYAN ICE HIGHWAY • RHYTHM MADNESS AT THE THRISSUR PURAM • TREKKING TO THE SOURCE OF THE GANGES • EATING A BANANA-LEAF LUNCH IN CHIDAMBARAM • THE DANCING GODDESS OF KERALA • TRACKING THE TURTLE ARRIBADA AT ORISSA • WATCHING THE SUN RISE OVER ACHYUTARAYA TEMPLE • VISITING THE TAJ BY MOONLIGHT • BIRDING BY RICKSHAW AT KEOLADEO • EXPLORING THE THAR DESERT BY CAMEL • WALKING TO "PARADISE" AT GOKARNA • DRIVING OVER THE ROOF OF THE WORLD • **ENVISIONING A LOST CIVILIZATION AT AJANTA** • ON THE EDGE IN THE ANDAMANS • SUFI GROOVES: QAWWALI AT NIZZAMUDDIN • TRACKING TIGERS IN BANDHAVGARH • CRUISING THE KERALAN BACKWATERS • SEEING RED DURING HOLI • CRICKET MAYHEM AT EDEN GARDENS • CATCHING THE SEA BREEZE AT ELSEWHERE • STAYING WITH A FAMILY IN THE HIMALAYAS • BEATING THE DROUGHT IN THE THAR • SADHU-SPOTTING AT THE KUMBH MELA • CHRISTMAS SHOPPING IN KUTCH • HOPPING ON BOARD FOR A KERALAN SADYA • GETTING SWEPT AWAY AT DURGA PUJA • TAKING TEA IN DHARAMSALA • LOWERING THE FLAG AT THE INDIA–PAKISTAN BORDER • **SACRED PEAKS: TREKKING IN THE HIMALAYAS** • HIGH IN HAPUTALE • RIDING WAVES IN THE INDIAN OCEAN • LAKESIDE ROMANCE IN RAJASTHAN • CATCHING THE PERFECT WAVE IN THE MALDIVES • BAREFOOT BLISS AT SONEVA GILI • INDIA'S ACROPOLIS: A SHRINE TO THE FISH-EYED GODDESS • **RIDING THE ROCKET ACROSS THE GANGES DELTA** • EMBARKING ON AN ELEPHANT SAFARI AT KAZIRANGA • WATCHING THE PONIES AT THE WORLD'S HIGHEST POLO TOURNAMENT • CLIMBING ADAM'S PEAK • CROWD-WATCHING AT KARTIK PURNIMA • CYCLING THE KARAKORAM HIGHWAY • PARIKRAMA AT THE GOLDEN TEMPLE • TRIPPING THROUGH

THE INDIAN SUBCONTINENT

809–861

WATCHING THE PONIES
AT THE WORLD'S HIGHEST 848
POLO TOURNAMENT

PAKISTAN

SACRED PEAKS: 830
TREKKING IN THE HIMALAYAS

NEPAL

VISITING THE TAJ 852
BY MOONLIGHT

RIDING THE ROCKET 854
ACROSS THE GANGES DELTA

INDIA

BANGLADESH

ENVISIONING A LOST 816
CIVILIZATION AT AJANTA

BOLLYWOOD GLITZ 836
AT THE MUMBAI METRO

ANDAMAN
ISLANDS

EATING A BANANA-LEAF LUNCH 860
IN CHIDAMBARAM

THE DANCING GODDESS 823
OF KERALA

HIGH IN HAPUTALE 831

SRI LANKA

BAREFOOT BLISS 838
AT SONEVA GILI

MALDIVES

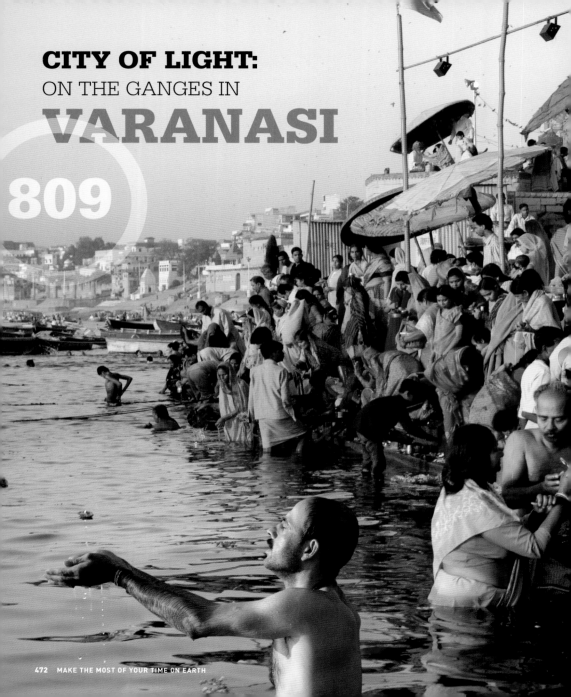

CITY OF LIGHT:
ON THE GANGES IN
VARANASI

809

INDIA The sun had barely risen above the riverbanks, but already the cremation ghats were hard at work. Four corpses, tightly bound in cotton and still soaked from their final cleansing dip in the Ganges, were laid out on wood pyres, ghee and garlands of orange marigolds piled on top of them. While gangs of small, dark, muscular men fed the flames, grieving relatives looked on, murmuring prayers with palms pressed together and heads bowed. The surrounding buildings were black with soot.

Varanasi – or Kashi ("City of Light"), as it was known in ancient times – is Hinduism's holiest city. Infamous across India for its squalor, its old core is a teeming, tangled warren of narrow alleyways with intricately carved doorways opening on to hidden, high-walled courtyards and shrines. Wander around for long enough and you'll eventually emerge at the ghats, or sacred stone steps, which spread around the mighty bend in the river here. From dawn until dusk, they present a constantly animated canvas of bathers, sadhus, tourists, hawkers, stray cows and priests plying their age-old trade under ragged parasols – all set against a magnificent backdrop of crumbling temples and palaces.

The best way to enjoy the spectacle is to jump in a rowing boat at Asi Ghat, in the south of the old city, just before sunrise. Paddling north as the first rays of sunlight infuse the riverfront with a reddish glow, you glide past the dark stupas of Buddha Ghat, Rewa Ghat's distinctive leaning towers, and the candy-striped steps of Vijayanagar Ghat. Manikarnika, the cremation ghat, is where the boatmen generally turn around.

Out on the river, visitors are insulated from the hassle of guides and trinket sellers, but not necessarily from Varanasi's still less savoury aspects. Poor Hindus who can't afford enough wood for their pyres will often have their charred remains shoved unceremoniously into the water – it's not unusual to find your boat bumping into a bloated body part, or even something eating one.

The ghats themselves are, however, most atmospheric just before dark. Watching the priests' cane lanterns flickering to life and mingling with the reflections of the afterglow, Kashi feels every inch the mystical "Threshold of Eternity" it has always been for Hindus.

810 WATCHING THE SUN RISE OVER ACHYUTARAYA TEMPLE

INDIA When Vijayanagar, capital of India's last Hindu empire, was ransacked by a Muslim army after the Battle of Talikota in 1565, the devastation was total. Few temples, palaces, houses or human lives were spared. It was the sixteenth-century equivalent of a nuclear holocaust.

Today, the site still lies largely deserted and in ruins – save for the mighty Virupaksha Temple at its heart, in the village of Hampi. Ranged around a bend in the Tungabhadra River, the small bazaar village and archeological remains occupy a landscape of surreal beauty. Hills of smooth granite boulders, eroded through time, are separated from each other by swathes of brilliant green banana groves, which conceal colonnaded walkways leading to hidden temples and bathing tanks. Because they were so comprehensively destroyed, the monuments possess an aura of greater antiquity than they perhaps deserve, but this only adds to the charisma of the place.

You can spend days wandering between sites, clambering up flights of rock-cut steps to reach forgotten shrines, deciphering mythological friezes on the walls of collapsed palaces, or catching coracles across the river to visit caves inhabited by dreadlocked sadhus. The definitive Hampi experience, however, has to be watching the sun rise from Matanga Hill, just east of the village's long, straight bazaar. Having scaled the flight of steps leading to the tiny temple crowning its summit, a wondrous view opens up. Immediately below you, the gopuras and walled enclosures of the Achyutaraya Temple rise through the morning mist like a vision from a lost world, framed by a vista of boulder hills stretching to the horizon.

And if that weren't a perfect enough way to start your day, an entrepreneurial chai-wallah has set up shop on the temple rooftop, so you can enjoy the awesome spectacle over a cup of delicious hot tea.

811 JOURNEYING OVER THE ROOF OF THE WORLD

INDIA–TIBET "Unbelievable is it Not!" reads a road sign at Tanglang La – at 5360m the highest point on the Manali–Leh highway. Looking north from the thicket of prayer flags fluttering above the pass, you'll probably find yourself agreeing. Between you and the white line of the Karakorams in the distance stretches a vast, bone-dry wilderness of mountains and snow-dusted valleys – not a view you'd normally expect from a bus window.

The 485-kilometre route from Manali in Himachal Pradesh to Leh in Ladakh is the great epic among Indian road journeys. With an overnight stop at altitude under a makeshift parachute tent en route, it takes two days to cover, carrying you from the foothills of the Himalayas to the margins of the Tibetan Plateau. Weather conditions can be fickle – blizzards descend even in mid-summer – and facilities along the way are rough and ready, to say the least. But the privations pale into insignificance against the astonishing scenery.

The first, and most formidable, of the obstacles to be crossed

is Rohtang La, "Pile of Bones Pass". Straddling one of the most sudden and extreme climatic transitions on the planet, Rohtang overlooks lush green cedar woods and alpine meadows on one side, and on the other a forbidding wall of chocolate- and sand-coloured scree, capped by ice peaks trailing plumes of spindrift.

Once across, settlements are few and far between. Nomadic shepherds and their flocks are sometimes the only signs of life on gigantic mountainsides streaked purple, red and blue with mineral deposits. Packed under snow for most of the year, the road surface deteriorates as you gain altitude, crumbling to loose shale and dizzying voids.

You cross Tanglang La late on the second afternoon, reaching the first Ladakhi villages soon after. Swathed in kidney-shaped terraces of ripening barley, each is surveyed by its own fairy-tale Buddhist monastery, with golden finials gleaming from the rooftops in sunlight of an almost unearthly clarity.

812 ELBOWING THROUGH THE CROWDS FOR ESALA PERAHERA

SRI LANKA In terms of noise and colour, there's nothing else quite like Kandy's Esala Perahera, an extravaganza dating back to the fourth century AD and the early days of Buddhism in Sri Lanka. Held over the last ten days of the Buddhist lunar month of Esala to honour the Buddha's tooth – according to legend, around 300 AD one of the Buddha's teeth was snatched from his funeral pyre by a devotee and smuggled to Sri Lanka, where it was laid in a golden urn and carried around in celebratory procession – the festival involves a series of spectacular night-time peraheras (parades) with drummers, dancers, torch-bearers, whip-crackers, fire-eaters and over a hundred costumed elephants.

The parades start between 8pm and 9pm, though you'll need to be in place at least an hour before. As dusk approaches, the flood of humanity lining the route turns into a solid, almost impenetrable mass. The smell of jasmine, incense, frangipani – not to mention the spicy picnic suppers everyone is tucking into – is intense, and the trees, shop fronts and streetlamps drip with tinsel and coloured lights.

You'll hear the perahera before you see it. Depending on the night, there might be up to a thousand drummers, and the boom of their instruments carries far across the city, heightening the sense of anticipation that precedes the arrival of the elephants – scores of them, decorated in golden balaclavas, beautiful silks and silver thread. Surrounding them are brightly attired dancers, drummers or torch-bearers, each either carrying a bundle of sticks that have been dipped in oil or swinging burning coconut husks from chains. Troupes of dancers, acrobats and musicians accompany the pachyderm procession, along with men yielding mighty whips, which they crack every minute or so, supposedly to scare away demons.

Near the head of the parade is the mighty Maligawa tusker elephant, the beast entrusted with the job of carrying the Tooth Relic (or a replica thereof). Kitted out more ostentatiously than all the other elephants put together, he marches through the streets with stately dignity, his appearance triggering wild cheering in the crowds, many of whom have waited for hours just to catch a glimpse of him.

INDIA In defiance of its old Rajasthani name, Marusthali (Land of Death) the Thar is the most densely populated of the world's great deserts. From the cities on its fringes all the way to the India–Pakistan border, the vast sand flats spreading across the northwest of the subcontinent are dotted with myriad tiny mud and thatch villages, most of them many kilometres from the nearest stretch of tarmac.

A train line and national highway wind in tandem to Jaisalmer, the Thar's most remote and beautiful citadel town, but from there on, the only way to reach the desert's more isolated settlements is by camel.

Riding out into the scrub, 2m off the ground, with the honey-coloured ramparts and temple towers of Jaisalmer fort receding into the distance, you enter another kind of India – one of wide, shimmering vistas, endless blue skies and, when the rolling gait of your camel ceases, profound stillness. The landscape is no great shakes: apart from a few picture-book dunes blistering up here and there, the Thar is monotonously flat.

Rather, it's for the flamboyance of the desert settlements that most visit this stark borderland. Perhaps as compensation for the sandy drabness of their world, the villagers adorn their children, their animals, houses, carts, shrines – and themselves – in elaborate style. Adobe walls are enlivened with elegant ochre and red geometric patterns; kitchen utensils with squiggly green and blue lacquerwork; moulded mud interiors, clothes and furniture with fragments of sparkling mica, cowry shells or embroidery.

Packs of jubilant children scamper out of every village as soon as a line of camels hoves into view. And the same pack follows you out again afterwards, which is perhaps why trekking camps tend to be in the middle of nowhere, well beyond foraging range. At sunset, saddle sore and a little sunburnt, you can sit back and reflect on the day's encounters as the desert glows red in the dying light. Sprawled on a rug beside a flickering campfire, with a pan of smoky dal and rice bubbling away under the starriest of skies, the Thar can feel a lot less like a "Land of Death" than a wholesome, blissful retreat.

EXPLORING THE
THAR DESERT
BY CAMEL

813

814 SEEING RED DURING HOLI

INDIA Holi is one of the most vibrant Indian festivals. It has its origins in Hinduism, but revellers today span the entire country, regardless of their religion, caste or class. Although a springtime festival, and hence a celebration of the arrival of the harvest season, Holi is essentially about colour, and everyone gets involved, showering friends, family and passers-by with multicoloured powders, and assaulting complete strangers with water balloons and spray guns. No one seems to mind.

Holi reaches its vigorous climax on the full-moon day of the Hindu month of Phalgun, but the build-up generally begins a few days earlier, when devout Hindu families get together in the evening to perform the formal sprinkling-of-colour ceremony. On the second day of the festival, Puno, bonfires are lit as part of the community celebrations, and people gather around the flames in festive bonhomie.

Celebrations peak on the final day, Parva. Children rush around squirting everyone with dyed water from their water guns, and people gather on the streets, smearing each other with powder called abeer and gulal – soon no one is recognizable, lost beneath the layers of

colour that cake their faces and bodies. Holi has always been chaotic, but these days things are more intense than ever, with eggs and mud baths added to the mix. Competing with the mayhem are the sounds of the dholaks, or Indian drums, as revellers belt out the songs of the season.

Although Holi is celebrated all over India, it's primarily a North Indian festival. And while colour may be the common feature, each region adds its own unique touch to the spectacle. Partying in the Uttar Pradesh towns of Mathura, Vrindavan, Barsana and Nandgaon lasts all week, with each major temple devoted to Radha and Krishna commemorating the occasion on a different day. The same region also hosts Lathmaar Holi, a particularly boisterous sort of battle of the sexes. Jaipur, in Rajasthan, holds an annual elephant festival, and Manipur festivities last six days, blending into the ancient Yaosang festival that follows.

Participating in Holi is not always your choice to make, especially in the north, where it's hard to avoid being dragged into the festivities. If you'd rather stay clean, remaining indoors is your best option – just

815 RIDING WAVES IN THE INDIAN OCEAN

SRI LANKA If you find yourself contemplating your next surfing trip, chances are wild elephants, Tamil Tigers, tea plantations, Buddhist temples and a political climate pre-heated by twenty years of civil war aren't high on your list of essential ingredients. But in Sri Lanka you'll find the following in spades, too: warm water, a tropical setting, friendly locals, perfect waves and beachside cafés so close to the water's edge that your feet get wet at high tide.

Lying like a teardrop off the southern tip of India, Sri Lanka is an Indian Ocean wave-magnet. Most of the surfing action takes place in two main regions on its southern coastline, Hikkaduwa and Arugam Bay, conveniently out of reach of hostilities between government forces and Tamil separatists (the LTTE or Tamil Tigers) on the north of the island – though you might encounter a few armed personnel and police checkpoints en route to Arugam Bay.

First stop is Hikkaduwa, 90km south of Colombo on the southwest coast. Surfers come from all over the planet to surf the dozen or so reef breaks around here, and for good reason. Unlike other world-class surfing destinations around the world, the waves aren't life-threatening, crowded or dominated by overprotective locals. This side of the island is also peacefully Buddhist with cultural offerings galore, and spicy local food for after-surf feasts.

Sri Lanka's pièce de résistance, however, is Arugam Bay, on the southeast coast. Where else could you surf peeling point breaks (promising 400-metre rides on a good day) without a wetsuit, for hours on end, in such laid-back company, then paddle in to the beach for more sunscreen and a snack of roti, bananas and coconut juice? For fifty cents one of the local kids might even scale a palm tree, knock down a coconut and hack it open with a machete for you.

816 ENVISIONING A LOST CIVILIZATION AT AJANTA

INDIA Even now, with the approach road marred by postcard stalls and car parks, the Ajanta Caves in northern Maharashtra have about them the aura of a lost world. Hollowed out of the sides of a horseshoe-shaped ravine, deep in an arid wilderness zone that has always been forbiddingly remote, the complex remains hidden from view until you're almost directly beneath it. When Lt Alexander Cunningham of the 16th Bengal Lancers stumbled on the site by chance during a tiger hunt in 1813, the excavations had lain forgotten for more than a thousand years – their floors a midden of animal bones and ash from aboriginal hunting fires, their exquisite frescoes blackened by soot.

These days, the worn, rock-cut steps to the caves are fitted with metal handrails, and electricity has replaced the candles used by Cunningham's party, but from the instant the guide first swings his arc light over the murals adorning the walls you're plunged into another time. It's a moment few visitors forget. Once your eyes have adjusted to the swirls of earthy red, yellow, blue and black pigments, scenes of unimaginable sophistication emerge from the gloom:

sumptuous royal processions; elaborate court and street scenes; snowcapped mountains; sages; musicians; stormy seascapes and shipwrecks; marching armies; and a veritable menagerie of animals, both real and imagined.

But it's the intimacy of the art that really captivates. The beautifully fluid tableaux seem to glow with life. Kohl-rimmed eyes light up; the well-toned torsos, draped with jewellery, still look sexy; dance poses ooze sensuous grace, humour and vitality; and you can almost smell the aroma of a lotus blossom being raised by the smiling Bodhisattva Avalokitesvara in Cave 1 – India's own Mona Lisa.

For the pilgrims who would have filed past these sacred treasures thousands of years ago, the art would have fired the imagination with a power equivalent to that of modern cinema. These must have been the Bollywood movies of their era, complete with resplendently bejewelled heroines and strong, compassionate heroes, backed up by a supporting cast of thousands – and if the images are anything to go by, the soundtrack would have been amazing.

817 SUFI GROOVES: QAWWALI AT NIZZAMUDDIN

INDIA The shrine, or Dargah, of the Sufi mystic Nizzamuddin Auliya, India's most revered Muslim saint, is one among many ancient vestiges rising from the modern sprawl of south Delhi. Sandwiched incongruously between a six-lane flyover and a faceless concrete suburb, it stands at the centre of a warren of narrow alleyways, mosques, onion-domed tombs and shanty huts. To step into this medieval enclave is to enter a kind of parallel reality where little has changed since Nizzamuddin's burial here in 1325.

From all over the city, large crowds descend on the Dargah on Thursday evenings to worship at the saint's candle-lit mausoleum. Rubbing shoulders with the devotees are always a collection of Sufi ascetics, or pir zadas, dervishes, henna-bearded Islamic scholars, and priests, who rock back and forth over worn copies of the Koran, murmuring prayers, chatting or fanning braziers of incense.

A sudden drum roll announces the start of the evening's Qawwali performance. As many as a dozen qawwals may be lined up, sitting cross-legged before the entrance to the tomb in long Peshwari frockcoats and lamb's-wool hats. A couple play harmonium, one

will play tabla; the rest provide clapping percussion and chorus, taking it in turns to sing lead.

The qawwals' job is to inspire hal – spiritual ecstasy – among the worshippers. They do this by singing songs of devotion to Nizzamuddin, to God and the Prophet; songs whose rhythms and melodies have the power to move even those who may not understand a single word of their poetry. As the music gradually picks up pace and volume, the crowd becomes more and more moved by its hypnotic beats. Hands rise into the air, heads turn towards the darkening sky and, if the hal is upon them, dervishes slip into trances and start to spin or convulse, possessed by adoration of the saint. Such gatherings can last all night, breaking up only at dawn after one final, tumultuous cadence.

It's a testament to the spirit of tolerance at the heart of Sufism that among the worshippers at Nizzamuddin's tomb are invariably members of all Delhi's faith communities: Sikhs, Hindus and Buddhists, as well as Muslims. In this age of religious fundamentalism, the unifying power of Qawwali is more in demand than ever.

818 CYCLING THE KARAKORAM HIGHWAY

PAKISTAN TO CHINA The Karakoram Highway – touted along its length as "The Eighth Wonder of the World" – is the ride of a lifetime for any Himalaya-hungry cyclist. Known to aficionados as the KKH, it was originally a feeder for the fabled Silk Route across Central Asia; today tarmac has replaced goat track, but it still threads its way up from near sea-level in Pakistan to the highest official border crossing in the world – the 4700-metre Khunjerab Pass into western China.

The highway officially starts in Hassan Abdal, a dusty railroad town west of Pakistan's capital, but if you begin in Islamabad itself, you can finish the first day's ride in Taxila – one of the most significant Buddhist sites in the world. Ahead down the highway lie the plains, where the temperature exceeds a brain-melting 50°C in summer; in this kind of heat you have to travel when it's coolest, so at the dawn call to prayer, it's time to ride.

The going only gets tougher when you finally reach the hills – these are Himalayan foothills, after all. Now the gauntlet of Indus Kohistan, or "Valley of the Ungovernables", stands between you and the mountains; here the road teeters hundreds of metres above the raging Indus River and the locals carry guns like handbags. Emerge unscathed and pedal past the roadside Buddha carvings at Chilas as you approach the densest concentration of 8000-metre mountains in the world: snowy giants such as Nanga Parbat and K2, and picturesque peaks such as Rakaposhi – held by many to be the most beautiful mountain in the world. The icy breath of glaciers, lying just centimetres from the road, pushes you up and over Khunjerab Pass, past the Pamirs and down into China's Xinjiang Province for noodles and a dust-down in the busy desert town of Kashgar.

819 TRACING THE TURTLE ARRIBADA AT ORISSA

INDIA We'd known they were on their way since breakfast time, when news that the arribada had formed a couple of kilometres out to sea had crackled through our shortwave radio from the spotter ship. First reports suggested that numbers were good. The Indian coastguard had forecast a steady on-shore breeze blowing from the Bay of Bengal until dawn, and the military firing range nearby, forewarned of the invasion, had agreed to suspend artillery tests and cut its lights. After a week of scanning the eastern horizon, the stage was set for one of the world's great wildlife spectacles.

The first olive ridleys reached us around sunset. After their epic swim across half of the planet's oceans, the pregnant females arrive exhausted and silent, allowing the surf to wash them as far up the incline as possible before starting their struggle with the undertow and soft sand. Within half an hour, the beach is entirely covered; a huge undulating sweep of hump-backed shells, glistening under a full moon.

An estimated 240,000 marine turtles crawled on to Gahirmatha beach that night, watched by barely thirty or so people from the Greenpeace Turtle Witness Camp.

By the time they'd laid their batch of eggs, many were too drained to move, submitting with watery-eyed indifference to the attentions of us onlookers. Then, as if in response to some pre-arranged signal, the whole arribada suddenly started lumbering seaward again, leaving behind them an empty beach crisscrossed with myriad prints.

The cool of early morning allowed us a few hours' sleep back at camp before we too had to begin our journeys homewards, in the opposite direction: via the crowded cities of coastal Orissa. Bumping along in the back of a local bus, I tried to work out where I'd be in forty days' time when the tiny turtle hatchlings would emerge from their nests and scuttle into the waves to start their long and perilous swim to the Pacific.

820 ON THE EDGE IN THE ANDAMANS

INDIA There had been an unseasonal downpour and the jungle was literally steaming. Slicks of red mud had spilled over the road in places, repeatedly forcing the bus into first gear. Every time it slowed I noticed the policemen riding shotgun at opposite ends of the vehicle un-shoulder their Enfield rifles and study the forest like hawks. Through the 1990s, the Andaman Trunk Road, which links the largest islands in this remote archipelago 1000km off the east coast of India, was repeatedly attacked by Jarawa aboriginal people, angry at encroachments on their territory by settlers and loggers. Arrows and spears had rained through bus windows; travellers had been killed and maimed.

Since then, relations between the Jarawa and the mostly Tamil incomers from the mainland had calmed down, but the two still kept their distance. Waiting at a ferry jetty, my fellow passengers fell into stony silence as three Jarawa men paddled out of the mangroves in a dugout. More African- than Asian-looking, they all wore bands of frayed cotton around their heads. Not a glance, let alone a greeting, was exchanged.

The far north of the Andamans has about it the air of a frontier zone. Infrastructure of any kind is minimal, and accommodation basic. The beaches, however, are out of this world. Permits restrict which islands you're supposed to visit, but local fisherman are happy to take you out in boats to little islets not patrolled by the coast guard, where you can camp wild on shell-white sand beside turquoise bays fringed with coral reefs.

Smith Island is one of the most exquisite. A twenty-minute crossing from the tiny port of Arial Bay, it was uninhabited last time I was there, save for a small colony of deeply tanned Westerners living out an Alex Garland fantasy on a remote sandbar. The talk was all of wild elephants, secret springs and the wonders visible off the reef: marine turtles, dugongs and giant manta rays that swooped out of the blue depths like spectres.

After a couple of nights grilling fish over driftwood fires, I began to understand why most had thrown away their permits and decided to stay until the rains came. In fact, it wouldn't surprise me if some were still there, paddling around Jarawa-style.

INDIA After several failed attempts, my quest to see the perfect wild tiger – any wild tiger, in fact – took me to Bandhavgarh national park in the heart of Madya Pradesh. I wasn't optimistic. India's tiger population is suffering from a poaching epidemic and numbers are thought to have fallen as low as 500, down from 50,000 at the beginning of the 1950s. But Bandhavgarh (which has the highest relative tiger density of all India's reserves) exceeded all my wildest dreams.

On our first drive, we saw two cubs lying quietly in a dried-up riverbed, enjoying the evening sun. Next morning, having trans-shipped to the back of an elephant, I saw their mother from three metres up, looking down at a huge, baleful face, framed in the long grass like a Rousseau painting. It was a strange, almost eerie experience, and when we had to move on, I felt a huge sense of loss.

The following evening, as we headed back from the park, a large male crossed the road in front of our jeep, so close that we almost collided with him. He paused for a second to look at us from the side of the road, then made off into the bush – we heard him roaring as he went deeper into the forest, checking his territory for intruders.

The last sighting was on my final day. We had parked by the side of a small lake, its perimeter surrounded by undergrowth, and with a steep, clear slope leading to the water's edge. As we waited, a single fully grown female came out of the trees, sauntered down the slope, went down on her haunches and stretched out her neck to drink. After five minutes, she pushed back and sloped off into the brush. Three hours later, still dazed by the experience, I was on an overnight train back to Delhi. As we rumbled through the night, I reflected that at a time when India's tigers are threatened as never before, this iconic animal is alive and flourishing – in Bandhavgarh at least.

821
TRACKING
TIGERS
IN BANDHAVGARH

822 TREKKING TO THE SOURCE OF THE GANGES

INDIA Of all India's holy rivers, the Ganges – or "Ganga" as it's known in Sanskrit – is considered by Hindus to be the holiest. And of all the sacred sites along its course, the most sacred is the spot, high in the Garhwal Himalaya, where its waters first see the light of day.

Aside from bringing you much spiritual merit (a mere wind-borne droplet of Ganga water is believed to purge the body of a hundred lifetimes of sin), the pilgrimage to the river's source provides the fastest possible route into the heart of the world's highest mountain range. Winding through rhododendron and deodar cedar forests, a paved road runs nearly all the way from the Indian plains to Gangotri, at an altitude of 3200m.

From here on, you have to join the ragged procession of pilgrims and ash-smeared sadhus as they cover the final twenty-kilometre leg: a long day's walk over a moonscape of grey dust and scree. Laden with sacks of offerings and supplies, many chant the 108 honorific titles of the river as they walk: "Imperishable", "A Sun Among the Darkness and Ignorance" or "Cow Which Gives Much Milk". And for once, the earthly splendour of the surroundings still lives up to its mythology.

Having crossed a rise on the valley floor, the full glory of the Gangotri Glacier is suddenly revealed, snaking away to a skyline of smouldering black and white snow peaks. A 400-metre vertical wall, grey-blue and encrusted with stones, forms the awesome snout of the ice floe – Gau Mukh, the "Cow's Mouth". For the community of sadhus who live semi-naked in this freezing spot year-round, nearly 4000m above sea level, there's nowhere on earth more uplifting. Come here at dawn, and you'll see them plunging into the icy water surging from the foot of the glacier, wringing it out of their long dreadlocks and settling down on the eroded rocks of the riverbank to meditate or practise yoga.

Even without the magnificent mountain backdrop the source would be one of the most enthralling places on earth. But with the crystal-clear mountain light, the rituals and the vast amphitheatre of rock and ice rising on all sides, the atmosphere is nothing short of transcendental.

823 THE DANCING
GODDESS
OF KERALA

INDIA A sudden intensification of the drumming and cymbal rhythms heralds the appearance of the Teyyam. The crowd of villagers falls silent. Bare-chested and wrapped in white cotton lunghis, the men and boys stand on one side, the women, in coloured silk saris with garlands of jasmine strung in their hair, stand on the other. Excitement, tempered with apprehension, flickers across their faces, turning in an instant to wide-eyed awe as the deity finally emerges from behind the village shrine.

It's hard to convey the electric mix of terror and adoration the Teyyam's costume inspires. A huge confection of gold-painted papier-mâché, metal jewellery, appliqué hangings, cowry-shell anklets and ornate necklaces, surmounted by a vast corona of silver foil and crimson fur, its focal point is an elaborately made-up face with curly chrome fangs protruding from its mouth.

This is as close to the goddess as some of these people will ever get. Age-old caste restrictions still bar them from access to Kerala's most revered Tantric shrines, but at this moment Muchilôttu Bhagavati, a local form of the Hindu goddess of death and destruction, Kali, is herself manifest among them, her spirit glaring through the Teyyam's bloodshot eyes, animating its every move and gesture.

Twisting and spinning through a succession of poses in the firelight, the apparition really does feel like a visitor from another realm. Temple drumming and chants accompany her graceful dance around the beaten-earth arena, which grows in intensity through the night, culminating in a frenzied possession. Only when the first daylight glows through the palm canopy does the deity retire, blessing her devotees as she does so.

824 LOWERING THE FLAG AT THE
INDIA–PAKISTAN BORDER

INDIA & PAKISTAN Relations between India and Pakistan have long been tense and bloody, but a trip out to Wagha in the Punjab on the Indian side of the border will make you wonder whether it's nothing but a sibling rivalry.

It's a short walk from the car park to the border, and you'll pass the customs and passport offices before reaching the tiered seating for the daily lowering of the flag ceremony, pitched somewhere between an Olympic event and a school concert.

There was already a large crowd assembled when I arrived, and I sought out an inconspicuous seat on the far end of the bleachers. The border area was punctuated with tall, mustachioed, plumed sentinels looking splendid in their red-and-gold trimmed khaki uniforms. Several turbaned young men were gathered near the front of the guards, looking smart in their tailored trousers and crisp white shirts and dancing with their arms around each other with as much enthusiasm as if their team had won the cricket. A group of middle-aged Israeli women joined in for a bit of pan-continental unification-style dancing, much to the bemusement of the Indian men.

Excitement among the crowd began to build. Chants of "Hin-doo-stan" on our side were matched in volume by the equally growing numbers of Pakistanis – somewhat less colourfully attired than their Indian counterparts, in their white kurtas and skull caps – shouting "Pak-is-tan" like a call and response game from the other side of the divide. This went on for some time, heightening the air of anticipation before the Indian guards began to march – not too dissimilarly to Basil Fawlty, with the flamboyance of flamenco dancers – along the famed border gate to the flag and eventually lowered it. Not to be outdone, the Pakistanis countered with their own colourful march, though on this occasion it was clear the Indian guards won the day. Totally surreal to a Westerner's eyes, the grandiose choreography was a reassuring symbol of good-natured nationalistic pride right at the heart of an age-old conflict.

825 CLIMBING ADAM'S PEAK

SRI LANKA Sacred sites are easily accessible in Sri Lanka; you'll barely move a step without tripping over giant Buddha statues, temples ancient and modern and rock paintings. But the most rewarding of all requires a night-time expedition to the summit of Adam's Peak. At 2243m, it is far from the highest mountain on the island, but as the holiest it draws thousands of pilgrims each year, all of whom pant their way up 4800 stone steps to worship at the indentation in the rock at the top. Most of the pilgrims are Buddhists, who believe it is the footprint of the Buddha. However, this is an all-purpose religious peak: Muslims attribute the footprint to Adam, Hindus to the god Siva and Christians to St Thomas. In fact, pilgrimages here pre-date all the religions and have been taking place for thousands of years.

It's a seven-kilometre path from Dalhousie up through the cloud forest where leopards are said to prowl. Rock steps and handrails guide pilgrims up the steepest sections although none of it is especially scary. From May to November you may well have the mountain to yourself, and the averagely fit take around four hours for the climb. In the pilgrimage season from December to April, when the weather is also at its best, the path is illuminated by a necklace of lights and endless tea stalls offer refreshment along the way. However, get behind an ancient grandmother and this may be the longest night of your life.

At the top offer a prayer in the tiny temple around the footprint, ogle the sunrise and then head across to the opposite side of the summit to take in a remarkable phenomenon – if you are lucky. The ethereal sight of The Shadow of the Peak occurs when the rising sun casts the perfectly triangular shadow of the mountain onto the clouds below for a few short minutes. It's a magical view to carry in your mind through the pain of the next few hours, when knees and thighs howl in protest throughout the descent and during the next couple of days when your gait becomes an inelegant waddle.

826 HOPPING ON BOARD FOR A KERALAN SADYA

INDIA It's hard to imagine a more romantic way to enjoy the extraordinary flavours of India's deep south than drifting across a lagoon just after sunset, against a backdrop of palms, mosque minarets and temple towers.

Aside from the slosh of the oarsman's pole punting you gondolier-style through the shallows, the only sounds likely to accompany your lantern-lit pukka feast – sadya in Malayalam – are the drone of tree frogs and cicadas, and the occasional blast of a Bollywood soundtrack from some village hidden behind the foliage lining the banks.

Sadyas are normally celebratory meals for Christmas or harvest festivals, but you're more likely to encounter them cruising through the Kuttinad backwaters in Kerala. On board, as on land, certain rules dictate the approach. Sadyas are nearly always served on glossy green plantain leaves and eaten with the fingertips. Strict Ayurvedic conventions govern both the placement of dishes and condiments, as well as the combinations of ingredients and spices used.

Once everything is arranged in rows around a central mound of fluffy reddish-white rice, proceedings kick off with a helping of tangy lentil stew called parippu. Next come the main courses, each one with its own distinctive flavour. Depending on the religion or caste of your cook, fish, lamb, clams or squid may be the prime ingredient. Vegetarian standards – what South India is known for – include avial (greens dressed in a creamy coconut sauce); thoran (vegetables steamed with grated fresh coconut); various chips (upperies) made by deep-frying jackfruit or bananas; and sambar, a fiery, watery stew. Coconut and yoghurt temper the incendiary effects of green chilies, while tamarind imparts a subtly sour taste.

Before the leaves are thrown unceremoniously into the water, one final course is whisked out of the kitchen. Prepared from boiled moong beans enriched with cardamom, cashew nuts and cane sugar, papayasa is Kerala's best-loved dessert – not least because it soothes the chili burn and promotes sound sleep.

827 GETTING SWEPT AWAY AT DURGA PUJA

BANGLADESH Hindus constitute just nine percent of Bangladesh's population, but the Durga Puja in Dhaka is at least as gripping as its Indian counterparts. Indeed, a consciousness of minority status seems to amplify the devotees' passion, and the close-knit Hindu enclaves concentrate the celebrations, creating a rarefied, otherworldly atmosphere. The enclaves, however, are certainly not ghettos, and the Puja is not exclusively for Hindus. Here is a festival at once a religious event and a vibrant carnival enjoyed by people of all faiths alike.

The centrepieces of the individual pujas – religious rituals that show respect to Hindu gods and goddesses – are the beautiful, exquisitely painted clay effigies of Durga, best seen in Shankharia Bazaar, the largest Hindu quarter in Old Dhaka, where the drama of street life at Puja time is intense. Here, among the warren of crowded lanes, the intertwining of lives seems to create a network of human connections so dense you can almost feel its ethereal fabric. A canopy of saffron drapes filters and softens the light, bathing the entire bazaar in an amber glow, and the numerous sites

of worship, the market stalls, the artisans, the creaking wooden Ferris Wheels, the troupes of singers, musicians and dancers – sometimes performing on a bamboo dais under which you walk – all of this gives the impression of a fantastic elongated temple having opened its doors to a throbbing street fair.

On the evening of the tenth day, the Puja erupts into an outpouring of frenzied activity. Galvanized by the eerie fanfare of conch-shell horns and the rolling thunder of ceremonial drums, columns of chanting devotees swarm towards Sadarghat, carrying aloft their effigies. Tens of thousands of people line the riverbank and crowd around the ghat as a relentless succession of Durgas arrives at the water's edge, where priests superintend their consecration and anoint their bearers with a smear of sandalwood ash. The goddesses are then loaded aboard diminutive boats that pitch and roll violently as the accompanying men dance and punch the air. In mid-stream the precious cargo is given to the water, and the sodden appearance of the returning men – delirious as they clamber up the steps of the ghat – hints at the mayhem beyond the reach of the light.

828 THE JUGGERNAUTS OF PURI

INDIA There are chariot festivals in other parts of India, but as the home of Lord Jagannath and one of the most significant stops on the Hindu pilgrimage trail, the one held in Puri, in the state of Orissa, is by far the biggest. They build three vast chariots from scratch here every June, garishly painted and draped with coloured cloth, and a crowd of thousands pulls them from the Jagannath temple to the outskirts of town and back again – a magnificent, devotional procession that is joined by thousands more. Orissa may be one of India's poorest states, but this is one of the country's greatest events by any standards – and just for good measure, the passion of its followers and the size of the chariots has bestowed on the English language the word "juggernaut".

829 MORNING PRAYERS AT DISKIT MONASTERY

INDIA To join in morning puja (prayers) in a Buddhist monastery in the Nubra Valley, in Ladakh, high in the Himalayas, is to enter frozen time.

It's cold outside, even though the sun has hit the valley floor. Long, cool shadows fall over yawning monks and novices flagged in plum-coloured robes. Incense is lit and syncopated chanting, more football terrace than enlightened warbling, begins.

Breakfast – butter tea dispensed from a dented kettle and porridge from a galvanized bucket – momentarily interrupts the rhythmic mantra. The simple, moving chorus starts once more, but with puja over there's a stampede past jewelled doors for a morning game of soccer.

830

NEPAL Seeing the Himalayas from the air feels almost vo-yeuristic, as if you're cheating by being at the same altitude. However, I couldn't resist pressing my nose against the win-dow as we began our descent to Kathmandu, an amber glow radiating from the snowy peaks above the valley as the sky turned from black to purple, then blue. It was October and the monsoon clouds had cleared – perfect trekking time.

A week later I was heading into the foothills of the spectacular Annapurna range with Jhamka and Baburam, my guide and porter. I'd considered going it alone, but, as each day passed, I was increasingly glad of their companionship, learning Nepali songs and the names of plants and animals we encountered along the way – everything from marijuana to macaques. As we moved from low-level bamboo forest to the steeper trails, I caught my first glimpse of Machupuchare or "Fishtail Mountain", named after its distinctive double summit. Just shy of 7000m, it's an altitudinal also-ran by the warped standards of Nepal, but has an atmosphere all of its own – even from this distance, with a classic pyramidal shape that ticks every box. Aloof, proud and elegant, it's revered by Hindus, and off-limits to climbers.

The cool air began to thin as we continued into the "sanctuary", a natural ampitheatre carved out by a long-departed glacier and home to Annapurna Base Camp (a mere 4130m up). Early the next morning, as the sun inched over the black ridge above us, we witnessed the gradual illumination of Annapurna – at 8091m, a legend among climbers in that it was the first eight-thousand-metre peak to be conquered. Finally putting away my camera, a sad realization dawned – it was time to head back down to earth.

HIGH IN HAPUTALE

SRI LANKA Sri Lanka has many unexpected sights, but few are as surreal as early morning in Haputale. As dawn breaks, the mists that blanket the town for much of the year slowly dissipate, revealing the huddled shapes of dark-skinned Tamils, insulated against the cold in woolly hats and padded jackets, hawking great bundles of English vegetables – radishes, swedes, cabbages and marrows – while the workaday Sri Lankan town slowly comes to life in the background, with its hooting buses and cluttered bazaars. As the mists clear and the sun rises, the tangled ridges of the island's hill country come slowly into view to the north, while to the south the land falls dramatically away to the lowlands below, with the far-off view of the coast and its sweltering Indian Ocean beaches faintly visible in the distance. As an image of Sri Lanka's unexpected juxtapositions, Haputale has few peers, and to stand shivering on a hilltop within a few degrees of the equator, watching a scene reminiscent of an English market town crazily displaced in time and space, is to understand something of the cultural and physical contradictions of this fascinatingly diverse island.

The contradictions continue in the countryside beyond Haputale, as the road twists and turns up into the sprawling British-era plantations of the Dambatenne Tea Estate, whose antiquated factory is filled with the ingenious Victorian mechanical contraptions which are still used to process the leaves brought in from the surrounding estates. For the British visitorparticularly, there is always the faint, strange nostalgia of seeing the legacy of one's great-great-grandparents preserved in a distant and exotic tropical island. But there is also the subversive awareness that the hillsides of Haputale, once colonized by British, have now reached out and quietly conquered distant parts of the world in their turn, filling the teabags and chai shops of countries as varied as England, Iran and India with a taste that is purely and uniquely Sri Lankan.

832 SLIDING ALONG THE HIMALAYAN ICE HIGHWAY

INDIA On the frozen river, silence has substance. It's tangible because it means the way ahead is solid, and therefore safe. More than the crack of splintering ice, travellers on this hazardous artery – the only winter route through the Great Himalayan range from the remote region of Zanskar to Ladakh, in the Indus Valley – learn to dread the lap of open water. "This one Tsarak Do . . . 'Running Place'". My guide, Namgyal Tenzing, wrapped in a wine-coloured wool *goncha*, ice dusting his hat and eyelashes, peers upriver through a mist of falling crystals. "Very cold place. Zanskar people is running here. Never stop. No good." This, however, is precisely what I and my three Zanskari companions are about to do.

After eight hours skidding over shattered plate ice, our only chance of shelter turns out to be a rock hollow on the opposite bank. But between us and it, the ice is tinged tell-tale green, and we can all hear the gurgles of a living river beneath our feet.

The crossing, however, turns out to be straightforward, and in no time at all we're huddled around a driftwood fire that spits wild sparks into the night. Later, as we lie wedged together in the cave, I can hear freshly formed ice fizzing downstream, and the mountains, ghost-like against the star-strewn sky, begin to glow with the first moonlight.

Depending on weather conditions, it can take anywhere between four and ten days – or even longer – to cover the length of the frozen river, which the locals call Chaddar. Given the dangers involved, it's amazing that so many use it to escape their snowbound homeland in midwinter. But for foreigners, the route repays its rigours ten times over. Quite apart from being one of Asia's last true adventures, it offers the chance to experience the inner Himalaya as few outsiders see it: medieval Buddhist monasteries and thatched-roof villages, half-buried under fresh snow powder snow; frozen waterfalls; herds of ice-encrusted yaks; and monks performing masked cham dances – all set against a vast amphitheatre of white peaks.

There are two talismanic words you'll be glad to hear, loud and often, along the way. Stepping gingerly out onto the river the morning after our freezing night in the cave, Namgyal strikes the surface with his stick, scrutinizes the spangle of blue bubbles beneath and calls out gala dukh! – "good ice!".

833 CATCHING THE PERFECT WAVE IN THE MALDIVES

THE MALDIVES Imagine having a perfect warm water tropical reef break to surf with just a few friends, each wave peeling with mechanical precision across a reef populated by bright turquoise parrot fish, turtles and even manta rays.

You take turns skimming across the aquamarine surface for 150m before kicking out with a whoop of sheer joy to paddle back out for more of the same. The waves break fast and regular and barrels are frequent – get inside and shelter from that hot sun! And you know that almost certainly the next day will provide you with waves of equal quality, parading north from the ever-present storms of the distant Roaring Forties.

In these ever-crowded days such surf conditions are rare indeed, but head off on a surf charter in the Maldives and they can become a reality. If your yacht anchors up off the break of your choice early enough in the morning, chances are that even the busier breaks near the capital island of Malé will be yours for the taking. When the late risers paddle out, simply clamber back onto your floating hotel and enjoy a leisurely breakfast while you sail away to more distant, isolated breaks.

A two-week surf trip here in peak surf season (July & Aug) can easily net you fourteen consecutive days of head-high (or bigger) surf. You'll never need to wear more than board shorts, a rash vest and plenty of sun cream, and it's quite easy to get in five sessions a day since you're literally living next to the break.

Downtime is spent snorkelling the Maldives' famed reefs, chilling out on deck with a book, or snoozing as the warm tropical sea breeze wafts across your surfed-out frame. There's also the chance to visit Malé, but don't expect to be clubbing and pub crawling – this is a Muslim nation so booze is forbidden. And anyway, who needs it when you'll be up at 5.30am the next morning to catch yet more of those perfect waves?

834 RHYTHM MADNESS AT THE THRISSUR PURAM

INDIA Kerala is famous for its extravagant festivals, and none is more grand – or more frenetic – than the annual Puram in the central Keralan town of Thrissur. Caparisoned elephants, ear-shattering drum orchestras, lavish firework displays and masked dance dramas are common to all of them, but at Thrissur the scale of proceedings – not to mention the suffocating pre-monsoon heat – creates an atmosphere that can, to the uninitiated at least, seem to teeter on the brink of total insanity.

Two rival processions, representing the Tiruvambadi and Paramekkavu temples, form the focal point. Each lays on a phalanx of fifteen sumptuously decorated tuskers, ridden by Brahmin priests carrying silver-handled whisks of yak hair, peacock-feather fans and bright pink silk parasols. At the centre of both lines, the elephants' attendants bear golden images of their temple deity, like soccer players brandishing a trophy from an open-top bus victory parade. Alongside them, ranks of a hundred or more drummers mesmerize the crowd with rapid-fire beats, accompanied by cymbal crashes and wailing melodies from players of the double-reeded khuzal.

The melam passes through four distinct phases of tempo, each double the pace of the last, with the fastest rhythm of all acting as a cue for those astride the elephants to stand up and brandish their feather fans and hair whisks in coordinated sequences. Meanwhile, the cymbals crash louder, the khuzals reach fever pitch and kompu trumpets blast away at their loudest and most dissonant.

Just at the point you think things couldn't get any more tumultuous, fireworks explode in the background – to great roars from the crowd. Many people punch the air, some randomly, while others are clearly talam branthans, or rhythm "madmen", whose thrusts follow every nuance of the drum patterns. When the fastest speed is played out, the slow march returns and the procession edges forward another few steps before stopping to begin the whole cycle again.

835 LAKESIDE ROMANCE IN RAJASTHAN

INDIA India is teeming with wonderful places to stay, many of them tiny, old family-run homes transformed into romantic bolt holes. It is rare, however, to find a large modern-day hotel with equal measures of soul, style and glamour. The arrival of Biki Oberoi's vilas properties in the state of Rajasthan has changed all that, creating a circle of confidence for nervous "but-won't-I-get-ill?" neophytes as well as a new kind of experience for old India hands.

These über-luxurious hotels are facing the future armed with spas, fancy food and twenty-first-century cocooning comforts. Udaivilas, situated in the achingly romantic city of Udaipur, is reached by canopied boat across shimmering Lake Pichola – arrive at dusk for the full effect. The grand Mewar-style building is a blaze of tinkling fountains, butter-coloured domes, reflective marble pools, pavilions and balconies. At night, flickering candles reflected in the water, the whole place evokes a bygone era of palaces and princes.

Despite all the must-do sightseeing in the area, it is hard to leave the hotel. Peacocks roam in the gardens, telepathic staff couldn't be cheerier, the shop is pashmina central and rooms offer divine decadence. The beds are vast, the marble baths deep, and local furniture and fabrics are beautifully crafted. You can even enjoy your very own mini infinity-edged pool, perfect for lazy lengths, with views of the City Palace, and a telescope to boot. If all this isn't enough, the hotel's Banyan Tree spa is a haven of ayurveda and aromatherapy. Every treatment begins with a foot scrub in rose-scented water, after which you can be wrapped in tomato or scrubbed with rice, enjoy marvellous massages or go yogic with the experts. As for the food – rejoice in fresh vegetables picked from the garden and fabulous meals ranging from fragrant curries to sophisticated Thai extravaganzas. Old hand or neophyte, you'll feast like there is no tomorrow – here is a hotel that satisfies everybody.

836 BOLLYWOOD GLITZ AT THE MUMBAI METRO

INDIA If you've never seen a Bollywood movie before, think John Travolta and Olivia Newton-John in *Grease*, then pump up the colour saturation, quadruple the number of dancing extras, switch the soundtrack to an AR Rahman masala mix and imagine Indo-Western hybrid outfits that grow more extravagant with every change of camera angle.

Like their classic forerunners of the 1970s and 80s, modern Bollywood blockbusters demand the biggest screens and heftiest sound systems on the market, and they don't come bigger or heftier than those in the recently revamped Metro cinema in Mumbai, the *grande dame* of the city's surviving Art Deco picture houses. A palpable aura of old-school glamour still hangs over the place, at its most glittering on red-carpet nights when huge crowds gather in the street outside for a glimpse of stars such as Shah Rukh Kahn or Ashwariya Rai posing for the paparazzi in front of the iconic 1930s facade.

A sense of occasion strikes you the moment you step into the Metro's foyer, with its plush crimson drapery and polished Italian marble floors. The recent refit has transformed the auditorium into a state-of-the-art multiplex, complete with six screens, lashings of chrome and reclining seats, but the developers had the good sense to leave the heritage features in the rest of the building intact. Belgian crystal chandeliers still hang from the ceilings, reflected in herringbone-patterned mirrors on the mid-landing, with original stucco murals lining the staircases.

While the Metro may have had a makeover, the same quirky conventions that have styled Indian cinema for decades still very much hold sway – in spite of Bollwood's glossier modern image and bigger budgets. So while the waistlines have dropped and cleavages become more pronounced, the star-crossed hero and heroine still have to make do with a coy rub of noses rather than a proper kiss.

Down in the stalls of the Metro, meanwhile, the new decor hasn't subdued behaviour in the cheaper seats. Shouting at the screen, cheering every time the hero wallops someone, and singing along with the love songs are still very much part of the flimi experience – even if overpriced popcorn has supplanted five-rupee wraps of peanuts.

837 CROWD-WATCHING AT KARTIK PURNIMA

INDIA In this era of "Readymade Suitings and Shirtings", traditional Indian dress is definitely on the decline. There is, however, one place you're guaranteed to see proper old-fashioned finery at its most elaborate and flamboyant. Each year, during the full-moon phase of Kartika month, tens of thousands of Rajasthani villagers hitch up their camel carts and converge on the oasis of Pushkar, on the edge of the Thar desert, for a bathe in the town's sacred lake, whose waters are said to be especially purifying at this time. As well as a redemptive dip, the festival also provides an opportunity to indulge those other great Rajasthani passions: trading livestock, arranging marriages – and generally strutting one's stuff.

Kartik Purnima has in recent times been rebranded as the Pushkar Camel Fair by the region's entrepreneurial tourist office. For sure, the vast sea of neatly clipped beige fur undulating in the dunes around the town during the festival presents one of India's most arresting spectacles. But it's the animals' owners who really steal the show. Dressed in kilos of silver jewellery, flowing pleated skirts and veils dripping with intricate mirrorwork and embroidery, the women look breathtaking against the desert backdrop, especially in the warmer colours of evening, when the sand glows molten red and the sky turns a fantastic shade of mauve. The men go for a more sober look, but compensate for their white-cotton dhoti loincloths and shirts with outsized, vibrantly coloured turbans and handlebar moustaches waxed to pin-sharp points.

Traditional Rajasthani garb looks even more wonderful against the backdrop of Pushkar's sacred steps, or ghats, spread around the lake. For the full effect, get up before dawn, when the drumming, conch-blowing and bell-ringing starts at the temples, and position yourself on one of the flat rooftops or peeling whitewashed cupolas overlooking the waterside. When the sun's first rays finally burst across Nag Pahar ("Snake Mountain") to the east, a blaze of colour erupts as thousands of pilgrims gather to invoke Brahma, the Supreme Creator Being of Hindu mythology, by raising little brass pots of sacred water above their heads and pouring them back into the lake. It's a scene that has changed little in hundreds – even thousands – of years.

Barefoot
Bliss
AT SONEVA GILI

838

THE MALDIVES For being in, on and with the sea, the wonderful water-world of the Maldives is hard to beat. A necklace of palm-topped, sandy white islands in the Indian Ocean, from your sea-plane they look for all the world like Tiffany-blue floating poached eggs. Wonderfully secluded, these amazing atolls are home to some of the most luxurious, beautiful and expensive hotels in the world, each occupying its own small island.

Soneva Gili epitomizes the very best in barefoot luxury. If your idea of a hot hotel is marble bathrooms, golf courses and tables groaning under the weight of silver, you've got the wrong place. We're talking Robinson Crusoe meets World of Interiors, a simple idyll finessed with lavish touches.

At *Gili* your shoes are gently removed upon arrival, the clocks are set an hour forward for maximum sunshine and your food, spa, CD and pillow preferences are all established ahead via email. The wooden villas are castaway fantasies, spacious and deeply private,

with walk-in wardrobes for all those clothes you'll never wear, breezy day rooms and two bathrooms – one inside, one beneath the stars. Stay in a villa on stilts over the shimmering sea and you can row your own little canoe back to your room, sleep outdoors lulled by a balmy breeze and order room service by speedboat – very James Bond.

Most pleasures here seem to be horizontal – sunbathing, swimming, snorkelling, scuba diving. You can also be dropped off at a deserted island for the day (hammocks and picnics provided), head off for a day of pampering at the spa, or simply chill in the pristine peace of your private pool.

The food is also sensational, much of it grown in the resort's own vegetable garden, with bread straight from the oven, sushi and oysters, zingy fresh fish and French wines. Feast in the candlelit privacy of your veranda or on a remote starlit sand-spit that's here today, gone tomorrow.

INDIA'S ACROPOLIS: A SHRINE TO THE FISH-EYED GODDESS

839

INDIA Rising from the surrounding plains of tropical vegetation like man-made mountains, the great temples of the Chola dynasty utterly dominate most major towns in Tamil Nadu. For sheer scale and intensity, though, none outstrips the one dedicated to the Fish-Eyed Goddess, Shri Meenakshi, and her consort, Sundareshwara, in Madurai. Peaking at 46m, its skyscraping gopuras stand as the state's pride and joy – Dravidian India's Empire State, Eiffel Tower and Cristo Redentor rolled into one. The towers taper skywards like elongated, stepped pyramids, every inch of their surfaces writhing with an anarchic jumble of deities, demons, warriors, supernatural beasts, curvaceous maidens, pot-bellied dwarves and sprites – all rendered in Disney-bright colours, and topped with crowns of gigantic cobra heads and gilded finials.

Joining the flood of pilgrims that pours through the gateways beneath them, you leave the trappings of modern India far behind. A labyrinth of interconnecting walkways, ceremonial halls and courtyards forms the heart of the complex. Against its backdrop of 30,000 carved pillars unfolds a never-ending round of rituals and processions. Day and night, cavalcades of bare-chested priests carry torches of burning camphor and offerings for the goddess, accompanied by drummers and musicians blasting out devotional hymns on Tamil oboes. Shaven-headed pilgrims prostrate themselves on the greasy stone floors as queues of women clutching parcels of lotus flowers, coconuts and incense squeeze through the crush to the innermost sanctum.

Perhaps the most amazing thing of all about the Meenakshi Temple is that these rituals have taken place in the same shrines, continually and largely unchanged, since the time of ancient Greece. Nowhere else in the world has a classical civilization survived into the modern era, and nowhere else in India are the ancient roots of Hinduism so tangible. It's as if Delphi or the Acropolis were still centres of active worship in the dot-com era.

840 WATCHING A KATHAKALI PERFORMANCE IN KOCHI

INDIA "Clang", goes the rusty bell, "clang", and the blanket posing as a curtain begins to shake.

It's dark in the theatre – the limited illumination from the candles at the front of the stage is just enough to catch the mirror-work on what I assume must be part of a costume shuffling in the wings – and the air is heavy with sandalwood incense.

"Clang", goes the bell again. The blanket is thrust to the ground and a brighter candle appears stage right, but it's the centre of the stage that draws my attention now, for there stands a nightmareish version of the Sugar Plum Fairy. His face is a gaudy green with cherry-red lips and eyes accented with kohl, his bodice a huge gold bib – from which his many skirts puff out like a tutu made from a tablecloth. His headgear is not unlike a Middle Eastern water pipe with a halo of gold and jewels. As we watch, his eyes flicker and flutter and his mouth contorts into a variety of grins and grimaces. Who is he? Why, the prince out hunting cobra, of course.

We had come to Ernakulum, in Kerala, to see a Kathakali, or "story play" performance, an ancient Hindu method of recounting tales from the Ramayana and Mahabarata. In this wordless theatre every concept or emotion has a corresponding facial or hand position – the performer contorts his face from one painful-looking, blinking attitude to another while gesticulating around the stage.

841 TAKING TEA IN DHARAMSALA

INDIA The bowl is placed gently in my hands. I look down at the thick, yellow liquid and sniff. It smells oily and rancid: yak butter tea. Three Tibetan women with browned, etched faces sit, like me, cross-legged on the floor. It's quiet except for their deep slurps – this is the equivalent of their morning coffee. The Himalayas loom all around us here in Dharamsala, the mountain home of the Dalai Lama and the Tibetan government in exile. The sun climbs in the sky, and I look out the window as the snowy peaks slowly come in to focus. My Tibetan friends smile at me encouragingly. I close my eyes and gulp the tea: congealed fat catches in my throat and salt puckers my lips. I force a few more sips, then cradle the bowl in my lap. An acquired taste, to be sure.

Yak butter tea, they say, was made for life in the mountains – fat to insulate you against the chill, salt for rehydration and black tea to keep you going. Our days in Dharamsala start at dawn. We gather on the rooftop, facing in the four sacred directions, the colorful prayer flags whipping over our heads. It's winter, and from here we can see the white mist swirling through the shivering pines, and down the village's steep stone streets. The wind whips past maroon-clad monks circling the Buddhist temple, and around the spinning gold-and-red-prayer wheels. It chills us as we later trek the mountain trails, the altitude leaving us breathless. Not until the sun sets do we return home, where we stretch our weary limbs, and warm up near the stove. A cup of yak butter tea, I think, would hit the spot.

PARIKRAMA
AT THE GOLDEN TEMPLE

INDIA The gates of the Sikhs' holiest shrine, the Golden Temple in Amritsar, are open to all. Given the desecrations inflicted on the complex by the Indian army in 1984 and 1987, this is an extraordinary fact, and vivid testament to the spirit of inclusiveness and equality at the heart of Sikhism.

Originating in the sixteenth century, the youngest of India's three great faiths drew its converts mainly from the oppressed and disenchanted underclasses of Islam and Hinduism. Philosophically and stylistically, it's very much an amalgam of the two, and nowhere is this hybridity more apparent than in the architecture of the shrine that forms the nerve centre of the temple.

Seemingly afloat on a serene, rectangular lake, the temple's centrepiece, the Harmandir, is adorned with a quintessentially Sikh fusion of Mughal-style domes and Hindu lotus motifs. Smothered in gold leaf, it looks at its most resplendent shortly after dawn, when sunlight begins to illuminate its gilded surfaces and the reflections in the lake shimmer to sublime effect. Before approaching it, pilgrims are supposed to bathe and then perform a ritual parikrama, or circumambulation of the gleaming marble walkway surrounding the lake. En route, returning Sikh expats in sneakers and jeans rub shoulders with more orthodox pilgrims wearing full-length shalwar-camises, beehive turbans and an armoury of traditional sabres, daggers and spears. Despite the weaponry on display, the atmosphere is relaxed and welcoming, even dreamy at times, especially when the temple musician-priests are singing verses from the Adi Granth, Sikhism's holy text, accompanied by tabla and harmonium.

Perhaps the most memorable expression of the temple's open-hearted spirit, though, is the tradition of offering free meals at the Guru-ka-Langar, a giant communal canteen next to the temple entrance. Foreign tourists are welcome to join the ranks of Sikh pilgrims and the needy from neighbouring districts who file in and sit together cross-legged on long coir floormats. After grace has been sung, the massive job of dishing up thousands of chapatis and buckets of spicy, black-lentil dal begins. By the time all the tin trays have been collected up and the floors swept for the next sitting, another crowd will have gathered at the gates for the cycle to begin again.

843 TRIPPING THROUGH THE PHALGUN FESTIVALS

NEPAL Kathmandu is blessed with not just one but two religions that seriously like to party. The month of Phalgun (starting late January or early February) is the time to see them at their wildest. Buddhists kick off the spring with the Tibetan New Year festival, Losar, most spectacular in the settlements at Boudha. Roughly two weeks later, come back for Hindu Shivarati: this is the call for the god's followers to head for Pashupatinath, site of one of Hinduism's holiest temples, where thousands of pilgrims and holy men bathe, fast, pray – and get stoned out of their minds. Then, during Holi, or Phalgun Purnima, join Kathmandu's youth as they take to the streets, throwing water bombs and red powder in a ritual laden with springtime sex symbolism.

You shouldn't expect anything austerely enlightened during Losar, the three final days of the old Tibetan year: this is Tantric country. Tibetans and Sherpas have a simple formula of boozing and feasting, with fireworks (to chase off the old year's devils) and ritual throwing of tsampa barley flour. Colourful, symbolic ceremonies take place on the morning of the last day, with yellow-hatted lamas gathering en masse around the main stupa at Boudha. It isn't too hard to get yourself invited to an evening feast.

You can really let it rip during Shivarati. Shivaites veer to the wilder side of Hinduism, and Shivarati is the night when they seriously let go. During the four-day build-up to the main event, and especially on the night itself, the place to be is on the east bank of the Bagmati River. The paved area facing the ghats is a sort of royal enclosure – though nudity and dreads are more de rigueur than a hat. From the terrace above you can look down on the pilgrims massing around the Pashupati temple. Around dusk, a gun salute rolls across the city. Oil lamps and fires light the woods of Gorakhnath, on the east bank, where saffron-robed sadhus and nagas (naked sadhus) camp on mats, drawing on chillum pipes and practising austerities. The yogis' freak show would be disturbing anywhere else, but in the middle of Shivarati it seems fairly cool to coat yourself in ash and lift weights with your penis. Through the night, the pounding of drums, wailing of flutes and chanting of Shiva's many names carries in the smoky air.

Holi, about another two weeks later, really hums during the raising of the chir pole in Kathmandu's Basantapur Square. This six-metre expression of virility is pulled up by a frantic crowd at the beginning of the ceremony. Eight days later, it's burnt at the Tundikhel parade ground in the centre of town, attended by the army in full Gorkhali costume. White-clad, scarlet-stained Newaris, Marwaris and other ethnic groups pray, beat drums and grab hot ashes with which to bless their homes. Later that night, you can join the hardcore as they head down to the strange buffalo sacrifices and burnings at Itum Bahal, deep in old Kathmandu – a fitting end to your trip through the Phalgun Festivals.

844 SNOWBOARDING IN KASHMIR

INDIA The subject of a long-standing bitter territorial dispute between India and Pakistan, Kashmir was dubbed "the most dangerous place on earth" after a particularly heated period in the 1990s involving not-so-veiled nuclear threats between the two countries. A few other places have since clinched that dubious title, but talk of the region still largely remains focused on its politics, obscuring the fact that Kashmir, with its verdant valleys and towering mountains, makes the Alps look like a cheap film set.

It's on those mountains that perhaps its biggest secrets – at least to snowboarding junkies – can be found. The Himalayas jut into Kashmir from Nepal, boasting light, dry powder in absurd quantities, but very few visitors around to take advantage of it. Its remoteness means that, if you're lacking a plane ticket, you might have to travel for days on a combination of trains, buses and jeeps filled with chickens to see for yourself.

Thankfully it doesn't disappoint. Kashmir, or rather the small ski town of Gulmarg, seems set to explode onto the ski resort radar. Opened in 2005, its gondola is, at just shy of 4000m, the third highest in the world, and the powdery terrain that spreads out before it is limitless and untracked.

From the top, head to Apharwat's high northwest and southeast shoulders, before descending the mountain's multiple ridges, faces and bowls. Or descend over the backside of the mountain on a 1700-metre run that takes you through forests dotted with snow-leopard and hill-fox tracks.

Topping it off are some very unresort-like qualities: you'll ride a pony back to a hot shower and a warm bed; if it's chicken for dinner you can pick one from the yard. The secret won't keep for long.

845 WATCHING ELEPHANTS BATHE AT PINNAWALA

SRI LANKA I picked up their ground vibrations first: a low rumbling from the dirt track behind. Soon after, shrill trumpet calls announced the arrival of the elephants at the Ma Oya River in Sri Lanka. In a scene straight out of *The Jungle Book*, a herd of gentle giants stomped into the shallow, fast-flowing river for their mid-morning bath. I was perched on a rock by the water's edge at a prime spot to get close to Pinnawala's elephants; perhaps perilously so, if the three-ton animals decided to charge. But there was little time for reflection – the water fun was about to begin.

The sociable, fun-loving nature of the magnificent creatures at Pinnawala Elephant Orphanage belies their troubled past. The Sri Lanka Wildlife Department founded the 24-acre sanctuary in 1975 to protect and nurture abandoned and injured elephants. Today, the enclosure is home to around sixty and is one of the few places in the world where you can watch elephants roaming freely and bathing in a river – an experience you won't soon forget.

The playful calves splashed, wallowed and rolled onto their sides, allowing the mahouts to give their wafer-thin ears and tree-trunk legs a good scrubbing. The elephants sucked water up through their six-litre trunks, squirted it into their mouths and hosed down their enormous backsides, a ritual they repeated again and again. Soon those that couldn't wait for lunch wandered off into the jungle on the opposite bank to forage for roots and leaves. Though I'd been rooted to the spot for more than an hour, I still couldn't tear myself away.

846 WALKING TO "PARADISE" AT GOKARNA

INDIA Goa tends to be where most people head when they fancy a beach break. There is, however, one special little town a couple of hours further south down the coast, where you can hit the sands without feeling like you've left India entirely behind.

As the site of one of the country's most revered Shiva shrines, Gokarna has been an important Hindu pilgrimage destination for thousands of years. Like a lot of India's religious centres, it's locked in a charismatic time warp: worn and dilapidated, but full of old-world atmosphere. Brahmin priests still saunter around bare-chested, swathed in white or coral-coloured lunghis, and the main market street is always thronged with stray cows and bus-loads of pilgrims squelching their way from the town's sacred beach to the temples after a purifying dip in the sea.

A lone Rama temple, overlooking Gokarna's seafront from the edge of a headland wrapped in waxy green cashew bushes, marks the start of a path to an altogether different kind of beach scene. Backed by coconut groves and forested hills, the series of beautiful bays to the south is where the hardcore hippy contingent forced out of Goa by the 1990s charter boom regrouped and put down roots.

Of all of them, Om Beach, where a pair of twin coves and their rocky outcrops replicate the sacred Hindu symbol for "Oneness and Peace", is the most famous. Further south, the path continues beyond steep, grassy clifftops dotted with miniature palms and red laterite boulders to a string of even more gorgeous side coves with names like "Full-Moon" and "Paradise". This far away from civilization, the jungle descends right to the sand line, while the sea crashes in wild and clean. Fish eagles patrol the foreshore and dolphins regularly flip out of the waves.

Admittedly, the kind of ersatz Indian behaviour beloved in these hideaways isn't for everybody. But if the ostentatious chillum-smoking, yoga posing and mantra-chanting does start to grate, rest assured you can always slip one of the local fishermen a fifty-rupee note and have him whisk you back to town to watch the real thing.

847 DRIVING OVER THE HIGHEST NAVIGABLE PASS ON THE PLANET

INDIA Everest is for serious mountaineers. But those who like sedentary adventure don't have to be left out: take four wheels instead, and cross the highest navigable pass on the planet.

A road vehicle can't get any higher than the 5602-metre Khardung La peak in Ladakh, although your blood pressure might when an army truck lumbers towards you on the single muddy track. The scraping of metal and your tightly held breath divides life from oblivion.

The summit is revelatory. You're light-headed because of the thin oxygen, and your heart still pounds because of the near-death experience; the high on reaching such altitude coupled with astonishing views is incredible.

848

WATCHING THE PONIES AT THE
WORLD'S HIGHEST
POLO TOURNAMENT

PAKISTAN The highest and most isolated polo tournament in the world, the Shandur Polo Tournament is staged every July in the Shandur Pass, in the far north of Pakistan, between six teams from each end of the pass. It's a fantastically remote place for a sporting event, 3700m up and nine hours' rocky and precipitous drive from Chitral to the west or thirteen hours from Gilgit in the east – you have to either be a keen polo fan, or determined traveller, to make the journey. But around ten thousand people do so every year, including the Pakistani president. Whether you like polo or not, the trip is unforgettable, and the tournament, surrounded by some spectacular mountain scenery, completely unique.

849 CATCHING THE SEA BREEZE AT ELSEWHERE

INDIA Few places in Asia have changed as dramatically over the past few decades as Goa. Since the advent of direct charter flights from northern Europe in the 1980s, this former Portuguese colony on India's tropical southwest coast has been struggling to keep its nose above the rising tide of concrete. It's no Costa Blanca – high-rise hotels are few and far between – but the distinctive Indo-Portuguese way of life that once prevailed here has been almost completely submerged.

Only one stretch of the white-sand beaches that extend along its coastline has escaped development. Flanked by palms and wispy casuarinas trees, the solitary colonial-era house *Elsewhere* rises from the dunes near the village of Mandrem, looking exactly as it did a century or more ago, when the great-grandfather of the present owner, local fashion photographer Denzil Sequeira, bought it as a hot-season retreat.

Rather than sell or lease the land behind it to a hotel chain, Denzil decided to renovate one of the derelict houses as an exclusive seaside bolt hole – in traditional Goan style. High-pitched terracotta roofs with jackwood beams allow the sea breezes blowing through the shuttered windows to circulate – so no air-conditioning is necessary – while the pillared veranda, painted in earthy reds and limewash, is possibly the loveliest spot on India's entire southwestern shoreline. Down on the beach, fish eagles flap lazily over the surf, and olive marine turtles nest unmolested beside traditional wooden outriggers.

A week here for a small group will cost you a lot less than it would in one of the snazzy charter complexes further south. The impact is minimal (no electricity generators, water-guzzling pools or lawns) and the experience of Goa infinitely more authentic. Villagers plod past picking cashew fruit or coconuts, and *Elsewhere*'s resident chef buys fish literally straight off the boat just after dawn.

Reclining on an antique Portuguese planter's chair, you can watch the sun setting over the Arabian Sea, secure in the knowledge that your luxury break is actually helping to protect this little corner of paradise.

850 STAYING WITH A FAMILY IN THE HIMALAYAS

INDIA As one of the holiest Hindu pilgrimage sites in the Indian Himalayas, Baijnath is busy year-round, but over the festival of Makar Sankranti, in mid-January, all hell breaks loose as villagers from the surrounding valleys pour in to town for the famous annual livestock fair. Most desirable among the animals traded on the muddy market ground here are the ponies brought in by the nomadic Bhotiyas, who pasture them on the grasslands of the Tibetan Plateau before leading them down to market in the winter.

The names, uses and cost of other exotic merchandise – borax, musk pods, dried apricots and salt horns – are explained to me by my companions from the village of Sonargaon, a few hours' bus ride further north into the mountains. I've been staying with a family for a month as part of a grassroots volunteer programme called ROSE (Rural Organization for Social Elevation), and this trip to the bright lights of the Makar Sankranti fair has been one of its highlights.

ROSE was set up as a development initiative to alleviate some of the hardships of rural life in the Kumaon region, where around 75 percent of people are landless farmers. Paying guests of the scheme get to work on a range of community-inspired projects that funds raised by them beforehand – along with bed-and-board money – help to pay for. During my stay I lent a hand to digging new latrines, planting trees and delivering smokeless, wood-free stoves to deforested villages. I also helped out with daily chores in the fields and at home: feeding the cattle, planting barley and potatoes and fixing roofs ahead of the summer rains.

Working alongside your hosts in this way leaves a vivid sense of how such small improvements might make a real difference. But the stay wasn't all toil. At the end, the eldest son from my host family arranged for a team of porters to trek with us further north into the mountains, to the snout of the Pinadri Glacier, overlooked by some of the highest peaks in the entire Indian Himalaya.

851 BEATING THE DROUGHT IN THE THAR

INDIA "People in the villages use only around fifteen litres of water for their daily bath, but a western shower uses two or three times that," explains our host, Ramesh, to a middle-aged Swiss lady who's confused by the presence of a large plastic bucket and mug in her bathroom. He hands her a copy of the lodge's "Advice to Visitors", in which the process of how Rajasthanis wash is elucidated, step-by-step: "1. They first soak themselves, taking water from the bucket with the mug; 2. Then they apply soap; 3. Finally, they rinse themselves". The Swiss lady seems delighted, and skips off to enjoy a water-saving sluice-over.

Saving water, as you soon find out, is a way of life in Shekhawati, a drought-prone region on the fringes of Rajasthan's great Thar desert. Average rainfall here has dropped over the past decade to less than 300mm per year – a quarter of the Indian norm. Ensuring visitors waste as little as possible, as well as efficiently harvesting what does fall in the annual monsoons, are thus high priorities at Ramesh Jangid's self-styled "eco-hotel", *Apani Dhani*.

Fusing traditional Rajasthani construction methods with modern renewable-energy technology, Ramesh created his small campus of baked-mud and thatch roundel "huts" for visitors to use as a homely base from which to explore the surrounding region. Solar panels provide hot water and lighting in the huts, and the meals served under cascades of bougainvillea in the central courtyard are cooked with organic produce from the garden, using biogas. And any waste – from potato peelings to the little dry-leaf plates you eat off – is composted or recycled.

In the village of Shekhawati, as in others, camels can still be seen hauling water from deep pits in the sand – a spectacle that must be much harder to enjoy after a water-squandering shower than a soak in Ramesh's old-fashioned bucket bath.

VISITING THE
TAJ
BY MOONLIGHT

852

INDIA When it comes to viewing the Taj Mahal, there isn't really an unflattering angle or wrong kind of weather. Even the Dickensian smog that can roll off the Jamuna River in mid-winter only serves to heighten the mystique of the mausoleum's familiar contours. The monsoon rains and grey skies of August also cast their spell; glistening after a storm, the white marble, subtly carved and inlaid with semi-precious stones and Koranic calligraphy, seems to radiate light.

The world's most beautiful building was originally commissioned by the Mughal emperor Shah Jahan in the 1630s as a memorial to his beloved wife, the legendary beauty Arjumand Bann Begum, or Mumtaz Mahal ("Elect of the Palace"), who died giving birth to their fourteenth child. It is said that Shah Jahan was inconsolable after her death and spent the last years of his life staring wistfully through his cusp-arched window in Agra Fort at her mausoleum downriver.

The love and longing embodied by the Taj are never more palpable than during the full-moon phase of each month, when the Archeological Survey of India opens the complex at night. For once, the streams of visitors flowing through the Persian-style Char Bagh Gardens leading to the tomb are hushed into silence by the building's ethereal form, rising melancholically from the river bank.

Shah Jahan's quadrangular water courses, flanking the approaches, are specially filled for full-moon visits, as they would have been in Mughal times. The reflections of the luminous walls in their mirror-like surfaces seem to positively shimmer with life, like the aura of an Urdu devotional poem or piece of sublime sitar music. At such moments, it's easy to see why the Bengali mystic-poet Rabindranath Tagore likened the Taj Mahal to ". . . a teardrop on the face of Eternity".

EMBARKING ON AN ELEPHANT SAFARI AT KAZIRANGA

INDIA Never ride an elephant on an empty stomach. Lolloping along 3m off the ground atop a bristly pachyderm before breakfast can induce a kind of motion sickness – which is why I happened to be chewing a day-old chapati when I had my most memorable wildlife encounter ever.

We'd been at Kaziranga, in the northeastern state of Assam, for a couple of days. The monsoon rains had petered out and the Brahmaputra, whose waters completely flood the park for several months each summer, had receded, leaving in their wake an abundance of small lakes, marshes and reedbeds teeming with birds and animals. In the space of half an hour, we'd sighted chital and sambar, nilgai (blue bulls), bison, wild elephant and, before the last wisps of straggling mist had disappeared from the treetops, our first rhino of the day.

Emerging slowly from a stand of elephant grass to our right, she'd stopped, raised an imperious horned nose to the air and ambled blinking into the sunlight, followed by her inquisitive calf and two more adults. Camera shutters whirred as the family group made its way to the banks of a nearby waterhole, by now each with a snowy white egret perched on its back.

Then something amazing happened. Our elephant, Laxmi, started shivering – not from the cold, but with naked fear. The mahout raised a hand, pointing to a break in the grass just next to where the rhinos had first appeared. There, frozen in mid-step, its striped face staring straight up at us, was a huge tiger. Unable to turn tail unnoticed, she instead decided to brazen the moment out and crept with feigned nonchalance in front of us, barely a few metres away.

Seeing tigers and rhinos in such proximity is an experience you'd never be able to have anywhere else. Established for over a century, Kaziranga is one of the world's richest wildlife sanctuaries; around 80 percent of the planet's total Indian rhino population lives within its borders, and the current tiger density is the highest in the country.

Back at the waterhole, the rhinos had got scent of our big cat and ushered their calf away. After a yawn and stretch, the tiger soon slunk off too, leaving us with plenty to savour on our long plod back to breakfast.

854 RIDING THE ROCKET ACROSS THE GANGES DELTA

BANGLADESH The arterial rivers Ganges and Jamuna, merging 60km west-southwest of Dhaka, feed hundreds of subsidiary rivers that radiate across the vast Ganges Delta, dissecting the land into a series of contiguous islands. This is the final stage in the odyssey of divine water, infused with an essence of the subcontinental millions who have used and venerated it along its courses.

A Conrad-esque journey aboard one of the Rocket service's paddle-wheeled boats is a way of joining the flow of life on this awesome network of waterways. Your odyssey begins in the evening at Sadarghat, Dhaka's teeming main hub for river traffic, approached through the atmospheric and labyrinthine Old Quarter. From the ghat – perhaps the most compelling location in the capital – you can take in the panorama of bustling activity playing itself out on land and water against the backdrop of the striking cityscape on the far bank. An intoxicating blend of the old and the new, lingering fragments of the pastoral offer a languid counterpoise to the frenetic effervescence of the urban sprawl. People bathe among beds of water hyacinth, swarms of gondolier-like craft weave among wallowing cargo vessels, and the call of the muezzin reverberating across the metropolis provides a stirring accompaniment to the ferment of voices rising from the riverside market.

Night descends soon after you clear the city limits, so your first proper sight of rural Bangladesh is likely to come on the following morning. The unfurling vista is one of verdant fields – a galaxy of greenery bejewelled with the women's multi-hued clothing – children cavorting in the shallows, fishermen, dolphins and a thousand other ingredients forming a truly mesmerizing rolling canvas.

Rocket boats are not pleasure cruisers that cocoon their passengers, but working parts of the transport infrastructure bringing you up close to the surrounding world. The nine stops between Dhaka and Khulna, when the boat comes alive with the transfer of people, animals and goods, offer the rare privilege of seeing in detail riverside habitations, ranging from clusters of huts nestled in pockets of jungle to the port of Mongla with its towering cranes and echelons of ocean-going freighters.

855 CHRISTMAS SHOPPING IN KUTCH

INDIA It had taken me an hour of skidding around sandy lanes in the humid late-November heat to find the place. Road signs are nonexistent in Kutch, and addresses vague, yet everyone seems to know exactly where you're headed, waving you in the right direction even before you've had time to stop your bike and ask.

I needn't have had any misgivings about turning up uninvited at the house of a renowned lacquerworker – they seemed to be expecting me. "Sit, sit," said a smiling granddaughter, spreading a mat on the beaten-earth floor next to the maestro. Glasses of hot chai appeared, along with a carved wooden spoon which the old man, his head wrapped in a huge white turban, started to spin on a lathe he manipulated with his toes. As its handle whirred, bands of brightly dyed wax were applied from zinc crayons, then deftly mixed into swirling patterns. "Fifty rupees!" announced the granddaughter when the wax had cooled. I didn't seem to have much choice in the matter, but considered the spoon a bargain anyway.

Kutch, a pan-shaped island off the northwest coast of Gujarat, is scattered with countless tiny craft villages – a legacy of the local ruling family's welcoming refugee policy. Over the centuries, castes and tribal minorities fleeing persecution were permitted to settle here, bringing with them a wealth of arts and crafts traditions.

I rode north next to visit a Harijan ("Untouchable") village famed for its embroidery. A gaggle of young girls, sumptuously attired in rainbow-woven bodices and silver neck rings, greeted me at the edge of their compound. Prompted by their shyer older sisters and mothers, they unfurled rolls of multicoloured stitchwork, sparkling with tiny mirrors. Later, they took me to a neighbouring Muslim village, where I watched a master block-printer make some of the most gorgeous textiles I'd ever seen, and finished up buying copper bells from a blind music teacher.

Buying work direct from the producers is a great way to really get under the surface exoticism of life in this remote corner of India. What's more, Kutchi craft villages offer a stimulating alternative to Christmas shopping at the mall – the lacquered spoon was a big hit with the in-laws.

856 SADHU-SPOTTING AT THE KUMBH MELA

INDIA At first I thought it was a severed head, smeared with cow dung, ash and sandalwood paste. But then its eyelids fluttered open. A murmur of amazement rippled through the crowd of onlookers. Buried up to his neck, dreadlocks coiled into a luxurious topknot, the sadhu then began to chant. Around him, smoke curled from a ring of smouldering camphor lamps, fed periodically by a couple of saffron-clad acolytes whose task it was to hassle the crowd for baksheesh.

"How many days is Baba-ji sitting in this way?" I asked one of them.

"Eight years, more than," came the reply.

You see many extraordinary things at the Maha Kumbh Mela, India's largest religious festival, held once every twelve years around the confluence of the Ganges, Jamuna and (mythical) Saraswati Rivers near Allahabad. But the penances performed by these wandering Hindu holy men are the ones that make you wince the most.

Standing on one leg or holding an arm in the air until it withers are two popular self-inflicted tortures. Sticking skewers through the genitals or dangling heavy bricks from the penis are others. Most sadhus who gather at the Kumbh, however, gain celestial merit in less ostentatious ways. For them, the simple act of bathing at the confluence during the festival is the fastest possible track to liberation from the cycle of rebirth.

The monastic orders, or Akharas, to which they belong erect elaborate tented camps ahead of the big days. Watching each process to the river banks in turn, led by their respective pontiffs enshrined on gilded palanquins and caparisoned elephants, is the great spectacle of the Allahabad Kumbh. Stark naked, their bodies rubbed with ash and vermillion, the lines of dreadlocked sadhus march military-style through the early-morning mist, brandishing maces, spears, swords, tridents and other traditional weaponry associated with their Akhara.

When they finally reach the waterside, the shivering ranks break into an all-out sprint for the shallows, ecstatically shouting invocations to the Hindu gods, Shiva and Rama. Arguments over pecking order often erupt between rival Akharas, and those traditional weapons are sometimes put to traditional uses, turning the foreshore into a bloodbath. Onlookers should avoid getting too close.

857 HAULING IN DINNER IN GOA

INDIA Though a cable winch (or a modern boat) would be more efficient, the Goan fishermen of Benaulim bring in their catch the old-fashioned way – and, if you're strolling by, they'll surely wave you over to help. Two long ropes stretch all the way up the beach, with heavy branches attached at intervals; on the other end is their net, sometimes floating 0.5km from the shore and visible only as a massive swirl of water and seabirds. You and eleven fishermen, six to a rope, brace your backs against the branches and take straining steps in reverse toward the line of palms.

The old wooden fishing boat that rests on the sand, with the Portuguese name *Bom Jesus* painted on its prow, is both a reminder of the tiny state's colonial past and evidence of its peculiar culture. Like most of India, Goa had a sophisticated indigenous society for more than a millennium before Europeans arrived, but its modern character is the result of spice-hunter Vasco da Gama's landing here at the turn of the fifteenth century. Though the Indian army finally drove the Portuguese out in the 1960s, Goans today are proud of their unique identity: partly Lusophone, largely Catholic and with an intriguing and delicious fusion of Portuguese and Indian cuisine. These traits have attracted travellers to Goa for decades, as much to admire its cathedrals and colonial architecture as to throw massive raves on its famously lovely beaches.

It's not party time in Benaulim, though; the sand slips out beneath your feet and you must be conceding 3m for every one you gain. Either the waves don't want to give up their bounty so easily, or the fish aren't keen on being dinner. Groaning, yelling, laughing and grimacing, your team could keep at this for hours until the net is hauled in, though by this point you may have turned over your position to someone else. Stick around, though, and you'll see what's likely to end up on your plate that evening in a fish curry or caldinha.

858 CRICKET MAYHEM AT EDEN GARDENS

INDIA Indians take their cricket very seriously. Bollywood may tug the nation's heart strings, but it's the exploits of the national cricket team that quicken its pulse – often to an unnerving degree. Whole cities grind to a halt for the culmination of test matches, and wars have nearly broken out after tussles with arch-rival Pakistan.

And if cricket is India's game, then Kolkata's Eden Gardens is its most hallowed ground. Attending a test or one-day international in the massive stadium – the oldest and biggest in the country – can feel like going to watch a gladiatorial combat at the Colosseum and cup final at the Bernabéu rolled into one. The crowds are vast, nudging 100,000 at capacity, and they're more voluble than any other in the world, unleashing deafening roars and fusillades of firecrackers every time their team takes to the field.

Stepping into such a cauldron for the first time can be an intimidating experience. But once on the terraces the atmosphere turns out to be a lot more welcoming than you'd expect. Kolkatans seem delighted and flattered that you've travelled all the way to the Eden Gardens for what, by the law of averages, will probably be a sound drubbing for your team.

Watching the last day of the second test against Australia in 2001, the locals in the stands around us spent as much time plying us with food from their tiffin tins as cheering their side on. To our shame, they knew our bowlers' and batsmen's stats better than we did, and even pressed handfuls of firecrackers into our hands for the rare occasions when one of their own wickets fell.

As it turned out, we had little to celebrate that day. India pulled off one of the most dramatic comebacks in cricket history to steal the match, and left the field to a tumult that, even by the standards of Eden Gardens, was exceptional. As the final wicket was taken, tens of thousands of flares, firework rockets, drums, trumpets and air-horns unleashed an ear-splitting racket into clouds of sulphurous smoke and beer spray. At once terrifying and hilarious, it was anarchy on a scale that would have left the grandees at Lord's apoplectic.

As one resplendently mustachioed gentleman next to me shouted, "Mister, you are thinking 'this is just not cricket!'"

859 CRUISING THE KERALAN BACKWATERS

INDIA Kerala's Kuttinad backwaters region is, in every sense, a world apart from the mainstream of Indian life. Sandwiched between the Arabian Sea and the foothills of the Western Ghat Mountains, its heart is a tangled labyrinth of rivers, rivulets and shimmering lagoons, enfolded by a curtain of dense tropical foliage. This natural barrier screens Kuttinad from the roads, railways and market towns that dominate the rest of the coastal strip, making it blissfully tranquil for such a densely populated area.

Innumerable small vessels glide around Kuttinad, but easily the most romantic way to explore it is in a kettuvallam, or traditional Keralan rice barge. Hand-built from teak and jackwood and sporting canopies made from plaited palm leaves, they're beautiful craft – whether propelled along gondolier-style using long poles or by less environmentally friendly diesel engines.

Views constantly change as you cruise along. One minute you're squeezing through a narrow canal clogged with purple water hyacinth; the next, you're gliding over luminous, placid lakes fringed by groves of coconut palms. Every now and then, a whitewashed church tower, minaret or temple finial will reveal the presence of a hidden village. Some settlements occupy only the tiniest parcel of land, barely large enough for a small house. Others have their own boatyards, vegetable gardens and ranks of cantilevered Chinese fishing nets dangling from the river bank.

Dozens of kettuvallam cruise firms compete for custom in towns such as Alappuzha and Karunnagapalli, some offering top-of-the-range rice barges complete with designer cane furniture, gourmet kitchens and viewing platforms scattered with cushions and lanterns. Alternatively, you could eschew such luxury in favour of a more authentic mode of transport: one of the stalwart municipal ferries that chug between Kuttinad's major towns and villages. Aside from saving you the equivalent of the average annual wage of most of your fellow passengers, arriving in one of these oily beasts won't provoke the frenzied response from local kids that can shatter the very tranquillity that makes Kuttinad so special.

860 EATING A BANANA-LEAF LUNCH IN CHIDAMBARAM

INDIA "Step in!", reads the sign, "for: idly-wada-dosai-utthapam-appam-pongal . . . and rice plate!". You might not know what any of these promised gastronomic delights are, but the aromas of freshly cooked spices, smoky mustard oil, simmering coconut milk and sandalwood-scented incense billowing into the street are enticement enough to do just as the sign says.

In the temple towns of Tamil Nadu, where regional cooking styles have been refined over centuries in the kitchens of the great Chola shrines, "meals" or "rice-plate" restaurants are where most working men – and travellers – eat. Some are swankier than others, with air-conditioning instead of paddle fans, but none serve tastier or more traditional south Indian food than *Sri Ganesa Bhawan*, in the shadow of the famous Nataraja temple in Chidambaram.

For lunch, space in the old-fashioned dining room is always at a premium – you'll probably find yourself squeezing on to a table of pilgrims, hair neatly oiled and caste marks smeared over their foreheads, who'll greet you with a polite wobble of the head. Once seated, a boy in a grubby cotton tunic will unroll a plantain leaf, which you sprinkle water on. This acts as a signal for a legion of other, older boys in less grubby tunics to swing into action, depositing ladles of rice, fiery rasam broth and lip-smacking curries on to your glossy green plate.

The various dishes are always consumed in the same set order, but chances are you won't have a clue what this is – much to the amusement of your fellow diners, who will by now be watching you intently. Mixing the various portions together with the rice, yoghurt, buttermilk and sharp lime pickle, and then shovelling them into your mouth with your fingers, requires a knack you won't get the hang of straight away. Not that it matters in the least. Underscored by the tang of tamarind, fried chilli, fenugreek seeds and fresh coconut, the flavours will be surprising, delicious and explosive, regardless of how you combine them.

861 BIRDING BY RICKSHAW AT KEOLADEO

INDIA "Sir-Madam. Indian helicopter for safari?" The joke was an old one we'd heard a hundred times in Agra, but the cycle rickshaw-wallah's English was impeccable. And he certainly seemed to know his birds. "All 220 resident species and 140 migrants I can identify: painted stork, brahminy duck, purple sunbird, laughing thrush, jungle babbler, Indian roller, blue-tailed bee-eater, common drongo …" "Ok, ok – let's go!"

As it turned out, our "pilot-cum-guide", Amar Singh, was worth every rupee of his fee. Keoladeo, India's famous bird park on the Rajasthan–Uttar Pradesh border, is largely roadless. But though this former royal hunting reserve spread over 29 square kilometres of misty wetlands is closed to motorized traffic, the dusty tracks that skirt its marshes, lagoons and lakes, edged by acacia and slender tamarind trees, are perfect terrain for bicycles. Moreover, Amar knew exactly where the largest congregations of birds were to be found.

Bouncing through early-morning fog on the back of a dilapidated Indian cycle rickshaw is a novel way to spot wildlife, and one that's possibly unique to Keoladeo. Elephant-back it isn't, but the trusty Indian helicopter allows you to get really close to the flocks of pelicans, brightly coloured ducks and herons and egrets that paddle through the shallows.

The park is a whirl of movement. Electric-blue kingfishers flash past your nose; paradise flycatchers with exquisite long white tails pull aerobatic stunts directly overhead; and ospreys flap dripping wet out of the water only a few metres away, huge fish writhing in their talons.

Most striking of all, though, are Keoladeo's human-sized Saras cranes, giant blue-grey birds with scarlet heads and yellow beaks that creep in slow motion through the reed beds, usually in pairs, and often barely a stone's throw from the rickshaw. And then there's the constant cacophony on all sides – of birds feeding, nesting, mating, grooming, or just squawking from the tree tops.

The racket eases off as you enter the southern limits of the park, half an hour's pedalling from the main gates. We'd come to this far-flung corner of Keoladeo in search of black buck and sambar deer, and might well have stayed long enough to spot some had Amar not told us a solitary tiger had been sighted here only the week before, hunting at the water's edge. I found myself suddenly wondering how fast a cycle-rickshaw could go at full pelt.

MISCELLANY

FIVE GREAT
PLACES TO STAY

Banyan Tree Maldives Vabbinfaru, Maldives. Quietly elegant villas on a stunning coral atoll.

Boulder Garden, Sinharaja Rainforest, Sri Lanka. A superbly comfortable eco-hotel set in virgin rainforest.

Imperial Hotel, New Delhi, India. Stately Raj-era-style hotel, in the heart of the capital.

Lake Palace Hotel, Udaipur, India. A Rajput fantasy of domes and cusped arches, seemingly afloat on Lake Pichola.

Umaid Bhavan, Jodhpur, India. Gigantic royal palace with fabulous Art Deco interiors.

BETELMANIA

Wherever you go in India you'll see people spitting long squirts of expectorated betel juice on to pavements, street corners and walls. The ubiquitous crimson spittle is a by-product of the country's number one bad habit: chewing paan, a preparation based on areca nut and intensified with tobacco and lime paste. At any given time, hundreds or millions of Indians may be under its mildly narcotic influence.

RELIGION

More than 82 percent of India's population follows **Hinduism** – less an orthodox faith than an amalgam of disparate religious rituals and practices dating back four or five millennia. **Islam** came to India, via Afghanistan and Central Asia, in the tenth and eleventh centuries and is the now the religion of 12 percent of Indians. The rest of the population comprises Sikhs, Jains, Buddhists and Christians. In Nepal Hindus also dominate, comprising around 75 percent of the population, while the Buddhist community makes up 20 percent; **Tibetan Buddhism** is most widely practised. In Pakistan, 96 percent of the population are Muslims (of which nearly 77 percent are Sunni Muslims) and the remainder Shi'a; Bangladesh is 80 percent Muslim; and in Sri Lanka, nearly 77 percent of the people are followers of **Buddhism**.

"Man is made by his beliefs. As he believes, so he is"

Bhagavad Gita

TOP FIVE
RELIGIOUS SITES

Golden Temple, Amritsar, India Holiest shrine of the Sikhs.

Sabarimala Forest shrine to the God Ayappa, India Deep in the Western Ghat mountains, the shrine receives 1.5 million devotees during the festival of Makara Sankranti each December and January.

Sri Dalada Maligawa, Sri Lanka The major Buddhist temple in Sri Lanka, said to house the Tooth of Buddha.

Swayambhunath Temple, Nepal The oldest and most beautiful temple in the Kathmandu Valley, which you access via 365 steps.

Varanasi, India Every Hindu hopes to make at least one pilgrimage to India's most sacred city, on the banks of the Ganges, and to have their ashes scattered there after cremation.

AYURVEDA

Ayurveda, literally "Science of Life", is a four-thousand-year-old holistic healing system still widely practised in India. It recognizes three constitutional types: **Vatta** (wind); **Pitta** (heat); and **Kapha** (earth and water). Disease is regarded as an imbalance between these three elements, so it's the imbalance rather than some infection that's treated, using a mixture of herbal remedies, massage, dietetics and lifestyle counselling.

"The butterfly counts not months but moments, and has time enough"

Rabindranath Tagore

BORDER CONFLICT

Since Partition in 1947, India has become embroiled in four major military confrontations with neighbour Pakistan, in addition to dozens of minor skirmishes. The conflict is fuelled by ongoing border disputes over Kashmir. In 2001, the two nuclear powers seemed on the verge of all-out war after Muslim extremists, allegedly armed by Pakistan, stormed the Indian parliament building. An estimated one million men at arms were involved in the ensuing standoff.

"It is the habit of every aggressor nation to claim that it is acting on the defensive"

Jawaharlal Nehru

SUCH GREAT
HEIGHTS

Mount Everest, in the Himalayas on the border between Nepal and China, is the world's highest peak at 8848m. Attaining the summit has long been the **ultimate mountaineering challenge**. Sir Edmund Hillary and Tenzing Norgay, a Sherpa mountaineer from Nepal, were the first people to complete the ascent in 1953. Other Everest records include the first ascent by a woman (in 1975) and by a blind person (2001). Climbing Everest has now become something of an aspiration for wealthy professionals – the current going rate for the venture is just under $55,000/£30,000.

However, scaling Everest is a dangerous endeavour, and at the close of 2004, 179 people had lost their lives in the attempt, a fatality rate of nine percent. About one-third of the total deaths is comprised of the local Sherpa population, many of whom serve as guides. For them, Everest has **spiritual significance** and there are many taboos relating to it, one of which is a ban on sex for anyone attempting the summit – it is thought to bring bad luck.

FIVE INDIAN DISHES TO DIE FOR...

- **Biryani**: tender lamb slow-baked in spicy saffron rice – a speciality of Hyderabad
- **Paturi maach**: steamed Bengali bekti fish in mustard and green chilli sauce
- **Malai kofta**: cheese and potato dumplings served in a creamy lentil gravy – a typical north Indian Mughlai favourite
- **Pepper-garlic crab**: mouthwatering Konkan seafood speciality
- **Masala dosa**: rice- and lentil-flour pancake with a tangy potato filling, originally from the temple town of Udipi, Karnataka

...AND WHERE TO TRY THEM

- **Dum Pukht**, Hyderabad: old recipes from the tables of the Nizams, including legendary biryanis
- **Sonargaon**, Kolkata: top-notch Bengali home cooking on silver platters
- **Bukhara**, New Delhi: often voted the world's best tandoori restaurant
- **Konkan Café**, Mumbai: amazing flavours from the southwest coast
- **Saravana Bhavan**, Chennai: definitive southern cuisine

THE INDIAN SUBCONTINENT IN FICTION

Arundhati Roy *The God of Small Things* (1997). Booker Prize winner about a well-to-do Keralan family caught up in the snobberies of high-caste tradition.

R K Narayan *A Malgudi Omnibus* (1994). Three of India's best-loved short novels, set in the imaginary south Indian town of Malgudi.

Rohinton Mistry *A Fine Balance* (1996). Long-time Canadian resident Mistry mines the 1970s Bombay of his childhood for this, his finest novel.

Michael Ondaatje *Anil's Ghost* (2000). Anil, a young anthropologist, returns to Sri Lanka, the land of her birth, and becomes engulfed in a murder mystery.

Salman Rushdie *Midnight's Children* (1980). The story of a man born at the very moment of Independence, whose life mirrors that of modern India itself. It won for Rushdie the Booker of Bookers in 1993.

Vikram Seth *A Suitable Boy* (1993). A virtuoso novel, anatomizing north Indian society in the Nehru era through a mother's search for an appropriate match for her daughter.

"An eye for an eye makes us all blind"

Mohandas K Gandhi

NUMBER CRUNCHING

340 million: the number of voters in India, the world's largest democracy.

2.5 million: the number of refugees in Pakistan, displaced by war in Afghanistan.

10: the number of members of the royal family assassinated by the Crown Prince of Nepal in 2001, before he took his own life.

15,000: the number of guests at former Tamil Nadu Chief Minister Jayalalitha's son's wedding.

7th: the population of Bangladesh is the world's seventh largest; its 144,000 square kilometres make it one of the most densely populated countries.

200 million: the estimated number of cows in India.

7258m: the lowest point of the Indian Ocean.

FIVE BOLLYWOOD CLASSICS

Pather Panchali ("Song of the Long Road"; 1955) Bengali director Satyajit Ray's 1955 debut, often dubbed "the greatest Indian film ever made".

Mother India (1957) Bollywood classic whose lead actors, Nargis and Sunil Dutt, caused a scandal by later marrying – Sunil had played Nargis's son in the film.

Sholay (1975) This spaghetti western-inspired flick was the most successful Bollywood movie of all time, starring the legendary "Big B" himself, Amitabh Bachchan.

Monsoon Wedding (2001) Mira Nair's witty depiction of a swanky Punjabi wedding in Delhi.

Devdas (2002) The highest grossing Bollywood blockbuster of the past decade, featuring megastars Aishwarya Rai, Shahrukh Khan and Madhuri Dixit.

HOLY FESTIVALS

- **Hinduism:** Kumbh Mela, India. Massive bathing ritual held in rotation on the banks of four sacred rivers. The 2001 Kumbh at Allahabad attracted 70 million worshippers.
- **Islam:** Mela Chiraghan. Lahore, Pakistan. A three-day annual festival of light to mark the death of the Sufi poet and saint Shah Hussain.
- **Jainism:** Mahamastakabhisheka Ceremony, Sravanabelgola, India. Vast quantities of milk, gold leaf and paints (including some from a helicopter) are poured over the colossus of Gomateshvara. Staged every 12 years, with the next scheduled for 2017.
- **Buddhism:** Esala Perahera, Kandy, Sri Lanka. A spectacular extravaganza held in honour of the Buddha's tooth, with drumming, dancing and a hundred costumed elephants. Held for ten days, usually in late July and early August.
- **Christianity:** Exposition of Saint Francis Xavier's remains, Old Goa, India. Every ten years, Catholics from all over the world travel to Goa for a glimpse of the supposedly incorruptible corpse of the "Apostle of the Indies". The next one's in 2014.

MUSIC
FIVE MUST-HAVE CDS

Asha Bhosle The Rough Guide to Bollywood Legends: Asha Bhosle (Rough Guides Music). Greatest hits from the most recorded artiste in history.

Salamat Ali Khan and sons Ragas Gunkali, Saraswati and Durga (Nimbus). Sublime ragas from Pakistan's late master of khayal singing.

Hariprasad Chaurasia Hari-Krishna: In Praise of Janmashtami (Navras). India's flute maestro at his most sublime.

Lata Mangueshkar The Rough Guide to Bollywood Legends: Lata Mangueshkar (Rough Guides Music). Retrospective from the "Nightingale of India", Asha Bhosle's elder sister, and the Queen of Bollywood playback singing.

Ravi Shankar Ravi Shankar & Ali Akbar Khan in Concert (Apple). Inspired sarod and sitar duet by two living legends of Indian classical music.

THE KINGS OF KOMODO • DAWN OVER KELIMUTU IN FLORES • FEELING FRUITY IN THE MEKONG DELTA • CLEANING UP AFTER THE KHMER ROUGE: TACKLING POL POT'S LEGACY WITH VSO • PEEKING AT PARADISE IN ARU • BUDGET BEACH CHIC • SNAKE EVERY WHICH WAY IN HANOI • COUNTING FISH IN THE SULU SEA • BOROBUDUR: THE BIGGEST BUDDHIST STUPA IN THE WORLD • **GOING APE IN BORNEO** • MOONLIT MEANDERS THROUGH HOI AN • FINDING PEACE AMONG THE WILDLIFE IN KO LIBONG • MEETING THE RELATIVES: ORANG-UTAN ENCOUNTERS IN SUMATRA • **VOLCANIC ACTIVITY: SUNRISE ON MOUNT BROMO** • TRYING TO SOLVE THE PUZZLES AT THE PLAIN OF JARS • DANCING UNDER A FULL MOON • FIREWORKS FEVER AT BUN BANG FAI • BUNAKEN'S MARINE MEGALOPOLIS • UNDERWATER AT SIPADAN ISLAND • THE BUZZ AROUND CHIANG MAI • CREATURES OF THE NIGHT • **HIKE THROUGH HISTORY ALONG THE KOKODA TRAIL** • JUNGLE BOOGIE IN SARAWAK • ALL ABOARD THE EASTERN & ORIENTAL EXPRESS • MEETING THE AMERICAN KILLER HEROES • CONQUERING SOUTHEAST ASIA'S HIGHEST PEAK: MOUNT KINABALU • BALINESE THEATRICS • ROAMING RAINY PENANG • THE HILLS ARE ALIVE: TRIBAL TREKKING • MIXING SAND AND SPICE ON KO SAMUI • EXPLORING MALAPASCUA BY BANCA • FIGHT NIGHT IN BANGKOK • JOINING THE PARTY AT AN IBAN LONGHOUSE • IRONING OUT THE KINKS • PADDLING INTO SECRET LAGOONS • **TAKING THE SLOW BOAT DOWN THE MEKONG** • SHOPPING AT CHATUCHAK WEEKEND MARKET • VISITING THE TUOL SLENG GENOCIDE MUSEUM • ISLAND-HOPPING IN THE BACUIT ARCHIPELAGO • PARTYING AT THE ATI-ATIHAN FESTIVAL • KARST AND CREW: STAYING OVERNIGHT ON HA LONG BAY • **A NIGHT IN THE RAINFOREST** • SAFFRON AND GOLD: FALLING UNDER THE SPELL OF LOUANG PHABANG • CLIMBING THE STAIRWAY TO HEAVEN IN BANAUE • DIVING THE TUBBATAHA REEF • ACQUIRING THE TASTE: COOKERY LESSONS • THE KINGS OF KOMODO • DAWN OVER KELIMUTU IN FLORES • FEELING FRUITY IN THE MEKONG DELTA • PEEKING AT PARADISE IN ARU • **SNAKE EVERY WHICH WAY IN HANOI** • BUDGET BEACH CHIC • COUNTING FISH IN THE SULU SEA • BOROBUDUR: THE BIGGEST BUDDHIST STUPA IN THE WORLD • GOING APE IN BORNEO • MOONLIT MEANDERS THROUGH HOI AN • FINDING PEACE AMONG THE WILDLIFE IN KO LIBONG • **DANCING UNDER A FULL MOON** • TRYING TO SOLVE THE PUZZLES AT THE PLAIN OF JARS • VOLCANIC ACTIVITY: SUNRISE ON MOUNT BROMO • FIREWORKS FEVER AT BUN BANG FAI • BUNAKEN'S MARINE MEGALOPOLIS • UNDERWATER AT SIPADAN ISLAND • THE BUZZ AROUND CHIANG MAI • CREATURES OF THE NIGHT • JUNGLE BOOGIE IN SARAWAK • ALL ABOARD THE EASTERN & ORIENTAL EXPRESS • MEETING THE AMERICAN KILLER HEROES • **EXPLORING THE TEMPLES OF ANGKOR** • CONQUERING SOUTHEAST ASIA'S HIGHEST PEAK: MOUNT KINABALU • BALINESE THEATRICS • ROAMING RAINY PENANG • THE HILLS ARE ALIVE: TRIBAL TREKKING • MIXING SAND AND SPICE ON KO SAMUI • EXPLORING MALAPASCUA BY BANCA • FIGHT NIGHT IN BANGKOK IRONING OUT THE KINKS • PADDLING INTO SECRET LAGOONS • SHOPPING AT CHATUCHAK WEEKEND MARKET • **ISLAND-HOPPING IN THE BACUIT ARCHIPELAGO** • VISITING THE TUOL SLENG GENOCIDE MUSEUM • TAKING THE SLOW BOAT DOWN THE MEKONG • PARTYING AT THE ATI-ATIHAN FESTIVAL • KARST AND CREW: STAYING OVERNIGHT ON HA LONG BAY • SAFFRON AND GOLD: FALLING UNDER THE SPELL OF LOUANG PHABANG • A NIGHT IN THE RAINFOREST • CLIMBING THE STAIRWAY TO HEAVEN IN BANAUE • DIVING THE TUBBATAHA REEF • ACQUIRING THE TASTE: COOKERY LESSONS • **JOINING THE PARTY AT AN IBAN LONGHOUSE** • THE KINGS OF KOMODO • DAWN OVER KELIMUTU IN FLORES • FEELING FRUITY IN THE MEKONG DELTA • CLEANING UP AFTER THE KHMER ROUGE: TACKLING POL POT'S LEGACY WITH VSO • PEEKING AT PARADISE IN ARU • BUDGET BEACH CHIC • SNAKE EVERY WHICH WAY IN HANOI • COUNTING FISH IN THE SULU SEA • MEETING THE RELATIVES: ORANG-UTAN ENCOUNTERS

SOUTHEAST ASIA

862–912

SNAKE EVERY WHICH WAY
IN HANOI
887

862 TAKING THE SLOW BOAT
DOWN THE MEKONG

THAILAND

LAOS

VIETNAM

CAMBODIA

PHILIPPINES

EXPLORING
THE TEMPLES **907**
OF ANGKOR

903 ISLAND-HOPPING IN THE
BACUIT ARCHIPELAGO

894
DANCING UNDER
A FULL MOON

BRUNEI

866 A NIGHT IN
THE RAINFOREST

MALAYSIA

SINGAPORE

875 JOINING THE PARTY
AT AN IBAN LONGHOUSE

899 GOING APE IN BORNEO

INDONESIA

PAPUA
NEW GUINEA

VOLCANIC ACTIVITY: **908**
SUNRISE ON MOUNT BROMO

EAST
TIMOR

HIKE THROUGH HISTORY
ALONG THE KOKODA TRAIL **910**

TAKING THE
SLOW BOAT
DOWN THE
MEKONG
862

LAOS Cargo-hold hell used to be the order of the day for travellers taking the slow boat through Laos, squashed between chickens and sacks of rice. But the ride's become so popular that there are now specially designed backpackers' boats running the 300-kilometre route from the Thai border east to Louang Phabang. They even have proper seats and a toilet – both pretty handy when you're spending two long days on the river. It's still a cramped, bottom-numbing experience though, with over a hundred passengers on board, and an average speed that's very slow indeed.

In truth you wouldn't expect a trip on Southeast Asia's longest and most important river to be plain sailing. Here in northern Laos, approximately halfway down the river's 4000-kilometre journey from its source on the Tibetan plateau to its delta in southern Vietnam, the Mekong is dogged by sandbanks and seasonal shallows. It can be tough to navigate, as passengers in the hurtling, accident-prone speedboats often discover. Better to take it slowly; bring a cushion and enjoy the ride.

Little about the river has changed over the decades. The Mekong has always been a lifeline for Laos, Southeast Asia's only landlocked nation, and villagers continue to depend on it for fish, irrigation and transport, even panning its silt in search of gold. Limestone cliffs and thickly forested hills frame its banks, with riverside clearings used for banana groves, slash-and-burn agriculture and bamboo-shack villages. The largest of these, Pakbeng, marks the journey's mid-point, where everyone disembarks for a night on dry land. A ramshackle place for such an important river port, Pakbeng offers an unvarnished introduction to Laos, with rudimentary guest-houses and just four hours of electricity a day. Roll on the civilized comforts of Louang Phabang, a mere eight hours downriver.

863 SHOPPING AT CHATUCHAK WEEKEND MARKET

THAILAND Want to feel like a local on a weekend in Bangkok? Then you need to go shopping. Specifically, you need to go to Chatuchak Weekend Market and spend a day rifling through the eight thousand-plus stalls of what some claim to be the world's biggest market. It's certainly a contender for the world's sweatiest and most disorientating, with a quarter of a million bargain-hunters crammed into an enormous warren of alleyways, zones, sections and plazas. The maps and occasional signs do help, but much of the pleasure lies in getting lost and happening upon that unexpected must-have item: antique opium pipe, anyone?

Alongside the mounds of second-hand Levis and no-brand cosmetics you'd expect to find in Southeast Asia's most frantic flea market, there's also a mass of traditional handicrafts from Thailand's regions. Fine silk sarongs from the northeast, triangular cushions and mulberry-paper lamps from Chiang Mai, and hill-tribe jewellery and shoulder bags are all excellent buys here. But what makes Chatuchak such a shopaholic's dream is its burgeoning community of young designers. Many of Asia's new fashion and interior design ideas surface here first, drawing professional trend-spotters from across the continent. The clothing zone is the obvious beacon, with its hundreds of mini-boutiques displaying radical-chic outfits and super-cute handbags, while the lifestyle zone brims over with tasteful ceramics and sumptuous furnishings.

Need a break from the achingly fashionable? Then wander through the pet section, perhaps lingering to watch Bangkokians' poodles getting their weekly grooming treatments, before enjoying a blast of natural beauty among the orchids and ornamental shrubs. You can treat your tastebuds for a handful of change at any number of foodstalls specializing in everything from barbecued chicken to coconut fritters, and there's even a tiny jazz café for that all-important chillout between purchases. And don't let your feet call a premature end to the day: simply get yourself along to the foot-massage stall in Aisle 6, Zone B.

864 KARST AND CREW: STAYING OVERNIGHT ON HA LONG BAY

VIETNAM Spend a night afloat among the limestone pinnacles of Ha Long Bay, and you'll witness their many moods as their silhouettes morph with the moonlight, mist and midday sun. Scores of local boat companies offer this experience, for the spectacularly scenic bay is a World Heritage site and Vietnam's top tourist destination.

Regularly referred to as the eighth natural wonder of the world, the 1500 square kilometres of Ha Long Bay contain nearly two thousand islands, most uninhabited outcrops that protrude evocatively from the Gulf of Tonkin. Their intriguingly craggy profiles have long inspired poets, wags and travel writers to wax lyrical about Italianate cathedrals, every type of creature from fighting cock to bug-eyed frog, even famous faces, but the bay's creation myth is just as poetic. "Ha Long" translates as "the dragon descending into the sea", for legend tells how the islets were scattered here by the celestial dragon as a barrier against invaders.

Even the most imaginative visitor might tire of interpreting the shapes for a full two days, so overnight trips offer different angles on rock appreciation. As well as lounging on island beaches by day and swimming the phosphorescent waters by night, there are plenty of caves and floating villages to explore, and endless fresh seafood to enjoy. Some tours allow you to paddle yourself around in a kayak, while others feature forest treks and cycle rides on Cat Ba Island, the largest in the bay.

865 PARTYING AT THE ATI-ATIHAN FESTIVAL

THE PHILIPPINES You need serious stamina for the three days and nights of non-stop dancing that mark the culmination of Ati-Atihan, the most flamboyant fiesta in the fiesta-mad Philippines. No wonder the mantra chanted by participants in this marathon rave is hala bira, puera pasma, which means "keep on going, no tiring". If you plan on lasting the course, start training now.

Ati-Atihan, which takes place during the first two weeks of January in Kalibo – an otherwise unimpressive port town on the central Philippine island of Panay – actually lasts for two weeks. But it's the final three days that are the most important, with costumed locals taking to the streets in a riot of spontaneous partying, music and street dancing. And it's this the tourists come for – 72 sleepless hours of alcohol-fuelled, intoxicating mayhem acted out to the deafening ranks of massed tribal drums.

Don't expect to just stand by and watch – the locals have an unwritten rule that there are no wallflowers at Ati-Atihan – and if you don't take part, they'll make you. Even if all you can muster is a drunken conga line, you can take the edge off your nerves with a few glasses of lambanog, a vigorous native aperitif made from leftover jackfruit or mango fermented in cheap containers buried in the earth – the "zombie flavour" is especially liberating.

Ati-Atihan is still partly a religious festival, held to celebrate the child Jesus (Santo Nino). In recent years it has morphed into a delightful hodge-podge of Catholic ritual, indigenous drama and tourist attraction. It's the one time of the year when Catholic Filipinos aren't afraid to push the boat out, especially for the final-day fancy dress parade that sees thousands of people in costumes so big and brash they almost block the street.

If you're feeling a little rough after all this, do what many others do and head up the coast to the beautiful little island of Boracay, where you can sleep off your hangover on one of the finest beaches in the world.

866 A NIGHT IN THE RAINFOREST

MALAYSIA You probably won't get much sleep on your first night in Taman Negara national park – not because there's an elephant honking on your chalet doorstep or the rain's dripping through your tent, but because the rainforest is unexpectedly noisy after dark. High-volume insects whirr and beep at an ear-splitting pitch, branches creak and swish menacingly, and every so often something nearby shrieks or thumps. Taman Negara is a deceptively busy place, home to scores of different creatures including commonly sighted macaques, gibbons, leaf monkeys and tapir, as well as more elusive tigers, elephants and sun bears. Not to mention some three hundred species of birds and an inordinate insect population.

Many rainforest residents are best observed after dark, either on a ranger-led night walk or from one of the twelve-bed tree-house hides strategically positioned above popular salt licks. But a longer guided trek also offers a good chance of spotting something interesting and will get you immersed in the phenomenally diverse flora of Taman Negara, which supports a staggering 14,000 plant species, including 75-metre-high tualang trees, carnivorous pitcher plants and fungi that glow like lightbulbs. The rewarding six-hour Keniam–Trenggan trail takes you through dense jungle and into several impressive caves, while the arduous week-long expedition to the cloudforests atop 2187-metre-high Gunung Tahan involves frequent river crossings and steep climbs. With minimal effort, on the other hand, you can ascend to the treetops near park headquarters, via a canopy walkway. Slung thirty metres above the forest floor between a line of towering tualang trees, this swaying bridge offers a gibbon's perspective on the cacophonous jungle below.

867 CLIMBING THE STAIRWAY TO HEAVEN IN BANAUE

THE PHILIPPINES Lay them out end-to-end and they'd stretch from Scandinavia to the South Pole. No wonder the tribes of Ifugao province, in the beautiful northern Philippines, call the Banaue rice terraces their stairways to heaven.

The terraces are one of this country's great icons, hewn from the land two thousand years ago by tribespeople using primitive tools, an achievement that ranks alongside the building of the pyramids. They are a truly awesome sight. Cut into near-vertical slopes, the water-filled ledges curve around the hills' winding contours, their waters reflecting the pale green of freshly planted rice stalks. And unlike other old wonders of engineering, the terraces are still in the making after two millennia. Employing spades and digging sticks, countless generations of Ifugao farmers have cultivated rice on thousands of these mountainside paddies. Constantly guarding them against natural erosion, they have fortified the terraces with packed-earth and loose-stone retaining walls, supporting an elaborate system of dykes.

A few kilometres up the road from Banaue town is a popular lookout point that offers a sweeping vista down a wide valley with terraces on both sides. It's a great view, but it's not the only one. The only way to really get to know the landscape is on foot. Dozens of narrow paths snake their way past thundering waterfalls into a dazzling green hinterland of monolithic steps. If you're looking for rural isolation and unforgettable rice-terrace scenery, the fifteen-kilometre trek from Banaue to the remote little tribal village of Batad simply shouldn't be missed. Batad nestles in a natural amphitheatre, close to the glorious Tappia Waterfall. Accommodation here is basic, but it doesn't matter. In the semi-dark, after a long trek and a swim in the falls, you can sit on your verandah, listening to the hiss of cicadas and the squawk of giant bats, transfixed by the looming silhouettes of the surrounding mountains.

868 MIXING SAND AND SPICE ON KO SAMUI

THAILAND Ko Samui is perhaps an unlikely spot to learn the art of Thai cooking. Given the choice between spending endless hours lapping up rays on a speck of sand, palms and waterfalls in the Gulf of Thailand and arming oneself with a sharp cleaver to take on a mound of raw pork and fiery chilies hardly seems worthy of debate – especially when the best plate of food you're likely to have in your life costs about a buck at the local market.

Yet the packed schedule at the Samui Institute of Thai Culinary Arts suggests otherwise. The school focuses on central Thai food, considered the classic style among the country's four regional cuisines with its coconut-milk curries and flavoursome balance of hot, sour, salty and sweet. The classes begin with a discussion of the ingredients (and how to substitute for those hard to find outside of Southeast Asia), work up to hands-on wok skills and end with a feast of your own making, an array of stir fries, curries and soups.

Walk into the school's unassuming shophouse just off Samui's Chaweng Beach and you may wonder whether you've been shanghaied into a tropical Iron Chef gone awry. A sea of tiny bowls bursting with cumin seeds, tamarind, coriander root, galangal and shrimp paste lie scattered across the prep tables, and you've got a little more than two hours to whip up three dishes. But before panic sets in, the lead chef calmly explains how to chiffonade a kaffir lime leaf, and soon enough, you're grinding out a proper chili paste in a mortar and pestle with the steady hand of a market lady who's been at it for fifty years. It can't be this easy, can it? Chop a few more chilies, toss in an extra dash of fish sauce, swirl the wok and – aroy mak – you've just duplicated that tom yum kai (spicy shrimp soup) you saw at the market. So what if it cost a few dollars more?

869 DIVING THE TUBBATAHA REEF

THE PHILIPPINES If you're looking for some of the most adventurous and thrilling scuba diving in the world, never mind Southeast Asia, Tubbataha Reef Marine Park in the Sulu Sea is the place to start. Well out of sight of land and almost two hundred kilometres southeast of Puerto Princesa in Palawan, this World Heritage site is only accessible on live-aboard boats when seas are favourable between March and June. Its very isolation means it's not overrun by package-tour divers, and even during these peak months you'll probably be on one of only a handful of small boats in the area. The reef – actually a grouping of dozens of small reefs, atolls and coral islands covering more than 300 square kilometres – is one of the finest in the world, with daily sightings of the big pelagics that all divers dream of.

Rise at dawn for a quick dive among the turtles and small sharks before breakfast. Afterwards there's time for a visit to Shark Airport, where sharks "take off" from sandy ledges like planes, before it's back to the boat for lunch and a snooze. You can do deep dives, night dives, drift dives, all kinds of dives. Or you can simply fossick gently along some of the shallower reefs, home to so many varieties of coral and fish that it's hard to know where to look next. For a real buzz, dive deep over one of the many coral walls that seem to plunge into infinity and hang out for a few minutes with giant manta rays, black-tip reef sharks and, just possibly, cruising hammerheads. You also stand a good chance of getting up close and personal with a whale shark, the harmless gentle giants of the sea known in the Philippines as butanding.

Of course, there's life beyond diving at Tubbataha. For a change of scene, you can snorkel around some of the atolls, picnic on the beach at the ranger station, or just kick back on deck and watch dolphins and tuna perform occasional aerial stunts.

CONQUERING SOUTHEAST ASIA'S HIGHEST PEAK:

MOUNT
KINABALU

MALAYSIA It's a hell of a slog up Malaysian Borneo's Mount Kinabalu, but every year thousands of visitors brave the freezing conditions and risk of altitude sickness to reach the 4095-metre-high summit. The reward is a spectacular dawn panorama across granite pinnacles rising out of the clouds below you – and the knowledge that you've conquered the highest peak between the Himalayas and New Guinea.

Your two-day expedition up the southern ridge begins at Kinabalu Park headquarters, where you meet your obligatory guide and gulp at the multiple jagged peaks ahead. You need to be equipped as for any mountain hike, prepared for downpours and extreme chill at the summit, but Kinabalu's appeal is that any averagely fit tourist can reach the top. The steady climb up to the Laban Rata mountain huts is a five-hour trek along a well-tramped trail through changing forest habitats. Beyond 1800m you're in dense cloudforest, among a thousand species of orchids, 26 types of rhododendron and a host of insect-hungry pitcher plants. By 2600m most of the vegetation has given up, but you stagger on to 3300m and the long-awaited flop into bed. Day two starts at 2.30am for the final push across the glistening granite rock face to Low's Peak, Kinabalu's highest point. It's dark and very cold; for three hours you see no further than the beam of your headtorch and, despite the handrails and ropes, the climb is tough; some have to turn back because of pounding altitude headaches. But when you finally reach the summit, your spirit rises with the sun as the awesome view comes into focus, your every horizon filled with the stark grey twists of Kinabalu's iconic peaks, the mile-deep chasm of infamous Low's Gully at your feet.

871 CANDLES IN THE WIND: THE LOY KRATHONG FESTIVAL OF LIGHT

THAILAND In the days leading up to Thailand's annual Loy Krathong Festival of Light, pretty little baskets fashioned from banana leaves and filled with orchids and marigolds begin to appear at market stalls across the country. On festival night everyone gathers at the nearest body of water – beside the riverbank or neighbourhood canal, on the seashore, even at the village fishpond. Crouching down beside the water, you light the candle and incense sticks poking out of your floral basket, say a prayer of thanks to the water goddess, in whose honour this festival is held, and set your offering afloat. As the bobbing lights of hundreds of miniature basket-boats drift away on the breeze, taking with them any bad luck accrued over the past year, the Loy Krathong song rings out over the sound system, contestants for the Miss Loy Krathong beauty pageant take to the stage and Chang beer begins to flow.

872 SHOPPING WITH THE WOMEN OF THE FLOWER HMONG HILL TRIBE

VIETNAM Even if you're not planning to splash out on an exuberantly embroidered shoulder bag or an extra line of braiding for the hem of your skirt, watching Flower Hmong hill tribe women rifle through stalls for the perfect accessory is well worth the ride up to the Sunday market in Bac Ha. Flower Hmong women have an extraordinarily fancy taste in clothes, with a special penchant for machine-embroidered brocades in electric shades – camellia pink, lime green, tangerine, delphinium blue – which they wear everyday, in the fields, at home and when coming to town. The net effect of all that colour crowded around the frippery stalls is exhilarating – and the bags make great souvenirs too.

873 GETTING DAZZLED AT BANGKOK'S GRAND PALACE

THAILAND As befits a former royal residence, there's bling aplenty at the Grand Palace, whose main temple, Wat Phra Kaeo, dazzles with its shimmering walls and gables covered all over in gilt and coloured glass mosaics. Join the hundreds of Thai pilgrims and step inside to pay homage to the teeny Emerald Buddha, the holiest icon in the country. The figurine is just sixty centimetres high, elevated atop a towering golden pedestal, and is dressed according to the season: a golden shawl in winter, a monk's robe for the monsoon and a crown for summer. Things get even more surreal in the colonnades that encircle the temple, where an exuberant kilometre-long mural depicts the complicated ups and downs of the Ramayana story, an ancient epic tale of good versus evil, whose cast includes a monkey king, a demon with ten heads and a lot of otherwordly air-borne creatures.

874 FIGHT NIGHT IN BANGKOK

THAILAND The Thai people are predominately Buddhist, and through much of their country Siddhartha's spirit is palpable. Even in the noisy and overcrowded capital city, hard-faced nationals will soften their features and treat visitors with a respect given all living creatures. The exception that proves the rule is the brutal national sport of muay thai, or Thai boxing – where knees batter ribs while gamblers wager their salaries on who will fall, and when.

Vendors surround Bangkok's Lumphini Stadium three nights out of seven, peddling wares and heated snacks to patrons streaming into a theatre of controlled violence. Past the ticket booth is a mere hint of a lobby, its walls pierced with numbered archways too small for the seating areas behind them. A rhythmic thudding from deeper inside triggers a bottleneck at the edges of the arena's heart, the narrow entryways imparting a final suggestion of order before releasing spectators into the clamour beyond. In the ring the pre-fight display has already begun. Like many of the martial arts, muay thai has its roots in national defence, and the fighters perform awkward dances before the bell in honour of a kingdom never conquered by foreign invaders.

Drums pulse behind tense woodwinds as the early rounds get underway, each fighter cautiously feeling for weakness in his opponent's defence. The crowd is equally patient, watching carefully for an advantage they can use against the bookmakers. At the end of the second round all hell breaks loose. In the stands men are waving and shouting, signaling with contorted hands the amounts they're (not so) willing to lose. Within two minutes the fighters must retake the ring, and when they meet there are no more feints or dodges. Each attack is without pause. The music quickens. Blows are harder now, exchanged at a furious rate. The crowd raises its voice at every strike. Against the shin, into the ribs. Ferociously. Relentlessly. And then, in a long second felt by a single fighter, a step backward and to the left reveals enough space to slip an instep up and through the loser's jaw. Patrons make good on their markers while a stretcher carries away the unconscious also-ran. With ten fights a night, there's simply no time for compassion.

875 JOINING THE PARTY AT AN IBAN LONGHOUSE

MALAYSIA It's always polite to bring gifts to your hosts' house, but when visiting a Sarawak longhouse make sure it's something that's easily shared, as longhouses are communal, and nearly everything gets divvied up into equal parts. This isn't always an easy task: typically, longhouses are home to around 150 people and contain at least thirty family apartments, each one's front door opening on to the common gallery, hence the tag "a thirty-door longhouse" to describe the size. These days not everyone lives there full time, but the majority of Sarawak's indigenous Iban population still consider the longhouse home, even if they only return for weekends.

Many longhouses enjoy stunning locations, usually in a clearing beside a river, so you'll probably travel to yours in a longboat that meanders between the jungle-draped banks, dodging logs being floated downstream to the timber yards. Look carefully and you'll see that patches of hinterland have

been cultivated with black pepper vines, rubber and fruit trees, plus the occasional square of paddy, all of which are crucial to longhouse economies.

Having firstly met the chief of your longhouse, you climb the notched tree trunk that serves as a staircase into the stilted wooden structure and enter the common area, or ruai, a wide gallery that runs the length of the building and is the focus of community social life. Pretty much everything happens here – the meeting and greeting, the giving and sharing of gifts, the gossip, and the partying. Animist Iban communities in particular are notorious party animals (unlike some of their Christian counterparts), and you'll be invited to join in the excessive rice-wine drinking, raucous dancing and forfeit games that last late into the night. Finally, exhausted, you hit the sack – either on a straw mat right there on the ruai, or in a guest lodge next door.

876 MEETING THE RELATIVES: ORANG-UTANS IN SUMATRA

INDONESIA Sandwiched between the raging Bohorok River and the deep, silent, steaming jungle, the Bukit Lawang Orang-utan Sanctuary, on the vast Indonesian island of Sumatra, offers the unique opportunity of witnessing one of our closest and most charming relatives in their own backyard.

Having crossed the Bohorok on a precarious, makeshift canoe, your first sight of these kings of the jungle is at the enclosures housing recent arrivals, many of whom have been rescued from the thriving trade in exotic pets, particularly in nearby Singapore. It's here that the long process of rehabilitation begins, a process that may include learning from their human guardians such basic simian skills as tree-climbing and fruit-peeling.

Most of these activities are done away from the prying cameras of tourists, but twice a day park officers lead visitors up to a feeding platform to wait, and to watch. The sound of rustling foliage and creaking branches betrays the presence of a rangy, shaggy silhouette making its languid yet majestic way through the treetops. Orang-utans literally force the trees to bend to their will as they swing back and forth on one sapling until the next can be reached. Swooping just above the awestruck audience, they arrive at the platform to feast on bananas and milk, the diet kept deliberately monotonous to encourage the orang-utans – all of whom have been recently released from the sanctuary – to look for more diverse flavours in the forest.

Once the ape has proved that it's capable of surviving unaided, it will be left to fend for itself in the vast, dark forests of north Sumatra. Its rehabilitation will be considered complete. Sadly, at Bukit Lawang there never seems to be a shortage of rescued apes to take its place.

877 COUNTING FISH IN THE SULU SEA

THE PHILIPPINES Emperors, damsels, parrots and snappers – they were all down there in the Sulu Sea off the Philippine island of Palawan. I scribbled their names on an underwater slate as we drifted over the reef, air bubbles rising twenty metres to the humid surface.

It was my second week of identifying fish – their features now familiar after a week of lectures and tests on reef ecology – on an expedition run by Coral Cay Conservation (CCC); others in my survey team were noting corals, sponges and invertebrates. The hump-headed shape of a Napoleon Wrasse, almost two metres long and most often found on dinner plates in the Far East, had me writing in large capitals. I tugged on the survey rope to alert the others, just in time to see it disappear among the rocks below.

As we began our ascent, we heard the familiar metallic "plink" of dynamite fishing in the distance, and it wasn't too difficult to picture the damsels, parrots and snappers being blasted out of their hiding places, to float – dazed and injured – into the waiting nets above.

Back at base – an almost clichéd tropical island idyll – we entered our data into special forms used to provide a picture of the reef's diversity and to create sustainable development plans for local communities. As dusk fell and gas lamps were lit, we began our nightly ritual, heading down to the beach to rate the sunset. Walking back along the sandy path, iguanas rustling either side, I wondered whether Napoleon would still be there tomorrow.

878 SAFFRON AND GOLD: FALLING UNDER THE SPELL OF LOUANG PHABANG

LAOS The pace of life is deliciously slow in Louang Phabang, but if you opt for a lie-in you'll miss the perfect start to the day. As dawn breaks over this most languorous of Buddhist towns, saffron-robed monks emerge from their temple-monasteries to collect alms from their neighbours, the riverbanks begin to hum and the smell of freshly baked baguettes draws you to one of the many cafés. It's a captivating scene whichever way you turn: ringed by mountains and encircled by the Mekong and Khan rivers, the old quarter's temple roofs peep out from the palm groves, its streets still lined with wood-shuttered shophouses and French-colonial mansions.

Though it has the air of a rather grand village, Louang Phabang is the ancient Lao capital, seat of the royal family that ruled the country for six hundred years until the Communists exiled them in the 1970s. It remains the most cultured town in Laos (not a hard-won accolade it's true, in this poor, undeveloped nation), and one of the best preserved in Southeast Asia – now formalized by its World Heritage status. Chief among its many beautiful temples is the entrancing sixteenth-century Wat Xiang Thong, whose tiered roofs frame an exquisite glass mosaic of the tree of life and attendant creatures, flanked by pillars and doors picked out in brilliant gold-leaf stencils. It's a gentle stroll from here to the graceful teak and rosewood buildings of the Royal Palace Museum and the dazzling gilded murals of neighbouring Wat Mai.

When you tire of the monuments, there are riverside caves, waterfalls and even a whisky-making village to explore, and plenty of shops selling intricate textiles and Hmong hill-tribe jewellery. Serenity returns at sunset, when the monks' chants drift over the temple walls and everyone else heads for high ground to soak up the view.

879 UNDERWATER AT SIPADAN ISLAND

MALAYSIA Every diver who comes to Sipadan will see something that they haven't seen before. Famous for its large resident population of green and hawksbill turtles as well as healthy numbers of reef sharks and magnificent coral, Sipadan is Malaysia's only oceanic island. Sitting in the Sulu Sea off the northeastern coast of Borneo, it's also a great base for exploring the nearby shoals of Kapalai and the island of Mabul, well-suited for voyeurs who are tantalized by the mating habits of mandarin fish and frogfish and other cryptic reef dwellers like sea-wasps. Above water, on Mabul you'll also meet the indigenous "sea-gypsies" – the Badjao – who live either in stilt-houses perched over the lagoon or on their tiny fishing boats which ply the Sulu Sea as far as the Philippines.

880 THE BUZZ AROUND CHIANG MAI

THAILAND The motorbikes of Chiang Mai are beautiful things. Renting them is easy and cheap, and they let you get around like a local, even if you have a poor sense of direction. Pick a morning, strap on your fisherman pants from the night market and, if you're brave, make room for a friend. Fly east to hilltop Wat Doi Saket to have your mind blown by trippy murals teaching Buddhist morality – illustrated with traffic signs. Buzz back along the "Handicraft Highway" to visit paper, celadon, wood and silk workshops. South of the city, get lost among the ancient chedis of Wiang Kum Kam, then rocket north to canoodle with baby elephants and watch their mothers make modern art at Mae Sa Elephant Camp. Once you've got the hang of all this, zip west up Doi Suthep mountain for lovely views of the countryside you've just explored. If the bike's motor hasn't turned your legs to jelly, climb the 300 stairs to Wat Phra That Doi Suthep, ding the bells in the courtyard for good luck – and beware speeding songthaew buses on the way back down.

881 BUNAKEN'S MARINE MEGALOPOLIS

INDONESIA The reefs at Bunaken Marine Park on Sulawesi teem with over 400 species of hard corals, rare pygmy seahorses, glorious gobies, decorator crabs and hairy frogfish. Coral walls, currents upwelling from deep nearby waters and huge schools of plankton feeders draw in gobs of different fish species, not to mention hordes of divers. Strict environmental regulations and cooperation with the local community have made Sulawesi, and the surrounding islands, one of the world's best diving destinations, and underwater photographers and marine biologists consistently rate Bunaken and the nearby Lembeh Strait as the globe's busiest macro-critter capital.

THE KINGS OF KOMODO

INDONESIA There are few expeditions more disquieting than visiting Indonesia's Komodo Island. Approaching by boat, it appears staggeringly beautiful – the archetypal tropical hideaway. But doubts about the sagacity of what you're about to do surface as soon as you step ashore and discover that you're sharing the beach with the local deer population: if they're too frightened to spend much time in the interior, is it entirely wise for you to do so?

Your unease only grows at the nearby national park office, as you're briefed about the island's most notorious inhabitant. From the tip of a tail so mighty that one swish could knock a buffalo off its feet, to a mouth that drips with saliva so foul that most bite victims die from infected wounds rather than the injuries themselves, Komodo dragons are 150kg of pure reptilian malevolence.

They are also – on Komodo at least – quite numerous, and it doesn't take long before you come across your first dragon, usually basking motionless on a rock or up a tree (among an adult dragon's more unpleasant habits is a tendency to feed on the young, so adolescents often seek sanctuary in the branches).

So immobile are they during the heat of the day that the only proof that they're still alive is an occasional flick of the tongue, usually accompanied by a globule of viscous drool that drips and hangs from the side of their mouths. Indeed, it's this docility that encourages you – possibly against your better judgement – to edge closer, until eventually those of sufficient nerve are almost within touching distance.

And it's only then, as you crouch delicately on your haunches and examine the loose folds of battle-scarred skin, the dark, eviscerating talons and the cold, dead eyes of this natural-born killer, that you can fully appreciate how fascinating these creatures really are, and that there is nothing, but nothing, so utterly, compellingly revolting on this planet.

882

883 FEELING FRUITY IN THE MEKONG DELTA

VIETNAM If you're looking for a classic Southeast Asian scene, Vietnam's Mekong Delta, south of Ho Chi Minh City, will do the trick. This is an area of vivid green rice paddies, conical-hatted farmers and lumbering water buffaloes; of floating markets and villages built on stilts. Lush orchards overflow with mangoes, papayas and dragonfruit; plantations brim with bananas, coconuts and pineapples. And through it all wind the nine tributaries of the Mekong River, their canals and tributaries nourishing this fruitbasket of Vietnam, the waters busy with sampans, canoes and houseboats. It is the end of the run for Asia's mighty Mekong, whose waters rise over four thousand kilometres away in the snows of the Tibetan plateau and empty out here, into the alluvial-rich plains fringing the South China Sea.

For the fifteen million people who live in these wetlands, everything revolves around the waterways, so to glimpse something of their life you need to join them on the river. Boat tours from the market town of My Tho will take you to nearby orchard-islands, crisscrossed by narrow palm-shaded canals and famous for their juicy yellow-fleshed sapodilla fruits. At Vinh Long, home-stay programmes give you the opportunity to sample the garden produce for dinner and spend the night on stilts over the water. Chances are your host-family catch fish as well – right under their floorboards in specially designed bamboo cages, so the daily feed is simply a matter of lifting up a plank or two. Next stop should be Can Tho, the delta's principal city, to make the ride out to the enormous floating market at Phung Hiep. Here at the confluence of seven major waterways, hundreds of sampans bump and jostle early each morning to trade everything from sugar cane to pigs – and of course mountains of fruit.

884 PEEKING AT PARADISE IN ARU

INDONESIA So here I was in the middle of the jungle in Aru, at the end of the end of everywhere in the southeastern Indonesian province of Maluku, trying to find cenderawasih, the greater bird of paradise. These are gorgeous creatures, about the size of a thrush and with a similarly brown body, but one topped by a metallic green cap and, in males, a fantastic fountain of long, fluffy-looking golden feathers, which are proudly swished and shaken in territorial dancing displays.

But they were proving elusive: this was my fourth attempt within a year, after the others had ended in ferry strandings, political violence and a plane crash. I had now spent three days being taken ever-deeper into the forest's vine-tangled depths by hunters who I could barely communicate with, leaving me with tick bites aplenty but no sign of birds of paradise. We hadn't even heard their noisy "wok-wok-wok-wok" call, which sounds as melodic as a tin alarm clock going off, and has caused locals to brand them burung bodoh, the stupid bird, because the racket makes them easy to track down and shoot.

But I was having fun, and now it was 6am on day five, my last, and I was being led into the forest once again by the sixty-year-old Bapak Gusti. He'd collared me in the village the evening before and casually mentioned that he owned a tree, just a short walk away, where the birds displayed every morning. I had nothing to lose by this point; my only worry was that this – like all the other "short walks" I had undertaken here – would actually last six hours, and the boat out would leave without me. But I was wrong: within twenty minutes, he had led me to a tree where, on a bare branch 30m up in the canopy, three male birds of paradise were displaying their hearts out, their plumage glowing as bright as the sunlight which brushed the treetops.

885 EXPLORING MALAPASCUA BY BANCA

THE PHILIPPINES The view as you approach the tiny island of Malapascua by sea is one you'll never forget. It sits exquisitely in an emerald sea like some tremulous flying saucer, the palm trees of its jungled interior ringed by a halo of blindingly white sand. This is Bounty Beach, as idyllic as they come.

Difficult as it may be, summon the willpower to move from your shady hammock and explore beyond – you'll be further rewarded with picturesque inlets and coves where you can play ultimate castaway, with a few home comforts. The best way to explore is by hiring a banca, a native wooden pumpboat with spidery bamboo outriggers. A boatman and a couple of boatboys will come as part of the package, and they'll know exactly where to take you.

Start with Carnassa Beach, a secluded envelope of sugary sand banded by low hills on three sides with dwarf coconut palms for shade. On the fourth side is the sea, its gin-clear waters perfect for snorkelling among the reef fishes and the occasional inquisitive turtle. From there chug north to Coconut Beach, a sunny crescent of sand backed by a coconut grove where you can drink fresh buko (coconut milk) and find a shady spot for a well-earned siesta.

For the ultimate sundowner, continue on to the unnamed curve of beach beyond the island's little lighthouse. From here you can gaze westward, chilled San Miguel beer in hand, as the tropical sun slips lazily below the horizon. South of here is Logon Beach, where the locals will rustle up some grilled fish for your dinner. Wash it down with a grog or two of local rum, and spend the night in simple huts made from native grass.

Next morning, set out at dawn for the two-hour banca trip to Calangaman, a stunningly gorgeous dumbbell-shaped slither of sand seemingly in the middle of nowhere. The islet's only residents are a handful of fisherfolk who can help you prepare an unparalleled "catch of the day" beach barbecue. Just don't forget the cold drinks.

986 BUDGET
BEACH-CHIC

THAILAND Old-school travellers complain that Thailand has gone upmarket, swapped its cheap sleeps for identikit villas and sacrificed the beach-shack-and-hammock vibe for apartments with swimming pools. They've got a point. Thailand is prospering: new boutique hotels entice you with minimalist curves and luxurious fabrics, and at $150 a night, a five-star suite can seem like an affordable indulgence.

But the rudimentary bamboo beach huts still exist and arguably there's no better way to experience the pleasures of Thailand's gorgeous strands. With over 3000km of coastline and scores of accessible islands you've got plenty of beaches to choose from, the default option being squeaky white sand and luminous turquoise water. Staying in a wooden hut you're often all but camping: you'll see the sand beneath your feet through the slats of the wonky planked floor; you'll hear the waves lapping the shoreline just a few metres from your ill-fitting front door; and there's no need for a fan when you prop open the woven rattan shutters and let the breeze waft through. Make your own shell mobiles, hang your sarong as a door curtain and string up your hammock. It's your very own eco home and worth every bit of the modest daily sum that buys you residency.

887 SNAKE EVERY WHICH WAY IN HANOI

VIETNAM When the man bringing your meal to the table is missing most of his fingers and the main ingredient is not only still alive but also long and writhing and – hang on, is that a cobra? Well, that's when you know this is no ordinary dining experience. Eating at one of Hanoi's snake restaurants is as much a theatrical performance as a meal out.

The decor is way over the top. From a grungy side-street you enter a world of exuberant woodwork with mother-of-pearl inlay glowing in the lantern light. Bonsai plants are scattered artfully while off to the side glass jars containing snake wine hint at what's to come.

When everyone's settled, the snake handler – he with very few fingers – presents the menu. He kicks off with cobra, the most expensive item on the menu (and a choice photo-op), then runs through the other options, all very much alive and hissing.

Traditionally, your chosen snake is killed in front of you, though it will be dispatched off-stage if you ask. The guest of honour (lucky you?) then gets to eat the still-beating heart. The Vietnamese say it contains a stimulant and that the meat is an aphrodisiac. The jury's out on both counts, however, because of the copious amounts of alcohol everyone consumes. By way of an aperitif you get two small glasses of rice wine, one blood red, the other an almost fluorescent, bile-ish green . . . which is exactly what they are.

Things get decidedly more palatable as the meal starts to arrive. In a matter of minutes your snake has been transformed into all manner of tasty dishes: snake soup, spring rolls, dumplings, filets, even crispy-fried snake skin. Absolutely nothing is wasted. It's washed down with more rice wine, or beer if you'd rather, and to round things off, fresh fruit and green tea – no snake sorbet forthcoming.

888 PADDLING INTO SECRET LAGOONS

THAILAND The first time you enter a *hong* you're almost certain to laugh with delight. The fun begins when your guide paddles you across to the towering karst island and then pilots your canoe through an imperceptible fissure in its rock wall. You enter a sea cave that reeks of bats and gets darker and darker until suddenly your guide shouts "Lie back in the boat please!" Your nose barely clears the stalactites and you emerge, toes first, into a sun-lit lagoon, or hong, at the heart of the outcrop.

Hong ("rooms" in Thai) are the pièce de résistance of southern Thailand's Phang Nga Bay. Invisible to any passing vessel, these secret tidal lagoons are flooded, roofless caves hidden within the core of seemingly solid limestone islands, accessible only at certain tides and only in sea canoes small enough to

slip beneath and between low-lying rocky overhangs. Like the islands themselves, the hong have taken millions of years to form, with the softer limestone hollowed out from the side by the pounding waves, and from above by the wind and the rain.

The world inside these collapsed cave systems is extraordinary, protected from the open bay by a turreted ring of cliffs hung with primeval-looking gardens of inverted cycads, twisted bonsai palms, lianas, miniature screw pines and tangled ferns. And as the tide withdraws, the hong's resident creatures – among them fiddler crabs, mudskippers, dusky langurs and crab-eating macaques – emerge to forage on the muddy floor, while white-bellied sea eagles hover expectantly overhead.

889 ROAMING RAINY PENANG

MALAYSIA It's tropically hot and raining in Penang's old town centre, Georgetown, the water hitting the road so hard that it makes a haze at about knee height. People are jumping the flooded gutters and running for cover under the collonaded shopfronts but there's not much room thanks to the squadrons of motorbikes parked here. Under this heavy downpour, you couldn't imagine a better evocation of colonial outpost gone to seed: wet, narrow lanes link the faded, mildewed buildings, their tops sprouting moss and small bits of vegetation.

At first, Georgetown gives little away about the people who actually live here; you can see the same century-old buildings all across Southeast Asia from here to the Philippines. But as you wander about you begin to notice the distinct shapes of the temples, the unique scripts and the different market and restaurant smells that mark out each community of the Chinese, Hindu, Burmese and Thai settlers. Weirdly, the British – in control here for so many years – and the indigenous Malay seem barely represented; just the seafront skeleton of Fort Cornwallis and

plush Eastern & Oriental hotel, and a night market where Malay youths parade their motorcycles and run stalls selling Nonya (Malay-Chinese) dishes.

About the only thing tying the communities together on this betel nut-shaped island (after which it's named) is the hot, sticky weather, and the way that everyone here seems to be under constant threat from the jungle that lurks in the background, just waiting to reclaim the city. Ride the funicular railway to the top of Penang Hill and you can see the reality of this: Penang's modern sprawl of towerblocks and expressways is laid out beneath you but up here there are huge trees, orchids, groves of bamboo and palms, greenery and red earth – not the wilds exactly, but only one step away from it. Down at the base of the hill, a walk around the Botanic Gardens only reinforces the feeling; here there are even monkeys, snakes and flying lizards. You can't help feeling that despite the development, Penang never really got anywhere, or at least, never fulfilled the first European colonists' expectations – though maybe it's just the heat and the heavy, waterlogged air.

890 TRYING TO SOLVE PUZZLES AT THE PLAIN OF JARS

LAOS After three hours trudging along steep forest paths, you come to a surreal sight. Hundreds of megalithic stone jars, large enough for a man to a crouch into, are strewn all around. They were made by a vanished civilization and their presence indicates that the mountains were prosperously settled at the time. This group of 416 jars is the largest at the aptly-named Plain of Jars, whose current tally stands at 1900 jars in 52 clusters, plus fifteen jar-making sites. Today, with the recent discovery of several jars, the Xieng Khoung province is on the rise again, this time as a tourist hub.

Little is known about the jar-makers, except that the plateau was a strategic and prosperous hub for trade routes extending from India to China. Nearly 2000 years ago, possibly earlier according to new evidence, these jars functioned as mortuary vessels: a corpse would be placed inside the jar until it decomposed down to its essence, then cremated and buried in a second urn with personal possessions (one burial was recently excavated). Now all that remains here are the empty jars, set in clusters on the crests of hills, an imposing and eerie legacy.

At Phukeng, you can see where the jars were made. Dozens of incomplete jars lie on the mountainside where they were abandoned after cracking during construction. It's a sight that evokes the magnitude of the effort: after many weeks spent gouging a jar from a boulder with hammer and chisel, the creators then had to haul the load of several tons (the largest jar weighs six tons) across the undulating, grassy, pine-studded landscape to the "cemetery" 8km away. How the jars were transported is another puzzle that serves to thicken the enigma that pervades the Plain of Jars.

891 BALINESE THEATRICS

INDONESIA On the island of Bali, a Hindu enclave in the Muslim majority nation of Indonesia, the gods and spirits need regular appeasing and entertaining. Offerings of rice and flowers are laid out twice a day in tiny banana-leaf baskets and on special occasions there is ritual music and dancing. Temple festivals are so frequent here that you've a good chance of coming across one, but there are also dance performances staged for tourists at the palace in Ubud, the island's cultural hub. Even though the programme has been specially tailored, there is nothing inauthentic about the finesse of the palace performers. And the setting – a starlit courtyard framed by stone-carved statues and an elaborate gateway – is magnificent.

Every performance begins with a priest sanctifying the space with a sprinkle of holy water. Then the gamelan orchestra strikes up: seated cross-legged either side of the stage, the twenty-five musicians are dressed in formal outfits of Nehru jacket, traditional headcloth and sarong. The light catches the bronze of their gongs, cymbals and metallophones, the lead drummer raises his hand, and they're off, racing boisterously through the first piece, producing an extraordinary syncopated clashing of metal on metal, punctuated by dramatic stops and starts.

Enter the dancers. Five sinuous barefooted young women open with a ritualistic welcome dance, scattering flower petals as an offering to the gods. Next, the poised refinement of the Legong, performed by three young girls wrapped in luminous pink, green and gold brocade, the drama played out with gracefully angled hands, fluttering arms and wide flashing eyes. Finally it's the masked Barong–Rangda drama, the all-important pitting of good against evil, with the loveable, lion-like Barong stalked and harassed by the powerful widow-witch Rangda, all fangs and fingernails. With typical Balinese pragmatism, neither good nor evil is victorious, but, crucially, spiritual harmony will have been restored on the Island of the Gods.

892 VISITING THE TUOL SLENG GENOCIDE MUSEUM

CAMBODIA Everyone over thirty in Cambodia has lived through the genocidal Khmer Rouge era. The woman who runs your guest house in downtown Phnom Penh; the moto driver who tried to rip you off on the ride down from the Thai border; your Angkor temples tour guide; your waiter at the seaside café in Sihanoukville. At the Tuol Sleng Genocide Museum you'll learn something of what that means.

A former school on the outskirts of Phnom Penh, Tuol Sleng, code-named S-21, was used by the Khmer Rouge to interrogate perceived enemies of their demented Marxist-Leninist regime. During the Khmer Rouge rule, from 1975 to 1979, some fourteen thousand Cambodians were tortured and killed here, often for the crime of being educated: for being a teacher, a monk, or a member of the elite; for wearing glasses; for being a discredited cadre. We know this because the Khmer Rouge were meticulous in their documentation. When the Vietnamese army arrived at S-21 in January 1979 they found thousands of mugshots of former prisoners, each of them numbered, along with reams of typed "confessions".

Those black and white photographs fill the downstairs walls of the museum today. There are rows and rows of them: men, women, children, even babies. Only seven prisoners survived S-21; one of them, Ung Pech, became the museum's first director. When the museum opened to the public in 1980, thousands of Cambodians came here to look for evidence of missing relatives.

The interior of the prison has in part been left almost as it was found. Tiled floors, classrooms crudely partitioned into tiny cells, shackles, iron bedsteads and meshed balconies. Elsewhere, graphic paintings by another survivor, Vann Nath, depict the torture methods used to extract confessions; some of these confessions are also reproduced here. Once they'd been coerced into admitting guilt, prisoners were taken to the Choeung Ek Killing Fields and murdered. Choeung Ek, 12km southwest, is now the site of another memorial. Both are important to see for yourself.

893 THE HILLS ARE ALIVE: TRIBAL TREKKING

THAILAND Exhilarating though the ridgetop views often are, it's not the scenery that draws travellers into the hills of northern Thailand, but the people who live in them. There are some four thousand hill-tribe villages in the uplands of Chiang Mai and Chiang Rai provinces, peopled by half a dozen main tribes whose ancestors wandered across from Burma and China. They have subsistence-farmed up here for two hundred years and continue to observe age-old customs and beliefs, making visiting them a fascinating, and popular, trip.

The trekking between villages is moderately taxing – you're in the hills after all – but the trails are well worn and a good guide will bring the landscape alive, pointing out medicinal plants and elusive creatures along the way. The highlights, though, are the villages themselves, clusters of stilted bamboo huts close by a river, invariably wreathed in wood-smoke and busy with free-ranging pigs and chickens. Village architecture varies a little between tribes, particularly where animist shrines and totems are concerned, for each group lives by distinct traditions and taboos. But the diverse costumes are more striking: the jangling headdresses of the Akha women decorated with baubles hammered out of old silver coins; the intricately embroidered wide-legged trousers worn by the Mien; the pom-poms and Day-Glo pinks and greens favoured by the Lisu. Many hill-tribeswomen make their living from weaving and embroidering these traditional textiles and buying direct is a good way of contributing to village funds.

894

DANCING UNDER A FULL MOON

THAILAND The tourist party season in Southeast Asia traditionally gets underway at the end of the year with huge, head-thumping parties at Hat Rin Beach on Thailand's Ko Pha Ngan island. Hat Rin has firmly established itself as Southeast Asia's premier rave venue, especially in the high season around December and January, but every month of the year at full moon travellers flock in for the Full Moon Party – something like *Apocalypse Now* without the war. Tens of thousands of party fiends from all corners of the world kick up the largely good-natured, booze- and drug-fuelled mayhem, dancing the night away on the squeaky white sand.

To make the most of a Full Moon Party, get yourself to Hat Rin at least a couple days in advance. That way you'll be able to maximize the stunning beach location, soak up the growing buzz as the crowds pour in and, more importantly, snag yourself somewhere to stay. Most partygoers make it through to the dawn, and some can still be seen splashing in the shallow surf towards noon, when the last of the beach DJs pull the plug.

895 JUNGLE BOOGIE IN SARAWAK

MALAYSIA Afternoon, the first day of Sarawak's Rainforest Music festival. People are mingling ahead of show time when the famous Malagasy band Tarika will perform. For now though, a local Melinau musician with a hat made of bark and bird feathers strums the lute-like sape as we wander around the site, comprising a dozen small longhouses which open daily for demonstrations of local culture. The music mingles with the screech of tropical birdlife, the scampering of chickens and the sing-a-long refrains of local children.

As evening progresses, crowds arrive from the nearby city Kuching, primed for the evening's fun. We first gorge ourselves on a Dyak feast of local delicacies: baked fish in banana leaves, spicy fried pork, rice and a salad dressed in lime and chili. Dusk swiftly becomes night as the festival hits its stride with sets from international folk, jazz and world fusion artists. I'm reminded of WOMAD in the early days, and expect to spot a beady-eyed Peter Gabriel on the lookout for new talent, hunting perhaps an upriver Iban rapper with a fleet of gongs and pipes for accompaniment.

By the time the opening night of the three-day jamboree draws to a close, and with the tropical heat cooled by a refreshing south-westerly, we are on our feet jiving crazily to Tarika lead singer Hanitra's robust evocations. We have made – or at least bumped into – many new friends from all over the world. Some have been coming to the festival for years, know the bands and appreciate the attention this little outpost of Malaysian camaraderie gets over this hot, hot weekend. Others, though, confess to not knowing what has hit them – how is it that all this world-class music is being performed in a tiny little jungle enclave at the bottom of a narrow road in a place called the Damai Peninsula?

We head for bed, luckily a comfortable hotel room with a balcony that's only a five-minute stagger away, to awake not just to a hangover but to the delicious promise of another two days of groovesome beats deep in the jungle.

896 FIREWORKS FEVER AT BUN BANG FAI

LAOS & THAILAND On the full moon in May it's time to light the fuse and stand well clear throughout Laos, as rocket fever grips the nation, and countless home-made contraptions are launched skywards to ensure good rain and a healthy crop as part of the Bun Bang Fai festival. Vientiane is the place to be, although you'll find smaller events going on all over the country. Buddhist monks are the most expert rocket scientists, using bamboo tubes – up to 5m in length – stuffed with gunpowder, decked in coloured ribbons and capped by a paper dragon's head. For the layman, PVC piping is a less traditional but equally effective material.

As it's something of a fertility festival, there's much bawdy singing and dancing through the day, and come the evening everyone assembles in raucous crowds by the Mekong to watch the launchings. There's serious "mine-is-bigger-than-yours"-type competition between builders, and those whose efforts fail to go off or flop badly face ridicule, and often wind up getting pushed into the river.

Bun Bang Fai is also celebrated in Yasothon, in Thailand's dense, less touristed northeast interior, close to the Laotian border. The fireworks safety book is thrown out of the window as the locals work their way through crates of Singha beer, and handcrafted rockets are let off with dangerous enthusiasm all over town.

897 MOONLIT MANOEUVRES THROUGH HOI AN

VIETNAM Once a month, on the eve of the full moon, downtown Hoi An turns off all its street lights and basks in the mellow glow of silk lanterns. Shopkeepers don traditional outfits; parades, folk opera and martial arts demonstrations flood the cobbled streets; and the riverside fills with stalls selling crabmeat parcels, beanpaste cakes and noodle soup. It's all done for tourists of course – and some find it cloyingly self-conscious – but nevertheless this historic little central Vietnam town oozes charm, with the monthly Full Moon Festival just part of its appeal.

Much of the town's charisma derives from its downtown architecture. Until the Thu Bon River silted up in the late eighteenth century, Hoi An was an important port, attracting traders from China and beyond, many of whom settled and built wooden-fronted homes, ornate shrines and exuberantly tiled Assembly Halls that are still used by their descendants today. Several of these atmospheric buildings are now open to the public, offering intriguing glimpses into cool, dark interiors filled with imposing furniture, lavishly decorated altars and family memorabilia that have barely been touched since the 1800s. Together with the peeling pastel facades, colonnaded balconies and waterside market, it's all such a well-preserved blast from the past that Unesco has designated central Hoi An a World Heritage site.

The merchant spirit needs no such protection, however: there are now so many shops in this small town that the authorities have recently imposed a ban on any new openings. Art galleries and antique shops are plentiful, but silk and tailoring are the biggest draws. Hoi An tailors are the best in the country, and for $200 you can walk away with an entire custom-made wardrobe – complete with Armani-inspired suit, silk shirt, hand-crafted leather boots and personalized handbag. And if you've really fallen under Hoi An's spell, you might find yourself also ordering an ao dai, the tunic and trouser combo worn so elegantly by Vietnamese women.

BOROBUDUR: THE BIGGEST BUDDHIST STUPA IN THE WORLD

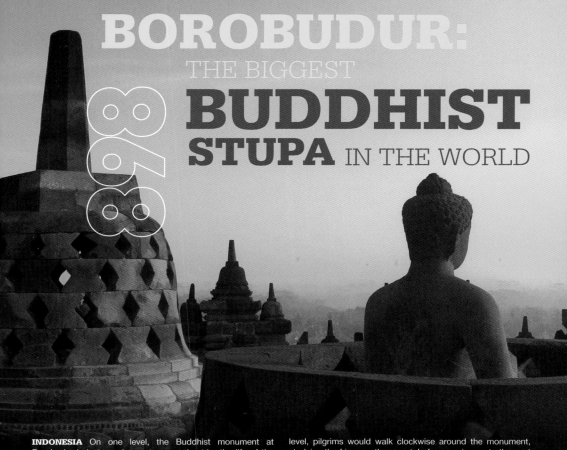

INDONESIA On one level, the Buddhist monument at Borobudur is just one huge stone comic strip: the life of the Buddha told in a series of intricate reliefs carved around a gigantic stupa-shaped structure rising from central Java's fertile plains. But it's also a colossal representation of the Buddhist cosmic mountain, Meru. Built sometime around the ninth century AD by the short-lived Saliendra dynasty, occupying some two hundred square metres of land and incorporating 1.6 million blocks of local volcanic rock, it is the largest monument in the southern hemisphere.

Much of Borobudur's appeal, however, comes not from its enormity but from the little details: the delicately sculpted reliefs, eroded down the generations but still identifiable and alive with warriors, maidens, the devout and the debauched, as well as elephants, turtles and other creatures. Beginning at ground level, pilgrims would walk clockwise around the monument, studying the frieze as they went, before moving up to the next level. Borobudur can be viewed as one enormous 34.5-metre-high educational tool; a complete circuit would take the pilgrims and monks, most of whom would have been illiterate, through the life of the Buddha. Starting from his earthly existence, represented by the friezes on the first four tiers, it ends with his attainment of Nirvana – or "nothingness" – at the tenth and top level, here represented by a large, empty stupa. The friezes on the first four "earthly" tiers are, on an artistic level, the most remarkable, but it is the upper five galleries that tend to linger in the memory, as the outside walls disappear, allowing you to savour the views over the lush Javanese plateau to the silent, brooding volcanoes beyond.

INDONESIA They're orange, they hang in trees, but they're not a fruit. Hairy rubber balls of creatures with a judo grip and a sense of humour, orang-utans are our nearest evolutionary cousins and the original "men of the forest". Like all the great apes, they're becoming extremely rare, and are found only on the huge island of Borneo, but there are still places where it's possible to see them fairly easily, in something approaching their natural state.

A research centre dedicated to reintroducing baby orang-utans orphaned by the pet trade into the wild, Camp Leakey is about five hours by klotok boat up the Sekonyer river from the tiny port of Kumai. It's a wonderful journey, past banks fringed with the huge fronds of nipa palms, then along increasingly narrow, tea-coloured tributaries flanked by ever-thicker jungle. Sitting on the klotok's flat roof as it chugs slowly along, there's a lot to look out for – the log-like head of a gharial crocodile, sinking without a ripple as the boat nears; proboscis monkeys making wild leaps between branches and occasionally jumping straight into the water for a swim, their oversized noses bobbing along; and the quiet shadows of gibbons moving swiftly through the treetops. And there, it's your first view of an orang-utan, a great blob of orange fur hanging on to a rattan vine above the water, trying to grab a pandanus fruit. Docking at a boardwalk a few minutes later, you're met by another one, much younger, who grabs you with an irresistibly strong but gentle hand, and climbs onto your back to hug you like a rucksack. There's no shifting him, so you carry him up to the boardwalk to a clearing where the orphans get a feed of bananas every evening.

He hitches a ride until a ranger appears, and then jumps down and scoots off towards the dozen others waiting impatiently for their supper to arrive. And once it does, and he's eaten his fill, it's straight up into the treetops for a snooze without a backward glance.

899 GOING APE IN BORNEO

900 IRONING OUT THE KINKS

THAILAND One of the many great things about having a Thai massage is that there's no oil or lotions involved, so you don't need to strip off and there's none of that embarrassing tussle with paper knickers; you can also get your massage pretty much anywhere. This could be at a temple – in particular at the famous Wat Pho in Bangkok, historic centre of Thai massage therapy – at a hotel spa, or, most enticingly (and cheaply), on the beach. A two-hour session under a palm tree will cost you no more than $10, the soothing soundtrack of gently lapping waves will be genuine, and you should emerge feeling like you've had a good yoga workout, both relaxed and energized, but without having made any of the effort yourself.

It can come as a shock the first time a Thai masseur uses his or her elbows on your back, then brings heels, feet and knees into play, pulling and pushing your limbs into contorted yogic stretches. But it's all carefully designed to exert a gentle pressure on your vital energy channels, and it's what distinguishes the Thai approach from most other massage styles, which are more concerned with tissue manipulation.

Thais will visit a masseur for conditions that might send others scuttling to the pharmacist – to alleviate fevers, colds and headaches, for example. But healthy bodies also benefit; it's said that regular massage sessions produce long-term well-being by stimulating the circulation and aiding natural detoxification. And it's certainly an idyllic way to while away a few languorous hours on the beach.

901 DAWN OVER KELIMUTU IN FLORES

INDONESIA There's something magnificently untamed about Flores. As with almost every island in this part of the Indonesian archipelago, Flores is fringed by picture-postcard beaches of golden sand. But to appreciate its unique charms you have to turn away from the sea and instead face the island's interior. Despite its relatively small size (a mere 370km long and, in places, as narrow as 12km), only the much larger Indonesian landmasses of Java and Sumatra can boast more volcanoes than this slender sliver of lush land.

Unsurprisingly, perhaps, Flores' jagged volcanic spine has played a major part in the island's development. The precipitous topography contributes to the island's torrential wet seasons, which in turn provides a tropical countenance – not for nothing did the Portuguese name this island "Cabo das Flores", the Cape of Flowers. The rugged peaks have also long separated the various tribes on the island – an enforced segregation that has ensured an inordinate number of different languages and dialects, as well as many distinct cultures.

The highest volcanic peak on the island is the towering 2382m Gunung Ranaka, while its most volatile is the grumbling, hotheaded Ebulobo on Flores' south coast. But the prince among them is Kelimutu.

Though just 1620m high, the volcano has become something of a pilgrimage site. Waking at around 4am, trekkers pile onto the back of an open-sided truck for the thirty-minute ride up the volcano's slopes, from where a short scramble to Kelimutu's barren summit reveals the mountain's unique attraction: three small craters, each filled with lakes of startlingly different colours, ranging from vibrant turquoise to a deep, reddish brown. With the wisps of morning mist lingering above the water's surface and the rising sun bouncing off the waters creating an ever-changing play of light and colour, dawn over Kelimutu is Indonesia at its most beguiling.

902 CREATURES OF THE NIGHT

SINGAPORE Darkness engulfs the sky, blanketing trees, the path and those out walking. From the mysterious shadows, sounds of people – breathing, treading on twigs, murmuring in the distance – filter through. Then suddenly an intimidating roar penetrates the din. Welcome to Singapore Zoo's night safari, the world's first nocturnal zoo.

Walk one of three trails – fishing cats, forest giants and leopards – or jump on a tram and travel two road loops to catch oblivious nocturnal creatures going about their usual business. You might find the shadowy corners of the trails a little disorientating, especially when you look up to find yourself face-to-face with a giant flying squirrel. Unlike other zoos, there aren't any big cats lazing around waiting for a keeper to bring them their meal. Here you'll witness them actually prowling around hunting for their supper – this is about as close to a real safari as you can get within the confines of a zoo.

The safari park is broken into eight geographical zones, home to over 1000 animals. In addition to the zones, there's an animal show, a fragrant walk (over 4000 plants line your entrance to the zoo) and cultural performances (including highlights from Borneo tribal performers). Many of the walk-through exhibits are likely to get your heart pumping faster: the forest giant's trail, home to plants of all shapes and sizes, also has flying lemurs, owls and tree shrews, so if you're at all uneasy about having a creature come within centimetres of you, this is not the exhibit – or the zoo – for you.

ISLAND-HOPPING IN THE
BACUIT ARCHIPELAGO

903

THE PHILIPPINES If you thought Alex Garland's tropical-island classic *The Beach* was inspired by Thailand, think again; it was the Philippines, particularly the spectacular islands and lagoons of the Bacuit archipelago in Palawan, where tourists are still relatively thin on the ground but surely won't be for long. It's not hard to see why Garland was so bewitched by this place: 45 stunning limestone islands rise dramatically from an iridescent sea. Most have exquisite palm-fringed beaches, so you shouldn't have too much trouble finding your own piece of paradise for the day. All you need to do is pack yourself a picnic, hire yourself an outrigger boat – known locally as a banca – and ask the boatman to do the rest.

Start by chugging gently out to Miniloc Island, where a narrow opening in the fearsomely jagged karst cliffs leads to a hidden lagoon known as Big Lagoon, home to hawksbill turtles. A couple of minutes away, also at Miniloc, is the narrow entrance to Small Lagoon, which you have to swim through, emerging into a natural amphitheatre of gin-clear waters and the screech of long-tailed macaques.

Other islands you shouldn't miss? Well, take your pick. Pangalusian has a long stretch of quiet beach; Tres Marias has terrific snorkelling along a shallow coral reef; and Helicopter Island (named after its shape) has a number of secluded sandy coves where your only companions are monitor lizards and the occasional manta ray floating by.

The culmination of a perfect day's island-hopping should be a sunset trip to Snake Island, where you can sink a few cold San Miguels (take them with you in an ice box), and picnic on a slender, serpentine tongue of perfect white sand which disappears gently into shallow waters that are ideal for swimming.

904 ALL ABOARD THE EASTERN & ORIENTAL EXPRESS

SINGAPORE– BANGKOK First, tea is served. In a fancy teapot, with biscuits, by a butler dressed in pristine white uniform. You stare lazily out of the window as porters labour in the crushing afternoon humidity, blissfully cool in your air-conditioned cabin. Then the train eases out of the station: the skyscrapers of Singapore soon fall away, and you're across the Straits of Johor and into the lush, torpid palm plantations of Malaysia.

This is the *Eastern & Oriental Express*, the luxurious train service that plies between Singapore and Bangkok, the last remnant of opulent colonial travel in Southeast Asia – evoking the days of posh British administrators, gin-sloshed planters and rich, glamorous dowagers rather like the set of the Merchant Ivory movie.

To be fair, you're more likely to meet professionals from San Francisco or Hong Kong on the train today. There are a couple of stops to break the three-day journey – a rapid but absorbing trishaw ride through old Penang, and an evocative visit to the Bridge over the River Kwai – but it's the train itself that is the real highlight of the trip.

If you feel the need to stretch your legs, the observation car offers a 360° panorama of the jungle-covered terrain, and there's a shop selling gifts to prove you've been (and rub it in). Then there's the elegant dining car. Eating on the train is a real treat, superb haute cuisine and Asian meals prepared by world-class chefs. Many choose to wear evening dress to round off the fantasy and after dinner retire to the bar car, where cocktails and entertainment await, from mellow piano music to formal Thai dance. A word of warning: after all this, reality hurts. Standing on the chaotic platform of Bangkok's Hualampong station, you might want to get back on board.

905 FINDING PEACE AMONG KO LIBONG'S WILDLIFE

THAILAND Ko Libong is much more than a beach: it has one of richest wildlife habitats in the region. Among its mudflats, you'll notice waves of baby crabs, in battalions of thousands-strong, and seashells, too, in congregations so concentrated that it's nearly impossible to avoid stepping on them. Then, the kingfishers swoop down from the mangrove trees to nab crabs. Soon, in high tide, the dugongs take their turn to feed; these voracious consumers of seagrass are endangered everywhere in Southeast Asia, and Libong's herd, which numbers 150, is one of the region's largest.

Chances are you'll be the only tourist around: this island in Thailand's southern Trang province has only two resorts and a handful of beaches, the best of which is Had Tung Ya, a long golden strip, fronted by an azure sea and backed by dense mountain-forest that is the domain of wheeling eagles.

But just being here is experience enough – and the peacefulness is infectious. Trills of birds wake you in the morning, just as the rubber farmers bring in their load from the hills and the fishermen head out to sea in colourful boats. The inhabitants are part of Libong's rugged quality: descendants of sea gypsies, they have modest ambitions and live in quaint wooden houses they decorate with flowering plants and pet birds singing in cages. You may get the urge to quit your office job and do likewise.

906 MEETING THE AMERICAN KILLER HEROES

VIETNAM The Vietnam War may have been a disaster for the people of Vietnam, but these days it's big business. Take the Cu-Chi Tunnels, a 200-kilometre underground maze 64km northwest of Ho Chi Minh City. Here, over thirty years ago, the Vietcong fought a bitter guerilla war against the Americans, creating a secret underground world of smokeless kitchens, field hospitals and "American Killer Heroes".

Wandering around the site today you'll find a carnival-like atmosphere: you can buy lighters made from bomb shells and fire AK-47 machine guns at a shooting range for US$1 per bullet.

Our guide down the tunnels was Mr Anh, an elderly gentleman who had a wry sense of humour and a blunt way of speaking about the war. Squeezing in after him, we crawled along the restored 100m section – "widened for foreigners" as he told us with a grin. It's claustrophobic nevertheless, unnervingly narrow, but the suffocating heat is a real surprise – how they managed to fight down here is unimaginable. Then there's the camouflaged punji stake pits, used to impale hapless attackers; and the tunnels that got thinner the further you went in, to trap "fat Americans" said Mr Anh as he demonstrated how Vietcong would take bayonets and finish them off.

At the end of the tour we watched the site's official video, rich in propaganda, where the "war crimes" of the US forces are described in typically vivid, Cold War language, while the Vietcong are praised: you had to kill at least twelve Americans to be an American Killer Hero. Mr Anh seemed to find the whole thing mildly amusing. It was only later, back in Ho Chi Minh City, that a friend explained Anh's disarming levity toward the violence that he lectured about.

"Mr Anh was there", he said. "He was a famous American Killer Hero".

I was astounded.

"It's true." he said. "Over 40,000 Vietnamese died at Cu-Chi Tunnels, and all his friends with them. It's too much pain. What else can he do but laugh?"

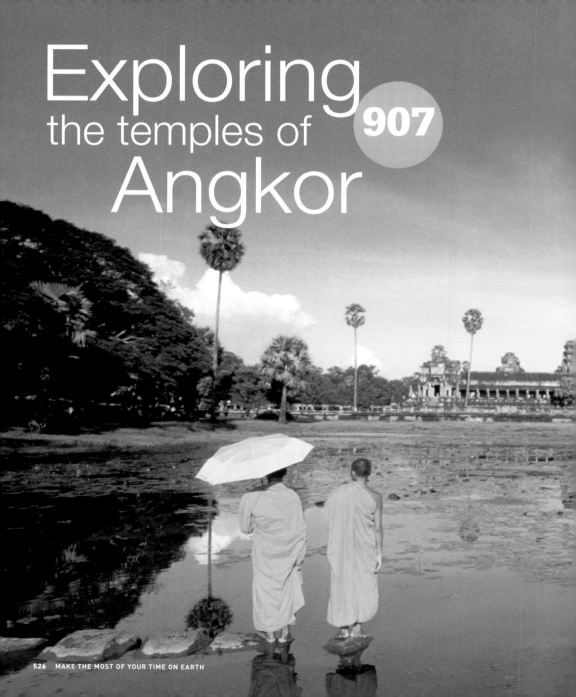

Exploring
the temples of
Angkor

907

CAMBODIA The sun was setting on the town of Siem Reap as I clung to the back of my moto driver. Threading our way through traffic, we rode out until town finally gave way to forest and we entered the Angkor site. In front of us were the iconic lotus-bud towers of Angkor Wat, looking like giant pine cones, resplendent in the light. Sunset is the best time to view west-facing Angkor Wat, from the top of nearby temple-mountain, Phnom Bakheng, when the greying stone of the towers glow red under the glare of the dying sun.

The secret of Angkor is to explore the galleries and enclosures at your own pace. Wander the corridors and you'll stumble across aged monks performing blessings on curious tourists; wafting bundles of burning incense over their body and loudly clapping a cupped palm across their back. The outer walls of the temple are covered with bas-reliefs retelling stories of Hindu battles and mythology, whose intricately etched bodies are worn smooth by the fingers of thousands of hands. And all around is the echo of children playing in the cool passageways and juvenile hawkers who sell cold drinks and trinkets out of plastic carrier bags.

The next morning I went back to see Angkor Thom, with its lichen covered towers of the Bayon revealing exquisite faces carved into rock. Fat, curvaceous lips smiling benevolently beneath half-closed eyes. Thick jungle once shrouded this lost twelfth-century Khmer kingdom: the site of which is amazing. Its painstaking restoration involved numbering and cataloguing each stone block before setting it back into its original position. The destructive force of nature and time on stone is no more evident than at Ta Prohm, the temple left to the jungle. Here huge tree trunks, hard as cement, spill out over the scattered blocks like the creamy bellies of snakes. It's a wonderfully peaceful place, and once you're done exploring the doorways and curious shapes of the forest over boulder, sit back, kick off your shoes and listen to the noise of insects whirring in the sun and birds squawking in a soothing blend of background noise.

908 VOLCANIC ACTIVITY:
SUNRISE ON MOUNT BROMO

INDONESIA It's not the most famous, the most active or the biggest volcano in the world, but Indonesia's 2392-metre-high Mount Bromo is one of the world's most picturesque – in a dusty, post-apocalyptic sort of way. The still-smoking and apparently perfectly symmetrical cone rises precipitously out of a vast, windswept, sandy plain. This is the Sea of Sand, actually the floor of an ancient crater (or caldera), stretching up to ten kilometres in diameter and with walls some three hundred metres high.

Though the locals will try to persuade you to take their horse, it's an easy enough walk to the summit, with no climbing ability required. Setting off an hour before sunrise, you follow a path across the Sea of Sand to the foot of Bromo's vertiginous cone. A small matter of 249 concrete steps up past crowds of others with the same idea – it's one of Java's most popular attractions – leads to the crater rim and a view down onto the fumaroles belching noxious sulphuric fumes. But the rewards of climbing Bromo are not olfactory, but visual: for if the gods of climate and cloud-cover are on your side, a flamboyant golden sunrise awaits, casting its orange glow over the vast emptiness of the sandy basin, with Java's lush green landscape stretching to the horizon beyond.

909 LONG LIVE THE EMPEROR: THE IMPERIAL MAUSOLEUMS OF HUÉ

VIETNAM The broad, peaceful outer courtyard sweeps you past an honourary guard of immaculate stone mandarins towards the first of a series of elegantly roofed gateways, through whose triple doorways you get a perfectly framed view of Emperor Minh Mang's mausoleum complex. Archways look wistful in peeling ochre paint; slatted lacquer-red shutters offer tantalizing angles on lotus ponds, pavilions and artfully placed bonsai trees; and ceramic rooftop dragons add a touch of kitsch in pastel pinks, greens and yellows. Look carefully and you'll see the Chinese character for "longevity" picked out in blue, and red and gold – Minh Mang, who designed his own mausoleum, left nothing to chance.

910 HIKE THROUGH HISTORY ALONG THE KOKODA TRAIL

PAPUA NEW GUINEA As you trek along Papua New Guinea's Kokoda Trail, winding north 96km from Owers' Corner to Kokoda, it can feel like every step has its own story. During World War II, Australian troops used the route to prevent the Japanese, who had landed on the northern beaches, from taking Port Moresby on the southern coast. Though the trail's military pedigree attracts both war buffs and nostalgics, it's also justly famous for some of the most rugged and remote terrain in the South Pacific. Climbing up to 2200m as it tops the Owen Stanley Range, the path traverses orchid-decked jungles, lush river valleys and the settlements of the Koiari and Orokaiva tribes. Like the help these people gave Allied troops during the war, the smiles you share with the villagers won't easily be forgotten.

911 SNACKING YOUR WAY THROUGH THE DAY: THE ALLURE OF THAI STREET FOOD

THAILAND Half the fun of foreign travel is trying new food – roast duck curry, sticky rice with mango, even deep-fried locusts. Throughout Thailand, the best places to try such delights are frequently the street stalls (many of which just specialize in a single dish) and night markets you'll find in nearly every town and city. It's safe to eat at almost any hot-food street stall; any doubts you might have should be dispelled by seeing just how little time it takes to flash-fry beef in oyster sauce or throw together a coconut chicken soup. Things don't tend to sit around for long.

Thais snack throughout the day, scoffing slices of pomelo fruit dipped in a sugar, salt and chili mix as a mid-morning refresher, perhaps a stick of chicken satay on the way home from work, then onto steaming bowls of noodles or sticky rice and mouth-blasting som tam (green papaya and chilli salad) and nearly anything else from the vast and varied night market later in the evening. Follow their cue, experimenting wherever you can – at these prices, you can certainly afford to.

912 CLEANING UP AFTER THE KHMER ROUGE: TACKLING POL POT'S LEGACY WITH VSO

CAMBODIA Thirty years after Pol Pot's notorious Khmer Rouge, VSO (Voluntary Service Overseas) now runs one of its largest country programmes in Cambodia, with ninety volunteers working to improve health and education systems and help build secure livelihoods. I joined their programme in Kampong Cham, working with an NGO to help improve local school curriculum through creative techniques such as art therapy and dance. The aim is to encourage children to express themselves and in time challenge the legacy of the Khmer Rouge, who left behind them a culture of fear and conformity.

Part of my role in schools was encouraging communication between boys and girls. Marital breakdown and domestic violence are common and high school drop-out rates for girls especially are high; tackling this together with local leadership seemed to me a really tangible benefit of volunteering. We would mix boys and girls in the classroom so they could talk to each other more freely, and then introduce art or dance activities where they would role-play everyday life and talk about what they had learned.

Over the year, I was inundated with invitations to people's homes and was even befriended by Buddhist monks keen to get me on board as a catalyst for reopening a street children's centre. I was eager to learn and feel at home myself and this sharing process affected me as much as my local counterparts, challenging the taboos of my own culture in return.

Towards the end of the placement, my Khmer became pretty fluent, giving me an insight into local life that I would have missed otherwise. I loved listening to conversations about me on the bus – "Where is she from?", "Why is she on her own?", "I think I've seen her around on her bicycle", and my personal favourite, "Doesn't she have a nice nose?" – and I'd pipe up half way through the journey speaking my Khmer and the whole bus would fall about laughing.

MISCELLANY

RELIGION

Buddhism is the predominant faith in Cambodia, Laos, Singapore, Thailand and Vietnam. Buddhist **monks** are forbidden to have any close contact with women, which means, if you are female, that you mustn't sit or stand next to a monk (even on a bus), brush against his robes, or hand objects directly to him. When giving something to a monk, the object should be placed on a nearby table or passed to a layman who will then hand it to the monk.

Indonesia is the largest Islamic nation in the world. The most orthodox region of the country is in North Sumatra; elsewhere, local Islamic practices often display animist, Buddhist and Hindu influences. Most of Indonesia's many tribal communities are animists, especially in West Papua, Sumatra and Kalimantan. Though their beliefs and customs vary widely, animists share the view that nearly everything in the world has a spirit, in particular trees, plants, rocks and rivers.

TASTE SENSATIONS

Amok dt'ray in Cambodia.
Fish curry made with a rich coconut sauce and baked in banana leaves.

Làp in Laos.
A salad of raw minced meat spiced up with garlic, chill and fish sauce.

Lechon in the Philippines.
Roast pig stuffed with pandanus leaves.

Nem in Vietnam.
Fresh spring rolls stuffed with herbs, crabmeat, rice vermicelli and beansprouts.

Tom yam kung in Thailand.
Fragrantly spiced hot and sour prawn soup.

And if you dare, **durian** in Thailand or Malaysia.
This fruit, somewhat of an acquired taste, has a foul smell – somewhere between detergent and dogshit.

PLACES TO STAY

Amandari, Bali, Indonesia. Tastefully understated villa compounds overlooking Ubud's lush Ayung River valley.
Swissôtel The Stamford, Singapore. The second tallest hotel in the world offers stunning views and classy rooms.
The Datai, Langkawi, Malaysia. Harmonious retreat that's surrounded by rainforest but beside the beach.
Grand Hotel D'Angkor, Siem Reap, Cambodia. Historic, colonial-era opulence close by the Angkor ruins.
The Tongsai Bay, Ko Samui, Thailand. Set in beautiful grounds fronting a private beach.

CAN I KICK IT?

In Thailand, **muay thai** (Thai boxing) enjoys a following similar to football in Europe. It's a bloodsport – with a spiritual component – in which all parts of the body, except the head, can be used to strike the opponent; the assaults can take place against any part of the body save the groin. Every province has a stadium and the biggest bouts are broadcast every Sunday afternoon on TV, watched by large noisy crowds in noodle shops around the country.

ECONOMICS

The average per capita income in **Singapore** is around US$28,000. In **Laos** it's US$300. **Vietnam** has the second fastest-growing economy in the Asia-Pacific region, after China. In 2006, just 12 years after the US lifted their trade embargo against their old enemy, Vietnam was accepted into the World Trade Organization as its 150th member nation.

> *"It makes you laugh with delight to think that anything so fantastic could exist on this earth"*
>
> **Somerset Maugham on the temples of Bangkok**

THE MIGHTY MEKONG

The **Mekong** is one of the great rivers of the world, the twelfth longest on the planet. From its source 4920m up on the east Tibetan Plateau it roars down through China's Yunnan province, then snakes its way a little more peaceably through Laos, by way of the so-called Golden Triangle, where Burma, Thailand and Laos touch. From Laos it crosses Cambodia and continues south to Vietnam, where it splinters into the many arms of the Mekong Delta before flowing into the South China Sea, 4184km from where its journey began.

POPULATIONS

Brunei 372,000
East Timor 925,000
Singapore 2.7 million
Laos 6 million
Cambodia 12 million
Malaysia 23 million
Burma 47 million
Thailand 63 million
Vietnam 83 million
The Philippines 87 million
Indonesia 200 million

COLONIALISM AND INDEPENDENCE

Thailand is the only Southeast Asian country **never to have been colonized** by a European nation. Historically, the major Western players in the region have been: France, in Laos, Cambodia and Vietnam; Britain, in Burma, Malaysia and Singapore; and the Netherlands, in Indonesia.

Timor Leste (East Timor) became the world's **newest nation** on May 20, 2002, having finally won autonomy from Indonesia. It had previously been under Portuguese rule for four centuries until Indonesia invaded the territory in 1975.

In 1898, America fought Spain for **control of the Philippines** and won. The Philippines finally gained independence on July 4, 1946.

THE GREAT RAILWAY BAZAAR

The Jungle Railway, Malaysia.
A fourteen-hour ride through mountainous jungle between Gemas and Kota Bharu.

The Death Railway, Thailand.
An amazing feat of engineering with a tragic history, built by World War II PoWs along the scenic River Kwai valley.

Eastern and Oriental Express,
Thailand, Malaysia and Singapore.
Elegant, wood-panelled carriages, a panoramic viewing car and cordon-bleu meals makes this the most luxurious – and expensive – way to travel the 52 hours between Bangkok and Singapore.

Reunification Express, Vietnam.
Chug gently down the length of Vietnam, from Hanoi in the north to Ho Chi Minh City in the south, in around 34 hours.

Phnom Penh to Battambang, Cambodia.
Cambodia's only train runs just once a week, takes up to fifteen hours to cover the 290-kilometre journey, and is predictably basic: many passengers bring their own hammocks.

ETIQUETTE

In Buddhist, Islamic and Hindu cultures, the **head** is considered the most sacred part of the body and the **feet** the most unclean. This means that it's very rude to touch another person's head or to point your feet either at a human being or at a sacred image. Be careful not to step over any part of a person who is sitting or lying on the floor without first offering an apology. Shoes are nearly always taken off before going inside a home or place of worship.

BUILDING SPECS

When designing a **traditional house** on the Indonesian island of Bali, the architect begins by noting down the vital statistics of the head of the household. The house-compound's walls, for example, must be the sum of a multiple of the distance between the tips of the householder's middle fingers when the arms are outstretched, plus the distance from his or her elbow to the tip of their middle finger, plus the width of their fist with the thumb stretched out. The different structures of the compound are believed to reflect the human body: the family shrine is the head, the main pavilions are the arms, the courtyard is the navel, the kitchen and rice barn are the legs and feet, and the garbage tip is the anus.

LANGUAGES

Bahasa Malay and its near-identical offshoot **Bahasa Indonesia** are among the easiest languages to master. They are written in Roman script, have no tones and use a straightforward grammar. Verbs have no tenses and nouns take no articles, with plurals simply a question of saying the word twice: thus "car" is mobil, and "cars" mobil-mobil, sometimes written mobil2.
The **Tai family** of languages includes Thai; Lao; Shan (Tai Yai), spoken in Burma; Phuan, spoken in Laos and parts of Thailand; and Tai Leu spoken by the Dai minority of China's Yunnan province. All are tonal languages, making them difficult for Westerners to master. Thai has five tones – low, middle, high, falling and rising – by which the meaning of a single syllable can be altered in five different ways. Using four of the five tones you can make a sentence from just one syllable: "mái mài mâi má" means "New wood burns, doesn't it?".

TRADITIONAL THERAPIES

In Laos, it's common to go for a **herbal sauna** before having a traditional massage. The herbs in question include tamarind, carambola, lemongrass and eucalyptus, though exact recipes are closely guarded.

The most famous traditional beauty treatment in Indonesia is the exfoliation rub, **mandi lulur**, which is based on a paste made from turmeric. Javanese brides are said to have a lulur treatment every day for the forty days before their wedding ceremonies.

LOCAL CRAFTS

Batik sarongs and shirts from Malaysia and Indonesia.
Silk Lustrous sheens and beautiful designs in Thailand, Laos, Vietnam and Cambodia.
Woodcarvings from Indonesia. Kalimantan and West Papua produce unusual tribal carvings, Bali makes contemporary figurines.
Triangular pillows from Thailand. Buy one with attached cushions to use on a chaise longue or as a spare bed.
Conical hats The trademark Vietnamese all-weather headgear.

"If the Tiger does not stop fighting the Elephant, the Elephant will die of exhaustion"

Ho Chi Minh anticipates Vietnam's victory over the US

FESTIVALS

What	When	Where
Ati-Atihan Mardi Gras-style extravaganza	mid-Jan	Kalibo, the Philippines
Thaipusam Hindu festival of ritual body piercing	Full moon, Jan or Feb	Singapore and Kuala Lumpur, Malaysia
Sumba Pasola Fierce battles between hundreds of costumed horsemen, held to restore cosmological balance	Feb or March	Sumba, Indonesia
Gawai Dayak All-night drinking and games in the longhouses to celebrate the end of the rice harvest	June	Sarawak, East Malaysia
Loy Krathong Palm-leaf baskets full of flowers and candles are floated on rivers and shorelines to honour the water goddess	Full moon, Oct or Nov	Thailand

WHAT LIES BENEATH: SNORKELLING AT THE GREAT BARRIER REEF • SLIP INTO BROOMETIME • FILLING UP IN AUCKLAND • WATCHING FOOTY AT THE MCG • LAST FRONTIER: WORKING ON A CATTLE STATION • WINE-TASTING IN THE BAROSSA VALLEY • BUZZING OVER THE BUNGLES • GETTING TO GRIPS WITH ABORIGINAL ART IN ALICE SPRINGS • INDULGE YOUR TASTEBUDS AT QUEEN VICTORIA MARKET • SEA KAYAKING AROUND SHARK BAY • CANYONEERING IN KARIJINI • WALKING ON THE WILD SIDE AT THE SYDNEY MARDI GRAS • VISITING THE CITY OF FESTIVALS • ISLAND DREAMING: SAILING THE WHITSUNDAYS • RAINFOREST VIBES IN THE DAINTREE • SUPPING WINE IN SUN-DRENCHED MARLBOROUGH • PEDALLING INTO THE HEART OF MANIOTOTO • ROCK STEADY: ADMIRING THE SHIFTING SHADES OF ULURU • RIDING THE GHAN TO DARWIN • SETTING SAIL AMONG THE BLISSFUL BAY OF ISLANDS • PLATYPUS-WATCHING: LOOKING FOR DUCK-BILLED MAMMALS • KIWI-SPOTTING IN TROUNSON KAURI PARK • DISCOVERING YOUR OWN MIDDLE EARTH • TAKING A TRIP TO HELL ON EARTH • WITNESSING THE POWER OF THE HAKA • CRUISING DOUBTFUL SOUND • RAFTING THE RAPIDS OF THE WILD WEST COAST RIVERS • TRAMPING THE MILFORD TRACK • SCUBA DIVING THE WRECKS AT THE POOR KNIGHTS ISLANDS • DODGING EMBERS ON MOUNT YASUR • RELAXING AT THE SEASIDE IN ART DECO NAPIER • TUCKING INTO A HANGI • EXPLORING WAITOMO'S EERIE UNDERGROUND WORLD • GETTING HANDS-ON AT WELLINGTON'S TE PAPA • HELI-HIKING ON FRANZ JOSEF GLACIER • TAKING THE PLUNGE WITH AJ HACKETT • QUEENSTOWN'S WINTER WONDERLAND • COAST TO COAST WITH THE TRANZALPINE • DOING THE CROCODILE ROCK AT KAKADU NATIONAL PARK • CELEBRATING MOOMBA WATERFEST • MOTORBIKING DOWN THE WILD WEST COAST • RIVER OF NO RETURN: RAFTING THE FRANKLIN • DRIFTING WITH JELLYFISH IN MICRONESIA • FROM PRISON TO PARADISE ON L'ILE DE PINS • SYDNEY HARBOUR-MASTERING • HUNTING NODDY BIRDS • DOUBLE-CROSSED IN THE SOUTH SEAS • SWIMMING WITH WHALE SHARKS AT NINGALOO • LEARNING TO SURF ON THE GOLD COAST • MEETING THE CROCS AT SHADYCAMP • HAVING A FAR-FLUNG FLUTTER AT THE BIRDSVILLE RACES • KNOCKING BACK KAVA • FOUR-WHEELING THROUGH CROC COUNTRY: CAIRNS TO CAPE YORK • ROAD TRIP DOWN UNDER: PERTH TO DARWIN TO ADELAIDE • SPYING ON PENGUINS AND ALBATROSSES ALONG THE OTAGO PENINSULA • GOING ORGANIC IN THE NORTHERN TERRITORY • RAFTING THE WILDS OF TASMANIA • HELI-SKIING THE SOUTHERN ALPS • TAKING IN THE VIEWS ON THE TONGARIRO CROSSING • OCEAN TO OCEAN, CAPE TO CAPE: ACROSS AUSTRALIA BY 4WD • DISCOVERING THE SECRETS OF KINGS CANYON • WALK ROUND ULURU • RIVER DEEP, MOUNTAIN HIGH: BUSHWALKING THE OVERLAND TRACK • LAZING ABOUT AT HOT WATER BEACH • WAITANGI: RELIVING THE BIRTH OF A MODERN NATION • WATCHING WHALES IN KAIKOURA • PADDLING THROUGH ABEL TASMAN NATIONAL PARK • FOLLOWING IN GAUGUIN'S FOOTSTEPS • TALL-SHIP SAILING IN THE INDIAN OCEAN • GETTING HIGH ON THE GILLESPIE PASS • HORSING AROUND ON AN AUSSIE BEACH • HELI-BIKING BEN CRUACHAN • WALKING THROUGH THE WOODS IN WAIPOUA KAURI FOREST • A WORLD AWAY ON THE LANDSBOROUGH RIVER • WHAT LIES BENEATH: SNORKELLING AT THE GREAT BARRIER REEF • SLIP INTO BROOMETIME • FILLING UP IN AUCKLAND • WATCHING FOOTY AT THE MCG • WINE-TASTING IN THE BAROSSA VALLEY • THE LAST FRONTIER: WORKING ON A CATTLE STATION • BUZZING OVER THE BUNGLES • GETTING TO GRIPS WITH ABORIGINAL ART • INDULGE YOUR TASTEBUDS AT QUEEN VICTORIA MARKET • SEA KAYAKING AROUND SHARK BAY • CANYONEERING IN KARIJINI • WALKING ON THE WILD SIDE AT THE SYDNEY MARDI GRAS • VISITING THE CITY OF FESTIVALS • ISLAND DREAMING: SAILING THE WHITSUNDAYS • RAINFOREST VIBES IN THE DAINTREE • SUPPING WINE IN SUN-DRENCHED MARLBOROUGH • PEDALLING INTO THE HEART OF MANIOTOTO •

AUSTRALIA, NEW ZEALAND & THE SOUTH PACIFIC

913–991

MARSHALL ISLANDS

Caroline Islands

PALAU

FEDERATED STATES OF MICRONESIA

NAURU

Line Islands

SOLOMON ISLANDS

TUVALU

KIRIBATI

W. SAMOA
Wallis & Futuna
American Samoa

Marquesas Islands

Society Islands

Tuamotu Archipelago

WHAT LIES BENEATH: SNORKELLING AT THE GREAT BARRIER REEF

Coral Sea Islands Territory

VANUATU

FIJI

Tahiti

TONGA

FOLLOWING IN GAUGUIN'S FOOTSTEPS

982

New Caledonia

934

980

Cook Islands

French

SWIMMING WITH WHALE SHARKS AT NINGALOO REEF

KNOCKING BACK KAVA

DODGING EMBERS ON MOUNT YASUR

Polynesia

961

GETTING TO GRIPS WITH ABORIGINAL ART

930

Pitcairn Island

AUSTRALIA

928

WINE-TASTING IN THE BAROSSA VALLEY

SETTING SAIL AMONG THE BLISSFUL BAY OF ISLANDS

922

NEW ZEALAND

HELI-HIKING ON FRANZ JOSEF GLACIER

945

969

SPYING ON PENGUINS AND ALBATROSSES ALONG THE OTAGO PENINSULA

913
BUZZING OVER THE
BUNGLES

AUSTRALIA If you've never been in a helicopter then a flight over Purnululu National Park – or the Bungle Bungles as most people call it – makes a great initiation. This mass of orange and black striped beehive-like domes is amazing enough at ground level, but leaning out of the doorless cockpit, your foot on the landing rail, you'll have a grin as wide as the Fitzroy River as you swoop and soar over the maze of 200-metre-deep chasms between the "bungles". At one point you launch low off the plateau and in an instant the ground disappears, sending your stomach spiralling.

Each dome ranges from 10 to 40m high but in total cover just a small part of the park's 25,000 square kilometres of lightly wooded hills and grassland. To local Aboriginal people Purnululu has been a sacred site for millennia, but the wonders of this remote region of northwestern Australia were only fully acknowledged in the 1980s when a TV crew came across it while filming a documentary about over-grazing. Recognizing these curious rock formations to be geologically unique, Purnululu National Park was created in 1987, with access purposely limited to small aircraft or high-clearance vehicles able to negotiate the twisting 53km access track.

The origin of the domes is still unclear. The theory of a meteor impact shattering the rock into the now weathered segments takes a knock when one sees mini-bungle formations elsewhere in the Kimberley. More mundane, but more likely, it's a result of deposition, uplifting and subsequent erosion. The banding, on the other hand, is a clear illustration of aeons of alternating sediments: the orange deposits (iron oxide) are not porous while the rock above and below holds water and supports the growth of black lichen, which forms a fragile crust.

And "fragile" may well describe your knees as you climb out of the helicopter and wobble across the launch pad. Now you've seen them from the air it's time for a closer inspection on foot.

914

WALKING ON THE WILD SIDE AT THE
SYDNEY
MARDI GRAS

AUSTRALIA The Sydney Gay & Lesbian Mardi Gras Parade is a party of the rarest and most uninhibited kind; it's the single largest night-time parade in the world and draws a bigger crowd than any other annual event in Australia, with about six thousand participants and half a million spectators. In essence, it's a full-on celebration of gay culture, and a joyous demonstration of pride; but it's enjoyable for people of any sexuality, provided partial nudity, g-strings, wild unleashings of inhibitions, senseless acts of kindness, random acts of love and lewd innuendo don't offend.

The parade route runs from Hyde Park, through the city's gay quarter, to Moore Park, and before the start the waiting crowd is whipped into a not-so-subtle frenzy over several hours by the presiding marshals. Searchlights, flares, fireworks, strobes and dance music from all the nearby clubs bring the throng to a fever pitch of anticipation – a perfect build-up to the gleaming Harley Davidsons of the Dykes on Bikes, who have heralded the start

of the parade for many years. Vast floats, effigies and marching troupes follow in their wake – everything from two hundred drag Madonnas in cowgirl hats spilling out of the longest stretch limo you've ever seen, to three hundred Barbara Cartlands in pink-sequined evening gowns, or mist-enshrouded boats carrying Thai princes and princesses, to six hundred bootscooters of every gender, age and size.

Afterwards, Australia's biggest parade is followed by Australia's biggest party at Moore Park Entertainment Precinct. Tickets sell out fast, and scalpers loiter out the front touting tickets at exorbitant prices. Whatever your sexuality, it's a pretty decadent affair, and – how can we put this? – voyeurs are not encouraged. But even if you can't get in, or just can't afford it, there are lots of places with plenty going on after the Parade. Just wander along the gay strip and the chances are you'll find every bar is jumping, and just as much fun as the last.

915 ISLAND DREAMING: SAILING THE WHITSUNDAYS

AUSTRALIA There's a distinct feeling of déja-vu cruising in a sailboat among the Whitsunday Islands. Presently it comes to you: you've been here many times, in your lottery fantasies. This tropical idyll of turquoise seas lapping ivory sands against a backdrop of dense green foliage is ingrained in our imagination, be it some Jungian folk memory or saturation advertising. The Beach before it all turned sour. Paradise.

Just over 1200km north of Brisbane, this compact archipelago of 70-odd islands lies just off Airlie Beach, a young-at-heart resort described by locals as "a drinking town with a sailing problem". Out at sea you have a delectable menu of islands to choose from: Hayman, which offers resorts so posh staff scurry unseen along tunnels; others like Long Island are more affordable; or you might prefer the Molle Islands, home to little more than a couple of basic campsites. Most are uninhabited.

Sheltered by the Great Barrier Reef, the Pacific swell is dampened, but reliable light breezes remain, making the Whitsundays a sailing haven, and at an affordable price. Choose between a sedate three-day cruise, where you can laze aboard a spacious and comfortable crewed boat, or get stuck in and crew on a huge racing "maxi yacht" catering for partying backpackers.

Either way life becomes sybaritically simple. By day you commune with turtles, dolphins and even whales – up from the Antarctic to give birth before heading south again. Or go snorkelling on the lookout for morays and parrotfish (the northeastern tip of Hook Island is best). Come sunset you moor in one of the many unnamed bays while the chef prepares a fresh seafood meal. A shower is as simple as diving into the surrounding water, and your bed is the deck of the boat or the sand on the beach.

916 CRUISING DOUBTFUL SOUND

NEW ZEALAND The smell of frying bacon wafting from the galley brings the boat awake. And what a place to wake up. Deathly still, there's mist clinging to the sides of the cliffs which hem in Doubtful Sound; the only movement comes from one lone soul who has borrowed one of the boat's kayaks and is out exploring the shoreline. Cruises on Milford Sound may be more famous, but Doubtful Sound, in the far southwest corner of the South Island, is equally spectacular and, being off the main tourist route, is a more intriguing place to visit. Just getting out here is half the fun. First a cruise across Lake Manapouri, a deep, glacier-hewn body of water that appears pristine, though it has been harnessed for power generation. You can even join a tour into the bowels of the earth to see the station, though it does seem at odds with the wilderness experience. Finally, a bus ride carries you over the

670-metre high Wilmot Pass from where you get your first glimpse of Doubtful Sound, a hairline thread of water forcing its way 20km inland from the Tasman Sea. So narrow is the fjord that explorer Captain Cook, who named the place, didn't actually enter – he felt it was so confined that he was doubtful he would be able to get out again.

After a hearty breakfast we're underway again, gently exploring narrow channels where the thick forest creeps right down to the shoreline. Before long we're joined by a small group of bottlenose dolphins. It is hard to work out if these are our friends from yesterday come back to play, or others from the resident pod. Either way, they seem to be having a great time riding the bow wave on their side gazing up at us as we lean over the rail.

917 RAINFOREST VIBES IN THE DAINTREE

AUSTRALIA Ancient rainforests cascading onto barely touched beaches, natural spa treatments, gourmet restaurants, beachside bungalows and world-class snorkelling on the Great Barrier Reef. The area around the Daintree River, between Port Douglas and Cape Tribulation in northern Queensland, is graced with some of the most spectacular landscapes, diverse flora and fauna, and unique eco-resorts in Australia.

Part of the appeal is that Daintree's wild beauty has not been totally sanitized. Estuarine crocodiles still cruise among the mangrove swamps, the forests harbour plants with vicious stinging leaves, and the Coral Sea is home to box jellyfish, though fortunately only during the torpid wet season. Bright blue butterflies share the breeze with a variety of birds, from the giant, emu-like cassowary to kingfishers whose luminescent liveries will stop you in your tracks.

Decisions get no more fraught than choosing papaya or mango for breakfast or opting for either sustained relaxation or a bit of wilderness exploration. A wildlife-spotting boat trip up the Daintree River is a rewarding compromise, or a walk through the Mossman Gorge may give you an appetite for a crocburger (yes, it does taste like chicken). Alternatively, just head to the beach with a sarong and the latest copy of Australian *Hello* magazine. For the widest range of restaurants and cafés, base yourself in Port Douglas, also a good departure point for exploring the reef. Better still, push the boat right out and indulge yourself with a stay at the Daintree Eco Lodge and Spa. Set beside the river and surrounded by lush jungle, it offers exclusive treehouse accommodation and is renowned for its luxurious spa treatments. And there's no need to put ambient relaxation tunes on your iPod: the mellow sounds of the world's oldest living rainforest are music enough.

918 ROCK STEADY: ADMIRING THE SHIFTING SHADES OF ULURU

AUSTRALIA Lounging on one of its pristine beaches, it's easy to forget that most of Australia is a vast wilderness of flat, sun-scorched earth, an ancient outback populated by a few hardy farmers and the continent's Aboriginal peoples. At its heart, marooned in an endless desert of Mulga scrub and hummock grass, lies the colossal red monolith of Uluru, also known as Ayer's Rock after Sir Henry Ayers, the chief secretary of South Australia when Europeans "discovered" it in the 1870s.

Its different names reflect a split personality: Ayer's Rock is testimony to the power of global tourism, clambered over, photographed from every angle from sunrise to sunset, and viewed by plane, bus and helicopter; Uluru is also the sacred place of the Aboriginal Anangu people, alive with myth and magical power. You can climb Ayer's Rock, or sip champagne, eat at vast barbecues and have breakfast while admiring it. But as you do so be aware that Uluru is littered with marks, gullies and bumps that represent tribal creation stories, a trove of ancient knowledge that sums up the Anangu concept of tjukurpa.

In truth, it's hard not to have a little of both experiences here. Protected within the Uluru-Kata Tjuta National Park, Uluru is owned by the Anangu and leased back to the government. The park's bright Cultural Centre sheds light on their belief systems and stories, while their tours take you close to – but not onto – the rock, and put it into an Aboriginal context.

In the end, it's impossible not to be captivated simply by its sheer size. The Anangu plead with visitors not to climb it, but they have never tried to enforce a ban. And although the carnival of tour buses and jeeps that assemble every morning and late afternoon to snap the rock's colourful transformation at sunrise and sunset can be off-putting, watching the sandstone's chameleon-like change – from a thousand shades of earthy golds and ochres, to pinks and copper-tones, and, finally, a deep, ruby-red – is truly unforgettable.

919 PEDALLING INTO THE HEART OF MANIOTOTO

NEW ZEALAND Dunedin's magnificent Victorian railway station is a suitably grand setting for the beginning of our train and cycle journey into the heart of New Zealand's isolated Maniototo region. With bikes stashed in the guard's van we board one of the refurbished 1920s wooden carriages of the Taieri Gorge Railway and are soon leaving the suburbs behind. The palpable strain on the engine signals the start of the climb into the hinterland, leaving the roads and houses behind. Tunnels burrow though bluffs and steel girder bridges span the gaps, and we hang out on the open footplates between carriages to get a better view.

It's a great trip, but my cycling legs are getting itchy. Two hours later we pull into Pukerangi, nothing but a tiny weatherboard stationhouse in the middle of nowhere. Bikes are unloaded and we prepare for the ride ahead: 160km to the town of Cromwell.

The train has done most of the work for us, and the terrain from here on is fairly flat. This is the Otago Central Rail Trail, which loops through the Maniototo region, an open expanse of three shallow valleys separated by the Lammerlaw and the Rock and Pillar ranges.

When the trains stopped coming to these parts the region entered terminal decline, but the popularity of the rail trail has changed all that. Wanting to show our appreciation we're tempted to stop at one of the revitalized country pubs, but instead follow a sign off the trail to a little shop selling homemade cakes and great espresso. Life is good.

For our second night on the trail we'll stay in a comfortable B&B, but tonight we've opted for some rustic, converted shearers' quarters. They're still 30km ahead, so we get back on our bikes and start pedalling.

920 RIDING THE GHAN TO DARWIN

AUSTRALIA In 2003 the Ghan train finally reached Darwin, about a hundred years behind schedule. Constructing a reliable rail link between these two towns took up most of the last century but around the start of the new millennium the government decided to plug the 1500-kilometre gap from Alice to Darwin and so a legendary transcontinental railway journey was completed.

For most of the two-day northbound ride the train passes through uninhabited Outback, far from the highway and sporadic settlements. Just a couple of hours out of Adelaide and you're already lost on the vast Nullarbor Plain. Night falls and bleached saltpans glow eerily in the moonlight as you tuck yourself in to your comfy four-berth cabin. Next morning the view from the dining car reveals classic Outback colours: clear blue skies, grey-green scrub and rich orange sand. While you stare, doze or read the train passes close to the geographical centre of the continent, and by lunchtime squeezes through the West MacDonnell Ranges into the likeable desert town of Alice Springs for a couple of hours' break.

Past Alice, the Ghan works its way through the ranges before spilling out onto the featureless 1000-kilometre Tanami Desert. The sun sets as you near Wycliffe Well roadhouse, famous for its UFO sightings. You peer keenly into the blackness but see only your reflection and so turn in. Dawn delivers you to the tropical Top End. Trees have reappeared for the first time since Adelaide, here interspersed with countless two-metre-high termite mounds. The town of Katherine marks another first on this epic journey – the only flowing river for over 2000km – and then it's just an hour or two to journey's end in Darwin.

Sure, you could've flown here in a few hours, or driven and arrived feeling like week-old roadkill. But by rolling into town on the Ghan your carbon footprint is the size of a possum's front paw. And that is something to feel good about.

921

SUPPING WINE
IN SUN-DRENCHED MARLBOROUGH

NEW ZEALAND When Marlborough's Cloudy Bay sauvignon blanc hit the international wine shelves in the late 1980s its zingy fruitiness got jaded tongues wagging. All of a sudden New Zealand was on the world wine map, with the pushpin stuck firmly in the north of the South Island. Half a dozen regions now boast significant wine trails, but all roads lead back to Marlborough, still the country's largest grape growing area, protected by the sheltering hills of the Richmond Range, and blessed with more than 2400 hours of sunshine a year.

Cellar doors around the region are gradually becoming more sophisticated, with their own restaurants and specialist food stores, but the emphasis is still mainly on the wine itself. And tasting it. To squeeze the very best from the area start by visiting Montana Brancott, the biggest and most established operation hereabouts. Take their winery tour to get a feel for how wine is made nowadays, then stick around for a brief lesson on wine appreciation. Even those familiar with the techniques will learn something of the qualities Marlborough winemakers are trying to achieve.

Next visit Cloudy Bay. Of course you'll want to try the famous sav, still drinking well today and available for tasting. Somehow it always seems that little bit fresher and fruitier when sampled at source out of a decent tasting glass.

Come lunchtime, head for Highfield Estate with its distinctive Tuscan-style tower and dine in the sun overlooking the vines. A plate of pan-seared monkfish is just the thing to wash down with their zesty sauvignon blanc.

SETTING SAIL AMONG THE **BLISSFUL BAY OF ISLANDS**

NEW ZEALAND We've lowered the sails, dropped anchor beside a gorgeous crescent of golden beach, and it's time for a swim before lunch. The waters are warm and clear in Northland's Bay of Islands, perfect territory for some gentle cruising and a touch of snorkelling. Our anchorage is just off Roberton Island where an isthmus is almost severed by a pair of perfectly circular blue lagoons. Mask on, I'm off to find the undersea nature trail where points of interest have been marked on plaques. It is fun but atypical of a region where nature in its rawest form is more usual.

After a lunch of fresh barbecued fish on deck we move slowly on past Black Rocks, bare islets formed from columnar jointed basalt – these rise only 10m out of the water but plummet a sheer 30m beneath, allowing us to inspect them at close quarters. We're aboard the *R Tucker Thompson*, a modern replica of a gaff rigged, square topsail schooner built in Northland in the style of a North American Halibut schooner. A majestic sight from afar, with the sails pushing out towards the open ocean, its even better aboard. You can help set the sails, ride the bowsprit, climb the rigging or just laze on deck playing the ship's guitar.

Occasionally dolphins will come and ride the boat's bow wave, but to really get close and personal with these fascinating mammals you need to get out on Carino, a smaller, modern yacht licensed for dolphin swimming. If a pod is spotted nearby, a handful of swimmers are immediately in the water splashing about and humming, trying to attract the dolphins' interest. Ever curious, dolphins seem to love the attention and are soon darting around, close but somehow always just out of reach.

923 KIWI-SPOTTING IN TROUNSON KAURI PARK

NEW ZEALAND They're elusive creatures, these kiwi. In fact, New Zealand's national bird is so rare that it's almost never seen other than at the half-dozen places where guided night safaris raise the odds considerably. Heading out on foot, you hear the piercing cry of the male cutting through the inky darkness, closely followed by the husky female reply, but neither has yet seen fit to show its pointy face. The eeriness of their plaintive calls is enhanced by the ghostly presence of kauri trunks, vast walls of bark climbing to the dense canopy high above, with an understorey of slender tree ferns further blocking out the stars.

I can sense the kiwi are nearby, but these things can't be rushed. Not so long ago you'd have been lucky to hear them at all, as introduced stoats, rats, possums and feral cats and dogs had decimated numbers. But Trounson is one of several "mainland islands" where this diminutive relative of the ostrich is being brought back from the brink of extinction, with intensive trapping and poisoning keeping predator numbers low enough to allow indigenous species to flourish. And it's not just kiwi that benefit. Our guide introduces us to the ruru – a native owl known as the "morepork" for the sound of its haunting call – as well as the palm-sized, carnivorous kauri snail and the scary-looking, grasshopper-like weta, which can grow up to 10cm long. They're not dangerous, but no one wants to get too close.

Finally, a gentle scuffling in the leaf litter comes closer and we get our first glimpse of a North Island brown kiwi, its slender beak probing the ground for food. Seemingly unconcerned by our presence, it wanders closer, its shaggy pelt looking more like fur than feathers. Then someone makes an unexpected move and the kiwi takes fright, skittering off into the darkness. Initial disappointment soon fades as another makes itself visible. That's it for the night, but even two sightings seems a rare privilege.

924 PLATYPUS-WATCHING: ON THE LOOKOUT FOR A DUCK-BILLED MAMMAL

AUSTRALIA There are plenty of animals that you just couldn't make up – think of squid, for instance, with their ten arms, jet-propelling body, human-like eyes, parrot's beak and communication system that consists of rapid changes of colour. So it's a little surprising that when the first dried, stuffed specimens of Australia's platypus were examined by British scientists in the early nineteenth century, they insisted it was a badly thought-out hoax made from bits of other animals sewn together. In fact, it was even weirder than they realized: not only do platypus genuinely look like a cross between a duck and an otter, but they lay eggs, requiring a whole new scientific order of mammals – monotremes – to be created.

All the more reason, then, to head up to the hills of eastern Australia and make a point of tracking one down. Platypus live in rivers and are reasonably common, but as they're extremely timid, vanishing at the slightest movement, you'll need a lot of patience to see one – dusk and dawn are the best times to look. And as they're under 30cm in length, your first reaction on seeing one will be "they're not as big as I thought". One of the best ways to track them is to follow the trail of mud rising off the bottom of a stream, caused as their rubbery bills rummage along the bottom in search of shrimps and beetles. Once they've found a beakful they bob to the surface to eat, lying flat on their fronts with their webbed feet splayed as they chew and glance nervously around – then it's a swift roll headfirst down to the bottom again. In winter, you might see a courting pair chasing each other around the water in tight circles; after mating, the female walls herself into a burrow, dug into the bank above the waterline, to wait for the young to hatch. And if you're lucky, you might see the young following her in a line, each holding on to the tail of the one in front.

925 DISCOVERING YOUR OWN MIDDLE EARTH

NEW ZEALAND When Peter Jackson decided to film the Lord of the Rings trilogy entirely in New Zealand, he couldn't have known what a lasting impact it would have on his homeland. Even five years on, the country's scenery seems inextricably linked with that of Middle Earth. Familiar scenes abound. The black scoria cone of Ngauruhoe in Tongariro National Park is easily recognizable as the formidable Mount Doom. In the centre of the South Island, a smallish hill, Mount Sunday, rises from a wide valley – this is Edoras, the fortress city of the Rohan people. Getting there involves a gorgeous drive into the high country with the snowy Southern Alps as a backdrop. You can see the hill from the road, but it is worth trekking across the fields to reach the summit, where you can close your eyes and imagine the bleats of the sheep are the cries of hordes of invading orcs. Although New Line Cinema went to great lengths to ensure that film sets were dismantled, Hobbiton managed to partially survive. You can now tour the partly restored set on a rolling green sheep farm (ahh, the Shire) a few kilometres outside the rural town of Matamata. Here, you can stand under the Party Tree where Bilbo Baggins held his eleventy-first birthday party, with the village pond behind you and a semicircle of hobbit holes cut into a shallow bowl in the undulating hills in front.

Plenty of tours can take you to movie locations, but the pleasure is not so much in visiting the scene as meeting people who were involved in some way. Chances are your driver was an orc, or your helicopter pilot flew influential crew members around, or you may even meet one of the horses used for the battle at Pelennor Field. Precioussssssss encounters indeed.

926
WITNESSING THE
POWER
OF THE HAKA

NEW ZEALAND Few spectacles can match the terrifying sight of the All Blacks performing a haka before a test match. You feel a chill down your spine fifty metres away in the stands; imagine how it must feel facing it as an opponent. The intimidating thigh-slapping, eye-bulging, tongue-poking chant traditionally used is the Te Rauparaha haka, and like all such Maori posture dances it is designed to display fitness, agility and ferocity. This version was reputedly composed early in the nineteenth century by the warrior Te Rauparaha, who was hiding from his enemies in the sweet potato pit of a friendly chief. Hearing noise above and then being blinded by the sun when the pit covering was removed he thought his days were numbered, but as his eyes became accustomed to the light he saw the hairy legs of his host and was so relieved he performed the haka on the spot. It goes:

Ka Mate! Ka Mate! (It is death! It is death!)
Ka Ora! Ka Ora! (It is life! It is life!)
Tenei te ta ngata puhuru huru (This is the hairy man)
Nana nei i tiki mai whakawhiti te ra (Who caused the sun to shine)
A upane, ka upane! (Step upwards! Another step upward!)
A upane, ka upane! (Step upwards! Another step upward!)
Whiti te ra! (Into the sun that shines!)

Over the last decade or so, descendants of tribes once defeated by Te Rauparaha took umbrage at the widespread use of this haka at rugby matches and consequently a replacement, the Kapa o Pango (Team in Black) haka, was devised. Numerous Maori experts were consulted over what form the haka should take but controversy still surrounds the final throat-slitting gesture, which is supposed to symbolize the harnessing of vital energy. It remains to be seen whether Kapa o Pango will replace the traditional haka, be used on special occasions (as apparently planned), or fade from view. But whichever you manage to catch, both versions still illicit that same spine-tingling response.

927 CELEBRATING MOOMBA WATERFEST

AUSTRALIA Held every March over the Labour Day weekend, the Moomba Waterfest turns the stereotypical Aussie reputation for making everything a giant piss-up on its head. Driven by civic pride, this fifty-year-old event is a deliberately wholesome family occasion, and gives Melbourne a chance to show off and prove that it's the match of its more international rival, Sydney. The key events are the opening night's huge fireworks display over the Yarra River; the Garden Party at the city's Treasurey Gardens, where you can rock away the afternoon to Aboriginal bands or spend an hour trying to master the intricacies of the didgeridoo at one of the many music workshops. The parade passes down Swanston Street on the Monday, featuring Melbourne's iconic trams dressed up to the nines, and people don budgie suits and giant puppet outfits to stalk passers-by.

928 WINE-TASTING IN THE BAROSSA VALLEY

AUSTRALIA While it's still said that "real men drink beer", nowadays many a true-blue Aussie bloke can tell his Shiraz from his Cabernet, his Semillon from his Riesling. And a wine-tasting weekend is now as much part of the Australian lifestyle as a barbecue in the backyard.

By far the best-known wine region in Australia is the Barossa Valley, an hour's drive northeast of Adelaide; it is also one of Australia's oldest – some of the vines planted over 150 years ago still bear fruit today. The valley's Mediterranean climate and soil are perfect for producing full-bodied reds and robust whites. Almost every Barossa winery has a Shiraz or Shiraz blend on their books – strong, dark wines with a full-fruited aroma and a round, velvety structure, while Riesling is the staple among the Barossa whites, rounded and full-flavoured with passionfruit and lime aromas.

The Winemaker Trail takes you through Barossa's picturesque hamlets and across rolling hills to its sixty wineries, many of which offer tastings and cellar door sales. Among the big-name establishments, Wolf Blass and Jacob's Creek are perennially popular, but also worth checking out is Bethany Wines, run by the same family for six generations, and up-and-coming Two Hands.

For the novice, wine-tasting can be a daunting experience. Try the wine in the order suggested by the winery, moving from whites and sparkling to reds, following the five S's of wine-tasting: See (study the colour); Swirl (allows the wine to breathe); Sniff (our sense of smell is more acute than our sense of taste); Sip; Savour (swirl around in the mouth to appreciate the flavour). Swallowing is optional; if you're visiting a lot of wineries it's probably better to spit out. Chances are you will walk away with a few bottles of your favourite — and a brand new vocabulary to boot.

929
TRAMPING THE
MILFORD TRACK

NEW ZEALAND You're going to get wet on this tramp. In fact it would be disappointing if you didn't. When the heavens open it seems like the hills are leaking; every cliff-face springs a waterfall and the rivers quickly become raging torrents.

The Milford Track lies in Fiordland National Park, most of which gets at least five metres of rain a year, making it one of the wettest places in the world. But unless you are really unlucky it won't rain the whole time. Blue skies reveal a wonderment of magical scenery best seen from Mackinnon Pass, the highest point of the tramp, at 1073m. Deep glaciated valleys drop steeply away on both sides while weather-worn mountains rear up all around. It is a great place to eat your lunch, always keeping a wary eye out for kea, New Zealand's cheeky alpine parrot, who will be off with your sandwiches given even a quarter of a chance.

From here you can see most of the Milford Track route. Behind you is the valley of the Clinton River, along which you've just spent a day and a half tramping, after being dropped off by a small launch on the shores of Lake Te Anau. Ahead is the Arthur River, where the rain puts on its best display with two spectacular waterfalls. The story goes that when blazing the route in 1880, explorers Donald Sutherland and John Mackay came upon one magnificent fall, and tossed a coin to decide who would name it on the understanding that the loser would name the next one. Mackay won the toss but rued his good fortune when, days later, they stumbled across the much more famous and lofty Sutherland Falls, at 580m the tallest in New Zealand..

GETTING TO GRIPS WITH
ABORIGINAL ART

AUSTRALIA There's no need for in-flight entertainment when you're flying across Australia because the view from the plane is always arresting. The endless, barely inhabited Outback looks spectacular from the air, a vast natural canvas of ivory-coloured salt pans, clumps of grey-green scrub, and sienna, ochre and russet sands, scored by the occasional dead-straight line of an oil exploration track or the wiggle of a long-dried watercourse. It's like one enormous abstract picture and, in part at least, that's what informs many Aboriginal artworks, particularly the so-called dot paintings.

At the heart of many Aboriginal traditions are practices for surviving in the extreme conditions of Outback Australia and the need to pass on this knowledge to descendants. Historically, one way of doing that has been to draw a map in the dust, detailing crucial local features such as sacred landmarks, waterholes and food sources. These sand paintings are elaborate and take days to create; they are also sacred and to be viewed only by initiated clan members before being destroyed. But in the early 1970s, a teacher at Papunya, northwest of Alice Springs, began encouraging young Aborigine kids to translate their sand-painting techniques on to canvas. In fact it was the elders who took to the idea – without divulging culturally secret information, of course – and a new art form was born.

Those early Papunya artists have been superseded by painters from throughout the central desert, the most successful experimenting with innovative abstract and minimalist styles in their bid to woo international collectors. Alice Springs now has two dozen art galleries devoted to Aboriginal art, with paintings priced between Aus$40 and Aus$40,000. Browsing these galleries is one of the highlights of a visit to Alice and even if you don't bring a picture home, you'll come away with a different perspective on the Outback.

931 QUEENSTOWN'S WINTER WONDERLAND

NEW ZEALAND Queenstown is definitely the place to be in winter. For a start it has some of the best skiing and boarding in New Zealand with two excellent fields right on its doorstep. It is also extremely picturesque, snuggled alongside the waters of Lake Wakatipu and hemmed in by snowcapped mountains, not least the aptly named Remarkables. So far so standard for ski resorts, but in Queenstown you can also partake in "summer" activities at the same time. Suitably wetsuited, whitewater rafters run the Shotover and Kawarau rivers, and the bungy site above the town comes alive most nights in winter for floodlit leaps.

Always popular with Kiwis, Queenstown also draws Australians and addicts from the northern hemisphere who can't get enough action in their own ski season. As for the slopes, they're bald. None of your slaloming through trees here: this is all open vistas (and high winds when it blows). With more than 400 vertical metres of skiing and the longest pedigree of any Kiwi skifield,

Coronet Peak is probably the more popular of the two fields. The Remarkables maxes out at 500 vertical metres and has its adherents, as much for the fine off-piste terrain as for the forgiving groomed slopes.

By world standards, Kiwi fields are quite primitive. Sure they have fast quad chairlifts and the like, but on-site facilities are limited to a few restaurants and bars. But that means you get to spend more time back in Queenstown where the après ski is second to none. The restaurants are easily the match of those in Auckland and Wellington and the nightlife ranges from lively dance clubs to chic joints where you need to know the doorman to get in.

The season typically runs from early June into October, but the time to come is the last week of June for the Queenstown Winter Festival – a real riot with heaps of activities, crazy stunts and, of course, plenty of carousing.

932 SEA KAYAKING AROUND SHARK BAY

AUSTRALIA The Peron Peninsula in Shark Bay, on the northwest coast of Western Australia, is well known for its regular dolphin visitations, and a beachside resort at Monkey Mia has grown around the spectacle.

But there's much more to this UNESCO-listed reserve than meeting Flipper and the family, and the sheltered conditions make the Shark Bay area ideal for a sea kayaking adventure.

Paddling in a bay named after the ocean's deadliest predator may sound as sensible as skinny-dipping in Piranha Creek. Sure, there are tiger sharks out in the depths, but the abundant sea life means they're fed well enough not to bother you in the shallows. Besides the pleasures of gliding serenely across bottle-green waters and camping beneath paprika-red cliffs on

whichever deserted beach takes your fancy, marine-life spotting adds a "sea safari" element to your trip. Don't be surprised if before long a green turtle passes under your kayak, followed by rays the size of a tablecloth. And where there are rays there are usually sharks, but only frisky babies less than a metre long, maturing in the shallow nurseries before heading out to sea.

Battling the winds around Cape Peron there's a good chance you'll encounter dugongs grazing in the sea grass meadows, and as you cruise down the sheltered side of the peninsula flocks of cormorants, terns and pelicans will take to the air. Finally, if you've not seen any already, bottlenosed dolphins are a guaranteed sight at Monkey Mia, which is also a great place for a day paddle.

933 CANYONEERING IN KARIJINI

AUSTRALIA Canyoneering through Karijini National Park is an Indiana Jones-style adventure through a rarely seen wonderland of towering red rock canyons, trickling waterfalls and hidden pools. Be prepared for half a day of walking then crawling, wading then swimming, climbing along ledges and up waterfalls and then jumping into freezing pools.

Part of the experience includes Knox Gorge; descending the steep track into the ravine you've little idea of what waits ahead. Paths and ledges peter out and you're forced to swim across a couple of pools until the walls narrow suddenly into a shoulder-wide slot that never sees direct sunlight. You enter the chasm, bridging over jammed boulders, deafened and disoriented by water running through your legs until it seems there is no way ahead. There is, but to continue you must hurtle blindly down

the "do-or-die" Knox Slide into an unseen plunge pool below. Amazed that you've survived that, you now make a six-metre jump or abseil off the next waterfall to emerge into the broad sunlit waters of Red Gorge, the park's main canyon.

From here you swim, wade and scramble over the debris washed down by the last cyclone until you reach the Four Gorges area. Hundreds of feet above, tourists at Oxer's Lookout point and stare, wondering how on earth you got there. Meanwhile, you're wondering how you're going to get out. The secret is to ascend the stepped ledges alongside Weano Falls and follow the canyon upstream until you emerge at Handrail Pool in the regular tourist zone. Once you're out, all that remains is to stagger over to Oxer's Lookout yourself and peer down in amazement at what you've just achieved.

DODGING EMBERS ON MOUNT YASUR

934

VANUATU The walk up Tanna's continuously erupting Mount Yasur takes about ninety minutes. A notice at the bottom warns against approaching the crater when there's a particular level of activity; usually it's safe to move on.

The climb goes through tropical forest: rainwater trickles down every tree, then gushes down the path. Suddenly the forest gives way to a grim desert of rock and mud extending to the summit. The temperature drops markedly; a cool, dank mist blows in from the sea.

Yasur announces itself the closer you get. Every few minutes, there's a loud boom, then a few lesser booms. Just below the summit, a battered letterbox proclaims itself the world's only Volcano Post – it's quite literally a chance to send postcards from the edge.

At the rim, a pleasant waft of heat rises up and drives the mist away. But the booms accompany tremendous eruptions of red-hot rocks – pyroclasts – that crash into the edge of the crater, and either fizzle or explode. The louder eruptions cause the ground to shake. Often the balls of fire soar high into the air; you'll have to guess where they're going to land. Most people, it seems, get lucky.

935 FROM PRISON TO PARADISE ON L'ILE DES PINS

NEW CALEDONIA If you have to go into exile somewhere, it might as well be the South Pacific, and this blob of an island, on the I'lle des Pins – Island of Pines – which measures just fourteen by eighteen kilometres, is a particularly bearable spot.

The island was a French penal colony in the nineteenth century, and is still French Territory, and it's interesting to share the impressions of one of the convicts transported here in the 1870s, following the collapse of the Paris Commune. Having acknowledged that he had ended up in a paradise, he immediately adds, with obvious bitterness, "but I saw nothing of its beauty" – and yearned only for the monochromes of northern France.

The modern-day visitor comes to I'lle des Pins by choice of course, and can hardly fail to notice its beauty: stunning coastlines, with hot, white sand; warm, limpid water, pale blue as far as the reef, and a deeper blue beyond. The classic South Sea paradise.

The most obvious place to test the water has to be the island's "la piscine naturelle", or natural swimming pool, where the sea enters a shallow bay through a narrow defile between jagged rocks and creates a calm, pristine pool, lined by sun-baked sand. You can wallow in safety while listening to the waves breaking in the distance.

But there's one thing stopping it all from becoming a cliché: the eponymous araucaria pines. Although the island can offer a good few swaying palms as well, it's these dark, spindly posts, soaring bolt upright into the sky, and adorned by minimal vegetation, that dominate, define and distinguish this place. And their forbidding, stark rigidity, in marked contrast to the friendly sway of the palms, creates a certain ambivalence. Do they really belong in paradise?

Before you leave, take in the island's ruined prison and monument and be thankful that you get to come and go as you please.

936 RELAXING AT THE SEASIDE IN ART DECO NAPIER

NEW ZEALAND With enough to keep you entertained but not so much to wear you out, Napier, a small provincial city on the east coast of the North Island, is perfect for a few days of leisure.

Its chief attraction is its small-scale Art Deco architecture, the result of a uniform building programme after the place was devastated by an earthquake in 1931. Hundreds of lives were lost as fires swept through the rubble of the town. But Napier rose from the ashes adopting the precepts of the Art Deco movement prevalent at the time, albeit in a more subdued style informed by the Great Depression still biting hard. Today you'll see an unusually harmonious downtown of asymmetric buildings popping with chevrons, ziggurats, fountains (a symbol of renewal) and lightning flashes. While predominantly Art Deco, Napier's buildings were also given elements of earlier styles and the city ended up with a palimpsest of early-twentieth-century design, combining aspects of the Arts and Crafts movement, the Californian Spanish Mission style, Egyptian and Mayan motifs, the stylized floral designs of Art Nouveau, the blockish forms

associated with Charles Rennie Mackintosh, and even Maori imagery. A case in point is the ASB Bank, its exterior adorned with fern shoots and a mask form from the head of a taiaha (a long-spear fighting club), while its interior has a fine Maori rafter design.

The up-and-coming harbour area of Ahuriri has perhaps Napier's finest example, the National Tobacco Company Building, which exhibits a decorative richness seldom seen on industrial buildings. The facade merges Deco asymmetry and the classic juxtaposition of cubic shapes and arches with the softening Art Nouveau motifs of roses and raupo (a kind of Kiwi bulrush).

But Napier's not just pretty architecture, it's also an idyllic seaside setting. Take a stroll along the beachside Marine Parade, an antipodean imprint of a classic British seafront with an aquarium, a sunken flower garden and an excellent modernized lido-style pool complex, and don't miss the curvaceous bronze statue of Pania of the Reef, a legendary Maori sea-maiden whose body now forms the rocky shoals just offshore.

937 TUCKING INTO A HANGI

NEW ZEALAND A suitably reverential silence descends, broken only by munching and appreciative murmurs from the assembled masses – the hangi has finally been served. This traditional Maori fare, similar to the luau prepared by the Maori people's Polynesian kin in Hawaii, is essentially a feast cooked in an earth oven for several hours. It can't be found on restaurant menus – but then again a hangi is not just a meal, it's an event.

To begin, the men light a fire, and once it has burned down, specially selected river stones that don't splinter are placed in the embers. While these are heating, a large pit is dug, perhaps two metres square and a metre and a half deep. Meanwhile the women are busy preparing lamb, pork, chicken, fish, shellfish and vegetables (particularly kumara, the New Zealand sweet potato).

Traditionally these would be wrapped in leaves then arranged in baskets made of flax; these days baking foil and steel mesh are more common.

When everything is ready (the prep can take up to three hours), the hot stones are placed in the pit and covered with wet sacking. Then come the baskets of food followed by a covering of earth which serves to seal in the steam and the flavours. There's a palpable sense of communal anticipation as hosts and guests mill around chatting and drinking, waiting for the unearthing. A couple of hours later, the baskets are disinterred, revealing fall-off-the-bone steam-smoked meat and fabulously tender vegetables with a faintly earthy flavour. A taste, and an occasion, not easily forgotten.

938 HAVING A FAR-FLUNG FLUTTER AT THE BIRDSVILLE RACES

AUSTRALIA Come September, locals flee the dusty desert township of Birdsville, as a six-thousand-strong crowd descends for a weekend of hard drinking and, if they sober up for long enough to work out the odds, the chance to win a packet on the ponies running in the Birdsville Races. This is the archetypal, good-natured Aussie piss-up, in a bizarre Outback setting. The racegoers are a mix of young cowpokes making the most of their one opportunity of the year to whoop it up and meet folks they're not related to, and townies who have just driven 1400km from the coast on atrocious roads to get there. Even by Australian standards, that's a long way to go for a drink. Although you might see the odd fist-fight between drunken mates on account of the effort involved in reaching Birdsville, nobody has anything to prove by the time they arrive, and there's nothing left for it but to down a slab and party.

The Birdsville Races (officially known as the Birdsville Cup Carnival) kick off on Friday, though most people skip the trackside opening ceremonies in favour of spending the day easing themselves onto a liquid diet. After dark, the town fires up in fairground mode, with a host of sideshow attractions – whip-cracking competitions, guess my weight, arm wrestling, you name it – setting up along the main street. A huge, mainly male crowd materializes at the fundraising auction, impatiently watching all sorts of farm junk going under the hammer as they wait for the real attraction: the draw at the end to win a T-shirt off the back of a stripper.

Saturday is the day to hit the racetrack – a baking hot, shadeless stretch of dust and gravel 3km west of town. The races end mid-afternoon, when everyone retires for a wash-and-brush-up before heading back to town to celebrate – or drown their sorrows.

939 WATCHING WHALES IN KAIKOURA

NEW ZEALAND It's 7.30am and we're just a kilometre off the coast of Kaikoura. I can still see the wharf where we embarked, backed by the snowcapped Seaward Kaikoura range, and yet below us is 1000m of ocean. This is exactly the sort of territory that many whale species like to call home. Most places in the world, a whale-watching trip involves hours powering out to sea to the whales' migration route, but here the whales are virtually on the doorstep.

Sperm whales and dusky dolphins are year-round residents, while blue whales, pilot whales, and especially humpback whales all pass through. Regular visitors include southern right whales, so named because whalers found them to be the "right" whales to kill – they floated after being harpooned.

Weather permitting, trips run several times a day, and you're typically out among the leviathans within minutes. (Tour operators are so confident you'll see a whale that they'll refund 80% of your fee if you don't.) On the short journey out, big video screens have taken us into the virtual "World of the Whales" and their life in the depths of the Kaikoura Canyon and beyond, but we're here to see the real thing. Right on cue, someone spots a plume of spray, then a short dorsal fin. It is a humpback. The previously half-awake boat comes alive as everyone crowds the rails, camera in hand. Out of the corner of my eye I just catch a thirty-tonne barnacled beast surge out of the water, almost clearing the waves, with sheets of brine pouring off its sides. It crashes back with a surface-rending splash. We're all thrilled at our good fortune and anticipating even greater displays when the whale decides it has had enough, and with a wave of its tail bids us adieu.

940 DOUBLE-CROSSED IN THE SOUTH SEAS

RAROTONGA The Cook Islands are not synonymous with hiking. Nor would you expect them to be; that's not why people make the journey to these South Sea idylls. But the cross-island walk in Rarotonga is plenty of motivation to do more than just your usual seaside saunter.

Most head out on a guided walk, not least because the trek is hard going. It certainly was for us; we just spotted the track on a map and set off . . . from the finish line rather than the beginning. We noted the sign that read, "It is advised you start the cross-island walk from the other side", but encircling the island would take ages. This seemed the quickest way.

As we started inland the temperature rose and the vegetation became fragrant. Before long the unmarked trail took us through tall, subtropical forest where tree roots had fashioned themselves into easy-to-climb stairs. It was like walking through a carved tunnel in an old cathedral. But soon we found ourselves scaling sheer slopes using any available tree root or liana for leverage. The vegetation got pricklier and sparser; still, we powered on and found our way to the top of the ridge, where the Needle, Te Rua Manga, stands. From here we could see the island's tallest peak as well as the golden beaches below and, in all directions, the infinite crystal sea.

Rather than continue cross-island, we doubled back – and soon found out why you're advised to head in this direction. For one, we finally saw the signposts on trail. And two, the hike up to the ridge is much steeper the way we did it. Getting back to base proved a whole lot easier than coming up.

941 SCUBA DIVING THE WRECKS AT POOR KNIGHTS ISLANDS

NEW ZEALAND Jacques Cousteau championed the Poor Knights Islands as one of the top ten dive sites in the world – fairly weighty praise from a man with his extensive marine knowledge. And with their warm currents, visibility regularly around 30m and a host of undersea attractions his judgement is understandable. Dive boats spread themselves over fifty recognized dive sites that jointly cover New Zealand's most diverse range of sea life (including subtropical species) such as Lord Howe coralfish and toadstool grouper, found nowhere else around the coast. Near-vertical rock faces drop 100m through a labyrinth of caves, fissures and rock arches teeming with rainbow-coloured fish, crabs, soft corals, kelp forests and shellfish. Blue, humpback, sei and minke whales also drop in from time to time, and dolphins are not uncommon.

A typical day might include an hour-long cruise out to the islands followed by a drift dive through a sandy-bottomed cave populated by stingrays and lit by shafts of sunlight. After lunch on board and perhaps some time paddling one of the boat's kayaks you'll head around the coast to a second dive spot, maybe working your way along a technicolour wall of soft corals and a few nudibranchs.

As if that weren't enough, the waters north and south of the reserve are home to two navy wrecks, both deliberately scuttled. The survey ship *HMNZS Tui* was sunk in 1999 to form an artificial reef, and it was so popular with divers and marine life that the obsolete frigate Waikato followed two years later. These form part of a Northland wreck trail which includes the remains of the Greenpeace flagship Rainbow Warrior, bombed by French government agents in 1985, just before it set out to campaign against French nuclear testing in the Pacific.

942 INDULGE YOUR TASTEBUDS AT QUEEN VICTORIA MARKET

AUSTRALIA A visit to Queen Victoria Market, or "Vic Market", located on the northern fringe of the city centre, is a superb introduction to Melbourne's vibrant food culture and will have you rubbing shoulders with everyone from government ministers to the city's best chefs. Running for 128 years, it's one of the oldest markets in Australia, and is liveliest on the weekends when buskers compete with spruiking stallholders for your attention.

For foodies there are three main areas: the Deli section, the Meat and Fish Hall, and the fruit and vegetable market. The Deli is characterized by its strong smells and its shops selling regional specialities such as fine local cheeses, including the Jindi Triple Cream Brie and Milawa's tasty goat varieties, as well as lesser-known fusions like kangaroo biltong (South African-style dried meat). Arriving hungry you'll find the free tastings will put a stop to the pangs as quickly as they tempt you to lighten your wallet. Greek, Italian, French and Polish stalls stock everything from marinated octopus to juniper sausage, while speciality butchers sell emu and crocodile, in addition to the usual quail, rabbit and venison. If you're looking for more traditional meat offerings, head to the Meat and Fish Hall. Here, competition is fierce, with dozens of butchers supplying prime cuts of meat from a leg of lamb to Japanese-style Wagu beef, and fishmongers stalls groan under an impressive display of fish and shellfish on ice, including northern Australian wild Barramundi, Victorian crayfish and fresh Tasmanian oysters.

The fruit and vegetable market reflects the seasons, dominated by root vegetables in winter and stone fruits in summer – the proximity of Southeast Asia means exotic fruits like mangosteens, rambutan and the pungent-smelling durian are also available.

If you're after something less epicurean, however, try the German Bratwurst shop for a sauerkraut and mustard covered sausage, or the American Doughnut Van, serving up bags of jam-filled doughnuts.

Vic Market is a fantastic way to experience the many cultures that make Melbourne what it is today – and to get a taste for where it's going.

943

EXPLORING WAITOMO'S
EERIE UNDERGROUND WORLD

NEW ZEALAND Waitomo, a tiny town in rolling sheep country, sits on a veritable Swiss cheese of limestone, with deep sinkholes, beautifully sculpted tunnels and wild organ pipes of stalactites all lit up by ghostly constellations of glowworms.

Traditionally the way to see all this is on a gentle stroll through some of the shallower caverns where the Victorian explorers named the flowstone formations after animals, mythical creatures and household items. Coloured lights pick out the salient features before you take an other-worldly ride in a dinghy across an underground lake; the green pinpricks of light above your head resembling the heavens of some parallel universe.

Ever the adventure pioneers, New Zealand has also created another method of exploring the caves – blackwater rafting. Decked out in wetsuit, helmet and miner's lamp you head underground with a truck inner tube, then sit in it and float through the gloom. The few rapids are gentle and safe but the blackness gives that extra frisson of uncertainty.

Assorted trips up the ante with hundred-metre-long abseils, waterfall jumping and even a little subterranean rock climbing. Or you could try a straightforward traditional caving trip. With small groups there's a genuine feeling of exploration as you negotiate tight squeezes, find your way into pristine rooms full of gossamer straws and maybe even fully submerge through sumps to access yet deeper recesses.

944 GETTING HANDS-ON AT WELLINGTON'S TE PAPA

NEW ZEALAND Since 1998, Wellington's magnificent waterfront has been dominated by the Museum of New Zealand, which is always known by its shortened Maori name of Te Papa, loosely translated as "Our Place".

A far cry from the stuffy glass cases of the old museum it replaced, Te Papa exudes a radical modern approach not just in the design of the building itself but in the way the exhibits invite interaction and involvement. Like any good museum it works on several levels and yet, despite its size, it never feels overwhelming. You can easily waltz through in a couple of hours and get a comprehensive overview of what makes New Zealand tick. To make the most of your visit, linger over the superb Maori section with its robustly carved war canoe, traditional houses, collections of fearsome war clubs and intricately worked jade jewellery. Displays showcase how people have migrated to New Zealand, first using the stars to navigate the Pacific in double-hulled canoes, later in sailing ships, and more recently as immigrants from east Asia. And you shouldn't miss the marae, a Maori meeting place that is dramatically different from the red, black and white wood carvings you'll see elsewhere. Here semi-mythological figures are fashioned from warped plywood and shaded in an eye-catching array of pastel tones.

With more time on your hands, there's plenty to keep you occupied – drawers reveal smaller artefacts, a gallery showcases the best in Kiwi painting and sculpture, and "sound posts" encourage you to tune into wide-ranging views about the ongoing debate on New Zealand's founding document, the Treaty of Waitangi.

Te Papa is a great place for kids too, with all kinds of interactive, hands-on displays, the chance to experience what it felt like to be in New Zealand's most powerful earthquake and even some high-tech rides.

Almost a decade after its opening, over a million people pass through Te Papa's doors every year. Not bad, considering the country only has a population of four million.

945 HELI-HIKING ON FRANZ JOSEF GLACIER

NEW ZEALAND After the chopper banks away and the thwump-thwump-thwump of the rotors has receded down the glacier, I'm left standing in a beautiful white silence. With half a dozen others and a guide I've got the next couple of hours to explore the upper reaches of Franz Josef glacier, one of a pair of blinding rivers of ice that cascade almost to sea level on the western side of the South Island's Southern Alps. In Maori legend these are Ka Riomata o Hinehukatere – "The Tears of the Avalanche Girl". The story goes that the beautiful Hinehukatere so loved the mountains that she encouraged her lover, Tawe, to climb alongside her. He fell to his death and Hinehukatere cried so copiously that her tears formed the glaciers.

The guide checks everyone has put on their crampons correctly and, stout stick in hand, we set off slowly working our way through a labyrinth of seracs (ice towers) and crevasses. It is a bit of a shock to the system and initially nerve-wracking as I gaze down into the blue depths of the glacier with teetering blocks of ice looming above. But the guide seems to know what she's doing, continually assessing the changes on this fast-moving glacier. Most of the hikers have never been anywhere like this before so she charts a course that is safe but keeps us on our toes. Just as I am beginning to feel comfortable she ratchets up the exposure along a knife-edge ridge, just to make sure we're keeping our wits about us.

The ridge leads to a series of ice caves, features you couldn't hope to experience on hikes lower down the glacier. Deep blue and gently sculpted, they're wonderfully enticing and the guide leads us through. A little scrambling, crouching and sliding against the slippery walls and we've made it. Feeling confident, a couple of us are keen for something more challenging and we're shown a narrow hole that looks way too small to get through. Stripping off as much clothing as the temperature will allow we manage to worm our way into a glorious glowing grotto where we sit for a few minutes before struggling elated (and cold) back to the surface.

All too soon we hear the beat of the helicopter coming to whisk us back to town. Still, that means a steaming cup of hot chocolate is only fifteen minutes away – much needed after these dazzling few hours on the ice.

946 TAKING THE PLUNGE WITH AJ HACKETT

NEW ZEALAND Ever since speed skiers and general daredevils AJ Hackett and Henry van Asch invented commercial bungy jumping, New Zealand has been its home, and Queenstown its capital. So if you're going to bungy what better place than here? And if it's the classic experience you're after, then the original Kawarau Suspension Bridge is your spot. At 43m it's only a modest jump by modern standards, but you're guaranteed an audience to will you on and then celebrate your achievement.

Diving off tall towers with vines tied around your ankles has been a male rite of passage in Vanuatu for centuries, but modern bungy started with the nutty antics of the Oxford University Dangerous Sports Club in the 1970s. The next leap forward was AJ Hackett's bungy off the Eiffel Tower in 1987. He was promptly arrested but soon started commercial operations in Queenstown.

So are you going solo or double? Dunking or not? Shirt on or shirt off? Decisions made, you stroll out onto the bridge (looking oh so casual) while pumping rock or hip-hop starts building the adrenaline. Wrapping a towel around your ankles for protection, they'll attach the cord while feeding you some jocular spiel about the bungy breaking (it won't) or not being attached properly (it will be). You'll then be chivvied into producing a cheesy (or wan) grin for the camera before shuffling out onto the precipice for the countdown.

Three. Two. One. Bungy!

RIVER OF NO RETURN:

RAFTING THE FRANKLIN

AUSTRALIA Determine when you come and the river decides how long you'll stay. You're going to be wet through, cold, and challenged by rapids with names like The Cauldron, Thunderush and Jawbreaker. And that's exactly why you're here.

The plan: you and nine others, including two all-knowing river guides, are to spend a week paddling, pinballing and peacefully drifting more than 100km through southwest Tasmania, one of the wildest and remotest parts of Australia. All the gear's provided: two inflatable rafts, camping equipment, wetsuits, helmets (to be worn at all times), waterproof-paddling jackets (unflatteringly called "cags") and, most importantly, lifejackets. The rest is up to the river.

Rafting the Franklin is one of the world's last true wilderness experiences, not least because the river has such a fearsome reputation. Its banks are so steep and its catchment so vast that any rain upstream (and it's plentiful in Tasmania) can cause river levels to rise 10m overnight, turning benign rapids into life-or-death obstacles for all but the most experienced river-travellers (that's where the guides come in); sometimes the team will even be forced to carry the fully laden rafts and gear along precarious, cliff-hugging tracks that skirt the most dangerous sections of river.

The good news is that no matter what the conditions – high water, low water, or somewhere in between – you're in for the ride of your life. Most of the whitewater is Grade 3 and 4, but there are plenty of still and silent pools where you might spot a platypus or drift past stately 2000-year-old Huon pine trees.

It's humbling to spend days in such a place, travelling along the river by day and camping on its edges at night. And in losing track of time and the days of the week, you gain something else: that rare relief of being nobody of consequence in true wilderness.

947

948 VISITING THE CITY OF FESTIVALS

AUSTRALIA Rock up any time in Adelaide and chances are there's an arts festival on somewhere. The Adelaide Festival of Arts is the big one, established in 1960 by a forward-thinking journalist who hoped to replicate Scotland's Edinburgh Festival down under, today it attracts a diverse range of international and Australian performers, with free concerts and open-air film performances, and energizes the city from late February to mid-March every even-numbered year.

A lively avant-garde Fringe festival parallels this event, and recently the Adelaide Film Festival has joined in too, premiering Rolf De Heer's Ten Canoes, the first Australian feature to be filmed in an indigenous language. There's even an Adelaide Festival of Ideas held every July in odd years, addressing prescient economic, cultural and environmental topics.

The Fringe kicks off with a street parade down Rundle Street followed by music and comedy at venues around town, all oiled by the 24-hour licensing laws. Previous artists have included Inga Liljeström, described as "Bjork, Portishead and Marianne Faithfull on the set of a David Lynch film", and the Musafir Gypsies of Rajasthan, whose music fuses with acrobatics and magic in the tradition of ancient desert wanderers. Jazz trumpeter Vince Jones has also performed, as well as the Pat Metheny Trio and the Amsterdam Sinfonietta, playing Shostakovich and Mozart. Theatre may range from a groundbreaking "shoe opera" about Imelda Marcos, Shakespeare and Ibsen to an adaptation of Peter Goldsworthy's black comedy, Honk If You Are Jesus.

Still uninspired? Then perhaps the annual Womadelaide music weekend held in early March in the Botanic Park is for you. Attracting over 70,000 visitors, it's a great place to encounter home-grown talent as well as international artists such as Baaba Maal, the Abdullah Ibrahim Trio and Gilberto Gil. Recently the Saltwater Band from Arnhemland performed alongside reggae journeyman Jimmy Cliff and Miriam Makeba. In short, if you can't find something to stimulate your interest in Adelaide, call an ambulance quick, you could well be dead.

949 MOTORBIKING DOWN THE WILD WEST COAST

NEW ZEALAND The beach lies just a few wheel revolutions away, its fine sand bleached nearly white and strewn with dark driftwood. The waves tumble towards the shore, their foam glinting platinum in the morning light. The road is flat. You turn the throttle; as the bike surges your adrenalin leaps too. Lick your lips and you can taste the salty spray of the sea beneath your visor. Travellers in their hulking RVs couldn't hope to understand.

You've set out from Karamea – the end of the road at its northern extreme – to cruise south down New Zealand's wild West Coast. At Westport, you take a detour for coffee at The Bay House, Tauranga Bay's scenic café, and watch the seals sunning themselves on the rocks.

As you continue your journey, the roadside rata trees are in full scarlet bloom. You stop at Punakaiki where the "pancake rocks" lie piled high like the breakfast of giants; at high tide the ocean rises in their caverns and blasts violent geysers through their blowholes.

You pass the historic gold-mining town of Hokitika and the serene lakes of Wahapo and Mapourika, which reflect the snowcapped mountains of the Southern Alps in colours of dazzling intensity. At Haast you must leave the coast to head inland; the coastal road dead-ends 50km south of there. You skim round the bends of Haast Pass, shifting your weight one way then the other. Wild lavender grows on the verge of the road to Queenstown and from your bike its scent is sharp and clear. You weave around the turquoise waters of Wanaka and Hawea lakes, coming to Queenstown – but you'll leave its thrills to others; more excitement lies ahead. It's back to the coast then on toward Milford Sound, the winding road lined by sheer granite cliffs down whose face streaky white waterfalls thunder. You turn the throttle a little further and roar towards the fjord.

950 DRIFTING WITH JELLYFISH IN MICRONESIA

PALAU They're all around you – literally millions of pulsating golden mastigia, like a swarm of squishy tennis balls in zero gravity. As you move your limbs to keep yourself afloat in this warm lake on one of Palau's Rock Islands, the jellyfish brush softly against your skin, then waft away as endless others take their place. They can barely sting – eons spent in this saltwater lake without a single predator have weakened their defenses – so there's no need to avoid them, and you couldn't even if you tried. And though beautiful, these creatures aren't as fragile as they look; the depths where they spend the night contain high levels of hydrogen sulfide, which is toxic to humans.

951 ASCENDING Q1 IN SURFERS PARADISE

AUSTRALIA Whereas most tall towers offer visitors 360-degree views of sprawling urban minutiae, you'd be lucky to see one single example of human existence from nearly half of the views at the Q1 Tower. The thing that separates the 323-metre Q1 Tower (the tallest residential tower in the world) from other super-tall towers is its beachside location. The entire eastern face looks out over nothing except ocean and sky. The best time to go is around sunset, when you can enjoy a master-crafted cocktail in its top floor bar and viewing area whilst watching the finger-like shadows reach out across the ocean as the sun drops behind the Q1's older and shorter neighbours.

952 RIVER DEEP, MOUNTAIN HIGH: BUSHWALKING THE OVERLAND TRACK

AUSTRALIA The country's best-known long-distance bushwalk leads from Tasmania's highest peak to Australia's deepest lake across a magnificent alpine wilderness, unbroken by roads and adorned by brooding lakes, glacier-carved cirques and thundering waterfalls.

Stormy skies are frequent on Tassie, but even on the ground there's no shortage of drama with features named after their classical Greek counterparts – Mount Eros, the Acropolis and Lake Elysia – providing a fitting backdrop to the Olympian landscape. And though much of the 65-kilometre trail is boardwalk with bridged creeks, there's no escaping several muddy interludes – be prepared to get wet.

This is Tasmania, so fresh drinking water is plentiful and need not be carried; the daunting task is lugging enough food and stove fuel for the duration. Once you accept that, the exhilaration of wandering completely self-sufficient through the mountain wilderness fills you with a sense of deep satisfaction. Up above, currawongs and eagles cut through the skies, while below you quolls and wallabies abound.

It takes about a week to tramp across the Overland's stirring range of landscapes, though you'll want to add a day or two for side trips to waterfalls, lakes and scrambling up peaks such as Mount Ossa, Tasmania's highest at 1617m, overlooking forests of King Billy pines and carpeted in fragrant wildflowers in early summer. Even then you're sure to have rain and even snow at some point, and eventually you'll stagger aboard the Lake St Clair ferry, aching, mud-caked but happy, for an uncelebrated return to civilization.

953 HUNTING NODDY BIRDS

NAURU The Minister for the Environment is a much faster runner than me. He weaves through the knife-blade sharp, crenellated edges of the coral pinnacles that cover almost the entire interior of the miniscule Pacific island of Nauru. Hiding in among the mined-out phosphate ruins that have turned this once-thriving island into a basket case is the noddy bird. Recent generations have forgone the traditional delicacy of eating its liver and intestines in favour of imported pies and steaks from Australia. Now, as Nauru comes to terms with bankruptcy, traditional island pursuits are being rediscovered.

The island's vast deposits of phosphate were mined and exported in the mid-twentieth century to the point where, at one stage in the 1970s, Nauru's people enjoyed the highest per capita income on the planet. But profits were squandered by epic corruption and terrible investments. Now all the phosphate has gone, the workers have fled, the machinery is broken, everyone is bankrupt and nobody ever comes to Nauru.

Baron Waqa, environment head of this wasteland, has, like everyone else on the island, forgotten how to mimic the uniquely gravelly calls of the noddy bird. Hiding behind a pinnacle at sunset with a huge net raised above him, he turns on a 1980s cassette player that has a recording of this small yet bilious creature. Waving our nets about frantically, it is only after around twenty minutes that a black blur comes in my direction. Stumbling wildly, I fall off my perch, badly cutting my arm. Baron, an old hand at this, manages to snare four in his net, which he swiftly plucks out feet first before breaking their necks.

The idea is to roast them on a barbecue in little rolls. There's very little meat, but what there is is intensely rich and gamey, not unlike pheasant or partridge. "This is so much better for us than frozen pizza", Baron tells me as we polish off our meagre yet tasty haul. As the rest of the world advances further, it seems that economic collapse has forced Nauruans to reach back into their past.

954 COAST TO COAST WITH THE TRANZALPINE

NEW ZEALAND New Zealand's South Island is vertically split by the Southern Alps, a snow-capped spine of 3000-metre-high mountains. Only three road passes breach this barrier, and just one rail line – the TranzAlpine. Slicing 225km across the South Island from Christchurch, the island's biggest city, to the small West Coast town of Greymouth, this unassuming train offers one of the most scenic train journeys in the world.

Don't come looking for a luxury experience. This certainly isn't the Orient Express, but any shortcomings of the train itself will fade into the background when you take a look out of the window – the scenery is mind-bogglingly spectacular, especially in winter, when it's at its most dramatic with the landscape cloaked in snow.

As the train eases out of Christchurch, urban back gardens give way to the open vistas of the Canterbury Plains, a swathe of bucolic sheep country carved into large paddocks. After an hour the rail line cuts away from the main highway and charts its own course past the dry grasslands of the Torlesse Range, gradually climbing all the while.

The west of the South Island gets huge amounts of rain, the east very little. Here you're in a transition zone, and with every kilometre you'll notice the character of the vegetation change. Subalpine tussock gives way to damp beech forests before heading into the dripping West Coast rain forest, thick with rampant tree ferns. Step onto the open-air viewing carriage for an even more intimate experience; photo opportunities abound.

At the little alpine community of Arthur's Pass you enter the eight-kilometre-long Otira Tunnel, burrowing under the high peaks and emerging at the former rail town of Otira. After losing height quickly along the cascading Taramakau River the train cuts to the tranquil shores of Lake Brunner before the final run down the Grey River to Greymouth.

955

SYDNEY HARBOUR-MASTERING

AUSTRALIA The urge to emigrate always surfaces when you take the public ferry across Sydney Harbour: the views from the deck not only encompass the city's two biggest icons – the Sydney Harbour Bridge and the Sydney Opera House – but also the stuff of daily Sydney life. Who wouldn't want to live in a harbour-view apartment, drop by one of the countless sandy beaches on the way home from work or learn to sail? Perhaps best of all, you could be taking this ferry on your daily commute from downtown Sydney to a home in Manly (12km north), a suburb which has not one but two beaches of its own, one facing the harbour, the other overlooking the high-rolling surf of the Pacific Ocean.

Fittingly, the Manly ferry sets off from alongside Sydney's oldest neighbourhood, The Rocks, site of the first permanent European settlement in 1788 and now a sort of neighbourhood theme park, with its preserved homes, museums and twee cafés. A few minutes later the ferry chugs you within waving distance of the

Bridge and all eyes swivel right for captivating views of the shell-shaped Opera House, with sea-sparkle in the foreground.

Want a different perspective of the harbour? Sign up for the Bridge Climb, a three-and-a-half-hour tour that takes you on to the girders of Sydney Harbour Bridge itself, and up to the summit of its eastern arch, 134m above the harbour waters. Once primed and prepped, you're clad in a regulation steel-grey jumpsuit and clipped on, steeplejack-style, to the railings, as you negotiate ladders and catwalks in the footsteps of your tour leader. Aside from awesome high-level vistas, you get to learn about the construction of its mammoth 503-metre-long arch, completed in 1932. Seventy-five years on and the Harbour Bridge is still the enduring symbol of the Sydney good life, linking the city's energetic business and historical districts with those ever-so-desirable North Shore suburbs across the water.

AUSTRALIA You're only going to do this once, so do it right and see it all. Across the tropical north from Cape Leveque, Western Australia to Cape York on Queensland's northern tip, it's a two-month, 8000-kilometre adventure via the Northern Territory's striking Central Deserts.

Broome, on the dazzling turquoise Indian Ocean is a great place to start, right beside the pearly sands of Cable Beach. The journey kicks off with the suspension-mashing 700-kilometre Gibb River Road; starting near Derby, it cuts through the Kimberley region's untamed ranges, known as Australia's "Alaska". Along the way, turn-offs tempt you to idyllic waterfalls like the Bell Creek Gorge where water rolls off a series of ledges into shallow inviting pools.

The Gibb finally spits you out at Kununurra township, where you can stock up on provisions and, hopefully, team up with another vehicle for the stretch ahead. Now comes the lonely 1500-kilometre all-dirt stage into the Territory and down to Alice Springs, notable for the only traffic lights en route until Cairns.

Exploring Alice's hinterland and weaving among the majestic ghost gum trees along the shady Finke River track to Uluru (Ayers Rock) is an adventure in itself. Moving on from the Rock, scoot eastwards to the solitary Mount Dare homestead; fill up here and then head out across the dune fields of the Simpson Desert to join the pilgrimage to the legendarily remote *Birdsville Hotel*, Australia's best-known bush pub.

Have a drink, then head any which way northeast across Queensland's flat dusty interior. It's time to get ready for the 1000-kilometre creek-crossing climax of your journey: the "Trip to the Tip". Between you and the Pacific lies one of the most ecologically diverse habitats on the planet: creeper-draped rainforest teeming with tombstone anthills and dayglo snakes.

Watching the sunset over Cape York, your journey is complete; the red dust is now in your blood and what you've missed of the Australian outback is a very short list indeed.

956

OCEAN TO OCEAN, CAPE TO CAPE: ACROSS AUSTRALIA BY 4WD

957 TAKING A TRIP TO HELL ON EARTH

NEW ZEALAND You'll no doubt smell Rotorua before you even reach the city limits. It isn't known as the "Sulphur City" for nothing, and the bad-egg smell gets everywhere. Thankfully you get used to it after an hour or so.

The whole city sits on a thin crust of earth underlain by a seething cauldron of waters and superheated steam that seem desperate to escape. Walking around you'll see puffs of vapour rising out of people's backyards, and stormwater drains venting sulphurous jets. Crypts predominate in the cemeteries as graves can't be dug into the ground, and on the shores of Lake Rotorua gulls are relieved of the chore of sitting on their ground-built nests – the earth is warm enough to incubate without assistance.

Half a dozen spectacularly active areas are home to some dramatic geothermal wonders. Tourists have been flocking for over a century to see the Pohutu geyser, which regularly spouts to 20m; around the turn of the millennium it performed continuously for an unprecedented 329 days. It still spouts several times a day, a spectacular show that's heralded by the Prince of Wales Feathers geyser. Mineral deposits turn lakes wild shades of orange and green, and steam forces its way through the earth to form boiling mud pools patterned with myriad concentric circles.

Weary bones are also well-catered for in Rotorua – just about every motel and campground has a hot pool in which to soak. Make a point of seeking out genuine mineral ones filled by therapeutic geothermal waters, whether it be hydrothermal pampering in sophisticated resorts or back-to-basics natural pools out in the woods under the stars.

958 DOING THE CROCODILE ROCK IN KAKADU NATIONAL PARK

AUSTRALIA "He was right by the base of that paperbark tree when the croc got him," says Nerida, our guide, as we unpack our picnic lunch on the edge of the West Alligator River. We're only a few hours drive out of Darwin and already this is her third crocodile tale, each new anecdote regaled with greater enthusiasm than the one before. Her eyes twinkle mischievously as she watches us quickly retreat back up the bank. "The poor guy didn't even have time to blink," she continues, with a deadpan delivery honed over countless tours. It's hard to tell if she has spiced up the story for us or not, but there's no doubting the reverential tone in her voice. Out here, I begin to understand, the crocodile is still king.

Nearly everyone you meet in Kakadu National Park has got a croc story to tell. And it's easy to see why: Kakadu is archetypal outback – Crocodile Dundee was filmed amongst the gum trees here – and it exudes a feeling of raw nature. Acres of bleached eucalypti stand silhouetted against a rich sapphire sky; fertile floodplains and billabongs, laced with water lilies and swollen from the recent rain, teem with some of the park's exotic wildlife: large goanna lizards, the blue-winged kookaburra, rare wallaroos and, of course, the saltwater crocodile, the park's most notorious resident.

After a few days spent exploring its woodlands, wetlands and sandstone escarpments, I was beginning wonder if I would leave Kakadu without seeing a quick glimpse of jagged tail. But stopping off on our drive back to Darwin for a cruise on the Adelaide River, I got it. The water was brown and still, and as our boat chugged upstream, a rugged outline broke the surface a few metres up ahead, scything through the water towards us. "A croc like that won't have got that old and that big without being more than a little clever," declares Nerida, checking that everyone onboard has their arms tucked firmly inside the boat. I just stare, transfixed, as nearly two hundred million years of immutable natural history glides slowly off into the distance.

959 GETTING HIGH ON THE GILLESPIE PASS

NEW ZEALAND Clinging to the sheer cliff turtle-style with a 15kg pack that defied gravity, I knew I couldn't afford to put a foot wrong: one slip on the scree and I'd plummet 500m. Forget bungee jumping and speed boats – if you want white-knuckle New Zealand, climb the Gillespie Pass. Below me, the steely grey crags of the Young Basin were shrinking, while above me the almighty 2,200m bulk of Mount Awful loomed large. When it comes to names, the Kiwis certainly know how to pick 'em.

After a series of tight switchbacks, I finally reached the Gillespie Pass: a rocky saddle speckled with brilliant wildflowers and random patches of snow. The tremendous panorama of the Southern Alps spread out in front of me, their peaks piercing the sky. Up here, only a lonesome kea shattered the silence with its shrill squawk. The feeling of being alone above the world was beyond words and a million miles away from New Zealand's more populated hikes. This was hardcore. As if to prove my point, a bitter wind blew across from Mount Awful where threatening storm clouds were gathering. A hostile reminder that Siberia lay ahead.

The Siberia Valley is cold. Incredibly cold. The sort of cold that even when you're cocooned in a -10°C sleeping bag creeps in and chills you to the bone. The star-studded, moonlit night illuminated the ice-cold river and the summit of Mount Dreadful (presumably Mount Awful's little brother). Frozen and sleepy, the final test of my mettle was the uphill climb to Crucible Lake the next morning. The boulder-strewn trek was tough, but the lake awesome: a glacier-gouged crater filled with turquoise water and chinking icebergs. It looked like an alpine pasture struck by a meteorite. New Zealand boasts many great walks, but if you're seeking the real deal, this has got to be it.

LEARNING TO
SURF
ON THE GOLD COAST

AUSTRALIA Mastering the art of riding a wave is not as tricky as it looks, and the southernmost coast of Queensland is one of the best surfing nurseries on the planet. Here the swell along the 40km beach from Coolangatta to South Stradbroke Island is untamed by the Barrier Reef's wave-dampening atolls further north. Between those two points you can't miss the high-rise blight of Surfers Paradise, Australia's domestic holidaymaking "Costa", but as far as you're concerned it's the reliable and easy surf that matters.

With tropical cyclones animating the Pacific swell, summer is the time to watch the surfing pros, while the temperate winter is the time to learn. From April to October the regular waves break safely over sand here and the warm, waist-deep water makes it all the more pleasurable. If you've got a good sense of balance, you'll be at an advantage; though most surf schools promise to have you at least standing on the board by the end of a typical two-hour session, and surfing properly in a day or two.

Catching a wave is the name of the game, something that you can teach yourself anytime on a short boogie board. The next big step on a full-size board is getting from prone to on your feet and arms out. Soon enough you'll be moving over the water and adopting the classic stance, even if the wave's only halfway up your shin. Get it right and you'll experience a taste of the bigger rush, the raw surge of adrenaline which is what surfing's all about. But everyone's got to start somewhere and for the novice surf junkie the beaches around Surfers Paradise couldn't be more aptly named.

SWIMMING WITH
WHALE
SHARKS

AT NINGALOO REEF

AUSTRALIA Once a year the world's largest fish makes an appearance at the Ningaloo Reef fringing Western Australia's North West Cape. Its arrival is strategically timed with a moonlit night in late summer when coral polyps spawn en masse, ejecting millions of eggs into the tropical waters. Guided by some arcane instinct on their northbound migration from the polar depths, the hungry whale sharks are waiting, mouths agape.

More whale than shark, this fifteen-metre-long gentle giant is twice the size of the great white of Jaws fame but entirely harmless to humans. It survives by ingesting all the krill, plankton and seasonal spawn that its metre-wide mouth can scoop in. For the whale shark the weeks that follow the coral spawning are equivalent to being locked up in a sweetshop for a night.

Not surprisingly the North West Cape has become the world's prime destination for diving and snorkelling with these seasonal

stars of Ningaloo. Spotter planes search for the telltale shadows and radio the boats below, which race into position ahead of the shark: after what may have been many hours of waiting, suddenly it's all action as you hurriedly don your kit. On the boat's rear platform they give the signal and you leap in, fins kicking hard, following the lead diver. As the bubbles clear a solitary grey silhouette looms out of the murk, its back speckled with white spots. With lazy sweeps of its tailfin, this oceanic behemoth glides gently by and for a couple of minutes, using your own fins, you do your best to keep up. This silent encounter with a shark longer than the boat you just jumped off should trigger alarm bells but strangely, as you swim alongside, you're mesmerized by its benign bulk until it dives effortlessly down into the abyss. You rise to the surface elated at having crossed paths with the biggest shark on the planet – and lived to tell the tale.

962 LAZING ABOUT AT HOT WATER BEACH

NEW ZEALAND Like beaches? Like soaking in hot springs? Combine the two at Hot Water Beach, where the receding tide reveals bath temperature water welling up through the sands. It's a beautiful thing to experience, but timing is crucial. Arrive at full tide and there'll be hardly anyone around. Sure the beach is a gorgeous strand of golden sand, but this part of New Zealand doesn't lack for gorgeous beaches.

Sometime around mid-tide you can wander down to the water edge and wriggle your toes down to feel the primal warmth below. An hour or so later families, backpackers and just about anyone with a sybaritic bent will be stopping in at the local shop renting a shovel and joining the throng on the beach. There's quite a communal spirit as people dig into the sand to create a network of shallow pools bolstered by sand embankments. You might have to pick your spot to find the optimum temperature, and at least part of the time you're likely to have surges of cool sea water easing the warmth. Hang around too long and the incoming tide gradually eats away at your defences – it's a good idea to enlist some dam-building kids to stem the tide for as long as possible if you can.

When you feel like you've cooked enough, you can always take a refreshing plunge in the sea. Be careful though, as this isn't the safest beach. Pacific breakers create powerful undertows and even strong swimmers should bathe with caution. With two low tides a day, chances are one will be at a convenient time. Perhaps the best are those that fall in the evening close to full moon: take down a bottle of wine and settle in to gaze up at the stars.

963 ROAD TRIP DOWN UNDER: PERTH TO DARWIN TO ADELAIDE

AUSTRALIA Who can resist the appeal of the open road? The lonesome highway, good company, and your favourite track on the stereo. Allowing hostel happy-hours to merge into weeks or getting lobstered under the ozone hole is all very well, but it's a big country out there, one which is full of adventure.

Let's say you settle for an easy-going two-month trip of around 8000km, from Perth to Darwin and down to Adelaide. Once out of the city you can count the number of traffic lights all the way to your final destination on the fingers of one hand. It's the open road all right; any more open and you'd fall right through it.

Don't expect too much until you can get past Kalbarri or even Monkey Mia, 1000km from Perth. Near here you cross the 26th parallel and a sign proclaims: "Welcome to the Nor'West"; now you're in the real Outback. Be warned: you'll need to fill up your tank at every roadhouse from here on out, and you may end up camping in lay-bys, so be prepared; it's all part of the adventure.

North of Carnarvon, lovely Coral Bay is worth the diversion, as is swinging inland to explore the awesome gorges in Karijini National Park. Chilling in laid-back Broome is compulsory, too, before heading across the top to Northern Territory's capital, Darwin, still 2000km away and nearer to Singapore than Sydney. Whatever the season, wet or dry, it's hot here, day and night.

From Darwin you head south down the barrel of the 3000km Stuart Highway. Triple-trailer roadtrains almost blow you off the road and the stark, dusty landscape makes you ponder, "Just how many anthills are there in the Northern Territory?" As you near the Central Desert, crisp horizons stretch out. The air feels fresher, the locals less deranged. You don't want to miss seeing Uluru or a night spent underground in the opal-mining town of Coober Pedy. Then Adelaide, and right on cue your long-suffering wagon's doors fall off. Patch it up and sell it on. It did it once and it can do it again.

964 A WALK ROUND ULURU

AUSTRALIA As you cruise westwards along the Lasseter Highway, you get your first glimpse of Uluru over cinnamon-red dunes while still 50km distant. Slowly the ochre-coloured monolith invades the empty horizon; it's hard to look at anything else. Then, just past the Uluru-Kata Tjuta National Park gates, you turn a bend, and suddenly it fills your field of vision. You simply have to stop and take a picture.

The Rock means different things to different people. To the Pitjanjarra people who've lived in its shadow for 20,000 years, "Uluru" is the name of a seasonal waterhole near the summit, formerly revealed only to initiates of the Mala wallaby clan during secret ceremonies. To them the mountain is no Mecca-like shrine, but a vital, resource-rich landmark at the intersection of various trails in the region. These "songlines" criss-cross the desert and any conspicuous natural features found along them were put into songs celebrating the "Dreaming" or Creation, to help memorize the way and so "learn the country".

To most tourists Uluru – or Ayers Rock (as it was named by explorer William Gosse in 1873 to honour his benefactor) – is still a climb to be conquered or a radiant landmark to be photographed en masse from the Sunset Viewing Area. But a far better way of getting into the spirit of the place is to take the nine-kilometre walk through waist-high grass around its base. Geologically the massif is a series of near-vertical strata inexplicably thrust up above all around it. Looking rather like a weathered loaf of sliced bread, its grooves and cliffs vary with your perspective. Approaching the "slices" end-on reveals smooth gullies carved into the rock and feeding waterholes like Mutijulu Springs shaded by groves of casuarina oaks. A few kilometres further the steep flanks harbour caves and bizarre scalloped formations, some of them sacred sites fenced off from visitors: every bend in the track offers another startling profile. When you're back at the start of the circuit, hot and sticky from the sun, you can be satisfied that you've experienced the Rock and not merely stood on top of it.

965 GOING ORGANIC IN THE NORTHERN TERRITORY

AUSTRALIA It's 5am; dawn's mellifluous chorus of the early-waking birds propel me into consciousness even before the sun can wrap its (not so temperate) fingers around the eucalypts. The air, fresh with lemon and lime, wafts through the mosquito-net mesh that passes for the windows of my tin shack. Perfect timing – I can just about fit in a spot of breakfast before work.

Thus begins a typical day down on Wilderness Organic Farm, 50km north of Katherine in Australia's Outback, Northern Territory. Part of WWOOF (World-Wide Opportunities on Organic Farms), which was set up by Sue Coppard in 1971 and now has national organizations in 24 countries, Wilderness takes in willing workers for anything from a week to several months, providing them with a bed for the night and three meals a day (organic, of course) in exchange for five hours of daily work – anything from planting capsicum and tomato seedlings, mulching lemon plants and harvesting mangoes to painting farm buildings, cooking and baking. Anything, basically, that might need doing in the daily life of a sub-tropical, Outback agricultural establishment. And by "smoko", an archaic Aussie term for mid-morning tea break, you'll be glad you got the hard graft out of the way during the cooler part of the day, as temperatures soar to 40°C by 11am.

There's certainly never a dull moment when you're working and living with locals, migrant workers and backpackers from all over the world, swapping stories (and a few toasted marshmallows) around the campfire. Besides, work will be nothing but a distant memory by the time you've cooled off in the Edith River after lunch, eaten barbecued kangaroo with homebrewed mango wine for dinner, and been lulled to sleep by a symphony of cicadas under a star-puckered black canvas at night.

966 PARIS IN THE PACIFIC

NEW CALEDONIA With its French food, wine and language, this island 1500km east of Australia brings a trés sophistiqué touch to the timeless, laidback South Pacific.

Visit the giant department store Geant-Sainte-Marie in the bustling capital to pick up some top-notch brie and a bottle of quality red. While staking out a sunny picnic spot, you'll pass clusters of Melanesian local kids playing soccer on the beach. Afterwards, snorkel the second largest barrier reef in the world, before heading to one of the many cafés and restaurants dotted along the Baie de Citron in Nouméa. Sit back and relax with an aperitif while watching the beautiful people stroll by – it's much like Paris, but with a beach view.

967 DIVING THE COOLIDGE

VANUATU There is no other wreck on earth like the *SS President Coolidge*, sunk in 1942 during wartime off the island of Espiritu Santo in Vanuatu. This 210-metre-long troop ship (and ex-luxury cruiser) is so huge you could dive here for a year and not see the half of it. Fin down the guide line into the deep blue, ending at the stern; from there, it's over the hull to where a hatch has been cut in the side. You're in darkness, following flashlight beams and rising bubbles along claustrophobic corridors. Forty-five deep metres and vision is shutting down like somebody pulled the plug; you adjust and the lights come back on. Down past dials, panels and machinery – the engine room – then there's a flash of grey and blue and you're on the sand outside the wreck, 60m down with half your air left. Time for a mellow ascent to the surface.

968 TAKING IN THE VIEWS ON THE TONGARIRO CROSSING

NEW ZEALAND Alpine tundra, barren volcanic craters, steaming springs and iridescent lakes – the sheer diversity on the Tongariro Crossing makes it probably the best one-day tramp in the country. The wonderfully long views are unimpeded by the dense bush that crowds most New Zealand tracks, and from the highest point you can look out over almost half the North Island with the lonely peak of Mount Taranaki dominating the western horizon.

The hike crosses one corner of the Tongariro National Park – wild and bleak country, encompassing the icy tops of nearby Mount Ruapehu, which is, at 2797m, the North Island's highest mountain. Catch the Crossing on a fine day and it is a hike of pure exhilaration. The steep slog up to the South Crater sorts out the genuinely fit from the aspirational, then just as the trail levels out, Mount Ngauruhoe (2291m) invites the keen for a two-hour side-trip up Ngauruhoe's scoria slopes. The reward is a stupendous view down into the gently steaming crater, and a longer one of the rest of the Crossing. Getting back on track is a heart-pounding hell for leather scree run back down the mountain coving, in fifteen minutes what took you an hour and a half to ascend.

The gaping gashes and sizzling fissures around Red Crater make it a lively spot to tuck into your sandwiches and ponder the explosive genesis of this whole region. From here it is mostly downhill past Emerald Lake, its opaque waters a dramatic contrast to the shimmering surface of Blue Lake just ahead. With the knowledge you've broken the back of the hike you can relax on the verandah of Ketetahi Hut gazing out over the tussock to glistening Lake Taupo in the distance. Rejuvenated, you pass the sulphurous Ketetahi Hot Springs on the final descent, down to the green forest and the welcome sight of your bus. Tired but elated you settle back in the seat dreaming of a good feed and the chance to relive the events of the day over a couple of beers.

969 SPYING ON PENGUINS AND ALBATROSSES ALONG THE OTAGO PENINSULA

NEW ZEALAND There's a knee-high, yellow-eyed penguin preening itself less than five metres away from me, and fifteen metres beyond him a sheep is grazing in lush meadows. It's an odd juxtaposition, probably one only to be found in New Zealand where, despite a lack of icebergs and tidewater glaciers, penguins abound. With two penguin species, a colony of seals and the world's only mainland Royal albatross colony, the Otago Peninsula is a fantastic place for a day's wildlife watching.

They're shy creatures, these penguins, but here at Penguin Place they're barely aware of our presence. We're shoulder-deep in a dugout trench draped with camouflage netting, half a dozen of us huddled together in a strategically positioned hide overlooking fields, patches of wetland and a golden beach. As we walked over the hills to the trenches we saw a couple of penguins slowly waddling up the beach returning home from their day's fishing, but it's only in the hides that we get to see them up close as they do their ablutions. Most of the four or five birds out this afternoon are just grooming and watching the world go by, but the setting feels so intimate that I could watch for hours.

Dragging ourselves away, we head 10km up the road to Pilot's Beach where we wander among southern fur seals sprawled languidly along the shore. We'll be back here after dark to watch more penguins (little blues this time) toddle up the beach to their nesting holes in the bank.

On the hill above the beach, Taiaroa Head, we're guided into another hide, this one the converted remains of a WWII viewing tower. High on this grassy headland we can look out over a couple of dozen of Royal albatrosses – a truly majestic bird with up to a 3.5-metre wingspan. Quite a sight in full flight. It's mid-summer and the chicks are growing nicely, but are still vulnerable and spend most of their time tucked under a parent's wing. With binoculars you can see their fluffy heads poking out, desperate to learn more about the big world out there. They'll get their chance soon enough and spend their lives circling the globe before returning here every two years to breed.

970 HELI-SKIING THE SOUTHERN ALPS

NEW ZEALAND As the helicopter pulls away from the snow you begin to get a sense of scale. Five perfect powder tracks recently laid down by you and your companions look increasingly lonely in this wide mountain bowl. Climbing higher they disappear altogether, replaced by mindblowing views over the tops of New Zealand's Southern Alps. It is already clear that this will be no ordinary day's skiing.

Now you are deposited at the top of a razorback ridge. You grab a last look at the jagged peaks piercing a deep blue sky then launch down a chute, putting in half a dozen quick turns. Soon the slope begins to ease and you're back out onto the treeless mountain basin shredding the knee-deep powder.

No tows, no groomer tracks, no queues, no crowds – just you, a guide and three or four companions creating multiple S-curves on a pure white canvas. With runs dropping 600 to 800 metres it is as exhausting as it is exhilarating, and when you reconvene near the snowline your tired bodies struggle to recuperate before the return of the helicopter. And then it is back to the top for one more very long run before a welcome lunch break out on the slopes.

DISCOVERING THE SECRETS OF
KINGS CANYON

AUSTRALIA If you're looking for adventure amidst the awe-inspiring scenery of Australia's Red Centre, you'd be hard-pushed to find somewhere that can match the spectacle of Kings Canyon in Watarrka National Park.The pale orange walls of the sandstone canyon were carved out during a more humid climatic epoch, thousands of years ago. Today it lies in a scrubby semi-desert of scurrying lizards and gnarled trees. The main attraction here is the six-kilometre walk taking you up and around the canyon's rim. Along the way you'll uncover a variety of wildlife and their habitats, from rocky crevices to palm-filled gorges, and can wander off the track as close as you dare to the very edge of the 100m cliffs.

Early morning is the best time to head out, starting from the car park you begin with a fifteen-minute stepped ascent that will get your heart pumping. But don't be put off; at the top the worst is over and from here the trail leads through the "Lost City", a maze of sandstone domes where interpretive boards fill you in on the surrounding geology and botany.

Back on the signed track you clamber down into a palm-filled chasm which you cross via an impressive timber bridge. Spinifex pigeons and other birds dart overhead, while on the far side there's an easily missed ten minute detour downstream to a shady pool. Most tour groups are content to sit here, eating their snacks, but the highlight of the walk and a secret known to few, is looking out from the very throat of the canyon above a dry waterfall. You can get there either by wading knee-deep round the right bank of the pool, scrambling over the rock above, or simply gritting your teeth and swimming across. Peering from the brink you get a perfectly framed view of the sunlit south wall and the canyon far below. Returning to the bridge, the walk takes you back to the very rim of the overhanging south wall above the jumbled rocks, before descending gently back to the car park.

972 FOUR-WHEELING THROUGH CROC COUNTRY: CAIRNS TO CAPE YORK

AUSTRALIA Most of us have little use for 4WDs, but in a particular corner of Australia these all-terrain machines can provide the sort of adventure they were truly built for. Cape York, Australia's northernmost point, is over 1000km from Cairns, with challenging driving that will demand concentration and an understanding of your vehicle's abilities as you gingerly inch across tidal creeks inhabited by crocodiles.

From Cairns head out along the scenic Captain Cook Highway to Cooktown: the last settlement of any size on your "Trip to the Tip". Choose either the coastal route via Cape Tribulation, where Cook's Endeavour nearly sank in 1770 or, for a real adventure, the infamous "CREB Track" out of Daintree. Here's your chance to play with the transfer levers as you run along the CREB's tyre-clawing gradients to the *Lion's Den Hotel*, a classic "bush pub" dating back to 1875.

Past Cooktown the Lakefield National Park is Queensland's answer to Kakadu, with "magnetic" anthills aligned north–south to avoid overheating in the noonday sun, 180 species of birds and a rich colony of flying foxes.

But there's more. A tough, creek-ridden diversion leads east to the Iron Range National Park, where the creeper-festooned rainforests don't recede until Chilli Beach campsite on the Coral Sea. Ecologically this extraordinary park has more in common with New Guinea and is famed for the nocturnal green python and brilliant blue-and-red eclectus parrot.

Back on the main road die-hards avoid the newer bypasses to follow the Old Telegraph Track's numerous creek crossings. Eventually you arrive at Twin Falls, with its safe swimming holes, before reaching the 100-metre-wide Jardine River, a once demanding crossing now made easier by the nearby ferry. Then suddenly the road runs out near a rocky headland overlooking the Torres Straits. A sign marks the tip of mainland Australia and the end of your journey.

973 A WORLD AWAY ON THE LANDSBOROUGH RIVER

NEW ZEALAND There's something about the South Island's Landsborough River that bends the mind. The water's crystal clarity binds the light so the river becomes a luminous ribbon slicing through the mountains. It's pure, too: whenever you get thirsty rafting the Landsborough, simply dunk your cup in the ice cold water and drink it down.

A chopper dropped us deep in New Zealand's Southern Alps. Glacier-laden mountains stood in stark relief against the blue sky. It would take three days to reach civilization, if all went well.

The sun held sway for two days, igniting the river's intense turquoise colour, but the water was subject to changing moods. We tackled fuming rapids hungry to consume our meagre raft, followed by idyllic calm stretches where the forest loomed close and lofty mountains crowded the sky.

Each evening we set up camp beneath ancient beech trees swaying with moss and inhabited by curious native birds. A green silence settled over the forest as night fell, and we wandered beyond camp to where glow-worms pierced the darkness like earthbound stars, clustered in constellations amongst the dense undergrowth.

Our final day on the river, low storm clouds swallowed the mountaintops and a cold headwind bit through our wetsuits. The river rose to a muddy grey torrent and each paddle stroke took effort. We put our heads down and paddled into the wind, pitched in a silent battle against the elements.

It was with a mixture of relief and disappointment that we saw the waiting minibus came into view on shore. New Zealand's wilderness has a way of making you think the rest of the world no longer exists.

974 HELI-BIKING BEN CRUACHAN

NEW ZEALAND The helicopter dropped its load on the mountaintop and swooped back down into the valley. Patches of snow lay on the ground, clouds hung low overhead and the air had a crisp, alpine bite. In every direction thrusting peaks stood in ranks, punctuated by fertile green valleys. The small group of downhill mountain bikers watched the helicopter diminish into a speck and breathed in a deep gulp of alpine air before donning helmets, gloves and body armour. They pointed their front tyres downhill and let gravity take care of the rest.

Ben Cruachan, a 2000m peak tucked behind the Remarkables, the mountain range that flanks the picturesque resort of Queenstown, is a favourite of many backcountry mountain bikers. It's no surprise why: it offers 1600 metres of pure downhill

adrenalin. And that's after the rush of flying up to the top.

The riders followed a rough 4WD road down the ridgeline from the summit. It was littered with loose shale, demanding both balance and patience to navigate. After a few kilometres the bikers veered left onto a technical single track snaking down a steep valley. The higher reaches of the track were fast and fun; further down, shallow water races cut across the trail and bucked riders over the handlebars or submerged their tyres in bogs.

Two hours after alighting on the mountain's summit, the riders hit the final gravel stretch. They raced each other downhill, sliding around corners and using their bike's full suspension to bunny hop rocks and potholes, before rolling up breathless on the valley floor.

975 WAITANGI: RELIVING THE BIRTH OF A MODERN NATION

NEW ZEALAND On February 6 1840, representatives of the British Crown and several dozen northern Maori chiefs met in a marquee on the lawns in front of the Waitangi Treaty House to sign the Treaty of Waitangi. The Maori chiefs were rightly suspicious of British motivations and it remains debatable whether they knew they were signing away their sovereignty. It was a tense time, but sign they did, and the Treaty became not just New Zealand's founding document, but the cornerstone of the country's race relations to this day.

Arriving at the Treaty Grounds, you walk straight out onto that hallowed lawn with its views out over the Bay of Islands and its historic flagpole where Maori and British flags still fly. Inquisitive foreign visitors, and Kiwis in search of their heritage, gravitate towards the 1834 Treaty House itself, all neat white weatherboards and rooms containing material on the early colonial period.

When the Maori arrived for the signing, most would have come by canoe – but few would have been as big as Ngatoki Matawhaorua, now in residence down by the shore. The world's largest wooden war canoe, it stretches more than 35m from prow to gloriously carved sternpost and took over two years to carve from a pair of massive kauri tree trunks. Eighty warriors are needed to paddle it during its annual outing on the anniversary of the signing of the Treaty.

Lolling-tongue carved figures with iridescent seashell eyes greet you at whare rununga, or Maori meeting house, up beside the lawn – the only pan-tribal meeting house in the country.

For a deeper understanding of the whare rununga's significance, return in the evening for the stirring Night Show. Through heartfelt dance, song and storytelling you'll get a primer in the richness of Maori legend and history and learn a good deal about modern Maori life and how the Treaty remains so essential to it.

976 TALL-SHIP SAILING IN THE INDIAN OCEAN

AUSTRALIA Slung over a yardarm, the deck, some 30m below your feet, seems impossibly tiny. The ship rolls, giving you a glimpse of the sky before listing towards the sea. On either side your shipmates are strung out along the yardarm like flags, everyone fumbling with the knots that keep the ship's sails neatly folded in the rigging. As you watch the thick, creamy-coloured canvas fall away and fill with wind, it is impossible not to think of the generations of seafarers who have sailed these waters before you.

The Indian Ocean stretches from the shores of Africa to the coast of Australia, washing up against India and Indonesia along the way, and has been a scene of conflict and adventure for centuries. Luckily, life on board these days is a lot more comfortable, with hot showers, a private bunk and wonderful food, but everyone is still expected to take a turn at scrubbing the decks, taking helm and standing a watch. In fact, you can be called on deck at any time of the day or night to dress the yards, propelled from bunk to rigging in a matter of minutes.

Shuffling along the yardarm towards the safety of the mast, the harness around your waist that clips onto the rigging is little comfort as the ship surges forward in the wind. Narrow rigging ladders run up and down the masts but also out over the bowsprit that sticks out of the front of the ship. From here you can feel every rise and fall of the waves, your legs dangling over the foaming water, mere feet from the dolphins that leap just in front of the ship's bow.

In every direction there is nothing but an empty horizon, yours the only ship in a vast ocean.

977 PADDLING THROUGH ABEL TASMAN NATIONAL PARK

NEW ZEALAND Some people hike along the coast of Abel Tasman National Park, others cruise through its glassy waters, but by far the best way to explore New Zealand's smallest and most intimate national park is by sea kayak. The sheltering arm of Farewell Spit ensures the waters are seldom rough, so even completely inexperienced paddlers can head out for several days in relative safety.

Above all, this type of trip is about enjoying yourself at a relaxed tempo. And not only can you take to the shore at a pace that exactly suits you, but also the kayak can carry the load of all the wine, beer and tasty delicacies you'll want to bring along. A wide choice of golden beaches with designated camping spots are at your disposal to stop and indulge in your goodies, spend the afternoon lazing on the sand, explore rock pools or take a dip. Pack a mask and snorkel so you can watch the shoals of fish weaving among the rocks and kelp beds.

It is tempting to stay put for one more lazy day, but there are still more winding estuaries to paddle. You can also explore vestiges of human occupation that date back 150 years, before this area was set aside as protected land. The stub of a wharf marks the spot where granite was quarried and you can search out the quarry and grub surrounds looking for the foundations of quarrymen's huts.

One essential stop is the Tonga Island Marine Reserve, where the rocks come slathered with seals. These playful creatures have been known to come up to swimmers and cavort for a while before deciding there is something more entertaining happening elsewhere.

When you crave something a little more sophisticated than dinner cooked over a camp stove, wend your way up the delightful estuary of the Awaroa River, where a few lodges inhabit patches of private land. Stop in for a sandwich and an espresso or a beer on the deck; if you're feeling flush and hankering for white linen you can stay the night. A perfect finale to a glorious few days of relaxation.

FOLLOWING IN
GAUGUIN'S
FOOTSTEPS

TAHITI Palms drooping languidly towards the ocean, vivid clumps of pink hibiscus and great patches of melon yellow and luminescent green. The "primitivism" Paul Gauguin found so appealing in Tahiti may be long gone, but the mesmerizing landscapes he painted are still here. The botanical gardens outside his museum are often deserted in the mornings: lounge under the canopy of a plump banana plant and imagine the artist creating his raw, expressive paintings, just across the river.

In 1891, Gauguin sailed to the Pacific to escape "everything that is artificial and conventional". His hut in Mataiea on the south coast of Tahiti no longer stands, but the absorbing Musée Gauguin nearby has exhibits about his life and work. To continue the trail you must fly to the fertile, ridge-backed island of Hiva Oa, where Gauguin made his final journey in 1901. Here you'll find a re-creation of his florid *Maison du Jour,* another small museum and finally, the rustic stone tomb where he was buried in 1903, appropriately sprinkled with bright yellow and ruby-red flowers.

978

979 HORSING AROUND ON AN AUSSIE BEACH

AUSTRALIA Beaches are an Australian way of life. For the most part, it's a nation of surfers, bronzed gods and goddesses strolling around in Speedos and barely-there bikinis, sizzling sun-lovers who enjoy nothing better than a dip in the ocean. But surely there's something else to the beach, something more than donning a wetsuit and jumping on a board, or rotating on a towel like a rotisserie chicken?

On a mission to discover an alternative, a friend and I headed to Blazing Saddles, a trail-ride company close to Victoria's Great Ocean Road. Jen drew the short straw and mounted the archetype of group horses – the slow one which enjoys regular toilet stops. Saddled up and helmets on, we headed through Angahook-Lorne State Park and marvelled at the profuse birdlife and lush scenery. We headed across the famous coastal road and hooves began to sink into the soft sand. I drew a deep breath, gave my horse a squeeze and headed off along the beach, forgetting my lack of experience and knowledge of all things equestrian, blinded by the waves to one side of me and the park on the other.

Suddenly, without warning, my steed began to speed along the sand, the coast unraveling before me. Panic sunk in – how do I get this creature to stop? Then it dawned on me, an oddly soothing idea: I could ride forever.

We eventually slowed down to a more leisurely pace, instigated by an incident which saw me being dragged, one foot in a stirrup, along the sandy beach and finally dislodging myself after half a kilometre. Even with the fall, the beauty of the soft white sands, juxtaposed with the nearby State Park, left me feeling that this was my piece of beach heaven. The bronzed brigade can keep their tanning lotions and surf clubs; I prefer the wind in my hair and the freedom that comes from riding in one of the most picturesque parts of the world.

980 KNOCKING BACK
KAVA

FIJI First, you'll be invited to join the group, languidly assembled around a large wooden bowl. Then, a grinning elder will pass you a coconut shell, saying "tovolea mada" – "try please". You take a look – the muddy pool in the shell looks like dirty dishwater, but what the hell, you sip anyway. And then the taste hits you, a sort of medicinal tonic tinged with pepper. Resist the urge to spit it out and you'll gain the respect of your hosts. Keep drinking, and you'll start to get numb lips, feel mildly intoxicated and if you're lucky, end up as tranquil as your new friends.

It's hard to forget the first time you try kava. Known as yaqona in Fiji, it's made from fresh kava root and has been imbibed for hundreds of years, remaining a potent link to the island's past. For the locals, sharing kava is a long-time social ritual, and it's common for families and friends to drink together at weekends or special occasions – getting invited to join them is one of the island's highlights.

Fiji's past also once included cannibalism, but visitors have long been off the menu, and you can safely take a trip to one of the traditional villages, such as Navala on the main island of Viti Levu, where you'll see houses, or bure, made of bamboo and leaves. The island's rich cultural heritage includes a blend of Polynesian and Melanesian, with nearly half the population of Indian origin. Suva, the capital, is filled with curry houses and even Hindu temples and, given the island's British colonial past, you'll come across numerous evocative colonial remains straight out of a Graham Greene novel, along with magical church choirs that are a harmonious blend of Victorian melodies and tribal soul. Still, if you want to get to the heart of Fiji, drinking kava is a good place to start.

981 WALKING THROUGH THE WOODS IN
WAIPOUA KAURI FOREST

NEW ZEALAND It may seem odd to drive for miles just to look at a bunch of old trees, but the kauri forests of New Zealand's North Island are special. To start with, the kauri trees are staggeringly, sensationally large. The tallest, Tane Mahuta (God of the Forest), towers some fifty metres above the earth; it's the same height as Nelson's Column in London's Trafalagar Square. Its long, straight trunk soars neck-achingly upwards, a smooth, brown cylinder unhindered by branches. Then, from near the top, spiky boughs spray outwards, covered in thousands of tiny, dark-green, oval leaves. The branches look feeble, gnarled and thin compared to the monumental proportions of the trunk, and they betray the tree's age like the wrinkles etched onto an old man's face. But

this tree is older than any man by far. It's reckoned to have started life some two thousand years ago; humans wouldn't even land here for another thousand years.

A walk through this protected sanctuary – European loggers and the gum trade greatly thinned the kauri ranks – takes you from Tane Mahuta to Te Matua Ngahere (Father of the Forest). This tree isn't as tall as Tane Mahuta, but it is phenomenally fat, more than sixteen metres wide. Personality oozes from every crack in its ancient bark. How many before you walked beneath its branches? Which now-extinct birds rested on its boughs? The tree replies with a far-distant rustle of leaves and continues its millennia-long watch.

982 WHAT LIES BENEATH: SNORKELLING AT THE GREAT BARRIER REEF

AUSTRALIA "It's like being in another world!" may be the most predictable observation following a close encounter with the Great Barrier Reef, but it's only when you've come face to face with the extraordinary animals, shapes and colours found beneath the ocean's surface that you realize you've truly entered a watery parallel universe. And as a curious thick-lipped potato cod nudges your mask, you might also wonder, "who exactly is watching who here?" The Great Barrier Reef follows Australia's continental shelf from Lady Elliot Island, in southern Queensland, 2300km north to New Guinea. Its northern reaches are closer to land so, while it's 300km to the main body from Gladstone, Cairns is barely 50km distant, making this the best place for reef day-trips. Scuba diving may get you more quality time down below, but a well-chosen snorkelling location can reveal marvels no less superb without all the bother of training, equipment and lengthy safety procedures. Though commonly called the world's biggest life form, the Great Barrier Reef is more an intricate network of patch reefs than a single entity. All of it, however, was built by one animal: the tiny coral polyp which grows together to create modular colonies – corals. These in turn provide food, shelter and hunting grounds for a bewildering assortment of more mobile creatures.

Rays, moray eels and turtles glide effortlessly by, while fish so dazzling they clearly missed out on camouflage training dart between caves to nibble on coral branches, and slug-like nudibranchs sashay in the current. It all unfolds before you one breath at a time, a neverending grand promenade of the life aquatic.

983 SLIP INTO BROOMETIME

AUSTRALIA The laid-back, romantic appeal of Broome stems partly from its uniqueness along the west Australian coastline. In many thousands of kilometres no other town matches its alluring combination of beautiful beaches and relative sophistication. Grotty, industrial Port Hedland, the next town, is 600km and many more light years away.

From its earliest days, Broome's had an ethnically diverse population: Timorese, Malays and Chinese came in their thousands to get rich quick when the pearl industry boomed here in the late 1800s. The world's largest oysters prospered in the tidal waters and shells were originally shovelled off the beach. With the invention of the diving helmet, Asian divers kept the supply going, but along with frequent cyclones the new-fangled technology caused many deaths, as a stroll around the town's different ethnic cemeteries reveals. Pearl farming continues today offshore, from securely guarded pontoons, and Broome remains the best place to buy these gems, particularly along Dampier Terrace.

The old Chinatown has been tastefully renovated, its once grubby tin-shack bordellos are now trendy boutiques, while a mile away the former master pearlers' bougainvillea-shrouded villas house galleries and coffee shops. Nearby, the 1916 Broome Picture House, the world's oldest open-air cinema, is still going strong. Bats flutter across the latest release on screen as you watch under starlight from communal canvas benches; the new air-con cinema round the corner just misses the point. Nature has further blessed Broome with heavenly Cable Beach; here a contented indolence permeates your bones as palm fronds waft lazily in the breeze. The classic vista from Gantheume Point lays red cliffs over ivory sands and a sea so hypnotically turquoise it should carry a health warning. A few years ago some bright spark cooked up the "Stairway to the Moon", the occasional "staircase" illusion created by the moon rising over the low-tide mudflats when viewed from Town Beach. It sounds better than it looks but you don't mind, you're on Broometime after all.

984 WATCHING FOOTY AT THE MCG

AUSTRALIA A Saturday "arvo" at the Melbourne Cricket Ground (MCG) reveals Melbourne at its best. All ages, races and classes are united by one passion: Australian Rules, or "footy" as it's known in this sports-mad city. Footy is Melbourne's religion, and the locals have been passionate followers since the 1850s, when it was first invented here to keep cricketers fit in winter.

Every weekend the nearby railway stations and roads are clogged with fans heading in to "barrack" for their team. If you plan to see a game, choose one between traditional rivals such as Essendon and Carlton, two of Melbourne's oldest teams; the atmosphere will be electric with a guaranteed full house, split 50/50. The scene is tense but never violent, rowdy but not without humour and you'll see just as many women as men cheering on their team.

The fun begins with rousing traditional team songs as players run onto the field, breaking through huge crepe-paper banners, while in the stalls big men wave pompoms in team colours. Though it lacks the ferocity of rugby or the theatrics of soccer, footy is a very physical game -- with kicking, catching, handpasses, footpasses, tackles, bounces, bumps and no offside rules -- and it requires great strength, athleticism and endurance. The players, who are usually long and lean, have been known to run up to twenty kilometres in a match lasting 120 minutes and divided into quarters.

Feeling confused by all the action? Any fan sitting next to you will be happy to fill you in on the finer points. Should you choose to support their team, you're likely to gain a lifelong mate. After all, nothing makes a devotee of a religion happier than a successful conversion.

985 MEETING THE CROCS AT SHADYCAMP

AUSTRALIA Evolving in isolation over millions of years, Australia's idiosyncratic wildlife is the stuff of Disney cartoons. The island continent has given us the bounding kangaroo and the duck-billed platypus (thought to be a hoax when introduced to Victorian society), and who can resist those cuddly koalas? Up in the "Top End" of the country, the shores of the Van Diemen Gulf east of Darwin hold a log-jam of big crocodiles. Though the saltwater or estuarine crocodile is not unique to north Australia, the size they can reach here is exceptional – they're the biggest examples of the world's largest reptiles.

Croc farms around the country allow you to safely poke fun at these gnarled, primeval beasts; many favourites are huge, battle-scarred "rogue crocs" brought into captivity after menacing some remote community. But take away the fencing and a one-to-one wild encounter with the jagged Silurian scowl of a mature saltie will send a quiver of fascinated revulsion across your skin. The best place for a guaranteed fence-free encounter is the tidal barrage at Shady Camp, an old buffalo-hunting base on the Mary River, north of the Arnhem Highway. Here the ebb and flow of the rich tropical sludge gives the resident reptiles all the sustenance they need: fat barramundi or catfish; gangly storks or ibis – sometimes snatched from the air; and feral water buffalo trapped in monsoonal mud. The menu even includes fellow crocs and, of course, you and me.

Territory lore is full of tales of menacing croc attacks and now, nearly half a century after commercial hunting was banned, those Sixties baby-boomers are reaching maturity of eight metres or more and a ton in weight. As you putter among the Shady Camp lilies in your rented outboard, just inches above the occluded surface, sun-baking salties open one eye, slide down the muddy banks and disappear into the water: a timid or provocative response? Hopefully you'll never find out.

986 FILLING UP IN AUCKLAND

NEW ZEALAND Balinese black sticky rice with tropical fruit, coconut cream and palm sugar. Cured salmon bagel with Japanese pickles and wasabi cream cheese. Lemon and dill potato hash cakes with asparagus, poached eggs and smoked paprika hollandaise. Is your mouth watering yet? How about banana and chocolate loaf with berry preserve and yogurt or maybe brioche french toast with blueberries and coffee mascarpone?

These aren't the offerings of a swanky New York hotel breakfast menu but pickings from a handful of Auckland's cafés. Invariably, you'll also be treated to superb coffee and the service will be casual and friendly, with a minimum of ceremony. Is it any wonder then that Aucklanders' favourite thing to do is to head out on the weekend to the dozens of suburban eateries dishing up such sumptuous selections? Although cafés are a particular Auckland speciality, at the ready for a laid-back meal or a simple coffee and slice of homemade carrot cake, often until late evening, Auckland's dynamic food scene is such that you'll be spoilt for choice if you're after a more formal meal too.

Globe-trotting chefs return to New Zealand's shores brimming with innovative Pacific-Rim versions of more traditional dishes. And what's more they have the very best of nature's offerings to play with. This clean, green land produces not only the top-notch lamb the country is so famous for but just about every fruit and vegetable that will withstand the Kiwi climate. Ingredients once alien in these parts are now cultivated; groves of olive trees produce oil that rivals any imported varieties, oak trees have been planted to establish a truffle industry and cheese-makers tired of replicating traditional European varieties now create their own concoctions, often with great aplomb. Let's not forget either, that with harbours on both the Pacific and Tasman coasts, Auckland is particularly blessed with its seafood. When it's all expertly put together and served with a smile, you'd be hard pressed to dine out better anywhere in the world. Who's hungry?

987 RAFTING THE RAPIDS OF THE WILD WEST COAST RIVERS

NEW ZEALAND Standing on a cold riverbank on a misty morning might not sound like much fun, especially when you know that soon you are going to get very wet. Such considerations evaporate when a chopper swoops around the side of a mountain and picks up your small team and its raft.

Seconds later you're in a plastic bubble skimming the tops of the ancient West Coast forests as you follow the river upstream. From above the river looks tame enough, but the reality is something else altogether. In no time you're in untouched wilderness, the fear building as the guides pump up the rafts and run you through the safety drill. And this is no litigation-conscious cover-your-back spiel; there's big water up ahead so guides and guests are mutually reliant for everyone's safety. You can expect around five hours on the water, often getting out to scout upcoming rapids, picking a line then paddling like hell to punch through a wave or avoid a hole. Some of the most thrilling and scenic whitewater trips in the world are offered here (many only explored in the last twenty years) – dramatically steep, they spill out of the alpine wilderness fed by the prodigious quantity of rain that guarantees solid flows. The steepness of the terrain means you're in Grade IV–V territory, so this isn't the right choice for novices. Companies in Rotorua and Queenstown run excellent low-cost trips for first-timers, but connoisseurs will delight in the challenges of West Coast rafting. It's truly heart-thumping stuff, making the wind-down time in a classic rural pub afterwards all the more enjoyable.

988 HIKING SYDNEY'S SPIT TO MANLY WALKWAY

AUSTRALIA The ten-kilometre harbour-side hike that runs through bush, above ragged cliffs and via sandy beaches is surely the world's most scenic city walk – and all of it is along the fringes of Sydney's northern suburbs. You begin at Spit Bridge, which spans the Middle Harbour, and end, an exhilarated three hours later, at the ferry wharf in Manly. Officially known as the Manly Scenic Walkway, the route is well-signed and dead easy to navigate – just keep the sea on your right and let your eyes feast on the scalloped sandstone coastline and the enviable colonial homes that get this view day in and day out. If you're not quite ready for a dip at Clontarf Beach, just 1500m into the walk, you'll surely be tempted when you reach secluded little Washaway Beach, a popular nudist spot. Tramping up to Grotto Point and later on to Dobroyd Head, through unadulterated forest that's protected as Sydney Harbour National Park, you get fabulous panoramas of the Harbour and its ocean jaws, the North and South heads.

989 ART MEETS NATURE ON WAIHEKE ISLAND

NEW ZEALAND Artists, writers and craftspeople have long flocked to Waiheke Island, which lies 35min from Auckland by ferry. It may be the relative isolation that appeals, or perhaps the captivating combination of sandy beaches, verdant native bush, neatly rowed vineyards and alluring eateries. Whatever the reason, creative types thrive in this laidback environment and there's ample opportunity to view the fruits of their labour around the island. Arguably, the best is at Connells Bay Centre for Sculpture. Here, a 2km track through bush and farmland takes you past a medley of stark sculptural works, which amalgamate effortlessly with the surrounding lush vegetation, often framed by awe-inspiring vistas of the Hauraki Gulf beyond – a true union of art and nature.

990 PARAGLIDING OVER THE PADDOCKS

AUSTRALIA Early starts are required to get the best out of paragliding over the vast farmland behind Mount Tambourine in Southern Queensland. The cool morning air, calm and still, gradually heats and begins to show signs of releasing every free-flyer's addiction – thermals. Bubbles of rising warm lift the lucky ones clear off the ground's pull and rewards them with breathtaking views out over the plains towards the Great Dividing Range. Once at cloud base, the hopeful pilots take in the view of rich green pasture intersected by old red dusty scars and wait for 2pm, checking their watches anxiously until the strong coastal breeze hits like a wall and accelerates them and their gliders towards the horizon.

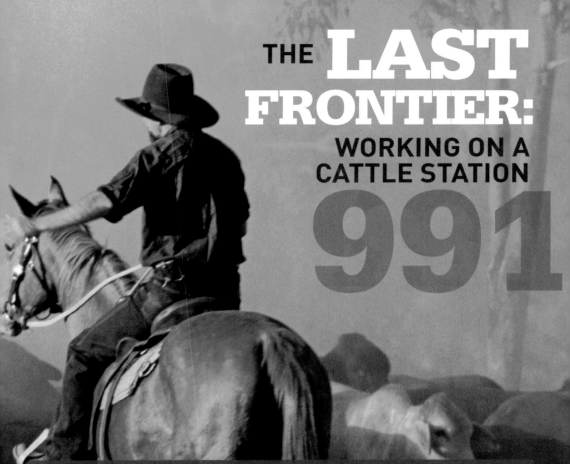

THE LAST FRONTIER:
WORKING ON A CATTLE STATION

991

AUSTRALIA Working on a Kimberley cattle station will be "hard yakka" as they say out here: hard graft for long hours and low pay. You'll be sharing a bunkhouse and meals with rangy stockmen, and objects like TV, telephones, the Internet and even the radio are luxuries you'll have to learn to live without.

But when it's over and the aches have subsided, you'll look back with satisfaction. Instead of passively consuming you'll have participated in an iconic Australian activity immortalized in books like Mary Durack's *Kings in Grass Castles*. You'll have learnt how to brand a bull, built up plenty of muscle, and experienced life in the fabled "Nor'west".

The Kimberley is Australia's last frontier, a place where cattle stations run to a million acres and are on the margins of manageability. The rugged landscape and climate (which in turn floods then burns) make this the harshest cattle country in Australia. But eager hands are always sought so you'll be welcomed, particularly if you've an aptitude for working with horses or motorbikes. With a bit of luck you'll be part of the annual muster, when cattle are tracked down and driven in from the four corners of the property for transport to market. Most stations use horses, dirt- and quad bikes for this, all coordinated from above by helicopters equipped with radios, but you'll be just as useful on foot, coaxing the nervy beasts into mobile yards or triple-trailer roadtrains. You may even get a ride in a bullcatcher, a stripped-down jeep that literally chases, knocks down and half parks on top of the biggest bulls so you can rope them up and drag them into the trailers.

As the theme song of the famous TV show Rawhide put it: "Don't try to understand 'em. Just rope, throw, and brand 'em. Soon we'll be living high and wide. Rawhide!"

MISCELLANY

AUSTRALIA'S FIRST PEOPLE

It is thought the ancestors of today's Aboriginal people arrived on the Australian continent via the Indonesian archipelago at least 40,000 years ago, though the date is probably much earlier. This makes today's descendants part of the world's oldest surviving culture. There were an estimated 750,000 Aboriginal people at the time of colonization in 1787. Following the disastrous impact of this, today's population has recovered to around 450,000 or 2.5 percent of Australia's population.

Aboriginal Dreamtime explains how creative forces shaped the landscape, how humans were created, provides verbal maps of tribal territory and links natural features to the actions of Dreamtime ancestors, who often had both human and animal forms. These stories were often passed down in the form of drawings on the ground or on cave walls, or as dot paintings in the Central and Western deserts.

Maori New Zealand

The precursors to New Zealand's Maori population arrived sometime between AD1200 and 1300. It has always been a strongly verbal culture, and oratory remains highly revered in formal situations. Anyone standing up to speak at a hui (meeting) or tangi (funeral) will first claim their right to speak for their people by reciting their whakapapa (genealogy). This is often followed by a reverential nod to the iwi's (tribe's) local mountain, river or bay and maybe a short legend from the iwi's past.

A BED TO SLEEP IN
FIVE GREAT AUSTRALIAN HOTELS

Adelphi Hotel, 187 Flinders Lane, Melbourne A striking exterior and an ultramodern interior featuring abstract designs make this one of Melbourne's most stylish choices.
The Bush Camp, Faraway Bay, Kimberley, NT Only accessible by small plane or boat, it's a remote coastal wilderness retreat with basic cabins and great food.

Dunk Island Resort, Mission Beach, Qld Low-key resort on a rainforest-clad humpbacked island fifteen minutes by ferry from Mission Beach or an hour's flight from Cairns. Forest walks, snorkelling, heavenly beaches – and it's kid-friendly too.
Intercontinental, 117 Macquarie St, Sydney Get high with stunning harbour views from the top thirty floors of this elegant five-star hotel.
Latitude 131°, Ayers Rock Resort, NT A tucked-away upmarket bush-camp with a handful of luxury tented cabins set among the dunes, all with views of Uluru.

FIVE GREAT NEW ZEALAND LUXURY RETREATS

Blanket Bay Lodge, Glenorchy. An A-list hangout with fabulous Lord of the Rings scenery. Seclusion and discretion guaranteed.
Huka Lodge, Taupo. Consistently rated among the world's finest lodges since 1984, when it was the first of its kind in New Zealand.
Kauri Cliffs Lodge, Kerikeri. Gorgeous sea views and New Zealand's finest golf course.
Treetops Luxury Lodge and Estate, Rotorua. Low-key luxury in a wonderful forest setting.
Wharekauhau, Featherstone. Elegant, Edwardian-style lodge on a large farm ten minutes by helicopter from Wellington.

"I like [her]…and I think she liked me"

Former Australian Prime Minister Paul Keating's uncharacteristically generous appraisal of the Queen

HIGHS, LOWS AND VOLCANOES

Australia is the world's flattest continent with only six percent of its land mass rising above 600m. The highest point is Mount Kosciuszko in NSW, at just 2228m. The lowest point is the usually dry Lake Eyre in South Australia at around 15m below sea level. New Zealand sits astride the Pacific and Australian tectonic plates, on the Pacific Ring of Fire. The major faultline runs from the actively volcanic White Island in the north, through steamy Rotorua and Taupo, through shaky Wellington and down the length of the Southern Alps in the South Island.

SPORT

Australians' love of sport and gambling are closely related though gambling probably came first. The game of **two-up** was brought to Australia by English and Irish convicts and soon spread across the country. It's basically heads or tails but with two coins, thrown up off a wooden "kip". The coins must land as two heads or two tails for the betters of either to win. The greater odds of 4:1 against plain old 2:1 with heads or tails are what gives two-up its edge.

Rugby union is more of a religion than a sport in New Zealand. A single All Black defeat elicits much hand wringing and calls for the head of the coach. Fortunately, that doesn't happen very often. However, the team habitually underperforms at the quadrennial Rugby World Cup and hasn't won the competition since the inaugural event in 1985, despite always seeming to enter as favourites. In 2011, when the country is hosting the event, the All Blacks hope to live up to expectations.

POLITICS

Exchanges between Australian politicians are famously robust and never more so than during the era of Labour Prime Minister, Paul Keating (1991–97). His withering insults flung across the floor of Canberra's New Parliament House became the scourge de jour, and were of course particularly barbed when aimed at opposition leaders. The performance of one-time Liberal leader John Hewson was once likened to "being flogged with a warm lettuce" while the current PM John Howard was described as "… a dead carcass, swinging in the breeze, but nobody will cut it down to replace him."

"Foam will always find its way to the shore"

Solomon Island proverb

FESTIVAL	WHEN AND WHERE
Waitangi Day National holiday with formal events, such as the ceremonial launching of the world's largest war canoe, at Waitangi.	**Feb 6**; throughout New Zealand
Te Mira Ura/Dancer of the Year Competition The highlight of a week-long festival, with plenty of traditional costumes and music.	**April**; Rarotonga, Cook Islands
Laura Aboriginal Dance Festival Electrifying celebration of Aboriginal culture.	**June in odd numbered years**; Laura, QLD, Australia
Matariki Celebration of the Maori New Year with street performances, tree planting and hangi (a traditional Maori feast) nights.	**June**; throughout New Zealand
Beer Can Regatta Beachside race with boats composed entirely of beer cans.	**July, third Sunday**; Darwin, Australia
Melbourne Cup The entire country stops for this 146-year-old horse racing event.	**November, first Tuesday**; Melbourne, Australia

STAYING ALIVE

Australia harbours some of the world's deadliest creatures. Crocodiles come in two types; the misleadingly named saltwater or **estuarine crocodile** can grow to 7m, ranges far inland (often in freshwater), and is the only Australian animal that constitutes an **active threat to humans**; the smaller, shy, inoffensive freshwater crocodile feeds on fish and frogs. Three quarters of the world's most venomous **snakes** can be found in Australia – although the small number of people that actually dwell in prime snake habitats means that India experiences thousands more fatalities a year. Two spiders whose bites can be fatal are the **Sydney funnel-web**, a black, stocky creature found in the Sydney area, and the **small redback**, a relative of the notorious **black widow** of the Americas, usually found in dark, dry locations all over Australia (ie outdoor toilets, under rocks and timber logs). The tropical coastal waters attract venomous **box jellyfish** during the summer months, these are saucer-sized jellyfish with long tentacles up to 3m long, whose venom can cause **rapid unconsciousness** and, in severe cases, **paralysis** of the heart muscles.

GREAT SCREEN MOMENTS
FROM THE OUTBACK TO THE SUBURBS

Babakiueria (1988). Culture-reversing spoof about Aboriginal colonizers coming ashore to disrupt a beachside "barbecue area".

Muriel's Wedding (1994). Set in fictional Porpoise Spit on the less fictional Gold Coast, Toni Collette made her big screen debut in this pre-*Kath and Kim* satire on the ghastlier side of suburban Australia.

Picnic at Hanging Rock (1975). Three young ladies mysteriously disappear on Valentine's Day 1900 while on a school outing. The disturbing sense of eeriness is aided by a Gheorghe Zamfir's panpipe soundtrack.

Wake in Fright (1970). Deliverance Down Under; a teacher can't escape a beer-sodden, roo-shooting, Outback-town-from-hell.

Walkabout (1971). Dad shoots his brains out during a barbie and leaves his two kids to wander the Outback until an Aboriginal boy befriends them and leads them to safety.

REEL NEW ZEALAND

Once Were Warriors (1994). A brutal tale of a South Auckland Maori family in the 1970s.

The Piano (1993). Brooding story of a mute Scottish émigré who uses the piano to express herself.

Sione's Wedding (2006). Entertaining comedy about four Auckland Samoan lads trying to get steady girlfriends.

Whale Rider (2002). Engaging story of a young girl who defies the patriarchal Maori elders with heart-warming results.

The World's Fastest Indian (2005). Uplifting biography of back shed motorbike mechanic Bert Munro who lived his high speed dreams.

SOAP OPERA LOCATIONS

The soapy teenage angst and surfie bonhomie of *Home and Away* has long revolved around Palm Beach in Sydney's northern beaches, with the Barrenjoey Lighthouse and headland regularly in shot. Melbourne is famous for being the filming location of *Home and Away*'s competitor, the veteran soapie *Neighbours*; Ramsay Street, Erinsborough is actually Pin Oak Court in Vermont South, while the cool international-hit TV series, *The Secret Life of Us* was filmed around St Kilda.

MEET AND GREET

The traditional greeting in Tuvalu in the South Pacific is a face pressed to the cheek, and a deep sniff.

OCEANIA ODDITIES

Pitcairn Island, in Polynesia, has a mere 67 residents, making it the least populated inhabited island (save for private islands) in the world. Tonga, also part of Polynesia, stands alone in the South Pacific for never having been colonized by Europeans. The phrase "As phony as a three-dollar bill" would mean very little in Rarotonga, the biggest of the Cook Islands; the bill is part of their currency.

BEHOLD THE NORTHERN LIGHTS • BEDDING DOWN IN AN IGLOO • SNORKELLING WITH ORCAS • TREKKING ACROSS THE ARCTIC CIRCLE • SCRAMBLING UP OBSERVATION HILL • STUMBLING UPON A POLAR OASIS • SPOTTING SEALS AND SKUAS • KAYAKING AMID ICEBERGS • VOYAGING INTO THE ICY UNKNOWN • BEHOLD THE NORTHERN LIGHTS • BEDDING DOWN IN AN IGLOO • SNORKELLING WITH ORCAS • **TREKKING ACROSS THE ARCTIC CIRCLE** • SCRAMBLING UP OBSERVATION HILL • STUMBLING UPON A POLAR OASIS • SPOTTING SEALS AND SKUAS • KAYAKING AMID ICEBERGS • VOYAGING INTO THE ICY UNKNOWN • BEHOLD THE NORTHERN LIGHTS • BEDDING DOWN IN AN IGLOO • SNORKELLING WITH ORCAS • TREKKING ACROSS THE ARCTIC CIRCLE • SCRAMBLING UP OBSERVATION HILL • STUMBLING UPON A POLAR OASIS • SPOTTING SEALS AND SKUAS • KAYAKING AMID ICEBERGS • VOYAGING INTO THE ICY UNKNOWN • BEHOLD THE NORTHERN LIGHTS • BEDDING DOWN IN AN IGLOO • SNORKELLING WITH ORCAS • TREKKING ACROSS THE ARCTIC CIRCLE • SCRAMBLING UP OBSERVATION HILL • STUMBLING UPON A POLAR OASIS • SPOTTING SEALS AND SKUAS • KAYAKING AMID ICEBERGS • VOYAGING INTO THE ICY UNKNOWN • BEHOLD THE NORTHERN LIGHTS • BEDDING DOWN IN AN IGLOO • SNORKELLING WITH ORCAS • TREKKING ACROSS THE ARCTIC CIRCLE • SCRAMBLING UP OBSERVATION HILL • STUMBLING UPON A POLAR OASIS • SPOTTING SEALS AND SKUAS • KAYAKING AMID ICEBERGS • **VOYAGING INTO THE ICY UNKNOWN** • BEHOLD THE NORTHERN LIGHTS • BEDDING DOWN IN AN IGLOO • SNORKELLING WITH ORCAS • TREKKING ACROSS THE ARCTIC CIRCLE • SCRAMBLING UP OBSERVATION HILL • STUMBLING UPON A POLAR OASIS • SPOTTING SEALS AND SKUAS • KAYAKING AMID ICEBERGS • VOYAGING INTO THE ICY UNKNOWN • BEHOLD THE NORTHERN LIGHTS • **BEDDING DOWN IN AN IGLOO** • SNORKELLING WITH ORCAS • TREKKING ACROSS THE ARCTIC CIRCLE • SCRAMBLING UP OBSERVATION HILL • STUMBLING UPON A POLAR OASIS • SPOTTING SEALS AND SKUAS • KAYAKING AMID ICEBERGS • VOYAGING INTO THE ICY UNKNOWN • BEHOLD THE NORTHERN LIGHTS • BEDDING DOWN IN AN IGLOO • SNORKELLING WITH ORCAS • TREKKING ACROSS THE ARCTIC CIRCLE • SCRAMBLING UP OBSERVATION HILL • STUMBLING UPON A POLAR OASIS • SPOTTING SEALS AND SKUAS • KAYAKING AMID ICEBERGS • VOYAGING INTO THE ICY UNKNOWN • BEHOLD THE NORTHERN LIGHTS • BEDDING DOWN IN AN IGLOO • SNORKELLING WITH ORCAS • TREKKING ACROSS THE ARCTIC CIRCLE • SCRAMBLING UP OBSERVATION HILL • STUMBLING UPON A POLAR OASIS • SPOTTING SEALS AND SKUAS • KAYAKING AMID ICEBERGS • VOYAGING INTO THE ICY UNKNOWN • BEHOLD THE NORTHERN LIGHTS • BEDDING DOWN IN AN IGLOO • SNORKELLING WITH ORCAS • TREKKING ACROSS THE ARCTIC CIRCLE • **SCRAMBLING UP OBSERVATION HILL** • STUMBLING UPON A POLAR OASIS • SPOTTING SEALS AND SKUAS • KAYAKING AMID ICEBERGS • VOYAGING INTO THE ICY UNKNOWN • BEHOLD THE NORTHERN LIGHTS • BEDDING DOWN IN AN IGLOO • SNORKELLING WITH ORCAS • TREKKING ACROSS THE ARCTIC CIRCLE • SCRAMBLING UP OBSERVATION HILL • STUMBLING UPON A POLAR OASIS • SPOTTING SEALS AND SKUAS • KAYAKING AMID ICEBERGS • VOYAGING INTO THE ICY UNKNOWN • BEHOLD THE NORTHERN LIGHTS • BEDDING DOWN IN AN IGLOO • SNORKELLING WITH ORCAS • TREKKING ACROSS THE ARCTIC CIRCLE • SCRAMBLING UP OBSERVATION HILL • STUMBLING UPON A POLAR OASIS • SPOTTING SEALS AND SKUAS • **KAYAKING AMID ICEBERGS** • VOYAGING INTO THE ICY UNKNOWN • BEHOLD THE NORTHERN LIGHTS • BEDDING DOWN IN AN IGLOO • SNORKELLING WITH ORCAS • TREKKING ACROSS THE ARCTIC CIRCLE • SCRAMBLING UP OBSERVATION HILL • STUMBLING UPON A POLAR OASIS • SPOTTING SEALS AND SKUAS • KAYAKING AMID ICEBERGS • VOYAGING INTO THE ICY UNKNOWN • BEHOLD THE NORTHERN LIGHTS • BEDDING

THE POLAR REGIONS

992–1000

PACIFIC OCEAN

180°

80°

Arctic Circle

ARCTIC OCEAN

90°

North Pole

90°

BEDDING DOWN IN AN IGLOO 993

TREKKING ACROSS THE ARCTIC CIRCLE 995

KAYAKING AMID ICEBERGS 999

60°

ATLANTIC OCEAN

0°

ATLANTIC OCEAN

SOUTHERN OCEAN

0°

INDIAN OCEAN

Antarctic Circle

80°

VOYAGING INTO THE UNKNOWN 1000

90°

South Pole

90°

SCRAMBLING UP OBSERVATION HILL 996

PACIFIC OCEAN

60°

SOUTHERN OCEAN

180°

992 BEHOLD THE NORTHERN LIGHTS

SWEDEN They appear as shimmering arcs and waves of light, often blue or green in colour, which seem to sweep their way across the dark skies. During the darkest months of the year, the Northern Lights, or Aurora Borealis, are visible in the night sky all across northern Sweden. Until you see the light displays yourself, it's hard to describe the spectacle in mere words – try to imagine, though, someone waving a fantastically coloured curtain through the air and you've pretty much got the idea.

What makes the Northern Lights so elusive is that it's impossible to predict when they're going to make an appearance. The displays are caused by solar wind, or streams of particles charged by the sun, hitting the Earth's atmosphere. Different elements produce different colours, blue for nitrogen, for example, and yellow-green for oxygen.

The best place to view these mystical performances is north of the Arctic Circle, where temperatures are well below freezing and the sky is often at its clearest – two conditions that are believed to produce some of the most spectacular sightings.

For the quintessential Northern Lights experience, pack a couple of open sandwiches topped with smoked reindeer meat and a thermos of hot coffee to keep out the chill, then take a snow-scooter tour deep into the forests of Lapland – Kiruna, Sweden's northernmost city, is the best base. Park up beside a frozen lake and train your eyes on the sky. Try this between mid-December and mid-January, when there's 24-hour darkness north of the Arctic Circle, and the chances are you won't have to wait long for your celestial fix.

993 BEDDING DOWN IN AN IGLOO

CANADA Tucked away between rolling hills and vast stretches of tundra in northern Quebec lie a series of igloos. These domed shelters were built by sealskin-clad Inuit elders, who carved snowblocks from windswept snowdrifts, using homemade snow knifes and skills passed on from their ancestors. Igloos have long played a vital role in the lives of Inuit across northern Canada, where generations have gathered to share food, sing, dance and socialize while seeking refuge from the unforgiving elements of the Arctic winter. Today, igloos continue to safeguard hunters and have become the latest trend for adventure seekers.

To enter an igloo, you crawl through a narrow tunnel leading to the large domed enclosure. Sunlight, streaming in from a window fashioned from a block of clear river ice, fills the room to reveal a scene from *Nanook of the North*, the world's first documentary film released in 1922. A raised sleeping platform

of snow, covered with willow mats and caribou skins, occupies the back half of the structure. Here, you sit back, remove your heavy parka and take it all in. Children giggle and play with a husky pup, while an elderly woman tends to the flame of her qulliq, a crescent-shaped lantern carved from soapstone and fuelled by seal blubber. A short while later you join the others around a plastic bag placed on the igloo floor where dinner is served. On the menu tonight: caribou stew and frozen Arctic char, eaten raw and considered a delicacy in this icy corner of the world.

After dinner and a round of cards you lie back in your sleeping bag and stare up at the spiraling blocks of snow while listening to muffled laughter and talking from the elders. Within minutes the sounds of the kids throat-singing and the gentle flicker of the burning qulliq lull you to sleep.

NORWAY As you slide quietly over the side of the boat and put your face in the freezing water, it's hard to breathe – not just because your teeth are chattering, but also because there, below you in the blue, are six or seven killer whales that seem as curious about you as you are about them.

Tell your friends you're going snorkelling with "killer whales" north of the Arctic Circle in winter and they're likely to think you're a few minnows short of a school. But though orcas, as they're more properly known, have been known to eat prey larger than humans – including seals, dolphins, sharks, and even other whales – the ones in northern Norway mainly eat fish.

Prime orca-viewing time is October through January, when migrating shoals of herring lure 600–700 orcas to Tysfjord in northern Norway. You might even have a chance to see them feed. Norway's orcas have perfected a fishing technique called "carousel feeding": they herd the unsuspecting herring into a tight ball using air bubbles as a visual net, slap the ball with their tails to stun 10–15 fish at a time, then scoff them one by one.

Sure it's cold (winter water temperatures hover around 40°F, 4°C), but there's plenty of gear to keep you warm: dry suit, warm inner suit, mask, snorkel, gloves and booties. And yes, you might feel a tad vulnerable drifting on the surface of the North Atlantic surrounded by a bunch of five-tonne marine mammals, a small rubber Zodiac your only back-up. But all that's forgotten as soon as you spot a dorsal fin breaking the surface – and you realize you didn't just become dinner.

995 TREKKING ACROSS THE ARCTIC CIRCLE

CANADA Bouncing along in a wooden kamotik, a traditional Inuit sled pulled by a snowmobile, you might have serious doubts as you think of what lies ahead: polar bears, hypothermia, avalanches and blizzards. You may question your sanity about trekking all the way to the Arctic Circle Marker in Auyuittuq National Park on Baffin Island. But in the end, you won't regret it for a moment.

Home to ten-thousand-year-old glaciers, towering granite mountains and awesome icy landscapes, Auyuittuq (pronounced "I-you-we-took") is an extraordinary place to explore on foot. Most visitors come during the summer months to trek 97km through the scenic Akshayuk Pass, a traditional corridor used by Inuit for thousands of years.

The guide drops you on the frozen shores at the Overlord Warden Station, the southern gateway to the park. Dwarfed by rugged snow-covered mountains, you are left alone to battle the elements. Within minutes the loud drone of the snowmobile disappears. Adrenaline pumping, you begin the 15km trek to the Arctic Circle, along the glacier-scoured terrain of the Weasel River Valley.

Guided by inuksuit, stone markers built by Inuit to navigate the land, you cross the turquoise-blue ice of braided streams along the base of sheer cliffs a kilometre high and over boulders of every shape and size conceivable. The scale of your surroundings is immense beyond belief.

Nearly five hours after starting out, you'll catch the first glimpse of the holy grail in the distance atop a gravel bed: a lonely inukshuk bearing a simple sign with the words "Arctic Circle" written in English, French and Inuktitut. Without fanfare or a welcome party you have reached your destination. A few moments surrounded by the great Arctic stillness is all the reward you need.

996 SCRAMBLING UP OBSERVATION HILL

ANTARCTICA Ice-locked into the France-sized Ross Ice Shelf lies Ross Island, a primary base for the British expeditions to Antarctica of a century ago. Many reminders of their efforts remain, including a stirring monument at the summit of the 230m Observation Hill, or "Ob Hill," so named because it was used as a lookout for ships returning to the ice; today station residents climb it for a view of their utterly alien, white environs.

The first third of the extinct volcano consists of loose scree, which must be scrambled up until you reach a road that winds partially around the hill to a decommissioned nuclear power plant. Here, most climbers turn to look for the first time at their temporary home – much like a new Manhattanite walks to the middle of the Brooklyn Bridge before gazing back at the city's towers. McMurdo Station, America's chief Antarctic research facility, looks like a small mining town from this vantage point,

with homey curls of steam puffing from each building.

Ob Hill's next two thirds must be bounded up, billy-goat-style, over large, haphazardly strewn rocks. About 75m from the top a small, boulder-topped peninsula flattens out in front of the climber, offering the chance to take a breather and peer out at the frozen McMurdo Sound and, further off to the left, the imposing Royal Society mountain range. To the right looms the smoking cone of Mount Erebus, the world's southernmost active volcano.

Not until you nearly reach the top do you see the solid wooden cross which stands as a memorial to Captain Scott and his men. The stout cross is inscribed with a line from Tennyson's Ulysses, which serves as a sobering reminder of the sacrifices made so that the climber can stand here today: "To strive, to seek, to find, and not to yield."

997 STUMBLING UPON A POLAR OASIS

CANADA Traveling by skidoo, you and your Inuit guide venture onto the sea ice off the coast of Baffin Island in Canada's eastern Arctic for a day's outing. Three hours later you spot a small body of water completely surrounded by ice and shrouded in mist. Nestled between two rocky islands this mysterious marine "lake" is teeming with life – hundreds of eider, oldsquaw and guillemot ducks dive for food while in the distance a ringed seal keeps a close watch. Fresh tracks of an Arctic fox circle the perimeter of the ice edge where only days earlier a local hunter had spotted a wandering polar bear. You have stumbled upon a polynya.

Polynyas are areas of open water bordered by thick sea ice that recur year after year in the same location. There are a few dozen scattered throughout the Arctic Archipelago, ranging in size from less than a hundred metres across to a massive 40,000 square kilometres. A combination of wind and strong ocean currents keep these areas free of ice year-round. Although they account for less than five percent of the entire surface area of the Arctic Ocean, their presence is crucial to the survival of countless species of marine organisms.

As the spring sun glares down onto the reflective icy surface and penetrates deep into the water, billions of microscopic plankton suddenly burst into life, thanks to incoming solar radiation. This influx of energy triggers a chain of events many naturalists describe as one of the greatest spectacles in the Arctic. Millions of migratory seabirds and ducks join bowhead whales and large pods of narwhal and beluga to feed in the nutrient-rich waters.

Standing at the edge of the ice, and surrounded by a symphony of sound and colour, you begin to scan the horizon for more signs of life. A flock of at least three hundred king eiders flutter by while the telltale spray from a pod of beluga signal their return to the surface. This flurry of activity almost distracts you from spotting the two-metre spiralled ivory tusk of a narwhal as it pierces through the calm waters of this remarkable polar oasis.

998 SPOTTING SEALS AND SKUAS

ANTARCTICA Upon arrival, one is struck by the pristine desolation: everywhere, as far as the eye can see, is pure white. There are no trees, no plants, no smells and very little movement of any kind, save for the blowing snow. But the continent is not just one "big dead place", as it has been described – rather it's populated by all sorts of unique beasties, from seals to skuas. You just have to know where – and when – to look.

At the American McMurdo Station, on Ross Island, you'll occasionally spot short, fat Adelie penguins waddling in a self-important huff through town, looking like nattily attired, curious tourists. But the best place to spot them is out on the white, flat, endless expanse of sea ice where you'll see one rushing headlong, like the White Rabbit in Alice's *Adventures in Wonderland*, toward some very important date for which they are, invariably, late. The resident seals – fat, grey, impassive yet graceful – laze about in threes or fours out on the vast stretches of ice. Sometimes pups – aptly named, considering their happy, dog-like faces – are snuggled with the adults, who raise up from their flop and stare at you purposefully if you get too close.

And then there are the skua birds, scavengers that look like dirty gulls, and with no natural predators. They are utterly unafraid of humans, and will walk right up to you, entirely unruffled – or, if you're carrying food, the daring devils might even attempt to divebomb you. But you take it all in stride, revelling in the chance to see these cantankerous creatures in their natural habitat – after all, you're the visitor; they, unlike humans, have no problem surviving and indeed thriving in the harsh wilds of Antarctica.

999 KAYAKING AMID ICEBERGS

NORWAY The ice cliffs gleamed platinum blue and towered above us as high as a fifty-storey skyscraper. We floated in our kayaks, cold even in our drysuits, but enthralled. Every few minutes the glacier calved, sending newborn icebergs out into the fjord. A loud crack and a deep rumble, then a huge sheet of ice dropped into the sea. We braced for the wave, inhaling the salt spray as we rose and fell with the swell.

Chastened, we paddled back into the fjord. I felt the sun warm my face as we emerged from the shadow of the glacier. Everything sparkled in the sunlight and our paddles scraped and crunched through the ice. We passed a giant iceberg, sailing like a swan in stately splendour, a flock of kittiwakes perched on its head.

I heard a plop and in the water before us was a round face, with huge eyes and whiskers. We lifted the paddles and glided in silence. "A ringed seal", whispered our guide in the next boat. Curious, the seal swam alongside the kayaks for a few moments, before retiring to sunbathe on a floating chunk of ice.

Soon I would become blasé about seals, saving my excitement for walruses, lying on the beach next to the bones of their ancestors. Or the enormous bird cliffs streaked pink with guano, home to about a million black-and-white guillemot. Or the minke whale, breaching by the stern of the ship.

The polar bears were the biggest thrill of all. We approached them only in motorized dinghies and kept a respectful distance. Once we attracted the attention of an old male, his fur yellowed and gouged with scars. He stood on the pebble beach and sniffed the air, then plunged into the water and started swimming towards us. Thankfully we had an engine not just an oar, and we beat a hasty retreat.

1000

VOYAGING INTO THE
UNKNOWN

ANTARCTICA Over a hundred years after the initial exploration of the continent, journeying to Antarctica still feels like stepping off the known world. Take a cruise to the crooked finger of land which points northward to South America and you'll encounter the other-planetary landscape and mysterious draw of this land beyond time – for the most part still beyond civilization's reach.

Once through the Drake Passage – reputed to be the roughest body of water in the world – you feel the frozen land long before you actually see it. As you cross the invisible line of the Antarctic Convergence, a ribbon of coldwater current which circumnavigates the continent, the temperature plummets. Huge tabular icebergs appear – interpreting their fantastic shapes is at least half the fun. In the Gerlache Strait, sudden charcoal tors soar vertically from the water up to 450m and glaciers tumble vertically into the sea. From the ship you can brush against their hummocked layers of ice and try your hand at cataloguing their colours: cobalt, indigo and mint.

The tar-black Antarctic water teems with marine life: humpback and killer whales are fairly common, and if there is sea-ice around you are guaranteed to see the silver-gold crabeater and nonchalant Weddell seals who can hardly be bothered to vacate a floe even as the ship splits it in two. Myriad penguins emit a serenade of squawks as the ship passes and albatrosses and petrels are stalwart chaperones, flying level with the ship for days at a stretch.

Go ashore at the abandoned British Base B at Deception Island, flattened by a volcanic eruption, and the British Antarctic museum at Port Lockroy, where a preserved-in-aspic 1950s base is on display, complete with tinned fruitcake and rice pudding from the explorer era.

On the whole, however, the Antarctic is a monumentally empty place, and a cruise down the peninsula gives you only a glimpse of this uninhabited continent, larger than Australia – but it's enough to draw you in. Even as it emits a froideur, there is an odd magnetism to the Antarctic; you'll feel its pull long after you've left.

MISCELLANY

HOW TO BUILD AN IGLOO

• Pack down a large, circular base area with snowshoes or skis, using a hand saw to cut blocks about 1m wide, 0.5m high and 20cm deep.

• Make the base layer of the igloo nearby, digging down into the snow to form the lower half of the igloo and an arched entrance tunnel.

• The second row of blocks should be cut bevelled at the bottom so the layers slant inward, toward the middle until the igloo is about shoulder height.

• Cover the hole at the top with one single block, enlarge the inner chamber and build the entrance in the same manner as the main hut.

• Cut a couple of vents for circulation and bed down for the night!

SOUTHERN LIGHTS

From March to September, outside the period when Antarctica experiences 24-hr daylight, the Aurora Australis, or Southern Lights, can be seen in the skies above the continent. These curtains of coloured light are one of the greatest spectacles on earth.

THE GREAT INUIT "SNOW" MYTH

The idea that the Inuit of the Arctic have over 100 words for "snow" is actually a complete fabrication. The confusion lies in how you define a word. The Inuit language group uses an extraordinary system of multiple, recursively addable derivational suffixes for word formation called postbases, which are added to roots to compose compounding words. Whereas English has one root word for "snow" – which is used for "snowball", "snowflake" and "snowstorm" – the Inuit have four: aput (snow on the ground); gana (falling snow); piqsirpoq (drifting snow); and qimuqsuq (a snow drift). Therefore, the 100-plus words the Inuit use are actually just compounds; the reality is that the Inuit have around the same number of words for "snow" as the English.

POLAR EXPLORERS

With cruise ships now regularly visiting Antarctica in the Southern Hemisphere's summer, it is easy to think the highest, coldest, windiest and driest continent has gone soft. But the South Pole was first reached less than a century ago. Some notable explorers include:

Roald Amundsen, Norway Leader of the first team to reach the South Pole, on December 14, 1911; he then made a successful return.

Robert Scott, UK Reached the South Pole 35 days after Amundsen. His party died of starvation just eleven miles short of a large food cache on the return journey.

Ernest Shackleton, Anglo-Irish Aboard the ship *Endurance*, Sir Ernest Henry Shackleton and crew attempted to sail across Antarctica, between the Weddell Sea and the Ross Sea, in 1914. This goal had to be abandoned when the ship was crushed by a floe of pack ice short of the continent. Shackleton then led his crew on an epic 639-day journey by sledge and boat to Elephant Island, just off the Antarctic Peninsula. From here he sailed with some of the men to South Georgia Island in the Falklands, where help was sought. Miraculously, not a man on the expedition was lost.

Edward E. Byrd, USA Byrd and three others were the first to fly over the South Pole in 1929.

Edmund Hillary, New Zealand In 1958 the Everest conqueror led the third party to reach the South Pole overland, and the first with land vehicles, in this case converted Ferguson tractors.

Boerge Ousland, Norway Ousland became the first person to cross Antarctica unsupported (in 64 days), using a sled, skis and a sail in 1997.

> *"Better a live donkey than a dead lion"*
>
> **Ernest Shackleton, after failing to reach the South Pole by 100km in 1909**

THE ARCTIC CIRCLE

The Arctic Circle is an imaginary line that marks the latitude above which the sun does not set on the day of the summer solstice (usually June 21) and does not rise on the day of the winter solstice (usually December 21). North of this latitude, periods of continuous daylight (known as the "Midnight Sun") or night last up to six months at the North Pole. The position of the Arctic Circle depends on the tilt of the earth's axis relative to the plane of its orbit around the sun, which is known as the "obliquity of the ecliptic". The average value of the tilt is currently decreasing by about 1.2cm per year, causing the Arctic Circle to drift towards the North Pole by some fifteen metres each year.

TAKE YOUR THERMALS

The coldest place on earth is Vostok, Antarctica: it's registered at a fairly chilly -89°C/-129°F.

> *"Water that does not move is always shallow"*
>
> **Sami proverb**

ON THE WING

The longest migration on earth is undertaken by Arctic terns: they fly 40,000km from the Arctic to the Antarctic – and back again.

THE ANTARCTIC TREATY

The Antarctic Treaty came into operation in 1961, having been ratified by the twelve countries involved with Antarctic science. It now has 44 signatories including the US, and aims to protect and preserve this unique wilderness, banning mineral extraction and military activity and promoting scientific discovery.

SMALL PRINT

THINGS YOU NEED TO KNOW
AUTHOR CREDITS
INDEX

BRITAIN & IRELAND

001 Punts can be hired from stations at Mill Lane, Magdalene Bridge and Jesus Green, and at other points in the city centre.

002 For information about matches and museum entry, go to ⊛www.gaa.ie.

003 Pick up a copy of the free Visitor Guide (☎01822/890414) or contact the Dartmoor National Park Visitor Centre (☎01822/890414, ⊛www.dart-moor-npa.gov.uk) for details of guided walks.

004 Trains run from Glasgow to Mallaig on the mainland, from where there's a ferry service to Skye, and from Inverness to Kyle of Lochalsh, which is linked by a road bridge to the island.

005 For entry hours and admission fees to Conwy Castle, see ⊛www.cadw.wales.gov.uk.

006 Tickets for Hogmanay are available from October from the Hub on Castlehill (☎0131/473 2000, ⊛www.thehub-edinburgh.com).

007 *Frash* 186 Ladypool Road (☎0121 753 3120); *Adil* 148–150 Stoney Lane (☎0121 449 0335); *Zeb's Miripuri Cuisine* 250 Ladypool Road (☎0121 449 8909).

008 For more info, go to ⊛www.pcnpa.org.uk.

009 From June to September, you need to book well ahead for accommodation – and especially for the *Hell Bay Hotel* on Bryher (☎01720/422947, ⊛www.hellbay.co.uk).

010 Two to try: *Stein's Fish & Chips*, South Quay, Padstow, Cornwall (☎01841/532700, ⊛www.rick-stein.com), and the *Magpie Café*, 14 Pier Rd, Whitby, Yorkshire (☎01947/602058).

011 *The Palace*, 21 Fleet St; *Mulligan's*, 8 Poolbeg St; *Ryan's*, 28 Parkgate St; Guinness Storehouse, off Belleview; ⊛www.guinness-storehouse.com.

012 Borrowdale is in the heart of the Lake District, running south of Keswick for eight miles. Parking is limited so catch the local bus from Keswick.

013 For opening hours and entrance fees, see ⊛www.durhamcathedral.co.uk.

014 For details of the festival's events, check the organizers' website ⊛www.stpatricksday.ie.

015 Ferries to Rum run daily from Mallaig and, in summer, from Arisaig. To stay in Kinloch Castle, phone ☎01687/462037 or see ⊛www.hostel-scotland.co.uk.

016 Book ghost tours through the York tourist office (☎01904 550099, ⊛www.visityork.org).

017 Bonfire Night is held on November 5, unless this falls on a Sunday, when it moves to November 6. For more info, contact the town's tourist office (☎01273 483448, ✉lewestic@lewes.gov.uk).

018 Tickets for Glastonbury usually go on sale in early April; snap them up online at ⊛www.glaston-buryfestivals.co.uk.

019 For more information on Mourne, see ⊛www.mourenalive.com.

020 Hay-on-Wye straddles the English–Welsh border, twenty miles from Hereford. Murder & Mayhem, 5 Lion Street; The Poetry Bookshop, Ice House, Brook Street; Hay Cinema Bookshop, Castle Street.

021 For entrance hours and exhibition details, contact the British Museum at ☎020/76351555 or go to ⊛www.thebritishmuseum.ac.uk.

022 Most people tackle Snowdonia from Idwal Cottage youth hostel, near the A5.

023 Oxford is northwest of London and easily accessible by bus from Victoria Station (1hr 30min) or train from Paddington Station (1hr).

024 For a picnic lunch on the beach, stock up at the wonderful Picnic Fayre deli in Cley.

025 Speyside's Malt Whisky Trail (⊛www.maltwhis-kytrail.com) points you in the direction of eight distilleries offering guided tours.

026 For info on the best riding in Wales, go to ⊛www.mbwales.com or ⊛www.adventure.visitwales.com.

027 Common Ridings is held on the first Friday and Saturday of June. For more details, see ⊛www.haw-ickcallantsclub.co.uk.

028 Royal Ascot begins on the third Tuesday in June. For tickets, contact ☎0870/7227 227 or check out ⊛www.ascot.co.uk.

029 For more information on the Barrow itself, and for details of barge-rental companies, see ⊛www.barrowvalley.org.

030 The largest breaks occur at the September and March equinoxes. Go to ⊛www.severn-bore.co.uk and ⊛www.boreriders.com for more details.

031 Most people walk the Pennine Way in 2 to 3 weeks, covering daily distances of 12 to 20 miles.

032 For more info, and to book a course, see ⊛www.bushcraftexpeditions.com.

033 *Irish Music Magazine* (✉mag.irish-music.net) makes a good starting point for nationwide session searches.

034 Highland Games are held throughout July and August – the big gatherings include Braemar (⊛www.braemargathering.org) and Cowal (⊛www.cowal-gathering.com).

035 TT race week is the first week of June; for more information, see ⊛www.iomtt.com.

036 ⊛www.nottinghill.co.uk has a wealth of information on the carnival

037 You can rent bikes at several points around the New Forest, with helmets, child seats and other equipment included in the price.

038 Big E's Belfast Taxi Tours (☎079/6847 7924, ⊛www.big-e-taxitours.com).

039 As long as you come equipped with a decent wetsuit, winter is the best time for surfing in Britain, with higher and more regular waves.

040 Players need to enter a ballot to get a tee-off time – visit ⊛www.standrews.org.uk or call ☎01334 477036.

041 A ferry runs to Mull from the west-coast port of Oban (6 or 7 daily; 46min).

042 For more on Edinburgh's festivals and the Military Tatoo, go to ⊛www.edinburghfestivals.co.uk.

043 For further information about Connemara, go to ⊛www.connemara.net.

044 For club nights, check out *Fabric* (⊛www.fab-riclondon.com); *Ministry of Sound* (⊛www.ministry-ofsound.co.uk); and *St Matthew's Church* (⊛www.babalou.net).

045 Boats run out to the Skelligs, usually between May and September, from several points on the Kerry coast, including Ballinskelligs and Portmagee.

046 Trains (5hr) run from Glasgow on the West Highland Line to Fort William and then onto Mallaig.

047 ⊛www.tate.org.uk/modern has current opening hours and details of exhibitions.

048 Cooper's Hill's Cheese-Rolling starts at noon on the end-of-May holiday Monday See ⊛www.cheese-rolling.co.uk for more.

049 The SETT tank is located in Gosport, near Portsmouth. For details see ⊛www.royal-navy.mod.uk/server/show/nav.3097.

050 For information on tickets, go to ⊛www.bbc.co.uk/proms or call ☎020/7589 8212.

051 The Brú na Boinne visitor centre (⊛www.herit-ageireland.ie) is 10km southwest of Drogheda in Co. Meath. The Loughcrew Cairns, near Oldcastle, are accessible only with your own transport – pick up the key for Cairn T at Loughcrew Gardens (⊛www.loughcrew.com).

052 *The Barrowland* is at 244 Gallowgate, Glasgow (☎0141/552 4601, ⊛www.glasgow-barrowland.com).

053 The London Marathon is held on a Sunday in mid-April; see ⊛www.london-marathon.co.uk.

054 For a closer look at the Aber Valley Male Voice Choir, see ⊛www.aber-valleymvc.co.uk.

055 For more info see ⊛www.manutd.com.

056 ⊛www.galwayoysterfest.com has event information and booking forms.

057 The website ⊛www.isleofbarra.com has the full lowdown on the island of Barra.

058 The website ⊛www.visit-fortwilliam.co.uk has a webcam permanently trained on Ben Nevis as well as plenty of information on climbing the mountain.

059 For more information, check out ⊛www.eden-project.com – or the unofficial, but useful, ⊛www.eden-project.co.uk.

WESTERN EUROPE

060 The Dutch motoring organization, the ANWB publish a series of 16 cycle maps that covers the whole country. Bike rental costs around €30 a week.

061 For more on cowfighting go to ⊛www.switzerland.isyours.com/e/guide/valais/cowfighting.html.

062 The Casements du Bock are open daily between March and November from 10am to 5pm.

063 Go to ⊛www.polostmoritz.com for full details.

064 A single, one-way, first-class ticket from Gloggnitz to Murzzuschlag costs €17. Tickets can be booked at ⊛www.oebb.at.

065 The Office de Tourisme in Épernay (⊛www.ot-epernay.fr) has information on touring the town's champagne houses.

066 For more info, check out ⊛www.oktoberfest.de.

067 *Tipis Indiens* is 42km from Lourdes. For reservations, go to ⊛www.tipis-indiens.com.

068 Further details can be found at ⊛www.ot-mont-saintmichel.com.

069 Château de Brissac, Brissac-Quincé (⊛www.chateau-brissac.fr); Château de Chémery, Loir-et-Cher (⊛chateaudechemery@wanadoo.fr); Manoir de la Rémonière, near Azay-le-Rideau (⊛www.manoird-elaremoniere.com).

070 See ⊛www.casinomontecarlo.com for opening times.

071 For more information, visit ⊛www.pontdugard.fr.

072 The Glacier Express runs daily between St Moritz and Zermatt: full details at ⊛www.glacierexpress.ch.

073 Mozartwoche (⊛www.mozarteum.at); Stiftskeller St Peter (⊛www.mozartdinnerconcert.com); Fortress concerts (⊛www.mozartfestival.at); Mozart Requiem at the Kollgienkirche (⊛www.salzburg-concerts.com).

074 Cap d'Agde is on France's Mediterranean coast, 60km southwest of Montpellier. For more information visit ⊛www.naturist.de.

075 For opening times and prices for the Eiffel Tower, see ⊛www.tour-eiffel.fr.

076 Numerous canoe rental companies set up along the Dordogne in summer offering rental by the day or half-day.

077 France's skiing season runs from January to mid-April. For more on winter sports, visit ✆www. skifrance.fr.

078 For opening times and massage costs, see ✆www.roemisch-irisches-bad.de.

079 The Streif run is in the resort of Kitzbühel (✆www.kitzbuhel.com); the most convenient airport is Munich.

080 Berlin's Love Parade is held annually on the second or third Saturday in July. Check out ✆www. loveparade.de for more information.

081 Ferries from Santa Teresa di Gallura in Sardinia run daily, year round. Corsica's airport is at Figari, 17km north of Bonifacio. For more, go to ✆ww.boni-facio.fr.

082 The Verzasca Dam lies just east of Locarno, in southern Switzerland. Visit ✆www.trekking.ch for more information.

083 For more on the museums, visit ✆www.chez. com/renoir/cagnes.htm, ✆www.musee-matisse-nice. org, or ✆www.antibes-juanlespins.com/eng/culture/musees/picasso.

084 Opening times can be found at: ✆www.kunsthaus graz.at, ✆www.neuegalerie.at and ✆www.forum.mur.at.

085 *Café Central*, 1, Herrengasse 14; *Café Landtmann*, 1, Dr-Karl-Lueger-Ring 4; *Café Hawelka*, 1, Dorotheergasse 6.

086 For information on how to get to Brittany and where to stay, visit ✆www.brittanytourism.com.

087 See ✆www.carnavaldebinche.be for more information.

088 Tickets for French rugby league matches cost around €10 and can usually be bought at the gate.

089 The cycling trails in the Upper Danube Valley are mostly flat and well signposted. Valley Bike (✆www. valleybike.de) in Hausen am Tal near Beuron rents mountain bikes.

090 For more on St Tropez, see ✆www.ot-saint-tropez.com.

091 ✆www.austrianchristmasmarkets.co.uk has the full lowdown (and links) on Austria's Christmas markets.

092 The Route de Alignments follows the course of the three main alignments. There's a visitor centre at the Alignements de Kermario (✆www.carnac.com).

093 Fribourg is the best place to try a classic style moitié-moitié; the pick of the bunch is the excellent *Gothard* at 18 Rue du Pont-Muré.

094 Tours of the winery are available for ten people or more; see ✆www.hofkellerei.li for details.

095 The website ✆www.vogel-gryff.ch has everything you need to know on the festival, though sadly not much in English.

096 The Louvre's "nocturnes" are on Wednesdays and Fridays. See ✆www.louvre.fr for more information.

097 ✆www.montreuxjazz.com has information on schedules, tickets and everything else.

098 You can find opening times, prices and other information at ✆www.aec.at.

099 See ✆www.chateau-guillaume-leconquerant.fr for opening hours and entry prices.

100 Lunch is traditionally the main meal of the day in France, and is usually between noon and 2pm.

101 Check ✆www.musee-orsay.fr for entry prices and opening times.

102 Loschadej's Huskypower (June–Oct; ✆www. huskypower.ch) operates on the Diablerets glacier, in southwestern Switzerland.

103 The cathedral is open April–June & Sept 8.30am–

7.15pm; July & Aug 8.30am–7.45pm; Oct–March 9am–5.45pm. Entrance is free.

104 The Route du Cidre is a 40-kilometre loop in the Pays d'Auge. For more information, visit ✆www.cal-vados-tourisme.com.

105 Sarlat main food market takes place on Saturday 8am–1pm.

106 A number of operators offer tandem paragliding in the Zillertal, including Tandemflug Austria (✆www. tandemflug.at) and Action Club Zillertal (✆www.ac-tion-club-zillertal.com).

107 *Godiva*, Place du Grand Sablon 47– 48; *Pierre Marcolini*, rue des Minimes 1; *Wittamer*, Place du Grand Sablon 12; *Planète Chocolate*, rue du Lombard 24.

108 The castle is a 20-minute walk from Hohenschwangau, in south Bavaria. See ✆www.neu-schwanstein.de.

109 Go to ✆www.elfstedentocht.nl for history, photos and details of upcoming races.

110 ✆www.rijksmuseum.nl, ✆www.vangoghmuseum. nl, ✆www.stedelijk.nl, ✆www.cobracafe.com.

111 There's usually no entry fee for fêtes and village festivals, but there tends to be a small charge for food and drink.

112 Rudolf Albiez in Radolfzell harbour rents kayaks (✆www.bootsvermietung-radolfzell.de).

113 Local tourist offices and Maisons du Vin provide lists of producers offering vineyard visits. Most visits are free, though more famous châteaux may charge a small fee.

114 The Monaco Grand Prix is held annually at the end of May. For tickets, visit ✆www.formula1.com.

115 The GR20 stretches for some 170km and is open from June until mid-October. Most people need between 10 and 13 days to complete it.

116 Grotte de Pech-Merle (✆www.quercy.net/pech merle) is two hours' drive north of Toulouse.

117 *La Becasse*, rue Tabora 11; *Cantillon Brewery*, rue Gheude 67; *La Mort Subite*, rue Montagne-aux-Herbes Potageres 7; *'t Spinnekopke*, Place Jardin aux Fleurs 1; *Delirium*, Impasse de la Fidelité 4a.

118 The Normandy landing beaches stretch west from the mouth of the River Orne near Caen to the Cotentin Peninsula south of Cherbourg. Informative tours are offered by the Caen Memorial (✆www. memorial-caen.fr).

119 Whitepod is located near Villars, in southwestern Switzerland. See ✆www.whitepod.com for details.

120 Ladurée (✆www.laduree.fr) is at 16 rue Royale.

121 Château de Peyrepertuse sits above the village of Duilhac. See ✆www.chateau-peyrepertuse.com.

122 Amsterdam's main clubs lay on special Queen's Day nights – pick up a copy of the freebie *Amsterdam Weekly* when you arrive.

123 The Cresta Run is open from December to March. See ✆www.cresta-run.com for more.

124 *Café Moskau* (✆www.das-moskau.com); *Tresor* (✆www.tresorberlin.de); *SO36* (✆www.so36.de); *Russendisko* (✆www.russendisko.de); *KitKat Club* (✆www.kitkatclub.de); *Tom's* (✆www.tomsbar.de); *Newton* (✆www.newton-bar.de); *Bar am Lützowplatz* (✆www.baramluetzowplatz.de).

125 *Lasserre* is at 17 Av Franklin Roosevelt (✆www. restaurant-lasserre.com). Men must wear a jacket and tie.

126 You can rent snowshoes and poles from the Haus der Natur in Feldberg. Check out ✆www.natur-park-suedschwarzwald.de for more details on the trails and maps.

127 Las Fallas is held annually March 12–19: see ✆www.fallasfromvalencia.com for more details.

128 Check ✆www.sierranevadaski.com, ✆www. baqueira.es and ✆www.altocampoo.com for up-to-date info.

129 *Arzak*, Avda Alcalde Elosegui 273 (✆943 278 465, ✆www.arzak.es).

130 Tours of Marqués de Riscal ✆www.marques-deriscal.com) are bookable in advance, but Roda (✆www.roda.es) and Ysios (✆www.byb.es) run theirs by appointment; for Muga, see ✆www.bodegasmuga. com.

131 The Guggenheim is in Bilbao's Abandoibarra district; see ✆www.guggenheim-bilbao.es.

132 Morella is served by buses from both the resort town of Vinaròs and the regional capital of Castellón de la Plana; the castle is open daily.

133 Sintra is just 45 minutes from Lisbon's Rossio or Sete Rios train stations.

134 Peak tapas times are noon–2pm and 8–10pm.

135 The Museo del Prado (✆www.museoprado.es) is on Paseo del Prado; the nearest metros are Atocha and Banco de España.

136 The official programme is available from newsstands in Seville; local newspapers also print timetables and maps.

137 FRS (✆www.frs.es) run ferries between Tarifa and Tangier (up to 7 daily; 35min).

138 The two nearest metro stations to Las Ramblas are Plaça Catalunya and Liceu.

139 Both parks are free but vehicular access to Aigüestortes is prohibited.

140 The Algarve Surf School and Camp at Praia do Amado, near Carrapateira (✆0282/624 560, ✆www. algarvesurfschool.com) runs surf camps year-round.

141 Jerez de la Frontera lies 85km south of Seville, with which it has regular bus connections.

142 In Madrid: *Corral de la Morería* c/Moreriacutea 17; *El Corral de la Pacheca* c/Juan Ramón Jiménez 26; *Calle 54* Paseo de la Habana 3; *La Soleá* c/Cava Baja 34. In Seville: *Los Gallos* Plaza de Santa Cruz; *La Carbonería* c/Levies 18; *Casa Anselma* c/Pagés del Corro 49.

143 Earthwatch (✆www.earthwatch.org) recruits and supplies volunteers to established conservation projects around the world.

144 For opening hours and entry fees, see ✆www. sagradafamilia.org.

145 Almost every Galician town has a decent pulpería. For some of the best percebes, try the hamlet of San Andrés de Teixido or the nearby port of Cedeira.

146 Go to ✆www.portoturismo.pt for more on the São João festival and on Porto itself.

147 *La Boqueria* has its own website – ✆www. boqueria.info – and is open Monday–Saturday 8am–8.30pm.

148 The official festival website ✆www.fiberfib.com has all the details you need on lineups, tickets. etc.

149 The tourist board website ✆www.azores.com has lots of details on the islands, including material on fishing.

150 Sabores a Bacalhau, Rua da Pimenta 47, Parque das Nações (✆0218 957 499; closed Tues).

151 Check ✆www.infocordoba.com for up-to-date

entry costs and other details.

152 The mobile tourist office in Plaza del Castillo has a timetable of events and map. See ⊛www.sanfermin.com for more information.

153 See ⊛www.surfline.com for information on local swells.

154 The site ⊛www.feriadesevilla.andalunet.com has more on the festival.

155 You'll find paradores throughout Spain; for further information check the detailed website ⊛www.parador.es.

156 The official carnival website – ⊛www.carnaval tenerife.es – has history and and photos as well as up-to-date info on the next carnival.

157 The nearest main town to Astigarraga is San Sebastien. The cider season lasts mid-Jan–May. Devotees should check out ⊛www.sagardotegiak.com.

158 Gracia lies to the north of central Barcelona. Take the metro to either Diagonal or Fontana stations.

159 The Puig de Maria monastery is open Tuesday–Sunday 10am–1pm & 4–7pm and admission costs €4.

160 The website ⊛www.latomatina.com has info on tomatina tours and plenty of photos and videos of the event.

161 Opening hours and entry costs can be found on the respective websites for Texas Hollywood (⊛www.fort-bravo.com) and Western Leone (⊛www.western-leone.com).

162 Haro's Wine War takes place on June 29; see ⊛www.haro.org for more details.

163 Go to ⊛www.deia.info for information on Deia in English.

164 The closing parties take place in the last three weeks of September; *DJ* and *Pacha* magazines have listings.

165 ⊛www.salvador-dali.org has details of opening hours and entry fees.

166 *Café Majestic*, Rua de Santa Catarina, Porto; *Café Aliança*, Rua Dr. F. Gomes 6–11, Faro; *Antiga Confeitaria de Belém*, Rua de Belém 90, Belém, Lisbon.

167 Check the English-language listings guide *24-7 Valencia* or the clubbier Spanish-language *alb* (*A Little Beat*); both are free

168 Situated on c/Concha Espina, the Bernabéu has its own metro stop (Line 10) and is served by various buses. Credit card hotline: ☏902 324 324.

169 Daily four-hour bus tours depart from the reception centre at El Acebuche, 4km north of the coastal resort of Matalascañas (☏959 430 432).

170 Tram 28 runs from roughly 6am to 11pm. Check ⊛www.carris.pt for fares.

171 La Gomera lies 28km from Tenerife and is served by at least ten ferries a day.

172 Rio Honor de Castilla/Rio de Onor is a twenty-minute taxi ride from the Leonese fortress town of Puebla de Sanabria.

173 Credencials (or Pilgrim's Passport) are available from Roncesvalles Monastery for a few euros, entitling you to free or very cheap hostal accommodation.

174 The Alhambra is open throughout the year; advance booking recommended (⊛www.alhambratickets.com).

175 Most mansions are restricted to exterior viewing. WOMAD (⊛www.womad.org) is held during the first fortnight in May.

176 Details of walking companies are available on the tourist-board website ⊛www.madeiratourism.org.

177 Carrer d'Avinyo runs south from c/de Ferran to-

wards the harbour.

178 ⊛www.picoseuropa.net has Spanish-only info. ⊛www.asturiaspicosdeeuropa.com is a useful English-language site.

SCANDINAVIA

179 Trains run from Kiruna to Abisko. Bus routes will take you back to civilisation from various points, including Kvikkjok.

180 The Tourist Information Centre in Reykjavik (☏345/562-3045, ⊛www.visiticeland.com) can provide information on guides and tour companies.

181 Try Ulriksdals Wärdshus, Slottspark (☏08 85 08 15), ten minutes' north of Stockholm in Solna.

182 Most public swimming pools in Finland have a sauna: check out Kotiharjun (Tues–Fri 2–8pm, Sat 1–7pm) on Harjutorinkatu street in Helsinki.

183 Geirangerfjord is in southwestern Norway, 9hr by bus from Bergen. Nærøyfjord and Lustrafjord are respectively 3hr and 5hr from Bergen.

184 The Lofoten islands can be reached by car ferry, passenger boat and plane from Bodø, in northern Norway.

185 The Westmann Islands Festival is held on the first weekend in August; shuttle flights run from Reykjavik to Heimaey.

186 Katka Husky Safaris (⊛www.wildlaplandsafaris.fi) run trips near Rovaniemi in Finnish Lapland.

187 *Noma* is at Strandgade 93,1401. Reservations can be made on ☏045 3296 3297 or at ⊛www.noma.dk.

188 See ⊛www.hurtigruten.com for fares and sailing schedules.

189 For more information on the area, see ⊛www.east.is.

190 The website ⊛www.hamletsommer.dk has all you need on Hamlet at Kronborg.

191 Diving Iceland (☏0354 663 2858, ⊛www.dive.is) organizes snorkelling trips into Silfra.

192 Most cross-country ski areas offer lessons and have skis and boots available for hire. For more information on the Peer Gynt Ski Region, go to ⊛www.peergyntskiregion.com; for Voss, see ⊛www.visitvoss.no.

193 Jotunheimen Nasjonalpark is accessed via Gjendesheim, 90km southwest of Otta. The Lake Gjende boat runs from late June to mid-Sept (☏061 23 85 09).

194 A Båtluffarkortet pass gets you 5 days of unlimited ferry travel; alternatively, you can hire a sailboat from any number of outfits in Stockholm. Visit ⊛www.skargardsstiftelsen.se for accommodation on the islands.

195 Skagens Museum (☏45 98 44 64 44, ⊛www.skagensmuseum.dk); Brøndum's Hotel (☏45 98 44 15 55, ⊛www.broendums-hotel.dk).

196 See ⊛www.gotland.travel for more on the Gotland Medieval Week and the island in general.

197 Kuhmo is close to the airports of Kajaani or Kuopio. See ⊛www.visitfinland.com or ⊛www.erapiira.fi for more details.

198 For opening hours and entrance fees, see ⊛www.tivoli.dk.

199 Ferries travel daily to Bornholm from Ystad, in southern Sweden (1hr 15min), and from Køge, south of Copenhagen (overnight).

200 Seljalandsfoss is 140km east of Reykjavik, just off Route 1. The falls are on the itineraries of most south-coast tours, including those offered by Iceland

Excursions (⊛www.icelandexcursions.is).

201 A number of Copenhagen restaurants offer Christmas dinner specials; for details, check with the tourist office, 1 Gammel Kongevej (☏45 33 25 74 00, ⊛www.visitcopenhagen.com).

202 Alcohol in Reykjavík is extremely expensive: a beer in a bar costs at least €7, and in a club you can expect to pay in the region of €9.

203 Breakfast at the *Grand Hotel*'s *Veranda* costs SEK235. Reservations on ☏08679 3586 or ⊛www.grandhotel.se.

204 *Laekjarbrekka* is at Bankstraeti 2 (☏0551 4430, ⊛www.laekjarbrekka.is).

205 Puffins are best viewed on an organized boat tour from Tórshavn; see ⊛www.visittorshavn.fo/uk for a list of operators.

206 *The Utter Inn* is situated at Lake Malaren, in Vasteras, a hour or so from Stockholm and costs around SK3000 a night. From the UK, call ☏0871 855 6912 for more details.

207 Myvatn is about six hours by road from Reykjavik, and two hours from the nearest town, Akureyri. Buses run in summer; you'll have to hire a car during the rest of the year.

208 Jukkasjärvi is 17km from Kiruna, the nearest domestic airport. Double rooms start at SEK2240. You can book online at ⊛www.icehotel.com.

SOUTHEAST EUROPE

209 Pescasseroli lies on the single paved road that runs through the heart of the park, and is fairly well served by buses.

210 For more information on Capri, see ⊛www.caprionline.com.

211 ⊛www.visitzagori.com has more information on the Zagori region and ⊛www.greecetravel.com/hiking/vikos has details on how to hike the Vikos Gorge.

212 The restaurant is at Via dei Macci 111 (☏055/200.1492; ⊛www.teatrodelsale.com.

213 ⊛www.np-plitvicka-jezera.hr is the official website for the Plitvice Lakes, though it's only in Croatian.

214 The Guča festival takes place over 4 or 5 days in August. See ⊛www.guca.co.yu.

215 San Luigi dei Francesi on Via della Scrofa.; Santa Maria del Popolo on Piazza del Popolo.; Sant'Agostino on Piazza Sant'Agostino.; Museo e Galleria Borghese; booking obligatory on ☏06.328.10 or ⊛www.galleriaborghese.it.

216 *Tri Volta*, *Ghetto* and *Puls* are officially only open until midnight, but tend to keep on serving as long as they feel they can get away with it.

217 ⊛www.comune.marinadigioiosaionica.rc.it has details on the area and the so-called Riviera del Bronzi.

218 *Andergraund* is at Pariski 1a (daily 10am–4am). Strahinjiča bana, Obiličev venac and Njegoševa ulica, offer the greatest concentration of bars and cafés.

219 The Duomo is on Via Duomo, 10 minutes' walk from the city's main train station.

220 See ⊛www.pompeisites.org for more info.

221 There is an airport in Mostar but it serves few international destinations. It's easier to fly into Sarajevo, or to Dubrovnik or Split in Croatia. Regular bus services run to Mostar from all three cities.

222 See ⊛www.postojna-cave.com for more information.

223 ⊕www.parks.it/parco.nazionale.gran.paradiso; ⊕www.pngp.it; ⊕www.granparadiso.net.

224 The city walls are open daily (summer 9am–7.30pm; winter 10am–3pm), and cost 40Kn.

225 There are particularly well-known, and extremely popular, midnight mass celebrations on the islands of Crete, Ídhra, Corfu and Pátmos. Ferries and accommodation will be very busy; book well in advance if you want to spend Easter at Loutró.

226 There are tours of the Palazzo Farnese every Monday and Thursday at 3pm, 4pm and 5pm. Book in advance, either by email to ⊕visitefarnese@france-italia.it, or by going to the consular office at Via Giulia 251 (⊕06.6889.2818).

227 The Colosseum is open daily from 9am and closes at 4.30pm in winter. Tickets cost €9.

228 See ⊕www.slovenia.info for more information.

229 Marsaxlokk is easily reached by public transport from the capital Valletta (approx 35 minutes, bus 27).

230 Climbing Stromboli is permitted only with a registered guide. Contact Magmatrek, Via Vittorio Emanuele, in Stromboli (⊕www.magmatrek.it) for further details.

231 Tamburini, via Caprarie 1, ⊕051.234.726, ⊕www.tamburini.bo.it; Café de Paris, Piazza del Francia 1, ⊕051.234.980; Nu Lounge, via dei'Musei 6, ⊕051.222.532, ⊕www.nulounge.com.

232 To see anything, you need to stake your claim by lunchtime in the standing-room only area of the piazza; ⊕www.initaly.com/ads/palio/palio.htm has info on limited seated tickets.

233 Captain Morgan runs trips from Sliema Marina on board beautifully crafted Turkish gullets. ⊕www.captainmorgan.com.mt. Alternatively, Gozo Channel Company runs a ferry from Cirkewwa on Malta and Mgarr on Gozo, to San Niklaw Bay on Comino (a short distance from the Blue Lagoon) between mid-March and mid-November. ⊕www.gozochannel.com

234 Sicily's main airports are at Palermo and Catania. Frequent ferries cross over the Straits of Messina from the Italian mainland, carrying both trains and cars.

235 The best time to hear the nightingales sing in Aïdhónia is from spring to early summer. The only way to really explore the island's green interior is on foot; so bring sturdy walking boots, long trousers, repellent to ward off bloodthirsty mosquitoes and plenty of sunscreen.

236 Hostel Celica is located on Metelkova ulica. See ⊕www.souhostel.com for more information.

237 The Buzet tourist office (⊕385 52 662-343, ⊕www.buzet.hr) has details of the Buzetska Subotina festival. Toklarija, Sovinjsko polje 11 ⊕052/663-031.

238 The Aspendos Festival takes place for 3 to 4 weeks, starting in mid-June. Contact the Antalya Tourist Office on ⊕692 5220 or ⊕312 311 24 30 or ⊕aspendosfestival@kultur.gov.tr to find out what's on, when.

239 Information and tickets for performances are available from the tourist offices at Taormina (⊕www.gate2taormina.com) and Siracusa (⊕www.apt-siracusa.it).

240 See ⊕www.carnevalediivrea.it for more info.

241 Mystra can be reached by bus from Sparti or Neos Mystras. It's open 8am–pm (2pm in winter). Entrance is €5.

242 The starting point for almost all Greek island travels is Athens' port at Pireás. Timetables change constantly, and are subject to the weather, so the only truly accurate information is at the port, on the day:

simply turn up and buy a ticket.

243 Check out ⊕www.galleriaborghese.it/nuove/infourbino.html for more information.

244 From Sultanahmet take a tram to Karaköy then the Tünel funicular railway to the bottom of Independence Street; both close at 9pm. Return to Sultanahmet by taxi after midnight.

245 The top-name fashion stores are concentrated in the "Quadrilatero d'Oro" or "Golden Quadrilateral".

246 See ⊕www.cenacolovinciano.it for more.

247 Buses run regularly to Durres from Tirana and take about an hour.

248 See ⊕www.firenzemusei.it for the Uffizi's entry fees and opening times.

249 For opening hours, ticket prices and further information on Malta's megalithic sites, visit ⊕www.heritagemalta.org The Fat Lady and other artifacts found on the sites are housed in the National Museum of Archaeology, Valletta, open 9am to 5pm most days of the year, adults Lm3, concession Lm2.50 ⊕www.heritagemalta.org/archaeologymuseum.html.

250 Only ten males are admitted to Mt Áthos each day, for a maximum of four days. Contact the Mount Athos office in Thessaloníki (⊕2310 252578, ⊕2310 222424).

251 For details of the Venice carnival, go to ⊕www.carnevale.venezia.it or ⊕www.carnivalofvenice.com.

252 The Amalfi Coast is in Italy's Campania region in the southwest of the country. See ⊕www.amalficoastweb.com for further details.

253 Paestum is open 9am–7pm; €6. It can be reached by bus from Naples and Salerno.

254 Cecil Studios offers life model posing; contact ⊕055 285102 or ⊕www.charlescecilstudios.com.

255 Donizetti is at Via Gombito 17a, Da Mimmo at Via Colleoni 17 and Caffè Funicolare on Piazza Mercato delle Scarpe (all closed Tues).

256 Fire-walking festivals take place towards the end of May in the villages of Langadas, Ayia Eleni, Meliki and Ayios Petros in northern Greece.

257 Ostia Antica can be reached from Rome's Termini station. Trains take approx 50min.

258 Epidavros is open daily 8am–7pm (winter until 5pm). Entrance costs €6. Plays are performed June–Aug on Fri and Sat eves.

259 You'll need a full day to explore Meteora ⊕www.meteora-greece.com); the town of Kalampaka, 20min by bus, is your best bet for an overnight stay.

260 Information on tickets and other Biennale practicalities is available at ⊕www.labiennale.org.

261 From May to September, there are ferries twice daily between Vathy and Sami, Kefalonia (1hr), and once daily between Frikes and Nidri, Lefkas (1hr 30min).

262 For more on Reinhold Messner, check out ⊕www.reinhold-messner.de.

263 Göreme and Ürgüp have regular bus connections to cities all over Turkey, although you often get dropped in the town of Nevsehir – 20km to the west – even if you have a ticket to Göreme.

264 For more on Mevlana Celaddin Runi, see ⊕www.mevlana.net.

265 The Sistine Chapel is part of the Vatican Museums: see ⊕www.vatican.va for more information.

266 For more got to ⊕www.cinqueterre.it and ⊕www.cinqueterre.com. To walk the Blue trail you need to pay a small fee.

267 Visit the tourist office, 24 via Vittorio Emanuele (⊕0832.332.463, ⊕www.pugliaturismo.com) for more

information.

268 Rafting is available between April and September; Tara Tours (⊕www.tara-grab.com) offer half day excursions for €65.

269 The truffle season runs from the end of September to the beginning of November, and Alba celebrates with its own fair for gourmets. More information can be found at ⊕www.tuber.it.

270 The mud baths are accessible by boat only. See ⊕www.dalyan.co.uk/tourist for more information.

271 New bars and cafés are constantly springing up in Tirana – follow the crowds for a good idea of what's hot.

272 The Gruppo Guide Alpine ⊕www.guidecortina.com offers guided day trips; or you can stay at scenic mountain huts and go from one route to another.

273 Da Genio, Salita San Leonardo 61, Genova ⊕010.588.463; Matricianella, Via del Leone 2, Roma ⊕06.683.2100; Bellini, Via Santa Maria di Costaninopoli 80, Napoli ⊕081.459.774

274 For information on what's on, visit ⊕www.zagreb-touristinfo.hr, although you're best advised to go to the sites of individual clubs.

275 The best map to use is Road Edition's no 31 Olympos, 1:50, 000.

276 Direct flights from the UK go to Iráklion and Haniá. Otherwise fly to Athens, from where it's a half-hour flight or comfortable overnight ferry ride.

277 Troy is best accessed from Çanakkale. Tours cost 26YTL upwards, and dolmuşes leave every twenty minutes.

278 Reserve a ticket by phoning ⊕049.201.0020, or online at ⊕www.cappelladegliscrovegni.it.

279 Venice's tourist season is an all-year affair, so book your room well in advance. The tourist office's website (⊕www.turismovenezia.it) gives details of accommodation of all types.

280 Hotel Danieli is at Riva degli Schiavoni 4196; reservations at ⊕www.luxurycollection.com/danieli.

281 You can find out more about how to stay at Studenica at ⊕www.hotelstudenica.co.yu or by calling ⊕036 836.222.

282 Istanbul's Kapali Çarşi is open Monday-Saturday 9am–7pm and admission is free.

283 St John's Co-Cathedral (Mon–Fri 9.30am–12.30pm & 1.30–4.15pm, Sat 9.30am–12.30pm).

284 The coastal resorts are easily accessed by bus from Podgorica, the Montenegron capital, or from Dubrovnik. See ⊕www.visit-montenegro.com.

285 The perfect Roman pizza: Ai Marmi, Viale di Trastevere 53–59. The perfect Neapolitan pizza: Di Matteo, Via dei Tribunali 94.

286 ⊕www.kirkpinar.com has everything you need to know about the Kirkpinar championships, past and present.

287 ⊕www.ohrid.org.mk has more on the lake and town.

288 Go to the official tourist board website (⊕www.turismo.toscana.it) for more info on Tuscany.

EASTERN EUROPE

289 Hotel Gellert, Szent Gellért tér, District XI, Budapest (⊕889-5500, ⊕www.danubiushotels.com/en/budapest-hotels/danubius-hotel-gellert-budapest).

290 The churches are scattered across a remote part of Slovakia – to best way to reach them is to hike or hire a bicycle.

291 *Na Spilce* is open daily 11am–10pm. For a guided tour, ring ☎377 062888 or see ⊕www.beerworld.cz.

292 Check out ⊕www.zemaitijosnp.lt for more about the tours. Hostel-style accommodation can be arranged from €10 per person.

293 For a virtual excursion of the park in English, see ⊕www.vvcentre.ru/eng/about_us/excursion.

294 Kraków Tourist Board ⊕www.krakow.pl; Sunday flea market (Gielda staroci), Hala Targowa, Massolit, ul. Felicianek 4 ⊕www.massolit.com.

295 See ⊕www.ukraine-travel-advisor.com/simferopol-airport.html for more information.

296 Hourly buses go from Braşov to Bran Castle. For Poienari, take a bus from Curtea de Argeş to Arefu, from where it's 4km to the footpath that leads up to the castle. *Casa Dracula*, the restaurant occupying Dracula's birthplace, is at Str Cositorarilor 5.

297 Alberta iela lies in the Centrs district of Rīga; see ⊕www.rigatourism.com.

298 The White Nights last from June 11 to July 2.

299 The Municipal Museum, inside the Poznański palace at ul. Ogrodowa 15 (Tues & Thurs 10am–4pm, Wed 2–6pm, Fri–Sun 10am–2pm), provides an overview of the city's industrial heritage.

300 The best time to see Kiev's chestnut flowers in bloom is May.

301 *The Military Pub* is at No.7, Kiev Street (nightly until 6am).

302 The Rákóczi cellar in Tokaj is at Kossuth tér 15 (mid-March to mid-Oct daily 10am–6pm); the cellar in Sá'rospatak is at Erzsébet utca tér 26 (same times); a tasting of six wines plus nibbles costs around €8.

303 Red Square can be reached from Ploshchad Revolyutsii, Aleksandrovskiy Sad, Biblioteka Imeni Lenina and Borovitskaya metros.

304 Zakopane is around 3 hours by train or bus from Kraków.

305 The Hermitage is on Palace Square, near Nevsky Prospekt metro. Ordering a ticket online (⊕www.hermitage.org) gives you a voucher allowing you to jump the queue.

306 The Jewish State Museum is at Pylimo 4 and Pamenkalnio 12. Paneriai lies 10km southwest of the city centre.

307 České Budějovice is 150km south of Prague. Masné kramy is just off the old town square on Krajinská. The brewery is 2.5km north of the old town: call ☎387 705 111 or see ⊕www.budweiser.cz for more information.

308 In Kovachevitsa, *Kapsuzovi Kushti* (☎899 403 089, ✉kapsazovs_houses@yahoo.com) offers fully equipped rooms and has a fantastic restaurant. Or contact Sofia-based Zig-Zag Holidays (☎980 3200, ⊕www.zigzagbg.com) for accommodation throughout Bulgaria.

309 The nearest town to Mount Elbrus is Mineralnya Vody, a short flight from Moscow or Munich; it's a 4-hour bus ride from the airport to the Baksan Valley at the base of Elbrus. For more information on the climb, visit ⊕www.elbrus.org.uk.

310 Wolf- and bear-tracking excursions can be organized with Roving Romania (⊕www.roving-romania.co.uk).

311 The tourist information office is at ul. Jozefa 7 (⊕www.krakow.pl). The Cracovia stadium lies west of the town centre on al. Focha.

312 Auschwitz is named after the Polish town of Oświęcim, around 50km west of Kraków – buses between the two are frequent. The Auschwitz-Birkenau Museum & Memorial is free; see ⊕www.auschwitz-muzeum.oswiecim.pl for the latest opening hours.

313 See ⊕www.urbanrail.net/eu/mos/moskva.htm for information on ticket prices and routes.

314 See ⊕www.transylvaniancastle.com for details of tours and accommodation.

315 The Lahemaa National Park lies an hour's drive east of Tallinn. The National Park visitors' centre (☎0372 329 5555, ⊕www.lahemaa.ee) is in Palmse.

316 St Vitus Cathedral in Prague Castle is open daily. Charles Bridge can be visited any time of the day or night. For more on St John, see ⊕www.sjn.cz.

317 Tiraspol can be accessed on regular buses from Chisinau, the capital of Moldova, or Lviv in the Ukraine.

318 ⊕www.brasovtravelguide.ro has more information on Braşov and the Juni.

319 From Plovdiv take a bus from the Yug terminal to the town of Haskovo (1hr 30min) to catch the 3pm bus to Madzharovo (2hr). The Nature Information Centre (☎03720/345, ✉marin.kurtev@bspb.org) arranges guided tours of the reserve.

NORTH AFRICA

320 The Pyramids are 11km west of Cairo and can be reached by bus or taxi. The site is open daily: summer 6.30am–midnight; winter 7am–8pm.

321 Several operators specialize in camel-trekking; try Siroko Travel (⊕www.sirokotravel.com).

322 The base for the Hoggar is the modern town of Tamanrasset. Point Afrique (⊕www.point-afrique.com) organizes expeditions.

323 Fes' Festival of Sacred Music is held over a week each June; see ⊕www.fesfestival.com.

324 Most Tassili treks are part of an organized tour; see ⊕www.sahara-overland.com. Written confirmation of your place on a tour is required to obtain an Algerian visa.

325 Troglodyte accommodation ranges from Matmata's deluxe *Hôtel Diar el Barbar* (☎75 240 074) to simple guesthouses in Douiret and Toujane.

326 Leptis Magna is 3km east of Khoms, though it makes an easy day-trip from Tripoli.

327 There's a wide choice of accommodation around the Jemaa, notably riads done out as boutique hotels.

328 Travellers' Tales runs their week-long travel-writing workshop in Morocco every year in late March. Check ⊕www.travellerstales.org.

329 You can rent a car in Tangier or Ceuta. For more, see ⊕www.sahara-overland.com.

330 Tanta is 95km north of Cairo. The moulid of Sayyid Ahmed al-Badawi takes place over eight days in October.

331 Aswan lies 900km south of Cairo. The Aswan tourist office can recommend felucca captains and prices.

332 For more information, go to Red Sea Diving College (⊕www.redseacollege.com).

333 The only permitted travel to Jebel Acacus is with a tour; try Wahat Umm Algouzlan, 1st Circle Road, Al-hdaiq, Benghazi (☎61 2223420, ✉info@libyato.com).

334 Mount Sinai is on the Sinai Peninsula in eastern Egypt. Tours can easily be arranged from Cairo and Alexandria.

335 Dougga is just over 100km from Tunis; to get there by public transport, take the bus from Tunis to Taboursouk and transfer to a louage.

336 For details on trekking in the Atlas Mountains, see ⊕www.visitmorocco.org.

337 The Bibliotheca Alexandrina is at El Shatby 21526. See ⊕www.bibalex.org for more.

338 The Marathon des Sables takes on average 6–7 days to complete the 243km between Erfoud and Tazaine in southern Morocco.

339 There are now flights to Ghadames from Tripoli, or you can take a bus via Nalut.

340 For upmarket accommodation, try the *Ville Nouvelle*, while there's a cluster of budget places around Bab Boujeloud.

341 A variety of tajines are available from places all over Morocco, from hole-in-the-wall eateries to up-market restaurants.

342 Non-Muslims are not expected to fast. Restaurants in the big hotels serve breakfast and lunch behind closed doors.

343 Douz is 9 hours by bus from Tunis. The Festival of the Sahara takes place every December.

344 Luxor is 700km south of Cairo. Boats cross the Nile, from where you can proceed by bus or taxi to the Valley of the Kings.

345 You can stay at several refurbished kasbahs along the route; the most atmospheric is Aït Ben Skoura (☎0212 4485 2116, ⊕www.kasbahbenmoro).

346 *Auberge Chez Tihri* (⊕www.tuaregexpeditions.com) lies 2km north of Merzouga.

347 Essaouira is 170km from Marrakesh. Buses leave daily from the gare routière.

348 *The Fishawi Café* is behind the *El Hussein* hotel in Khan-el-Khalili and is open 24hr.

349 The usual jumping-off point for the Ubari lakes is Tekerkiba, where there are a couple of places to camp and eat; otherwise there's a youth hostel in nearby Fjeij.

350 Tlemcen is a town of around 180,000 people, close by the Moroccan border, and is well connected with the rest of Algeria by bus and train, as well as by air with Algiers.

351 The best time to cross the desert is between November and March.

352 For information on travelling to Beni Abes and Timimoun, visit ⊕www.algeria.embassyhomepage.com.

353 As well as the Medina, spare some time for Tripoli's wonderful Jamahiriya museum – one of the world's best archeological collections.

354 For information on tours to the area, see ⊕www.sahara-overland.com.

WEST AFRICA

355 Check out clubs *Thiossane*, to see if Youssou N'Dour is in town; *Le Kily* (also called *Kilimandjaro*), home to local superstar Thione Seck; or *Just 4 You*, for Orchestra Baobab. The monthly *221* magazine has all the latest listings.

356 You can also reach Timbuktu along the river from Mopti, or by light aircraft from Bamako.

357 Bus services run along the main coastal highway from Accra.

358 Treks on Mount Cameroon can be arranged in Buea, 70km from Douala, through the Mount Cameroon Inter-communal Ecotourism Board (☎332.20.38, ⊕www.mount-cameroon.org).

359 TAP (Air Portugal) fly once a week from Lisbon to São Tomé; see ⊕www.flytap.com for details.

360 Prime bird-watching areas include the Tanbi Wetlands, Abuko Nature Reserve, Brufut Woods, Marakissa and Janjanbureh. Birdfinders (☻www.birdfinders.co.uk) offer specialist tours to The Gambia.

361 You can get around the islands by ferry, but voyages can be rough and slow; alternatively, buy a multi-coupon domestic air ticket on TACV (☻www.tacv.cv), the national airline.

362 Yankari can get crowded at weekends, especially over Christmas and Easter. The park lodge has basic rooms (reserve ahead on ☎077/543 674).

363 The most popular trek is from Banani to Kani Kombolé and takes roughly two days.

364 The WWF office at Yokadouma (☎629.59.31 or 529.24.84, ☻www.panda.org), 612km from the capital of Yaoundé, can arrange treks with Baka guides into all three of southeastern Cameroon's national parks.

365 Sanyang Beach is an easy taxi ride from Banjul and the resort towns of Kololi, Kotu, Fajara and Bakau.

366 The festival takes place in early January at Essakane. For tickets and more information, go to ☻www.festival-au-desert.org.

367 For practical information, see ☻www.ibike.org.

368 Tour agencies in Agadez can organize camel treks.

369 Parc National du Banc D'Arguin is two hours from Nouadhibou, near the Moroccan border. Randonnées Tours in Nouakchott (☎0222 525 9535, ☻rt@toptechnology.mr), run bird-watching tours.

370 Trains run three times a day in each direction, but only two of these services – the 12.10pm from Zouérat and the 2.40pm Nouadhibou – have passenger carriages.

371 The national airline TACV (☻www.tacv.cv) offers flights to Fogo.

372 Passenger-carrying pirogues (dug-out canoes) leave Bissau twice weekly for the two main Bijagós islands of Bubaque and Bolama.

373 Djenné is 30km from the main road between the Malian capital, Bamako, and the junction town of Mopti. The interior of the mosque is open to muslims only.

374 In season (Aug–Dec) boats leave Koulikoro every Tuesday at 10pm.

375 Ouidah is an hour's taxi ride from Cotonou. The Temple of the Python is open daily.

376 A useful source of general tourist information is ☻www.visitsierraleone.org.

377 Chinguetti is 2 days' drive from the capital, Nouakchott. A dozen or so families maintain libraries in their homes, preserving some 6000 manuscripts in total.

378 Djado is a 3-day jeep drive from Agadez, the largest city in northern Niger.

CENTRAL & EAST AFRICA

379 Large two-bed safari tents at *Red Chilli Rest Camp* (☻www.redchillihideaway.com/paraa.htm) cost Ush25,000.

380 Queen Elizabeth National Park is 5 hours from the capital, Kampala. Accessing the cave is best done with a local guide.

381 The journey between Kinshasa and Kisangani takes two weeks. Alternatively, Go Congo (www.gocongo.com) runs an adventure tour in a 34-metre river cruiser.

382 See ☻www.malewariverlodge.com for more in-formation.

383 Lamu is served by domestic flights and by buses from Malindi and Mombasa.

384 It's possible to book your journey locally or you can reserve a place in advance with ☻www.eastafricashuttles.com/train.htm.

385 *Chole Mjini* is reached by dhow from Mafia Island, which is itself a short flight from Dar es Salaam. For rates and bookings, see ☻www.africatravelresource.com.

386 *Maia Resort and Spa* (☻www.maia.com.sc) is on Mahé island. A stay costs from €1530 per night.

387 For further information on Kahuzi-Biega National Park, contact the Gorilla Organisation (☻www.gorillas.org).

388 Injera has a slightly sour taste, and is best accompanied with a drink of tej (a honey wine) or Ambo (a brand of fizzy water).

389 Many resorts offer turtle-watching trips in season; one of the easiest places to see them is Cousine Island.

390 A three-day pass covering all eleven churches costs around Br165. Hiring a guide is worthwhile, at around Br110 per day.

391 You can visit Langoué Bai with World Primate Safaris (☻www.worldprimatesafaris.com), whose trip includes a stay at *Langoué Bai Camp*, a rustic forest base run by Wildlife Conservation Society researchers.

392 The closest town to Mount Elgon is Kitale. The entrance fee for Mount Elgon National Park is US$20 per day.

393 Several white water-rafting companies operate out of Jinga; try Adrift (☻www.adrift.ug) or Nile River Explorers (☻www.raftafrica.com).

394 The best time to see the migration in the Serengeti is between December and July; for the river crossings, visit in June (Grumeti) and July or August (Mara). Check out ☻www.wildwatch.com/sightings/migration.asp for up-to-date reports on the location of the herds.

395 Zanzibar is a 20-minute flight from Dar es Salaam, and under 3 hours by ferry.

396 Frégate Island (☻www.fregate.com) is a 20-minute helicopter hop from the international airport on Mahé. Villas cost from €2400 per night for two people on a full-board basis (3 nights min stay).

397 The best times to make the ascent of Kilimanjaro are January to mid-March and June to October. Climbers must sign up with a trekking agency. Treks last 6 to 8 days.

398 *Chumbe Island Eco-Lodge* (☻www.chumbeisland.com) is reached by boat from Zanzibar. All profits from the lodge go back into the conservation of the island.

399 Kibale Forest National Park is best reached from Fort Portal, either on local buses or with organized day tours.

400 Rooms at *Giraffe Manor* (☻www.giraffemanor.com) cost from US$290. Giraffe Centre (☻www.giraffecenter.org).

401 Standard practice at meat bars is to go to the kitchen and order by weight direct from the butcher's hook or out of the fridge. *Carnivore* (☻www.carnivore.co.ke), on Longata Road, is Nairobi's best-known and biggest nyama choma bar.

402 Meroë is a two-day train ride north of the capital, Khartoum.

403 Crater safaris are easily arranged in Arusha, several hours' drive to the east.

404 *Il Ngwesi* is approximately 90 minutes' rough drive from the nearest road. See ☻www.lets-go-travel.net for more information and rates of bandas.

405 A guide and scout can be hired at the entrance to the national park. Avoid the rainy season (June–Sept).

406 Access is easier by public transport than in your own vehicle: get to Mpanda by rail, then catch a vehicle to the village at the park headquarters. Armed rangers cost US$20 per day (plus park entrance of US$20/day).

407 Pemba Island is easily accessed from Zanzibar, either by ferry or by air.

408 Balloon flights are offered by several of the larger safari camps and lodges in Kenya; they'll come and pick you up if you're staying elsewhere in the Maasai Mara.

409 Ferries to the islands leave from Bukakata; timings are erratic, so be prepared to hang around.

410 For more, see ☻www.zanzibar.net.

411 See ☻www.operation-loango.com for more info on Loango National Park.

SOUTHERN AFRICA

412 Only a handful of game reserves in South Africa are large enough to accommodate free-ranging lions. Madikwe (☻www.tourismnorthwest.co.za/madikwe) is one, though you can only visit if staying at one of its private lodges.

413 The Zululand Birding Route (☻www.zbr.co.za) can provide guides to help you explore the area.

414 For more about the island of Mauritius, see ☻www.mauritius.net.

415 Anjajavy is 120km north of Majunga. It's a very remote spot, accessible by air only – *Anjajavy Hotel* runs a regular transfer from the capital, Antanarivo.

416 The "Big Baobab" is situated about three and half hours away from Johannesburg. For more, go to ☻www.bigbaobad.co.za.

417 An early morning hot-air-balloon safari over the desert near Sossusvlei, followed by a champagne breakfast on the ground, costs N$2750 per person with NamibSky Adventure Safaris (☻www.balloonsafaris.com).

418 For more information about Kande Beach, go to ☻www.kandebeach.com.

419 Bull Seals are rarely seen outside of the breeding season (Oct). Nov–Dec is the best time to see baby seals.

420 Most lodges in the Okavango Delta run mokoro safaris. Visit ☻www.okavango-delta.net for more information.

421 Hiking along the canyon itself is only allowed from May to September to avoid flash flood accidents. Numbers are limited: book as far in advance as you can at ☻www.nwr.com.na.

422 *Tendele Camp* (☻www.drakensberg-tourism.com/tendele-camp-royal-natal.html) offers bungalows with mountain views. For more information on hiking in the Drakensberg, visit ☻www.drakensbergtourism.com.

423 Etosha National Park is located about 400km north of Namibia's capital, Windhoek. The 3 national park rest camps have shops, fuel and plentiful accommodation, from cottages to camping.

424 Visit ☻www.kawazavillage.co.uk for more information. Bookings can be made through ☻www.robinpopesafaris.net.

425 In a 4WD, you can reach the Makgadikgadi Pans from the main tar road between Nata and Maun: the two largest pans, Sowa and Ntwetwe, lie to the south; Nxai Pan to the north.

426 Nyika Plateau National Park lies 350km north of Malawi's capital, Lilongwe. It's a long slog by road to the top, or a short flight to Chelinda, the park headquarters, where there's a campsite, chalets, an upmarket lodge and mountain bikes for hire.

427 Ongava Game Reserve is in the far north of Namibia. Staying at *Ongava Tented Camp* (⊕ www.ongava. com) costs from N$1340 per person per night.

428 *Bulungula Lodge* (⊕ www.bulungula.co.za) has dorms for R80 (per person) and twin rooms for R200.

429 Volunteers on Azafady's ten-week Pioneer programme are required to raise a minimum donation of £2000. For more, see ⊕ www.azafady.org.

430 It takes about 12 hours to drive between Cape Town and Jo'burg on the N1: the tiny towns of Richmond and Hanover are roughly halfway. See ⊕ www. northerncape.org.za for more.

431 *Guludo Beach Lodge* (⊕ www.bespokeexperience. com) costs from US$205 per person per night.

432 Botswana has two great elephant-safari operations: Elephant Back Safaris at *Abu Camp* (⊕ www. abucamp.com), and Living with Elephants (⊕ www. livingwithelephants.org).

433 A Tsitsikamma Canopy Tour costs R395 per person from Stormsriver Adventures (⊕ www.stormsriver. com) .

434 Since rainfall and temperatures vary from year to year, it's impossible to be sure when and where the show of flowers will be at its peak, but the best displays are usually from mid-August to mid-September.

435 Vamizi is reached via international flights to Dares-Salaam and then a private charter flight to Mozambique. For more on *Vamizi Lodge*, see ⊕ www. maluane.com.

436 Tsimanin Droa is accessible by air only. *Anjajavy Hotel* (⊕ www.anjajavy.com) runs a regular transfer from the capital, Antananarivo.

437 Contact *Jan Harmsgat Country House B&B* at ⊕ www.jhghouse.com.

438 A good place to arrange treks is *Malealea Lodge* (⊕ www.malealea.co.ls), an hour's drive south of the capital Maseru.

439 The river is at its lowest between mid-July and mid-January. Safari Par Excellence (⊕ www.safpar. com) runs trips out of Livingstone.

440 Malolotja Nature Reserve is 30 minutes' drive from Mbabane, Swaziland's capital, and 90 minutes from Matsapha airport.

441 New Year and Easter are the big Rustler's Valley events, but there are two or three other parties held between September and April each year. See ⊕ www. rustlers.co.za for more info.

442 You can dive in Lake Malawi all year round, but it's important to be wary of bilharzia (schistosomiasis): avoid reedbeds in calm water close to shore.

443 To make the most of the mountain, book a place on one of Hoerikwaggo Trails' guided hikes (⊕ www. hoerikwaggotrails.co.uk).

444 Resorts on the Bazaruto Archipelago usually include charter flights in their packages. The Mozambican airline LAM flies to Beira, Nampula (from where buses leave for Ilha do Moçambique) and Pemba, the main town in Cabo Delgado.

445 For tours, try Papyrus (⊕ 01405 785 232, ⊕ www. papyrustours.co.uk), the Ultimate Travel Company (⊕ 020/7386 4646, ⊕ www.ultimatetravelcompany.co.

uk) or Wildlife Worldwide (⊕ 0845 130 6982, ⊕ www. wildlifeworldwide.com).

446 *Palmwag Rhino Camp* is run by Wilderness Safaris (⊕ www.wilderness-safaris.com) in conjunction with Save the Rhino (⊕ www.rhino-trust.org.na).

447 See ⊕ www.zambiatourism.com/travel/places/ victoria.htm for more on the Falls.

448 Calabash Tours (⊕ www.calabashtours.co.za) in Port Elizabeth and Cape Capers (⊕ www.tourcapers. co.za) in Cape Town run township tours.

449 Zambia's South Luangwa National Park is one of Africa's best walking-safari destinations. Outfits operating there include The Bushcamp Company (⊕ www. bushcampcompany.com).

450 For more details on becoming a wildlife ranger go to ⊕ www.krugerpark.co.za.

451 Shipping vessels leave 12 times a year from Cape Town to Tristan da Cunha. To enquire about permission to visit the island, go to ⊕ www.tristandc.com

452 Many wineries around Stellenbosch, Franschhoek and Paarl open their cellars to the public from November to March: see ⊕ www. stellenbosch tourism.co.za for more information.

453 Ncwala is held across Swaziland each December, lasting for 3 weeks.

454 A package trip includes guided nature walks and 4WD excursions. The only accommodation is *Skeleton Coast Camp* (⊕ www.wilderness-safaris.com), a luxury tented camp reachable by air.

455 Numerous outfitters can be hired in Antananarivo or at Miandrivazo; Belaza Tours (⊕ www.gassitours. com) offers a variety of tours of the river.

THE MIDDLE EAST

456 Buses run to Masada from Jerusalem, Tel Aviv, Beersheba and Eliat. Entrance costs around NLS59 if you take the cable car or NLS25 if you brave the walk.

457 Aleppo is 350km north of Damascus and is accessible by plane, train and bus. Most shops in the souk are open 9am–6pm (closed Fri).

458 Abu Shukri's is at the fifth station of the cross on the Via Dolorosa, near the Damascus gate.

459 Khasab Travel and Tours (⊕ www.khasabtours. com) runs half- and full-day cruises on the Musandam fjords; otherwise, try Shaw Travel (⊕ www.shawtravel. com), who include the Musandam fjords in some of their Oman itineraries.

460 There are hotels and/or public beaches on the eastern shore near Swaymeh (Jordan); and on the western shore at Ain Feshka (in the Palestinian Territories), Ein Gedi and Ein Bokek (both in Israel).

461 Shibam is roughly 500km east of Sana'a, most easily reached by air.

462 Hama is 47km north of Homs, served by trains and buses between Damascus and Aleppo.

463 The *Emirates Palace* (⊕ www.emiratespalace. com) is on the Corniche, 1km outside Abu Dhabi city centre.

464 Salalah is 1000km southwest of Muscat, served by regular worldwide flights.

465 Visit the Museum of Pearl Diving in Manama for an insight into the tradition.

466 Acre is 25km north of Haifa, served by buses and trains from there and Tel Aviv.

467 Khor al-Adaid lies 75km south of Doha, the Qatari capital. No roads run even close. The only way to get here is in a 4WD vehicle organized by any of several tour companies based in Doha: see ⊕ www.

gulf-adventures.com or ⊕ www.nettoursdubai.com.

468 Races in Wahiba – 190km from Muscat – are held on Fridays and public holidays in the winter.

469 Buses from Beirut to Baalbek take between two and three hours – see ⊕ www.baalbeck.org.lb for details.

470 Tawi Attair is located in southwest Oman. You'll need a 4WD to access the area, which you can hire in nearby Salaha.

471 Visit the Krak des Chevaliers as soon as it opens (8.30am) to avoid the crowds. Entrance costs approx S£320.

472 Socotra lies 500km south of the Yemeni coast, reached most easily by scheduled flights from Aden or Sanaa. For more go to ⊕ www.socotraisland.org and ⊕ www.friendsofsoqotra.org.

473 Check out ⊕ www.bethlehem-city.org for information on where to stay.

474 See ⊕ www.saudiembassy.net for information on visas: a tiny number of tourist visas are issued each year, but only to organized groups.

475 Palmyra is 220km northeast of Damascus. The site is unfenced, though some of the temples have set hours (generally 8am–sunset; S£300).

476 Operators offering dolphin-watching cruises include ⊕ www.arabianseasafaris.com, ⊕ www.oman-diving.com and ⊕ www.zaharatours.com

477 Tour operators worldwide offer diving packages to the Red Sea, and dive centres in Aqaba offer PADI and other international diving courses. Try ⊕ www. seastar-watersports.com, ⊕ www.rdc.jo, ⊕ www.aquamarina-group.com or ⊕ www.diveaqaba.com.

478 Hammam Nur ad-Din (daily 8am–midnight) is strictly men-only. Hammam al-Qaimariyya (daily 7am–midnight) is one of several in Damascus with women-only hours (noon–5pm).

479 The Hammam Abhar is open Mon, Wed & Thurs for men and Tues, Fri & Sat for women; entrance is 100YR.

480 Most shops in the Deira Gold Souk follow similar hours (daily 9am–10pm).

481 Persian voyages (⊕ www.persianvoyages.com) can organize a trip to Iran. All visitors require a visa.

482 Even when Israel and Palestine are consumed by conflict, Tel Aviv often seems a world away, but it's best to check the situation before you travel.

483 In Lebanon, the country's finest mezze restaurants are in the town of Zahlé.

484 Wadi Rum lies 300km south of Amman. The best online resource is ⊕ www.jordanjubilee.com.

485 For further information, see ⊕ www.burj-al-arab. com.

486 Tours of the Arab Organizations Headquarters Building can be booked by emailing ⓒ adnang@earth-link.net.

487 Habiba, Jabri and Zalatimo (⊕ www.zalatimo sweets.com) have numerous stores across Amman.

488 Check out ⊕ www.rscn.org.jo for more information.

489 Wadi Shab is on the coastal rough between Muscat and Sur and requires a 4WD vehicle to access.

490 The Baptism Site (daily 8am-sunset; JD5; ⊕ www.baptismsite.com) is signposted from the Amman-Dead Sea highway.

491 *B018* is located 2km north of the centre of Beirut just off the Dora highway. It opens at 9pm and is in full swing by 3am.

492 The I-Imam Mosque, Sheikh Lotfollah Mosque and Ali Qapu Palace are all open daily (approx 8am–sunset; IR30,000).

493 The mosque is open to visitors daily 8am–5pm (until 7pm during the summer), but it is closed on Friday mornings. Entry is IR30,000.

494 Petra (daily 6am–sunset) is 240km south of the Jordanian capital, Amman. The adjacent town of Wadi Musa has restaurants and hotels.

495 Kuwait Camel Racing Club is in Kabad, an hour's drive west of Kuwait City. Races are held every Thursday afternoon; call ahead for the schedule (☎539 4015).

496 There are numerous tour companies in Qatar who offer 4WD trips into the desert; Arabian Adventures (⊕www.arabianadventureqatar.com) are well established and drivers often speak English.

497 Serjilla lies 7km east of Bara. The nearest facilities are in Idleb.

498 Habalah is located about 75km from Abha.

USA

499 South Beach occupies the southernmost part of Miami Beach; Ocean Drive runs south–north for 10 blocks.

500 Visit ⊕www.cubs.com for Wrigley Field ticket information. *Murphy's Bleachers*, 3655 North Sheffield Ave(⊕www.murphysbleachers.com); *Sheffield's*, 3258 North Sheffield Ave (⊕www.sheffieldschicago.com).

501 The Empire State Building, 350 Fifth Ave (daily 8am–midnight; ⊕www.esbnyc.com).

502 Two of the most experienced stormchasing operators are Violent Skies (⊕www.violentskiestours.com) and TRADD (⊕www.traddstormchasingtours.com).

503 The Monument Valley Visitors' Center (⊕www.navajonationparks.org) is off Hwy-163 in Arizona, near the Utah border.

504 Visit ⊕www.mardigras.neworleans.com for more information on the festivities.

505 *Russ and Daughters*, 179 E Houston St (☎212/475-4880, ⊕www.russanddaughters.com).

506 Dr Wilkinson's Hot Springs, 1507 Lincoln Ave, Calistoga (☎707/942-4102, ⊕www.drwilkinson.com); Mount View Spa, 1457 Lincoln Ave, Calistoga (☎707/942-6877, ⊕www.mountviewspa.com); Jack London State Historic Park, Glen Ellen (⊕www.jacklondonpark.com); *The French Laundry*, 6640 Washington St, Yountville (☎707/944-2380, ⊕www.frenchlaundry.com).

507 The parkway starts at Rockfish Gap near Waynesboro, Virginia, just off I-64, and ends 469 miles later near Cherokee, North Carolina, on Hwy-441.

508 Direct flights connect Lihue on Kauai with Honolulu, San Francisco and Los Angeles. Visit ⊕www.hawaii.gov/dlnr/dsp/NaPali/na_pali.htm for information on hiking in the Na Pali Coast State Park.

509 US Capitol (Mon–Sat 9am–4.30pm; ⊕www.aoc.gov/cc/visit); White House (⊕www.whitehouse.gov/history/tours); Supreme Court (Oct–April arguments 10am & 11am; ⊕www.supremecourt.us.gov).

510 The round-trip hike to the top of Half Dome is 17 miles (9–12hr; 4800ft ascent).

511 Walking tours cover everything from local architecture to legends; visit ⊕www.savannahvisit.com.

512 The most popular entrance to Glacier National Park (⊕www.nps.gov/glac) is near the town of West Glacier, off Hwy-2.

513 Ceremonial dances are performed at Taos Pueblo (⊕www.taospueblo.com) about 10 times a year.

514 Several stores in town offer bike rentals and or-ganize shuttles to trailheads; the best times to visit are spring and fall.

515 For information on the event, visit ⊕www.halloween-nyc.com. Some of the best costume-supply shops include Abracadabra Magic & Costumes, 19 W 21st St (☎212/627-5194, ⊕www.abracadabrasuperstore.com); Creative Costume Company, 242 W 36th St (☎212/564-5552, ⊕www.creativecostume.com); and Ricky's, 44 E Eighth St (☎212/254-5347, ⊕www.rickys-nyc.com).

516 Old Coal Mine Museum, 2814 Hwy-14, Madrid (☎505/438-3780, ⊕www.turquoisetrail.org/oldcoalmine); *Mine Shaft Tavern*, 2846 Hwy-14, Madrid (☎505/473-0743, ⊕www.themineshafttavern.com).

517 For more information, go to ⊕www.cassadaga.org.

518 Blazing Saddles Bike Rentals & Tours is at 2715 Hyde St at Beach (☎415/202-8888, ⊕www.blazingsaddles.com).

519 A crab feast is best in a backyard or church basement, but Annapolis's *Cantler's Riverside Inn*, 458 Forest Beach Rd (☎410/757-1467, ⊕www.cantlers.com), or *Kelly's*, 2108 Eastern Ave (☎410/327-2312) and *Costas Inn*, 4100 Northpoint Blvd (☎410/477-1975), both in Baltimore, will do the trick.

520 The Strip, a 4-mile stretch of hotel-casinos along Las Vegas Boulevard (8 of the 10 largest hotels in the world call Vegas home), is the city's beating heart.

521 *Two Lights Lobster Shack*, 225 Two Lights Rd, Cape Elizabeth (5 miles south of Portland; ☎207/799-1677).

522 For more on Cannon Beach, visit ⊕www.cannon-beach.net.

523 The festival takes place in May in Molokai on the western tip of the island. Admission is free.

524 Alaska Sea Kayakers (☎907/472-2534, ⊕www.alaskaseakayakers.com), in Whittier, rents sea kayaks and run guided day-trips and multi-day tours.

525 Visit ⊕www.appalachiantrail.org for more information on hiking the AT.

526 Several companies, including Celebrity (⊕www.celebritycruises.com), Holland America (⊕www.hollandamerica.com) and CruiseWest (⊕www.cruisewest.com) run cruises through Alaska's Inside Passage.

527 Cedar Point (☎419/627-2350, ⊕www.cedarpoint.com) is open daily 10am–10pm from late-May to early Sept.

528 The route is largely snow-free between early June and early September. A permit is required and reservations are recommended.

529 The Crazy Horse Memorial (⊕www.crazyhorse.org) is located in South Dakota's Black Hills, on Hwy-16/385.

530 *Pat's*, 1237 E Passyunk Ave (☎215/468-1546, ⊕www.patskingofsteaks.com); *Geno's*, 1219 S Ninth St (☎215/389-0659).

531 Fish-throwing is from 11am to around noon at Pike Place Market, 1st Ave and Pike St (⊕www.pikeplacemarket.org).

532 The Harvard University Events & Information Center (9am–4.45pm Mon–Sat during the academic year and daily in summer; ☎617/495-1573, ⊕www.news.harvard.edu/guide), the Holyoke Center Arcade, 1530 Massachusetts Avenue, Cambridge.

533 Visit ⊕www hanggliding.com for details.

534 Kilauea is part of Hawaii Volcanoes National Park (⊕www.nps.gov/havo).

535 The official website, ⊕www.burningman.com,

has ticket information, photos and a helpful "First-Timers' Guide".

536 The first two weeks of October are prime leaf-viewing time, but you can usually see the colours change throughout the month – ⊕www.foliage-vermont.com should keep you updated.

537 Green Tortoise (⊕www.greentortoise.com) runs trips throughout North and Central America.

538 The Steamship Authority (☎508/693-9130, ⊕www.steamshipauthority.com) and Hy-Line Cruises (☎1-800/492-8082, ⊕www.hy-linecruises.com) run ferries to Nantucket from Hyannis, Cape Cod.

539 The Department of Environmental Conservation (⊕www.dec.ny.gov) has lists of public campgrounds.

540 Concerts are every Saturday night at the Carter Family Memorial Music Center (⊕www.carterfamilyfold.org) in Hiltons.

541 The Austin American-Statesman Bat Observation Center is on the southeast side of the bridge.

542 To experience life on the road in true Golden State-style, rent a convertible; you can slip behind the wheel of a Chevrolet Corvette with San Francisco-based Specialty Rentals (⊕www.specialtyrentals.com).

543 The Everglades (⊕www.nps.gov/ever) are best visited during the dry season (Nov–April).

544 Blue Star Brewing Company, 1414 South Alamo, San Antonio (☎210/212-5506, ⊕www.bluestarbrewing.com). Maps and itineraries are available at San Antonio Missions National Historic Park (⊕www.nps.gov/saan).

545 Jockey's Ridge State Park, US 158 Bypass, Mile 12.5. Kitty Hawk Kites/Carolina Outdoors (☎252/441-4124) provides instruction and equipment.

546 For a detailed introduction to the world of RV travel, visit ⊕www.gorving.com.

547 In Lockhart: *Kreuz Market*, 619 N Colorado St (☎512/398-2361, ⊕www.kreuzmarket.com); *Black's Barbecue*, 215 N Main St (☎512/398-2712, ⊕www.buyblacksbbq.com). In Luling: *City Market*, 633 E Davis St (☎830/875-9019). Near Driftwood: *The Salt Lick*, 18001 FM 1826 (☎512/858-4959, ⊕www.saltlickbbq.com). In Taylor: *Louie Mueller BBQ*, 206 W 2nd St (☎512/352-6206, ⊕www.louiemuellerbbq.com).

548 Book huts through the 10th Mountain Division Hut Association (☎970/925-5775, ⊕www.huts.org). Paragon Guides (☎970/926-5299, ⊕www.paragonguides.com) run mountain-biking and cross-country skiing trips between the huts (from $990 for three days).

549 For Bourbon Trail information, visit ⊕www.kybourbon.com.

550 The New York City marathon takes place every November; to register go to ⊕www.nycmarathon.org.

551 *Jules' Undersea Lodge*, Key Largo Undersea Park, 51 Shoreland Drive, MM-103.2, Key Largo (☎305/451-2353, ⊕www.jul.com).

552 The Field of Dreams is owned by two neighbouring farms: see their respective sites ⊕www.fieldofdreamsmoviesite.com and ⊕www.leftandcenterfod.com.

553 *Galatoire's*, 209 Bourbon St (☎504/525-2021, ⊕www.galatoires.com). Jackets required for men after 5pm and all day Sunday.

554 Alabama state capitol, 600 Dexter Ave (☎334/242-3935); Dexter Avenue Church, 454 Dexter Avenue (⊕www.dexterkingmemorial.org); Civil Rights

Memorial, 400 Washington Ave (@www.tolerance.org/memorial); Rosa Parks Museum, 252 Montgomery St (☎334/241-8615, @montgomery.troy.edu/rosaparks/museum).

555 The A-train runs from Queens through Brooklyn and Manhattan to Inwood–207th Street.

556 *La Posada*, 303 E Second St, Winslow (☎928/289-4366, @www.laposada.org).

557 For more info on Fantasy Fest, check out @www.fantasyfest.net.

558 The "Ghosts of Charleston" tour (☎1-800/979-3370, @www.tourcharleston.com); *Planter's Inn* (☎1-800/845-7082, @www.plantersinn.com).

559 For more information, visit @www.nps.gov/pore.

560 Visit @www.alta.com and @www.snowbird.com for full details on lift tickets, accommodation and transport.

561 For more information on wolf-watching in Yellowstone, visit @www.yellowstoneassociation.org.

562 Graceland, 3734 Elvis Presley Blvd, Memphis (☎800/238-2000, @www.elvis.com/graceland).

563 The Indianapolis 500 (@www.indy500.com) is held over Memorial Day weekend at the Indianapolis Motor Speedway (@www.brickyard.com); you'll need to pre-order tickets.

564 Brooks Falls (@www.nps.gov/katm) is a 20-minute walk from Brooks Camp. Getting to Brooks Camp from Anchorage involves a flight to the town of King Salmon, then a short float-plane flight.

565 Grand Canyon National Park (@www.nps.gov/grca) is in northern Arizona. The South Rim is open 24 hours a day, 365 days a year, the North Rim from mid-May to mid-October.

CANADA

566 The Lake Louise Visitor Reception Centre in Lake Louise Village (☎403/522-3833 or 522-1264) has trail information.

567 See @www.quebecregion.com for visitor information.

568 For information on travelling to Gwaii Haanas National Park Reserve and Haida Heritage Site, see @www.pc.gc.ca/gwaiihaanas.

569 The aurora borealis is visible in Yellowknife about 296 nights per year – see @www.northernfrontier.com.

570 Contact CMH Heli-Skiing (☎403/762-7100 or 1-800/661-0252, @www.cmhski.com).

571 The city's biggest food festival is the Taste of the Danforth, held the second weekend of August (@www.tasteofthedanforth.com).

572 Afternoon tea starts at noon at the *Empress Hotel*, 721 Government St (☎250/389-2727, @www.fairmont.com/empress).

573 Expédition Agaguk in Havre-Saint-Pierre (☎418/538-1588, @www.expedition-agaguk.com) rents equipment and provides guides for trips around the islands.

574 Camping programmes run mid-May to mid-Sept. Advance reservations are essential (☎403-553-2731, @www.head-smashed-in.com).

575 The ice road is usually only open from February to April – see @www.inuvik.ca for more up-to-date info.

576 Go to @www.bcadventure.com for details of 25 back-country ski lodges.

577 The journey from Vancouver to Toronto takes 3 days: VIA Rail trains (@www.viarail.ca) depart from Vancouver on Tues, Fri and Sun at 5.30pm.

578 The P'Tit Train du Nord takes 3–4 days, starting in Saint-Jérôme and ending in Mont-Laurier (@www.transportduparclineaire.com).

579 Dawson City is a 1hr 15min flight from Whitehorse. *Diamond Tooth Gertie's Gambling Hall* is at 4th Ave and Queen St; the *Sourdough Saloon* is at 2nd Ave and Queen.

580 Gatherall's Puffin & Whale Watch Tours offers daily trips to the Witless Bay Ecological Reserve (@www.gatheralls.com).

581 Plan at least a year in advance for the annual Stampede: visit @www.calgarystampede.com.

582 See @www.internationaldesfeuxloto-quebec.com for schedule and ticket information.

583 Truro, Moncton and Saint John are good bases for trying to see a tidal bore – @www.pc.gc.ca/fundy.

584 Little Manitou Lake lies beside the small town of Watrous. The Manitou Springs Resort (☎306/946-2233 or 1-800-667-7672, @www.manitousprings.ca) is adjacent to the lake.

585 The Hudson Bay train runs from Winnipeg to Churchill 3 days a week – see @www.viarail.ca for details.

586 See @www.algonquin.on.ca for canoe rental details.

587 Tundra buggy trips cost around C$80 per day, or you can book an all-inclusive five-day bear-spotting package with Wildlife Adventures – @www.wildlifeadventures.com.

588 See @www.westsidesurfschool.com and @www.surfsister.com for lessons.

589 Cycling the 10.5km Seawall takes about an hour; you must ride in a counterclockwise loop – see @www.vancouverbikerental.com.

590 The website @www.westcoasttrailbc.com has most of the details you need.

591 Go to @www.gbcountry.com for lots of info and links on Georgian Bay.

592 Tickets need to be bought in advance for nearly all matches; check the club websites via links at @www.nhl.com.

593 *The Maid of the Mist* leaves every 15–30min and The Journey Behind the Falls tour lasts 30–45min – see @www.niagaraparks.com.

594 For further info, consult @www.gov.pe.ca/visitorsguide.

595 The race's official website (@www.yukonquest.com) has past and future race details.

596 Tours with Brewster Vacations (@www.brewster.ca) include a ride on an Ice Explorer on the Columbia Icefield and a night's stay in a Jasper hotel.

THE CARIBBEAN

597 See @www.barbados.org/cropover.htm for information.

598 See @www.junkanoo.com for information.

599 The safest way to explore Port-au-Prince is by using drivers who work from the main hotels; they can be hired by the hour or the day.

600 Check @www.bvitourism.com/virgin-gorda for more.

601 @www.grenadagrenadines.com has more details on St George's.

602 *La Guarida*, at Concordia 418, e/Gervasio y Escobar, Centro Habana (☎7/863 7351 and 866 9047), is open daily, noon to midnight.

603 The main parades in the capital, Port of Spain,

take place on the Monday and Tuesday before Ash Wednesday.

604 It's best to explore the cave with a knowledgeable guide; check with the Gerace Research Center (@www.geraceresearchcenter.com) for more information.

605 Fly into Puerto Plata's international airport, from where it's a 4-hour bus ride to Samaná village. Check with Victoria Marine (☎809/538-2494) for a whale-watching boat tour.

606 The Pitons Tour Guide Association (☎758/459-9748) leads hikes of Gros Piton from the Interpretive Centre in Fond Gens Libre, near Soufrière.

607 Plenty of guides organize treks up to Boiling Lake; Seacat and his partner Roots also arrange excursions throughout the island. Contact them on ☎767/448-8954 or at @seacat55@hotmail.com.

608 To book at *Goldeneye*, visit @www.islandout-post.com.

609 To visit the makers of Ron de Barrilito, contact the tourist office at La Casita in Old San Juan (☎787/722-1709). Casa Don Q faces the marina near La Casita, across from Pier 1, while the Casa Bacardi Visitor Center (☎787/788-8400, @www.casabacardi.org) lies across San Juan Bay.

610 For more information, see @www.skedaddle.co.uk/p2p.asp.

611 The international airport at Puerto Plata is 20km west of Cabarete. All the major windsurfing and kiteboarding equipment manufacturers have schools and equipment rental along the town's main strip.

612 Arikok National Park lies 20km east of the capital city of Oranjestad.

613 *La Casa de las Tradiciones*, in Santiago de Cuba, features live *son* and other varieties of Cuban music.

614 The official festival website (@www.reggaesumfest.com) has full details of the event.

615 @www.infobonaire.com has lots of info on snorkelling.

616 *Cafeteria Mallorca*, c/San Francisco 300 (☎787/724-4607); *Restaurante El Jibarito*, c/Sol 280 (☎787/725-8375).

617 *Sunshine's* is on Pinney's Beach, on the northwest corner of the island, and is open 7 days a week for lunch and dinner during high season (mid-Dec to mid-April); @www.nevisisland.com has more info.

618 The Santo Domingo Tourist Office has event information (☎4 809/221-4660).

619 The main transport hub in the Exuma Cays is Staniel Cay, easily reached from Nassau; for trips departing from Great Exuma, you can fly into George Town from Florida. Outfitters – see @www.kayakbahamas.com – run guided tours through the cays.

620 There are several places to stay in the rainforest, from budget cabins for US$35 a night to luxury villas for US$150 upwards. See @www.elyunque.com for more.

621 *Crescent Moon Cabins* (☎767/449-3449, @www.crescentmooncabins.com) is located halfway between the capital Roseau and Melville Hall Airport.

622 From the northern city of Cap Haitian, you can take a private taxi or the public bus to the town of Milot, where you'll start your ascent to the Citadelle.

623 For info on Treasure Beach, visit @www.treasurebeach.net. For more on BREDS, visit @www.breds.org.

624 For more info, check @www.divecayman.ky.

625 *La Guacara Taina*, Av Mirador del Sur, Santo Domingo (☎809/530-0671).

626 There are no direct flights to St Barts from the North American or European mainland; you'll have to fly to St Martin and then catch an island-hopper to St Jean Airport, which lies snug in the centre of the island's inner curve. Try ⊕www.saint-barths.com for information on villa rentals.

MEXICO & CENTRAL AMERICA

627 Tortuguero National Park is 3–4hr north of Limón by boat. Independent travellers must buy tickets for the park and arrange for a certified tour guide.

628 You can reach Chamula and Zinacantán by bus from San Cristóbal. A permit from the town's tourist office is needed to enter the church in Chamula.

629 Rail services depart from Los Mochis and Chihuahua daily. Tickets are available from individual train stations or direct from Ferrocarril Mexicano (⊕www.chepe.com.mx).

630 Puerto La Libertad is 34km south of San Salvador; there are frequent buses. In La Libertad, you can rent boards from *Mango's Lounge* and *Punta Roca*; *Hotel Horizonte Surf Resort* rents boards in El Zonte.

631 Utila has several daily flights and a daily ferry connection with La Ceiba on the mainland. Utila Dive Center (⊕www.utiladivecenter.com) is a highly recommended dive operator.

632 Xochimilco is 28km southeast of Mexico City, reachable from Tasqueña station.

633 Frequent lancha boats buzz across Lago Atitlán between each village.

634 You can take a bus from Belize City to San Ignacio, the nearest town to *Blancaneaux* (⊕www.blancaneaux.com).

635 Saturday is market day in Oaxaca. The Mercado de Abastos is near the second-class bus station on Periférico.

636 Zacatecas (8hr by bus from Mexico City) typically has 3 or 4 callejóneadas every Friday and Saturday around 8pm.

637 Chichén Itzá is about 4hr from Cancún.

638 *Morgan's Rock* (⊕www.morgansrock.com) is north of San Juan del Sur, a 2hr drive from Granada. Rates include three daily meals and two daily tours.

639 There are frequent buses to Liberia, the capital of Guanacaste province, from San José.

640 It's best to visit Corcovado during its dry season (Dec–March). Places in the park's ranger stations need to be booked 6 weeks ahead (☎506/257-2239, ⊕azucena@ns.minae).

641 The town of Pátzcuaro, on the shores of Lago Pátzcuaro, is the main staging point for boat trips to Janitzio; boats run throughout the night. Accommodation for the Day of the Dead should be booked at least 6 months in advance.

642 Antigua's main bus terminal is next to its market; set off for Chimaltenango, from where a directo leaves to Nebaj.

643 Guerrero Negro is easily reached by bus from Tijuana or La Paz. There are numerous operators offering whale-watching tours in Guerrero Negro and the town of San Ignacio, 150km to the south.

644 Boats from Sittee River and Dangriga travel to the reef at least once a week; each caye within Glover's central lagoon has a dive operator that organizes tours or rents equipment.

645 To visit Isla Barro Colorado, contact the Smithsonian Institute in Panama City (☎507/212 8026,

⊕www.stri.org).

646 Several distilleries around Tequila run tours; the most popular is José Cuervo (⊕www.cuervo.com). *La Maestranza* is at Maestranza 179, in Guadalajara.

647 Bonampak is a short hike from the village of Lacanjá Chansayab. You can also ride directly to the site in a Lacandón-run van from the Frontier Highway.

648 Antigua is served by regular buses from Guatemala City. The tourist office in Antigua (☎832 0763) has maps.

649 Several companies offer trips to Lamanai down the New River, including Jungle River Tours, 20 Lover's Lane, Orange Walk (☎501/302-2293, ⊕lamanaimayatour@btl.net).

650 A leisurely ride from Tijuana to La Paz with plenty of rest will take around a month.

651 Tour operators in both Loreto and La Paz offer outfitting, guided expeditions and accommodation, with La Paz providing more rental options for the independent kayaker.

652 There are hourly bus services to Ensenada from Tijuana. *Tacos Fenix* is on Calle Espinosa, at Calle Juárez.

653 San Francisco el Alto is 1hr by bus from Quetzaltenango.

654 Most of the adventure holiday companies offer Costa Rica as a family trip; try Explore! Family Adventures (⊕www.exploreworldwide.com).

655 The best place to see the butterflies is in the butterfly sanctuary near the village of El Rosario (mid-Nov to mid-March daily 9am–5pm; ☎01-800/450-2300, ⊕www.turismomichoacan.gob.mx).

656 Find out more about *Maruba* at ⊕www.marubaspa.com. Doubles start at about US$200 a night.

657 Minibuses (5am–6pm) run from the towns of El Remate and Flores to Tikal National Park approximately every 30 minutes. There are three hotels in the park, and both towns also have plentiful accommodation.

658 Regular daily flights leave Panama City for several islands in Kuna Yala.

659 Four boats a day leave San Carlos for El Castillo. Two boats a week (Tues and Fri 5am; 10hr) travel the whole length of the river to the Caribbean Sea.

660 Puebla's best restaurants are *La Guadalupana*, 5 Oriente 605, and *Mesón Sacristía de la Compañia*, 6 Sur 304. You can buy mole paste at the Mercado 5 de Mayo.

661 Cozumel has scores of dive operators who will take you to Palancar Reef; Deep Blue (☎987/872-5653, ⊕www.deepbluecozumel.com) is recommended.

662 The entire house may be rented for a (very negotiable) $26,000 per week, all-inclusive. Contact the owners at ⊕casamagna@amansala.com or ☎011 52 9841 000 805.

663 Caye Caulker lies 35km northeast of Belize City; regular boats travel here from Belize City and San Pedro, on Ambergris Caye.

664 Allow at least 6 months to cross the Pacific. See ⊕http://cruisenews.net for websites dedicated to voyages currently underway.

665 Every September, Guadalajara hosts performers from all over the world for the Festival de los Mariachis (⊕www.mariachi-jalisco.com).

666 All buses between Dangriga and Punta Gorda pass Maya Centre. The Saqui family (⊕nuukcheil@btl.net) and the Chun family (⊕www.mayacenter.com) offer comfortable accommodation and can arrange trips into the reserve.

667 Parque Nacional Soberanía is a 45min drive from Panama City.

668 There are 10 ferries daily from San Jorge, which is a short taxi from the town of Rivas, to Ometepe.

669 Major cruise lines operate tours from Colón to Panama City, and from Panama City to Colón.

670 The nearby town of Copán Ruinas has plenty of accommodation, although Santa Rosa de Copán, around 50km east, is a much nicer place to stay.

671 The market is open every day and most traders accept US dollars.

672 The Palacio National is open daily 9am–5pm and entry is free.

673 Cenote Zací in Valladolid is in the block formed by calles 34, 36, 37 and 39. Dzitnup and Samula are 7km west of Valladolid on Hwy-180. There are also cenotes along the Carribean coast.

SOUTH AMERICA

674 Getting into the High Chaco is difficult and not to be attempted alone. FAUNA Paraguay (⊕www.faunaparaguay.com) offers expert-led eco-tours.

675 For more information, visit ⊕www.galapagospark.org. Visitors have to pay a US$100 national park entrance fee on arrival.

676 *Bodega Catena Zapata*, in Luján de Cuyo (⊕www.catenawines.com).

677 Visitors are admitted to terreiros, with "mass" usually beginning in the early evening. Trousers and long skirts should be worn, preferably white. For information on ceremonies in Salvador, contact the Federação Baiana de Culto Afro-Brasileiro, Rua Portas do Carmo 39 (☎3326-6969).

678 Qoyllur Riti happens every year in early May just before Corpus Christi. You can arrange transport to the start of the trek near the town of Ocongate with tour companies in Cusco.

679 Isla Navarino is most easily reached by plane from Punta Arenas or Ushuaia. The best map is in the *Circuito Dientes de Navarino*, available in Punta Arenas.

680 It's much easier to fly to Cartagena than take the bus, as military roadblocks can cause lengthy delays.

681 The Plaza de Ponchos market in Otavalo is open every day, but is most impressive on Saturdays.

682 Guided treks run to Torres del Paine from Puerto Natales, or you can travel to the park by bus or Zodiac inflatable.

683 Los Llanos is about an hour's flight from Caracas. The easiest time to find anacondas is the dry season (Nov–May).

684 Rafting trips can easily be arranged in Cusco. The rapids on the Urubamba are Class III and suitable for beginners.

685 *El Ombú* (⊕www.estanciaelombu.com); *Cabaña Las Lilas*, Av Alicia M de Justo 516.

686 Ica is a 6-hour bus ride from Lima; you can take a bus or taxi from Ica to Huacachina. Most of the cafés along the lagoon's shoreline rent sandboards.

687 The Pantanal's dry season (April–Oct) is the best time to spot wildlife; a dozen lodges offer tours with gaucho guides, or try Green Track (⊕www.greentrack.net).

688 You can only hike the Inca Trail as part of an organized tour group. Book well in advance.

689 *Academia da Cachaça*, Rua Conde Bernadotte 26, Leblon, Rio de Janeiro (☎21/2529-2680, ⊕www.academiadacachaca.com.br).

690 The Teatro Amazonas, which hosts an annual opera festival at the end of April, can be visited on a guided tour.

691 Wilderness Explorers (@www.wilderness-explorers.com), in Georgetown, offers day-trips by plane to the falls. Kaieteur Falls are at their most dramatic during the wet season (April–Aug).

692 Tapati begins every year at the end of January. For more information, consult the Chilean tourist board site @www.sernatur.cl.

693 One-day bike trips are easy to arrange with operators in La Paz; the original and best is Gravity Assisted Mountain Biking (@00591 2313849, @www.gravitybolivia.com).

694 You can see the Valley of the Moon on a tour from San Pedro – there are lots of tour operators, and you can expect to pay around CH$4000 a head.

695 You can reach the Falklands by air via Santiago in Chile or fly direct from the UK with the RAF from Brize Norton in Oxfordshire.

696 Punta del Este's Laguna del Sauce airport is only 30min from Buenos Aires' Aeroparque Jorge Newbery. November and March are best for avoiding crowds.

697 The visitors' centre for the Paraguayan side of the Itaipú dam is about 20km north of Ciudad del Este. Visits are by guided tour only (Mon–Fri 9.30am, 1.30pm & 3pm, Sat 9.30am).

698 Although only in Portuguese, @www.estradareal.org.br offers local information about the Estrada Real.

699 For information about getting to the Juan Fernández archipelago, visit @www.islarobinsoncrusoe.cl (Spanish only). The *Refugio Náutico* on Robinson Crusoe Island (@refugionautico@123.cl) offers accommodation and seal trips.

700 *Termas de Puyuhuapi* (@67 325103, @www.patagonia-connection.com) offers transfers from Balmaceda airport, 5hr south of Puyuhuapi.

701 Volcán Cotopaxi is in the Parque Nacional Cotopaxi, accessed from the Panamericana 41km south of Quito. Fully qualified guides are available through operators in Quito or Riobamba.

702 Tours to the Central Surinam Nature Reserve can be organized through STINASU (@www.stiansu.sr), who manage the country's protected areas.

703 Flights over the Nazca Lines cost around US$50 for a 45min flight.

704 Trips are easy to arrange in towns like Manaus in Brazil, Iquitos in Peru, or Rurrenabaque in Bolivia.

705 Boats to the Isla del Sol depart every morning from the town of Copacabana.

706 The national park information centre is open daily 8am–8pm; @02962/493004.

707 For stays on a coffee finca, contact Ecoguías in Bogotá (@www.ecoguias.com).

708 One of the best times to be in La Paz is for the Fiesta del Gran Poder – held in late May or early June.

709 Ferries depart daily every 30min from Puerto Montt in the Lake District to Chacao at Isla Grande's northern tip.

710 Potosí is some 500km southeast of La Paz. Koala Tours, located opposite the Moneda, run 4-hour trips into the mines.

711 The popular Playa El Agua and Playa Puerto Cruz, at the northern tip of Isla Margarita, are regularly patrolled by oyster vendors.

712 A bus runs from Avenida América in Quito to Mitad del Mundo. For Inti Ñan, turn left from the Mitad

del Mundo, walk uphill a few hundred metres and then follow signs left again.

713 Lençois is roughly 6hr by bus from Salvador da Bahia. Once there, hook up with Lentur (@75/3334-1271, @www.lentur.com.br) for day-trips in the park.

714 Fishing licences are available in Rio Grande, from the Asociación de Pesca con Mosca at Montilla 1040 (@02964/421268).

715 "Moto Rent" shops (@www.guiacolonia.com.uy/motorent) are abundant in the Barrio Histórico; golf carts and bicycles are also available.

716 You can only hike the Inca Trail on a tour or with a licensed guide. Two of the best operators in Cusco are SAS (@www.sastravel.com) and United Mice (@www.unitedmice.com).

717 Most tourist lodges near Iquitos, Puerto Maldonado and Pucallpa in Peru can arrange visits to shamans. Otherwise, finding a legitimate shaman can be difficult.

718 Homestays on Anapia can be arranged at the jetty in Puno, a 2hr boat ride from the island, or as a package; try Insider Tours (@www.insider-tours.com).

719 Lauca National Park (@www.visit-chile.org) is 160km east of Arica.

720 The Cordillera Real is a few hours' drive from La Paz – guides and equipment can be organized here or in Sorata.

721 The football year is split into two seasons (late July–early Dec and late Jan–early June) in both Brazil and Argentina. Tickets are available on match days, but buy ahead for the big games.

722 Lan Chile (@www.lan.com) makes the 5-hour flight to Easter Island 3 times a week from Santiago.

723 *Colomé* (@www.estanciacolome.com) is in the far northwest corner of Argentina, 200km from the nearest airport at Salta. Arrange transport through Salta's Marina Turismo (@www.marina-semisa.com.ar).

724 There are daily flights to Fernando de Noronha from Recife and Natal; the hotel (@3619 0028; @www.pousadamaravilha.com.br) is a 5min drive from the airport.

725 The teleférico in Caracas leaves from the intersection between avenidas Principal de Maripérez and Boyacá, a 15min taxi ride north from the centre.

726 Elephant seals are at their most active Sept–Nov, which is also the best time for whale watching.

727 The 700km route takes 4–5 days in a 4WD pickup truck, available for rent in Iquique. You need to carry petrol, spare tyres, a tent, a stove and plenty of food and water.

728 Boi Bumba takes place for 3 days every June. Visit @www.boibumba.com for more information.

729 Most Colca Canyon trips leave from Arequipa, approximately 5hr away.

730 Carnival takes place from the Friday before Ash Wednesday. Tickets for the Sambódromo can cost anywhere from US$200 for the bleachers to more than US$1000 for a covered box.

731 Expeditions to the Salar by 4WD are easily arranged with local tour operators in Uyuni, 12hr from La Paz.

732 Jan and Feb are the best months to drive the Carretera. *Casa Ludwig*, Av Otto Uebel, Puyuhuapi (@67/325220, @www.contactchile.cl/casaludwig); *El Reloj*, Baquedano 828, Coyhaique.

733 There are many ceviche-appropriate parks in and around Lima – Country Club el Bosque (Carretera

Panamericana Sur Km 44.45; @51/01 346-0018) has picnic tables, tennis courts and a swimming pool.

734 Visit @www.cnes-csg.fr for launch dates. If you want to watch from the closer sites, request an invitation by writing to: CNES-Centre Spatial Guyanais, Service Communication, BP 726, 97387 Kourou Cedex. You are free to use another site, 15km from the launch, without invitation.

735 The nearest town to the Perito Moreno Glacier is El Calafate; the official website @www.elcalafate.gov.ar is a mine of information on how to visit.

736 Ski season lasts from late May until early October, with the peak season from mid-July to early August.

737 *Hotel Centinela* (@56 64 391 326, @www.hotel-centinela.cl) is on Lago Llanquihue, 5km from Puerto Octay.

738 Trips to the Cuyabeno Wildlife Reserve, a good spot for piranha-fishing, can be organized through Safari in Quito (@www.safari.com.ec).

739 Montecristi is about 3hr by road from Guayaquil, Ecuador's biggest city.

740 The municipal installations at Mamalluca (@www.mamalluca.org) are easily accessible from the city of Vicuña.

741 Venues and times of milongas are constantly changing, so seek local advice; a good place to start is @www.tangodata.com.ar, which has weekly listings.

742 The best close-up experience to be had is in the Parque Nacional, outside Puerto Iguazú (Argentina), and the rainy summer season (Nov–March) is the best time to go. For more information, consult @www.iguazuargentina.com.

743 For information on hang-gliding in Rio, email @justfly@alternex.com.br or call @2268-0565.

744 Tupiza Tours, inside the *Hotel Mitru* (@www.tupizatours.com), can organize trips to San Vicente.

745 The Associacao de Capoeira Mestre Bimba, Rua das Laranjeiras 1, is Salvador's foremost dance school and sometimes has classes open to tourists.

746 Go to @www.iloveyerba.com to find out more about the life-enhancing benefits of maté.

CENTRAL AND NORTHERN ASIA

747 Cranes visit Caohai between November and March. Weining is most easily reached by bus from Anshun, western Guizhou's main town (5hr). Caohai is a 20min walk south of town.

748 Tsukiji (Mon–Sat) is on the Hibiya subway line but if you want to catch the auctions – which start at 5am and require a permit – you'll need to take a taxi.

749 Passenger boats run year-round through the Three Gorges, though spring and autumn provide the most colourful scenery. Tour-boat berths are best booked through online agents such as @www.chinahighlights.com.

750 The Terracotta Army (daily 8am–6pm) is 28km east of Xi'an and can be reached in one hour on bus #306 from Xi'an's train station.

751 You can reach Harbin from Beijing by train (9 daily; 17hr) or plane (13 daily; 1hr 30min). The Winter Ice Festival lasts from January 5 until February 5.

752 The official @www.mongoliatourism.gov.mn website is a good if rather dull first stop for all things Mongolian.

753 Two of Chengdu's busiest teahouses are at Renmin Park in the city centre, and Wenshu Temple, 1.5km north off Renmin Zhong Lu.

754 For tips on where to cycle in the Yangshuo area, see ◉www.yangers.com.

755 See ◉www.dragonboat.org.hk for more details.

756 Li River cruises depart Guilin daily year-round and can be organized through CITS (☎0773/2861623, ◉www.china4seasons.com).

757 Check ◉mazu.taichung.gov.tw for details.

758 Datong, in the centre of Guangzhou, is the busy, noisy dim sum experience par excellence.

759 There are several tour companies that run tours of the DMZ; the best is USO (◉www.uso.org/korea).

760 Kyoto is the place to sample kaiseki cuisine – try Nakamura-ro or Hyotei.

761 Jinghong is the main town of the region, reachable in an hour from Kunming by air, or around 16hr by bus.

762 The best time for horse trekking is late June to mid-September. Boojum Expeditions (◉www.boojum.com) offers trekking from Ulaan Baatar.

763 The Naked Man festival generally falls between Jan and March, but it's best to confirm dates at ◉www.seejapan.co.uk.

764 Though the exact dates vary each year, the sakura usually blossoms in late March or early April.

765 The Longmen Caves (daily 7am–6.30pm) are 13km south of Louyang city, reached from Louyang's train station on bus #81.

766 There are several jjimjilbang in every Korean city of note, and any tourist office or taxi driver will be able to direct you to one.

767 The Jokhang opens daily 8am–6pm. As with all Tibetan temples, circuit both the complex and individual halls anti-clockwise.

768 Shilin Night Market in Taipei is opposite Jiantan MRT station, and is open daily.

769 For more information, check ◉eng.templestay.com.

770 Many sections of the Great Wall are accessible as day-trips from Beijing: regular tourist buses run to Badaling (daily 9am–4.30pm), Mutianyu (daily 8am–4pm) and Simatai (daily 8am–4pm).

771 Taketomi-jima is reached by ferry from Ishikagi on Ishikagi-jima, which has direct flights to Tokyo and Osaka.

772 The Japan Rail Pass (◉www.japanrailpass.net) must be purchased before arriving in Japan as it's only available to foreign visitors.

773 For more information on yurt stays, check out ◉www.cbtkyrgyzstan.kg.

774 Several companies offer all-inclusive tours to North Korea, but one of the best is Koryo Group (◉www.koryogroup.com).

775 To reach Huang Shan, you need to take a train, bus or plane to Tunxi, 50km southwest, and then a minibus to the mountain's base at Tangkou. Further minibus taxis run from Tangkou up the mountain to the start of trails at Ciguang Ge or Yungu Si. See ◉www.huangshantour.com.

776 The full trek takes at least 2 days, though 3 is recommended. Spring and autumn are the best months for walking as summer can be wet, with potentially dangerous landslides.

777 You can see snow monkeys throughout Japan, but your best chances are in Jigokudani, or "Hell's Valley".

778 Buses take around 8 hours and run daily from Ganzi to Dêgê.

779 The Bund is south of Suzhou Creek on the western bank of the Huangpu River.

780 Visitors to Bhutan must be part of an arranged tour. Many companies offer treks in the country, among them Himalayan Kingdoms (◉www.himalayankingdoms.com) and Karakoram Experience (◉www.keadventure.com).

781 Six basho a year take place in alternate months. Tokyo's tonsil-twisting Ryogoku Kokugikan arena is the main venue, with tournaments in Jan, May and Sept. The March, July and Nov basho take place in Ōsaka, Nagoya and Fukuoka, respectively.

782 Kashgar's Yekshenba Bazaar takes place every Sunday about 2km from the city centre off Ayziret Lu.

783 Macau is a 4km-long peninsula jutting out from the Chinese mainland about 60km west of Hong Kong. The border with China is open 7am–midnight, and there are hourly ferries around the clock from Hong Kong.

784 Gyeongju is served by buses and trains from all over Korea.

785 Emei Shan is in Sichuan, 150km south of Chengdu. Buses run from Chengdu's Xinnanmen bus station through the day to Baoguo township, at the foot of the mountain (2hr 30min); you can also catch a train from Chengdu to Emei town (10 daily; 2hr) and a minibus from there to Baoguo (20min).

786 Central is on the north shore of Hong Kong Island, easily reached from anywhere in Hong Kong via the MTR, or on the Star Ferry from Kowloon (◉www.starferry.com.hk).

787 Kyoto is the best place to sample the ryokan experience. Book well in advance for Hiiragiya (◉www.hiiragiya.co.jp) or Yoshikawa Ryokan (☎075/221-5544).

788 The Forbidden City (summer 8.30am–5pm, winter 8.30am–4.30pm) is in the centre of Beijing, immediately north of Tian'anmen Square.

789 No independent travel is allowed to North Korea, but Koryo Tours (◉www.koryogroup.com) operates regular tours.

790 The Chengdu Giant Panda Breeding research Base (◉www.panda.org.cn) is located 10km outside Chengdu in Sichuan province.

791 Wudang Shan is in northwestern Hubei; from the nearest train station at Shiyan (25km west), catch a bus to Wudang town at the bottom of the mountain and then a minibus to Nanyan temple, about halfway up. A tiring 2hr track leads from Nanyan to the summit.

792 Getting to the craters is a difficult, bumpy ride across sand dunes into the desert. Experienced drivers can be found in Darvaza, on the highway between the capital of Ashgabat and the Uzbek border town of Konye-Urgench.

793 Contact CITS in Kaili (☎0855/8222506, ◉www.qdncits.com), who can advise on dates, accommodation and guides.

794 The gardens are scattered through the centre of town, though you'll need taxis if you plan to visit a lot in one day (daily 7.30am–4.30pm).

795 Gyeongbokgung is best accessed by subway, at the station of the same name. The north end of Insadong-gil is most easily reached from Anguk, one station east of Gyeongbokgung on the same line.

796 The Peak is on Hong Kong Island. The tram runs daily 7am–midnight; get to the lower Tram terminal on Garden Road by bus #15C from outside the Star Ferry terminal.

797 For details, check ◉www.taipei101mall.com.tw.

798 You can buy tickets at the CITS office in the Beijing International Hotel, but you'll have to get a transit visa for Russia as well. See ◉www.transib.net for information.

799 ◉www.azerbaijan24.com has more on how important tea and the chaihana is to Azerbajanis.

800 Quanjude Roast Duck restaurant, 32 Qianmen Dajie, Beijing ☎010/6701 1379.

801 It takes 2 months to walk the 1400km between the 88 temples on the Shikoku pilgrimage route. Zentsu-ji is just outside the small port of Marugame, in the north of the island.

802 The carpet museum is open daily except Sun 10am–6pm; the market takes place on Sundays.

803 Tianyuanki Guesthouse, 73 Ming Qing Jie (☎00354/5680069).

804 For packages, check out Elemental Adventure (☎0870 738 7838, ◉www.eaheliskiing.com).

805 Contact the Kyoto Tourist Information Centre (☎075/343-6655 or 344-3300) for event information.

806 Apart from adjusting to the altitude, there's little that's technically difficult about climbing Fuji. During the climbing season, regular buses connect Kawaguchi-ko station with the fifth station.

807 Kronotsky Reserve is accessed by helicopter from Petropavlovsk; entrance is restricted and by permit only. The Valley of the Geysers is closed from mid-May to early July to protect breeding and nesting activity. July and August offer the best weather.

808 Beidaihe is on the east China coast, about 2hr 30min from Beijing by train (7 daily). The beaches stretch for around 5km along the south side of a broad peninsula, easily walkable from town or reached by buses #6 or #34.

THE INDIAN SUBCONTINENT

809 Boat rides cost anything between Rs100 and Rs500, depending on demand and your ability to haggle.

810 Hampi is a 30min bus ride from the town of Hospet, which is served by mainline trains from Hyderabad, Goa and Bangalore.

811 The Manali–Leh Highway is officially open between June 21 and September 15, although buses tend to run as long as the passes remain free of snow.

812 Esala Perahera takes place in Kandy over 10 days, usually in late July and early August. See ◉www.daladamaligawa.org for info.

813 Camel treks can be arranged through any Jaisalmer hotel or tourist office. Early Dec–end Jan is the best time to go.

814 Holi goes for about 4 days in February or March. The website ◉www.mathura-vrindavan.com has information on the festival in the North Indian towns of Mathura and Vrindavan.

815 Sri Lanka is a year-round surfing destination: the surf's up at Arugam Bay April–Oct, then Nov–April at Hikkaduwa.

816 The Ajanta Caves are open daily 9am–5.30pm. Most visitors base themselves in the city of Aurangabad, 108km southwest, travelling by bus or jeep taxi.

817 Nizzamuddin is 6km south of Connaught Circus along the Mathura Road. Visitors should dress modestly and cover their heads.

818 The Karakoram Highway runs between Islamabad, Pakistan and Kashgar, China. It takes about a month to cycle the full 1300km. Spring and autumn are the best seasons to ride.

819 Gahirmatha beach can only be reached with your own transport – ask at the OTDC tourist office in Puri to see if the turtles are expected before you set off.

820 You can fly to the Andaman Islands from Chennai (Madras) . You can also get there by ferry via Chennai or Kolkata (3–5 days).

821 To see tigers in Bandhavgarh, contact Discovery Initiatives (❂www.discoveryinitiatives.com).

822 Gangotri is accessible from May to October. Most visitors stay at the state-run Tourist Bungalow, in Bhojbasa, 5km from the glacier.

823 Teyyattam rituals are held across the north of Kerala from November through March. The simplest way to find one is to visit the tourist office in Kannur (Cannanore).

824 Buses leave Amritsar for Wagha every 45 minutes, although it's worth booking a taxi for the round trip.

825 Dalhousie is 30km southwest of Hatton, which is on the main rail line from Colombo and Kandy.

826 Sadya feasts play a central role in the annual Onam harvest festival, held in early September.

827 The Durga Puja falls in September or October, depending on the lunar cycle – try searching for the dates on ❂www.bangladeshonline.com/tourism.

828 Z, on CT Rd near the beach, is the place to stay for backpackers in Puri (☎06752/222554).

829 Diskit is a 6hr bus journey from Leh, but there's only one bus a week.

830 Nepal's main trekking season runs from late September to late November. Given the unpredictable security situation, trekking alone is not recommended.

831 Haputale can be reached by train from Colombo (9hr) and Kandy (5hr 30min). Accommodation is limited to a handful of guesthouses: try the excellent *Amarasinghe Guest House* (☎075/226-8175).

832 The frozen river is practicable for around 6 weeks during January and February; a few trekking agencies in Leh offer it as a package.

833 Pure Vacations (❂www.purevacations.com) offers 14-day surf charters to the Maldives.

834 Puram usually takes place in late May; check with the state tourist office, ❂www.keralatourism.org, for exact dates.

835 For reservations at *Udaivilas* call ☎294 243 3300 or visit ❂www.oberoiudaivilas.com.

836 Mumbai's Metro Cinema is at Dhobi Talao Junction, at the top of Azad Maidan, a short cab ride from CST (VT) Station. For tickets, go to ❂www.adlabscinemas.com.

837 Kartik Purnima is usually held in early November. Check ❂www.rajasthantourism.gov.in for the exact dates.

838 The island is 15 minutes by speedboat from Male airport. Prices start from US$1000 per night for a Villa Suite.

839 Madurai, in the south of Tamil Nadu, can be reached by plane from Mumbai (3hr 20min) or the state capital, Chennai (1hr).

840 Kathakalis are usually performed as part of Ernakulam's annual festival in Jan/Feb.

841 Dharamsala is 12hr from Delhi by bus and there's usually several every day.

842 Both the Golden Temple and Guru-ka-Langar are open 24hr. Although meals are served free of charge, small donations are welcomed.

843 All of the festival sites are within a few kilometres of each other, and Kathmandu. See ❂www.nepalhomepage.com/society/festivals for more.

844 From Srinagar it's a 2hr, 200km taxi ride to Gulmarg. Dec–April is the best time to visit.

845 The Pinnawala Elephant Orphanage is 3km from the Rambukkana junction on the Colombo–Kandy road; bath times are at 10am and 2pm.

846 Gokarna is most easily accessible via the Konkan Railway, which connects Mumbai with Kerala.

847 The Khardung-La pass is north of Leh, on the way to Diskit – see #829.

848 The Shandur Polo Tournament takes place every year during the second week of July. A tent village is set up at the Pass during the tournament.

849 *Elsewhere* (❂www.aseascape.com) comfortably accommodates six people. A week at the house costs US$1000–4000 depending on the season.

850 Other than for the festival, the best time to visit Kumaon is in early spring (March–April) and late summer (Sept–Oct).

851 For more information on *Apani Dhani*, visit ❂www.apanidhani.com. Excursions around Shekhawati can be arranged on arrival.

852 The Taj Mahal is open from 6am to 7pm daily except Friday. Over the 4 days of a full moon, you can also visit between 8pm and midnight when tickets must be booked a day in advance at the main entrance.

853 Kaziranga is 217km east of the Assamese capital, Guwahati. The park is open from November to April. Elephant rides depart daily between 5 and 7am.

854 Operated by the Bangladesh Inland Water Transport Corporation, the Rocket service covering the 354km route between Dhaka and Khulna runs all year.

855 Bhuj, the capital of Kutch, is accessible by train from Ahmedabad. Guides and transport for trips out to the craft villages north of town can be arranged with the tourist officer in Bhuj's Aina Mahal Museum.

856 The last Kumbh Mela to take place at the sacred confluence near Allahabad was in January 2007. In 2010, the honour will be enjoyed by the town of Haridwar, 214km northeast of Delhi.

857 Benaulim is 15min by public bus from Margao, Goa's "second city".

858 Unless you have a local contact, expect to queue for tickets for test matches at Eden Gardens days in advance.

859 Kettuvallam cruises can be arranged through most upscale hotels.

860 *Sri Ganesa Bhawan*, on West Car St (no phone), serves lunch between 11.30am and 2.30pm.

861 Keoladeo is open year round, but the best time to visit is between October and March.

SOUTHEAST ASIA

862 Slow boats leave when full and run from Houayxai on the Thai–Lao border to Louang Phabang, and vice versa.

863 Chatuchak Weekend Market (Sat & Sun 7am–6pm) is in north Bangkok, near Mo Chit Skytrain and Kamphaeng Phet subway stations.

864 Most people arrange all-inclusive tours of the bay from Hanoi, about 150km away. April–Oct is the best time to visit.

865 Kalibo is a one-hour flight south of the Philippine capital, Manila. Hotels are usually full for Ati-Atihan, so book well in advance. See ❂www.ati-atihan.net for information.

866 Taman Negara (❂www.wildlife.gov.my) is 250km from Kuala Lumpur and can be reached by bus or, more enjoyably, by train and boat.

867 It's a bumpy 7hr bus ride from Manila to Banaue, where guides for treks can be hired.

868 Classes are held twice daily at SITCA, on Soi Colibri (☎077 413172, ❂www.sitca.net).

869 Philippines-based dive operators such as Scuba World (❂www.scubaworld.com.ph), Dive Buddies (❂www.divephil.com) and Asia Divers (❂www.asiadivers.com) organize trips out of Puerto Princesa.

870 Kinabalu Park headquarters (❂www.suterasanctuarylodges.com) issues permits and organizes guides and porters. Book accommodation in advance. Kinabalu Park is a 2hr bus ride from Kota.

871 One of the best places to experience Loy Krathong is in Sukhothai, the first Thai capital, 400km north of Bangkok, where the ruins of the ancient capital are lit up by fireworks.

872 Bac Ha is visitable on a day-trip from the northern Vietnamese hill town of Sa Pa.

873 Wat Phra Kaeo, or the Grand Palace, is open daily 8.30am–3.30pm.

874 Lumphini Stadium, on Thanon Rama IV, stages fights on Tues, Fri and Sat eves. Take the subway to Lumphini station or the Skytrain to Sala Daeng and then a taxi.

875 The easiest way to arrange a night in a longhouse is via a tour company based in the Sarawak capital, Kuching: Borneo Transverse (❂www.borneotransverse.com.my) or Borneo Adventure (❂www.borneoadventure.com).

876 Bukit Lawang is a 3hr bus ride from Medan. The sanctuary is only open to visitors during the twice-daily feeding sessions at 8am and 3pm.

877 CCC sends teams of volunteers to survey some of the world's most endangered coral reefs and rainforests. For more info, visit ❂www.coralcay.org.

878 Louang Phabang is served by flights from Bangkok, Chiang Mai and Vientiane. You can also reach it by bus and boat from Vientiane and by boat from the Thai–Lao border at Chiang Khong/Houayxai.

879 For more information on diving Sipadan, check ❂www.visitborneo.com.

880 Queen Bee, at 5 Thanon Moonmuang near Tha Pae Gate (☎053 275525, ❂www.queen-bee.com), has reliable motorbikes and insurance coverage.

881 For more information, check ❂www.divenorthsulawesi.com.

882 Most trips to Komodo (❂www.komodonationalpark.org) are organized from Labuanbajo, on the coast of neighbouring Flores.

883 My Tho is a 90min bus ride from Ho Chi Minh City. Homestays can be arranged at local tourist offices or through Sinhbalo Adventure Travel in Ho Chi Minh City (❂www.cyclingvietnam.net).

884 Aru's major settlement, Dobo, is 2 days from the Maluku district capital, Ambon, with Pelni, the Indonesian state shipping line.

885 You can rent a car and driver or take a bus to Maya, the northernmost town on mainland Cebu. Regular ferries run from Maya to Malapascua.

886 Thailand's best old-style beach huts are *KP Huts*, scattered through a shoreside coconut grove on Ko Chang (☎84 099 5100); *Island Hut* on Ko Mak (☎87 139 5537); and *Bee Bee Bungalows* on Ko Lanta (☎81 537 9932, ☹www.diigii.de).

887 Hanoi's most famous snake restaurants are in the suburb of Le Mat, including the reliable *Quoc Trieu* (☎04/827 2988).

888 Phang Nga Bay covers some 400 square kilometres of coast between Phuket and Krabi. A reputable sea-canoeing trips operator around the bay is John Gray's Sea Canoe (☹shoreside.johngray-seacanoe.com).

889 Penang lies just off Malaysia's west coast, connected to the nearest mainland centre of Butterworth by a bridge. For more information, check out ☹www.tourismpenang.gov.my.

890 Daily public buses connect Luang Prabang and Vientiane with Phonsovan. *Auberge De La Plain De Jars* (☎auberge_plainjars@yahoo.fr) is the province's best hotel, with private wooden bungalows.

891 Dance performances are staged nightly at Ubud Palace, about 30km from Bali's international airport.

892 The Tuol Sleng Genocide Museum (daily 7.30–11.30am & 2–5pm) is off Street 13 on the southern fringes of Phnom Penh.

893 Insensitive tourism has caused many problems in hill-tribe villages, and exploitation by travel companies is widespread, so choose your trekking company wisely. In Chiang Mai, both Eagle House (☹www.eaglehouse.com) and the Trekking Collective (☹www.trekkingcollective.com) are recommended operators.

894 ☹www.fullmoon-party.com gives the dates of forthcoming parties and news of big-name DJs.

895 The yearly festival takes place in the first half of July; check ☹www.rainforestmusic-borneo.com for more details.

896 Visit ☹www.tourismlaos.gov.la for tourist information.

897 Hoi An is around 700km south of Hanoi. The nearest airport and train station are in Da Nang, a 30km taxi ride away.

898 Borobudur (daily 6am–5.30pm; ☹www.borobudurpark.com) is served by frequent buses from Yogyakarta, 40km southeast, and can be visited as a day-trip. An overnight stay, however, allows you both to watch the sunset and to visit early the next day before the crowds arrive.

899 Kumai is about an hour from Pangkalanbun, where you must first pick up permits for your visit from the police and PKA (National Parks) office, then arrange a klotok. More information can be found at ☹www.orangutan.org.

900 Bangkok's Wat Pho has been the leading school of Thai massage for hundreds of years, and masseurs who train there are considered the best in the country. Wat Pho runs massage courses in English (☹www.watpomassage.com).

901 Regular flights from Bali serve Flores' 3 main airports, Labuanbajo, Maumere and Ende.

902 For further information on Singapore Zoo's night safari, check out ☹www.nightsafari.com.sg.

903 There are daily flights from Manila to El Nido, departure point for the archipelago, with SEAIR (☹www.flyseair.com) and Islands Transvoyager Incorporated.

904 Singapore to Bangkok costs around US$2000 one way – see ☹www.orient-express.com.

905 Regular buses travel from Trang to Had Yao, where you can get a boat to Ko Libong. The *Libong Nature Beach Resort* (☎0818946936, ☹www.

trangsea.com) is the better of the two resorts in Libong.

906 For further details on exploring the tunnels, check ☹www.cuchitunnel.org.vn.

907 The Angkor site is 5km from Siem Riep; to visit you need a pass valid for 1 day (US$20), 3 days (US$40) or 7 days (US$60).

908 Mount Bromo is the main attraction of East Java's Bromo-Tengger-Semeru National Park. Most people stay in the nearby village of Cemoro Lawang, a 2hr bus drive from Probolinggo on Java's north coast.

909 The Minh Mang mausoleums are part of Hué's imperial city, which is open daily 7am–5pm.

910 The website ☹www.kokodatrail.com.au has lots of information on the Kokoda Trail.

911 Chiang Mai and Bangkok have the most diverse array of street stalls in Thailand; good night markets include those in Bangkok's Chinatown and Anusarn Market, off Thanon Chang Klan in Chiang Mai.

912 VSO is an international development agency operating in over thirty countries. For more information, visit ☹www.vso.org.uk.

AUSTRALIA, NEW ZEALAND & THE SOUTH PACIFIC

913 The park is 110km north of Halls Creek (allow 3hr) and is open April–Dec, weather permitting.

914 For more information, visit ☹www.mardigras.org.au.

915 Aussie Adventure Sailing (☹www.aussiesailing.com.au) offers outings on classic tall ships; Southern Cross (☹www.soxsail.com.au) has tours on maxi-yacht racers.

916 Trips start from Te Anau or Manapouri in Fiordland National Park. Real Journeys (☎03/249 7416, ☹www.realjourneys.co.nz) run excellent cruises.

917 Daintree Village is a 110km drive north of Cairns; Port Douglas is a well-established holiday town 70km north of Cairns. For information on accommodation visit ☹www.daintree-ecolodge.com.au or ☹www.ca-petribbeach.com.au.

918 Aboriginal guided tours are run by Anangu Tours (☹www.ananguwaai.com.au) in the Uluru-Kata Tjuta National Park (daily: June & July 6.30am–7.30pm, Dec–Feb 5am–9pm).

919 The Taieri Gorge Railway (☎03/477 4449, ☹www.taieri.co.nz) runs from from Dunedin to Pukerangi, where you start on the Otago Central Rail Trail (☹www.centralotagorailtrail.co.nz).

920 *The Ghan* (☹www.gsr.com.au) leaves Adelaide for Darwin every Friday and Sunday at 5.15pm and takes 48 hours.

921 Visit ☹www.marlboroughtours.co.nz or ☹www.winetoursbybike.co.nz for more information.

922 For more information, see ☹www.northlandnz.com.

923 Visit ☹www.kauricoast.co.nz for further details.

924 Broken River, in Eungella National Park, has a viewing platform built over the river; the platypus, fairly used to being watched by humans, aren't too timid here. The park lies 80km inland from the coastal city of Mackay and is easily reached by road.

925 For a broad guide to locations, visit ☹www.filmnz.com/middleearth/locations/index.html; for tours visit ☹www.hobbitontours.com.

926 For more information on the All Blacks, visit ☹www.allblacks.com or ☹www.haka.co.nz.

927 For more information, visit ☹www.melbourne.vic.gov.au.

928 Check ☹www.southaustralia.com for more details on the region.

929 For more information, visit ☹www.ultimatehikes.co.nz.

930 For more on Alice Springs, see ☹www.alice-springs.net.au.

931 ☹www.queenstown-nz.co.nz is a decent one-stop source of all things Queenstown.

932 Visit ☹www.australiaadventures.com for more information.

933 Visit ☹www.australianexplorer.com for further details.

934 A tour to Tanna, including a trip to Mount Yasur, can be arranged with any number of agencies in Vanuatu's capital of Port Vila.

935 To stay on the island, try the *Nataiwatch* bungalows, which go for around €70 (☹www.nataiwatch.com).

936 The Art Deco Shop, 163 Tennyson St (daily 9am–5pm), offers a free Deco video and sells maps for self-guided Art Deco walks.

937 The ideal way to experience a hangi (pronounced "hungi") is as a guest at a private gathering of extended families. The alternative is to join one of the commercial affairs; visit ☹www.worldofmaori.co.nz for more information.

938 Check out ☹www.birdsvilleraces.com for more information.

939 All boat-based whale-watching trips are run by the Maori-owned Whale Watch Kaikoura (☎03/319 6767, ☹www.whalewatch.co.nz); book in advance.

940 Organized hikes can be arranged with Pa's Treks (☎jillian@pasbungalows.co.ck).

941 The Poor Knights Islands are a marine reserve 25km off the east coast of Northland. For more information, visit ☹www.diving.co.nz

942 Check ☹www.qvm.com.au for further details.

943 Most people take a walking tour through Waitomo Glow-worm Caves (daily 9am–5pm). The most adventurous tours are with Absolute Adventure who don't offer tubing or long abseils but give an authentic caving experience.

944 Te Papa (☹www.tepapa.govt.nz) is open daily 10am–6pm and until 9pm on Thursday.

945 For reliable service at the best prices, try The Guiding Company (☎0800/800 102, ☹www.nzguides.com).

946 AJ Hackett Bungy (☎0800/286 495, ☹www.ajhackett.com) operate three bungy sites around Queenstown.

947 Rafting trips on the Franklin begin and end in Hobart and guides are recommended. World Expeditions runs 9-day rafting trips between November and April; for more information, go to ☹www.worldexpeditions.com.au, ☹www.franklinrivertasmania.com, ☹www.raftingtasmania.com or ☹www.tas-ex.com.

948 Full details on the web at ☹www.adelaidefestival.org.au, ☹www.adelaidefringe.com.au, ☹www.adelaidefilmfestival.org, ☹www.womadelaide.com.au.

949 Motorbike hire and guided tours are available from Ian and John Fitzwater at ☹www.gotournz.com.

950 Go to ☹www.visit-palau.com for more details.

951 Q1's official website is ☹www.q1.com.au.

952 Most walkers tackle the track north – south to get the potentially bad weather behind them; it's the mandatory direction between November and April. See ❸www.overlandtrack.com.au for more information.

953 Our Airline runs flights from Brisbane to Nauru (❸www.southpacific.org/map/airnauru.html). There are two hotels on the island; *OD-N-Aiwo Hotel* is the cheapest.

954 The TranzAlpine (❸www.tranzscenic.co.nz) operates daily from Christchurch to Greymouth and back, taking around 4hr 30min in each direction.

955 For more, visit ❸www.sydneyferries.info.

956 For a long trip, you're best buying a 4WD bushcamper. Visit ❸www.exploreoz.com for good advice and information on outback four-wheeling.

957 For more, visit ❸www.rotoruanz.com.

958 The website ❸www.deh.gov.au/parks/kakadu is a mine of information about the park.

959 You should be fit and have a head for heights to hike the Gillespie Pass in the Mount Aspiring National Park. For further information, contact the Makarora Visitor Centre, Haast Highway 6, Makarora (☎03 443 8365, ❸www.doc.govt.nz).

960 For lessons, try Surfers Paradise Free Ride Surfing School (❸www.freeridesurfing.com.au), Cheyne Horan School of Surf (❸www.cheynehoran.com.au) or Australian Surfer (❸www.australiansurfer.com).

961 The best time to see whale sharks is between April and July. Licensed operators include Three Islands (❸www.whalesharkdive.com) and Exmouth Diving Centre (❸www.exmouthdiving.com).

962 The Otago Peninsula starts in the suburbs of New Zealand's main southern city, Dunedin. It is an easy and scenic drive to all the spots mentioned including Penguin Place (☎03/478 0286, ❸www.penguinplace.co.nz) and the Royal Albatross Centre (tours late Nov to mid-Sept daily; ❸www.albatross.org.nz).

963 Rent a 20-year-old station wagon with travelling gear for the trip. For old cars, hostel ads are better than used-car dealers.

964 For more information, visit ❸www.environment.gov.au/parks/uluru.

965 For more information, check out WWOOF's wesbite at ❸www.wwoof.org.

966 You can fly to New Caledonia from Auckland, Brisbane, Melbourne and Sydney with Aircalin (❸www.aircalin.nc).

967 The tourist board site (❸www.vanuatutourism.com) has more on the wreck, including a dive map.

968 The 16km-long Tongariro Crossing involves around 750m of ascent and 1000m of descent and typically takes 6–8hr. The climate between November and April makes these the most popular months.

969 Reaching Otago from Dunedin is easy with your own transport, but lots of people run decent tours – try ❸www.elmwildlifetours.co.nz. or ❸www.wildearth.co.nz.

970 Harris Mountains Heli-Ski (☎03/442 6722, ❸www.heliski.co.nz) offer heliskiing and heliboarding around Queenstown, Wanaka and near Mount Cook. The season runs June–Oct.

971 Kings Canyon is 400km from Alice Springs, on the way to Uluru. Allow 2.5 hours to enjoy the walk and take plenty of water. You can camp, lodge and eat at the *Kings Canyon Resort*, 10km past the canyon (❸www.kingscanyonresort.com.au).

972 You can rent a fully equipped 4WD bushcamper in Cairns; allow at least a fortnight for the return trip. Travel is only possible out of wet season from May to November.

973 Queenstown Rafting (☎0800 723 8464,❸www.rafting.co.nz) offers multi-day guided trips down the Landsborough River; trips run from mid-Nov to end of March.

974 Helicopter to the top of Ben Cruchuan with Vertigo Bikes (❸www.vertigobikes.co.nz) in Queenstown.

975 During the day, visit the Waitangi Visitor Centre and Treaty House (daily: Oct–March 9am–6pm; April–Sept 9am–5pm; ❸www.waitangi.net.nz). In the evening, book ahead for the Night Show (Oct–March Mon, Wed, Thurs & Sat 8pm; ☎09/402 5990, ❸www.culturenorth.co.nz).

976 The *STS Leeuwin II* is an 1850s-style tall ship based in Fremantle, Western Australia. The Leeuwin Ocean Adventure Foundation (❸www.leeuwin.com) operates voyages throughout the year along the Australian coast and the Indian Ocean.

977 Most people rent kayaks in Marahau or one of the other small towns at the southern end of the park. For lodge accommodation, visit ❸www.awaroalodge.co.nz.

978 The Musée Gauguin (☎689/57 10 58) is open daily 9am–5pm. Hiva Oa is one of the Marquesas Islands, most easily reached by domestic flight on Air Tahiti (❸www.airtahiti.aero).

979 Blazing Saddles in Aireys Inlet, Victoria (❸www.blazingsaddlestrailrides.com), offers trail rides seven days a week.

980 Nadi, on Viti Levu, is a major South Pacific hub, while the capital, Suva, on the southeast coast, is served by a smaller airport. *Home Stay Suva* (265 Prince's Rd, ☎679/337 0395) is the best deal in the capital, a colonial home with magnificent views.

981 Waipoua Kauri Forest is 50km north of Dargaville; Tane Mahuta and Te Matua Ngahere both lie close to the road and are accessible via a series of boardwalks.

982 For more information, visit ❸www.greatbarrierreef.aus.net.

983 There are frequent flights to Broome from Perth and other state capitals. See also ❸www.broomevisitorcentre.com.au.

984 For more information, visit ❸www.mcg.org.au.

985 *Shady Camp* is 200km east of Darwin (last 60km is 2WD dirt road). Some Kakadu tours include an excursion here, but you can easily rent a boat nearby for 2 hours (☎08/8978 8937).

986 Try *Benediction*, 30 St Benedicts St, Newton (☎09/309 5001); *Atlas*, 285 Ponsonby Rd (☎09/360 1295); *Occam*, 135 Williamson Ave, Grey Lynn (☎09/378 0604) or *La Zeppa*, 33 Drake St (☎09/379 8167).

987 For more information, visit ❸www.activities.nz.com/rafting.

988 You can pick up a free map of the walkway from the Manly Visitor Centre on Manly Wharf.

989 There are ferries to Waiheke from Auckland's Ferry Building and Half Moon Bay.

990 To get an early start on Mount Tambourine, book in at the cosy *Polish Place* (☎07/5545 1603; ❸www.polishplace.com.au).

991 For more information, visit ❸www.outback-australia-travel-secrets.com.

THE POLAR REGIONS

992 In Kiruna, stay at the comfortable *Vinterpalatset* (❸www.vinterpalatset.se), which has rooms for SEK1000–1500.

993 Spending a night in an igloo can be arranged in any Nunavik or Nunavut community – see ❸www.nunavik-tourism.com or ❸www.nunavuttourism.com.

994 The local Tysfjord tourst office runs snorkelling safaris between October and mid-January for 1600Kr per person. See ❸www.tysfjord-turistsenter.no for more.

995 You can get more infomation on the Auyuittuq National Park on ☎867/473 2500 or at ❸www.pcgc.ca. All visitors must register with Parks Canada.

996 Ocean Adventures (❸www.oceanadventures.co.uk) operate a 30-day cruise that visits McMurdo station and several of the area's historic huts.

997 There are numerous polyanas throughout Canada's Arctic, and each village has outfitters who can arrange trips. Komeaortok Tours (❸ktoursoutfitting@yahoo.ca) arranges visits by snowmobile from Pangnintung, an hour's flight from Iqaluit, the capital of Nunavut.

998 The website ❸www.antarcticconnection.com has lots of info on Antarctic birds and wildlife and much else besides, including trips and cruises.

999 ❸www.spitsbergentravel.no is the best all-round travel site or try Aurora Expeditions (❸www.aurora expeditions.com).

1000 There are many Antarctic cruise operators but one of the best is Exodus (❸www.exodus.co.uk).

AUTHOR CREDITS

001 Nick Jones
002 Paul Gray
003 Robert Andrews
004 Donald Reid
005 Paul Whitfield
006 Donald Reid
007 Charles Campion
008 Alf Alderson
009 Mark Ellingham
010 Robert Andrews
011 Paul Gray
012 Paul Whitfield
013 Lucy White
014 Mark Connolly & Paul Gray
015 Donald Reid
016 Lucy White
017 Al Spicer
018 Robert Andrews
019 Tim Ecott
020 Katy Ball
021 Sarah Eno
022 Paul Whitfield
023 Sarah Eno
024 Mark Ellingham
025 Donald Reid
026 Alf Alderson
027 Dave Dakota
028 Lucy White
029 Keith Drew
030 Alf Alderson
031 Chris Scott
032 Dave Abram
033 Geoff Wallis
034 Helena Smith
035 Polly Evans
036 Polly Thomas
037 Robert Andrews
038 Paul Whitfield
039 Robert Andrews
040 Mark Robertson
041 Donald Reid
042 Donald Reid
043 Paul Gray
044 Melanie Kramers
045 Paul Gray
046 Donald Reid
047 Rob Humphreys
048 Martin Dunford
049 Tim Ecott
050 Natasha Foges
051 Paul Gray
052 James Smart
053 Keith Drew
054 Caitlin Fitzsimmons
055 Keith Drew
056 Dave Dakota & Paul Gray
057 William Sutcliffe
058 Kerry Walker
059 Diana Jarvis
060 Martin Dunford
061 Martin Dunford
062 Emma Gibbs
063 Martin Dunford
064 Greg Langley
065 Kevin Fitzgerald
066 Martin Dunford
067 Dave Abram
068 Chris Straw
069 James McConnachie
070 Neville Walker
071 Helena Smith
072 Martin Teller
073 Neville Walker
074 Ross Velton
075 Helen Marsden
076 Jan Dodd
077 James Smart
078 James Stewart
079 Keith Drew
080 Diana Jarvis

081 Dave Abram
082 Matthew Teller
083 Stephen Keeling
084 Jon Bousfield
085 Neville Walker
086 Ross Velton
087 Martin Dunford
088 Mick O'Hare
089 Kerry Walker
090 Neville Walker
091 Lucy White
092 Stephen Keeling
093 Matthew Teller
094 Natasha Foges
095 Martin Dunford
096 Ruth Blackmore
097 Martin Dunford
098 Lucy White
099 Ross Velton
100 Jan Dodd
101 Sarah Eno
102 Matthew Teller
103 James McConnachie
104 Ross Velton
105 Jan Dodd
106 Emma Gibbs
107 Martin Dunford
108 Keith Drew
109 Martin Dunford
110 Martin Dunford
111 Helen Marsden
112 Kerry Walker
113 Jan Dodd
114 Martin Dunford
115 Dave Abram
116 Stephen Keeling
117 Martin Dunford
118 Ross Velton
119 Matthew Teller
120 Ruth Blackmore
121 Stephen Keeling
122 Martin Dunford
123 Lucy White
124 Neville Walker
125 Ruth Blackmore
126 Kerry Walker
127 Brendon Griffin
128 Brendon Griffin
129 Brendon Griffin
130 Brendon Griffin
131 Brendon Griffin
132 Brendon Griffin
133 Matthew Hancock
134 Brendon Griffin
135 Brendon Griffin
136 Brendon Griffin
137 Brendon Griffin
138 AnneLise Sorensen
139 Brendon Griffin
140 James Smart
141 Brendon Griffin
142 Brendon Griffin
143 Harriet Mills
144 Brendon Griffin
145 Brendon Griffin
146 Matthew Hancock
147 AnneLise Sorensen
148 James Smart
149 Martin Dunford
150 Matthew Hancock
151 Brendon Griffin
152 Martin Dunford
153 Keith Drew
154 Damien Simonis
155 AnneLise Sorensen
156 Christian Williams
157 Keith Drew
158 Jeffrey Kennedy
159 Kerry Walker
160 Dave Dakota & Damien Simonis
161 Brendon Griffin

162 Martin Dunford
163 AnneLise Sorensen
164 Iain Stewart
165 Brendon Griffin
166 Matthew Hancock
167 Brendon Griffin
168 Brendon Griffin
169 Brendon Griffin
170 Matthew Hancock
171 Christian Williams
172 Brendon Griffin
173 Brendon Griffin
174 Brendon Griffin
175 Brendon Griffin
176 Matthew Hancock
177 AnneLise Sorensen
178 Brendon Griffin
179 James Proctor
180 Felicity Aston
181 Roger Norum
182 James Proctor
183 Keith Drew
184 Phil Lee
185 David Leffman
186 Adrian Mourby
187 Oliver Schwaner-Albright
188 Keith Drew
189 Tim Ecott
190 Nikki Birrell
191 Keith Drew
192 Alf Alderson
193 Keith Drew
194 Roger Norum
195 AnneLise Sorensen
196 Tim Ecott
197 Keith Drew
198 Caroline Osborne
199 AnneLise Sorensen
200 Todd Obolsky
201 AnneLise Sorensen
202 James Proctor
203 Tim Ecott
204 Todd Obolsky
205 Kate Thomas
206 Keith Drew
207 David Leffman
208 Keith Drew
209 James McConnachie
210 Jeffrey Kennedy
211 Martin Dunford
212 Martin Dunford
213 Martin Dunford
214 Norm Longley
215 Martin Dunford
216 Jon Bousfield
217 Jeffrey Kennedy
218 Norm Longley
219 Martin Dunford
220 Martin Dunford
221 Polly Evans
222 Norm Longley
223 Jeffrey Kennedy
224 Norm Longley
225 John Fisher
226 Martin Dunford
227 Martin Dunford
228 Norm Longley
229 Megan McIntyre
230 Ros Belford
231 Mark Ellwood
232 Martin Dunford
233 Megan McIntyre
234 Robert Andrews
235 Kerry Walker
236 Norm Longley
237 Jon Bousfield
238 Terry Richardson
239 Robert Andrews
240 Martin Dunford
241 Martin Dunford
242 John Fisher

243 Jonathon Buckley
244 Terry Richardson
245 Lucy Ratcliffe
246 Stephen Keeling
247 Ross Velton
248 Jonathon Buckley
249 Megan McIntyre
250 Marc Dubin
251 Richard Schofield
252 Sarah Eno
253 Martin Dunford
254 Lucy White
255 Matthew Teller
256 Natasha Foges
257 Martin Dunford
258 Martin Dunford
259 Natasha Foges
260 Jonathon Buckley
261 Kerry Walker
262 Martin Dunford
263 Martin Zatko
264 Barnaby Rogerson
265 Martin Dunford
266 Philippa Hopkins
267 James McConnachie
268 Norm Longley
269 Siobhan Donaghue
270 Martin Dunford
271 Emma Gibbs
272 Greg Witt
273 Martin Dunford
274 Jon Bousfield
275 Lucy White
276 Jon Bousfield
277 Greg Langley
278 Jonathon Buckley
279 Jonathon Buckley
280 Jonathon Buckley
281 Martin Dunford
282 Martin Dunford
283 Victor Borg
284 Norm Longley
285 Martin Dunford
286 Martin Dunford
287 Martin Dunford
288 Jonathon Buckley
289 Andrew Rosenberg
290 Rob Humphreys
291 Mick O'Hare
292 Jon Bousfield
293 Lily Hyde
294 Jon Bousfield
295 Lily Hyde
296 Norm Longley
297 Jon Bousfield
298 Dan Richardson
299 Jon Bousfield
300 Kate Thomas
301 Rob Crossan
302 Norm Longley
303 Alison Murchie
304 James Smart
305 Dan Richardson
306 Alison Murchie
307 Rob Humphreys
308 Jon Bousfield
309 Kate Thomas
310 Norm Longley
311 Jon Bousfield
312 Stephen Keeling
313 Lily Hyde
314 Alison Murchie
315 Jon Bousfield
316 Rob Humphreys
317 Martin Zatko
318 Keith Drew
319 Dan Richardson
320 Michael Haag
321 Adrian Mourby
322 Richard Trillo
323 Dan Jacobs
324 Chris Scott

325 Dan Jacobs
326 Dan Jacobs
327 Dan Jacobs
328 Roger Norum
329 Chris Scott
330 Dan Jacobs
331 Matthew Teller
332 Kate Berens
333 Victor Borg
334 Juliana Barnaby
335 Caitlin Fitzsimmons
336 Adrian Mourby
337 Juliana Barnaby
338 Keith Drew
339 Victor Borg
340 Dan Jacobs
341 Mark Ellingham
342 Matthew Teller
343 James Smart
344 Matthew Teller
345 Keith Drew
346 Dave Abram
347 Katy Ball
348 Michael Haag
349 Chris Scott
350 Richard Trillo
351 Chris Scott
352 Richard Trillo
353 Richard Trillo
354 Chris Scott
355 Richard Trillo
356 Richard Trillo
357 Richard Trillo
358 Lone Mouritsen
359 Rob Crossan
360 Emma Gregg
361 Richard Trillo
362 Richard Trillo
363 Emma Gregg
364 Lone Mouritsen
365 Emma Gregg
366 Miranda Davies
367 Richard Trillo
368 Chris Scott
369 Roger Norum
370 Anna Paynton
371 Richard Trillo
372 Ross Velton
373 Emma Gregg
374 Suzanne Porter
375 Eliza Reid
376 Richard Trillo
377 Chris Scott
378 Chris Scott
379 Marie Javins
380 Nick Maes
381 Richard Trillo
382 Richard Trillo
383 Richard Trillo
384 Richard Trillo
385 Keith Drew
386 Emma Gregg
387 Stanley Johnson
388 Marie Javins
389 David Leffman
390 Beth Wooldridge
391 Emma Gregg
392 Richard Trillo
393 Nick Maes
394 Keith Drew
395 Jens Finke
396 Tim Ecott
397 Henry Stedman
398 Keith Drew
399 Nick Maes
400 Tim Ecott
401 Richard Trillo
402 Chris Scott
403 Jens Finke
404 Richard Trillo
405 Richard Trillo
406 Richard Trillo

407 Nick Maes
408 Richard Trillo
409 Nick Maes
410 Nikki Birrell
411 Richard Trillo
412 Donald Reid
413 Keith Drew
414 Richard Trillo
415 Nick Maes
416 Rob Crossan
417 Emma Gregg
418 Nikki Birrell
419 Keith Drew
420 William Sutcliffe
421 Richard Trillo
422 Adrian Mourby
423 Mike Unwin
424 Justin Francis
425 Mike Unwin
426 Mike Unwin
427 Keith Drew
428 Tony Pinchuck
429 Dave Abram
430 Donald Reid
431 Dave Abram
432 Emma Gregg
433 Emma Gregg
434 Emma Gregg
435 Tim Ecott
436 Nick Maes
437 Nick Maes
438 Donald Reid
439 Emma Gregg
440 Mike Unwin
441 Gregory Mthembu-Salter & Tony Pinchuck
442 Emma Gregg
443 Emma Gregg
444 Ross Velton
445 Nick Garbutt
446 Keith Drew
447 Nikki Birrell
448 Emma Gregg
449 Emma Gregg
450 Keith Drew
451 Rob Crossan
452 Emma Gregg
453 Keith Drew
454 Emma Gregg
455 Claus Vogel
456 Marie Houghton
457 Matthew Teller
458 Matthew Teller
459 Keith Drew
460 Matthew Teller
461 Matthew Teller
462 Matthew Teller
463 Matthew Teller
464 Matthew Teller
465 Emma Gibbs
466 Matthew Teller
467 Matthew Teller
468 Roger Norum
469 Roger Norum
470 Roger Norum
471 Michael Haag
472 Matthew Teller
473 Dan Jacobs
474 Matthew Teller
475 Matthew Teller
476 Matthew Teller
477 Matthew Teller
478 Matthew Teller
479 Roger Norum
480 Matthew Teller
481 Matthew Teller
482 Dan Jacobs
483 Matthew Teller
484 Matthew Teller
485 Daisy Finer
486 Diana Jarvis

487 Matthew Teller	575 Polly Evans	661 Zora O'Neill	750 David Leffman	838 Daisy Finer	926 Paul Whitfield
488 Matthew Teller	576 Alf Alderson	662 Mark Fass	751 David Leffman	839 Dave Abram	927 Martin Dunford
489 Roger Norum	577 Megan McIntyre	663 AnneLise Sorensen	752 Martin Dunford	840 Diana Jarvis	928 Chris Scott
490 Matthew Teller	578 Felicity Aston	664 Sarah Trefethen	753 David Leffman	841 AnneLise Sorensen	929 Paul Whitfield
491 Keith Drew	579 Janine Israel	665 Polly Rodger Brown	754 Lucy Ridout	842 Dave Abram	930 Chris Scott
492 Matthew Teller	580 Claus Vogel	666 Rob Coates	755 Martin Dunford	843 James McConnachie	931 Paul Whitfield
493 Roger Norum	581 Christian Williams	667 Keith Drew	756 David Leffman	844 Flip Byrnes	932 Chris Scott
494 Matthew Teller	582 Ross Velton	668 Jonathan Yevin	757 Stephen Keeling	845 Kerry Walker	933 Alec Simpson
495 Marie Javins	583 Melissa Graham	669 Lily Fink	758 David Leffman	846 Dave Abram	934 Peter Chapple
496 Holly Wademan	584 Christian Williams	670 Diana Jarvis	759 Martin Zatko	847 Nick Maes	935 Peter Chapple
497 Matthew Teller	585 Janine Israel	671 Andrew Rosenberg	760 Jan Dodd	848 Martin Dunford	936 Paul Whitfield
498 Matthew Teller	586 Claus Vogel	672 Tim Ecott	761 Polly Evans	849 Dave Abram	937 Paul Whitfield
499 Ross Velton	587 Christian Williams	673 Zora O'Neill	762 David Leffman	850 Dave Abram	938 David Leffman
500 Stephen Timblin	588 Phil Lee & Anna Roberts Welles	674 Paul D Smith	763 Rob Crossan	851 Dave Abram	939 Paul Whitfield
501 JD Dickey		675 Harry Ades	764 Martin Zatko	852 Dave Abram	940 Diana Jarvis
502 Keith Drew	589 Janine Israel	676 Joshua Goodman	765 David Leffman	853 Dave Abram	941 Paul Whitfield
503 Stephen Keeling	590 Steven Horak	677 Caroline Lascom	766 Martin Zatko	854 Richard Wignell	942 Chris Scott
504 Sean Harvey	591 Phil Lee	678 James Read	767 David Leffman	855 Dave Abram	943 Paul Whitfield
505 Andrew Rosenberg	592 Christian Williams	679 Keith Drew	768 Stephen Keeling	856 Dave Abram	944 Paul Whitfield
506 JD Dickey	593 Phil Lee	680 James Read	769 Anna Fifield	857 Seph Petta	945 Paul Whitfield
507 Stephen Keeling	594 Phil Lee	681 Harry Ades	770 David Leffman	858 Dave Abram	946 Paul Whitfield
508 Greg Ward	595 Polly Evans	682 Richard Danbury	771 Simon Richmond	859 Dave Abram	947 Chris Scott
509 JD Dickey	596 Christian Williams	683 Keith Drew	772 Jan Dodd	860 Dave Abram	948 Chris Scott
510 Paul Whitfield	597 Adam Vaitilingam & Ross Velton	684 Rosalba O'Brien	773 Anna Fifield	861 Dave Abram	949 Polly Evans
511 Zora O'Neill	598 Gaylord Dold & Natalie Folster	685 Rosalba O'Brien	774 Martin Zatko	862 Lucy Ridout	950 Seph Petta
512 JD Dickey		686 Hal Weitzman	775 David Leffman	863 Lucy Ridout	951 Scott Stickland
513 Zora O'Neill	599 Hannah Hennessy	687 Polly Rodger Brown	776 David Leffman	864 Lucy Ridout	952 Chris Scott
514 Christian Williams	600 Andrew Rosenberg	688 Dilwyn Jenkins	777 Martin Zatko	865 David Dalton	953 Rob Crossan
515 Don Bapst	601 Andrew Rosenberg	689 Oliver Marshall	778 David Leffman	866 Lucy Ridout	954 Paul Whitfield
516 Megan Kennedy	602 Matt Norman	690 Polly Rodger Brown	779 David Leffman	867 David Dalton	955 Chris Scott
517 Jeffrey Kennedy	603 Polly Thomas	691 Ross Velton	780 Lesley Reader	868 Jeff Cranmer	956 Chris Scott
518 Shea Dean	604 Chris Hamilton	692 Andrew Benson	781 Martin Zatko	869 David Dalton	957 Paul Whitfield
519 Zora O'Neill	605 Sean Harvey	693 James Read	782 David Leffman	870 Lucy Ridout	958 Keith Drew
520 Andrew Rosenberg	606 Steven Horak	694 Steven Horak	783 David Leffman	871 Martin Dunford	959 Kerry Walker
521 Sarah Hull	607 Chris Hamilton	695 Rob Crossan	784 Martin Zatko	872 Lucy Ridout	960 Martin Dunford
522 Andrew Rosenberg	608 Polly Thomas	696 Andrew Benson	785 David Leffman	873 Lucy Ridout	961 Lucy Ridout
523 Andrew Rosenberg	609 Stephen Keeling	697 Paul D Smith	786 David Leffman	874 Sean Mahoney	962 Paul Whitfield
524 Paul Whitfield	610 Dave Abram	698 Oliver Marshall	787 Jan Dodd	875 Lucy Ridout	963 Chris Scott
525 Sara Lieber	611 Sean Harvey	699 Andrew Benson	788 David Leffman	876 Henry Stedman	964 Chris Scott
526 Paul Whitfield	612 Claus Vogel	700 Melissa Graham	789 Anna Fifield	877 Andy Turner	965 Diana Jarvis
527 Steven Horak	613 Seph Petta	701 Harry Ades	790 David Leffman	878 Lucy Ridout	966 Nikki Birrell
528 Paul Whitfield	614 Polly Thomas	702 Seph Petta	791 David Leffman	879 Tim Ecott	967 David Leffman
529 Stephen Keeling	615 Claus Vogel	703 Seph Petta	792 Anna Fifield	880 Christina Markel	968 Paul Whitfield
530 Jeff Cranmer	616 Stephen Keeling	704 James Read	793 David Leffman	881 Tim Ecott	969 Paul Whitfield
531 JD Dickey	617 Sarah Eno	705 James Read	794 David Leffman	882 Henry Stedman	970 Paul Whitfield
532 Sarah Eno	618 Sean Harvey	706 Keith Drew	795 Martin Zatko	883 Lucy Ridout	971 Lucy Ridout
533 Jeffrey Kennedy	619 Natalie Folster	707 Andrew Rosenberg	796 David Leffman	884 Flip Byrnes	972 Alec Simpson
534 Greg Ward	620 AnneLise Sorensen	708 Seph Petta	797 Stephen Keeling	885 David Dalton	973 Holly Wallace
535 Cali Alpert & Brad Olsen	621 Steven Horak	709 Steven Horak	798 Simon Lews	886 Lucy Ridout	974 Holly Wallace
	622 Chris Hamilton	710 Holly Wallace	799 Nick Middleton	887 Jan Dodd	975 Paul Whitfield
536 Caroline Lascom	623 Polly Thomas	711 Dave Dakota	800 David Leffman	888 Lucy Ridout	976 Felicity Aston
537 Hunter Slaton	624 Tim Ecott	712 Hal Weitzman	801 Martin Zatko	889 David Leffman	977 Paul Whitfield
538 Sarah Hull	625 Megan Kennedy	713 Seph Petta	802 Keith Drew	890 Victor Borg	978 Stephen Keeling
539 Andrew Rosenberg	626 Sean Harvey	714 Keith Drew	803 Lucy Ridout	891 Lucy Ridout	979 Megan McIntyre
540 Madelyn Rosenberg	627 Jean McNeil	715 Megan Kennedy	804 Alf Alderson	892 Lucy Ridout	980 Stephen Keeling
541 Madelyn Rosenberg	628 Caroline Lascom	716 Keith Drew	805 Martin Dunford	893 Lucy Ridout	981 Polly Evans
542 Keith Drew	629 Richard Arghiris	717 Hannah Hennessy	806 Simon Richmond	894 Paul Gray	982 Chris Scott
543 Sarah Eno	630 Polly Rodger Brown	718 Dave Abram	807 Greg Witt	895 Charles de Ledesma	983 Chris Scott
544 Megan Kennedy	631 Iain Stewart	719 James Smart	808 David Leffman	896 Martin Dunford	984 Chris Scott
545 Andrew Rosenberg	632 Polly Rodger Brown	720 James Smart	809 Dave Abram	897 Lucy Ridout	985 Anne Dehne
546 Steven Horak	633 Iain Stewart	721 Rosalba O'Brien	810 Dave Abram	898 Henry Stedman	986 Paul Whitfield
547 Zora O'Neill	634 Kate Berens	722 Melissa Graham	811 Dave Abram	899 David Leffman	987 Paul Whitfield
548 Christian Williams	635 Caroline Lascom	723 Andrew Benson	812 Dave Dakota & Gavin Thomas	900 Lucy Ridout	988 Lucy Ridout
549 Stephen Timblin	636 Paul Whitfield	724 Daisy Finer		901 Henry Stedman	989 Nikki Birrell
550 Charles Lyons	637 Zora O'Neill	725 Hal Weitzman	813 Dave Abram	902 Megan McIntyre	990 Scott Stickland
551 Mark Ellwood	638 Daisy Finer	726 Keith Drew	814 Reem Khokar	903 David Dalton	991 Chris Scott
552 Keith Drew	639 Jean McNeil	727 Melissa Graham	815 Louise Southerden	904 Stephen Keeling	992 James Proctor
553 Samantha Cook	640 Polly Rodger Brown	728 Alex Robinson	816 Dave Abram	905 Victor Borg	993 Claus Vogel
554 JD Dickey	641 Paul Whitfield	729 Hannah Hennessy	817 Dave Abram	906 Stephen Keeling	994 Louise Southerden
555 Alice Park	642 Iain Stewart	730 Caroline Lascom	818 Laura Stone	907 Karoline Densley	995 Claus Vogel
556 Greg Ward	643 Polly Rodger Brown	731 Keith Drew	819 Dave Abram	908 Henry Stedman	996 Hunter Slaton
557 Mark Ellwood	644 Rob Coates	732 Andrew Benson	820 Dave Abram	909 Lucy Ridout	997 Claus Vogel
558 Megan Kennedy	645 Keith Drew	733 Seph Petta	821 Stanley Johnson	910 Seph Petta	998 Hunter Slaton
559 Christina Markel	646 Paul Whitfield	734 Ross Velton	822 Dave Abram	911 Lucy Ridout & Andrew Rosenberg	999 Caitlin Fitzsimmons
560 Stephen Timblin	647 Zora O'Neill	735 Andrew Benson	823 Dave Abram		1000 Jean McNeil
561 Stephen Timblin	648 Iain Stewart	736 Roger Norum	824 Diana Jarvis	912 Rob Coates	
562 Zora O'Neill	649 AnneLise Sorensen	737 Hannah Hennessy	825 Lesley Reader	913 Alec Simpson	Miscellanies: Emma Kirby;
563 Caroline Lascom	650 Tom Kevill-Davies	738 Toby Nortcliffe	826 Dave Abram	914 Chris Scott	Matthew Teller; Brendon
564 Paul Whitfield	651 Gregory Witt	739 Hal Weitzman	827 Richard Wignell	915 Chris Scott	Griffin; Roger Norum;
565 Stephen Keeling	652 Jason Clampet	740 Andrew Benson	828 Martin Dunford	916 Paul Whitfield	Stephen Keeling; Norm
566 Janine Israel	653 Iain Stewart	741 Rosalba O'Brien	829 Nick Maes	917 Chris Scott	Longley; Richard Trillo; JD
567 Christian Williams	654 Mark Ellingham	742 Andrew Benson	830 Andy Turner	918 Stephen Keeling	Dickey; Seph Petta; Polly
568 Janine Israel	655 Polly Rodger Brown	743 Joe Tyrrell	831 Gavin Thomas	919 Paul Whitfield	Rodger Brown; James
569 Christian Williams	656 AnneLise Sorensen	744 Steven Horak	832 Dave Abram	920 Chris Scott	Read; David Leffman; Dave
570 Christian Williams	657 Iain Stewart	745 Andrew Rosenberg	833 Alf Alderson	921 Paul Whitfield	Abram; Lucy Ridout; Chris
571 Megan McIntyre	658 James Read	746 Keith Drew	834 Dave Abram	922 Paul Whitfield	Scott; Helena Smith.
572 Janine Israel	659 Polly Rodger Brown	747 David Leffman	835 Daisy Finer	923 Paul Whitfield	
573 Felicity Aston	660 Polly Rodger Brown	748 Keith Drew	836 Dave Abram	924 Dave Leffman	
574 Oliver Marshall		749 David Leffman	837 Dave Abram	925 Paul Whitfield	

INDEX

ALBANIA
Bunkering down in Durres 144
Making the party last all night in Tirana 155

ALGERIA
Discovering rock art on the Tassili N'Ajjer Plateau... 190
Exploring Beni Abbés & Timimoun 203
Hiking in the Hoggar 189
Seeing the old city of Tlemcen 201
Trans-Sahara by motorbike.................................... 202

ANTARCTICA
Scrambling up Observation Hill 581
Spotting seals and skuas....................................... 582
Voyaging into the unknown.................................... 583

ARGENTINA
Beefeater's paradise: the Argentine parrilla 399
Fly-fishing in Tierra del Fuego............................... 412
Getting soaked at Iguazu...................................... 427
Going downhill in the Andes 425
Putting the boot in on the Falkland Islands 404
Swept off your feet in Buenos Aires 426
Tackling the Fitz Roy Massif 409
Taking a ring-side seat at the Península Valdés ... 418
Walking on ice: the Perito Moreno glacier 424
Watching a football match...................................... 415
Wine and horses at Estancia Colomé..................... 417
Wine tasting in Mendoza.. 394

ARUBA
Arikok National Park: the Caribbean Outback 356

AUSTRALIA
Ascending Q1 in Surfers Paradise 555
Buzzing over the Bungles 534
Canyoneering in Karijini... 547
Celebrating Moomba Waterfest 544
Discovering the secrets of Kings Canyon.............. 566
Doing the Crocodile Rock in Kakadu
     National Park 560
Four-wheeling through croc country:
     Cairns to Cape York.. 576
Getting to grips with Aboriginal art 560
Going organic in the Northern Territory 564
Having a far-flung flutter at the Birdsville Races... 550
Hiking Sydney's spit to Manly Walkway 574
Horsing around on an Aussie beach...................... 570
Indulge your taste buds at Queen Victoria market .. 551
Island dreaming: sailing the Whitsundays............. 537
The last frontier: working on a cattle station 575
Learning to surf on the Gold Coast 561
Meeting the crocs at Shady Camp 573
Ocean to ocean, cape to cape: across
     Australia by 4WD 559
Paragliding over the paddocks 574
Platypus-watching: on the lookout for a
     duckbilled mammal 541
Rainforest vibes in the Daintree 537
Riding the Ghan to Darwin 538
River deep, mountain high: bushwalking
     the Overland Track... 556
River of no return: rafting the Franklin 554
Road trip Down Under: Perth to Darwin
     to Adelaide 563
Rock steady: admiring the shifting shades
     of Uluru 538
Sea kayaking around Shark Bay 547
Slip into Broometime.. 538
Swimming with whale sharks at Ningaloo Reef..... 562
Sydney Harbour-mastering 574
Tall-ship sailing in the Indian Ocean 568
Visiting the City of Festivals 555
A walk round Uluru... 563
Walking on the wild side at the Sydney
     Mardi Gras 536

Watching footy at the MCG 572
What lies beneath: snorkelling at the
     Great Barrier Reef... 572
Wine-tasting in the Barossa Valley........................ 544

AUSTRIA
Ars Electronica Centre: losing grip on reality......... 60
Catching the cultural zeitgeist in Graz 55
Defying gravity on the Semmering Railway 44
Kaffee und Kuchen in a Viennese Kaffeehaus...... 56
Kayaking across borders on Lake Constance 68
Listening to Mozart in Salzburg 48
Paragliding in the Zillertal...................................... 65
Skiing the Streif 52
Treating your senses at a Christkindlmarkt............ 58

AZERBAIJAN
Tea in the Land of Fire... 463

THE BAHAMAS
The Cave of Indescribable Horrors 353
Doing Junkanoo 351
Sea kayaking in the Exumas 359

BAHRAIN
Pearl diving in the Persian Gulf............................. 273

BANGLADESH
Getting swept away at Durga Puja 482
Riding the Rocket across the Ganges Delta.......... 496

BARBADOS
Celebrating Crop Over 350

BELGIUM
Gorging on chocolates in Brussels 65
Having a beer in Brussels 71
Joining the Gilles at the Binche Carnival 56

BELIZE
Easing into the New Year on Caye Caulker 384
Floating down the New River to Lamanai.............. 377
Indulging in the jungle... 379
Paddling Glover's Reef.. 374
Rustic luxury in the Belizean forest....................... 369
Searching for jaguars in Cockscomb Basin
     Wildlife Sanctuary 386

BENIN
Demystifying voodoo in Ouidah 219

BHUTAN
Sharing ancient roads with yak herders................ 542

BOLIVIA
Exploring silver mines in the Andes 411
Ice climbing in the Cordillera Real 414
Light show in La Paz.. 409
Making a pilgrimage to the Isla del Sol.................. 408
Mountain-biking the World's Most
     Dangerous Road 403
On the trail of Butch Cassidy and the
     Sundance Kid 429
Traversing the Salar de Uyuni 422

BONAIRE
Snorkelling with turtles.. 358

BOSNIA
Back from the brink: the bridge of Mostar........... 131

BOTSWANA
Crossing the Makgadikgadi Plains......................... 250
Learning about elephants in the Botswanan bush...253
Tricky topography: the Okavango Delta.............. 247

BRAZIL
Capoeira up close 429
Downing caipirinhas in Rio de Janeiro.................. 401
Drifting down the Amazon..................................... 407
Flying down to Rio 428
The frenzy of Boi Bumba 418

Going to the opera at Teatro Amazonas 402
Honouring the Orixas in Salvador 395
Lost in time on the Royal Road 405
The secret sensation of Pousada Maravilha 417
Seeking heat in the Chapada Diamantia 412
Show no restraint at Carnival 421
Trekking through the Pantanal 401
Watching a football match 415

BRITISH VIRGIN ISLANDS
Bathtime in Virgin Gorda 351

BULGARIA
High on a hill with a lonely goatherd.................... 178
Vulture watching in the Madzharovo
     Nature reserve.. 183

CAMBODIA
Exploring the temples of Angkor.......................... 526
Cleaning up after the Khmer Rouge: tackling
     Pol Pot's legacy with VSO 529
Visiting the Tuol Sleng genocide museum 518

CAMEROON
Conquering Mount Cameroon 209
Cycling a ring road with a difference 212
Seeing the jungle through the eyes of the Baka... 211

CANADA
In awe of the Aurora Borealis................................ 333
Beaching it with a literary classic.......................... 345
Bedding down in an igloo...................................... 580
Camping beneath Head-Smashed-In
     Buffalo Jump.. 335
Catching a wave on Vancouver Island.................. 341
Coasting on the P'tit Train du Nord 336
Crossing the prairies by train 336
Cruising Georgian Bay 343
Cycling around Stanley Park 342
Driving the Icefields Parkway 345
Eating your way around the world in Toronto........ 334
Exploring ancient culture on Haida Gwaii............ 333
Following the Yukon Quest 345
Form a lasting impression at Niagara Falls........... 344
Getting lost within the walls of Vieux-Quebec...... 332
Hiking around Lake Louise..................................... 331
The Ice Road from Inuvik to Tuktoyaktuk 335
Lighting up the sky in Montreal............................. 339
Paddling your way through Algonquin
     Provincial Park 340
Redefining remote on the Hudson Bay train........ 340
Reliving the Wild West at the Calgary Stampede . 338
Sea kayaking in the Mingan Archipelago.............. 334
Seeing old rivals in an ice-hockey game............... 343
Ski from the sky in the Rockies 333
Spying whales and spotting puffins in the Atlantic...337
Staying afloat on Little Manitou Lake 339
Striking it lucky in Dawson City 336
Stumbling upon a polar oasis............................... 582
Taking afternoon tea in Victoria............................ 334
The thrill of back-country skiing............................ 335
Tracking down polar bears in Churchill................. 341
Trekking across the Arctic Circle........................... 581
Watching the tide roll away in the Bay of Fundy .. 339

CAPE VERDE
Island hopping off the African Coast 210
Peaking on Fogo 216

CAYMAN ISLANDS
Deepest blue: diving Bloody Bay Wall 361

CHILE
Across the Altiplano 418
Braving the wind in Torres del Paine...................... 398
Crashing out by Lago Chungará............................ 414
Driving the Carretera Austral................................. 422
Enjoying isolation at the Termas de Puyuhapi...... 406

Frolicking with fur seals....................................... 405
The Giants of Rapa Nui.. 416
Going to church in Chiloé..................................... 410
A royal welcome at Hotel Centinela....................... 425
Seeing the sun rise in the Valley of the Moon 403
Stargazing on Cerro Mamalluca............................ 426
Tapati: fun and games on Easter Island................ 403
Trekking at the End of the World........................... 397

CHINA

Beach lounging in Beidaihe 467
Beaten and bruised at Wudang Shan.................... 459
Blown away by the Great Wall............................... 448
Celebrating the Dragon Boat Races....................... 438
Cracking the Ice Festival...................................... 436
Cruising the Three Gorges 434
Double happiness at the Tianyuki Guesthouse 464
Dwarfed by Hong Kong's skyscrapers.................... 456
Faces from the past: Xi'an's Terracotta Army......... 435
Getting lost in the Forbidden City.......................... 456
Getting soused at Sisters' Meal Festival 459
Gorging on dim sum in Guangzhou........................ 441
Joining the pilgrim's trail at Emei Shan................. 455
Jousting for a taste of Beijing duck....................... 463
Losing track of time: Beijing to Moscow on the
    Trans Siberian Railway..................................... 462
Losing your shirt in Macau.................................... 455
On foot through Tiger Leaping Gorge..................... 450
Peaking early in Hong Kong................................... 460
Quality space: admiring Suzhou's gardens............ 460
Riding by bus to Dêgê 452
Shopping at the mother of all markets 454
Stalking cranes at Caohai 434
Step aerobics: climbing Huang Shan 450
Strolling the Shanghai Bund 452
Taking tea in Chengdu 437
They eat shoots and leaves: meeting pandas
    in Chengdu.. 458
A trek back in time in rural Yunnan....................... 442
Two wheels good: biking around rural Yangshuo... 437
Unscrolling the Li River 440
Visiting Henan's Mona Lisa 444

COLOMBIA

Navigating the narrow streets of Cartagena.......... 397
Wake up and smell the coffee: the Zona Cafetera .. 409

COSTA RICA

A Costa Rica family adventure............................. 378
Galloping through Guanacaste 371
Trekking in Corcavado National Park..................... 372
Turtle-watching in Tortuguro 366

CROATIA

Getting lost in Diocletian's Palace 129
Joining the truffle trail in Buzet 131
Navigating the nocturnal underworld in Zagreb 156
Treading the boardwalks at Plitvice Lakes............ 127
Walking Dubrovnik's walls.................................... 133

CUBA

Classic Cuban cars and cuisine............................ 352
Meet the People: Fair Trade and Fruit Passion..... 356
Land of the Midnight Son 357

CZECH REPUBLIC

Drinking Pilsner from its home-town taps 169
Supping a real Bud in České Budějovice 177
The tale and the tongue of St John of Nepomuk . 181

DEMOCRATIC REPUBLIC OF CONGO

Cruising the Congo 225
The gorillas of Kahuzi-Biega 227

DENMARK

Christmas in the Happiest Place in the World 119

Creative cuisine at Nordic NOMA 114
Danish delights: Tivoli's fairground attractions 118
Seeing the light at Jutland's edge......................... 117
A toast to Vikings in Bornholm 118
Watching Hamlet in Kronborg Slot........................ 114

DOMINICA

Sniffing sulphur at Boiling Lake 355

DOMINICAN REPUBLIC

Going underground in Santo Domingo.................... 361
Kiteboarding in Cabarete 356
Living it up at Fiesta de Merengue........................ 359
Savouring the familiar at Crescent Moon 359
Whale-watching in Samaná 353

ECUADOR

Equitorial differences in Quito 411
Natural rejection in the Galapagos........................ 394
Piranha-fishing in the jungle................................. 425
Retail therapy at Otavalo crafts market 397
Seeing the sun rise from Volcán Cotopaxi............. 406
Visiting the last Panama-hat weavers.................... 426

EGYPT

A walk of repentance: climbing Mt Sinai 195
Diving in the Red Sea coral gardens 193
Drifting down the Nile... 193
Enjoying the view from the Fishawi Café............... 201
Gilf Kebir: the land of the English Patient............. 203
Greeting the Pharaohs in the Valley of the Kings ... 199
Losing yourself in a good book at the
    Bibliotheca Alexandrina 196
Ramadan nights 198
The mould of Sayyid Ahmed al-Bedawi................. 192
The Pyramids at Giza.. 189

EL SALVADOR

Surfing at La Libertad... 367

ENGLAND

Be humbled in Durham 15
Burning rubber at the Isle of Man TT..................... 25
Catching the Last Night of the Proms 33
Chasing cheese in Gloucester 33
Clubbing in London... 31
Cycling in the New Forest 28
Daydreaming in Oxford 19
Dressing up for Royal Ascot 22
Enjoying the seasons of the Scillies...................... 13
Experience Glastonbury 18
Feeling insignificant at the British Museum 19
Finding heaven on earth at the Eden Project 37
Fish and chips: the true English favourite.............. 14
Free-diving in the Royal Navy's SETT.................... 33
Get lost in the Balti Triangle 12
Gunpowder, treason and plot: Lewes Bonfire Night.. 17
Hiking the Pennine Way 23
Hitting the streets for Notting Hill Carnival 26
Holkham magic 20
Hunting ghosts in York.. 16
Learning to survive in deepest Dorset 24
Pounding the streets of London 34
Punting on the Cam 8
Rambling on Dartmoor.. 10
Surfing in Newquay... 28
Surfing the Severn Bore.. 22
Take a stroll from St Paul's to Tate Modern 32
Wandering Borrowdale in the Lake District 15
Watching a football match at the
    Theatre of Dreams 35

ESTONIA

Beavering away in Lahemaa National Park 181

ETHIOPIA

Dropping in on the churches of Lalibela............... 229

Share and share alike: making a meal of injera 228
Trekking in the Simien Mountains 237

FAROE ISLANDS

Puffin and pantin' 205

FIJI

Knocking back kava.. 570

FINLAND

Feeling the heat in a Finnish sauna 111
Going to the dogs in Finnish Lapland.................... 113
White-water rafting with a difference.................... 117

FRANCE

Art after dark: an evening in the Louvre................. 60
Assembling a picnic from Sarlat market................ 64
Battling the elements on the Brittany coast........... 56
Braving the heights of Bonifacio............................ 54
Canoeing down the Dordogne 51
Cathar castles of Languedoc-Roussillon 73
Champagne tasting in Épernay............................. 44
Climbing Mont-St-Michel...................................... 46
Communing with Carnac's prehistoric past........... 59
Cool camping in the French Pyrenees................... 45
Deluxe dining in Paris.. 75
Exploring the Prehistoric cave art of Pech-Merle ... 71
Getting naked in Cap d'Agde 48
Going to the medieval movies 61
Hiking Corsica's GR20 70
Impressionist paintings at the Musee D'Orsay 63
The jewel of Berry: Cathedrale St-Etienne............ 63
Living the high life in St-Tropez............................ 57
Lording it in the Loire Valley 46
Lunch in a rural restaurant 62
Macaroons fit for her majesty 72
Making a statement at a game of treize 57
On the art trail in the Cote D'Azur......................... 55
Partying the night away at a summer fête 68
Paying your respects in Normandy......................... 71
Sloping off to the French Alps 52
Swimming under the Pont du Gard 47
Taking a trip up the Eiffel Tower............................ 49
Washing it down with cider in Normandy 64
Wine-tasting in Bordeaux...................................... 68

FRENCH GUIANA

Catching a launch at the Centre Spatial Guyanis... 423

GABON

Languoué Bai: the Last Place on Earth 229
Surf's up: watching hippos hit the waves............. 239

THE GAMBIA

Admiring the catch on Sanyang Beach 212
Twitcher's delight: watching hornbills 210

GERMANY

Berlin by night 75
Big Foot: snowshoeing through the Black Forest .. 75
Downing a stein or ten at the Oktoberfest............ 44
Feeling the love in Berlin...................................... 53
Freewheeling in the Danube Valley 57
The Friedrichsbad: the best baths in Baden-Baden.. 52
Kayaking across borders on Lake Constance 68
Schloss Neuschwanstein: the ultimate
    fairytale castle 66

GHANA

The Gold Coast: sun, sea and slave forts............. 208

GREECE

Classical drama at Epidavros................................ 148
Conquering Mount Olympus.................................. 156
Greek Island-hopping... 142
In the footsteps of Odysseus on Ithaca................ 150
Listening for nightingales on Samos..................... 139
Lose yourself at Mystra.. 141
Monasteries suspended in the air........................ 149

Monastic Mount Áthos...145
Ring of fire: walking on hot coals...................148
Seeing legends come alive in Crete...................157
The Zagóri and Vikos Gorge............................126
This is the light: Easter celebrations in Loutro... 133

GRENADA
Spice shopping in St George's 351

GUATEMALA
All aboard the chicken buses..............................373
Circling Lago Atitlán 369
Dawn at Tikal...380
Heading to market in the Guatemalan Highlands.....378
Observing Semana Santa in Antigua 376

GUINEA-BISSAU
Running around in the Bijagós Islands 216

GUYANA
Looking down on Kaieteur Falls...........................402

HAITI
Experiencing the extremes of Port-au-Prince.......351
In search of the Citadelle 360

HONDURAS
Chasing whale sharks near Utila.........................367
Stelae stories of Copán....................................388

HUNGARY
Golden mouldie: drinking Tokaj in ancient cellars .. 174
Soothe your troubles at the Hotel Gellert 168

ICELAND
Debunking myths in Kverkfjöll............................110
Dressing up for the Westmann Islands Festival.....113
Partying all night in Reykjavík 119
Seljandsfoss: behind the glass curtain 119
Soaking in Lake Mývatn's hot springs 121
Testing your tastebuds in Reykjavík...................120
Trekking to Door Mountain 114

INDIA
Beating the drought in the Thar 494
Birding by rickshaw at Keoladeo 499
Bollywood glitz at the Mumbai Metro....................486
Catching the sea breeze at Elsewhere................494
City of light: on the Ganges in Varanasi...............472
Cricket mayhem at Eden Gardens.........................498
Crowd-watching at Kartik Purnima.......................486
Cruising the Keralan backwaters 498
The dancing goddess of Kerala 480
Driving over the highest navigable pass
    on the planet...492
Eating a banana-leaf lunch in Chidambaram.......499
On the edge in the Andamans 478
Embarking on an elephant safari at Kaziranga.....496
Envisioning a lost civilization at Ajanta 477
Exploring the Thar Desert by camel.....................475
Hauling in dinner in Goa....................................497
Hopping on board for a Keralan sadya................482
India's Acropolis: a shrine to the fish-eyed
    goddess..488
Journeying over the roof of the world..................474
The juggernauts of Puri....................................482
Lowering the flag at the India-Pakistan border..... 481
Parikrama at the Golden Temple.........................490
Rhythm madness at the Thrissur Puram 485
Sadhu-spotting at the Kumbh Mela......................497
Seeing red during Holi.....................................476
Sliding along the Himalayan Ice highway 485
Snowboarding in Kashmir..................................491
Staying with a family in the Himalayas 494
Sufi grooves: Qawwali at Nizzamuddin.................477
Taking tea in Dharamsala..................................489
Tracing the turtle arribida in Orissa....................478
Tracking tigers in Bandhavgarh..........................479
Trekking to the source of the Ganges.................480
Visiting the Taj by moonlight 495

Walking to "Paradise" at Gokarna 492
Watching a kathakali performance in Kochi 489
Watching the sun rise over Achyutaraya Temple.. 474

INDONESIA
Balinese theatrics 518
Borobudur: the biggest Buddhist stupa
    in the world 521
Bunaken's marine megalopolis 512
Dawn over Kelimutu in Flores 523
Going ape in Borneo 522
The kings of Komodo.......................................513
Meeting the relatives: Orang-utans in Sumatra 511
Peeking at paradise in Aru................................514
Volcanic activity: sunrise on Mount Bromo............528

IRAN
Carving a path through Persepolis 280
Soaking up the Masjid I-imam............................287
Taking tea in Isfahan 286

IRELAND
Barging down the Barrow 22
On the fiddle: attending a traditional Irish
    music session 24
Following the Oyster Trail in Galway..................... 36
Getting away from it all on Skellig Michael............ 31
Losing yourself in Connemara 30
Painting the town green on St Patrick's Day 16
Supping Guinness in Dublin.............................. 15
Watching the hurling at Croke Park 10
Winning the prehistoric lottery 34

ISRAEL & THE PALESTINIAN
TERRITORIES
Checking out the Bauhaus architecture in Tel Aviv..281
Christmas at the Church of the Nativity in
    Bethlehem 277
Fighting off the cats in Acre 273
Masada: conquering Herod's hilltop palace 270
Walking around the Old City of Jerusalem 271

ITALY
All you can eat – with music! 126
Beans and oranges in Ivrea 141
Bears and boars: trekking in Abruzzo
    National Park 126
Braving the midday sun in Lecce........................153
Carnival in Venice..146
Celebrating the Biennale..................................150
Chewing the fat: a glutton's tour of Bologna.......137
Classical studies in Sicily 141
Climb every mountain: Reinhold Messner 150
The Colosseum in winter..................................136
Divine madness in Calabria..............................129
Doing penance in the Sistine Chapel...................153
Enjoying Da Vinci's Last Supper 144
Feasting in Bergamo 255
Finding yourself on Capri 126
Getting the measure of the Medicis....................144
Getting your kit off in Florence...........................147
Going with the flow in Naples............................130
Hiking the Via Ferrata.....................................155
Live like a doge: one night at the Danieli.............158
Living it up on the Amalfi Coast.........................147
Looking for pasta heaven.................................156
Ostia Antica..148
Paradise regained: exploring Italy's oldest
    National Park 133
The peace of Paestum 147
Playing for high stakes at Siena's Palio 138
Sharing the Loves of the Gods at the
    Palazzo Farnese...135
Shopping with style in Milan 143
Snuffling for truffles in Piemonte.......................155
Solving the mysteries of Pompeii.......................130
Spotting Giotto in Padua..................................157
Touring the Tuscan hilltowns,............................162

On the trail of Caravaggio 129
Venice: Europe's first modern city? 158
Visiting Federico's Palace in Urbino....................143
Visiting the home of pizza 151
Walking the Cinque Terre 153
Watching worlds collide in Sicily........................139
Working out a lava on Stomboli's slopes.............137

JAMAICA
Finding inspiration at Goldeneye 355
Grooving at Reggae Sumfest..............................358
Discovering treasure on Jamaica's coast 361

JAPAN
Bathing with snow monkeys...............................451
Chasing temples in Shikoku...............................463
Climbing Fuji...467
A floral wave of cherry blossoms........................764
Getting naked in Inazawa..................................442
Past meets present at Gion Matsuri 466
Relaxing in tropical Taketomi-Jima.....................449
The ritual of a kaiseki meal 441
Sitting ringside at a sumo tournament.................453
Sushi at 300kph: riding the shinkansen...............449
Sweet dreams Japanese-style 456
Tskukiji: where seafood gets serious 434

JORDAN
Bedouin camping at Wadi Rum 283
Blazing a trail at Dana Nature Reserve 285
Diving the Gulf of Aqaba 278
Floating on the Dead Sea 272
Getting acquainted with Arabic sweets 285
Taking a dip in the River Jordan 286
Walking the Siq to Petra 288

KENYA
Following the Greatest Show on Earth 230
Getting up up close and personal with a giraffe... 234
The Great African Meat Feast.............................234
Hot-air ballooning over the Maasai Mara..............408
Mount Elgon: the elephants of Kitum Cave...........230
Mountain-biking with the herds 225
A night on the equator with Kenya Railways 226
Sustainable safaris with the Maasai....................237
Wandering Lamu Island.....................................225

KUWAIT
The Arab Organizations Building: an office
    with attitude..285
Robot camel-back racing...................................289

KYRGYZSTAN
Living the nomadic life 449

LAOS
Fireworks and fever at Bun Bang Fai....................520
Saffron and gold: falling under the spell
    of Louang Phabang 511
Taking a slow boat down the Mekong..................504
Trying to solve puzzles at the Plain of Jars...........517

LATVIA
Eccentric architecture: wandering the
    streets of Rīga 172

LEBANON
Beirut's bunker bar...286
Feasting on Lebanese mezze 281
Feeling dwarfed by Baalbek...............................274

LESOTHO
Pony-trekking in the Mountain Kingdom 256

LIBYA
Exploring the dune lakes of Ubari.......................201
Getting to know the souks of Tripoli 203
Keeping cool in the old town of Ghademes 196
Mountains and mirages in Jebel Acacus 194
Strolling through the ruins of Leptis Magna...........191

LIECHTENSTEIN
Tasting wines that are fit for a prince...................... 59
LITHUANIA
Discovering Jewish Vilnius 177
Pondering Armageddon at the Plokštine
    Missile Base 169
LUXEMBOURG
Going underground in the Casements du Bock 43
MACEDONIA
Sampling the grilled trout of Lake Ohrid.............. 161
MADAGASCAR
Digging and dancing on a Pioneer Programme.... 252
The earth music of Tsimanin Droa 255
Jungle operatics: the lemurs of
    Andasibe-Mantadia...................................... 260
Tsingy: a forest of limestone peaks...................... 245
Up the Tsiribihina in a dugout canoe 265
MADEIRA
Above the clouds on Pico Ruivo........................... 105
MALAWI
Counting fish in Lake Malawi 259
A taste of the sweet life at Kande Beach Bar....... 246
On your bike: cycling through the Nyika Plateau.. 250
MALAYSIA
Conquering Southeast Asia's highest peak:
    Mount Kinabalu 508
Joining the party at an Iban longhouse 510
Jungle Boogie in Sarawak 520
A night in the rainforest....................................... 506
Roaming rainy Penang 517
Underwater at Sipadan Island.............................. 512
THE MALDIVES
Barefoot bliss at Soneva Gili 487
Catching the perfect wave in the Maldives........... 485
MALI
Destination Timbuktu 208
Journeying up the River Niger 218
Partying with the Tuareg at the Festival in
    the Desert 212
Sacred space: the Grand Mosque in Djenné....... 217
Trekking in Dogon country 211
MALTA
Comino's Blue Lagoon... 139
Europe's most ancient temples............................ 145
Grand Master Flash 160
Something fishy in Marsaxlokk 137
MAURITANIA
Bird-watching in the Banc d'Arguin 214
Riding the wagons on the world's longest train.... 216
Visiting the ancient libraries of Chinguetti............ 219
MAURITIUS
Trou aux Cerfs: inside the crater.......................... 245
MEXICO
Being serenaded by mariachis in Guadalajara 384
Biking the Baja Peninsula 377
Climbing El Castillo at Chichén Itzá..................... 370
Diving at Palancar Reef 383
Floating through Xochimilco 368
A glimpse of the murals at Bonampak.................. 375
Honouring the dead in Janitzio 372
Hopping aboard the Copper Canyon Railway 367
Kayaking in the Sea of Cortés 377
Making peace with tequila in Tequila 374
Market day in Oaxaca 365
Meeting the monarchs in Michoacán.................... 379
Mexico City's murals... 388
Sampling fish tacos in Ensenada......................... 378

Taking a dip in the Yucatán's cenotes 389
A taste of mole poblano in Puebla....................... 382
Touring the Zapatista heartland 366
Vacation like a drug lord in Tulum....................... 384
Wandering the back alleys of Zacatecas 370
Whale-watching in Baja California 373
MICRONESIA
Drifting with jellyfish in Micronesia...................... 555
MOLDOVA
Nightclubbing back in the (old) USSR 174
MONACO
Playboys and petrolheads: the Monaco Grand Prix..69
Shaken but not stirred in Monte-Carlo 47
MONGOLIA
Horsing about with the Mongols........................... 442
Naadam: the Manly Games 437
MONTENEGRO
Chilling out on the Montenegrin coast.................. 160
Rafting the Tara Canyon...................................... 154
MOROCCO
Around the world at the Festival of Sacred Music 189
Driving the Route of A Thousand Kasbahs............ 199
Going over the top in the Atlas Mountains 195
Haggling in the souks of Fes 197
Hanging out in the Jemaa El Fna......................... 191
Hitting the road across the Sahara 192
Idling the day away in Essaouira 201
Learning the art of travel writing in Marrakesh 192
Mopping up a Moroccan tajine............................. 198
Slogging over sand dunes in the Marathon des
    Sables 196
Staying with a family in Merzouga 200
MOZAMBIQUE
Giving something back at Guludo Beach Lodge.. 252
Rediscovering the forgotten coast 260
Vamizi Island: paradise with principles 255
NAMIBIA
Cape Cross colony: the seal deal 246
Dreaming in colour: ballooning over the Namib ... 246
Enjoying the show in Etosha National Park 249
Exploring the Skeleton Coast 265
Going bush in Ongava Game Reserve 251
Hiking through the Fish River Canyon 248
Tracking rhino in Damaraland 261
Watching the desert bloom in Namaqualand 255
NAURU
Hunting noddy birds.. 556
NEPAL
Sacred peaks: trekking in the Himalayas.............. 483
Tripping through the Phalgun Festivals................. 491
THE NETHERLANDS
Cranking up the volume on Queen's Day 73
Cycling in the Dutch courtyside........................... 42
Skating the superhuman race 67
Spending the day in Amsterdam's Museum Quarter..67
NEW CALEDONIA
From prison to paradise on L'ile des Pins 549
Paris in the Pacific... 564
NEW ZEALAND
Art meets nature on Waiheke Island 574
Coast to coast with the TranzAlpine 556
Cruising Doubtful Sound 537
Discovering your own Middle Earth...................... 541
Exploring Waitomo's eerie underground world 552
Filling up in Auckland 573
Getting hands on at Wellington's Te Papa 553
Getting high on the Gillespie Pass....................... 560

Heli-biking Ben Cruachan 567
Heli-hiking on Franz Josef glacier........................ 543
Heli-skiing in the Southern Alps........................... 565
Kiwi-spotting in Trounson Kauri Park.................... 541
Lazing about at Hot Water Beach......................... 563
Motorbiking down the wild west coast.................. 555
Paddling through Abel Tasman National Park 568
Pedalling into the heart of the Maniototo 538
Queenstown's winter wonderland 547
Rafting the rapids of the wild West Coast rivers .. 573
Relaxing at the seaside in Art Deco Napier 549
Scuba diving the wrecks at Poor Knights Islands 551
Setting sail among the blissful Bay of Islands....... 540
Spying on penguins and albatrosses along the
    Otago Peninsula.. 565
Supping wine in sun-drenched Marlborough........ 539
Taking a trip to hell on earth 560
Taking in the views on the Tongariro Crossing 564
Taking the plunge with AJ Hackett 543
Tramping the Milford Track 545
Tucking into a hangi 549
Waitangi: the birth of a modern nation 568
Walking through the woods in Wipoua
    Kauri Forest.. 571
Watching whales in Kaikoura 550
Witnessing the power of the haka 543
A world away on the Landsborough River........... 567
NICARAGUA
Handmade hammocks in Masaya 388
Isla de Ometepe by motorcycle........................... 387
Revel in eco-luxury at Morgan's Rock 370
Riding down the Rio San Juan 382
NIGER
Getting back to basics with the People of the Veil . 213
NIGERIA
Soaking in Wikki Warm Springs............................ 211
NORTH KOREA
A little local flavour in Pyongyang........................ 450
Eyeballing soldiers in the "Scariest Place
    on Earth".. 441
Viewing the Arirang Mass Gymnastics Festival ... 457
NORTHERN IRELAND
See the Belfast murals... 28
Walking in the Mountains of Mourne 18
NORWAY
A to B by cross-country ski 116
Cruising the coolest coast in Europe 114
Fjord focus: touring the western waterways.......... 112
Hiking the Besseggen Ridge................................. 116
Kayaking amid icebergs....................................... 582
Living the quiet life in Lofoten 113
Snorkelling with orcas 581
OMAN
Bobbing about in the Musandam fjords 271
Camel racing in the Wahiba Sands....................... 274
Frolicking with dolphins off Muscat 278
On the incense trail in Arabia Felix 273
Swimming the Wadi Shab 286
Tawi Attair: the "singing" sinkhole........................ 274
PAKISTAN
Cycling the Karakoram Highway............................ 478
Lowering the flag at the India–Pakistan border 481
Watching the ponies at the world's highest polo
    tournament.. 493
PANAMA
Bird-watching on the Pipeline Road 387
Encountering Kuna culture................................... 382
Family sailing across the Pacific........................... 384

From sea to shining sea: cruising the
Panama Canal...387
Isla Barro Colorado: the appliance of science......374

PAPUA NEW GUINEA
Hike through history along the Kokoda Trail.........529

PARAGUAY
Itaipú: plugging the world's biggest dam..............404
Watching wildlife in the Chaco..............................394

PERU
Celebrate Qoyllur Riti 396
Chasing condors in Colca Canyon 419
Communing with a Shaman...................................414
Following ancient footsteps on the Inca Trail 401
Life on the quiet side: homestays on Lago Titicaca..414
Rafting on sacred waters in the Urubamba Valley....398
Sandboarding at Huacachina..............................400
Savouring ceviche in Lima 423
Soaring over the Nazca Lines 406
The Road to Ruins: Machu Picchu 413

THE PHILIPPINES
Climbing the stairway to heaven in Banaue 506
Counting fish in the Sulu Sea...............................511
Diving the Tubbataha Reef 507
Exploring Malapascua by banca...........................514
Island-hopping in the Bacuit Archipelago...........524
Partying at the Ati-Atihan Festival........................505

POLAND
Burrowing for bargains in Kraków.........................170
Crossing cultural boundaries in Kraków 179
Hiking in the Tatras...175
Horrors of the Holocaust: visiting Auschwitz.......179
Mills and malls: on the industrial heritage
trail in Łódź...173

PORTUGAL
Clearing your calendar for bacalhau......................91
Exploring mystical Sintra.......................................84
Learning to surf on the Atlantic coast....................86
In search of the perfect tart 100
Stop! It's hammer time at the Festa de São João.. 90
Tram #28: taking a ride through Lisbon's historic
quarters...102

PUERTO RICO
Feasting your way through old San Juan 358
The nocturnal symphony of El Yunque.................359
Sugar and spice: touring rum makers...................355

QATAR
Off-roading for real: across the sand dunes to
Khor al-Adaid...289
Sand-skiing in the dunes 273

RAROTONGA
Double-crossed in the South Seas 551

ROMANIA
On the Dracula trail in Transylvania......................171
Reclaiming the streets at the Pageant of the Juni.. 182
Staying with a real-life Transylvanian count..........181
Tracking carnivores in the Carpathian Mountains 178

RUSSIA
Losing track of time: Beijing to Moscow on the
Trans Siberian Railway.......................................462
A mindblowing museum: St Petersburg's
Hermitage...176
Mount Elbrus: climbing Europe's mightiest peak . 178
St Petersburg's wild White Nights.........................173
Soviet exhibitionism in Moscow 170
Skiing in the Land of Fire and Ice 465
Standing at the heart of Mother Russia................174
Taking a trip on the Moscow metro 180

ST BARTHÉLEMY
Living it up like a celebrity on St Barts 361

ST KITTS & NEVIS
Shrimp BBQ and Rum punch in Nevis 358

ST LUCIA
High Adventure in the West Indies........................354

SÃO TOMÉ & PRÍNCIPE
In search of the best chocolate in the world 210

SAUDI ARABIA
Discovering Mada'in Saleh....................................277
Visiting the "hanging village" of Habalah.............289

SCOTLAND
Breathing in the sea air in Tobermory 30
Calling in the heavies at the Highland Games........25
Flying with BA to Barra and beyond 36
Gigging in Glasgow...34
Highland fling: getting personal with Ben Nevis .. 36
Hogmanay: seeing the New Year in, Scottish style.. 12
Horsing around at the Common Ridings 21
Playing the Old Course at St Andrews 29
Soaking up the Edinburgh Festival 30
A taste of rum in Kinloch Castle 16
A taste of Skye..10
Toasting bad weather in the Scottish Highlands ... 21
Trundling along the West Highlands Railway.........31

SERBIA
Balkan brass madness in Guča 128
Having a blast in Belgrade 130
Studenica and the magical monasteries.............158

SEYCHELLES
Fulfilling fantasies on Frégate Island....................231
Swimming with turtles in the Indian Ocean 229
Unwinding at Maia Resort and Spa.....................226

SIERRA LEONE
Take a walk in the rainforest 219

SINGAPORE
All aboard the Eastern & Oriental Express...........525
Creatures of the night 523

SLOVAKIA
Wooden churches: "mass" tourism with a twist...169

SLOVENIA
Locked up in Ljubljana: Hostel Celica 140
Stalagmites, stalactites and a human fish 132
Tackling old Mr Three Heads 136

SOUTH AFRICA
Across the Great Karoo...252
Birding in the Greater St Lucia Wetlands..............245
Climbing Table Mountain......................................260
Eating the fat of the land in Klein Karoo 255
Getting hot and bothered on the Drakensberg.....249
Getting out of your tree at the world's
smallest pub...246
Learning the ways of a wildlife ranger 263
Looking for lions in Madikwe 244
On a swing and a prayer: flying through the
Tsitsikamma Forest canopy...............................254
Rustic rocking at Rustler's Valley Festivals...........259
Sampling wines in the Western Cape 264
Touring a township 263
Tracing Mandela's roots in the Eastern Cape......251
Watching the desert bloom in Namaqualand 255

SOUTH KOREA
Buddhist boot camp at Haeinsa Temple..............447
Eyeballing soldiers in the "Scariest Place on
Earth" 441
Getting steamy in a Jjimjilbang............................445
Sauntering through Seoul 460

Walking among Silla royalty 455

SPAIN
Alpargatas: the soul is in the sole........................105
Browsing La Boqueria 91
Castle in the sky: over the Meseta to Morella 84
Counting dolphins in the Mediterranean................88
Cruising through the Coto de Doñana.................101
Cycling for the soul: el Camino de Santiago 103
Dancing in the streets of Gracia 94
Dancing till dawn at Benicàssim............................91
Discovering the Conquistadors' spoils 104
A drop of the Bard's stuff: sipping sherry
Spanish style..87
Dropping in at Mundaka...93
Fair play at the Feria 93
Flamenco: backstreets and gypsy beats 88
Gawping at the Guggengheim 82
Getting lost in the Pilgrim's Palace 93
Going for your guns in Almería 96
Heading for the heights in the Picos de Europa... 105
Hiking in the Pyrenees 86
La Rioja: land of the rising vine 81
Living without sleep in Valencia 100
The lost streets of Rio Honor de Castilla 103
Marvelling inside the Mezquita 92
Modernisme and mañana: Gaudí's
Sagrada Famalia...89
Moorish Granada: exploring the Alhambra...........104
Painting the town red at La Tomatina 95
Playing with fire at Las Fallas 80
Poetic license in Deià 97
Portraits and Purgatory at the Prado 85
Pray Macarena! Easter in Seville...........................85
Pulpo addiction: going gastro in Galicia 89
Roaming Las Ramblas 86
Running with the bulls 93
Seeing stars in San Sebastián 81
Skiing under a Spanish sun 81
Surfing the Coast of Light: from Tarifa to Tangier... 85
Surreal life at the Dalí Museum 98
Tapas-crawling in Madrid 84
Waging wine war in La Rioja 97
Washing away the cider house blues 94
Watching Real Madrid at the Bernabéu.................101

SRI LANKA
Climbing Adam's Peak..481
Elbowing through the crowds for Esala Perahera .. 474
High in Haputale..484
Riding waves in the Indian Ocean 477
Watching elephants bathe at Pinnawala...............491

SURINAME
Bird-watch and be watched...................................406

SWAZILAND
Dancing with the king at Big Ncwala....................264
Malalotja: a big place in a small country 259

SWEDEN
Behold the Northern Lights....................................580
Breakfasting with the stars at the Grand Hotel... 120
Chilling out in the Icehotel....................................121
Lapping up life in Lapland.....................................110
Navigating a Swedish smörgåsbord
Sleeping with the fishes at Utter Inn 120
Summer sailing in the Stockholm archipelago 114
Visiting Visby's vikings..117

SWITZERLAND
Bungeeing off the Verzasca Dam 55
Cow-fighting at the Combat des Reines 43
The Cresta Run: sledging with a difference............74
Gathering friends for a Swiss fondue 59
Getting groovy at the Montreux Jazz Festival 60

Horsing about at the Polo World Cup on Snow 43
Kayaking across borders on Lake Constance 68
Lounging aboard the Glacier Express.................... 48
Mush! Mush! Husky sledding in the Swiss Alps 63
Snow wonder: podding it up in the Swiss Alps..... 72
Vogel Gryff: there's no place like Basel................. 59

SYRIA
Bargaining in the Aleppo souk 271
Haunting the Dead Cities 289
Hearing the groans in Hama 272
Krak de Chevaliers: the finest castle in the world .. 275
Relaxing in a Damascus hammam........................ 278
Sunset over Palmyra 277

TAHITI
Following in Gauguin's footsteps........................ 569

TAIWAN
Filling up on little eats 445
Shooting to the top of the world's tallest building.. 461
Walking with the Queen of Heaven...................... 440

TANZANIA
Climbing Kilimanjaro 233
Following the Greatest Show on Earth 230
The Great African Meat Feast 234
Losing the crowds at Katavi National Park........... 237
Playing Tarzan on Chole Island 226
Reef encounter: eco-living on a Tanzanian Island.. 234
Wildlife-spotting in the Ngorongoro Crater.......... 236

THAILAND
All aboard the Eastern & Oriental Express........... 524
Budget beach-chic.. 515
Candles in the water: the Loy Krathong
   Festival of Light.. 509
Dancing under a full moon................................ 519
Fight night in Bangkok...................................... 510
Finding peace among Ko Libong's wildlife 525
Fireworks fever at Bun Bang Fai........................ 520
Getting dazzled at Bangkok's Grand Palace 509
The hills are alive: tribal trekking...................... 518
Ironing out the kinks.. 523
Mixing sand and spice on Ko Samui 507
Paddling into secret lagoons 516
Shopping for Thailand at Chatuchak
   Weekend Market.. 505
Snacking your way through the day: the allure of
   Thai street food.. 529

TIBET
Circuiting the Jokhang 445
Driving over the highest navigable pass
   on the planet.. 492
Journeying over the Roof of the World................. 474
Morning prayers at the Diskit Monastery 482

TRANSDNIESTR
Spending a night in Europe's Twilight Zone.......... 182

TRINIDAD
"Get on bad" in Trinidad.................................... 352

TRISTAN DA CUNHA
Swigging the most remote beer on earth 264

TUNISIA
Camel fighting at The Festival of the Sahara........ 199
Camel trekking in the Sahara............................. 189
Exploring the Roman ruins at Dougga................. 195
Touring troglodyte villages 191

TURKEY
A night out on Independence Street.................... 143
Called by Rumi: dervishes in Istanbul................. 152
Cappadocia: land of the fairy chimneys 151
Getting down and dirty in Dalyan 155
Inside a metaphor: Troy.................................... 157

Music, dance and drama in ancient Aspendos 140
Shop till you drop in Istanbul 159
Striking oil in Edirne 161

TURKMENISTAN
Visiting the pits of hell 459

UAE
The Burj Al Arab shows off in Dubai................... 284
Flaunting it at the Emirates Palace 272
Shopping in the City of Cold............................. 280

URUGUAY
Experiencing the two sides of Punta del Este 404
Exploring Colonia del Sacramento by scooter 412
Taking time over maté....................................... 429

UGANDA
Camping with hippos in Murchison Falls
   National Park.. 224
Meeting the cheeky monkeys of Kibale................ 234
The real bat cave... 225
Storytelling on the Ssese Islands........................ 239
White water-rafting at the source of the Nile 230

UKRAINE
Counting colours in Kiev................................... 173
Trial by trolleybus: Simferopol to Yalta............... 170

USA
Angling for brown bears in Alaska 323
Attending a ceremonial dance at Taos Pueblo 302
Aura cleansing in Old Florida............................. 303
Bed, barracuda and breakfast: Jules'
   Undersea Lodge 318
Biking the Golden Gate Bridge 304
Biking the San Antonio Mission Trail 315
Burning Man Festival 310
California in a convertible: driving the length of
   Highway 1 313
Castles made of sand: acting like a kid on
   Cannon Beach 305
Catching a baseball game at Wrigley Field 294
Cedar Point: the roller-coaster capital of the world...307
Celebrating Fantasy Fest in Key West 320
Chasing storms in Tornado Alley 295
Checking the progress of the Crazy Horse
   Memorial 308
Choosing the right Philly cheesesteak.................. 308
Cruising the Inside Passage................................ 306
Eating barbecue in Texas Hill Country................. 316
Finding paradise on Kauai's north shore 300
Gazing at a Nantucket sunset............................. 311
Getting in line at Mardi Gras 298
Going batty in Austin.. 312
Going to the sun in Glacier National Park 302
Halloween in NYC 303
Hang-gliding in the outer banks.......................... 315
In high spirits on the bourbon trail 316
Hiking Half Dome in Yosemite............................ 301
Hiking the Chilkoot Trail 308
Hit the hut: attending nature's boot camp............ 316
Hitting the track at the Indianapolis 500.............. 322
Jumping through hoops to see the hula................ 305
Leaf-peeping along Route 100 311
Leaving it all behind on the Appalachian Trail 306
Lost for words at the Grand Canyon 325
Lunching on Creole cuisine in New Orleans.......... 319
Making a mess with Maryland crabs 304
Making like King Kong at the Empire
   State Building.. 294
Mighty Real in Las Vegas.................................. 305
A night at the lobster pound 305
On the road with the Green Tortoise................... 311
Paying homage to country music 312
Playing ball at the Field of Dreams 318

Primal Point Reyes... 320
Reconsidering the Wild West in Monument Valley ..296
Riding high on the Blue Ridge Parkway 299
Riding the Slickrock in Moab 302
Running the New York City marathon................... 317
Scoping out the scene on Ocean Drive................ 294
Sea kayaking in Prince William Sound................. 306
Seeing the Bay Area from atop Mount Tam.......... 309
Setting up camp in the Adirondacks 312
Sidestepping ash and lava on Kilauea................. 309
Skiing at Alta and Snowbird............................... 321
Sleeping near the corner in Winslow 320
Spending a weekend in Wine Country................... 299
Spooked in the old south.................................. 320
Strolling through downtown Savannah 301
Taking the A-Train through Manhattan................. 319
Touring Alaska by RV 315
Touring Graceland 322
Tracing civil rights history in Montgomery 319
Travel the Turquoise Trail.................................. 303
The quintessential snack in America's
   food capital.. 298
Up close with Alligators on the Anhinga Trail 314
Visiting Harvard Yard.. 309
Watching the fish fly at Pike Place Market 308
Witnessing power in action on Capitol Hill 301
Wolf-watching in Yellowstone National Park........ 322

VANUATU
Diving the Coolidge.. 564
Dodging embers on Mount Yasur 548

VENEZUELA
Getting high in Caracas 417
Searching for the perfect oyster on Isla Margarita... 411
Size matters: in search of the world's
   longest snake.. 398

VIETNAM
Feeling fruity in the Mekong Delta 534
Karst and crew: overnighting in Ha Long Bay 505
Long live the emperor: the imperial
   mausoleums of Hué...................................... 529
Meeting American Killer Heroes.......................... 525
Moonlit meanders through Hoi An 520
Shopping with the women of the Flower
   Hmong Hill Tribe.. 509
Snake every which way in Hanoi 516

WALES
Go West: walking the Pembrokeshire Coast Path.. 13
Hiking in Snowdonia 19
Hoarding books in Hay-on-Wye........................... 18
Mountain biking Welsh trails 21
Into the Valley: hearing a Welsh choir 35
Walking the walls of Conwy Castle...................... 11

YEMEN
Mud-brick marvels: experiencing the traditional
   architecture of Sana'a, Tarim and Shibam 272
Wandering Old San'a 279
Searching for dragon's blood.............................. 276

ZAMBIA
In at the deep end: whitewater-rafting on the
   Zambezi 258
Living with the Kunda.. 249
Taking a walk on the wild side 263

ZANZIBAR
Dinner at Moses' place 239
That's magic: Pemba's Djinn.............................. 237
Touring the Spice Island 230

ZIMBABWE
The smoke that thunders at Victoria Falls 262